**10**<sup>th</sup>

EDITION

# CONSUMER
# BEHAVIOR

## ROGER D. BLACKWELL

## PAUL W. MINIARD
*Florida International University*

## JAMES F. ENGEL
*Eastern College*

**THOMSON**

**SOUTH-WESTERN**

Australia · Brazil · Canada · Mexico · Singapore · Spain · United Kingdom · United States

# THOMSON
™
## SOUTH-WESTERN

Consumer Behavior, Tenth Edition
Roger D. Blackwell, Paul W. Miniard, James F. Engel

**VP/Editorial Director:**
Jack W. Calhoun

**Publisher:**
Melissa Acuna

**Executive Editor:**
Neil Marquardt

**Sr. Developmental Editor:**
Mardell Glinski-Schultz

**Marketing Manager:**
Nicole Moore

**Production Project Manager:**
Brian Courter

**Manager of Technology, Editorial:**
Vicky True

**Technology Project Editor:**
Pam Wallace

**Web Coordinator:**
Karen Schaffer

**Manufacturing Coordinator:**
Diane Lohman

**Production House:**
G & S Book Services

**Printer:**
Seng Lee Press

**Art Director:**
Stacy Jenkins Shirley

**Internal Designer:**
Beckmeyer Design

**Cover Designer:**
Beckmeyer Design

**Cover Images:**
© Getty Images

**Photography Manager:**
Deanna Ettinger

**Photo Researcher:**
Terri Miller

Library of Congress Control
Number: 2005933698

For more information about our
products, contact us at:
Thomson Learning Academic
Resource Center
1-800-423-0563

Thomson Higher Education
5191 Natorp Boulevard
Mason, OH 45040
USA

# Brief Contents

# Contents

## SUMMARY

682

# About the Authors

**Roger D. Blackwell** is a recently retired Professor of Marketing and Logistics from the Fisher College of Business at The Ohio State University. He is also President of Roger Blackwell Associates, Inc., a consulting firm in Columbus, Ohio, through which he has worked with many of America's most successful companies.

Dr. Blackwell was named Outstanding Marketing Educator in America by Sales and Marketing Executives International and received the Alumni Distinguished Teaching Award, the highest award given by The Ohio State University, and in 2004 he was the first inductee to the Central Ohio Marketing Hall of Fame. In 2005, he received three additional teaching awards, reflecting the depth of knowledge and enthusiasm for teaching that make him a favorite among students.

Dr. Blackwell received his B.S. and M.S. degrees from the University of Missouri and his Ph.D. from Northwestern University. He also received an honorary doctorate from the Cincinnati College of Mortuary Science. He resides in Columbus, Ohio, and serves on numerous boards of both privately and publicly held corporations. He is the author or coauthor of a number of best-selling business books including *Consumer Driven Health Care* (2005), *Brands That Rock* (2003), *Customers Rule* (2001), *From Mind to Market* (1997), and *From the Edge of the World* (1995). His research has been published in the *Journal of Marketing Research*, *Journal of Advertising Research*, *Journal of Marketing*, *Journal of Retailing*, and other publications.

**Paul W. Miniard** earned his B.S., M.A., and Ph.D. at the University of Florida and is currently the BMI Professor of Marketing at Florida International University. Previously, he was a tenured member of the faculties at the University of South Carolina and The Ohio State University.

Dr. Miniard is well known through his published research in the areas of advertising and consumer behavior. His research has appeared in a number of leading journals, including *Journal of Advertising*, *Journal of Advertising Research*, *Journal of Business Research*, *Journal of Consumer Psychology*, *Journal of Consumer Research*, *Journal of Experimental Social Psychology*, *Journal of Marketing*, *Journal of Marketing Research*, *Journal of Public Policy & Marketing*, *Journal of the Academy of Marketing Science*, and *Marketing Letters*. He has received a number of honors and awards for his research, service, and teaching at both the undergraduate and graduate levels. He also serves as a consultant and expert witness in areas involving advertising and consumer behavior.

**James F. Engel** earned his B.S. at Drake University and obtained his Ph.D. at the University of Illinois, Urbana. Professor Engel has a distinguished name in the study of consumer behavior. He was honored by his peers in 1980 as the founder of the field when he was named one of the first two Fellows of the Association for Consumer Research. He received a similar citation with the prestigious Paul D. Converse Award of the American Marketing Association. These honors were given in recognition of his pioneering research (which he began in 1960), his original role as senior author of this textbook, and other forms of leadership.

Dr. Engel is the retired Distinguished Professor of Marketing and Director of the Center for Organizational Excellence at Eastern College, St. Davids, Pennsylvania. In his career, Professor Engel shifted his emphasis from consumer goods marketing to the application of nonprofit marketing principles to religious organizations worldwide. He has served as a consultant and management development specialist with hundreds of organizations in more than sixty countries.

# Preface

Just as customer-centric organizations put the consumer at the center of all activities, you are the primary focus of this book. That means that *Consumer Behavior* is written with you, the reader, in mind, and that its concepts and principles are explained in terms understandable to you. It also means that the topics have been selected to provide you a foundation for analyzing consumer behavior and to be managerially and personally relevant in a wide variety of activities throughout your career. Many books give an overview of consumer behavior topics, but *Consumer Behavior* describes the topics in sufficient detail that you can apply them to your career and your life. In most instances, the topics in the book are accompanied by real examples from real organizations to help you see the relevance of theory in developing the strategy and tactics that create effective marketing programs.

"Consumer behavior is everything and everything is consumer behavior" would be a fitting motto for this book because nearly every part of life involves the consumption of goods and services. The study of consumer behavior focuses on questions such as, "Why do people spend their time and money on activities such as enjoying meals with family or friends, participating in sports, donating blood and body organs, and visiting restaurants and stores for something other than food and functional necessities?" Once you understand how to answer questions like these, you'll have a basis for knowing how to influence people's consumption choices.

*Consumer Behavior* focuses on *why* as well as *how* consumers make specific decisions and behave in certain ways—what motivates them, what captures their attention, and what retains their loyalty (i.e., what turns customers into "fans" of an organization). Getting answers to questions about why people buy and consume requires an examination of many different aspects of consumers and their behaviors, from their motivations, personalities, knowledge, and attitudes to the process by which they make their purchase and consumption decisions. This examination also includes understanding things as far-reaching as the consumer's culture and macroeconomic conditions as well as the influences exerted by the consumer's peers and family. You will not only be able to apply this knowledge to nearly any career you choose, but you can also apply it to your personal decisions, making you a wiser consumer. In this regard, an important new feature of the book called "Buyer Beware" appears in each chapter to raise your awareness of how the marketplace works. You're probably very interested in how much income you'll earn following graduation, but in the long term, what you will have as a consumer is determined by more than what you earn. It will also depend on what you save. By learning this Buyer Beware material, you will save even more money.

## Learn from Every Discipline and Everyone

Consumer behavior is an applied discipline that borrows from every discipline that contributes to understanding consumers. When the first edition of *Consumer Behavior* was published in 1968, the "discipline" of consumer behavior was in its infancy and there was no choice except to borrow from the best of other disciplines helpful in understanding consumers—psychology, economics, sociology, anthropology, and the few consumer behavior–oriented marketing studies that existed at that time. To bring together information from all of these disciplines, the authors developed a model to provide a "roadmap" or blueprint for assimilating all of this diverse knowledge to understand consumer decision making. This blueprint became known as the EKB model, named after James Engel, David Kollat, and Roger Blackwell, the author team for the first edition of *Consumer Behavior*. Refined in the second edition, the model soon became the organizing framework for most books in consumer behavior, for the consumer behavior chapter in most marketing textbooks, and for marketing programs in many organizations. When Paul Miniard joined the team for the fifth edition published in 1986 following David Kollat's departure after the third edition, the model became the EBM model to reflect his contributions. You'll still find the seven-stage model (composed of need recognition, search, pre-purchase evaluation of alternatives, purchase, consumption, post-consumption evaluation, and divestment) in its latest version in this tenth edition of *Consumer Behavior*, now referred to as the consumer decision process (CDP) model.

## Ten Times Better

As you study this text, you'll be part of what is for us a significant milestone—the publication of the tenth edition of *Consumer Behavior*. Nearly forty years have passed since the first edition of *Consumer Behavior* was published, an event of some historical significance itself because it marked the publication of the first business textbook devoted to this subject. Since that time, the author team has made numerous changes to the book, striving to improve its informational content while making it even more reader friendly, understandable, and, dare we say, even enjoyable to read. In the ninth edition, for example, we introduced a novel approach to covering many of the psychological processes that affect consumer behavior. In the past, the book had included a section called "Psychological Processes" in which the chapters focused on various theories and mental processes, followed by a consideration of their practical relevance and business implications. Today we employ an approach (see the section called "Influencing Consumer Behavior") that begins with the pragmatic requirements for influencing consumer behavior, such as making contact with consumers, shaping their product opinions, and helping them to remember, and then introduces the theories and concepts relevant to these various requirements and those that influence consumers. The ninth edition also introduced the use of cases. This edition contains a whole new set of cases, many applicable to global strategic situations, which provide students the opportunity to apply the knowledge gained from the text. We continue this legacy of continuous improvements, the particulars of which are described next. It is our hope that this latest edition of *Consumer Behavior* is at least ten times better than its pioneering predecessor first published in 1968.

For those familiar with previous editions, you'll find a number of changes in this version of *Consumer Behavior*. First and foremost are the aforementioned new Buyer Beware vignettes. This material offers an entirely new dimension to readers. In addition to educating them about how to do a better job in analyzing and influencing consumer behavior, the book now—through this Buyer Beware material—educates readers about how to be better consumers. Also new to this edition are vignettes labeled "Consumer Behavior and Marketing" and "Market Facts." The former provides contemporary examples of how the actions of a variety of companies and industries are shaped by consumer behavior, and the latter furnishes the reader with an up-to-date understanding of various aspects of the marketplace.

Another special feature unique to this edition is the introduction of the "Honor Roll of Consumer Researchers." The knowledge contained within this book largely comes from the efforts of consumer researchers who publish their work in academic journals and other scholarly outlets. In recognition of their efforts, we have included a special section near the beginning of the book that identifies the research productivity of certain individuals who have published in the two leading journals devoted to consumer research, the *Journal of Consumer Psychology* and the *Journal of Consumer Research,* over the past twenty years.

Although *Consumer Behavior* is still largely entrenched in its tried-and-true theoretical foundation, the authors have always strived to anticipate where the field is going in the future, and this edition continues that forward-thinking goal. We address new applications of consumer behavior theory by addressing e-commerce and the influences of the Internet and other technologies on consumer behavior in the many places it is relevant, but especially in Chapters 4 and 14. Indeed, you'll find many new topics throughout the tenth edition, including viral marketing, e-mail marketing, mobile marketing, blogging, podcasting, advergaming, self-knowledge, phishing, framing, perceived scarcity, customer lifetime value, and many others. Bayesian analysis has been around for several centuries, but has recently gained widespread interest among marketers. That's why you'll find a new section on that topic in this edition, in Chapter 2, now focused on the topic of "Creating Marketing Strategies for Customer-Centric Organizations." Perceptual mapping has long been a staple in the market researcher's tool bag, but is now covered for the first time in Chapter 9.

This tenth edition of *Consumer Behavior* offers a deeper look at a number of topics. In this regard, certainly one of the most significant changes from the prior edition has been the expanded coverage of consumption. Recently, a number of important research articles have furthered our understanding of consumption, and the knowledge gained from this research has been incorporated into this edition. Moreover, *Consumer Behavior* has always been at the forefront of describing consumption in minority market segments, among the first to incorporate African American, Latino, gay and lesbian, French-Canadian, and Asian consumer behavior into a widely used text. You'll find even more coverage of these topics, especially Latino markets, in this edition, beginning with the opening vignette in Chapter 1.

Customer relationship management (CRM) programs are now a "must" for nearly every marketing organization and are a new addition to this edition, along with expanded coverage of loyalty programs and data mining. The largest business in the world—now approaching one-third of a trillion dollars in sales and a major employer of college graduates in marketing and other majors—is Wal*Mart, and you'll find increased discussion of the reasons for its success throughout the book. In the United States, health care currently accounts for more than 15 percent of all the goods and services produced in the nation, and for freshmen entering college that number is projected to be nearly 20 percent by the time they graduate. With nearly one out of five consumer dollars spent on this service, you can see why the topic is discussed throughout this edition, along with other services that are now more important than cars, computers, and other products in creating jobs in the U.S. and other economies. You'll also find an increasing emphasis in this edition on the macroeconomic effects of consumer behavior. Brand strategies and the creation of brand equity are topics of increasing attention among marketers, and you'll see an expansion of these topics in the tenth edition, including ideas on how to turn ordinary customers into "fans."

Just as no person is an island, neither is an organization seeking to sell to consumers. *Consumer Behavior* describes marketers as part of a *demand chain* that starts with the mind of the consumers and works back through the supply chain to include retailers, intermediaries, manufacturers, and facilitating agencies (such as advertising agencies or logistics providers), all focused upon delighting customers. Understanding customer-centric organizations is relevant to creating profitable marketing organizations, but increasingly it is also relevant to understanding why some nations are more productive than others in providing goods and services as diverse as cars and groceries or banking and health care. Nations around the globe are moving increasingly toward consumer-driven economies, an additional reason for understanding the behavior of people as consumers.

Because this book has been translated into many languages and studied in many nations, but also because marketers in one nation increasingly must understand consumers in many nations, the book is written from a global perspective. The tenth edition uses examples from companies in Europe, Asia, Africa, and Australia as well as the Americas. These examples are chosen to reflect the interests of readers around the world, including those who use the book in one of its various translations, including Russian, Portuguese, Japanese, Korean, French, and Spanish.

Despite the many changes made from the previous edition, one thing has not changed in this edition: the authors' commitment to providing comprehensive references to scholarly research on consumer behavior. Although many readers may be less interested in the specifics of who wrote which articles reporting which research underlying the principles and theories described in this book, this research is important in establishing credibility for the concepts and conclusions you will study. *Consumer Behavior* provides references in the endnotes to many of the articles and research reports that support and amplify the principles presented in the text.

## Practicing What We Preach

In *Consumer Behavior*, customer-centricity is described as the process of developing products, services, and strategies based on listening to consumers to provide what they want. That's what we've tried to do in this edition—listen to our customers and adapt accordingly. We give many thanks to our colleagues who have taken the time to write to us over the years and tell us what they would like to see in future editions, and thanks also to the many friends who have contributed to the success and evolution of this book in a more formal way as reviewers. Our students also have been invaluable in providing feedback about what they like and what can be improved.

In an ongoing effort to be customer friendly and marketing oriented, we encourage you to submit questions or comments to either author about his respective chapters. Paul Miniard was the primary author of Chapters 4, 6, 8, 9, 10, 14, 15, and 16, and Roger Blackwell was the primary author of Chapters 1, 2, 3, 5, 7, 11, 12, and 13. Roger can be reached by phone (614-457-6334) or by e-mail at rblackwell @rogerblackwell.com. Paul can be reached by phone (305-348-3322) at his FIU office or by e-mail at miniardp@fiu.edu.

## Text Supplements

The tenth edition of *Consumer Behavior* includes a comprehensive set of supplements designed to enhance student learning and comprehension as well as aid in instructor presentation of text materials.
IRCD (ISBN: 0-324-27207-3)

The instructor's CD-ROM provides all key ancillaries for ease in preparing for classes and customizing lectures, presentations, and assessment. Included on the IRCD is the instructor's manual, ExamView testing software and PowerPoint as described below.

*Instructor's Manual:* Prepared by Paul Miniard, Shazad Mohammed, and Alan Ayers, the instructor's manual includes chapter outlines, answers to discussion questions, lecture notes, and teaching suggestions.

*ExamView®:* The ExamView test creation software is an easy-to-use, windows-based program that allows instructors to create exams and quizzes from a bank of multiple choice, true/false, and essay questions. Instructors can preview and edit test questions as well as add their own. Questions can be scrambled and printed in various formats for easy text and quiz preparation. The questions were prepared by Paul Miniard and Shazad Mohammed.

*PowerPoint®:* Classroom lectures and discussions come to life with this presentation created by Paul Miniard and Shazad Mohammed. Organized by chapter, this program includes key material from each chapter along with figures, and tables from the text.

*Videos* (ISBN: 0-324-27209-X) Closely tied to the text, this video package features real-world organizations and events related to *Consumer Behavior.* Segments featuring concepts directly from chapter materials are included for dynamic classroom presentations.

*Website: http://blackwell.swlearning.com* This site includes information for both instructors and students that includes consumer behavior–related links, along with links to business sites and other resources of interest to people who are learning about or teaching a consumer behavior course.

*Distance Learning:* For professors interested in supplementing classroom presentations with online content or in setting up a distance learning course, Thomson South-Western, along with WebCT, can provide the industry's leading online courses. WebCT provides tools to help you manage course content, facilitate online classroom collaboration, and track your students' progress. For more information on this service, please contact your local sales representative. To view a demo of any of our online courses, go to webct.harcourtcollege.com.

*The Business Company Resource Center,* available through our product support website, provides online access to a wide variety of global business information including current articles and business journals, detailed company and industry information, investment reports, stock quotes, and much more. Debbie Laverie of Texas Tech University has written questions to accompany each chapter, providing students with an opportunity to do research and apply what they have learned.

## Our Hats Go Off to . . .

The authors owe a great intellectual debt to James Engel, whose name is retained on this edition to recognize his role as senior author in previous editions. David Kollat left the academic world to shape retail strategy at Limited Brands, but his contributions to understanding consumer behavior have been monumental and greatly appreciated.

This text is a culmination of efforts, assistance, research, and guidance from colleagues around the world. Foremost in importance are the thousands of researchers whose labors provide the essential content of knowledge about consumers and whose works are cited throughout the book. Our colleagues in the Association for Consumer Research have shaped our thinking about all aspects of consumer behavior. We are particularly fortunate to have outstanding colleagues at Ohio State University and Florida International University to stimulate our intellectual and pedagogical endeavors. We appreciate the assistance and helpful suggestions of Professors Neeli Bendapudi, Greg Allenby, Mike Barone, Jim Burroughs, Robert Burnkrant, Peter Dickson, Rao Unnava, Leslie Fine, Pat West, Curt Haugtvedt, William Lewis, and Deepak Sirdeshmukh.

Our thanks also go to the following colleagues who participated in an important pre-revision survey that helped shape the new edition: Barry Babin, University of Southern Mississippi; Zuzana Brochu, University of Vermont; James Dixon, Bowie State; Fred Ede, Benedict College; Peggy S. Gilbert, Southwest Missouri State University; Prnjal Gupta, University of Central Florida; Lynda Maddox, George Washington

University; Lynnea Mallalieu, Iowa State; Sue O'Curry, DePaul University; Esther Page-Wood, Western Michigan University; Kim Robertson, Trinity University; Larry Seibert, Indiana University Northwest; Ekkehard Stephan, University of Cologne; Jeff Stoltman, Wayne State University; Gail Tom, California State University; and Linda Wright, Mississippi State University.

A special thanks goes to Alan Ayers, Director of Consulting Services at Roger Blackwell Associates, for his extensive research on many of the innovative retail concepts featured in the book, as well as countless hours of copyediting and coordinating communication, to Professor Steve Burgess, who gave detailed critiques and suggestions for Roger Blackwell's chapters, and to Susanne Krohn and Jeremy Ericson for their research assistance. Professor Brian Wansink provided invaluable assistance to Paul Miniard in developing his understanding of consumption, assistance that greatly enhanced the thoroughness of Chapter 6 in particular. The authors wish to acknowledge the many hours spent by Shazad Mohammed, a doctoral student at Florida International University, in compiling the information needed for developing the "Honor Roll of Consumer Researchers." We received outstanding support from Mardell Glinski Schultz, the Senior Developmental Editor for *Consumer Behavior,* as well as Neil Marquardt, Executive Editor, and Brian Courter, Production Project Manager, at Thomson South-Western publishing. A special thanks goes to Deanna Ettinger for overseeing permissions and image selection, and to Terri Miller and Susan Van Etten for their tireless efforts in securing these permissions and identifying replacement images. Finally, we are very indebted to Jamie Armstrong for her assistance during the copyediting phase of the book and to Mark Smith, who served as copyeditor on this edition. His command of the English language and attention to even the smallest details has improved the book significantly. We also appreciate the help we received from the many executives and staff of the business organizations described in the book, including Lizzie Babarczy at Hitwise, Inc., who provided their valuable time and knowledge to be sure we "got it right" for the future leaders of the world.

On a personal note, we thank the people in our lives who support and assist us in all that we do. Roger Blackwell acknowledges the influence of his father, who taught him the joy of being a teacher, and his mother, who taught him the insights of a businessperson, as well as his children Becca, a fountain of creativity, and Christian, who practices with excellence a family tradition of four generations of teachers (and to Frances, the mother of Josette, Lindsey, and Jude—who no doubt will be teachers in the future). Thank you also to Mary Hiser for her ability and patience and to Kelley Hughes. Paul Miniard extends his appreciation to his wife, Shirley, and his daughter, Valeska, for their support, patience, and understanding during the many months he "lived" in the office working on this revision. And he is eternally grateful to his parents, Ernest and Shirley, who taught him the value of education and who supported him during his nine years as an undergraduate and graduate student at the University of Florida. Finally, he wishes to acknowledge the lifelong influence of Professor Joel Cohen, his mentor and exemplar during his days at the University of Florida, and Professor Peter Dickson, his best friend ever since their days as doctoral students.

## A Joy

The time a student spends studying at a university is a mere moment in the course of a lifetime of learning. A proverb states that "the wise teacher makes learning a joy." We hope this text helps make learning about consumer behavior a knowledge base that will serve you well as you enter the workforce and begin a lifetime of learning. But understanding and relating to people is fun, and studying consumer behavior from this text might turn out to be something you consider fun. Our desire is that it will be a book that for you will make learning a joy.

# Honor Roll of Consumer Researchers

You might wonder how the authors of a book you are beginning to read know all the concepts and principles written on the following pages. We don't, of course. We study the published research of our colleagues and attempt to summarize their research in a way that's easy to read, easy to understand, and easy to learn. We can't include research from every source, so we focus primarily on those journals considered to be the foundation of knowledge about consumer behavior and marketing.

Which consumer researchers have been the most active in generating knowledge about consumer behavior in recent times? One way to answer this question is to examine research productivity in terms of the number of articles published that pertain to consumer behavior. Of course, such articles appear in many different journals across a range of disciplines, from psychology to sociology to finance to home economics, and even more. Many of these articles are cited throughout the text. But it would take far more time and resources than currently available for us to examine the consumer-oriented research that has appeared across these literatures. It was possible, however, to examine the productivity of those individuals that have published in the two leading journals devoted to consumer research: the *Journal of Consumer Psychology (JCP)* and the *Journal of Consumer Research (JCR)*.

We therefore counted the number of articles authored or coauthored by an individual in these two journals over the twenty years from 1985 to 2004. Listed below are the names of researchers who contributed at least one article during this time period in either *JCP* or *JCR*. We wish to reemphasize that this analysis is limited by its narrow focus on two journals during a specific time frame. A broader assessment of research productivity, or even a different assessment procedure such as citation analysis (which examines the frequency a particular article is cited in other published articles), would lead to a different list of names. Even so, there is no denying the contributions made by the individuals identified here.

We divide our list of researchers publishing in *JCP* or *JCR* between 1985 and 2004 into three categories in recognition of their level of contribution: Highest Honors (those individuals who have authored or coauthored ten or more articles, a truly exceptional accomplishment), High Honors (those who've authored or coauthored between four and nine articles), and Honors (those authoring or coauthoring three or fewer articles).

Highest Honors (researchers with ten or more articles in *JCP* or *JCR*, 1985–2004)

| | | | |
|---|---|---|---|
| Kardes, Frank R. | | 16 | |
| Holbrook, Morris B. | 15 | Simonson, Itamar | 12 |
| Janiszweski, Chris | 15 | Thompson, Craig J. | 12 |
| Belk, Russel W. | 14 | Peracchio, Laura A. | 11 |
| Kahn, Barbara E. | 14 | Aaker, Jennifer L. | 10 |
| Alba, Joseph W. | 13 | John, Deborah Roedder | 10 |
| Maheswaran, Durairaj | 13 | Morwitz, Vickie G. | 10 |
| Mick, David Glen | 13 | Nowlis, Stephen M. | 10 |
| Bearden, William O. | 12 | Raghubir, Priyar | 10 |
| Lynch, John G., Jr. | 12 | Sherry, John F., Jr. | 10 |
| Meyers-Levy, Joan | 12 | Wyer, Robert S., Jr. | 10 |

High Honors (researchers with four to nine articles published in *JCP* or *JCR*, 1985–2004)

| | | | | |
|---|---|---|---|---|
| Batra, Rajeev | 9 | Price, Linda L. | 6 |
| Folkes, Valerie S. | 9 | Sanbonmatsu, David M. | 6 |
| Herr, Paul M. | 9 | Shavitt, Sharon | 6 |
| Hoch, Stephen J. | 9 | Stern, Barbara B. | 6 |
| Johar, Gita Venkataramani | 9 | Sujan, Mita | 6 |
| Menon, Geeta | 9 | Unnava, H. Rao | 6 |
| Baumgartner, Hans | 8 | Urbany, Joel E. | 6 |
| Hirschman, Elizabeth C. | 8 | Wooten, David B. | 6 |
| Hoyer, Wayne D. | 8 | Barone, Michael J. | 5 |
| Lichtenstein, Donald R. | 8 | Bloch, Peter H. | 5 |
| Pechmann, Cornelia | 8 | Brinberg, David | 5 |
| Posavac, Steven S. | 8 | Burroughs, James E. | 5 |
| Ratneshwar, S. | 8 | Campbell, Margaret C. | 5 |
| Richins, Marsha L. | 8 | Cronley, Maria L. | 5 |
| Shimp, Terrence A. | 8 | Drolet, Aimee | 5 |
| Sternthal, Brian | 8 | Gregan-Paxton, Jennifer | 5 |
| Wallendorf, Melanie | 8 | Grewal, Dhruv | 5 |
| Brucks, Merrie | 7 | Holt, Douglas B. | 5 |
| Chakravarti, Dipankar | 7 | Howard, Daniel J. | 5 |
| Chernev, Alexander | 7 | Huber, Joel | 5 |
| Fitzsimmons, Gavan J. | 7 | Hutchinson, J. Wesley | 5 |
| Goldberg, Marvin E. | 7 | Iacobucci, Dawn | 5 |
| Heath, Timothy B. | 7 | Kellaris, James J. | 5 |
| Keller, Kevin Lane | 7 | Keller, Punam Anand | 5 |
| Luce, Mary Frances | 7 | Kernan, Jerome B. | 5 |
| Phaum, Michel Tuan | 7 | Kirmani, Amna | 5 |
| Schmitt, Bernd H. | 7 | Kozinets, Robert V. | 5 |
| Schwartz, Norbert | 7 | Krishnan, H. Shanker | 5 |
| Shiv, Baba | 7 | Lehman, Donald R. | 5 |
| Stayman, Douglas M. | 7 | McQuarrie, Edward F. | 5 |
| Tybout, Alice M. | 7 | Meyer, Robert J. | 5 |
| Ariely, Dan | 6 | Monroe, Kent B. | 5 |
| Arnould, Eric J. | 6 | Moore, William L. | 5 |
| Bagozzi, Richard P. | 6 | Ozanne, Julie L. | 5 |
| Bettman, James R. | 6 | Payne, John W. | 5 |
| Block, Lauren G. | 6 | Priester, Joseph R. | 5 |
| Childers, Terry L. | 6 | Reed, Americus, II | 5 |
| Dhar, Ravi | 6 | Reingen, Peter H. | 5 |
| Escalas, Jennifer Edson | 6 | Schlosser, Ann E. | 5 |
| Gorn, Gerald J. | 6 | Sen, Sankar | 5 |
| Homer, Pamela M. | 6 | Sengupta, Jaideep | 5 |
| Jacoby, Jacob | 6 | Srivastava, Joydeep | 5 |
| Johnson, Eric J. | 6 | Staelin, Richard | 5 |
| Lowrey, Tina M. | 6 | Swait, Joffre | 5 |
| Marmorstein, Howard | 6 | Swasy, John L. | 5 |
| Miniard, Paul W. | 6 | Tavassoli, Nader T. | 5 |
| O'Guinn, Thomas C. | 6 | West, Patricia M. | 5 |
| Oliver, Richard L. | 6 | Zhang, Shi | 5 |
| Park, C. Whan | 6 | Adaval, Rashmi | 4 |

| | |
|---|---|
| Ahluwalia, Rohini | 4 |
| Anand, Punam | 4 |
| Anderson, Eugene W. | 4 |
| Beatty, Sharon E. | 4 |
| Broniarczyk, Susan M. | 4 |
| Burton, Scot | 4 |
| Chatterjee, Subimal | 4 |
| Cohen, Joel B. | 4 |
| Cole, Catherine A. | 4 |
| Dahl, Darren W. | 4 |
| Dickson, Peter R. | 4 |
| Duhacheck, Adam | 4 |
| Edell, Julie A. | 4 |
| Grayson, Kent | 4 |
| Gurhan-Canli, Zenyep | 4 |
| Heckler, Susan E. | 4 |
| Hui, Michael K. | 4 |
| Inman, J. Jeffrey | 4 |
| Irwin, Julie, R. | 4 |
| Johnson, Michael D. | 4 |
| Kahle, Lynn R. | 4 |
| Kamakura, Wagner A. | 4 |
| Kamins, Michael A. | 4 |
| Kleine, Robert E., III | 4 |
| Kleine, Susan Schultz | 4 |
| Lastovicka, John L. | 4 |
| Leclerk, France | 4 |

| | |
|---|---|
| Loken, Barbara | 4 |
| Mackenzie, Scott B. | 4 |
| Mazursky, David | 4 |
| Mitchell, Andrew A. | 4 |
| Moorman, Christine | 4 |
| Morrin, Maureen | 4 |
| Mothersbaugh, David L. | 4 |
| Munch, James M. | 4 |
| Muthukrishnan, A. V. | 4 |
| Netemeyer, Richard G. | 4 |
| Osselaer, Stijn M. J. van | 4 |
| Otnes, Cele C. | 4 |
| Pan, Yigang | 4 |
| Petty, Richard E. | 4 |
| Ratchford, Brian T. | 4 |
| Rindfleisch, Aric | 4 |
| Rose, Randall L. | 4 |
| Schul, Yaacov | 4 |
| Schumann, David W. | 4 |
| Shapiro, Stewart | 4 |
| Soman, Dilip | 4 |
| Steenkamp, Jan-Benedict E. M. | 4 |
| Teel, Jesse E. | 4 |
| Wells, William D. | 4 |
| Winer, Russell S. | 4 |
| Wright, Peter | 4 |
| Zinkhan, George M. | 4 |

Honors (researchers with one to three articles published in *JCP* or *JCR*, 1985–2004)

| | |
|---|---|
| Allen, Chris T. | 3 |
| Anderson, Paul F. | 3 |
| Arnold, Stephen J. | 3 |
| Basu, Kunal | 3 |
| Bechwati, Nada Nasr | 3 |
| Brown, Christina L. | 3 |
| Burke, Raymond R. | 3 |
| Burnkrant, Robert E. | 3 |
| Calder, Bobby J. | 3 |
| Carlson, Les | 3 |
| Chattopadhyay, Amitava | 3 |
| Cook, Alan D. J. | 3 |
| Cote, Joseph A. | 3 |
| Coupey, Eloise | 3 |
| Cox, Anthony D. | 3 |
| Deighton, John | 3 |
| Desarbo, Wayne S. | 3 |
| Dube-Rioux, Laurette | 3 |
| Erdem, Tulin | 3 |

| | |
|---|---|
| Faber, Ronald J. | 3 |
| Fazio, H. Russell | 3 |
| Fischer, Eileen | 3 |
| Fisher, Robert J. | 3 |
| Fleming, Monique A. | 3 |
| Fornell, Claes | 3 |
| Fournier, Susan | 3 |
| Friestad, Marian | 3 |
| Gaeth, Gary J. | 3 |
| Goodstien, Ronald C. | 3 |
| Gupta, Sunil | 3 |
| Haugtvedt, Curtis R. | 3 |
| Hawkins, Scott A. | 3 |
| Hill, Ronald Paul | 3 |
| Hoffman, Donna L. | 3 |
| Houghton, David C. | 3 |
| Houston, Michael J. | 3 |
| Jain, Shailendra Pratap | 3 |
| Jewell, Robert D. | 3 |

| | | | | |
|---|---|---|---|---|
| Klein, Noreen M. | 3 | Brown, Steven P. | 2 |
| Kuss, Alfred | 3 | Brown, Tom J. | 2 |
| Leong, Siew Meng | 3 | Brumbaugh, Anne M. | 2 |
| Levy, Sidney J. | 3 | Brunel, Frederic F. | 2 |
| Locander, William B. | 3 | Burke, Marian Chapman | 2 |
| Loewenstein, George F. | 3 | Carmon, Ziv | 2 |
| Luna, David | 3 | Carpenter, Gregory S. | 2 |
| MacInnis, Deborah J. | 3 | Celsi, Richard L. | 2 |
| Macklin, M. Carole | 3 | Chaiken, Shelly | 2 |
| Mandel, Naomi | 3 | Chakravarti, Amitav | 2 |
| Mantel, Susan Powell | 3 | Churchill, Gilbert A., Jr. | 2 |
| Markman, Arthur B. | 3 | Clemons, D. Scott | 2 |
| Mazumdar, Tridib | 3 | Cooper, Lee G. | 2 |
| McCarthy, Michael S. | 3 | Corfman, Kim P. | 2 |
| Meyvis, Tom | 3 | Cotte, June | 2 |
| Millbert, Sandra J. | 3 | Coursey, Don L. | 2 |
| Moon, Youngme | 3 | Cowley, Elizabeth | 2 |
| Moreau, C. Page | 3 | Cox, Dena | 2 |
| Mowen, John C. | 3 | Creyer, Elizabeth H. | 2 |
| Mukherjee, Ashesh | 3 | Cunha, Marcus, Jr. | 2 |
| Murray, Jeff B. | 3 | Curasi, Carolyn Folkman | 2 |
| Murray, John P., Jr. | 3 | Curry, David J. | 2 |
| Novak, Thomas P. | 3 | Dacin, Peter A. | 2 |
| Page, Christine M. | 3 | Davis, Harry L. | 2 |
| Peterson, Robert A. | 3 | DeBerry-Spence, Benet | 2 |
| Pollio, Howard R. | 3 | Deshpande, Rohit | 2 |
| Rao, Akshay R. | 3 | Dholakia, Utpal M. | 2 |
| Ratner, Rebecca K. | 3 | Diehl, Kristin | 2 |
| Rook, Dennis W. | 3 | Dillon, William R. | 2 |
| Rose, Gregory M. | 3 | Dowling, Grahame R. | 2 |
| Ross, William T., Jr. | 3 | Engle, Randall W. | 2 |
| Ruth, Julie A. | 3 | Fedorikhin, Alexander | 2 |
| Sawyer, Alan G. | 3 | Feick, Lawrence | 2 |
| Schindler, Robert M. | 3 | Feinberg, Richard A. | 2 |
| Schouten, John W. | 3 | Fishbein, Martin | 2 |
| Scott, Linda M. | 3 | Fisher, Gregory W. | 2 |
| Sherman, Steven J. | 3 | Forehand, Mark R. | 2 |
| Shrum, L. J. | 3 | Frederick, Donald G. | 2 |
| Simmons, Carolyn J. | 3 | Frenzen, Jonathan K. | 2 |
| Strahilevitz, Michal | 3 | Friedman, Monroe | 2 |
| Wanke, Michaela | 3 | Gardner, Meryl P. | 2 |
| Ward, James C. | 3 | Gengler, Charles | 2 |
| Warlop, Luk | 3 | Gershoff, Andrew D. | 2 |
| Wernerfelt, Birger | 3 | Gibbs, Brian J. | 2 |
| Wilkes, Robert E. | 3 | Glazer, Rashi | 2 |
| Williams, Patti | 3 | Godek, John | 2 |
| Wong, Nancy Y. | 3 | Goodwin, Cathy | 2 |
| Wood, Stacy L. | 3 | Gould, Stephen J. | 2 |
| Yi, Youjae | 3 | Gourville, John T. | 2 |
| Boulding, William | 2 | Graham, John L. | 2 |
| Briley, Donnel A. | 2 | Greenleaf, Eric A. | 2 |
| Britton, Julie Edell | 2 | Grier, Sonya A. | 2 |

| | | | | |
|---|---|---|---|---|
| Grossbart, Sanford | 2 | Nayakankuppum, D. J. | 2 |
| Ha, Young-Won | 2 | Nedungadi, Prakash | 2 |
| Hartwick, Jon | 2 | Obermiller, Carl | 2 |
| Hastak, Manoj | 2 | Okada, Erica Mina | 2 |
| Haubl, Gerald | 2 | Olsen, Jerry C. | 2 |
| Haugtvedt, Curtis P. | 2 | Ostrom, Amy | 2 |
| Hauser, John R. | 2 | Park, Jong-Won | 2 |
| Helgeson, James G. | 2 | Pavia, Teresa M. | 2 |
| Ho, Edward A. | 2 | Peck, Joann | 2 |
| Hong, Sung-Tai | 2 | Penaloza, Lisa | 2 |
| Hornik, Jacob | 2 | Pieters, Rik G. M. | 2 |
| Hsee, Christopher K. | 2 | Pitts, Robert E. | 2 |
| Huffman, Cynthia | 2 | Powell, Martha C. | 2 |
| Hyatt, Eva M. | 2 | Purohit, Devavrat | 2 |
| Hyun, Yong J. | 2 | Raj, S. P. | 2 |
| Isen, Alice M. | 2 | Ray, Michael L. | 2 |
| Iyer, Easwar S. | 2 | Reilly, Michael D. | 2 |
| Jaccard, James J. | 2 | Romeo, Jean B. | 2 |
| Joachimsthaler, Erich A. | 2 | Rothschild, Michael L. | 2 |
| Joiner, Christopher | 2 | Russel, Cristel Antonia | 2 |
| Joy, Annamma | 2 | Russo, Edward J. | 2 |
| Kalyanaram, Gurumurthy | 2 | Schurr, Paul H. | 2 |
| Kasser, Tim | 2 | Scott, Carol A. | 2 |
| Kates, Steven M. | 2 | Sheldon, Kennon M. | 2 |
| Kent, Robert J. | 2 | Shocker, Allan D. | 2 |
| Kidwell, Blair | 2 | Sirdeshmukh, Deepak | 2 |
| Kim, John | 2 | Smith, Daniel C. | 2 |
| Krishna, Aradhna | 2 | Smith, Robert E. | 2 |
| Krishnamurthi, Lakshman | 2 | Smith, Ruth Ann | 2 |
| Krishnamurthy, Parthasarathy | 2 | Snyder, David J. | 2 |
| Kumar, Anand | 2 | Solomon, Sheldon | 2 |
| Lee, Angela Y. | 2 | Sood, Sanjay | 2 |
| Lee, Julie Anne | 2 | Spangenberg, Eric R. | 2 |
| Levin, Irwin P. | 2 | Spiggle, Susan | 2 |
| Lurie, Nicholas H. | 2 | Spira, Joan Scattone | 2 |
| Machleit, Karen A. | 2 | Sprott, David E. | 2 |
| Madden, Thomas J. | 2 | Stewart, David W. | 2 |
| Malaviya, Prashant | 2 | Stuart, Elnora W. | 2 |
| Mason, Charlotte H. | 2 | Teas, R. Kenneth | 2 |
| McCabe, Deborah Brown | 2 | Thorson, Esther | 2 |
| McCracken, Grant | 2 | Tian, Kelly Tepper | 2 |
| McGill, Ann L. | 2 | Tsiros, Michael | 2 |
| Mehta, Raj | 2 | Viswanathan, Madhubalan | 2 |
| Menon, Satya | 2 | Wansink, Brian | 2 |
| Middlestadt, Susan E. | 2 | Warshaw, Paul R. | 2 |
| Mitchell, Deborah J. | 2 | Wedell, Douglas H. | 2 |
| Mitra, Anusree | 2 | Whittler, Tommy E. | 2 |
| Mittal, Vikas | 2 | Xia, Lan | 2 |
| Moore, David J. | 2 | Yadav, Manjit S. | 2 |
| Moschis, George P. | 2 | Yoon, Carolyn | 2 |
| Myers, John G. | 2 | Zeelenberg, Marcel | 2 |
| Nakamoto, Kent | 2 | Zhao, Rongrong | 2 |

Aaker, David A. 1
Aalst, Marcel van 1
Abdul-Muhmin, Alhassan G. 1
Abe, Shuzo 1
Abeele, Piet Vanden 1
Achenreiner, Gwen Bachmann 1
Ackerman, David 1
Ackerman, Lee J. 1
Adamowicz, Wiktor 1
Aggarwal, Pankaj 1
Agrawal, Jagdish 1
Agrawal, Nidhi 1
Agrawal, Sanjeeve 1
Ahtola, Olli T. 1
Ahuvia, Aaron C. 1
Ajzen, Icek 1
Albaum, Gerald 1
Alden, Dana L. 1
Allen, Douglas E. 1
Allison, Scott T. 1
Alon, Anat 1
Alpert Frank H. 1
Andrade, Eduardo B. 1
Andrews, J. Craig 1
Ansari, Asim 1
Antil, John H. 1
Antonides, Gerrit 1
Aparicio, Manuel, IV 1
Applbau, Kalman 1
Appleby, Drew C. 1
Areni, Charles S. 1
Argo, Jennifer J. 1
Armstrong, Gary M. 1
Armstrong, J. Scott 1
Arnold, Todd J. 1
Arora, Neeraj 1
Arsel, Zeynep 1
Artz, Nancy 1
Askegaard, Soren 1
Au, Kevin 1
Avnet, Tamar 1
Babin, Barry J. 1
Bahn, Kenneth D. 1
Baker, William E. 1
Balakrishnan, P. V. (Sundar) 1
Balasubramanian, Siva K. 1
Ball, Dwayne A. 1
Bamossy, Gary 1
Baralou, Lawrence W. 1
Bardley, Samuel D., III 1
Bargh, John A. 1
Barlow, Todd 1

Barnes, Paul 1
Barrickman, P. J. 1
Barwise, T. Patrick 1
Basil, Michael D. 1
Basuroy, Suman 1
Baumeister, Roy F. 1
Bazerman, Max H. 1
Beggan, James K. 1
Bell, David R. 1
Beltramini, Richard F. 1
Bergadaa, Michelle 1
Bergami, Massimo 1
Bergen, Mark E. 1
Bhalla, Gaurav 1
Bhargava, Mukesh 1
Bian, Wen-Qiang 1
Bierley, Calvin 1
Bijmolt, Tammo H. A. 1
Biocca, Frank 1
Biswas, Abhijit 1
Bither, Stewart W. 1
Black, William C. 1
Blair, Irene V. 1
Blari, Edward 1
Blazing, Jennifer 1
Bless, Herbert 1
Bloom, Paul N. 1
Bodur, H. Onur 1
Boller, Gregory W. 1
Bolton, Ruth N. 1
Bone, Paula Fitzgerald 1
Boninger, David S. 1
Bonsu, Samuel K. 1
Borgmann, Albert 1
Boush, David M. 1
Brannon, Laura A. 1
Brasel, Adam S. 1
Braun, Kathryn A. 1
Brendl, C. Miguel 1
Brenner, Lyle 1
Briesch, Richard A. 1
Brinol, Pablo 1
Bristol, Terry 1
Bristor, Julia M. 1
Brock, Timothy C. 1
Bronnenberg, Bart J. 1
Brooks, Charles M. 1
Brooks, Michael A. 1
Brown, Jacqueline Johnson 1
Brown, William J. 1
Bryant, Jennings 1
Bryant, W. Keith 1

| | | | |
|---|---|---|---|
| Buchan, Nancy R. | 1 | Dawson, Scott | 1 |
| Buchanan, Bruse | 1 | De Wilde, Els | 1 |
| Buckley, M. Ronald | 1 | De Zwaan, Martina | 1 |
| Bucklin, Randolph E. | 1 | Dean, Dwane H. | 1 |
| Buhl, Claus | 1 | Debevec, Kathleen | 1 |
| Burnett, Melissa S. | 1 | Decarlo, Thomas E. | 1 |
| Burns, Mary Jane | 1 | Dekleva, Christine | 1 |
| Burroughs, W. Jeffrey | 1 | DeMoss, Michelle | 1 |
| Buyukkurt, B. Kemal | 1 | Denison, Daniel R. | 1 |
| Cacioppo, John | 1 | Denton, Frank | 1 |
| Camargo, Eduardo G. | 1 | Denzin, Norman K. | 1 |
| Camon, Ziv | 1 | Desai, Kalpesh Kaushik | 1 |
| Chakraborty, Goutam | 1 | Dholakia, Ruby Roy | 1 |
| Chandon, Pierre | 1 | Diamond, William D. | 1 |
| Chandran, Sucharita | 1 | Dick, Alan | 1 |
| Chandrashekaran, Murali | 1 | Donthu, Naveen | 1 |
| Chapin, Kathryn | 1 | Dornoff, Ronald J. | 1 |
| Cheema, Amar | 1 | Douglas, Susan P. | 1 |
| Chen, Hong C. | 1 | Drew, James H. | 1 |
| Chiang, Kuan-Pin | 1 | Dreze, Xavier | 1 |
| Choi, S. Chan | 1 | Driver, B. L. | 1 |
| Christenson, Gary A. | 1 | D'Rozario, Denver | 1 |
| Cline, Thomas W. | 1 | Durvasula, Srinivas | 1 |
| Cohen, Lizabeth | 1 | Dutta-Bergman, Mohan J. | 1 |
| Coon, Gregory S. | 1 | Earl, Peter E. | 1 |
| Costa, Arnold | 1 | Eaton, John P. | 1 |
| Costley, Carolyn | 1 | Edwards, Elizabeth A. | 1 |
| Cote, Jane | 1 | Ehrenberg, Andrew S. C. | 1 |
| Coulter, Robin A. | 1 | Einwiller, Sabine | 1 |
| Cowley, Ayn E. | 1 | Ekstrom, Karin M. | 1 |
| Craik, Fergus I.M. | 1 | Ellen, Pam Scholder | 1 |
| Creek, Kelly Jo | 1 | Elliott, Michael T. | 1 |
| Cripps, John D. | 1 | Elliott, Richard | 1 |
| Crockett, David | 1 | Endler, Norman S. | 1 |
| Crosen, Rachel T. A. | 1 | Erb, Hans-Peter | 1 |
| Cross, Gary | 1 | Erevelles, Sunil | 1 |
| Csikszentmihalyi, Mihaly | 1 | Erickson, Gary M. | 1 |
| Currim, Imran | 1 | Eroglu, Sevgin A. | 1 |
| Dabholkar, Pratibha A. | 1 | Esteban, Gabriel | 1 |
| Dalakas, Vassilis | 1 | Fan, Xiucheng | 1 |
| Dame, Jill Ann | 1 | Farley, John U. | 1 |
| Danko, William D. | 1 | Farquhar, Peter H. | 1 |
| Darden, William R. | 1 | Faulds, David J. | 1 |
| Dardis, Rachel | 1 | Feltham, Tammi S. | 1 |
| Darke, Peter R. | 1 | Fennis, Bob M. | 1 |
| Darley, William K. | 1 | Fern, Edward F. | 1 |
| Das, Enny H. H. J. | 1 | Filiatrault, Pierre | 1 |
| Das, Samar | 1 | Fine, Leslie, M. | 1 |
| Daugherty, Terry | 1 | Firat, A. Fuat | 1 |
| Davies, Anthony | 1 | Fishe, Raymond P. H. | 1 |
| Dawar, Niraj | 1 | Florsheim, Renee | 1 |
| Dawson, Ian | 1 | Ford, Gary T. | 1 |

| | | | |
|---|---|---|---|
| Kerr, David | 1 | Lonial, Subhash C. | 1 |
| Kim, Dong Ki | 1 | Lord, Kenneth R. | 1 |
| Kim, Juyoung S. | 1 | Louviere, Jordan J. | 1 |
| Kim, Woo-Sung | 1 | Lozada, Hector | 1 |
| Kim, Young Chan | 1 | Lutz, Richard J. | 1 |
| Kirby, Patrick N. | 1 | Lux, David S. | 1 |
| Kisielius, Jolita | 1 | Lynn, Michael | 1 |
| Kivetz, Ran | 1 | Lysonski, Steven | 1 |
| Klein, David M. | 1 | MacCannell, Dean | 1 |
| Knasko, Susan C. | 1 | MacEvoy, Bruce | 1 |
| Knight, Susan J. | 1 | Mackie, Diane M. | 1 |
| Kolbe, Richard H. | 1 | MacLachlan, Douglas L. | 1 |
| Koltesky, Susan | 1 | Maiorelle, Melissa J. | 1 |
| Konakayama, Akira | 1 | Maloy, Kate | 1 |
| Koomen, Willem | 1 | Malter, Alan J. | 1 |
| Kopalle, Praveen K. | 1 | Malthouse, Edward C. | 1 |
| Kornish, Laura J. | 1 | Manchander, Puneet | 1 |
| Koslow, Scott | 1 | Manchander, Rajesh V. | 1 |
| Kover, Arthur, Jr. | 1 | Mangold, W. Glynn | 1 |
| Krish, Rajan | 1 | Manning, Kenneth C. | 1 |
| Kristel, Orie V. | 1 | Mano, Haim | 1 |
| Kropp, Frederic | 1 | Manolis, Chris | 1 |
| Kumar, Ajith | 1 | Maoz, Eyal | 1 |
| Kuntze, Ronald J. | 1 | Markus, Hazel | 1 |
| Kwak, Hyokjin | 1 | Martin, Brett A. S. | 1 |
| Lacher, Kathleen T. | 1 | Martin, Ingrid M. | 1 |
| Laczniak, Russel N. | 1 | Martinec, Radan | 1 |
| Lane, Paul M. | 1 | Martino, Victor | 1 |
| Larsen, Val | 1 | Mason, Marlys J. | 1 |
| Lau-Gesk, Loraine G. | 1 | Mathwick, Charla | 1 |
| Laverie, Debra A. | 1 | Matta, Shashi | 1 |
| Lavin, Marilyn | 1 | Mattila, Anna | 1 |
| Law, Sharmistha | 1 | Matulich, Erika | 1 |
| Lawson, Robert | 1 | Mauser, Gary A. | 1 |
| Lee, Yih Hwai | 1 | Mayhew, Lenn E. | 1 |
| Lefkoff-Hagius, Roxanne | 1 | Mazis, Michael B. | 1 |
| Leigh, Thomas W. | 1 | Mazzon, Jose Alfonso | 1 |
| Leonard-Barton, Dorothy | 1 | McAlexander, James H. | 1 |
| Levav, Johnathan | 1 | McAlister, Leigh | 1 |
| Levin, Aron M. | 1 | McCullough, James | 1 |
| Lewis, Philip A. | 1 | McDaniel, Stephen W. | 1 |
| Li, Hairong | 1 | McGrath, Mary Ann | 1 |
| Li, Wai-Kwan | 1 | McGraw, A. Peter | 1 |
| Liefeld, John | 1 | McGuire, William J. | 1 |
| Lim, Jeen-Su | 1 | McKenzie, Karyn | 1 |
| Lin, Hi-Yuan | 1 | McQueen, Josh | 1 |
| Lin, Ying-Ching | 1 | McSweeney, Frances K. | 1 |
| Lindquist, Jay D. | 1 | Meeds, Robert | 1 |
| Lipkus, Isaac M. | 1 | Mela, Carl F. | 1 |
| Little, John D. C. | 1 | Meloy, Maragret G. | 1 |
| Liu, Raymond R. | 1 | Menasco, Michael B. | 1 |
| Lodish, Leonard M. | 1 | Mermis, Maria | 1 |

| | | | |
|---|---|---|---|
| Messner, Claude | 1 | Patrick, Vanessa M. | 1 |
| Metcalf, Barbara L. | 1 | Patterson, Maggie Jones | 1 |
| Meyvis, Tom | 1 | Patton, Charles | 1 |
| Midgley, David F. | 1 | Paul, Pallab | 1 |
| Millard, Robert T. | 1 | Pavelchak, Mark A. | 1 |
| Milliman, Ronald E. | 1 | Perner, Lars | 1 |
| Mitchell, James | 1 | Perr, Andrea L. | 1 |
| Mizerski, Richard | 1 | Peter, Anil C. | 1 |
| Mobley, Mary F. | 1 | Peter, J. Paul | 1 |
| Moe, Wendy W. | 1 | Peters, Cara Okleshen | 1 |
| Mohr, Lois A. | 1 | Peterson, Steven P. | 1 |
| Molina, David J. | 1 | Petroshius, Susan M. | 1 |
| Moore, Danny L. | 1 | Phillips, Diane M. | 1 |
| Moore, Elizabeth S. | 1 | Pluzinski, Carol | 1 |
| Moore, Ellen M. | 1 | Podsakoff, Philip M. | 1 |
| Moore, Marian Chapman | 1 | Pollay, Richard W. | 1 |
| Moore, Melissa | 1 | Pontes, Manuel C. | 1 |
| Moorthy, Sridhar | 1 | Pounds, Julia C. | 1 |
| Morgan, James N. | 1 | Pracejus, John W. | 1 |
| Morgan, Michael S. | 1 | Prelec, Drazen | 1 |
| Morris, Louis A. | 1 | Pruyn, Ad Th.H. | 1 |
| Morris, Michael W. | 1 | Pullig, Chris | 1 |
| Morrison, Michelle | 1 | Punj, Girish N. | 1 |
| Mukhopadhyay, Anirban | 1 | Puri, Radhika | 1 |
| Mulani, Narendra | 1 | Puto, Christopher P. | 1 |
| Muniz, Albert M., Jr. | 1 | Qualls, William J. | 1 |
| Murray, Kyle B. | 1 | Raghunathan, Rajagopal | 1 |
| Narayanan, Sunder | 1 | Ragsdale, E. K. Easton | 1 |
| Nasco, Suzanne A. | 1 | Rajecki, D. W. | 1 |
| Nelson, Kim A. | 1 | Raju, P. S. | 1 |
| Nelson, Paul | 1 | Ramachander, S. | 1 |
| Newman, Bruce I. | 1 | Raman, Kalyan | 1 |
| Niedrich, Ronald W. | 1 | Ramanathan, Suresh | 1 |
| Noel, Hayden | 1 | Ramaswami, S. | 1 |
| Nolan, Catherine A. | 1 | Ramaswamy, Sridhar N. | 1 |
| Nordhielm, Christie L. | 1 | Ramaswamy, Venkatram | 1 |
| Norman, Andrew T. | 1 | Rao, C. P. | 1 |
| Notani, Arti Sahni | 1 | Rao, Vithala R. | 1 |
| Novernsky, Nathan | 1 | Reeves, Bryon | 1 |
| Nuttavuthisit, Krittinee | 1 | Reid, Katherine A. | 1 |
| O'Curry, Sue | 1 | Reinartz, Werner J. | 1 |
| Ofir, Chezy | 1 | Ridgway, Nancy M. | 1 |
| Olney, Thomas J. | 1 | Rigdon, Edward | 1 |
| Olsen, G. Douglas | 1 | Rimer, Barbara K. | 1 |
| Olshavsky, Richard W. | 1 | Riney, Bobye J. | 1 |
| Ornstein, Stanley I. | 1 | Ritchie, Robin J. B. | 1 |
| Oropesa, R. S. | 1 | Ritson, Mark | 1 |
| O'Shaughnessy, John | 1 | Robertson, Thomas S. | 1 |
| Oswald, Laura R. | 1 | Robinson, Michael | 1 |
| Painton, Scott | 1 | Roehm, Michelle L. | 1 |
| Palan, Kay M. | 1 | Roggeveen, Anne L. | 1 |
| Park, Kiwan | 1 | Romer, Daniel | 1 |

| | | | |
|---|---|---|---|
| Rosa, Jose Antonio | 1 | Snell, Jackie | 1 |
| Roseberg, Edward | 1 | Snyder, Rita | 1 |
| Rosen, Dennis L. | 1 | Soberon-Ferrer, Horacio | 1 |
| Rosenstien, Alvin J. | 1 | Soll, Jack B. | 1 |
| Rossiter, John B. | 1 | Sommer, Robert | 1 |
| Roth, Martin S. | 1 | Spaulding, Melinda | 1 |
| Rottenstreich, Yuval | 1 | Spears, Nancy | 1 |
| Rozin, Paul | 1 | Spence, Mark T. | 1 |
| Rubin, Rose M. | 1 | Spreng, Richard A. | 1 |
| Russel, Gary J. | 1 | Sproles, George B. | 1 |
| Ryu, Gangseog | 1 | Srinavasan, Narasimhan | 1 |
| Saegert, Joel | 1 | Srivastava, Rajendra K. | 1 |
| Salisbury, Linda Court | 1 | Srul, Thomas K. | 1 |
| Sam Min, Kyeong | 1 | Stamey, Mark | 1 |
| Sarin, Rakesh K. | 1 | Stapel, Diedreck A. | 1 |
| Sauer, Paul L. | 1 | Steckel, Joel H. | 1 |
| Saxton, Mary Jane | 1 | Stephens, Debra | 1 |
| Schau, Hope Jensen | 1 | Stiving, Mark | 1 |
| Scheurich, Jim | 1 | Storm, Diana | 1 |
| Schmittlein, David | 1 | Strebel, Judi | 1 |
| Schneier, Wendy L. | 1 | Stuenkel, Kathleen J. | 1 |
| Schwartz, Albert | 1 | Sudharshan, D. | 1 |
| Scott, Cliff | 1 | Sudman, Seymour | 1 |
| Sethuraman, Raj | 1 | Suri, Rajneesh | 1 |
| Sexton, Richard J. | 1 | Swaminathan, Vanitha | 1 |
| Shahin, Kimary N. | 1 | Swan, John E. | 1 |
| Shamdasani, Prem N. | 1 | Swan, Suzzane | 1 |
| Shandler, Bruce | 1 | Swinyard, William R. | 1 |
| Shapiro, Jon M. | 1 | Szykman, Lisa R. | 1 |
| Sharma, Arun | 1 | Talpade, Salil | 1 |
| Sharma, Subhash | 1 | Talukdar, Debabrata | 1 |
| Sheppard, Blair H. | 1 | Tambyah, Siok Kuan | 1 |
| Shermohamad, Ali | 1 | Tan, Chin Tiong | 1 |
| Sherrell, Daniel L. | 1 | Tangpanichdee, Vanchai | 1 |
| Sheth, Jagdish N. | 1 | Tansuhaj, Patriya S. | 1 |
| Shirai, Miyuri | 1 | Tasaki, Lori H. | 1 |
| Shugan, Steven M. | 1 | Tepper, Kelly | 1 |
| Shulman, David | 1 | Tetlock, Philip E. | 1 |
| Sieben, Wanda A. | 1 | Thakor, Mrugank V. | 1 |
| Siebler, Frank | 1 | Thomas, Gloria Penn | 1 |
| Siegel, Harvey | 1 | Tietje, Brian C. | 1 |
| Silk, Tim | 1 | Tormala, Zakary L. | 1 |
| Silver, Steven D. | 1 | Touchstone, Ellen E. | 1 |
| Simonson, Yael | 1 | Trifts, Valerie | 1 |
| Sin, Leo Yatming | 1 | Tripp, Carolyn | 1 |
| Singh, Leher | 1 | Troester, Maura | 1 |
| Singh, Surendra N. | 1 | Troutman, Tracy | 1 |
| Sirsi, Ajay K. | 1 | Tsal, Yehoshua | 1 |
| Sivaraman, Anuradha | 1 | Tse, David K. | 1 |
| Smith, Darlene B. | 1 | Twitchell, James B. | 1 |
| Smith, Karen H. | 1 | Urbany, Glen A. | 1 |
| Smith, Scott M. | 1 | Ursic, Anthony C. | 1 |

| | | | | |
|---|---|---|---|---|
| Ursic, Michael L. | 1 | Wilke, William L. | 1 |
| Ursic, Virginia L. | 1 | Williams, Carol J. | 1 |
| Van Auken, Stuart | 1 | Wilton, Peter C. | 1 |
| Van Houwelingen, Jeannet H. | 1 | Wirtz, Jochen | 1 |
| Van Ittersum, Koert | 1 | Witkowski, Terrence H. | 1 |
| Van Raaij, W. Fred | 1 | Wogalter, Michael S. | 1 |
| Vannieuwkerk, Renee | 1 | Woltman Elpers, | |
| Varey, Carol | 1 | Josephine L. C. M. | 1 |
| Velthuijsen, Aart S. | 1 | Wong, John K. | 1 |
| Venkatesh, Alladi | 1 | Woodruff, Robert B. | 1 |
| Verhoef, Peter C. | 1 | Woodside, Arch G. | 1 |
| Verzer, Robert W., Jr. | 1 | Wright, Alice A. | 1 |
| Vogt, Christine A. | 1 | Yagci, Mehmet I. | 1 |
| Volker, Carol B. | 1 | Yeung, Catherine W. M. | 1 |
| Wagner, Janet | 1 | Yi, Sunghwan | 1 |
| Wang Jing | 1 | Yorkston, Eric | 1 |
| Wang, Cheng Lu | 1 | Yu, Fang | 1 |
| Warren, Wendy L. | 1 | Yu, Shihti | 1 |
| Wathieu, Luc | 1 | Zaichkowsky, Judith Lynne | 1 |
| Webster, Cynthia | 1 | Zajonc, R. B. | 1 |
| Wegener, Duane T. | 1 | Zatlman, Gerald | 1 |
| Weigold, Michael F. | 1 | Zauberman, Gal | 1 |
| Weilbaker, Dan C. | 1 | Zeithaml, Valarie | 1 |
| Weiner, Bernard | 1 | Zettelmeyer, Florian | 1 |
| Wertenbroch, Klaus | 1 | Zhang, Jiao | 1 |
| Westbrook, Robert A. | 1 | Zhang, Yan | 1 |
| White, Tiffany Barnett | 1 | Zhao, Xiande | 1 |
| Whitney, John C., Jr. | 1 | Zhou, Nan | 1 |
| Wiener, Joshua Lyle | 1 | Ziamou, Paschalina (Lilia) | 1 |
| Wilk, Richard, R. | 1 | | |

We appreciate the work of our colleagues who have contributed to the stream of research on consumer behavior and marketing, thus making it possible for us to write *Consumer Behavior,* tenth edition.

Roger Blackwell
Paul W. Miniard

# Introduction to Consumer Behavior

## PART 1

Every day in nearly every way, consumer behavior is woven into the fabric of our lives, confronting each of us with a multitude of important decisions. Whether you're deciding on a college major, a career to pursue, food to eat, clothes to wear, a television show to watch, or an Internet site to visit, you are participating in the activities most important to the study of consumer behavior.

Chapter 1 lays the foundation for studying these types of decisions by identifying the activities included in consumer behavior and the methods consumer analysts use to observe, record, and analyze consumer reactions, behaviors, and trends. These activities affect many areas of your life as well as the lives of others. They also provide information you can use to not only develop marketing strategy and influence consumers to buy from the organization in which you work, but also use to become a smarter consumer yourself.

Chapter 2 describes how to create customer-centric organizations, incorporating consumer behavior into strategic planning for both nonprofit and for-profit organizations. In today's hypercompetitive business environment, delighting consumers is required to remain competitive, regardless of the size or scope of the organization. Some of the most successful firms are striving to become *customer-centric*, which involves organizing every activity around the needs and behavior of key customers. That's accomplished by identifying consumers' needs, formulating strategies to fulfill those needs, and monitoring changing trends through consumer research and analysis to keep consumer behavior at the top of all executives' list of priorities. At the forefront of implementation is the concept of segmentation—the reality that, although they may share some similarities, people are not all alike. The most effective organizations focus on consumer groups with similar *behavior*, not just common characteristics.

As you read this text, ask yourself how its content relates to your life and career. You may find that consumer behavior touches and mirrors your daily life more than any other course you will take. Welcome to what we hope will be a great adventure and a lifelong topic of interest.

# Chapter 1

# Consumer Behavior and Consumer Research

## Opening Vignette

It's 7:00 a.m. and a sudden blare of music by Vicente Fernandez radiates through the bedroom from a Panasonic clock radio. A human hand reaches out from beneath a sea of Polo flannel sheets bought on sale at T.J. Maxx and fumbles for the "off" button, just as an advertisement for Donatos Pizza begins on the radio. Another day in the life of Carlos, a twenty-year-old university student, has begun.

Carlos races downstairs to see his younger brother and sister fighting over the last Pop Tart and his mother stuffing Oscar Mayer Lunchables into their backpacks. Carlos lives with his family not far from campus, deciding to save the money he makes from his part-time job as a restaurant reviewer for a Spanish-language newspaper to help his family pay rent. Rather than take time to eat breakfast at home, Carlos rushes to campus, picking up coffee and a muffin at Starbucks while listening to Chalino Sanchez and Ramon Ayala on his iPod. "Too bad Starbucks doesn't have *pan dulce* like the *concha* my grandmother makes in Mexico City," he mutters.

After attending his accounting class, Carlos remembers that today his consumer behavior class is featuring a visiting professor from IMSA University in Barcelona, Spain, lecturing on cross-cultural consumer behavior. At the beginning of the class, the professor greets all the students in English, but then turns to the Latino students, sitting together, and thanks them for the honor of being invited to speak: "*Gracias por invitarme a esta universidad. Es un honor estar aqui con todos vosotros.*" Carlos notices the reaction of some of his friends when the professor refers to the students using the expression "*con vosotros*" instead of "*con ustedes.*" The professor then looks at the textbook the students are using and says, "This is the same book we use in my consumer behavior class, except ours is in Spanish, of course, and it's titled *Comportamiento del Consumidor.*"

After classes, Carlos heads to the newspaper office, where his task today is to study the growing number of restaurants featuring cuisine from various parts of the world and to write reviews that will interest the increasing number of Spanish-speaking residents in the city. "Maybe they would be interested in that new Ethiopian restaurant or a description of the subtleties of *sake* at a Japanese restaurant," he thinks to himself. Although sometimes he'd rather be with his girlfriend Angelica, he decides that gaining work experience during college is more important; besides, earning money has its advantages.

Because his mother's birthday is tomorrow and he hasn't yet bought anything for her, Carlos calls 1-800-FLOWERS and orders flowers to be delivered the next morning. He knows his mother likes flowers but she would not spend the money to buy them for herself. The sales associate describes in Spanish what the arrangement will look like, increasing Carlos' confidence that he's made a good selection.

Before heading home from work, Carlos's cell phone rings, playing a clip of his favorite music. It's a friend from school, Jamal, who asks, "Whassup?" "*Nada, amigo mio*," Carlos replies and listens to Jamal say, "Usher is here for a concert next month—you should expand your horizons and go with me." Carlos's phone rings again a few minutes later—it's his mother asking him to buy some *leche* on the way home. Instead of dealing with a large supermarket, he stops at a neighborhood CITGO station where he also buys some gas. "Helps the Venezuelans," he thinks to himself. Even though Carlos knows the milk costs less at Aldi, the convenience is worth it—especially after a long day.

Carlos arrives home after the rest of the family has left together, knowing they wanted him to join them for dinner at his uncle's house. Hungry and tired, he remembers the advertisement on the radio when he woke up and orders a Donatos "No Dough" pizza. Like many other Americans, he's counting carbs, even though his family thinks it's silly. Once the pizza arrives, Carlos turns on the television and watches a *Cristina* show his sister told him about, recorded earlier on TiVo. After eating, he goes to his room and turns on his computer to check e-mail, hoping to get a message from an Italian cyber-friend whom he met in a global chat room. He then checks the progress of the stocks in which he invested through E*Trade. Monitoring and trading stock became a hobby after one of his professors convinced Carlos he needed to start an IRA early if he planned on retiring as a multimillionaire,

and because Carlos believes the Social Security program older people rely on is unlikely to be there when people his age grow old. He's even started an HSA (Health Savings Account) for himself and has encouraged his older brother and sisters to do the same. Finally, he searches the online archives of the *Journal of Consumer Research* and the *Journal of Consumer Psychology* for information on a report for his consumer behavior class. Just after midnight, Carlos places his iPod in its new docking station and drifts off to sleep to the music of Diego Torres and Virginia Lopez.

---

Carlos's story is just one example of a day in the life of a typical American consumer in his age group and life stage.

From the time we learn to walk and talk, we are involved in consumer behavior on a daily basis. Whether we go to a retail store, shop via catalog or the Internet, eat breakfast at home or stop by McDonald's, we are functioning as living, breathing consumers. Just like Carlos, all of us face a myriad of consumer decisions ranging from which brands to buy, where and how to buy them, and how to use the products we buy.

If you consider all the encounters we have each day with products, brands, and advertisements, not to mention the people in our lives, you begin to understand something about the scope of the subject called *consumer behavior.* Far more than just a specialized area of marketing, consumer behavior affects nearly every aspect of life.

## What Is Consumer Behavior?

**Consumer behavior** is defined as *activities people undertake when obtaining, consuming, and disposing of products and services.* Simply stated, consumer behavior has traditionally been thought of as the study of "why people buy"—with the premise that it becomes easier to develop strategies to influence consumers once a marketer knows the reasons people buy specific products or brands.

Three primary activities are included in the definition of consumer behavior—obtaining, consuming, and disposing.

- **Obtaining** refers to *the activities leading up to and including the purchase or receipt of a product.* Some of these activities include searching for information regarding product features and choices, evaluating alternative products or brands, and purchasing. Consumer behavior analysts examine these types of behaviors, including how consumers buy products—do they shop at specialty stores, at shopping malls, or on the Internet? Other issues might include how consumers pay for products (with cash or credit cards), whether they buy products as gifts or for themselves, whether consumers transport products or have them delivered, where consumers get information about product and store alternatives, and how brands influence consumers' product choices.
- **Consuming** means *how, where, when, and under what circumstances consumers use products.* For example, issues relating to consumption might include decisions about whether consumers use products at home or at the office. Do they use products according to instructions and as intended or do they find their own unique ways of using products? Is the experience of using the product entertaining or purely functional? Do they use the entire product before disposing of it or is some of it never consumed?
- **Disposing** refers to *how consumers get rid of products and packaging.* Consumer analysts might examine consumer behavior from an ecological standpoint: How do consumers dispose of product packaging or product remains? Are products biodegradable? Can they be recycled? Consumers might also choose to extend the life of some products by handing them down to younger children, donating them to charity thrift shops, or selling them on eBay.

These three activities are depicted in Figure 1.1, which also shows how many variables affect the process of consumer behavior. Each of these influences will be discussed throughout the text, but are introduced here to show how "individual and unique" a consumer's behavior can be and how these influences can explain why you or Carlos make decisions as a consumer.

**Consumer behavior** also can be defined as *a field of study that focuses on consumer activities.* As the study of consumer behavior has evolved, so has its scope. Historically, the study of consumer behavior focused on buyer behavior, or "why people buy." More recently, researchers and practitioners have focused on **consumption analysis,** which refers to *why and how people use products* in addition to *why and how they buy.* Consumption analysis is a broader conceptual framework than buyer behavior because it includes issues that arise after the purchase process occurs—issues that often affect how people buy and the satisfaction they receive from their purchases.

Consumer behavior should be the primary focus of every aspect of the firm's marketing program. This is central to the **marketing concept**—*the process of planning and executing the conception, pricing, promotion, and distribution of ideas, goods, and*

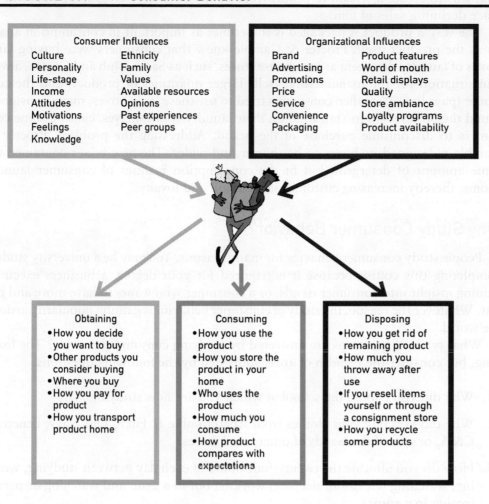

| Consumer Influences | | Organizational Influences | |
| --- | --- | --- | --- |
| Culture | Ethnicity | Brand | Product features |
| Personality | Family | Advertising | Word of mouth |
| Life-stage | Values | Promotions | Retail displays |
| Income | Available resources | Price | Quality |
| Attitudes | Opinions | Service | Store ambiance |
| Motivations | Past experiences | Convenience | Loyalty programs |
| Feelings | Peer groups | Packaging | Product availability |
| Knowledge | | | |

**Obtaining**
- How you decide you want to buy
- Other products you consider buying
- Where you buy
- How you pay for product
- How you transport product home

**Consuming**
- How you use the product
- How you store the product in your home
- Who uses the product
- How much you consume
- How product compares with expectations

**Disposing**
- How you get rid of remaining product
- How much you throw away after use
- If you resell items yourself or through a consignment store
- How you recycle some products

*services to create exchanges that satisfy individual and organizational objectives.* The key element in marketing is the *exchange* by the marketer of something of such value that the customer will pay the price that meets the needs and objectives of the seller. A consumer's satisfaction with an exchange depends on his or her satisfaction with *consumption* of the product as well as the exchange of money. Consumers only want to pay for products and services that satisfy their needs, a process unlikely to occur unless the firm thoroughly understands how buyers *consume* or *use* a particular product.

Consumption is a key to understanding why consumers buy products. When wireless phones with built-in cameras were introduced, they produced low-resolution images and were cumbersome to use. As a result, adoption was slow and sales were disappointing. However, when manufacturers began producing camera phones with higher-quality images that consumers could easily "point and shoot" to friends and family, consumers traded their old phones and increased their consumption of wireless services such as network minutes. Observing that camera phones were popular at rock concerts, marketers added audio recording capabilities so consumers could transmit photos and music simultaneously. When digital cameras sold in greater numbers than traditional film cameras, Kodak saw sales of film, from which a high proportion of its profits were derived, plummet. After decades of promoting "Kodak memories," Kodak introduced personal printers that made creating digital prints convenient and affordable in an attempt to resurrect sales of "memories"—permanent images consumers can share with friends and family as well as on the Internet. For Kodak, the goal was to create a stream of profits from hardware and photographic paper to replace declining sales of film.

The way a product is packaged is sometimes as important in consumption analysis as the product itself. Procter & Gamble knew that consumers were buying large boxes of laundry detergent at warehouse stores, such as Sam's Club and Costco, a win-win situation for the manufacturer (sells larger quantities of product) and the consumer (pays less). Yet when consumers tried to *use* these large boxes, many consumers found the boxes were too tall to fit on their laundry room shelves, causing some consumers to discontinue purchase of the brand. Addressing the problem, Procter & Gamble redesigned its boxes to be shorter and wider. The new boxes contained the same amount of detergent, but fit the consumption realities of consumer laundry rooms, thereby increasing customer satisfaction and loyalty.

## Why Study Consumer Behavior?

People study consumer behavior for many reasons. You may be a university student completing this course because it is required for your degree, a business executive gaining insight into consumer trends, or a consumer who wants to have more and pay less. Whatever the reason, the study of consumer behavior is gaining popularity around the world.

What types of questions are answered by studying consumer behavior? The list is long, but consider the breadth of areas addressed by the following questions:

1. Why did you choose the school at which you are now studying?

2. Why did you buy your clothes from Abercrombie & Fitch, Old Navy, Benetton, C&A, or any of thousands of other retail stores?

3. How do you allocate the twenty-four hours of each day between studying, working, watching television, sleeping, working out in a gym, and watching or participating in a sport?

4. Do you usually cook your food from scratch, microwave it, or buy it already cooked in a restaurant to eat there or take home? Why do you eat certain types or brands of food most often?

5. If you had the choice of attending a sports event, visiting a museum, attending a concert, or spending the evening with games and Internet chats on your computer, which would you choose?

6. When you graduate and buy a car, do you plan on buying it new or used? Which model or make will you most likely choose? Will you lease it or buy it?

7. Which ads do you like and which do you dislike? How do they influence your purchase decisions?

8. Did you donate blood this year? Do you give time or money to help people with personal, medical, or economic problems, or do you leave those problems for other people to solve?

9. Did you vote in the last election? For whom and why?

10. Compared to other people earning the same income as you, do you save more or less money than they do? Do you make financial decisions based on what pleases you now or what will provide the biggest payoff in the future?

Although you may be able to answer these questions as they apply to you, understanding the reasons that cause others to answer them differently is more difficult. But that's what consumer analysts and marketers must understand when chasing ever-precious consumers. A firm's ability to attract consumers, satisfy and retain them, and sell more to them affects greatly a company's profitability. Consider question 6. If you were an executive at Toyota or General Motors, how much would you pay to know how the millions of new car buyers each year would answer? Beyond corporate bottom lines, look at question 9 and consider how valuable it would be for a political candidate to know why large numbers of citizens have voted as they have.

The relevance and importance of each of these questions vary from one organization to another. Retail executives want to know how millions of consumers would answer question 7, but this type of consumer information also helps nonprofit organizations better serve the public. Knowing how consumers prefer to spend their time, as indicated in question 5, might help sports teams and arts organizations better promote and position their offerings. Or if a health agency's mission focuses on increasing the nation's blood supply or reducing the incidence of HIV/AIDS, it could concentrate its study of consumer behavior in finding answers to question 8.

Collectively, the issues identified in this list of questions represent the breadth of issues included in the study of consumer behavior and in this book. These issues also serve as a good starting point to begin examining the more-important-than-ever subject of consumer behavior.

## Consumer Behavior Determines the Economic Health of a Nation

Every day, in every country around the globe, an election is held. The election is not about which political parties will be leading a nation. Rather, consumers are voting on which nations and firms win, and they do it with their dollars, euros, and yen. With their money, consumers elect the retailers and other marketers they want to survive and be profitable enough to provide jobs for a nation's citizens. With their votes, consumers determine which people will have good jobs or bad jobs, and which will have no jobs at all. Ultimately, consumers determine which companies will have rising share prices (attracting capital, improving technology, and creating jobs for college graduates) and which will go out of business. On a macroeconomic level, when consumers "vote" with their money, they determine whether workers in China and India should have more jobs or whether work should go to Europe and North America. In the United States, consumers are responsible for two-thirds of the nation's economy. They determine which nations obtain needed capital and revenue, yielding jobs and prosperity.

## Consumer Behavior Determines the Success of Marketing Programs

People who study consumer behavior generally desire to influence or change the behavior of consumers in some way. Some marketers, such as consumer products manufacturers, want to use *marketing* to influence brand choice and purchase, whereas others, such as public health advocates, use *demarketing* to influence people to stop smoking or abstain from illegal drugs.

### "THE CONSUMER IS KING"

Today, businesses around the world recognize that "the consumer is king." Knowing why and how people consume products helps marketers understand how to improve existing products, what types of products are needed in the marketplace, and how to attract consumers to buy their products. In essence, consumer behavior analysis helps firms know how to "*please the king*" and directly impact bottom-line profits. Without customer satisfaction, organizations are unlikely to increase sales and, without increased sales, organizations won't have resources to invest in customer service centers, special sales promotions, or sales training—important components of customer satisfaction programs. Rather than attempting to influence consumers, the most successful organizations develop marketing programs influenced by consumers.

Consumer behavior studies consumers as *sources of influence* on organizations. Today, the most successful organizations are described as *customer-centric,* which means that they attempt to focus everyone in the organization on satisfying customers. Customer-centricity involves a total marketing approach to product development, innovation, research, logistics, and communication. By allowing consumers to influence the organization to have the products, prices, promotions, and operations consumers will buy, customer-centric organizations are more likely to delight customers, create brand loyalty, and increase revenues and profits.

As a practical philosophy of managing successful organizations, **marketing** is *the process of transforming or changing an organization to have what people will buy* (at a profit, in the case of for-profit organizations). Marketing works well when the organization is influenced by the needs and wants of consumers instead of consumers influenced by the desires of marketers.

## "ONLY THE CUSTOMER CAN FIRE US ALL"

Until the time of his death, Wal*Mart founder Sam Walton visited each store every year to talk with associates and customers, gather information, and formulate ideas on how to improve Wal*Mart. It was a strategy that took him from one small store in Rogers, Arkansas, to a chain large enough to challenge and eventually beat Sears and Kmart at the retailing game they helped invent while sealing the demise of long-established firms such as Montgomery Ward. Even after Wal*Mart became a public corporation and Sam Walton became a billionaire, he continued to walk through his stores and talk to his associates. He would remind everyone from cashiers to senior executives that "the only person who can fire us all is the customer."

Walton spoke the truth. He believed that consumers ultimately determine which organizations thrive and which ones fail. He understood that when consumers make purchase decisions, they are voting for the candidates they want to survive in today's hypercompetitive retail marketplace. Walton's philosophy created a customer-centric culture in which everyone in the organization, including suppliers, is expected to find ways to cut costs and transfer the savings to the wallets of customers instead of the "bottom line" of the firm. In the long run, Walton's customer-centric philosophy created the largest corporation in the world, believed by many to eventually become the world's first trillion-dollar corporation.

The power of the consumer is immense, and the desire of major firms to understand consumers is huge. The most successful entrepreneurs will tell you how costly and challenging it has become to recruit new customers; therefore, they focus on *relationship marketing,* or how to keep existing customers in the long run by establishing relationships based on mutual cooperation, trust, and commitment to value-added exchanges. Whether the strategy is offering special products and services or a customer loyalty card, the goal is the same: keep customers so satisfied that they will not only return but also will recruit friends to be customers. To accomplish this goal, firms must truly understand customers and the reasons for their behavior.

## Consumer Behavior Determines the Economic Health of Everyone

Your decisions as a consumer determine your own economic health, which may be the most important reason to study consumer behavior. It's why you'll find boxes throughout this book marked "Buyer Beware," which give examples of how to make more effective consumption decisions while avoiding deceptive practices harmful to consumers. Anyone can benefit from money-saving strategies and tips on how to be "better shoppers," but educational programs should be based on research into motivation and behavior if they are to be relevant in the real world of consumer life. Consumer economists, home economists, and specialists in consumer affairs are among the leading researchers of how and why people consume products.

Public policy leaders and social commentators study consumer behavior to alleviate problems such as overconsumption and underconsumption. Overeating, overspending, drug and alcohol abuse, and excessive gambling are behaviors that individuals and social agencies wish to minimize, whereas exercising, reading, and eating nutritional foods are generally encouraged. Understanding these issues from a consumer perspective helps policy makers, consumer interest groups, and businesses

**FIGURE 1.2** Government and Non-Profit Groups Use Consumer Behavior to Spread Their Messages

develop the best methods to reach consumers with information and assistance. The U.S. Department of Homeland Security encourages business leaders to be prepared for terrorism or other crises, as you can see in Figure 1.2.

As another example, consider the consumer compulsion toward obesity, which is a growing health problem in the United States. Today more than 31 percent of U.S. adults are obese, up from 13 percent in 1962.[1] While another health problem, cigarette smoking, causes more than 400,000 premature deaths each year, smokers today make their choices in a marketing environment saturated with information about the health risks as well as generally negative reinforcement from nonsmokers. Warning labels, advertising restrictions, lawsuits, bans in public places, cessation programs, and high taxes have substantially reduced adult smoking rates. Now, consumers, employers, health care providers, the government, and marketers are going after obesity with the same determination. The Centers for Disease Control and Prevention (CDC) has declared obesity an epidemic, the nation's second-leading actual cause of death and a primary factor in many others. Today, 127 million American adults (about two-thirds of adults) and 9 million children and teens are considered overweight or obese, and 58 million live with serious obesity-related health conditions. Obesity is not only a direct cause of illnesses such as cancer, high blood pressure, heart disease, diabetes, stroke, and osteoporosis, but it also seriously exacerbates all other medical conditions with direct health care costs exceeding $100 billion per year, according to the American Obesity Association (www.obesity.com).

## Burger King President's Challenge Program:
### Bringing fitness and activity to schools

FIGURE 1.3a  Burger King Partners with the Public Sector to Promote Health and Fitness

## Burger King "Food and Fashion"
### Salad Pouch: The Ultimate Lunch Accessory

FIGURE 1.3b  Burger King Associates Healthier Food Choices with High Fashion

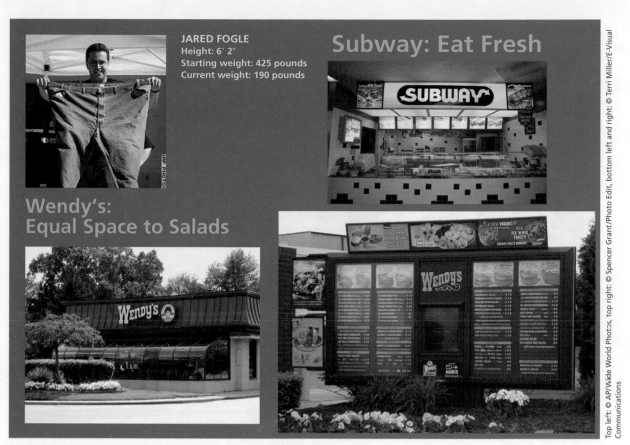

JARED FOGLE
Height: 6′ 2″
Starting weight: 425 pounds
Current weight: 190 pounds

Subway: Eat Fresh

Wendy's:
Equal Space to Salads

**FIGURE 1.3c** Leading Fast Food Chains Raise Awareness of Healthy Food Choices

Figure 1.3a shows how public and private sectors can work together on this consumer problem. The President's Challenge Program, a public sector educational program, is extended in influence by the private sector, in this instance Burger King. Notice in Figure 1.3b that Burger King is also promoting a product—salad pouches with less calories and fat—targeting a fit, fashionable consumer. In Figures 1.3c and 1.3d you see educational programs by other quick service restaurants (QSRs) attempting to raise consumer awareness of healthier menu items. Subway grew to a chain with more outlets than McDonald's with the help of Jared Fogle, who was successful enough at losing weight by eating at Subway to become its primary television spokesperson. Wendy's featured its "Garden Sensations" salads so sensationally that it attracted consumers desiring healthier choices from sit-down restaurants to Wendy's. As a result, the share of Wendy's total sales from salads grew from less than 3 percent to more than 12 percent. McDonald's responded with its own healthier choices, including fresh fruit and yogurt, and by giving away 5 million pedometers to promote not only its salads but also exercise as a sensible way to reduce weight. QSRs are considered by many to be part of the obesity problem, but visionary marketers also can be part of the solution—provided they have a solid understanding of consumer behavior.

## Consumer Behavior Helps Formulate Public Policy

Organizations and individuals interested in public policy must understand the needs of consumers when formulating policies relating to economics, social welfare, family planning, or nearly any other subject. They also need to know how to predict the behavioral changes that will follow their policies. When the Federal Reserve changes interest rates, what is the effect on demand for homes, cars, investments, and other

Adult Happy Meals comprised of a salad, bottled water and a pedometer to encourage physical activity.

Milk or apple juice optional in kid's meals.

Apple slices (with low-fat caramel sauce on the side) substituted for fries.

"We are going to serve 35 million pounds of apples that Americans didn't have last year."

—Dr. Cathy Kapica, McDonald's Global Director of Nutrition

**FIGURE 1.3d** McDonald's Encourages Adults and Children to Be Physically Active

products? Will government-mandated warning labels cause consumers to buy less or more of a product? For years, economic policy has recognized the importance of such questions, but the amount of research in this area has been limited. In recent years, public policy has changed to emphasize a shift *from* government protection and education to guarantee consumer welfare *to* protection resulting from competitive markets.

The cornerstone of a market-driven economy is the right of any consumer to make an informed and unrestricted choice from an array of alternatives. When this right is curtailed by business abuse, governments are expected to influence consumer choice by curbing deception and other unfair trade practices.

## Consumer Behavior Affects Personal Policy

Possibly the most important reason you should be interested in consumer behavior is the effect it will have on your own life. Personal policy includes how you behave (toward others and in buying situations), your values and beliefs, and how you live your life. Will you marry and have children or remain single? Will you spend your income on material goods or donate it to charity? Will you spend all of your income when you earn it or will you save part of it for future consumption?

A person's economic quality of life is determined by personal policy. Once you truly understand consumer behavior, you will realize that what you have in life is determined more by how much you save (and how little you spend) than how much you earn. As you read Buyer Beware 1.1, consider not only the tactical issue of whether to buy a car or lease it, but how the personal policy decisions of Carlos and Richard determine how much money they have to spend on other needs and wants.

Retailers appeal to different consumers with different spending and saving behaviors. Supermarkets such as Kroger and Wild Oats Market offer consumers a wide variety of produce, meat, gourmet foods, and prepared entrees in attractive stores with bright lighting and wide aisles. Though a consumer may spend an average of $130 to $150 per cart of groceries at these retailers, other consumers choose to shop at lower-priced stores, such as Aldi (the German-based, global grocery giant that caters to "smart" consumers—see www.aldi.com). Instead of paying $3.69 for a leading brand of cereal at the supermarket, Aldi customers pay $1.39 for the Aldi captive brand. Although quality is not sacrificed (the cereal often comes from the same manufacturer, is made with the same formula, and is packaged in a box similar to the highly advertised brand), the Aldi consumer has fewer brand choices and less ambience. When the Aldi shopper checks out, however, the total bill is $70 to $80, leaving money for entertainment, gasoline, and other products the consumer may enjoy more than basic food. You can learn more about how retailers offer low prices on high-quality goods by studying the Aldi case at the back of this text.

Consumers can choose how and where they spend their incomes, and the choices they make determine who is most able to buy goods and services. When it comes

## Will You Be Upside Down?

Remember Carlos from the opening vignette? After college graduation, one of the biggest consumer decisions facing him will be buying a car. At the dealership, he may be asked to lease rather than buy and offered lower monthly payments if he leases. Carlos should be aware, however, that lease payments are based on an assumed value of the car at the end of the lease period. If the dealer inflates the assumed value at the end of the lease, Carlos may be "upside down," with the actual value less than the assumed value and Carlos owing more than he believed he would pay on the lease. Even worse, Carlos may not realize that if he chose a loan instead of a lease, he will own the car at the end of the agreed period, driving it in the future for no additional cost except maintenance. If he leases the car, at the end of the lease period he has nothing except the need to buy another car.

Consider what happens if Carlos buys the car, but his friend Richard chooses a lease. After Carlos and Richard graduate, let's say they both secure jobs paying approximately $40,000 a year. Both want and need a car, and decide on a Honda costing around $20,000 with a modest down payment and monthly payments of $500 for 48 months. Carlos obtains information from *Consumer Reports* and other sources when buying the car and follows advice on maintaining it properly, changing oil and performing maintenance at specified times, and keeping the car clean inside and outside. Richard, on the other hand, does none of

these and, by the end of four years, owns an unreliable, dirty, and dented car, and decides to buy or lease another car, continuing the $500 monthly payments. Because Carlos takes care of his car, it is reliable and attractive at the end of four years. Instead of buying a new car, he invests the $500 per month in a mutual fund for the next six years, knowing that almost any car that is well maintained will last for ten years and 100,000 miles and that some manufacturers even provide a warranty for ten years.

At the end of six more years, Carlos's investment has increased to well over $50,000, with which he can buy a new $20,000 car and still have $30,000 continuing to compound in his investment account. Even if both consumers earn the same amount of income throughout life, Carlos will amass more assets due to his consumption behavior. How these consumers spend, save, and consume will determine how much health care they can buy when they are older, how much they can invest in the stock market, and what kinds of cars and homes they can buy in the future. By saving the $500 per month on car payments (and applying this type of consumption behavior to other areas as well), Carlos might choose to retire earlier, buy a house, or eventually buy a Porsche—without earning more than Richard, illustrating that it's not what consumers earn so much as what consumers save that determines how much they have.

to purchasing casual clothing, housewares, and small appliances, consumers often choose mass retailers such as Wal*Mart and Target over traditional department stores such as Macy's and Dillard's. The cost savings may require consumers to give up some perks like carpeted aisles, recessed lighting, and mall-based locations, but if you could choose between making 30 percent more income by working additional hours or decreasing your expenses by 30 percent with smarter consumer decisions, which would you prefer? If you worked more hours for greater pay, some of your income would be taxed, but there's no tax on "earnings" from smarter consumer decisions.

By understanding success in consumer behavior terms, marketers also can understand how to appeal to specific consumers. For example, Cadillac and Mercedes are positioned as symbols of economic success, attracting consumers who have achieved affluence or want to be perceived as having done so. Socially, you might be viewed as more successful if you bought a parka at Abercrombie & Fitch for $159 than if you paid $9.98 at Steve & Barry's (www.steveandbarrys.com), but it's your personal definition of "success" that determines your choice as a consumer. Understanding how consumers make such decisions may influence your own financial success, however, in a marketing career.

## Evolution of Consumer Behavior

Look at the myriad products available to consumers and you quickly realize that consumers face choices every hour of the day and night. Red blouses or blue shirts? Music by OutKast or Norah Jones? Hybrid cars, pick-up trucks, or sports utility vehicles? Shares of stock in Home Depot, Ford, or Dell, bought from a broker, an employer, online, or at a bank? Heinz ketchup or picante salsa, bought from a supermarket, a Wal*Mart Supercenter, or a convenience store? Consumers face an almost infinite number of possibilities, but who determines the final selection of what is available for consumers to snatch off retail shelves? That also has changed over time, as consumers force marketers to evolve from supply chains to demand chains.

### Who Determines What Consumers Can Buy?

Everyone involved in determining what consumers are able to buy are included in a **supply chain,** defined as *all the organizations involved in taking a product from inception to final consumption.* These organizations typically include *manufacturers* (who turn raw materials into products); *wholesalers* (or other forms of distributors who procure products, house them, and distribute them to the point of sale); *retailers* (who sell them to final users through stores, directly or on the Internet); and *consumers* (who buy and consume the products). The supply chain also includes many *facilitating organizations* such as advertising and research firms, financial institutions, and transportation or logistics firms. The focus and power within the supply chain to determine what is offered to consumers has shifted throughout history, as summarized in Figure 1.4.

From the early days of the American colonies until the U.S. Civil War, traders—a type of wholesaler—served as the connector between European products and U.S. markets. It was these distributors who determined whether consumers were offered red dresses or blue shirts or barrels containing shovels or sugar. Consumers had little influence on the process. Europeans may question why the United States is so marketing oriented, but historian Walter McDougall describes its origins in *Freedom Just Around the Corner.*[2] He explains that English trading companies left a culture more entrepreneurial than if the French or Spanish had controlled the emerging nation. Entrepreneurial values (described by McDougall as "hustling") still influence the economy and dominate the marketing environment of the United States.

**FIGURE 1.4**  Who Decides What Products Will Be Available
for Choice by Consumers?

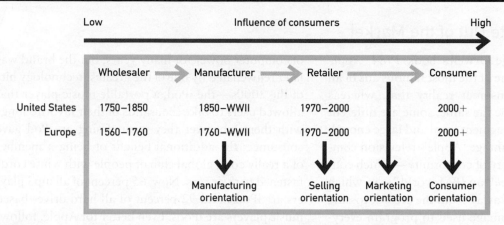

Manufacturing emerged in the mid-1800s and blossomed during the Civil War, giving rise to the power of manufacturers in the supply chain in the late 1800s until the latter part of the twentieth century. Manufacturers such as Procter & Gamble had the ability to decide which products to make, the colors and sizes of packages, how they should be advertised, and where retailers should place them on shelves. Whether the product was soap, shoes, or automobiles, manufacturers dominated what was produced and made available for consumers to buy.

Power began to shift again after World War II, when retailers took more control of the supply chain. By the end of the century, mega-retailers such as Wal*Mart, IKEA, Home Depot, and Target were not only larger than many of the manufacturers and wholesalers of the past but they were also closer to the increasingly elusive consumer. Retailers began to enforce their views about what products to manufacture, how they should be packaged, where they should be inventoried, and how they should be priced and sold. Retailers dominated the supply chain because they provided the essential connection between production and consumption.

In the twenty-first century, power has shifted yet again, fueled somewhat by the quantity and quality of information about consumers and their behavior, much of it obtained from point-of-sale (POS) data. Increased competition and slowing population growth has also created an environment in which too many marketers are chasing too few customers, who are bombarded with time pressures and thousands of advertisements per day. The new "boss" in the new millennium rules Sony, Procter & Gamble, and Microsoft. The same boss gives orders to retailers as large and global as Wal*Mart and Carrefour or as small as the independently owned shops in your hometown. Even wholesalers such as Cardinal Health (pharmaceuticals) and Ingram Micro (computers and electronics) and integrated producers and distributors like BP and ExxonMobil must take orders from the boss. The boss, of course, is the *consumer*—thus making the study of consumers and consumer behavior more important than ever.

Just as the consumer is the focus and basis of marketing strategy, so too is the consumer the focal point for building a customer-centric supply chain, called a demand chain.[3] Rather than building and operating their supply chain from manufacturer to market, the best firms are creating chains based on consumers' needs, wants, problems, and lifestyles. Understanding consumers is a driving force in customer-centric supply chains, whether the chain is supplying consumer goods such as grocery and apparel, health care services from physicians and hospitals, cultural experiences at a performance or art gallery, or financial services from a bank or broker.

## Apple Takes a Byte Out of the Market

Borrowing from George Orwell's book *1984,* Apple Computer developed one of the most famous ads of all time based on the consumer reality that, whereas many consumers may be the same, some are different enough to be a market segment loyal and large enough to yield a strategic advantage. Apple's television commercial depicted a society of conformity—which consumers understood to be "an IBM world"—in which a young woman breaks away from the crowd, tossing a hammer through an image used to program everyone to behave the same. The ad ran only once, during the 1984 Super Bowl, but it positioned Apple forever as an innovator in what may be the most influential ad ever to appear on television.

Nonconformist but highly reliable operating systems, software, and a mouse were enhanced by Apple's colorful and contemporary product design, with its distinctive icon inviting consumers to "take a bite out of the Apple." Great design and slick, starkly simple advertising campaigns supported the sale of gigabytes

of computer power for many years, but the brand was later rejuvenated by one of the greatest technology hits of the 2000s—the iPod, a portable music player that allowed users to take thousands of their favorite songs with them wherever they went. Using an iPod gave consumers the additional benefit of being a member of a really cool, global club of people with white cords fastened to their ears. Now, 65 percent of all mp3 players are iPods, and 92 percent of all hard drive–based music players are iPods. Even better for Apple, following their purchase of an iPod, 6 percent of consumers purchased an Apple computer and 7 percent plan to buy one in the next twelve months. The original iPod can hold up to ten thousand songs, featuring Apple's patent-pending "click wheel" and up to twelve hours of battery life. The iPod mini, a lower-priced and smaller version, holds up to one thousand songs. All iPods work in conjunction with Apple iTunes, an online service that offers fans a digital jukebox on a Mac or Windows computer. Apple wasn't first with a hard-drive music player, but it capitalized on small size and

**From the creators of iPod** The new iMac G5

iPod puts all your music in your pocket. The new iMac G5 puts an entire computer in an ultra-slim display. From $1,299.

Life is random.

Meet iPod shuffle. 240 songs. A million different ways. From $99. PC+Mac.  iPod shuffle

a well-designed interface to deliver the message of portability and freedom to its consumers.

Apple doesn't license its operating system to competitors, but encourages partner firms to introduce accessories that will fit its customers' consumption behavior. Accessories for the iPod range from a $20 plastic carrying case to a $300 snowboarding jacket with iPod controls built into the sleeve. There are speaker systems from JBL and Bose, high-end headphones from Shure, and a wall-mounted unit from Sonance. Germany's Goldster Audio designed the most expensive accessory, a vacuum tube amplifier and matching set of full-range speakers to add a rich and warm texture to the iPod's digitized sound, costing over $4,000. Looking to the future, Apple is focused on establishing the iPod as an automotive accessory, striking deals with BMW and Nissan to wire music players directly to car stereos, and adapters from car stereo firms Pioneer, Alpine, and Clarion are now on the market.

Moving from market segmentation to mass market was the next step in the type of skimming strategy described in most marketing courses. In 2005, Apple introduced the iPod shuffle, a bare-bones mp3 player holding 120-plus songs and priced well below competitors' prices for similar products. Apple is betting that there are enough low-budget buyers to penetrate the mass market without cannibalizing its loyal fans, and that many of them will want to move up to pricier iPods after becoming hooked on the iTunes Music Store. The iPod shuffle and a similar strategy for the new MacMini computer caused massive media attention and a soaring price for Apple stock.

Source: Adapted from various sources including Deborah Vince, "Ad Campaign, Simplicity Drive Sales of Apple iPod," *Marketing News* (December 15, 2004), 18; "Apple's Bold Swim Downstream," *Business Week* (Jan. 24, 2005), 33–35; and "Accessories at the Core of Apple's Plans for the iPod," *Financial Times* (January 31, 2005), 16.

As a result of the convergence of changing market forces, including increased competition, changing consumer lifestyles, power shifts within the supply chain, and the influence of the consumer, business orientation changed from a *manufacturing focus* to a *marketing focus*. Throughout this book, you'll find boxes titled "Consumer Behavior and Marketing," which provide examples of how marketers use consumer behavior and trends to develop marketing strategy. In the first one, Consumer Behavior and Marketing 1.1, you can see how Apple Computer developed its original positioning strategy with one of the world's most famous ads, but later rejuvenated its sales and its brand by creating new products such as the iPod (evolving from computers to music) with new designs and prices that appealed to new segments of consumers. Apple's strategy offers functionality that satisfies consumer needs, but differentiates the brand with emotional appeal and personality appealing to consumer desires and lifestyles. (You can also read more details about iPod in Market Facts 4.1 in Chapter 4.)

### Shifting from Supply to Demand

Business strategy in the twentieth century focused on supply, but in the twenty-first century it focuses on demand. Imagine, if you will, the challenges facing Henry Ford in the early 1900s when the Model T swept the market. When Ford could sell all the cars it could make, Mr. Ford made the famous statement: "You can get it in any color as long as it is black." That statement accurately reflected the focus of that time—producers dictated what was sold, and business strategy was based on a *manufacturing orientation*, centered primarily on *how to make products*. Today's consumer researcher wasn't needed back then, but today's auto marketers face marketing pressures from a variety of competitive challenges, including automotive superpowers such as Daimler-Chrysler and a greatly segmented market that demands variety, from ecological Smart Cars (produced by a partnership between Mercedes and Swatch), to Sebring convertibles, Dodge trucks, Jeep SUVs, and the $375,000 Maybach luxury sedan.

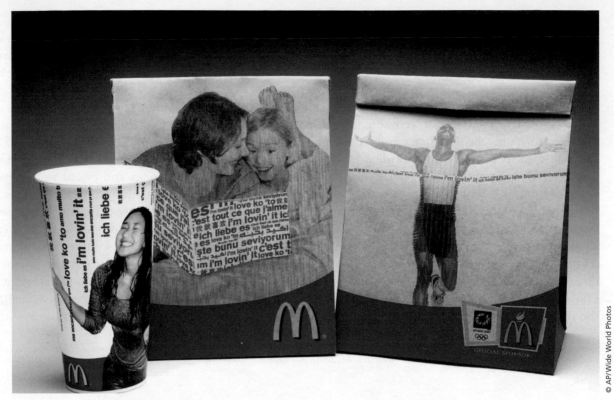

FIGURE 1.5 McDonald's Provides the Same Unique Selling Proposition Worldwide

Henry Ford's management skills and market understanding suited an earlier era, but today he would need, among other things, a crash course in consumer behavior.

### From Manufacturing to Selling

The earliest contributions to consumer behavior occurred in the 1920s when production capacity began to outrun demand and the challenge shifted from *how to manufacture goods* to *how to sell them*. As competition intensified, advertising agencies emerged as important institutions, and universities began offering courses on selling, advertising, and other marketing areas. Advertising agencies and universities relied on the accumulated wisdom of experience rather than behavioral science to influence consumers, with the one exception of *behaviorism*.

In the 1930s, learning theorist John B. Watson applied the practical aspects of this psychological approach to advertising and highlighted the importance of repetitive advertising to build awareness and brand preference. Using this principle, the Ted Bates advertising agency devised the phrase *unique selling proposition (USP)* in the 1940s and 1950s to describe the importance of selecting a benefit of the product and repeating that phrase so often that consumers uniquely associate that benefit with a particular brand. McDonald's has successfully marketed itself in different countries by identifying its USP as fast, consistent service in clean facilities and convenient locations, which provides consumers time to enjoy friends, family, and activities. Another USP is fun, as illustrated not only by the company's spokesperson, Ronald McDonald, but also by its global ad campaign "I'm lovin' it," shown in Figure 1.5.

### From Selling to Marketing

For a few years after World War II, it was easy to predict what consumers (who were catching up from the scarcity experienced during the Depression and war years) would buy—anything firms could produce. The age of scarcity ended in the United

**FIGURE 1.6**    Evolution of Business Orientation and
Consumer Behavior Studies

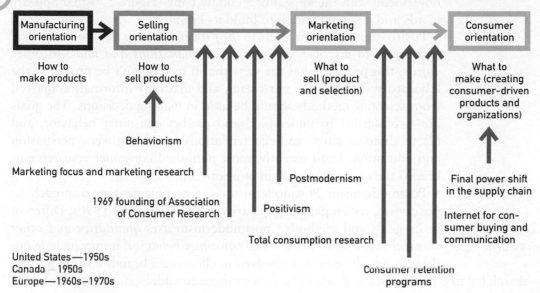

```
Manufacturing  →  Selling  →  Marketing  →  Consumer
orientation        orientation   orientation    orientation

How to          How to       What to        What to
make products   sell products sell (product  make (creating
                              and selection) consumer-driven
                                             products and
                                             organizations)

                Behaviorism

Marketing focus and marketing research       Final power shift
                                             in the supply chain
          1969 founding of Association        Internet for con-
          of Consumer Research   Positivism   sumer buying and
                                              communication
                  Total consumption research

United States—1950s                          Consumer retention
Canada—1950s                                 programs
Europe—1960s–1970s

                              Postmodernism
```

States and Canada by the 1950s and in most of Western Europe during the 1960s and 1970s, ushering in the **marketing era.** During this new era, productive capacity far exceeded demand, requiring the study of consumer behavior to grow beyond its roots in economics into a meaningful discipline. Although price once dominated the study of consumer behavior by economists, modern-day marketers began to focus on many other dimensions affecting consumer choice, such as quality, convenience, image, and advertising, aiding the transition of organizations to *having what consumers would likely buy.* Figure 1.6 details this evolution in the study of consumer behavior.

Ask Wal*Mart executives what they sell in their stores, and you may get the answer, "Nothing." According to senior management, Wal*Mart is not in the business of *selling things* to consumers; it's in the business of *buying what people need to consume,* whether it's clothing, food, or gasoline. Wal*Mart's positioning as a purchasing agent for consumers led to enormous success by the end of the twentieth century. Today at Wal*Mart's headquarters in Bentonville, Arkansas, you'll also find a Product Development Department with more than 250 people—many who studied consumer behavior and retailing—conducting research to determine what consumers want to buy, and thus guiding manufacturers in what to make.

Switching from sales to a marketing orientation required more sophisticated tools to understand consumers and what products or services will satisfy them. Marketing activities expanded with the speed and force of a nuclear blast throughout the most successful firms around the globe. Behavioral sciences took center stage and provided a toolbox of theories and methodologies borrowed by innovative marketing organizations, including:

• **Motivation research:** Marketers were hungry for new insights, and one of the tastiest theories was motivation research, derived from psychoanalytic theories of Sigmund Freud. Led by its chief proponent, Ernest Dichter,[4] the world of Freud and psychoanalysis found its way to the marketplace during the 1960s, with publications such as Vance Packard's *Hidden Persuaders.*[5] The goal of motivation researchers was *to uncover hidden or unrecognized motivations through guided interviewing.* One widely reported finding from the motivation research era was

**FIGURE 1.7** "Nothin' Says Lovin' Like Somethin' from the Oven"

that women bake cakes out of the unconscious desire to give birth. (Yes, you read this correctly.) Perhaps that's why Pillsbury created the Dough-boy™ icon with the appeal of a cuddly baby (Figure 1.7) that appears in ads and on merchandise to build its brand.

- **Positivism:** Positivism refers to *the process of using rigorous empirical techniques to discover generalizable explanations and laws.* In other words, this process takes the view that if results can't be proven in the laboratory, the data are not useful, and that only information derived from scientific methods should be used in making decisions. The goals are twofold: (1) to understand and predict consumer behavior, and (2) to discover cause-and-effect relationships that govern persuasion and education. Until recently, most published consumer research embraced the research paradigm of positivism.
- **Postmodernism:** Postmodernism is a complementary approach to positivism, which gained popularity in the 1980s and 1990s. Different in its goals and methods,[6] **postmodernism** *uses qualitative and other research methods to understand consumer behavior.* It may include understanding the emotion involved in choosing a brand. Postmodern research led to ethnographic and other research methods to understand daily life and the influence of the culture on how people consume products.[7]

### Customer-Centric Organizations in Demand Chains

Whereas a **marketing orientation** focuses on *how an organization adapts to consumers,* customer-centricity extends this focus to *how all organizations in a demand chain adapt to changing consumer lifestyles and behaviors.* Organizations such as Limited Brands, Wal*Mart, and Dell achieved much of their success because they are organized around a comprehensive **consumer orientation,** bringing product design, logistics, manufacturing, and retailing together as a customer-centric demand chain. Additionally, a comprehensive consumer orientation recognizes that consumers shape many aspects of society, including government, social programs, health care, and other areas of life. A comprehensive consumer perspective is helpful in nations such as China, India, and Russia as they move from centrally planned economies toward more market-based systems, with cooperation between all entities of a supply chain working together for the comprehensive good of all members.

Much of the remainder of this book focuses on issues affecting customer-centric firms. To succeed, firms need to sharpen their skills in areas such as information technology, customer retention programs, consumption research, consumer buying decisions, branding, and Internet strategies. And they will have to hone their already developed skills in advertising, communication, and marketing migrated to a multimedia, multichannel world increasingly linked together by the Internet.

## How Do You Study Consumers?

In a hypercompetitive global marketplace, the need increases for valid, accessible, and practical information about consumer motivation and behavior. The question is how to obtain that information by applying theories, problem-solving methods, and techniques to identify and solve marketing problems.[8] To help do this, marketers have turned to behavioral sciences to collect and interpret information about consumers, often with advanced information technology. Regardless of method, the goal is to understand how to study consumer behavior and implement a strategy that is best for specific situations.

Studying consumer behavior is much like studying medicine, an applied science using knowledge from disciplines such as chemistry, biology, psychology, and engineering. If you are a runner suffering from pain in your knee, your physician might try to research and diagnose the problem with an X-ray. If the problem is with cartilage rather than bones, the physician may order an MRI (magnetic resonance imaging) for more information. Before deciding how to fix the problem, the physician will do additional research, including taking a medical history.

The study of consumer behavior is similar, an applied science drawing from disciplines such as economics, psychology, sociology, anthropology, and statistics. To understand consumer behavior, you need to know what is going on inside a consumer's mind just as thoroughly as a surgeon understands what is going on inside your knee. But understanding why consumers behave the way they do is just the beginning. You must also have the skill of a surgeon in applying that knowledge to product development, advertising, retailing, and all other areas of the marketing mix. Getting inside the minds of consumers requires the theoretical and methodological equivalents of X-rays and MRIs.

## Methods of Studying Consumer Behavior

No single solution exists for conducting consumer research; consumer analysts need many methods to "get into the minds of consumers." The methods sometimes include conducting experiments to determine changes in buyer behavior based on special product offers and coupons or asking questions through interviews and focus groups. Other times, consumer research borrows from anthropology and sociology, studying consumers in a less formal, more natural setting,[9] exploring people's homes, offices, cars, and closets, to understand how consumers use products or invent ways to solve problems. These methods can be classified into three major methodological approaches: (1) observation, (2) interviews and surveys, and (3) experimentation.

## OBSERVATION

An **observational approach** to consumer research consists primarily of *observing consumer behaviors in different situations*. Sometimes researchers monitor behaviors in their natural settings, such as watching consumers use products and eat foods in their homes, but other times they monitor behavior in laboratory settings. This process might include observing how consumers react to different advertisements, packaging, or colors in a research facility. At other times, consumer analysts are more like Peter Falk, if you've ever watched reruns of the *Columbo* detective episodes, in which Falk shows up in his battered, barely running car, wearing an old, stained raincoat and figures out what nobody else can apparently see. How did he do it? Usually by noticing small but crucial sensory clues that went unnoticed by the police. Like good detectives, good consumer analysts observe the sight, sound, touch, taste, and smell sensations that build or erode consumer trust and brand loyalty. To understand how to tap into the powerful children's market, for example, marketers may visit playgrounds, schools, or sports venues and watch children's subconscious responses to products and displays through observational research.[10]

**In-home observation** *places marketers inside people's homes to examine exactly how products are consumed*. The observation may be done with personal interviews and surveys, video cameras, or other technologies that measure actual experience with a product. For example, a major cereal manufacturer seeks volunteer families who agree to have video cameras (activated by motion detectors) installed in their kitchens. When a family member enters the kitchen, the camera begins recording the events.

From these tapes, the manufacturer can observe how much milk is used in a cereal bowl, whether the milk is whole or skim, whether consumers drink the milk afterward, what other items are consumed with the cereal, and other consumption details that lead to improved products or packaging. Perhaps crunchier cereal needs to be developed for skim milk households, an example of adapting an existing product to fit better the changing tastes and consumption patterns. Children might also have difficulty pouring milk or preparing their own breakfasts, prompting changes in milk cartons or the introduction of a plastic "bowl" of cereal to make consumption easier for children and portability easier for adults. Eating in the car on the way to work has made Kellogg's NutriGrain cereal bars and Slim-Fast popular with some consumers by allowing them to eat on the go.

**Shadowing** is *a method in which a researcher accompanies or "shadows" consumers through the shopping and consumption processes,* asking questions about each step of the process. Usually answers are recorded on audio or video tape. By understanding why and how consumers move through the shopping process, marketers can begin to identify ways to solve the problems encountered by consumers. The result is more satisfied customers, who in turn develop brand or store loyalty. Some retailers use security cameras to monitor consumer movement through the store, the number of brands examined in a shelf, and what consumers do when stock-outs occur. This type of observation is the research methodology used in best-selling books on consumer behavior by Paco Underhill.[11]

**Physiological observational methods** increasingly are used by consumer researchers, involving techniques borrowed from medicine, psychology, and other sciences. These include cameras to measure eye movement, galvanic skin response (GSR), and MRI (you'll see an example in Chapter 9 of how MRI is used to understand the differences between Pepsi and Coke consumers). The same methodologies used to observe how pilots look for dots on a radar screen or how airport security agents screen bags for concealed weapons can be applied to the study of how consumers scan retail shelves. Because such observations produce large amounts of data requiring complex statistical analysis, they have been shown by Professors van der Lans, Pieters, and Wedel to be useful in modeling how consumers look for favored brands on overstocked retail shelves,[12] which in turn can help marketers to design more effective retail displays. The use of physiological methods of consumer research continues to grow because it overcomes some of the limitations of traditional and more widely used research methods. Dan Hill, one of the leading proponents of psychophysiological research, summarizes both of these approaches in Market Facts 1.1. (As you study this book, you'll see a number of Market Facts boxes, usually reporting data from market studies, although Market Facts 1.1 focuses on *methods* of conducting market studies.)

## INTERVIEWS AND SURVEYS

Consumer analysts also gather information from consumers by conducting surveys and interviews. **Surveys** are *an efficient way of gathering information from a large sample of consumers by asking questions and recording responses.* Surveys can be conducted by mail, telephone, Internet, or in person, with each method having some advantages and disadvantages. Many surveys done in person are *mall intercepts*—interviewing people in shopping malls. The advantage of this method is that researchers can ask consumers more detailed questions, show product samples or different ads, and ask opinions. Yet this method may be expensive and subject to **interviewer bias,** in which *responses are influenced by the interviewer or by an individual's desire to please the interviewer. Telephone surveys* also allow researchers to obtain a lot of information quickly from consumers; however, the questions and topics covered must be fairly simple, and it's difficult to reach consumers who screen their calls or use only

# Strengths and Weaknesses of Traditional and Psychophysiological Research Methods

## TRADITIONAL METHODS

### Focus Groups

Good for brainstorming, immediate surface-level emotional and verbal input, and sensing what's socially acceptable.

Exploratory, descriptive, offers opportunity for showing stimuli, to establish rapport and probe.

Major weakness is bias of both group dynamics and moderator's influence.

Risk of securing what is expected, acceptable, "fits the agenda." Low likelihood of accessing feelings or unconscious reactions. Gain only mediated filtered public responses.

### Surveys

Opportunity to gauge attitudes, gain statistics for simple analysis.

Except by Internet, usually conducted in abstract, so no sensory stimuli. Because it gains input retrospectively, it risks the fallacies of memory.

Chance to misrepresent feelings or failure to gain access to them. Low commitment level by participants.

Problem of leading questions and ambiguous phrasing. Solicits general response, not specifics of emotions.

### Choice Modeling

Rigorous diagnostic exercises to pinpoint and isolate influential variables. Rigorous data sorting.

Uses past behavior to predict future behavior.

Data may not be sufficient, accurate, up to date, or relevant.

No ability to access nonverbal, unconscious responses. Research is conducted in the abstract, without sensory clues.

Interrelations of independent variables could make it unreliable to interpret.

### Observation

What people do is more reliable than what they say. Behavior will involve both conscious and unconscious impulses.

Conducted in real time, with loads of sensory data. Follows the narrative of what people do.

Involves translation or self-interpretation of data.

In interviews, it risks leading questions and ambiguous phrasing. What does the behavior mean? Difficult to know "why" people do what they do.

## PSYCHOPHYSIOLOGICAL METHODS

### Biofeedback

Chance to gain direct, unfiltered access to transitory emotional states and unconscious reactions.

Precise, objective, real-time readings of otherwise subtle, even invisible reactions.

Use of sensors creates some degree of self-consciousness and physical inhibition.

### Facial Coding

Gains real-time access to emotional response, so you can learn the motivational potency of stimuli.

Accesses both conscious and unconscious reactions, often through brief, micro-expressions involuntarily revealed.

Need to draw participant pool correctly to allow for gender differences. Best to phrase the questions so they invite spontaneous reactions.

### Eye Tracking

Opportunity to gauge with some real-time precision what catches the eye, how quickly, and how long the subjects focus on it.

Can't access appeal except through verbal solicitation of reactions.

### Vocal Analysis

Helps sense energy level apparent in response. Considerable evidence that emotion produces change in respiration, phonation, and articulation.

Gets at intangibles, available tonally.

Ability to read emotions with accuracy is possibly limited to sadness and anger.

Need to separate impact of elocution and dictation from signal read-out transcript.

cell phones. *Mail questionnaires* allow consumer researchers to gather a lot of information, without interviewer bias; however, this approach takes longer to complete because of the lag between sending them and receiving them from consumers. *Internet surveys* increasingly are used with the same types of questions formerly collected by telephone, personal, or mail surveys. Internet surveys have the advantage of speed in completion, ease of data entry, and the possibility for complexity in questionnaire design and interactivity between questions, depending on consumer responses. These advantages, combined with the decline in response to telephone surveys, lead some researchers to believe this method will replace most telephone surveys.[13] The major issue is whether people who respond to Internet surveys are representative of those who don't respond, or those who do not have Internet access.

**Focus groups** are one of the most common methods used to delve into a variety of consumer and consumption issues. Focus groups usually consist of *eight to twelve people involved in a discussion led by a moderator skilled in persuading consumers to discuss thoroughly a topic of interest to the researcher.* Compared to surveys, focus groups can probe in depth very specific aspects of how consumers prepare to buy, decide to purchase, and use products.

**Longitudinal studies** involve *repeated measures of consumer activities over time to determine changes in their opinions, buying, and consumption behaviors.* A common method of collecting data is through membership clubs or customer loyalty programs, such as those operated by airlines, grocery chains, and other marketers. An airline, for example, can measure trips by its frequent fliers to study their consumption behaviors in terms of overseas versus domestic travel, repeated trips to the same city, special meal requests, and seat preferences, just to name a few. These data create profiles of the consumption styles of key market segments, which can be used with targeted communication, improved product and service offerings, and perhaps cooperative marketing programs with hotels or restaurants.

Many other types of longitudinal studies are designed to understand consumer behavior over time, usually supplied by specialized research organizations such as Information Resources, Inc. (IRI). Most studies are conducted in retail stores at the point-of-sale and collect what is called POS data, but IRI also maintains a representative panel of consumers who agree to set up a scanner at home to record the UPC code of every product purchased at the end of each day, as well as the outlet at which it was purchased. This makes it possible to measure changes in consumption of major product categories, as well as market share shifts by brand and retail outlet. Other organizations, such as National Panel Data (NPD) and Retail Forward (ShopperScape) collect detailed purchase and consumption data from diaries collected electronically from consumers, making it possible to track changes in product usage and brand share across time periods.

## EXPERIMENTATION

**Experimentation,** as a research methodology, *attempts to understand cause-and-effect relationships by carefully manipulating independent variables* (such as number of advertisements, package design, methods of communication) *to determine how these changes affect dependent variables* (such as purchase intent or behavior). A **laboratory experiment** is conducted in a *physical environment* (either commercial or academic facilities) *that permits maximum control of variables being studied.* A **field experiment** *takes place in a natural setting such as a home or a store.* An example is a retailer that mails several versions of a coupon with variations in price, presentation, and copy to measure the most effective combination. If you are reading this book as a requirement for a marketing or psychology course, it is likely that consumer behavior research involving all of the above methods is occurring at your school. At the beginning of this book, you read the Honor Roll of Consumer Researchers, which describes many of the contributors to these studies. Not all involve experiments, but leading journals most frequently include experiments rather than other research methods.

The "best" research is done by researchers who ask the "right" questions—those that truly reflect the issues important in developing marketing strategy—and formulate the valid, reliable, and cost-efficient ways to answers those questions. The best researchers are frequently those who look at the same data as others, but "see" what few others see—the underlying reasons why people buy and use products.

## CONSUMPTION RESEARCH

Consumption research focuses on how people use products rather than how they buy them, and can involve any of the research methods described. This approach often requires researchers to get inside people's homes or other places to understand how lifestyles, values, and societal trends affect usage in daily living. Figure 1.8 shows how Campbell's Soup at Hand fits into varied usage patterns of consumers.

Consider the problem facing a marketing manager who wants to increase sales of a household appliance such as a dishwasher. How can a firm like Whirlpool increase sales in the U.S. market when most families who can afford a dishwasher already own one? Expanding in less-developed countries probably won't work because labor costs are so low that upper-income families can hire domestic help to cook, who will also wash the dishes. Traditional marketers might try price-cutting, which will increase the number of households that can afford to buy a dishwasher but decrease revenue among high-income consumers, or they might sell in other countries where the need for dishwashers is increasing. Although both might be reasonable, analyzing consumption patterns of high-income consumers offers another way to expand consumption of the product category.

The next time you are in your kitchen, observe how the appliance is used and how consumers compensate for product shortcomings. Researchers might find that many households contain kitchens with dishwashers full of clean dishes and sinks full of dirty dishes. Ask most consumers what the biggest problem with their dishwashers is and they will say, "It doesn't unload itself." Consumers can load a few dishes at each meal until it's finally full. But consumers' lifestyles are so busy, they don't have time to empty dishwashers, causing sinks to end up full of dirty dishes in households with consumers who live in "time poverty."

If you're a marketing manager at Whirlpool, understanding consumption patterns might lead to the conclusion that one way to increase the total size of the market is to position the product to a segment of affluent, time-constrained households that will buy two dishwashers. The marketing plan needs to reach designers and architects serving consumers who are looking to save time by not putting clean dishes into kitchen cupboards. Instead, dishes remain in the "clean" dishwasher to be used as needed and then returned to the empty dishwasher. Once this dishwasher is full and the other one empty, the process is reversed, allowing one dishwasher to be used as a storage cabinet for

**FIGURE 1.8** Understanding How Consumers Use Products Is Key to Innovation

*Courtesy of The Campbell Soup Company, Model: Tara Dakidas, Photographer: Markus Paulsen*

clean dishes while the other is the receptacle for dirty dishes. Not only does the consumer gain time for more valuable activities, but the marketer increases demand by focusing on how people use the product. Understanding how consumers *use* products often leads to improved understanding of how they *buy* products.

## The Underlying Principles of Consumer Behavior

Before reading the remainder of this book, it is important to outline and review a few underlying principles that shape this text. These principles have become mottos for some of the most successful organizations. The principles might seem basic, but they often are misunderstood or ignored.

### The Consumer Is Sovereign

Peter Drucker, world-renowned professor and perhaps the most influential business writer, said it well, "There is one valid definition of business purpose: *to create a customer.*"[14] And marketing executives agree that it is much easier to create a customer if you have what consumers want to buy.

Consumer behavior, as a rule, is purposeful and goal oriented. Products and services are accepted or rejected to the extent that they are perceived as relevant to needs and lifestyles. The individual is fully capable of ignoring everything the marketer has to say. It all comes down to a simple point: It is easier for a firm to change its marketing programs to fit the preferences of consumers than to expect consumers to change their preferences to fit the needs of a marketer. Firms that survive and thrive learn that the consumer reigns.

### The Consumer Is Global

"The world is our marketplace" might be the new creed for consumers and organizations that must understand consumers who watch global television networks and search the World Wide Web to satisfy basic consumer needs and decision processes that are nearly universal. The new global consumer buys the same brands, from the same types of retailers, and for the same reasons in many countries throughout the world. Whether it is South Africa, Taiwan, Russia, or Australia, researchers are using the same methods and theories to conduct research and analyze consumer behavior. Even though there are differences between cultures and consumer decisions, as consumers become more global the similarities are much greater.

### Consumers Are Different; Consumers Are Alike

In school, children often learn to focus on the *differences* (primarily outward in appearance) that distinguish people, but marketing practitioners focus on the similarities, always looking for groups of people who have the same needs and basic behaviors wherever they may live and whatever they do. Marketers must dive deeper in their understanding of consumer behavior to identify groups of people—called **market segments**—spanning demographic characteristics and geographical boundaries. Consumer analysts focus on *similarities within groups of consumers, while recognizing the differences between groups.* When these segments exist *across national boundaries,* it's described as **intermarket segmentation.**[15] Look at Figure 1.9 and you'll see consumers who superficially appear to be different. Probe into their behavior, however, and you'll see more similarities, in this case behavior that causes them to respond to brands in similar ways. In this example, the segment is global, composed of consumers who respond to brands in similar fashion. It probably matters little what the country of origin of the brand may be or where the consumer might live.

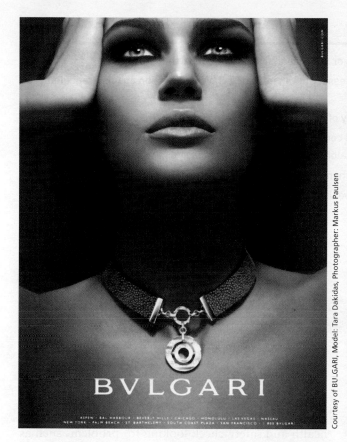

**FIGURE 1.9** What Similar Behaviors Would You Expect to Find Among These Consumers?

| 1. | The right to safety—protection against products or services that are hazardous to health and life. |
| 2. | The right to be informed—provision of facts necessary for an informed choice; protection against fraudulent, deceitful, or misleading claims. |
| 3. | The right to choose—assured access to a variety of products and services at competitive prices. |
| 4. | The right to be heard (redress)—assurance that consumer interests receive full and sympathetic consideration in formulation and implementation of regulatory policy, and prompt and fair restitution. |
| 5. | The right to enjoy a clean and healthful environment. |
| 6. | The right of the poor and other minorities to have their interests protected. |

**BUYER BEWARE 1.2**

## Do You Know Your Rights?

When you rent an apartment, many landlords will check your credit rating. It's essential, they argue, to protect against fraud. They may also check your employment history and criminal records. Be sure to check your own credit report, which usually can be done online, before you look at apartments. If you've had problems with credit or landlords in the past, it is usually best to be upfront and offer an explanation for what happened. Some landlords are willing to make exceptions if you have credible explanations.

As a consumer, you may also take steps to protect against landlord fraud. One way is to ask in writing for any promises to fix problems or to refund security deposits. Then be sure you store that document in a safe, accessible place. You also should do a complete health and safety check looking for problems such as disrepair. A quality apartment often indicates a quality landlord. Oral promises to fix problems often lead to disputes.

If you have problems, get help from the local association of apartment owners, city or county officials, and perhaps the Better Business Bureau.

Source: Based on Jennifer Plotnick, "Renters, Tenants Should Know What They're Getting Into," *Knight-Ridder Tribune Business News* (April 16, 2005), 1.

### The Consumer Has Rights

Consumer needs are real. They are expressed in the purchases consumers make and in the purchases they choose to forego. Leo Bogart, a well-known marketing strategist, stated that the combined effect of the thousands of advertisements consumers face each year is a constant reminder of material goods and services they don't have. Individuals are motivated toward more consumption, acquisition, and upward mobility, and society is driven to produce and innovate.[16] Sometimes, however, fraud and manipulation occur, and in response to such events, the Consumer Bill of Rights was written,[17] as shown in Table 1.1.

Rights are absolute, inviolable, and nonnegotiable. Outright deception, poor product quality, nonresponse to legitimate complaints, pollution, and other actions are nothing less than violations of legitimate rights. A shift toward higher demands for moral and ethical behavior appears to be taking place, even in the face of violations of such standards by business and political leaders. Manufacturers and retailers increasingly are faced with vigorous protest when their actions go against social consensus. When you read Buyer Beware 1.2, consider what consumers sometimes must do to protect their rights.

The right way to think about consumer behavior includes high standards concerning deception, fraud, or lack of consumer information. What do you think—do firms generally increase their profits by deceiving or cheating consumers? Though high standards for consumer information and prevention of consumer deception are justifiable for personal and moral reasons, these standards also help the long-term profitability of organizations. Research by Dr. James Collins and Dr. Jerry Porrous in their best-selling *Built To Last* indicates that firms with clear, visionary standards of right and wrong are the ones that earn the highest profits and have the best-performing stock.[18] Call it values or call it ethics, the best firms are those that place the safety, social, and physical well-being of their customers ahead of corporate profits.

Sometimes skeptics criticize companies for advertising, accusing them of trying to persuade consumers to buy products or services that they might not need. Some call it social irresponsibility. There are times, however, when *not* advertising a product or service could be considered socially irresponsible. If a company develops a product to help consumers quit smoking or overcome obesity, consumers would be worse off if they didn't know about the product or were withheld the right to buy the product. More generally, any company that believes it produces products or services that consumers either need or desire has a responsibility to inform and educate consumers about that product. Failure to do so may also result in the failure of the firm. In contrast, if a firm produces a bad product, it will find that effective advertising only accelerates the demise of the product and perhaps the firm.

## Challenges for the Future

More than thirty-five years have passed since the field of consumer research was born, evolving from various disciplines in behavioral sciences. More than ever before, the need to understand consumers and consumer behavior has become a hot topic around the globe, from boardrooms and executive suites to universities and health care providers. Now, we find ourselves with new challenges:

1. Gathering and interpreting correctly the information that organizations need to meet the sophisticated needs of organizations in the twenty-first century

2. Developing effective consumer research methods to keep abreast of the rapid changes in consumer trends and lifestyles

3. Understanding consumer behavior from a broader perspective as an important part of life in its own right

Fasten your seatbelt as we fly into the midst of a sophisticated base of theory and methodology for the remainder of this book. Consumer behavior is dynamic and exciting, and one thing is for sure—the rate at which consumers are changing and at which marketing is adapting will only accelerate in the future. Mastering this subject will require a long-term commitment to the study of consumers—how their lifestyles and needs are changing, how family structures and relationships are changing, and how purchase behaviors and consumption patterns are changing. Although this book is designed to make you a better marketer by illustrating how firms use consumer research to enhance marketing strategies, mastery of this subject can help make you a better consumer as well.

## Summary

Research into consumer motivation and behavior has assumed significance in contemporary societies worldwide. In the past thirty-five years, a large and growing multidisciplinary field of study has emerged. A concern of businesses, consumer economists, and others is to find more effective strategies to influence and shape behavior. The best firms are searching for ways to gather and analyze consumer information to help develop winning strategies. As a result, consumer research is of premier importance in this applied world.

Just as business orientation evolved throughout the years (from a manufacturing orientation to consumer orientation), so has the study of consumer behavior evolved, sometimes fueling and sometimes keeping pace with the changes in organizations. One thing is for certain, consumer behavior is more important than ever in today's consumer-focused world, making consumer analysts valuable to any type of organization. Some consumer analysts have a more holistic perspective referred to as *postmodernism* and are focusing efforts on studies of consumption to understand how humans think and behave in this important life activity. When we factor in the more recent expansion of inquiry across cultural borders, the result is a rich and growing field of research. In addition to exploring why people buy certain products, consumer behavior also focuses on the study of how consumers *use* products. Consumption research provides marketers with insights to guide new product development and communication strategies.

The perspective of this book is primarily, although not exclusively, that of the field of marketing. As a result, our central concern is the practical relevance of principles and findings to business strategies. Once you accept the premise that it is important to study consumers, the question of how best to study them arises. Various research methods are used today to get into the minds of people to understand why they behave in certain ways. These methods include observational research, interviews and surveys, and experimentation. Although research provides insight into marketing planning and corporate strategy, it also serves as the basis for consumer education and protection, and furnishes important information for public policy decisions.

## Review and Discussion Questions

1. Discuss Sam's Walton's statement that "only the customer can fire us all." Do you agree with this statement, and how do you relate consumer behavior to this statement?

2. Which of the following decisions should be considered legitimate topics of concern in the study of consumer behavior: (a) selecting a college, (b) purchasing a life insurance policy, (c) smoking a cigarette, (d) selecting a church to join, (e) selecting a dentist, (f) visiting an auto showroom to see new models, or (g) purchasing a college textbook. Explain the importance or potential application of each.

3. Think of a product you recently bought and used. Using a consumption analysis approach, describe what product or packaging features could be improved based on an examination of how it is consumed.

4. Examine current advertisements for consumer products and select one for a new product. Will this product succeed in the long run in the consumer marketplace? What factors determine success?

5. A family has just come into the local office of a lending agency, asking for a bill consolidation loan. Payments for a new car, television, stereo, bedroom set, and central air conditioning have become excessive. The head of the family does not have a steady source of income, and real help is now needed. Is this an example of purposeful consumer behavior, or has this family been manipulated into making unwise purchases?

6. If it is true that motivations and behavior can be understood through research, is it also true that the marketer now has greater ability to influence the consumer than would have been the case in an earlier era?

7. What contribution does the analysis of consumer behavior make to the fields of finance, production, insurance, and top management administration?

8. Would it be equally necessary to understand consumer behavior if the economic system were not one of free enterprise? In other words, is the subject matter of this book only of interest to those in capitalistic systems, or does it also have relevance for socialist and communist societies?

9. Health care costs are soaring in the United States, higher than any other nation in the world. What could an understanding of consumer behavior and marketing do to solve this problem?

# Notes

[1] Michael Arndt with Adrienne Carter and Catherine Arnst, "Needed: More Bite to Fight Fat," *Business Week* (January 31, 2005), 36.

[2] Walter A. McDougall, *Freedom Just Around the Corner* (New York: Harper-Collins, 2004).

[3] Roger Blackwell, *From Mind to Market* (New York: HarperBusiness, 1997).

[4] Ernest Dichter was a prolific writer. Perhaps the most representative of his contributions is *The Strategy of Desire* (New York: Doubleday, 1960).

[5] Vance Packard, *The Hidden Persuaders* (New York: Mackay, 1957).

[6] A definitive source on this subject is John F. Sherry, "Postmodern Alternatives: The Interpretive Turn in Consumer Research," in Thomas S. Robertson and Harold J. Kassarjian, eds., *Handbook of Consumer Behavior* (Englewood Cliffs, NJ: Prentice Hall, 1991), 548–591.

[7] For an example of ethnographic research on how shoppers develop and imagine the social relationship when selecting goods, see Daniel Miller, *A Theory of Shopping* (Ithaca, NY: Cornell University Press, 1998).

[8] Naresh Malhotra, *Marketing Research: An Applied Orientation,* 3rd ed. (Upper Saddle River, NJ: Prentice Hall, 1999). Also see references on marketing research such as Joseph Hair Jr., Robert P. Bush, and David J. Ortinau, *Marketing Research: Within a Changing Information Environment* (New York: McGraw-Hill/Irwin, 2002); and David Aaker, *Marketing Research* (New York: Wiley, 2004).

[9] Joshua Macht, "The New Market Research," *Inc.* (July 1998), 88–94.

[10] Tom McGee, "Getting Inside Kids' Heads," *American Demographics* (January 1997), 53.

[11] Paco Underhill, *Why People Buy: The Science of Shopping* (New York: Simon and Schuster, 2000); and Paco Underhill, *The Call of the Mall* (New York: Simon and Schuster, 2004).

[12] Michel Wedel and Rik Pieters, "Eye Fixations on Advertisements and Memory of Brands: A Model and Findings," *Marketing Science,* 19 (Fall 2000), 297–312; and Ralph van der Lans, Rik Pieters, and Michel Wedel, "Eye Movement Analysis of Target Search," working paper, 2004.

[13] Seymour Sudman and Edward Blair, "Sampling in the Twenty-First Century," *Journal of the Academy of Marketing Science,* 27 (Spring 1999), 269–277.

[14] Peter E. Drucker, *The Practice of Management* (New York: Harper & Row, 1954), 37.

[15] Salah Hassan and Roger Blackwell, *Global Marketing: Perspectives and Cases* (Chicago: Dryden Press, 1994), 53.

[16] Leo Bogart, "Where Does Advertising Research Go from Here?" *Journal of Advertising Research,* 9 (March 1969), 10.

[17] For a fascinating history, see Robert J. Lampman, "JFK's Four Consumer Rights: A Retrospective View," in Scott E. Maynes, ed., *The Frontier of Research in Consumer Interest* (Ames, IA: American Council on Consumer Interests, 1998), 19–26.

[18] James Collins and Jerry Porrous, *Built to Last* (New York: HarperBusiness, 1997).

# Chapter 2

# Creating Marketing Strategies for Customer-Centric Organizations

## Opening Vignette

Did you know that Gene Simmons, the makeup-wearing, tongue-wagging leader of the rock group KISS, and Sam Walton, the straitlaced founder of the world's largest corporation, are "soul mates"? You're probably thinking, "What could this pair possibly have in common besides both starting their businesses in the 1960s?" Well, the answer is strategy. Simmons and Walton used the same understanding of why consumers buy (and what strategy would assure that consumers would buy from them) to become two of the most effective merchandisers in the world.

Wal*Mart, the world's largest corporation (based on sales) is headquartered in the Ozark mountain town of Bentonville, Arkansas (population: 19,730), not far from its first store in Rogers, Arkansas. Seeing customers through the eyes of founder Sam Walton, this "little David" conquered the "Goliaths" of American retailing—Montgomery Ward, Kmart, and Sears. While other retailers focused on their "bottom lines," Wal*Mart organized everything in the firm, including technology, employees, merchandise, and logistics, in such a way that pleased its customers. As a result of this customer-centric approach, Wal*Mart ranked first in J. D. Power & Associates' national survey of customer satisfaction and achieved annual sales of nearly $300 billion (putting Wal*Mart well on its way to becoming the world's first trillion-dollar corporation).

With food sales approaching $162 billion, Wal*Mart eclipses the combined total sales of the next three largest grocery retailers—Kroger, Safeway, and Albertson's—yet Wal*Mart's commitment to low prices causes local grocery prices to drop about 14 percent when Wal*Mart enters a new market (saving money for customers who don't even shop there). Analyzing consumer behavior to determine what additional items consumers might like to buy at low prices, Wal*Mart constantly expands its mix of products and services to now include appliances, gasoline, auto maintenance, banking, and even chiropractic clinics in some stores. The ability to evolve and change in response to consumer demand also is a trait shared by KISS.

Although the members of KISS were raised in New York, the group achieved little success in large cities, where it faced competition from groups with more musical talent. Gene Simmons admits that "we're not the best musicians," but when KISS concentrated on rural fairs and small town venues, its pyrotechnics, platform shoes, and makeup were far more exciting than the alternatives available to teenagers at the time—which in some cases were limited to someone loudly playing their car stereo in the parking lot of the local Sonic drive-in. Just like Wal*Mart, KISS built its base of fans in small segments neglected by major bands, using its "KISS Army" to persuade radio stations to play its music and gradually achieve the scale of visibility needed to enter larger venues, including New York's Madison Square Garden. Like Wal*Mart, KISS became champion merchandisers, identifying what customers would buy for what price and selling 2,500 different items ranging from KISS-branded T-shirts and pens to action figures and condoms.

Like KISS, Wal*Mart didn't attack the likes of Sears and Kmart "head-on" but rather followed the classic military strategy of guerilla warfare by flanking a superior force—in KISS and Wal*Mart's case, by building strength in small segments of consumers. Wal*Mart "conquered" rural communities, keeping overhead costs low while building volume that allowed it to negotiate low prices from suppliers. The giants of retailing focused on metropolitan areas and largely ignored such market segments, considering them too small to be profitable. As a result, Wal*Mart's competition was weak. After circling cities, however, Wal*Mart infiltrated its small-town values of friendly people and low prices, first to the suburbs, then to major urban areas and eventually to other nations to become the world's largest retailer. Whereas department stores emphasized high margins on their merchandise, Wal*Mart's customer-centric strategy was based on the belief that it's more profitable to make a little on a lot. Today Steve & Barry's (clothing) and Aldi (groceries) are following a similar strategy, concentrating on rural or lower-income consumers to build strength for growth in mass markets.

Much of Wal*Mart's success can be attributed to the values and vision of founder Sam Walton, who thrived on change, whether it was changing consumer behavior or advances in technology. When Wal*Mart learned that Kmart and other retailers often frustrated customers by being out of stock on advertised items, it made massive investments in RFID (Radio Frequency Identification Devices) to track inventory moving through its warehouses, traveling in its trucks, and sitting in the back of its stores to make sure its customers weren't disappointed when they looked for Tide detergent, Gillette razors, and Ol' Roy dog food at Wal*Mart. Today RFID tags are placed only on case and pallet shipments, but when the cost is low enough for tags to be placed on individual items, consumers could potentially push their shopping carts through an "antenna" that automatically detects and totals all items, bypassing the manual checkout lines that now frustrate time-strapped shoppers.

Customer-centricity strategies need technology to facilitate data warehousing, data mining, and logistics. Wal*Mart's RetailLink is the largest private database in the world, designed to track what consumers are buying, reduce overhead, offer lower prices, and increase customer satisfaction. When a Wal*Mart customer buys a box of Pampers baby diapers, the "cha-ching" of the cash register is heard all the way in Bentonville—thanks to rapid and sophisticated electronic data interchange (EDI) transmission—where data is stored in a 460-terabyte warehouse. To put that in perspective, the Internet has less than half as much data, according to experts. The "cha-ching" of Wal*Mart's cash registers is also heard at the Cincinnati headquarters of Procter & Gamble, the manufacturer of Pampers. Cooperative sharing of data with supply chain partners to schedule manufacturing and delivery more efficiently is a big part of building effective marketing strategies in customer-centric organizations.

## The Century of the Consumer

You're living in what could be called the century of the consumer, because what consumers buy determines which firms survive or thrive. Today's consumers have more power than ever before, fueling two-thirds of the U.S. economy. More important than ever is **consumer analysis**, *the process of understanding consumer trends, global consumer markets, models to predict purchase and consumption patterns, and communication methods to reach target markets most effectively*. This chapter focuses on the concepts, methods, and skills that you, as a consumer analyst, will need to be effective in formulating and implementing marketing strategies in customer-centric organizations. These concepts and methods include customer relationship management, market segmentation, brand strategy, customer retention and loyalty programs, and global marketing and communication strategies.

### What Is Strategy?

Some people believe that marketing involves manipulating consumers, but when marketing is successful, the organization is really the one that gets manipulated. **Strategy,** a *decisive allocation of resources (capital, technology, and people) in a particular direction,* is essential to this process. In customer-centric organizations, the direction in which resources should be committed is determined by consumers. The job of consumer analysts is to understand consumers well enough to predict what direction they will lead the organization. The process is similar in business-to-business (B2B) marketing organizations because industrial demand is ultimately created by consumer demand. For B2B marketers, the challenge is not only to understand the minds of customers, but also to understand the minds of customers' customers.

At a more operational level, marketing strategy is a long-range, time-phased plan designed to achieve, usually at a high rate of return on investment, a market position so advantageous that competitors can retaliate only at prohibitively high costs.

### What Are Customer-Centric Organizations?

**Customer-centricity** is *a strategic commitment to focus every resource of the firm on serving and delighting profitable customers*. It involves producing new or improved products with evolving marketing methods focused on core, but sometimes changing, market targets.

Customer-centricity is vividly illustrated at Amazon.com, whose original mission in 1995 was to be "the Earth's largest bookstore." Today, Amazon's mission is to be "the Earth's most customer-centric organization" (you can view this description in the Investor Relations section of www.amazon.com). CEO Jeff Bezos has explained that customer-centricity involves "starting with the mind of customers and working backward in the supply chain." Since inception, Amazon has spent $1.1 billion on technology compared to $700 million on customer acquisition and $300 million on fulfillment assets. Obsession with consumers has created a strategy for Amazon more profitably tied to its role as a B2B services provider than as a retailer, illustrating how customer-centricity causes a firm to refocus both its markets and its products, often facilitated by technology.

A summit of leading retailers, technology firms, and academic researchers on customer-centricity (sponsored by Cisco Systems and Dartmouth's Tuck School of Business) addressed the question, "What does it mean to be a customer-centric organization?" [1] The characteristics of such an organization include the following.

## SHARED VISION AND VALUES

The essence of customer-centricity is not software to aid in customer relationship management (CRM). It's a vision, a set of values, and a belief that the future of the firm is embedded in the minds of consumers. If senior management is not *obsessive* about delighting customers, don't expect the phrase "customer-centricity" to do much for the organization.

## CROSS-FUNCTIONAL INTEGRATION

Customer-centricity breaks down "silos" in organizations, focusing everyone on core customers. Customer-centricity is achieved by marketing and sales, customer call centers, and CRM software linked closely to production, human resources (HR), and finance. Providing all functional areas with easily understandable information on all other business functions is a characteristic of customer-centricity and a major challenge for information technology (IT).

## SYSTEM-WIDE SIMULTANEOUS TRAINING

A wise Texan once said, "You can't no more do what you ain't been taught, than you can go back to where you ain't been." In small organizations, this concept involves face-to-face interaction of *all* the members of the team from the CEO down to front-line sales people and truck drivers. In large organizations, it means total organizational meetings, on a global basis, probably delivered by satellite, Internet, or other technologies—catapulting IT to the forefront of the HR role in customer-centric organizations.

## CUSTOMER-BASED METRICS

Progress toward customer-centricity requires changing from metrics based on product lines, geographic divisions, or business units—including profitability, productivity, and customer satisfaction—to metrics based on core customers and segments. It means marketers, especially retailers, need to change from tracking "comp store" sales to "comp customer" sales.

## From Market Analysis to Market Strategy: Where Does Consumer Behavior Fit?

The goal of a customer-centric organization is to provide consumers with more *value* than its competitors. **Value** is the *difference between what consumers give up* (time, money, or other resources) *for a product and the benefits they receive.* In today's value-conscious environment, sellers must develop and communicate the overall value of their products.[2]

Quality, often thought to be synonymous with value, is not enough to sustain competitive advantage in today's environment,[3] but the combination of other components of value, such as brand, image, price, and product features, does provide an advantage. It must be clear, however, how these components communicate value to customers.[4] For example, both Nike and Reebok athletic shoes provide the same basic functions and quality. However, Nike's shoes might have a special air-cushioning feature in their soles, the brand endorsement of Michael Jordan, and bear the famous "swoosh" logo. Reeboks might feature a nighttime reflector and a lower price. Consumers choose products that provide the greatest value—not necessarily in terms of cost savings, but in terms of overall benefits, which might include the approval of peers.

**Marketing strategy** involves *the allocation of resources to develop and sell products or services that consumers will perceive to provide more value than competitive*

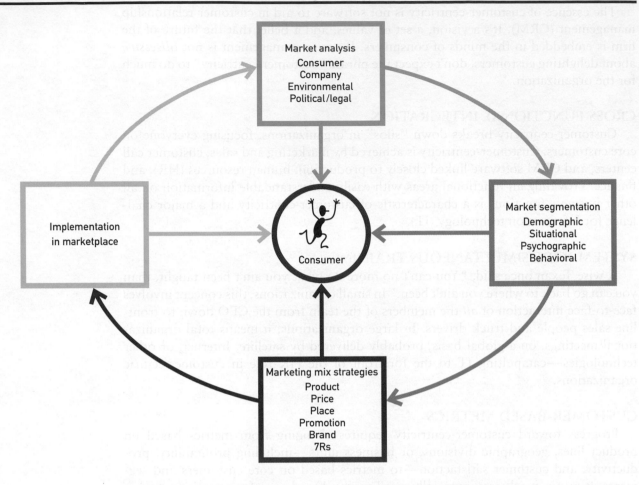

Market analysis
Consumer
Company
Environmental
Political/legal

Market segmentation
Demographic
Situational
Psychographic
Behavioral

Implementation
in marketplace

Consumer

Marketing mix strategies
Product
Price
Place
Promotion
Brand
7Rs

*products or services.* The process includes *market analysis, market segmentation, brand strategy,* and *implementation,* with the study of consumers at the core. As seen in Figure 2.1, the consumer relates directly with each of these areas of strategy formulation and implementation. To reap the rewards of consumer research and market planning, marketers must understand how consumer behavior fits into the marketing process. What roles do consumers and consumer behavior have in market analysis, marketing strategy, and the entire marketing process? Figure 2.1 shows four major steps of marketing any product or service and introducing it to the marketplace.

### Market Analysis

**Market analysis** is the *process of analyzing changing consumer trends, current and potential competitors, company strengths and resources, and the technological, legal, and economic environments.* All these factors add dimension and insight to the potential success of a plan for a new product or service.

## CONSUMER INSIGHT AND PRODUCT DEVELOPMENT

When marketers attempt to get consumers to buy their products, most of the time they fail. Kuczmarski & Associates studied the success rates of 11,000 new products launched by 77 different companies and found that only 56 percent were still on the market five years later.[5] Group EFO Ltd. reports even more discouraging results, with only 8 percent of new product concepts offered by a group of 112 leading manufacturers and retailers reaching the market, 83 percent of which failed to meet marketing objectives.[6]

Why is this failure rate so high? The answer is simple and straightforward—a new product must satisfy customers' needs, wants, and expectations, not those of a management team, and they must do it better than existing solutions. Although formal analyses might point to product life cycles, poor performance, or ineffective communication, often the bottom-line issue is a failure to understand the intended market. For instance, many firms don't understand how targeted consumers are likely to react to new products. Different consumers possess different levels of innovativeness, affecting which advertising and positioning strategies will be most effective. For example, highly innovative consumers attach more importance to stimulation, creativity, and curiosity,[7] characteristics that marketers can use to target product offerings and advertising to specific segments. Organizations around the world continue to spend billions of dollars annually on product concepts that would never be introduced to the marketplace if they had been more closely tested against consumer insight.

**Consumer insight** can be defined as *an understanding of consumers' expressed and unspoken needs and realities that affect how they make life, brand, and product choices.*[8] This concept combines *facts* (either from primary or secondary research, sales data, or customer information) with *intuition,* resulting in an *insight* that can lead to a new product, existing product innovation, brand extension, or revised communication plan. As companies turn to consumer feedback for new product guidance and ideas, researchers and marketers search for ways to channel *ideation* (the process of forming and relating ideas) to allow consumers to be more focused and productive, providing better information to marketers.[9]

In the century of the consumer, marketers need to understand market reality, sometimes through participant observation.[10] Anyone in the firm can conduct research, including the CEO. Eastman Kodak executive Raymond H. DeMoulin was in a Tokyo fish market early one morning when he observed a photographer trying to pry open a film container with his teeth while holding his camera. This observation quickly led to a packaging change enabling consumers to open containers of Kodak film with one hand.[11] Even though he had no clipboard or computerized data reports in front of him, DeMoulin conducted consumer research that morning—the enlightened use of observation, which then was blended with experience and intuition (creative insight) to build practical, workable marketing strategy. As with other corporate initiatives, the greater perceived importance placed on consumer insight by top management, the more likely it is to affect product development strategies. You can see how market analysis without consumer insight led to disaster for Toys "R" Us and other firms in Consumer Behavior and Marketing 2.1.

## CONSUMER ENVIRONMENT

When marketers study the *consumer environment,* they examine many issues, including demographic trends; personal and group influences; consumers' knowledge, attitudes, and motivations; the process by which consumers make their purchase and consumption decisions; and changing consumer needs, wants, and lifestyles. The relationship between the consumer in the middle of the model in Figure 2.1 and the market analysis stage is an important one. Understanding changes in the consumer environment can lead to new product ideas, product adaptations, new packaging, or even new services to help consumers meet their changing needs. For example, consumers are spending more time working than in the past, including longer commutes.

## Retail Strategy Is Not Kids' Play

When U.S. toy retailer Toys "R" Us decided to expand sales by opening stores in Australia, the market statistics made it appear as easy as kids' play. Australia is a high-income market of 17 million consumers, known as a culture to be highly interested in its children. With a toy purchase rate 30 percent less than in the United States, Toys "R" Us smelled market opportunity.

It entered the market and reportedly lost over $100 million, because it lacked consumer insight into the consumption patterns in a nation that has mostly good weather all year. Toys "R" Us achieved success for many years in the United States and Germany, but those nations are much colder than Australia. When children play outside, as they do in Australia, they don't require as many toys.

Toys "R" Us also failed to understand the local competition. Coles Myer, operator of Kmart and Target in Australia, anticipated the threat and made large investments to fend off Toys "R" Us, developing a new chain of its own called "Just for Kids." As Australia's leading retailer, Coles Myer had better access to local real estate and moved quickly to get the best locations—a critical move considering the adage that the three most important variables in retail are "location, location, and location."

The other local competitor, Big W (operated by Woolworths of Australia, no longer related to the former U.S. retailer), analyzed the market and realized that Toys "R" Us gets 80 percent of its sales and profits from 20 percent of its SKUs. Big W sent buyers to the United States to buy heavily in this 20 percent, stocked these items in its stores, and slashed prices so much that neither Just for Kids or Toys "R" Us could be profitable on their core merchandise. Big W, which operates in Australia with the same or greater efficiency that Wal*Mart operates in the United States, made money while Toys "R" Us lost $100 million and Just For Kids lost $250 million before closing its stores.

In the United States, Toys "R" Us faced similar problems in dealing with Wal*Mart. Maybe consumer analysts at Wal*Mart's Bentonville, Arkansas, headquarters were watching what happened in Australia! Marketing strategy without consumer insight yields poor strategy.

This changing environment creates an opportunity for more iPod accessories to be licensed for use in automobiles, as you read in Consumer Behavior and Marketing 1.1 in Chapter 1.

### CORPORATE STRENGTHS AND RESOURCES

Developing marketing strategy is a process of balancing market opportunities with corporate resources and strengths. This process involves examining the financial stability and resources of the company, as well as its technological, personnel, managerial, production, research, and marketing abilities. How much can the company invest of these various resources into the development and marketing of this product? Great opportunities may exist but a firm may simply lack key resources to pursue them and determine that lesser opportunities more closely fit the firm's capabilities. What resources does the company lack, and how might it overcome its weaknesses internally or through relationships with strategic partners? For example, Procter & Gamble once developed everything internally, but today 35 percent of its innovations are based on licensing and strategic acquisitions.

## CURRENT AND POTENTIAL COMPETITORS

A thorough market analysis also examines *current and potential competitors*. A traditional approach to this type of analysis focuses strategic thinking on staying ahead of the competition, which might include looking at existing competitive products and figuring out how to add a feature that might make a product "just a little better" in the mind of consumers. Other, more innovative firms pay less attention to matching or beating their rivals, but focus instead on using innovation to weaken or make competitors irrelevant in the marketplace.[12] How does a firm accomplish this, how easy will it be for competitors to enter the market, and how will current competitors react?

Firms can construct alternative *scenarios* to anticipate reactions of current competitors and anticipate how firms, though not necessarily competitors at present, might respond with similar products. Think how Toys "R" Us's strategy in CBM 2.1 might have been different if it understood better the competition it faced in Australia.

## MARKET ENVIRONMENT

Marketers also must examine the condition of the overall *market environment* into which the product or service will be introduced. Factors such as the state of the economy, government regulations, physical conditions, and technology play an important role in the potential success of a product or service. If the economy is not good—unemployment is high, inflation is high, or wages are declining—introducing relatively expensive products may fail. Although segments of the market may buy high-end products regardless of overall economic conditions, volume may be too small to justify introduction or price and distribution strategies may need to be changed. Legal and governmental factors that must be considered, especially when selling in global markets, include local ordinances, tariffs and trade agreements, and currency fluctuations. Physical conditions, including a country's political stability and infrastructure reliability, the availability of technology, and overall personal health (including the prevalence of HIV/AIDS and obesity), are all factors that create both market problems and strategic opportunities for firms that understand them.

Natural disasters such as hurricanes and ice storms may disrupt the sales of many firms, but they also generate opportunities for retailers who have a strategic plan. Home Depot and Lowe's are known for quickly turning such disasters into opportunities by, for example, moving inventories of plywood, generators, and drinking water to consumers in Florida in the hours following a hurricane. You might believe that marketers can't do anything about the weather, but consumer analysts now employ strategic weather services (such as www.flashweather.com) that provide long- and short-term forecasts, giving retailers and manufacturers the ability to increase stocks of snow blowers before especially cold winters or of sprinklers before dry summers.

All of the elements in the marketing environment affect consumer needs and ability to buy. Many also affect consumer mood and willingness to buy, both at a macro-level affecting total retail sales and at a micro-level affecting specific products and retailers. Market Facts 2.1 describes some trends that affect consumer mood and marketing tactics in the U.S. market.

## Consumer Mood Affects Marketing Strategy

Consumer analysts focus on understanding consumer mood because mood affects buying and consumption. Consumers tend to cycle between buying more of what they *need* versus what they *want,* depending on their moods. When consumers are happy and feel that times are good, they are much more likely to buy items that they want, regardless of how much they really need them, which causes sales of luxury cars, jewelry, vacations, and "white tablecloth" restaurants to soar. The converse is true when consumer moods shift downward. Product positioning, sales forecasts, and marketing strategy should therefore reflect factors that can be forecast with contingency plans for those more difficult to anticipate. The following are some factors that consumer analysts seek to understand as mood determinants.

- *Stock market:* When the stock market falls, consumers feel financially vulnerable (even though their income might be the same or even higher than the previous year), often causing a pullback in buying and slow growth or declines in retail sales.
- *Media:* As the media bombards people with stories about layoffs, unemployment, corruption, and violence, consumers become as depressed as if these things were happening to them. Some consumers resort to "tuning out" the media, and some marketers avoid placing ads in media during news events likely to elicit negative moods.
- *Workplace:* In the wake of corporate bankruptcies and downsizing, trust between management and employees is sometimes strained, which causes employees to transfer their fears and low morale to peers while providing poor service to customers.
- *Peers and family:* Financial and health challenges can either strain or strengthen relationships with family or peers, depending on the emotional maturity of the individual. Divorce, depression, and family strife may influence individual buying patterns and motivations.

- *Changing self-concepts:* Obesity is now America's number-one health problem, and when people don't feel good about their bodies, they are less likely to be in the mood to try on clothes, follow fashion trends, or participate in physical activities.
- *Personal security:* When people fear terrorist or random sniper attacks, their initial reaction is to stay home, which causes declining retail sales. Safety concerns may make catalog or online shopping more attractive and create market opportunities for security products.

People look for ways to change their moods and escape the pressures of daily life. For some consumers, the solution is shopping. Just as marketers are sometimes the "victims" of consumer mood, so they can be change agents of consumer mood, creating havens of comfort in neighborhood restaurants, shopping malls, and community events to which consumers may want to flock. Engaging consumers through all of their senses—from colors that convey happiness and security and scents that are inviting— makes them want to spend more time in stores. Special sales may use price as an enticement to leave home for the mall, but so do friendly faces, helpful associates, good lighting, and security measures. When disasters or attacks occur, marketing leaders need to spend time in their stores and with their employees, talking to them, reassuring them, and spending time with them in recreational activities and community projects to rebuild trust. Marketers may not be able to change the environmental factors that create depressed consumer mood, but they can create places people want to be and *the reassurance of familiar brands and products.* Ultimately, consumer mood changes, and marketers that invest in an emotional relationship with their customers, even when they aren't buying, reap rewards when mood and financial circumstances turn upward.

Source: Adapted from Roger D. Blackwell, "Understanding Consumer Mood," *RIS News* (December 2002), 10.

**FIGURE 2.2**    Consumer-Centric Marketing Strategy:
Market Segmentation

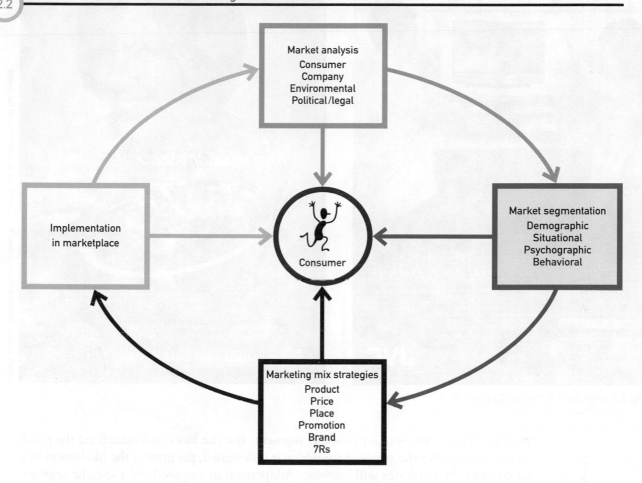

## Market Segmentation

The next step in creating market strategy, highlighted in Figure 2.2, is **market segmentation,** the *process of identifying groups of people who behave in similar ways to each other, but somewhat differently than other groups.* Look at the ads in Figure 2.3 and consider how you would describe how these people would behave in situations other than using the products shown. Some variables used to identify segments are described in Table 2.1. Identifying groups of people with similar *behavior* enables product, packaging, communications, and other elements of the marketing mix to be focused on creating a special appeal that meets the group's specific needs.

A **market segment** is *a group of consumers with similar behavior and needs that differs from those of the entire or mass market.* The need for segmentation is rooted in the fact that people are different—if all humans were identical in their preferences and behaviors, every product would be the same. But because people differ so much in their motivations, needs, and decision processes, custom-tailoring products and services maximizes consumer satisfaction.

The goal in measuring market segments is to allocate consumers into categories that minimize variance within groups and maximize variance between groups. By identifying market segments that are similar in their behavior, products can be developed that are closely matched to the preferences of that group. By maximizing variance between segments, a differential advantage is obtained that, ideally, will be so appealing that it will command a premium price greater than the cost of catering to the

**FIGURE 2.3** What Other Behaviors Can You Infer?

specialized preferences of a particular segment. But the more individualized the product and the smaller the segment for which it is designed, the greater the likelihood that the costs to the marketer will increase. Adaptation to the needs of a specific segment may require a higher price than consumers in that segment are willing to pay. For example, custom-tailored clothing and custom-designed homes meet the needs of discriminating consumers, but they carry with them higher price tags, making it difficult to compete with the lower prices of mass-produced products. The intersection of these multiple characteristics and influences is shown in Figure 2.4.

The opposite of market segmentation is **market aggregation** or **mass marketing,** which occurs *when organizations choose to market and sell the same product or service to all consumers.* This strategy may be effective in emerging economies where there exists pent-up demand for basic products and services. Consumers in these markets want functional benefits at the lowest possible prices, which usually calls for a standardized product, produced at low cost in long, homogeneous production runs and sold through basic distribution channels with few added features.

Although some firms still choose a market aggregation approach, the reality is that mass markets are going the way of the dinosaur in industrially advanced countries. In North America, Europe, and some Asian markets, it may not be too bold to say that there are no more mass markets, only variations in the size of market segments. This is due to the following factors.

- Affluence: Consumers can afford products that are more customized to suit their individual tastes, needs, and lifestyles.
- Consumer databases: Product designers have the information required to address variations in consumers' consumption and behavior patterns, and marketers have the information needed to advertise and communicate with individual consumers.

- Manufacturing technology: Production processes can be computer controlled and tailored to smaller production runs without corresponding cost increases.
- Multiple distribution channels: Multiple methods of retailing, including direct sales and the Internet, allow distribution to be closely related to the needs and desires of specific segments.

## IDENTIFYING SEGMENTS

In marketing strategy applications, it is essential to remember that segmentation is based on identifying and appealing to consumers with similar behavior, not necessarily similar characteristics. When consumer analysts use consumer characteristics for segmentation, it's because they are correlates, or "proxies," for behavior—not because the characteristics are determinants of why people buy. For example, market segments that buy a stereo priced at $3,000 are much different from those that buy a stereo priced at $300. Not only will the product and price be different, based upon different music-listening behavior, but the distribution channels and promotional

| TABLE 2.1 | How to Segment Consumer Markets | |
|---|---|---|
| **CONSUMER CHARACTERISTICS** | | |
| **Demographics** | | |
| Age | Education | Marital status |
| Gender | Family size | Occupation |
| Ethnicity | Nationality | Religion |
| Income | Life stage | Living arrangements |
| **Psychographics** | | |
| Activities | Interests | Opinions |
| **Purchase and consumption behaviors** | | |
| Shopping location preferences | Brand loyalty | |
| Frequency of purchase | Benefits sought | |
| Media used | How used | |
| Price sensitivity | Rate of use | |
| **Values** | | |
| **Culture** | | |
| **Personality** | | |
| **GEOGRAPHICAL CHARACTERISTICS** | | |
| National boundaries | | |
| State and regional boundaries | | |
| Urban versus rural | | |
| Zip code | | |
| **SITUATIONAL CHARACTERISTICS** | | |
| Work versus leisure usage | | |
| Time | | |
| Where used | | |

FIGURE 2.4    Defining Markets on Multiple Characteristics

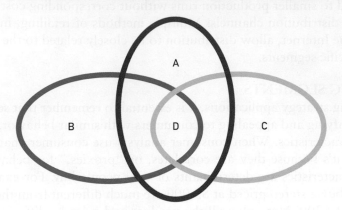

A: Demographic Segment (based on two demographic variables)
    Age 30–34, female, $40,000–$50,000 income
B: Consumption Behavior
    Eat vegetarian meals 7–10 times per week
C: Situational Characteristics
    Cook dinner at home 5 times per week
D: Intersection—Defining Market Segment
    Age 30–34, female, $40,000–$50,000 income
    Eat vegetarian meals 7–10 times per week
    Cook dinner at home 5 times per week

components of the marketing mix likely will be different. At first glance, one might conclude (falsely) that the segments buying the $3,000 stereo would all be high income and the segments buying the $300 stereo would be low income. In fact, a few low-income consumers might buy the expensive stereo (leaving other needs and wants unfulfilled), and many high-income consumers might buy the lower-priced stereo (providing future savings for consumption of other things).

Measuring behavior for the purpose of developing a targeted marketing mix is difficult, but it's relatively easy to measure consumer characteristics such as income, age, or gender. Therefore, the basis for developing marketing strategy frequently relies on these types of consumer characteristics (shown in Table 2.1) because they are often correlated with consumer behaviors. Demographics, psychographics, purchase and consumption behaviors, geographical characteristics, and situational factors are the variables typically used to define segments of potential customers with similar behavior. These variable-based segments overlap, as you can see in Figure 2.4, yielding a highly targeted segment, which may improve the predictability and sensitivity of how segments will respond to specific types of advertising, promotions, product variations, and distribution channels.

## ADDRESSING THE NEEDS OF MARKET SEGMENTS

Consumers are becoming more sophisticated, demanding more customized products to fit their individual needs, preferences, and tastes. The quest to be consumer driven has led many successful firms to offer products or services tailored to different market segments—a costly and complex undertaking, especially as consumers and their needs grow increasingly diverse. **Mass customization,** *customizing goods or services for individual customers in high volumes and at relatively low costs,* is one way for firms to efficiently offer unique value to customers. Making mass customization pay off in terms of *value to the company* requires understanding what type of customization *customers value the most,* which varies in different situations.[13] Marketers can obtain this type of information from customer databases, sometimes offering incentives to encourage customers to give information.

The ultimate form of market segmentation and customization is creating and marketing to segments of one. This process was popularized in the best-selling book, *The One To One Future*.[14] In that book, authors Martha Rogers and Don Pepper describe a florist in Bowling Green, Ohio, who specializes in selling flower arrangements and small gifts—just as most flower shops of similar size. But instead of waiting for customers to call or visit to place an order, this store relies on its database for proactive marketing. When a customer places an order, his or her contact and billing information is recorded along with what was ordered, for whom, and for which occasion. If a customer sends yellow roses for her mother's birthday on October 13, the flower shop contacts the customer a few weeks prior to that date the following year and asks if a similar bouquet should be sent this year. Although the shop sells flowers, it really sells gift solutions and convenience. With this style of individual-based marketing, this otherwise simple florist creates loyal and delighted customers. On a global scale, the same process is used by Amazon.com, which sends promotional messages to "segments of one," reflecting personal preferences in music and books, and even a "personal store" for frequent customers.

## PROFITABILITY OF MARKET SEGMENTATION

The ultimate goal of segmentation is increased customer satisfaction and profitability. Increased profitability occurs when the economic value to consumers is higher than the cost of creating the value. For example, a computer program might be adapted to the special needs of some users and positioned based on benefits most desired by this specific segment.[15] If the costs of adaptation were expensive but caused the program to be worth hundreds or even thousands of dollars of value to many users, the higher price that could be charged compared to a standardized product might yield millions of dollars of additional profitability.

Adding value by identifying profitable market segments is a process that created fortunes for Michael Dell in the computer industry and made Ft. Myers, Florida–based Chico's one of America's fastest growing and most profitable retailers, as you can read in Consumer Behavior and Marketing 2.2. At Chico's, even the in-store music is selected to attract core segments. Shoppers hear tracks like "Head Over Heels"—a mellow, Latin-flavored jazz tune by Matt Bianco—but never songs, like "New Sensation," by INXS, that are "too hard and too fast" to appeal to Chico's core customers, who prefer a mixture of adult pop, cool jazz, foreign vocals, and 1960s pop. (For details, see www.visualstore.com.) If you understood Chico's market segmentation strategy well enough to invest $10,000 in its stock (New York Stock Exchange symbol: CHS) five years earlier, your investment would have been worth $110,230 in 2005. Understanding segmentation is profitable for investors as well as marketers!

Segmentation can also help not-for-profit firms reduce their promotional expenditures and increase their revenues. Consider the example of BalletMet, a nationally recognized ballet company based in Columbus, Ohio. BalletMet tracks the purchase and attendance behaviors of its subscribers and regular ticket buyers and analyzes which types of performances they prefer. BalletMet has three major productions each year—popular and well-known performances, such as *Swan Lake, Cinderella,* and *The Nutcracker*—as well as an entire series of smaller performances ranging from the poignant to the poetic and appealing to different niche audiences. Instead of advertising all events to everyone in the database, BalletMet sends special promotions to those patrons most likely to attend a particular event. This not only reduces the cost of direct mail but significantly increases response rates. BalletMet also provides flexibility in its season ticket packages, allowing consumers to purchase the combination of performances that most appeals to them, and plans special events in relation to each performance. A performance that appeals for families, for instance, may have a pre-performance briefing

## Chico's

Exterior of a Chico's store

Chico's aims to reach its target market—female consumers between the ages of thirty-five and fifty-five, with household income over $75,000—with products featuring "unique styles and patterns, comfort, easy care and contemporary style in a fun, friendly atmosphere." Chico's starts by determining what's important to its core customers and designs its clothes, accessories, catalogs, and stores from the "mind up."

### What Makes Chico's Unique?

*Unique sizing:* Chico's clothes come in one of four sizes: 0, 1, 2, and 3. Clothes are grouped by "outfits" and "mix-and-match" garments that complement one another. Most outfits are sold as separate items, because not all women are shaped alike. Some women require different sizes for top and bottom, but Chico's product strategy allows consumers to build a completely coordinated wardrobe, one piece at a time.

*Comfort construction:* Pants and skirts have elastic waists, and jackets are "unconstructed and untailored." Free-flowing garments (as opposed to

tailored or tight-fitting clothes) do not call unwanted attention to the figures of consumers who may feel insecure with their bodies.

*Exclusivity:* Chico's clothes are not carried in any other store or catalog. Designs are inspired from cultures around the world.

*Easy wear, easy care:* All garments are machine washable and wrinkle-free. No ironing is required! This saves time-strapped consumers hundreds of dollars annually on dry cleaning. The wash-and-wear "Traveller's Collection" is "easy to pack and unpack."

*Starter's kit:* Chico's recommends that new customers start with five basic black garments (a skirt, pants, jacket, and two tank tops). Women can add additional coordinated garments and accessories to their "collection" over the years.

After $500 in purchases, shoppers become "Passport Club" members and receive the benefits listed for life. There is no time limit to accumulate the $500 in purchases and no expiration date to the program.

| | Permanent members | Preliminary members |
|---|---|---|
| Members | 1,100,000 | 3,600,000 |
| Average purchase | $113 | $73 |
| Purchase frequency | Four to seven times per year more than preliminary members | |
| Percentage of total sales | 73 | 20 |

As of 2005, Chico's operated nearly five hundred stores and expects to open three hundred more in the coming years. Stores operate at a 30 percent margin, and for the past twenty-seven of twenty-nine quarters, have experienced an 11 percent average increase in same store sales.

that explains what the ballet is about and describes the costumes and lighting. By contrast, a ballet that appeals to a mature audience may offer cocktails and hors d'oeuvres with the dancers after the performance.

## CRITERIA FOR CHOOSING SEGMENTS

How does a firm choose which segment it should target when many potential segments have been identified? Determining the attractiveness of a market segment involves analyzing segments based on the following four criteria.

- **Measurability** refers to the *ability to obtain information about the size, nature, and behavior of a market segment*. Consumers may behave in similar ways, but those behaviors must be directly measurable (or with close correlates) to formulate and implement marketing mix strategies.
- **Accessibility** (or reachability) is the *degree to which segments can be reached*, either through targeted advertising and communication programs or through multiple retail channels.
- **Substantiality** refers to the *size of the market*. Small segments may not generate enough volume to support development, production, and distribution costs that would be involved in satisfying these segments. Generally more substantial segments make better market targets.
- **Congruity** refers to *how similar members within the segment exhibit behaviors or characteristics that correlate with consumption behavior*. The more congruous a segment, the more efficient are product offerings, promotion, and distribution channels directed specifically to that segment.

Segmentation methods and strategies are continuously refined by marketers. In an era characterized by increasing market diversity resulting in market fragmentation,[16] segmentation strategy (based on data mining), customized manufacturing technology, and targeted distribution allows firms to reach smaller but potentially more profitable segments. In recent years, the analytical process has begun to move from traditional statistical methods to Bayesian methods.

## Bayesian Analysis

Answering the question of "why people buy" increasingly involves a centuries-old statistical technique called Bayesian analysis—a tool for exploring the human mind and defining market segments that has attracted the attention of marketers in recent years. Marketing researchers have long used probability theory to explain how consumers may react to marketing strategy, but in recent years have turned for help to Thomas Bayes, an eighteenth-century mathematician and theologian. He formulated an equation that expresses uncertainty using the same kind of language that describes the outcome of a coin toss or a roll of the dice in probability terms. The newer, and sometimes controversial, application of Bayes's theorem involves taking an educated guess about the likelihood of something happening, and then gradually making the prediction better by factoring in the results from rigorous, controlled scientific experiments. For classical statisticians, for whom controlled experiments were the only legitimate source of information, allowing for "educated guesses" was viewed as scientific heresy. As consumer analysts recognized that human decisions are often nonlinear, multifaceted phenomena that are nearly impossible to analyze with classical statistical methods, they turned to Bayesian statistical techniques.

Bayesian statistical techniques can analyze massive amounts of data, typically collected from point-of-sale (POS) scanner data, facilitated by large-scale computers that

## Bayesian Analysis Probes the Human Mind

Most scientific advances that are heralded as breakthroughs are really the result of years of incremental progress. "But modern Bayesian statistics really is a breakthrough, because it replaces complex equations with simple ones that computers can perform over and over," says Professor Greg Allenby at Ohio State University. Along with researchers at Harvard, Duke, Carnegie Mellon, and the University of Chicago, Allenby is one of the growing number of marketing analysts who use Bayesian statistics to understand what consumers really want and then develop effective marketing strategies to give it to them. Using market surveys to understand how consumers think is usually too broad of an approach that yields only shallow results. Allenby says it's like "a puddle a mile wide and an inch thick." Although experiments in laboratory settings can dive deep into individual behavior, they can do so only one consumer at a time. The challenge with testing on a large-scale basis, however, is that it requires massive amounts of data.

A problem with most marketing models is that they assume people think in a linear fashion when they decide to buy something—as if thought A leads directly to thought B, which leads to purchase. Unfortunately, as purchase data reveal, the human mind is decidedly nonlinear. Merging psychology, statistics, and marketing into a focus on how the human mind works for specific choices, such as how people react to a new product is a more attainable goal.

As an example of the kind of questions Bayesian analysts would like to answer, Allenby offers the simple analogy of a company that wants to introduce a new brand of ketchup. To be successful, the company needs to know more than which brands of ketchup sold well in the past. Shoppers, he says, will consider a series of questions, consciously or subconsciously, that will decide the purchase: What's special about this new ketchup? Will it help get the kids to eat? Will it go with what I'm serving? Is it priced to suit my budget? "To really understand whether a new product will sell at the grocery store, you have to think not just about the particular product, but about broad issues like family and time pressures and financial pressures and the meaning of dinner." Allenby's colleague, psychologist Trisha Van Zandt, uses the same methodology to study how people buy automobiles. "Greg talks ketchup. I talk cars," she says. "It's the same thing." Van Zandt explains that ketchup-sized decisions are similar to Toyota-sized ones. Consumers think about a product, gather information over time, marking ticks in a kind of mental "yes" or "no" column until they feel they know enough to buy, or not buy. More "ticks" may be required before consumers commit to buy a Toyota, but the process is the same, and Bayesian statistical techniques allow marketers to identify segments—perhaps in the "tails" of the distribution of choices in the total market—that marketers can identify and then serve with tailored products, product attributes, and communication strategies.

Source: Based on an interview with Professor Greg Allenby, Ohio State University, 2005.

identify patterns of behavior that identify segments based on how the human mind affects behavior rather than external consumer characteristics, such as demographics.[17] See Market Facts 2.2 for more on Bayesian analysis.

### Marketing Mix Strategies

Marketing strategy (highlighted in Figure 2.5) involves a plan to meet the needs and desires of specific target markets by providing value to that target better than competitors. Such a plan must specify the essential components of the marketing mix, often described as the four P's (product, place, price, and promotion). Consumer research is critically important in developing segmentation strategy as well as formulating the marketing mix, and both also are affected by the decision process of consumers, as you will see in Chapter 3.

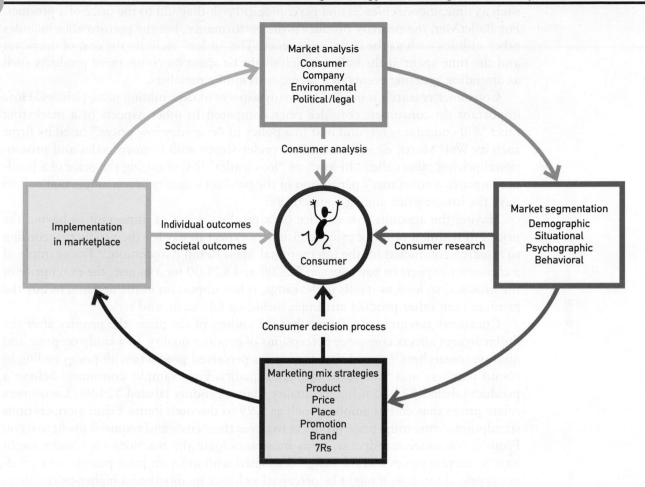

The first element of the marketing mix is **product,** which includes *the total bundle of utilities (or benefits) obtained by consumers in the exchange process.* Products include both goods and services with both tangible and intangible attributes. Products may be purchased for a variety of reasons ranging from satisfying a basic need (e.g., food) to indulging in something that just feels good (e.g., massage). Internally, a firm analyzes its capabilities and the costs associated with producing, distributing, and selling the product. Externally, however, the focus in product development is on how consumer behavior will affect the product. What form of the product best serves consumption patterns for the target segment? What packaging will best attract consumers and satisfy their transportation, usage, and disposal of the product? How will consumers compare this product to competitive or substitute products? Marketers must answer these questions and monitor consumption patterns, with product innovations following consumption trends closely.

The second element of the marketing mix is **place** (or distribution). In this phase, firms decide the *most effective outlets through which to sell their products and how best to get them there.* Where will consumers expect and want to buy this product—through mass retailers, electronic retailing, direct selling, or catalogs? An expensive or highly complex product like jewelry might sell better in a specialty store in which consumers receive personal assistance with product choice and operations instructions, whereas simple, everyday products might sell better in mass retail outlets.

The third element of the marketing mix is **price,** or the *total bundle of disutilities (costs) given up by consumers in exchange for a product.* Disutility usually refers to cash paid (or credit card debt incurred) for the product, but includes other disutilities such as time, inconvenience, and psychological risk that add to the price of a product. For BalletMet, the primary product is the performance, but the performance includes other utilities such as the social experience. The "price" includes the cost of the ticket and the time spent at the ballet, which might be spent on competitive products such as attending sporting events or a picnic with family members.

Consumer research is needed for many aspects of determining price policies. How important do consumers consider price compared to other aspects of a marketing mix? Will consumers respond best to a policy of "everyday low prices" (used by firms such as Wal*Mart), or will consumers prefer stores with frequent sales and promotional pricing (also called "hi-low" or "loss leader")? Can raising the price of a product improve a consumer's perception of the product's quality? How important is it to have the lowest price among competitors?

Having the absolute lowest price on a product is not as important as having the price fall within a range of prices consumers expect to pay for the product, according to research conducted for the International Mass Retail Association.[18] For example, if a consumer expects to pay between $25.00 and $28.00 for a blouse, the exact price of the product, so long as it falls in the range, is less important in the decision to buy the product than other product attributes including fabric, fit, and style.

Consumer research also shows that the ending of the price (the pennies after the dollar figure) affects consumer perceptions of product quality. In a study on price and quality, researchers[19] found that consumers perceived products with prices ending in round numbers and $.00 to be of higher quality. For example, consumers believe a product labeled $25.00 is higher quality than a product labeled $24.98. Consumers relate prices that end in numbers such as $.99 to discount items. From an operations standpoint, firms must price products to cover their costs and required profit margin. From a consumer standpoint, firms must anticipate the reactions consumers might have to certain prices and the image associated with different price points—if a product is priced too low, it might be perceived as lower quality than a higher-priced item.

The final element of the marketing mix is **promotion**, *including advertising, public relations, sales promotion, and personal sales.* In much of the rest of this text, you will see how organizations must determine what messages they want to send to which consumers, which forms of communication will best reach specific segments, what type of communication should occur during the various stages of the purchase and consumption processes, and how different product attributes should be positioned through different forms of media.

No discussion on marketing strategy would be complete without a discussion of *brand strategy.* Brands are discussed throughout the text because they are critically important to successful marketing strategies and are influenced by many areas of consumer behavior. They warrant special discussion here because a firm's brand or portfolio of brands is a company asset highly correlated with the firm's ability to achieve superior margins, profitability, and price-to-earnings (P/E) ratio. The more consumers equate a brand with their personal preferences, the more likely they are to be loyal to that product or company, and probably at a premium price. And if a product benefit is conveyed in a brand name, consumers are more likely to recall the advertised benefit claim.[20] Brands, done right, provide an emotional connection between a firm and its customers.

## The Value of Brands in Marketing Strategy

It doesn't matter whether you go to work for a manufacturer, distributor, or retailer, a nonprofit organization or a for-profit corporation, or the Rolling Stones or

Maroon 5—building brands will probably be an essential part of your marketing career. Some brands, such as McDonald's and Victoria's Secret, are highly successful. Some were once stellar in consumer acceptance, but turned disastrous—Montgomery Ward and Kmart come to mind—and others simply were "put out to pasture" like Borden's famous "Elsie the Cow." But regardless of how good or bad, every firm, every institution, and every person is a brand. Even government leaders are brands—consider how the "brands" of U.S. Presidents Bill Clinton and George W. Bush or New York City Mayor Rudolph Giuliani evolved during their terms of office.

A brand is perhaps the greatest asset of any company that doesn't appear on its balance sheet. Because accountants find the concept of a "brand" difficult to quantify, it is often thought of as an abstract marketing concept that involves a logo, a tagline, and large expenditures. But a **brand** is much more than that. It is *a product or product line, store, or service with an identifiable set of benefits, wrapped in a recognizable personality,* carrying with it a connection between product and customers.[21] It is the difference between a watch and a Rolex, a car and a Lexus, a cup of coffee and a Starbucks latte. It is the difference between the Eagles and Flock of Seagulls or a host of other rock and roll wannabes. In the language of business, music stars are brands—some are the Cokes and Lexuses of music and others are the Shasta colas and Yugos. In the language of music, some brands are an Aerosmith or Dave Matthews Band and others are the garage band you love, but no one else knows.

Developing brands that create brand equity requires excellence with both the functional elements and emotional elements of the brand. The **functional elements** of a brand include performance, quality, price, reliability, and logistics. In other words, does the brand *solve a problem as expected and do what it is supposed to do?* The **emotional elements** include image, personality, style, and evoked feelings. In other words, does the brand *create an emotional connection between customers and the product or firm?*[22] Southwest Airlines is similar to other airlines in its use of jets in transporting customers between two points (functional elements) but in the mind of customers, it is differentiated by having "lighthearted fun" and being "no frills" (emotional elements).

Although a powerful brand creates an image and an identity for a product or a company, it also connotes a **brand promise,** describing *what consumers can expect in exchange for their money.* If the promise is kept, brands save customers the time spent deciding between various alternatives because there is little question in the minds of consumers as to final outcome of their decision. But when the promise is not fulfilled, consumers are often dissatisfied and switch to another brand more likely to deliver on its promise, as rapidly as one number-one song replaces another.

Contrary to the perception among accountants that a brand is just a "marketing expense," branding affects the financial well-being of the entire company, and when executed properly, branding sends a unified image and message throughout the firm and throughout the marketplace. The P/E ratio and market capitalization of a public firm often is dramatically higher if it has a powerful brand or a strong portfolio of brands. For private firms, the value of its brands may have a profound influence on the continuing success and liquidation value of the firm. The difference in profitability between firms with powerful brands and those with weak brands is known as **brand equity**—*the difference in value created by a brand less the cost of creating the brand.* It may be measured as the difference between market capitalization and book value, but when brands "rock" they create investor value that lasts for decades. Creating brand equity is not a static concept or merely a marketing goal. Rather, it is a dynamic process that requires brands to be engaged in conversation with customers. This type of two-way relationship implies mutual transfer of information, from the brand to the customer and from the customer to the brand.

When a brand is successfully deployed, a it takes on an identity of its own that causes the relationship between brands and consumers to go beyond information flow to become emotion flow. Do consumers see a brand as being competent, exciting, sophisticated or rugged? **Brand personality** is *the reflection consumers see of themselves or think they will develop by using a brand.* For example, Target, Costco, Harley-Davidson, and similar brands evoke such intense emotions among their fans that they can overcome the lower prices, greater convenience, or better fuel efficiency of their competitors. Rather than focusing on relationships with customers that are primarily economic in nature, recent research focuses on those involving high levels of social exchange (described as "the identity salience model" of relationship marketing).[23] Many financial analysts missed the ground floors of stocks like Chico's, Starbucks, and Google because they underestimated the impact of emotional connections between brands and customers and failed to see the relationship between these brands and the culture of the core customers they serve.

Brands also offer protection both to firms that own a brand and consumers who buy a brand. The brand equity of a firm can be protected legally under provisions of the Lanham Act, the Federal Trademark Registry, and other legislation with firms such as Coca-Cola diligent in both their protection of the meaning of its brand to customers as well as the prevention of other firms from using a name, trade dress, or slogans that might cause confusion among consumers. **Brand protection** also extends to consumers. *By promising a certain outcome, brands reduce the risk to consumers that a product or service may not deliver as expected.* For example, guests at Hampton Inn are promised "100% Satisfaction Guaranteed." If, for any reason, a guest is dissatisfied with his or her stay, and management is unable to resolve the issue to the guest's satisfaction, the guest does not pay for the room. This protects consumers from a restless night while providing a mechanism for the hotel to assure its guests are satisfied.

Part of the success of eBay is due to member feedback, the diligence of the firm's legal department in preventing fraud, and a secure payment mechanism (PayPal), all of which protect both buyers and sellers who rely on eBay's digital marketplace to exchange value.

The goal of marketing strategy in customer-centric organizations should be to transform ordinary customers into "friends," and for the most successful brands, to delight customers and friends so well that they become "fans." Just as with rock groups, the best brands develop fans who will endure hardships, pay high prices for the live experience of a concert, and enlist their friends to join them at the concert—whether the concert is an Usher performance, the customer service at Nordstrom, coffee at Starbucks, or believing "there is no substitute" for the driving performance of a Porsche. This process of converting customers to "fans" is shown in Table 2.2.

## The Seven Rs of the Marketing Mix

Superior implementation of marketing strategies can be achieved through a checklist we call the seven Rs of the marketing mix—research, rate, resources, retailing, reliability, reward, and relationship. "R" is the right letter for success in customer-centric organizations, because it also stands for relationship marketing, the science and art of acquiring and retaining customers. Table 2.3 summarizes the seven Rs and what each factor means from the organization's and the consumer's point of view. Recent developments in technology enable two of these—customer relationship management (discussed later in this chapter) and loyalty programs (discussed in Chapter 8)—to become part of the required skill set for marketers in customer-centric organizations.

## 2.2

**TABLE 2.2**  Converting Customers into Fans

| CUSTOMERS | FRIENDS (REPEAT CUSTOMERS) | FANS |
|---|---|---|
| Are price driven | Are value driven | Are experience driven |
| Shop opportunistically | Shop purposefully | Shop for pleasure |
| Want you to sell them products | Want products and good service | Want personalized advice and solutions |
| Need a reason to buy from you | Prefer to buy from you | Are devoted to you and are yours to lose |
| Are surprised by good service | Have a history of good experiences with you | Automatically assume you will delight them |
| Drop you if they're disappointed | Tell you if they're disappointed and give you a chance to respond | Tell you if they're disappointed, want you to fix it, and are anxious to forgive and forget |
| Are indifferent to your company | Feel a connection with you, rationally and/or emotionally | Actively invest time, emotion, attention, and money in their relationship with you |
| Don't think or talk about your firm | Recommend your firm casually | Evangelize about your firm |

Source: Adapted from Roger Blackwell and Tina Stephan *Brands That Rock: What Business Leaders Can Learn from the World of Rock and Roll* (New York: Wiley, 2003).

## 2.3

**TABLE 2.3**  The Seven Rs of the Marketing Mix

| | ORGANIZATION | CONSUMER |
|---|---|---|
| Research | Formulate methodology<br>Conduct research<br>Analyze research | Participate in research<br>Provide information and access to mind of the market |
| Rate | Speed to market | Speed through shopping process<br>Usage rates of products |
| Resources | Commitments to project: financial, personnel, etc.<br>Cost: effect on pricing | Payment for product: money, time, attention, energy, and emotions<br>Scarcity of resources |
| Retailing | Which outlets to sell products?<br>Location in store and shelf position | Where they expect to buy product and where they like to shop |
| Reliability | Dependency on supply chain members<br>Avoiding product recalls | Product quality and consistency<br>Reliability of retailer<br>Access to company for questions or product problems |
| Reward | Program to increase purchases and loyalty | Reward from using product<br>Reward programs |
| Relationship | Relationships within supply chain<br>Relationships with customers<br>Customer satisfaction | Loyalty to brand and store<br>Feeling valued and special<br>Customer satisfaction |

The final stage of marketing strategy in customer-centric organizations is *implementation*. Even if you understand perfectly why consumers behave as they do and are successful in developing strategies based on that understanding, the best strategies are rendered worthless without superior implementation in the marketplace. The ability to implement marketing programs with distinction at the point of interaction with consumers transforms strategy into reality. The following characteristics of the twenty-first century are likely to present the marketing profession with major opportunities and threats that have important implications for strategy implementation.[24]

## Customer Loyalty and Retention Strategies

Recent developments in marketing strategy place more attention on customer retention than new customer acquisition because it is generally less expensive to hold onto present customers than to attract new ones. In the industrialized countries of North America, Europe, and Japan, where population grows slowly, customer loss can be disastrous because there are fewer new consumers to replace those who leave. Therefore, customer loyalty based on genuine and ongoing satisfaction is one of the greatest assets a firm can develop. Loyal customers are the fans that generate superior margins and recruit additional customers for a firm or a brand. At the same time, evidence shows that many consumers are becoming less loyal and more resistant to brands, indicating that many firms have little or no deep emotional connection with consumers. Marketing academics and practitioners have focused on customer retention, but it can also be highly profitable to win back customers who have lapsed or defected.[25]

What is causing this decline in loyalty, and what does it mean to organizations? As consumers are given more choices, distinctions between brands fade, and people try new things.[26] Consumers feel entitled to try new brands, especially if they don't feel "rewarded" for remaining loyal, and they perceive many brands to be equal in terms of quality and value received. As a result, switching behavior (also known as defection) increases, as do complaints, cynicism toward the concept of loyalty, and litigious activities.[27] Marketers have moved from a world in which a static understanding of customers (e.g., demographics, psychographics, current satisfaction, current purchase patterns) is sufficient to understanding customers in a dynamic, changing environment in which future expectations (of themselves and of the firm) determine whether they continue to do business with a firm. If a firm wants to retain current customers, customer expectations of future benefits should be the primary focus.[28] Table 2.4 describes some of the ways that firms are acquiring, retaining, and delighting their best customers.

To address the problem of customer defection, researchers are beginning to use changes in customer transaction patterns as a basis for identifying likely defectors (even before defection occurs)[29] and gearing promotions or special incentives to these consumers. Software to manage these relationships is called customer relationship management.

### Customer Relationship Management

Customer relationship management (CRM) is a process for managing all the elements of the *relationship* a firm has with its customers and potential customers. In recent years, a large number of organizations have developed software to support this process. The most widely used (but very basic) program is Microsoft Outlook, which comes standard with most versions of the Windows operating system. More advanced CRM software known as contact management (CM) products include ACT! and GoldMine (used by many retailers). Another type of CRM software is known as sales

TABLE 2.4          Strengthening Customer Relationships

**2.4**

The following list highlights some strategies to acquire, retain, and delight an organization's best customers.

- *Make individualized marketing a reality.* Build-A-Bear Workshop provides a "hands-on" retail entertainment experience that allows children to create their own stuffed toys by picking the body, eyes, filling, clothing, shoes, and accessories. After the toy is "manufactured," the customer receives a personalized "birth certificate" for their new friend. Operating nearly two hundred locations, including a 21,000-square-foot flagship store in New York City and a location in Paris's world-famous Galeries Lafayette department store, Build-A-Bear is innovative in its collection of personal information on customers and the products they buy. This allows the company to send postcards on the child's birthday or for Christmas, offering coupons or other incentives to return to the store and buy additional outfits, accessories, or even "friends" for their toys.

- *Institute a total quality control policy.* Total quality control (TQC) or total quality management (TQM) is an operating philosophy that has its roots in the late 1970s, when Japanese companies took to heart the teachings of W. Edwards Deming. Deming called for a total

commitment to excellence from top management, exemplified by an effective system of quality circles (groups of employees regularly meeting to help solve problems), an employee suggestion system, wide use of statistical quality control principles, a goal of "zero defects," and ongoing training programs. A commitment to quality helps ensure that the products a firm produces will satisfy its customers and therefore foster trust between the parties and promote repeat sales. Marketers also use "Six Sigma" techniques developed at Motorola and General Electric, which use statistical analysis to reduce the level of defects in a process incrementally until there are none.

- *Introduce an early warning system to identify problems.* By the time a customer shows up as a cancellation in a system, attempted retention measures are too late. Early warning systems identify customers who buy less and prompt marketing efforts to reach them before they are lost customers. The system identifies potential defectors with behavior analysis and surveys, knowing that monitoring quality and performance must occur through the eyes of the consumer. In its simplest form, continually learning what the customer

expects in quality and performance and monitoring customer response—through focus groups, regular surveys, or salespeople—provides information needed for firms to strengthen customer relationships.

- *Build realistic expectations.* Satisfaction is based on an assessment of how consumers' expectations about a product are met. A consumer purchasing a cellular phone based on its offer of "clearest reception in the entire metropolitan area," who later finds geographical limits on the phone's range, will be unhappy with the purchase, the product, and the brand because of the unrealistic advertising claim. Exaggeration, which often leads to dissatisfaction, undermines other organizational programs designed to enhance loyalty and promote repeat purchase.

- *Provide guarantees.* Product guarantees have grown robustly through the years, taking some of the perceived risk out of buying a particular brand or product. Although there is evidence that guarantees have greater effects on evaluations of new brands, all companies can use them to encourage a sale and begin a relationship with a customer.

force automation (SFA), with leading applications including SalesLogix, Salesforce .com, and myNextSale. Comprehensive CRM solutions such as Siebel, Onyx, and Epiphany are widely used by consumer analysts in larger organizations. (For additional information, many of these firms offer free demonstrations on their websites, including www.epiphany.com). Many add-on products also are available for the major enterprise system providers such as SAP, Oracle, and Microsoft Business Solutions (Great Plains), among others.

The CRM solution used by Wal*Mart and other retailers and many financial firms is part of an analytical and data mining package known as Teradata by NCR. A favorite analytical package of marketing researchers for determining which customer segments are most valuable and how to reach them is offered by SAS Institute. Many books have been written on CRM,[30] and you can also find up-to-date information on current developments at www.destinationCRM.com as well as at the websites of individual application providers.

Although CRM can take many forms, the following are the basic steps in implementing CRM.

1. Identify all customers and the nature of contacts with them

2. Identify which types of customers are most profitable
    by sales
    by profit contribution

3. Identify and understand behaviors of the most profitable customers
    how to encourage behaviors of most profitable customers
    how to encourage those behaviors among other segments of the customer base
    how to cross-sell other products to customers

4. Manage contacts with most profitable customers

5. Manage activities of the firm that will please the most profitable customers, including both strategies and tactics

Customer acquisition and retention are not independent processes. Historically, consumer behavior and marketing strategy focused more on the process of acquiring customers, a process that can be biased and misleading in determining the profitability of marketing strategy. Today, modeling of this process emphasizes retention, including understanding the financial impact of not accounting for the effect of acquisition on customer retention.[31]

One of the benefits of CRM is an enhanced ability to calculate the **customer lifetime value (CLV)** defined as *the value to the company of a customer over the whole time the customer relates to the company.*[32] CLV is an important metric in long-term strategies to acquire, grow, and retain the "right" customers in customer relationship management programs. Whether marketing strategy is focused on business-to-consumer (B2C) or business-to-business (B2B) customer targets, the most profitable marketing strategies should focus on the value of the customer.[33]

Should a company "fire" its unprofitable customers? Some companies that understand CLV do exactly that when they determine certain customers are costing them money and time.[34] For example, several years ago banking industry giants like Wells Fargo and Washington Mutual began to identify customers who kept low balances and took advantage of free checking by making excessive transactions, teller visits, or calls to customer service. Computer systems flagged these customers so that they would incur service charges for overdrafts and other activities that normally might be waived for more profitable customers. Auto insurers act similarly when they cancel the policies of consumers who file excessive claims.

A company has to be careful to protect its reputation as providing superior service to *all* customers, but other subtle ways can be used to discourage unprofitable customers. Best Buy, for instance, seeks to discourage customers who abuse store policies by buying merchandise at full price, applying for manufacturers' rebates, and then

## Serving the $25,000 Customer at Max & Erma's

*Courtesy of Max & Erma's*

Max & Erma's, a casual restaurant chain with locations from Richmond, Virginia, to St. Louis, Missouri, is known not only for its food but for its emphasis on customer service. Described in restaurant guides as the "inventor of the gourmet hamburger," Max & Erma's goal is to serve the best burgers in America and help guests enjoy their dining experience so much they can't wait to come back. The functional element of the brand—its outstanding food and service—is complemented by its "hometown favorite" personality, even though it is a regional chain.

Analysis of its credit card transactions and consumer surveys enabled Max & Erma's to determine that the "lifetime value" of frequent customers who are "fans" of the restaurant is over $25,000. Management concluded that it is more profitable to serve existing customers more frequently than to acquire new ones. Whether the customers are soccer moms with minivans full of eager athletes, college students on a date, or baby boomers who dine out frequently, Max & Erma's trains its personnel and organizes its operations to create fans that transcend nearly all generations but have one thing in common—a CLV of $25,000.

Breaking through any negative images "chain restaurants" might carry with them, Max & Erma's deco-

rates each store differently, featuring the work of local artists and highlighting community sports teams and heroes, and in some stores, local menu favorites. The personality of the firm, however, is derived from innovative local promotions directed by Bonnie Brannigan, vice president of marketing for Max & Erma's. Some stores open to the fanfare of the local high school band marching through the streets, stopping traffic on its way to the store ribbon-cutting ceremony—generating TV and newspaper coverage more effective and less expensive than paid media advertising.

Max & Erma's designs its stores to become a favorite among consumers by looking at behavior rather than demographics. The music, a boomer-friendly selection that appeals to all ages, plays throughout, but at levels over which people can carry on a conversation. It also offers an eclectic food selection—one that cuts across tastes and themes—that allows children, teens, parents, and grandparents to find something they like. Because the wide selection of menu items doesn't fall under just one category of "Italian" or "Mexican," for example, people can eat there more often. As a result, Max & Erma's boasts twice as many "frequent" customers as its competitors, and yet maintains lower advertising expenditures.

later returning the merchandise so they can repurchase it at the discounted returned-merchandise price. These money-losing practices were curbed by charging a 15 percent restocking fee on returns and selling returned merchandise online, not in its stores. A list was maintained of customers who made excessive returns and these customers were warned that in the future their returns might not be accepted. Studies indicate that as many as 20 percent of customers are unprofitable, so using CRM to eliminate them can free time and resources to serve the 80 percent or more of customers who make money.

In a retail setting, much of the loyalty and trust achieved with customers can be attributed to frontline employees, especially when they exhibit "negative" performance to customers.[35] That's why the casual dining chain Max & Erma's places so much emphasis on personnel training to pamper its customers with high CLV, as described in Consumer Behavior and Marketing 2.3 (on p. 57).

## Global Marketing Strategy

Marketing strategy increasingly must be developed in a global marketplace. Corporations such as Coca-Cola, IBM, Toyota, Nestlé, Sony, and Unilever derive more than 50 percent of their sales outside their countries of origin, requiring a global perspective in strategic planning. Even a small neighborhood retailer may find itself in competition with firms either owned or stocked by global corporations carrying brands from all over the world. In addition, 80 percent of the 100,000 companies that export goods from the United States are small businesses.[36] Your career will probably depend to a large degree on your ability to "think globally" as you develop marketing strategy. Thinking globally involves the ability to understand markets beyond one's own country of origin with respect to the following.

1. Sources of demand: selling to markets throughout the world

2. Sources of supply: sourcing materials, expertise, and management from around the world

3. Methods of effective management and marketing: learning from firms around the world how best to manage and market globally[37]

### Global Market Analysis and Strategy

Global market analysis starts with understanding markets on a global basis in terms of people. What are their needs, ability and authority to buy, and willingness to spend? How do they differ from consumers to whom we already sell? As highlighted in Consumer Behavior and Marketing 2.4, today's consumers have the opportunity to choose from a myriad of foreign-made and globally branded products found in stores from London to São Paulo or on the Internet. But consumers also must choose from ideas, advertisements, and friends representing a diversity of nations and cultures. Cultural, ethnic, and motivation variables affect how consumers make purchase decisions, thus increasing the need for consumer analysts and researchers to help design global marketing strategies. Firms look to consumer analysts to help identify growing populations and segments of consumers economically able to buy products, and strategies for how to reach them effectively. This chapter discusses global marketing and consumer behavior from a strategy standpoint, Chapter 7 focuses on global consumer and population trends, and Chapter 11 focuses on cultural and ethnic variables.

## A Snapshot of Global Retailing

Walk down Oxford Street in London and you'll notice a new marketplace on every block. You can choose from a myriad of retail concepts, including those from some of the most famous traditional English retailers, such as Boots, Selfridges, and Marks & Spencer. Step inside Selfridges, however, and you step into a global bazaar featuring merchandise from around the world with brands ranging from Sony (Japan) to Miele (Germany) in the household goods department, and Lindt (Switzerland) to Mars (United States) in the food court. When you shop in Boots, which now sells far more than the traditional pharmaceutical products of a "chemist," you will be served with cash registers and computer software that is among the most technologically advanced in the world, designed and produced in several different countries. And when you shop at Marks & Spencer, you can find popcorn, tortilla chips, or other packaged treats, which in fact were probably produced by Wyandot Snacks in Marion, Ohio.

Venture further into London's shopping scene and you likely will see store signage in languages as diverse as Arabic and Japanese, and hear other shoppers speaking in French, Yiddish, Afrikaans, German, and nearly every other language of the world. With the removal of double-decker buses and the replacement of black taxis with yellow ones, this shopping experience could occur in New York City along Fifth Avenue. Except for variations in proportion, consumers can scan Manhattan's shopping district and find many of the same stores (or at least types of stores), brands, and languages. Even more important—from the perspective of this book—chances are you would find some of the same consumers.

### Can Marketing Be Standardized?

Firms facing global markets must ask the question: Is it possible to use one marketing program in all target countries? Or are distinct marketing programs required for each country? Many strategic considerations in terms of cost, brand image, advertising message and methods, and effectiveness must be evaluated before deciding the best solution for a particular product. If marketing programs must be modified to each culture, firms will fail if they do not develop specific products, promotions, and organizations for each country. Enormous economies of scale and advantages of unified brand image are achieved, however, if the marketing program is standardized.

At the most basic level, marketers must ask which of the following they believe is greater: the differences or the similarities among consumers of different countries and different cultures. If you agree that consumer behavior is subject to cultural universals, then you might agree with the position that advertising can be standardized. This position has intrigued marketers ever since Erik Elinder first raised it in 1965,[38] and the debate over its validity intensified with a controversial article by Ted Levitt that described the globalization of the marketplace.[39] In either instance, the reality is that inherent cultural differences exist between consumers from different cultures and these differences must be addressed at some level of the marketing plan.

**Cross-cultural analysis** is the *comparison of similarities and differences in behavioral and physical aspects of cultures.* Included are "meaning systems" of consumers in a nation that are intelligible within the cultural context of that country. Marketing practitioners need cultural empathy to be able to predict how consumers will buy and use new products and to avoid blunders when entering a new market. **Cultural empathy** refers to *the ability to understand the inner logic and coherence of other ways of life and refrain from judging other value systems.*

Communication with consumers can occur at different stages of the purchase process, including at the time of sale. **Ethnograpy,** *describing and understanding consumer behavior by interviewing and observing consumers in real-world situations,* can help analyze the subtle ways buyers and sellers interact in the marketplace and can be useful in business negotiation processes. The more that is known about the cultures of the parties involved in the transaction (different styles and habits), the greater the likelihood of success, even in such specific marketing tactics as negotiation between buyers and sellers.[40] Communication prior to sale, in the form of advertising, also is affected by cultural variables. These variables shed light on various issues, including which attributes of a new product are likely to be more valued than others, which language should be used in the ads, and who might be an effective spokesperson for the brand or product. First through television and now over the Internet, communications must reach people around the world with similar appeals for similar products, but still maintain the ability to communicate to consumers with their own unique cultural identities and characteristics, sometimes requiring the formulation of specialized communication programs.

### Intermarket Segmentation

Whether targeting European consumers or consumers around the globe, many successful global marketers identify and reach consumers through **intermarket segmentation**—*the identification of groups of customers who transcend traditional market or geographic boundaries.* Intermarket segments consist of people who have similar patterns of behavior regardless of where they live. When intermarket segmentation is adopted at a strategic level, marketing strategies focus on similar customer behavior wherever it is found in the world rather than on national boundaries as definitions of markets.

Intermarket segmentation plays a key role in understanding the similarities and differences between consumers and countries that become the foundation of marketing standardization—an international marketing strategy that more organizations are adopting.[41] A study of twenty-seven multinational enterprises (MNEs), including General Foods, Nestle, Coca-Cola, Procter & Gamble, Unilever, and Revlon, found that 63 percent of the total marketing programs could be rated as "highly standardized."[42] These marketers have built successful strategies on the principle that "people are basically the same around the globe" even though they may vary in specific traits often influenced by structural elements such as economic resources, urbanization, and population age. The challenge is to build the core of the marketing strategy on the universals rather than on the differences.

An example of this strategy is the focus on the desire to be beautiful. In a sense, young women in Tokyo and Berlin are sisters not only "under" the skin but "on" their skin, lips, fingernails, and even in their hairstyles. Refer back to Figure 1.9 in Chapter 1 for examples. Consequently, these women are likely to buy similar cosmetics as well as luxury accessories, promoted with similar appeals.[43] Appeals to universal images, such as mother and child, freedom from pain, and glow of health, may cut across many boundaries.

### Localization Based on Differences

The European Union (EU) continues to fine-tune its functioning as a single market. With the introduction of the euro to an increasing number of nations, firms increasingly are defining market segments to consist of similar types of customers and cultures throughout Europe rather than groups within a specific country. But as more businesses treat the EU as one common market, will the cultural identities of each country disappear? Will the French become less "French" if treated as a generic "European"? The answer depends on whether a firm's implementation of marketing strategies is based on the similarities among consumers or the differences between consumers.

True localization of marketing strategies requires different products and ads in every country of the world. Although this is economically inefficient and impractical, it is important to examine the needs and wants of specific markets and to adapt products, packaging, and advertising based on the differences between markets and the consumer behavior patterns of the target markets. Therefore, going global and acting local has become the choice of many marketers.

Before Japanese cars were introduced in the United States, the cars had to be redesigned so that the steering wheels were on the left side. How many Americans would have bought Hondas had the steering wheel been on the "wrong" side? You might think that medicines would be the same around the world because they are used for the same human species. Yet it is not uncommon to see the same medicine dispensed according to local preferences: capsules in the United States and Canada, tablets in England, injections in Germany, and suppositories in France.

## Global Advertising Effectiveness

In a global business environment, many firms turn to advertising to communicate with new consumers around the world. This can be done through either globalized or localized advertising campaigns. Global campaigns focus on sending the same message to all consumers around the world. Localized campaigns adapt messages to the norms of the different cultures addressed in a particular market.

Global advertising agencies can be efficient in implementing globalized advertising campaigns that relay the same message to each market regardless of geographical location. At first, Nestlé found difficulties in promoting its Nescafé line to consumers in different cultures because the definition of coffee is different for many people. Japan has a tea culture, France, Germany, and Brazil like ground coffee, and the United Kingdom has embraced instant coffee. Nestlé decided to sell "coffeeness" around the world rather than selling coffee. By selling the aroma and feelings associated with coffeeness and allowing consumers to decide what coffee means to them, Nescafé has overcome cultural differences and linked Nescafé advertising in fifty countries, perhaps unintentionally preparing the world for another global coffee brand, Starbucks.

Some advertising messages and specific product characteristics tend to be suited better than others for a globalized advertising approach. The following is a summary of these characteristics.

1. The communications message is based on similar lifestyles.

2. The appeal of the ad is to basic human needs and emotions.

3. The product satisfies universal needs and desires.[44]

Regardless of advertising approach, implementation of the campaign in a new market can be successful only if the strategic landscape of that market is understood. For example, firms in the United States typically spend about 3 percent of sales on advertising. In Australia, the advertising-to-sales ratio is typically between 7 and 8 percent, in Sweden about 5 percent, in Mexico a little more than 5 percent, and in Canada between 4 and 5 percent.[45] An American company entering Australia may under budget for advertising according to local practices, which could decrease the effectiveness of its campaign because of lower levels of exposure. In Japan, comparative advertising

**TABLE 2.5**       Which Form of Advertising Do You Find Most Effective?

| | UNITED STATES (%) | UNITED KINGDOM (%) | GERMANY (%) | CHINA (%) | RUSSIA (%) | JAPAN (%) | FRANCE (%) | CANADA (%) | TOTAL (%) |
|---|---|---|---|---|---|---|---|---|---|
| Television | 65.1 | 66 | 44.1 | 68.1 | 62 | 68.5 | 53.4 | 60.3 | 60.94 |
| Radio | 3.9 | 3.1 | 1.6 | 0.8 | 1.7 | 0.5 | 2.4 | 2.2 | 2.03 |
| Newspaper or magazine | 16.7 | 17.8 | 13.4 | 10.8 | 12.6 | 10.7 | 17.9 | 17.8 | 14.71 |
| Internet | 5.3 | 8 | 9.3 | 14.4 | 9.8 | 12.7 | 9.4 | 5.7 | 9.33 |
| Billboard or posters | 1.3 | 2.6 | 4.3 | 4.1 | 7.3 | 1.6 | 10.6 | 2.5 | 4.29 |
| Inserts | 7.7 | 2.5 | 27.3 | 1.8 | 6.6 | 6 | 6.3 | 11.5 | 8.71 |
| Total | 12.5 | 12.5 | 12.5 | 12.5 | 12.5 | 12.5 | 12.5 | 12.5 | 100 |

Source: Global Market Insite: "Which Form of Advertising Do You Find Most Effective?" GMI Poll, December 8, 2004. Global Market Insite (GMI, Inc.) Mercer Island, WA. Copyright 2004 Global Market Insite, Inc.

is not permitted by the Advertising Code, which explains, "Let us avoid slandering, defaming and attacking others."[46] Marketing programs in Japan are strongly influenced by Confucianism, which places high value on self-esteem, reciprocity, and harmony. Values are also derived from Buddhism, and this leads to a need for simplicity and a dominant aesthetic sense as well as loyalty and satisfaction in interpersonal relationships.

Values associated with American brands may not be shared by consumers in many parts of the world. According to the 2003 Pew Research Center (which consists of 16,000 people in twenty countries), 53 percent of Europeans claim that the United States is a threat to world peace, which is a reason U.S. firms may not want to emphasize U.S. culture and values in marketing programs.[47] The individualistic values that make America so successful economically may be unappealing in markets with a more collectivist culture. So should American brands act locally to avoid negative consumer reactions? A recent Research International Study in Latin America found that any brand that more than 50 percent of respondents identified as American was seen more negatively than others.[48] Only 35 percent of people say they trust American brands, according to a survey of global consumers by NOP World in June 2004, and just 15 percent associate American brands with honesty, meaning that the global strategy of U.S. firms should focus on attributes of the brand and should probably deemphasize its U.S. origins. Even Nestlé, based in a nation known for mountains, chocolates, precision watches, and political neutrality, does not emphasize its Swiss origin in its marketing strategies used throughout the globe. Global strategies must be localized to some extent, as you might conclude from Table 2.5, which shows perceptions of the most effective type of advertising in several nations. Television rules in each of these countries, however, and there is consistency in rankings of effectiveness, despite considerable variation in the importance of specific types of advertising, such as the use of newspaper inserts in Germany.

## OVERCOMING LANGUAGE PROBLEMS

Language problems must be overcome to standardize marketing programs and avoid blunders such as these: In a Paris hotel, a sign requests that guests "Please leave your values at the desk." In Bangkok, a dry cleaner's advertising suggests that customers "Drop your trousers here for best results." In a Norwegian cocktail lounge, the message may have been a bit confused on a sign that says, "Ladies are requested not to have children in the bar." An English slogan for Coors beer, "Turn it Loose," in Spanish became "Suffer from Diarrhea."[49]

A useful technique for overcoming language problems is **back-translation.** In this procedure, *a message* (word or a series of words) *is translated from its original language to the translated language and then back to the original by several translators.* The purpose of the iterations is to attempt to achieve conceptual equivalency in meaning by controlling the various translation biases of translators.[50]

## GLOBAL BRANDING

Brand names should be evaluated from a cross-cultural perspective even if currently used only in domestic markets. Thinking globally includes considering the possibility that the brand will someday be extended to other countries, as well as making it more appealing to diverse cultures within the current country. Coined names are increasing in popularity among Fortune 500 companies because they do not need to be translated. This makes names like Exxon and Accenture very effective in a global market, along with the Japanese electronics firm Pioneer, truly a pioneer since it selected the English brand in the 1930s.

Among the questions that need to be answered before settling on an English brand name are the following.

1. Does the English name of the product have another meaning, perhaps unfavorable, in one or more of the countries where it might be marketed?

2. Can the English name be pronounced everywhere? For example, Spanish and some other languages lack a *k* in their alphabets, an initial letter in many popular U.S. brand names.

3. Is the name close to that of a foreign brand, or does it duplicate another product sold in English-speaking countries?

4. If the product is distinctly American, will national pride and prejudice work against the acceptance of the product?

Global brands can have substantial advantages for creating awareness for a product or brand worldwide, especially when they are easily recognized and trusted. Sometimes helpful associations occur as well. Students in Japan reportedly have caused sales of KitKat chocolate bars to soar, because although it is a global brand, the name resembles a Japanese expression—"kitto katsu"—used by students to wish each other luck before exams. The phrase has been translated roughly as "I hope you will win." KitKat took advantage of this fortunate meaning of its brand by introducing a range of flavors designed especially for the sweet-toothed Japanese market, including green tea, passion fruit, white chocolate, and lemon cheesecake.[51]

Although global brands often work well, many companies are realizing that globalization is not an all-or-nothing proposition. There are many parts to a brand: the name, symbol, slogan, and associations. Many marketers, including Coca-Cola, are finding that, although they have a global brand, not all portions of the brand are global. Diet Coke is sold in the United States, but the same product is sold as Coca-Cola Light in Europe because of restrictions on using the word *diet* when no medicinal connotation is intended. Customer-centric marketers globalize those elements for which there is a payoff in cost or impact, but let other elements of a product's brand equity be customized to local markets.

# Summary

Customer-centricity is a strategic commitment to focus every resource of the firm on serving and delighting profitable customers. It involves producing new or improved products with evolving marketing methods focused on core, but sometimes changing, market targets. The characteristics of customer-centric organizations include shared vision and values, cross-functional integration, system-wide simultaneous training, and customer-based metrics.

Strategy involves a decisive allocation of resources in a particular direction. Resources include capital, technology, people, and effort all focused on a course of action in a particular direction. In customer-centric organizations, the direction in which resources should be committed is determined by consumers. The job of consumer analysts is to understand consumers well enough to understand what direction they will lead the organization. Marketing strategy involves the allocation of resources to develop and sell products or services that consumers will perceive to provide more value than competitive products or services. The process includes market analysis, market segmentation, brand strategy, and implementation, with the study of consumers at the core.

Market analysis is the process of analyzing changing consumer trends, current and potential competitors, company strengths and resources, and the technological, legal, and economic environments, with particular emphasis on developing *consumer insight*. The next step in creating market strategy is market segmentation, which is the process of identifying a portion of the total market that behaves in similar ways to other members of a group, but somewhat differently than other groups. The opposite of market segmentation is market aggregation or mass marketing—when organizations choose to market and sell the same product or service to all consumers.

Determining the attractiveness of a market segment involves analyzing segments based on four criteria. Measurability refers to the ability to obtain information about the size, nature, and behavior of a market segment. Accessibility (or reachability) is the degree to which segments can be reached, either through various advertising and communication programs or through multiple channels of retailing. Substantiality refers to the size of the market. Congruity refers to how similar members within the segment exhibit behaviors or characteristics that correlate with consumption behavior. Identifying market segments and answering the question of "why people buy"

increasingly involves a centuries-old statistical technique called Bayesian analysis, a tool that has attracted attention of marketers in recent years.

Developing marketing strategy also must include a plan to specify the essential components of the marketing mix, often described as the four P's (product, place, price, and promotion). A brand is perhaps the greatest asset of any company not to appear on its balance sheet. It is a product or product line, store, or service *with an identifiable set of benefits, wrapped in a recognizable personality,* carrying with it a connection between product and customers. Brands include *functional* and *emotional* elements, delivering promise, personality, and protection to consumers.

The final stage of marketing strategy in customer-centric organizations is *implementation*. Customer acquisition and retention strategies increasingly involve new technologies such as customer relationship management (CRM) and loyalty programs.

Developing customer-centric strategies increasingly requires understanding of buying and consumption decisions on a global basis. Cross-cultural analysis, the systematic comparison of similarities and differences in the behavioral and physical aspects of cultures, provides an approach to understanding market segments both across national boundaries and between groups within a society. The process of analyzing consumers on a cross-cultural basis is particularly helpful in deciding which elements of a marketing program can be standardized in multiple nations and which elements must be localized.

## Review and Discussion Questions

1. What does it mean to be a "customer-centric" organization?
2. What are some of the most important changes in the consumer environment in the United States? How are these likely to impact marketing strategy? How would you expect them to differ in other nations?
3. Why does market segmentation exist? Is the use of market segmentation strategies by organizations harmful or helpful to consumers and to society?
4. What are some of the most common bases used for market segmentation?
5. What criteria for selecting segments should be used by an organization in deciding which segments to target?
6. How and why is Bayesian statistical analysis useful in marketing strategy?

7. Using the concept of consumer insight and marketing mix, choose a product that has been introduced to the market in the last two years and explain why you think it has succeeded.

8. Suppose you are the marketing manager for a new Ford Focus hybrid automobile. How would you use intermarket segmentation to develop marketing strategies for Ford?

9. In reference to your answer to question 5, how would you best communicate to the target audience? Describe your promotion campaign for Ford.

## Notes

1 "Enabling a Customer-Focused Organization," Thought Leadership Summit on Digital Strategies, Center for Digital Strategies, Tuck School of Business at Dartmouth (September 2003).

2 Dhruv Grewal, Kent B. Monroe, and R. Krishnan, "The Effects of Price-Comparison Advertising on Buyers' Perceptions of Acquisition Value, Transaction Value, and Behavioral Intentions," *Journal of Marketing* (April 1988), 46–59.

3 Robert B. Woodruff, "Customer Value: The Next Source for Competitive Advantage," *Journal of the Academy of Marketing Science,* 25 (Spring 1997), 139–154.

4 A. Parasuraman, "Reflections on Gaining Competitive Advantage through Customer Value," *Journal of the Academy of Marketing Science,* 25 (Spring 1997), 154–161.

5 C. E. Morris, "Why New Products Fail," *Food Engineering,* 65 (June 1993), 129.

6 Cyndee Miller, "Survey: New Product Failure Is Top Management's Fault," *Marketing News* (February 1, 1993), 2.

7 Jan-Benedict E. M. Steenkamp, Frenkel ter Hofstede, and Michel Wedel, "A Cross-National Investigation into the Individual and National Cultural Antecedents of Consumer Innovativeness," *Journal of Marketing,* 63 (April 1999), 55–69.

8 Kristina Stephan and Roger Blackwell, *Consumer Insight,* prepared for Kodak, Inc. (September 1999).

9 Jacob Goldenberg, David Mazursky, and Sorin Solomon, "Toward Identifying the Inventive Templates of New Products: A Channeled Ideation Approach," *Journal of Marketing Research,* 36 (May 1999), 200–210.

10 Evert Gummersson, "Implementation Requires a Relationship Marketing Program," *Journal of the Academy of Marketing Science,* 26 (July 1998), 242–249.

11 "Shoot Out at the Check-Out," *Economist* (June 5, 1993), 69.

12 W. Chan Kim and Renee Mauborgne, "Value Innovation: The Strategic Logic of High Growth," *Harvard Business Review* (January/February 1997), 103.

13 James H. Gilmore and B. Joseph Pine II, "The Four Faces of Mass Customization," *Harvard Business Review* (January/February 1997), 91.

14 Martha Rogers and Don Pepper, *The One To One Future* (New York: Bantam, Doubleday, 1997). Also see Don Pepper and Martha Rogers, *Managing Customer Relationships: A Strategic Framework* (New York: Wiley, 2004).

15 Frenkel Ter Hofstede, Jan-Benedict E. M. Steenkamp, and Michel Wedel, "International Market Segmentation Based on Consumer Product Relations," *Journal of Marketing Research,* 36 (February 1999), 1–17.

16 Jagdish Sheth and Rajendra Sisodia, "Revisiting Marketing's Lawlike Generalizations," *Journal of the Academy of Marketing Science,* 27 (Winter 1999), 71–87.

17 Examples include Greg Allenby, Robert Leone, and Lichung Jen, "A Dynamic Model of Purchase Timing with Application to Direct Marketing," *Journal of American Statistical Association,* 94 (June 1999), 365–374; and Faming Liang and Wing Hung Wong, "Real-Parameter Evolutionary Monte Carlo with Application to Bayesian Mixture Models," *Journal of the American Statistical Association,* 96 (June 2001), 653–666.

18 Roger Blackwell and Kristina Blackwell, "Changing Consumption Trends," International Mass Retail Association, 1997.

19 Mark Stiving, Greg Allenby, and Russell Winter, "An Empirical Analysis of Price Endings with Scanner Data," *Journal of Consumer Research,* 24 (June 1997), 57–67.

20 Kevin Lane Keller, Susan E. Heckler, and Michael J. Houston, "The Effects of Brand Name Suggestiveness on Advertising Recall," *Journal of Marketing,* 62 (January 1998), 48–57.

21 Adapted from Roger Blackwell and Tina Stephan, *Brands That Rock: What Business Leaders Can Learn from the World of Rock and Roll* (New York: Wiley, 2003).

22 C. B. Bhattacharya and Sankar Sen, "Consumer-Company Identification: A Framework for Understanding Consumers' Relationships with Companies," *Journal of Marketing,* 67 (April 2003), 76–89.

23 Dennis Arnett, Steve German, and Shelby Hunt, "The Identity-Salience Model of Relationship Marketing Success: The Case of Nonprofit Marketing," *Journal of Marketing,* 67 (April 2003), 89–106.

24 Nigel Piercy, "Marketing Implementation: The Implications of Marketing Paradigm Weakness for the Strategy Execution Process," *Journal of the Academy of Marketing Science,* 26 (Spring 1998), 222–236.

25 Jacquelyn Thomas, Robert Blattberg, and Edward Fox, "Recapturing Lost Customers," *Journal of Marketing Research,* 41 (February 2004), 31–46.

26 Steve Schriver, "Customer Loyalty: Going, Going . . . ," *American Demographics* (September 1997), 20–21.

27 Ibid.

28 Katherine N. Lemon, Tiffany White, and Russell S. Winer, "Dynamic Customer

Relationship Management: Incorporating Future Considerations into the Service Retention Decision," *Journal of Marketing,* 66 (January 2002), 1–14.

[29] Michael M. Pearson and Buy H. Gessner, "Transactional Segmentation to Slow Customer Defections," *Marketing Management,* 8 (Summer 1999), 17–23.

[30] Jill Dyché, *The CRM Handbook: A Business Guide to Customer Relationship Management* (Boston: Addison-Wesley, 2001); Janice Reynolds, *A Practical Guide to CRM* (New York: CMP Books, 2002); Paul Greenberg, *CRM at the Speed of Light,* 3rd ed. (New York: McGraw-Hill, 2004).

[31] Jacquelyn S. Thomas, "A Methodology for Linking Customer Acquisition to Customer Retention," *Journal of Marketing Research,* 38 (May 2001), 262–269.

[32] John Hogan, Donald Lehmann, Mario Merino, Rajendra Scrivastava, Jacquelyn S. Thomas, and Peter Verhoef, "Linking Customer Assets to Financial Performance," *Journal of Service Research,* 5 (August 2002), 26–38; Werner Reinartz and V. Kumar, "The Impact of Customer Relationship Characteristics on Profitable Lifetime Duration," *Journal of Marketing,* 67 (January 2003), 77–99.

[33] Rajkumar Venkatesan and V. Kumar, "A Customer Lifetime Value Framework for Customer Selection and Resource Allocation Strategy," *Journal of Marketing,* 68 (October 2004), 106–125.

[34] Larry Selden and Geoffrey Colvin, *Angel Customers and Demon Customers: Discover Which Is Which and Turbo-Charge Your Stock* (New York: Portfolio, 2003).

[35] Deepak Sirdeshmukh, Jagdip Singh, and Barry Sabol, "Consumer Trust, Value, and Loyalty in Relational Exchanges,"

*Journal of Marketing,* 66 (January 2002), 15–38.

[36] "Three Small Businesses Profit by Taking on the World," *Wall Street Journal* (November 8, 1990), B2.

[37] Salah Hassan and Roger Blackwell, *Global Marketing Perspectives and Cases* (Fort Worth, TX: Dryden Press, 1993), 3.

[38] Erik Elinder, "How International Can European Advertising Be?" *Journal of Marketing,* 29 (April 1965), 7–11.

[39] Theodore Levitt, "The Globalization of Markets," *Harvard Business Review,* 61 (May/June 1983), 92–102. For the contrasting perspective, see Yoram Wind, "The Myth of Globalization, *Journal of Consumer Marketing,* 3 (Spring 1986), 23–26.

[40] Brian Mark Hawrysh and Judith Lynne Zaichkowsky, "Cultural Approaches to Negotiations: Understanding the Japanese," *European Journal of Marketing,* 25 (1991), 51.

[41] Robert D. Buzzell, "Can You Standardize Multinational Marketing?" *Harvard Business Review,* 46 (November/December 1986), 102–113; Theodore Levitt, "The Globalization of Markets," *Harvard Business Review,* 61 (May/June 1983), 92–102; "Multinationals Tackle Global Marketing," *Advertising Age* (June 25, 1984), 50ff. Also see "Marketers Turn Sour on Global Sales Pitch Harvard Guru Makes," *Wall Street Journal* (May 11, 1988), 1.

[42] Ralph Z. Sorenson and Ulrich E. Wiechmann, "How Multinationals View Marketing Standardization," *Harvard Business Review,* 53 (May/June 1975), 38–56. Also see William H. Davidson and Philippe Haspeslagh, "Shaping a Global Product Organization," *Harvard Busi-*

*ness Review,* 60 (July/August 1982), 125–132.

[43] Arthur Fatt, "The Danger of 'Local' International Advertising," *Journal of Marketing,* 31 (January 1967), 60–62.

[44] Roger Blackwell, Riad Ajami, and Kristina Stephan, "Winning the Global Advertising Race: Planning Globally, Acting Locally," *Journal of International Consumer Marketing,* 3 (April 1991), 108.

[45] Charles E. Keown, Nicolas Synodinos, Laurence Jacobs, and Reginald Worthley, "Can International Advertising Be Standardized?" World Congress of the Academy of Marketing Sciences, Barcelona (1987).

[46] This section abstracted from Dentsu Incorporated, *Marketing Opportunity in Japan* (London: McGraw-Hill, 1978), 84–114. Dentsu is one of the largest advertising agencies in the world.

[47] Ruth Mortimer, "Yankee Doodle Branding," *Brand Strategy* (January 2005), 24–27.

[48] Ibid.

[49] Kevin Lynch, "Adplomacy Faux Pas Can Ruin Sales," *Advertising Age* (January 15, 1979), S–2ff; and "When Slogans Go Wrong," *American Demographics* (February 1992), 14.

[50] Richard W. Brislin, "Back-Translation for Cross-Cultural Research," *Journal of Cross-Cultural Psychology,* 1 (September 1970); Oswald Werner and Donald T. Campbell, "Translating, Working through Interpreters and the Problems of Decentering," in Raoul Naroll and Ronald Cohen, eds., *A Handbook of Method in Cultural Anthropology* (Garden City, NY: National History Press, 1970), 298–420.

[51] BBC News, February 5, 2005.

# Consumer Decision Making

Buying and using goods and services occurs as the result of consumer decision making. That's why marketers need a systematic, comprehensive way to understand how and why consumers make decisions. Part II of the text is designed to give you a model and methodology to develop that understanding.

Chapter 3 introduces a model of the consumer decision process, which features the seven major stages of decision making and the variables that affect activities in each stage. The model shows how consumers purchase products to solve problems and highlights the activities that occur before, during, and after the purchase of a product. Take special time to understand this model as it is presented—it has served as a point of study in the field of consumer behavior for hundreds of thousands of students and for marketing strategists and business organizations worldwide. The model also provides the structure for the remainder of this book.

Chapter 4 focuses on the *pre-purchase* stages of the decision process model—recognition, search, and evaluation. This part of the process begins with need recognition, or what causes consumers to begin searching for a product, service, or solution to fulfill their needs and wants. The focus then shifts to the consumer's internal and external search for information. Where do consumers get information about how to satisfy their needs? How long do they search for information useful for making decisions before they are ready to evaluate their alternatives? Understanding consumer needs leads to the next topic of the chapter: pre-purchase alternative evaluation. As you'll see, consumers can evaluate product and service alternatives in many different ways during decision making.

Chapter 5 examines *purchase*—how and where consumers buy products, and what factors influence their purchase behaviors. This chapter explores the various retail options available to consumers and the strategies that successful retailers implement to compete for consumer patronage, including the increasing use of electronic marketing and e-commerce.

Chapter 6 focuses on the *post-purchase* stages in the consumer decision process—consumption and post-consumption evaluation. Consumption consists of how and when consumers use products, including whether or not they use them as instructed and intended, and whether they use them soon after purchase or store them for later use. Decision making does not stop with consumption, however, because there is likely to be continued evaluation of the product or service leading to feelings of satisfaction or dissatisfaction, which have significant implications for customer retention.

# Chapter 3

# The Consumer Decision Process

## Opening Vignette

By focusing on middle-income women as a core market target, J. C. Penney CEO Allen Questrom knew the retailer had identified an opportunity to serve well a market segment largely ignored by competitors. Wal*Mart thrived on low prices for the masses and Neiman Marcus prospered in the luxury market, but old-style department stores like Macy's and Dillard's had achieved little success adapting brands popular with younger women, like Tommy Hilfiger and Ralph Lauren, to the needs of middle-aged career women. Although Chico's was successful with specialty stores, Questrom recognized an opportunity for Penney to attract married women ages thirty-five to fifty-four, with children and an average of $69,000 median household income. Many bought casual clothing for family members at Target and other discount stores but also perceived Penney to be a retailer of quality products at fair prices. To be successful, Penney needed to understand the minds, search and evaluation processes, and consumption decisions of this "missing middle."

To do so, Penney began in-depth research with a telephone survey of nine hundred women, asking them about their casual clothes. To drill down into the consumption process, Penney researchers videotaped interviews lasting up to six hours with thirty women, recording everything from their feelings about fashion to what was hanging in their closets. Re-searchers shadowed women on shopping trips to J. C. Penney and a competitor and asked the women to clip words and images from magazines and glue them to posters in ways that expressed their feelings about what casual clothing meant to them.

When interviews were conducted in consumers' homes, one woman pointed to a cartoon image of SpongeBob SquarePants, with his typically strung-out expression, and said, "This is me, my stress with shopping." The consumer explained further that she disliked short shorts and skirts, exposed midriffs or cleavage, and spaghetti straps on tank tops because they didn't enhance her figure. But the consumer said that being alluring is still important, to a degree. "You can still be a mom, but you still want to be cute and a little bit hip. You're not dead yet, and you're not a grandma—you still want to be in the game."

J. C. Penney found the two biggest "no-no's" among target consumers were being "matronly" and having "sex-kitten looks." The women said they wanted to look stylish and that they craved options that hinted at sensuality without being too tight. Quality is also important, an attribute long associated with Penney and something for which this market segment is willing to pay a premium. Participants studied clothing labels and touched garments to assess fabric and construction, expressing a preference for styles that let them make a "personal statement."

Based on these research findings, Penney recruited world-renowned designer Nicole Miller to design well-styled clothes with good quality and a good price. Penney also launched a private-label brand called "W—Work to Weekend," reflecting the lifestyle and consumption realities of its market target. As a mom who leads a busy lifestyle, Miller understood what women needed. As a result, she became directly involved in designing products, not just lending her name. Penney launched its new products for spring 2005 targeted to the "missing middle" who

want clothes that are stylish, but not overly trendy; form-fitting, but not too tight; and made with high-quality fabrics, good stitching, and interesting buttons.

Source: Ellen Byron, "New Penney: Chain Goes for 'Missing Middle,' " The Wall Street Journal, February 14, 2005, B1ff. © 2005 by Dow Jones & Co. Reproduced with permission of Dow Jones & Co., Inc., in the textbook format via Copyright Clearance Center, Inc.

Remember the key elements of this opening vignette; throughout this chapter you'll see how they represent many of the elements of a model of how consumers make decisions about nearly every product they buy and use.

## The Consumer Decision Process Model

You've just arrived at the airport in a strange city and have rented a car to get to your hotel. If you don't know how to get there, you could use a set of printed directions listing the steps you need to take (left at High Street, left at second light onto North Broadway, and so forth) or you could consult a road map. Directions seem easier at first glance, but what happens when you encounter a detour, decide to go somewhere else, or simply get lost along the way? A list of streets is fairly useless when change occurs, but a road map can still show you to where you need to go.

In the disruptive, discontinuous markets of contemporary and future business environments, a road map of how consumers make purchase decisions is more reliable than a set of directions. The **consumer decision process (CDP) model**, a simplified version of which is shown in Figure 3.1, represents a *road map of consumers' minds that marketers and managers can use to help guide product mix, communication, and sales strategies*. The model captures the activities that occur when decisions are made in a schematic format and shows how different internal and external forces interact to affect how consumers think, evaluate, and act.

No one buys a product unless they have a problem, a need, or a want, and the CDP model shows how people solve the everyday problems that cause them to buy and use products of all kinds. The CDP model, in its earliest state, was developed by Professors Engel, Kollat, and Blackwell at The Ohio State University, and was known as the EKB model, which served as the foundation for earlier editions of this textbook. As the textbook evolved, so did the model, which was renamed the EBM model to acknowledge the work of Professor Paul W. Miniard, who joined the team as coauthor of the text. The goal in creating this model was to analyze how individuals sort through facts and influences to make logical and consistent decisions.

**FIGURE 3.1**  How Consumers Make Decisions for Goods and Services

As the model shows, consumers typically go through seven major stages when making decisions: need recognition, search for information, pre-purchase evaluation, purchase, consumption, post-consumption evaluation, and divestment. Though marketing textbooks and consumer researchers sometimes employ slightly different terms or consolidate some of the stages, the study of consumer behavior focuses primarily on these seven stages and how various factors influence each stage of consumers' decisions. By understanding the stages in the consumer decision-making road map, marketers can discover why people are or are not buying products and what can be done to get them to buy more or buy from a specific supplier.

The first half of this chapter focuses on each stage of the CDP model. Pay special attention to how Figures 3.2, 3.4, 3.5, 3.7, 3.9, 3.11, 3.12, and 3.14

build on one another to create the complete CDP model. To make these concepts more understandable, below each figure is a running example of how a college student in need of a car might move through each stage.

## Stage One: Need Recognition

The starting point of any purchase decision is a customer need (or problem). **Need recognition** occurs when *an individual senses a difference between what he or she perceives to be the* ideal *versus the* actual *state of affairs.* Consumers don't just walk into a store and say, "I notice you have things to sell. I have some extra money I would like to spend, so just give me something and charge it to my credit card." Consumers buy things when they believe a product's ability to solve a problem is worth more than the cost of buying it, thereby making recognition of an unmet need the first step in the sale of a product. Need recognition, sometimes called problem recognition, is shown in Figure 3.2 and is one of the focal topics of Chapter 4.

In addition to needs, consumers have desires, as is the case with "Joe College" in Figure 3.2. But realistically, marketers must examine desires under a microscope of constraints, including consumers' ability and authority to buy. While marketers strive to fulfill the desires of their consumers, they must keep costs in line with what their target markets can afford. Consumers are willing to sacrifice some of their desires to buy affordable products that meet their needs and their budget, though they might still aspire to fulfill their desires at a time in the future when they are able to afford it.

**FIGURE 3.2**     Need Recognition

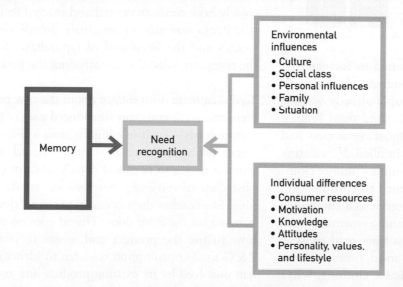

Sometimes when we least expect, we recognize a need. For instance, Joe College, a university student, is driving to class, and his car breaks down in the middle of the road. Smoke pours out from underneath the hood, and hissing noises rise from the engine. A local mechanic examines the car, fixes it temporarily, but suggests the student look for a new car. The student has a problem—he needs to obtain some form of reliable transportation—and has entered the consumer decision-making process. He returns home and sees his neighbor, who just bought a new Volkswagen Passat. After talking about his predicament, Joe sits in the new car. That sigh-invoking new car scent only increases his desire to buy a car. He closes his eyes and visualizes himself driving through campus in a Porsche 911—but desires and needs aren't always the same. While we don't always get what we desire, we usually manage to get what we need. Joe College has just begun the purchase process for a car. Stay tuned.

## Solving the Dry-Cleaning Problem

Care For Your "Dry Clean Only" Clothes Right At Home!

Dryel® allows you to clean and freshen your "dry clean only" clothes in your own dryer in just 30 minutes for *less than $1 a garment.*

**The Dryel Process is 4 easy steps**

● Remove Stains
● Load Bag
● Tumble in Dryer
● Hang Garments

Now, MAYTAG® has a dryer with a Dryel setting that offers optimal results through ideal time and temperature.

Exclusively at BEST BUY

www.dryel.com or call 1-800-214-8913

*Prices set by retailer

Save $2.00

On ONE Any Size Dryel® "Dry Clean Only" Starter Kit Or Refill

By permission of Dryel

Recently, Procter & Gamble wanted to increase the proportion of clothing that consumers cleaned with its products. Although many people already washed their clothes with Tide or Cheer (and used Bounce fabric softener in their dryers), most consumers had additional cleaning needs not fulfilled by existing P&G products. To identify consumers' unmet clothing care needs, the company turned to consumption research, in which marketers interviewed thousands of consumers about their cleaning methods and products. P&G found that consumers tend to wear their "dry-clean only" garments more times between cleanings than they do their washable clothing. Why? Many problems were discovered, including high dry-cleaning costs, wear and tear on garments that were taken to commercial dry-cleaners, and a lack of time to take and retrieve clothing from the dry-cleaner.

All these consumer *problems* led to the introduction of Dryel. Dryel is a garment-cleaning kit designed to let consumers do their own dry-cleaning at home in their dryers—an *alternative* to buying services from a retail dry-cleaner. Consumers can remove stains and freshen their clothing by placing garments in special applicator bags that release a cleaning solvent during the process.

P&G tested the at-home dry-cleaning alternative, and consumers responded favorably. They were pleased with the quality of the product, the ease of *consuming* or *using* the product, and how their clothes looked and smelled after cleaning. Consumers also liked the convenience of *purchasing* Dryel at grocery stores and discount retailers. All these factors contributed to the overall *satisfaction* that consumers felt with the product and the at-home cleaning process. By studying closely how consumers used and reacted to the product, P&G was able to anticipate overall satisfaction ratings and the likelihood of repurchase, leading to the company's decision to introduce the product.

To disseminate *information* about the new product to consumers, the company introduced a set of television commercials—each one highlighting a different consumer problem solved by Dryel. One ad features a woman racing to her local dry-cleaner, jumping over obstacles, to retrieve a garment she needs that evening. She reaches the store only to see a "closed" sign hanging on the front door. The ad goes on to explain how to use the product and where to purchase it. P&G used consumption research to identify a problem unsolved by its existing product line and formulated product and distribution strategies to solve a consumer problem formerly addressed primarily by dry-cleaning businesses.

Marketers must know consumers' needs—if they know where consumers "itch," they have a better idea of where to "scratch" with new and improved products, more effective communication programs, and more user-friendly distribution channels. Firms sometimes make the mistake of developing new products based on what they are able to manufacture or sell rather than based on what consumers want to buy. Products and services that don't solve consumer problems fail, no matter how dazzling the technology or how much is spent on advertising aimed at convincing consumers to buy them.

Even stellar manufacturers like Procter & Gamble have made the mistake of flooding the market with unnecessary product variations. In the 1980s, P & G experienced slowed sales growth because of a major consolidation among retailers and a deluge of competitive knockoff products. The company fought back by introducing hundreds of slightly new but not-so-different products, such as thirty-five varieties of Bounce fabric softeners. In its defense, the company said its goal was to offer consumers more choices, but unfortunately the choices didn't address any unmet needs. After years of confusing consumers and encouraging retailers to stock products that consumers didn't want to buy, A. G. Lafley, P & G's president and CEO, began slashing the number of product variations to meet consumer desires more closely based on interviews and sales reports, a process expected to be repeated with P & G's $57 billion acquisition of Gillette in 2005. Among other actions, P & G sold off slow-growing brands such as Jif and Crisco to concentrate on markets it knew would be growing because of changing demographics, such as health and beauty aids, while also repositioning brands such as Old Spice to target another growing segment of young consumers known as Generation Y. Consumer Behavior and Marketing 3.1 describes how understanding consumer needs and problems led to an entirely new product called Dryel, but Figure 3.3 shows how an existing brand, Old Spice, was "spiced up" to appeal to younger consumers who perceive Old Spice's image today to be in the "Red Zone." P & G's brand reinvention for Old Spice increased its market share from 1 percent to 21 percent, becoming the nation's number-one selling men's deodorant. Lafley's strategies created a 132 percent increase in P & G's stock from the time he took over in 2000 through 2005.[1]

Pottery Barn once fell into the category of retailers that had added too many items to its selection and expanded the size of its stores so much that it became unprofitable. Overinventoried in many slow-moving product categories, Pottery Barn reduced its SKUs (stock keeping units) by 30 percent. The new look? Cleaner, simpler, and more consumer-friendly stores that carry what consumers want. Before understanding purchase behavior, Pottery Barn followed the lead of other retailers that simply put more products on their shelves, hoping that consumers would find something they needed and buy it. The problem is that such wide selections sometimes confuse consumers and increase buying and operations costs substantially, reducing total margins. That's why the best

**FIGURE 3.3** In the "Red Zone": Old Spice's Appeal to Younger Consumers

Courtesy of The Procter & Gamble Company

retailers focus on limiting their SKUs with "category management" programs—stocking only the items it knows consumers will buy—and achieving faster inventory "turns."

Retailers and manufacturers alike must monitor consumer trends because, as consumers change, so do their problems and needs. Some influences most likely to alter the way consumers look at problems and the ways to solve them are family, values, health, age, income, and reference groups. Spotting changes in these variables is often the key to new marketing opportunities. Thirty-year-old consumers with families need to buy more detergent and shampoo (usually in larger quantity packages) than do consumers in their seventies, who may be living alone and in smaller homes with less storage space. As consumers move through different life stages, their needs and buying habits for many items can be expected to change. Desire also increases with the expectation of rising income; that's why Ford sends information about its Ford Focus and other models to graduating university seniors anticipating their first salaried jobs, but who also may be receptive to fuel-efficient vehicles.

Marketers often communicate a need, thereby raising consumers' awareness of unperceived needs or problems. Many years ago, Listerine mouthwash used advertising to increase the awareness of halitosis and in the process dramatically increased mouthwash sales. Listerine did not create the problem of bad breath; it simply raised awareness and offered a solution to the problem. Can marketers create needs? Not really, but they can show how a product meets unperceived needs or problems consumers may not have considered before.

## Stage Two: Search for Information

Once need recognition occurs, consumers begin searching for information and solutions to satisfy their unmet needs. Search may be **internal**, *retrieving knowledge from memory or perhaps genetic tendencies,* or it may be **external**, *collecting information from peers, family, and the marketplace* (see Figure 3.4). Sometimes consumers search passively by simply becoming more receptive to information around them, whereas at other times they engage in active search behavior, such as researching consumer publications, paying attention to ads, researching on the Internet, or venturing to shopping malls and other retail outlets. Search refers to a receptivity of information that solves problems or needs, rather than a search for specific products. Look at Buyer Beware 3.1 and you'll see that information directed toward needs may cause people to buy products about which they were unaware prior to receiving information (in that example, prescription drugs), but may also alienate or embarrass consumers who don't identify with those same needs.

Sometimes consumers are thrust unexpectedly into the search process, prompted by situational factors beyond their control. When a car suddenly breaks down or gets a flat tire, consumers must search for information just as they would for planned purchases. But the urgency of the situation might restrain the amount of time available to search. When a refrigerator suddenly stops working, consumers need a replacement quickly—they can't afford to search as extensively as they would if they were planning the purchase (when building a new house, for instance)—and the immediate availability of buying a new one is considered more important than any money saved by repairing the old one.

The length and depth of search is determined by variables such as personality, social class, income, size of purchase, past experiences, prior brand perceptions,[2] and customer satisfaction. If consumers are delighted with the brand of product they currently use, they may repurchase the brand with little, if any, search behavior, making

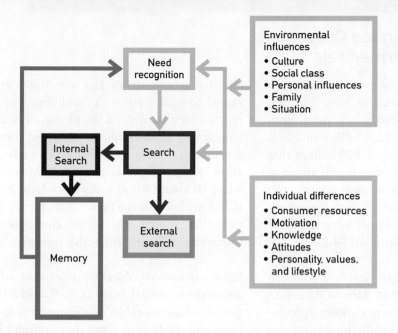

Environmental influences
- Culture
- Social class
- Personal influences
- Family
- Situation

Need recognition

Internal Search

Search

External search

Memory

Individual differences
- Consumer resources
- Motivation
- Knowledge
- Attitudes
- Personality, values, and lifestyle

Joe College has begun his quest for information. To his surprise, he begins to notice dozens of television and magazine ads about autos and begins to digest them. He can afford to spend up to $6,000 on a used car and decides to search the classified ads in the newspaper and car dealers' websites for options. He talks to friends about their cars—what features they like best, how satisfied they are with the performance, and where they bought them. After days of searching, he's gathered information on models he can afford, including who sells them, how much they cost, gas mileage, and so on.

it more difficult for competitive products to catch their attention. That's why successful firms place such a high priority on keeping customers satisfied and creating long-term "fans." When consumers are unhappy with current products or brands, search expands to include other alternatives.

## SOURCES OF INFORMATION

As in the case of the student car buyer, consumers search a variety of sources to obtain the information they need to make product choices with which they are comfortable. These sources can be categorized as (1) marketer-dominated or (2) non-marketer-dominated, as shown in Figure 3.5. *Marketer-dominated* refers to anything that the supplier does for purposes of information and persuasion, such as using advertising, salespeople, infomercials, websites, and point-of-sale materials.

Search is not limited to these marketer-dominated sources. Consumers also seek information from sources over which marketers have little control, yet are critically important to consumers. *Non-marketer-dominated* sources include friends, family, opinion leaders, and the media. Many of these influences come in the form of word-of-mouth; others come from having consulted objective product rating sources such as *Consumer Reports*, government and industry reports, or news stories in the mass media or on the Internet.

Increasingly, information search is occurring on the Internet. Although some searches on the Internet may take a fairly long time, others are much speedier,

## Does Advertising Embarrass Consumers and Cause Them to Overmedicate?

Direct-to-consumer advertising of prescription drugs is legal only in the United States and New Zealand, but it is skyrocketing in the United States, rising from $800 million spent in 1996 to $2.7 billion in 2001. Eighty-six percent of the more than $20 billion that drug companies spend on advertising is still aimed at doctors, but a Kaiser Family Foundation report, conducted by Harvard researchers, estimates that every extra dollar spent on direct-to-consumer advertising for pharmaceuticals results in an additional $4.20 in sales.

This advertising can benefit public health. An American Medical Association survey of African American physicians found that "people were making appointments with doctors to ask about something (they saw in an ad) that might be important for their life, like high blood pressure." The ads may inform people of the availability of help for conditions they didn't know were treatable or were too shy to mention to their doctors, such as overactive bladder, or even depression and anxiety.

The downside is that advertised, brand-name pharmaceuticals may be more expensive than older, equally effective generic drugs and sometimes are not warranted to treat a patient's condition. The advertising may create a burden on the physician to explain to a patient why a drug might be okay, but something they don't need, sometimes resulting in an adversarial situation. Russell Roberts at George Mason University adds, "If I want to eat really spicy food because I love it, but my body doesn't react well, there's a drug I can take, but should my fellow employee pay for it (through employer-paid health insurance)?"

Some consumers object to television ads that talk about controversial subjects such as erectile dysfunction at the dinner table, causing parents to explain the birds and the bees at times they consider inappropriate. Don Sexton, professor at Columbia University, commented on this problem, saying, "Marketing is most effective when it speaks to you personally, but with broadcasting, the audience can be broad and varied, so if a product is targeted at men and women of a certain age, there can be other people in the room. If people are mildly embarrassed, I'd be sorry about that, but I personally feel advertising follows along with where the culture goes."

Source: Adapted from Anita Manning, "Plugged into Prescription Drugs," USA Today, Februrary 15, 2005, D1ff. © 2005 USA Today, a division of Gannett Co., Inc.

depending on how the website is designed.[3] Some researchers surmise that if online retailing decreases the cost of searching for price information, consumers will become more price sensitive.[4] Other studies have shown that by altering web design and making it easier to search for and compare quality information, consumers will become less price-sensitive and more likely to purchase quality products.[5] It is the execution of the website that influences how consumers will use it in the consumer decision process. Getting people to a website is sometimes difficult, done with search engines such as Google or with "pop-up" ads that consumers bemoan but advertisers maintain because they are effective. Most marketers now print their website addresses on shopping bags, invoices, business cards, mass media products, and other sources to get people to visit their websites. Some marketers even purchase ads in magazines they know their target market reads, as you see in Figure 3.6, an ad designed to direct consumers to websites of firms such as Acura and Subway. When rising prices increase the importance of purchase decisions, consumers may turn to the Internet as a source of information, as has occurred with gasoline in Buyer Beware 3.2.

Some consumers prefer the old-fashioned approach to search, called shopping. Many consumers think walking and browsing through malls is fun, whereas others

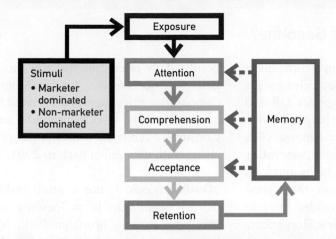

During the decision process, Joe will encounter a wide range of information on vehicle models, options, and prices from paid advertisements via television, direct mail, and the newspaper (marketer- dominated) to feedback from family, friends, and reviews in such publications as *Car and Driver* (non-marketer-dominated).

think it is a chore. Understanding when search is fun and when it is a chore provides valuable information for retailers. For example, the search for microwave oven information and alternatives probably doesn't excite many consumers. The most effective marketing channel for this product minimizes the time and effort required to obtain information. By contrast, many consumers of new cars enjoy the process of going to auto shows, reading automobile magazines, and test-driving new models.

While in-store information search is appealing to some consumers, others prefer catalog shopping—a simplified version of the traditional shopping experience. One of the reasons for the popularity of catalogs among consumers is that the typical catalog page provides more information for less effort than does the typical retail store. Victoria's Secret, which dominates the catalog field, allows consumers to scan hundreds of fabric, style, and color alternatives quickly without leaving home or turning on a computer. Searching its catalogs, filled with pictures of beautiful models in interesting settings, is also an entertaining way to identify the latest fashion designs and is the key element driving sales to both the stores and website of Victoria's Secret, the largest and most profitable business unit of retailing giant Limited Brands.

## INFORMATION PROCESSING

As a consumer is exposed to information resulting from external search, he or she begins to process the stimuli. Figure 3.7 highlights the following steps involved in processing information.

1. *Exposure.* First, information and persuasive communication must *reach* consumers. Once exposure occurs, one or more of the senses is activated and preliminary processing begins.

2. *Attention.* After exposure, the next step is to allocate (or not allocate) information-processing capacity to the incoming information. The more relevant the message and its content, the more likely the consumer will pay attention. Consumers frequently ignore commercial persuasion at this stage and engage in selective attention.

FIGURE 3.6 Example of Ads Directing Consumers to Visit Websites

## Are You Paying Too Much for Gasoline?

To cope with rising energy prices, many people make a "mental note" of daily prices as they drive by gas station marquees, buying gas when prices fall and telling their friends when they spot a bargain. However, the price of gasoline is also just a mouse click away. A relatively new Internet website, www.Gas Buddy.com, contains the comparative highs and lows of gasoline at gas stations throughout the United States and Canada. The website provides links to 173 separate websites, including www.FloridaState GasPrices.com and www.OrlandoGasPrices.com, which provide prices at local pumps throughout a given state or metropolitan area. The prices— grouped in categories such as "highs" and "lows"— are updated every forty-eight hours.

The latest prices are provided by volunteer "price spotters" who are registered online at GasBuddy.com.

Besides daily prices, the free site also offers unleaded gasoline price averages for local markets as well as comparative prices across the United States and Canada, on a daily, weekly, monthly, and yearly basis. Consumers can track trends in gas prices using price charts with data going back to 2001.

"GasBuddy.com is not a profit-making website for us," says cofounder Jason Toews, a computer consultant who lives in Brooklyn Park, Minnesota. "We have some ads, but those are only to help pay for the site. Our basic goal is to help consumers share information about low-priced fuel and find the lowest priced stations." Toews and cofounder Dustin Coupal, an ophthalmologist from Saskatoon, Saskatchewan, created the site after finding few service stations provided prices over the phone.

Source: Excerpted from Tony Natale, "Website Allows Consumers to View Gas Prices Online," *Knight Ridder Tribune Business News* (April 15, 2005), 1. Copyright 2005 by Knight Ridder Tribune Business News. Reproduced with permission of Tribune Media Services.

**FIGURE 3.7**     Information Processing: Exposure Through Retention

Although Joe has been exposed to volumes of information on market choices, not all information catches his attention. He may discard some of the direct mail without reading it, and he may "tune out" certain radio or television commercials. For the messages that do capture his attention, he analyzes their content according to what he already knows from his experience or other messages. If an advertisement shows a used Yugo as fast and chic, for instance, he might discount the credibility of the message, regarding it as inconsistent with his observations and media portrayals of the car. If he "accepts" the message, however, not only will his opinions and attitudes be change or reinforced, but he will remember the information for later use in decision making.

FIGURE 3.8 Advertising That Creates an Image for a Brand

3. *Comprehension.* If attention is attracted, the message is further analyzed against categories of meaning stored in memory. The marketer hopes that accurate comprehension will occur.

4. *Acceptance.* Once comprehension occurs, the message can be either dismissed as unacceptable (a common outcome) or accepted. The goal of the message is to modify or change existing beliefs and attitudes, but the message must be accepted before this can happen. There is a good chance of at least some change occurring if acceptance within the system or structure occurs.

5. *Retention.* Finally, the goal of any persuader is for this new information to be accepted *and* stored in memory in such a way that it is accessible for future use.

Everyone is exposed to a barrage of messages competing for their attention, but individuals comprehend, accept, and retain only a few. Brand equity and favorable brand image in the minds of consumers help firms get their messages into this subset. Information processing is discussed in detail in Chapters 14 through 16. A substantial amount of advertising, especially for apparel and luxury brands, breaks through the processing stages with an appealing photograph and the primary purpose of creating an image for the brand, usually one that hopes to appeal to the aspirations of the target consumer. Figure 3.8 for Calvin Klein is an example.

## Stage Three: Pre-Purchase Evaluation of Alternatives

The next stage of the consumer decision process is evaluating alternative options identified during the search process, as shown in Figure 3.9. In this stage, consumers

## FIGURE 3.9    Alternative Evaluation

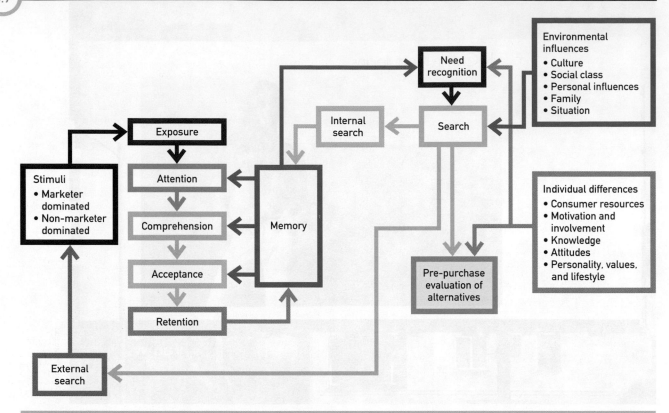

After searching for information and compiling a list of models and requirements, Joe begins to compare his alternatives. He evaluates specific models based on a set of attributes he compiled earlier, including safety, reliability, price, warranty, gas mileage, and number of beverage holders. He also considers things like how he will feel owning and driving the car and evaluates where he might buy the car, comparing the various dealers and the atmosphere each one provides. Although he feels some pressure to make a decision, he has access to his father's car for a few weeks while he finds a car to match his needs and financial constraints; therefore, he takes his time to evaluate thoroughly all the information and alternatives at this stage. The list narrows to a few alternatives, and he prepares to buy one of them.

seek answers to questions such as "What are my options?" and "Which is best?" when they evaluate and select from various products or services. Consumers compare what they know about different products and brands with what they consider most important, to narrowing the field of alternatives before they finally resolve to buy one of them.

Consumers use new or preexisting evaluations stored in memory to select products, services, brands, and stores that will most likely result in their satisfaction with the purchase and consumption. Different consumers employ different **evaluative criteria**—*the standards and specifications used to compare different products and brands.* How individuals evaluate their choices is influenced by both individual and environmental influences (see Figure 3.9). As a result, evaluative criteria become a product-specific manifestation of an individual's needs, values, lifestyles, and so on. But consumers must also evaluate *where* they are going to purchase the desired product, and they apply relevant evaluative criteria to the retail outlets from which they will buy.

Some attributes upon which alternatives are evaluated are *salient,* and some are *determinant,* yet both affect marketing and advertising strategy. Consumers think of **salient attributes** such as *price, reliability, and factors that probably vary little between similar types of products,* as potentially the most important. How alternatives differ on determinant attributes (in the case of a car, details such as style, finish, and type of cup holders) usually *determine which brand or store consumers choose,* especially when they consider the salient attributes to be equivalent. Knowing that people who don't like the attributes of coffee are unlikely to evaluate Starbucks as a place to visit, the firm hopes to create a reason among consumers who do like the attributes of chocolate—with a "sub brand" called Chantico (shan-TEE-ko), as you can see in Figure 3.10.

Consumers often monitor attributes such as quantity, size, quality, and price. Further, changes in these attributes can affect their brand and product choices. If consumers recognize a price increase in a brand that they prefer, they often evaluate the *motive* (the more consumers believe price increases are due to increasing profits, the more "unfair" the increase is perceived)[6] of the price increase to determine whether the price change is fair or not. Perceived unfairness reduces shopping intentions.[7]

Some research focuses on the attributes affecting the choice process for experience goods, such as entertainment. Movies serve as a good category to research because they are experience goods that are hard to evaluate prior to viewing.[8] Although variables, such as word-of-mouth and newspaper

**FIGURE 3.10** Chocolate Chantico Increases Starbucks' Appeal to Non–Coffee Drinkers

reviews, have been identified as critical influencers on consumer choice of movies,[9] other psychological variables, such as emotional expectations and latent product interest, also play an important role in choice. The finding that new movie choice is influenced by emotional expectations, not by cognitive assessment of product attributes, recognizes the importance of emotions in certain areas of consumer behavior.[10] When evaluating alternatives and making trade-offs between product attributes, emotion-laden trade-offs complicate how trade-offs are made and what value is assigned to attributes during the choice process.[11]

When it comes to deciding where to purchase, consumers may evaluate purchasing from one store over another based on consumer traffic within the store, cleanliness of the store, how often the store is out of stock of the needed item, and how many checkout lanes are available. When retailers achieve equivalence on salient attributes such as price and quality, consumers make choices based on "the details" such as ambience or personal attention given to the customer.

## Stage Four: Purchase

The next stage of the consumer decision process is purchase, shown in Figure 3.11. After deciding whether or not to purchase, consumers move through two phases. In the first phase, consumers choose one retailer over another retailer (or some other form of retailing such as catalogs, Internet, or direct sales). The second phase involves in-store choices, influenced by salespersons, product displays, electronic media, and point-of-purchase (POP) advertising.

A consumer might move through the first stages of the decision process according to plan and intend to purchase a particular product or brand. But consumers

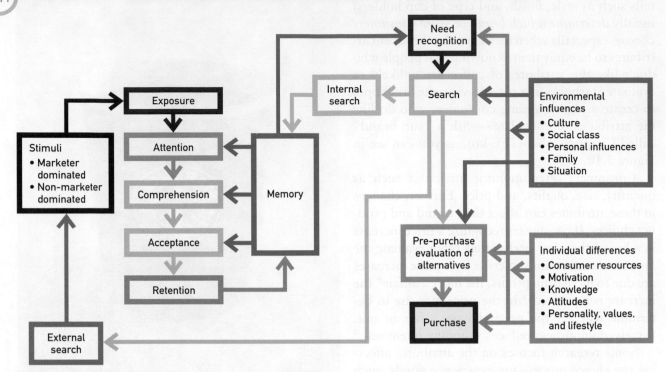

After evaluating his choices, Joe is ready to buy a car. But before he makes the purchase, he must choose a used car lot. He goes to the first lot and browses. A good salesperson should convert the browse into a buy. A bad salesperson might convert an intended purchase into a lost sale. The student knows he wants a reliable, four-door, preferably red car that is priced under $6,000 and that he can afford to pay $300 per month. Many things can kill the deal right now and cause him to leave the lot without purchasing a car. If the student has credit problems, a good dealer will find a way to make the car affordable, either with a lease option or by extending the number of payments. If the dealer doesn't have the right model, color, and accessory package in stock, the purchase process can die. That's why dealers carry hundreds or thousands of cars in inventory. Joe finds a used Volkswagen Jetta that he likes and can afford, and he buys the car.

sometimes buy something quite different from what they intended or opt not to buy at all because of what happens during the purchase or choice stage. A consumer may prefer one retailer but choose another because of a sale or a promotional event at a competitor's store, hours of operation, location, or traffic-flow problems. Inside the store, the consumer may encounter a salesperson or end-of-aisle display providing a compelling reason to buy a different product or brand, use a coupon or price discount, fail to find the intended product or brand, or lack the money or right credit card to make the purchase. The best retailers manage the overall attributes and image of the store to achieve preferred patronage among the market target and to manage, in micro detail, all aspects of the in-store shopping experience.

### Stage Five: Consumption

After the purchase is made and the consumer takes possession of the product, consumption can occur—the point at which consumers use the product. Figure 3.12 highlights both the consumption and post-consumption evaluation stages. Consumption can either occur immediately or be delayed. For example, if a consumer sees a sales promotion for frozen entrees, he or she may "stock up," buying more than can be used in the normal time frame of consumption and requiring the consumer to "warehouse" the product in his or her freezer. How consumers use products also affects how satisfied they are with the purchases and how likely they are to buy that particular

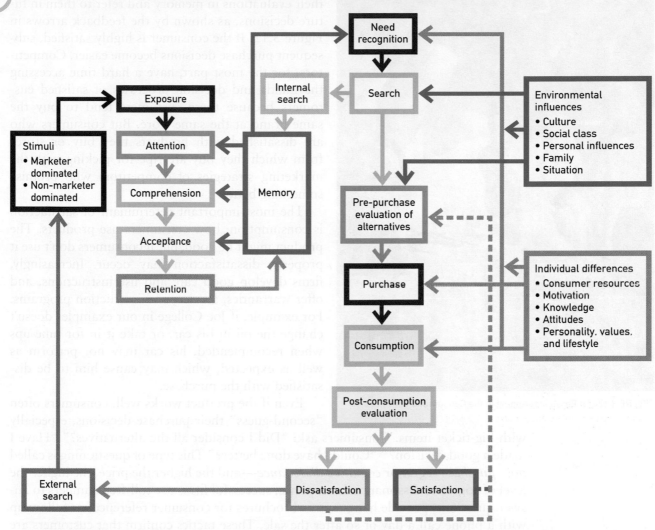
**FIGURE 3.12** Consumption and Post-Consumption Evaluation

As Joe drives his car off the dealer's lot, he thinks, "What have I done?" He gets a sinking feeling in his stomach, while his brain searches for reasons to justify his purchase decision. The dealer that sold him the car understands what the student is feeling and will follow up with a letter in a few days assuring him he made a good decision. (New car buyers might receive free road-side service or leather registration portfolios to relieve their post-purchase concerns.) As for the student, as each problem-free day passes, he feels better about his decision and the process. The car performs well and gets good gas mileage—and his girlfriend likes it, too. Buying a car wasn't so bad after all. In fact, if he had to do it again, he would probably go back to the same dealer.

product or brand in the future. How carefully they use or maintain a product also may determine how long the product will last before another purchase is needed. Figure 3.13 shows how North Face highlights the consumption stage in one of its ads. Not only does the ad appeal to functional attributes of the brand, shown with photography of the shoe's sole, it appeals to the emotional attributes of the brand, highlighting the hedonic benefit of "taking any fork in the road."

Stage Six: Post-Consumption Evaluation

The next stage of consumer decision making is post-consumption evaluation, in which consumers experience a sense of either satisfaction or dissatisfaction. **Satisfaction** occurs *when consumers' expectations are matched by perceived performance. When experiences and performance fall short of expectations,* **dissatisfaction** occurs. These

Heed the call of the ultra.

THE NORTH FACE

NEVER STOP EXPLORING
www.thenorthface.com

High in the Dolomites, Dean Karnazes and Topher Gaylord rely on their Men's Resilience as they head toward no place in particular. Near Cortina, Italy. Photo: Dan Patitucci

**FIGURE 3.13** An Emotional Appeal in the Consumption of Shoes

outcomes are significant because consumers store their evaluations in memory and refer to them in future decisions, as shown by the feedback arrows in Figure 3.12. If the consumer is highly satisfied, subsequent purchase decisions become easier. Competitors, for the most part, have a hard time accessing the minds and decision processes of satisfied customers because these customers tend to buy the same brand at the same store. But consumers who are dissatisfied with products they buy or stores from which they buy are ripe for picking with the marketing strategies of competitors who promise something better.

The most important determinant of satisfaction is consumption: how consumers use products. The product might be good, but if consumers don't use it properly, dissatisfaction may occur. Increasingly, firms develop good care and use instructions, and offer warranties, service, and instruction programs. For example, if Joe College in our examples doesn't change the oil in his car, or take it in for tune-ups when recommended, his car may not perform as well as expected, which may cause him to be dissatisfied with the purchase.

Even if the product works well, consumers often "second-guess" their purchase decisions, especially with big-ticket items. Consumers ask: "Did I consider all the alternatives?" "Have I made a good decision?" "Could I have done better?" This type of questioning is called *post-purchase regret* or *cognitive dissonance*—and the higher the price, the higher the level of cognitive dissonance. In response, successful firms use toll-free numbers to answer questions, provide hang-tags or brochures for consumer reference, or follow up with a phone call a day or so after the sale. These tactics confirm that customers are satisfied and provide additional information to comfort consumers.

Emotions play an important role in how someone evaluates a product or transaction. An emotion can be defined as a reaction to a cognitive appraisal of events or thoughts. An emotion is accompanied by physiological processes, is often expressed physically (in gestures, posture, or facial expressions), and may result in specific actions to cope with or affirm the emotion.[12] For example, satisfaction with a car has been found to be dependent on a combination of attribute satisfaction and dissatisfaction and positive (joy) and negative (anger, guilt, or contempt) effects or emotions.[13]

Just as consumers compare prices and evaluate the fairness of exchange in the alternative evaluation stage, so do they revisit these issues during post-purchase evaluation. Some research indicates that how consumers view the fairness of the exchange *over time* affects current and future usage behavior. Price and usage also affect their overall evaluations of the fairness of the exchange. In turn, these evaluations affect overall satisfaction and future usage.[14]

### Stage Seven: Divestment

Divestment is the last stage in the consumer decision process model, shown in Figure 3.14. Consumers have several options, including outright disposal, recycling, or remarketing. When the student in the example is finished using the car he purchased, he has to dispose of it somehow. He can choose to sell (remarket) it to another con-

PART 2 [ CONSUMER DECISION MAKING

**FIGURE 3.14** Divestment

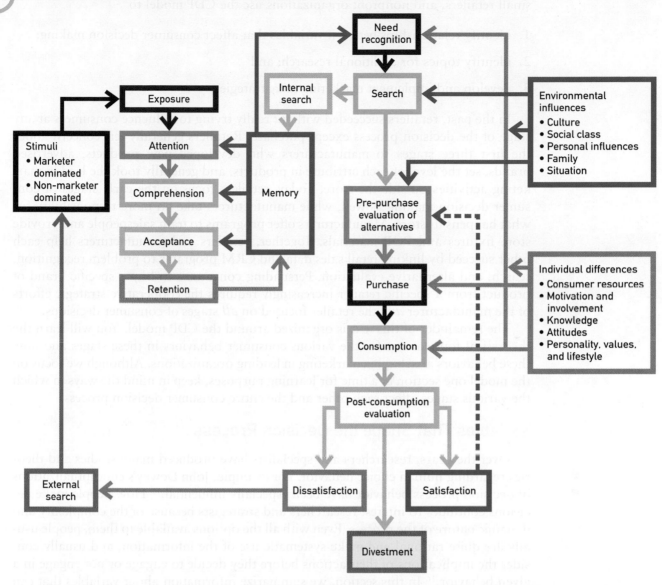

After years of driving his car, Joe decides he needs a new one—preferably a sports car. He has many options available for getting rid of his old car. He could trade it for credit toward a new car, or he could sell it himself through classified ads in his local newspaper. He has also heard that he can donate the car to various charitable organizations and deduct the value of the car from his personal income taxes. Though all of these divestment methods are feasible, he decides that since his sister is starting college and needs a reliable car, he will sell it to her for a very reasonable price, which he can, in turn, apply toward his new car purchase.

sumer, trade it in for another vehicle, or take it to the junkyard. With other products, consumers find themselves having to dispose of packaging and product literature as well as the product itself. In these situations, recycling and environmental concerns play a role in consumers' divestment methods. For many products, auctions on eBay offer an opportunity to divest of products and earn a little cash at the same time.

## How Organizations Use the CDP Model

One of the goals of the CDP model is to help marketers study consumers by examining how consumers proceed through the decision model (adapted for a particular product or service) and ask questions, such as those at the end of the chapter in

Table 3.1. Manufacturers such as Procter & Gamble and General Motors, large and small retailers, and nonprofit organizations use the CDP model to

1. identify relationships between variables that affect consumer decision making;

2. identify topics for additional research; and

3. develop and implement marketing mix strategies.

In the past, retailers succeeded without really trying to influence consumers at any stage of the decision process except purchase. Retailers generally left concern about the first three stages to manufacturers who developed new products, advertised brands, set the level of each attribute in products, and generally took the lead in marketing activities outside the store. Today, retailers focus on the early stages of consumer decision making as well, while manufacturers take on more responsibility for what happens in-store. Manufacturers offer programs to train salespeople and provide store fixtures and POP materials. Together, retailers and manufacturers help each other succeed by linking retail sales data and CRM programs to problem recognition, search, and alternative evaluation. Persuading consumers to buy a specific brand of product from a specific retailer increasingly requires the cooperative strategic efforts of the manufacturer *and* the retailer focused on *all* stages of consumer decisions.

The remainder of this text is organized around the CDP model. You will learn the theoretical foundations for the various consumer behaviors in these stages and how these behaviors are shaping marketing in leading organizations. Although we focus on the model one section at a time for learning purposes, keep in mind the ways in which the various stages affect each other and the entire consumer decision process.

## Variables That Shape the Decision Process

Over the years, researchers and specialists have produced many studies and theories regarding human choice behavior. For example, John Dewey's conceptualizations of decision process behavior have been especially influential.[15] How people make decisions continues to interest researchers and strategists because of the complexity and dynamic nature of the process. Even with all the options available to them, people usually are quite rational and make systematic use of the information, and usually consider the implications of their actions before they decide to engage or not engage in a given behavior.[16] In this section, we summarize information about variables that can influence decision making.

Consumer decision making is influenced and shaped by many factors and determinants that fall into these three categories: (1) individual differences, (2) environmental influences, and (3) psychological processes. A summary of these variables follows, but each is covered in depth in later chapters, with Part III focusing on individual differences, Part IV on environmental influences, and Part V on influencing consumer behavior. Refer to Figure 3.14 to see how all the stages of the CDP model are affected by these variables.

### Individual Differences

Five major categories of individual differences affect behavior: (1) demographics, psychographics, values, and personality; (2) consumer resources; (3) motivation; (4) knowledge; and (5) attitudes.

- **Demographics, psychographics, values, and personality:** How people differ affects decision processes and buying behavior. You will read about these influences in depth in Chapter 7. These variables make up what has come to be known as *psy-*

*chographic research,* which probes into those individual traits, values, beliefs, and preferred behavior patterns that correlate with behavior in market segments.

• **Consumer resources:** Each person brings three primary resources into every decision-making situation: (1) time, (2) money, and (3) information reception and processing capabilities (attention). Generally, the availability of each has distinct limits, thus requiring some careful allocation. Chapters 5 and 7 provide guidelines to help you assess the implications of limited resources on consumer motivation and behavior.

• **Motivation:** Psychologists and marketers alike have conducted a wide variety of studies to determine what takes place when goal-directed behavior is energized and activated. Chapter 8 discusses motivation in detail.

• **Knowledge:** Knowledge is defined in Chapter 9 as information stored in memory. It encompasses a vast array of items such as the availability and characteristics of products and services; where and when to buy; and how to use products. A primary goal of advertising and selling is to provide relevant knowledge and information to consumers so as to assist them with decision making, especially in extended problem solving.

• **Attitudes:** Behavior is influenced strongly by attitudes toward a given brand or product. An attitude is simply an overall evaluation of an alternative, ranging from positive to negative. Once formed, attitudes play a directive role on future choice and are difficult to change. Nevertheless, attitude change is a common marketing goal, as you will see in Chapter 10.

## Environmental Influences

Consumers live in a complex environment. In addition to individual variables, their decision process behavior is influenced by environmental factors, including (1) culture, (2) social class, (3) family, (4) personal influence, and (5) situation.

• **Culture:** In the study of consumer behavior, culture refers to the values, ideas, artifacts, and other meaningful symbols that help individuals communicate, interpret, and evaluate as members of society. Chapter 11 provides a comprehensive overview of cultural issues from both a global and an ethnic perspective.

• **Social class:** Social classes are divisions within society that are composed of individuals sharing similar values, interests, and behaviors. You will see this discussed in Chapter 11 as well. Socioeconomic status differences may lead to differing forms of consumer behavior (for example, the types of alcoholic beverages served, the make and style of car driven, and the styles of dress preferred).

• **Family:** Since the field of consumer research was founded, the family has been a focus of research. You will learn in Chapter 12 that the family often is the primary decision-making unit, with a complex and varying pattern of roles and functions. Cooperation and conflict often occur simultaneously with interesting behavioral outcomes.

• **Personal influence:** As consumers, our behaviors often are affected by those with whom we closely associate. This is referred to as *personal influence* and is discussed in Chapter 13. Consumers often respond to perceived pressure to conform to the norms and expectations provided by others—seeking and taking their counsel on buying choices, observing what others are doing as information about consumption choices, and comparing their decisions to those of others.

• **Situation behaviors** change as situations change. Sometimes these changes are erratic and unpredictable, such as a medical emergency, and at other times, they can be predicted by research. Situation is treated as a research variable in its own right and is discussed in various chapters.

Finally, those who wish to understand and influence consumer behavior must have a practical grasp of three basic psychological processes: (1) information processing, (2) learning, and (3) attitude and behavior change.

- **Information processing:** Communication is a bottom-line marketing activity. Therefore, consumer researchers have long been interested in discovering how people receive, process, and make sense of marketing communications. Information processing research, discussed in Chapters 14 through 16, addresses *the ways in which information is retrieved, transformed, reduced, elaborated, stored, recovered, and retrieved.* Exposure and attention is covered in Chapter 14, comprehension and acceptance in Chapter 15, and retention in Chapter 16.
- **Learning:** Anyone attempting to influence the consumer is trying to bring about learning—*the process by which experience leads to changes in knowledge and behavior.* Learning theory is important to understanding consumer behavior, especially for those products and services bought with less reflection and evaluation. You'll learn how classical conditioning functions in Chapter 15, how cognitive learning occurs in Chapter 16, and how operant condition functions in Chapter 5.
- **Attitude and behavior change:** Changes in attitude and behavior are an important marketing objective that reflect basic psychological influences and have been the subject of decades of intensive research. Chapter 15 reviews this literature from the perspective of designing effective promotional strategies.

## Types of Decision Process

The extent to which each of the stages in Figure 3.14 is followed in the precise form and sequence suggested can vary from one situation to the next. Sometimes consumers undertake a complex decision process requiring substantial amounts of time and energy. More common, however, are rather simplistic processes in which relatively little time and effort are devoted to the decision.

### Decision Process Continuum

One way to think about these variations is to imagine a continuum of decision-making complexity ranging from high to low (see Figure 3.15). In situations in which consumers are making a decision for the first time, actions must be based on some form of problem solving. When this process is very complex, it is called extended problem solving. Limited problem solving represents a lower degree of complexity. For convenience, we refer to the process along the middle of the continuum as midrange problem solving.

In Figure 3.15, we allow for the fact that most consumer purchases are made on a repeated basis. When this is the case, the individual may engage in problem solving once again. Alternatively, he or she may greatly simplify the decisions by foregoing any deliberation of purchase alternatives and simply choosing the same brand purchased previously. This represents habitual decision making, the least complex of all decision processes.

### Initial Purchase

When the initial decision is made by extended problem solving, enduring buying patterns based on brand loyalty are often established. However, limited problem solving leads to inertia-based habits—it's easier to do the same thing again than switch. The reasons for these distinctions will be discussed in this section.

**FIGURE 3.15**    Consumer Decision Process Continuum

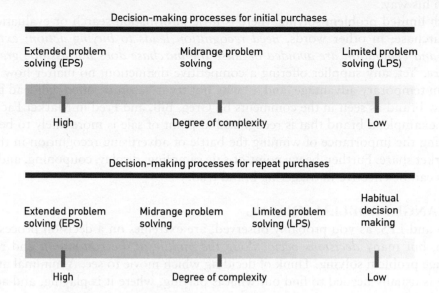

Decision-making processes for initial purchases

Extended problem solving (EPS)     Midrange problem solving     Limited problem solving (LPS)

High          Degree of complexity          Low

Decision-making processes for repeat purchases

Extended problem solving (EPS)     Midrange problem solving     Limited problem solving (LPS)     Habitual decision making

High          Degree of complexity          Low

## EXTENDED PROBLEM SOLVING

When the decision process is especially detailed and rigorous, **extended problem solving (EPS),** or *problem solving of a higher degree of complexity that influences consumers' actions,* often occurs. EPS is commonly used by consumers purchasing automobiles (as in the example of Joe College), expensive clothing, stereo equipment, and other major products or services for which the costs and risks of a wrong decision are high. Sometimes EPS is fueled by doubts and fears; other times it is based on lack of experience and information about an expensive, significant, or high-involvement purchase. Regardless of the reason, these consumers are open to information from various sources and are motivated to undertake the effort required in making "the right choice."

When EPS is activated, all seven stages in the decision process are likely to be followed, although not necessarily in that exact order. Consumers engaging in EPS generally evaluate many alternatives, consulting a wide variety of product information sources and research options on how and where to make the purchase.

In short, a high degree of thought and evaluation usually precede the act of purchase and use because of the importance of making the right choice. The process of analysis and reflection, however, does not cease after purchase and use. If the item purchased is perceived as falling short of expectations, the outcome can be substantial, and often vocal, dissatisfaction. The desired outcome is satisfaction, expressed as positive recommendations to others and the intention to repurchase should the occasion arise.

## LIMITED PROBLEM SOLVING

The other extreme of the decision-making continuum is **limited problem solving (LPS),** or *problem solving of a lower degree of complexity that influences consumers' actions.*[17] In most situations, consumers have neither the time, the resources, nor the motivation to engage in EPS. It is far more common to simplify the process and sharply reduce the number and variety of information sources, alternatives, and criteria used for evaluation. Market Facts 3.1 shows excerpts from a focus group demonstrating how this process occurs.

Several of the men in the focus group express sentiments such as "buy a brand that I recognize" or "buy the cheapest brand,"[18] both examples of "simple rules" that may drive consumers' choices. One focus group member squeezes the very last use out of his toothpaste tube, makes a mental note to stop at the supermarket on the way home, happens to see a special on a new brand that he recognizes, picks up a large tube, and goes on his way.

With **limited problem solving**, there is little information search or evaluation before purchase; in other words, *need recognition leads to buying action; extensive search and evaluation are avoided because the purchase does not assume great importance.* Yet, any supplier offering a competitive distinction, no matter how small, can gain temporary advantage, and a "why not try it" attitude often will lead to trial of a new brand as seen in the comments by Greg, Bill, and Fred in Market Facts 3.1.

For example, a brand that is recognized at point of sale is more likely to be tried, indicating the importance of winning the battle of advertising recognition in the war for market share. Further, heavy point-of-sale sampling, display, couponing, and other devices can be effective in triggering brand trial.

## MIDRANGE PROBLEM SOLVING

EPS and LPS, as you probably observed, are extremes on a decision process continuum, but many *decisions occur along the middle of the continuum* and require **midrange problem solving.** Think of deciding which movie to see. A minimal amount of time is usually needed to find out what is playing, where it is playing, and at what time. Because several options look promising, there is a need to evaluate them, often by consulting reviews on the Internet or the recommendations of a friend. All this can be accomplished quickly with only moderate deliberation.

---

Most purchases are repeated over time. When repeat purchases occur, two possibilities can happen: (1) repeated problem solving, and (2) habitual decision making.

## REPEATED PROBLEM SOLVING

Repeat purchases often require continued problem solving. Several factors can lead to this outcome, including dissatisfaction with a previous purchase (often resulting in brand switching) and retail stockouts (when the retailer doesn't have product available). In this type of purchase behavior, the buyer must weigh the consequences of investing time and energy in finding another alternative.

## HABITUAL DECISION MAKING

It's far more likely that repeat purchases will be made on the basis of habits or routines that simplify life for the consumer. Habitual behavior takes different forms, depending on the decision process followed in the initial purchase: (1) brand or company loyalty, and (2) inertia.

• *Brand or company loyalty:* Consumers have certain expectations about the products they buy and the retailers from whom they purchase. The satisfaction that consumers experience when their expectations are met or exceeded often results in loyalty to a product or retailer. For the most part, consumers want to reward these companies with continued use over time—that is, brand or company *loyalty,* which can be highly resistant to change.

Marketers covet high loyalty and often do everything possible to maintain it. Anyone who tries to dislodge loyal purchasers of a brand of 35mm film such as Fuji faces a tough challenge. This loyalty is often based on both the high-involvement nature of photography among consumers who take their photography seriously enough to still use analog cameras and their belief that Fuji offers the brightest color and image quality. Such buyers have no incentive to change unless there is a demonstrable competitive breakthrough. In fact, many firms reward customers for their continued patronage with loyalty programs, as you'll read in Chapter 8, with great success for airlines, hotels, and retailers such as Chico's.

• *Inertia:* Toothpaste is a product category in which there is limited brand loyalty. Where any degree of loyalty does exist, it mostly consists of several brands, all of which are about equal. Buying habits of this type are based on *inertia* and are unstable. Although there is little incentive to switch, this may occur quite readily when prices are lowered with a coupon or another brand is promoted as offering something new, as Mentadent attempts to do with a difference in whitening, shown in Figure 3.16.

### Impulse Buying

The so-called **impulse purchase,** *an unplanned, spur-of-the-moment action triggered by product display or point-of-sale promotion,*[19] is the least

**FIGURE 3.16** Ad for Mentadent Highlights Special Whitening Feature

complex form of LPS but differs in some important ways. The following are its characteristics.[20]

1. a sudden and spontaneous desire to act accompanied by urgency

2. a state of psychological disequilibrium in which a person can feel temporarily out of control

3. the onset of conflict and struggle that is resolved by an immediate action

4. minimal objective evaluation, with emotional considerations dominating

5. a lack of regard for consequences

Although the careful reasoning characteristic of EPS are absent, the indifference that accompanies LPS is also absent. A high sense of emotional involvement and urgency, in effect, short-circuits the reasoning process and motivates immediate action.

### Variety Seeking

Consumers often express satisfaction with their present brand but still engage in brand switching. The motive is variety seeking, which occurs most often when there are many similar alternatives, frequent brand shifts, and high purchase frequency.[21] This activity can occur simply because someone is bored with his or her current brand choice, or it can be prompted by external cues such as store stock-outs or coupons that

FIGURE 3.17 Martha Stewart Brings Style to KMart Stores

PART 2 [ CONSUMER DECISION MAKING

promote switching and can vary with product category and consumer commitment (loyalty) to brands.[22] After seeing its once strong brand lose some of its appeal, KMart sought to rejuvenate it with high-profile designers, such as Martha Stewart, shown in Figure 3.17.

## Factors Influencing the Extent of Problem Solving

The extent of the problem-solving process consumers undergo in different purchase situations depends on distinctive factors such as (1) degree of involvement, (2) degree of differentiation between alternatives, and (3) amount of time for deliberation.

### Degree of Involvement

The degree of *personal involvement* is a key factor in shaping the type of decision process that consumers will follow. **Involvement** is *the level of perceived personal importance and interest evoked by a stimulus within a specific situation.*[23] To the extent that a consumer is involved, the consumer acts *to minimize the risks* and *to maximize the benefits* gained from purchase and use.

Involvement ranges from low to high. The degree of involvement is determined by how important consumers perceive the product or service to be. Simply stated, the more important the product or service to a consumer, the more motivated he or she is to search and be involved in the decision. Involvement becomes activated and felt when intrinsic personal characteristics (needs, values, self-concept) are confronted with appropriate marketing stimuli within a given situation.[24] Furthermore, involvement seems to function in comparable ways across cultures, although the specific products and modes of expression vary somewhat.[25] How involved are consumers in their purchase decisions for a product such as multivitamins? Several decades ago, when multivitamins were being advertised fairly heavily in mainstream media, consumers were given information on the importance to their health and the convenience of taking all their vitamins in one daily dose. Over time, choosing and purchasing multivitamins went from being a medium- to high-involvement purchase to a low-involvement decision. But various factors, such as the interest in herbal medicines and the evolution of self-medication, sparked the opportunity for Bayer's One-A-Day vitamins to provide new information to consumers and increase the degree of involvement in the decision to purchase. One-A-Day now has a variety of herbal additives available to consumers—ranging from ginkgo (for memory) to ginseng (for energy)—involving consumers more in their purchase decisions, as well as distinct formulas for different segments and life stages of consumers including children, people watching their weight, and adults over the age of fifty.

Several factors exist that determine the degree of involvement consumers have in making a decision. Research on the factors that generate high or low involvement is extensive and is summarized in the following section. Take time to review the factors and understand how they play a role in the various purchase decisions you make.

### PERSONAL FACTORS

Degree of involvement tends to be higher when the outcome of the decision affects the person directly. Personal factors include self-image, health, beauty, and physical condition. Without activation of need and drive, there will be no involvement, and involvement is strongest when the product or service is perceived as enhancing self-image.[26] When that is the case, involvement is likely to be enduring and to function as a stable trait, as opposed to being situational or temporary.[27] For example, the purchase of cosmetics tends to be a high-involvement decision because it affects directly a consumer's self-image and looks. A consumer's physical handicap also affect how involved he or she is in buying a home. Are there steps leading up to the house? Is there a bedroom on the first floor, and are doorways wide enough to accommodate a wheelchair?

## PRODUCT FACTORS

Products or brands also become involving if there is some perceived risk in purchasing and using them. Many types of perceived risk have been identified, including physical (risk of bodily harm), psychological (especially a negative effect on self-image), performance (fear that the product will not perform as expected), and financial (risk that outcomes will lead to loss of earnings).[28]

The greater the perceived risk by consumers, the greater is the likelihood of high involvement. When perceived risk becomes unacceptably high, there is motivation either to avoid purchase and use altogether or to minimize risk through the search and pre-purchase alternative evaluation stages in extended problem solving. For example, consumers may become highly involved in the choice and purchase of a physician, especially when surgery is required, because of the high perceived risk.

## SITUATIONAL FACTORS

Situational (or instrumental) involvement includes factors such as whether the product is purchased for personal use or as a gift, and whether it is consumed alone or with others. Situational involvement changes over time: it may be strong on a temporary basis and wane once purchasing outcomes are resolved.

This is often the case with fads such as trendy clothing items in which involvement is high initially but quickly diminishes once the item is worn and fashions begin to change. Changing situational involvement also happens when an otherwise uninvolving product takes on a different degree of relevance because of the manner in which it will be used.[29] For example, a big difference can exist in the perceived importance between a brand of bath gel purchased for home use and that given as a gift.

Finally, involvement can increase when social pressures are felt. For example, research indicates that consumers act quite differently when purchasing wine for ordinary personal consumption than when serving it at a dinner party.[30] Consumers may feel pressure to buy a more expensive or well-recognized wine when entertaining with friends than when eating alone.

## Perceptions of Difference among Alternatives

Marketers find that EPS is more probable when choice alternatives are seen as differentiated.[31] The more similar choices are perceived to be, however, the greater the likelihood that consumers will spend less time on problem solving. Consider what happens when a consumer is shopping and finds that Bounce fabric softener is out of stock. If the consumer perceives the Snuggle brand to be similar, she or he will spend less time choosing the available alternative than if the difference between the two is perceived to be great.

## Time Availability

Two time-related factors also affect the degree of involvement in a decision: how much time a consumer has to devote to solving the problem and how quickly the decision needs to be made. Joe College, our car buyer, spent a lot of time evaluating various cars because he had access to his father's car and didn't need to make a purchase right away. But if he had been stranded without any transportation, he may have had to make a much faster decision. In this case, the situation places a time constraint on the decision. Another consumer might want a new car but does not have much time to read brochures, talk with friends, and test-drive various brands because of job- and family-related time constraints. That consumer may be less involved in the decision because of the time constraints that he or she brings to the situation. As a general rule, therefore, EPS is followed when time pressures are low.

### Consumer's Mood State

Consumer mood can strongly influence information processing and evaluation.[32] Consumer mood state—how people feel at a particular moment—influences the affective component of attitudes (this will be discussed in Chapter 10). At a macro-level of consumer behavior, however, if consumers generally are in a good mood and look forward to shopping for a Christmas gift, they may spend more time in the shopping mall looking for the perfect gift. Others may dislike holiday shopping and spend as little time as possible in the shopping process, often turning to the Internet for quick and easy solutions. Today, many consumers solve their problems with gift cards.

At times, a positive effect on mood can cause consumers to reduce the length and complexity of the decision process,[33] but at other times mood can have exactly the opposite effect.[34] Look at the decision process of purchasing funeral services. If purchased before the need occurs (as is the case with prearranged funerals), consumers may spend more time looking at alternative choices. If purchased at the time of need, however, the family may feel distraught and emotional, thus choosing to shorten the decision process. Though it is not always clear *how* mood will affect consumer behavior, it can affect buying and consumption, as you read in Market Facts 2.1.

## Diagnosing Consumer Behavior

The primary focus of this chapter has been the consumer decision process, with an emphasis on the CDP model as a framework for examining how consumers make decisions. Table 3.1 features a guide for strategic thinking that incorporates the materials covered in this chapter, including the consumer decision process, types of decisions, and degree of involvement. The guide is a list of questions that will help in formulating diagnostic marketing research and developing communication and marketing strategies.

## Need Recognition

1. What needs and motivations are satisfied by product purchase and usage? (i.e., What *benefits* are consumers seeking?)
2. Are these needs dormant or are they presently perceived as felt needs by prospective buyers?
3. How involved with the product are most prospective buyers in the target market segment?

## Search for Information

1. What product- and brand-related information is stored in memory?
2. Is the consumer motivated to turn to external sources to find information about available alternatives and their characteristics?
3. What specific information sources are used most frequently when search is undertaken?
4. What product features or attributes are the focus of search when it is undertaken?

## Pre-Purchase Evaluation of Alternatives

1. To what extent do consumers engage in alternative evaluation and comparison?
2. Which product and/or brand alternatives are included in the evaluation process?
3. Which product evaluative criteria (product attributes) are used to compare various alternatives?
   a. Which are most salient in the evaluation?
   b. How complex is the evaluation (i.e., using a single attribute as opposed to several in combination)?
4. What are the outcomes of evaluation regarding each of the candidate purchase alternatives?
   a. What is believed to be true about the characteristics and features of each?
   b. Are they perceived to be different in important ways, or are they seen as essentially the same?
5. What kind of decision rule is used to determine the best choice?

## Purchase

1. Will the consumer expend time and energy to shop until the preferred alternative is found?
2. Is additional decision process behavior needed to discover the preferred outlet for purchase?
3. What are the preferred models of purchases (i.e., retail store, in the home, or in other ways)?

## Consumption

1. How is the consumer using the product?
   a. For intended purpose?
   b. As recommended in usage/care instructions?
   c. To solve some problem the product was not designed for?
2. What other products are used in conjunction with the product?
3. Where is the product stored when not in use?
4. What is normal frequency of usage and duration of consumption?
5. In relationship to purchase, where and when does the consumption occur?
6. How are household members, peers, and others involved in consumption?

## Post-Consumption Evaluation

1. What degree of satisfaction or dissatisfaction is expressed with respect to previously used alternatives in the product or service category?
2. What reasons are given for satisfaction or dissatisfaction?
3. Has perceived satisfaction or dissatisfaction been shared with other people to help them in their buying behavior?

TABLE 3.1          (Continued)

4. Have consumers made attempts to achieve redress for dissatisfaction?

5. Is there an intention to repurchase any of the alternatives?

   a. If no, why not?

   b. If yes, does intention reflect brand loyalty or inertia?

**Divestment**

1. When does the consumer divest of the product?

   a. When the product is either completely consumed or used?

   b. When the consumer tires of it?

   c. When a better alternative comes along?

2. How does the consumer dispose of the product?

   a. Does he or she throw away the product at home or somewhere else?

   b. Does the consumer recycle the product or resell it?

   c. Does the consumer donate the product to a nonprofit organization or give it to a friend?

3. How does the consumer dispose of the packaging?

4. What role does concern for the environment play in the divestment choice?

## Summary

The purpose of this chapter has been to introduce you to the nature of consumer decision making and the influences on this process. The consumer decision process (CDP) model provides a "road map" of how consumers find their way in a world of consumption decisions.

Consumer decisions, analyzed with the aid of the CDP model, move through the following stages: (1) need recognition, (2) search for information, (3) pre-purchase evaluations of alternatives, (4) purchase, (5) consumption, (6) post-purchase alternative evaluation, and (7) divestment. As consumers move through these stages, marketers have an opportunity to react to and influence behavior with effective communication and marketing strategies that address each of these stages and the variables that affect each stage. Purchase and consumption are affected by a complex set of factors that influence and shape decision process behavior, including *individual differences* and *environmental influences*.

Decision processes can range from extended problem solving (which can be viewed as one end of a problem-solving continuum) to limited problem solving (the opposite end of the spectrum). EPS is characterized by intensive search for information and complex evaluation, whereas LPS represents far less motivation to search widely for information and engage in alternative evaluation.

When the occasion arises for repeat purchases, many consumers quickly develop habitual decision processes. Sometimes they are brand loyal and repeat their initial choice in subsequent purchases. This often occurs when there is high perceived involvement. When high involvement is not present, habits are likely to be built on loyalty or inertia. If a consumer has no reason to switch, a repurchase will be made. But the consumer also is prone to switch if there is incentive to do so. This frequently occurs when there is low involvement and little commitment to prefer one alternative to another.

Several factors influence decision process behavior in terms of degree of involvement. Determinants of involvement include (1) personal factors, (2) product factors, and (3) situational factors.

## Review and Discussion Questions

1. Some analysts argue that consumers really do not pursue any kind of decision process but make their selections more or less randomly without any apparent reasoning. What is your position on this issue? Why?

**Chapter Summary**

2. Define the terms *extended problem solving* and *limited problem solving.* What are the essential differences? What type of decision process would you expect most people to follow in the initial purchase of a new product or brand in each of these categories: toothpaste, flour, men's cologne, carpeting, toilet tissue, bread, light bulbs, a digital camera, a sports car?

3. Referring to question 2, is it possible that the decision process could differ widely from one consumer to another in purchasing each of these items? Explain.

4. How might a manufacturer of automatic washers and dryers use a decision process approach to better understand how consumers purchase these products?

5. Which of the following types of products do you think are most likely to be purchased on the basis of brand loyalty and on the basis of inertia: laundry detergent, motor oil, lipsticks, shoe polish, soft drinks, lawn care products, and spark plugs?

6. Assume you are responsible for marketing a new digital camera. You are competing against Kodak and Nikon, which have built substantial brand loyalty. What strategies could you suggest to make market inroads?

7. Assume you have been hired as a marketing consultant to suggest an advertising strategy for a new brand of dry cat food. Which of the types of decision processes discussed in this chapter do you believe is likely with most prospective buyers? Why do you say this? What difference will this make in marketing strategy?

8. In Buyer Beware 3.1, you read about the possibility of consumers buying prescriptions they might not need and the fact that advertising to consumers for such products is legal only in the United States and New Zealand. Do you think advertising of prescription drugs should be prohibited in the United States or other countries? Why or why not?

## Notes

[1] Richard Siklos, "Procter's Lafley Is the Best a Man Can Get," *Sunday Telegraph* (January 31, 2005).

[2] Sridhar Moorthy, Brian T. Ratchford, and Debabrata Talukdar, "Consumer Information Search Revisited: Theory and Empirical Analysis," *Journal of Consumer Research,* 23 (March 1997), 263–277.

[3] Abeer Y. Hogue and Gerald Lohse, "An Information Search Cost Perspective for Designing Interfaces for Electronic Commerce," *Journal of Marketing Research,* 36 (August 1999), 387–394.

[4] J. Alba, J. Lynch, B. Weitz, C. Janisqewski, R. Lutz, A. Sawyer, and S. Wood, "Interactive Home Shopping: Consumer, Retailer, and Manufacturer Incentives to Participate in Electronic Marketplaces," *Journal of Marketing,* 61 (July 1997), 38–53.

[5] John Lynch and Dan Ariely, "Interactive Home Shopping: Effects of Search Cost for Price and Quality Information on Consumer Price Sensitivity, Satisfaction with Merchandise Selected and Reten-

tion," working paper, Marketing Department, Duke University (1999).

[6] Robert Franciosi, Praveen Kugal, Roland Michelitsch, Vernon Smith, and Gang Deng, "Fairness: Effect on Temporary and Equilibrium Prices in Posted-Offered Markets," *The Economic Journal,* 105 (July 1995), 938–950.

[7] Margaret C. Campbell, "Perceptions of Price Unfairness: Antecedents and Consequences," *Journal of Marketing Research,* 18 (May 1999), 187–199.

[8] Mohanbir Sawhney and Jehoshua Eliashberg, "A Parsimonious Model for Forecasting Gross Box Office Revenues of Motion Pictures," *Marketing Science,* 15 (1996), 113–131.

[9] Jehoshua Eliashberg and Steven Shugan, "Film Critics: Influencers or Predictors?" *Journal of Marketing,* 61 (April 1997), 68–78.

[10] Ramya Neelamegham and Dipak Jain, "Consumer Choice Process for Experience Goods: An Econometric Model and Analysis," *Journal of Marketing Research,* 36 (August 1999), 373–386.

[11] Mary Frances Luce, John W. Payne, and

James R. Bettman, "Emotional Trade-Off Difficulty and Choice," *Journal of Marketing Research,* 36 (May 1999), 143–159.

[12] Richard P. Bagozzi, Mahesh Gopinath, Prashanth Nyer, "The Role of Emotions in Marketing," *Journal of the Academy of Marketing Science,* 27 (Spring 1999), 184–206.

[13] Richard Oliver, "Cognitive, Affective, and Attribute Bases of the Satisfaction Response," *Journal of Consumer Research,* 20 (December 1993), 418–430.

[14] Ruth N. Bolton and Katherine N. Lemon, "A Dynamic Model of Customers' Usage of Services: Usage As an Antecedent and Consequence of Satisfaction," *Journal of Marketing Research,* 36 (May 1999), 171–186.

[15] John Dewey, *How We Think* (New York: Heath, 1910).

[16] Icek Ajzen and Martin Fishbein, *Understanding Attitudes and Predicting Social Behavior* (Englewood Cliffs, NJ: Prentice-Hall, 1980).

[17] Harold E. Kassarjian, "Consumer Research: Some Recollections and a

Commentary," in Richard J. Lutz, ed., *Advances in Consumer Research,* 13 (Provo, UT: Association for Consumer Research, 1986), 6–8.

[18] Wayne D. Hoyer, "Variations in Choice Strategies across Decision Contexts: An Examination of Contingent Factors," in Lutz, *Advances,* 23–26.

[19] Francis Piron, "Defining Impulse Purchasing," in Rebecca H. Holman and Michael R. Solomon, eds., *Advances in Consumer Research,* 18 (Provo, UT: Association for Consumer Research, 1991), 512–518.

[20] Dennis W. Rook and Stephen J. Hoch, "Consuming Impulses," in Elizabeth C. Hirschman and Morris B. Holbrook, eds., *Advances in Consumer Research,* 12 (Provo, UT: Association for Consumer Research, 1985), 23–27.

[21] Itamar Simonson, "The Effect of Purchase Quantity and Timing on Variety-Seeking Behavior," *Journal of Marketing Research,* 27 (May 1990), 150–162; Wayne D. Hoyer and Nancy M. Ridgway, "Variety Seeking as an Explanation for Exploratory Purchase Behavior: A Theoretical Model," in Thomas C. Kinnear, ed., *Advances in Consumer Research,* 11 (Provo, UT: Association for Consumer Research, 1984), 114–119.

[22] Hans C. M. Van Trijp, Wayne D. Hoyer, and J. Jeffrey Inman, "Why Switch? Product Category—Level of Explanations for True Variety-Seeking Behavior," *Journal of Marketing Research,* 33 (August 1996), 281–292.

[23] John H. Antil, "Conceptualization and Operationalization of Involvement," in Kinnear, *Advances,* 204.

[24] Richard L. Celsi and Jerry C. Olson, "The Role of Involvement in Attention and Comprehension Processes," *Journal of Consumer Research,* 15 (September 1988), 210–224.

[25] See James Sood, "A Multi-Country Research Approach for Multinational Communication Strategies," *Journal of International Consumer Marketing,* 5 (1993), 29–50; Dana L. Alden, Wayne D. Hoyer, and Guntelee Wechasara, "Choice Strategies and Involvement: A Cross-Cultural Analysis," in Thomas K. Srull, ed., *Advances in Consumer Research,* 16 (Provo, UT: Association for Consumer Research, 1989), 119–125.

[26] Meera P. Venkatraman, "Investigating Differences in the Roles of Enduring and Instrumentally Involved Consumers in the Diffusion Process," in Michael J. Houston, ed., *Advances in Consumer Research,* 15 (Provo, UT: Association for Consumer Research, 1988), 299–303.

[27] Robin A. Higie and Lawrence E. Feick, "Enduring Involvement: Conceptual and Measurement Issues," in Srull, *Advances,* 690–696.

[28] See George Brooker, "An Assessment of an Expanded Measure of Perceived Risk," in Kinnear, *Advances,* 439–441; John W. Vann, "A Multi-Distributional, Conceptual Framework for the Study of Perceived Risk," in Kinnear, *Advances,* 442–446.

[29] Russell W. Belk, "Effects of Gift-Giving Involvement on Gift Selection Strategies," in Andrew Mitchell, ed., *Advances in Consumer Research,* 9 (Ann Arbor, MI: Association for Consumer Research, 1981), 408–411.

[30] Judith L. Zaichkowsky, "Measuring the Involvement Construct," *Journal of Consumer Research,* 12 (December 1985), 341–352.

[31] Giles Laurent and Jean-Noel Kapferer, "Measuring Consumer Involvement Profiles," *Journal of Marketing Research,* 22 (February 1985), 41–53.

[32] Consumer research was strongly influenced in 1980 by the finding that feelings and mood (affective responses) operate independently from cognitive responses. See Robert Zajonc, "Feeling and Thinking: Preferences Need No Inferences," *American Psychologist,* 35 (February 1980), 151–175. This article was followed by an influential article by Mitchell and Olson. See Andrew Mitchell and Jerry Olson, "Are Product Attribute Beliefs the Only Mediator of Advertising Effects on Brand Attitudes?" *Journal of Marketing Research,* 18 (August 1981), 318–322.

[33] Meryl Paula Gardner, "Mood States and Consumer Behavior: A Critical Review," *Journal of Consumer Research,* 12 (December 1985), 281–300.

[34] Haim Mano, "Emotional States and Decision Making," in Marvin E. Goldberg, Gerald Gom, and Richard W. Pollay, eds., *Advances in Consumer Research,* 17 (Provo, UT: Association for Consumer Research, 1990), 577–589.

# Chapter 4

## Pre-Purchase Processes: Need Recognition, Search, and Evaluation

### Opening Vignette

The health care system in America is sick. On average, American adults receive only half of the recommended care that's proven to be effective. Significant deficiencies exist in such critical areas as early cancer detection and the treatment of diabetes. Too many cancers are detected at a late stage, leading to suffering and premature death. Only about 20 percent of patients with diabetes receive all the recommended tests to ward off complications. By one account, such problems are responsible for 57,000 avoidable deaths each year!

Part of the solution to this tragic situation must come from a better-informed, more health-literate consumer. An estimated 90 million American adults have limited health literacy. These adults have difficulty in following instructions on drug labels, interpreting hospital consent forms, even understanding a doctor's diagnosis and instructions. Beyond these knowledge deficiencies, there are real concerns about the adequacy of the information currently available to consumers. At least one consumer group has recommended the goal of enhancing consumers' "health search literacy" by improving their "ability to locate and retrieve quality information on the Internet." And even those consumers who do find ratings of hospitals and doctors report placing little weight on such information. In one survey, 25 percent reported seeing ratings for hospitals, but only 3 percent said they used it when making a decision. Of the 10 percent who found doctor ratings, only 1 percent considered this information when making their choices.

Sources: Excerpted and adapted from Katherine H. Capps, "Align with Trusted Sources to Satisfy Consumers' Appetites for Health Information," *Dermatology Times* (May 2004), 76; Laura Landro, "Health & Family—The Informed Patient: Consumers Need Health-Care Data," *Wall Street Journal* (January 29, 2004), D3; Lauran Neergaard, "Many Can't Tell What the Doctor Ordered," *Miami Herald* (April 9, 2004), A7; "Most Consumers Ignore Health Ratings," *Wall Street Journal Online* (October 11, 2002), B2.

Enhancing consumers' propensity to acquire and utilize information to make better health-related decisions is part of the solution to the health care crisis facing America today.[1] More generally, information search and evaluation of choice alternatives, whether these alternatives involve doctors, medicines, hospitals, or any other good or service, are fundamental stages of the consumer decision-making process. This chapter covers these stages. But before consumers start searching and evaluating their decision options, a reason to even begin the decision process must exist. The reason stems from consumers recognizing an unfulfilled need. We refer to this first stage in the process as **need recognition,** defined as *the perception of a difference between the desired state of affairs and the actual situation sufficient to arouse and activate the decision process.*

## Need Recognition

Figure 4.1 illustrates what happens during need recognition. Need recognition depends on how much discrepancy exists between the actual state (the consumer's current situation) and the desired state (the situation the consumer wants to be in). When this difference meets or exceeds a certain level or threshold, a need is recognized. For example, a consumer currently feeling hungry (actual state) and wanting to eliminate this feeling (desired state) experiences need recognition when the discrepancy between the two states is of sufficient magnitude. If the difference is below the threshold level, however, need recognition does not occur.

Thus, need recognition occurs when changes in either the actual or desired state cause them to be noticeably out of alignment. These two fundamental causes of need recognition are displayed in Figure 4.2. To illustrate each, consider the consumer with a ten-year-old television set. Although this consumer had been hearing about plasma television sets for quite some time, he had never actually seen one until he visited a friend who had just purchased one. The consumer could hardly believe the superior picture quality plasma offers relative to his current television. This exposure to a plasma TV may cause him to redefine the picture quality he desires when watching television. Alternatively, he still may experience need recognition even if he never sees a plasma television set, such as when his current TV experiences a breakdown.

Consumers' desired and actual states change for a variety of reasons. What we desire in our younger years often changes as we grow older. Whereas today many male baby boomers get a haircut as soon as their hair starts touching their ears, in their younger days need recognition never crossed their mind even though their hair was touching their shoulders! Consider the childless couple who has little need for the products necessary for raising children. After discovering that they will soon be parents, however, they will experience a change in their actual state. Products that previously were irrelevant to them now become essential.

Anyone who has gone too long since his or her last meal knows that the simple passage of time can lead to an unpleasant deterioration in the actual state. Similarly, as

**FIGURE 4.1**   The Need Recognition Process Centers on the Degree of Discrepancy

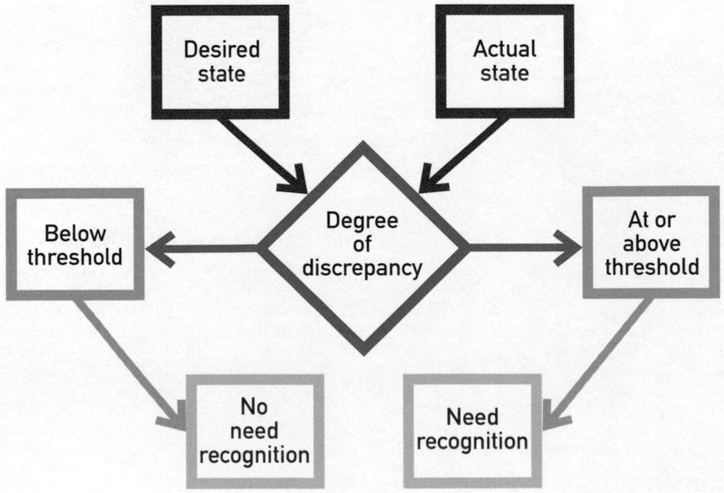

4.1

**FIGURE 4.2**     Changes in Either the Desired State or the Actual State Trigger Need Recognition

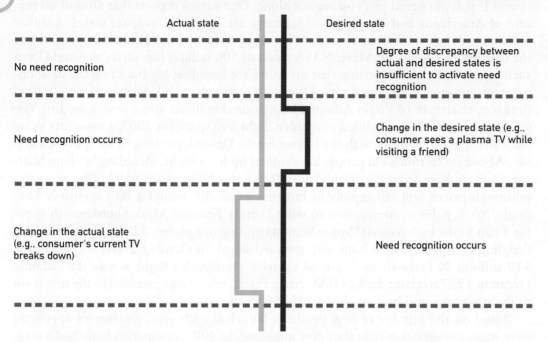

the American population ages, the health of many people will deteriorate. Those experiencing some degree of vision loss will climb from 3.3 to 5.5 million over the next two decades.[2] A need may be recognized simply because consumers have depleted their existing product inventory. The last slices of bread were toasted for breakfast, and more bread is needed for tonight's dinner. In this instance, need recognition is triggered by an anticipated need in the immediate future resulting from a change in the current situation.

Although need recognition often occurs for reasons outside a company's control, this certainly does not preclude the possibility for businesses to influence need recognition. Indeed, activating need recognition is often an important business objective that, when neglected, can have unfavorable consequences for individual companies and entire industries. In the following sections, we discuss the practical value of understanding need recognition and describe some of the ways in which companies attempt to influence it.

## The Need to Understand Need Recognition

One potential benefit of understanding need recognition is that it may reveal a market segment with unsatisfied desires (i.e., the actual state falls substantially short of the desired state), thereby providing businesses with new sales opportunities. Proctor & Gamble discovered that existing air fresheners left much to be desired in several ways. Consumers quickly adapt to scents and are unable to smell them in as little as half an hour. Getting an even distribution of the scent throughout the room was problematic. And consumers complained that scents often smelled artificial. These limitations drove P&G to develop Febreze Scentstories, a scent machine resembling a CD player that "plays" one of five different scents every thirty minutes. These scents, such as "Relaxing in the Hammock" and "Wandering Barefoot on the Shore," are dispersed throughout the room by a tiny fan inside the device. "Nobody could have articulated Scentstories," says Steve McGowan, a product-development manager for Febreze, "but if you really watch the consumer, they'll tell you what they wish."[3]

The existence of unsatisfied needs and desires today lays the foundation for the new businesses and product innovations of tomorrow. Would you like to travel into outer space? If you answered yes, you are not alone. One survey reports that around 60 percent of Americans and 70 percent of Japanese are interested in space travel. Another indication of consumers' fascination with outer space is that within three months of the Pathfinder landing on Mars, NASA received 500 million hits on its website! Given such interest, it's not surprising that investors are spending big bucks on the development of commercial space flight. Microsoft cofounder Paul Allen and Sir Richard Branson, chairman of Virgin Atlantic, have poured millions into a new company, Virgin Galactic, that has scheduled its maiden flight into space for 2007, a mere fifty years since the space age began with the former Soviet Union launching of its Sputnik satellite. About seven thousand people have signed up for a flight, including William Shatner, Captain Kirk from the original *Star Trek* series.[4] The price? $190,000 per person (although prices will fall rapidly as business expands). Sound a bit expensive? Certainly. Yet it pales in comparison to what Dennis Tito and Mark Shuttleworth spent for a trip to the International Space Station orbiting our planet: $20 million each! This fledgling company took a huge step forward when, in October 2004, it claimed the $10 million X Prize (reminiscent of Charles Lindbergh's flight across the Atlantic Ocean in 1927 to claim the $25,000 Orteig Prize), which was awarded to the first team to fly into space and back aboard a reusable craft.[5]

Based on the number of new products launched each year, consumers appear to have more unmet needs than they ever imagined. In 2003, companies launched a staggering total of 34,000 new products in the food, drink, and beauty categories alone. Yet only 2 percent of these new products reach the $100 million mark in first-year sales, the level considered the threshold for success. And marketing costs often surpass $50 million when introducing a new product to the market. Clearly the new product business is a risky and expensive one.[6]

An analysis of need recognition may also reveal barriers to an existing firm's success. Consider the furniture industry.[7] During the 1970s, Americans bought dinettes once every twelve to thirteen years. In the 1990s, the average replacement rate was every twenty-one years. Consumers began spending less and less on their furniture. What is responsible for this state of affairs? Although pointing the finger at a single culprit would be overly simplistic, there is no denying that the industry's failure to adequately stimulate need recognition is a major reason. Take a look at Figure 4.3, which summarizes the findings from a national study of furniture buyers about what prompted them to buy new furniture.[8] Which of these reasons do you think can reasonably be linked to the industry's efforts to attract new customers? Nearly all of them reflect circumstances outside of the industry's influence. Perhaps those indicating that they "wanted a new model or style" felt this way because of the industry's marketing efforts. For good measure, we could even throw in those consumers who reported that they "saw it and liked it." Yet together these represent less than 20 percent of new furniture buyers. As one industry executive observes, "The auto industry has convinced Americans to buy $25,000 cars that they throw away every three years, but the furniture industry still sells bedroom sets that people pass down to their kids." Another industry observer adds, "We haven't done a great job of attracting the consumer."

Until the furniture industry can motivate consumers to redecorate more often, the industry's future does not look rosy. Stop for a moment and think about the basic strategies that might be pursued in this situation. In particular, what implications are suggested by viewing need recognition as depending on whether consumers perceive a meaningful difference between their current and ideal states? How can companies stimulate need recognition?

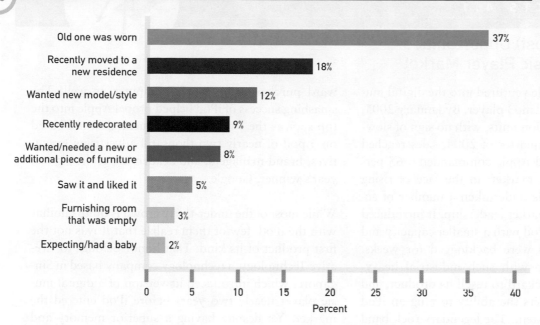

Source: Joella Roy, "The Consumer Purchasing Process—Part 1," www.furninfo.com (June 1, 2002). Reprinted with permission from the author.

## Influencing Need Recognition

To illustrate some of the options for activating need recognition, let's stay with the furniture example. Apparently, many consumers are rather content with keeping the same set of furniture for many years, even decades. What they currently own is deemed sufficient. They do not experience a strong enough desire for something new and different that it leads them to replace their existing furniture.

One way of activating consumers' needs for new furniture is to change their desired state. That is, offer them something to die for! Develop and promote new styles, designs, and fabrics. One recent attempt in this direction has been the introduction of 36-inch dining tables, a half-foot taller than the traditional height of these tables.[9]

More generally, product improvements and innovations may cause need recognition by altering consumers' desires. This was certainly the case when Pfizer introduced Listerine PocketPaks in 2001. These mouthwash strips offered consumers an entirely new way of freshening their breath, and the product racked up $175 million in first-year sales.[10] The same thing is happening today with the advent of mp3 players, such as Apple's iPod (see Market Facts 4.1 and Figure 4.4), high-definition television (HDTV), and on-board navigation systems for automobiles. These new products and improvements to long-established products have been successful because they offer desirable benefits. These products have redefined consumers' desired states.

Returning to the furniture industry, another option—one that must be handled very delicately so as not to offend consumers—is to influence how consumers perceive their actual state. The objective would be to undermine consumers' perceptions about the adequacy of their existing furniture. Advertising could suggest, perhaps in a humorous way, the possibility that one's present furniture is in greater need of retirement than recognized previously. Show consumers how much more attractive and enjoyable their homes will be when refurbished with new furniture. To the extent that such advertising was successful in causing consumers to question the adequacy and attractiveness of their existing furniture, they would experience greater need recognition.

## Captured (and Lost) Opportunities in the Digital Music Player Market

In October 2001, Apple ventured into the digital music market with its iPod mp3 player. By January 2005, sales surpassed 10 million units, with no sign of slowing down. In the last quarter of 2004, sales reached 4.58 million units, and Apple commanded a 65 percent share of the U.S. market. In the face of rising competition, Apple has undertaken a number of actions to maintain its market leadership. It introduced a mini version of the iPod with a smaller capacity and a lower price. Orders were backlogged for weeks. Apple also teamed up with such industrial heavyweights as Hewlett-Packard to resell its product, and BMW now offers drivers the ability to plug an iPod into the car's audio system. The legendary rock band U2 was featured in an iPod advertising campaign, and a special "U2 edition" of the iPod was introduced in late 2004. In 2003, Apple rolled out the iTunes Music Store, which sells downloads for 99 cents per song. Sales already have exceeded 100 million songs. "Clearly, Apple has taken over the digital-music market," says Charlie Wolf, an analyst at Needham & Company. "The iPod has become a cult. It's a phenomenon." And iPod's success has rubbed off on Apple's computer business. More than one million Apple computers were shipped in the fourth quarter of 2004, a 26 percent increase over the same quarter in 2003. Sales for the iMac line of computers nearly tripled. According to one analyst, "This is the first proof positive that the halo effect is real," reflecting the notion that iPod buyers become predisposed toward purchasing an Apple computer as well. The smashing success of iPod helped propel Apple into the top spot as the world's most influential brand based on a poll of nearly two thousand advertising executives, brand managers, and academics, replacing last year's winner, Google.

While most of the under-thirty crowd is quite familiar with the iPod, few of them realize that it was not the first product of its kind. That honor belongs to Creative Technology, a technology company based in Singapore, which introduced its version of a digital music player nearly two years before iPod entered the market. Yet despite having a superior memory and battery life and a price as much as 30 percent less than iPod, Creative's entry has continued to lose worldwide market share, from 31 percent in 2001 to 17 percent in 2003 (versus 54 percent at that time for iPod). Why? According to Creative's founder and chief executive, Sim Wong Hoo, "We were first, but Apple has more [money] to splash around." Others see more to the story. "The Creative brand is popular among PC-crazed people who pay a lot of attention to the quality of sound and graphics on their computer," says Jonathan Koh, an analyst at Singapore brokerage firm, UOB Kay Hian. "But the mp3 has become more of a consumer item, and the way that you market to these people is totally different. This is a much wider audience."

Sources: Laurie Flynn, "Apple's Profit Quadruples, Thanks to iPod," *New York Times* (January 13, 2005), C1; Rachel Konrad, "Apple Profits Quadruple as iPod Sales Surge," www.washingtonpost.com (January 12, 2005); Walter S. Mossberg, "Mating iPod and BMW Is a Brilliant Concept, But First Try Is Crude," *Wall Street Journal* (August 5, 2004), B1; Cris Prystay, "When Being First Doesn't Make You No. 1," *Wall Street Journal* (August 12, 2004), B1; Pui-Wing Tam, "Apple's Net Soars on Strong iPod, Sales," *Wall Street Journal* (April 15, 2004), A3; Pui-Wing Tam, "Apple, Paced by Sales of iPod, Sees Profit and Revenue Surge; Digital-Music Operations Exceed Best Expectations of Analysts—and Company," *Wall Street Journal* (October 14, 2004), B4; Nick Wingfield, "Price War in Online Music; RealNetworks Targets iTunes With 49-Cents-a-Song Sale; A Taste of What's Ahead?" *Wall Street Journal* (August 17, 2004), D1; Nick Wingfield and Ethan Smith, "U2's Gig: Help Apple Sell iPods," *Wall Street Journal* (October 20, 2004), D5; "Apple Voted Most Influential Brand," http://www.cnnmoney.com (January 31, 2005).

Altering consumers' perceptions about their actual state thus represents another way for companies to influence need recognition. Let's take the example of personal computers. When consumers were asked about their computer's vulnerability to online threats, about three-fourths of them were confident that their computer was safe from viruses and hackers. Researchers then visited their homes and examined their computers. **Spyware,** which is *software that's downloaded onto a computer without*

FIGURE 4.4 New Product Innovations Can Activate Need Recognition by Changing Consumers' Desired State

*the permission of the owner and that collects personal information such as the user's online activities, financial records, and passwords,* was found in 80 percent of the computers. The antivirus software had not been updated for at least seven days on two-thirds of the computers. The same percentage of computers lacked any type of protective firewall program. One person in the study discovered that his computer was infested with more than one thousand spyware programs![11] It's safe to assume that the majority of participants in this study changed their perceptions about the actual state of their computers and, as a consequence, experienced need recognition.

Simply reminding consumers of a need may be sufficient to trigger need recognition. Consumers browsing a retailer's aisles may encounter a display that reminds them of a previously recognized but since forgotten purchase need. Dentists send patients due for a checkup and cleaning a simple reminder in the mail that it's time to schedule an appointment. Helping consumers remember their needs is something we will discuss again in Chapter 16.

Manufacturers have even modified their products to stimulate need recognition. Although most toothbrushes wear out in three months, consumers typically replace them only once a year. Toothbrush maker Oral-B introduced a patented blue dye in the center bristles that gradually fades during usage. The absence of the blue dye indicates that the toothbrush is no longer effective and needs replacement.[12]

A basic distinction among efforts to activate need recognition is whether they attempt to stimulate primary demand (representing the total sales of a product category) or selective demand (representing the sales of each competitor within the product category). Companies seeking to grow the size of the total market for a product (i.e., stimulate primary demand) are attempting to elicit generic need recognition.[13] **Generic**

This Sunday, we'll see who wants it more.

It's winner take all on game day, and only the strong survive. That's why milk's 9 essential nutrients are part of every competitor's game plan.

got milk?

**FIGURE 4.5** The Milk Industry Focuses on Generic Need Recognition

**need recognition** occurs *when the need for an entire product category is stimulated.* More than a billion dollars is reportedly spent each year by industries attempting to build primary demand.[14] Past and present efforts have been undertaken by the apple, avocado, beef, catfish, cotton, egg, milk, orange juice, and pork industries.

Efforts to activate generic need recognition are often undertaken by industries in which consumers perceive minimal differences between competitors. Take the example of milk. For most consumers, milk is perceived as a commodity product. One brand tastes pretty much the same as another. It is extremely difficult for a particular milk producer to convince consumers that its milk is superior to its competitor's milk. Instead, milk producers have pooled their resources and invested millions of dollars into advertising designed to activate generic need recognition and build primary demand. Figure 4.5 contains one of the industry's current advertisements from its "got milk?" campaign that started in 1994.[15] We will return to this campaign in Chapter 6 as one example of the potential benefits offered by understanding consumers' product consumption. But for now check out Consumer Behavior and Marketing 4.1, which details PepsiCo's current strategy of building demand for its brand of bottled water, Aquafina, by encouraging generic need recognition.

The potential value of growing a product market need not be limited to product categories composed of relatively undifferentiated brands. According to Jack Trout, a well-known marketing consultant, "If you are the leader, it is a lot better to broaden the category even though that might help the other guys who are nibbling away at you. What you want to do is build a market as big as you can and then defend it with a vengeance, like Coke and Hertz do."[16] Thus, even in product markets containing differentiated brands, the market leader may find it profitable to stimulate primary demand. This ultimately depends on whether the leader attracts and keeps a sufficient share of the new business.

**Selective need recognition** occurs *when the need for a specific brand within a product category (selective demand) is stimulated.* Marketing efforts that involve this type of need recognition focus on persuading consumers that their needs will be satisfied by a particular brand. The advertisement in Figure 4.6 is likely to activate selective need recognition for Colgate Total by educating American consumers with diabetes about their actual state (that they are twice as likely to develop gingivitis) and touting the product's unique effectiveness in combating this problem ("the only toothpaste that reduces gingivitis by up to 88 percent"). More generally, comparative advertising that describes the advantages of the advertised brand over its competition should be especially effective for activating selective need recognition.[17]

## Drink More Water!

Some people drink alcohol as if it were water. Now some bottled water companies actually want them to do so. In an advertising campaign that debuted during the summer of 2004, PepsiCo's Aquafina has beer drinkers opting for water rather than suds. The commercial shows people singing, dancing, and carousing at an English pub and a German beer garden. Rather than chugging frothy lagers, the exuberant folks are chugging Aquafina. Aquafina's new ads will try to push sales of all water by using a new tagline, "Drink more water." Other bottled water companies have pursued similar themes. An ad for Coca-Cola's Dasani shows attractive young people swigging Dasani at a nightclub.

Aquafina's new ads are a noticeable departure from their predecessors. One ad from the previous year showed black and white images of an artist, skier, and guitar player drinking the water. The ad carried the tagline, "Aquafina. Purity Guaranteed." But rather than pushing the brand, the new ads are pushing the entire product category. Why? Both Pepsi and Coke have struggled to forge a strong identity for their flagship brands, particularly because many consumers shop based on price. "It's been tougher to build brand and loyalty in the category because water is generic in composition," says Michael Bellas, chief executive of Beverage Marketing, a research, data, and consulting firm. So now the focus is on promoting the entire category, a marketing strategy category leaders often use. Aquafina has 11.3 percent of the wholesale bottled-water category in the United States, with $936 million in sales in 2003. Next is Coke's Dasani with a 10 percent share and $834 million in sales.

Dissatisfied with the level of creativity in the entire water category, Pepsi wants to jazz up its Aquafina commercials. Dave Burwick, chief marketing officer for PepsiCo North America, says most bottled-water advertising has been lackluster industry wide. Branding experts point out that creative output in the bottled-water category pales in comparison with that in other categories, such as soda and beer—two ad sectors known for highly entertaining commercials. Aquafina hopes to change this as well as the beverage of choice of many American consumers.

Source: Excerpted and adapted from Suzanne Vranica, "Partyers Knock Back a Few . . . Aquafinas," *Wall Street Journal* (July 13, 2004), B4.

## Search

Simply because consumers have experienced need recognition does not necessarily mean that they will proceed through the decision process. This depends on the importance of the need at the time it is activated. A hungry consumer, for instance, may not think that the rumblings in his or her stomach merit immediate action. It also depends on whether consumers believe that a solution to the need is within their means. Many consumers desire owning an expensive automobile, but lack the money necessary for satisfying this desire.

Nonetheless, consumers often proceed through the decision-making process following need recognition. **Search,** the second stage of the decision-making process, represents the *motivated activation of knowledge stored in memory or acquisition of information from the environment about potential need satisfiers.* As this definition suggests, search can be either internal or external. **Internal search** involves *scanning and retrieving decision-relevant knowledge stored in memory.*[18] **External search** consists of *collecting information from the marketplace.*

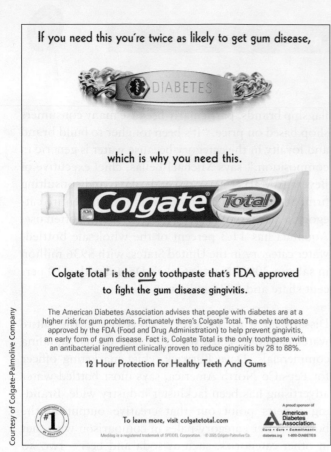

If you need this you're twice as likely to get gum disease,

DIABETES

which is why you need this.

Colgate Total

Colgate Total® is the only toothpaste that's FDA approved to fight the gum disease gingivitis.

The American Diabetes Association advises that people with diabetes are at a higher risk for gum problems. Fortunately there's Colgate Total. The only toothpaste approved by the FDA (Food and Drug Administration) to help prevent gingivitis, an early form of gum disease. Fact is, Colgate Total is the only toothpaste with an antibacterial ingredient clinically proven to reduce gingivitis by 28 to 88%.

12 Hour Protection For Healthy Teeth And Gums

#1 RECOMMENDED MOST BY DENTISTS

To learn more, visit colgatetotal.com

A proud sponsor of American Diabetes Association. Cure • Care • Commitment diabetes.org 1-800-DIABETES

Medilog is a registered trademark of SPEIDEL Corporation. © 2005 Colgate-Palmolive Co.

**FIGURE 4.6** This Advertisement Activates Selective Need Recognition

## Internal Search

As indicated by Figure 4.7, consumers experiencing need recognition begin their search internally. Many times a past solution is remembered and implemented. For this reason, consumers often have little need for undertaking external search before a purchase, even for major expenditures such as furniture, appliances, and automobiles.[19] More than half of the consumers participating in one study reported relying solely on their existing knowledge when choosing an auto repair service.[20]

Interestingly, consumers may rely on existing knowledge about one product category when making decisions about another product category. For instance, consumers might assume that their knowledge about traditional film-based cameras applies to an unfamiliar digital camera being considered for purchase. There are, however, some potential limitations of doing this (e.g., when existing knowledge is ill suited for the domain to which it is applied), which may cause consumers to make suboptimal choices.[21]

While knowledge relevant to the recognized need is essential, more is required before internal search can be successful. Consumers must be confident in their knowledge as well. Those in their fifties, for instance, will have considerable experience in many different product categories. Yet for product categories characterized by large interpurchase times (the

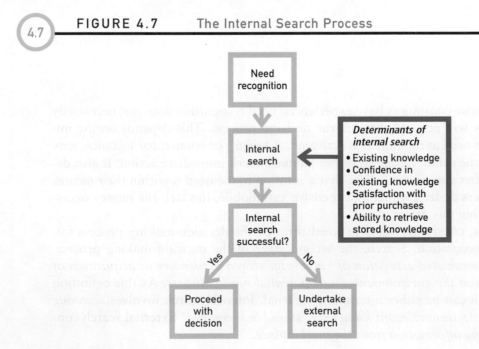

4.7    **FIGURE 4.7**    The Internal Search Process

Need recognition

Internal search

Internal search successful?

Yes — Proceed with decision

No — Undertake external search

**Determinants of internal search**
- Existing knowledge
- Confidence in existing knowledge
- Satisfaction with prior purchases
- Ability to retrieve stored knowledge

amount of time between purchase occasions) during which there are significant product changes in prices and features, or new brands and stores, these experienced consumers may not feel confident in relying on their current knowledge to make a purchase decision. Some degree of external search will be needed, even if it's only to evaluate the adequacy of one's existing knowledge. The degree of satisfaction with prior purchases also determines the consumer's reliance on internal search. If the consumer has been satisfied with the results of previous buying actions, internal search may suffice.[22] Finally, internal search is dependent on consumers' ability to retrieve their knowledge. Not all that is stored in our memory is accessible at the moment we try to remember it, as you well know from the times you have been unable to recall the answer to a test question, only to have this answer pop into your head at a later time. And some knowledge may fade away, especially in product categories associated with large interpurchase times in which a long time has passed since consumers used this knowledge.

### External Search

When internal search proves inadequate, the consumer may decide to collect additional information from the environment. *External search motivated by an upcoming purchase decision* is known as **pre-purchase search.** This type of external search differs from **ongoing search,** in which *information acquisition takes place on a relatively regular basis regardless of sporadic purchase needs.*[23] The car enthusiast who enjoys reading automotive magazines for their own sake is engaging in ongoing search. Consumers who read the same magazines because of a forthcoming purchase are conducting pre-purchase search.

The primary motivation behind pre-purchase search is the desire to make better choices. Similarly, ongoing search may be motivated by desires to develop a knowledge base that can be used in future decision making. Ongoing search also occurs simply because of the enjoyment derived from this activity.[24] Consumers may browse the World Wide Web without having specific purchase needs, simply because it's fun for them to do so.

The decision to undertake pre-purchase search requires consumers to make a number of additional decisions in executing their search behaviors. What should be searched? Where should the consumer search? How much search should be undertaken? We now turn to each of these questions.

## WHAT TO SEARCH?

Consider Amy, a high school student who has firmly decided to further her education. Less certain, however, is what option she should pursue. She is very familiar with the local university and what it has to offer. Her best friend, who graduated high school the year before and decided to attend this university, has supplied a wealth of information about this option. Far less familiar are universities outside of her community which, at best, she knows only by name. Then there are those educational alternatives that would require far less time commitment. Amy's been bombarded by materials from a variety of technical schools promoting their one-year and two-year vocational programs. Maybe she should learn more about these options.

Amy is struggling with a fundamental pre-purchase search decision: which choice alternatives should she search? We refer to this as the **external search set**—*those choice alternatives that consumers gather information about during pre-purchase search.* While Amy possesses sufficient knowledge about her local university (i.e., internal search is sufficient for this option), such is not the case for any other educational alternative she might consider when making her final decision. Consequently, Amy will need to decide on her search set. She may even decide that search is needed to help her finalize her search set. Depending on the consumer's experience and the importance of the decision, consumers may invest a considerable amount of effort into identifying the search set members. Amy might talk to others, such as her high school teachers, browse the World Wide Web, or check out a book from the library as sources of information useful in forming her search set. For other decisions, this set will be determined far more easily. Consumers could, for instance, simply decide to restrict their search sets to whatever products are offered by their local retailer.

Beyond deciding on their search sets, consumers must also decide what they wish to learn about each of the search set members. Returning to Amy and her educational decision, what information would be important to her? This question was asked of students seeking information on college websites. The results are presented in Figure 4.8. Not surprisingly, information about courses and majors, costs, and academic programs topped the list of what was most important to students. Faculty's egos, on the other hand, certainly were not bolstered by the fact that information about the faculty was at the bottom of the list.

While we might normally think of information acquisition as involving sight (such as when we read product labels or search the Internet) and sound (such as when we

**FIGURE 4.8**  Information on College Websites That Is Very Important to Students

4.8

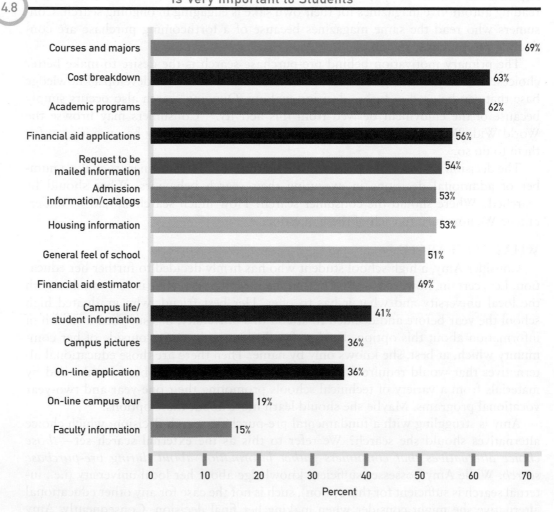

Source: Arundhati Parmar, "Student e-union: Colleges Write Textbook on Internet Marketing," *Marketing News* (April 1, 2004), 13–14. Reprinted with permission from American Marketing Association.

PART 2 [ CONSUMER DECISION MAKING

talk to others or listen to a commercial), consumers may rely on any of the five senses (sight, hearing, taste, touch, and smell) in acquiring product information. Consumer researchers have recently focused on **haptic information**, which represents *information acquired by touch*.[25] As with other types of information, consumers vary in their propensity to gather haptic information. Touching a product to assess its hardness, texture, and weight is vital for some; less so for others. Restrictions in the ability to collect haptic information, as in the case of Internet-based search, may be somewhat compensated by the provision of written descriptions conveying haptic information.[26] Similarly, product packaging that enables consumers to touch the product, such as the cut-out portion of the packaging for Paper Mate's DynaGrip pens that allows one to feel the pen's grip, should be effective in appealing to haptically motivated consumers.

## WHERE DO CONSUMERS GO FOR INFORMATION?

Deciding what information about which choice alternatives is only part of the decisions consumers make during pre-purchase search. Consumers must also decide where they will collect this information. Is the purchase decision such that the desired information can be gathered within a retail store?[27] Or is it better to rely on information sources outside of the store? Beyond their in-store versus out-of-store location, informational sources can be further distinguished based upon their personal (e.g., salespeople, friends) versus impersonal nature (e.g., product labels, magazines). The information sources available to consumers as a function of these particular characteristics are summarized in Table 4.1.

Not surprisingly, consumers are far more likely to rely upon the opinions of other individuals than information sources with vested interests in their decisions. Unlike an advertisement or a salesperson, a friend or coworker usually has little to gain or lose by what we decide. In contrast, consumers have a healthy degree of skepticism about information that originates from sources controlled by businesses. Such information, however, does not fall on deaf ears. In a study of three thousand consumers, many of them reported that advertising had the strongest influence on what they purchased while shopping for groceries. For a breakdown of different media sources' influence on grocery shopping and how this has changed recently, see Table 4.2.

Unfortunately, this study of grocery shopping is silent about the role played by personal sources of information. Yet it is well known that consumers frequently turn to these sources when searching for information. Indeed, *other consumers respected for their expertise in a particular product category,* referred to as **opinion leaders**[28] or

TABLE 4.1 — Consumers' Sources of Information

|  | IN-STORE | OUT OF STORE |
|---|---|---|
| Personal | Sales personnel | Family and friends |
|  | Other shoppers | Coworkers |
|  |  | Experts, opinion leaders, and influentials |
|  |  | Internet forums and bulletin boards |
| Impersonal | Product labels | Advertising |
|  | Store signage | Catalogs |
|  | Point-of-purchase materials | Magazines |
|  | (e.g., displays, advertising circulars) | Television and radio shows |
|  |  | Websites |

**TABLE 4.2**      Which Form of Media Has the Strongest Influence on Consumers' Grocery Decisions?

| YEAR | ADVERTISING INSERTS/ CIRCULARS | TV | ADS ON PAGE OF NEWSPAPER | CATALOGS | MAGAZINES | DIRECT MAIL | RADIO | INTERNET | E-MAIL |
|------|------|------|------|------|------|------|------|------|------|
| 1998 | 23% | 26% | 16% | — | 9% | 4% | 6% | — | — |
| 2000 | 23% | 23% | 22% | — | 5% | 4% | 4% | 4% | — |
| 2002 | 22% | 22% | 19% | 10% | 6% | 4% | 3% | 4% | — |
| 2004 | 28% | 22% | 18% | 6% | 5% | 4% | 3% | 1% | 1% |

Source: Deborah L. Vence, "I Saw an Ad for That!" *Marketing News* (June 15, 2004), 4.

influentials,[29] are often consulted for their opinions and advice. Can you guess what topic influentials reported being asked about most often in a recent study covering nineteen product and service categories? The number one category, and the category showing the largest increase in activity over the past couple of years, is health. Sixty percent reported being asked for their advice on health problems, a 16 percent increase since 2001.[30]

Nor is personal influence limited to face-to-face encounters. Internet forums and bulletin boards have enabled consumers to communicate with each other online. One study shows that consumers become more interested in the product category when they gathered information from Internet forums and bulletin boards than corporate websites.[31] The importance of these personal sources of information is such that we devote much of Chapter 13 to this topic. For now, however, we turn our attention to an information source that has been in existence for a relatively short amount of time yet has profoundly changed consumer behavior.

## THE INTERNET AND CONSUMER SEARCH

Thinking about taking a vacation? Taking a business trip out of town? Do you need to book a flight? How about a hotel? Increasingly, consumers are turning to the Internet for answers to these questions. The travel industry accounts for about one-third of the money spent online.[32] Companies such as Expedia .com (see Figure 4.9) have prospered as more and more consumers become familiar with the World Wide Web. And to learn about the "father" of the World Wide Web, read Market Facts 4.2.

If you asked consumer behavior experts to identify the most profound influences on consumer behavior in recent times, we imagine that virtually all of them would include the Internet. Most consumers had never even heard of the World Wide Web a decade ago. It was July 1995 when Amazon.com got things started by selling its first book. Yet according

**FIGURE 4.9** Expedia.com Wants You to Search Their Site

## Tim Berners-Lee, Father of the World Wide Web

In 2004, the first Millennium Technology Prize, worth $1.2 million in cash, was awarded to Tim Berners-Lee for creating the World Wide Web. The price committee outlined the award to be given for "an outstanding innovation that directly promotes people's quality of life, is based on humane values, and encourages sustainable economic development." "Isn't this like a definition of the World Wide Web?" asked Pekka Tarjanne, chairman of the prize committee.

Berners-Lee first proposed the Web in 1989 while developing ways to control computers remotely at CERN, the European nuclear research lab near Geneva. He never got the project formally approved, but his boss suggested he quietly tinker with it anyway. He fleshed out the core communication protocols needed for transmitting Web pages: the HTTP, or hypertext transfer protocol, and the so-called markup language used to create them, HTML. By Christmas Day in 1990, he finished the first browser, called simply "WorldWideWeb." Although his inventions have undergone rapid changes since then, the underlying technology is precisely the same.

Berners-Lee says he never would have succeeded if he had charged money for his inventions. "If I try to demand fees . . . there would be no World Wide Web," says Berners-Lee. "There would be lots of small webs." The prize committee agreed, citing the importance of his decision never to commercialize or patent his contributions to the Internet technologies he had developed, and recognizing his revolutionary contribution to humanity's ability to communicate. Despite his prize, he remains modest about his achievements. "I was just taking lots of things that already existed and added a little, little bit," he says. "Building the Web, I didn't do it all myself. The real exciting thing about it is that it was done by lots and lots of people, connected with this tremendous spirit." "No one doubts who the father of the World Wide Web is, except Berners-Lee himself," says Tarjanne.

Source: Excerpted in part from Mans Hulden, "Internet Inventor Named First Winner of Technology Prize," *Miami Herald* (June 16, 2004), A4.

to a Disney Online study, the Internet is the information source that moms would miss the most.[33] Indeed, as Ken Goldstein, vice president and managing director of Disney Online observes, "When we decided to put vacation planning online at Disney 4 to 5 years ago, focus group moms said, 'I'd *never* make a big decision like that without an actual person involved.' Now they'll plan, book and charge their Disney World vacation without ever talking to a travel agent. That's a *huge* behavioral change."[34]

Consumers also recognize the substantial impact the Internet has had on their shopping behaviors. DoubleClick, a marketing consulting firm with twenty-three offices around the world, surveyed two thousand consumers in December 2003 about their purchases in a variety of product categories and the impact of the Internet on their purchase decisions. Figure 4.10 summarizes the participants' responses to the question, "Has the Internet changed the way you make purchase decisions about this type of product compared to five years ago?" Most consumers answered in the affirmative for most of the product categories. Even in the product category with the lowest score, prescription drugs, more than 40 percent of consumers believed that the Internet has changed their decision process.

One reason the Internet is dramatically changing consumer behavior is that it helps us search much more easily and efficiently than ever before.[35] A few clicks on the computer screen and we're driving down the information highway. And to make life easier, technology does most of the work for us. Just type what you're looking for, and any one of the available search engines will quickly point you in the right direction (see Market Facts 4.3 for a look at how the popularity of particular search engines

**FIGURE 4.10**  Consumers' Ratings of How Much the Internet
Has Influenced Their Purchase Decisions

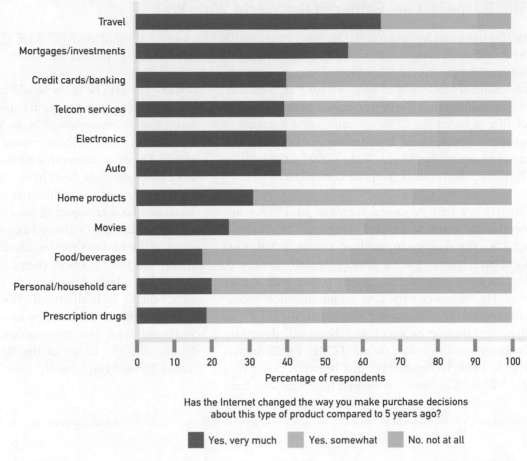

Has the Internet changed the way you make purchase decisions
about this type of product compared to 5 years ago?

■ Yes, very much   ■ Yes, somewhat   ■ No, not at all

Source: DoubleClick, "Catalyst for Change: 64% Say the Internet Has Altered Purchase Decision," www.doubleclick.net (March 2004).
Copyright DoubleClick, Inc. All rights reserved.

changed dramatically in a very short time, and see Consumer Behavior and Marketing 4.2 to learn about search engines' importance in determining a website's success).

To better appreciate just how much the Internet permeates everyday life, consider the following statistics.

- In December 2004, more than 132 million consumers, representing nearly 82 percent of American Internet users, turned to the Web for help in meeting the demands of the holiday season.[36]
- Online consumer spending (excluding auctions) in the United States reached $117 billion in 2004, a 26 percent increase from the year before.[37]
- Sixty-eight percent of American adults use the Internet. In Canada, the figure is 71 percent.[38]
- During the fall semester of 2004, college students spent an average of 15.1 hours a week online. Males averaged 15.4 while females averaged 14.8 hours.[39]
- The time American mothers spend on the Internet (13.2 hours per week), including time spent writing e-mails, nearly doubles the time they spend in front of the television (7.6 hours per week).[40]
- These same moms use the Internet most often as a source of information (86 percent place it ahead of TV and newspapers). Moreover, they trust it more than the information acquired from TV, radio, and magazines.[41]

- On a "typical day," 16 percent of U.S. Internet adult users are researching a product or service they intend to buy.[42] And in April 2004, 37 million people visited a website, such as Shopping.com, that compares the prices of products offered by different websites.[43]
- In the United Kingdom, 85 percent of consumers report using the Internet for research prior to purchasing a car or visiting a dealership.[44] Sixty percent of those looking to buy a house use the Internet to search for properties.[45]
- It is projected that, by 2008, 30 percent of all sales transacted in bricks-and-mortar stores will be researched online initially.[46]

## MARKET FACTS 4.3

## Press "Search"

Which search engine is the most popular choice? According to the Internet tracking company WebSide-Story, it's Google. Based on a sample size of 25 million browsers, WebSideStory examined the number of referrals generated on March 23, 2004, by each of the big three U.S. search engines—Google (based in Mountain View, California), Yahoo (Sunnyvale, California), and MSN (Redmond, California). WebSideStory then compared these numbers with those from the same day in 2001, 2002, and 2003 to see if things had changed. They had. In 2001 and 2002, Yahoo was consumers' top choice. Yet despite spending more than $1 billion acquiring search companies, Yahoo lost the top spot by 2003, with the gap between Google and Yahoo becoming even greater the following year. Indeed, Google's rapid ascent to the top spot has been most impressive. Listed below is the percentage of referrals for each engine from 2001 to 2004.

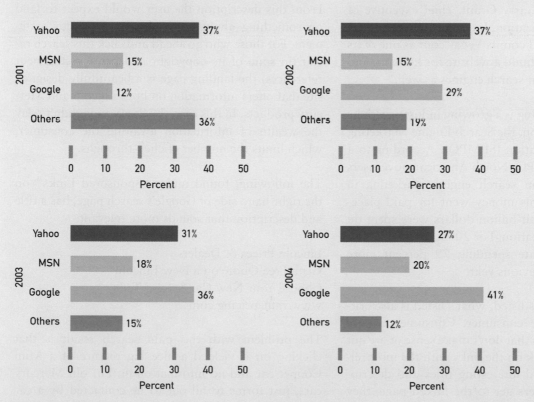

Sources: Catherine Arnold, "If You're Looking," *Marketing News* (June 1, 2004), 4; Michael Bazeley, "Amazon Tests Search Engine," *San Jose Mercury News* (April 15, 2004), 1.

## Companies Sometimes Fall Short of Optimizing Their Presence on the Internet

Searching online is how nearly 85 percent of Internet users find websites. When consumers type a word or phrase into their favorite search engine, they get a series of pages containing site recommendations in the form of titles and descriptions. These results include paid sponsored links and editorial results. Yet only 7 percent look past the first couple of pages of search results, which means if a listing is not on the first page or two, it probably will not be seen. For this reason, companies are quite interested in where they appear in the search results, and often hire companies that specialize in this line of work. Because search engines rank Web pages once a month based on secret mathematical algorithms, achieving a high ranking in the search listings remains a bit of a mystery. But there are some guidelines, with the simplest being to add links to similar websites or get other sites to link to you. More links means higher rankings. Quality counts as well. The better company you keep, the more important you seem. According to Garry Grant, chief executive of Search Engine Optimization, Inc., a firm that starts its billing at $10,000 and counts Vegas.com as one of its clients, "You have to build a website for humans, and you have to build it for search engines as well."

Search engine marketing is a growing industry with its own trade organization, the Search Engine Marketing Professional Organization (SEMPO). According to a report issued by SEMPO, North American advertisers spent $4.1 billion on search engine marketing in 2004. The bulk of this money went for paid placement, but nearly a half-billion dollars were spent on search engine optimization. For 2005, search marketing agencies anticipate spending 79 percent more money than in the previous year.

Beyond where a site is listed, what's listed is also critical in attracting the consumer. Consumers ignore titles and descriptions that don't make sense or are not compelling. They click on the links with the most relevant, persuasive, and interesting titles and descriptions. When consumers get to the linked page, they ask, "Does this page have the information I'm looking for?" If not, one click of the "back" button and they're quickly browsing somewhere else.

How companies manage their presence online will influence what consumers do during this search process. A company can spend millions of dollars in television advertising, generating thousand of searches. But if the titles and descriptions that appear on the search results page are not convincing or interesting (or the company is not listed or is not listed early enough), the consumer will end up on someone else's website. For example, at one time a search of "Lincoln Mercury" on Google generated the following title and description in the editorial search results:

Lincoln & Mercury
Copyright 2003 Ford Motor Company
Privacy Statement

From this description the user would expect to land on something about copyrights or a privacy statement. For those who go ahead and click this search result (in spite of its copyright and privacy statement references) the landing page is a beautifully designed site that offers information on both Lincoln and Mercury products. In this case, the description didn't relay the wealth of information awaiting the consumer, which limits the number of click-throughs.

The following, found under "Sponsored Links" on the right-hand side of Google's search page, has a title and description that sounds more relevant:

Lincoln Prices & Dealers
Get a Free Quote on a New Lincoln
Choose Your New Car & Save Today
www.valuepricing.com

The problem with this paid search result is that clicking on it yielded a nice big picture of a Mini Cooper car and no information on Lincoln Mercury cars, just forms to fill out to be contacted by a car salesperson.

Sources: Excerpted and adapted from Ross Fadner, "Report: Search Soars to $4 Billion," www.mediapost.com (December 15, 2004); Gerry Grant, "Search Optimization Campaigns Build Brand," *Marketing News* (September 29, 2003), 22; and Erika D. Smith, "Businesses Must Make Sure Their Web Sites Can Be Seen by Search," *Akron Beacon Journal* (September 6, 2004), 1.

Our understanding of consumer behavior and the Internet is in its infancy.[47] Even something as fundamental as estimating the extent of Internet penetration has been problematic, with competing measurement services reporting highly divergent estimates.[48] Nonetheless, descriptive research such as that provided by comScore, with its global panel of more than 2 million consumers that allow the company to track their browsing and transaction behaviors, has certainly added to our understanding. comScore recently examined the search and buying behavior of Internet users who conducted a search for consumer electronics or computers at one of the top twenty-five search engines.[49] The particular words or phrases used by consumers in guiding the search engines fell into three major categories: generic terms representing product categories (e.g., camera, plasma television), specific retailers (e.g., Best Buy, Gateway .com) and specific products (e.g., Canon digital camcorder, HP notebook). More than 70 percent of the searches used generic terms. Specific retailers accounted for about 20 percent, and specific products represented around 10 percent. The study's findings also challenged the notion that consumers typically follow a **"funnel" search strategy**, in which they *begin their Internet search with generic terms but eventually refine their search with terms focusing on specific products*. Most consumers did start with the generic terms, but only a relatively small portion of them refined their subsequent search using product-specific terms. As the report notes, this is important because many companies invest solely in product-specific keywords. This strategy reaches those using such specific terms during search, but it misses those who do not.

So what terms are used most often by consumers when they are searching for products and retailers? To answer this question, we turned to Hitwise (www.hitwise.com), a major Internet market research company that monitors the search activities of 25 million Internet users as they interact with over a half-million websites. At our request, Hitwise prepared a list of the terms most frequently used by Americans when searching the Internet.[50] These results, based on a sample of 10 million consumers, were broken down into three main categories: those listing a retailer, those listing a specific brand within a product category, and those listing a product using non-brand-specific terms. This sampling was done for two different four-week time periods: the first ending July 17, 2004, which gives us a glimpse at consumer search during the summer, and the second ending December 25, 2004, which reflects search during the prime holiday season. Do you want to venture a guess about the most searched terms in each category? The answers can be found in Table 4.3, which presents the top twenty in each category during each time period.

Notice that some retailers and products show up more than once in the top twenty. This happened because different consumers looking for the same retailer or product used slightly different search terms. So eBay shows up as ebay, ebay.com, and www .ebay.com, and PlayStation 2 appears as playstation 2, ps2, playstation 2 console, playstation2, and sony playstation 2. If you compare the search terms across the two time periods, you'll see considerable overlap in the terms for the retail and non-branded product categories. This is not the case, however, for the branded product category. Christmas shopping leads consumers to search for branded products unlike those searched during the summer, especially in the video games category.

Do you know which websites attract the most visitors? How about which websites are the fastest growing? Again we turn to comScore for answers to these questions. Tables 4.4 and 4.5 summarize comScore's findings for two different months during 2004. Notice that the three most popular websites remained the same between the two time periods and had considerable distance between themselves and the rest of the field. And of the top ten, Ask Jeeves gained the most ground, jumping from number twenty in March to number seven in December. Yet it was not the fastest-growing website on the Internet. As revealed by Table 4.5, that distinction went to the World

## June 20–July 17, 2004

| RANK | RETAILER | BRANDED PRODUCT | NONBRANDED PRODUCT |
|------|----------|-----------------|--------------------|
| 1 | ebay | barbie | furniture |
| 2 | ebay.com | ashley furniture | sporting goods |
| 3 | walmart | yugioh | cell phones |
| 4 | home depot | pocket bikes | tires |
| 5 | best buy | yugioh cards | auto parts |
| 6 | target | borders books | lingerie |
| 7 | sears | ipod | books |
| 8 | amazon.com | atkins diet | digital cameras |
| 9 | circuit city | motorola v600 | coupons |
| 10 | lowes | bratz | flowers |
| 11 | amazon | norton anti virus | free music downloads |
| 12 | www.ebay.com | dell computer | used books |
| 13 | ikea | amazon books | shoes |
| 14 | dell | oakley sunglasses | fireworks |
| 15 | costco | nike shoes | free internet |
| 16 | barnes and noble | yu-gi-oh | posters |
| 17 | bed bath and beyond | nike shox | auctions |
| 18 | walmart.com | joann fabrics | digital camera |
| 19 | target.com | phantom fireworks | rims |
| 20 | toys r us | harbor freight tools | music |

## November 28–December 25, 2004

| RANK | RETAILER | BRANDED PRODUCT | NONBRANDED PRODUCT |
|------|----------|-----------------|--------------------|
| 1 | ebay | playstation 2 | digital cameras |
| 2 | walmart | nintendo ds | sporting goods |
| 3 | best buy | ipod | toys |
| 4 | target | terrain twister | books |
| 5 | circuit city | borders books | lingerie |
| 6 | ebay.com | xbox | prom dresses |
| 7 | amazon.com | ugg boots | flowers |
| 8 | sears | barbie | auto parts |
| 9 | toys r us | napa auto parts | digital camera |
| 10 | amazon | tyco terrain twister | tires |
| 11 | home depot | build a bear | furniture |
| 12 | walmart.com | bratz | cell phones |
| 13 | overstock.com | ps2 | shoes |
| 14 | target.com | yugioh | auctions |
| 15 | dell | playstation 2 console | used books |
| 16 | lowes | playstation 2 | mp3 players |
| 17 | kmart | uggs | coupons |
| 18 | www.ebay.com | yugioh cards | jewelry |
| 19 | toysrus | sony playstation2 | portable dvd players |
| 20 | barnes and noble | fossil watches | posters |

**TABLE 4.4**     The Ten Most-Visited Websites in March and December 2004

| MARCH 2004 | | DECEMBER 2004 | |
|---|---|---|---|
| 1. Yahoo! sites | 110.8 | 1. Yahoo! sites | 119.5 |
| 2. Time Warner Network | 110.6 | 2. Time Warner Network | 114.9 |
| 3. MSN-Microsoft sites | 109.7 | 3. MSN-Microsoft sites | 113.5 |
| 4. eBay | 69.7 | 4. Google sites | 71.7 |
| 5. Google sites | 65.0 | 5. eBay | 66.5 |
| 6. About/Primedia | 39.0 | 6. Amazon sites | 48.2 |
| 7. Terra Lycos | 37.3 | 7. Ask Jeeves | 41.4 |
| 8. Amazon sites | 35.5 | 8. About/Primedia | 38.4 |
| 9. Viacom Online | 26.9 | 9. Wal*Mart | 34.0 |
| 10. Walt Disney Internet Group | 25.2 | 10. Symantec | 33.9 |

Source: "comScore Media Metrix Announces Top 50 U.S. Internet Property Rankings for March 2004," www.comscore.com/press/release .asp?press=447 (April 22, 2004); "Holiday Festivity Drove Web Activity in December, According to comScore Media Metrix Top 50 Online Property Ranking," www.comscore.com (January 17, 2005).

Note: Numbers represent the total number of unique visitors in millions.

**TABLE 4.5**     The Ten Fastest-Growing Websites in March and December 2004

| March 2004 | | |
|---|---|---|
| WEBSITE | NUMBER OF VISITORS (IN MILLIONS) | MONTHLY INCREASE (%) |
| 1. World Wrestling Entertainment | 2.8 | 52 |
| 2. Sportsline.com sites | 6.8 | 48 |
| 3. Miniclip.com | 3.9 | 44 |
| 4. Marriott | 3.2 | 44 |
| 5. Homeagain.com | 3.1 | 44 |
| 6. Mars, Inc. | 3.1 | 36 |
| 7. Fox Sports Interactive Media | 2.9 | 30 |
| 8. Fidelity Investments | 3.8 | 25 |
| 9. Intercontinental Hotels Group | 3.1 | 25 |
| 10. Homedepot.com | 5.8 | 23 |

| December 2004 | | |
|---|---|---|
| WEBSITE | NUMBER OF VISITORS (IN MILLIONS) | MONTHLY INCREASE (%) |
| 1. Donotcall.gov | 7.4 | 317 |
| 2. KB Toys | 5.0 | 54 |
| 3. Radioshack.com | 3.1 | 53 |
| 4. Limited brands | 6.9 | 50 |
| 5. Deutsche Telekom | 6.9 | 49 |
| 6. UPS sites | 14.1 | 49 |
| 7. Drugstore.com | 4.3 | 48 |
| 8. GSI Network | 11.8 | 47 |
| 9. 1-800-FLOWERS | 3.3 | 44 |
| 10. USPS.com | 11.6 | 39 |

Source: "comScore Media Metrix Announces Top 50 U.S. Internet Property Rankings for March 2004," www.comscore.com/press/release .asp?press=447 (April 22, 2004); "Holiday Festivity Drove Web Activity in December, According to comScore Media Metrix Top 50 Online Property Ranking," www.comscore.com (January 17, 2005).

Wrestling Entertainment (formerly the World Wrestling Federation before a lawsuit by the World Wildlife Fund forced a name change) in March and the donotcall.gov website (for those wishing to place their phone numbers on the list that prevents them being contacted by telemarketers) in December.

Of course, consumers use the Internet to search for much more than information about products. Indeed, do you know which word is the most searched? Would you believe *horoscopes?* And what celebrities are the most searched? In 2004, that honor went to Britney Spears (with Paris Hilton nibbling at her heels).[51] On a more practical note, consumers often turned to the Internet for health information. When they do, two-thirds use a search engine as their primary point of entry—not to identify the "best" website, but because they want to locate multiple websites so they can determine what information is repeated across the sites. Such consistency enhances their confidence in the information's validity.[52]

## HOW MUCH DO CONSUMERS SEARCH?

The answer to this question is, "It depends." Sometimes we invest substantial amounts of time and effort into collecting information for a pending purchase decision. Take, for example, buying a home. Few, if any, of the purchase decisions made during our lifetime will exceed the amount of search undertaken while shopping for a new home. When one of the authors of this book decided it was time for a new house, he devoted hundreds of hours over several months to searching the market. With the aid of his real estate agent, a list of existing homes for sale that met certain criteria (location, price, size, and so on) was developed. Many days were then spent visiting these homes.

Eventually, after examining dozens of existing homes, he reluctantly decided to build a new home. He had heard many complaints from others that had gone through this experience, including his own parents. He also realized that this would greatly complicate matters. Numerous decisions unique to building a new home must be made. Should you hire an architect to draft plans for the home? Perhaps it would be better to find a builder that offers a variety of models that can be customized. Should one builder do everything? Or should certain parts of the home (e.g., flooring, pool, landscaping) be handled by subcontractors? What about options and upgrades? Builders offer options for certain features that must be decided upon (e.g., the type of material for the kitchen counter tops). And nearly anything can be upgraded for the right price.

Fortunately, few purchase decisions are as challenging as the decision to buy a home. Think about your last trip to the grocery store. If you are like most grocery shoppers, the time you spent making each individual purchase decision can be measured in seconds! Consumers have little patience in locating what they want. According to Anthony Adams, vice president of marketing research at Campbell Soup, "After about forty-five seconds, we find that consumers just give up."[53] Even less time is taken once the shopper arrives at the proper location. On average, about twelve seconds passes from the moment a consumer stops next to where the product sits on the shelf and places the chosen item in his or her grocery cart.[54]

Earlier in the chapter we covered the most popular websites on the Internet. Now let's take a look at some findings from the third quarter of 2004 about how much search takes place once the consumer arrives at a website. On average, consumers viewed 10.3 pages during each site visit versus 7.7 pages the previous year. However, this page increase was also accompanied by a considerable decline in the average time spent on each page, from forty-three seconds in 2003 to twenty-nine seconds in 2004.[55] Do the math and this works out to an average time spent on each site of five minutes in 2004, down 10 percent from the five and a half minutes in 2003.

**FIGURE 4.11**    Number of Stores Visited by Furniture Buyers

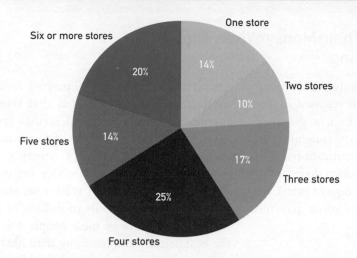

Source: Joella Roy. "The Consumer Purchasing Process—Part 1." www.furninfo.com (June 1, 2002).

Now let's take a look at a search activity that takes far greater effort than searching the Internet—visiting retail stores. How many stores do consumers visit when shopping for furniture? The same study that yielded the information presented in Figure 4.3 also examined this question. On average, consumers visited 3.2 stores when making their decisions about what to buy.[56] This average, however, conceals considerable variability in the amount of store search. Figure 4.11 shows the distribution of store visitations. Whereas one out of seven buyers made their purchase decisions after visiting a single store, one-fifth of them examined at least six stores before making their decision.

Why do some furniture shoppers search only a single store whereas others continue their search for many more stores before making their final decision? According to a **cost versus benefit perspective,** *people search for decision-relevant information when the perceived benefits of the new information are greater than the perceived costs of acquiring this information.*[57] Consumers will search until the benefits no longer outweigh the costs. The primary benefit is making better purchase decisions, either identifying the superior product or finding the right product at a cheaper price. Presumably, then, those furniture buyers that stopped after visiting a single store did not believe that further search would be worthwhile. Yet consumers often fail to fully appreciate the benefits of search, especially the value of searching for lower prices (see Buyer Beware 4.1).

Search costs include the time and effort that must be expended and vary directly with how easily information can be acquired. Making it easier for consumers can lead to greater search. Such was the case with the unit price information available in grocery stores.[58] Unit price information is typically presented on separate tags along the grocer's shelf. Acquiring this information becomes much easier when it is consolidated and presented on a single list. For this reason, consumers' purchases reflected greater search and use of unit price information presented on a list than on separate tags.

As noted earlier, making better purchase decisions is the primary benefit of prepurchase search. This benefit depends on **perceived risk,** representing *consumers' uncertainty about the potential positive and negative consequences of the purchase decision.* Generally speaking, as the perceived risk of a purchase decision increases, so does search. By searching more, consumers hope to reduce the chances of making a purchase they'll regret.

## Many Consumers Forego Their Money When They Forego Comparison Shopping

Most consumers underestimate the value of comparison shopping, according to research released by the Consumer Literacy Consortium (CLC), a group of consumer education leaders from government, non-profit, consumer, and business organizations. The CLC has concluded that consumers often do not realize that, for most products, a wide range of prices are available and, therefore, consumers often pay too much for the items they buy.

To assist consumers in their comparison shopping, the CLC is releasing a revised and updated version of its popular brochure, "66 Ways to Save Money." Consumers have requested 1.4 million copies of earlier editions of the brochure, which offers simple, straightforward, money-saving tips on twenty-eight types of products. CLC estimates that, by acting on these simple tips, the typical American household can cut its expenses by more than $1,000 a year.

According to an Opinion Research Corporation International survey of American adults, the typical consumer needs about a 10 percent price savings to persuade them to comparison shop for most products. For gasoline, auto insurance, color televisions, long-distance phone service, and new and used cars, consumers said they need savings of 10 percent or more to make shopping around worthwhile. For car rentals, plane tickets, and life insurance the price difference required to motivate shopping around was substantially higher at 25 percent.

Yet many consumers do not shop around. For example, nearly 60 percent of female car buyers do no research about financing options. They "often forget about shopping for financing, which can be a mistake costing thousands of dollars over the life of the loan," says Joni Gray, consumer advice editor at Kelley Blue Book.

An important reason why consumers do not shop around is the perception that it's not worth the effort. They rationalize that the savings potential will not be greater than the desired 10 percent savings needed to motivate action. "The fact is that shopping around for most products will yield savings far greater than 10 percent," said Jack Gillis, director of public affairs at Consumer Federation of America, an advocacy, research, education, and service organization. "The 50 percent of consumers who don't shop around are losing out on thousands of dollars of potential savings. By luck some of these people will stumble onto the best priced item, but more than likely half of them will pay far more than they should."

In the fall of 2002, students at Virginia Tech University participated in a comparison-shopping study to determine typical price savings gained by shopping around and the time it took to discover these savings. For each of four products listed below, thirty-seven students called three sellers. The median price savings for each of these products represented the median price difference for all thirty-seven sets of price differences.

### Search Time and Savings for Selected Products

| Product | Median savings | Search time (minutes) |
|---|---|---|
| Round trip flight, Washington, D.C.–Chicago | $125 | 21 |
| Round trip flight, Houston–Los Angeles | $139 | 15 |
| Car rental (two days) | $ 26 | 21 |
| Color television | $100 | 16 |

"Shopping, especially by phone or on the Internet, is easier than most consumers realize," said Robert Krughoff, president of Consumers' Checkbook, a nonprofit consumer information resource. "For many products and services, consumers can save themselves between $1 and $9 for every minute they devote to shopping. That is a much higher rate of return than most of us get on the job and, of course, you don't have to pay taxes on money you save."

Sources: Excerpted in part from Donna Harris, "Poll: Female Buyers Lack Confidence," *Automotive News*, 79 (October 18, 2004), 29; "New Report Shows Consumers Underestimate Value of Comparison Shopping," www.consumerfed.org/041603compare.html (April 16, 2003).

**FIGURE 4.12**     Consumers' Knowledge and the Amount of External
Pre-Purchase Search: An Inverted-U Relationship

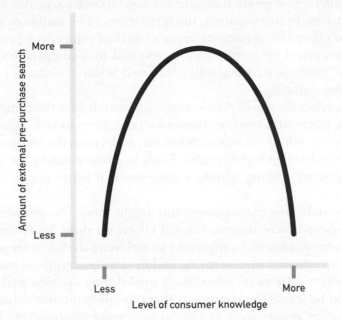

When consumers perceive significant differences between products but are uncertain about which product is best for their needs, search becomes more likely.[59] Similarly, as potential consequences become more important, perceived risk increases, thereby leading to greater search. A poor choice is easier to live with when the price is cheap, but not so when you are spending thousands of dollars. Consequently, consumers invest more effort into search as the price of the product increases.[60]

External search, like internal search, depends on what consumers know. The less you know, the more you search, right? Not necessarily. Those possessing very limited knowledge may actually search less than their more knowledgeable counterparts. Why? It is true that the uninformed have a greater need for information, but they are less able to conduct a useful search. They lack the prerequisite knowledge needed to guide their search in the proper direction and to comprehend acquired information. Those more informed have the knowledge needed to undertake a meaningful and productive search. Consequently, they will search more than unknowledgeable consumers. At some point, however, greater knowledge reduces search, because less need exists for external information and consumers can search more efficiently. Thus, there is what's called an inverted-U relationship between knowledge and external search.[61] This relationship is diagrammed in Figure 4.12.

## The Value of Understanding Consumer Search

Companies benefit from an understanding of consumer search in many ways. When, as noted earlier, Campbell Soup realized the unwillingness of consumers to devote more than forty-five seconds in locating what they want, the company streamlined its soup selections so that shoppers could locate items as quickly as possible.[62] In this instance, the company modified the breadth of its product line in response to the constraints imposed by consumers' search behavior.

Pricing decisions may also benefit. Companies want to know how much they should charge to maximize their profitability. They also need to know how much attention they should give to the prices charged by competitors in setting their own prices. As a rule of thumb, a company should pay as much attention to the prices of its competitors as do consumers in its target market. Consider the retailer that competes with a couple other retailers in its area. If consumers typically compare the prices charged by retailers, this would highlight the need to pay particular attention to the competition's prices. In this situation, the retailer would be unable to sell items comparable to those offered by its competitors at a less than competitive price. For this reason, grocery executives are more likely to respond to a competitor's price cuts for "high-visibility" items (e.g., soda, milk, bananas) when consumers engage in more price comparison shopping.[63]

In contrast, reduced levels of price comparison search offer the company more flexibility in setting prices. It is not uncommon for consumers to visit a single retailer before making their purchase decisions. When this is the case, the retailer can more easily get away with charging higher prices. Thus, by understanding the emphasis given to price by consumers during search, a company can better appreciate consumers' price sensitivity.

Consumer search also carries important implications for promotional strategy. Ideally, a firm should focus its promotional efforts on those areas most likely to be searched by target consumers. Companies can feel more confident about the potential payoff of their investments in advertising and in-store promotional materials if these represent important sources of information used during decision making. These investments would be wasted on consumers that rely solely on internal search.

Sometimes other people serve as critical sources of information. A pharmacist's opinion about the product best suited for relieving certain symptoms often leads to selecting the recommended product. Friends' opinions may be instrumental, particularly when they are perceived as being well informed about the product. Promotional efforts would be focused on gaining a favorable opinion among those serving as valued information sources.

Because what happens during search may determine what happens during purchase, it is also important for companies to understand the relationship between various search activities and the particular brand purchased. That is, beyond understanding the frequency and nature of different activities, we also need to understand if and how each activity influences consumers' choices. Each time a company discovers that search of a particular kind enhances the odds of its product being purchased, the company has uncovered another opportunity for gaining more customers.

One way to do this is to survey recent product buyers about their search behaviors. Respondents can be classified into different search segments based on the amount and nature of their search. The percentage of consumers choosing the company's brand within each search segment could be identified. The company would then test whether this percentage differs significantly across the search segments.

To illustrate, suppose that a company discovered that consumers who consulted a doctor during search were much more likely to buy the company's product (e.g., 35 percent of this search segment buys from the company) than those who did not acquire information from a doctor (e.g., only 10 percent of this segment buys from the company). If so, clearly the company should encourage this search activity. One example of using advertising to encourage consumer search of a particular nature appears in Figure 4.13. Notice how the ad asks the reader to talk to her or his doctor about the product. The wisdom of this request ultimately depends on whether consumers are more likely to purchase the advertised brand after talking to these sources.

On the other hand, suppose that a company finds that consumers are much less likely to buy the company's product if they engage in a specific search activity. When this happens, clearly the company has substantial incentive *not* to encourage this type of search. Less defensible, however, are attempts to discourage search. Indeed, such efforts may actually backfire. Consider the bad press Ibiley School Uniforms received

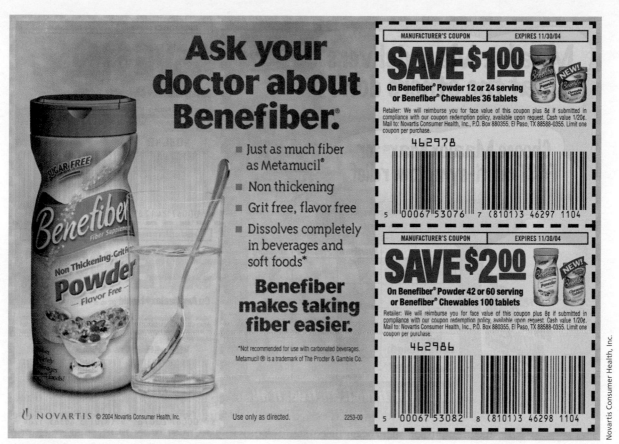

**FIGURE 4.13** This Ad Encourages Consumer Search

when a newspaper published a story about its advertising, which claimed, "Hey, school uniforms are never on sale, and you have to go to Ibiley anyway!" [64] The problem was that consumers didn't have to go to Ibiley. School board policy allowed parents to buy uniform components anywhere. Yet this was not how consumers interpreted Ibiley's advertising. As one consumer explained, "Listening to that I believed I *had* to buy the uniforms there. They're misleading people with that ad." Ibiley's president replied, "It's not misleading, it's true. They have to come to Ibiley because we're the best company to go to. That's just my way of advertising, telling them we're the best company with the best quality." Apparently being the best company does not include having the best prices. The newspaper article contained numerous price comparisons between the prices charged by Ibiley and its competitors for a variety of boys' and girls' garments. For the overwhelming majority, Ibiley charged more. We imagine Ibiley's competitors really enjoyed reading the paper that day!

## Pre-Purchase Evaluation

Ultimately, the likelihood of a product being purchased depends on whether it is evaluated favorably by consumers. In deciding which products and brands to buy, consumers rely heavily on their evaluations of the alternatives available for choice. Disliked alternatives are quickly rejected, if not ignored completely. Liked alternatives may be considered and compared, with the one receiving the most positive evaluation being chosen.

*The manner in which choice alternatives are evaluated* is the focus of our third stage of the consumer decision-making process, **pre-purchase evaluation.** Although we

**FIGURE 4.14**     The Pre-Purchase Evaluation Process

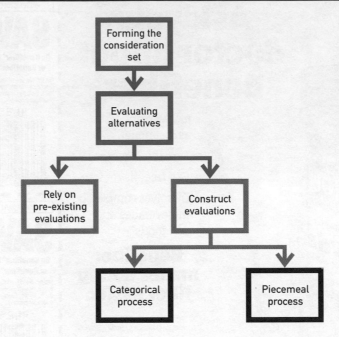

present search and pre-purchase evaluation as "separate" stages for pedagogical reasons, recognize that the two stages are intricately intertwined during decision making. The acquisition of product information from one's environment, for instance, normally leads to some evaluation (e.g., "these prices are too high") that may then guide subsequent search (e.g., "let's check the store across the street").

Just as consumers have various decisions to make during the search stage of decision making, this is also the case during pre-purchase evaluation. Should all possible offerings in the marketplace be considered, or should consideration be restricted to some subset of the offerings? Of those alternatives deemed worthy of consideration, how should they be evaluated? These fundamental aspects of the pre-purchase evaluation process are represented in Figure 4.14, which provides a roadmap of where we're going in this section.

## Determining Choice Alternatives

When making purchase decisions, we normally have a number of possibilities from which to choose. Yet we may not consider all alternatives that are available to us. It is highly unlikely that, the next time you decide to eat out, you'll consider all the restaurants in your area. Instead, you'll probably make a choice after considering only a subset of available restaurants.

*Those alternatives considered during decision making* compose what is known as the **consideration set** (also known as the **evoked set**).[65] As suggested by the information presented in Table 4.6, the consideration set typically contains only a subset of the total number of alternatives available to the consumer. Recognize that these results represent the average size of the consideration set. Some consumers have even larger consideration sets. For others, the consideration set is smaller. Consumers extremely loyal to a particular brand will have only this brand in their consideration set. Not only does the size of the consideration set vary between consumers and product categories, it may also vary as a function of consumers' search behavior. Car buyers searching the Internet, for instance, consider more cars than those who do not turn to this source of information.[66]

| PRODUCT CATEGORY | AVERAGE CONSIDERATION SET SIZE | PRODUCT CATEGORY | AVERAGE CONSIDERATION SET SIZE |
|---|---|---|---|
| Analgesic | 3.5 | Frozen dinners | 3.3 |
| Antacid | 4.4 | Insecticides | 2.7 |
| Air freshener | 2.2 | Laundry detergent | 4.8 |
| Bar soap | 3.7 | Laxative | 2.8 |
| Bathroom cleaner | 5.7 | Peanut butter | 3.3 |
| Beer | 6.9 | Razors | 2.9 |
| Bleach | 3.9 | Shampoo | 6.1 |
| Chili | 2.6 | Shortening | 6.0 |
| Coffee | 4.0 | Sinus medicine | 3.6 |
| Cookies | 4.9 | Soda | 5.1 |
| Deodorant | 3.9 | Yogurt | 3.6 |

Source: John R. Hauser and Birger Wernerfelt. "An Evaluation Cost Model of Consideration Sets." *Journal of Consumer Research* 16 (March 1990). 393–408.

Earlier in the chapter we introduced the notion of the external search set, which, depending on a couple of things, is not necessarily synonymous with the consideration set. First, consumers need not only consider those alternatives that are searched externally. Indeed, some, perhaps all, of the members of the consideration set may come from internal search. Moreover, depending upon the information obtained, some of the alternatives searched externally may not be deemed worthy of consideration. Thus, only when the consideration set is limited to each of the members of the external search set would the two sets be identical.

Because failure to gain entry into the consideration set means that a competitor's offering will be purchased, gaining consideration for one's product is essential. The importance of gaining consideration is well appreciated by Jim Ivey, the CEO at Savin Corporation, a manufacturer of office copiers. "With all the competitors and all the brands, making sure you are on the consideration list is most important," he says. Sometimes an entire industry finds itself in need of consideration. Such was the case for the horse racing industry. According to Rick Baedeker, the vice president of marketing for the National Thoroughbred Racing Association, horse racing had "slipped in the mind of the consumer. It's not that they think badly of us. They just don't think of us." [67]

Fortunately, companies have at their disposal a variety of ways for gaining consideration from their target customers. One way is to simply ask. How many times have you ordered a hamburger at a fast-food restaurant only to be asked if you would also like some fries? Likewise, shoppers who have just chosen a suit to purchase are likely to be asked by the salesperson if they want to consider accessory items (see Buyer Beware 4.2 for more about the "helpful" salesperson). Simply requesting consideration is common in the marketplace.

What if you were in the market for a loan and encountered the flyer in Figure 4.15? Unless you have more money than you know what to do with, it's almost certain that you would include BankAtlantic in your consideration set of possible lenders. An even

## "You Want Me to Look at What?"

Suppose you're at a store trying to decide which of two different brands you will purchase. Your dilemma stems from uncertainty about whether the higher-quality brand is worth its higher price. Perhaps you would be better off buying the lower-priced, lower-quality brand. As you deliberate, the salesperson suggests a third option for you to consider. This brand offers noticeably higher quality. Of course, it does so at a much higher price than the others. Is this addition to your consideration set likely to influence which brand you purchase?

It certainly is. Beyond the possibility that you might end up buying the most expensive alternative, the probability is that it has significantly enhanced the chances of you choosing the mid-priced alternative over the least expensive option. It is for this reason that some retailers follow the "good-better-best" approach in stocking their product lines. "I've always believed in the good-better-best theory in quality and price point," says Ronnie Haun, senior product line manager at Tucker Rocky Distributing. "A premium helmet can add substantial profit to a counter sale or new bike sale. At the very least, having premium helmets in a dealership increases the ceiling. Suddenly the better [mid-price point] helmets are not perceived as so expensive." [1]

Consumer researchers have documented this outcome in their examination of what is known as the compro-mise effect. The **compromise effect** *occurs when an added alternative causes a preexisting option to become more attractive as it now represents a compromise choice amongst the set of alternatives.* [2] In our example, the mid-priced, mid-quality brand is a compromise between the lower-priced, lower-quality brand and the higher-priced, higher-quality brand.

Altering what is chosen by what is added is not limited to compromise effects. There's also the attraction effect. According to the **attraction effect,** *the attractiveness of a given alternative and its odds of being chosen are enhanced when a clearly inferior alternative is added to the set of considered alternatives.* [3] If, for example, the salesperson suggests you look at a more expensive brand of comparable quality to the mid-priced brand, its obvious inferiority (much greater cost without appreciable benefits) to the mid-priced brand makes the latter more attractive.

Moreover, consumers are likely to be receptive to the salesperson's attempts to expand their consideration sets. In what has been termed the "lure of choice," recent research shows that consumers prefer more choices rather than fewer choices, regardless of whether the added choices allow the person to improve the ultimate outcome. [4] So be careful the next time you allow a salesperson to recommend what you should look at. Sometimes free advice has a hidden price.

[1] Mary Slepicka, "How to Beat Internet Sales," *Dealernews* (2004), 12.

[2] Itamar Simonson, "Choice Based on Reasons: The Case of Attraction and Compromise Effects," *Journal of Consumer Research,* 16 (September 1989), 158–174.

[3] Joel Huber, John W. Payne, and Christopher Puto, "Adding Asymmetrically Dominated Alternatives: Violations of Regularity and the Similarity Hypothesis," *Journal of Consumer Research,* 9 (June 1982), 90–98; Joel Huber and Christopher Puto, "Market Boundaries and Product Choice: Illustrating Attraction and Substitution Effects," *Journal of Consumer Research,* 10 (June 1983), 31–44; Barbara Kahn, William L. Moore, and Rashi Glazer, "Experiments in Constrained Choice," *Journal of Consumer Research,* 14 (June 1987), 96–113; Sanjay Mishra, U. N. Umesh, and Donald E. Stem Jr., "Antecedents of the Attraction Effect: An Information-Processing Approach," *Journal of Marketing Research,* 30 (August 1993), 331–349; Yigang Pan and Donald R. Lehmann, "The Influence of New Brand Entry on Subjective Brand Judgments," *Journal of Consumer Research,* 20 (June 1993), 76–86; Srinivasan Ratneshwar, Allan D. Shocker, and David W. Stewart, "Toward Understanding the Attraction Effect: The Implications of Product Stimulus Meaningfulness and Familiarity," *Journal of Consumer Research,* 13 (March 1987), 520–533.

[4] Nicola J. Brown, Daniel Read, and Barbara Summers, "The Lure of Choice," *Journal of Behavioral Decision Making,* 16 (2003), 297–308.

more powerful version of this tactic is seen in the car dealerships that advertise that they will buy the car for you if you can find a competitor offering a lower price. Companies in the enviable position of being able to make such offers will receive far greater consideration than those unable to do so.

Another way, then, businesses gain consideration is to offer consumers incentives for taking a look at what they are selling. A coupon offering a sizable price reduction might do the trick. Perhaps a free gift will work. We will further consider the ability of incentives to influence consumers in Chapter 8.

Sometimes it will take changing the product itself before consumers will view it as worthy of consideration. After all, products lacking something deemed necessary by the consumer have little reason to be considered. If a consumer is in the mood for blackened fish but a certain seafood restaurant does not offer this on its menu, the restaurant will receive neither her consideration nor her money. Or suppose this consumer walks into a furniture store and asks the salesperson to show her what's available in a certain style or fabric. If that just so happens to be a style or fabric excluded from the store's product line, then the store will be excluded from the consumer's consideration set.

## Constructing the Consideration Set

Suppose you were hungry and decided to eat out tonight. In this instance, you could go about constructing a consideration set in at least two ways. You could undertake external search, such as scanning the restaurants listed in the yellow pages, mentally noting those worth further consideration. A more likely scenario, however, would involve an internal search through memory, which will probably yield several possibilities. In the latter situation, the consideration set would depend on your *recall of choice alternatives from memory,* known as the **retrieval set.**[68]

Not all the alternatives retrieved from memory or available at the point of purchase will necessarily receive consideration. When there are preexisting evaluations, consumers may screen the alternatives based on how favorable they are about each one. After all, if you know that your taste buds are terrified by a particular restaurant's cuisine, there's no sense giving the restaurant a moment's thought. Instead, consumers will largely limit their consideration to those alternatives toward which they are favorably predisposed.

Obviously, consumers cannot construct a consideration set based on an internal search of memory without prior knowledge of at least some alternatives. Yet, particularly for first-time buyers in the product category, consumers may lack knowledge about what alternatives are available to choose from. When this occurs, the consideration set may be developed in one of several ways. The consumer might talk to others, search through the yellow pages, consider all brands available at a local store, and so on. Thus, external factors such as the retail environment have a greater opportunity to affect the consideration set of less knowledgeable consumers.[69]

The manner in which the consideration set is constructed can shape marketing strategy. Consider those situations in which consumers construct a consideration set based on an internal memory search. When this occurs, the odds of a given offering being chosen depend on its being recalled from memory. Accordingly, when consideration sets are based on internal search, it is very important that consumers are able to *recall* the company's offering.

At other times, *recognition* rather than recall becomes more important in determining the consideration set. Take the consumer who quickly scans the shelf at a grocery store to determine what is available and makes a choice among those brands that he or she recognizes, ones that look familiar. Recognition of alternatives available at the point of purchase would therefore determine the consideration set. Beyond making sure its offering is available at the store, a company would also want to teach consumers about what its product packaging looks like so that it can be easily recognized.[70]

**FIGURE 4.15** Offering Incentives to Gain Consideration

As indicated in Figure 4.14, determining the consideration set is only part of pre-purchase evaluation. In addition, consumers must decide how these considered alternatives will be evaluated. Basically, two options exist for doing this: (1) rely on preexisting product evaluations stored in memory, or (2) construct new evaluations based on information acquired through internal or external search.

## RELYING ON PREEXISTING EVALUATIONS

Which do you prefer, Coke or Pepsi, McDonald's or Burger King, Colgate or Crest? Most American consumers would find it rather easy to answer this question. This is because their prior consumption of these products has led to the formation of evaluations that are stored in memory. If the relevant evaluations are retrieved during internal search, then each can be compared to determine which considered alternative is most liked.

Obviously, consumers' ability to use this decision strategy depends on the existence of preexisting evaluations. These preexisting evaluations may be based on prior purchase and consumption experiences with a product. At other times, evaluations may be based on indirect or secondhand experiences, such as the impressions we might form after hearing our friends talking about a product.

The extent to which these preexisting evaluations are based on direct versus indirect experiences is important. Because consumers are more confident in evaluations derived from actual product usage, they'll be more likely to use these preexisting evaluations when making their purchase decisions. Such is the case for many of the purchase decisions made in the grocery store, and this is the reason that shoppers are able to make many of their selections in only a few seconds.

## CONSTRUCTING NEW EVALUATIONS

In many circumstances, consumers may be unable or unwilling to rely on their preexisting evaluations for making a choice. Unless you are more than a casual bowler, it is unlikely that you hold any preferences concerning urethane versus reactive resin bowling balls. Inexperienced consumers making a first-time purchase decision will typically lack preexisting evaluations.

Even experienced consumers possessing preexisting evaluations may elect not to use these evaluations. After decades of purchasing and driving automobiles, older consumers are likely to hold rather strong feelings about different automobile makers. Nonetheless, if considerable time has elapsed since they made their last purchase, they may question whether they are adequately informed about today's offerings.

Consumers can construct evaluations by two basic processes. According to a **categorization process**, *evaluation of a choice alternative depends on the particular category to which it is assigned*. In contrast, under a **piecemeal process**, *an evaluation is derived from consideration of the alternative's advantages and disadvantages along important product dimensions*. We discuss each process next.

**The Categorization Process** One aspect of human knowledge is the existence of mental categories. Categories can be very general (motorized forms of transportation), or they can be very specific (Harley-Davidson motorcycles). Typically, these categories are associated with some degree of liking or disliking. Moreover, the evaluation attached to a category may be transferred to any new object assigned to the category.[71]

This same process can be used when consumers are forming their initial evaluations of a product.[72] To the extent that the product can be assigned membership to a particular category, it will receive an evaluation similar to that attached to the category.

If consumers perceive a new product they encounter at the grocery store as just another health food, then they may simply evaluate it based on their liking of health foods in general.

Accordingly, when consumers rely on a categorization process, a product's evaluation depends on the particular category to which it is perceived as belonging. Given this, companies need to understand whether consumers are using categories that evoke the desired evaluations. Indeed, how a product is categorized can strongly influence consumer demand. For example, what products come to mind when you think about the "morning beverages" category? To the soft drink industry's dismay, far too few of us include sodas in this category. Several attempts have been made at getting soft drinks on the breakfast table, but with little success.[73]

**Brand extensions,** in which a *well-known and respected brand name from one product category is extended into other product categories,* is one way companies employ categorization to their advantage. Brand extensions are a common business practice. Disney took a name built on cartoon characters and amusement parks and extended it to the cruise line industry. Kimberly-Clark, the maker of Huggies, the best-selling brand of disposable diapers in the United States, has extended the Huggies' name to disposable washcloths and liquid soap for babies, and will soon start selling a line of Huggies toiletries.[74] The hope is that consumers' favorable opinions about the core brand will transfer to the company's new extension, whether it be a cruise ship or a washcloth. Some believe this is wishful thinking. According to one corporate identity consultant in New York, "The Huggies and Pampers brand names are specific to a product—a diaper. Just because mothers buy other products for infants and children doesn't mean the brand names would work for these other products."[75]

So what does existing research say about this consultant's reservations about brand extensions? Will consumers transfer their positive feelings about a well-established brand name into a new product category? They will, depending on how similar the extension product category is to the core brand's product category.[76] As shown in Figure 4.16, when the core brand's name is extended into a category seen as similar to the

**FIGURE 4.16**    The Transference of Attitude toward the Core Brand to Its Extension Depends on the Extension's Similarity to the Core Brand

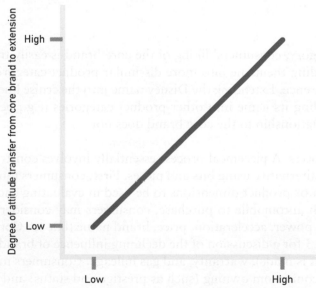

Degree of attitude transfer from core brand to extension

Degree of similarity between core brand and extension

## Brand Names and Logos Are Losing Their Appeal

Everywhere you look, the picture is the same: Consumers are paying less and less attention to a product's name when making their purchase decisions. When eight thousand consumers were questioned in late 2000, 48 percent said brand names were extremely important when choosing holiday gifts. Three years later, the number had dropped by a third to 32 percent. When a different survey asked seventy-five hundred consumers whether the importance of brands and trademarks had changed when selecting apparel items, 57 percent reported that labels and logos had become less important to them, and only 10 percent felt they were more important than before. Interestingly, women were nearly eight times more likely than men to report that names and logos had become less important. And what consumers are saying mirrors what they are buying. Consider store-branded products, which are sold under a retailer's private label as opposed to a national or regional brand name. Sales of store-branded products in the twenty best-selling categories have grown at a much faster pace (22 percent) than have total sales in these product categories (15.6 percent). Moreover, a survey of grocery shoppers revealed that 70 percent wished that store brands were as commonly available as the national brands

and 54 percent plan on buying more store-branded products in the future.

So what accounts for this decline in consumers' preference for national brands? Part of the blame lies in the economic hardships many consumers were experiencing during this time period. The higher price of the heavily marketed brand names drove many consumers to their lower-priced counterparts. Given that discounting their prices and reducing their profitability is rarely an attractive option, companies can do little to address this problem other than wait for more prosperous times to return. But this is only part of the story. This erosion in consumer preference for national brands has also occurred because of changes in consumers' perceptions about the relative quality of the branded alternatives. Once upon a time most consumers believed that national brands offered higher quality. In the same survey of grocery shoppers noted above, 59 percent thought store-branded products charged less but still offered national brand quality. Little wonder that these shoppers have defected from the national brands in favor of the store brands. And until the makers of the nationals reverse such beliefs, the situation is only going to get worse for them.

Sources: Shelly Branch, "What's in a Name? Not Much According to Clothes Shoppers—House-Brand Bargains Edge Out Designer Threads, Marketing Survey Finds," *Wall Street Journal* (July 16, 2002), B4; Clayton Collins, "Why the Lure of Logos Wears Thin," *Christian Science Monitor* (June 18, 2004), 11; Tracie Rozhion, "Brand Names Are Paying the Price for a Change in Shopping Trends," *New York Times* (December 10, 2003), C1: Sandra Yin, "Shelf Life," *American Demographics*, 26 (March 2004), 16.

core brand's category, consumers' liking of the core brand is easily transferred to the extension. Extending the name into more dissimilar product categories, however, reduces this transference. Extending the Disney name into the cruise line industry makes sense, but extending its name into other product categories (e.g., beer or cigarettes) that have little relationship to the core brand does not.

**The Piecemeal Process** A piecemeal process essentially involves constructing an evaluation of a choice alternative using bits and pieces. First, consumers must determine the particular criteria or product dimensions to be used in evaluating choice alternatives. In deciding which automobile to purchase, consumers may consider such criteria as safety, reliability, power, acceleration, price, brand name (but see Consumer Behavior and Marketing 4.3 for a discussion of the declining influence of brand name), country of origin (where it is made), warranty, and gas mileage. Consumers may also consider the feelings that come from owning (such as prestige and status) and driving (such as exhilaration and excitement) the car.

Decisions involving "noncomparable" alternatives may require the consumer to use more abstract criteria during evaluation.[77] Consider the consumer faced with choosing among a refrigerator, a television, and a stereo. These alternatives share few concrete attributes (price is an exception) along which comparisons can be made directly. Comparisons can be undertaken, however, using abstract dimensions such as necessity, entertainment, and status.

Next, consumers need to evaluate the strength or weakness of each considered alternative along the particular criteria deemed important in making their choice. Is the product's price acceptable? Does the product provide the desired benefits? Is the warranty strong enough?

In many cases, consumers already have stored in memory judgments or beliefs about the performance of the choice alternatives under consideration. The ability to retrieve this information may affect which alternative is eventually chosen.[78] Consumers lacking such stored knowledge, however, will need to rely on external information in forming beliefs about an alternative's performance.

In judging how well an alternative performs, consumers often use cutoffs.[79] A **cutoff** is simply a *restriction or requirement for acceptable performance*. Consider price. Consumers usually have an upper limit for the price they are willing to pay. A price that exceeds this limit will be viewed as unacceptable.[80] Likewise, consumers may reject a food item because it exceeds the number of calories they are prepared to consume.

Consumers may rely on certain signals when judging a product. **Signals** are *stimuli used to make inferences about the product*. It's common to find consumers using particular product features, such as the name it carries, to infer the quality of the product. Many of us would perceive the quality of a watch much differently depending on whether it carries the Rolex or Timex brand name. Higher prices are often interpreted as an indicator of higher quality.[81] Conversely, price promotions or discounts may have the opposite effect.[82]

A product's warranty may serve as a signal.[83] Companies that fail to recognize the signaling power of certain attributes may unnecessarily sell themselves short. Once upon a time Whirlpool washing machines received the best ratings by *Consumer Reports*, a publication dedicated to providing unbiased assessments of product quality.[84] Yet the signal sent by its warranty, which was clearly inferior to the warranty offered by some of its competitors, and no better than the warranty offered by other competitors, suggested otherwise. One can only wonder how many sales Whirlpool lost because of the weak signal sent by its warranty.

Even how a product is packaged may be interpreted as a signal of the product's quality. A certain supermarket learned this lesson the hard way when it decided to package its fresh fish in plastic wrap rather than displaying it unwrapped on crushed ice. Consumers no longer perceived the fish as fresh and sales declined. As seen in Figure 4.17, the wine industry is expanding the use of boxed packaging to higher-quality, even award-winning, vintages.[85] Why? Boxes are cheaper, more compact, easier to carry, and, once opened, preserve the wine far longer than their glass counterparts. Yet all of these advantages may not matter if consumers view the box as a signal of an inferior wine.

Signals can come in other forms beyond a product's attributes. Simply putting a product's price on a sign serves as a potent bargain signal to shoppers. One pricing executive reports that such signs enhance sales by 50 to 60 percent, so long as the retailer doesn't overdo it.[86]

The final step in a piecemeal process involves using one's judgments about the performance of the considered alternatives to form an overall evaluation of each alternative's acceptability. Consumer researchers have identified a number of ways in which

**FIGURE 4.17** Boxed Wines: Is the Packaging Perceived by Consumers as a Product Benefit or a Signal of an Inferior Product?

consumers may do this. A fundamental distinction between these evaluation strategies is whether they are compensatory or noncompensatory.

*Noncompensatory Evaluation Strategies* Common to this set of evaluation strategies is that a product's weakness on one attribute *cannot* be offset by its strong performance on another attribute. Consider snack foods. Manufacturers have the capability of meeting consumers' desires for healthier snacks by cutting the amount of oil and salt in the products. But eliminate too much of these ingredients and the snacks taste lousy. Although the reformulated product will score high marks on nutritional considerations, this strength cannot overcome the weakness in the product's taste. According to Dwight Riskey, a psychologist and vice president of market research at Frito-Lay, "Consumers won't sacrifice taste for health in snacks."[87]

Noncompensatory evaluation strategies come in many different forms.[88] According to a **lexicographic strategy**, brands are compared initially on the most important attribute. If one of the brands is perceived as superior based on that attribute, it is selected. If two or more brands are perceived as equally good, they are then compared on the second most important attribute. This process continues until the tie is broken.

The **elimination by aspects strategy** resembles the lexicographic approach. As before, brands are first evaluated on the most important attribute. Now, however, the consumer imposes cutoffs. The consumer may, for example, use cutoffs such as "must be under $2" or "must be nutritious."

If only one brand meets the cutoff on the most important attribute, it is chosen. If several brands meet the cutoff, then the next most important attribute is selected and the process continues until the tie is broken. If none of the brands are acceptable, the consumer must revise the cutoffs, use a different evaluation strategy, or postpone choice.

**TABLE 4.7**     Hypothetical Brand Ratings

| | | BRAND PERFORMANCE RATINGS | | | |
|---|---|---|---|---|---|
| ATTRIBUTE | IMPORTANCE RANKING | BRAND A | BRAND B | BRAND C | BRAND D |
| Taste | 1 | Excellent | Excellent | Very Good | Excellent |
| Price | 2 | Very Good | Good | Excellent | Fair |
| Nutrition | 3 | Good | Good | Poor | Excellent |
| Convenience | 4 | Fair | Good | Good | Excellent |

Cutoffs also play a prominent part in the **conjunctive strategy.**[89] Cutoffs are established for each salient attribute. Each brand is compared, one at a time, against this set of cutoffs. Thus, processing by brand is required. If the brand meets the cutoffs for *all* the attributes, it is chosen. Failure to meet the cutoff for any attribute leads to rejection. As before, if none of the brands meet the cutoff requirements, a change in either the cutoffs or the evaluation strategy must occur. Otherwise, choice must be delayed.

To illustrate the operation of these strategies, consider the information presented in Table 4.7. This table contains attribute-performance ratings (from excellent to poor) for four different brands of food and attribute-importance rankings (where 1 is most important). Which brand would be chosen if a lexicographic strategy were used? The answer is brand A. A comparison on the most important attribute, taste, produces a tie between brands A, B, and D. This tie is broken on the next most important attribute, price, because brand A has the highest rating of the three brands. Notice, however, what happens with a slight change in the attribute-importance rankings. For instance, if price were more important, brand C would be chosen.

Choice based on elimination by aspects would depend on the particular cutoff values imposed by the decision maker. Suppose the minimum acceptable values for taste and price were "excellent" and "very good," respectively. Brand A would again be chosen. But if the cutoff for taste was lowered to "very good" and the cutoff for price was raised to "excellent," then brand C would be selected.

To illustrate the conjunctive strategy, assume that the consumer insists that the brand receive a rating of at least "good" on each attribute. In Table 4.7, brand A is rejected because of its inadequate rating (i.e., does not meet the cutoff requirement of "good") on convenience, whereas brand C is inadequate on nutrition. Brand D is eliminated by the unacceptable price rating. Only brand B meets all the cutoff requirements and therefore would be evaluated as an acceptable choice.

*Compensatory Evaluation Strategies* Did you notice the plight of poor brand D in Table 4.7? Despite its excellent ratings in three of the four salient attributes (including the most important attribute), brand D never emerged as the top brand. Why? Its poor price performance, that's why. Indeed, none of the noncompensatory strategies permitted the brand's poor rating on price to be offset by its otherwise excellent performance.

This is not the case for compensatory evaluation strategies. Now a perceived weakness of one attribute may be offset or compensated for by the perceived strength of another attribute. Two types of compensatory strategies are the simple additive and weighted additive.

Under **simple additive**, the consumer simply counts or adds the number of times each alternative is judged favorably in terms of the set of salient evaluative criteria. The alternative having the largest number of positive attributes is chosen. The use of simple additive is most likely when consumers' processing motivation or ability is limited.[90]

A more complex form of the compensatory strategy is the **weighted additive**. The consumer now engages in more refined judgments about the alternative's performance than simply whether it is favorable or unfavorable. These judgments are then weighted by the importance attached to the attributes. A weighted additive strategy is equivalent to the multiattribute attitude models described later in Chapter 10.

At this point, let's stop and consider what all this means for the practitioner. What value does knowledge about the particular evaluation strategy used during decision making have for the development of marketing strategies?

Fundamentally speaking, marketers need to understand evaluation strategies because they affect consumer choice. An understanding of the strategy (or strategies) used by a company's customers may suggest actions that maintain or facilitate customers' use of this strategy. For example, if customers use a lexicographic strategy with product quality being the most important attribute, the company may find it profitable to implement an advertising campaign stressing the importance of product quality and the quality of the company's product.

Understanding evaluation strategies is also important for identifying the appropriate actions for improving consumers' product evaluations.[91] To illustrate, suppose that brand C in Table 4.7 improved its taste perception from "very good" to "excellent." This change makes considerable sense if consumers use a lexicographic strategy because it would lead to brand C being chosen. Suppose, however, that consumers use a conjunctive strategy with cutoffs of "good." Improving the product's taste would be of little value because its nutritional rating of "poor" is unacceptable. Instead, enhancing the brand's nutritional performance would be critical.

Changing consumers' evaluation strategies provides marketers with another mechanism for influencing choice. In some cases, this might involve changing the importance of product attributes. For example, assuming a lexicographic strategy, the maker of brand C in Table 4.7 might try to alter the importance consumers attach to taste and price. A lexicographic strategy with price being the most important attribute would lead to the selection of brand C, whereas this strategy would lead to brand A being chosen when taste is most important.

Changing the cutoffs is another mechanism for altering choice. As illustrated by the example in the prior discussion of elimination by aspects, changes in the minimum acceptable values for taste and price resulted in the selection of different brands from Table 4.7.

## How Good Are We at Evaluating Alternatives?

Numerous examples indicate that consumers have little to brag about when it comes to figuring out which alternative is best for them. A classic demonstration of this involved offering grocery shoppers the opportunity to win a sizable amount of money if they could choose which of two brands was the best buy.[92] Doing so simply required shoppers to calculate each brand's unit price and choose the lowest. But to complicate matters, the brand having the higher unit price was described as being on sale. Nonetheless, even at the sale price, its unit price was still greater. Apparently, many shoppers interpreted this sale as a signal that the more expensive brand was a better buy. In this instance, the signal was misleading, and shoppers made the wrong choice.

As noted earlier in the chapter, consumers often rely upon certain signals, such as a product's price, to make inferences about the product's quality. Yet such signals may not be accurate indicators. Consider blenders that range in price from a low of $15 to as much as $600. In a test of six models, a $25 model outperformed competitors priced four to six times higher.[93] Signals that are related imperfectly to actual quality will mislead those consumers choosing to rely upon these inaccurate signals.

Beyond relying upon imperfect signals, many consumers display their limited ability to make wise product assessments by the choices they make in the marketplace. Consumers unable to afford buying the product outright but wishing to avoid the high interest rates of buying it on credit often opt for what is known as "renting to own." The consumer pays a weekly or monthly fee to lease the product with an option to

## BUYER BEWARE 4.3

### Extended Warranties: How Much Are You Willing to Pay for Peace of Mind?

We've all been through the routine. Just as the salesperson is about to wrap up our purchase, we're asked if we'd like to buy an extended warranty. Such warranties are offered on a vast array of items, from cars to refrigerators to cell phones. And little wonder. Their 60–70 percent profit margins, versus the 10 percent or so margins on the merchandise itself, make them extremely attractive to retailers. So if they're this profitable for the seller, how good a deal can they be for the buyer?

According to David Helm, deputy editor of *Consumer Reports,* "The odds are against you ever needing to use an extended warranty." The magazine surveyed 38,000 of its readers on which of their home appliances and electronics were repaired during the first three years after purchase—the lifespan of many extended warranties. For thirty- to thirty-six-inch televisions, the repair rate was a meager 7 percent. Only 8 percent of analog camcorders, electric ranges, dishwashers, and top-freezer refrigerators were repaired. Desktop computers needed the most repairs, with 39 percent getting repaired in the first three years.

So the odds of needing a repair for many products during their first three years are not good, but extended warranties may not be worth their price for other reasons. Many products that do break down in their early years do so in their first ninety days due to manufacturing problems or faulty parts. These breakdowns are covered by the manufacturer's free warranty. Warranties may come with certain exceptions and rules that make them difficult to redeem. The cost of a repair may be similar to (or even less than) the price of the warranty. The average cost of the warranty for a projection television, for example, was about the same as the repair cost in the *Consumer Reports* survey. And for some product categories, such as those falling in price or improving in quality, you might be better off buying one of the latest models than using a warranty to repair the version you purchased a couple of years ago.

Nonetheless, extended warranties are not without their virtues. For very expensive items, many prefer not to place so much money at risk. *Consumer Reports* recommends considering extended warranties for certain products, such as expensive treadmills and computers. And then there's the psychological benefit. As one consumer explains, "I'd rather have the warranty and the peace of mind, rather than have to worry about losing out or not having the money to replace or fix something you've spent a lot of money on."

Sources: Adapted from "Extended Warranty? Ho, Ho, No!" *Consumer Reports: Publisher's Edition Including Supplemental Guides,* 68 (December 2003), 9; Jeff D. Opdyke, "Love & Money: Product Insurance: Have I Been Stupid?" *Wall Street Journal* (August 15, 2004), 2; Kelly K. Spors, "Consumer Watch: No, Thanks, on That Extended Warranty," *Wall Street Journal* (January 11, 2004), 4.

buy. And pay they do! By the time the customer exercises the option to buy and completes all the required payments, the average interest rate is 100 percent and ranges as high as 275 percent.[94] Or consider the phone industry. Discount carriers now offer long-distance telephone rates for as low as three to four cents a minute. Yet at least 10 million Americans are paying between thirty-five to forty cents a minute for their long-distance calls.[95]

Limitations in evaluating choice alternatives are particularly pronounced among functionally illiterate consumers deficient in language and number skills.[96] These consumers neglect unit price considerations when making choices between brands of varying sizes and prices. They will prefer the offering that has the lower total price even when the larger, "more expensive" option represents a greater value for their money by virtue of its lower unit price. More generally, many functionally illiterate consumers will focus on a single dimension, whether it is price or some other attribute, such as the size or shape of a package, when judging the choice alternatives. In doing so, these consumers ignore other aspects of the product that, if considered, might lead to very different choices.

Consumers' ability to accurately evaluate choice alternatives is important for their own welfare as well as society's. Every time we make a poor decision, we pay the price, although we may not even be aware of this. Consider credit insurance, which covers the borrower's financial obligation if he or she becomes disabled or dies. According to Consumers Union, publisher of *Consumer Reports,* consumers overpay for the coverage they receive by $2 billion a year![97] Similarly, consumers may be wasting their money when they purchase extended warranties. To learn why, read Buyer Beware 4.3.

Nor is it in society's best interests for its members to consume inefficiently. Such inefficiencies mean that we are not getting as much out of our resources as we could or should. Consequently, public policy makers are very interested in helping consumers make better purchase decisions. The nutritional labels on today's food packaging that were mandated by legislation are a good example of this. Helping the individual helps us all.

## Summary

The decision process begins when a need is activated and recognized because of a discrepancy between the consumer's desired state and actual situation. Understanding need recognition may reveal unfulfilled desires, thereby indicating potential business opportunities. Sometimes businesses influence need recognition as a way of stimulating product purchase.

The search for potential need satisfiers follows need recognition. If an internal search of memory provides a satisfactory solution to the consumption problem, consumers don't need to seek information from their environment. Often, however, some degree of external search is needed. Consumers have a variety of information sources at their disposal, and the Internet has affected the way many consumers search and shop. Consumers will search so long as the perceived benefits of the collected information outweigh the costs of acquiring it. Efforts to enhance consumer search may be warranted so long as such search enhances the odds of the product being purchased.

Pre-purchase evaluation represents the decision-making stage in which consumers evaluate considered alternatives to make a choice. Sometimes preexisting evaluations are retrieved from memory and acted upon. At other times, consumers have to construct new evaluations to make a choice. Understanding how these evaluations are made may reveal a number of opportunities for businesses to influence consumer behavior.

**Chapter Summary**

## Review and Discussion Questions

1.  What are the basic strategies available for companies seeking to influence need recognition?
2.  Imagine that you have been hired by a life insurance company to serve as a consultant. The company is especially interested in your opinions about what it might do to (1) convince consumers that currently do not own life insurance that they should have a life insurance policy, and (2) encourage existing policy holders with inadequate levels of coverage to increase their coverage. Which stage of the decision-making process is most relevant here? How would you proceed in deciding what the company should do?
3.  Explain how each of the following factors might affect consumer search: (a) brand loyalty, (b) store loyalty, (c) uncertainty about which brand best meets consumers' needs, and (d) the importance consumers place on paying a low price.
4.  Figure 4.11 indicates that a nontrivial number of consumers made their furniture purchases after shopping a single store. What is the significance of this search segment? That is, what opportunities does it offer and what constraints does it impose?
5.  A recent study has classified consumers into one of three segments based on the amount of search they did when making their purchase decisions. For each segment, the percentage buying your brand versus competitive brands was examined. The results are as follows:

|  | Percentage buying: | |
| --- | --- | --- |
| AMOUNT OF SEARCH | YOUR BRAND | COMPETITORS' BRANDS |
| Minimal | 3 | 97 |
| Moderate | 9 | 91 |
| Extensive | 17 | 83 |

What implications do these results carry for marketing strategy?

6.  The results of a consumer research project examining whether target consumers' brand preferences at the time of need recognition carried over to actual purchase has just arrived on your desk. Consumers just beginning their decision process were asked about their preferences for the company's brand and two competitors' brands. These results, as well as each brand's share of purchases, are as follows:

| BRAND | CONSUMERS' PREFERENCE AT TIME OF NEED RECOGNITION (%) | SHARE OF PURCHASES (%) |
| --- | --- | --- |
| Company's brand | 50 | 30 |
| Competitor A | 30 | 50 |
| Competitor B | 20 | 20 |

What conclusions would you reach from this information?

7.  This chapter indicates that offering incentives is one way for a product to gain consideration during consumer decision making. How else might a product try to enter the consideration set?
8.  A restaurant is trying to decide on the appropriate method for assessing consumers' consideration set when they are deciding where to eat out. One person has argued for a recall method in which consumers are asked to remember the names of restaurants without any memory cues. Another person recommends a recognition method in which consumers are given a list of local restaurants and asked to circle the appropriate names. Which method would you recommend? Would your answer change if consumers normally consulted the yellow pages in making the decision?
9.  A company that currently offers a product warranty quite similar to the warranties offered by competitors is considering the merits of increasing the warranty's coverage. A market study was undertaken to examine consumer response to an improved warranty. College students were shown the product accompanied by either the original warranty or the improved warranty. Students perceived the improved warranty as much better. Moreover, the product's quality was rated higher when it was paired with the improved warranty. Although the company viewed these results as very encouraging, concerns were raised about the appropriateness of using college students, most of whom have yet to make a purchase in the product category. Consequently, the study was replicated using older consumers possessing greater purchase experience. As before, the improved warranty was seen as providing much better coverage. Quality judgments, however, were unaffected by the warranty. How can you explain this difference between the two studies' findings concerning the warranty's influence on perceived product quality? Further, do you believe that the company should offer the improved warranty?

# Notes

[1] For a much broader perspective on the solution to this crisis, see Roger D. Blackwell and Tom Williams, *Consumer-Driven Health Care: How a Health Savings Account May Save Your Job and Solve America's Two Trillion Dollar Crisis* (Book Publishing Associates 2005).

[2] Lindsey Tanner, "Surge in Vision Loss Predicted by Researchers," *Miami Herald* (April 13, 2004), A9.

[3] Deborah Ball, Sarah Ellison, and Janet Adamy, "Just What You Need! It Takes a Lot of Marketing to Convince Consumers What They're Lacking," *Wall Street Journal* (October 28, 2004), B1.

[4] Hannah Karp, "Branson's 'Rebel' Persona Places Halo over UK Megacompany," *Wall Street Journal Europe* (November 15, 2004), A7.

[5] This paragraph is based on the following sources: Dina Elboghdady, "Far-Out: Former Astronaut Wants to Start a Space Airline," *Miami Herald* (August 7, 1997), A9; Victoria Griffith and Clive Cookson, "X Marks the Spot—in Space," *Miami Herald* (October 9, 2004), C2; Kenneth Miller, "Your Spaceship Awaits," *Life* (October 22, 2004), 6–9; Robin Stansbury, "Space Tours No Longer Are Sci-Fi," *Miami Herald* (April 12, 1998), J1, J4; "Cheick Diarra," *Fast Company* (September 1999), 136; "Like Grandpa, Like Grandson," *Miami Herald* (July 1, 1999), A2.

[6] The statistics cited in this paragraph come from Ball, Ellison, and Adamy, "Just What You Need!"

[7] This discussion of the furniture industry is based on the following sources: Cheryl Russell, "The New Consumer Paradigm," *American Demographics* (April 1999), 50–58; Jennifer Steinhauer, "Traditions Hurting Some Big Names in Furniture Industry," *Miami Herald* (September 14, 1997), F8; Teri Agins, "Furniture Firms Try Show Biz to Woo Public," *Wall Street Journal* (November 12, 1993), B1, B6.

[8] Joella Roy, "The Consumer Purchasing Process—Part 1," www.furninfo.com (June 1, 2002).

[9] Cheryl Lu-Lien Tan, "Elevating the Family Dinner; Furniture Makers Hope Tall Tables Ignite Sales; Finding Chairs That Fit," *Wall Street Journal* (November 4, 2004), D8.

[10] Ball, Ellison, and Adamy, "Just What You Need!"

[11] Ted Bridis, "Internet Users: Think Your Secure Surfing Net? Click Again," *Miami Herald* (October 25, 2004), A1.

[12] Ian MacMillan and Rita Gunther McGrath, "Discovering New Points of Differentiation," *Harvard Business Review* (July/August 1997), 133–145.

[13] For an insightful examination of advertising designed to influence generic need recognition, see Amitav Chakravarti and Chris Janiszewski, "The Influence of Generic Advertising on Brand Preferences," *Journal of Consumer Research*, 30 (March 2004), 487–502.

[14] Ibid.

[15] Paula Mergenhagen, "How 'got milk?' Got Sales," *Marketing Tools* (September 1996), 4–7.

[16] Raju Narisetti, "Rubbermaid Ads Pitch Problem Solving," *Wall Street Journal* (February 4, 1997), B6.

[17] For research on comparative advertising, see Dhruv Grewal, Sukumar Kavanoor, Edward F. Fern, Carolyn Costley, and James Barnes, "Comparative versus Noncomparative Advertising: A Meta-Analysis," *Journal of Marketing*, 61 (October 1997), 1–15; Cornelia Droge and Rene Darmon, "Associative Positioning Strategies through Comparative Advertising: Attribute versus Overall Similarity Approaches," *Journal of Marketing Research*, 24 (November 1987), 377–388; Kenneth C. Manning, Paul W. Miniard, Randall L. Rose, and Michael J. Barone, "Understanding the Mental Representations Created by Comparative Advertising," *Journal of Advertising*, 30 (Summer 2001), 27–39; Paul W. Miniard, Randall L. Rose, Michael J. Barone, and Kenneth C. Manning, "On the Need for Relative Measures When Assessing Comparative Advertising Effects," *Journal of Advertising*, 22 (September 1993), 41–58; Paul W. Miniard, Randall L. Rose, Kenneth C. Manning, and Michael J. Barone, "Tracking the Effects of Comparative and Noncomparative Advertising with Relative and Nonrelative Measures: A Further Examination of the Framing Correspondence Hypothesis," *Journal of Business Research*, 41 (February 1998), 137–143; A. V. Muthukrishnan, Luk Warlop, and Joseph W. Alba, "The Piecemeal Approach to Comparative Advertising," *Marketing Letters*, 12 (February 2001), 63–73; Cornelia Pechmann and S. Ratneshwar, "The Use of Comparative Advertising for Brand Positioning: Association versus Differentiation," *Journal of Consumer Research*, 18 (September 1991), 145–160; Cornelia Pechmann and David W. Stewart, "The Effects of Comparative Advertising on Attention, Memory, and Purchase Intentions," *Journal of Consumer Research*, 17 (September 1990), 180–191; Joseph R. Priester, John Godek, D. J. Nayakankuppum, and Kiwan Park, "Brand Congruity and Comparative Advertising: When and Why Comparative Advertisements Lead to Greater Elaboration," *Journal of Consumer Psychology*, 14 (2004), 115–123; Randall L. Rose, Paul W. Miniard, Michael J. Barone, Kenneth C. Manning, and Brian D. Till, "When Persuasion Goes Undetected: The Case of Comparative Advertising," *Journal of Marketing Research*, 30 (August 1993), 315–330; Shailendra Pratap Jain and Steven S. Posavac, "Valenced Comparisons," *Journal of Marketing Research*, 41 (February 2004), 46–58.

[18] Internal search has received relatively little attention in the consumer behavior literature. For exceptions, see James R. Bettman, *An Information Processing Theory of Consumer Choice* (Reading, MA: Addison-Wesley, 1979), 107–111; Gabriel J. Biehal, "Consumers' Prior Experiences and Perceptions in Auto Repair Choice," *Journal of Marketing*, 47 (Summer 1983), 87–91. For research on how

internal search may affect external search, see Girish Punj, "Presearch Decision Making in Consumer Durable Purchases," *Journal of Consumer Marketing,* 4 (Winter 1987), 71–82.

[19] John D. Claxton, Joseph N. Fry, and Bernard Portis, "A Taxonomy of Prepurchase Information Gathering Patterns," *Journal of Consumer Research,* 1 (December 1974), 35–42; David H. Furse, Girish N. Punj, and David W. Stewart, "A Typology of Individual Search Strategies among Purchasers of New Automobiles," *Journal of Consumer Research,* 10 (March 1984), 417–431; David E. Migley, "Patterns of Interpersonal Information Seeking for the Purchase of a Symbolic Product," *Journal of Marketing Research,* 20 (February 1983), 74–83; Joseph W. Newman, "Consumer External Search: Amount and Determinants," in Arch G. Woodside, Jagdish N. Sheth, and Peter D. Bennett, eds., *Consumer and Industrial Buyer Behavior* (New York: North Holland, 1977), 79–94.

[20] Biehal, "Consumers' Prior Experiences and Perceptions in Auto Repair Choice."

[21] Gregan-Paxton and her colleagues have made considerable progress in understanding consumers' propensity to engage in such transference of knowledge. See Jennifer Gregan-Paxton, "The Role of Abstract and Specific Knowledge in the Formation of Product Judgments: An Analogical Learning Perspective," *Journal of Consumer Psychology,* 11 (2001), 141–158; Jennifer Gregan-Paxton and Page Moreau, "How Do Consumers Transfer Existing Knowledge? A Comparison of Analogy and Categorization Effects," *Journal of Consumer Psychology,* 13 (2003), 422–430; Jennifer Gregan-Paxton, Steve Hoeffler, and Min Zhao, "When Categorization Is Ambiguous: Factors That Facilitate the Use of a Multiple Category Inference Strategy," *Journal of Consumer Psychology* (2005), forthcoming.

[22] Geoffrey C. Kiel and Roger A. Layton, "Dimensions of Consumer Information Seeking Behavior," *Journal of Marketing Research,* 18 (May 1981), 233–239.

[23] Peter H. Bloch, Daniel L. Sherrell, and Nancy M. Ridgway, "Consumer Search: An Extended Framework," *Journal of Consumer Research,* 13 (June 1986), 119–126.

[24] Ibid.

[25] Joann Peck and Terry Childers, "To Have and to Hold: The Influence of Haptic Information on Product Judgments," *Journal of Marketing,* 67 (April 2003), 35–48.

[26] Ibid.

[27] For a recent study of consumer in-store search behavior, see Mark Cleveland, Barry J. Babin, Michel Laroche, Philippa Ward, and Jasmin Bergeron, "Information Search Patterns for Gift Purchases: A Cross-National Examination of Gender Differences," *Journal of Consumer Behaviour,* 3 (September 2003), 20–47.

[28] James H. Meyers and Thomas S. Robertson, "Dimensions of Opinion Leadership," *Journal of Marketing Research,* 9 (February 1972), 41–46.

[29] Becky Ebenkamp, "Keeping Up with the Joneses," *Brandweek,* 45 (April 19, 2004), 20.

[30] Ibid.

[31] Barbara Bickart and Robert M. Schindler, "Internet Forums as Influential Sources of Consumer Information," *Journal of Interactive Marketing,* 15 (Summer 2001), 31–40.

[32] Leslie Walker, "Suddenly, Retail Clicks," *Washington Post* (June 3, 2004), E1.

[33] Becky Ebenkamp, "Surfing with Mom," *Brandweek,* 45 (March 8, 2004), 26.

[34] Ibid.

[35] Brian T. Ratchford, Myung-Soo Lee, and Debabrata Talukdar, "The Impact of the Internet on Information Search for Automobiles," *Journal of Marketing Research,* 40 (May 2003), 193–209.

[36] "Holiday Festivity Drove Web Activity in December, According to comScore Media Metrix Top 50 Online Property Ranking," www.comscore.com (January 17, 2005).

[37] "Online Holiday Spending Surges beyond Expectations, Driving E-Commerce to Record Annual Sales of $117 Billion," www.comscore.com/press/release.asp?press=546 (January 10, 2005).

[38] Bob Tedeschi, "More Canadians Than Americans Use the Internet, But They Do Far Less of Their Shopping There," *New York Times* (January 26, 2004), C5.

[39] "Time Spent Online Continues to Grow," www.studentmonitor.com (January 21, 2005).

[40] Ebenkamp, "Surfing with Mom."

[41] Ibid.

[42] Mark Dolliver, "People Keep Expanding Their Internet Activity," *Adweek,* 45 (April 19, 2004), 35.

[43] Walker, "Suddenly, Retail Clicks."

[44] "Car Buyers Turn to the Web for Research," *New Media Age* (April 15, 2004), 15.

[45] "Six Out of Ten House-Hunters Use the Web for Research," *New Media Age* (December 11, 2003), 12.

[46] Richard A. D'Errico, "Online Shopping Grows, But May Not Be Every Business' Cup of Tea," *Business Review* (February 27, 2004), 19.

[47] For recent research, see Gerald J. Gorn, Amitava Chattopadhyay, Jaideep Sengupta, and Shashank Tripathi, "Waiting for the Web: How Screen Color Affects Time Perception," *Journal of Marketing Research,* 41 (May 2004), 215–225; Charla Mathwick and Edward Rigdon, "Play, Flow, and the Online Search Experience," *Journal of Consumer Research,* 31 (September 2004), 324–332; Kenneth C. C. Yang, "Effects of Consumer Motives on Search Behavior Using Internet Advertising," *Cyber Psychology & Behavior,* 7 (2004), 435–447.

[48] Kate Fitzgerald, "Debate Grows Over Net Data," *Advertising Age,* 75 (March 15, 2004), 4–5.

[49] "comScore Study Reveals the Impact of Search Engine Usage on Consumer Buying," www.comscore.com/press/release.asp?id=526 (December 13, 2004).

[50] A special thanks to Lizzie Babarczy at Hitwise for her assistance in preparing this material for our use.

51 Gavin O'Malley, "Diets, Denim, and Divas Dominate AOL Search," www.media post.com (December 15, 2004).

52 Linda Holiday and Bruce Grant, "On the Web: If You're Not Everywhere, You're Nowhere," *Pharmaceutical Executive,* 23 (December 2003), 102–105.

53 Patricia Braus, "What Is Good Service?" *American Demographics* (July 1990), 36–39.

54 Peter R. Dickson and Alan G. Sawyer, "The Price Knowledge and Search of Supermarket Shoppers," *Journal of Marketing,* 54 (July 1990), 42–53. Also see Wayne D. Hoyer, "An Examination of Consumer Decision Making for a Common Repeat Purchase Product," *Journal of Consumer Research,* 11 (December 1984), 822–829.

55 Ross Fadner, "Study: Retailers' Search Engines Dry Online Purchases," www.mediapost.com (November 3, 2004).

56 Joella Roy, "The Consumer Purchasing Process—Part 1," www.furninfo.com (June 1, 2002).

57 Joel E. Urbany, "An Experimental Examination of the Economics of Information," *Journal of Consumer Research,* 13 (September 1986), 257–271. Also see Narasimhan Srinivasan and Brian T. Ratchford, "An Empirical Test of a Model of External Search for Automobiles," *Journal of Consumer Research,* 18 (September 1991), 233–242.

58 J. Edward Russo, "The Value of Unit Price Information," *Journal of Marketing Research,* 14 (May 1977), 193–201; J. Edward Russo, Gene Krieser, and Sally Miyashita, "An Effective Display of Unit Price Information," *Journal of Marketing,* 39 (April 1975), 11–19.

59 Urbany, "An Experimental Examination of the Economics of Information." Also see Joel E. Urbany, Peter R. Dickson, and William L. Wilkie, "Buyer Uncertainty and Information Search," *Journal of Consumer Research,* 16 (September 1989), 208–215; Calvin P. Duncan and Richard W. Olshavsky, "External Search: The Role of Consumer Beliefs," *Journal of Marketing Research,* 19 (February 1982), 32–43.

60 Kiel and Layton, "Dimensions of Consumer Information Seeking Behavior."

61 James R. Bettman and C. Whan Park, "Effects of Prior Knowledge and Experience and Phase of the Choice Process on Consumer Decision Processes: A Protocol Analysis," *Journal of Consumer Research,* 7 (December 1980), 234–248.

62 Braus, "What Is Good Service?"

63 Joel E. Urbany and Peter R. Dickson, "Consumer Information, Competitive Rivalry, and Pricing in the Retail Grocery Industry," working paper, University of South Carolina (1988).

64 Maria A. Morales, "It Pays to Shop Around for Uniforms," *Miami Herald* (July 20, 1997), B1, B2.

65 For research on consideration sets, see Joseph W. Alba and Amitava Chattopadhyay, "Effects of Context and Part-Category Cues on Recall of Competing Brands," *Journal of Marketing Research,* 22 (August 1985), 340–349; Juanita J. Brown and Albert R. Wildt, "Consideration Set Measurement," *Journal of the Academy of Marketing Science,* 20 (Summer 1992), 235–243; Tulin Erdem and Joffre Swait, "Brand Credibility, Brand Consideration, and Choice," *Journal of Consumer Research,* 31 (June 2004), 191–198; John R. Hauser and Birger Wernfelt, "An Evaluation Cost Model of Consideration Sets," *Journal of Consumer Research,* 16 (March 1990), 393–408; Frank R. Kardes, Gurumurthy Kalyanaram, Murali Chandrashekaran, and Ronald J. Dornoff, "Brand Retrieval, Consideration Set Composition, Consumer Choice, and the Pioneering Advantage," *Journal of Consumer Research,* 20 (June 1993), 62–75; Michel Laroche, Chankon Kim, and Takayoshi Matsui, "Which Decision Heuristics Are Used in Consideration Set Formation?" *Journal of Consumer Marketing,* 20 (2003), 192–209; Prakash Nedungadi, "Recall and Consumer Consideration Sets: Influencing Choice Without Altering Brand Evaluations," *Journal of Consumer Research,* 17 (December 1990), 263–276; John H. Roberts and James M. Lattin, "Development and Testing of a Model Consideration Set Composition," *Journal of Marketing Research,* 28 (November 1991), 429–440.

66 Ratchford, Lee, and Talukdar, "The Impact of the Internet on Information Search for Automobiles."

67 Maricris G. Briones, "And They're Off," *Marketing News* (March 30, 1998), 1, 14.

68 Alba and Chattopadhyay, "Effects of Context and Part-Category Cues on Recall of Competing Brands."

69 Joseph W. Alba and J. Wesley Hutchinson, "Dimensions of Consumer Expertise," *Journal of Consumer Research,* 13 (March 1987), 411–454.

70 Wayne D. Hoyer and Stephen P. Brown, "Effects of Brand Awareness on Choice for a Common, Repeat-Purchase Product," *Journal of Consumer Research,* 17 (September 1990), 141–148.

71 Carolyn B. Mervis and Eleanor Rosch, "Categorization of Natural Objects," in Mark R. Rozenzweig and Lyman W. Porter, eds., *Annual Review of Psychology,* 32 (Palo Alto, CA: Annual Reviews, 1981), 89–115.

72 Mita Sujan, "Consumer Knowledge: Effects on Evaluation Strategies Mediating Consumer Judgments," *Journal of Consumer Research,* 12 (June 1985), 31–46.

73 Robert M. McMath, "The Perils of Typecasting," *American Demographics* (February 1997), 60.

74 Jane L. Levere, "The Makers of Huggies and Pampers Are Seeking to Extend Their Brands into Children's Toiletries," *New York Times* (January 18, 2005), C8.

75 Ibid.

76 For research on brand extensions, see David A. Aaker and Kevin Lane Keller, "Consumer Evaluations of Brand Extensions," *Journal of Marketing,* 54 (January 1990), 27–41; Subramanian Balachander and Sanjoy Ghose, "Reciprocal Spillover Effects: A Strategic Benefit of Brand Extensions," *Journal of Marketing,* 67 (January 2003), 4–13; Michael J. Barone and Paul W. Miniard, "Mood and Brand Extension Judgments: Asymmetric Effects for Desirable and Undesirable Brands," *Journal of Consumer Psy-*

*chology,* 12 (2002), 283–290; Michael J. Barone, Paul W. Miniard, and Jean Romeo, "The Influence of Positive Mood on Consumers' Evaluations of Brand Extensions," *Journal of Consumer Research,* 26 (June 2000), 386–400; Paul A. Bottomley and Stephen J. S. Holden, "Do We Really Know How Consumers Evaluate Brand Extensions? Empirical Generalizations Based on Secondary Analysis of Eight Studies," *Journal of Marketing Research,* 38 (November 2001), 494–500; David M. Boush and Barbara Loken, "A Process-Tracing Study of Brand Extension Evaluation," *Journal of Marketing Research,* 28 (February 1991), 16–28; Kevin Lane Keller and David A. Aaker, "The Effects of Sequential Introduction of Brand Extensions," *Journal of Marketing Research,* 29 (February 1992), 35–50; Richard R. Klink and Daniel C. Smith, "Threats to the External Validity of Brand Extension Research," *Journal of Marketing Research,* 38 (August 2001), 326–335; Vicki R. Lane, "The Impact of Ad Repetition and Ad Content on Consumer Perceptions of Incongruent Extensions," *Journal of Marketing,* 64 (April 2000), 80–91; Barbara Loken and Deborah Roedder John, "Diluting Brand Beliefs: When Do Brand Extensions Have a Negative Impact?" *Journal of Marketing,* 57 (July 1993), 71–84; Tom Meyvis and Chris Janiszewski, "When Are Broader Brands Stronger Brands? An Accessibility Perspective on the Success of Brand Extensions," *Journal of Consumer Research,* 31 (September 2004), 346–357; C. Whan Park, Sandra Milberg, and Robert Lawson, "Evaluation of Brand Extensions: The Role of Product Feature Similarity and Brand Concept Consistency," *Journal of Consumer Research,* 18 (September 1991), 185–193; Vanitha Swaminathan, Richard J. Fox, and Srinivas K. Reddy, "The Impact of Brand Extension Introduction on Choice," *Journal of Marketing,* 65 (October 2001), 1–15.

[77] James R. Bettman and Mita Sujan, "Effects of Framing on Evaluation of Comparable and Noncomparable Alternatives by Ex-

pert and Novice Consumers," *Journal of Consumer Research,* 14 (September 1987), 141–154; Kim R. Corfman, "Comparability and Comparison Levels Used in Choices among Consumer Products," *Journal of Marketing Research,* 28 (August 1991), 368–374; Michael D. Johnson, "Consumer Choice Strategies for Comparing Noncomparable Alternatives," *Journal of Consumer Research,* 11 (December 1984), 741–753; Michael D. Johnson, "Comparability and Hierarchical Processing in Multialternative Choice," *Journal of Consumer Research,* 15 (December 1988), 303–314; Michael D. Johnson, "The Differential Processing of Product Category and Noncomparable Choice Alternatives," *Journal of Consumer Research,* 16 (December 1989), 300–309; C. Whan Park and Daniel C. Smith, "Product-Level Choice: A Top-Down or Bottom-Up Process?" *Journal of Consumer Research,* 16 (December 1989), 289–299.

[78] Gabriel Biehal and Dipankar Chakravarti, "Information Accessibility as a Moderator of Consumer Choice," *Journal of Consumer Research,* 10 (June 1983), 1–14; Gabriel Biehal and Dipankar Chakravarti, "Consumers' Use of Memory and External Information in Choice: Macro and Micro Perspectives, *Journal of Consumer Research,* 12 (March 1986), 382–405; John G. Lynch Jr., Howard Marmorstein, and Michael R. Weigold, "Choices from Sets Including Remembered Brands: Use of Recalled Attributes and Prior Overall Evaluations," *Journal of Consumer Research,* 15 (September 1988), 169–184.

[79] For research on cutoff usage, see Barton Weitz and Peter Wright, "Retrospective Self-Insight on Factors Considered in Product Evaluations," *Journal of Consumer Research,* 6 (December 1979), 280–294; Peter L. Wright and Barton Weitz, "Time Horizon Effects on Product Evaluation Strategies," *Journal of Marketing Research,* 14 (November 1977), 429–443.

[80] Susan M. Petroshius and Kent B. Monroe, "Effects of Product-Line Pricing Charac-

teristics on Product Evaluations," *Journal of Consumer Research,* 13 (March 1987), 511–519.

[81] William B. Dodds, Kent B. Monroe, and Dhruv Grewal, "Effects of Price, Brand, and Store Information on Buyers' Product Evaluations," *Journal of Marketing Research,* 28 (August 1991), 307–319; Gary M. Erickson and Johnny K. Johansson, "The Role of Price in Multi-Attribute Product Evaluations," *Journal of Consumer Research,* 12 (September 1985), 195–199; Michael Etgar and Naresh K. Malhotra, "Determinants of Price Dependency: Personal and Perceptual Product Evaluations," *Journal of Consumer Research,* 8 (September 1981), 217–222; Zarrel V. Lambert, "Product Perception: An Important Variable in Price Strategy," *Journal of Marketing,* 34 (October 1970), 68–76; Irwin P. Levin and Richard D. Johnson, "Estimating Price-Quality Tradeoffs Using Comparative Judgments," *Journal of Consumer Research,* 11 (June 1984), 593–600; Kent B. Monroe, "The Influence of Price Differences and Brand Familiarity on Brand Preferences," *Journal of Consumer Research,* 3 (June 1976), 42–49; Akshay R. Rao and Kent B. Monroe, "The Effect of Price, Brand Name, and Store Name on Buyers' Perceptions of Product Quality: An Integrative Review," *Journal of Marketing Research,* 26 (August 1989), 351–357.

[82] Priya Raghubir and Kim P. Corfman, "When Do Price Promotions Affect Brand Evaluations?" *Journal of Marketing Research,* 36 (May 1999), 211–222.

[83] William Boulding and Amna Kirmani, "A Consumer-Side Experimental Examination of Signaling Theory: Do Consumers Perceive Warranties as Signals of Quality?" *Journal of Consumer Research,* 20 (June 1993), 111–123.

[84] "Washing Machines," *Consumer Reports* (February 1991), 112–117.

[85] Michelle Locke, "Top Wines Uncorked," *Miami Herald* (June 25, 2004), C1.

[86] Terry C. Evans, "Editorial," *Home Channel News,* 30 (March 8, 2004), 11.

87 Robert Johnson, "In the Chips," *Wall Street Journal* (March 22, 1991), B1–B2.

88 For a discussion of other forms of noncompensatory evaluation strategies, see James R. Bettman, *An Information Processing Theory of Consumer Choice* (Reading, MA: Addison-Wesley, 1979), 181–182.

89 For a study of the conjunctive decision rule, see David Grether and Louis Wilde, "An Analysis of Conjunctive Choice: Theory and Experiments," *Journal of Consumer Research,* 10 (March 1984), 373–385.

90 Joseph W. Alba and Howard Marmorstein, "The Effects of Frequency Knowledge on Consumer Decision Making," *Journal of Consumer Research,* 14 (June 1987), 14–25.

91 Peter L. Wright, "Use of Consumer Judgment Models in Promotion Planning," *Journal of Marketing,* 37 (October 1973), 27–33.

92 Noel Capon and Deanna Kuhn, "Can Consumers Calculate Best Buys?" *Journal of Consumer Research,* 8 (March 1982), 449–453. Also see Catherine A. Cole and Gary J. Gaeth, "Cognitive and Age-Related Differences in the Ability to Use Nutritional Information in a Complex Environment," *Journal of Marketing Research,* 27 (May 1990), 175–184.

93 Valli Herman-Cohen, "Mixed Up About Blenders? You Can't Judge by Price," *The Herald* (October 16, 2003), 22.

94 Melanie Eversley, "Interest Rising in Regulations on Rentals," *Miami Herald* (August 21, 1997), C1, C3.

95 Shawn Young, "Bad Phone Deals Haunt Consumers," *Wall Street Journal* (September 16, 2004), D9.

96 Madhubalan Viswanathan, Jose Antonio Rosa, and James Edwin Harris, "Decision Making and Coping by Functionally Illiterate Consumers and Some Implications for Marketing Management," *Journal of Marketing,* 69 (2005), 15–31.

97 Marcy Gordon, "Groups Urge Consumers to Pass on Credit Insurance," *Miami Herald* (March 18, 1999), A19.

# Chapter 5

# Purchase

## Opening Vignette

Farmacias Similares is one of the world's fastest-growing drugstore chains, based in Mexico City and stocking only generic drugs, many of which it manufactures. Six 20-milligram tablets of omeprazole, a popular antacid used to treat ulcers, heartburn, and other conditions, sells for $3.50 at Farmacias Similares, versus $20 at a conventional pharmacy for the same dose of Prilosec, the patent-protected product made by the U.K.'s AstraZeneca. Next door to most of the stores is a medical clinic (run by a private foundation and subsidized by the chain) staffed by doctors who charge $2 a visit and write prescriptions for the generic drugs the store carries.

The son of a pharmacist, Victor González started this alternative approach to health care marketing in 1997. By 2005, the chain grew to more than 3,100 drugstores (the majority of which have medical clinics) in Mexico and Central America. Before Farmacias Similares, generic drugs were available only in government-run hospitals and clinics, forcing the 50 million Mexicans without health insurance to pay top dollar for name-brand drugs at private pharmacies. Many of Mexico's poor, who can't afford the $30 or more charged for a visit to private clinics, see González as a champion of their cause.

Farmacias Similares gets attention for its brand—a bald cartoon character named "Dr. Simi" who bears a big white mustache, fluffy white eyebrows, and a white lab coat—and for its eye-catching pinup girls called "Simi Chicas" appearing on billboards, in newspaper ads, and in their own calendar endorsing Simi-branded diapers, Simi prepaid phone cards, Simi condoms, and Simi tequila shot glasses. To further build the brand, over two thousand store employees regularly dress in 7-foot-tall Dr. Simi costumes and one of the Simi Chicas, Romanian-born actress Joana Benedek, hosts a television information and talk show called the *Dr. Simi Hour.*

Effective supply chain management is part of the company's success. González owns the manufacturing firm Laboratorios Best, which supplies about 20 percent of the generic products sold by the retail chain, with the rest purchased from other domestic manufacturers. Whereas some national health leaders call González a marketing genius, others attack the business model claiming that the drugs it sells are inferior and less potent than brand-name pharmaceuticals and that they can endanger patients. González responds by saying that he's a champion of the poor and by assuring the public that new laws will require all generic drugs to be tested for potency. Meanwhile, Dr. Simi appeals to moms and kids, Simi's Chicas appeal to men, and low prices appeal to the masses.

Source: Adapted from David Luhnow, "In Mexico, Maker of Generics Adds Spice to Drug Business," *Wall Street Journal* (February 14, 2005), A1ff. Copyright 2005 by Dow Jones & Co. Reproduced with permission of Dow Jones & Co., Inc., in the format textbook via Copyright Clearance Center, Inc.

Where people buy, what they buy, and—as you may have concluded in this opening vignette—*whether* consumers are able to buy is influenced by retailing. Understanding how consumers respond to and reward retailers with patronage, determines which firms—both retailers and their suppliers—prosper. That's why the next logical step in understanding consumer behavior is purchase—how consumers make choices between and within retail offerings.

"Dr. Simi" welcomes consumers to Farmacias Similares.

Joana Benedek, one of "Simi's Chicas," hosts the *Dr. Simi Hour.*

## To Buy or Not to Buy

To buy or not to buy? That is the question answered in stage four of the CDP model. In the *purchase decision process*, consumers decide:

1. Whether to buy

2. When to buy

3. What to buy (product type and brand)

4. Where to buy (type of retailer and specific retailer)

5. How to pay

Many factors influence these shopping decisions, including in-store promotions, store ambience and cleanliness, level of service, price, value, logistics, and overall retail experience. Retailers compete with each other on these various attributes to win the patronage of consumers. Consumers, in turn, must sift through the options made available to them and decide not just which product and brand to buy, but where and how to buy it. For some purchases, consumers may never enter a store, purchasing instead from the Internet, a catalog, or a direct salesperson.

The first hurdle is the decision to purchase. Consumers always face the option of aborting the process for many reasons, including changed motivations and circumstances, new information, or lack of available products, thereby deferring the decision.[1] Once the decision to buy has been made, various outcomes can occur. For example, a consumer may enter the Abiyuki district in Tokyo with the intention of buying a Sony television set but leave with a Panasonic television *and* a Bosch dishwasher. The decision to buy can lead to a **fully planned purchase** *(both the product and brand are chosen in advance)*, a **partially planned purchase** *(intent to buy the product exists but brand choice is deferred until shopping)*, or an **unplanned purchase** *(both the product and brand are chosen at point of sale)*.

### Fully Planned Purchase

Marketers promote brand and store loyalty with advertising and other programs that encourage consumers to plan their purchases. Research indicates that purchase planning is more likely to occur when involvement with the product is high[2] (as with autos) but can occur with lower-involvement purchases (groceries) as well. Whether or not purchasing occurs as planned is affected by in-store factors, such as knowledge of store layout and design, and time pressures that restrict browsing and in-store decision making.[3] Planned purchasing may also be interrupted or diverted by marketing tactics that might switch consumers from their preferred brand, including *product samples, price reductions, coupons, point-of-purchase displays, or other promotional activities*. How marketing efforts affect purchase depends on loyalty. Studies indicate that coupon ads that provide useful product information work well with consumers who are interested in switching brands, but attractive pictures are more effective with consumers who are loyal to a competitive brand.[4]

### Partially Planned Purchase

Consumers may plan the products they intend to purchase but delay choice of brand or specific styles or sizes of the product until they are in the store or on a website. When involvement is low, consumers often resort to buying one of the brands they know and like. The final brand or style decision may be influenced by price reductions or special displays and packaging.[5]

## Unplanned Purchase

Studies indicate that 68 percent of items bought during major shopping trips and 54 percent on smaller trips are unplanned.[6] These "impulse" sales, bought by consumers in an often whimsical manner, can be prompted by POP displays, a sale price on a related product,[7] or just by seeing a new product in the store. Impulse buys also show that consumers use in-store influences to guide product and brand choices made within the store.[8] Shoppers often intentionally use product displays and materials from catalogs as a surrogate shopping list. In other words, a display can remind a consumer of a need and trigger a purchase, perhaps of something they have seen on television or a website.

## Purchase Factor

When and if a purchase occurs is affected by *timing factors* such as seasonality; thus, a demand chain must be able to provide products such as air conditioners, snow blowers, umbrellas, and seasonal apparel when consumers need them, or the purchase may never occur. Similarly, retailers increase their profits by predicting, promoting, and supplying the right amount of inventory for Christmas, Hanukkah, Cinco de Mayo, and other holiday purchase needs. Further, some promotions that offer refunds or other future benefits in exchange for "effort" by the consumer (such as saving receipts for rebates or using a loyalty card) seem attractive at the time of brand choice but not as attractive later, when they have to complete the required tasks.[9] These promotions may accelerate the timing of purchase.

Timing also affects the price, and therefore the likelihood, of a purchase. For example, a student who intends to purchase an airline ticket to visit family members during spring break may not be able to purchase the ticket if he or she waits too long to book a reservation on the Internet at an affordable price. Timing factors were a primary driver behind the birth and success of convenience stores, such as 7-Eleven and WaWa, which recognized that consumers want to buy milk, beer, gas, and other products whenever they want. A factor in the success of e-tailers is the ability to offer twenty-four-hour-a-day shopping opportunities. Consider the websites of Best Buy, Nordstrom, Babies "R" Us, Target, and other firms that rely on the expertise and infrastructure of Amazon.com for their online presence.

When making a purchase, a consumer must also decide how to pay. Although cash and checks are still used for many purchases, many consumers pay with plastic—often influenced by credit card grace periods or the convenience of debit cards. But be careful as a consumer in how you use credit cards (see Buyer Beware 5.1). Marketers often prefer consumers to use debit and credit cards or checks from which they can *create a database of names for developing continuous communications and relationships with the consumer,* a process called **data mining** or data-based marketing.[10] The largest retailer credit card database once belonged to Sears, with 44 million household accounts (nearly half of the households in the United States at that time). Before spinning it off as a separate entity in 1999, Sears earned more profit from its credit card operations than all $30 billion of sales in its retail stores.[11]

In this chapter, you will learn more about purchase—specifically, retail applications and strategies. Think carefully about how you and other consumers make purchase decisions. You may find that you understand your own purchases better, allowing you to receive more value for your purchase dollars. If you work for a retailer, you obviously are interested in how the purchase and retail processes occur and how to influence consumers to buy from your store.

## Do You Use a Credit Card or Does It Use You?

Decades ago, introductory marketing textbooks contained a chapter on credit. Its purpose was twofold: to teach marketers, primarily retailers, how to increase sales by offering credit while, hopefully, controlling the costs of offering and collecting credit. The other purpose was to warn consumers that they would pay more for what they buy if they use credit instead of saving until they could pay cash. Ultimately, the research clearly demonstrated, consumers who use credit to make their purchases cannot buy as many goods as those who save until they can pay cash.

Most Americans over the age of eighteen with a job (or a cosigner) have a credit card, although credit cards are less common in Europe and other areas of the world. But beware! If you don't pay the entire balance off by the required date, you'll pay a very high interest rate by using a credit card, usually 14–36 percent or even more with high interest rates activated by missing payments and incurring late fees. Don't be fooled by special introductory rates, and always read the fine print describing what happens after the introductory period or if you fail to strictly obey the payment terms. One of the worst things you can do as a consumer is to pay only the minimum payment—you might need fourteen to thirty years to pay off credit card debt that way and you could end up paying several times the purchase price of the product.

Debit cards can be as big a mistake as credit cards and sometimes worse. They don't have the same fraud protection as credit cards, so if someone steals your debit card, they may clean out your bank account before you can notify the bank, causing your outstanding checks to start bouncing and leaving you penniless for weeks before the stolen funds are returned to your account. Debit cards often carry high fees when using ATM machines at banks other than your own, and they don't allow you to earn interest as you do with the "float"

obtained with credit cards or checks. Moreover, if you don't carefully balance your checkbook, it's possible to create costly overdrafts by using your debit card when there is an insufficient balance available to cover the charges. Banks and retailers promote the use of debit cards because of their lower operating expenses, but consumers must be wise in how they use them.

Wise consumers know that credit cards should be used for only two purposes: (1) expenses you know you'll pay entirely by the required date of the bill; and (2) emergencies or investments that couldn't otherwise be acquired.

There are some reasons to use credit cards—obtaining a printed record of expenses, for example, or obtaining airline miles, free gasoline, grocery rebates or other perks marketers don't give for cash purchases, as long as you pay the entire amount by the required date. And some necessary purchases are so large, such as a refrigerator or a washing machine (which may save you money in the long run compared to using a laundromat), you have no choice except to buy it on credit—but pay it off as quickly as possible. It's also okay to ask a retailer for a cash discount if you don't use a credit card—sometimes they will comply on larger purchases.

Having a credit card for traveling is usually essential to pay for tickets or auto repairs or other true emergencies. But if you are maxed to the limit on your credit card, it won't be available for emergencies. The next time you're tempted to put a pizza on your credit card, ask yourself if it wouldn't be better to pay cash, which probably causes most consumers to buy less when they see their hard-earned cash vanishing. If you aren't sure you will pay off the entire balance when you receive the next bill, maybe you should just fix a peanut butter sandwich.

## Retailing and the Purchase Process

Retailing is the process of uniting consumers and marketers, the culmination point of efforts by supply chain partners to meet the demands of consumers. Completing the purchase process requires consumers to react with retailers of some type.

| PERSONAL MOTIVES | SOCIAL MOTIVES |
|---|---|
| Role playing | Social experiences outside the home |
| Diversion | Communication with others who have similar interests |
| Self-gratification | Peer group attraction |
| Learning about new trends | Status and authority |
| Physical activity | Pleasure of bargaining |
| Sensory stimulation | |

Source: Excerpted from Edward M. Tauber, "Why Do People Shop?" *Journal of Marketing* 36 (October 1972), 46–59.

## MARKET FACTS 5.1

### The Thrill of the Bargain

As consumers continue to trawl through the complexities of shopping for bargains, the whole relationship between spending and saving comes into question. Are people buying specials in order to spend more or are they spending more in order to save? What is clear is that the simple relationship of thrift as a means toward the end goal of an overall saving does not hold for most shoppers. It is just as reasonable to see thrift as the end in itself, that people are going shopping in order to have the experience of saving money. For some people the thrill is in the bargain, and it almost doesn't matter how much one spends to achieve it. It is also clear that, although the forms of thrift differ considerably across class and income group, thrift itself is as important a factor in shopping for the wealthy as it is for the poor. After all, it is a common cliché that the rich are rich because they are thrifty.

Source: Daniel Miller, "Making Love in Supermarkets," in *A Theory of Shopping* (Ithaca, NY: Cornell University Press, 1998), 61.

### Why People Shop

Whether consumers buy from bazaars, flea markets, or department stores, the most basic question to answer when examining purchase behavior is "why do people shop?" The most obvious answer is "to acquire something," but consumers shop for many other personal and social reasons, as described in Table 5.1. For some consumers, shopping alleviates loneliness, dispels boredom, provides escape and fantasy fulfillment, and relieves depression. Others view shopping as a sport (with the goal of beating the system) or a modern form of the primal "hunt" (with the shopper acting as "the great provider"). The search for savings is not limited to low-income consumers; "finding bargains" is a reason in itself for shopping, as you can read from an ethnographic analysis of shopping motives in Market Facts 5.1.

Some consumers don't like to shop, with about 20 percent of the population avoiding the marketplace whenever possible.[12] These consumers are largely oblivious and unresponsive to marketing efforts positioning retailing as a "fun experience," perhaps embracing Internet buying or other forms of direct marketing as a way to make

## Cabela's

AS THE
**WORLD'S FOREMOST OUTFITTER,**
WE PASSIONATELY SERVE PEOPLE WHO ENJOY THE
OUTDOOR LIFESTYLE BY DELIVERING INNOVATION,
QUALITY AND VALUE IN OUR PRODUCTS AND SERVICES.

**CORE VALUES**
SUPERIOR CUSTOMER SERVICE • INTEGRITY AND HONESTY
QUALITY PRODUCTS AND SERVICES • RESPECT FOR INDIVIDUALS
EXCELLENCE IN PERFORMANCE

Cabela's is the nation's largest direct marketer—and a leading specialty retailer—of hunting, fishing, camping, and related outdoor merchandise. Since its founding in 1961, Cabela's has grown to become one of the best-known outdoor recreation brands in the United States, recognized as the "World's Foremost Outfitter." Through its direct business and a growing number of destination retail stores, Cabela's offers a wide selection of outdoor products at competitive prices and superior customer service. The firm is an integrated multichannel retailer, offering customers a seamless shopping experience through its catalog, website, and retail locations. Cabela's marketing strategy is effective at reaching consumers in rural areas, who have the greatest demand for outdoor products but the least retail access to Cabela's huge assortment, with its catalog and online offerings. Yet, the company's approach also provides an experience likely to attract consumers to an entertaining destination with gun museums, taxidermy displays, and thousand-gallon aquariums, which are also useful in demonstrating products and solving a wide variety of consumption problems.

shopping quicker, easier, and less personally involving. Some firms, such as outdoors outfitter Cabela's, deliver this type of experience for consumers, as you see in Consumer Behavior and Marketing 5.1. In the case of Cabela's, consumers can choose how they deal with the company—online, telephone, mail, or at its retail stores, which are top-notch educational and entertainment attractions featuring native fish aquariums, wildlife displays, gun museums, restaurants, and gift shops.

Marketers should determine how their core customers think of shopping—is it fun for them or is it a chore they must complete? If consumers shop for social interaction or some of the other reasons highlighted in Table 5.1, they are more likely to enjoy shopping than consumers who just buy products. If shopping is considered to be work, marketers should strive to make the shopping process easier—with quicker checkout lines, easier-to-read store guides and maps, easier-to-navigate aisles, and conveniently located staple products. If shopping is considered fun, however, the goal is to provide more reasons to visit the store and stay in it longer, as Cabela's has done in stores that evoke feelings of the great outdoors. For many consumers, shopping is both functional and fun, depending on the product and the retailer. The challenge for consumer analysts is to know which consumers and in which situations shopping is one or the other and develop retail formats to fit each situation or segment.

You can analyze where Internet retailing is appropriate and where it is not by analyzing motivations for shopping. Online grocers such as Webvan and Peapod failed partly because of the higher logistics costs their business model incurred, but also because many consumers—most, as it turned out—consider grocery shopping a fun social occasion to walk through pleasant-smelling and appealing stores to see products, compare labels, get ideas, obtain information,[13] and perhaps sample products. Compare the online retailing experience with the in-store experience offered by Fresh Market, Whole Foods, Wild Oats, Stew Leonard, and other specialty food retailers or innovative grocery chains and you'll understand why e-grocers had difficulty taking market share from location-based retailers that provide a superior shopping experience. Internet grocery retailing is profitable only in special circumstances (see Consumer Behavior and Marketing 5.2) and then only when it fits both the logistics of markets and lifestyles of consumers.

## CONSUMER BEHAVIOR AND MARKETING 5.2

## Why Webvan Went Bust

"We believe we had a brilliant concept. We were just ahead of our time," said Webvan spokesperson Bud Grebey at the announcement of the cessation of its operations and the demise of the Internet grocer, which had raised $1 billion in IPO financing. A careful analysis shows the opposite, however. In fact, Webvan was about forty years behind its time.

Why? Because just adding Internet ordering to the "pick-pack-ship" model of home delivery common in the 1950s and 1960s does not deem the Webvan strategy futuristic. Images of dairy and bread companies delivering groceries to the door are appropriate in a Norman Rockwell print from that era, but these images don't fit today's consumers' lifestyles or the economic realities of distribution in the twenty-first century.

Adding bandwidth or giving consumers access to the Web on their cell phones only addresses the *e* part of e-commerce—it doesn't change the reality of an average $30–35 delivery cost for complex, heterogeneous orders in large metropolitan areas. Add Webvan to the heap of failed dot-coms that focused so much on the *e* side of the equation that they neglected the *commerce* portion.

The basic flaws of the Webvan business model are not in the technology—in fact, many of its customers were satisfied with the ordering and delivery systems. Ask consumers and many say they like the idea of having someone pick, pack, and deliver their groceries, but few are willing to pay the true costs associated with the service, especially working professionals who often are not home during the day when delivery is economical for the company.

In contrast, Fresh Direct, a New York wholesaler that added Internet ordering, operates in a few zip codes in Manhattan with trucks already delivering to small retailers in the same area. As an experienced food distributor, its food comes directly from farms, dairies, and fisheries in the region, so the food is several days fresher and less expensive than at the high-priced neighborhood stores of Manhattan. The company's fully refrigerated, state-of-the-art warehouse (minutes from Manhattan in Long Island City) lets it meet standards difficult to achieve by retailers. Because customers don't shop in its warehouse, Fresh Direct can maintain different environments for each type of food sold including seven different "climates" for handling produce, ensuring that the bananas are as happy as the potatoes. By applying the "pizza delivery" concept of a limited delivery area in a competitive environment that contains no Wal*Mart Supercenter, Fresh

*(continued)*

Direct can offer consumers a superior alternative, perhaps at a lower price.

Here are a few lessons that can be learned from the demise of Internet grocers such as Webvan.

- *Redefine e-commerce businesses as commerce-e initiatives.* The Webvan saga illustrates that the disadvantages of not mastering the functions of inventory management, sourcing, transportation and distribution, customer attraction and retention, warehousing, and logistics outweigh the advantages of mastering Internet ordering technology.
- *Don't absorb the costs of functions consumers are willing to do for free.* After years of availability of phone-in orders and home delivery, the vast majority of consumers have chosen to shop for groceries in stores. And when they do, they perform the picking (from shelves) and delivery functions at no cost to the retailer. Webvan took on these functions for consumers at an IPO-funded loss to increase trial and acceptance of the service. How could Webvan compete effectively in the long term against stores that get consumers to perform these functions for free?
- *Don't offer consumers a new technology unless it solves their problems better than their current solution.* Technology determines only what can be *offered* to consumers, but consumers determine which technologies are *accepted.* The same holds true for e-tailing. Most consumers migrate to Internet buying only when they are dissatisfied with present solutions, but studies show that 75–80 percent of consumers like today's grocery stores, leaving only 20–25 percent potentially receptive to online buying and home delivery. In cities like New York, with a highly dense population and low quality and quantity of grocery store alternatives, the opportunity for Internet ordering and delivery is greater than in most markets, especially among affluent consumers living in high-rise apartments with a doorperson to accept deliveries.
- *Create e-tail strategies that match the lifestyle realities of consumer segments.* Once commonplace, home delivery of bread, milk, and other food products gave way to large, departmentalized grocery stores because of lifestyle shifts, many triggered by more women working outside the home. This led to the reality still true today—most consumers with money to spend on extras like home delivery aren't home during the day and have limited windows of time to accept deliveries. They also consume fewer groceries than other segments because they dine out more than they eat at home. The Webvan model required high sales volume for survival, which best matches the requirements of the "heavy user" segment of grocery shoppers. High-volume households, although diverse in many ways, tend to have lower incomes, large families, less computer access, and more motivation to buy at low prices. Webvan's appeal was greatest among a small segment of dual-income households that had someone to accept deliveries during the day.
- *Don't enter a low-price and highly efficient industry with a high-cost and inefficient strategy.* In a mature industry such as the grocery industry, the major chains are consolidating into a few very efficient giants. Their purchasing power, market coverage, and economies of scale can easily outmuscle miniscule e-tailers. Opportunities for new firms to enter and transform an industry usually occur when existing firms have high margins, are inefficient, or both. Webvan had to compete with grocery giants, such as Kroger, Albertsons, Safeway, and Publix, that operate with 25–27 percent margins and net profits that average 1.08 percent—stores that were facing difficulty themselves surviving against super-efficient Aldi, Wal*Mart, and Costco.

Webvan's fate was foreseeable to consumer analysts who understood why the home delivery system vanished thirty years ago and who examined market realities and the marketing principle of shifting functions to their most efficient level in channels of distribution, often the consumer. In the end, consumers vote with their wallets for the solutions that best meet their needs and wants. Webvan lost the election, but not without providing lessons useful for studying the future of Internet marketing.

Sources: Adapted from Roger Blackwell, "Why Webvan Went Bust," *Wall Street Journal* (July 16, 2001); "50 Coolest Websites," *Time* (June 1, 2004); and "Web Grocer Hits Refresh," *PC Magazine* (May 18, 2004).

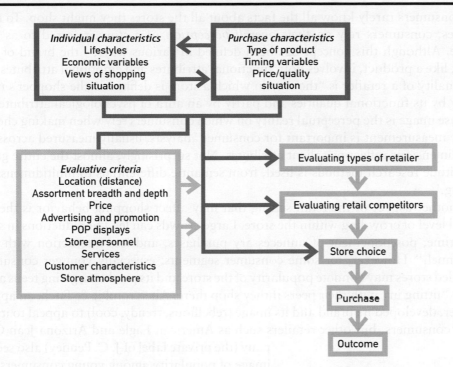

## The Purchase Decision Process

Looking closely at retailers that prosper and those that fail discloses much about how consumers decide where and how to purchase. In the choice process, consideration of *which type of retail concept* (Internet, direct mail, catalog, or location-based retailers) usually precedes choosing *which type of store* (mass retailer, hypermarket, department store, specialty store, and so on) and *which specific retailer to patronize* (Wal*Mart versus Target). Figure 5.1 shows how consumers usually decide whether to buy from a discount store or a department store before choosing between Wal*Mart and Target or between Saks and Nordstrom. In reality, however, retail choice is often an interactive process in which *type of outlet* and *specific retailer* affect each other.

The process of choosing a specific store involves matching consumer characteristics and purchase characteristics with store characteristics. An individual may use different criteria to evaluate which store best meets his or her needs depending on the type of purchase. Consumers compare retail and store options based on how they perceive each will perform on the various criteria.

Consumers don't always go through the entire series of choices, from retail concept to competitive retailers to specific store choice. Past experience and store image might take consumers right to the specific store choice. If you've purchased jeans at Express or the Gap in the past and liked the product and the experience, you may proceed from purchase need to store selection immediately. But if you are buying something for the first time or had a bad experience previously, then you may evaluate more alternatives.

Consumers in different market segments form images of stores based on their perceptions of the attributes they consider important. Research indicates that customers can quickly name a store (that is, retrieve from long-term memory) when asked what store comes to mind for specific attributes such as "lowest overall prices" and "most convenient." [14] These top-of-mind responses are associated strongly with customers' primary store choices within each segment of the market. Thus, it's very important to understand how images of retailers develop to place a store at the "top of the mind" within each consumer segment.

Consumers rarely know all the facts about all the stores they might shop. To make choices, consumers rely on *their overall perception of a store,* referred to as **store image.** Although this concept has been defined in various ways,[15] the brand of a retailer, like a product, involves both functional attributes and emotional attributes. The personality of a retailer is "the way in which a store is defined in the shopper's mind, partly by its functional qualities and partly by an aura of psychological attributes."[16] Because image is the perceptual reality on which consumers rely when making choices, image measurement is important for consumer analysts, usually measured across several dimensions reflecting salient attributes. Not surprisingly, almost the entire gamut of attitude research methods is used, from semantic differentials to multidimensional scaling.[17]

Another aspect of the retail setting that may affect shopping behavior is the perceived level of crowding within the store. Large crowds can lead to reductions in shopping time, postponement of unnecessary purchases, and less interaction with sales personnel.[18] However, for some consumer segments, especially younger consumers, crowded stores may connote popularity of the store and its products, giving teens a feeling of "fitting in" with their peers if they shop there. Abercrombie & Fitch, an apparel retailer, developed its brand and its image (rebellious, trendy, cool) to appeal to its targeted consumers, but other retailers such as American Eagle and Arizona Jean Company (the private label of J. C. Penney) also seek an image of popularity among young consumers, just not as "edgy" as A&F. Look at each example in Figure 5.2 and describe how you believe consumers would perceive the image of each retailer, based on these ads. These retailers base their appeal on functional attributes of quality products as well as on an emotional connection with the culture of their target market. Forever 21, a mall retailer targeting teenage girls, may be perceived as trendy and low priced, even if consumers believe the products sold are more likely to be "disposable fashions." Which of these store images best fits your own personal preferences? You may also want to check sales reports to see which of these retailers is currently most successful, based on "comps" (sales in retail stores open for more than a year).

## Determinants of Retailer Success or Failure

Although determinants of store choice vary by market segment and by product class, the most important attributes determine which retailers succeed and which ones fail. These determinants fall into the following categories, as noted in Figure 5.1: (1) location, (2) nature and quality of assortment, (3) price, (4) advertising and promotion, (5) sales personnel, (6) services offered, (7) physical store attributes, (8) nature of store clientele, (9) point-of-purchase displays, and

**FIGURE 5.2a** Which Store Image Is Most Appealing to You?

**FIGURES 5.2b and c** Which Store Image Is Most Appealing to You?

(10) consumer logistics. Each of these variables is important in determining consumer choice, although the weight given them varies by market segment.

## Location

For most consumers, location is perceived in terms of time and hassle as well as actual distance. Cognitive maps or consumer perceptions of store locations and shopping areas are more important than actual location[19] because they represent the distance and time consumers *perceive* they have to travel to reach and shop at the store. Consumers generally overestimate both functional (actual) distance and time.

Variations between cognitive and actual distance are related to factors such as ease of parking in the area, quality of merchandise offered by area stores, checkout procedures, display and presentation of merchandise, and ease of driving to an area. Other factors that affect the cognitive maps of consumers include the price of merchandise and helpfulness of salespeople.[20] In some markets, a good location may be defined by the ability to walk or take public transportation. In Japan, for example, some retailers are called "railroad retailers" because they are clustered near major rail stations that nearly all consumers use for commuting to work. When retailers are equidistant from a consumer's origin, consumers choose retailers that are more clustered.[21]

## Nature and Quality of Assortment

Depth, breadth, and quality of assortment are important determinants of store choice. This is especially true for stores located in shopping centers.[22] One reason specialty stores such as Chico's, bebe, and Victoria's Secret have been so successful is their ability to design and present dominant assortments, whether defined on the basis of classification, end use, or lifestyle (Figure 5.3a).[23] These specialty stores have narrow but deep selections, usually appealing to a specific niche or segment of consumers. By developing "fans" for one line of merchandise, a retailer may be able to extend its appeal in one line, such as apparel, to another product line, such as fragrances at Victoria's Secret (see Figure 5.3b).

Dominant assortment of merchandise is also critical to the success of mass merchandisers known as "category killers," which specialize in one category of merchandise. Examples include Home Depot and Lowe's (home improvement), Virgin Megastores (music), Circuit City (electronics), LensCrafters (eyeglasses), and Staples (office supplies). Category killers and niche retailers competed effectively with department stores, which typically have slower inventory turns, high operating expenses, and larger inventory losses, but are experiencing more difficulty competing with value merchants such as Wal*Mart with their relentless emphasis on efficiency, cost reduction, and disciplined inventory management.

## Price

The importance of price as a determinant of store patronage varies by type of product. Supermarkets have placed great emphasis on price since the 1930s, when King Kullen on Long Island, New York, pioneered the concept. The importance of price depends on the nature of the buyer. Some customers preferring factors such as convenience will, in effect, trade off that consideration against higher prices.[24] Keep in mind that it is the consumer's perception of price that is usually more important than actual price.[25] So, if "total price" involves time spent commuting to the retail location and waiting in line, the consumer may still judge the store that doesn't require these activities as cheaper even if it charges more.

Price may be the most misunderstood variable in retailing. When Wal*Mart overtook Sears as the largest retailer in the United States, Sears cut its prices in a failed

FIGURE 5.3a  Specialty stores like bebe appeal to highly defined customer segments.

FIGURE 5.3b  Victoria's Secret's New Fragrances on Display

attempt to win back customers. What Sears failed to understand is that Wal*Mart not only has the policy of "Everyday Low Prices," it also has human resource policies to implement their customer policy ("Treat every customer as a guest") and logistics systems (increasingly based on radio frequency identification [RFID] technology) to ensure that the products consumers want are on the shelves when consumers want them. Consumer analysts must take care to avoid confusing "lowest price" with "acceptable range of price" as a determinant of store choice. Market Facts 5.2 shows that consumers prefer prices that are within an acceptable range (combined with other attributes that consumers prefer) to prices that are always lowest. A common mistake of retailers is to emphasize lowest price to appeal to the minority of consumers who value lowest price the most at the expense of losing the majority of consumers who prefer other attributes to lowest price.

For many years, retailers often relied on price to build patronage, a strategy that is increasingly questioned, despite its widespread use.[26] Price promotion may only shift demand from one time period to another for a store, or from one brand to another within the store without increasing a store's total sales. Nevertheless, price advertising is frequently used to maintain competitive parity, based on a belief that market share between competing retailers is influenced by advertising the lowest price. Although a segment of consumers is affected by price advertising, loyalty may last only until the next set of advertised prices attracts that segment elsewhere. Detailed scanner data on sales and changes in price are now available for all types of consumer goods, making it easier for marketers to discover what works[27] and to turn information into strategic customer-focused actions.[28]

Marketers need to address how market segments respond to short-term changes in brand prices and promotions.[29] Questions about the relative effectiveness of price promotions, advertising, sales promotion, and so forth are increasingly analyzed with scanner data.[30] Research indicates that price promotions and, to a lesser degree, in-store displays have brand substitution effects but also store substitution effects on a retailer and its competitors. Ultimately, consumers rely on their overall image of a retailer to filter the effects of price advertising.[31]

## MARKET FACTS 5.2

## The Importance of Price in Product Decisions

**How Consumers React to the Importance of Paying the Lowest Price Versus Paying a Price in the Range They Expect to Pay\* in Brand Choice**

| Product Category | Lowest Price (%) | | | Price Range (%) | | |
|---|---|---|---|---|---|---|
| | Total | Female | Male | Total | Female | Male |
| Television | 57 | 55 | 59 | 80 | 84 | 74 |
| Prescriptions | 63 | 64 | 60 | 58 | 62 | 53 |
| Sweatshirts | 58 | 60 | 56 | 75 | 79 | 70 |
| Jeans | 59 | 59 | 60 | 74 | 79 | 68 |

\* Research indicated that women evaluate products more on expected price range and men evaluate more on lowest price.

Source: Roger Blackwell and Tina Blackwell, *Understanding Your Customer, Part I* (International Mass Retail Association, 1997), 24.

## Advertising and Promotion for Positioning of the Retail Brand

Advertising and other forms of promotion are important tools to create a retail brand—a summary of consumer perceptions about the store and overall image. Advertising to create a retail brand includes image and information. When a retailer creates its initial image in a market or attempts to position itself differently than in the past, the advertising should emphasize image. **Image advertising** uses *visual components and words that help consumers form an expectation about their experience in the store and about what kinds of consumers will be satisfied with the store's experience.* You can observe that objective in the ad in Figure 5.4, which positions an image of class, style, and sophistication. **Information advertising,** on the other hand, *provides details about products, prices, hours of store operation, locations, and other attributes that might influence purchase decisions,* as seen in the weekly circular shown in Figure 5.5.

Retail advertising appears to be evolving to an emphasis on image advertising and nonprice information instead of the price advertising that was often the practice of retailers in the past. If consumers need specific information about locations or hours of operation and perhaps prices, such information is usually available at the retailer's website. This frees funds for brand building or positioning advertising in broadcast and print media.

**FIGURE 5.4** Image Advertising: Class, Style, and Sophistication

The focus of retailing has also evolved to focus on marketing. Historically, retail firms emphasized merchandising—buying the right merchandise, displaying and stocking it correctly, and pricing and taking markdowns at the right time. Most retailers gave little attention to marketing activities outside the store, except for price advertising. In an effort to change perceptions of the store and attract consumers, however, retailers are now adding marketing activities, such as special hours and services for preferred customers and communicating with segments through computerized databases, often tied to loyalty programs and CRM programs, as you read in Chapter 2.

### Sales Personnel

*You Win with People!* was the title of Ohio State University head football coach Woody Hayes's book on winning—a philosophy as true in retailing as it is in football. Although much of retailing is now characterized by self-selection without the intervention of a salesperson, knowledgeable and helpful salespeople are still important when choosing a store or shopping center.[32] European stores recognize the importance of personal selling, typically hiring individuals who attend apprentice programs and complete specific educational and test requirements. In the United States, the low unemployment rates associated with the Internet boom of the late 1990s caused retailers to hire minimally qualified and minimally trained personnel, who frequently failed to meet consumer expectations. When the economy softened, retailers were able to hire

**FIGURE 5.5** Information Advertising: Weekly Sales Circular

better personnel and many began to revamp and upgrade their training and motivation programs to improve customer service. One innovative firm has been the Cracker Barrel Old Country Store, which offers a combination of onsite and distance learning to its associates. Store personnel who are motivated to advance in the organization complete modules on topics ranging from customer service to store operations that eventually groom employees to advance as trainers, supervisors, and store managers.

What makes a salesperson effective? Research shows that although personal characteristics of salespeople (such as personality, temperament, age, and appearance) have some relationship to performance, skill levels and motivation are even more important.[33] These characteristics can be influenced through increased training and experience, visionary leadership, and corporate culture.

What this means is that sales success is determined by two factors: (1) the relationship during the transaction, and (2) the persuasion strategies used.[34] The salesperson's ability to win a buyer's confidence and successfully complete a negotiation process is affected by the following.

- *Perceived knowledge and expertise.* A salesperson's ability to exert persuasive influence is affected by his or her perceived expertise. When salespeople are seen as knowledgeable, consumers are more likely to buy a product based on their trust and confidence in the associate.[35]
- *Perceived trustworthiness.* A buyer's prior beliefs about a seller's trustworthiness affect the entire negotiation process. Buyer-seller agreements, as well as buyer willingness to make concessions, are enhanced when high levels of perceived trustworthiness are present. Bargaining toughness is viewed more positively when trust is strong.[36]
- *Customer knowledge.* Several recent studies have shown that the more familiar a salesperson is with his or her customer, the more likely he or she is to close a sale.[37] Knowledgeable sales associates can describe and classify different types of customers (including knowledge about traits, motives, and behavior) and have information about other sales experiences to guide them in similar situations.
- *Adaptability.* A sophisticated customer knowledge structure, in turn, seems to be related to adaptability. With this structure in place, a salesperson is able to respond to individual customer needs and changing expectations.

Even though consumer confidence in retail salespeople is often low, some stores find ways to recruit, train, and motivate high-quality sales personnel. Home Depot achieved success as a do-it-yourself home-improvement store partly because of its policy of training salespeople to walk the floors and help consumers, communicated to customers with its slogan, "You can do it. We can help." Its salespeople are often recruited from the building trades (including plumbers, carpenters, and electricians) and encouraged to spend time helping customers,[38] explaining to them what products they need to complete their projects.

People are also at the center of the strategy of Starbucks, the mega-star of the world of coffee and snacks, and one of the world's fastest growing specialty retailers. The firm provides stock options, even for its part-time workers, and tremendous training programs. The result? Employee turnover that is half or less than that of other food operations. CEO Howard Schultz explains, "Our only sustainable competitive advantage is the quality of our work force. We're building a national retail company by creating pride in—and a stake in—the outcome of our labor."[39] Following this example, when Domino's Pizza observed service problems, it implemented a program in 2005 to reduce turnover among management, believing well-trained and motivated managers are the key to better frontline personnel. Even when a firm maintains policies that are fair and customer-centric, it depends on its employees to implement the policies. When employees don't implement the policies, not only is the image of the firm harmed, but consumers may also be harmed, as you can see in Buyer Beware 5.2, which describes the continuing problem of discrimination by some firms.

## Services Offered

Convenient self-service facilities, ease of merchandise return, delivery, credit, and overall good service have all been found to be considerations affecting store image. This varies depending on the type of outlet and consumer expectations. For instance, Neiman Marcus and other upscale department stores provide personal shoppers to assist customers in assembling complete outfits, including accessories and shoes. A personal shopper will also proactively call a customer when the store receives merchandise that may coordinate well with his or her existing wardrobe. Harrods and Selfridges in the United Kingdom, C&A in Belgium, and Coles Myer in Australia are just a few of the firms that focus on providing excellent service to attract consumers. Consumer Behavior and Marketing 5.3 describes how Loblaws, Canada's largest supermarket chain, has become a leader and innovator in providing consumer services ranging from financial services to fitness centers, as well as nonfood products and its highly successful store brand President's Choice.[40] Although many consumers buy manufacturers' brands because of the uncertainty associated with buying private label brands,[41] Loblaws reduces this perceived risk by delivering an overall satisfying experience to its customers.

## Physical Store Attributes

Elevators, lighting, air conditioning, convenient and visible washrooms, layout, aisle placement and width, parking facilities, carpeting, and architecture affect store image and choice. *The physical properties of the retail environment designed to create an effect on consumer purchases* are often referred to as **store atmospherics**.[42] From the marketer's perspective, a store's atmospherics can help shape both the direction and duration of consumers' attention, and increase the odds that a consumer will purchase products that otherwise might go unnoticed. The retail environment can also express store character and image to consumers. Finally, the store setting can elicit particular emotional reactions, such as pleasure and arousal, that can influence the amount of time and money consumers spend while shopping.[43]

Atmospherics can involve multiple senses to attract consumer purchase behavior, forming a "gestalt" of perception in which consumers perceive cues from the environment holistically and rate retailers higher when the cues are congruent.[44] Music can affect purchase in several ways.[45] Music played in a store at a low volume may

## Dealing with Discrimination

Discrimination against African American, Latino, and other consumers continues to be a major problem. In a study by the Association of Community Organizations for Reform Now (ACORN), African American consumers were twice as likely as whites to be denied home loans. The study found that 20 percent of black mortgage applicants were rejected in 2003, compared to only 10 percent of whites. For Latino applicants, the denial rate was 17 percent. "There continues to be redlining," said Brian Kettering, an official of ACORN.

Milwaukee was the toughest place for minorities to obtain loans, according to the ACORN study of 120 metropolitan areas, with blacks rejected four times as often as whites and Latinos denied three times as often. However, other lenders, such as Fannie Mae and Freddie Mac, have stepped forward to seek minority borrowers with education efforts and pools of cash designated for minority borrowers, recognizing their growing importance as states such as California and Texas become a majority of minorities.

The discrimination may be subtle rather than the blatant redlining of the past, but today's lenders find other ways to deny loans. Although credit scores exclude race and income in their calculations, African Americans and Latinos may be less likely to have credit cards, affecting the credit scores that influence mortgage loans. One large title insurance company, First American Corporation of California, tries to address that problem through alternative credit scoring for buyers who lack traditional credit histories. Some lenders have sought to teach minorities about qualifying for mortgages, although decades of discrimination have left lasting effects, creating a need for marketers to train personnel well to avoid such practices. Consumers who recognize the potential for discrimination must arm themselves with information and resist intimidation when it occurs.

Other types of loans sometimes also discriminate against minorities, according to class action suits alleging discrimination in car loans by banks and automobile company financing units. The suits allege that car dealers tend to mark up loans more frequently and aggressively with black borrowers than with white borrowers, and that the banks' policies enable the discrimination. A study used by plaintiffs found that African American car buyers paid loan markups averaging $1,229 each compared to $867 a loan for white consumers with similar credit histories. Class action suits and the settlements they sometimes stimulate are methods consumers use to fight discriminatory practices.

Sources: Based on Jeff Ostrowski, "Blacks Are More Likely to Face Rejection For Mortgages, Study Shows," *Knight-Ridder Tribune Business News* (October 15, 2004), 1; and Lee Hawkins Jr., "Banks Are in Talks About Bias Suits Over Auto Loans," *Wall Street Journal* (January 17, 2005), A3.

encourage more social interaction between shoppers and sales staff. Faster or slower music may affect perceptions of time spent in the store, and classical music may give a more upscale or higher-priced image.[46] Music tempo (slow versus fast) also affects shopping. Research indicates that slow-tempo music increases both shopping time and expenditures compared with fast-tempo music in grocery stores.[47] In restaurants, patrons spent nearly 25 percent more time and nearly 50 percent more on bar purchases when the tempo of the music being played was slow.[48]

Colors within the store can also influence consumers' perceptions and behavior. Consumers have rated retail interiors using cool colors as more positive, attractive, and relaxing than those using warmer colors, which are sometimes most suitable for a store's exterior or display windows to draw customers into the store.[49] Although color may not affect perceptions of merchandise quality, it does affect how up to date consumers believe merchandise displays are.

## Loblaws Supermarkets Wow Customers with Extras

When you enter its front doors, Loblaws wants you to shed all your views on what a grocery store should or shouldn't be. Of course, Canada's largest food distributor (with over 1,000 stores and several formats) sells all the grocery and produce items found in grocery stores throughout the world, but the extras it offers wow consumers and industry experts alike. The leader in the ancillary service arena, Loblaws rents store space to dry-cleaners, beer and liquor stores, and coffee shops, and it offers in-store pharmacies and banking centers to its customers. Though other stores have followed suit, Loblaws upped the ante by offering financial services and video game and cell phone sales outlets, and leasing space to clothing chain Club Monaco in some of its stores.

Loblaws raised the bar of service extras by including a 7,000-square-foot fitness club in some stores and by increasing its newest stores to 140,000 square feet, incorporating many features of European hypermarkets. Loblaws' GoodLife Fitness Club lets consumers work out, take aerobics classes, sit in a sauna, leave their children in the day care center, and buy their groceries for the day or week in one visit. And time-pressured female consumers, who look for creative ways to juggle a multitude of responsibilities and pressures, like the concept so much that the company plans

to roll out GoodLife Fitness clubs throughout Canada. For years its President's Choice brand, which has an emphasis on high quality and design and is on over two thousand products, has achieved higher market share than manufacturers' brands in most categories, accounting for over 25 percent of store sales as of 2005. Loblaws also offers a "blue line" of products to especially target consumers concerned with the environment and staying healthy, and the company is a leader in ethnic and organic products, appealing to Canada's increasingly diverse population.

Loblaws' strategy is to build customer loyalty and sales with superior ancillary services in addition to great products. And the strategy is working. Even now that U.S. giants Costco and Wal*Mart have entered the Canadian market, Loblaws continues to post rapid growth. "They're like a social laboratory, always trying things out, modifying, making sure the adjacencies are right," said John O. Winter, president of John Winter Associates, a Toronto retail consulting firm. "Every time you go into one of their stores, you find something new. The newest ones have bands playing, cooking classes—and my daughter has had her birthday party there for the last three years. There are all these things to bring you in. It's one-stop shopping taken to the ultimate."

Sources: Based partly on Joel A. Baglole, "Loblaw Supermarkets Add Fitness Clubs to Offerings," *Wall Street Journal* (December 27, 1999), B4; Susan Thorn, "Loblaws 84 Years Old, Still Canada's Biggest Grocer By Far," www.icsc.org (June 2003); and company statistics from www.loblaws.com.

### Store Clientele

The type of person who shops in a store affects consumer purchase intention because of the tendency to match one's self-image with that of the store. One West Coast computer store is known for its rude sales personnel and junky appearance, but thousands of technology buffs throng to the store because of its wide selection of merchandise and public perceptions that it is the preferred store of techies.[50]

Some customers may also avoid stores because they do not want to associate with or be associated with the store or who they perceive is the store's clientele. Some people may prefer specialty stores over mass marketers, such as dollar stores or Wal*Mart, for that reason, although it appears that the number of consumers who consider it smart to shop at value-oriented retailers is increasing. Young consumers may avoid a retailer because it has "too many old people there," and some older consumers may avoid stores that attract "too many young people." Restaurants frequently reflect a trendy belief about what type of people are likely to be the clientele and thus offer positive or negative reasons for patronage. Some consumers may avoid restaurants that are believed to attract children, whereas other market segments are attracted to restaurants that are kid-friendly.

## Point-of-Purchase Materials

Point-of-purchase (POP) displays and signs can increase the odds of capturing consumers' attention, and thereby stimulate purchase and increase sales.[51] Some reports indicate that up to 70 percent of purchase decisions in grocery and drug stores are made in store aisles, often aided by the prompt of a POP attention grabber.[52]

For agencies specializing in creating POP displays and campaigns, times are lucrative for several reasons. First, POP materials are inexpensive compared to other forms of promotion. Second, they reach people where they buy the products. And third, they add atmosphere to retail stores. Moreover, informative and easier-to-use POP materials can partly help offset declines in the quantity and quality of retail salespeople.[53] This is when a YES (which stands for "Your Extra Salesman") POP unit might come in handy. This kind of unit, which hangs on the shelf, works like a window shade. Product information is printed on a self-retracting shade that rolls down from a canister unit.[54] POP designers are pushing the envelope of creativity even further by using digitally enhanced in-store marketing materials, including the following.

### E-THEATER

"Retailing is theater," Stanley Marcus once observed, but now it's e-theater. That's what customers experienced on Friday nights in the summer of 2005 in more than 2,600 Wal*Mart stores when AOL televised its original Broadband Rocks concert series on the Wal*Mart Television Network, an in-store television system operated by Premier Retail Networks. National attractions can become local events and help convert customers into fans with the undeniable power of music, sports, and celebrities. Malls and retailers use live performances during holidays to attract customers and create moods that stimulate sales. Now that process is digitally enabled. Whereas television, sports, and news once kept customers at home, today e-theater draws them back into stores.

### d-POP

Digital point of purchase (d-POP) is emerging in major discount chains, grocery chains, and restaurants. A d-POP device consists of one or several digital flat-panel displays, which communicate through moving text, images, video, and sound effects. One of the first uses of d-POP was by Donatos Pizza in explaining its low-carb "NoDough" pizza, tortilla sandwiches, and other menu innovations to customers. Not only did the display sway consumers to purchase the promoted items, it sparked conversation and contributed to consumer interest in trying new items on their next visit. Whereas traditional POP involves a battle to get stores to place displays properly and on schedule (which can then be moved or torn down by competitors) and usually take months from inception to implementation, d-POP gets 100 percent compliance in nanoseconds because new "signs" are installed via the Internet from corporate headquarters.

## COMPUTER-ENHANCED MERCHANDISING

An example of digitally enhanced in-store marketing is the Isee2 program of Brussels-based Overseas Diamonds, Inc., which installs a "Beauty Box" in jewelry retailers allowing customers to compare the appearance of diamonds. A large, magnified image of the diamond appears on an adjacent computer monitor, demonstrating the diamond's clarity, color, and cut to consumers. The ability for consumers to see the fine details of a diamond focuses their attention on the attributes of beauty and light that are most important to consumers while also building trust in the store and greater satisfaction in the sale. Using a separate "ID Box," the unique ID number of a diamond (laser-engraved to deter thieves and thwart terrorists who use diamonds as currency), can be linked to a website that provides the diamond's "birth certificate," which shows its country of origin, when it was mined, and its progress through the supply chain. The Isee2 system works only with high-quality diamonds that are subject to close-up examination; stores that use the apparatus report price premiums as high as 80 percent over similar commodity diamonds.

## DIGITAL SELF-SERVICE

Self-checkouts rang up $128 billion of purchases in 2004, and the IHL Consulting Group forecasts a rise to $1.3 trillion by 2007. Grocery chains now report self-checkout accounting for as much as 15 to 40 percent of sales in some stores using very clunky technology, but RFID tags placed on individual items will soon allow customers to pass their carts through "antennae" instantly registering and totaling their purchases. RFID tags were introduced in retailers at the case and pallet level, but are expected to be placed on individual items when costs fall to one cent per tag, meaning the mess of cash registers, cashiers, and baggers at the front of stores will be replaced with better store design and more customer-centric merchandising.

## Consumer Logistics

Consumption analysis focuses on more than what people buy; it examines how people shop at stores. **Consumer logistics**[55] is the *speed and ease with which consumers move through the retail and shopping process,* from the time they begin the shopping process to the time they take products home. Consumer logistics examines store characteristics (such as signage, lighting, customer service, and checkout), keeping peoples' shopping behaviors in mind. It contains seven primary consumer stages: (1) preparation to shop; (2) arriving at the store; (3) entering the store; (4) movement through the store; (5) checkout; (6) travel home and home-warehousing; and (7) inventory stock-outs, which prompt repurchase. These stages, as seen in Table 5.2, cover location of stores, store layouts, aisle width, POP displays, checkouts, traffic in the store, customer service and personnel, payment methods, signage, and safety of stores from the consumer's perspective. Retailers can use this list to segment and organize research they have done on these topics and how they affect store sales and consumer satisfaction.

The purchase process is facilitated, positively or negatively, by consumer logistics. For example, in-store traffic flow can affect sales. Crowding in a store often causes people to be less satisfied, and widening aisles may help to increase consumer willingness to buy, especially in shopping situations that require shopping carts. If this is not physically possible, providing consumers with some choice about handling the crowded conditions may cause them to be more positive about the store.[56] Offering an

| 1. PREPARATION | 2. ARRIVING AT STORE | 3. ENTER STORE | 4. MOVING THROUGH THE STORE | 5. CHECKOUT | 6. GOING HOME AND STORAGE | 7. INVENTORY REPLENISHMENT |
|---|---|---|---|---|---|---|
| • Coupons | • Outstore environment | • Greeters | • Layout of products | • Amount of time in line | • Getting out to car | • Needed to start process again |
| • Advertising | • Parking lot | • Getting and separating carts | • Changes in product locations | • Number of people in lane | • Ease of exiting parking lot | • Satisfaction/ dissatisfaction with product, brand, store |
| • Shopping circulars brands | • Safety— patrol on duty | • Entry—cluttered or clean | • Signage for sections | • Choosing "best" line | • Products in car | |
| • Lists—getting products and stores on list | • Signage | • Cameras | • Lighting | • Size of aisles | • Where put items at home | |
| • Planning route to travel | • Lighting | • First stops | • Music | • Self-checkout | • Pantry loading | |
| • Point of departure | • Clientele | • Comfort with size | • Store personnel | • Payment methods | • Disposal problems | |
| • Bundling of stops | • Crowded | • Familiarity | • Assistance/help mechanisms | • Loading on belt | | |
| • Hours of operation | • Weather | • Ability to see through store | • Product selection | • Monitoring prices | | |
| • Perception of how busy it will be | | | • Carts | • Price checks/ accuracy | | |
| • Needs of products | | | • Aisles | • Redeeming coupons | | |
| • Looking at catalog from store if available | | | • Promotions or POP | • Bagging | | |
| • Perceptions about store | | | • Price evaluations | • Scanning prices | | |
| | | | • Brand evaluation | • Security | | |
| | | | • Who shopping with them | • Hairpins | | |
| | | | • Size of store | | | |
| | | | • Handicaps | | | |
| | | | • Reading labels | | | |
| | | | • Traffic in store | | | |

express checkout lane for small purchases is an option, with the self-checkout lanes eventually dominating when RFID is economically feasible. When that happens, stores can be redesigned, replacing cash registers in the front of the store with seasonal or other high-margin product lines.

In general, stores are adding technology, personnel, and training to increase service and decrease the time consumers spend waiting in the store and at checkout. Target, Kohl's, and other retailers place barcode scanners throughout their stores for shoppers who want to verify the current price. If a product is not marked or is on sale, consumers can decide whether to buy or not before they reach the checkout lane. Waiting in line is a frustrating experience for consumers, especially when they see unused resources, such as empty tables in a restaurant or closed checkout lanes in a grocery store.[57] Offering some sort of distraction while people wait (such as small impulse items and magazines to read) or moving personnel from the back of the store to open more checkout lanes when needed makes the shopping experience more satisfactory and increases the likelihood of repeat patronage. You can see how many of the items discussed in this section affect the consumer logistics process.

What consumers expect and demand from a purchase situation changes depending on what type of store they are visiting. For example, as time pressures on consumers increase, they search for ways to increase the efficiency of their shopping patterns.[58] Let's now take a look at *where* consumer purchases are occurring around the world and how retailers are adapting their strategies to meet changing consumer behaviors.

## The Changing Retail Landscape

Consumers want to purchase goods and services from a variety of retailing formats. This creates the opportunity for successful marketers to implement **multichannel retailing**—*reaching diverse consumer segments through a variety of formats based on their lifestyles and shopping preferences*. Multichannel retailing includes many alternatives: location-based retailing, direct selling, direct marketing, and Internet retailing. Most retailers find that their best customers are those that use multiple formats. It's easier for marketers to change their retail format to fit the lifestyles of consumers than trying to change the lifestyles and behavior of consumers to fit existing or emerging formats. Less successful retailers rely on merchandising techniques and markdowns to move goods rather than changing to have what consumers want.[59]

### Location-Based Retailing

Consumers buy most products from retailers that have a physical location—a store that's free-standing or housed in a mall, strip center, central market, or central business district. Location-based formats include specialty stores, grocery and drug stores, and convenience stores. In recent years, value-oriented retailers, such as "category killers," discount stores, superstores, and hypermarkets, have experienced the greatest growth.

#### VALUE-ORIENTED RETAILERS

Value retailers usually offer consumers lower prices than other forms of retailing because of the large economies of scale generated by their high sales volume.[60] Many consumers also find them convenient because they can buy many different types of products in one store or see a large selection of items, in the case of the "category killers" (also called "big-box" stores).

One form of location-based retailing that thrives in nations other than the United States is the **hypermarket**. These stores *incorporate breakthrough technology in handling materials from a warehouse-operating profile that provides both a warehouse feel for consumers as well as strong price appeal*. Examples include Carrefour, based in France and found in nations throughout the world, Gigante in Mexico, LuLu in the Middle East, and Pick 'n Pay in South Africa. Although the United States does not have true hypermarkets, many of the principles of this form of retailing have been incorporated by Meijer and Wal*Mart Supercenters, as well as big-box stores such as Lowe's and Home Depot.

#### THE SHOPPING MALL

On average, U.S. consumers are visiting malls less often than they used to, and when they do, they visit about half the number of stores that they used to—three and a half stores per trip as opposed to seven.[61] Diminished leisure time, traffic congestion, increased stress levels, economic fears, concerns about security, and Internet shopping are some of the causes of the decline.

Yet this has not stopped U.S. developers from building new retail space. In the 1970s, there existed eight square feet of retail space per person, and today that number has increased to more than twenty square feet. Similar trends are occurring in Europe and Australia, although the amount of retail space per person is still much lower in other nations than in the United States.

Regional shopping malls have progressed dramatically since J. C. Nichols built the first one, Country Club Plaza, in Kansas City in 1922. The United States currently has 28,500 shopping centers—far more than any other nation—up from 2,000 in 1957. Although the Country Club Plaza is still the premier shopping venue for Kansas City, the ultimate mall today is found in Edmonton, Alberta, Canada. The West Edmonton Mall, generally recognized as the world's largest, was the first mega-mall, with 5.2 million square feet and 800 stores and services. It features a 5-acre World Waterpark (the largest indoor water park in the world), 19 movie theaters, a hotel, 110 food outlets, dozens of amusement rides, an ice rink, a miniature golf course, a chapel, a car dealership, and a zoo. Consumers travel from across North America to shop and play for a few days in this destination shopping center.

Others have followed suit. Bluewater, Europe's crown jewel of shopping centers, can be found seventeen minutes outside London and two hours from Paris via the Chunnel rail link. Another giant, the Mall of America in suburban Minneapolis, boasts 520 stores (including Bloomingdale's, Macy's, and Nordstrom) as well as Camp Snoopy (the nation's largest indoor amusement park) and Underwater Adventures (a 1.2-million gallon walkthrough aquarium). In 2005, the 4.2-million-square-foot mall announced an expansion phase, expecting to almost double its size.

The newest versions of shopping centers are frequently described as *lifestyle centers*. An example is Easton in Columbus, Ohio, which features almost four million square feet of retail space built around a "Town Center" designed to act as a gathering place for shoppers, where consumers can eat, be entertained, and watch their children play in the large outdoor fountains. Easton celebrates the traditional shopping patterns found in small towns across North America a century earlier. Instead of enclosed malls that control consumer activities and traffic patterns, Easton incorporates an outdoor shopping district, in which pedestrians and vehicles coexist, with a "retailtainment" mall featuring a movie theater, food court, and specialty merchants. The complex includes innovative local restaurants and stores such as Brio Italian Bistro and Max & Erma's, night clubs and taverns focused on different age groups, as well as national chains such as Cheesecake Factory, Crate & Barrel, and Nordstrom. It also includes value retailers as perimeter stores (including CompUSA, Target, and PETsMART) in addition to luxury apartment homes, an ice-skating rink, soccer fields, and a twenty-four-hour fitness center. Easton and other lifestyle centers are more than just a place to shop—they are a "place to be."

## Direct Marketing

A growing percentage of consumers' shopping and buying activities now occur in some place other than a store. **Direct marketing** refers to *the strategies used to reach consumers somewhere other than a store* (e.g., in the home, office, or on an airplane). Direct marketing is growing in the United States and in most developing countries of the world, including China, India, and some countries in Africa. Compared with the general population, in-home shoppers are somewhat younger with slightly higher household incomes, have above average education and income, and are more likely to live in smaller towns or rural areas. Most are active retail shoppers who shop at home for reasons other than deliberate avoidance of the store or shopping mall.[62] Yet direct marketing is also of interest to older consumers, home-bound or disabled consumers, and other special segments of the population. The items most frequently ordered are apparel, magazines, home accessories, home maintenance and kitchen equipment, and home office supplies.

There are six methods of direct marketing: (1) direct selling; (2) direct mail ads; (3) direct mail catalogs; (4) telemarketing; (5) direct response ads; and (6) interactive electronic media, including notably, the Internet. Direct marketing, in all its forms, involves direct contact with consumers. Although credit cards, loyalty programs, and scanner data are increasingly making it possible for stores to collect data about consumers, direct marketing offers the possibility of selecting specific target markets through the use of specialized mailing lists, databases, or media. This permits customized appeals and creative strategy based on the lifestyles and needs of the target market segments.

## DIRECT SELLING

**Direct selling** is defined as *any form of face-to-face contact between a salesperson and a customer away from a fixed retail location.* Although accurate statistics are hard to come by, direct personal selling now accounts for about 2 percent of all general merchandise sales and mostly takes place in the home or workplace. You may have met with a sales consultant, or hosted a party for Amway, Mary Kay, Pampered Chef, Creative Memories, or others. Avon's door-to-door selling method might seem like a blast from the past, the company still relies on its sales force for about 98 percent of its sales.[63] However, Avon will also spend up to $90 million in global advertising to promote its website.[64] The Longaberger Company utilizes nearly 60,000 independent home consultants located in all U.S. states who sell its handcrafted baskets, pottery, wrought iron, fabric accessories, specialty foods, and other products directly to customers. Look at Consumer Behavior and Marketing 5.4 and you may think you're looking at one of its baskets, but it's actually the corporate headquarters—a giant basket-shaped building from which the $833 million enterprise is controlled.

### CONSUMER BEHAVIOR AND MARKETING 5.4

## Longaberger—The Power of Direct Selling

Courtesy of The Longaberger Company Home Office, Newark, Ohio

Situated on a parklike setting off State Route 16 in Newark, Ohio, the basket-shaped corporate headquarters of the Longaberger Company is visited by thousands each year, including Longaberger home consultants, customers, and tourists who desire a closer look at the one-of-a-kind structure. Although bankers and contractors initially balked at the idea of an office building shaped like a basket, the building's notoriety has turned into one of many successful marketing tools for the company because it frequently appears in magazines, travel guides, and television programs.

Longaberger is the premier maker of American-made handcrafted baskets and other quality home and lifestyle products. Annual sales of 8 million baskets and a total of 30 million pottery, dinnerware, wrought-iron, and other home products are accomplished by nearly 70,000 independent home consultants nationwide who sell Longaberger products directly to customers. Led by CEO Tami Longaberger, the company was ranked the eighteenth largest woman-owned U.S. company by *Working Woman* magazine in 2001.

## DIRECT MAIL ADS

Shopping in response to direct mail appeals has been shown to meet real consumer needs, such as availability of merchandise, convenience, low price, and better quality. Although many people often assume wrongly that direct mail is an unwanted invasion into the home, polls consistently show that well over half of consumers welcome direct mail, open it, and read it—although interest declines with increasing education and income levels.

## DIRECT MAIL CATALOGS

Catalog buying has experienced dramatic growth in recent years, averaging about 7 percent per year growth in sales (at least twice as high as location-based retailers). According to studies, more women than men shop from catalogs, more than two-thirds of catalog shoppers have attended college, they're technology savvy, and they spend more time and money on leisure events. In North America, catalogs currently appeal to upscale consumers, whereas in many other countries the catalog is preferred more by downscale consumers.

## TELEMARKETING

Nearly 20 percent of direct response orders now are triggered by a telephone call (referred to as outbound telemarketing). Homes can be targeted with great demographic precision using census data available within geographic zip codes. In spite of the irritation reported by many consumers and their willingness to place their names on the national "do not call" registry, some firms are successful with telemarketing if the callers are skillful and sensitive. **Inbound telemarketing**, on the other hand, refers to the *use of a toll-free number to place orders directly*. The heaviest users are younger, better-educated families with higher incomes and children at home.[65] Telemarketing works best with present customers (a customer database indicates prospects' interests and preferences), often generated from catalog or direct mail.

## DIRECT RESPONSE ADS

About 20 percent of in-home purchases are stimulated each year by newspaper, magazine, and yellow pages ads that call for a direct response such as the return of an order form. But big growth in this category is occurring in television home shopping both in the United States and abroad. The on-screen sell seems to work well with a variety of products, especially when there is a need for demonstration. When Kodak introduced its new Cameo zoom lens camera on the QVC shopping network, 9,700 were sold in just seventy minutes.[66] Kodak also benefited from pitching its related products at the same time.

Add up all these trends and you may conclude that the polarity of retailing described in Market Facts 5.3 describes much of what is happening and can be expected to happen to retail trade and service marketing in the future.

## Purchase Behavior in the E-Commerce Revolution

The glamour child of direct marketing today is e-commerce. Just as the industrial revolution radically changed the nature of work, created enormous wealth, altered family structure, spawned new lifestyles, and eventually affected even the primary form of government throughout the world, the e-commerce revolution brought about changes no less profound, especially for *digital* products (such as e-tickets, stock trades, and mp3s) rather than *molecular* products, which much deal with the logistics costs of transporting physical products.

## The Increasing Polarity of Trade

As a child, do you remember going downtown to a large department store during the holidays, gazing in awe and wonder at the lights and decorations before telling Santa which of the many toys on display you wanted for Christmas? In Los Angeles, you might have gone to Bullock's, in Philadelphia to John Wanamaker, or in Cleveland to Higbee's (icon of the film *A Christmas Story*). Nearly every major city had at least one department store that was all things to all people. Go to those same stores today, however, and you won't find any toys. In many cities, you won't even find the department store—just an abandoned building.

Department stores, like many other middle-of-the-market retailers, went the way of dinosaurs because they were prey for what Harvard Business Professor Malcolm McNair called the "wheel of retailing." This process involves innovative, specialized retailers entering markets to compete against large, established stores with broad product lines. Retail profitability is determined by a combination of margin and inventory turnover. Whereas traditional department stores have high overhead and attain only moderate sales volume on their large inventories, the new competitors carry a limited number of items and sell them in large quantities, providing not only higher turnovers, but also higher margins due to volume discounts and a more efficient supply chain. When department stores could no longer match the low prices offered by these new entrants, consumers began to leave in favor of stores like Wal*Mart, Costco, and Home Depot.

In the United States, the greatest sales growth is found among mass retailers that offer low prices based on high efficiency, but growth is also seen among specialty stores who find "riches in the niches" at specialty stores such as Chico's, Victoria's Secret, Pottery Barn, and other well-operated independents. A few traditional department stores, such as Milwaukee-based Kohl's, became efficient enough to compete against the new mass retailers, and others such as Seattle-based Nordstrom carved out a niche focusing on exclusive brands and superior customer service, but most have not changed fast enough to survive the "shrinking big middle."

*Polarity of trade* describes the phenomenon of the shrinking middle, which is what happens when the most successful business models are those that provide basic services at a low cost to the masses or highly specialized services to selected niche markets. This phenomenon has resulted in the consolidation of banks, airlines, accounting firms, and many large department store chains into a handful of national players.

It's also why malls are now using stores like Target, Wal*Mart, and high-end retailers like Neiman Marcus to serve as "anchors," rather than department stores, which had been used in the past. "Department stores used to be the 800-pound gorilla, but what is an anchor and who is an anchor, have changed," comments Malachy Kavanah, a spokesperson for the International Council of Shopping Centers.

In the airline industry in recent years, TWA folded, United and US Airways entered bankruptcy, and American, Delta, and Northwest have been fighting to avoid bankruptcy. Yet one airline has been profitable for thirty-one years straight, has loyal employees who enjoy their jobs, and receives the highest levels of satisfaction in consumer polls. Its name is Southwest and its stock symbol says much about the reason for its success—LUV. JetBlue Airways has the same basic business model with the added advantage of newer aircraft equipped with in-seat televisions for long-haul flights.

Can quality and customer satisfaction be achieved by low-cost firms? Southwest and JetBlue are prototypes for innovative forms of marketing, demonstrating that low-cost providers can offer higher consumer satisfaction than traditional, high-cost, full-service firms. Consider the following ranking of airline quality using fifteen attributes considered important to consumers.*

1. JetBlue Airways
2. Alaska Airlines
3. Southwest Airlines
4. America West
5. US Airways

(continued)

6. Northwest Airlines
7. Continental Airlines
8. AirTran
9. United Airlines
10. ATA
11. American Airlines
12. Delta Air Lines

As you can see from the list, three of the top four airlines in customer satisfaction are low-cost carriers, with JetBlue achieving the best overall performance. These airlines are quickly grabbing market share from traditional network carriers because they're on time more often, bump fewer passengers, mishandle fewer bags, and generate fewer customer service complaints. In fact, Southwest is now the largest or second largest carrier (in terms of local passengers) in the majority of airports it serves. Nobody wants to cut costs if it compromises safety, but with newer aircraft and more focused processes, low-cost airlines actually have safety records as good as or better than their high-cost counterparts.

Hospitals and physicians' offices basically are retailers of health care products and services, subject to the same consumer-driven trends and demands as any other retailer. Increasing polarity can be expected in this industry as consumers drive more of their own health care purchases instead of insurance companies. In the future, some of today's large general hospitals may still exist, but in far more efficient forms. Others may be converted to retirement homes, specialized care facilities (perhaps for Alzheimer's patients) or, like some department stores, just boarded up. Specialty hospitals with focused expertise in heart surgery or orthopedics, nontraditional clinics focused on alternative medicine, and large national medical centers like Mayo Clinic offering high-quality care and integrated practice across a variety of disciplines will probably experience high growth. Mayo Clinic, while technically not a specialty hospital because of the breadth of its expertise, specializes in marketing to a national segment of patients attracted by its strength in diagnostic services.

The salient point is that the best service is often achieved by firms with the lowest costs, whether they are mass airlines like JetBlue and Southwest, mass retailers, or health care providers like MinuteClinic (now in some Target stores) and Mexico's Farmacias Similares, which was described in the opening vignette of this chapter.

Sources: Adapted from Jagdish Sheth and Rajendra Sisodia, *Rule of Three* (New York: Simon & Schuster, 2002); Clayton Christenson, *The Innovator's Dilemma* (Cambridge, MA: Harvard Business Press, 1997); Roger Blackwell and Tom Williams, *Consumer Driven Health* (Columbus, OH: Book Publishing Associates, 2005); and Ryan Chittum, "Anchors Away!" *Wall Street Journal* (March 1, 2005), B1.

* University of Nebraska at Omaha Aviation Institute and W. Frank Barton School of Business at Wichita State University, 2004.

The winners in "clicks and order" retailing, like their predecessors in "bricks and mortar" retailing, are customer-centric firms such as Amazon.com and eBay that know how to take care of customers better than competitors. The technology of websites determines what can be offered to consumers, but only consumers determine which forms of retailing technology are accepted. The challenge for consumer analysts is to make sense of this form of retailing. Table 5.3 applies the first four stages of the CDP model to e-commerce retailing and purchasing.

When examining how consumers make purchase decisions, one shortcoming of the Internet is the lack of the ability to touch and experience the product before purchase. At Printemps in Paris, one of the world's most famous department stores, consumers can go online and communicate with a salesperson at the store. The salespersons—called "Webcamers"—are equipped with ultra-lightweight laptop computers, wireless networking gear, and video cameras. They also wear rollerblades, allowing them to move quickly throughout Printemps' 1.5-million-square-foot flagship store (located on twenty-four floors in three buildings).[67] Consumers communicate online with salespeople who can show consumers the exact garment in which they're interested,

## Problem Recognition

*Which parts of shopping cause consumers problems that can be solved better on the Internet or through an e-tailer?*

• Not being able to go to a store when the store is open

• Store location is far away (either other city or country)

• Need special products that are not carried by many retailers (special sizes, out-of-print materials, personal preferences, or products for special medical needs)

*Example*   A consumer might have difficulty buying size 14 shoes from a traditional retailer that cannot afford to carry inventory of specialized products that don't turn quickly. An e-tailer or shopping directly from the manufacturer solves the problem better for the consumer than the existing retail channel. E-tailers may have a major advantage in solving problems for these consumers *by selling products that appeal to segments too small for location-based retailers.*

*Limitations*   Trying on the shoes for fit and comfort, an important part of buying, is a problem that e-tailing does not solve very well. Even when consumers are attracted to apparel and order it, the return rate is so high that location-based retailers may have lower costs than e-tailers.

## Search

*In which instances is the search process enhanced or simplified by the Internet?*

• Searching a wide variety of sources of information, perhaps on a global basis

• Identifying a specific product title, name, or brand and retailer selling the item

• Searching for information on competitive brands or on a topic of interest

• Ability to "shop" various retailers for products and prices

*Example*   In the past, if consumers were looking for a specific book or music CD, they might have to travel to several stores to find the title. The search process could involve several phone calls or trips to various stores. With the Internet, however, consumers can search online for the inventories of location-based retailers and choose to buy from the store or buy online. Also, accessing information about products or interests can be done from home rather than in the library.

*Limitations*   If consumers are not exactly sure what they are looking for, the search may be complicated if help is not available to narrow the search process. The search will lead to purchasing in countries where the postal service or commercial services can deliver the products easily and cheaply, especially if issues such as transportation charges, shipping damages, and customs and duties are not solved satisfactorily.

## Pre-Purchase Evaluation of Alternatives

*In which instances is the evaluation process enhanced or simplified by the Internet?*

• When comparing product prices across retailers (especially global locations)

• When comparing features of products

*Example*   E-tailing offers consumers advantages in comparing attributes of products offered by competitors, especially price. Numerous search programs and websites are available to compare prices after consumers have defined other attributes or brands that are in their consideration set.

*Limitations*   Two major issues make it difficult for consumers to evaluate alternatives on variables other than price. First, many of the data for such comparisons are not retrievable from the databases of competitors, who may actively avoid the disclosure of such data. The second problem is that many of the most important attributes cannot be compared digitally.

## Purchase

*When is purchasing on the Internet more efficient and preferred to other forms of purchase?*

• When you can't physically go to the store

• When calling is difficult or not convenient

• When the same order is repeated

*(continued)*

- When the consumer is familiar with the products being ordered
- When the consumer doesn't need the product immediately

*Example*  Consumers who have purchased shirts from L.L. Bean in the past, might find it convenient to visit the website and order additional shirts. The advantage is that this can be done anytime, day or night, without fear that the size will be wrong. Some similarities exist for nonperishable, staple items found in grocery stores.

*Limitations*  When a consumer walks through a grocery store to buy the average purchase of 18 items, the consumer uses about 21 minutes to search the store, select products, check out, and load the car. Can grocery e-tailing compare in time and assistance? Only if the e-tailer provides information about product selections and availability, provides "time utility," and offers a similar or lower price. If it is easier and more convenient to use an e-tailer, then consumers may be willing to absorb the higher costs of home delivery and a "hired shopper."

perhaps enlisting another person to model the garment. The store even has a global wedding and gift registry (www.printemps.com) available to its international customer base. The department store has experimented with other innovations, such as weekly fashion shows, twenty-four-hour-a-day shopping, and special presentations of merchandise similar to TV's Home Shopping Network.

Of the thousands of consumers who visit the website of an e-tailer, only a few actually purchase goods on the site. Consumers may develop favorable aesthetic experience (browsers) or find specific information (searchers), but if the website is not congruent with their goals, they may fail to purchase.[68] Even among consumers who make a decision to buy a product, place it into a "shopping cart," and provide their name, address, and credit card number, most terminate the process without completing a transaction. Although the reasons are not always clear, the consequence was that early e-tailers failed to make sustainable profits. As a category, catalog retailers have been more successful than either bricks and mortar stores or pure e-tailers, usually because they were better at operating customer call centers and logistics systems for small unit shipments and because they understood the types of products that customers are most willing to buy in locations other than location-based retailers. You can use Table 5.4 to analyze which consumer goods fit best to sell online. Looking at each of the attributes, you can easily see why specialty goods fit best for e-commerce among molecular products. Digital products such as e-tickets and music files don't have this problem and are therefore more successful online.

## Consumer Resources: What People Spend When They Purchase

Regardless of how or what consumers purchase, they have several budgets from which they spend to obtain products and services. Consumers spend money, time, and attention when they buy products. Therefore, all products can be viewed as having economic, time, and cognitive prices that consumers have to pay in the purchase process.

### Money and Time Budgets

We know from basic economics that the more money a person earns, the more he or she has to spend in the marketplace. Chapter 7 will highlight income trends for consumers around the world, but here we want to focus on how consumers use their resources to make purchases. Studies show that the more money people make, the busier they are, thus increasing the value of their time. Although people can make an infinite amount of money (at least in theory), they can have only twenty-four hours per day to

## TABLE 5.4 — Which Products Are Best for Selling Online?

| | CONVENIENCE GOODS | SHOPPING GOODS | SPECIALTY GOODS |
|---|---|---|---|
| Margins | | | |
| Inventory turns | | | |
| Price | | | |
| Ease of sourcing | | | |
| Now factor | | | |
| Price sensitivity | | | |
| Brand substitution | | | |
| Search and planning | | | |
| Ease of buying | | | |
| Product evaluation | | | |
| FIT FOR SELLING ONLINE: | LOW | LOW/MEDIUM | HIGH |

Source: Roger Blackwell and Tina Stephan, *Customers Rule! Why the E-Commerce Honeymoon Is Over and Where Winning Businesses Go from Here* (Crown/Random House, 2001), 86.

## FIGURE 5.6 — Concepts of Consumer Time Budgets

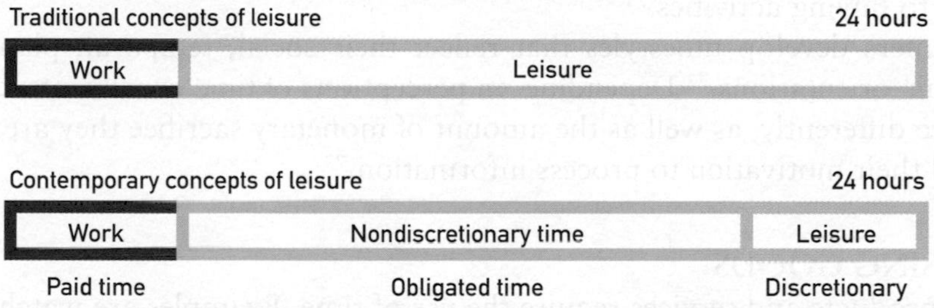

Traditional concepts of leisure — 24 hours

| Work | Leisure |
|---|---|

Contemporary concepts of leisure — 24 hours

| Work | Nondiscretionary time | Leisure |
|---|---|---|
| Paid time | Obligated time | Discretionary |

spend on activities as basic as sleeping and eating to playing sports, working, and shopping.[69] How consumers allocate that time depends on their *timestyles.*

Consumer time budgets, which people spend on life activities, used to be divided into two components: work and leisure. These budgets assumed that all time spent outside work was leisure. In contrast, a contemporary view of time, as indicated in Figure 5.6, divides time into three blocks: paid time, obligated time, and discretionary time. **Discretionary time** is leisure time[70]—*when individuals feel no sense of economic, legal, moral, social, or physical compulsion or obligation.* In recent years, as people work more hours and find themselves obligated to do more work or family activities, the amount of leisure time in American time budgets has decreased significantly. **Nondiscretionary time** includes *physical obligations* (e.g., sleeping, commuting, personal care, and so forth), *social obligations* (which increase with urbanization and the rising proportion of professional and white-collar occupations), *and moral obligations.* Physical and social obligations increase with increasing income.

Harried consumers cope with time-crunched lifestyles in many ways. Many people just cut back on sleep. Others spend less time doing what they really want to do or choose activities that take less time. Consumer decision making also takes time, as shown in Table 5.5. The amount of time consumers are willing to spend on shopping activities often decreases as the amount of money they make increases, increasing the

| TABLE 5.5 | Consumer Purchase Activities Involving Expenditure of Time |
|---|---|

| PRE-PURCHASE | PURCHASE | POST-PURCHASE |
|---|---|---|
| • Information gathering<br> • Conversation<br> • Misc. media use<br>  (e.g., *Consumer Reports*)<br> • Browsing, window shopping<br> • Other advertising<br>  (e.g., billboard)<br>• Search for "time-saving"<br> features<br>• Comparison shopping | • Buying<br> • By mail/telephone<br> • In the store<br> • Form of payment (e.g., cash,<br>  check, credit card)<br>• Related travel time and waiting<br> in line | • Information gathering and<br> learning on how to use product<br>• Filling out warranty forms<br>• Repairs and maintenance<br>• Actual use of the product and<br> continued use of the product<br>• Disposing of product (presorting<br> aluminum and plastic, driving to<br> the city dump, etc.) |

Source: John P. Robinson and Franco M. Nicosia, "Of Time, Activity, and Consumer Behavior: An Essay on Findings, Interpretations, and Needed Research," *Journal of Business Research* 22 (1991), 171–186.

importance of brands as a time-saving strategy for consumers. If a consumer trusts a brand, he or she can spend less time repurchasing the product. Factors such as the enjoyment of shopping may also influence the amount of time consumers are willing to devote to buying activities.[71]

Consumers develop timestyles that reflect their social, temporal, planning, and polychronic orientations.[72] Depending on perceptions of time constraints, consumers value price differently, as well as the amount of monetary sacrifice they are willing to make and their motivation to process information.[73]

## TIME-USING GOODS

Some products and services require the use of time. Examples are watching television, skiing, fishing, golfing, and playing tennis. How likely consumers are to purchase time-using goods depends on their time usage in a typical twenty-four-hour day. As consumers make more money, they are willing to spend more money on the precious time they do have. This shift has increased the market for travel, extreme sports, and eating out. For example, some consumers may choose to play tennis rather than golf, because tennis takes less time and involves more strenuous exercise.[74] As mentioned earlier in the chapter, shopping at an "experience" retailer like Cabela's or visiting a "lifestyle" shopping center can be a time-using expenditure consumers believe valuable in the allocation of their limited time resources because it meets several needs simultaneously.

## TIME-SAVING GOODS

Consumers can gain leisure time by decreasing nondiscretionary time expenditures with goods and services. Hiring a neighborhood teenager to cut the grass may provide a consumer with time for either more work (which might increase income) or more leisure. Child care, housecleaning, restaurants, and a wide array of other services are direct substitutes for time obligations, making them fast-growing markets in industrialized economies. Dishwashers (remember the two-dishwasher example in Chapter 1?) and microwave ovens are examples of how time-saving attributes create enormous market opportunities. This concept holds for foods and packaged goods. In fact, Minute Rice and Minute Maid even highlight their time benefits in their names.

## Polychronic Time Use

**Polychronic time** use involves *combining activities simultaneously,* such as eating while watching television or working with a laptop computer while traveling on an airplane. By combining activities, individuals use their time resources to accomplish several goals at the same time. This concept has also been called dual time usage and contrasts with *performing only one activity at a time* (**monochronic time** use). Computers and wireless technology facilitate polychronic time expenditures.

Many products are marketed to enrich the time budgets of consumers through polychronic time usage. Drive-through dry-cleaners, prepared meals bought at a supermarket, reading racks on exercise bikes, and beepers for dental patients who want to shop in nearby stores while waiting for appointments are just a few innovations driven by polychronic time trends.[75] Wireless phones diffused rapidly in part because they gave people the freedom to move while talking on the phone. Online radio and video services allow consumers to listen to their favorite music or programs while working on their computers.

## Time Prices

Products have economic prices as well as *time prices,* which are often featured as a product benefit in an ad. Such ads may state that a product requires only two hours to install. Some stores advertise wider aisles and more checkout lanes to tell consumers that it will take less time to shop than it did in the past. Harried consumers—those who feel rushed and pressured for time—visit fewer stores and make fewer comparisons by considering fewer brands and attributes than those who are relaxed shoppers.[76] Product attributes may communicate the ability to reduce the time price of a product. Examples include shampoo and conditioner in one, quick-dry paint, and fast-igniting charcoal.

## Cognitive Resources

Walking through a supermarket, you may see a lot of consumers looking up and down the aisles, scanning shelves, picking up products and comparing labels, spending minutes or even hours in the store, and often looking a bit confused. This is not a new form of ritual shopping behavior; it is an illustration that consumers have another resource from which they must spend to buy products and services—cognitive resources (these will be examined further in Chapter 14).

**Cognitive resources** represent the *mental capacity available for undertaking various information-processing activities.* Just as marketers compete for consumers' money and time, so do they compete for cognitive resources or the attention of consumers. **Capacity** refers to the *cognitive resources that an individual has available at any given time for processing information.*

The *allocation of cognitive capacity* is known as **attention.** Attention consists of two dimensions: direction and intensity.[77] *Direction* represents the focus of attention. Because consumers are unable to process all the internal and external stimuli available at any given moment, they must be selective in how they allocate this limited resource. Some stimuli will gain attention; others will be ignored. *Intensity* refers to the amount of capacity focused in a particular direction. Consumers will often allocate only the capacity needed to identify a stimulus before redirecting their attention elsewhere. On other occasions, consumers may pay enough attention to understand the gist of the ad. Sometimes consumers may give the ad their complete concentration and carefully scrutinize the message, such as spring breakers looking at the location and amenities of a resort destination.

Gaining the consumer's attention represents one of the most formidable challenges a marketer may face. Consumers are bombarded continually by many stimuli that compete for their limited mental capacity. Consumers already encounter hundreds of radio, television, magazine, newspaper, billboard, and Internet ads in a typical day, and the number is expected to increase as marketers develop new avenues for reaching consumers including video displays in shopping carts and visual merchandising technology (d-POP, as described earlier). Whether advertising or in-store marketing, success depends on gaining consumer attention.

## SHALLOW ATTENTION

Many products are simply not important enough to consumers to warrant a large investment of their limited cognitive resources, as is the case with low-involvement products. In many respects, consumers are cognitive misers, as they attempt to find acceptable rather than optimal solutions for many of their consumption needs.

## DANGER OF EXCEEDING COGNITIVE CAPACITY

Because capacity is limited, it is possible to provide too much information and exceed capacity.[78] What happens when information overload occurs? Some have speculated that too much information on packaging can cause confusion and cause consumers to make poorer choices, even though the information may make them feel better about their decisions.[79] Critics, however, disagree.[80] They maintain that information overload, though possible, is unlikely because consumers will stop processing information before they are overloaded.[81] One study, however, suggests that consumers may be unable to stop short of overloading when in an information-rich environment.[82]

The amount of attention a consumer gives to a product or specific purchase choice depends on factors such as involvement, situation, personality, and other variables. A group of consumers may spend a lot of time at a new and exciting product display in a supermarket—some consumers might be reading the labels because they are interested in nutrition and fat content; others might be reading about a contest associated with buying the product; and yet others might be reading preparation instructions. The reasons that people spend their time, money, and attention budgets on products vary depending on the characteristics of the individual.

## Communicating with Consumers: Integrated Marketing Communications

The final step in promoting purchase and taking retail strategy to consumers is to develop an **integrated marketing communications** (IMC) program.[83] Broadly, an IMC is *a systematic, cross-organizational marketing communication process that is customer-centric, data-driven, technically anchored, and branding effective.* Integrated marketing communications differ from traditionally programmed communications in the following ways.

1. IMC programs are comprehensive. Advertising, websites, personal selling, retail atmospherics and in-store programs, behavioral modification programs, public relations, investor relations programs, employee communications, and other forms are all considered in the planning of an IMC.

2. IMC programs are unified. The messages delivered by all media, including such diverse influences as employee recruiting and the atmospherics of retailers, are the same or supportive of a unified theme.

3. IMC programs are targeted. The public-relations program, advertising programs, and in-store and point-of-purchase programs all have the same or related target markets.

4. IMC programs have coordinated execution of all the communications components of the organization.

5. IMC programs emphasize productivity in reaching the designated targets when selecting communication channels and allocating resources to marketing media.

Studies indicate that only half of all promotions generate economic benefits to the advertisers, making the need for integrated advertising and promotion efforts important.[84] A firm's pricing and communications strategies are likely to mirror the strategies they pursue in conventional channels.[85] E-tailing provides opportunities to build brands on the Internet, as well as provide specific information to show consumers where to find that brand at a local dealer or retail outlet. Burton Snowboards, for example, developed an effective marketing program involving its website (www.burton.com), snowboarding events and sponsorships, and conventional media.

Advertising on the Internet has become a major medium, competing with television, radio, newspapers, magazines, outdoor, and other direct media that have been the preferred ways for consumers to search for information and products in the past. Google keywords, pop-ups, and other intrusions confront Internet users constantly, and you may be one of those who ask why advertisers spend so much money on them. The answer, of course, is that they are effective. Perhaps there is comfort, however, that most advertising resources are still spent on traditional media. As you saw earlier, the applications of the Internet for profitable e-commerce are constrained by marketing logistics and consumer lifestyles. As an information medium and part of an IMC program, Internet applications are nearly unlimited. It's probably correct to conclude that the Internet is still best for providing information rather than selling.

## Summary

Attracting consumers to buy more from a particular store includes performing well on the attributes that consumers think are most important—(1) location, (2) nature and quality of assortment, (3) price, (4) advertising and promotion, (5) sales personnel, (6) services offered, (7) physical store attributes, (8) nature of store clientele, (9) point-of-purchase displays, and (10) consumer logistics.

Increasingly, retailers are reaching consumers through a variety of formats. Multichannel retailing includes in-store and nonstore retailing. In-store retailing includes traditional stores, specialty stores, mass merchants, and factory direct stores, whereas out-of-store formats include direct selling, direct marketing, and electronic retailing. Even though many formats promote self-selection of products,

consumers still rely on personal sales assistance when available. The factors that differentiate successful salespersons from their counterparts are (1) perceived knowledge and expertise, (2) perceived trustworthiness, (3) knowledge of their customer, and (4) adaptability.

When consumers do make a purchase, they have several budgets from which to spend: time, money, and attention. The more money individuals earn, the more valuable their time becomes. Products and services classified by their time properties may be called time goods. Time-using goods require the use of time, whereas time-saving goods allow consumers to increase their discretionary time. Consumers also allocate attention to various activities in life. Because this capacity is limited, people must be selective in what they pay attention to and how much attention is allocated during information processing. Gaining con-

**Chapter Summary**

sumers' attention can be challenging for marketers, especially when the product is of limited importance. To gain consumer attention, marketers design IMC programs that communicate similar messages and images through various media in an effort to increase the bang for their promotional buck.

## Review and Discussion Questions

1. Define the term *store image* and explain why it is important as a concept for retail management. Choose one retailer and evaluate its image and how that image is portrayed in its advertising.

2. You are the marketing manager for a manufacturer of specialty watches designed for runners. Would you sell these items through retail stores or on the Internet (either alone or in combination with location-based retailers)? Why?

3. Many contend that interactive electronic media will revolutionize consumer buying patterns. What is your opinion? What advantages are offered? Will traditional retail shopping become largely obsolete?

4. Choose a retailer you frequent often. Evaluate the store based on the elements of consumer logistics. How would you change the store?

5. How might the relationship between time budgets and economic budgets affect the marketing strategy of a major retailer?

6. What are some of the trends affecting time budgets for most Americans? How do you think these trends will be changing in the future?

7. Create an IMC strategy for a specific brand of clothing. What promotional elements would you include, and what would be the look and feel and message?

## Notes

[1] Ravi Dhar, "Consumer Preference for a No-Choice Option," *Journal of Consumer Research*, 24 (September 1997), 215–231.

[2] Alain d'Asdtous, Idriss Bensouda, and Jean Guindon, "A Re-Examination of Consumer Decision Making for a Repeat Purchase Product: Variations in Product Importance and Purchase Frequency," in Thomas K. Srull, *Advances in Consumer Research*, 16 (Provo, UT: Association for Consumer Research, 1989), 433–438.

[3] C. Whan Park, Easwar S. Iyer, and Daniel C. Smith, "The Effects of Situational Factors on In-Store Grocery Shopping Behavior: The Role of Store Environment and Time Available for Shopping," *Journal of Consumer Research*, 15 (March 1989), 422–433.

[4] France Leclerc and John D. C. Little, "Can Advertising Copy Make FSI Coupons More Effective?" *Journal of Marketing Research*, 4 (November 1997), 473–484.

[5] For a careful analysis of the impact of retail promotions, see Rodney G. Walters, "Assessing the Impact of Retail Price Promotions on Product Substitution, Complementary Purchase, and Interstore Sales Displacement," *Journal of Marketing*, 55 (April 1991), 17–28.

[6] J. Jeffrey Inman and Russell Winer, "Impulse Buying," *Wall Street Journal* (April 15, 1999), A1.

[7] Pradeep K. Chintagunta and Sudeep Haldar, "Investigating Purchase Timing Behavior in Two Related Product Categories," *Journal of Marketing Research*, 35 (February 1998), 43–53.

[8] David I. Kollat and Ronald P. Willett, "Customer Impulse Purchasing Behavior," *Journal of Marketing Research*, 4 (February 1967), 21–31.

[9] Dilip Soman, "The Illusion of Delayed Incentives: Evaluating Future Effort-Money Transactions," *Journal of Marketing Research*, 35 (November 1998), 427–437.

[10] Laura Loro, "Data Bases Seen as 'Driving Force,'" *Advertising Age* (March 18, 1991), 39.

[11] Joseph B. Cahill, "Sears' Credit Business May Have Helped Larger Retailing Woes," *Wall Street Journal* (July 6, 1999), A1.

[12] James U. McNeal and Daryl McKee, "The Case of Antishoppers," in Robert E. Lusch et al., eds., *1985 AMA Educators' Proceedings* (Chicago: American Marketing Association, 1985), 65–68.

[13] Jack A. Lesser and Sanjay Jain, "A Preliminary Investigation of the Relationship Between Exploratory and Epistemic Shopping Behavior," in Robert E. Lusch et al., eds., *1985 AMA Educators' Proceedings* (Chicago: American Marketing Association, 1985), 75–81.

[14] Arch G. Woodside and Randolph J. Trappey III, "Finding Out Why Customers Shop Your Store and Buy Your Brand: Automatic Cognitive Processing Models of Primary Choice," *Journal of Advertising Research*, 32 (November–December 1992), 59–78.

[15] See Jay D. Lindquist, "The Meaning of Image," *Journal of Retailing*, 50 (Winter 1974/1975), 29–38; Robert A. Hansen and Terry Deutscher, "An Empirical Investigation of Attribute Importance in Retail Store Selection," *Journal of Retailing*, 53 (Winter 1977/1978), 59–72; Leon Arons, "Does Television Viewing Influence Store Image and Shopping Frequency?" *Journal of Retailing*, 37 (Fall 1961), 1–13; Ernest Dichter, "What's in an Image," *Journal of Consumer Marketing*, 2 (Winter 1985), 75–81.

[16] Pierre Martineau, "The Personality of the Retail Store," *Harvard Business Review*, 36 (January/February 1958), 47.

[17] For semantic differential, see G. H. G. McDougall and J. N. Fry, "Combining Two

Methods of Image Measurement," *Journal of Retailing,* 50 (Winter 1974/1975), 53–61. For customer prototypes, see W. B. Weale, "Measuring the Customer's Image of a Department Store," *Journal of Retailing,* 37 (Spring 1961), 40–48. For Q-sort, see William Stephenson, "Public Images of Public Utilities," *Journal of Advertising Research,* 3 (December 1963), 34–39. For Guttman scale, see Elizabeth A. Richards, "A Commercial Application of Guttman Attitude Scaling Techniques," *Journal of Marketing,* 22 (October 1957), 166–173. For multidimensional scaling, see Peter Doyle and Ian Fenwick, "How Store Image Affects Shopping Habits in Grocery Chains," *Journal of Retailing,* 50 (Winter 1974/1975), 39–52. For psycholinguistics, see Richard N. Cardozo, "How Images Vary by Product Class," *Journal of Retailing,* 50 (Winter 1974/1975), 85–98. For multiattribute approach, see Don L. James, Richard M. Durand, and Robert A. Dreves, "The Use of a Multi-Attribute Model in a Store Image Study," *Journal of Retailing,* 52 (Summer 1976), 23–32.

[18] Gilbert D. Harrell, Michael D. Gutt, and James C. Anderson, "Path Analysis of Buyer Behavior under Conditions of Crowding," *Journal of Marketing Research,* 17 (February 1980), 45–51. See also Michael K. Hui and John E. G. Bateson, "Perceived Control and the Effects of Crowding and Consumer Choice on the Service Experience," *Journal of Consumer Research,* 18 (September 1991), 174–184.

[19] David B. Mackay and Richard W. Olshavsky, "Cognitive Maps of Retail Locations: An Investigation of Some Basic Issues," *Journal of Consumer Research,* 2 (December 1975); and Edward M. Mazze, "Determining Shopper Movements by Cognitive Maps," *Journal of Retailing,* 50 (Fall 1974), 43–48.

[20] R. Mittelstaedt et al., "Psychophysical and Evaluative Dimensions of Cognized Distance in an Urban Shopping Environment," in R. C. Curhan, ed., *Combined Proceedings* (Chicago: American Marketing Association, 1974), 190–193.

[21] Charles Brooks, Patrick Kaufmann, and Donald Lichtenstein, "Travel Configuration on Consumer Trip-Chained Store Choice," *Journal of Consumer Research,* 31 (September 2004), 241–249.

[22] Hansen and Deutscher, "An Empirical Investigation"; Lindquist, "The Meaning of Image"; Gentry and Burns, "How Important"; and John D. Claxton and J. R. Brent Ritchie, "Consumer Prepurchase Shopping Problems: A Focus on the Retailing Component," *Journal of Retailing,* 55 (Fall 1979), 24–43.

[23] Walter K. Levy, "Department Stores—The Next Generation: Form and Rationale," *Retailing Issues Letter,* 1 (August 1987), 1.

[24] Robert H. Williams, John J. Painter, and Herbert R. Nicholas, "A Policy-Oriented Typology of Grocery Shoppers," *Journal of Retailing,* 54 (Spring 1978), 27–42.

[25] Kent B. Monroe, "Buyers' Subjective Perceptions of Price," *Journal of Marketing Research,* 10 (February 1973), 73–80.

[26] Joseph N. Fry and Gordon H. McDougall, "Consumer Appraisal of Retail Price Advertisements," *Journal of Marketing,* 38 (July 1974); V. Kumar and Robert P. Leone, "Measuring the Effect of Retail Store Promotions on Brand and Store Substitution," *Journal of Marketing Research,* 25 (May 1988), 178–185.

[27] Alan L. Montgomery and Peter E. Rossi, "Estimating Price Elasticities with Theory-Based Priors," *Journal of Marketing Research,* 36 (November 1999), 413–423.

[28] John Roberts, "Developing New Rules for New Markets," *Journal of the Academy of Marketing Science,* 28 (Winter 2000), 31–44.

[29] Randolf E. Bucklin, Sunil Gupta, and S. Siddarth, "Determining Segmentations in Sales Response Across Consumer Purchase Behaviors," *Journal of Marketing Research,* 35 (May 1998), 189–197.

[30] Greg Allenby, "Reassessing Brand Loyalty, Price Sensitivity, and Merchandising Effects on Consumer Brand Choice," working paper, 1993.

[31] Stephen K. Keiser and James R. Krum, "Consumer Perceptions of Retail Advertising with Overstated Price Savings," *Journal of Retailing,* 45 (Fall 1976), 27–36.

[32] "Service: Retail's No. 1 Problem," *Chain Store Age Executive* (January 1987), 19.

[33] Gilbert A. Churchill Jr., Neil M. Ford, Steven W. Hartley, and Orville C. Walker Jr., "The Determinants of Salesperson Performance: A Meta-Analysis," *Journal of Marketing Research,* 22 (May 1985), 103–118.

[34] This categorization has its roots in Peter H. Reingen and Arch G. Woodside, *Buyer-Seller Interactions: Empirical Research and Normative Issues* (Chicago: American Marketing Association, 1981).

[35] Arch G. Woodside and William Davenport Jr., "The Effect of Salesman Similarity and Expertise on Consumer Purchasing Behavior," *Journal of Marketing Research,* 11 (May 1974), 198–203. Also see Paul Busch and David T. Wilson, "An Experimental Analysis of a Salesman's Expert and Referent Bases on Social Power in the Buyer-Seller Dyad," *Journal of Marketing Research,* 13 (February 1976), 3–11.

[36] Paul H. Schurr and Julie Ozanne, "Influences on Exchange Processes: Buyers' Preconceptions of a Seller's Trustworthiness and Bargaining Toughness," *Journal of Consumer Research,* 11 (March 1985), 939–953.

[37] Siew Meng Leong, Paul S. Busch, and Deborah Roedder John, "Knowledge Bases and Salesperson Effectiveness: A Script-Theoretic Analysis," *Journal of Marketing Research,* 26 (May 1989), 164–178; Harish Sujan, Mita Sujan, and James R. Bettman, "Knowledge Structure Differences between More Effective and Less Effective Sales People," *Journal of Marketing Research,* 25 (February 1988), 81–86; and David M. Syzmanski, "Determinants of Selling Effectiveness," *Journal of Marketing,* 52 (January 1988), 64–77.

[38] Greg Gattuso, "Customer Rapport," *Direct Marketing* (January 1994), 46.

[39] Howard Schultz and Dori Yang, "Pour Your Heart Into It: How Starbucks Built A Company One Cup at a Time," (New York: Hyperion, 1999).

[40] Joel A. Baglole, "Loblaw Supermarkets Add Fitness Clubs to Offerings," *Wall Street Journal* (December 27, 1999), B4.

[41] Rajeev Batra and Indrajit Sinha, "Consumer-Level Factors Moderating the Success of Private Label Brands," *Journal of Retailing*, 76 (Summer 2000), 175–192.

[42] Philip Kotler, "Atmospherics as a Marketing Tool," *Journal of Retailing*, 49 (Winter 1973/1974), 48–63. Also see Robert J. Donovan and John R. Rossiter, "Store Atmosphere: An Environmental Psychology Approach," *Journal of Retailing*, 58 (Spring 1982), 34–57; Elaine Sherman and Ruth Belk Smith, "Mood States of Shoppers and Store Image: Promising Interactions and Possible Behavioral Effects," in Melanie Wallendorf and Paul Anderson, eds., *Advances in Consumer Research*, 14 (Provo, UT: Association for Consumer Research, 1987), 251–254.

[43] Peter Doyle and Ian Fenwick, "How Store Image Affects Shopping Habits in Grocery Chains," *Journal of Retailing*, 50 (Winter 1974/1975), 39–52.

[44] Anna Mattila and Jochen Wirtz," *Journal of Retailing*, 77 (Summer 2001), 272–290.

[45] For a review and analysis of music's usefulness to marketers, see Gordon C. Bruner II, "Music, Mood, and Marketing," *Journal of Marketing*, 54 (October 1990), 94–104.

[46] Richard Yalch and Eric Spangenberg, "Effects of Store Music on Shopping Behavior," *Journal of Consumer Marketing*, 7 (Spring 1990), 55–63.

[47] Ronald E. Milliman, "Using Background Music to Affect the Behavior of Supermarket Shoppers," *Journal of Marketing*, 46 (Summer 1982), 86–91.

[48] Ronald E. Milliman, "The Influence of Background Music on the Behavior of Restaurant Patrons," *Journal of Consumer Research*, 13 (September 1986), 286–289.

[49] Joseph A. Bellizzi, Ayn E. Crowley, and Rondla W. Hasty, "The Effects of Color in Store Design," *Journal of Retailing*, 59 (Spring 1983), 21–45.

[50] Rick Brooks, "Alienating Customers Isn't Always a Bad Idea, Many Firms Discover," *Wall Street Journal* (January 7, 1999), A1, A12.

[51] V. Kumar and Robert P. Leone, "Measuring the Effect of Retail Store Promotions on Brand and Store Substitution," *Journal of Marketing Research*, 25 (May 1988), 178–185; Gary E. McKinnon, J. Patrick Kelly, and E. Doyle Robison, "Sales Effects of Point-of-Purchase In-Store Signing," *Journal of Retailing*, 57 (Summer 1981), 49–63; Arch G. Woodside and Gerald L. Waddle, "Sales Effects of In-Store Advertising," *Journal of Advertising Research*, 15 (June 1975), 29–33.

[52] Ymiko Ono, "Wobblers and Sidekicks Clutter Stores, Irk Retailers," *Wall Street Journal* (September 8, 1998), B1, B4.

[53] John A. Quelch and Kristina Cannon-Bonventre, "Better Marketing at the Point of Purchase," *Harvard Business Review*, 61 (November/December 1983), 162–169.

[54] Howard Schlossberg, "P-O-P Display Designer Wants to Keep Shoppers Shopping Longer," *Marketing News* (November 11, 1991), 15.

[55] As defined in Roger Blackwell and Tina Blackwell, *Understanding Your Customer: Consumer Logistics*, International Mass Retail Association (1998).

[56] Michael K. Hui and John E. G. Bateson, "Perceived Control and the Effects of Crowding and Consumer Choice on the Service Experience," *Journal of Consumer Research*, 18 (September 1991), 174–184.

[57] Julie Baker and Michaelle Cameron, "The Effects of the Service Environment on Affect and Consumer Perception of Waiting Time: An Integrative Review and Research Proposition," *Journal of the Academy of Marketing Science*, 24 (Summer 1996), 338–349.

[58] Benedict Dellaert, Theo Arentze, Michel Bierlaire, Aloys Borgers, and Harry Timmermans, "Investigating Consumers' Tendency to Combine Multiple Shopping Purposes and Destinations," *Journal of Marketing Research*, 35 (May 1998).

[59] Roger D. Blackwell and Wayne Talarzyk, "Lifestyle Retailing: Competitive Strategies for the 1980's," *Journal of Retailing*, 59 (Winter 1983), 7–27.

[60] Frederick E. Webster, "Understanding the Relationships among Brands, Consumers and Resellers," *Journal of the Academy of Marketing Science*, 28 (Winter 2000), 17–23.

[61] "The Changing Face of Retail," *The Retailer* (Winter 1994), 6–15.

[62] See, for example, Peterson and Albaum, "Nonstore Retailing in the United States," International Academic Symposium on Nonstore Retailing, Berlin, Germany, September, 1993; Martin P. Block and Tamara S. Brezen, "A Profile of the New In-Home Shopper," in Rebecca Holman, ed., *Proceedings of the 1991 Conference of the American Academy of Advertising* (New York: Rebecca H. Holman, D'Arcy Masius Benton & Bowles, Inc., 1991), 169–173; Paul I. Edwards, "Home Shopping Boom Forecast in Study," *Advertising Age* (December 15, 1986), 88.

[63] Erin White, "Ding-Dong, Avon Calling (on the Web, Not Your Door)," *Wall Street Journal* (December 28, 1999), B4.

[64] Ibid.

[65] "Behavior and Attitudes of Telephone Shoppers," *Direct Marketing* (September 1987), 50.

[66] Riccardo A. Davis, "QVC Clicks for Kodak Cameras," *Advertising Age* (January 17, 1994), 17.

[67] Kevin J. Delaney, "Where the E in E-Shopping Stands for 'Extreme,'" *Wall Street Journal* (October 14, 1999), B1ff; and company websites, www.printemps.fr and www.webcamer.com.

[68] Ann Schlosser, David Mick, and John Deighton, "Experiencing Products in the Virtual World: The Role of Goal and Imagery in Influencing Attitudes versus Purchase Intentions," *Journal of Consumer Research*, 30 (September 2003), 184–199.

[69] This conceptual framework is developed originally in Justin Voss and Roger

Blackwell, "Markets for Leisure Time," in Mary Jane Slinger, ed., *Advances in Consumer Research* (Chicago: Association for Consumer Research, 1975), 837–845; and Justin Voss and Roger Blackwell, "The Role of Time Resources in Consumer Behavior," in O. C. Ferrel, Stephen Brown, and Charles Lamb, eds., *Conceptual and Theoretical Developments in Marketing* (Chicago: American Marketing Association, 1979), 296–311.

[70] Justin Voss, "The Definition of Leisure," *Journal of Economic Issues*, 1 (June 1967), 91–106.

[71] Howard Marmorstein, Dhruv Grewal, and Raymond P. H. Fishe, "The Value of Time Spent in Price-Comparison Shopping: Survey and Experimental Evidence," *Journal of Consumer Research*, 19 (June 1992), 52–61.

[72] June Cotte, S. Ratneshwar, and David Mick, "The Times of Their Lives: Phenomenological and Metaphorical Characteristics of Consumer Timestyles," *Journal of Consumer Research*, 31 (September 2004), 333–346.

[73] Rajneesh Suri, Kent Monroe, David Mick, and William Bearden, "The Effects of Time Constraints on Consumers' Judgments of Prices and Products," *Journal of Consumer Research*, 30 (June 2003), 92–105.

[74] Douglass K. Hawes, W. Wayne Talarzyk, and Roger D. Blackwell, "Consumer Satisfaction from Leisure Time Pursuits," in Slinger, *Advances*, 822.

[75] Carol Felker Kaufman, Paul M. Lane, and Jay D. Lindquist, "Exploring More than 24 Hours a Day: A Preliminary Investigation of Polychronic Time Use," *Journal of Consumer Research*, 18 (December 1991), 392–401.

[76] Aida N. Rizkalla, "Consumer Temporal Orientation and Shopping Behavior: The Case of Harried vs. Relaxed Consumers," in Robert L. King, ed., *Retailing: Its Present and Future*, 4 (Charleston, SC: Academy of Marketing Science, 1988), 230–235.

[77] Scott B. MacKenzie, "The Role of Attention in Mediating the Effect of Advertising on Attribute Importance," *Journal of Consumer Research*, 13 (September 1986), 174–195.

[78] James R. Bettman, "Issues in Designing Consumer Information Environments," *Journal of Consumer Research*, 2 (December 1975), 169–177.

[79] Jacob Jacoby, Donald Speller, and Carol Kohn Berning, "Brand Choice Behavior as a Function of Information Load," *Journal of Marketing Research*, 11 (February 1974), 63–69.

[80] Jacob Jacoby, Donald Speller, and Carol Kohn Berning, "Brand Choice Behavior as a Function of Information Load: Replication and Extension," *Journal of Consumer Research*, 1 (June 1974), 33–42; J. Edward Russo, "More Information Is Better: A Reevaluation of Jacoby, Speller, and Kohn," *Journal of Consumer Research*, 11 (November 1974), 467–468; William L. Wilkie, "Analysis of Effects of Information Load," *Journal of Marketing Research*, 11 (November 1974), 462–466; Jacob Jacoby, Donald E. Speller, and Carol A. K. Beming, "Constructive Criticism and Programmatic Research: Reply to Russo," *Journal of Consumer Research*, 1 (September 1975), 154–156; Jacob Jacoby, "Information Load and Decision Quality: Some Contested Issues," *Journal of Marketing Research*, 15 (November 1977), 569–573. Also see Debora L. Scammon, "Information Load and Consumers," *Journal of Consumer Research*, 4 (December 1977), 148–155; Naresh K. Malhotra, "Information Load and Consumer Decision Making," *Journal of Consumer Research*, 8 (March 1982), 419–430; Naresh K. Malhotra, Arun K. Jain, and Stephen W. Lagakos, "The Information Overload Controversy: An Alternative Viewpoint," *Journal of Marketing*, 46 (Spring 1982), 27–37; Naresh K. Malhotra, "Reflections on the Information Overload Paradigm in Consumer Decision Making," *Journal of Consumer Research*, 10 (March 1984), 436–440.

[81] Jacob Jacoby, "Perspectives on Information Overload," *Journal of Consumer Research*, 10 (March 1984), 432–435.

[82] Kevin Lane Keller and Richard Staelin, "Effects of Quality and Quantity of Information on Decision Effectiveness," *Journal of Consumer Research*, 14 (September 1987), 200–213.

[83] This section is based on Roger D. Blackwell, "Integrated Marketing Communications," in Gary L. Frazier and Jagdish N. Sheth, eds., *Contemporary Views on Marketing Practice* (Lexington, MA: Lexington Books, 1987), 237–250.

[84] Marnik G. Dekimpe and Dominique M. Hanssens, "Sustained Spending and Persistent Response: A New Look at Long-Term Marketing Profitability," *Journal of Marketing Research*, 36 (November 1999), 397–412.

[85] Florian Zettelmeyer, "Expanding to the Internet: Pricing and Communication Strategies When Firms Compete on Multiple Channels," *Journal of Marketing Research*, 37 (August 2000), 292–309.

# Chapter 6

# Post-Purchase Processes: Consumption and Post-Consumption Evaluations

## Opening Vignette

Businesses that focus on the purchase stage to the exclusion of the consumption stage in the decision-making process may end up selling themselves short. Consider health clubs, which often offer a price break to those willing to pay for a full year instead of signing up for a month at a time. The idea is to hook you for the whole year and get paid up front. Is that smart business? To find out, John Gourville, a Harvard Business School marketing professor, examined the records of two hundred members of a Colorado health club that offered annual, semiannual, quarterly, and monthly payment options. He found that those who paid up front exercised more frequently early in the year and gradually tapered off. Those who paid quarterly tended to exercise a lot in the first few weeks of the quarter. Those who paid monthly exercised most often during the year. Importantly, members were much more likely to be exercising in November and December, the time when the club would be trying to get them to renew their membership. A pair of economists from the University of California at Berkeley and Stanford University took this a step further by analyzing three years of records of nearly eight thousand members of three other health clubs. People on the monthly plan were 12.5 percent more likely to sign up for another year than those on the yearly plan.

So why does the type of payment plan influence consumption and the odds of repurchase? People tend to go to the gym when the memory of paying the bill is freshest. The psychological pain of paying the bill declines over time. "As it fades, you feel less of a need to justify the cost by going to exercise," explains Professor Gourville. Those paying monthly are constantly reminded of what they are spending for their membership, thus making them more likely to be using and, consequently, renewing their membership. The trick for businesses is to strike a balance between enticing consumers to make that initial purchase and encouraging them to use a product so they'll buy it again. Business often goes heavy on the first part because it's simpler to understand. But it's getting consumers to use—and buy again—that usually builds a business.

Getting consumers to use what they buy is a critical part of maintaining and building a company's sales. When consumers have stockpiled more than enough product in their household to meet their short-term needs, purchase is unlikely to occur until the existing supply is at least close to being depleted. In this situation, increasing consumption today will facilitate purchase tomorrow. Even more troublesome is when consumers fail to use a purchased product at all, thereby giving them little reason to buy again. Accordingly, companies often (and, if not, should) focus part of their marketing activities on encouraging consumption of their products rather than simply the purchase of their products, a point we'll return to later in the chapter. But this is only one of several key points that will be made about the importance of understanding consumers' consumption behaviors. As you will discover, there's much about this stage of the consumer decision process that helps businesses do a better job in serving their customers and enhancing their profitability.

This chapter starts with the consumption stage. Consumption represents a critical part of the decision process. For it is here that we usually can best evaluate what the product has to offer. How did the product perform? Did it deliver what was expected? Depending on the answers to these questions, consumers will develop more or less favorable evaluations of their consumption experiences. Post-consumption evaluations represent a critical stage of the consumer decision process and are discussed in the latter part of the chapter.

## Consumption

**Consumption** represents *consumers' usage of the acquired product.* Although this definition is simple, understanding consumption is much more complex. Indeed, there are a number of different ways to think about consumption. Let's start with consumption behavior itself.

### Consumption Behaviors

When is the last time you ate frozen pizza? Have you attended a professional football game in the past year? What about a collegiate football game? Do you watch Donald Trump tell contestants "You're fired" on the *Apprentice* TV program? Have you ever rode the ocean waves on a cruise liner? How often do you work out at a gym or health club?

Your answers to the preceding questions reveal whether or not you are a consumer of these products. **User** and **nonuser** are terms often used to distinguish between *those who consume the product* and *those who do not.* Take a look at Market Facts 6.1 for information about the size of the user and nonuser segments for colognes and perfumes in some of the markets around the world. You will find some intriguing differences between countries.

The number of people that fall into the user and nonuser categories is important to businesses in a couple of ways. Knowing the number of current users in a product category is one indicator of the market's attractiveness to the company. Generally speaking, the larger the market (i.e., as the number of users increases), the greater its attractiveness. The size of the nonuser segment, on the other hand, speaks to future growth opportunities. Converting nonusers into users is not a particularly attractive option for increasing sales when the market contains few nonusers. But as the number

---

## MARKET FACTS 6.1

### Cologne and Perfume Usage by Country and Gender

The global fragrance market is one of considerable diversity. In European markets, most consumers splash themselves with colognes and perfumes. This is not the case in Asian markets where the vast majority of consumers have yet to become product users. Another complicating factor is the user's gender. Whereas typically a greater percentage of females use perfume than males use cologne, this is not true in every country. Listed below is the size of the male and female user markets in various countries around the world.

| Country | Men (%) | Women (%) |
|---|---|---|
| China | 4 | 23 |
| France | 70 | 92 |
| Germany | 85 | 94 |
| Great Britain | 70 | 88 |
| Italy | 83 | 72 |
| Japan | 8 | 21 |
| Saudi Arabia | 53 | 84 |
| Spain | 80 | 94 |
| United States | 57 | 79 |

**FIGURE 6.1**    Consumption Behaviors: Users and Usage

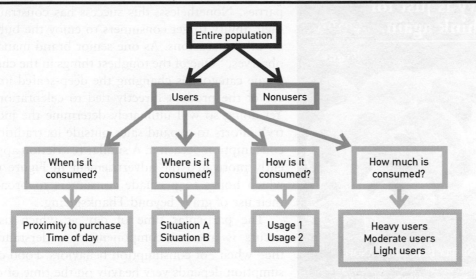

of nonusers increases, the potential payoff from courting nonusers becomes greater. Consider hair-growth products such as Rogaine. About three million American men use these products. Yet this is only a small fraction of the forty million men in the United States who have hereditary hair loss.[1] As hair-growth products improve, substantial opportunity exists for increasing the size of the user market. Similarly, cruise ships have an enormous nonuser market because about 90 percent of North Americans have yet to come onboard.[2]

An understanding of consumption behaviors requires more than simply distinguishing between those who consume and those who do not. Indeed, consumption behaviors can be characterized along a number of important dimensions, which are represented in Figure 6.1 and discussed subsequently.

## WHEN DOES CONSUMPTION OCCUR?

One fundamental characteristic of consumption behaviors involves when usage occurs. In many cases, purchase and consumption go hand in hand. That is, in making the purchase, we have committed ourselves to when consumption will occur. Buying tickets for a concert or sporting event, eating at a restaurant, and taking your car to the local car wash fall into this category. At other times, purchases are made without knowing precisely when consumption will occur. Food items bought during your last trip to the grocery store sit on a shelf or in the refrigerator until you decide to consume them.

When consumption decisions are made independently of prior purchase decisions (such as when you are choosing something from your pantry to munch on), a company may find it worthwhile to put some of its efforts into encouraging consumption rather than focusing exclusively on encouraging purchase. This was so for one food manufacturer that discovered many people left its product sitting in their pantries long after purchase had occurred. This discovery prompted the company to develop an advertising campaign that aired late at night encouraging consumers to consume the food as a late-night snack. Another example of encouraging consumption is provided by the wine industry. In response to declining wine consumption, a multimedia advertising campaign was launched featuring the slogan, "Wine. What are you saving it for?"[3]

Consider champagne makers who, in some ways, have become victims of their own success. They've done a wonderful job in positioning their product as an essential part of celebration activities. More than 50 percent of champagne sales take place at

**If you think gravy is just for Thanksgiving, think again.**

BOSTON MARKET
Home Style Meals

SIMPLY BEEF STROGANOFF

A classic made easy - just brown ground beef or beef strips and simmer with a jar of Boston Market® Classic Beef Gravy and sour cream. Serve over noodles.

Boston Market is a registered trademark of Boston Market Corporation ©H.J. Heinz Company, L.P. 2003. All rights reserved.

**FIGURE 6.2** Boston Market Attempts to Expand Gravy Consumption beyond Thanksgiving

year-end, the season of Christmas and New Year's parties. Nonetheless, this success has constrained their ability to get consumers to enjoy the bubbly on other occasions. As one senior brand manager observes, "One of the toughest things in the champagne category is changing the deep-seated imagery of the product directly tied to celebration."[4] Yet doing so will ultimately determine the industry's efforts to expand sales outside its traditional consumption occasion. A similar restriction apparently motivated the advertisement in Figure 6.2, which hopes to persuade consumers to broaden their use of gravy beyond Thanksgiving.

The particular time of day at which usage occurs is another component of understanding the "when" of consumption behaviors. Food consumption depends very heavily on the time of day. We rarely eat spaghetti for breakfast or pancakes for dinner. Orange juice is usually consumed at the breakfast table (see Consumer Behavior and Marketing 6.1 to learn about the challenges facing citrus marketers). In years past, the orange juice industry attempted to break out of this restriction with its famous advertising campaign slogan, "It isn't just for breakfast anymore." A similar theme was reflected in advertisements for Pop Tarts that proclaimed that the product was "not just for breakfast." Whereas some products hope to broaden their usage outside of the breakfast table, other products are trying to find their way onto this table. Pizza makers, for example, have marketed "breakfast pizzas," and soda manufacturers have offered enhanced caffeine soft drinks (e.g., the short-lived Pepsi A.M.) in an effort to gain a greater presence at the morning table.

When consumption occurs is especially important for those taking medications, the effectiveness of which depends on the time they're taken.[5] Some cholesterol medicines work better when given in the evening because they target a cholesterol-affecting liver enzyme that's most active at night. Asthma attacks frequently occur at night and typically are more severe at night. Some asthma patients have cut nighttime attacks in half by taking their medicine in the early evening, thus providing them with enough medication to make it through the night.

When people consume at different times, it may be useful to segment the market accordingly. Those responsible for marketing the Florida Keys have discovered noteworthy differences between tourists who visit during the summer versus those visiting during the more expensive winter months. Winter visitors typically are older and wealthier people who enjoy sightseeing, and are more likely to be white. Summer visitors tend to stay for shorter amounts of time (about four days on average) and are more likely to be found snorkeling in the reefs. Latinos and blacks are more likely to be visiting during the summer. Such information helps in targeting different segments more effectively and efficiently.[6]

Sometimes the answer to the question "when does consumption occur?" is "never." Such nonconsumption occurs when consumers purchase, but for one reason or another, fail to consume the product. An extreme example of purchase without consumption is the can of sardines that, over a time period covering more than twenty years, was transferred from grandmother to mother to daughter![7] According to one estimate, as much as 12 percent of the products bought for the pantry escape

## The Squeeze Is On

The citrus industry has been squeezing oranges and grapefruits for a very long time. Now, it's the industry's turn to be squeezed. According to Andrew W. LaVigne, executive vice president and chief executive of industry association Florida Citrus Mutual, "This year will probably be one of the most challenging we've had in twenty years."

The industry is being squeezed by both competitors and consumers. Competitive challenges loom large both domestically and internationally. The world's biggest orange producer, Brazil, is lobbying the United States to eliminate tariffs imposed on imported frozen orange juice concentrate. If this happens, consumers will see a lower retail price for orange juice, but Florida farmers claim it would decimate the domestic industry and the 90,000 jobs it generates. The tariff, these farmers say, levels the playing field against growers in developing countries that pay workers a fraction of U.S. wages and provide no health benefits.

Pressure is also being felt on the home front. A sheer tidal wave of thirst-quenching options is available to consumers today, many of them with low or no calories. "There's a stomach-share battle in the drink case," observes Dan Richey, president of Riverfront Groves in Vero Beach, Florida, and a state citrus commissioner. "The bottled-water craze has cannibalized some of our market."

Which leads us back to the consumer. This increased competition is at least partly responsible for the declining consumption of citrus products. Between 1997 and 1998, annual orange juice consumption was nearly six gallons per capita. By 2002–2003, per capita consumption was less than five gallons, representing a 17 percent decrease in just five years. Grapefruit juice has also lost 17 percent in annual consumption, but it has taken only three years for this to happen.

Once considered the king of the wholesome breakfast, vitamin C–laden orange juice is now disparaged by weight-conscious consumers as a high-sugar, high-calorie, high-carbohydrate villain. An eight-ounce glass of orange juice contains about 100 calories, 22 grams of sugar, and 26 grams of carbs. Trendy low-carbohydrate diets generally avoid high-calorie orange juice. Grapefruit, on the other hand, has suffered from a 1989 medical finding that an enzyme in the fruit and juice causes certain medicines to enter the bloodstream at higher doses than recommended. Pharmacists and doctors started suggesting that patients avoid grapefruit while on certain medications. Drug interaction fears have taken a slice out of some of grapefruit's biggest fans—senior citizens.

The grapefruit industry is undertaking a variety of actions in its efforts to regain lost business. For example, the industry is sponsoring research to further examine the breadth of potential drug interactions. According to Andrew Meadows, spokesperson for Florida's Citrus Department, "Our message is that while grapefruit does interact with some drugs, it doesn't interact with all. There was a lot of misunderstanding about that." The industry is also sponsoring research to explore grapefruit's health benefits. "There's always been a perception that grapefruit speeds up metabolism and is a positive thing for diabetics," says Meadows. "We want to prove that scientifically."

Another way the industry is trying to recapture lost sales involves altering the product and its packaging. Tropicana, a division of PepsiCo, has introduced Light'n'Healthy, a 70 percent orange juice drink with about one-third less calories, sugar, and carbs than 100 percent juice, thanks to added water and sweetener. Companies are also packaging citrus brands in grab-and-go single-serving bottles instead of the traditional refrigerator carton. Richey acknowledges, "We've got to be innovative to come up with products to meet the lifestyle of this dashboard-dining mentality."

A rethinking of the industry's advertising strategy has also taken place. In early 2001, officials decided to veer away from touting orange juice as a health food that reduces the chances of cancer, heart disease, and birth defects in an effort to "take orange juice out of the medicine cabinet." Instead, campaigns focused on

*(continued)*

young moms as the principal household shoppers and refrigerator gatekeepers. "We got away from the wholesomeness, natural message," says LaVigne. "We have to reclaim the breakfast spot and target the general nutrition of orange juice as probably the best wholesome product out there, maybe tying that in with obesity." Bob Crawford, executive director of the Florida Department of Citrus, says the organization is returning to the roots of orange juice by emphasizing its health benefits. So in 2004 the Florida Department of Citrus launched a $7 million national television campaign. "Our goal is to remind people that orange juice is the healthiest beverage you can drink," says Meadows.

Sources: Excerpted in part from Christina Hoag, "Ailing Citrus Industry Promotes 'Healthy' OJ," *Miami Herald* (April 20, 2004), C1; Christina Hoag, "The State of Citrus," *Miami Herald: Business Monday* (January 12, 2004), 22–25.

consumption and ultimately are discarded.[8] The primary reason this occurs is because consumers purchase products for an intended usage that never materialized (e.g., unmade recipes, buying something for guests who never show up).[9]

### WHERE DOES CONSUMPTION OCCUR?

When consumption does occur, the particular place or situation in which it occurs may shape consumer behavior. Beer sales, for example, are quite sensitive to whether consumption happens inside or outside the home. The majority of sales for domestic brews are generated by in-home consumption. In contrast, imported beers obtain the majority of their sales on premise (in bars and restaurants).[10] Apparently, many people believe that drinking imported beers projects a more favorable social image to those present during consumption.

The consumption of wine has grown by 24 percent the past decade, and is anticipated to grow nearly 30 percent between 2005 and 2008.[11] And if it does, America will become the top consumer of wine, surpassing France and Italy. Wine makers have been pushing their product in its boxed form recently. Boxed wine sales have grown at more than twice the pace of bottled sales.[12] Even so, consumer acceptance of boxed wines is unlikely to occur for all consumption situations. "I would not be able to handle well someone coming tableside with a towel over their arm and a 3-liter box," says one consumer. "It's just an image I'm not ready for."[13]

Failure to understand where consumption occurs can be a costly mistake. This lesson was learned by Wendy's when it offered drive-through breakfast meals containing scrambled-egg platters, made-to-order omelets, French toast, and pancakes. According to one company executive, "Customers raved about the product, but said, 'I can't travel with it,' and didn't buy it."[14] In contrast, Burger King avoided this problem by offering French toast sticks and miniature pancakes that could be easily held and dipped into maple syrup.

### HOW IS THE PRODUCT CONSUMED?

Different people may purchase the same product but consume it in different ways. Take rice, for example. Sometimes rice is used as an ingredient that's mixed with other food items (e.g., a casserole). Sometimes it's served by itself as a side dish. The particular brand of rice that's purchased often depends on how it will be used. When consumers intend to serve the rice as a side dish, they are more likely to buy an expensive brand. If, however, rice is destined to be used as an ingredient, consumers more often opt for a cheaper competitor. Do you know why these differences occur?

Many consumers believe that the higher-priced brand tastes better than the less-expensive competition. If they intend to serve the rice by itself, they are willing to pay more to enjoy the better taste. But when rice is mixed with other ingredients, its taste becomes less noticeable. For this reason, consumers do not feel justified in spending the additional money for something that goes largely unnoticed. Thus, a change in how the product will be consumed leads to a change in what is purchased.

Understanding how consumers use milk was an essential element in the development of the famous "got milk?" advertising campaign. Prior advertising by the industry depicted milk as something that was consumed alone. Yet milk is a product that typically is digested along with something else, such as cookies, brownies, cereal, or a sandwich. Consequently, the "got milk?" campaign reflected this reality by showing people suffering from a lack of milk while consuming certain food items. In one commercial, a ruthless businessman dies and fears that he has gone to hell. To his relief, he finds a plate of giant chocolate chip cookies and a refrigerator full of milk cartons. After munching on the cookies, he reaches for some milk, only to discover that all of the cartons are empty. Commercials like this helped the milk industry hold per-capita consumption steady after many years of declining use.[15]

Sometimes companies discover consumers using their products in new and innovative ways. A soap manufacturer realized that its sales in one rural region vastly exceeded what would be expected based on the population living in that area. After further investigation, it found that many of the local farmers were using the soap to protect their fruit trees from preying insects and animals. Simply hanging the soap from the limbs deterred the pests without harming the fruit. We'll come back to this topic when we discuss usage knowledge in Chapter 9.

One way companies can enhance their sales is to encourage consumers to use their products in more ways than those they have grown accustomed to. Such is the case for the ad in Figure 6.3, which encourages consumers to use a product traditionally associated with doing laundry for cleaning in the kitchen. This ad is an example of **usage expansion advertising**, which *attempts to persuade consumers to use a familiar product in new or different ways.*[16]

Usage expansion advertising can take several forms. The advertiser could simply link the product to the new usage situation (let's say, for example, eating soup for breakfast). Such advertising might also take a comparative format. The product could be compared to another product typically consumed in the new usage situation (e.g., comparing soup with hot cereal). Alternatively, the product's consumption in the new usage situation could be compared with its consumption in another usage situation commonly associated with the product (e.g., comparing soup for breakfast with soup for lunch). Which form do you think would be most effective? The answer, according to one study, is advertising comparing the different situations, which increased total product consumption by 168 percent versus only 50 percent for product comparison advertising and 106 percent for noncomparison advertising.[17]

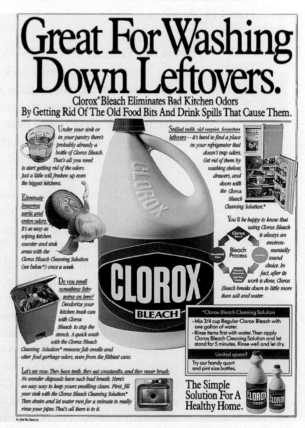

FIGURE 6.3 Companies Often Encourage Different Ways of Consuming Their Products

**FIGURE 6.4** Would Consumers Pour the Same Amount of Beverage into Each of These Glasses?

## HOW MUCH IS CONSUMED?

Consider the parents seeking to influence their children's consumption of a particular beverage. Perhaps they want their children to consume more milk. Maybe they seek to curb the consumption of soft drinks. Now look at the two different glasses appearing in Figure 6.4. These two glasses hold the same volume of liquid. They differ only in their shape. Do you think that young consumers would pour the same amount of beverage into each glass?

Answering this question was the focus of recent research by Wansink and van Ittersum.[18] In one study, young consumers from ages twelve to seventeen poured their own juice for breakfast into either the tall, slender glass or the short, wide glass. Those using the short, wide glass poured and consumed 74 percent more juice than did those using the tall, slender glass. That's right, 74 percent! Why? Despite their equivalence, the shorter glass is perceived to have a smaller capacity.[19] People therefore think that they need to pour more into the shorter glass to reach the desired amount. The same basic result was replicated in a different study using adults, although the magnitude of the difference (19 percent more in the shorter glass) was much less.

The amount of product used by consumers is also affected by their existing supply of the product. Research shows that consumers use less of a cleaning product as the amount remaining decreases.[20] Conversely, as consumers' stockpile of a product increases, they use more of the product.[21] Coupons that encourage stockpiling by requiring the purchase of more than one unit of the product have become increasingly popular and account for one-fourth of coupons distributed to consumers.[22] Carlene Thissen, president of Retail System Consulting, which works on electronic marketing in the supermarket industry, points out that "Hellman's wants you to stock up on Hellman's so you don't buy Kraft for a couple of months."[23] But now you know that, beyond preempting the competition, another potential benefit of promotional activities that encourage stock-piling is that they facilitate greater consumption of the stockpiled product.

In addition to making judgments about how much to consume of a product at a particular moment in time, such as when pouring orange juice into a glass, consumers also have to make judgments about how much they will consume in the future. For example, when deciding between different calling plans for their cell phones, consumers need to estimate their likely monthly usage. Decisions about gym memberships and movie-rental clubs also require consumers to judge whether they will use these services enough to justify their costs. Unfortunately, as discussed in Buyer Beware 6.1, consumers' miscalculations about their usage behaviors often ends up costing them money.

As you are well aware, consumers may differ substantially in their amount of consumption of a particular product. Some of you may drink bottled water all day long. Others may do so only occasionally. But did you know that differences in the amount of consumption provide businesses with a basis for segmenting the user market? This form of segmentation, called **usage volume segmentation**, typically *divides users into one of three segments: heavy users, moderate users, and light users.* Heavy users are those exhibiting the highest levels of product consumption. In the United States, 16 percent of adult consumers account for 88 percent of all wine consumption.[24] Light users are those who consume rather small amounts of the product. Moderate users fall in between these two extremes. In Chapter 2 we introduced the concept of customer lifetime value (CLV). Heavy users will possess a much greater CLV than moderate and light users. For this reason, heavy users are a desirable target market.

**BUYER BEWARE 6.1**

## Consumers' Overestimation of Consumption Can Be Costly

For more than a year, Rachel Hulin paid about $90 a month for a gym membership. She used it maybe four times in all—for a per-visit rate of roughly $315. "I felt sort of like an idiot," says the twenty-four-year-old photographer. "I think I signed up for it to try to make myself go." Ms. Hulin later dropped her membership and joined another less expensive gym at $55 a month. But she admits she hasn't gone there in a while either.

Research suggests consumers often pay too much for services ranging from gym memberships to movie-rental clubs because they overestimate how often they will use them. The studies, by a variety of economists around the country, are part of a growing movement to examine the role of self-control in spending, which affects everything from how you enroll in a 401(k) plan to whether you remember to use a gift card.

The harsh reality that people lack self-discipline rings true for many consumers. In a three-year study of about eight thousand gym membership records from the Boston area, about 80 percent of gym members with a monthly contract were paying significantly more than if they had gone on a pay-per-use basis. That's because members went to the gym an average of less than five times per month, far less than they thought they'd go. The result: average users paid $17 per workout—even though a $10 pay-per-use option existed. That adds up. Members were losing about $700 over the life of the gym contract, compared with the pay-per-use option. The researchers also found that people cancel their memberships months after they actually stop going, at a cost of several hundred dollars. "People take the monthly contract because they assume they are going to the club about two times a week or they hope the monthly option will motivate them to go more," says Ulrike Malmendier, an assistant professor of finance at Stanford's Graduate School of Business, who coauthored the study. "But they end up being overconfident."

Source: Excerpted in part from Rachel Emma Silverman, "Why You Waste So Much Money; Research Suggests That People Don't Use Services Like Gyms, Cell Phones Enough to Justify Cost," *Wall Street Journal* (July 16, 2003), D1.

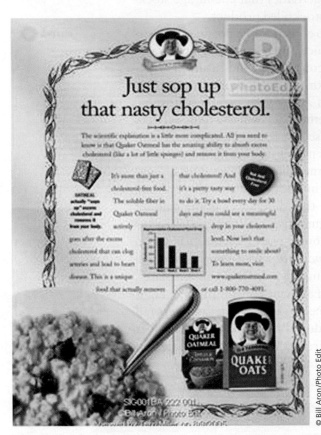

Courtesy of Cattleman's Beef Association

© Bill Aron/Photo Edit

**FIGURE 6.5** Advertising That Encourages More Product Consumption

Beyond its implications for identifying attractive market segments, businesses are also interested in the amount of consumption because enhancing how much consumers consume can translate into greater sales and CLV. Two basic strategies are available to businesses for increasing the amount of consumption. First, companies can try to enhance the frequency of consumption, or how often consumption occurs. So if consumers typically consume the product once a month, one might try to get them to use it once a week. Consider Murphy Oil Soap, a household cleaning product. It's advertising includes copy ("Murphy's Once A Week") explicitly calling for a frequency of usage greater than that undertaken by many of its users. The "got milk?" advertising campaign seeks to increase the frequency of consumption among current milk drinkers rather than converting nonusers into users.[25] Other examples appear in Figure 6.5. The Quaker Oats ad suggests that eating the product daily for 30 days could improve one's cholesterol level. The long-running "Beef, It's What's for Dinner" campaign should enhance beef's chances of being served more often at the dinner table.[26]

Businesses may also encourage more frequent consumption by modifying their products. Earlier we noted that champagne makers want to expand consumption beyond its traditional use during festive occasions. One way they're trying to accomplish this is by offering new products that taste more like wine in the hopes of getting more frequent consumption.[27] Camera film manufacturers have similar aspirations for their new, smaller-sized cameras, some of which are no larger than a credit card. Consumers may be more likely to carry these tiny cameras around with them, thereby leading to more opportunities to snap pictures.[28] Of course, taking pictures is one thing. Whether consumers actually turn these pictures into prints is another. Read Consumer Behavior and Marketing 6.2 to learn more about this.

## Print Me, Please!

Americans have fallen in love with their digital cameras. In 2004, Americans snapped around 22 billion digital images. Yet all is not rosy. The problem? Getting consumers to convert these digital images into hard copies. About two out of three images never knows what it feels like to be printed on paper. Why? Cost is one reason. Convenience is another. "It's easier to just share the pictures online with everyone," explains Courtney Nisbet, a stay-at-home mom in Palo Alto, California, who snaps twenty to thirty pictures of her three-year-old daughter every month but prints only a few of these. And with the introduction of new products that make keeping pictures in their digital form easier and more attractive, getting consumers to print them becomes all the more challenging.

The tendency among customers to save their digital images on a website or their home computers, rather than printing out hard copies, is changing the industry's financial picture. Manufacturers such as Hewlett-Packard and Canon typically lose money on digital cameras and other hardware, recouping their investment only when consumers buy ink cartridges to print images. Retailers that offer photo processing, meanwhile, are looking to digital photos to help replace their declining revenues from traditional film developing. The photo websites are in the same boat: they market themselves as services where you can share photos online, but their primary source of revenue is printing.

Companies are pursuing a variety of strategies designed to encourage consumers to print out their photos instead of just sharing them online or via computer slide shows. These strategies cover the three main ways that people develop digital pictures: on home printers, at a retail outlet, or via a specialized photo website. Hardware makers such as Hewlett-Packard and Canon have marketed various package deals. Hewlett-Packard offered a bundle of photo paper and ink cartridges that it says lowers the expense of home printing from a typical cost of sixty cents to twenty-nine cents per print. Canon provided price discounts for consumers purchasing its digital cameras and printers together.

During the 2004 Christmas season, the time of year when consumers are more likely to be snapping images of parties and present-opening sessions, retailers promoted a variety of deals. CVS, for example, offered a $5 coupon for its $19.99 single-use digital cameras. These cameras have a capacity of twenty-five digital pictures, but to get the photos out of the camera, you have to print them. You can't upload them to a website or save them on a computer.

Online photo websites courted consumers with easier ways to create greeting cards as well as gift merchandise. Snapfish, the online arm of District Photo, significantly increased the number of gift items on its site that can be personalized with a photo. It also cut the price of its photo giftbooks, which essentially are personal photo albums. A company called Shutterfly more than doubled the number of holiday-themed cards available on its website. The company also provided a direct-mail service that addresses and sends its customers' Christmas cards.

Ms. Nisbet, the Palo Alto mother, says she has noticed all the new offers, and plans to take advantage of them. She is going to print more than one hundred Christmas cards on Shutterfly, using a photo of her daughter standing in front of the Golden Gate Bridge. She says, "Its getting so easy now, it's . . . almost a no-brainer."

Source: Excerpted in part from Pui-Wing Tam, "Holiday Deals Target Digital Photos; Incentives Aim to Prod People to Actually Print Their Shots; 14 Billion Unprinted Images," *Wall Street Journal* (December 1, 2004), D1. Also see Pui-Wing Tam, "New Ways to View Your Digital Pictures; Aim Is to Get Camera Owners to Buy Yet Another Gadget; Toting Around 35,000 Photos," *Wall Street Journal* (January 26, 2005), D1.

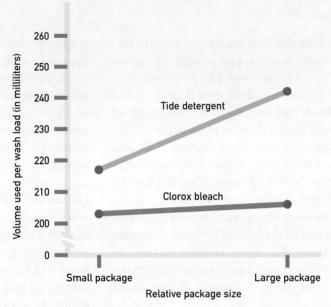

Source: Brian Wansink, "Can Package Size Accelerate Usage Volume?" *Journal of Marketing*, 60 (July 1996), 9.

The second strategy for increasing the amount of consumption involves getting users to consume more per consumption occasion. How might this be done? For packaged goods, the answer lies in the package. Wansink has shown that consumers may use more of a product when it's poured from a larger package.[29] One of his studies examined how much detergent and bleach people used at a laundromat. Some consumers were given these products in a large package; others received them in a small package. The results appear in Figure 6.6. As can be seen, consumers poured 11 percent more detergent into washing machines when the detergent was in the larger package. A significant change as a function of package size was not seen in the usage of bleach, however. Apparently concerns about the negative consequences of overusing the bleach negated the influence of package size. Thus, in some product categories the package size will not affect the amount consumed, but other categories will see that size matters. Indeed, beyond detergent, larger packages have been shown to increase consumers' usage of cooking oil, spaghetti, M&Ms, and household cleaners.[30] Similarly, moviegoers given a large container of free popcorn consumed more than those receiving free popcorn in a medium-sized container.[31]

Another way to increase how much is consumed per consumption occasion is to offer greater product variety. In one study, children were offered free jelly beans on a serving tray. The jelly beans were organized or grouped by color. The children consumed 137 percent more when the serving tray contained twenty-four different colors of jelly beans rather than six different colors. Similarly, adults consumed 123 percent more of the jelly beans as the number of colors present on the tray increased from six to twenty-four. Moreover, greater consumption will occur even if the actual product variety is unchanged so long as consumers think there is more variety. For example, rather than organizing the jelly beans by color, they could be all mixed together on the tray. This might create the illusion of greater variety when the actual variety is relatively limited. Sure enough, the children ate 81 percent more jelly beans when the six colors were presented in a disorganized rather than organized fashion. For adults, an increase of 75 percent occurred.[32]

Our focus so far has been on increasing consumption, but sometimes a reduction in consumption is the objective. Consumers on diets will certainly wish to reduce, even eliminate, their consumption of certain food items. Obviously, the best solution is to simply not have the product around. But if totally eliminating the product from one's surroundings is more than the person can bear, reducing its visibility and convenience (i.e., ease of consumption) will still help consumers achieve their objective of reduced consumption. In an interesting study of this, the visibility and convenience of chocolate candy was varied by changing the location of the candy container in the work environment.[33] Sometimes the container was sitting on the person's desk (visible and convenient). Sometimes it was inside the person's desk (convenient but not visible). And sometimes it was on a shelf away from the desk (neither visible nor convenient). The results (see Figure 6.7) clearly show the benefits to one's waistline by reducing the candy's visibility and convenience.

Those interested in consumer welfare often find themselves trying to get consumers to consume less. In recent years, substantial efforts have been undertaken to reduce the consumption of such things as cigarette smoking, illegal drug usage, and underage drinking. Current trends in obesity clearly underscore the importance of getting both younger and older consumers to, among other things such as developing more active lifestyles, eat less of certain foods. Presently about one out of every three American adults and one out of every six youngsters are seriously overweight.[34] Even more alarming is how rapidly obesity rates have changed. In just twenty years, they have doubled in younger children and tripled in teenagers.[35] This problem is not unique to America. About 7 percent of the adults in the United Kingdom were overweight in 1980, but the figure had risen to about 20 percent in 2004.[36] Food manufacturers that traditionally have targeted children with products perceived as contributing to this obesity problem have now become targets themselves. Critics point to the billions of dollars spent marketing to children and the tens of thousands of television commercials for unhealthy foods watched by children as significant contributors to the obesity problem.[37] Progress is being made. Companies such as Kraft, which has been at the front of its industry in initiating changes, are planning on scaling back on certain types of advertising.[38] Some product changes have been aimed at reducing the problem, such as cutting back on the amount of sugar and eliminating trans-fats altogether.[39] Nonetheless, some critics question whether these changes are enough.[40]

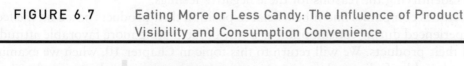

**FIGURE 6.7**   Eating More or Less Candy: The Influence of Product Visibility and Consumption Convenience

6.7

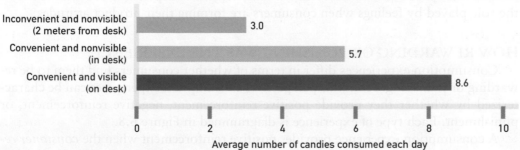

Source: James E. Painter, Brian Wansink, and Julie B. Hieggelke, "How Visibility and Convenience Influence Candy Consumption," *Appetite,* 38 (2002), 237–238.

In the preceding section, we focused on particular behavioral characteristics of consumption, such as when and where it takes place. We now turn to the consumption experience itself.

## HOW DOES IT FEEL?

A critical characteristic of many consumption behaviors is the particular feelings experienced during consumption.[41] How do you feel when you are eating your favorite candy? The last time you visited a dentist, how did you feel? What (if any) feelings do you experience when pouring laundry detergent into the washing machine?

Feelings come in many different shapes and sizes. They can be positive (e.g., excitement, pleasure, relief, sentimentality), or they can be negative (e.g., anger, boredom, guilt, regret). Sometimes they are overwhelming. More often they are experienced with much less intensity.

One of the most intense and inspiring things that I have experienced personally was during my first helicopter ride while vacationing in the Hawaiian Islands. I floated above an extinct volcano, lush with the vegetation that comes from growing in an area that receives the greatest amount of rainfall on our planet. I hovered next to spectacular waterfalls scattered in remote pockets throughout the island. I saw cliffs magnificently sculptured by the ocean winds. At one point, I found myself holding back tears of joy as I marveled at the wonders of nature before me.

Unfortunately, such consumption experiences are the exception rather than the rule. Many consumption behaviors are rather ordinary and experienced with little feeling. Pouring laundry detergent into the washing machine, taking vitamin pills, and pumping gas into a car are activities usually performed without much feeling.

Of course, even an ordinary consumption activity can evoke strong feelings when things go wrong. Have you ever had the dry-cleaner lose your clothes? What about having a trash bag filled with garbage break open, spilling its contents everywhere? Negative feelings, such as disappointment and regret, perhaps even anger, may arise whenever the consumption experience fails to measure up to what was expected.

Typically, negative feelings during product usage are undesirable from both the customer's and company's perspective. Although negative feelings may sometimes be an inherent part of the consumption experience (such as the nervousness and anxiety that accompanies getting a tooth pulled), often they are the result of failing to deliver what the customer wants and expects. Feelings such as disappointment, regret, frustration, and anger are clear indicators of a problem. Implementing corrective actions requires identifying the reasons for these negative feelings.

Sometimes companies find it beneficial to position their products based on the feelings experienced during consumption as a way of facilitating more favorable attitudes toward their products. We will return to this topic in Chapter 10, when we examine the role played by feelings when consumers are forming their product attitudes.

## HOW REWARDING OR PUNISHING WAS THE EXPERIENCE?

Consumption experiences differ in terms of whether consumers find them to be rewarding or punishing. From this perspective, consumption experiences can be characterized by whether they provide positive reinforcement, negative reinforcement, or punishment. Each type of experience is diagrammed in Figure 6.8.

A consumption experience provides **positive reinforcement** when the *consumer receives some positive outcome from product usage.* For example, many of us love to visit amusement parks because of the thrills and exhilaration experienced while riding certain attractions. **Negative reinforcement** occurs when *consumption enables consumers*

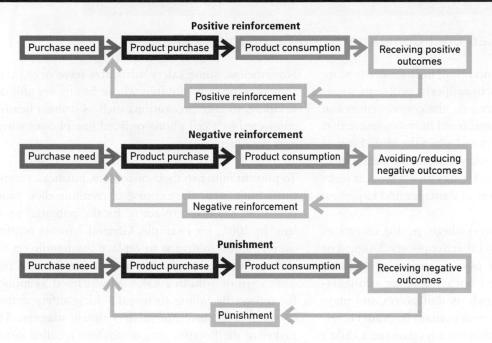

to avoid some negative outcome. Eye drops, for example, are used to remove the negative feelings caused by burning, irritated eyes. Sometimes both positive and negative reinforcement can happen during consumption. An air freshener can replace odors (negative reinforcement) with a refreshing smell (positive reinforcement).

Ideally, companies want their products to provide as much reinforcement as possible. Doing so means that customers are much more likely to become repeat buyers. Unfortunately, consumption experiences sometimes bring punishment. **Punishment** occurs when *consumption leads to negative outcomes.* Cosmetic surgeries that leave the person in worse shape than before the surgery are punishing indeed. A punishing consumption experience is unlikely to be tried again, particularly if the negative outcomes experienced during consumption outweigh any reinforcement that may have also been received. Unfortunately, as described in Buyer Beware 6.2, punishment does exist in the marketplace.

Companies offering negative-reinforcement products should recognize the existence of three distinct market segments for their products. Obviously, consumers currently experiencing the problem solved by the product are the primary target. Consumers who formerly suffered from the problem compose another market segment that may be receptive to appeals that encourage product use to ensure that the problem will not recur. Even consumers who have not faced the problem may be a viable segment. It may be possible to encourage product consumption as a means of reducing the odds that consumers would ever experience the problem. One commercial currently running on television features a young father talking about his family's history of hair loss. He explains that although he currently doesn't have a problem, he uses the advertised product to reduce the chances of future hair loss.

## DID IT CONFIRM OR DISCONFIRM EXPECTATIONS?

Another way to think about consumption experiences involves the degree to which the expectations carried by consumers into purchase and consumption are confirmed or disconfirmed. Consider the following comments from a person who had just completed a canoe trip around Biscayne Bay, Florida: "I was enticed into coming on

## Product Failures Can Cost Consumers and Companies Alike

Although it is in the best interest of businesses to ensure that their products perform properly, problems sometimes arise. And in some cases, the consequences can be dire. A paraplegic man suffered burns so severe that skin graft surgery was required when the heated seat of his 2004 Jeep Grand Cherokee malfunctioned and rose to more than 150 degrees. He has filed a lawsuit seeking more than $14 million in damages and expenses.

Potential dangers lurk everywhere, posing threats to consumers of all ages. Toys that are poorly designed or inadequately tested can pose a variety of risks to young children, ranging from choking or strangulation hazards, toxicity (such as nail polish and play-cosmetics for young girls that contain harmful chemicals), and being so loud that the toys damage a child's hearing. According to a report by the U.S. Public Interest Research Group, a consumer watchdog group, in 2003 there were eleven toy-related deaths and over 200,000 people ended up in the emergency room with toy-related injuries.

Even products as seemingly benign as cell phones are potential hazards. Over the last two years, consumers have filed eighty-three reports with federal safety officials of cell phones exploding or igniting into flames, usually because of a battery problem. Dozens of injuries have been reported, including burns to the face and other parts of the body. Moreover, laboratory research has shown that the electromagnetic fields typical of cell phones can cause damage to human cells. Even so, no scientific evidence yet shows that cell phones themselves will cause similar damage.

Nonetheless, some safety advocates have urged consumers, especially children whose brains are still developing, to take precautions such as using a headset connected to a cell phone or fixed line phones whenever possible.

To prevent injury to their customers, businesses sometimes must incur the expense of recalling their products from the marketplace to fix the potential problem. In 2005, for example, General Motors recalled over 700,000 minivans to replace the handle on the sliding doors, which had been found to injure a person's wrist or arm. In 2004, GM was fined $1 million for repeatedly failing to reveal vehicle safety defects to the federal government in a timely manner. The maker of the Bowflex fitness machine recalled nearly 800,000 machines in 2005 as a result of the injuries reported by customers because of either the seat breaking or the backboard bench collapsing.

These two products are only the tip of the iceberg when it comes to product recalls. The Consumer Product Safety Commission (CPSC), the federal agency responsible for such matters, made 279 recalls involving about 40 million product units in 2003. The CPSC website (www.cpsc.gov) is an invaluable information source for those seeking to keep abreast of product safety issues. The site contains information on over 4,000 product recalls and recall alerts. According to this website, consumer product-related incidents are responsible for more than $700 billion in damages to people and property each year. Now that is something to beware of!

Sources: David Pringle and Peter Grant, "Child-Cellphone Warning Stirs Debate," *Wall Street Journal* (January 13, 2005), D2; Camille Ricketts, "Heed Warnings on Toys, Group Advises Parents," *Miami Herald* (November 24, 2004), A6; Elizabeth Wolfe, "Cellphone Explosions Scrutinized," *Miami Herald* (November 24, 2004), A3; Greg Schneider, "GM Fined for Slow Reporting of Defects," www.washingtonpost.com (January 13, 2005); "Bowflex Fitness Machine Recalled Following Injuries," *Wall Street Journal* (November 17, 2004); "Exploding Cell Phones a Growing Problem," www.business.bostonherald.com (November 24, 2004); "GM Recalls 700,000 Minivans," www.washingtonpost.com (December 24, 2004); "Paraplegic Sues Chrysler Over Heated Seat," www.washingtonpost.com (December 17, 2004); "Study: Mobile Phone Radiation Harms DNA," www.cnnmoney.com (December 21, 2004); United States Consumer Product Safety Commission, *2003 Annual Report*, www.cpsc.gov.

this trip. I was told it would be easy and it was not. I was told it would be cool and it was not. I was told I would see lots of wildlife and I saw very little. I'm just glad it is over."[42] Obviously, the consumption experience did not live up to this person's expectations.

Of course, this is just one person's experience with a single, small, largely unknown company. So let's take a look at what thousands of consumers think about

TABLE 6.1

## Average Ratings of How Well Different Brands Are Meeting Consumers' Expectations

6.1

| BRAND | RATING |
|-------|--------|
| WD-40 spray lubricant | 7.99 |
| Reynolds Wrap aluminum foil | 7.93 |
| Heinz ketchup | 7.73 |
| Oreo cookies | 7.69 |
| Duracell batteries | 7.58 |
| Google.com | 7.44 |
| Barnes & Noble | 7.35 |
| Yahoo! | 7.07 |
| Wal*Mart | 6.99 |
| Best Buy | 6.88 |
| Visa | 6.75 |
| Microsoft.com | 6.42 |
| MasterCard | 6.30 |
| eBay | 6.24 |
| Nokia cell phones | 6.24 |
| Motorola cell phones | 6.18 |
| Discover | 5.73 |
| Verizon Wireless | 5.50 |
| Citibank | 5.49 |
| AT&T Long-Distance Services | 4.98 |

Source: "Reynolds Wrap Aluminum Foil Ranks #1 in Overall Brand Equity," Harris Interactive, www.harrisinteractive.com (June 22, 2004). Reprinted with permission from Harris Interactive, Inc. All Rights Reserved.

Note: The higher the number, the more expectations have been fulfilled, with 10 being the maximum score.

well-established products, services, and retailers financed by major corporations. Part of the EquiTrend system developed by Harris Interactive to assess brand equity (you'll learn more about this system in Chapter 10) includes an assessment of whether consumers believe that the product, service, or retailer fulfilled their expectations. Table 6.1 presents the average expectations ratings for twenty of the more than one thousand brands evaluated in the EquiTrend system.

Notice the substantial variation that exists among the brands in how well they are meeting consumers' expectations, ranging from WD-40, at the top with a score of 7.99 out of a possible 10, to AT&T long-distance services, at the bottom with a score of only 4.98. Note that the top of the list is dominated by branded products, with retailers and service providers lagging behind in how well they fulfill consumers' expectations. Clearly room for improvement exists for virtually all of these brands, although certainly more so for some than others. Not only is there room for improvement, but there's also the need. As we will discuss later in the chapter when we consider post-consumption evaluations, the extent to which the consumption experience confirms or disconfirms expectations usually has a powerful influence on the degree of customer satisfaction, which in turn affects the likelihood of repeat buying.

## SHAPING CONSUMERS' INTERPRETATION
## OF THE CONSUMPTION EXPERIENCE

Those interested in influencing consumer behavior will be happy to learn that consumers' interpretation of a consumption experience may depend on more than the consumption experience itself. For example, your opinion about a coffee's taste, such as whether or not it is bitter, can be affected by more than the coffee's actual bitterness. How? By altering your expectations about this product characteristic prior to tasting it. Suppose some of you are led to anticipate that a coffee are about to drink it is bitter tasting, but the rest of you are not led to expect this. All of you then drink the same coffee. A study testing exactly this situation showed that, when asked to rate the coffee's bitterness, those expecting a bitter coffee rated the coffee as more bitter than those not expecting bitterness.[43]

Another demonstration of this phenomenon is provided by a classic marketing research study showing that brand names create expectations that affect how a product, in this case beer, is judged following consumption. When the consumed brands were unlabeled (i.e., consumers tasted the brands without knowing their brand identities), consumers did not differentiate between the brands; they rated all the brands essentially the same. This was not the case when consumers tasted the brands and knew their brand identities (i.e., the brands were labeled). For some brands, consumers' ratings increased dramatically when the label was present during consumption. Thus, the expectation created by the brand label was powerful enough to alter consumers' interpretation of what their taste buds were telling them.[44] Findings such as these underscore the added benefits companies receive from having strong brand names for their products.

Expectations may not always bias post-consumption evaluations. Bias depends on the ambiguity of the consumption experience. In a study in which product quality could be judged unambiguously (in this case, a paper towel's ability to absorb water), the expectations of product quality created by an advertisement had no impact. Yet when product quality was difficult to evaluate (a polo shirt's quality), advertising-based expectations were influential.[45]

Consumers' interpretation of a consumption experience may also depend on their moods at the time of consumption.[46] But we will defer discussion of this until Chapter 10, where you will learn about how moods and feelings can shape consumers' attitudes.

### Consumption Norms and Rituals

**Consumption norms** represent *informal rules that govern our consumption behavior.* A suit and tie are the expected garb for businessmen. Gifts representing expressions of love are exchanged on Valentine's Day. A corsage is a fundamental part of a prom date.

Many consumption activities are ritualized. **Consumption rituals** are defined as "*a type of expressive, symbolic activity constructed of multiple behaviors that occur in a fixed, episodic sequence, and that tend to be repeated over time. Ritual behavior is dramatically scripted and acted out and is performed with formality, seriousness, and inner intensity.*"[47] At the time this chapter is being written, it's almost Thanksgiving, so let's use this U.S. national holiday to illustrate consumption rituals.[48]

The origins of Thanksgiving go back to 1621 when the Pilgrims invited the local Native Americans to a feast to celebrate a good harvest. This celebration has since become one of the most widely observed holidays in America. The script is all too familiar. Family and close friends converge to a single location for a day of relaxation, conversation, and, of course, eating. Turkey, mashed potatoes, stuffing, cranberries, and pumpkin pie will be found on many dining tables. Although most people think of

Thanksgiving as a day of family togetherness, it also represents symbolically a celebration of material abundance. The table is loaded with a greater variety of foods than found at nearly any other time during the year; plates are filled until they are overflowing, and the host or hostess often isn't happy until at least some of the participants announce that they have eaten too much! Figure 6.9 shows how one company reinforces its product's place during consumption rituals.

Holiday rituals are but one of many different types of consumption rituals. Most of us perform certain grooming rituals that are followed routinely when getting ready in the morning.[49] Gift-giving behavior can also be characterized as ritual.[50] And during football season, many fans engage in particular game-day rituals.

## Compulsive Consumption

Consumption behavior can take forms and directions that are decidedly counterproductive. The term **compulsive consumption** is defined as *a response to an uncontrollable drive or desire to obtain, use, or experience a feeling, substance, or activity that leads an individual to repetitively engage in a behavior that will ultimately cause harm to the individual and possibly others.*[51] The term *compulsive consumption* actually encompasses many forms of compulsive consumer behavior: compulsive buying, compulsive shopping, compulsive spending, compulsive depletion, compulsive using, and compulsive possession.[52] Each of these forms of compulsive consumption is defined in Table 6.2.

Compulsive consumption may occur for any one of a number of different reasons. It may occur as a way of bolstering the person's self-esteem.[53] Feeling depressed or inadequate may trigger it.[54] Fear may motivate it, such as those who hoard objects

**FIGURE 6.9** Reinforcing the Product's Place During Consumption Rituals

| | TABLE 6.2 | The Many Forms of Compulsive Consumption |
|---|---|---|

| CONCEPT | DEFINITION |
|---|---|
| Compulsive shopping | The compulsive drive to browse in the marketplace regardless of whether something is purchased |
| Compulsive buying | The compulsive drive to purchase something |
| Compulsive spending | The compulsive drive to dispose of one's money |
| Compulsive depletion | The compulsive drive to consume something until it is gone |
| Compulsive using or doing | The compulsive drive to use or do something |
| Compulsive possession | The compulsive drive to own something |

Sources: Derek N. Hassay and Malcolm C. Smith. "Compulsive Buying: An Examination of the Consumption Motive." *Psychology & Marketing*, 13 (December 1996), 741–752; Rajan Nataraajan and Brent G. Goff. "Manifestations of Compulsiveness in the Consumer-Marketplace Domain." *Psychology & Marketing*, 9 (January 1992), 31–44.

(a type of compulsive possession) out of fear that they may one day need them.[55] Even a person's family structure has been linked to compulsive consumption, with those growing up in single-parent families being more likely to engage in such behavior.[56]

Beyond shopping and buying, compulsive consumption can extend to such activities as exercising and gambling.[57] According to the National Gambling Impact Study Commission, over five million Americans have a gambling problem. This problem is not limited to adults. More than one million American adolescents ranging in age from twelve to seventeen are compulsive gamblers. Estimates of the economic cost of problem gambling are in the billions of dollars.[58] Compulsive consumption has also been linked to such problems as alcoholism, eating disorders, kleptomania, and drug abuse.[59]

The Internet has given birth to a new type of compulsive consumption: Web dependency. Web dependents average nearly forty hours a week on the Internet. Nearly half are homemakers and unemployed college students. Many spend most of their time in chat rooms where they often assume different identities. Letters seeking advice from newspaper columnists about Web dependency are common. And one mother was arrested for child endangerment after police discovered her children in a feces-littered playroom while she sat nearby in a spotless computer room.[60]

## Understanding Consumption through Ethnography

At this point you should have a pretty good understanding of the consumption stage of the decision-making process. We now want to say a few words about how businesses and researchers learn about consumers' product usage using ethnography. **Ethnography** involves *describing and understanding consumer behavior by interviewing and observing consumers in real-world situations*. Ethnography can take many forms. Table 6.3 describes the ethnographic techniques used by IDEO, a design firm whose client list includes AT&T Wireless Services, Gap, Hewlett-Packard, NASA, Nestlé, Prada, Procter & Gamble, and Samsung. "I think the world of them," says Procter & Gamble CEO Alan Lafley about IDEO. "They are a world-class strategic partner."[61]

| TABLE 6.3 | IDEO's Ethnographic Techniques |
| --- | --- |
| **TECHNIQUE** | **DESCRIPTION** |
| Shadowing | Observing people using products, shopping, going to hospitals, taking the train, using their cell phones |
| Behavioral mapping | Photographing people within a space, such as a hospital waiting room, over two or three days |
| Consumer journey | Keeping track of all the interactions a consumer has with a product, service, or space |
| Camera journals | Asking consumers to keep visual diaries of their activities and impressions relating to a product |
| Extreme user interviews | Talking to people who really know—or know nothing—about a product or service, and evaluating their experience using it |
| Storytelling | Prompting people to tell personal stories about their consumption experiences |
| Unfocus groups | Interviewing a diverse group of people (to explore ideas about sandals, for example, IDEO gathered an artist, a bodybuilder, a podiatrist, and a shoe fetishist) |

Source: Excerpted from Bruce Nussbaum, "The Power of Design," *Business Week* (May 17, 2004), 86–90.

## Ethnographic Analysis of the Miller Lite Drinker

To get a better handle on its customers, the Miller Brewing Company turned to its advertising agency, Ogilvy & Mather, one of the world's top agencies, and its ethnographers. As directors of OgilvyDiscovery, Emma Gilding and Johanna Shapira supervise a team of researchers who follow consumers for hours or days at a time, filming them in their native habitats. Their goal: to capture the telling moments that reveal what consumers actually do with products, rather than what they say they do.

One of their projects involved trying to decode the male-bonding rituals of twenty-something Miller Lite drinkers. Doing so required spending many hours observing men drinking in bars. As a videographer films the action, Gilding keeps tabs on how close the guys stand to one another. She sees that high-fiving is out, fist-pounding is in. She watches guys gather, disperse, then reconvene around the call for "Beer!" She eavesdrops on stories and observes how the mantle passes from one speaker to another, as in a tribe around a campfire.

Back at the office, a team of trained anthropologists and psychologists pore over more than seventy hours of footage. One key insight: Miller Lite is favored by groups of drinkers, whereas its main competitor, Bud Lite, is a beer that sells to individuals. That insight reinforced research that Tom Bick, Miller's senior brand manager, had been conducting independently. "We can see from our own demographics and focus groups that our drinker base was somewhat different than Bud's," he says. "But we couldn't put our finger on it." Ogilvy's research confirmed that the archetypal Miller drinker felt more comfortable expressing affection for friends than did the Bud Lite boys. "We felt the Bud guys were much more about impressing each other," Bick says. "The problem was, how do we convey that without completely going off the edge? We

don't want a campaign that got all sanctimonious. It's a beer ad."

Enter the Ogilvy creative team, which riffed on their own experience in bars. The result was a hilarious series of ads that cut from a Miller Lite drinker's weird experiences in the world—getting caught in the subway taking money from a blind musician's guitar case, and hitching a ride in the desert with a deranged trucker—to shots of him regaling friends with tales over a brew. Steve Hayden, Ogilvy's vice chairman and worldwide creative director, said the real-life video helped the team get the details just right: "In advertising, one of the hardest things to do is to recreate a world, from behavior to real human cadences and tones. The tape showed us, for example, that these guys don't speak in neat sentences or well-outlined paragraphs. It let us bring a level of verisimilitude to the execution that was just terrific."

Although the ads had high marks from audiences for their entertainment value and emotional resonance, they weren't as successful in driving sales. "What people got from that campaign was that it was about time with your best friends," says Bick. "The emotional side was very powerful. Its downfall was that it didn't work on a more fundamental level." That is, it didn't connect the emotional appeal with a compelling enough product message. But Bick isn't complaining. Indeed, he thinks it may be time to deploy another team to revalidate the initial findings and discover what's new. In fact, he's considering similar research for Miller Genuine Draft, Miller Lite's sister brand. "So much other research is done in isolation of social groups," he says. "But brands are adopted by a tribe of users." Ethnographic research "helped us to understand the Miller Lite drinker and his friends as genuine people." Now, he just needs to figure out how to sell those guys more beer.

Source: Excerpted in part from Linda Tischler, "Every Move You Make," *Fast Company* (April 2004), 73–75.

Manufacturers find ethnographic analysis useful in many ways. By observing how consumers use their products, companies may learn that consumers engage in certain activities that are counterproductive to maximizing product performance, which, in turn, can reduce their satisfaction with the product. In Consumer Behavior and Marketing 9.2 of Chapter 9, we describe how laundry detergent makers watched consumers doing their laundry and discovered certain limitations in consumers' usage knowledge. Ethnographic analysis may reveal problems or points of frustration when consumers' use of a product suggests ways of improving the product, or even provides the foundation for developing a new product. Observing consumers' cleaning habits helped Procter & Gamble launch its $1 billion Swiffer mop business.[62] Observation may even reveal novel ways that the product is used by consumers that can be used in promoting the product.

Ethnography is also valuable to retailers and advertisers. **Shop-a-longs,** *in which shoppers are accompanied by one or more observers,* can help retailers better understand which things seem to attract shoppers' attention and interest as well as which areas have room for improvement. One shop-a-long revealed that many women didn't especially enjoy shopping for lingerie at department stores.[63] Finding certain products wasn't always easy. Fitting rooms were often too small to accommodate the female friend accompanying the shopper. Even a place nearby for the friend to sit was uncommon. Advertisers find ethnographic analysis to be a powerful way of getting closer to the customer. Doing so enables them to develop messages with a stronger appeal. One example of this can be found in Consumer Behavior and Marketing 6.3 (on p. 209).

The emergence of ethnography in academic consumer research can be traced back to the mid-1980s. One of the most unique events in the history of consumer research occurred in the summer of 1986.[64] In what has become known as the Consumer Behavior Odyssey, a rotating group of academic researchers traveled across the United States and observed consumer behavior in a variety of marketplace settings, including swap meets, flea markets, festivals, and stores, as well as in consumers' homes. The observations and insights derived from the Odyssey provided the basis for journal articles[65] and conference presentations[66] that have helped ethnography grow into a major discipline within the field of consumer research. Ethnographers have applied their skills to understanding many facets of consumer behavior, ranging from Thanksgiving rituals[67] to rodeos[68] to bikers[69] to the homeless,[70] and more.[71]

## Post-Consumption Evaluations

As discussed in Chapter 4, evaluating choice alternatives is a fundamental part of the pre-purchase phase of the decision-making process. Evaluations also occur following purchase and consumption. We refer to these as post-consumption evaluations, and they represent the next stage of our decision-making process. Based on their consumption experience, consumers will reinforce or modify their attitudes toward the consumed object (Chapter 10 covers the concept of attitudes in considerable depth). Traditionally, both practitioners and academicians have focused on post-consumption evaluations in the form of *satisfaction* and *dissatisfaction,* representing whether product consumption is viewed as providing the consumer with a favorable or unfavorable experience.

How satisfied are American consumers with the products they consume? An entire industry of market research firms is devoted to answering this question. One of the most famous is J. D. Power & Associates, the focus of Market Facts 6.2. Unfortunately, the proprietary reports produced by these companies are rarely available for public consumption. Fortunately, publicly available information about the satisfaction

## J. D. Power & Associates

The name J. D. Power is virtually synonymous with the measurement of satisfaction in the world of marketing. Firms that have earned a J. D. Power award for outstanding customer satisfaction often feature the award in their advertising and promotional materials (if you look at Figure 6.15 you will find an example of the J. D. Power award being used in advertising). Back in 1968, David Power III founded J. D. Power & Associates (JDPA). In the beginning the firm focused on measuring the satisfaction of American new car buyers. Today, JDPA surveys consumers' levels of satisfaction in a variety of other industries, including telecommunications, health care, utilities, travel, insurance, and real estate. In 2003, it had research-only revenues of nearly $120 million in the United States, making JDPA the twelfth-largest market research firm in the country. For more information about J. D. Power & Associates, go to www.jdpower.com.

Source: Jack Honomichl, "Honomichl Top 50," *Marketing News* (June 15, 2004), H24. Reprinted with permission from American Marketing Association.

levels of American consumers is provided by the American Customer Satisfaction Index (ACSI), which has been produced by the University of Michigan Business School and its partners since 1994.[72] Tens of thousands of U.S. consumers are surveyed about their level of satisfaction with the products, services, and websites of approximately two hundred companies and fifty government agencies. The survey, administered on a quarterly basis, asks consumers to rate along a 0–100 point scale only those products, services, and websites that they've used in the past month. The average rating has been slowly increasing the past few years. In 2004, the average rating reached an average of 74, its highest level since 1995.[73] The satisfaction ratings of some of the companies are summarized from highest to lowest in Table 6.4.

Clorox and Heinz, two companies that make their livings in the supermarkets of America, head the list with a rather impressive score of 88. These were the top scores in the commercial sector, but ACSI has recorded even higher scores in the government sector. Coming in at an eye-popping 95 is the Veteran Administration's National Cemetery Administration. Nonetheless, consumers are not happy with all governmental agencies. Indeed, the Internal Revenue Service registered only a 52 among individual paper tax filers (interestingly, this score jumps to 78 for electronic tax filers). But back to the commercial sector and Table 6.4, notice the relatively poor scores attached to such well-known companies as McDonald's, US Airways, and Sprint. For reasons discussed shortly, these rather poor satisfaction ratings suggest a less than rosy future for these companies. Any such conclusions, however, should be tempered by how these scores (1) compare to the scores earned by competitors in the same industry, and (2) their trend over time. Let's examine why this is so.

Consider US Airways. The average rating for the airline industry in 2004 was 66. Against this average, US Airways' score of 62 doesn't look nearly as bad. Nonetheless, US Airways does not compete against an average; it competes against individual airlines. And against such competitors as Northwest (64), American (66), and Delta (67), its satisfaction score is not that far behind. But when compared to Southwest Airlines' score of 73, US Airways is clearly at a disadvantage. Moreover, the trend over time is particularly troublesome. In the past year, US Airways' scores have declined by 3 percent, from 64 to its current 62. (And if you think a 3 percent decline is rather minor, reserve such judgments until after you read in the next section of the chapter about the impact satisfaction has on a firm's financial value.) The decline is even more dramatic

**TABLE 6.4**     ACSI Satisfaction Scores by Company

| COMPANY | SCORE |
| --- | --- |
| Clorox | 88 |
| H. J. Heinz | 88 |
| Amazon.com | 84 |
| Coca-Cola | 83 |
| FedEx | 83 |
| Publix Supermarkets | 82 |
| Apple Computer | 81 |
| Campbell Soup | 79 |
| Miller Brewing | 79 |
| Nike | 78 |
| Hilton Hotels | 77 |
| Papa John's Pizza | 76 |
| Travelocity.com | 76 |
| *Average rating* | 74 |
| Southwest Airlines | 73 |
| Motorola | 70 |
| Taco Bell | 68 |
| Verizon Wireless | 68 |
| Ramada | 67 |
| Aetna Health Insurance | 66 |
| McDonald's | 64 |
| US Airways | 62 |
| Sprint PCS Group | 59 |
| Charter Communications | 56 |

Source: Fourth Quarter Scores 2003, First Quarter Scores 2004, Second Quarter Scores 2004, Third Quarter Scores 2004, ACSI—American Customer Satisfaction Index. www.theacsi.org. Reprinted with permission.

if we go all the way back to the first time the ACSI survey was administered, when US Airways scored a 72. These findings indicate that US Airways will be flying into a strong headwind unless the company turns things around.

Not only does satisfaction vary from one product to another, it may vary from one geographic region to another for the same product.[74] When a domestic automobile manufacturer examined its customers' satisfaction, considerable variation in the level of satisfaction was detected across the United States. Figure 6.10 depicts these results and reveals considerable variability in customer satisfaction from one geographic location to another. Those areas appearing darker in color indicate more satisfied customers, and those appearing lighter signify less satisfied customers. Identifying such variations allows businesses to specify those areas in greatest need of whatever actions are deemed necessary for improving customer satisfaction.

## The Importance of Customer Satisfaction

Why should companies be so concerned about customer satisfaction? Perhaps most obvious is that customer satisfaction impacts the odds of customers coming back for

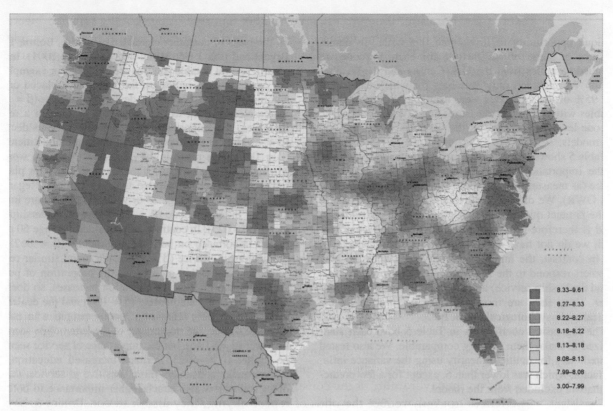

| | |
|---|---|
| | 8.33–9.61 |
| | 8.27–8.33 |
| | 8.22–8.27 |
| | 8.18–8.22 |
| | 8.13–8.18 |
| | 8.08–8.13 |
| | 7.99–8.08 |
| | 3.00–7.99 |

**FIGURE 6.10** Geographic Variations in Customer Satisfaction

Source: Vikas Mittal, Wagner A. Kamakura, and Rahul Govind, "Geographic Patterns in Customer Service and Satisfaction: An Empirical Investigation," *Journal of Marketing*, 68 (July 2004), 48–62.

more. But this is far from the only reason why companies should devote special attention to customer satisfaction. The purpose of this section is to describe the many reasons that make customer satisfaction so important.[75]

## IT INFLUENCES REPEAT BUYING

As just noted, customer satisfaction influences whether consumers will buy from the same company again. Consumers holding negative evaluations of the product following consumption are unlikely to buy again; those holding positive evaluations are much more likely to repurchase the product. Because it is typically cheaper to retain an existing customer than to recruit a new one,[76] companies have become very focused on ensuring that their customers have satisfactory consumption experiences. Nonetheless, unhappy customers are not uncommon. In 2002, America Online (AOL), the Internet service provider, averaged more than 200,000 customers per month becoming ex-customers.[77]

Importantly, the relationship between customer satisfaction and customer retention is not perfect.[78] According to an article published by the *Harvard Business Review*, "In business after business, 60 percent to 80 percent of lost customers reported on a survey just prior to defecting that they were satisfied or very satisfied. Most automakers . . . still see 90 percent of their customers claiming to be satisfied and 40 percent coming back to buy again."[79] Yet it should not be too surprising that many of the customers satisfied today take their business elsewhere tomorrow. After all, there are typically many competitors dangling attractive incentives as bait to lure away one's customers.

Although a satisfactory consumption experience does not guarantee loyalty, the likelihood that customers will remain loyal depends on their level of satisfaction. The

Xerox Corporation discovered that customers reported to be "totally satisfied" were six times more likely to repurchase its products than customers who reported simply being "satisfied."[80] For this reason, businesses have begun to realize that simply satisfying customers may not be enough. Rather, they should strive for "customer delight," which comes when customers are satisfied completely.[81] Consistent with this, the Enterprise Rent-A-Car company only counts those customers giving it the very highest rating in its satisfaction surveys in ranking its five thousand U.S. branches. And to ensure that these numbers were taken seriously, the company implemented a policy that managers could not be promoted unless the branch or branches under their charge equaled or exceeded the company's average scores, a policy the company CEO believes to be a major reason for the company's continued growth.[82]

## IT SHAPES WORD-OF-MOUTH AND WORD-OF-MOUSE COMMUNICATION

Beyond influencing consumers' future purchase behaviors, post-consumption evaluations affect other behaviors as well. *Discussing one's consumption experiences with other people* is a common activity, known as **word-of-mouth communication.** How many times have you heard people talking about their last vacation, seeing the latest movie, dining at some restaurant, or getting ripped off by some unscrupulous company? Conversations about consumption experiences are a common occurrence.

Obviously, the favorability of such word-of-mouth communication directly depends on the favorability of the consumption experience.[83] Negative consumption experiences not only reduce the odds of repeat buying, they also lead consumers to say unflattering things when discussing their experiences with others. Dissatisfied consumers sometimes go to great lengths to share their negative opinions with others, even complete strangers. Consider the unhappy renter who, at his own expense, copied and distributed hundreds of copies of the flyer in Figure 6.11.

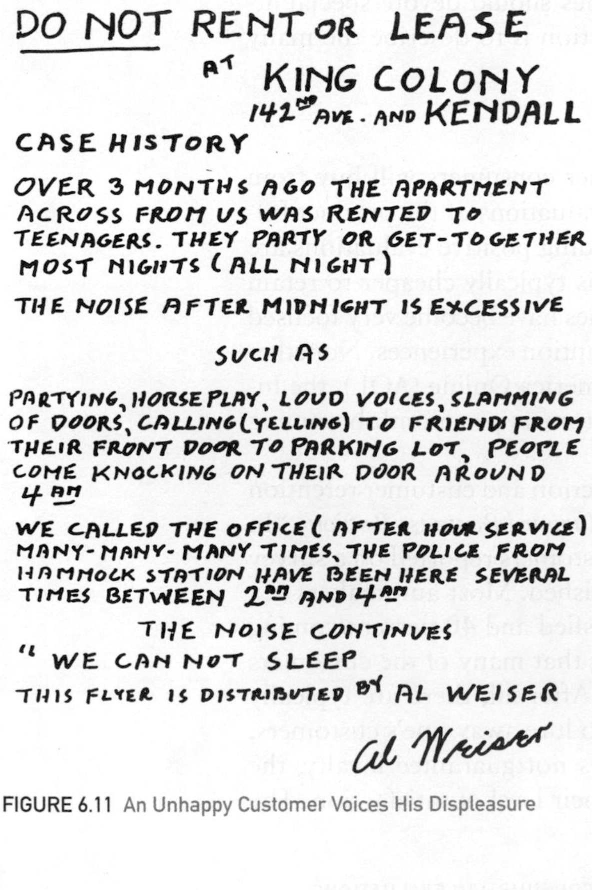

In April 2003, the Sloan School of Management at MIT hosted a conference focusing on the role of the Internet in facilitating communication among consumers and how businesses can cope with this rapidly expanding form of communication.[84] To better represent the uniqueness of *consumers communicating with each other over the Internet*, a new term has entered our vernacular: **word-of-mouse communication.**[85] And never has any mouse been this powerful. Whereas word-of-mouth communication may trickle down to the friend of your friend's friend, word-of-mouse builds like an avalanche with the speed of lightning. Here are two stories that provide testimony to the power of word-of-mouse.

First up is the story of the Neistat brothers, Casey and Van. When the battery in Casey's iPod began to fail, he contacted Apple for a replacement. To his dismay, he was told that the cost of replacing his battery would be so high that he was better off buying a new iPod. The brothers decided to document their experience in a three-minute film titled "iPod's Dirty Secret." The film begins with an audio of Casey talking to an Apple representative about this problem and learning that he will not be able to replace his battery at a reasonable price. The remainder of the film shows Casey spray painting the message "iPod's unreplaceable battery lasts only

DO NOT RENT OR LEASE
AT KING COLONY
142ND AVE. AND KENDALL

CASE HISTORY

OVER 3 MONTHS AGO THE APARTMENT ACROSS FROM US WAS RENTED TO TEENAGERS. THEY PARTY OR GET-TOGETHER MOST NIGHTS (ALL NIGHT)

THE NOISE AFTER MIDNIGHT IS EXCESSIVE

SUCH AS

PARTYING, HORSE PLAY, LOUD VOICES, SLAMMING OF DOORS, CALLING (YELLING) TO FRIENDS FROM THEIR FRONT DOOR TO PARKING LOT, PEOPLE COME KNOCKING ON THEIR DOOR AROUND 4 AM

WE CALLED THE OFFICE (AFTER HOUR SERVICE) MANY-MANY-MANY TIMES, THE POLICE FROM HAMMOCK STATION HAVE BEEN HERE SEVERAL TIMES BETWEEN 2ND AND 4AM

THE NOISE CONTINUES
"WE CAN NOT SLEEP

THIS FLYER IS DISTRIBUTED BY AL WEISER

Al Weiser

Courtesy of Mr. and Mrs. Al Weiser

**FIGURE 6.11** An Unhappy Customer Voices His Displeasure

**FIGURE 6.12**    Kryptonite's Ten-Day Experience with Word-of-Mouse on the Internet

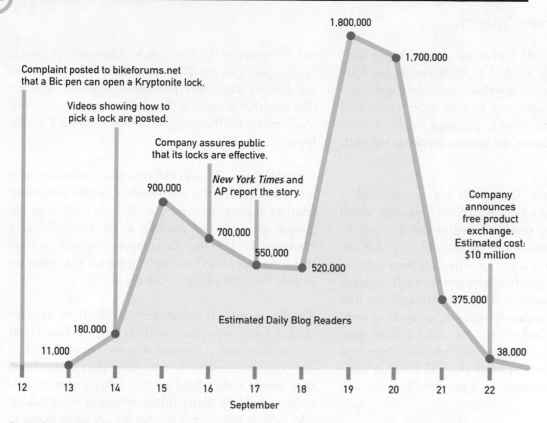

Complaint posted to bikeforums.net that a Bic pen can open a Kryptonite lock.

Videos showing how to pick a lock are posted.

Company assures public that its locks are effective.

*New York Times* and AP report the story.

Company announces free product exchange. Estimated cost: $10 million

1,800,000

1,700,000

900,000

700,000

550,000

520,000

375,000

180,000

11,000

38,000

Estimated Daily Blog Readers

12    13    14    15    16    17    18    19    20    21    22

September

Source: David Kirk Patrick and Daniel Roth, "Why There's No Escaping the Blog." *Fortune* (January 10, 2005), 44–50.

18 months" on numerous iPod posters. The brothers initially posted the film on the Web (which can be seen at www.ipodsdirtysecret.com) in late 2003, and told some of their friends about it. By the next day, they had 300 hits on their site. By the following day, the number had grown to 40,000. By the time I viewed the film on December 31, 2004, the counter on the website was at 1,704,333. Clearly few consumers can claim to have had this degree of word-of-mouth influence.

Our next example begins on September 12, 2004, when someone posted on a group discussion site for bicycle enthusiasts that the popular U-shaped Kryptonite lock could be opened easily with, of all things, a Bic ballpoint pen.[86] A couple days later, a video demonstration of this appeared on several blogs. **Blogs,** short for Web logs, are *websites that contain an online personal journal with reflections, comments, and often hyperlinks provided by the writer.*[87] As shown in Figure 6.12, the number of people who read a posting about Kryptonite exploded. Within ten days of the original posting, nearly 7 million people had seen something posted about this issue. Eventually, the makers of Kryptonite offered consumers a free lock in exchange for their defective one. The expected cost of doing so: $10 million.

Nonetheless, voicing your displeasure with companies and their products can be risky. As described in Buyer Beware 6.3, one couple has been sued by a company that created a website to inform other consumers about their unhappy experience with the company's product.

Note, then, that a company's ability to deliver a satisfying consumption experience will affect its success in retaining current customers as well as recruiting new ones. Disappointed customers may not only take their business elsewhere, but they may

## The Price of Free Speech

When Allen and Linda Townsend were unhappy with the spray-on siding applied to their house, the frustrated couple launched a website, complete with photographs, to complain and to give other unsatisfied customers a forum. Visitor postings to the website said the product, Spray on Siding, cracked, bubbled, and buckled.

For their efforts, the Townsends got slapped with a lawsuit by the product's maker. Alvis Coatings, which supplied the siding product used in the Townsends' $16,721 home remodeling project, claims that the couple's website infringes on the company's trademarks, defames its product, and intentionally misleads and confuses consumers. The complaint alleges that the name of the Townsends' website, spraysiding.com, "is confusingly similar" to the official Alvis site, sprayonsiding.com, as well as its trademark "Spray on Siding." Alvis is seeking more than $75,000 in damages in addition to unspecified punitive damages and attorney fees.

Though neither side was looking for a brawl over speech rights, the lawsuit is headed that way, says Paul Levy, an attorney for Public Citizen, which agreed to help represent the Townsends. Among other things, Levy argues that the Townsends have the right to use the domain name they purchased. Another attorney observes that a website that bashes a product is not likely to create the type of confusion alleged in the lawsuit.

Craig Hartman, Alvis's chief operations manager, says his company sued the Townsends only after months of fruitless dealings with the couple. "We truly want the people who use our product to be satisfied," says Hartman. He said that the company made three "formal generous offers" to the Townsends that were rejected. The lawsuit was a last resort.

The Townsends say one settlement offer from Alvis included a gag order barring them from talking about the product and a demand that the couple sell their site's domain name to the company. They decided that they would rather fight so that other potential customers could be better informed about the product. "As long as this stuff is on our house, we're going to talk about it," says Linda Townsend. "You could say we're very idealistic about this."

Source: Excerpted in part from Charles Odum, "Testing the Limits of Free Speech," *Fort Lauderdale Sun-Sentinel* (November 14, 2004), F3.

spread the word to others, thereby undermining the company's recruitment efforts. Satisfied customers become repeat buyers and are valuable messengers for reaching new prospects.

Some people have even suggested that a certain type of word-of-mouth communication may be the best indicator of customer loyalty, even better than whether consumers continue to repurchase the same product. After all, sometimes continued repurchasing simply indicates that it is too difficult or inconvenient for consumers to take their business elsewhere. Consequently, the extent to which a customer would recommend the product to other people has been argued to be a better indicator of true customer loyalty.[88] Indeed, loyalty in the form of customers recommending the product to others has been found to be more strongly related to the growth experienced by many companies across a variety of industries than any other type of loyalty measure.[89] One illustration of this relationship in the airline industry appears in Figure 6.13. For each airline company (the size of the circles representing the companies in Figure 6.13 vary according to the size of the company), a *net promoter* index is calculated, which represents the percentage of the company's customers labeled as *promoters* (those recommending it to others) minus the percentage of the company's customers labeled as *detractors* (those with unkind things to say). This index is then

**FIGURE 6.13** A Company's Promoters and Detractors Shape Its Future Growth

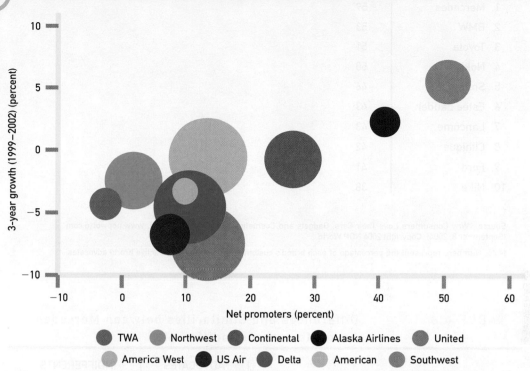

Source: Frederick Reichheld, "The One Number You Need to Grow," *Harvard Business Review* (December 2003), 47–54.

plotted against the company's three-year growth rate. Notice how the airline with the highest net promoter percentage, Southwest, is also experiencing the greatest growth.

So which brands enjoy the most promoters in their customer base? To answer this question, NOP World surveyed over thirty thousand customers of various brands across thirty countries and segmented them into four different categories: active brand advocates (their term for promoters), brand committed, fulfilled, and indifferent.[90] The ten brands with the highest percentage of advocates are listed in Table 6.5. In the top spot is Mercedes. It, along with the brand ranked second (BMW) and third (Toyota), enjoy having more than half their customer base being active brand advocates. Tim Wragg, global director of NOP World's Customer Management Center of Excellence, comments, "For businesses such as car manufacturers, it is evident that customers have a much deeper relationship than just driving their car. Once a brand strikes an emotional relationship with its customers, people talk about the brand, and this is very powerful."[91] And to better appreciate how active brand advocates differ from other consumers, take a look at Table 6.6. This table presents the results for Mercedes owners classified as advocates versus those from the indifferent segment in terms of their responses to various measures assessing their impressions of Mercedes. Not only do advocates perceive the brand as more reliable and offering superior technology, they also feel that the brand makes them part of a special group, a feeling completely absent among indifferents. Given the types of feelings and opinions held by the advocates, it's easy to see why they would serve as enthusiastic emissaries for the brand.

## DISSATISFACTION CAN LEAD TO COMPLAINTS AND LAWSUITS

Beyond spreading negative word-of-mouth, dissatisfied customers may also file formal complaints and lawsuits against the company. This, in turn, may generate negative publicity and absorb the time and resources required for defending the company

| TABLE 6.5 | The Ten Most Advocated Brands (percent) |
|---|---|

| | |
|---|---|
| 1. Mercedes | 59 |
| 2. BMW | 53 |
| 3. Toyota | 51 |
| 4. Nokia | 50 |
| 5. Sony | 46 |
| 6. Estée Lauder | 43 |
| 7. Lancôme | 43 |
| 8. Clinique | 42 |
| 9. Ford | 41 |
| 10. Nike | 38 |

Source: "Why Consumers Love Their Cars, Gadgets and Cosmetics Brands," NOP World, www.nopworld.com (September 8, 2004). Copyright 2004 NOP World.

Note: Numbers represent the percentage of each brand's customer base classified as active brand advocates.

| TABLE 6.6 | Differences and Similarities between Mercedes' Advocates versus Indifferents |
|---|---|

| | ADVOCATES | INDIFFERENTS |
|---|---|---|
| Has cutting-edge technology | 43 | 0 |
| Is reliable | 57 | 29 |
| Makes me feel part of a special group | 40 | 0 |
| Helps me strengthen bonds with other people | 23 | 0 |
| Has a vision I admire | 20 | 0 |
| Is a brand I trust | 63 | 43 |
| Makes me feel happy | 27 | 29 |
| Supports social issues that matter to me | 17 | 14 |

Source: Tim Wragg, "Nurturing Brand Advocates," *Brand Strategy* (November 2004), 36–37.

Note: Numbers represent the percentage agreeing with each statement.

in the courtroom and in the press. For example, Estée Lauder was sued by a consumer on the grounds that its La Mer brand of moisturizer, costing over $100 per ounce, made false claims in its advertising about the product's anti-aging benefits.[92]

What do consumers complain about the most? To answer this question, more than 400,000 complaints made to the member agencies of the Consumer Federation of America and the National Association of Consumer Agency Administrators were examined.[93] The results appear in Table 6.7. Topping the list are complaints about home-improvement contractors that provided poor workmanship or failed to fulfill contracts.

Although dissatisfaction is an essential prerequisite for complaint behavior, not every dissatisfied customer will complain.[94] Yet without knowing the customer's reasons for being unhappy, the task of taking corrective actions to avoid or minimize future unhappiness becomes all the more challenging. In addition, dissatisfied customers who don't voice their complaints are more likely to take their business elsewhere.[95] For these reasons, companies should take steps that enable unhappy customers to easily voice their concerns.[96] One car rental company advertises a toll-free number for just this purpose.

Dissatisfied customers may not complain for several reasons. Consumers may not feel compelled to complain when they are only mildly dissatisfied. Sometimes consumers do not hold the product directly responsible for their dissatisfaction. Instead, they may attribute a dissatisfying consumption experience to themselves (e.g., "I used it improperly") or to external circumstances that are beyond control (e.g., "Bad weather caused my flight to be delayed").[97] Even if consumers hold the product or retailer responsible, complaint behavior still may not occur when consumers don't believe it's worth their time and effort.[98]

For those who do take the time and effort to register their complaints, a sincere attempt to rectify problems can alleviate the dissatisfaction and potentially lead to even stronger intentions to repurchase.[99] The speed of response by the company to a complaint is important. Customers feel more satisfied when the response is quicker.[100] How easy companies make it for unhappy customers to resolve a problem is also important.[101] Among those unhappy customers who only needed one contact to resolve a problem, 41 percent of them ultimately were satisfied. If it takes two contacts, only 29 percent were satisfied. At three or more contacts, the numbers satisfied plummeted to only 6 percent. Now consider this: the average number of contacts consumers need to resolve problems with a financial institution was 5.5. In the telephone industry, the average is 5.6. Do you see the problem? What about the (in most cases, lost) opportunities?

Finally, the nature of the company's response is critical. For complaints involving monetary losses, customers' satisfaction with the company's response becomes greater as the percentage of the loss repaid by the company becomes greater.[102] Yet consumers' opinions about how well companies handle their complaints indicate that there's considerable room for improvement. In the American Customer Satisfaction Index discussed previously in the chapter, consumers are asked to rate companies on how well they handle complaints. The average score out of 100? A disappointing 57. And in fourteen out of seventeen industries it was determined that complaint handling was so

**6.7**

TABLE 6.7        Consumer Complaints: The Top Ten

1. Home improvement—bad workmanship and not living up to contracts.
2. Automobile sales of new and used cars—problems with warranties, advertising, financing, and undisclosed mechanical problems.
3. Automobile repairs—faulty repairs, cost overruns, and "ghost" repairs.
4. Credit—excessive interest and fees and predatory lending.
5. Telecommunications—disputes about contracts, solicitations, and undisclosed charges.
6. Collections and billing practices—unscrupulous debt collection tactics or inaccurate records.
7. Identity theft and deceptive practices—those using phony e-mails and websites.
8. Internet-related issues—e-commerce and scams.
9. Major purchases of household goods—defective goods and dishonored warranties.
10. Telemarketing and advertising sales practices—deceptive advertising, sales, and promotions.

Source: Kimberly Morrison, "Top 10 Consumer Complaints Include Telecom Frustrations, Contractor Complaints," *Knight Ridder Tribune Business News* (February 11, 2005), 1. Copyright 2005 by Knight Ridder Tribune Business News. Reproduced with permission of Tribune Media Services.

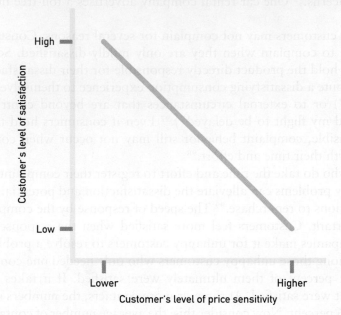

FIGURE 6.14    The Customer Satisfaction–Price Sensitivity Relationship

**FIGURE 6.14**    The Customer Satisfaction–Price Sensitivity Relationship

High —

Customer's level of satisfaction

Low —

Lower          Higher
Customer's level of price sensitivity

bad that customers were actually being driven away.[103] According to Ronald Goodstein, a marketing professor at Georgetown University, much of the problem can be traced back to companies' call centers. As he notes, call centers typically configure employee rewards based on the number of calls handled rather than whether the customer is left feeling satisfied.[104]

## SATISFACTION LOWERS CONSUMERS' PRICE SENSITIVITY

Typically, the more we value something, the more we're willing to pay for it. Given that products that produce satisfying consumption experiences will be valued more than those that don't, greater satisfaction with a product should lower consumers' price sensitivity.[105] In other words, the number of customers that switch to the competition in response to a company raising its price or competitors lowering their prices will be reduced as customer satisfaction increases. As consumers become less satisfied with the product, a company is less able to increase its price or have competitors lower their prices without losing customers. This negative relationship between price sensitivity and customer satisfaction is illustrated in Figure 6.14.

## IMPLICATIONS FOR CUSTOMER RECRUITMENT

For reasons already described, customer satisfaction is critical for customer retention, but it also may be useful for customer recruitment purposes. As evidenced by how often this tactic is used, advertisers apparently believe that providing evidence of a product's ability to satisfy its customers is worthwhile. Take a look at the advertisement for T-Mobile in Figure 6.15. It contains not one, not two, not even three, but four satisfaction awards from J. D. Power & Associates (the company we discussed in Market Facts 6.2). Beneath these awards appears the following text: "In two national studies by J. D. Power and Associates, T-Mobile ranked highest among wireless carriers. Plus, we ranked Highest for Call Quality in the Southeast region and Overall Wireless Satisfaction in all six regions of the study."

Beyond understanding the post-consumption evaluations of their own customers, companies may also find it useful to understand these evaluations of their competitors' customers. Doing so provides valuable guidance to the development of customer recruitment strategies. Efforts to steal business away from the competition are unlikely to succeed when competitors' customers are happy with their current company. Instead, there is usually a greater return from attacking the competitor serving a rather unsatisfied customer base. Unhappy customers are more willing to consider alternative offerings. And in mature markets in which few nonusers become users, a company's growth depends heavily on attracting the dissatisfied customers of the competition.

Of course, the recruitment of dissatisfied customers is important even for vibrant, growing markets. Consider what happened when AOL shifted from hourly fees to unlimited access for a flat rate for its Internet service. Customer usage increased so much that it became nearly impossible to gain access. Stories about frustrated customers, some of whom had taken their business elsewhere, became commonplace. AOL's competitors moved quickly to take advantage of the situation. A Super Bowl ad for CompuServe started off with a blank screen and the sound one hears when trying unsuccessfully to log onto the Internet with a dial-up modem. The ad closed by telling the viewer: "Looking for dependable Internet access? CompuServe. Get on with it." [106]

**FIGURE 6.15** Using Customer Satisfaction as Ammunition for Advertising

## IT ULTIMATELY AFFECTS SHAREHOLDER VALUE

Our preceding discussion about the importance of customer satisfaction has been building the case for why it should impact a firm's value in financial markets. For example, by virtue of its influence on customer retention and repeat buying, customer satisfaction helps firms to secure future revenues. Similarly, its influence on word-of-mouth should facilitate customer recruitment efforts while reducing costs (e.g., such as when free word-of-mouth diminishes the amount of expensive advertising needed). These effects should contribute to the firm's value.

For these and other reasons, Anderson, Fornell, and Mazvancheryl proposed and tested for a positive relationship between customer satisfaction and shareholder value.[107] Satisfaction scores from the ACSI were related to a capital market–based measure of the companies' value that incorporates their stock prices. This relationship was positive and statistically significant. Moreover, the study's analyses suggested that for a firm worth $10 billion, even the seemingly meager increase of 1 percent in the satisfaction of its customers can translate into an increase of nearly $275 million in the firm's value. In this light, that 3 percent decline in satisfaction scores for US Airways discussed earlier in the chapter acquires even greater significance.

### So What Determines Satisfaction?

Consumer researchers have devoted considerable attention to answering this question. It is beyond the scope of this chapter to provide a comprehensive review of the literature examining the determinants of satisfaction. Instead, we will focus on three major determinants of satisfaction.

## PRODUCT PERFORMANCE

Obviously, a critical determinant of satisfaction is consumers' perceptions of the product's performance during consumption. Poor performance and unfavorable consumption experiences usually guarantee that consumers will be dissatisfied with the product unless there are extenuating circumstances. In general, the more favorable a product's performance, the greater the customer's satisfaction.

## CONSUMPTION FEELINGS

We talked earlier in the chapter about how consumption may lead to a variety of feelings of differing favorableness and intensity. The feelings experienced during consumption are important in determining satisfaction.[108] Positive feelings enhance satisfaction; negative feelings reduce it.

## EXPECTATIONS

Last, but certainly not least, are the expectations consumers hold about the product and consumption experience. Perhaps the most well-known conceptualization in the satisfaction literature is Richard Oliver's **expectancy disconfirmation model**, which proposes that *satisfaction depends on a comparison of pre-purchase expectations to consumption outcomes.*[109] To illustrate, suppose that when you go for your doctor's appointment you are told that the doctor is running behind schedule and that you will be seen in a few minutes. A half-hour later, you finally see the doctor. Would you be very happy about waiting this long, especially after expecting a much shorter wait? Now suppose that you were initially told that it would be an hour before you would see the doctor. Would you feel any differently about having to wait a half-hour? Chances are you would. In this instance, your expectations were exceeded. Most of us would feel better about waiting a half-hour after expecting to wait an even longer time. Notice that even though the actual waiting time does not change between these two hypothetical situations, a change in what is expected makes a substantial difference in how satisfied consumers will be with their waiting experiences.

When comparing what is expected to what is received, three outcomes are possible. If the *product delivers less than expected,* **negative disconfirmation** occurs (see Buyer Beware 6.4 for some of my recent encounters with negative disconfirmation). **Positive disconfirmation,** on the other hand, exists when the *product provides more than expected.* Finally, **confirmation** takes place when the *product's performance matches expectations.* Confirmation produces greater satisfaction than exists following negative disconfirmation. Positive disconfirmation evokes the highest levels of satisfaction.

In the case of negative disconfirmation, consumers may also experience additional reactions. One is **regret.** Regret occurs *when consumers believe that an alternative course of action than the one chosen would have produced a better outcome.*[110] Accordingly, regret depends not only on the performance of the product chosen, but on the expected performance of products not chosen.[111] Consumers have less to regret when they believe that the products they didn't choose would have produced the same disappointing outcome as the chosen product. A more extreme reaction to negative disconfirmation is **rage,** which occurs *when consumers are extremely upset.*[112] One survey reports that about two-thirds of consumers who filed a complaint with a company experienced rage over how their complaint was handled.[113] Among those experiencing this emotion when dealing with a financial institution, over half said they did not return.[114] And nearly one in five consumers admitted that they wanted to extract some type of revenge from the institution.[115]

Finally, we need to emphasize that dissatisfaction may not arise solely because of negative disconfirmation with a product that fails to meet expectations. Consumers' expectations extend beyond the product to the company that produces it and supports

## Companies That Did Me Wrong

At the top of my list of wrongdoers is the Shutter Store, a southern Florida business that sells and installs hurricane shutters. In 2001, I paid this company $10,900 to install accordion shutters on my home. Fortunately, it wasn't until three years later that I needed them. To my dismay, less than forty-eight hours before a hurricane was projected to strike southern Florida, I discover that several of the shutter locks on the second floor of my home don't work. A simple nudge and the shutters pop open. I immediately call the Shutter Store. When I finally get through, I'm told that it's not possible for anyone to take care of this problem before the hurricane arrives. All the crews are busy, and once they have completed their current jobs, they will be sent home to take care of their own residences. While I'm certainly not pleased to hear this, it was not unexpected. Things certainly get rather hectic and crazy this close to a hurricane arrival. I'm told to call back the following week and someone will take care of the problem then. Fortunately, the hurricane veered north, and my area was spared. Nonetheless, it's just the beginning of hurricane season and I need to have this problem fixed. So I call back and am told someone will get in touch with me to take care of the problem. Six months later, after living through

one of the worst hurricane seasons in Florida's history, after numerous phone calls to the company and dealing with a woman with the worst set of customer skills I've ever encountered, my shutter locks are still not fixed. So when my neighbor told me that he wanted to get hurricane shutters like mine and asked me for the name and phone number of the company that installed my shutters, take a wild guess what I said to him.

Next up is Carnival Cruise Lines. I thought I had booked two cabins, one with an ocean view for my wife and me, the other across the hallway for our four-year-old daughter and her grandmother. That's what I had requested; that's what the Carnival Cruise Lines' booking agent told me I was getting. But that is not what we got. Our two cabins were located many floors apart. Even though the cruise was sold out, I had hoped that swapping cabins with other passengers would remedy the situation. Not possible, I was told. Carnival's solution? Discount coupons to be used when we booked another cruise with Carnival. Yeah, right. Last week I booked another cruise . . . with Royal Caribbean.

---

it. Even if the product performs as anticipated, failure to meet the expectations for the service that supposedly stands behind it is sufficient reason for customers to be unhappy. And a poorly performing product coupled with inadequate service is a recipe for disaster. When consumers were asked what is the biggest threat to being satisfied, the most frequent response, given nearly twice as much as the next most frequent answer (poorly trained employees), was the inability to talk with another human being about their problem or need (see Figure 6.16).[116] Poor product quality, indicative of unfulfilled expectations, was a distant third.

**Setting Consumers' Expectations** Consider the recent DHL ad proclaiming, "Now you can expect more." What does this really tell consumers about what they can expect from this company? It says to expect more, but more than what? More than what DHL had delivered previously? More than what competitors can deliver? It's not entirely clear, is it?

One decision facing companies is how specific they should be when setting consumers' expectations. Sometimes, as in the DHL advertisement, there is a lack of clarity about just what's being promised. At other times, companies are quite precise in the expectations they are attempting to set. Think about the differences you encounter when you have telephoned a company and are placed in a queue waiting for the next available service representative. Typically, you are told that your call will be answered

FIGURE 6.16

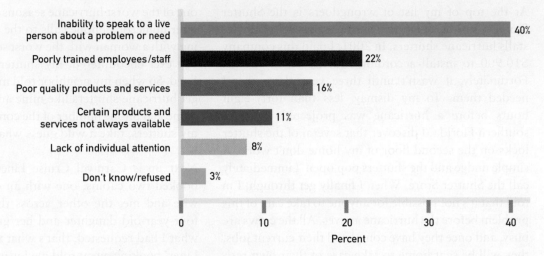

Question: Which of the following do you think is the biggest problem facing consumers today in terms of their satisfaction with products and services?

Inability to speak to a live person about a problem or need — 40%

Poorly trained employees/staff — 22%

Poor quality products and services — 16%

Certain products and services not always available — 11%

Lack of individual attention — 8%

Don't know/refused — 3%

Percent

Source: "Customer Satisfaction: Where's the ROI?" *Wirthlin Report* (December 2003), 5. Reprinted with permission from Harris Interactive, Inc. All Rights Reserved.

in the order in which it was received, but you have no idea how long that might take. Some customer service systems, however, give you a precise estimate on how long you will need to wait before talking to the service representative.

Both approaches have their merits and their limitations. Companies would presumably want to be perfectly clear about why you should do business with them, especially when these reasons present significant advantages over the competition. So why would any company not want to be precise about what you should expect? Sometimes this precision may not be possible, such as those companies lacking the technology necessary to tell you just how long you are going to be waiting on the phone before talking to the service representative. And in all cases, being specific means that customers can more readily evaluate whether the product fulfilled their expectations, thereby enhancing the chances of negative disconfirmation. Being a bit more vague about what is being promised gives the company a little more leeway in what it can deliver without triggering dissatisfaction. Nonetheless, so long as one delivers what one promises, and what is promised represents compelling reasons for product purchase, setting precise expectations should be preferable.

Even so, setting precise expectations may not be as straightforward as it seems. Some marketers recommend setting consumers' expectations as high as possible.[117] Because higher expectations means that more is being promised, consumers should be more likely to buy the product. In addition, as we noted earlier in the chapter, expectations can influence consumers' interpretation of the consumption experience. Higher expectations would mean that consumers are more likely to form more favorable impressions about the product following consumption. So what's the problem with setting expectations as high as possible given a product's performance level? Because doing so raises the risk of falling short and evoking negative disconfirmation and dissatisfaction. Setting expectations at the maximum of what can be delivered leaves no room for error.

One approach to this dilemma is exemplified by Levenger, a mail-order catalog company that specializes in "tools for serious readers" (writing instruments, items for a study, and so forth). The company's motto is "under-promise and over-deliver." In essence, the company seeks to exceed the expectations it creates among its customers.

By adopting a conservative approach when setting expectations (the "under-promise" part), the company improves its chances of evoking positive disconfirmation. The resulting improvement in customer satisfaction is hoped to increase customer retention and repeat buying. Nonetheless, some would argue that such a strategy ends up costing the company because, in comparison to setting higher expectations, it attracts fewer new customers and reduces the improvement in post-consumption evaluations stemming from expectations biasing the interpretation of the consumption experience.

**Shaping Consumers' Expectations** Once the decision has been made about what expectations need to be set in the marketplace, elements of the marketing mix need to be configured in a fashion consistent with the desired expectation mindset. What's said in the product's advertising obviously goes a long way toward shaping consumers' expectations. The various claims made about the product in an advertisement represent promises to the consumer that he or she will surely expect to be fulfilled. But advertised promises are far from being the only thing that determines consumers' expectations. A product's packaging also contributes to the expectations formed by

## CONSUMER BEHAVIOR AND MARKETING 6.4

## Managing Consumers' Expectations

According to one old saying, "what you see is what you get." Or is it? The packaging for telescopes is often adorned with pictures of celestial wonders. The box for one telescope, for example, shows pictures of colorful nebulae, comets, meteors, and star clusters. This led one purchaser of the product to believe that such images could be viewed by this telescope. "I expected to see the same kind of objects you could see on the box," said the buyer. Yet when he purchased the product and later looked through the eyepiece, he discovered the view was less impressive. Indeed, often what you see through a telescope is a small, nearly colorless image. Moreover, the pictures on telescope boxes usually are taken with digital cameras attached to the telescopes that produce images better than anything the human eye can observe through the telescope.

This disconnect between what consumers expect and what they receive has led to a series of lawsuits being filed against various telescope makers, including industry leaders Meade Instruments and Celestron, for allegedly using deceptive marketing. The lawsuits were filed in California by William Weilbacher, an attorney and amateur astronomer, on behalf of several fellow astronomers. In one suit filed in September 2003 against Orion Telescopes & Binoculars, Mr. Weilbacher took

aim at a catalog of the company, saying the company's telescopes "are totally incapable of providing actual views even remotely comparable to the pictures of the celestial objects as depicted on the catalog pages." In another lawsuit, Mr. Weilbacher sued a company called Cstar Optics over photography on the box of its products. He also alleged that the company was advertising magnifications that were too high for the telescopes.

The lawsuits were eventually settled out of court. Some of the manufacturers have altered their packaging to ensure that the photographs on their boxes reflected the capabilities of the actual telescope. Similar changes were made for the products being advertised in catalogs. Disclaimers noting that images are merely decorative are now being used. Rodney Wayne Harris, Cstar's vice president, concedes that "the lawyer had a valid point" about the magnifications claims. He has decided to change the magnifications claims and to use a disclaimer letting people know they can't see everything shown on the box.

So remember, what you see is not always what you get. Instead, as another old saying goes, "appearances can be deceiving."

Source: Reed Albergotti, "Star Wars: The Battle over Telescopes," *Wall Street Journal* (December 22, 2004), D1. Copyright 2004 by Dow Jones & Co. Reproduced with permission of Dow Jones & Co., Inc., in the textbook format via Copyright Clearance Center, Inc.

consumers.[118] Consumer Behavior and Marketing 6.4 describes how the packaging used for home telescopes created expectations that were not met, which resulted in lawsuits being filed.

Expectations may also depend on the product's price. A higher price usually leads to greater expectations about how the product will perform. As one executive in the sports industry observes, "Teams are charging top dollar for tickets, and athletes are getting top-dollar deals from the owners, and so fans' expectations are much higher. Everything has to be perfect for the fan, not just on the field or court or ice, but from the retail side as well."[119] One interesting illustration of this comes from a computer manufacturer that substantially reduced the number of features offered by its product, thereby enabling it to also reduce the product's price. As a result, product returns declined from about 12 to 5 percent. Apparently, consumers expected less and became less demanding at the lower price point.[120]

## ADDITIONAL INFLUENCES ON CUSTOMER SATISFACTION

Actual performance relative to expected performance is undeniably critical in shaping customer satisfaction, but additional methods are used by businesses to enhance the satisfaction of their customers. Creating loyalty programs (which we will discuss rather thoroughly in Chapter 8), offering online services, and developing personalized relationships with customers are some of the ways that companies can foster satisfaction. Would you believe that simply participating in customer surveys makes customers feel more satisfied? It's true. Take a look at Figure 6.17, which presents the findings from a survey that asked consumers who had participated in each of the activities listed in the figure whether such participation increased or decreased their satisfaction. Half of the consumers who had participated previously in a survey

**FIGURE 6.17**    Consumers' Perceptions of What Increases Their Satisfaction

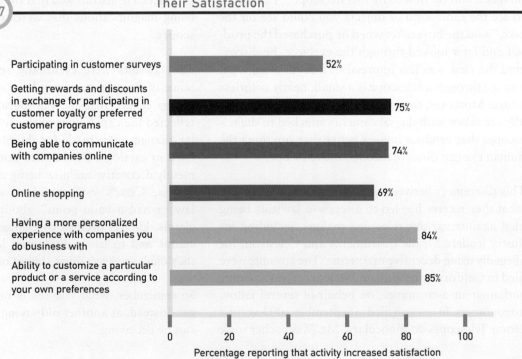

Source: "Customer Satisfaction: Where's the ROI?" *Wirthlin Report* (December 2003), 4. Reprinted with permission from Harris Interactive, Inc. All Rights Reserved.

PART 2 [ CONSUMER DECISION MAKING

reported feeling more satisfied with the company, presumably because it makes them feel that the company is interested in learning about their opinions to improve service. And this was the least effective of the activities examined in the survey. As these findings clearly show, consumers believe that the product, while essential, is not the only way of making them more satisfied.

## Summary

This chapter examines the last two stages in the consumer decision process—consumption and post-consumption evaluation. A fundamental part of market segmentation for many products involves distinguishing between users (those who consume) and nonusers (those who do not). It is also important to understand the dynamics of consumption: When does consumption occur? Where does it occur? How is the product consumed? How much is consumed? Beyond answering these questions, a thorough understanding of the consumption stage of the decision-making process further requires focusing on the consumption experience itself. This examination involves considering the types of feelings experienced during consumption, the extent to which consumption provides positive versus negative reinforcement, and whether pre-purchase expectations are confirmed.

Just as consumers form pre-purchase evaluations to help them decide which products should be purchased and consumed, they also form post-consumption evaluations about the consumed product. Typically, companies examine these post-consumption evaluations in terms of customer satisfaction. Understanding satisfaction is essential for several reasons. The level of satisfaction or dissatisfaction influences repeat buying, word-of-mouth (and word-of-mouse) communication, and complaint behavior. Further, an understanding of the satisfaction or dissatisfaction of competitors' customers enables a company to more effectively and efficiently steal business from the competition.

Consumers' satisfaction with a product depends heavily on its performance. But beyond this, satisfaction may further depend on what consumers expect. Companies must be careful that customers do not expect too much. Otherwise, customers end up being dissatisfied. If consumers expect too little, they may underappreciate what the product has to offer and, consequently, buy something else. Walking the line between promising too much and selling the product short is one of marketing's toughest challenges.

## Review and Discussion Questions

1. In the chapter, we discussed how one rice manufacturer discovered that many of its customers switched to a lower-priced competitor when using the rice as an ingredient rather than as a side dish. What suggestions do you have for this manufacturer concerning how it could encourage consumers to buy its brand when using rice as an ingredient?

2. Describe the different ways a company could segment a market based on consumption.

3. Consider the company who seeks to increase consumption of its product. What options are available to the company for achieving this objective?

4. Using the example of fast-food restaurants, apply the concepts presented in the "Consumption Behaviors" section. What implications might this analysis carry in developing business strategy for a particular restaurant?

5. In the chapter we discussed the problem many consumers are having with their weight. What lessons have you learned from the chapter that would be useful to someone watching their weight?

6. Related to question 5, one executive for a major food company believes that it is unlikely that advertising has contributed to children's obesity. His argument is based on the fact that although obesity rates vary widely across the country, advertising does not. What is your opinion about this executive's position and logic?

7. The chapter indicates that satisfaction may depend on consumers' expectations of product performance and the feelings experienced during consumption. How important do you believe each of these factors might be in determining satisfaction with the following products: scissors, an amusement ride, vitamin pills.

8. A business is interested in thoroughly understanding the opinions held by its customers following product consumption. Given this objective, what suggestions do you have about what should be examined?

9. Why are consumers' expectations important?

10. The motto of one consumer-products company is "under-promise and over-deliver." What are the potential advantages and disadvantages to the company living up to its motto?

## Notes

1. Yumiko Ono, "Pharmacia Bets New Rogaine Grows Sales," *Wall Street Journal* (August 4, 1997), B6.

2. Gregg Fields, "Vessels Revamp Cruise Industry," *Miami Herald* (November 12, 1999), C1.

3. Robert P. Libbon, "How Popular Is Wine These Days?" *American Demographics* (September 1999), 25.

4. Elizabeth Jensen, "Champagne Makers Are Hoping Chardonnay Adds Fizz to Sales," *Wall Street Journal* (March 21, 1997), B5.

5. Lauran Neergaard, "Research Finds Internal Clock Important in Drug Effectiveness, Health," *Miami Herald* (May 1, 1999), A11.

6. Marika Lynch, "Keys Might Be Losing Allure," *Miami Herald* (January 31, 1997), A1.

7. Brian Wansink, S. Adam Brasel, and Steven Amjad, "The Mystery of the Cabinet Castaway: Why We Buy Products We Never Use," *Journal of Family and Consumer Sciences,* 92 (2000), 104–107.

8. Ibid.

9. Ibid.

10. Kevin T. Higgins, "Beer Importers Upbeat about Future, Despite Warning Signs," *Marketing News* (October 25, 1985), 1ff.

11. Fred Tasker, "Raise a Glass: America Soaks up the Vino," *Miami Herald* (February 24, 2005), A1, A24.

12. Michelle Locke, "Top Wines Uncorked," *Miami Herald* (June 25, 2004), C1.

13. Ibid.

14. Judith Weinraub, "Breakfast! The Drive-Through Phenomenon," *Miami Herald* (February 6, 1997), E1, E3.

15. Paula Mergenhagen, "How 'got milk?' Got Sales," *Marketing Tools* (September 1996), 4–7.

16. Brian Wansink and Michael L. Ray, "Advertising Strategies to Increase Usage Frequency," *Journal of Marketing,* 60 (January 1996), 31–46.

17. Ibid. For additional research examining usage expansion advertising, see Brian Wansink, "Advertising's Impact on Category Substitution," *Journal of Marketing Research,* 31 (November 1994), 505–515.

18. Brian Wansink and Koert van Ittersum, "Bottoms Up! The Influence of Elongation on Pouring and Consumption Volume," *Journal of Consumer Research,* 30 (December 2003), 455–463.

19. Priya Raghubir and Aradna Krishna, "Vital Dimensions in Volume Perception: Can the Eye Fool the Stomach?" *Journal of Marketing Research,* 36 (August 1999), 313–326.

20. Valerie S. Folkes, Ingrid M. Martin, and Kamal Gupta, "When to Say When: Effects of Supply on Usage," *Journal of Consumer Research,* 22 (December 1993), 296–304.

21. Pierre Chandon and Brian Wansink, "When Are Stockpiled Products Consumed Faster? A Convenience-Salience Framework of Postpurchase Consumption Incidence and Quantity," *Journal of Marketing Research,* 39 (2002), 321–335. Also see Brian Wansink and Rohit Deshpande, "Out of Sight, Out of Mind: Pantry Stockpiling and Brand Usage Frequency," *Marketing Letters,* 5 (1994), 91–100.

22. Margaret Webb Pressler, "Use of Coupons Cuts Both Ways," www.washingtonpost.com (September 12, 2004).

23. Ibid.

24. Libbon, "How Popular Is Wine These Days?"

25. Mergenhagen, "How 'got milk?' Got Sales."

26. For research examining the relative effectiveness of alternative advertising strategies for enhancing product usage, see Wansink and Ray, "Advertising Strategies to Increase Usage Frequency."

27. Jensen, "Champagne Makers Are Hoping Chardonnay Adds Fizz to Sales."

28. Emily Nelson, "Camera Makers Focus on Tiny and Cute," *Wall Street Journal* (March 14, 1997), B1.

29. Brian Wansink, "Can Package Size Accelerate Usage Volume?" *Journal of Marketing,* 60 (July 1996), 1–14.

30. Ibid.

31. B. Wansink and S. B. Park, "At the Movies: How External Cues and Perceived Taste Impact Consumption Volume," *Food Quality and Preference,* 12 (2001), 69–74.

32. Barbara E. Kahn and Brian Wansink, "The Influence of Assortment Structure on Perceived Variety and Consumption Quantities," *Journal of Consumer Research,* 30 (March 2004), 519–533.

33. James E. Painter, Brian Wansink, and Julie B. Hieggelke, "How Visibility and Convenience Influence Candy Consumption," *Appetite,* 38 (2002), 237–238.

34. "Study on Eating Habits Is Upbeat, but Some Are Wary of the Results," *Wall Street Journal* (October 14, 2004), D3.

35. Caroline E. Mayer, "Group Takes Aim at Junk-Food Marketing; Industry Counters That Ads Targeting Children Decreased in Past Decade," *Washington Post* (January 7, 2005), E5.

36. "Food Brands Consider the Limits of Snacking," *Marketing Week* (October 7, 2004), 24.

37 Sarah Ellison, "Kraft Limits on Kids' Ads May Cheese Off Rivals; Company Plans to Stop Advertising Junk Food to Children Age 6 to 11," *Wall Street Journal* (January 13, 2005), B3; Melissa Healy, "Those Sugary Saturday Mornings; As Parents Call for Curbs on TV Ads Aimed at Kids, One Food Maker Is Promising to Change Its Marketing Strategies," *Los Angeles Times* (January 24, 2005), F1; Betsy McKay, "The Children's Menu: Do Ads Make Kids Fat?" *Wall Street Journal* (January 27, 2005), B1.

38 Ellison, "Kraft Limits on Kids' Ads May Cheese Off Rivals"; Healy, "Those Sugary Saturday Mornings; As Parents Call for Curbs on TV Ads Aimed at Kids, One Food Maker Is Promising to Change Its Marketing Strategies."

39 Caroline E. Mayer, "Putting a Healthy Spin on Processed Foods," *Washington Post* (January 10, 2005), A1.

40 Caroline E. Mayer, "Kraft to Curb Snack-Food Advertising," *Washington Post* (January 12, 2005), E1; Mayer, "Putting a Healthy Spin on Processed Foods."

41 Richard L. Oliver, "Cognitive, Affective, and Attribute Bases of the Satisfaction Response," *Journal of Consumer Research,* 20 (December 1993), 418–430; Robert A. Westbrook, "Product/Consumption-Based Affective Responses and Postpurchase Processes," *Journal of Marketing Research,* 24 (August 1987), 258–270; Robert A. Westbrook and Richard L. Oliver, "The Dimensionality of Consumption Emotion Patterns and Consumer Satisfaction," *Journal of Consumer Research,* 18 (June 1991), 84–91.

42 Geoffrey Tomb, "Parks Offer a 2-hour Glide to Serenity," *Miami Herald* (September 10, 1996), B1, B6.

43 Jerry C. Olson and Philip A. Dover, "Cognitive Effects of Deceptive Advertising," *Journal of Marketing Research,* 15 (February 1978), 29–38.

44 Ralph I. Allison and Kenneth P. Uhl, "Influence of Beer Brand Identification on Taste Perception," *Journal of Marketing Research,* 1 (August 1964), 36–39.

45 Stephen J. Hoch and Young-Won Ha, "Consumer Learning: Advertising and the Ambiguity of Product Experience," *Journal of Consumer Research,* 13 (September 1986), 221–233.

46 Paul W. Miniard, Sunil Bhatla, and Deepak Sirdeshmukh, "Mood as a Determinant of Post-Consumption Evaluations: Mood Effects and Their Dependency on the Affective Intensity of the Consumption Experience," *Journal of Consumer Psychology,* 1 (1992), 173–195.

47 Dennis W. Rook, "The Ritual Dimension of Consumer Behavior," *Journal of Consumer Research,* 12 (December 1985), 251–264.

48 For a classic article on this subject, see Melanie Wallendorf and Eric J. Arnould, "'We Gather Together': Consumption Rituals of Thanksgiving Day," *Journal of Consumer Research,* 18 (June 1991), 13–31.

49 Rook, "The Ritual Dimension of Consumer Behavior."

50 Russell W. Belk, Melanie Wallendorf, and John F. Sherry Jr., "The Sacred and the Profane in Consumer Behavior: Theodicy on the Odyssey," *Journal of Consumer Research,* 16 (June 1989), 1–38.

51 Thomas C. O'Guinn and Ronald J. Faber, "Compulsive Buying: A Phenomenological Exploration," *Journal of Consumer Research,* 16 (September 1989), 147–157. Also see Aviv Shoham and Maja Makovec Brencic, "Compulsive Buying Behavior," *Journal of Consumer Marketing,* 20 (2003), 127–138.

52 Rajan Nataraajan and Brent G. Goff, "Manifestations of Compulsiveness in the Consumer-Marketplace Domain," *Psychology & Marketing,* 9 (January 1992), 31–44.

53 O'Guinn and Faber, "Compulsive Buying: A Phenomenological Exploration."

54 Elizabeth C. Hirschman, "The Consciousness of Addiction: Toward a General Theory of Compulsive Consumption," *Journal of Consumer Research,* 19 (September 1992), 155–179.

55 Mirene E. Winsberg, Kristin S. Cassic, and Lorrin M. Koran, "Hoarding in Obsessive-Compulsive Disorder: A Report of 20 Cases," *Journal of Clinical Psychiatry,* 60 (September 1999), 591–597.

56 Aric Rindfleisch, James E. Burroughs, and Frank Denton, "Family Structure, Materialism, and Compulsive Consumption," *Journal of Consumer Research* 23, (March 1997), 312–325.

57 Alvin C. Burns, Peter L. Gillett, Marc Rubinstein, and James W. Gentry, "An Exploratory Study of Lottery Playing, Gambling Addiction and Links to Compulsive Consumption," in Gerald A. Gorn and Richard W. Pollay, eds., *Advances in Consumer Research,* 17 (Provo, UT: Association for Consumer Research, 1990), 298–305.

58 "Report for Congress on Gambling Addiction Stirs Debate with Gaming Industry," *Miami Herald* (March 19, 1999), A3.

59 O'Guinn and Faber, "Compulsive Buying: A Phenomenological Exploration."

60 Thomas G. Watts, "Caught in the Web: 'Dependents' Studied," *Miami Herald* (August 16, 1997), A10.

61 Bruce Nussbaum, "The Power of Design," *Business Week* (May 17, 2004), 86–90.

62 Ibid.

63 Linda Tischler, "Every Move You Make," *Fast Company* (April 2004), 73–75.

64 Harold H. Kassarjian, "How We Spent Our Summer Vacation: A Preliminary Report on the 1986 Consumer Behavior Odyssey," in Melanie Wallendorf and Paul Anderson, eds., *Advances in Consumer Research,* 14 (Provo, UT: Association for Consumer Research, 1987), 376–377.

65 Belk, Wallendorf, and Sherry, "The Sacred and the Profane in Consumer Behavior: Theodicy on the Odyssey."

66 Russell W. Belk, "The Role of the Odyssey in Consumer Behavior and in Consumer Research," in Melanie Wallendorf and Paul Anderson, eds., *Advances in Consumer Research,* 14 (Provo, UT: Association for Consumer Research, 1987), 357–361.

67 Wallendorf and Arnould, "'We Gather Together.'"

68 Lisa Penaloza, "Consuming the American West: Animating Cultural Meaning and Memory at a Stock Show and Rodeo," *Journal of Consumer Research,* 28 (December 2001), 369–398.

[69] John W. Schouten and James H. McAlexander, "Subcultures of Consumption: An Ethnography of the New Bikers," *Journal of Consumer Research,* 22 (June 1995), 43–61.

[70] Ronald Paul Hill, "Homeless Women, Special Possessions, and the Meaning of 'Home': An Ethnographic Case Study," *Journal of Consumer Research,* 18 (December 1991), 298–310; Ronald Paul Hill and Mark Stamey, "The Homeless in America: An Examination of Possessions and Consumption Behaviors," *Journal of Consumer Research,* 16 (December 1990), 303–321.

[71] Russell W. Belk and Janeen Arnold Costa, "The Mountain Man Myth: A Contemporary Consuming Fantasy," *Journal of Consumer Research,* 25 (December 1998), 218–240; Steven M. Kates, "The Protean Quality of Subcultural Consumption: An Ethnographic Account of Gay Consumers," *Journal of Consumer Research,* 29 (December 2002), 383–399; Albert M. Muniz Jr. and Thomas C. O'Guinn, "Brand Community," *Journal of Consumer Research,* 27 (March 2001), 412–432; Robert V. Kazinets, John F. Sherry Jr., Diana Storm, Adam Duhachek, Krittinee Nuttavuthisit, and Benet DeBerry-Spence, "Ludic Agency and Retail Spectacle," *Journal of Consumer Research,* 31 (December 2004), 658–672.

[72] Claes Fornell, Michael D . Johnson, Eugene W. Anderson, Jaesung Cha, and Barbara Everitt Bryant, "The American Customer Satisfaction Index: Nature, Purpose, and Findings," *Journal of Marketing,* 56 (October 1996), 7–18.

[73] Jane Spencer and Reed Albergotti, "Customer Satisfaction Index Climbs," *Wall Street Journal* (February 18, 2004), D2.

[74] Liz Flaisig, "Southern Regions Rank High in Customer Satisfaction," *Business Journal* (March 12, 2004), 4.

[75] Although not discussed in this section, satisfaction also has been linked to consumer spending growth. Spending slows down when satisfaction declines. See

Doris Hajewski, "Kohl's, Northwestern Mutual Top Customer Satisfaction Survey," *Milwaukee Journal Sentinel* (February 15, 2005), 1; Teresa F. Linderman, "Consumers Soured Shortly on Retailers during Last Year's Holiday Season," *Pittsburgh Post-Gazette* (February 15, 2005), 1.

[76] Claes Fornell and Birger Wernerfelt, "Defensive Marketing Strategy by Customer Complaint Management: A Theoretical Analysis," *Journal of Marketing Research,* 24 (November 1987), 337–346.

[77] Frederick Reichheld, "The One Number You Need to Grow," *Harvard Business Review* (December 2003), 47–54.

[78] Richard L. Oliver, "Whence Consumer Loyalty?" *Journal of Marketing,* 63 (Special Issue 1999), 33–44; Thomas A. Stewart, "A Satisfied Customer Isn't Enough," *Fortune* (July 21, 1997), 112–113.

[79] Frederick F. Reichheld, "Learning from Customer Defections," *Harvard Business Review* (March/April 1996), 56–69.

[80] Thomas O. Jones and W. Earl Sasser Jr., "Why Satisfied Customers Defect," *Harvard Business Review* (November/December 1995), 88–99.

[81] Kevin T. Higgins, "Coming of Age: Despite Growing Pains, Customer Satisfaction Measurement Continues to Evolve," *Marketing News* (October 27, 1997), 1, 12; Jones and Sasser, "Why Satisfied Customers Defect"; Steve Lewis, "All or Nothing: Customers Must Be 'Totally Satisfied,'" *Marketing News* (March 2, 1998), 11–12; Richard L. Oliver, Roland T. Rust, and Sajeev Varki, "Customer Delight: Foundations, Findings, and Managerial Insight," *Journal of Retailing,* 73 (Fall 1997), 311–336; Benjamin Schneider and David E. Bowen, "Understanding Customer Delight and Outrage," *Sloan Management Review,* 41 (Fall 1999), 35–45.

[82] Reichheld, "The One Number You Need to Grow."

[83] For research concerning word-of-mouth activity by consumers, see Marsha L. Richins, "Negative Word-of-Mouth by

Dissatisfied Consumers: A Pilot Study," *Journal of Marketing,* 47 (Winter 1983), 68–78.

[84] Nicholas Thompson, "More Companies Pay Heed to Their 'Word of Mouse' Reputation," *New York Times* (June 23, 2003), C4.

[85] According to the web site www.wordspy.com, the first published use of the phrase *word-of-mouse* was in John Zilber, "Of Mice and Menaces," *MacUser* (January 1991).

[86] David Kirk Patrick and Daniel Roth, "Why There's No Escaping the Blog," *Fortune* (January 10, 2005), 44–50.

[87] Jesse Oxfeld, "Blogs Rolling in 2005," *Editor & Publisher,* 138 (January 2005), 36–40.

[88] Reichheld, "The One Number You Need to Grow."

[89] Ibid.

[90] "Why Consumers Love Their Cars, Gadgets and Cosmetics Brands," www.nopworld.com (September 8, 2004).

[91] Ibid.

[92] Lauren Weber, "Estee Lauder, Other Firms, Face Suit Over Ads of Anti-Aging Products," *Knight Ridder Tribune Business News* (January 12, 2005), 1.

[93] Kimberly Morrison, "Top 10 Consumer Complaints Include Telecom Frustrations, Contractor Complaints," *Knight Ridder Tribune Business News* (February 11, 2005), 1.

[94] Richard L. Oliver, "An Investigation of the Interrelationship between Consumer Dissatisfaction and Complaint Reports," in Melanie Wallendorf and Paul Anderson, eds., *Advances in Consumer Research,* 14 (Provo, UT: Association for Consumer Research, 1987), 218–222.

[95] Claes Fornell and Nicholas M. Didow, "Economic Constraints on Consumer Complaining Behavior," in Jerry C. Olson, ed., *Advances in Consumer Research,* 7 (Ann Arbor, MI: Association for Consumer Research, 1980), 318–323.

[96] Fornell and Wernerfelt, "Defensive Marketing Strategy by Customer Complaint Management: A Theoretical Analysis." Perhaps surprisingly, efforts to encourage

one's customers to complain ultimately may cause companies to become less responsive to this form of customer feedback. Evidence indicating this possibility is reported by Claes Fornell and Robert A. Westbrook, "The Vicious Circle of Consumer Complaints," *Journal of Marketing,* 48 (Summer 1984), 68–78.

[97] For research on the role of attributions as a determinant of complaint behavior, see Valerie S. Folkes, "Consumer Reactions to Product Failure: An Attributional Approach," *Journal of Consumer Research,* 10 (March 1984), 398–409; Valerie S. Folkes and Barbara Kotsos, "Buyers' and Sellers' Explanations for Product Failure: Who Done It," *Journal of Marketing,* 50 (April 1986), 74–80; Valerie S. Folkes, Susan Koletsky, and John L. Graham, "A Field Study of Causal Inferences and Consumer Reaction: The View from the Airport," *Journal of Consumer Research,* 13 (March 1987), 534–539.

[98] Ralph L. Day, "Modeling Choices among Alternative Responses to Dissatisfaction," in Thomas C. Kinnear, ed., *Advances in Consumer Research,* 11 (Provo, UT: Association for Consumer Research, 1984), 496–499.

[99] Mary C. Gilly and Betsy D. Gelb, "Post-Purchase Consumer Processes and the Complaining Consumer," *Journal of Consumer Research,* 9 (December 1982), 323–328; Denise T. Smart and Charles L. Martin, "Manufacturer Responsiveness to Consumer Correspondence: An Empirical Investigation of Consumer Perceptions," *Journal of Consumer Affairs,* 26 (Summer 1991), 104–128.

[100] Gilly and Gelb, "Post-Purchase Consumer Processes and the Complaining Consumer"; Chow-Hou Wee and Celine Chong, "Determinants of Consumer Satisfaction/Dissatisfaction Toward Dispute Settlements in Singapore," *European Journal of Marketing,* 25 (1991), 6–16.

[101] Michael Sisk, "Fending Off Consumer Rage," *US Banker,* 115 (January 2005), 16.

[102] Gilly and Gelb, "Post-Purchase Consumer Processes and the Complaining Consumer."

[103] Caroline E. Mayer, "These Days, Consumers May As Well Keep Their Complaint to Themselves," *Washington Post* (March 28, 2004), F1.

[104] Ibid.

[105] Eugene W. Anderson, "Customer Satisfaction and Price Tolerance," *Marketing Letters,* 7 (July 1996), 19–30; Das Narayandas, "Measuring and Managing the Benefits of Customer Retention: An Empirical Investigation," *Journal of Service Research,* 1 (November 1998), 108–128.

[106] Jared Sandberg, "CompuServe Will Mock AOL's Woes in Super Bowl Ad," *Wall Street Journal* (January 24, 1997), B16; David Poppe, "AOL's Still Busy—Taking Cancellations," *Miami Herald* (January 31, 1997), C1, C3.

[107] Eugene W. Anderson, Claes Fornell, and Sanal K. Mazvancheryl, "Customer Satisfaction and Shareholder Value," *Journal of Marketing,* 68 (October 2004), 172–185.

[108] Laurette Dube and Bernd H. Schmitt, "The Processing of Emotional and Cognitive Aspects of Product Usage in Satisfaction Judgments," in Rebecca H. Holman and Michael R. Solomon, eds., *Advances in Consumer Research,* 18 (Provo, UT: Association for Consumer Research, 1991), 52–56; Laurette Dube-Rioux, "The Power of Affective Reports in Predicting Satisfaction Judgments," in Martin E. Goldberg, Gerald A. Gorn, and Richard W. Pollay, eds., *Advances in Consumer Research,* 17 (Provo, UT: Association for Consumer Research, 1990), 571–576; Richard L. Oliver, "Cognitive, Affective, and Attribute Bases of the Satisfaction Response"; Robert A. Westbrook, "Product/Consumption-Based Affective Responses and Postpurchase Processes"; Westbrook and Oliver, "The Dimensionality of Consumption Emotion Patterns and Consumer Satisfaction."

[109] Richard L. Oliver, "A Cognitive Model of the Antecedents and Consequences of Satisfaction Decisions," *Journal of Marketing Research,* 17 (November 1980), 460–469. See also Ruth N. Bolton and James H. Drew, "A Multistage Model of Customers' Assessments of Service Quality and Value," *Journal of Consumer Research,* 17 (March 1991), 375–384; Gilbert A. Churchill Jr., and Carol Suprenant, "An Investigation into the Determinants of Customer Satisfaction," *Journal of Marketing Research,* 19 (November 1983), 491–504; Ernest R. Cadotte, Robert B. Woodruff, and Roger L. Jenkins, "Expectations and Norms in Models of Consumer Satisfaction," *Journal of Marketing Research,* 24 (August 1987), 305–314; Richard L. Oliver and Wayne S. DeSarbo, "Response Determinants in Satisfaction Judgments," *Journal of Consumer Research,* 14 (March 1988), 495–507; David K. Tse and Peter C. Wilton, "Models of Consumer Satisfaction Formation: An Extension," *Journal of Marketing Research,* 25 (May 1988), 204–212; Robert B. Woodruff, Ernest R. Cadotte, and Roger L. Jenkins, "Modeling Consumer Satisfaction Using Experience-Based Norms," *Journal of Marketing Research,* 20 (August 1983), 296–304. Despite the substantial support this model has received, researchers have suggested model modifications. Some have argued for simplification on grounds that expectations may not always play a role in determining satisfaction (Susan Fournier and David Glen Mick, "Rediscovering Satisfaction," *Journal of Marketing,* 63 [October 1999], 5–23). Others have advocated more complex specifications (Ruth N. Bolton and Katherine N. Lemon, "A Dynamic Model of Customers' Usage of Services: Usage As an Antecedent and Consequence of Satisfaction," *Journal of Marketing Research,* 36 [May 1999], 171–186; Richard A. Spreng, Scott B. MacKenzie, and Richard W. Olshavsky, "A Reexamination of the Determinants of Consumer Satisfaction," *Journal of Marketing,* 60 [July 1996], 15–32).

[110] J. Jeffrey Inman, James S. Dyer, and Jianmin Jia, "A Generalized Utility Model of

Disappointment and Regret Effects on Post-Choice Valuation," *Marketing Science,* 16 (Spring 1997), 97–111; Michael Tsiros, "Effect of Regret on Post-Choice Valuation: The Case of More than Two Alternatives," *Organizational Behavior and Human Decision Processes,* 76 (October 1998), 48–69; Michael Tsiros and Vikkas Mittal, "Regret: A Model of Its Antecedents and Consequences in Consumer Decision Making," *Journal of Consumer Research,* 26 (March 2000), 401–417.

[111] Kimberly A. Taylor, Paul W. Miniard, and Mary Jane Burns, "The Influence of Choice Sets on Consumers' Post-Consumption Responses and the Moderating Role of the Consumption Experience," (2005), working paper.

[112] Sisk, "Fending Off Consumer Rage."

[113] Don Oldenburg, "Seller Beware: Customers Are Mad As Hell," *Washington Post* (September 9, 2003), C10.

[114] Sisk, "Fending Off Consumer Rage."

[115] Ibid.

[116] "Customer Satisfaction: Where's the ROI?" *Wirthlin Report* (December 2003), 1–7.

[117] Dan Meyers, "Set Expectations High to Win New Business," *Marketing News* (October 28, 2002), 48.

[118] Jennifer Lach, "The Price Is Very Right," *American Demographics* (April 1999), 44–45.

[119] Paul King, "Home Park Advantage," *Nation's Restaurant News* (March 29, 2004), 17.

[120] Herbert M. Myers, "Packaging Must Keep Promises Made to Buyers," *Marketing News* (July 6, 1998), 11–12.

# Individual Determinants of Consumer Behavior

Consumers are like diamonds. Each is extremely valuable to marketers, but no two are exactly the same. One person may have lots of time but little money, whereas the next person may have lots of money but little time. One buyer may have years of experience in purchasing and using a product. Another may be looking to try something new. And what motivates one person to buy is not necessarily what leads the next person to do so.

The existence of these individual differences makes life a bit more complicated for those wishing to influence consumers and their behaviors. After all, what works when selling to Jim may be ineffective when selling to Jennifer. Consequently, when developing a business strategy, it is important to understand the key characteristics of target consumers.

This section of the text focuses on some of the individual characteristics that are particularly useful for analyzing consumer behavior. Traditionally, companies have paid close attention to the demographic characteristics (e.g., age, income, marital status) of their target consumers. Chapter 7 discusses demographics as well as other psychographic and personality variables useful in understanding consumer behavior. Chapter 8 looks at consumer motivation and the diversity of needs that motivate purchase behavior. Consumers also differ in what they know and how they feel about products. Chapter 9 focuses on consumer knowledge. That knowledge, along with feelings, ultimately determines consumers' attitudes and intentions. Chapter 10 discusses the importance of understanding consumers' beliefs, feelings, attitudes, and intentions.

# Chapter 7

# Demographics, Psychographics, and Personality

## Opening Vignette

How does a company reach into the minds of consumers to create products and services that consumers want to buy? And how does it devise effective distribution and communication strategies to make those products and services easily accessible to consumers? The process starts with understanding everything about consumers, including their demographics, lifestyles, personal preferences, and behaviors. To do that, marketers are turning to customer-centric designers such as IDEO and the techniques you read about in the last chapter in Table 6.3. IDEO is a San Francisco firm known for designing such user-friendly products such as the Palm V, the Steelcase Leap Chair, and Zinio (technology that converts print magazines to a digital format, allowing Internet users to download and read them offline). IDEO also designed the first no-squeeze, stand-up toothpaste for Procter & Gamble's Crest as well as the Gripper—a large-handled Oral-B toothbrush that is easy for children to hold and control. IDEO helps clients by showing them the consumer world through the eyes of anthropologists, graphic designers, engineers, and psychologists. Other firms also use similar techniques. Design Continuum in West Newton, Massachusetts, for example, observed consumer cleaning habits to help P&G launch its $1 billion Swiffer mop business, and headed to construction sites to help Andersen create a new line of windows for the growing market of volume homebuilders.

Part of what firms such as IDEO do is to show global corporations how to focus on the consumer, says P&G CEO Alan Lafley, who teamed up with IDEO to create a more innovative company culture after taking his entire team of forty business-unit heads to San Francisco for an immersion that included sending everyone out shopping to understand consumer experiences ranging from funky, music stores to retailers appealing to low-income consumers as well as online purchasing. IDEO uses a process, involving the ethnographic techniques described in Table 6.3, in which corporate executives partner with the firm's cognitive psychologists, anthropologists, and sociologists to understand the consumer experience.

The creative process often occurs while brainstorming—an intense, idea-generating session analyzing data gathered by observing people. Rules of brainstorming are strict and are stenciled on the walls:

- *Defer judgment*—Don't dismiss any ideas.
- *Build on the ideas of others*—No "buts," only "ands."
- *Encourage wild ideas*—Embrace the most out-of-the-box notions because they can be the key to solutions.
- *Go for quantity*—Aim for as many new ideas as possible. In a good session, up to one hundred ideas are generated in sixty minutes.

- *Be visual*—Use yellow, red, and blue markers to write on 20-inch by 25-inch Post-its, which are then put on wall.
- *Stay focused on the topic*—Always keep the discussion on target.
- *One conversation at a time*—No interrupting, no dismissing, no disrespect, no rudeness.

Source: Based on Bruce Nussbaum, "The Power of Design: IDEO Redefined Good Design by Creating Experiences, Not Just Products," *Business Week* (May 17, 2004), 86–94.

## Analyzing and Predicting Consumer Behavior

Consumers have a perceptual map—a *gestalt,* as you read in Chapter 1—that influences every part of the way they live their lives, including their CDP (consumer decision process). At each stage of the CDP, personal variables such as gender, age, income, lifestyle, and personality affect how consumers make choices to buy and use goods and services. Your own personal variables influence your choices as a consumer, but your job as a consumer analyst or corporate strategist is to look beyond your own perceptual map and see life from the eyes of people who are different from you. As you do so, you will begin to understand how people spend time, choose friends, allocate financial resources to products or retailers, support social programs, and ultimately determine the effectiveness of an organization's marketing strategy. Firms like IDEO (described in the opening vignette) are experts at understanding the CDP of customers and potential customers, wherever they may live around the globe. This chapter will help you understand the most important variables of consumer behavior and how they are changing.

A logical place to begin is **demographics,**[1] defined as *the size, structure, and distribution of a population.* According to Canadian demographer David Foot, "Demographics explain two-thirds of everything. They help predict which products will be in demand and what school enrollments will be in the future. They also help forecast which drugs will be in fashion ten years down the road and which types of crime can be expected to increase."[2] Do your own demographics make you a "normal" consumer? Remember that *normal* is a statistical concept describing the characteristics of the majority of consumers and how they behave. Look at Table 7.1 to determine how you—and therefore the perceptual map you use to make consumer decisions—compare with the global village. Some of the facts in that table might surprise you, perhaps causing you to conclude that in some ways you are "abnormal."

Marketers use demographic analysis in two ways—as *market segment descriptors* (as described in Chapter 2) and in *trend analysis.* As descriptors of market segments, marketers match demographic and psychographic profiles of a segment with its consumer behaviors, keeping in mind that demographics are merely proxies for what really needs to be measured, behavior. When marketers need more information to understand behavior than can be extracted from demographics, they turn to additional variables (described later in the chapter) such as psychographics, personality, and personal values. When behavior correlates with demographics, strategists focus on changes that can be forecast about demographics, often quite reliably, to forecast trends in consumer behavior.

### Demographic Analysis and Social Policy

Demographic analysis is useful in analyzing policy questions related to **macromarketing,** *the aggregate performance of marketing in society.* Macromarketing evaluates marketing from society's perspective and seeks to understand the consequences of marketing actions and transactions in a society. How much food will be required to feed the population of a country in the future? If a tax cut is proposed, how will it affect consumer spending? What policies would cause consumers to save more and spend less on current consumption? Should consumers be encouraged to buy remarketed homes, cars, clothing, and sports equipment instead of new products, thereby using fewer natural resources but diminishing the need for human workers in factories that manufacture new products? Does affluence in one nation create more or less affluence

If the Earth's population were to shrink to a village of 100 people, with existing human ratios remaining the same, it would look like this.

- 61 would live in Asia, 12 in Europe, 14 in the Western Hemisphere, and 13 in Africa
- 50 would be female; 50 would be male
- 85 would be non-white; 15 would be white
- 67 would be non-Christian; 33 would be Christian
- 18 would be Muslim, 16 Hindu, 6 Buddhist, less than 1 would be Jewish, and 16 would be non-religious
- 60 percent of the entire world's wealth would be in the hands of only 6 people—mostly U.S. citizens
- 25 would be living on $1.00 a day or less
- 47 would be living on $2.00 a day or less
- 46 would live in urban areas
- 17 would live in substandard housing
- 41 would be without basic sanitation
- 14 would not be able to read
- 13 would be malnourished
- 4 would be Internet users
- 8 would be personal computer users
- 2 would be college educated

Sources: Original data from George F. Fussell Jr., Frank Russell Company, Tacoma, Washington (March 22, 1999). Update compiled by ZPGSEATTLE.org, now combined with Population Connection at www.popconnect.org (March 2005).

in other nations? Some consumer analysts subscribe to a mission statement that defines their vision as raising the average standard of living in the world. Understanding consumer behavior at the macromarketing level helps them accomplish that mission.

The root of macromarketing is in an area of study known as psychological economics.[3] When corporate executives or policy makers discuss such topics as the loss of jobs in an economy due to offshore outsourcing, they need to understand macromarketing. The fundamental principle of globalization is that when workers are competent in other places and the legal and logistics infrastructure is in place, work migrates to the lowest-cost producers. Congress can pass laws and unions can organize strikes to delay job movement, but neither can deny the laws of economics. If a domestic producer cannot increase its productivity, reduce its costs, develop better products than global competitors, or market its products to consumers who are willing to pay premium prices reflecting higher costs, that firm first loses profits, then loses jobs, and finally goes out of business.

A common solution to the outsourcing problem is to ask consumers to "buy American." Some observers ask, "Wouldn't consumers be willing to pay higher prices to support American workers?" From PCs to pantyhose, consumers who vote with their wallets on a daily basis respond, "No!" A few years ago, Wal*Mart tried to maintain a policy of "buy American," perhaps believing consumers would pay a little more for American-made products. When it lost business to competitors selling less expensive goods made in China or Bangladesh, however, Wal*Mart placed lower-priced imports next to its higher-priced American-made products and found that consumers almost always purchased the less-expensive goods. Consumers may say they prefer to buy American, but their true attitudes are reflected in their behavior every time cash registers ring up another "ka-ching" for imported goods. Understanding what is happening to jobs in the U.S. economy is dependent on understanding consumer behavior and how to develop products and marketing strategies that cause nations to prosper or decline. Ultimately, macromarketing decisions determine consumer demographics—income, births, and longevity (because of variables such as sanitation, pollution, and water supply)—for people in every nation. And the wealth that consumers have to spend is heavily influenced by how they spend the wealth they have.

## DEMOGRAPHICS AND INDUSTRIAL DEMAND

Consumer behavior, especially analysis of demographic trends, is also important for industrial or business-to-business marketing because industrial demand is ultimately derived from consumer demand. Will there be enough consumer demand for LTG (Liquid to Gas) fuels to justify the billions spent by oil companies to develop production plants in Qatar? Will automobile component manufacturer firms be successful in selling Honda or Ford the technologies required for hybrid cars? Will industrial distributors of conveyor belts and ball bearings be selling to manufacturing firms in North America, Europe, Asia, or Africa? The answers to all those questions are in the minds and wallets of consumers. Your job in any organization is to understand the minds of its customers. In an industrial firm, you must understand not only the customers' minds, but also the minds of the customers' customers.

## Changing Structure of Consumer Markets

Firms that fail to plan generally plan to fail. Planning, however, requires information about markets and their four main components:

- people with needs,
- ability to buy,
- willingness to buy, and
- authority to buy.

Understanding the demographics of markets, both now and in the future, is essential to understanding the types of products people will need, where they are likely to buy them, and the attributes most likely to delight them. Market analysis begins with understanding how people's needs relate to variables such as age and other demographic factors, but it also considers other individual variables such as personality, personal values, and lifestyles. Forecasting consumer *ability to buy* requires an understanding of economic resources—who has money now and who is likely to have it in the future from a global perspective. *Willingness to buy* is affected by the many variables described throughout this book, including the importance of brands. *Authority to buy* is addressed in Chapter 12 in its discussion of family and household influences, a situation that shares many similarities with the analysis of organizational buying behavior in which influence may officially reside in the purchasing department but is influenced by other people and departments within an organization.

### People: Foundation of Market Analysis

Although the title of this book is *Consumer Behavior*, it is really about *people* behavior. Therefore, the number and nature of people are the foundation of markets and market analysis. Demographic analysis answers such questions as: How many people will there be? What will be their age distribution? Where will they live? Combine demographics with data on purchasing power or wealth, and the result is **economic demographics**, *the study of the economic characteristics of a nation's population.*

Population trends are relatively reliable to predict compared with many other variables in the study of consumer behavior. There are unknowns, of course, such as natural calamities like tsunamis or hurricanes, wars, and epidemics like AIDS, all of which affect population projections in less predictable ways. Ordinarily, three variables determine the size and nature of population—births, deaths, and net migration. Births are usually the most important, but they are volatile and sometimes difficult to forecast.

## HOW MANY BABIES WILL BE BORN?

Several terms are used to describe and project future populations. **Birthrate** is the *number of live births per 1,000 population in a given year*. Birthrates should not be confused with **natural increase**, which is the *surplus of births over deaths in a given period*. The **fertility rate** is the *number of live births per 1,000 women of childbearing age* (defined as 15 to 44 years). **Total fertility rate** (TFR) is the *average number of children that would be born alive to a woman during her lifetime if she were to pass through all of her childbearing years conforming to the age-specific fertility rates of a given year*. TFR answers the simple question: how many babies are women having currently? In emerging markets, the number is high—8.0 in Niger, for example. Currently, in the United States, it's about 2.0. TFR is low across Europe and in Japan and most developed countries other than the United States. This is significant because the replacement rate—the number of births required to maintain current population levels—is 2.1 children, allowing for infant mortality. Because U.S. TFR is higher than most other industrialized nations, U.S. markets are highly attractive to global marketers, creating intense competition among global enterprises and providing one more reason for customer-centric marketing strategies.

**Population momentum**, which recognizes that *the future growth of any population will be influenced by its present age distribution*, is crucial for understanding the dynamics of population growth. That's why replacement-level fertility does not immediately translate into zero population growth. Even if fertility fell to that level currently, world population would continue to grow for several decades.

**Future Fertility Scenarios** Forecasting births decades into the future is difficult. Although *fecundity*, the physiologic capability of women to reproduce, is fairly predictable, *fertility*, which is actual reproductive performance, is less certain. The solution to the problem of forecasting babies—and thus, total population—is to provide several projections based on different fertility assumptions. In the United States, the Census Bureau calls these Series I (highest), assuming 2.7 children per woman; Series II (middle), assuming 2.1 children; and Series III (lowest), assuming 1.7. Before 1993, fertility in the United States had fallen to its lowest level in about fifteen years, but increased in the 1990s and stands now at about 2.0. If global fertility were to continue at a constant rate, the world population would be 12 billion by 2050, but that's not expected to happen. The middle assumption puts the forecast at 8 billion, but in 2003, for the first time, the United Nations Population Division issued its forecast that in the twenty-first century fertility will drop to 2.1 in developing nations and that, by 2050, three out of four countries in the less-developed regions, using the medium scenario, will be experiencing below-replacement fertility.[4] Using the low scenario, which some consumer analysts believe might occur because of AIDS (contributing to the death of women of childbearing age) and other factors, global population would peak in 2035 and then begin declining. Consumer analysts must pay close attention to changes in fertility because getting the right answer makes a big difference in projections of future markets, as you can see in Figure 7.1.

**FIGURE 7.1**   Estimated and Projected Population of the World,
1950–2050, by projection variant

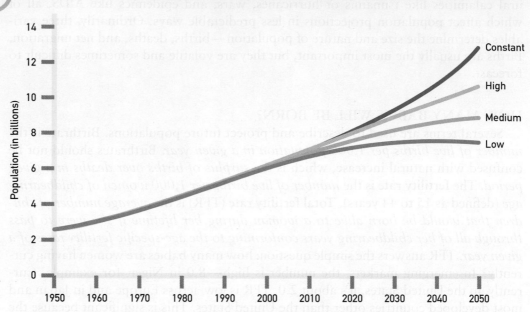

Source: Population Division of the Department of Economic and Social Affairs of the United Nations Secretariat, *World Population Prospects: The 2002 Revision Highlights* (New York: United Nations, 2003). Copyright United Nations.

**What Causes Babies?**  To predict how population size will change, marketers examine variables that determine birthrates. First is the *age distribution* of the population. Second is *family structure,* which involves facts such as the proportion of people who are married, proportion of women employed outside the home, and average age when people get married. The third cause of births is *social attitudes* toward family and children. Finally, birthrates are affected by *technology,* such as availability and cost of contraception, as illustrated in Market Facts 7.1, which looks at contraception in India. Affluence historically has caused low fertility, but now affluence is also causing declines in the age groups that typically produce babies. In developing countries, the relationship between affluence and HIV/AIDS in women of childbearing age could slow the growth of cities such as Bangalore, India, where affluence and urbanization of previously rural population groups has created an increase in infection rates. In thirty-eight highly affected countries of Africa, the population by 2015 is projected to be 91 million, or 10 percent lower, than it would have been without AIDS, causing population in the most affected nations (Botswana, Lesotho, South Africa, and Swaziland) to be projected lower in 2050 than it is today.[5] Fertility rates in the United States are projected to remain higher than in most advanced countries for several decades. By 2020, TFR in the United States is expected to be 2.03, higher than Canada at 1.44 and even greater than Mexico at 1.94.[6]

Although the *number* of children in a family affects buying and consumption patterns, *order effects* also affect consumption even when total births remain constant. First-order (firstborn) babies may generate $1,500 of retail sales, for example, whereas higher-order babies generate less than half that amount. One-child families are generally able to afford better food and health care and buy more products like personal computers, new clothing (instead of "hand me downs"), and services such as private education, ballet school, and sports lessons compared to families with more children. Also, childlessness has become a lifestyle of choice or necessity for an increasing number of consumers, releasing income for more and better restaurants, travel, leisure, higher education, and other products and services.

## MARKET FACTS 7.1

## Population Growth Fuels Birth Control Sales Efforts in India

In Mirazfari, a small village in the northern part of India, medicine man Sushil Bharati dispenses cough medicine and advice on karma from behind a small desk under a tree. In villages throughout India's poorest areas, Bharati and others like him are the center of life, and now they have become the center of a birth control marketing campaign called Butterfly. The program enlists the help of a network of medicine men to teach Indians about birth control pills and condoms, in exchange for free radio advertising, customer referrals, posters, and a percent of the profits from selling condoms. Although Mirazfari's 10,000 citizens are very poor and have on average eight children to feed, clothe, and house on an average income of $10 per month, the program is met with much skepticism.

The need to curb population growth is great in India, the population of which hit 1 billion in May 2000—surpassed only by China's 1.2 billion. In the past, the government tried to control growth with mandated sterilization; the government stopped this practice about three years ago, however, owing in part to pressure from human rights groups. Now Butterflies can be found plastered on billboards and building walls around the state of Bihar, and even on Bharati's prescription pads.

Though the program is aimed to improve the quality of life in India, it is also admittedly about branding and making money. Similar ventures, some sponsored by the U.S. government and others by private funds, are trying to reach India's women through established networks of professionals. But networks of all types are having a difficult time convincing women to try some method of birth control. Some believe the pill causes cancer, whereas others leave it up to their husbands to decide all matters. One key in fighting this battle is literacy and education. Three southern Indian states, in which literacy is much higher among women, have reached the replacement fertility rate of 2.1 children per couple. And signs do exist that even Bihar residents are beginning to try contraceptives.

Source: Miriam Jordan, "Selling Birth Control to India's Poor," *Wall Street Journal* (September 21, 1999), B1–B4. Copyright 2005 by Dow Jones & Co. Reproduced with permission of Dow Jones & Co., Inc., in the format textbook via Copyright Clearance Center, Inc.

**Ethnic Variations** Small variations in fertility rates among ethnic groups produce large differences in population. In the year 2010, fertility rates for various ethnic segments in the United States are expected to be African American (2.44), white (2.05), Asian (1.95), and Hispanic (2.98).[7] About 66 percent of all births currently are non-Hispanic white, but that percentage is predicted to decline to 42 percent in 2050, creating dramatic shifts for products that have markets concentrated among younger age groups. All other race and ethnic groups are expected to increase their share of births. Chapter 11 will examine further the characteristics and effects on marketing of the changing ethnic makeup of the population.

## HOW LONG WILL PEOPLE LIVE?

Life expectancy has increased dramatically in most countries, affected greatly by declines in infant mortality. A century ago, the average American died at the age of 47 years. Today, white females have the longest life expectancy at 79.9 years, and black males the shortest at 68.8 years. Black females have a life expectancy of 75.6 years, and white males a life expectancy of 74.5 years.[8] As people live longer, the need for in-home health care, nursing home facilities, senior activity centers, and special products increases, but many other products not usually associated with old age will also increase, as you'll see later in the chapter under the topic of the "Young-Again Market." To find out how long you personally are expected to live, read Buyer Beware 7.1. Beware of saving so little that your retirement income expires before you do.

## How Long Will You Live?

If you want an estimate of how many years you personally will live, use a Web browser to search for a "longevity calculator." Thousands are available, but "The Longevity Game" available on the Northwestern Mutual website (www.nmfn.com) shows the effect of each question you answer on your expected longevity. If you go to this website, look at the effects on your expected life of variables you control—such as eating fruits and vegetables, regular exercise, smoking, and traffic violations. Also look at ones you can't control such as your sex and the age of your parents currently or at their death. The longer you have lived already, the longer your expected longevity. But beware! Are

you saving enough now to support you during your expected life will your savings expire before you do? If some of your answers reduce the number of years you want to live, will you change them? Longevity calculators are useful planning tools for your lifestyle, behavior, and financial planning.

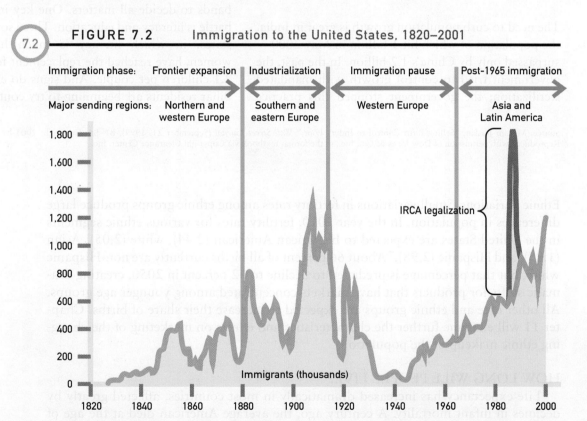

**FIGURE 7.2**     Immigration to the United States, 1820–2001

Source: Philip Martin and Elizabeth Midgley, "Immigration: Shaping and Reshaping America," *Population Reference Bureau Population Bulletin*, 58 (June 2003).

### HOW MANY PEOPLE WILL IMMIGRATE?

Immigration has been a major contributor to the U.S. population since its inception, as shown in Figures 7.2 and 7.3. An analysis by the Center for Immigration Studies of the Current Population Survey (CPS) indicates that more than 33 million immigrants (legal and illegal) live in the United States.[9] Unlike most of the past century, immigration

**FIGURE 7.3** Percentage of U.S. Population Growth from Immigration, 1900–1999

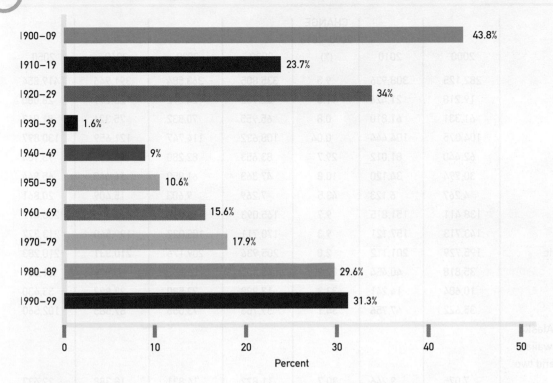

Source: Population Reference Bureau. www.prb.org/Content/NavigationMenu/PRB/Educators/Human_Population/Migration2/Migration1.htm

currently represents more than 30 percent of the population growth in the United States. As you can see from Figure 7.3, however, growth from immigration was even greater in the first few decades of the last century, with peaks and troughs of immigration flows since then.[10] The United States is becoming an immigrant society again, but today the relatively high impact of immigration on population growth is due more to low growth of the existing population than the absolute numbers of immigrants. Undocumented immigrants boost the numbers somewhat; some observers estimate that they boost the numbers by about one-third. Of significance in Figure 7.2 is also the issue of culture—as people immigrate from different countries than they did in the past, will the culture, norms, and values they bring with them affect consumer behavior in the United States, or will immigrants quickly assimilate? As you may remember from the opening vignette about Carlos in Chapter 1 of this book, the answer is some of both.

Immigration has significant effects on consumer markets, especially in nations such as the United States and Canada. Without immigration, the United States would rapidly become a nation of older consumers, much like Europe and Japan are already becoming. Any marketer selling to young consumers must plan strategies to reach customers increasingly from ethnic backgrounds associated with first- and second-generation immigration. Housing markets have grown rapidly in recent years, much of it fueled by immigration, especially in low- and middle-priced housing units. The demand for education, housing, food, clothing, and many other products and services requires consumer behavior to focus on the role of immigration as a foundation for those markets.

## Most Likely Population Scenarios

How many consumers will be in the U.S. market in the future? No one knows exactly, but Table 7.2 presents estimates prepared by the U.S. Census Bureau using the

TABLE 7.2

**Projections of U.S. Resident Population by Age, Sex, Race, and Hispanic Origin, 2000–2050 (in thousands except as indicated)**

| POPULATION OR PERCENT, SEX, AND AGE | 2000 | 2010 | CHANGE 2000–2010 (%) | 2020 | 2030 | 2040 | 2050 |
|---|---|---|---|---|---|---|---|
| Population total | 282,125 | 308,936 | 9.5 | 335,805 | 363,584 | 391,946 | 419,854 |
| 0–4 | 19,218 | 21,426 | 11.5 | 22,932 | 24,272 | 26,299 | 28,080 |
| 5–19 | 61,331 | 61,810 | 0.8 | 65,955 | 70,832 | 75,326 | 81,067 |
| 20–44 | 104,075 | 104,444 | 0.04 | 108,632 | 114,747 | 121,659 | 130,897 |
| 45–64 | 62,440 | 81,012 | 29.7 | 83,653 | 82,280 | 88,611 | 93,104 |
| 65–84 | 30,794 | 34,120 | 10.8 | 47,363 | 61,850 | 64,640 | 65,844 |
| 85+ | 4,267 | 6,123 | 43.5 | 7,269 | 9,603 | 15,409 | 20,861 |
| Male, total | 138,411 | 151,815 | 9.7 | 165,093 | 178,563 | 192,405 | 206,477 |
| Female, total | 143,713 | 157,121 | 9.3 | 170,711 | 185,022 | 199,540 | 213,377 |
| White non-Hispanic | 195,729 | 201,112 | 2.8 | 205,936 | 209,176 | 210,331 | 210,283 |
| Black | 35,818 | 40,454 | 12.9 | 45,365 | 50,442 | 55,876 | 61,361 |
| Asian | 10,684 | 14,241 | 33.3 | 17,988 | 22,580 | 27,992 | 33,430 |
| Hispanic | 35,622 | 47,756 | 34.1 | 59,756 | 73,055 | 87,585 | 102,560 |
| American Indian, Alaska native, Native Hawaiian, Pacific Islander, and two or more races | 7,075 | 9,246 | 30.7 | 11,822 | 14,831 | 18,388 | 22,437 |

Source: U.S. Census Bureau, "U.S. Interim Projections by Age, Sex, Race, and Hispanic Origin," www.census.gov/usinterimproj (March, 2005).

Note: Weighted interim middle series data.

cohort-component method, which uses assumptions about the components of population change (fertility, mortality, and international migration) to project population by age and sex. These projections show the total number of consumers growing from 282 million in 2000 to 308 million in 2010 and 419 million by 2050. There are, however, many structural conditions that may keep this from happening. Chapter 12 describes factors that may lead to lower fertility, and the difficulties in obtaining green cards and student visas since September 11, 2001, have affected immigration patterns. In the past, the importance of immigration on population growth was linked to higher fertility and yet, when you look at the nations with the lowest fertility (historically Catholic nations, such as Italy and Spain), continued birth rates may be a questionable assumption if Roman Catholic immigrants from Latin America adopt similar behavior in the future. Table 7.2 represents the latest projections available when this book was written and serves as the basis for the rest of the chapter. You may also want to visit the website of the U.S. Census Bureau (www.census.gov) or Statistics Canada (www.statcan.ca) to monitor changes in fertility, immigration, and longevity. Other useful sources include the Population Reference Bureau (www.prb.org), but as a consumer analyst your best strategy is to study the data and develop your own assumptions about what is likely to happen to fertility, immigration, and, ultimately, population size.

# Changing Age Distribution in the United States

Understanding the changing age distribution in North America and its effect on consumer behavior provides insight on the types of products and services that will be bought and consumed in the future, as well as on related behaviors, attitudes, and opinions.[11] Take time to look at Table 7.2 and see how the various age segments are likely to either increase or decline in the next decade. What does this mean to you if you're a marketer of children's toys, low-end furniture, reading glasses, healthy foods, or wheelchairs? As you read the following pages, think of ways that demographics affect a firm's current and future segmentation strategies. Also consider the macromarketing policy implications. For example, what are the effects on Social Security and Medicare of a nearly 30 percent increase this decade of the 45–64 age group, who in less than two decades will expect benefits to be paid by the relatively few consumers now in the 20–44 age group?

*Cohort analysis* is fundamental to understanding changing consumer markets—not only understanding the number of people in each age group but also the important influences on their lives, including media, peers, and parents. A **cohort** is *any group of individuals linked as a group in some way*—usually by age. The key to cohort analysis is examining the influences that are shared by most people in a specific group. For example, what's your favorite music? Chances are it's the music you loved during puberty and the years soon after that. It's likely that your own "puberty music" will be your favorite music throughout your life, and marketers who want to reach you and your cohort will evoke positive feelings toward their product by associating it with that music.[12] Can you remember where you were and what you were doing on September 11, 2001? Or when the United States invaded Iraq? What about the day O. J. Simpson or Michael Jackson was acquitted, or when Ronald Reagan was shot? If one of these events was your most vividly memorable moment, it's likely that you are part of a cohort of people who share many of the beliefs, lifestyles, and behaviors of that age group. Ultimately those influences affect consumer decision processes and the types of products, brands, and retailers consumers prefer when responding to a firm's marketing strategy.

## Children as Consumers

The number of young children may increase somewhat between 2000 and 2010 because of higher birth rates among immigrants, but the importance of children as consumers increases even more, with the high proportion of first-order babies generating high demand for quality products and services.[13] Many parents shop at Wal*Mart, especially those with larger families and lower incomes, whereas affluent first-child parents, often in their thirties and forties in two-career households, may shop more at specialty stores. Both of these developments create a polarity of retailing (see Chapter 5) for children's products that has already challenged Toys "R" Us. At specialty stores, older parents shop with high expectations for information and quality and a willingness to pay for designer labels, first at Baby Gap, then at Abercrombie & Fitch, and before long at the Apple Store. Chapter 12 discusses in detail the spending power of children in families. Most parents may do most of the buying, but children are often involved in family purchasing decisions, accompanying their parents to the store and reserving veto power over brands and products. In addition, children often have their own ability to buy, mirroring their increased allowances, giving businesses a golden opportunity to encourage a retail-consumer bonding that could last for a lifetime of purchases.[14]

Although Table 7.2 shows little increase in the 5–19 and 20–44 age groups in future years, the categories used by the Census Bureau mask a cohort of special interest to marketers. This cohort is referred to by various names (e.g., "Echo" Generation, "N" Gen—for *networked*), but most often it's called Generation Y, or simply Gen Y, to differentiate it from Generation X, the smaller cohort a decade older. Born in the 1980s and early 1990s, with 72 million members, Gen Y is the first group to challenge baby boomers in numbers and is 50 percent larger than Generation X. Teenagers are expected to spend nearly $200 billion and add 4 million new drivers each year throughout the 2000–2010 decade, creating a market not only for cars and gasoline, but also for music and entertainment, fast food, computers, cameras, cell phones, and many other products. Marketers are directing ads to teenagers, who are increasingly given the task of buying products for the family because they have more time and because they like shopping more than their parents do.[15] But when it comes to getting their attention, members of Gen Y expect marketers to be honest, use humor, be clear in message, and show them the product in ads.[16] Teen consumers tend to be fickle.[17] They are likely to switch brand preferences more quickly than other groups because of their high need to keep on top of trends and be accepted by their peers. Research indicates that what teens like best about shopping is being with their friends and that companies should focus some of their marketing efforts on opinion leaders within teen groups.[18]

Where does Gen Y spend its time? For many, the answer is the mall, not only as a place to shop, but as a place of employment and a gathering place to meet friends for entertainment and eating, especially if it is a lifestyle mall, as described in Chapter 3. It's also a teacher—a place to form brand preferences and learn how firms market. They have favorites, including Target and Wal*Mart, but Gen Y also likes specialty stores such as those in Figure 7.4, which can be "out" as rapidly as they are "in."

## Gen X—Young Adults

Generation X is often called the forgotten generation because its members are too young to be baby boomers, but too old to be baby boomers' children. Whereas Gen Y is an opportunity for high growth during the 2000s, the number of young adults between 25 and 34 is declining as a result of the baby bust from 1965 to 1980. As you can see in Table 7.2, the number of consumers from age 20 to 44 is more than 100 million, but it is projected to have essentially no growth. The entire young adult segment, however, is expected to increase slightly in this decade, because of the inclusion of older Gen Y consumers. The younger portion of the 20–44 segment is independent, not yet facing "grown-up" issues such as buying homes or saving for retirement. Much of this group doesn't have health insurance or a regular doctor[19]; its members live life for the present more than for the future and make up a large portion of the nation's 50 million consumers without health insurance (but have little need for anything more than "catastrophic" or high-deductible health insurance policies).

Consumers aged 25–45 are historically in a life stage when they form families, have children, and buy their first home and a new car. Due to declining growth, marketers of products that appeal to this age group (including diamond engagement rings, maternity clothes, and furniture) face flat or declining sales in upcoming years. To survive, many marketers will focus on taking market share from competitors or look to other cohorts for growth. This age group is also living at home longer and graduating, marrying, and starting families later than its parents did.[20] When they do leave home, Gen X'ers use credit cards to support their "habits" of microwaves, dishwashers, DVD players, and similar consumer goods, which they often buy from value-oriented retailers, such as Wal*Mart, Circuit City, and Best Buy. Despite their declin-

Where Gen Y Shops

**FIGURE 7.4** Specialty Stores Appealing to Gen Y

ing numbers, Generation X is an important market segment for many home-related products.

## Baby Boomers or "Muppies"

A pivotal point in history was 1996—the year baby boomers started reaching age 50, sparking an era of consumption freedom as their mortgages, car payments, and college education bills for their children began to subside. The next pivotal point in history will occur soon after 2010, when they begin to retire, sparking a new era of freedom from their working careers. *Baby boomers* refers to the large cohort of people born after World War II. The 74 million births that occurred between 1946 and 1964 have affected markets and all other aspects of society for decades. In the 1980s, marketers called them "yuppies"—young urban professionals—because of their high discretionary incomes and influence on market trends. Today, "yuppies" have become "muppies"—middle-aged urban professionals—creating even more profitable markets. These individuals are influencing everything from retailing and advertising to product development and the performance of the stock market.[21]

Baby boomers delayed getting married and having children to focus on their careers, the financial rewards of which created a permanent propensity to consume. They held power in the marketplace because of their numbers, and marketers aimed to satisfy their wants—quality, aesthetically pleasing, personally satisfying, natural, and, if possible, noncaloric products. Baby boomers buy more and save less than past generations, spending on products that past generations would have considered luxuries, such as consumer electronics, multiple cars, and household services. They want clothes that fit comfortably, yet are stylish, one of the reasons for Chico's success (see Figure 7.5).

**FIGURE 7.5** Chico's Is Successful Because It Understands the Minds of Middle-Aged Women

The lifestyle decisions of baby boom consumers are influenced greatly by trends in marriage, divorce, and consumption during the 1980s and 1990s. They don't need a new car, but if they buy one, it will be higher quality than what they accepted as young adults. It may also be one that restores some of the youth they don't want to concede to the next generation. Porsche, Lexus, and more recently Cadillac are auto brands that meet both criteria. When baby boomers buy homes or products for the home, they also face less immediacy and more ability to buy quality. Instead of the split-level home they might have preferred in younger years, they want a nicer but perhaps smaller home, along with a second home that might someday be used for retirement.[22] Such explains the development in many suburbs of luxury detached condos with full maintenance services as well as the construction boom at such destination resorts as Vail, Colorado, and Naples, Florida.

Table 7.2 shows that the 45–64 age group will grow by nearly 19 million consumers between 2000 and 2010, and most of these will be considered muppies. These consumers provide surging markets for luxury travel, restaurants, and the theater, which often means they need fashionable clothing and jewelry. Although they do not cook at home as often as their parents did, they remodel their homes to include gourmet kitchens (and large walk-in closets to store all of their "stuff").[23] They watch their waistlines and spend freely on spas, health clubs, cosmetics, salons, diet plans, and health foods. And they are a prime prospect for financial products oriented toward asset accumulation and retirement income.

The baby boomer population explosion that moves through markets has been compared to "a pig that's been swallowed by a python," inviting marketers to satisfy the needs, wants, and fantasies of 76 million people. Add to that the fact that many of them are still the primary purchasers, or at least primary payers, for a lot of children and grandchildren, and you begin to understand the need to connect with them. They not only affect the economy, they *are* the economy, representing the greatest share of the work force, the greatest share of income, and the greatest share of voting power and political influence. Boomers have freedom both to spend and to withhold spending. Since they already have enough housing, cars, and clothing, they not only have the freedom to spend on what they want, they have the freedom to withhold spending until they find exactly what they want, whether it's a Jaguar, a Hummer, or a Cadillac. Consumer Behavior and Marketing 7.1 describes additional opportunities for marketers created by baby boomers.

## What Will Baby Boomers Buy in the Next Ten Years?

Changing lifestyles and purchasing power of today's baby boomers will change their buying behavior and wants. Strategic planning of manufacturers, retailers, and service providers will be affected by these trends.

- *Maintenance and parts*—The old adage, "If I'd known I was going to live so long, I'd have taken better care of myself," might become the official motto of today's baby boomers. Consumers want to take care of their skin, joints, bones, and body parts, looking beyond doctors to retailers and manufacturers on how to do it. Sears, Wal*Mart, and Costco already sell eyeglasses, hearing aids, and prescriptions—are knees, hips, and hair far behind?

- *Crowded closets*—In a focus group about shopping, one consumer said that nothing comes into the house unless something goes out. Hoarding unnecessary junk like our grandparents from the Depression era did is "out," and so is the buying of things to fill up an empty house like the 25–34-year-olds of the past did. That's good news for marketers that sell what people want more than what they already have and bad news for those who just sell stuff they hope consumers will add to the stuff they already own.

- *Creative arts*—As people increase the number of years they have as empty nesters, they will likely look to activities such as crafts, cooking, and foreign language or arts courses to keep them fulfilled. This development is good news for retailers such as Michael's, Hobby Lobby, and JoAnn's and also for community colleges, universities, executive MBA programs, and schools offering adult education.

- *Style over fashion*—Young consumers need the safety in numbers of fashion apparel. MUPPIES (Mature Urban Professionals) choose styles of clothing that give them comfort and good fit, overcoming the need to look like their peers and don the latest fashion craze they felt during their younger years. Consumers will be loyal to the brands and retailers, like Chico's, that provide quality, stylish, comfortable clothing they can count on.

- *Services galore*—As consumers age and need fewer "things," the demand for services will increase. In addition to financial and travel services, consumers will want to buy more daily-chore home services and life-management planning services (including career and family advice).

- *Home reconfiguration*—In addition to beautifying their homes with nicer furniture and decor, consumers will likely begin changing their homes to adapt to their changing lifestyles. Many will look to stay in their homes longer, opting for first-floor master suites and laundry rooms and handicap-accessible doorways and bathrooms. And those with financial freedom may buy second homes.

The bottom line is that firms need to monitor these types of trends to anticipate how aging baby boomers are likely to change their wants and buying behavior.

Source: Adapted from Roger Blackwell and Tina Stephan, *Brands That Rock: What Business Leaders Can Learn From Rock and Roll* (New York: Wiley, 2003), 289.

Another rapid growth segment is the young-again market—consumers who have accumulated lots of chronologic age but who feel, think, and buy young. Other terms to describe this segment include *mature market, seniors,* and *elderly.* Table 7.2 shows that consumers from ages 65 to 84 are projected to grow 10.8 percent between 2000 and 2010, and consumers 85 and over will grow by 43.5 percent. Between 2010 and 2030, the 65–84 group is projected to leap from 34 million to 62 million, and between now and 2050, those over age 85 are projected to go from 4 million to 21 million, and all will be expecting Social Security and Medicare to be paid by increased taxes on the salaries of younger workers. It's an important group of consumers to understand because they will dominate the markets (and the voting booths) of the future.

**Cognitive age** is the *age one perceives one's self to be.* It is measured in terms of how people feel and act, express interests, and perceive their looks. Cognitively younger "older" women, for example, manifest higher self-confidence and greater fashion interests, are more work oriented, and have greater participation in entertainment and culturally related activities than women who see themselves as "old."[24] Cognitive age can be used in conjunction with chronological age to better target segments, create more effective content, and select the most efficient media channels.

Older families have more to spend, but less need to spend. Those on fixed incomes are thrifty and careful with the money they do spend[25] because inflation causes prices to increase, reducing their buying power. They have experience with shopping and are able to wait until they find a good value. Consumption patterns vary substantially between the retired and those still working,[26] and therefore some may respond more to coupons and be willing to shift their buying to off-peak times. Nevertheless, with home mortgages paid off or nearly so, no more college education to finance, and an inventory of appliances and furnishings, mature families are good prospects for luxury goods, travel-related products and services, health care, and a wide range of financial services.

Market segmentation is especially important in the mature market.[27] Most often, this is done on the basis of age, income, or work (retirement) status. Other segmentation variables are health, activity level, discretionary time, and engagement in society. Gender is also an important variable. Women outnumber men because of greater life expectancy, and many older (often widowed) women cannot earn an income, have inadequate or dangerous housing, and suffer social and economic isolation.[28]

Communicating with older consumers requires alterations of traditional materials and messages. Many consumers in this age cohort have difficulty processing information from traditional media, such as television and radio, because of declining sensory abilities.[29] Many don't see as well as they used to, creating the need for larger print and bright colors rather than pastels or earth tones, and others are annoyed by flashy television commercials with visual changes every few seconds. Older consumers are likely to be newspaper readers and AM talk radio listeners and are more likely to shop department stores than mass retailers, where they often find it difficult to park and to find what they need. They also tend to be more alert in the morning and therefore shop earlier than other consumers, making advertising and special services at stores more convenient for this segment when conducted in the morning.[30] Older consumers are pretty much like younger segments in their brand loyalty and shopping behavior[31] and respond equally well to younger or older role models, at least for age-neutral products such as coffee.[32] But there is a sensitivity to revealing their age. Therefore, an ad that blasts out in pictures or words that the product is for 60-year-olds won't work. Nor will advertising that is obviously directed to 30-year-olds. Figure 7.6 makes it obvious that a person's age is irrelevant; taking care of yourself is what's important. The most

FIGURE 7.6 Ad for Olay Shows Consumers How They Can Take Care of Themselves

effective way to get around the stigma of old age is to create affinities between a product and some interest of the mature generation. Figure 7.7 also illustrates how to market to the young-again segment. Many have a cognitively youthful age, to which Porsche appeals, but they have additional needs, including luggage and a desire to transport two or more adults that cannot be easily accommodated by the two-seat Porsche 911. The Cayenne SUV provides the same image, speed, and comfort as its predecessor sports coupes, hoping to convince affluent but older consumers, "There is no substitute."

## Macromarketing to an Aging Population

Clearly, the populations of the United States, Japan, Canada, and Europe are becoming older, which has enormous effects on macromarketing and social policy. After about 2010, massive numbers of consumers move to the age when traditionally they expect to retire, mostly with income from Social Security. At

**For those of us either blessed or cursed with the ability to tell the difference.**

For those in this select group, the rewards of the Cayenne S are immediate. Impressive power and torque perfectly matched with inspired road-holding capability. One drive and compromise is no longer an option. Porsche. There is no substitute.

The Cayenne S. Starting at $56,300.

PORSCHE

FIGURE 7.7 Porsche Cayenne Appeals to the "Young-Again" Segment

that time, millions of baby boomers will start visiting doctors and hospitals as often as they visit golf courses and cruise ships. Currently the United States spends 15 percent of its gross domestic product on health care (more than any other industrialized nation), with average expenditures exceeding $6,000 per person and increasing at double-digit rates. Unless things change, it's possible that federal spending on Social Security and Medicare could eventually consume as much of the nation's economy as the entire federal budget does now, consuming nearly the entire incomes of younger consumers.

Federal Reserve Board Chairman Alan Greenspan provoked a political tempest when he told members of the House Budget Committee that future Social Security and Medicare benefits must be reduced to prevent a fiscal calamity in decades to come. The ability to meet Social Security obligations has concerned people for years, but Greenspan warned that Medicare entitlements, which are "unknown" and "unlimited," are a much more serious concern than Social Security benefits, which are "defined" and "actuarially predictable." In addition, medical science not only leads to more expensive treatments, but allows people with chronic conditions to live longer, incurring greater lifetime health care costs. Experts forecast future deficits for Social Security and Medicare to be in the trillions, increasing each year nothing is done.

Baby boomers spent their money on the "good life" and failed to save much for either retirement income or increased medical costs. The rest of the nation will have to pay for their failure, deny them the benefits to which they thought they were entitled, or change the system. It seems unlikely the aging voters of America or their political leaders will deny health care and retirement benefits to people already receiving or nearing the age when they expect to receive benefits. One solution to reducing Medicare and Social Security deficits is to adjust further the age at which these benefits begin. If you think 65 is the normal retirement age for Social Security, and you were born before 1938, you are correct. If you were born later than that date, however, you might not be aware that the present schedule was changed a few years ago to make 67 the normal age for full Social Security benefits, with a sliding scale for retirement benefits depending on date of birth. That change requires changing the age people and organizations expect to retire, a major shift in cultural norms and work patterns. *Quasi-retirement* is one solution, helping employees, employers, and society by advancing the age of full retirement. A few firms are already using highly experienced workers who might otherwise retire to fill in for younger workers during vacations, sabbaticals, training, or maternity leaves. Other firms are "doubling up" by employing two quasi-retired workers for one job, recognizing their desire for increased leisure time and receiving, in return, the wisdom, reliability, and dedication of long-term employees. Less concerned about future promotions, quasi-retired workers might be especially useful for special projects that younger workers might be reluctant to accept with no clear career path.

When it comes to being able to pay for your health care in the future, don't count on your employer or the government. If you are reading this book and you're under the age of 50, the safest course of action is to start planning now for a future in which the government may not be a reliable source of retirement income beyond some minimal subsistence level. Not only are younger generations likely to grow frustrated with a significant portion of their income going to pay the medical expenses of older generations, they are also likely to demand changes in these government programs. Many will also set aside funds in their Health Savings Accounts while their health costs are low to be sure there is enough money to take care of them when they are old. The decision to save versus spend necessarily affects all other consumption decisions, demonstrating how demographics are very important to understanding your own future, the future of consumer markets, and macromarketing decisions.

## Changing Geography of Demand

The search for growing segments in a slow-growth society almost always leads to identifying domestic and global geographic areas of growth. *Where people live, how they earn and spend their money, and other socioeconomic factors*—referred to as **geodemography**—are critical to understanding consumer demand. The study of demand related to geographic areas assumes that people who live in proximity to one another also share similar consumption patterns and preferences. For example, one study found that consumer purchases from various channels or retail formats, such as grocery stores, drugstores, mass merchandisers, club stores, and convenience stores are related to the geodemographic characteristics of those consumers,[33] based on the geodemographic areas described in Market Facts 7.2.

### Segmenting Geographically

Which city do you believe is largest: San Jose or San Francisco? Columbus or Boston? If you picked San Jose and Columbus, you were correct because the question referred to cities. But San Francisco and Boston have larger metropolitan areas. Consumer analysts use a common language and set of terms to understand marketing strategies based on geodemographic variables. Cities are the most important unit of analysis in most marketing plans as well as fundamental in determining the prosperity of nations.[34] Suburbs have grown rapidly, but today **exurbs**—*areas beyond the suburbs*—are experiencing the fastest growth. Fast-growing counties are often nonmetropolitan or rural but adjacent to suburban or metropolitan areas. The **metropolitan statistical area** (**MSA**) is defined as *a free-standing metropolitan area, surrounded by nonmetropolitan counties and not closely related with other metropolitan areas*. A **primary metropolitan statistical area** (**PMSA**) is a *metropolitan area that is closely related to another city*. A *grouping of closely related PMSAs* is a **consolidated metropolitan statistical area** (**CMSA**). More than one-third of the people in the United States live in the country's twenty-two CMSAs.

Broadcast advertising is usually purchased by city or MSA (metropolitan statistical area), but many national magazines such as *Time* and *Business Week* also sell regional advertising sections on a state or city basis. In fact, some print media is moving toward editions based on such highly segmented geographic areas as zip codes. Cities are especially important for ethnic marketing. Whereas half of all Americans live in the fifty largest metro areas, more than 70 percent of Asians and Hispanics live in cities.

### Which States Are Growing?

Market trends vary substantially between states. Projections about which states are expected to grow the most are shown in Table 7.3. The greatest gains in population are concentrated in California, Texas, and Florida—states with not only the highest rates of foreign immigration, but also an influx of consumers relocating from other states. That's why retailers usually consider these states as prime candidates for new stores, whereas a state like North Dakota might be less attractive because it experienced an actual decline in population between 2000 and 2005.[35] There are pitfalls associated with concentrating only on growth. Idaho is expected to grow by 20 percent this decade, and Nevada is expected to grow by almost 40 percent. Yet these two states have relatively small populations, illustrating the trap of chasing the trend but ignoring the substance. A 10 percent market share in a no-growth market such as Ohio or Michigan may be preferable to a high market share in a rapid-growth but sparsely populated market like Alaska.

Geographic variables affect many components of a firm's marketing strategy. When firms' customers are located in geographically dispersed areas, it can be difficult to

## Geographic Areas, Defined by Spectra Lifestyle and Life–Stage Descriptions

### LIFESTYLE DESCRIPTIONS

**Upscale suburbs: 12.05 percent**
Major metro suburbs and urban fringe neighborhoods
Top-end incomes, educations, and occupations

**Traditional families: 9.45 percent**
Suburbs and outlying towns
Mixed white-collar and well-paid blue-collar occupations
Upper-middle incomes and educations
Typically dual-income households

**Mid/upscale suburbs: 9.88 percent**
Metro urban fringe locations
Mixed single-unit and apartment neighborhoods
Upper incomes and educations

**Metro elite: 9.30 percent**
Urban and urban fringe
Townhouse and high-rise apartment areas
Above-average incomes and occupations; very high educations
Younger, professional population

**Working-class towns: 13.69 percent**
Towns and outlying suburbs
Mixed lower-level white-collar and upper-level blue-collar occupations
Middle-class incomes and educations

**Rural towns and farms: 13.27 percent**
Mill, factory, and mining towns with rural farm areas
Middle to lower-middle incomes

Predominately blue-collar occupations with farming
Rust Belt mill towns and Midwestern farmers

**Mid-urban melting pot: 8.29 percent**
Major metro urban and urban fringe
Lower-level white-collar and service occupations
Mid to lower-middle incomes and strong ethnic presence

**Downscale rural: 12.19 percent**
Rural towns, hamlets, villages, and farming areas
Very low incomes and educations
Light industry, textiles, and agriculture
Strongly skewed to southeastern United States

**Downscale urban: 11.77 percent**
Densely populated urban areas, most common in northeastern United States
Very low incomes and educations
Lower-level blue-collar and service occupations
Strong ethnic presence

### LIFE-STAGE DESCRIPTIONS

| | |
|---|---|
| 18–34 with kids | 14.30 percent |
| 18–34 without kids | 12.75 percent |
| 35–54 with kids | 24.15 percent |
| 35–54 without kids | 14.44 percent |
| 55–64 | 13.34 percent |
| 65+ | 21.02 percent |

Source: Spectra (www.spectramarketing.com), quoted in J. Jeffrey Inman, Venkatesh Shankar, and Rosellina Ferraro, "The Roles of Channel-Category Associations and Geodemographics in Channel Patronage," *Journal of Marketing*, 68 (April 2004), 51–71.

manage service quality because its relative importance is likely to vary spatially. One solution is for managers to identify areas of high service responsiveness or areas in which overall satisfaction is low, but customers are highly responsive to improvements in service quality.[36] FSIs (free standing inserts), the flyers you receive in your home through the mail or the Sunday newspaper, are important tools for many marketers because they can be targeted to specific geographic areas, but the effectiveness of their

TABLE 7.3          Projections of the Total Population of States: 1995 to 2025

| SERIES A | JULY 1, 1995 | JULY 1, 2000 | JULY 1, 2005 | JULY 1, 2015 | % Δ 2005– 2015 |
|---|---|---|---|---|---|
| Alabama | 4,253 | 4,451 | 4,631 | 4,956 | 7.0 |
| Alaska | 604 | 653 | 700 | 791 | 13.0 |
| Arizona | 4,218 | 4,798 | 5,230 | 5,808 | 11.0 |
| Arkansas | 2,484 | 2,631 | 2,750 | 2,922 | 6.3 |
| California | 31,589 | 32,521 | 34,441 | 41,373 | 20.2 |
| Colorado | 3,747 | 4,168 | 4,468 | 4,833 | 8.2 |
| Connecticut | 3,275 | 3,284 | 3,317 | 3,506 | 5.7 |
| Delaware | 717 | 768 | 800 | 832 | 4.0 |
| District of Columbia | 554 | 523 | 529 | 594 | 12.3 |
| Florida | 14,166 | 15,233 | 16,279 | 18,497 | 13.6 |
| Georgia | 7,201 | 7,875 | 8,413 | 9,200 | 9.4 |
| Hawaii | 1,187 | 1,257 | 1,342 | 1,553 | 15.7 |
| Idaho | 1,163 | 1,347 | 1,480 | 1,622 | 9.6 |
| Illinois | 11,830 | 12,051 | 12,266 | 12,808 | 4.4 |
| Indiana | 5,803 | 6,045 | 6,215 | 6,404 | 3.0 |
| Iowa | 2,842 | 2,900 | 2,941 | 2,994 | 1.8 |
| Kansas | 2,565 | 2,668 | 2,761 | 2,939 | 6.4 |
| Kentucky | 3,860 | 3,995 | 4,098 | 4,231 | 3.2 |
| Louisiana | 4,342 | 4,425 | 4,535 | 4,840 | 6.7 |
| Maine | 1,241 | 1,259 | 1,285 | 1,362 | 6.0 |
| Maryland | 5,042 | 5,275 | 5,467 | 5,862 | 7.2 |
| Massachusetts | 6,074 | 6,199 | 6,310 | 6,574 | 4.2 |
| Michigan | 9,549 | 9,679 | 9,763 | 9,917 | 1.6 |
| Minnesota | 4,610 | 4,830 | 5,005 | 5,203 | 5.6 |
| Mississippi | 2,697 | 2,816 | 2,908 | 3,035 | 4.4 |
| Missouri | 5,324 | 5,540 | 5,718 | 6,005 | 5.0 |
| Montana | 870 | 950 | 1,006 | 1,069 | 6.3 |
| Nebraska | 1,637 | 1,705 | 1,761 | 1,850 | 5.1 |
| Nevada | 1,530 | 1,871 | 2,070 | 2,179 | 5.3 |
| New Hampshire | 1,148 | 1,224 | 1,281 | 1,372 | 7.1 |
| New Jersey | 7,945 | 8,178 | 8,392 | 8,924 | 6.3 |
| New Mexico | 1,685 | 1,860 | 2,016 | 2,300 | 14.1 |
| New York | 18,136 | 18,146 | 18,250 | 18,916 | 3.6 |
| North Carolina | 7,195 | 7,777 | 8,227 | 8,840 | 7.5 |
| North Dakota | 641 | 662 | 677 | 704 | 4.0 |
| Ohio | 11,151 | 11,319 | 11,428 | 11,588 | 1.4 |
| Oklahoma | 3,278 | 3,373 | 3,491 | 3,789 | 8.5 |
| Oregon | 3,141 | 3,397 | 3,613 | 3,992 | 10.5 |
| Pennsylvania | 12,072 | 12,202 | 12,281 | 12,449 | 1.4 |

(continued)

| SERIES A | JULY 1, 1995 | JULY 1, 2000 | JULY 1, 2005 | JULY 1, 2015 | % Δ 2005–2015 |
|---|---|---|---|---|---|
| Rhode Island | 990 | 998 | 1,012 | 1,070 | 5.7 |
| South Carolina | 3,673 | 3,858 | 4,033 | 4,369 | 8.3 |
| South Dakota | 729 | 777 | 810 | 840 | 3.7 |
| Tennessee | 5,256 | 5,657 | 5,966 | 6,365 | 6.7 |
| Texas | 18,724 | 20,119 | 21,487 | 24,280 | 13.0 |
| Utah | 1,951 | 2,207 | 2,411 | 2,670 | 10.7 |
| Vermont | 585 | 617 | 638 | 662 | 3.8 |
| Virginia | 6,618 | 6,997 | 7,324 | 7,921 | 8.2 |
| Washington | 5,431 | 5,858 | 6,258 | 7,058 | 12.8 |
| West Virginia | 1,828 | 1,841 | 1,849 | 1,851 | — |
| Wisconsin | 5,123 | 5,326 | 5,479 | 5,693 | 3.9 |
| Wyoming | 480 | 525 | 568 | 641 | 13.0 |

Note: Numbers in thousands. Resident population. For more detailed information, see Population Paper Listing #47, "Population Projections for States, by Age, Sex, Race, and Hispanic Origin: 1995 to 2025."

size, average discount, and allocation of the flyer to category and brand types varies by the demographics of trading area inhabitants.[37]

## Economic Resources

As you saw in Chapter 5, the three primary resources that consumers spend when purchasing are economic, temporal, and cognitive. An economic resource, or ability to buy, is a key demographic variable in explaining why, what, and when people buy. The combination of age and income is the most frequently used demographic variable to define segments.

Economic resources can be measured in various ways. **Income** is defined as *money from wages and salaries as well as interest and welfare payments.* Official measures do not include other kinds of compensation such as employer or government benefits. Although income determines what consumers *can* buy, it does not determine what they *want* to buy—many consumers might want a new Porsche, but few can afford to buy one. Market research questionnaires often ask about an individual's behavior, but also ask about household income as a determinant of the buying ability of an individual or their household unit.

The median household income was $43,318 in 2003, unchanged from the previous year. Compared to 1967, the first year for which data were collected, real median income is up 30 percent, but year-to-year numbers tend to rise and fall with the business cycle.[38] In 2003, the number of people in poverty increased compared to 2002 from 9.6 percent to 10 percent, but about half of the people in poverty in earlier years escaped that category in later years.[39] Over the past decades, while the rich were getting richer, the poor were getting richer as well, but at a much lower rate, leading to a greater disparity in incomes between rich and poor despite an increase in the real incomes of each. The income for the poorest families rose less than 1 percent between 1988 and 1998, but rose 15 percent for the richest quintile.[40] The top 20 percent of households accounted for 49.8 percent of all U.S. income in 2003.[41] Inequality is one of the reasons why many markets involve income as a useful variable for segmentation.

## Consumer Confidence

Consumers drive the economy, accounting for more than two-thirds of all economic activity in the United States and Canada. Consumption is heavily influenced by *what consumers think will happen in the future*, referred to as **consumer confidence**. Consumer confidence influences whether consumers will increase their debt or defer spending to pay off debt. Measures of consumer confidence are important to marketers making decisions about inventory levels, staffing, or promotional budgets. During late summer, for example, retailers closely examine consumer confidence about future economic conditions before placing inventory orders for the holiday season. If consumer confidence is high, holiday spending is usually strong.

Two organizations are known for their consumer confidence surveys. The Conference Board mail survey of five thousand households asks respondents to look six months ahead and focuses on availability of jobs. The University of Michigan Survey, which tends to be less volatile, questions five hundred households per month by telephone about such things as family finances and overall business conditions. The Conference Board survey conducted is based on responses to the following five issues.

1. Respondents' appraisal of current business conditions.

2. Respondents' expectations regarding business conditions six months hence.

3. Respondents' appraisal of the current employment conditions.

4. Respondents' expectations regarding employment conditions six months hence.

5. Respondents' expectations regarding their total family income six months hence.

For each of the five issues, there are three response options: positive, negative, and neutral.[42]

## Wealth

**Wealth** is a *measure of a family's net worth or assets in such things as bank accounts, stocks, and a home, minus its liabilities* such as home mortgage and credit card balances. Net worth influences willingness to spend, but not necessarily ability to spend, because much wealth is not liquid and cannot be spent easily. A correlation exists between income and net worth, but how much people accumulate over the years is more a function of how much they save than how much they earn.[43] In the late 1990s, the net wealth of most Americans rose substantially, due to the rise in the stock market, then dropped during an era of dot bombs and the technology bust. In the long run, consumers who invested in the mid-1990s who didn't get caught by the irrational exuberance of the late 1990s and who emphasized financial fundamentals in their decisions typically have seen their 401(k)'s and other investments more than double. Consumers who invested in the same fast-moving companies as their friends and who measured success by market share, first to market, or concepts other than profits, probably saw their 401(k) become a 201(k). Although consumers are segmented primarily on income rather than wealth, wealth is also important to consumer analysts because of its effect on consumer confidence, especially for luxury products.[44] In the fourth quarter of 2004, for example, Microsoft declared a cash dividend totaling $32 billion in payments to shareholders, rivaling the $38 billion the government paid out in federal income tax rebates in the summer of 2001, and boosting consumer income a record 3.7 percent that quarter.[45] The effect was to cause 2004 retail sales to soar, surprising consumer analysts who had not factored into their forecasts the effect of dividend-generating wealth on rising consumer disposable income.

Wealthy consumers spend their money on services, travel, and investments more than others. Because they place a premium on time, they value superior customer service, immediate availability, trouble-free operation of products, and dependable maintenance and repair services. They are targets for products that enhance the physical self, restore youthfulness (e.g., expensive cosmetics, skin care, cosmetic surgery, and spas), and protect and secure their property and themselves (e.g., security systems, security guards, and insurance).

## Targeting the Up Market

The up market, often referred to as the *superaffluent*, represents the top quintile of consumers in terms of income. These households often consist of two income earners who place high value on time because, for them, time is scarcer than money. They value extra services that some retailers provide to capture new customers.[46] They are good targets for jewelry, electronics and home entertainment systems, upscale cars (including SUVs and sports models), art, and entertainment. But just because this segment makes more money than other groups, marketers must not assume that they will spend all that they make and shop only at upscale stores and shopping centers. For many individuals in this group, saving money is as important as spending it. They shop discount stores,[47] use coupons, and wait for sales to buy products. Even downscale or bargain retailers such as Aldi, Big Lots, and dollar stores are frequented by individuals with above-average net worth. A few exceptions receive their money from the lottery or inheritance, but for the most part, the rich are rich because they work hard and save their money.

When planning a communications strategy, it's important to remember that the up market is more print oriented than other market segments. Readership of local weekday and Sunday newspapers and news magazines is higher and television viewership is lower—although this segment has a higher concentration subscribing to cable television and listening to public radio. Appealing to consumers with simple ads that promote image often works well, as you saw in the Porsche ad in Figure 7.7. This market also places more importance on the credibility of the source selling or promoting the product, which is why product reviews or news articles talking about a product or service may influence this group more than paid ads. But the new affluent are often frugal, as you see in Market Facts 7.3.

## Targeting the Down Market

Throughout the world, the majority of consumers are low income. Although the United States, Canada, and other industrialized countries have a vast middle class, the number of lower-income consumers is still high. Wal*Mart has found success by providing good products at reasonable prices to lower-income segments, which is why 82 percent of Americans shop at Wal*Mart. It focuses on offering attractive stores, stylish and up-to-date products, and friendly employees that treat customers with respect. Consequently, Wal*Mart has attracted a substantial portion of the up market into its stores as well as the down market. Closeout stores, such as Big Lots, T.J. Maxx, Marc's, and Tuesday Morning, make it possible for all income-level consumers to buy brand name products at low prices. These firms specialize in buying product overruns from manufacturers or the inventories of stores that are liquidating, offering products to consumers at deep discounts. Dollar stores are one of the fastest growing retail categories. Although consumers of all levels might sometimes shop there, their core market segment is lower-income consumers.

Consumers' income situations may change depending on inflation, recessions, or personal situations, such as changes in health, job, or marital status. Astute marketers

## Affluent Consumers Are Frugal

The term *new affluent* may seem synonymous with the young, wealthy set, the constituents of which lavishly spend their inherited riches. According to a recent poll, however, individuals within the 35–54 age range with high-income household incomes are shunning traditional images of wealth and luxury and looking for more value. The Visa Signature poll, conducted by research firm Fabrizio, McLaughlin & Associates, is based on the responses of eight hundred adults with annual household incomes of $125,000 or more, and an equal sample size of adults that demographically represents the country.

The new affluent consumers' frugal mindset may stem from most of its members' middle-class backgrounds. "A lot of these new affluent grew up middle class, with middle class roots," says Michael Weiss, president of Weiss Micromarketing Group. "They really work very, very hard to do well in their careers so they've emerged as a very level-headed group. They know how hard it is to make it, so they are very vigilant about spending their money wisely." In fact, study results indicate that new affluent consumers value instilling in their children traits like honesty and integrity—ranking these two qualities at the top of things that they want to pass on to their children—over money or status, which ranked at the bottom.

Additional findings imply that many new affluent consumers are uncomfortable with even being considered wealthy. Nine out of ten new affluent consumers surveyed considered themselves to be middle or upper-middle class, and 72 percent of respondents admitted that they are embarrassed by or dislike being identified as wealthy or well off, even though they acknowledge these terms are an accurate description of their financial status.

This customer segment may be on the hunt for bargain basement prices, more so than the general population. According to the poll, about three-quarters (72 percent of respondents) stated that they clip coupons—seven percentage points higher than the national average. Sixty-six percent reported that they regularly shop at club discount or warehouse stores, whereas less than half of the general population choose these shopping outlets, and 34 percent admitted that they have gone to garage sales. "[They are] not the Rockefellers of our parents' generation in how they spend in the marketplace. Businesses don't have to think that just because they are especially boutique they can't go after these new affluent consumers," Weiss says.

As these consumers continue to look for ways to cut costs and maximize their resources, marketers may need to retool their strategies. "They're into getting value and are more likely to respond to less-is-more promotions," Weiss says, such as frequent-flyer miles. For instance, 78 percent said they have a payment card that allows them to earn rewards and enjoy perks. Additionally, 57 percent responded that they select midrange hotels with reasonable prices, whereas just 13 percent contend that they opt for high-end hotels.

The new affluent cohort is applying more a middle class sensibility when in the marketplace, Weiss says, but they have not completely abandoned lavish spending. "Yes, owning a nice home is considered part of the good life, and yes, they describe themselves as early adopters of consumer electronics and they're buying luxury sedans and SUVs at higher than average rates. But after that, so much of what they do is almost commodity behavior," he says. "It's a flip side to the old line of F. Scott Fitzgerald that the rich are different from you and me. Today's affluent isn't so different than Joe and Jane Average in America today."

Source: Coreen Bailor, "The Young and the Rich: The New Thrifty," *Destination CRM* (February 9, 2005). Copyright 2005, CRM magazine/destinationCRM .com. Reprinted with permission www.destinationCRM.com.

## Changes in Income Cause Changes in Consumption

The average American family spent $40,817 on goods and services in 2003. Where did the money go? More than half of the budget went for the house (33 cents of every dollar) and car (19 cents). After paying for food (13 cents), medical bills (6 cents), a little booze (1 cent), and more, families had a nickel left to spend on entertainment.

Household spending has increased tenfold since 1950, according to the Bureau of Labor Statistics. Factor in inflation, and the increase is less dramatic. Spending, adjusted for inflation, rose from about $29,000 in 1950 to $37,000 in 1972. Since then, spending has seen smaller real increases.

Viewed over the long term, statistics prove a point: Americans' real income has increased, which leads to more consumption, which leads to changing priorities. The following is a primer on consumer spending patterns over the decades and a closer look at 2003, based on labor statistics data.

### Food

The most dramatic change in consumer spending is food's shrinking share of the wallet. Food accounted for 13 cents of each consumer dollar in 2003, down from 32 cents in 1950 and 43 cents in 1901. This is a big change—and fully expected as the nation's income grew. It confirms Engel's Law, the observation by nineteenth-century German statistician Ernst En-

gel that the proportion of income spent on food falls as income rises.

Rising income also means more dining out. Restaurant dining and takeout food accounted for 41 percent of food spending in 2003, up from 21 percent in 1960.

Rich and poor allocate the same amount of spending—about 5.5 cents of each dollar—on away-from-home meals, according to the bureau's latest Consumer Expenditure Survey. But the share of food budget devoted to dining out increases with wealth. The poorest fifth of families spent one-third of food budgets on away-from-home meals in 2003. The top fifth spent slightly more dining out ($4,535) than eating at home ($4,503).

### Housing

The drop in the food budget frees up income. Much of the extra money has gone into the American dreams of house and car.

Americans are buying more—and bigger—homes. The Census Bureau says 69 percent of families own homes today, versus 63 percent in 1965. The average new house today is 2,300 square feet, versus about 1,500 square feet in the mid-1960s and below 1,000 square feet in 1950, according to the National Association of Home Builders. These new rooms need to

react to economic changes, such as a recession, by promoting value. Many firms cut advertising during recessions, but firms with strong balance sheets and a long-term perspective on strategy practice contracyclical advertising and marketing. **Contracyclical advertising** is *the practice of increasing or at least maintaining advertising during economic slowdowns to gain market share when competitors cut promotional activity.* When the economy turns around, contracyclical spenders emerge with higher market share and profitability.

### Poverty

Poverty exists around the world, including the most advanced and industrialized nations. Although poor people in the United States make up about 10 percent of consumers, their incomes increase at much lower rates than upper income levels, which creates the growing inequality between rich and poor. Although homeless people and consumers with few economic resources are typically not big consumers,

be furnished. Add it up, and housing accounted for 33 cents of every dollar of consumer spending in 2003, up from 26 cents in 1950.

## Transportation

Transport costs took 19 cents of every consumer dollar in 2003, up from 15 cents in 1960. The reason is more—and more expensive—cars. One in seventeen Americans bought a new car in 2004, versus one in twenty-five in 1960, according to census data and sales figures from *Automotive News*. In 1960, a basic Ford sedan cost $2,257, or $14,000 in 2003 dollars. In 2003, the average transaction price for a new vehicle was about $25,000.

The annual Consumer Expenditure Survey shows how dependent auto marketers are on upper-income buyers. In 2003, households in the bottom three quintiles of income spent more money on used cars than new. The second-highest income group spent only a little more on new cars than used cars. Only the top 20 percent overwhelmingly splurged for that new car smell. The top fifth of households spent almost as much on new cars as the bottom 80 percent combined.

Rich and poor drive different wheels. Simmons' spring 2004 National Consumer Survey found lower-income households are 70 percent more likely than the average household to drive a Mercury, not good news for Ford's ailing up-market brand. The rich favor luxury brands BMW, Infiniti, and Lexus.

## Apparel

The average household spent 12 percent of its budget on apparel and shoes in 1950, but that fell to 8 percent in 1972, 6 percent in 1984, 5 percent in 1993, and 4 percent in 2003.

Inflation has been held in check by the rise of low-cost foreign production and discounters like Wal*Mart; $100 of clothing in 1984 would have cost $116 in 1993, and the same $116 in 2003, according to Consumer Price Index data. Households tend to allocate a similar share of the budget to clothes—4 percent to 5 percent—regardless of income.

## Entertainment

The share of money spent on entertainment has hovered around 5 percent since 1950, but priorities have shifted. Spending on consumer electronics has soared; spending on newspapers, magazines, and books has plummeted. The average household apportioned just 0.3 percent of spending ($127) for reading materials in 2003, down from 1 percent ($51, or $317 adjusted for inflation) in 1960.

The rich, who also are more educated, spend more money on print media and books than the poor do. But don't read too much into that. It turns out that households in every quintile of income spent the same average 0.3 percent of budget on reading in 2003. For publishers, that doesn't make cents.

Source: Bradley Johnson, "Families Spend Less on Food as They Pursue House, Car Dreams," *Advertising Age* (Midwest region edition), 76 (February 7, 2005), 1.

they are of interest to consumer analysts because they do buy some things. More important, consumer analysts are concerned with social policies that affect the educational levels, value systems, and economic policies for this segment, all of which have implications on all other segments.[48]

As you shift to thinking about global demographics, think through the information you've just learned and consider how marketing strategy must evolve continuously in response to changing markets. Market Facts 7.4 describes how changing income affects consumption expenditures. After reading that, consider what you would do if you were a strategist for a grocery, apparel, or leisure retailer or one of their suppliers. Unless management changes, the more successful a firm has been in the past, the more likely it is to fail in the future, because the future is rarely like the past. Most firms try to do better what they did well in the past, until they become unprofitable or go out of business, like Montgomery Ward. But some firms change. Read Consumer Behavior and Marketing 7.2 and consider how the founder of Limited Brands reacted to the market changes you've read about in the previous pages and in Market Facts 7.4.

## Limited Brands Adapt to Changing Consumption Decisions

Leslie Wexner, the man who turned The Limited, Abercrombie & Fitch, and Victoria's Secret into household names, has lost his faith in apparel. But he has a new source of inspiration: face cream. Ten years ago, apparel accounted for 70 percent of the sales of Limited Brands, Inc., Mr. Wexner's specialty retailing empire. Today, after shelving some clothing chains and investing heavily in its Victoria's Secret and Bath & Body Works divisions, 70 percent of Limited's sales come from skin-care products, cosmetics, and lingerie—businesses that tend to fluctuate less wildly than apparel. In its new strategy, Bath & Body Works and Victoria's Secret are the stars, while clothing chains Express and The Limited are laggards.

The new focus at Limited Brands reflects a big shift among consumers: clothes are increasingly out of fashion. After declining for three consecutive years, U.S. apparel sales nudged up 4 percent last year to $172.8 billion, according to market-research firm NPD Group. Apparel's share of consumer spending fell below 5 percent for the first time in 2003 and was 4.9 percent last year, according to consulting firm Customer Growth Partners. That's partly because discounters have driven clothing prices down, and partly because shoppers are spending more on things like electronics, home improvement, and spa services.

The Limited's early success was based on its ability to copy the designer products carried in department stores and create its own unique brands around them. But Wal*Mart, Target, and other discounters have proven to be equally crafty copycats. Now The Limited and its direct competitors, including the Gap, are feeling the pressure that specialty chains have brought to bear on department stores.

Victoria's Secret is adding hair and cosmetics lines to its beauty business. The lingerie company already offers three of the top ten selling fragrances in the United States, and Limited Brands has struck deals to sell a line of $26 candles with unusual scents (like fig and black currant) in trendy stores like Fred Segal Studio in Santa Monica, California, and Selfridges in London.

Mr. Wexner founded The Limited in 1963, choosing the name because his store's selection was limited to women's sportswear. By the 1980s, his company was the nation's largest specialty retailer. He also came to appreciate the emotional attachment shoppers have to strong brands, which played a big role in the rise of Express, with its international flavor, and Abercrombie & Fitch, which Mr. Wexner transformed from a sportswear and sporting-goods store into a trendy clothing chain focused on young adults. He began pushing Limited Brands to develop products more quickly, to stay ahead of competitors. The company has cut lead times for new Bath & Body Works products to as little as six months, from as much as two years.

© AP/Wide World Photos

Leslie H. Wexner, CEO of Limited Brands

© AP/Wide World Photos

Limited Brands operates over 1,000 stores.

Source: Based on Amy Merrick, "For Limited Brands, Clothes Become the Accessories," *Wall Street Journal* (March 8, 2005), A1.

## Global Market Opportunities: Reacting to Slow-Growth Market Conditions

Countries experiencing slow or no population growth often turn to global markets to find growth markets. If you work for a U.S.-based firm and are charged with growing sales by 20 percent, you have several options. You can increase market share in the United States—but your traditional markets may be decreasing and you may have saturated the best markets—or you can choose to expand to global markets.

The world population is approximately 6.1 billion and, as you observed in Figure 7.1, growing at a slowing rate with the possibility of reaching a stable or declining number of people. Wide variations, however, exist in the growth rate of specific global markets.

Measured by numbers of new consumers, the fastest-growing nation the world is India, expected to surpass China as the most populous nation before 2025. The top nations in the world, ranked by population, are shown in Table 7.4. As you can see,

**7.4**

**TABLE 7.4**      Top Twenty-Five Nations Measured by Total Population

| 1950 | 2000 | 2050 |
|------|------|------|
| 1. China | 1. China | 1. India |
| 2. India | 2. India | 2. China |
| 3. United States | 3. United States | 3. United States |
| 4. Russia | 4. Indonesia | 4. Nigeria |
| 5. Japan | 5. Brazil | 5. Indonesia |
| 6. Indonesia | 6. Russia | 6. Pakistan |
| 7. Germany | 7. Pakistan | 7. Bangladesh |
| 8. Brazil | 8. Bangladesh | 8. Brazil |
| 9. United Kingdom | 9. Japan | 9. Congo (Kinshasa) |
| 10. Italy | 10. Nigeria | 10. Mexico |
| 11. Bangladesh | 11. Mexico | 11. Philippines |
| 12. France | 12. Germany | 12. Ethiopia |
| 13. Pakistan | 13. Philippines | 13. Uganda |
| 14. Ukraine | 14. Vietnam | 14. Egypt |
| 15. Nigeria | 15. Egypt | 15. Russia |
| 16. Mexico | 16. Turkey | 16. Vietnam |
| 17. Spain | 17. Iran | 17. Japan |
| 18. Vietnam | 18. Ethiopia | 18. Iran |
| 19. Poland | 19. Thailand | 19. Turkey |
| 20. Egypt | 20. United Kingdom | 20. Sudan |
| 21. Philippines | 21. France | 21. Afghanistan |
| 22. Turkey | 22. Italy | 22. Thailand |
| 23. South Korea | 23. Congo (Kinshasa) | 23. Germany |
| 24. Ethiopia | 24. Ukraine | 24. Tanzania |
| 25. Thailand | 25. South Korea | 25. Yemen |

Source: U.S. Bureau of the Census: International Database (IDB).

major changes are projected. France drops out of the top 25, for example, by 2050. African nations and predominantly Muslim nations are among the fastest growing by percentage increase, with Indonesia, Pakistan, and Bangladesh projected to be in the top ten. From a marketing perspective, the greatest hope for "rich" countries in having growing markets for their products in the future is to assist in developing the "poor" countries to the point that they are rich enough to be economically strong, as well as populous, markets.

## Global Market Demographics and Attractiveness

The most attractive markets are countries that are growing both in population and in economic resources. Two relevant indicators of market attractiveness are natural increase (percentage increase in population each year, considering births and deaths) and life expectancy at birth (indicating overall quality of life), as seen in Table 7.5 for selected nations.

The search for both population growth and ability to buy takes consumer analysts increasingly to the Pacific Rim, the Indian Ocean Rim, parts of Asia, and Latin America. Despite rapid growth, many of these nations have relatively low income, in

**7.5**    TABLE 7.5      Populations of Selected Nations

| | MID-2004 POPULATION (MILLIONS) | TOTAL FERTILITY RATE | TOTAL LIFE EXPECTANCY | GNP PER CAPITA ($US) | PROJECTED POPULATION, 2025 (MILLIONS) | GROWTH, 2004–2025 (%) |
|---|---|---|---|---|---|---|
| **Africa** | | | | | | |
| Botswana | 1.7 | 3.5 | 36 | 7740 | 1.1 | −34 |
| Egypt | 73.4 | 3.2 | 68 | 3810 | 103.2 | 41 |
| Ethiopia | 72.4 | 5.9 | 46 | 780 | 117.6 | 62 |
| Kenya | 32.4 | 5.0 | 51 | 1010 | 39.9 | 23 |
| Nigeria | 137.2 | 5.7 | 52 | 800 | 206.4 | 50 |
| South Africa | 46.9 | 2.8 | 53 | 9810 | 44.6 | −5 |
| Zimbabwe | 12.7 | 4.0 | 41 | 2180 | 12.8 | 1 |
| **Latin America** | | | | | | |
| Argentina | 37.9 | 2.4 | 74 | 10190 | 45.9 | 21 |
| Brazil | 179.1 | 2.2 | 71 | 7450 | 211.2 | 18 |
| Chile | 16.0 | 2.4 | 76 | 9420 | 19.5 | 22 |
| Colombia | 45.3 | 2.6 | 72 | 6150 | 58.1 | 28 |
| Cuba | 11.3 | 1.6 | 76 | — | 11.8 | 4 |
| Mexico | 106.2 | 2.8 | 75 | 8800 | 131.7 | 24 |
| Peru | 27.5 | 2.8 | 69 | 4880 | 35.7 | 30 |
| Venezuela | 26.2 | 2.8 | 73 | 5220 | 35.3 | 35 |
| **Asia** | | | | | | |
| China | 1300.1 | 1.7 | 71 | 4520 | 1476.0 | 14 |
| India | 1086.4 | 3.1 | 62 | 2650 | 1363.0 | 25 |
| Indonesia | 218.7 | 2.6 | 68 | 3070 | 275.5 | 26 |
| Israel | 6.8 | 2.9 | 79 | 19000 | 9.3 | 37 |
| Japan | 127.6 | 1.3 | 82 | 27380 | 121.1 | −5 |
| North Korea | 22.8 | 2.0 | 63 | — | 24.7 | 8 |

comparison to nations in Europe that have static or declining populations but relatively high incomes. China and India are attracting the interest of world marketers because of the size of their population bases and the speed of their growth. Although low per-capita income is a disadvantage when selling most products in these countries, it is an advantage to firms looking to buy products from the lowest-cost source. Further, there are pockets of consumers who are able to buy many products, even in the poorest countries of the world. With large population size, the percentage of middle- to upper-income consumers does not have to be as high as in countries with smaller populations to create a substantial market.

The following market summaries illustrate the facts a consumer analyst should consider when evaluating the attractiveness of a market. In general, a thorough analysis extends beyond demographics to include market preferences.

## Consumer Behavior in Emerging Markets

Consumers have the same basic needs and follow many of the same purchase processes wherever they live, but there are plenty of differences as well. The rapid growth

**TABLE 7.5** (Continued)

| | MID-2004 POPULATION (MILLIONS) | TOTAL FERTILITY RATE | TOTAL LIFE EXPECTANCY | GNP PER CAPITA ($US) | PROJECTED POPULATION, 2025 (MILLIONS) | GROWTH, 2004–2025 (%) |
|---|---|---|---|---|---|---|
| Philippines | 83.7 | 3.5 | 70 | 4450 | 118.4 | 41 |
| Saudi Arabia | 25.1 | 4.8 | 72 | 12660 | 40.1 | 60 |
| Singapore | 4.2 | 1.3 | 79 | 23730 | 4.8 | 14 |
| South Korea | 48.2 | 1.2 | 77 | 16960 | 50.6 | 5 |
| **Europe** | | | | | | |
| Belgium | 10.4 | 1.6 | 79 | 28130 | 10.8 | 4 |
| Denmark | 5.4 | 1.8 | 77 | 30600 | 5.4 | 0 |
| France | 60.0 | 1.9 | 79 | 27040 | 63.4 | 6 |
| Germany | 82.6 | 1.3 | 78 | 26980 | 82.0 | −1 |
| Greece | 11.0 | 1.3 | 78 | 18770 | 10.4 | −5 |
| Hungary | 10.1 | 1.3 | 73 | 13070 | 8.9 | −12 |
| Italy | 57.8 | 1.3 | 80 | 26170 | 57.6 | 0 |
| Netherlands | 16.3 | 1.8 | 79 | 28350 | 17.4 | 7 |
| Poland | 38.2 | 1.2 | 75 | 10450 | 36.6 | −4 |
| Russia | 144.1 | 1.4 | 65 | 8080 | 136.9 | −5 |
| Sweden | 9.0 | 1.7 | 80 | 25820 | 9.9 | 10 |
| Switzerland | 7.4 | 1.4 | 80 | 31840 | 7.4 | 0 |
| United Kingdom | 59.7 | 1.7 | 78 | 26580 | 64.0 | 7 |
| **Oceania** | | | | | | |
| Australia | 20.1 | 1.7 | 80 | 27440 | 24.2 | 20 |
| **North America** | | | | | | |
| Canada | 31.9 | 1.5 | 79 | 28930 | 36.0 | 13 |
| United States | 293.6 | 2.0 | 77 | 36110 | 349.4 | 19 |

about which you just read has focused attention increasingly on emerging markets. Youthfulness is apparent, with large numbers of babies and children but lower life expectancy. In addition to high birthrates and strong population growth, low income is a marketing reality in many of these markets. Most emerging markets are largely rural, with consumers dependent on their own productivity for daily subsistence and on other countries for equipment, supplies, higher education, and sometimes even food. Marketing programs should focus on creating brand awareness (because competitors are entering the market as well) and stimulating product trial (hoping once consumers try the product, they'll use it regularly). Marketers may have to teach consumers about new products taken for granted in developed markets, such as deodorant. Although in many parts of the world, television has been blamed for contributing to societal problems, studies indicate that attention should be focused on the prosocial effects of entertainment television programs in developing countries.[49]

Many of the world's fastest growth markets are located in the Indian Ocean Rim (IOR), the confluence of the Indian and Atlantic Oceans near Cape Town, South Africa, and ending at Australia's southern coast. Led by its major trading nations—Singapore, United Arab Emirates, South Africa, Malaysia, Thailand, Indonesia, and India—IOR regional characteristics differ greatly to those of the historically industrialized nation and represent substantial growth potential for many global firms.[50] The political and economic power of the Middle East provides diverse and rapidly developing markets, fueled by financial and logistics centers such as Dubai and Qatar. In a continent of surging population, South Africa and Botswana are attractive markets because of their relatively high incomes and strong economies, despite their projected population declines. For many developing countries in the Middle East and Africa, tourism provides a significant source of external revenues. South Africa, known globally for its reformed political system and lavish safari and beachfront excursions, is in many ways both a developing and a developed nation. The home of open-heart surgery, digital reattachment, and other medical breakthroughs, South Africa consists of sophisticated markets in which the most advanced marketing strategies are applicable for specific segments with accelerating computer and Internet usage.[51] Read the Pick 'n Pay case at the back of this book for more details about retailing in South Africa.

India, projected to become the largest country in the world, is currently attracting worldwide interest among marketers. Although still considered poor by Western standards, the attractiveness of India is based on its infrastructure, its well-developed legal system, and its large numbers of well-educated doctors, engineers, and others needed for growth of a thriving middle class. Bangalore has become a world-standard city for productivity, technical innovation, new construction—and traffic jams.

India's middle class is the key to understanding its consumer markets and the success of firms such as McDonald's, which has adapted its products to local values.[52] India's middle class is larger than the total market of most European countries, including France.[53] Consequently, the demand for consumer goods is rising rapidly, with dramatic increases in sales of cars, motorbikes, scooters, and other durables increasing at the rate of 20 percent annually. Middle-class families may not live in luxury but they are buying a wide range of electronics, household goods, and a wardrobe of shoes, jewelry, and silk saris.

## Consumer Behavior in the Pacific Rim

The Pacific Rim provides some of the most attractive markets for growth-oriented firms. The area includes many low-income but fast-growing population bases in Southeast Asia, India, and China, as well as some of the older, more established markets like Australia and Japan.

## AUSTRALIA

Australia shares a number of characteristics with European and North American markets, including high income, an older population,[54] and a well-developed infrastructure. Australia is a diverse nation and has plenty of room to grow, with a majority of its population clustered around major cities in coastal areas, such as Melbourne, Sydney, and Perth. At one time, immigration was mostly European, but in recent years, nearly 50 percent of immigration has been Asian, contributing to the rapid population growth you saw in Figure 7.2. Marketers find Australia attractive because it also has a well-developed advertising and marketing research system, which can support new product and brand development with sophisticated strategies and execution, as well as excellent retailers such as Coles Myer (which operates both Kmart and Target stores in Australia, under license), David Jones, and Woolworths. Remember, however, the problems of Toys "R" Us in Consumer Behavior and Marketing 2.1 in Chapter 2.

## JAPAN

Although Japan is smaller in land area than California, its 127 million people consume more goods and services than any other country in the world, except the United States. Land is perhaps the most scarce and valuable resource in Japan, which also lacks petroleum and other natural resources. Yet its main assets are its culture and people, which have contributed to the development of its powerhouse economy.

Japanese people love their culture. Although some young adults are questioning the strict work and family ethics of their elders, there still exists a very strong Japanese traditional lifestyle and aesthetic sense. The Japanese have integrated modern technology into their traditional lives. Studies conclude that the fundamental philosophy for product designing and marketing in Japanese enterprises is to adapt high-tech products to the culture of the countries in which they are sold.[55]

In terms of marketing, the great majority of Japanese television commercials are directed toward affective (or emotional) rather than cognitive (or learning) components of attitude. Japanese consumers react more to beautiful background scenery or a television, music, or movie star than to product recommendations. Japanese viewers dislike argumentative sales talk; product information should be short and conveyed with a song that sets a mood. This is an important point to learn for foreign manufacturers accustomed to American hard-sell ads. Japanese advertising is more likely to develop a story, describe the expression of people, and enhance the mood of the product. The message usually comes at the end of the commercial, almost as an afterthought to the rest of the ad.

## CHINA

China is the world's most populous nation. The pent-up demand of 1.2 billion consumers excites marketers all over the world. In the past, most of China's imports have been industrial goods, but new government priorities caused marketers to consider the potential for consumer markets. China is creating a market-based economy from one that had been a planned communist system for decades, and this new economy is currently running a significant trade surplus with the United States. Many of China's urban factories are staffed by workers who have migrated from rural areas, sometimes returning to their hometowns to start families and using their accumulated savings to start entrepreneurial businesses.

With the increasing salaries of urban workers and the rise of new entrepreneurs in China's special economic areas, more people can buy a broader array of consumer goods.[56] What do Chinese consumers want to buy most? Refrigerators top the list in a study made in two of China's largest cities, Beijing (population 9.5 million) and Guangzhou (population 7 million), with washing machines a close second. Televisions are the most common owned electrical appliances. Rapid growth is projected for the Internet. With 79 percent of those online being male and 75 percent under age 30, many international firms see the Internet as an efficient marketing method reaching young, affluent, and educated Chinese.[57] In recent years, more than one million Chinese have become *dakuan,* or dollar millionaires, with approximately 5 percent of the population declared as affluent by Chinese standards. There exist many examples of individuals who have been able to develop their careers and live in lavish surroundings with luxury products, yet most citizens still live in crowded cities or poor farming villages. This also brings about changes in culture among the young, career-oriented generation of men and women whose focus is on independence and self-gratification.[58] Chinese teenagers are also challenging authoritarian rules, with the Rolling Stones and other groups playing to crowds of young people, confronting the traditional view that rock and roll is not good for China.[59]

## Latin America

Latin American markets have three major advantages for U.S. firms: rapid population growth, moderately high (compared to other emerging markets) incomes, and close proximity. Additionally, many managers of U.S. firms already speak Spanish. U.S., Canadian, and Mexican firms also benefit from the increasing economic flexibility of NAFTA (North American Free Trade Agreement). In addition to Central American countries, consumer analysts find attractive markets of affluent segments in Brazil, Venezuela, Colombia, Argentina, and Chile. American culture is present and growing in Brazil with the arrival of more American newspapers, magazines, automobiles, and fast-food restaurants. In Chile, American brands and retailers (like Liz Claiborne and Hallmark) appear frequently in shopping malls. American supermarkets have also influenced popular Chilean supermarkets, which are now among the best in the world with modern, fast-moving checkout lines and oversized snack food aisles—a sharp contrast to the more common central markets of days past. Consumer analysts should consider that low reported per-capita income levels often hide substantial market segments with high income levels. Although most consumers in Latin American countries might not be able to afford luxury or even mass market items, intermarket segmentation provides a basis for identifying segments that can afford items such as appliances, cars, designer clothing, travel, and specialty food items.

## Eastern Europe

Eastern European economies opened up for trade with the rest of the world in the 1990s. Some countries have had more success than others. Hungary and Poland have both received much interest from global marketers and from consumers (in the form of tourism). The attractiveness of Eastern European markets for global marketers is the similarity with preferences of Western consumers. The most desired durable products in Eastern Europe are Western cars, electronics, and microwaves, and the most desired nondurables are perfume, athletic shoes, and fashionable clothing. Television viewing is the most frequent leisure-time activity, making TV advertising viable. Because consumers have limited storage space at home and because few have cars, 85 percent of Eastern Europeans shop every day for food or other items.[60]

Companies such as Procter & Gamble are now significant marketers in countries such as Hungary, Poland, and Yugoslavia. Products include Pampers disposable diapers, Blend-a-Med toothpaste, Vidal Sassoon shampoo, Ariel laundry detergents (but observe the problem described in Consumer Behavior and Marketing 7.3), and a host of brands with proven track records in Western Europe. With assistance from international advertising agencies, P&G and successful Western European brands adapted

## The Challenge of Global Brand Management in a Changing Middle East

Arab activists are boycotting Western brands, giving rise to a new class of "spiritually correct" brands, as reported in the *Economist* (November 2, 2002). Among the most popular entries is Zam Zam Cola, named after a holy spring in Mecca, which now claims supermarket shelf space in Iraq, Bahrain, Qatar, and Saudi Arabia. Sales of Star Cola have risen by 40 percent in the past three months in the United Arab Emirates, and Cairo's Al Ahram Beverages has become one of the world's most profitable breweries by selling beer to Muslims (alcoholic varieties are discreetly home-delivered—*shhhh!*). Heineken recently acquired Al Ahram.

The trend is not limited to beverages, however, nor is it exclusive to American brands: shoppers are shying away from big European brands such as L'Oréal cosmetics and Nestlé, and protesters recently gathered outside Mercedes dealerships in Amman, Jordan. In Saudi Arabia, fast food chains such as KFC and Burger King have reported a 50 percent drop in sales since September 2000. Losses have forced McDonald's to close two of its six restaurants in Jordan. Procter & Gamble has been forced to defend its Ariel brand of laundry detergent from activists' charges that it is named for Israeli Prime Minister Ariel Sharon, and that its logo is really a star of David. A P&G spokesperson responds: "It's ridiculous. Ariel was around long before the Israeli leader. Our logo represents an atom's path, not a religion." In Egypt, meanwhile, souks (street markets) are selling Yasser Arafat Crisps.

Some observers say that the boycotts are hurting Arab economies, noting that most American brands are run with local talent and investment. Comments Ahmed Zayat of Al Ahram: "Arabs must learn the best practices and creativity of Western firms, not drive them away. If we want to be global, we need their muscle." Indeed, P&G, in Egypt, has spent $97 million on factories and also community projects—building schools, financing health education, and even paying for Muslims to make their pilgrimages to Mecca. Likewise, Coca-Cola is the second-biggest investor in Lebanon and Palestine. However, a Coke spokesperson says the company "is delaying hirings and investments because boycotts have dented confidence." Meanwhile, unemployment in the region is pegged at about 20 percent.

Source: Tim Manners, www.Reveries.com (November 5, 2002).

their strategies slightly and found rapid market adoption in the East. With the influence of television, movies, and products, tastes in this part of the world have now become quite similar to those found in Western Europe and in North America.

### European Single Market

The European Union (EU) is a market larger than the United States. In fact, it is the largest single market in the world. In addition to a common currency (the euro) to facilitate trade across the continent, people, money, and goods move freely across borders without passports, exchange controls, or customs.

As you saw in Table 7.5, population growth has become nonexistent in Europe. Responding to this problem, countries unified economically in an attempt to develop efficiency and profitability serving the massive population and buying power of the combined EU. Factories can be more efficient serving a market of 344 million people purchasing $4 trillion in goods and services. Efficiencies include logistics, financial arrangements, and marketing economies of scale. Borders between European countries may have only a sign noting the country and featuring the EU symbol prominently. National identity and cultures have not disappeared, however. In fact, some argue that as the push for a single market occurs, the more likely individuals are to cling to their identities.

The dominant economic force in the EU is Germany (with France playing a significant role in policy formulation), which capitalizes on trade opportunities with Eastern Europe and other nations. Although Brussels is the political capital of the EU, from a marketing perspective, Berlin has arguably become the capital of all of Europe. Germans may not have as high per-capita income as Switzerland and some other nations (see Table 7.5), but they do have nice homes, high-quality cars, good health care, fast highways, environmentally concerned cities ringed by green forests, and very good beer!

### Canada

Although Canada is the world's largest country at 3.9 million square miles, about 80 percent of all Canadians live within 200 kilometers of the United States–Canada border. This geography creates a market about 4,000 miles long and 125 miles wide. The fact that Canadian consumers are in a horizontal string in contrast to U.S. population clusters is a logistics problem in Canada. Some of these U.S. clusters, which are oriented to urban centers, overlap with major Canadian markets, especially in Ontario. Companies often can operate more efficiently by supplying Canadian markets from those efficient high-volume distribution circles than from Canada's thin linear supply line. As a consequence, international firms that operate in the northern United States and that use U.S. cities as distribution points to Canada may have lower costs than firms operating solely in Canada.[61]

## The Influence of Individual Differences on Consumer Behavior

The effects of variables such as age, income, and geography are important to understanding consumer behavior and developing marketing plans. Additional understanding can be obtained by analyzing the ways in which individual differences such as personality, values, and lifestyles affect consumer behavior. These influences are shown at the right side of the CDP model featured throughout this text.

## Personality and Consumer Behavior

Although consumer analysts can't look into the eyes of consumers, as the Swiss guide in Consumer Behavior and Marketing 7.4 does, and tell if they will buy Fords or Chevrolets, analysts can look at variables such as personality, values, and psychographics to predict the effects of individual variables on purchase and consumption. These individual differences pick up where demographics leave off and provide an understanding of characteristics more determinant of behavior. Everyone is different. Effective marketing and advertising programs are achieved with products and messages that have an especially strong appeal and cause consumers to think, "That product or message fits what I believe (values), the way I normally behave (personality), and my situation in life (lifestyle)." These variables are not more important than others you will study (such as knowledge, motivation, and attitudes), but lifestyles and the underlying personality they reflect are frequently more visible. When marketing communication is successful, a person feels that the communicator understands him or her and respects his or her individuality. A consumer's *need for uniqueness* (NFU) is achieved to some extent through the acquisition, utilization, and disposition of consumer goods for the purpose of developing and enhancing one's personal and social identity.[62] Research indicates that consumers with a high NFU and a willingness to select reasons that express their uniqueness and intellect are less responsive to marketing influence tactics, including sales promotions and advertising puffery.[63]

## Can You Handle It?

From the Swiss village of Zermatt, a first glance of the Matterhorn is chilling. Higher peaks can be seen nearby, but none stand so stark, so imposing as the defiant 14,692-foot granite pyramid, whispering "I dare you" to onlookers.

As many as two thousand people a year climb the Matterhorn during a short summer season from mid-July to mid-September. A corps of seventy-five expert guides makes the two-day adventure relatively safe for adults in good physical condition. Guides say men and women from thirty to forty-five years old are the best candidates because they have greater combined mental and physical strength than younger people. But there's no upper age limit—one man made the climb at age ninety. The climb itself takes two days, starting with a hike to the base camp. "Going down was very tough. I ran out of energy. Mental strength got me down," says Patricia Ruiz, a former IBM executive based in Paris who prepared by jogging up the steps to the top of the Eiffel Tower every day for six months.

The Matterhorn can be unforgiving. Each year, the mountain claims ten to twenty lives of those who failed to respect the safety rules. The worst candidates, guides say, are those who seek to prove something to others. The best are those who are driven by awe of the mountain and a reverence for nature. Ask any mountain guide to take you to the top, and he'll first look into your eyes and see which type you are. A guide explains, "I can usually tell standing in the office if someone can make it or not."

Source: Excerpted from Gail Schares, "A Peak Experience," *Business Week* (June 1, 1992), 118.

## Personality

Personality has many meanings. In consumer studies, **personality** is defined as *consistent responses to environmental stimuli.*[64] It is *an individual's unique psychological makeup, which consistently influences how the person responds to his or her environment.* Why do some people like to go to movies or walk during their free time and others like to run marathons or go skydiving? We often say it is because of personality. Consumer analysts approach the answer by employing three major theories: psychoanalytic, sociopsychological, and trait factor.[65]

### PSYCHOANALYTIC THEORY

Psychoanalytic theory recognizes that the human personality system consists of the *id, ego,* and *superego.*[66] The id is the source of psychic energy and seeks immediate gratification for biological and instinctual needs. The superego represents societal or personal norms and serves as an ethical constraint on behavior. The ego mediates the hedonistic demands of the id and the moralistic prohibitions of the superego. The dynamic interaction of these elements results in unconscious motivations that are manifested in observed human behavior. Sigmund Freud, the father of psychoanalytic theory, believed that personality is derived from the conflict between the desire to satisfy physical needs and the need to be a contributing member of society.

Psychoanalytic theory served as the conceptual basis for the motivation research movement described in Chapter 1 and was the forerunner of lifestyle studies. According to the philosophy of motivation researchers such as Dr. Ernest Dichter, consumer behavior is often the result of unconscious consumer motives, which can be determined through indirect assessment methods such as projective and related psychological techniques. The motivation research movement produced some extraordinary findings. For example, motivation researchers theorized that a man who buys a convertible sees it as a substitute mistress, and that men want their cigars to be odoriferous to prove their masculinity.[67] Similarly, consumers buy gourmet foods, foreign cars, vodka, and perfume to express individuality.[68] These examples are subject to serious questions of validity and provide little more than a starting place for marketing planning. A consumer's personality is a result of much more than subconscious drives. Yet, a great deal of advertising is influenced by the psychoanalytic approach to personality, especially its heavy emphasis on sexual and other deep-seated biological instincts.

## SOCIOPSYCHOLOGICAL THEORY

Sociopsychological theory recognizes the interdependence of the individual and society. The individual strives to meet the needs of society, whereas society helps the individual to attain his or her personal goals. The theory is therefore a combination of sociological and psychological elements.[69] Sociopsychological personality theory differs from psychoanalytic theory in two important respects. First, social variables rather than biological instincts are considered to be the most important determinants in shaping personality. Second, behavioral motivation is directed to meet those needs. For example, a consumer may buy a product that symbolizes an unattainable or socially unacceptable goal. Although the consumer might not admit why he or she bought the product, we know that the acquisition fulfills some subconscious "forbidden desire."

An example of sociopsychological personality theory is the Horney paradigm (based on theory developed by Karen Horney), which suggests that human behavior results from three predominant, interpersonal orientations: compliant, aggressive, and detached. Questions designed to measure these variables are referred to as a CAD scale.[70] Compliant people are dependent on others for love and affection, and are said to move toward others. Aggressive people are motivated by the need for power and move against others. Detached people are self-sufficient and independent, and move away from others.[71]

## TRAIT-FACTOR THEORY

Trait-factor theory is a quantitative approach to personality, which proposes that an individual's personality is composed of predispositional attributes called traits. A **trait** is *any distinguishable, relatively enduring way in which one individual differs from another.* Examples of such traits might be sociability, amount of internal control, or other individual difference variables.[72] Consumer analysts might find traits such as risk-taking, self-consciousness, and need for cognition[73] most useful in marketing planning. One researcher suggests a three-tiered framework that includes personality traits, personal concerns, focusing on goals and the strategies people use to achieve those goals, and life stories, the narratives people construct to integrate their past, present, and anticipated future.[74]

Three assumptions delineate the trait-factor theory. The first assumption is that traits are common to many individuals and vary in absolute amounts among individuals, and therefore can be used to segment markets. The second assumption is that these traits are relatively stable and exert fairly universal effects on behavior regardless of the environmental situation. Therefore, traits can predict a wide variety of behaviors. The final assumption asserts that traits can be inferred from the measurement of behavioral indicators.

Several standard psychological measures have been developed to inventory traits, such as the California Psychological Inventory and the Edwards Personal Preference Schedule (EPPS). Widely used for psychological testing, these tests are sometimes applied to marketing[75] but often produce mixed results. Modified tests are more likely to be useful for consumer research.[76]

Trait theory is perhaps most useful to marketing strategists in developing **brand personality**—the *personality consumers interpret from a specific brand*. Brands may be characterized in a variety of ways, such as old-fashioned, modern, fun, provocative, masculine, or glamorous. Some advertising addresses the tendencies of some consumers to buy and own products that are an extension of themselves or a reflection of who they would like to be. Three traits—emotional stability, agreeability, and the need for activity—account for 39 percent of the variance in the customer orientation of employees toward customers in service organizations.[77]

### Predicting Buyer Behavior

Trait-factor theory has been the primary basis of marketing personality research. A typical study attempts to find a relationship between a set of personality variables and assorted consumer behaviors such as purchases, media choice, innovation, fear and social influence, product choice, opinion leadership, risk-taking, and attitude change. In early research, personality was found to relate to specific attributes of product choice.[78] Research also indicated that people could make relatively good judgments about other people's traits and how they relate to automobile brands, occupations, and magazine choices.[79]

Predicting consumer behavior was often the objective of personality research in the early years. Studies attempted to predict brand or store preference and other buyer activity, but usually found only very small amounts of variance in product choice explained by personality.[80] Looking back from today's vantage point, these results are not surprising. After all, personality is but one variable in the consumer decision-making process. If any relationship were to be established, dependent variables (such as intention) would be better candidates than behavior. Even if personality traits were found to be valid predictors of intentions or behavior, these traits are difficult to use in marketing strategy for the following reasons.

1. People with common personalities can represent wide variations in demographic variables, and mass media is primarily segmented on a demographic basis.

2. Measures that isolate personality variables often don't demonstrate adequate reliability and validity.

Personality has been able to explain only about 10 percent of variance in behavior. Procter & Gamble conducted many studies several decades ago using personality as a segmentation variable. After three years of effort, the attempt was abandoned because the brand and advertising managers could not generate results that allowed them to develop marketing strategies any more effectively than with other methodologies.

The failure of personality measures to predict consumer behavior has stimulated development of more recent approaches. One approach is to relate personality measures to mediating variables or stages within the decision process, such as need recognition, and to understand the role of personality in information processing. Another approach incorporates personality data with information about individuals' social and economic conditions. And another approach is to use broader concepts such as values and psychographics.

## Personal Values

Examining consumers' values is another way to understand why consumers vary in their individual decision making. Like attitudes, values represent consumer beliefs about life and acceptable behavior. Unlike attitudes, values transcend situations or events and are more enduring because they are more central in the personality structure. Values represent three universal requirements of human existence: biological needs, requisites of coordinated social interaction, and demands for group survival and functioning.[81] Values express the goals that motivate people and the appropriate ways to attain those goals. Because people hold the same values but differ only in the importance they place on them, and because values play such a central role in cognition, values provide a powerful basis for understanding consumer behavior within and across cultures.[82] The enduring nature of values and their central role in personality structure have caused them to be applied to understanding many aspects of consumer behavior, including advertising cognitions, product choice, brand choice, and market segmentation.

Marketers may focus on individual or group values. When the importance of a value is so widely held that it becomes the way a market segment or group is identified, we refer to it as a social value.[83] When we study culture in Chapter 11, the focus will be on social values. **Social values** define *"normal" behavior for a society or group.* **Personal values** define *"normal" behavior for an individual,* and these values are the focus here. Remember as you read the next few pages, however, that the values of groups to which you belong (social values) will have a major influence on your personal values.

Personal values reflect the choices an individual makes from the variety of social values or value systems to which that individual is exposed. Your values concerning work, personal achievement, and social interaction, for example, may determine how much time you spend studying this text, and thus the grade you may get in this course, and more important, your career progression later in life. Although people are influenced by family, peer, and cultural values, individuals pick and choose which social values to emphasize when developing their own personal values.

## Rokeach Value Scale

Early research concerning values was influenced most by Milton Rokeach and his Rokeach Value Scale (RVS), although one study has shown that the concept of values is implicit or explicit in many of the psychological theories of Freud, Jung, Fromm, Adler, Horney, Erikson, Dichter, and others.[84] Rokeach believed that values are concerned both with the goals (end-state or terminal elements) and the ways of behaving (instrumental components) to obtain goals (see Table 7.6). His major contribution was to define values as enduring beliefs that specific modes of conduct or end states of existence are personally or socially preferable to opposing modes of conduct or end states of existence.[85] The RVS asks people to rank the importance of a series of goals and ways of behaving, which can be analyzed by gender, age, ethnicity, or whatever variable might be of interest in consumer analysis.

Several studies have linked personal values to brand choice, product usage, market segmentation, and innovative behavior.[86] In a study of car buying, researchers found consumption-related variables are related to family-oriented core values that stimulate motivation.[87] With low-involvement products such as deodorants, studies found that individuals who preferred Arrid to Right Guard, for example, were consumers who placed high importance on the measurement of "mature love" in the RVS.[88] In the past most applications used the RVS to describe the differences between segments defined a priori on demographic or other variables. More recently, consumer analysts are using values as the criterion for segmenting the population into homogeneous groups of individuals who share a common value system.[89]

## Schwartz Value Scale

The work of psychologist Shalom Schwartz has become very influential on values research in marketing and other behavioral sciences. Schwartz's research has focused on identifying a universal set of values and determining the structure of their relations.

| TABLE 7.6 | Rokeach Value Scale |
|---|---|

| TERMINAL (DESIRABLE END STATES) | INSTRUMENTAL (MODES OF CONDUCT) |
|---|---|
| A comfortable life | Ambition |
| An exciting life | Broad-minded |
| A sense of accomplishment | Capable |
| A world at peace | Cheerful |
| A world of beauty | Clean |
| Equality | Courageous |
| Family security | Forgiving |
| Freedom | Helpful |
| Happiness | Honest |
| Inner harmony | Imaginative |
| Mature love | Independent |
| National security | Intellectual |
| Pleasure | Logical |
| Salvation | Loving |
| Self-respect | Obedient |
| Social recognition | Polite |
| True friendship | Responsible |
| Wisdom | Self-controlled |

His Schwartz Value Scale (SVS) and Portraits Questionnaire (PQ) were designed to measure a comprehensive set of values thought to be held by nearly everyone.[90] Based on empirical studies of more than 100,000 people in more than sixty countries, the Schwartz theory proposes that values are trans-situational goals that serve the interest of individuals or groups and express one of ten universal motivations or value types, thereby challenging the simple Rokeach classification of instrumental and terminal values.[91] Schwartz argues that the meaning of an individual value is reflected in the pattern of its relations with other values, usually determined using an analytical technique called smallest space analysis (SSA). These relations of the ten value types, and the four higher-order value domains that contain them, represent a continuum of related motivations that give rise to a circular structure (see Figure 7.8). The pursuit of a specific value may be compatible or in conflict with other values. For example, caring for one's family (benevolence) is compatible with caring for the environment (universalism) but in conflict with placing one's own needs before those of others to achieve personal goals (achievement).

These motivations or value types are the guiding principles in consumers' lives. Table 7.7 defines the ten motivational value types and gives some exemplary values for each.[92] The SVS has been used to understand why some consumers prefer banks to competitive financial institutions as well as to compare brand preferences between market segments.[93]

## Values and Consumer Decision Process

Personal values help explain how we answer the question, "Is this product for me?" Values are particularly important in the need recognition stage of consumer decision making but also affect consumers in determining evaluative criteria, by helping to

FIGURE 7.8    Structural Relation of the Motivational Value Types

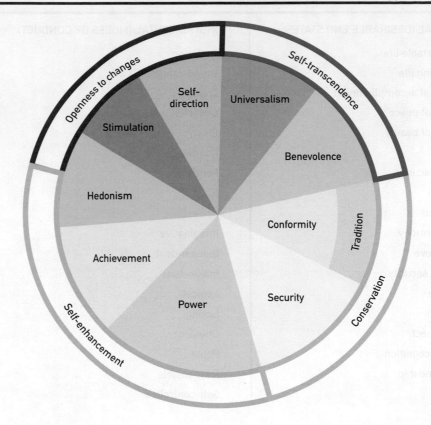

answer such questions as, "Is this brand for me?" Values influence the effectiveness of communications programs as consumers ask, "Is this situation (portrayed in the ad) one in which I would participate?" Values are enduring motivations or the "ends" people seek in their lives. In a sense, marketing often provides the "means" to reach these ends.

### Laddering

Understanding how values determine market demand can be facilitated by a technique called laddering. **Laddering** refers to *in-depth probing directed toward uncovering higher-level meanings at both the benefit (attribute) level and the value level.* Laddering seeks to uncover the linkages between product attributes, personal outcomes (consequences), and values that serve to structure components of the cognitive network in a consumer's mind.[94]

Figure 7.9 shows the *attributes* provided by wine coolers (e.g., carbonation, crisp, expensive, label, bottle, less alcohol, filling, smaller size) and how the consequences of those *benefits* (e.g., refreshing, thirst quenching, more feminine, avoid negatives of alcohol, impress others, and so on) relate to the *values* (e.g., self-esteem, accomplishment, belonging, family life) of varying market segments. Any of these perceptual maps of the value structures could lead the company to develop alternative marketing strategies. Although the attributes might be the same, the image that should be developed for those with the self-esteem value would emphasize impressing others, perhaps with a sophisticated image. The other image, however, would be developed for the family-life value, emphasizing socializing without the negatives of alcohol. Additional analysis may indicate the size of segments, the degree of overlap between segments, appeals that can be used to appeal to the widest number of consumers, and the level of abstraction that should be used in advertising and other elements of advertising strategy.[95] Recent advances in laddering theory focus on extending laddering to

TABLE 7.7     Definitions of the Ten Motivational Value Types in Terms of Their Goals and Specific Values That Represent Them

| VALUE TYPE | DEFINITION | EXEMPLARY VALUES |
|---|---|---|
| Power | Social status and prestige, control or dominance over people and resources | Social power, authority, wealth |
| Achievement | Personal success through demonstrating competence according to social standards | Successful, capable, ambitious |
| Hedonism | Pleasure and sensuous gratification for oneself | Pleasure, enjoying life |
| Stimulation | Excitement, novelty, and challenge in life | Daring, varied life, an exciting life |
| Self-direction | Independent thought and action—choosing, creating, exploring | Creativity, curious, freedom |
| Universalism | Understanding, appreciation, tolerance, and protection for the welfare of *all* people and for nature | Broadminded, social justice, equality, protecting the environment |
| Benevolence | Preservation and enhancement of the welfare of people with whom one is in frequent personal contact | Helpful, honest, forgiving |
| Tradition | Respect, commitment, and acceptance of the customs and ideas that traditional culture or religion provide | Humble, devout, accepting my portion in life |
| Conformity | Restraint of actions, inclinations, and impulses likely to upset or harm others and violate social expectations or norms | Politeness, obedient, honoring one's parents or elders |
| Security | Safety; harmony; and stability of society, of relationships, and of self | Social order, clean |

Source: Excerpted from Shalom H. Schwartz, "Are There Universal Aspects in the Structure and Contents of Human Values?" *Journal of Social Issues* 50, 4 (1994), 19–45.

research on a wider range of goal-directed behaviors and on new statistical techniques to aid in interpretation.[96]

## Lifestyle Concepts and Measurement

Lifestyle is a popular concept for understanding consumer behavior, perhaps because it is more contemporary than personality and more comprehensive than values. Lifestyle marketing attempts to relate a product, often through advertising, to the everyday experiences of the market target.

**Lifestyle** is a summary construct defined as *patterns in which people live and spend time and money*. These patterns reflect a person's activities, interests, and opinions (AIOs), as well as demographic variables discussed earlier. People use constructs such as lifestyles to construe the events happening around them and to interpret, conceptualize, and predict events as well as to reconcile their values with events. This type of construct system is personal but also changes continually in response to a person's need to conceptualize cues from the changing environment to be consistent with his or her own values and personality.[97]

Values are relatively enduring; lifestyles change more rapidly. Lifestyle researchers must, therefore, keep research methods and marketing strategies current. Some of the

FIGURE 7.9        Hypothetical Hierarchical Value Map
                  Wine Cooler Category

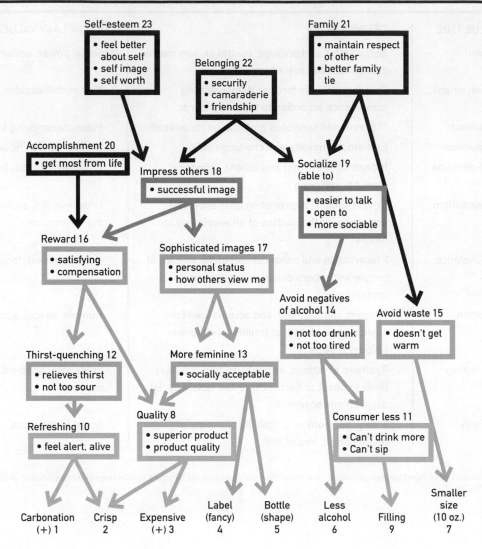

most effective advertisers track lifestyle trends of key market targets and reflect those lifestyles in their ads, as seen in Figure 7.10, which shows an active lifestyle mixed with family responsibility.

### Psychographics

**Psychographics** is an *operational technique to measure lifestyles; it provides quantitative measures and can be used with the large samples needed for definition of market segments.* In contrast, psychographics can also be used in qualitative research techniques such as focus groups or in-depth interviews. Psychographic measures are more comprehensive than demographic, behavioral, and socioeconomic measures—demographics profile *who* buys products, whereas psychographics focus on *why* they buy.

The term *psychographics* is often used interchangeably with **AIO measures**—*statements that describe the activities, interests, and opinions of consumers.* AIO components are defined by the following categories.

- *Activity:* an action such as bowling, shopping in a store, or talking on the telephone. Although these acts are usually observable, the reasons for the actions are seldom subject to direct measurement.

• *Interest:* the degree of excitement that accompanies both special and continuing attention to an object, event, or topic.

• *Opinion:* a spoken or written "answer" that a person gives in response to a "question." An opinion describes interpretations, expectations, and evaluations, such as beliefs about other people's intentions or anticipations concerning future events.[98]

Examples of each category are shown in Table 7.8.

### Market Segmentation

Psychographic studies are used to develop an in-depth understanding of market segments and sometimes to define segments—for example, single women between age twenty-five and thirty who actively participate in outdoor activities and care about nutrition. To identify significant lifestyle trends, researchers often ask consumers to answer AIO statements using a Likert scale. In one popular approach, consumers choose from five possible responses, ranging from strongly agree (scored $+2$) to strongly disagree (scored $-2$). Consumer responses can be analyzed by cross-tabulating each statement on the basis of variables believed important for market segmentation strategies, such as gender and age, or by looking at the mean response within these categories. If too many AIO statements are included in the research, analysts may have trouble understanding the basic structure of consumer lifestyles influencing purchase and consumption behavior. Thus, researchers often use techniques such as multidimensional scaling, principal components analysis, or exploratory factor analysis to reduce the number of related "dimensions" or "factors," based on their covariance or intercorrelations.[99]

Taking a psychographic approach, Procter & Gamble identified a core consumer insight into why people like to drink coffee and turned that into a brand appeal for

**FIGURE 7.10** Ad Showing a Mother Spending Quality Time with Her Child

© Susan Van Etten

| | TABLE 7.8 | | AIO Categories of Lifestyle Studies | | |
|---|---|---|---|---|---|
| **ACTIVITIES** | | **INTERESTS** | | **OPINIONS** | |
| Work | | Family | | Themselves | |
| Hobbies | | Home | | Social Issues | |
| Social Events | | Job | | Politics | |
| Vacation | | Community | | Business | |
| Entertainment | | Recreation | | Economics | |
| Club Membership | | Fashion | | Education | |
| Community | | Food | | Products | |
| Shopping | | Media | | Future | |
| Sports | | Achievements | | Culture | |

Folgers coffee. In its ads, Folgers appealed to consumers' memories of smelling coffee brewing in their homes when they were young. For the baby boomer generation, Folgers meant returning home to the safety and comfort of family. More recently, however, a younger, more mobile group of coffee drinkers was born—the Starbucks generation. Coffee didn't mean a return to home (which for many meant divorce and unhappy childhoods)—Starbucks, rather, became a status symbol and icon for freedom and success. This change also meant that a majority of coffee consumption was occurring outside the home. To compete, P&G introduced Millstone, a fresh-ground gourmet coffee (in gourmet flavors) positioned to reach this new coffee-shop lifestyle segment. P&G packaged the coffee in bags rather than cans, offered more flavors, and let consumers bring coffee-shop coffee and aroma home with a grocery store brand.

With psychographic analysis, marketers can understand their core customers' lifestyles better and develop packaging and communication programs that position products to their various lifestyle attributes. How does the marketer of a new pasta dinner kit want to show the product in an ad? Should it show how easy it is to make the pasta (showing the man of the house preparing it without making a mess in the kitchen), or should it show how delicious it is (having people consume it at an elegant dinner table with candlelight and flowers)? The idea is to go beyond standard demographics to position the product in line with the activities, hopes, fears, and dreams of the product's best customers. Psychographics have also been used to determine whether national brand promotions and store brands attract the same value-conscious consumers, which would aggravate channel conflict between manufacturers and retailers. Psychographic drivers of store brand use, in-store promotion use, and out-of-store promotion use [100] differ substantially, as store brand use is particularly associated with price consciousness, lower quality consciousness, and store loyalty, whereas out-of-store promotions are associated with higher shopping enjoyment and less pressure to conform to the expectations of others. [101] Patterns of searching online, time spent per search episode, and search frequency can also be studied using psychographics, which can be useful in Web design and planning communication strategies.

## VALS™

A widely used approach to lifestyle marketing is the Values and Lifestyle System (VALS™), which was developed at SRI International and shown in Figure 7.11. According to this approach, consumers buy products and services and seek experiences that fulfill their characteristic preferences and give shape, substance, and satisfaction to their lives. An individual's primary *motivation* determines what in particular about the self or the world is the meaningful core that governs his or her activities. Consumers are inspired by one of three primary motivations: *ideals, achievement,* and *self-expression.* Consumers who are primarily motivated by ideals are guided by knowledge and principles. Consumers who are primarily motivated by achievement look for products and services that demonstrate success to their peers. Consumers who are primarily motivated by self-expression desire social or physical activity, variety, and risk.

In addition to motivation, the other dimension of the VALS™ typology is *resources.* A person's tendency to consume goods and services extends beyond age, income, and education to include energy, self-confidence, intellectualism, novelty seeking, innovativeness, impulsiveness, leadership, and vanity. These personality traits in conjunction with key demographics determine an individual's resources. Different levels of resources enhance or constrain a person's expression of his or her primary motivation. You can visit the VALS™ website (www.sric-bi.com/VALS), both to determine your own VALS™ type as well as to see how marketers develop strategies using the basic VALS™ types shown in Table 7.9.

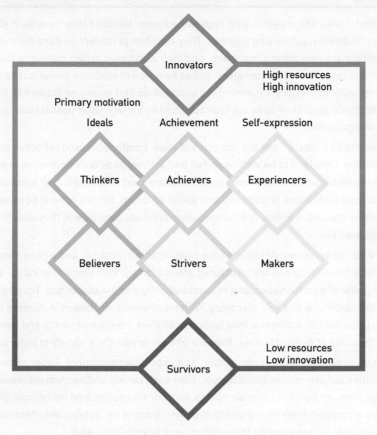

## LOV

An alternative to VALS™ is the List of Values (LOV) approach.[102] The LOV asks consumers to rate seven statements that were derived from the RVS. Although neither the RVS nor the LOV measures the comprehensive set of the universal values identified by Schwartz, both have proved useful in marketing research.[103] Researchers compared VALS™ with LOV and found that when used with demographic data, the LOV approach predicted consumer behavior better than VALS™.[104] When LOV is augmented with measures of more general values—such as materialism—the predictive power is further improved.[105]

## Global Lifestyles

Increased globalization of markets requires that marketing strategy increasingly be planned on a global basis. VALS™ and other approaches have been used to identify lifestyle segments across country borders,[106] and the VALS™ typology has been used successfully to segment Japanese and Canadian markets.[107] One of the most comprehensive studies of values on a wide range of topics in Europe was published by Sheena Ashford and Noel Timms.[108] Their study provides an understanding of European values, the differences between American and European values, and how values change over time. The study also shows that the overwhelming majority of people in each country say that they are happy. No significant differences exist between men and women in any of the countries surveyed, but some countries enjoy higher levels of happiness than others. Schwartz's values have been shown to be especially useful in

TABLE 7.9          VALS™ Types

- Innovators are successful, sophisticated, take-charge people with high self-esteem. Because they have such abundant resources, they exhibit all three primary motivations in varying degrees. They are change leaders and are the most receptive to new ideas and technologies. Innovators are very active consumers, and their purchases reflect cultivated tastes for upscale niche products and services. Image is important to Innovators, not as evidence of status or power but as an expression of their taste, independence, and personality. Innovators are among the established and emerging leaders in business and government, yet they continue to seek challenges. Their lives are characterized by variety. Their possessions and recreation reflect a cultivated taste for the finer things in life.

- Thinkers (formerly Fulfilleds) are motivated by ideals. They are mature, satisfied, comfortable, and reflective people who value order, knowledge, and responsibility. They tend to be well educated and actively seek out information in the decision-making process. They are well informed about world and national events and are alert to broaden their knowledge. Thinkers have a moderate respect for the status quo institutions of authority and social decorum, but are open to consider new ideas. Although their incomes allow them many choices, thinkers are conservative, practical consumers; they look for durability, functionality, and value in the products they buy.

- Achievers are motivated by the desire for achievement. Achievers have goal-oriented lifestyles and a deep commitment to career and family. Their social lives reflect this focus and are structured around family, their place of worship, and work. Achievers live conventional lives, are politically conservative, and respect authority and the status quo. They value consensus, predictability, and stability over risk, intimacy, and self-discovery. With many wants and needs, Achievers are active in the consumer marketplace. Image is important to Achievers; they favor established, prestige products and services that demonstrate success to their peers. Because of their busy lives, they are often interested in a variety of time-saving devices.

- Experiencers are motivated by self-expression. As young, enthusiastic, and impulsive consumers, Experiencers quickly become enthusiastic about new possibilities but are equally quick to cool. They seek variety and excitement, savoring the new, the offbeat, and the risky. Their energy finds an outlet in exercise, sports, outdoor recreation, and social activities. Experiencers are avid consumers and spend a comparatively high proportion of their income on fashion, entertainment, and socializing. Their purchases reflect the emphasis they place on looking good and having "cool" stuff.

- Like Thinkers, Believers are motivated by ideals. They are conservative, conventional people with concrete beliefs based on traditional, established codes: family, religion, community, and the nation. Many Believers express moral codes that are deeply rooted and literally interpreted. They follow established routines, organized in large part around home, family, community, and social or religious organizations to which they belong. As consumers, Believers are predictable; they choose familiar products and established brands. They favor American products and are generally loyal customers.

- Strivers are trendy and fun loving. Because they are motivated by achievement, Strivers are concerned about the opinions and approval of others. Money defines success for Strivers, who don't have enough of it to meet their desires. They favor stylish products that emulate the purchases of people with greater material wealth. Many see themselves as having a job rather than a career, and a lack of skills and focus often prevents them from moving ahead. Strivers are active consumers because shopping is both a social activity and an opportunity to demonstrate to peers their ability to buy. As consumers, they are as impulsive as their financial circumstances will allow.

- Like Experiencers, Makers are motivated by self-expression. They express themselves and experience the world by working on it—building a house, raising children, fixing a car, or canning vegetables—and have enough skill and energy to carry out their projects successfully. Makers are practical people who have constructive skills and value self-sufficiency. They live within a traditional context of family, practical work, and physical recreation and have little interest in what lies outside that context. Makers are suspicious of new ideas and large institutions such as big business. They are respectful of government authority and organized labor, but resentful of government intrusion on individual rights. They are unimpressed by material possessions other than those with a practical or functional purpose. Because they prefer value to luxury, they buy basic products.

- Survivors live narrowly focused lives. With few resources with which to cope, they often believe that the world is changing too quickly. They are comfortable with the familiar and are primarily concerned with safety and security. Because they must focus on meeting needs rather than fulfilling desires, Survivors do not show a strong primary motivation. Survivors are cautious consumers. They represent a very modest market for most products and services. They are loyal to favorite brands, especially if they can purchase them at a discount.

fast-changing transitional economies, such as those in Asia, Eastern Europe, and southern Africa, for relating value differences to the demographic characteristics of consumers and for explaining differences in lifestyle interests, brand loyalty, and innovative consumer behavior.[109] Studies in Taiwan indicate that lifestyle segments categorized as "experiencers," "traditionalists," and "self-indulgents" differ in their Internet usage and attitudes toward Internet advertising.[110]

## Summary

At every stage of the CDP, personal variables such as gender, age, income, lifestyle, and personality affect how consumers make choices to buy and use goods and services. Understanding these individual variables is foundational to understanding markets, which consist of people (and their needs), ability to buy, willingness to buy, and authority to buy. Understanding the size and behavior of market segments and forecasting trends in markets focuses on each of these variables. Analysis of these variables is called demographics, defined as the size, structure, and distribution of a population.

Key determinants of markets include variables described as (1) personality, (2) demographics, (3) psychographics, and (4) values. Demographic analysis increasingly focuses on how the populations of the world are changing by monitoring birth rates, death rates, immigration, and economic resources. Consumer behavior analysts are increasingly required to understand buying and consumption decisions on a global basis, especially the slow or declining population base of some of the most affluent nations. The search for markets that have both population growth and good or improving economic conditions often leads to the Pacific Rim, the Indian Ocean Rim (IOR), and Latin America. In the United States, most of the growth in markets is among older cohorts, especially muppies and the young-again generation.

Beyond demographics, consumer analysts need to examine personality, values, and lifestyles. Deciding what products to buy and use varies between individuals because of the unique characteristics possessed by each individual. Personality is defined as consistent responses to environmental stimuli. Three major theories or approaches to the study of personality include psychoanalytic, sociopsychological, and trait factor. Personal values also explain individual differences among consumers. One approach to understanding values is the Rokeach Value Scale (RVS), which identified values as terminal and instrumental, or the ends to which behavior is directed and the means of attaining those ends. Another approach is the Schwartz Value Scale (SVS), which identifies the value system that underlies motivations, and appears to have broad generality across disparate cultures.

Lifestyles are patterns in which people live and spend time and money. Lifestyles are the result of the total array of economic, cultural, and social life forces that contribute to a person's human qualities. Psychographics or AIOs measure the operational form of lifestyles. AIO stands for activities, interests, and opinions, and may be either general or product specific. VALS™ is a system used to segment American consumers into eight primary categories and can be helpful in guiding marketing communication and product positioning strategies. An alternative methodology is the List of Values (LOV).

## Review and Discussion Questions

1. Evaluate this statement: Analysis of consumer trends is obviously important for firms marketing consumer products but of limited value to industrial marketers.

2. Will there be more or fewer births in the future in the United States? What variables should be considered in answering this question?

3. Assume a marketer of major appliances is interested in the effects of the baby boomers on demand for the company's products. What are your conclusions, and what, if any, research should be conducted to answer the question more fully?

4. Analyze this statement: Maturity markets are growing in number very rapidly, but they are of little interest to marketers because they have little money compared with younger markets.

5. Which countries of the world will provide the best consumer markets in the next five to ten years? In the next ten to thirty years? Why?

6. How do you reconcile the belief that India represents an attractive market when reports indicate such a low per-capita GNP?

Chapter Summary

7. Assume that a manufacturer of shoes wishes a market analysis on how to enter the most profitable markets in Africa. What should be included in the report?

8. Clearly distinguish between the following terms: lifestyles, psychographics, AIO measures, personality, and values.

9. Using the VALS™ categories of lifestyle, choose a product and two different segments, and describe how the positioning and communication strategies would differ for the two segments.

10. Describe the trait-factor theory of personality and assess its importance in past and future marketing research.

11. Assume that you are developing an advertising program for an airline. How would you use laddering to assist in the development of the program?

12. How might personal values be used to segment markets for financial services? Could similar approaches be used in less-developed countries as well as industrialized markets?

## Notes

[1] An excellent, comprehensive book on this topic is Jacob Siegel and David Swanson, *The Methods and Materials of Demography* (New York: Elsevier Academic Press, 2004).

[2] David K. Foot, *Boom Bust & Echo* (Toronto: Macfarlane Walter & Ross, 1996), 2.

[3] George Katona, *Psychological Economics* (New York: Elsevier Scientific Publishing, 1975).

[4] United Nations, World Population Prospects, the 2002 Revision (February 26, 2003), 11.

[5] United Nations, World Population Prospects, the 2002 Revision (February 26, 2003), 11.

[6] United States Census Bureau population projections website; Ontario Ministry of Finance demographic trends website.

[7] John Knodel, "Deconstructing Population Momentum," *Population Today* (March 1999), 1–2.

[8] United States Department of Health and Human Services, Centers for Disease Control and Prevention, National Center for Health Statistics website.

[9] Steven Camarota, "Immigrants in the United States," Center for Immigration Studies, Population Reference Bureau (November 2002).

[10] Phillip Martin and Elizabeth Midgley, "Immigration: Shaping and Reshaping America," *Population Bulletin 2*, Population Reference Bureau, 58 (June 2003).

[11] "Projected Fertility Rates," U.S. Department of Commerce, Bureau of the Census, no. 98, page 79.

[12] Roger Blackwell and Tina Stephan, *Brands That Rock* (New York: Wiley, 2003).

[13] Joseph O. Rentz and Fred D. Reynolds, "Forecasting the Effects of an Aging Population on Product Consumption: An Age-Period-Cohort Framework," *Journal of Marketing Research*, 28 (August 1991), 355–360.

[14] James Heckman, "Say 'Buy-Buy,'" *Marketing News* (October 11, 1999).

[15] "Teens, Toddlers Intriguing Market," *Mass Merchandise Retailer* (October 19, 1998), 16.

[16] Heather Chaplin, "The Truth Hurts," *American Demographics* (April 1999), 68.

[17] Marcia Mogelonsky, "Product Overload?" *American Demographics* (August 1998), 65–69.

[18] Dennis H. Tootelian and Ralph M. Gaedeke, "The Teen Market: An Exploratory Analysis of Income, Spending, and Shopping Patterns," *Journal of Consumer Marketing*, 9 (Fall 1992).

[19] Alison Stein Wellner, "The Young and the Uninsured," *American Demographics* (February 1999), 73–77.

[20] Bob Losyk, "Generation X: What They Think and What They Plan to Do," *Futurist* (March/April 1997), 39–44.

[21] Harry Dent, *The Roaring 2000s* (New York: Simon & Schuster, 1998).

[22] For additional examples, see Dale Blackwell and Roger Blackwell, "Yuppies, Muppies and Puppies: They Are Changing Real Estate Markets," *Ohio Realtor* (August 1989), 11–15; Roger D. Blackwell and Margaret Hanke, "The Credit Card and the Aging Baby Boomers," *Journal of Retail Banking*, 9 (Spring 1987), 17–25.

[23] Carlos Tejada and Patrick Barta, "Hey, Baby Boomers Need Their Space, OK?" *Wall Street Journal* (January 7, 2000), A1–A6.

[24] Robert E. Wilkes, "A Structural Modeling Approach to the Measurement and Meaning of Cognitive Age," *Journal of Consumer Research*, 19 (September 1992), 292–301.

[25] George Moschis, "Marketing to Older Adults," *Journal of Consumer Marketing*, 8 (Fall 1991), 33–41.

[26] Thomas Moehrle, "Expenditure Patterns of the Elderly: Workers and Nonworkers," *Monthly Labor Review*, 113 (May 1990), 34–41.

[27] Paula Fitzgerald Bone, "Identifying Mature Segments," *Journal of Consumer Marketing*, 8 (Fall 1991), 19–32.

[28] Benny Barak, "Elderly Solitary Survivors and Social Policy: The Case for Widows," in Andrew Mitchell, *Advances in Consumer Research* (1984), 27–30.

[29] Ivan Ross, "Information Processing and the Older Consumer: Marketing and Public Policy Implications," in Mitchell, *Advances*, 31–39.

[30] Carolyn Yoon, "Age Differences in Consumers' Processing Strategies: An Investigation of Moderating Influences," *Jour-

nal of Consumer Research, 24 (December 1997), 329–342.

[31] Nark D. Uncles and Andrew S. C. Ehrenberg, "Brand Choice among Older Consumers," Journal of Advertising Research, 30 (August/September 1990), 19–22.

[32] Alan J. Greco and Linda E. Swayne, "Sales Response of Elderly Consumers to Point-of-Purchase Advertising," Journal of Advertising Research, 32 (September/October 1992), 43–53.

[33] Jeffrey Inman, Venkatesh Shankar, and Rosellina Ferraro, "The Roles of Channel-Category Associations and Geodemographics in Channel Patronage," Journal of Marketing, 68 (April 2004), 51–72.

[34] Jane Jacobs, Cities and the Wealth of Nations (New York: Random House, 1984).

[35] United States Census Bureau State Population Estimates, www.census.gov/popest/states (March 2005).

[36] Vikas Mittal, Wagner Kamakura, and Rahul Govind, "Geographic Patterns in Customer Service and Satisfaction: An Empirical Investigation," Journal of Marketing, 68 (July 2004), 48–63.

[37] Els Gijsbrechts, Katia Campo, and Tom Goossens, "The Impact of Store Flyers on Store Traffic and Store Sales: A Geomarketing approach," Journal of Retailing, 79 (Spring 2003), 1–16.

[38] Carmen DeNavas-Walt, Bernadette Procter, and Robert Mills, U.S. Census Bureau, Current Population Reports P60-226, Income, Poverty and Insurance Coverage in the United States (Washington, D.C.: U.S. Government Printing Office), 2004.

[39] Ibid.

[40] Shannon McCaffrey, "Income Gap for Families Is Widening, Report Says," Columbus Dispatch (January 18, 2000), A1–A2.

[41] Mittal, Kamakura, and Govind, "Geographic Patterns in Customer Service and Satisfaction."

[42] The Conference Board, www.conferenceboard.org.

[43] Thomas J. Stanley and William D. Danko, The Millionaire Next Door (New York: Pocket Books, 1998).

[44] Wendy Zellner, Rob Hof, Larry Armstrong, and Geoff Smith, "Shop Till The Ball Drops," Business Week (January 10, 2000), 42–44.

[45] Associated Press, "Microsoft Dividend Helps Boost Personal Income To Record Level," (January 31, 2005).

[46] Valarie A. Zeithaml, "Service Quality, Profitability, and Economic Worth of Customers: What We Know and What We Need to Learn," Journal of the Academy of Marketing Science, 28 (October 2000), 67–85.

[47] Marcia Mogelonsky, "Those With More Buy for Less," American Demographics (April 1999), 18–19.

[48] Octavio Blanco, "The Changing Face of Poverty," www.cnnmoney.com (December 30, 2004).

[49] William J. Brown, "The Use of Entertainment Television Programs for Promoting Prosocial Messages," Howard Journal of Communications, 3 (Winter/Spring 1992), 253–266.

[50] Steven Burgess, The New Marketing: Building Strong Marketing Strategies in South Africa (Cape Town, South Africa: Halfway House, Zebra Press), 1998.

[51] Nua Internet Surveys, Webchek: South African Teenagers Surge Online (December 17, 1999).

[52] Valerie Reitman, "India Anticipates the Arrival of the Beefless Big Mac," Wall Street Journal (October 20, 1993), B1.

[53] Anthony Spaeth, "A Thriving Middle Class Is Changing the Face of India," Wall Street Journal (May 19, 1988), A22.

[54] Grame Hugo, Australia's Changing Population: Trends and Implications (Oxford: Oxford University Press, 1987).

[55] Tohru Nishikawa, "New Product Development: Japanese Consumer Tastes in the Area of Electronics and Home Appliances," Journal of Advertising Research, 30 (1990), 30.

[56] Jerry Stafford, "Vast China Market Just Waiting to Be Researched," Marketing News (September 12, 1986), 1.

[57] Nua Internet Surveys, China Internet Network Information Center: Amount of Chinese Internet Users Explodes (January 21, 2000).

[58] Sandra Burton, "A New Me Generation," Time (November 29, 1993), 39.

[59] Leslie Chang, "Teenage Band Tries to Rock China," Wall Street Journal (July 21, 1999), B1.

[60] "Perestroika: The Consumer Signals," Euromarketing Insights, 2 (February 1991), 4. For statistical information on the European Community, see sources such as Brian Morris, Klaus Boehm, and Maurice Geller, The European Community (Berlin: Walter DeGruyter & Co., 1991); Secretariat of the Economic Commission for Europe, Economic Survey of Europe (New York: United Nations Publication, 1991); and Alan Tillier, Doing Business in Today's Western Europe (Chicago: NTC Business Books, 1992).

[61] Randall Litchfield, "Competitiveness and the Constitution," Canadian Business (August 1991), 18.

[62] Kelly Tian, "Consumers' Need for Uniqueness: Scale Development and Validation," Journal of Consumer Research, 28 (June 2001), 50–67.

[63] Itamar Simonson and Stephen Nowlis, "The Role of Explanations and Need for Uniqueness in Consumer Decision Making: Unconventional Choices Based on Reason," Journal of Consumer Research, 27 (June 2000), 49–69.

[64] H. Kassarjian, "Personality and Consumer Behavior: A Review," Journal of Marketing Research (November 1971), 409–418.

[65] For descriptions of major personality theories, see Walter Mischel, Introduction to Personality: A New Look (New York: CBS College Publishing, 1986); and Larry Hjelle and Daniel Ziegler, Personality Theories: Basic Assumptions, Research and Applications (New York: McGraw-Hill, 1987).

[66] For a marketing view of psychoanalytic theory, see W. D. Wells and A. D. Beard, "Personality and Consumer Behavior," in Scott Ward and T. S. Robertson, eds., Consumer Behavior: Theoretical Sources

(Englewood Cliffs, NJ: Prentice-Hall, 1973).

[67] The classic example of this literature is Ernest Dichter, *Handbook of Consumer Motivations* (New York: McGraw-Hill, 1964). For an example of motivation research by Dr. Dichter, see the "Swan Cleaners" case in Roger D. Blackwell, James E. Engel, and W. Wayne Talarzyk, *Contemporary Cases in Consumer Behavior* (Chicago: Dryden, 1990), 135–142.

[68] Jeffrey F. Durgee, "Interpreting Dichter's Interpretations: An Analysis of Consumption Symbolism in the *Handbook of Consumer Motivations*," in Hanne Hartvig-Larsen, David Glen Mick, and Christian Alstead, eds., *Marketing and Semiotics: Selected Papers from Copenhagen Symposium* (Copenhagen: Handelsh Jskolens Forlag, 1991).

[69] For a more complete explanation of this approach, see C. S. Hall and G. Lindzey, *Theories of Personality* (New York: Wiley, 1970), 154–155.

[70] J. B. Cohen, "An Interpersonal Orientation to the Study of Consumer Behavior," *Journal of Marketing Research*, 4 (August 1967), 270–278; J. B. Cohen, "Toward an Interpersonal Theory of Consumer Behavior," *California Management Review*, 10 (1968), 73–80. Also see Jon P. Noerager, "An Assessment of CAD: A Personality Instrument Developed Specifically for Marketing Research," *Journal of Marketing Research* (February 1979), 53–59.

[71] Ibid.

[72] A good introduction to the theory and techniques of this approach is found in A. R. Buss and W. Poley, *Individual Differences: Traits and Factors* (New York: Halsted Press, 1976).

[73] Curtis Haugtvedt, Richard E. Petty, and John T. Cacioppo, "Need for Cognition and Advertising: Understanding the Role of Personality Variables in Consumer Behavior," *Journal of Consumer Psychology*, 1 (1992): 239–260.

[74] Hans Baumgartner, "Toward a Personality of the Consumer," *Journal of Consumer Research*, 29 (September 2002), 286–291.

[75] Raymond L. Horton, "The Edwards Personal Preference Schedule and Consumer Personality Research," *Journal of Marketing Research*, 11 (August 1974), 335–337.

[76] Kathryn E. A. Villani and Yoram Wind, "On the Usage of 'Modified' Personality Trait Measures in Consumer Research," *Journal of Consumer Research*, 2 (December 1975), 223–226.

[77] Tom Brown, John Mowen, Todd Donavan, and Jane Licata, "The Customer Orientation of Service Workers: Personality Trait Effects on Self- and Supervisor Performance Ratings," *Journal of Marketing Research*, 39 (February 2002), 110–120.

[78] Mark I. Alpert, "Personality and the Determinants of Product Choice," *Journal of Marketing Research*, 9 (February 1972), 89–92.

[79] Paul E. Green, Yoram Wind, and Arun K. Jain, "A Note on Measurement of Social-Psychological Belief Systems," *Journal of Marketing Research*, 9 (May 1972), 204–208.

[80] The classic study of this topic is E. B. Evans, "Psychological Objective Factors in the Prediction of Brand Choice: Ford versus Chevrolet," *Journal of Business*, 32 (March 1959), 340–369.

[81] Shalom H. Schwartz, "Value Priorities and Behavior: Applying a Theory of Integrated Value Systems," in Clive Seligman, James M. Olson, and Mark P. Zanna, eds., *The Psychology of Values: The Ontario Symposium*, 8 (Mahwah, NJ: Lawrence Erlbaum, 1996), 1–24.

[82] Steven M. Burgess and Jan-Benedict E. M. Steenkamp, "Value Priorities and Consumer Behavior in a Transitional Economy," in Rajeev Batra, ed., *Marketing Issues in Transitional Economies* (Norwell, MA: Kluwer Academic Press, 1999), 85–105.

[83] Lynn R. Kahle, "Contemporary Research on Consumer and Business Social Values," *Journal of Business Research*, 20 (February 1990), 81–82; Lynn R. Kahle, "Social Values and Consumer Behavior: Research from the List of Values," in Seligman, Olson, and Zanna, eds., *The Psychology of Values*, 135–152.

[84] Steven M. Burgess, "Personal Values and Consumer Research: An Historical Perspective," in Jagdish N. Sheth, ed., *Research in Marketing*, 11 (Greenwich, CT: JAI Press, 1992), 35–80.

[85] Milton Rokeach, *The Nature of Human Values* (New York: Free Press, 1973), 5; also see M. Rokeach and S. J. Ball-Rokeach, "Stability and Change in American Value Priorities, 1968–1981," *American Psychologist*, 44 (May 1989), 773–784.

[86] Klaus G. Grunert, Suzanne C. Grunert, and Sharon E. Beatty, "Cross-Cultural Research on Consumer Values," *Marketing and Research Today* (February 1989), 30–39; J. M. Munson and E. F. McQuarrie, "Shortening the Rokeach Value Survey for Use in Consumer Research," *Advances in Consumer Research*, 15 (Association for Consumer Research, 1988), 381–386; S. W. Perkings and T. J. Reynolds, "The Explanatory Power of Values in Preference Judgments Validation of the Means-End Perspective," *Advances in Consumer Research*, 15 (Association for Consumer Research, 1988), 122–126; G. Roehrich, Pierre Valette-Florence, and Bernard Rappachi, "Combined Incidence of Personal Values, Involvement, and Innovativeness on Innovative Consumer Behavior," in *Is Marketing Keeping Up with the Consumer? Lessons from Changing Products, Attitudes and Behavior* (Vienna, Austria: ESOMAR, 1989), 261–279; D. K. Tse, J. K. Wong, and C. T. Tan, "Towards Some Standard Cross-Cultural Consumption Values," *Advances in Consumer Research*, 15 (Association for Consumer Research, 1988), 387–395; Pierre Valette-Florence and Alain Jolibert, "Social Values, A.I.O. and Consumption Patterns: Exploratory Findings," *Journal of Business Research*, 20 (March 1990), 109–122; Jan-Benedict E. M. Steenkamp, Frenkel Ter

PART 3 [ INDIVIDUAL DETERMINANTS OF CONSUMER BEHAVIOR

Hofstede, and Michel Wedel, "A Cross-National Investigation into the Individual and Cultural Antecedents of Consumer Innovativeness," *Journal of Marketing Research,* 36 (February 1999), 1–17.

[87]Donald E. Vinson, Jerome E. Scott, and Lawrence M. Lamont, "The Role of Personal Values in Marketing and Consumer Behavior," *Journal of Marketing,* 41 (April 1977), 44–50.

[88]Robert E. Pitts and Arch G. Woodside, "Personal Values and Market Segmentation: Applying the Value Construct," in *Personal Values and Consumer Psychology* (Lexington, MA: Lexington Books, 1984), 55–67.

[89]Wagner A. Kamakura and Jose Alfonso Masson, "Value Segmentation: A Model for the Measurement of Values and Value Systems," *Journal of Consumer Research,* 18 (September 1991), 208–218.

[90]Shalom H. Schwartz, Sonia Roccas, and Lelach Sagiv, "Universals in the Content and Structure of Values: Theoretical Advances and Empirical Tests in 20 Countries," *Advances in Experimental Social Psychology,* 25 (1992), 1–49; S. H. Schwartz, A. Lehmann, and S. Roccas, "Multimethod Probes of Basic Human Values," in J. Adamopoulos and Y. Kashima, eds., *Social Psychology and Cultural Context* (Newbury Park, CA: Sage Publications, 1999).

[91]Shalom H. Schwartz and Lelach Sagiv, "Identifying Culture-Specifics in the Content and Structure of Values," *Journal of Cross-Cultural Psychology,* 26 (March 1995), 96–112.

[92]Schwartz, Roccas, and Sagiv, "Universals in the Content and Structure of Values."

[93]S. M. Burgess and R. D. Blackwell, "Personal Values and South African Financial Services Brand Preference," *South African Journal of Business Management,* 25 (1994), 22–29.

[94]Thomas J. Reynolds and Jonathan Gutman, "Advertising Is Image Management," *Journal of Advertising Research,* 24 (February/March 1984), 27–36.

[95]Thomas J. Reynolds and Jonathan Gutman, "Laddering Theory, Method, Analysis, and Interpretation," *Journal of Advertising Research,* 28 (February/March 1988), 11–31.

[96]Richard P. Bagozzi and Pratiba A. Dabholkar, "Consumer Recycling Goals and Their Effect on Decisions to Recycle: A Means-End Chain Analysis," *Psychology and Marketing,* 11 (July/August 1994), 313–340; Richard P. Bagozzi and Pratiba A. Dabholkar, "Discursive Psychology: An Alternative Conceptual Foundation to Means-End Chain Theory," *Psychology and Marketing,* 17 (July/August 2000); see also the special issue of *International Journal of Research in Marketing* 12, 3, which was devoted to laddering, especially R. Pieters, H. Baumgartner, and D. Allen, "A Means-End Chain Approach to Consumer Goal Structures," *International Journal of Research in Marketing,* 12 (October 1995), 227–244.

[97]George A. Kelly, *The Psychology of Personal Constructs* (New York: W. W. Norton, 1955); also see Fred Reynolds and William Darden, "Construing Life Style and Psychographics," in William D. Wells, ed., *Life Style and Psychographics* (Chicago: American Marketing Association, 1974), 71–96.

[98]Reynolds and Darden, "Construing Life Style."

[99]Introductions to these multivariate techniques are available in J. F. Hair Jr., R. E. Anderson, R. L. Tatham, and W. C. Black, *Multivariate Data Analysis with Readings,* 5th ed. (Englewood Cliffs, NJ: Prentice-Hall, 1998); and George H. Dunteman, *Introduction to Multivariate Analysis* (Beverly Hills, CA: Sage Publications, 1984).

[100]Amit Bhatnagar and Sanjoy Ghose, "Online Information Search Termination Patterns across Product Categories and Consumer Demographics," *Journal of Retailing,* 80 (Fall 2004), 221–229.

[101]Kusum Ailawadi, Scott Neslin, and Karen Gedenk, "Pursuing the Value-Conscious Consumer: Store Brands versus National Brand Promotions," *Journal of Marketing,* 65 (January 2001), 71–90.

[102]Lynn R. Kahle, *Social Values and Social Change: Adaptation to Life in America* (New York: Praeger, 1983).

[103]Lynn R. Kahle, and Larry Chiagouris, eds., *Values, Lifestyles, and Psychographics* (Mahwah, NJ: Lawrence Erlbaum, 1997).

[104]Lynn R. Kahle, Sharon E. Beatty, and Pamela Homer, "Alternative Measurement Approaches to Consumer Values: The List of Values (LOV) and Values and Life Styles (VALS)," *Journal of Consumer Research,* 13 (December 1986), 405–409; see also Burgess, "Personal Values and Consumer Research: An Historical Perspective"; Matthew Perri III, "Application of the List of Values Alternative Psychographic Assessment Scale," *Psychological Reports,* 66 (July 1990), 403–406; Thomas P. Novak and Bruce MacEvoy, "On Comparing Alternative Segmentation Schemes: The List of Values (LOV) and Values and Life Styles (VALS)," *Journal of Consumer Research,* 17 (June 1990), 105–109.

[105]Kim P. Corfman, Donald R. Lehmann, and Sarah Narayanan, "Values, Utility, and Ownership: Modeling the Relationships for Consumer Durables," *Journal of Retailing,* 67 (Summer 1991), 184–204.

[106]Arnold Mitchell, "Nine American Lifestyles: Values and Societal Change," *Futurist,* 18 (August 1984), 4–13.

[107]Ian Pearson, "Social Studies," *Canadian Business,* 58 (1985), 67–73.

[108]Sheena Ashford and Noel Timms, *What Europe Thinks: A Study of Western European Values* (Aldershot: Dartmouth Publishing Company Limited, 1992).

[109]Burgess and Steenkamp, "Value Priorities and Consumer Behavior in a Transitional Economy"; Steven M. Burgess and M. Harris, "Values, Optimum Stimulation Levels and Brand Loyalty: New Scales in New Populations," *South African Journal of Business Management,* 29 (September 1998), 142–157.

[110]Kenneth Yang, "A Comparison of Lifestyle Segments toward Internet Advertising in Taiwan," *Journal of Marketing Communications,* 10 (September 2004), 195–212.

# Chapter 8

# Consumer Motivation

## Opening Vignette

Forget horsepower, fuel injection, or the time it takes to go from zero to sixty. These days, nothing revs in the automobile world like sales of options and accessories. What's your pleasure? Will it be blinding high-intensity discharge lights? A deaf-defying sound system? How about exterior lighting to highlight your handiwork? Maybe you prefer those flashy, spinning wheel covers? Don't worry, you are sure to find something that suits your fancy. Hundreds of companies now introduce thousands of customizing accessories for cars every year.

How big is the options and accessories market? The Specialty Equipment Market Association (SEMA) estimates the so-called aftermarket, where cars are customized after purchase, at $29 billion in retail sales. And some of the niches within this general market are growing extremely fast. For example, accessories sales in the "tuner" market—sport compact cars—has exploded. From $295 million in 1997, sales multiplied by nearly eightfold to $2.3 billion by 2002, fueled in part by the 2001 summer hit movie *The Fast & The Furious*, which earned over $200 million worldwide at the box office.

The lower end of the market, demographically, is dominated by young drivers. The MTV program *Pimp My Ride* has sparked, or at least reflects, the increasingly personal touch that young drivers are putting on their wheels. The show's theme song begins:

So you wanna be a playa?
But your wheels ain't fly
You gotta hit us up
to get a pimped-out ride.

In other words, if you decorate your car, you'll be more popular.

Accessorizing cars isn't strictly for the young. Older drivers, too, are plunking down big bucks for extras. Unlike the kids and grandkids, however, these motorists tend to favor interior gadgetry over exterior design statements. And the goal is generally a safer, simpler, and quieter driving experience. "They're making it like your car is your house," says one older consumer. "You never want to leave."

Increasingly, the aftermarket is a beforemarket, as auto makers themselves get in on the act, encouraging accessories firms to develop products tailor-made for new models. The redesigned Ford Mustang, for example, has fifty companies making customized products for it. "Margins are thin, so car dealers are looking to us as a new revenue stream," says Peter MacGillivray, a spokesman for SEMA.

Just one warning, say the experts. Before you plop down hundreds or thousands of dollars for that accessory that makes you cool, remember that it won't last forever. "The trends, they are always changing," says Michael Myers, president of Number One Parts International, an Atlanta-based company that specializes in the right stuff for the sixteen- to twenty-five-year-old driver.

Source: Excerpted in part from Gregg Fields, "Hot Wheels," *Miami Herald* (November 11, 2004), C1.

---

One of the most fundamental questions that companies must answer about consumer behavior is, "Why do people buy our product?" Answering this question requires understanding consumer motivation. **Consumer motivation** represents *the drive to satisfy both physiological and psychological needs through product purchase and consumption.*[1] Implementing the marketing concept of providing products that satisfy consumers' needs must first begin with an understanding of what these needs are.

As suggested by the chapter opener, consumers' purchases of a particular product are often motivated by several factors. In the car accessories aftermarket, some people buy for comfort and convenience. Others are motivated by the desire to turn their automobile into a fashion statement. At least some consumers hope that accessorizing their car will increase their social standing. This diversity in consumer motivation is what keeps marketers on their toes.

Although this chapter can't feasibly describe all the different types of needs that motivate consumers, it is possible and worthwhile to discuss some of these needs. In the following section, we review some of the more important needs that shape consumer behavior.

## Types of Consumer Needs

During the past century, psychologists and marketers alike have tried their hand at identifying and classifying needs.[2] Sometimes needs are classified into very broad, dichotomous categories (e.g., utilitarian/functional versus hedonic/experiential needs). Other times a very detailed list of needs is provided. What follows falls somewhere in between these two extremes.

### Physiological Needs

Physiological needs are the most fundamental type of consumer needs. Indeed, our very survival depends on satisfying these needs. We must have food and water. And it wasn't too long ago in the history of mankind that satisfying these needs absorbed substantial amounts of people's time and energy. Raising crops, scouring for wild fruits and berries, hunting, and fishing were activities undertaken by nearly everyone.

Although satisfying the need for food and water remains omnipresent for millions of people on our planet, those more fortunate live in a time in which these needs are fulfilled with relatively little effort. Entire industries have developed that cater to our physiological needs. Food producers and manufacturers, beverage makers, grocery stores, and restaurants have freed many consumers from worrying about where their next meal is coming from. And with home delivery, need fulfillment is only a phone call away.

Physiological needs involve more than what we eat and drink. Humans need to sleep, and many people will spend one-third or more of their lives sleeping. This need has given birth to many product categories, including beds, mattresses, sleeping bags, pillows, sheets, and various sleeping aids. Since the turn of the twenty-first century, premium mattress sales have seen excellent growth, fueled primarily by baby boomers, that segment of the population representing the 76 million people born between 1946 and 1964.[3] Memory foam mattresses, which conform to the shape of your body without using the inner springs of traditional mattresses, can cost between $1,000 to $3,000. A Dux bed from Sweden will run you between $4,000 and $7,000. A horsehair mattress from Hastens, another Swedish company, can set you back $20,000. One out of every five mattresses sold in the United States during 2003 cost at least $1,000. In Consumer Behavior and Marketing 8.1, you can find out more about a brilliant strategy that some mattress companies (as well as other product manufacturers) are using to convert consumers into customers.

Sexual needs are also part of our physiological needs. The initial success of the anti-impotency drug Viagra, with sales reaching $1 billion in its first year on the market, provides strong testament to the importance of our sexual needs.[4] Yet recent times have been much more challenging for Viagra. New competitors have entered the market, Levitra in 2003 and Cialis in 2004, and have begun whittling away at Viagra's market share. The flood of free samples used to attract potential customers has suppressed industry sales. In December 2004, doctors were handing out free samples rather than writing prescriptions 35 percent of the time. The net effect of increased competition in a flat market: Viagra's sales in the United States dropped 20 percent to under $900 million in 2004.[5]

### Safety and Health Needs

Once upon a time, mankind constantly worried about becoming some predator's next meal. Fortunately, those days are long gone. Even so, threats to our safety abound.

## Converting Consumers into Customers: A Valuable Lesson Courtesy of the Mattress Industry

Beyond consumers' reluctance to spend thousands of dollars for something that they have purchased in the past for a few hundred dollars, what do you think is likely to be the greatest barrier a seller of premium mattresses must overcome? Consumers' uncertainty about what it will be like to sleep on a mattress for a full night. It's one thing to lie on a mattress for a minute or two. It's quite another to do so all night long.

So how would you overcome this purchase barrier? Probably the most obvious answer is to offer customers a money-back guarantee. This is precisely what many companies do. Consumers are told that they can return the mattress for a full money refund within a specified time period. But there is usually one little catch: the pickup fee, which can range between $50 to $150 or more. And there are other considerations, such as where to store the original mattress that's being replaced while trying the new one, as well as the inconvenience of switching back and forth.

So how else might a company allow consumers to experience a full night's sleep on its expensive mattress? Simmons, a mattress seller that began selling 95-cent coil mattresses in 1876, has devised an ingenious answer to this question. The company partnered with Westin Hotels, owned by Starwood Hotels & Resorts, to stock Westin's hotel rooms with the Heavenly Bed. Hotel guests are then offered the opportunity to buy a Heavenly Bed. In just four years, Westin Hotels in the United States and Canada have sold former guests 4,000 of the Heavenly Bed setups, which cost about $3,000 for an entire ensemble. Westin has also sold 30,000 Simmons feather pillows at $65 to $75 each.

Others have followed suit. Sheraton Hotels, also part of Starwood, sells its Sweet Sleeper beds and bedding to former guests through a toll-free telephone number. And Tempur-Pedic, the maker of memory foam mattresses (which I recently purchased after sleeping on water beds for decades and absolutely love), has its own partnerships, helping the company achieve sales of over a half-billion dollars. Tempur-Pedic's website sends potential customers to a selection of hotels around the country where they can buy themselves a night of sleep on the foam mattress.

This relatively new kind of symbiosis allows hotel guests to test-drive products from beds to lighting to shower heads to hand lotions and then buy the products for their homes. This arrangement also allows companies to pitch their products in a relaxed and sometimes luxurious atmosphere. About four years ago, Moen asked the Marriott Courtyard across the street from its Ohio headquarters to let the faucet company test out its Revolution Massaging Showerhead in some of the guest rooms. Consumer reaction was so positive, the company said, that the hotel asked Moen to let it sell the showerhead right at the front desk before it was released to the market at large.

Sources: Excerpted in part from Joyce Gempertein, "Boomers Go Beddy-Buy; Can't Sleep Without $4,000 Mattresses and Water-Pocket Pillows," *Washington Post* (September 19, 2004), F1. Also see Amy Cortese, "The Sleep of Forgetfulness (And The Bed Remembers)," *New York Times* (September 12, 2004), 3, 8; Ron Lieber, "The Cranky Consumer: Taking a Mattress Home for a Test Drive; Once-Sleepy Industry Pushes New Beds, Relaxed Policies; Booking Time in a Nap Room," *Wall Street Journal* (May 18, 2004), D1.

Mother Nature, terrorists, criminals, drunk drivers, diseases and ailments new and old, product malfunctions, and simple human error jeopardize our health and safety. Safety needs motivate the purchase of firearms and other personal protection devices, hurricane shutters, home security systems, and residences within gated communities. During the 1990s, safety concerns fueled the sales of oversized sport utility vehicles (SUVs), trucks, and vans that made their drivers feel less vulnerable and in greater control. Concerns about safety may also be one reason why consumers are nonusers rather than users of a product. Some people avoid certain forms of transportation (e.g., flying) and entertainment (e.g., skydiving) because they worry about whether they'll safely survive the experience.

Prior to September 11, 2001, most tourists and travelers took safety and security for granted. No longer is this the case. When visitors to California were asked about the importance of safety and security when making their leisure travel decisions, the average rating, on a 10-point scale, was 8.9, with 55 percent giving the maximum importance score. International visitors were even more concerned. They averaged a 9.6, with 63 percent selecting the maximum score.[6]

The past few years have witnessed the emergence of new types of safety needs: protecting our computers and our personal information in cyberspace. Viruses are no longer something that applies only to human beings. Viruses pose serious threats to our computers and to our computer-dependent nation. A related danger has caused the introduction of a new word to the English vocabulary—**phishing**—to represent *online scams in which crooks pose as representatives of banks or companies sending e-mails soliciting credit card and other personal information from consumers.* These e-mails often contain links to genuine-looking websites for banks or some other company, but they are fake, created solely for the purpose of getting the desired information. One of the authors received a phishing e-mail notifying him that his e-mail address had been selected randomly from millions of e-mail addresses and that he had won the grand prize in a sweepstakes drawing worth hundreds of thousands of dollars. The message indicated that they were eagerly waiting (for the record, they're still waiting) for him to send certain personal information, including his bank account information, so that the prize money could be wired directly to his account. In 2003, losses due to phishing were estimated at a staggering $1.2 billion.[7] The rise in identity theft led Citibank to launch its ID Theft service, which was introduced to consumers in a series of captivating commercials in which victims of identity theft were shown lip-synching to the perpetrator's voice gloating about all of the goods purchased using the victim's name. We will return to the problem of phishing and what you can do to prevent "getting caught" in Chapter 14 (see Buyer Beware 14.2).

Even products whose primary function is to fulfill needs other than safety have still benefited from connecting to this need. Michelin tires, with its product slogan, "Because so much is riding on your tires," has consistently emphasized the importance of safety in its product positioning. Entire industries have addressed their ability to provide safety to users. The steel industry, for example, has emphasized the metal's safety in an effort to upgrade its image among American consumers.[8]

Ever since the 1950s, when Ford saw its sales decline following a year-long campaign promoting safety, there's been an industry-wide myth that safety doesn't sell.[9] That such a myth would persist is amazing given Volvo's decades-long reputation for safety.[10] And listening to what consumers have to say, promoting a product's safety simply makes sense in the automobile industry. The vast majority of consumers rate safety features such as air bags, automatic skid control, and the notification of emergency personnel when accidents occur as very important.[11] Noting these findings, General Motors chooses to convey its dedication to its customers' safety (see Figure 8.1). General Motors is not alone in its efforts. Lexus has promoted its new backup camera system, in which images of what's behind the vehicle are transmitted to the dashboard screen, as a valuable safety feature offered in some of its models.

As fundamental as the need for safety is, occasionally it's still necessary to remind consumers of this need. An excellent example of this is the recent advertising campaign that promotes safe driving among male SUV drivers. SUV rollover crashes take thousands of lives and cause tens of thousands of injuries each year. The majority of these rollovers involve males; the accidents also largely involve people between twenty and thirty-nine years old. So using the money obtained in a settlement with Ford, a

**FIGURE 8.1** GM Appeals to Consumers' Safety Needs

$27 million ad campaign targeting young men was launched. The ad shows young men riding a creature called the Esuvee, which resembles a woolly mammoth with headlights. The ad tells viewers, "Anybody can ride an Esuvee, but not everybody rides it right." As Connecticut attorney general Richard Blumenthal explains, "What we want to do through this campaign is to remove the halo that SUVs now have . . . the halo effect that makes young men particularly feel that they are invulnerable or invincible when they are behind the wheel of a sport utility vehicle." [12]

According to one old saying, "There's nothing more important than your health." One indication of how concerned people are about health is the frequency with which it shows up in New Year's resolutions. Table 8.1 reports Americans' New Year's resolutions from 2002 to 2005. "Losing weight or exercising more" has been at or near the top each of these years. When combined with those resolving to stop smoking or drinking alcohol, health concerns were behind the 2005 New Year's resolutions of more than 40 percent of those surveyed. [13]

Consumers' desires to improve their health are well founded. Some estimates suggest that dietary and lifestyle changes could prevent between three to four million cancer cases worldwide each year. Take, for example, colorectal cancer, the third most common cancer among Americans. The American Cancer Society estimates that more than 56,000 Americans die yearly from colon and rectal cancers. Yet the diets of many Americans significantly enhance their chances of getting these cancers. Those eating the equivalent of a hamburger a day are 30–40 percent more likely to develop these cancers than those eating less than half this amount. Heavy consumption of processed meats such as hot dogs raises the risk of colon cancer by 50 percent. [14]

So how well do Americans take care of their health relative to consumers living in other countries? One answer to this question is provided by Americans' average life expectancy relative to others. Another indicator is the average number of years lived

**TABLE 8.1**  Americans' New Year's Resolutions (percent)

| | 2005 | 2004 | 2003 | 2002 |
|---|---|---|---|---|
| Lose weight or exercise more | 30 | 27 | 29 | 30 |
| Pay off or pay down debt | 25 | 28 | 29 | 28 |
| Get a more secure or better job | 14 | 15 | 11 | 12 |
| Improve personal relationships | 12 | 13 | 11 | 13 |
| Stop smoking or drinking alcohol | 11 | 7 | 11 | 8 |
| Other | 3 | 4 | 4 | 3 |
| Nothing | 5 | 6 | 5 | 6 |

Source: Cambridge Consumer Credit Index, www.cambridgeconsumerindex.com (January 28, 2005). Copyright 2005 Cambridge Consumer Credit Index. All rights reserved.

**TABLE 8.2**  Average Life Expectancy and Average Number of Years Lived in Good Health: The Top Ten Countries

| COUNTRY | RANK | AVERAGE LIFE EXPECTANCY | COUNTRY | RANK | AVERAGE YEARS IN GOOD HEALTH |
|---|---|---|---|---|---|
| Japan | 1 | 81.9 | Japan | 1 | 75.0 |
| Switzerland | 2 | 80.9 | Sweden | 2 | 73.3 |
| Australia | 3 | 80.4 | Switzerland | 3 | 73.2 |
| Sweden | 3 | 80.4 | Italy | 4 | 72.7 |
| Canada | 5 | 79.8 | Australia | 5 | 72.6 |
| France | 6 | 79.7 | Spain | 5 | 72.6 |
| Italy | 6 | 79.7 | Norway | 7 | 72.0 |
| Singapore | 8 | 79.6 | Canada | 7 | 72.0 |
| Spain | 8 | 79.6 | France | 7 | 72.0 |
| Austria | 10 | 79.4 | Germany | 10 | 71.8 |

Source: Anthony Faiola, "Japanese Are Old Hands at Fitness," *Miami Herald* (October 28, 2004), A24. Copyright 2004 by the Miami Herald. Reproduced with permission of Tribune Media Services.

in good health. Table 8.2 lists the ten countries with the highest averages for each of these measures. And no, it's not a mistake that the United States does not appear on either list. Even if we expanded the lists to the top twenty countries, the United States would barely make one of them. The average life expectancy at birth for Americans is 77.3 years, which makes it twentieth in the world. The average years of good health is 69.3, making the U.S. twenty-third in the world.[15]

The need to maintain or improve our health, both mental and physical, is the foundation on which many professions and goods and services have been built. Doctors, dentists, nurses, laboratory technicians, dental assistants, medicines, hospitals, vitamins, exercise clubs and equipment, diet (see Buyer Beware 8.1) and health foods, and numerous diet- and health-related books, magazines, and television shows owe their existence to consumers' health needs. In 2004, Americans spent nearly a quarter of a trillion dollars ($235.4 billion, to be precise) on prescription drugs alone, an increase of more than 50 percent from $150 billion in 2000.[16] Products such as air-cleaning sys-

## Weight Lost or Lost Money?

As part of a crackdown on false and deceptive diet claims, the Federal Trade Commission sent letters to nine media companies reminding them to stop publishing advertisements for bogus weight-loss products. Letters went to *Cosmopolitan, Woman's Own, Complete Woman, USA Weekend, Dallas Morning News, San Francisco Chronicle, Cleveland Plain Dealer, Albuquerque Journal* and the Spanish-language magazine *TeleRevista*. These publications had run ads for products that were the targets of six lawsuits filed by the agency—pills, powders, green tea, topical gels, and patches that promised significant weight loss, even if consumers didn't decrease their food intake or increase their exercise. This incident was the first time the agency sent letters to publishers in conjunction with lawsuits against diet-product makers. The FTC estimates that Americans spend $37.1 billion a year on weight-loss products and says media firms have benefited substantially with their promotions.

The agency is seeking a halt to the ads and consumer refunds for such products as the "Himalayan Diet Breakthrough"—a dietary supplement of what the manufacturer called Nepalese Mineral Pitch, a paste-like material that "oozes out of the cliff face cracks in the summer season." The product, which costs $39.95 for a month's supply, promised consumers could lose as much as thirty-seven pounds in eight weeks if taken before lunch, dinner, and bedtime. With Chinese Diet Tea, dieters were told they could lose as much as six pounds a week if they drank a cup after each meal to neutralize the absorption of fattening foods. This product costs $24.95 for a thirty-day supply.

"These claims are about as credible as a note from the tooth fairy," says FTC chairperson Deborah Platt Majoras. "But they ran in the pages of well-known national magazines and big-city newspapers and on popular Internet sites, all of which lend an air of credibility to these outlandish claims."

Source: Caroline E. Mayer, "FTC Admonishes Media Not to Run False Diet Ads," *Washington Post* (November 10, 2004), A13. Copyright 2004 The Washington Post. Reprinted by permission.

tems, with industry sales expected to crack the half-billion dollar mark in the next few years, have prospered because of consumers' health needs.[17] Even such staples as milk have benefited from the growing number of health-conscious consumers around the world. In Consumer Behavior and Marketing 8.2, you can learn about the growing milk market in China as well as the challenges and opportunities this market presents.

You might remember our discussion in Chapter 6 (see especially Consumer Behavior and Marketing 6.1) about the challenges facing the citrus industry. One way orange juice producers have responded to these challenges is through the introduction of new products (such as the one featured in Figure 8.2) that are linked to consumers' health concerns.[18] The words used by fruit juice makers to describe their new products also reveals their desire to make their products more appealing to health-conscious consumers. Table 8.3 reports how often particular words and phrases appeared on a new fruit juice product in 2004.

The Red Lobster chain of restaurants has attempted to reverse its declines in sales and customer traffic by connecting with health-conscious consumers. The chain's new "Lighthouse Selections" menu displays nutritional information about thirty-three entrées, side dishes, and beverages. For years the chain has used the slogan, "For the seafood lover in you." This slogan has been modified to "For the healthy seafood lover in you" in its new advertising. "It's about time Red Lobster did this," says one restaurant analyst. "I would be very surprised if the change doesn't have a significant impact on sales." "They certainly needed to do something," adds another. "Red Lobster is an old brand that's been forgotten, especially by younger people. They have a real opportunity now to stand for something and be a healthy alternative." [19]

As people grow older, their health begins to deteriorate. Consequently, the health needs of older individuals are usually much more pressing than those of younger ones. And Americans, on average, are getting older. The tens of millions born during the population explosion following World War II through the mid-1960s (a group known as the baby boomer generation) are now moving into the fifty-plus age category. The beginning of the twenty-first century saw an unprecedented increase in the number of Americans over fifty. Industries and companies catering to consumers' health will reap the benefits that come from serving a growing market. For this reason, you can expect many companies to jump on the health bandwagon when promoting their products.

## CONSUMER BEHAVIOR AND MARKETING 8.2

## Milk Benefits from China's Movement toward a Healthier Consumer

A glass of milk may be part of the daily routine for people in developed countries, but the Chinese have long turned up their noses at it. Part of the reason is economic. Milk costs more than water or tea. Many also find the taste disagreeable or lack the enzymes needed to digest it. Milk was rarely found in Chinese refrigerators, and certainly never on restaurant menus.

But China is starting to get milk. There's been a basic change in the national diet that reflects larger shifts in the surging Chinese middle class. Production of milk in China nearly doubled during the five-year period ending in 2003. Its total milk production is still small compared with the West, but, with a population of 1.3 billion, China "is one of the fastest-growing markets in the world, and probably the fastest in absolute terms," says Thierry Vappereau, head of planning for Nestlé SA's China division. Shanghai Bright Dairy & Food Co., China's biggest dairy producer, delivers 2 million bottles of milk to customers each day, compared with 1,800 bottles a day five years ago when the service was launched.

Behind the milk movement is a fitness craze sweeping Chinese consumers. With increasing purchasing power, they are flocking to health clubs, reading health magazines, downing vitamins, and drinking milk in record numbers. As China plays economic catch-up with the developed world, authorities are also seeking to improve the country's health. In the last two years, China has launched a subsidized milk program for schoolchildren, and state-run television has aired programs on the benefits of drinking milk.

Among the hurdles all companies face is the fact that many Chinese can't stomach the milk. No official estimates exist for how many people in China are lactose intolerant, but the percentage is thought to be high. The National Institutes of Health (NIH) estimate as many as 50 million people in the United States have an inability to digest lactose, a natural sugar found in milk. Certain ethnic groups are more widely affected than others; some 90 percent of Asian Americans are lactose intolerant, according to the NIH.

Most of China's milk demand is in urban areas, where distribution channels exist and consumers have more income. So milk companies are targeting China's city dwellers and their kids. President Enterprises, one of Taiwan's top dairy companies, is focusing on malted milk, with toy giveaways at supermarkets. The company plans to roll out "milk tea" and "milk coffee" for the parents. Among Shanghai Bright's strategies are chocolate milk, cartoon-festooned milk cartons, and a national ad campaign featuring China's Olympic diving champion Tian Liang. "We're developing future customers," says a spokeswoman.

Source: Kath Chen, "Acquired Taste: New Craze Seizes China's Consumers: A Glass of Milk—Fitness Boom, Higher Income Make It a Growth Market; Advice for Sour Stomachs—Mr. Miao's Hangover Helper," The Wall Street Journal, February 28, 2003, A1. © 2003 by Dow Jones & Co. Reproduced with permission of Dow Jones & Co., Inc., in the textbook format via Copyright Clearance Center, Inc.

### The Need for Love and Companionship

By and large, humans are social creatures. Although the idea of being stranded all alone on a deserted island may appeal to a few, most of us would prefer to share the island with someone else. Virtually everyone needs love and companionship. And virtually every adult has found it, at least once. Table 8.4 shows the number of times American men and women report being in love during their adult life. Whereas nearly a quarter of the men report being in love five or more times, apparently women are more selective, as only one-ninth of them have reached this level of loving.

Dating services, social clubs, bars, vacation cruises, and resorts catering to singles on the prowl, and products that help us attract others during the dating game (from personal hygiene products to clothing to plastic surgery) thrive on this need. The Internet has proven to be fertile ground for the dating industry, which has experienced explosive growth in recent times (see Market Facts 8.1).

Moreover, products are often used as symbols of love and caring.[20] Flowers, candies, and greeting cards are often given as tokens of our affection for someone. So are jewelry and diamonds—two industries that have carefully cultivated their products' symbolic meaning. "Show her how much you care without saying a word," proclaims one jewelry advertisement. A brochure for diamonds begins with the statement, "All the ways to say 'I love you.'" One advertisement in Figure 8.3 portrays jewelry as "very small objects that express very large emotions." And, as illustrated by the other ad in Figure 8.3, even rather ordinary products, such as those found at the grocery store, sometimes are positioned as symbols of our caring for someone else.

**FIGURE 8.2** Appealing to Consumers' Health Needs

---

**TABLE 8.3**     Words and Phrases That Appeared on New Fruit Juice Products in 2004: Appealing to Consumers' Health Needs

| WORD OR PHRASE | NUMBER OF OCCURRENCES |
| --- | --- |
| Natural | 71 |
| No preservatives | 33 |
| Organic | 24 |
| No artificial color | 21 |
| No artificial flavor | 21 |
| Real | 18 |
| Pure | 17 |
| No artificial ingredients | 10 |
| No additives | 9 |
| No genetic modification | 8 |
| No artificial sweeteners | 4 |
| No chemicals | 4 |

Source: "Random Sampling: Apples and Oranges," *Marketing News* (October 15, 2004), 3. Reprinted with permission from American Marketing Association.

| TABLE 8.4 | Americans in Love | |
|---|---|---|

**In your adult life since you turned eighteen, have many times have you been in love?**

| | MEN (%) | WOMEN (%) |
|---|---|---|
| Once | 20 | 25 |
| Twice | 24 | 30 |
| Three times | 18 | 20 |
| Four times | 12 | 12 |
| Five or more times | 24 | 11 |

Source: Simona Covel, "The Heart Never Forgets," *American Demographics* (July/August 2003), 13.

## MARKET FACTS 8.1

## Looking for Love Online

The need for love and companionship has fed a thriving online industry catering to this need. Traditional dating services have not enjoyed a particularly favorable image, and personals posted in newspapers have had limited appeal, but consumers are flocking to websites that offer them the opportunity to find that special someone. Some 40 million Americans visited an online dating site in August 2003. And the revenue growth over the past couple years has been nothing short of phenomenal. From $72 million in 2001, revenues more than quadrupled to $302 million the following year. And 2003 wasn't too shabby either. Total revenues came in at a hair under $450 million, representing an annual growth of nearly 50 percent. Online

personals and dating services are the single largest category of consumer spending for online content, easily surpassing the $334 million spent on the number two product category, business and investment.

One of the earliest online dating sites was Match.com, founded in 1995. This site took six months to register its first 60,000 members. That's "something we now do in less than three days," says Trish McDermott, vice president of communications. As of January 2005, the Match.com website claimed to be "the world's largest dating site" with more than 8 million members and "twice as many marriages as any other site in the world."

Sources: Catherine Arnold, "How Marketers Capitalize on e-Motions," *Marketing News* (November 10, 2003), 1, 11–12; "U.S. Consumer Spending for Online Content Totals Nearly $1.6 Billion in 2003, According to Online Publishers Association Report," www.comscore.com/press/release.asp?press=455 (May 11, 2004).

The need for love and companionship partly explains why Americans own so many pets. Do you know what the most popular pet is in America? Hint: It likes to say "meow." Americans own 59 million cats. Fish are a close second at 55.6 million. Man's best friend ranks third, with Americans owning nearly 53 million dogs. Other popular pets include birds (12.6 million), rabbits and ferrets (5.7 million), rodents (4.8 million), horses (4 million), and reptiles (3.5 million).[21]

Tastes
Like
Somebody
Loves
You.

**FIGURE 8.3** Symbols of Love

## The Need for Financial Resources and Security

Money is the tool that the majority of us use for satisfying most of our needs. Money can't buy love, but it sure can buy a lot of other things. The extent to which consumers can afford to satisfy their current needs depends primarily on their paycheck. But what about their future needs when they have left the work force and their paychecks behind? At this point in a person's life, he or she will need financial security, which involves establishing adequate financial resources so that one's "golden years" live up to their name.

In America, the government offers some financial support to retirees in the form of Social Security payments. But these payments alone do not come close to providing sufficient financial resources for most retirees who wish to maintain their preretirement lifestyle and consumption patterns. Without personal savings, life during the golden years will not be golden. Yet, as you will read about in Chapter 9, millions of Americans working today probably will suffer from inadequate financial resources when they eventually retire because they failed to accurately understand the monetary requirements for a happy retirement.

The need for financial security also extends to our important others. As long as I'm alive and working, my family will be taken care of. But what about when I'm no longer here? For this reason, I, along with millions of other consumers, buy life insurance, which satisfies our need to ensure the financial security of our loved ones. Nonetheless, to the dismay of the insurance industry, many Americans have yet to protect their loved ones' financial security. In what is referred to as the "underinsurance problem," a little more than one-third of the individuals in the "prime needs segment" (those with a full-time job and at least one dependent) do not own any form of life insurance.[22] Another part of the underinsurance problem is that many of those who have purchased life insurance have relatively low levels of coverage. Whereas a quarter of life insurance owners have policies that equal or exceed five times their annual household income, nearly one-third own policies that would not replace even a single year of household income.[23] Compounding the problem is that 76 percent of those owning policies providing less than a year's worth of income replacement believe that their existing coverage is adequate.[24] And these individuals hold this belief even though most of them admit that they've taken none of the steps needed to determine their households' life insurance needs.[25] Educating consumers about the importance of owning life insurance and the coverage levels needed for providing adequate protection would certainly help the life insurance industry's future growth.

### Social Image Needs

Do you care what your loved one and family think of you? Are you concerned about how you are perceived by your friends and coworkers? Nearly everyone is. We want our family to be proud of us. We want to be seen as a good person. Some want to be viewed as successful and, perhaps, rich; others want to be seen as attractive and hip. Social image needs are based on a person's concerns about how he or she is perceived by others, and a desire to project a certain image to his or her social environment.

As you well know, and as advertisers constantly remind us (see Figure 8.4), a person's social image depends, at least in part, on the products that the person buys and consumes. Where we live, what we drive, the clothing we wear, and the music we listen to contribute to our social image. Even something as mundane as the bottled water we drink may be valued because it enables us to symbolically represent ourselves to others. The term **conspicuous consumption** is often used to describe *purchases motivated to some extent by the desire to show other people just how successful we are.*

Companies are continually reinforcing the notion that their products enable users to communicate their social image. "You can tell a lot about a man by his brand," announces an ad for Marlboro cigarettes. We are told, "Clothes may make the man but I prefer to see what's in his liquor cabinet," by one liquor ad. A jewelry ad shows a woman admiring another's engagement ring and saying, "What a big, beautiful diamond! Your fiancé must really be rich." Mel Prince, a marketing professor at Southern Connecticut State University, explains, "If someone's wearing a diamond, it's definitely on display. The larger it is, the more it reflects on his [the male buyer] status. That is important in this society, for a man to demonstrate that he has worth. The prestige of the consumer is reflected in the prestige of the diamond."[26]

Car makers often emphasize their products' ability to convey "who we are" by what we drive. The ad in Figure 8.5 tells you that you'll look "all that" driving the streets with this set of wheels. When George Murphy, senior vice president of global brand marketing at DaimlerChrysler, was asked about whether the com-

**FIGURE 8.4** Advertising Constantly Reminds Us That Our Possessions Define Who We Are

WITH ALL THIS, YOU'LL DEFINITELY BE ALL THAT.

trailblazer    IMAGINE ALL THIS AT YOUR FINGERTIPS — AVAILABLE TOUCH-SCREEN NAVIGATION SYSTEM,* XM SATELLITE RADIO, REAR-SEAT DVD ENTERTAINMENT SYSTEM, BOSE
PREMIUM SPEAKER SYSTEM, AND THE ULTIMATE IN SECURITY — A STANDARD ONE-YEAR ONSTAR SAFE & SOUND PLAN. YEAH, IT'S DEFINITELY ALL THAT. CLICK ON CHEVY.COM.

General Motors Corp. Used with permission, GM Media Archives

**FIGURE 8.5** Products That Make You Look "All That"

pany's Dodge Charger and its Chrysler 300 would be competing with each other, he responded, "No. They are completely different customers. The Chrysler (buyer) is much more enamored of a great interior and refinement. That is what the brand is and what the car is. Dodge is much more about power, Hemi, muscle, a sinister front end. If you want to make a statement about yourself being bold, on the edge, full of life, you'll get the Dodge. If you want people to think you are refined and upscale, you will buy a Chrysler. The positioning is night and day, and the customers are the same way."[27]

Serving as a beta tester, in which consumers use a company's new product prior to its actual release to see what problems may exist, is an important part of some consumers' social image. Clifford Nass, a communications professor at Stanford University whose research examines social responses to technology, explains, "Having special knowledge of technology is the latest way they demonstrate who they are." This opinion is echoed by Nicco Mele, who runs the Internet consulting firm EchoDitto. "There's a lot of cachet associated with being an early adopter. It's similar to how every time you're in a meeting, everyone wants to show off who's got the coolest new phone," says Mele.[28]

Just as some products will be viewed as contributing to or enhancing the consumer's social image, others will be viewed as not doing so or, even worse, hurting one's image. Wearing a Rolex watch will be viewed by many as an enhancement to the wearer's image; wearing a Timex will not. In the United Kingdom, McDonald's recently has been plagued by complaints about its food and its poor service. This situation has led to some consumers being unwilling to admit to their friends that they patronize the Golden Arches. Apparently, eating at McDonald's is not conducive to the social image these consumers wish to project. This is not good news for McDonald's. Indeed, as

## Two Different Industries Serving the Same Basic Need Are Heading in Opposite Directions

The toy industry is under siege. Retailers KB Toys and FAO Schwarz have been pushed into bankruptcy. The Toys "R" Us chain is contemplating leaving the business that made its name. Industry leader Mattel has experienced a staggering 26 percent drop in domestic sales of its cornerstone Barbie product line. Total industry sales are heading south at an increasing pace. In 2002, sales for the year were down 1 percent. The following year they dropped 3 percent. And heading into the end of 2004 sales were off another 5 percent.

What's going on? Several things. Children get bored with traditional toys at a younger age than ever before. Children are also growing up faster. As one toy consultant explains, "It's not that they're rejecting traditional toys, but there's a cultural shift. If you talk to kids, they want things like iPods. The role models they're looking up to are not sitting around playing Chutes and Ladders." There's another key factor: growing up in the digital age. It's only natural that children in today's environment would gravitate toward technological toys. This shift is compounded by the fact that parents have cut back on traditional toy purchases to afford the pricier electronic games and systems.

A strong indictment against traditional toy makers comes from Isaac Larian, president and chief executive officer of MGA Entertainment, the company behind the successful Bratz dolls. Larian says, "I don't see how companies that just make toys can survive. If I were an investor, I wouldn't want to invest in a company that just makes toys." What strategy is MGA pursuing to reduce its dependence on toys? Extending the Bratz property into a lifestyle brand by placing the Bratz name on a variety of products ranging from CD players to clothing to digital cameras to room decorations.

The traditional toy market is contracting, but the video game market is heading in the opposite direction. In 2004, U.S. videogame sales are expected to rise 10 percent to $7.8 billion. Industry leader Electronic Arts, with annual sales of nearly $3 billion, produced 22 games in 2002 that sold more than a million copies, and five others that sold more than 4 million apiece. The company publishes the all-time bestselling computer game, *The Sims*, which is essentially a digital dollhouse. Twenty-seven million copies have been sold in three years. Competitor Microsoft broke sales records in 2004 when its *Halo 2* raked in $125 million its first day on the market (see Figure 8.6).

their chief global marketing officer, Larry Light, laments, "We don't want to have closet loyalists."[29]

Consumers may sometimes differ in their opinions about how a product impacts their social image. What may be seen as an image enhancer by some may be viewed as hurting their image by others. This is so for tattoos. When asked how they would compare people with tattoos (which now represents around one-sixth of American adults) to those without, tattooed consumers, as one would certainly expect, often believed that tattoos enhanced the tattoo owner: 34 percent thought tattoos made the owner more sexy, 26 percent thought they made the owner more attractive, and 5 percent even thought tattoos made the owner more intelligent. Consumers without a tattoo, on the other hand, had very different opinions: 36 percent thought tattoos made the tattoo owner less sexy, 42 percent said they made the owner less attractive, and 31 percent perceived the owner as less intelligent.[30]

**FIGURE 8.6** When Microsoft Released *Halo 2,* Consumers Were Standing in Line Hoping for a Chance to Buy It

Within a month *Halo 2* had reached $250 million in sales. Yet all of these numbers pale in comparison to the all-time video game leader: Madden NFL. Since 1989, its first year on the market, Madden NFL has sold nearly 37 million units. At $50 a pop, its total sales are closing in on the $2 billion mark.

Source: Excerpted in part from Queena Sook Kim, "Toy Makers Outgrow Toys; With the Industry Reeling, Bratz Dolls Lead the Push into Electronics, Room Decor," *Wall Street Journal* (October 19, 2004), B1; Marcelo Prince, "Videogame's Break into the Big Time; Blockbuster Sales Rival Those of Movie Industry, But Costs Are Escalating," *Wall Street Journal* (December 21, 2004), B3; Jose Antonio Vargas, "Madden NFL Scores Again; Football Fans Lineup for Super Bowl of Videogames," *Washington Post* (August 12, 2004), C1; Andrea K. Walker, "In Digital Era, Toys Struggle to Survive," *Miami Herald* (December 19, 2004), E1, E2; May Wong, "The Art of the Game," *Miami Herald* (August 19, 2003), C8.

## The Need for Pleasure

There's a saying, "All work and no play makes Johnny a dull boy." Although some people may live for their work, most need pleasurable distractions. Without fun and excitement, life would be rather dull and boring indeed.

Consumers satisfy their need for pleasure in many different ways. Although our basic physiological requirements mandate the consumption of food, sometimes food consumption occurs even though we do not feel hungry. In such cases, we eat something simply because we wish to enjoy the consumption experience itself. A person who is feeling depressed may try to improve his or her mood by eating a favorite food.

The entertainment industry is built on consumers' need for pleasure. Television, movies, music, Broadway plays, fictional books, sporting events, amusement parks, bowling alleys, ocean cruises, and nightclubs are popular because of the pleasures they deliver. The same is true for the toy and electronic games industries (for a discussion of the changes going on in these industries, see Consumer Behavior and Marketing 8.3). In point of fact, many consumption activities are valued because of

### TABLE 8.5 Traffic Patterns at Online Fantasy Sports Sections

| MONTH | NUMBER OF VISITORS (MILLIONS) | REGULAR SEASON LEAGUE SCHEDULES | | | |
|---|---|---|---|---|---|
| | | MLB | NFL | NBA | NHL |
| October 2003 | 7.447 | | X | X | X |
| November 2003 | 7.413 | | X | X | X |
| December 2003 | 7.038 | | X | X | X |
| January 2004 | 2.997 | | | X | X |
| February 2004 | 2.355 | | | X | X |
| March 2004 | 3.797 | X | | X | X |
| April 2004 | 3.604 | X | | X | X |
| May 2004 | 3.104 | X | | | |

Source: "More Than 7 Million Americans Participate in Online Fantasy Sports." Comscore Media Metrix. www.comscore.com (July 19, 2004). Copyright 2004 comScore Networks, Inc.

Note: Number of visitors refers to visitors to the fantasy sports sections of Yahoo! Sports, CBS Sportsline, and ESPN.

the fun and excitement they offer (e.g., skydiving, riding roller coasters, white water rafting, hunting).

Millions of consumers have found pleasure online by participating in fantasy sports. For a small fee, you can create your own team using current professional players and compete against teams created by other competitors. How these players perform in their real world games relative to the performance of the players on opposing teams determines who wins. How popular is this pastime? It depends on what time of the year you're talking about. Table 8.5 indicates the number of visitors to certain fantasy sports sections of certain websites between October 2003 and May 2004. More than 7 million consumers were visiting the fantasy sports sections during football season. Following football season, typically less than half this number were visiting the sites. Male participants outnumbered their female counterparts by a ratio of three to one. One interesting statistic about fantasy sports participants: they are much more likely to earn six-figure incomes than the regular Internet user.[31]

Consumers also go online to find pleasure in the form of gambling. Nearly 2 million poker players could be found gambling online in January 2005.[32] The popularity of poker has exploded over the last few years. Much of this increase in popularity can be attributed to such poker television shows as the World Series of Poker on ESPN and the World Poker Tour on the Travel Channel. Tiny cameras installed at the table enable viewers to see players' "hole cards" (those cards that are turned face down during the hand) and are credited for much of the shows' popularity. Human interest stories—from the unknown accountant from Tennessee, Chris Moneymaker, winning the World Series of Poker in 2003 and claiming the first-place prize of $2.5 million, to Ben Affleck winning $360,000 at a poker tournament—serve as a powerful enticement for others. In just two years, the industry grew an astounding fifteen-fold. Websites that were making $300,000 a day in 2003 were making more than ten times that amount per day in 2005.[33] By one estimate, about $124 million was being wagered collectively in more than one hundred online poker rooms during a single twenty-four-hour period.[34]

The need to possess is a hallmark characteristic of our consumer society. Americans own more clothing than any culture in the history of mankind. The average American household has more cars (1.9) than drivers (1.8)![35] According to the American Moving and Storage Association, the typical family carted 5,645 pounds of belongings when they moved in 1977. By 2004, the average move weighed in at 7,700 pounds, an increase of 36 percent.[36] What accounts for this increase? Certainly much of it can be attributed to consumers' need to acquire more and bigger products. Here's a quick inventory of one twenty-nine-year-old lawyer's possessions: "I've got a sixty-one-inch TV which, diagonally, is one inch bigger than my own mother. I've got an eleven-speaker surround-sound system. I've got oversize plush couches and a monster-size kitchen with a huge bread maker and a commercial-size mixer. And I've got a large master bedroom with a walk-in closet that was the size of my bedroom in my old house."[37]

What's driving this need to possess? For one, comfort. According to the lawyer with the oversized possessions: "It's nice when you're done with your day to be able to come home and soak in the big tub, grill in your big backyard, and watch your sixty-one-inch TV. It allows you to escape the daily stress. You work hard; you want to enjoy your comforts."[38]

Although important, comfort is not the only reason behind this need to possess. We may wish to possess some objects simply because of their historical significance. As an extreme example, consider Todd McFarlane, a comic book artist and creator. He outbid all others during an auction and paid $3 million for a single baseball! Of course, it wasn't just any baseball. It was the seventieth home-run ball hit by Mark McGwire in 1998 when McGwire established the new major league record for home runs in a single season. "I blew my life savings on this," said McFarlane. "I'm not Donald Trump. I don't have a lot of cash."[39] Now imagine how he felt when Barry Bonds surpassed that record in 2001 by hitting seventy-three home runs!

Collectors know full well the power of their need to possess. During my younger days, I was an avid coin collector. For many years, I spent part of my lunchtime looking through the school cafeteria's cash register for coins to be added to my collection. I visited local coin dealers and purchased (my budget was a bit more limited than Todd McFarlane's) certain coins that could no longer be found in circulation. I routinely bought coin sets from the U.S. Mint. I even enlisted the help of my mother and sister. And the time I spent building my collection pales in comparison to the time I spent staring at my collection for no other reason than to admire its existence.

Many others have begun to experience this passion for coin collecting since 1999, when the U.S. Mint began issuing its statehood quarter series (see Figure 8.7). Each year, through 2008, five new quarters, one designed for each of the fifty states in the order that they joined the union, are released. The U.S. Mint estimates that 110 million Americans are collecting the quarters. One of the first quarters, that commemorating Connecticut, helped the Mint sell a record $2 million worth of

**FIGURE 8.7** Millions of Americans Have Felt the Need to Possess the Statehood Quarters

them in one day over its website. "This is probably the hottest collectible of the decade," says Michael White of the U.S. Mint.[40]

Objects may be valued because they make us feel connected to their prior owners. Consumers spent millions of dollars buying former possessions of famous individuals (e.g., Marilyn Monroe, Jacqueline Kennedy) during auctions held in the late 1990s. Possessions also play an important role in linking a person with his or her past. Objects may be acquired to preserve memories and to serve as a permanent nostalgic benchmark of a different time and place. Vacationers, for instance, often buy items (e.g., T-shirts, arts and crafts from local artists, and so on) to commemorate their travels.

At the extreme, possessions may become so important that we believe that they help define who we are. Have you ever heard the expression, "You are what you eat"? In this context, it's "You are what you own." One noted consumer researcher has even suggested, "That we are what we have is perhaps the most basic and powerful fact of consumer behavior."[41] From this perspective, consumers' **self-concept,** representing their *impressions of the type of person they are,* depends, at least in part, on what they possess.[42]

Finally, the need to possess plays an important role in impulse buying. **Impulse buying** occurs when *consumers unexpectedly experience a sudden and powerful urge to buy something immediately.*[43] Their need to possess is felt so strongly that it propels them to act quickly.

### The Need to Give

How many times have you heard about someone making it big and feeling the need to give something back? Sometimes it's the college graduate who, after earning millions

---

### BUYER BEWARE 8.2

## Do You Know Where Your Money Is Going?

In 2003, Americans made $241 billion in charitable donations. Yet only part of the money raised by telemarketers during average charitable campaigns actually goes to their intended causes, from defending human rights to helping police associations to making sure government doesn't waste money. According to a report released by Attorney General Tom Reilly, for each contributed dollar in 2003, 29 cents ended up in the hands of the charity.

"People should be mindful that, in some cases, large portions of their donations may not ultimately be going to the charitable program," says Reilly. "I urge people to be aware and ask questions so that they know just where their dollars will wind up."

Many people might not be so charitable with their money if they realize just how little goes to the intended charity. An extreme example is the campaign for the Association of Blind Citizens, which raised $2.9 million yet netted only $277,098, representing less than 10 percent of contributors' original donations.

Charities and telemarketers defend their practices, saying it's a simple fact of life that one has to spend money to make money. True enough. But not all charitable organizations spend the same proportion on making money. For example, according to the Christian Children's Fund's website (www.christian childrensfund.org), nearly 81 percent of its revenue is spent on children's services. A tad better than 29 cents on the dollar, we would say.

Source: Jay Fitzgerald, "Charities Lose 71 Percent of Donations: Fund-Raising Companies Get It, AG Says," www.business.bostonherald.com (December 10, 2004); Penelope Wang, "Making Your Generosity Pay," www.cnnmoney.com (December 22, 2004).

PART 3 [ INDIVIDUAL DETERMINANTS OF CONSUMER BEHAVIOR

of dollars during a highly successful career, returns to his or her alma mater and provides the money necessary for student scholarships or a new building. Or it's the pro athlete who returns to the neighborhood where he or she grew up and funds a facility dedicated to keeping at-risk kids out of trouble. The story may differ in its details, but the underlying constant is the need to give.

Have you ever donated to charity? (Whether your answer is yes or no, check out Buyer Beware 8.2.) Most of us have, often for no more reason than to help others less fortunate than ourselves. Yet such altruism may be only one reason for giving. Sometimes we give because of its implications for our social image. We do not want to be seen as cheap or uncaring, especially when the request for a donation comes from a friend or coworker. Donations, especially large ones, serve as symbols of the donor's wealth. Although some wealthy donors request anonymity, many do not. The success of charitable organizations' fund-raising activities heavily depends on their understanding the relative influence of these different reasons behind the need to give.

The need to give is not limited to money. This need also encompasses products (and gift cards—see Market Facts 8.2) that are given to others as gifts. Gift giving is an essential part of many holidays. Valentine's Day, Mother's Day, Father's Day, and the granddaddy of them all, Christmas, are celebrated, at least in part, through gift-giving rituals. Birthdays, anniversaries, and graduations are also traditional gift-giving occasions.

## MARKET FACTS 8.2

## Gift Cards Come of Age

Once upon a time gift cards were looked down upon. They were seen as an indication that the giver was unwilling to exert the effort to find a proper gift for the recipient. But that's no longer the case. Now they're viewed as the best way of ensuring that the recipient will get something that he or she really wants. And, when received as a Christmas gift, there's an added bonus to the recipient, depending on when they are redeemed. Many consumers redeem their gift cards in the week following Christmas, a time in which many retailers are running substantial price promotions. This effectively increases what consumers can get with their cards.

About three out of four Americans purchased a gift card during the 2004 holiday season. Estimates range between $17–20 billion or more for the amount spent on gift cards during this time. For the very first time, gift cards were expected to become the most popular holiday purchase, passing the longtime leader, apparel. And gift cards' popularity is not limited to the holiday season. Birthdays are the number one occasion for gift cards. In total, a record $55 billion was spent on gift cards in 2004.

An added bonus exists for retailers regarding gift cards. Do you know what it is? Is it that the majority of consumers don't redeem them, as is the case for rebates (as you will learn in Consumer Behavior and Marketing 8.4)? Nope, that's not it. Is it that many consumers end up spending more money when they're in the store redeeming their gift card? That's it. According to Laura Lambeth, spokeswoman for Paymentech, an electronic payment processor of gift cards, electronic checks, and credit and debt card transactions, consumers tend to spend as much as 40 percent more than the amount of the gift card during redemption.

Sources: Deborah Alexander, "Growing Popularity of Gift Cards Helps Keep Holiday Sales Season Going," *Knight Ridder Tribune Business News* (January 20, 2005), 1; Maria Halkias, "Gift Cards: Playing a Hot Hand," dentonrc.com (December 16, 2004); Ron Lieber, "The Cranky Consumer: The Secondary Market for Gift Cards; Sites Spring Up That Let Recipient's Trade Scrip; We Test the Different Options," *Wall Street Journal* (January 18, 2005), D1; Daniel Shoer-Roth, "Gift Cards Make the Season Jolly," *Miami Herald* (January 5, 2005), C1.

**FIGURE 8.8** This Ad Encourages Consumers to View the Product as a "Self-Gift"

Beyond giving to others, sometimes we feel the need to give to ourselves. We may do so in the form of **self-gifts**.[44] Self-gifts are *things that we buy or do as a way of rewarding, consoling, or motivating ourselves*. The gift may be as small as eating a favorite snack. Or it may be as large as buying a new car or taking an expensive vacation. A nationally representative survey that asked consumers about their holiday purchase plans found that one out of every four American adults was planning on buying a gift for themselves, although this varied as a function of the person's age. A little more than one-third of younger adults (from ages eighteen to thirty-four) planned to do so versus only 12 percent of those fifty-five years old or older.[45] Being aware of this inclination, companies often encourage consumers to view their products as self-gifts (see, for example, the ad in Figure 8.8).

### The Need for Information

Making reasoned choices requires being informed. And being informed requires information. As discussed in previous chapters, consumer decision making depends heavily on the information—both internal (what you already know) and external (what you may learn while searching the environment)—available to consumers at the time they make their choices. In the following chapter on consumer knowledge, we'll talk about the importance of internal information. But now we focus on how the need for information itself influences consumer behavior.

The purchase and consumption of many products can be attributed to consumers' need for information. Without this need, consumers would have little reason to watch news programs on television and even less reason to read the newspaper. Do-it-yourself books and shows would disappear. Colleges and universities would be out of business. A major reason the Internet has become so popular is that it enables consumers

**TABLE 8.6**     Consumers' Need for Financial Information
Takes Them to the Web

| WEBSITE | AUDIENCE (MILLIONS) | AVERAGE TIME AT SITE |
|---|---|---|
| CBS MarketWatch | 7.1 | 26:32 |
| Wall Street Journal Online | 3.4 | 31:38 |
| Motley Fool | 3.4 | 8:46 |
| Bankrate.com | 2.9 | 6:22 |
| TheStreet.com | 2.0 | 14:11 |

Source: Eric Dash, "Internet News Sites Are Back in Vogue," *New York Times* (January 24, 2005), C1. Copyright 2005 by the New York Times Co. Reprinted by permission.

to easily satisfy their informational needs.[46] As documented in Table 8.6, millions of consumers spend time browsing financial information websites.

Consumers' need for information is also important because of its role in the persuasion process. Suppose you are planning to make a first-time purchase in a particular product category and you encounter an advertisement for one of the brands in the category. Your need for relevant product information leads you to pay close attention to what the ad has to say. In contrast, suppose you encountered the ad at a time when you did not need the information it contains. In this case, you obviously have little reason to pay attention to the ad. And without attention, the ad has no chance of persuading you. Consequently, advertisers must use some sort of attention-getting device (e.g., a pretty face, a well-known celebrity, a talking animal or reptile) as a way of attracting your attention. We'll cover this topic in much greater depth in Chapter 14. And in Chapter 15, we'll discuss how the relative persuasiveness of different advertising elements (e.g., claims, pictures, music, and so on) depends on the need for information.

## The Need for Variety

According to one saying, "Variety is the spice of life." How true this is! As you well know, too much of the same thing over and over again can quickly become rather boring. This certainly applies to product consumption. I usually drink Diet Coke. But every once in a while I'll buy a non-cola-flavored soft drink at the grocery store just because I want something different tasting.[47] But this need for variety can get us in trouble. Recall from Chapter 6 how greater variety can lead to more consumption, as shown by the study in which people ate more M&Ms as the candies' variety in terms of colors was increased.[48]

This need for variety is partly responsible for the recent popularity of musical mobile telephones in Japan. As one twenty-one-year-old explains, "I think it is crazy for everyone to have the same or similar ringing tone." Over four million copies have been sold of a book that provides the numbers or symbols for programming the phone's ringing tone to produce a musical melody.[49] The need for variety helps explain why McDonald's sells more food in France than any other European country. Explains one eighteen-year-old French teenager, while eating some McDonald's fries, "Yes, there is other food around, but this is different, like food you want to eat as a break." Another young consumer adds, "It's good to get something that tastes completely different."[50]

**FIGURE 8.9** Appealing to Consumers' Need for Variety

Companies respond to consumers' need for variety in several ways. Food manufacturers may offer different versions of their original brand. In 2005, both Coca-Cola and Pepsi introduced flavored versions of their bottled waters in hopes of appealing to consumers thirsting for something different.[51] Food manufacturers may also promote different ways for preparing and serving their products. The need for variety is sometimes the focus of a product's advertising and positioning. The soft drink advertisement in Figure 8.9 proclaims, "All the Flavor. All the Variety. All for You." The advertising for one steak sauce depicted the product as something "deliciously different." An adventure tour may declare that it offers vacationers something different and unique, especially these days when tourists are, according to one tourist industry spokesperson, "looking for variety."[52]

## Motivational Conflict and Need Priorities

Fulfilling one need often comes at the expense of another need. Money spent satisfying one need leaves less for the rest. The time allocated to one need means there's less time for fulfilling others. These *tradeoffs in our ability to satisfy various needs* cause **motivational conflict**.

Motivational conflict can take one of three basic forms. **Approach-approach** conflict occurs when *the person must decide between two or more desirable alternatives* (e.g., between buying new furniture and taking a cruise). **Avoidance-avoidance** conflict involves *deciding between two or more undesirable alternatives* (e.g., between mowing the yard and cleaning the pool). The last type, **approach-avoidance,** exists when *a chosen course of action has both positive and negative consequences*. Cigarette consumption satisfies smokers' need for nicotine, but does so at the risk of their health. Users of the prescription painkiller Celebrex, taken to treat arthritis, have recently experienced approach-avoidance motivational conflict after a study found a greater risk of heart attacks among those taking high doses of the drug. "My family thinks I should stop taking it," says one consumer. "They say the pain would come back but I'd be alive. They see it in black-and-white. What I understand better than my family is that with every benefit there is a side effect, but not everyone gets the side effect."[53] As of the time this chapter was being written, whether Celebrex would be withdrawn from the market had yet to be determined, a decision complicated by the conflicting evidence about the medicine's health risks.[54]

Resolving motivational conflict requires people to prioritize their needs. Doing so means that people must decide on the relative importance of each of their needs. These decisions will be of both a short-term (which needs to satisfy now) and long-term (which needs to satisfy in the future) nature. The rumblings in your stomach may motivate you to satisfy your need for food at that moment. Concerns about financial security during retirement may motivate years of saving money.

Like most things, consumers differ in the priorities they assign to their needs. What is vital to one person may be trivial to another. In a survey of women aged twenty to fifty, 24 percent strongly agreed with the statement, "I am concerned about what others think of me."[55] For this group, the need to project a desirable social image will

**FIGURE 8.10** Maslow's Hierarchy of Needs

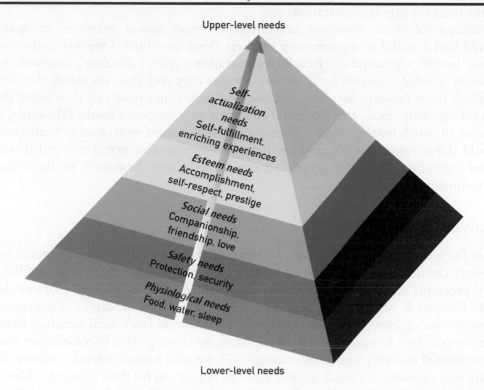

Upper-level needs

Self-actualization needs
Self-fulfillment, enriching experiences

Esteem needs
Accomplishment, self-respect, prestige

Social needs
Companionship, friendship, love

Safety needs
Protection, security

Physiological needs
Food, water, sleep

Lower-level needs

be very important, certainly more so than for those disagreeing with the statement. Those products perceived as better at fulfilling this need stand a much greater chance of being chosen and consumed, but only for those consumers for whom the need is an important priority.

One well-known approach to specifying the relative priority assigned to different needs is Maslow's hierarchy (see Figure 8.10). According to psychologist Abraham Maslow, some needs take precedence over other needs.[56] Physiological needs are the most basic in the hierarchy; they take top priority. Only after these needs have been fulfilled do people progress up the hierarchy to the next level of needs. In essence, then, Maslow's hierarchy orders needs from most important (represented at the bottom of the hierarchy) to those least important (represented at the top of the hierarchy).

Maslow's hierarchy is a useful concept because it reminds us that people attach different priorities to their needs. Nonetheless, his theory should not be seen as providing a definitive specification of what these priorities may be. Although Maslow's ordering may correspond with the priorities of many, it certainly does not reflect everyone's priorities in all situations. Sometimes people ignore lower-order needs in pursuit of higher-order needs. A mother's love may lead her to disregard her own safety when the life of her child is at risk. Others pursue careers that satisfy their need for accomplishment at the expense of their love relationships.

Differences in the importance consumers attach to various needs ultimately affect how they evaluate products being considered for purchase and consumption. Different needs lead consumers to seek different product benefits. Car buyers that are strongly motivated by a desire to project a certain image are looking for a different benefit from those more concerned about safety. Consequently, the evaluative criteria (see Chapter 4) used during decision making may change depending on what benefits are desired and what needs are to be fulfilled. Those concerned with image will place greater importance on a car's styling and social standing. A car's safety features (e.g., airbags, antilock brakes) and safety record are accorded greater emphasis for those motivated by the need for safe transportation.

Because of these variations in consumers' motivational priorities, companies should find it useful to segment their markets along these lines. One way to do this is to use benefit segmentation. **Benefit segmentation** involves *dividing consumers into different market segments based on the benefits they seek (i.e., the needs they want fulfilled) from product purchase and consumption.* Companies can then tailor their marketing efforts more effectively and efficiently to a segment's needs. Obviously, the manner in which bottled water is positioned to the segment motivated by health needs should differ from how it's positioned to the segment that perceives bottled water as an appropriate way for conveying something about themselves to their social environment.

## Motivational Intensity

Thus far we have ignored the issue of **motivational intensity,** which represents *how strongly consumers are motivated to satisfy a particular need.* Sometimes fulfilling a need preempts all else. At other times, motivational intensity is much more modest.

In Chapter 4, we noted that need recognition depends on the degree of discrepancy between one's current situation (where one is now) and one's ideal situation (where one wants to be). As need deprivation increases, need recognition becomes more likely. Motivational intensity also grows stronger. Those who haven't eaten for twenty-four hours will experience a much greater sense of urgency to fill their stomachs. Motivational intensity also depends on the need's importance. The needs most important to consumers are pursued more intensively.

Another way of thinking about motivational intensity is through the concept of involvement. Involvement represents the degree to which an object or behavior is personally relevant.[57] To the extent that some object or behavior is thought to satisfy important needs, the greater is its personal relevance. The more strongly motivated consumers are to satisfy their needs, the greater their involvement with potential sources of need satisfaction. Consumers motivated to project a favorable social image, for example, will be more involved with products perceived as satisfying this need than those who are not so motivated. In the same way, products that evoke higher involvement (those that are more personally relevant to our needs) will increase consumers' motivation to acquire and consume these products.

Involvement and motivational intensity are important because they determine the amount of effort consumers exert when trying to satisfy their needs. As intensity and involvement increase, consumers try harder to fulfill their needs. They become more attentive to relevant information. They undertake more thinking and respond differently to persuasive communications (see Chapter 15). External search becomes greater.[58] Consumers may also consider a larger number of choice alternatives for attaining need satisfaction.

Businesses sometimes craft their marketing programs with consumers' product involvement in mind. An excellent example of this is Nintendo's loyalty program (available at www.nintendo.com), which consists of three membership tiers. Those attaining the highest level of membership, called Sage, do so based on the depth of their involvement on Nintendo's website. "The feedback we're getting from this program has been outstanding so far," says Dan Owsen, Nintendo of America's online manager. "We've been able to identify a good core group to be our first Sages." Since the site's launch in December 2003, weekly registrants have tripled, and about 3 million unique visitors browse the site each month.[59]

## The Challenge of Understanding Consumer Motivation

Those interested in understanding consumer motivation must avoid the pitfall of believing that research is unnecessary because the reasons underlying purchase behavior are "obvious." To illustrate this point, we want to tell you a story about Mel Fisher. Mel searched for sunken treasure from a Spanish galleon that was sent to the bottom of the ocean by a hurricane in 1622. In 1985, after fifteen years of searching and enduring many personal hardships, including the loss of a son who died when one of the search vessels capsized, another of Mel's sons found the treasure forty-one miles off Key West. And what a treasure it was! Nearly $400 million in gems, gold, and silver. Almost overnight, Mel became a celebrity. He appeared as a guest on television talk shows, was featured in National Geographic specials, and his life story was told in a made-for-TV movie.

Stop and think for a moment about what motivated Mel in his quest for sunken treasure. What would you guess to be his reasons for doing so? The most obvious explanation for why Mel searched so many years and sacrificed so much is that he was motivated by the wealth he would attain if his search were successful. Yet those who knew him say otherwise. According to Madeleine Burnside, executive director of the Mel Fisher Maritime Heritage Society, "It was never about the value of the gold. It was always about the hunt and the excitement. After they found the main pile, they all actually got terribly depressed. Because it was about the search." Pat Clyne, vice president of Treasure Salvors and Mel's friend for nearly thirty years, has a similar opinion. "He's not like other people. He wasn't interested in money. The whole thing was the expedition, the puzzle."[60]

Similarly, the obvious reason for consumers' behavior may not always tell the whole story. Consider credit counseling services. What do you think is the primary reason behind consumers' use of such services? Many would probably guess that it has something to do with consumers overspending and having too much debt. Many would be wrong. The reason given most frequently involves consumers' frustration with the high rates and fees charged by lenders.[61]

Moreover, humans are complex creatures and engage in behaviors for reasons that sometimes are less than transparent. This truism also applies to consumer behavior. Indeed, the motivation for buying and consuming can be downright surprising sometimes, as the McCann-Erickson advertising agency learned when researching why Raid roach spray outsold Combat insecticide disks in certain markets. Most users agreed that Combat is a better product because it kills roaches with minimal effort by the user. So why did some of them still use roach spray? When the heaviest users of roach spray—low-income southern women—were asked to draw pictures of their prey, they portrayed roaches as men. "A lot of their feelings about the roach were very similar to the feelings they had about the men in their lives," says Paula Drillman, executive vice president at McCann-Erickson. The roach, like the man in their life, "only comes around when he wants food." Setting out Combat was easier, but it did not give them the satisfaction they derived from spraying roaches and seeing them die. "These women wanted control," Drillman explains. "They used the spray because it allowed them to participate in the kill."[62]

Understanding why people behave as they do is often a challenging endeavor. One reason this is so is that people may not be willing to disclose the real reasons behind their actions. Consumers may not feel comfortable divulging what makes them tick to others. The guy that buys a "muscle car" as a way of enhancing his own sense of masculinity may not wish to admit this. Similarly, how many charitable donors motivated by the need to display their wealth would be willing to admit this?

When people believe that their answers to a question may cast a less than favorable light on themselves, they may decide not to tell the truth. Rather, they provide answers that, to them, are socially acceptable. One compelling demonstration of this involves how consumers distort how much milk and alcohol they drink when asked to report on their consumption of these items. These self-reports are then compared with the empty milk and alcohol containers found in consumers' garbage cans. Many report drinking more milk than they actually do while underreporting their consumption of alcohol.

Another complicating factor is that people may not be able to tell us why they behave the way they do. Indeed, consumers spend millions of dollars each year at psychologists' offices to try and understand the reasons for their own feelings and actions. At the beginning of the twentieth century, Sigmund Freud and his followers introduced the idea of **unconscious motivation,** in which *people are unaware of what really motivates their behavior.* According to Ernest Dichter, considered by many to be the father of motivational research, "Knowing one's own motivations is one of the most difficult things, because we try to rationalize. Most of us try to explain our behavior in an intelligent way, when very often it is not."[63]

Nonetheless, motivational researchers have been probing consumers' psyche for decades. Dichter proposed long ago that women were using Ivory soap to wash their sins away before a date. He also suggested that convertible automobiles serve as substitute mistresses for sexually frustrated men.[64] And many years ago, motivational researchers were posed the question, "Why do women bake cakes?" According to some of the researchers, women baked cakes because of their unconscious desire to give birth. Perhaps it is for this reason that Pillsbury invented its famous "Doughboy" character (see Figure 8.11).

Another challenge to understanding consumer motivation stems from the reality that it can change. What motivates purchase today may not be what motivates purchase in the future. Consider consumers' motivation for using soap. As one executive explains, "It used to be 'I'm trying to make myself presentable to you.' Now it's more about 'Hey, I've got to wash you off of me.'"[65] What about going to the dentist? One dentist explains that when he started out, "people came to the dentist for health reasons. They were in pain. In the last five or six years, people come to the dentist, really, to enhance their smile. It's the No. 1 reason people go to the dentist."[66]

A change in consumer motivation can be good or bad news for business. If the change involves a particular need becoming more important to consumers, then businesses serving this need should benefit. Conversely, if a change is due to the need becoming less important, then businesses serving this need may suffer. In Japan, for example, female consumers' need to give "obligation chocolates" to their friends and coworkers on Valentine's Day (as opposed to "true-love" chocolates for their sweethearts) is declining, a trend that concerns both chocolate makers and retailers.[67]

## Motivating Consumers

As should be apparent from the numerous examples presented throughout this chapter, companies often try to motivate consumer buying by linking their products to important needs. There are, however, other ways for motivating consumers.

© AP/Wide World Photos

**FIGURE 8.11** Does the Pillsbury Doughboy Appeal to Consumers' Unconscious Needs?

Some of these methods were discussed previously in Chapter 4's coverage of the need recognition stage of decision making (e.g., the motivational power of reminding consumers of their needs). We now describe some others.

## Motivating With Money

A couple of weeks before Valentine's Day, Bailey Banks & Biddle jewelers mailed out the card appearing in Figure 8.12 to selected customers. On the left-hand page appears a carefully crafted message designed to touch base with, as we discussed previously in the chapter, consumers' need for love and affection (e.g., "you are sure to find the perfect symbol of your abiding love and devotion"). But the effectiveness of this promotional material is not limited to the left-hand page. For on the right-hand page appears one of the most powerful and popular tactics for motivating consumers: money! Whether it be in the form of price cuts, rebates, or coupons, money talks and consumers listen.[68] When, for example, Southwest Airlines slashed the average price charged for a one-way ticket on a certain route by 62 percent, the number of tickets sold skyrocketed by more than 800 percent![69]

Websites that offer consumers rebates for shopping at particular online retailers are popping up all over the Web. Here's how it works: you sign up for free at a rebate site and then shop at affiliated retailers. Your purchases are tracked automatically and once your earned rebate reaches a certain value, a check is sent to you. Rebates typically range from 4–8 percent. One of the best-networked sites is Butterflymall.com, which is connected to more than six hundred Web retailers, including Barnes and Noble, Target, and Circuit City.[70]

Nonetheless, motivating consumers through price is a dangerous proposition. One concern is that, although sales may increase, profitability may not. After all, at least

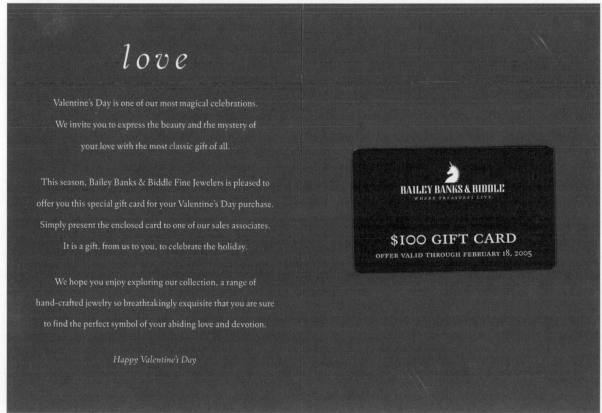

**FIGURE 8.12** Bailey Banks & Biddle Uses Money to Lure Customers into Its Store

some of the consumers who buy at the reduced price would have done so even at the full price. According to one estimate, current users of a product account for more than 70 percent of coupon redemption.[71] For each redemption, money is lost and profitability reduced. Consequently, unless the profit received from incremental customers (i.e., those who would not have purchased the product without the price reduction) is large enough to cover the losses incurred by selling to those who would have paid more, the company loses money. And attracting those who would have otherwise purchased another product requires a substantial discount. Charles Brown, vice president of marketing for NCH Marketing Services, a clearinghouse that processes coupons for retailers, and co-chairman of the Promotion Marketing Association's coupon council, advises that it takes about a 40 to 50 percent discount on a product before consumers will switch from the products they regularly purchase.[72]

Another concern with price reductions involves the type of customer they attract. Market research tests of rolling out new products with or without a coupon show that, of those who initially buy the product with a coupon, nearly one-fourth become repeat buyers. By comparison, nearly one-third of those who made their initial purchase without the coupon become repeat buyers.[73] As these findings suggest, consumers motivated today by price are less likely to become tomorrow's customers. Rather, they tend to give their business to whoever is offering the lowest price. Further, incentives based on price reductions have been found to increase the price sensitivity of both loyal and nonloyal consumers. As one market researcher explains, "Over time, price promotions train consumers, particularly nonloyal ones, to look for deals in the marketplace instead of encouraging them to be loyal to a given brand based on attributes other than price."[74] General Motors experienced this result in late 2004 when, in an effort to improve its profitability, the company reduced the discounts it was offering new car buyers by roughly 10 percent. Car shoppers responded by taking their business elsewhere. While Nissan enjoyed a monthly sales increase of 26 percent, GM's sales declined by nearly 17 percent.[75] Seeking to stop a slide in which its U.S. market share fell to a historical low of 24.6 percent, GM implemented another sales incentive plan the following month by offering rebates of up to $5,000 on select 2004 and 2005 models.[76]

Price reductions have another potential problem. As discussed in Chapter 4, consumers may use price as a signal of product quality. If so, then price reductions may produce a similar reduction in perceived quality of the product that, in turn, will undermine consumers' attitudes toward the product. Consistent with this reasoning, cutting the price has been found to reduce the favorability of consumers' attitudes toward the product.[77]

Despite these concerns, price reductions remain one of the most popular marketing tactics for motivating purchase behavior. Pick up any Sunday newspaper and you'll find sales galore. Even professional sports has relied on the power of cutting prices. When the National Basketball Association players' strike of 1999 ended, franchises slashed ticket prices for some seats to bring fans back to the arenas.[78] To learn more about why businesses are so fond of rebates and coupons, read Consumer Behavior and Marketing 8.4 and Buyer Beware 8.3.

## Providing Other Incentives

Reducing a product's price is just one of the ways businesses can sweeten a deal. Another way is to provide **premiums,** which is *when one product is offered as an incentive for the purchase of another product.* Sometimes the premium is offered for free; sometimes the premium is offered at a discounted price. Billions of children's meals have been sold by fast-food restaurants, many because they included toys. When

## Motivate with the Rebate

One popular business tactic for overcoming price barriers and motivating consumers is the product rebate. Consumers purchase the product at full price but receive a certain amount of money back once they have submitted the appropriate documents. The earliest known rebate was offered in 1914 by Ford for purchases of its Model T car. Rebates have since become a heavily advertised, high-dollar strategy to move merchandise, especially in the big-ticket world of consumer electronics. Rebates of more than $100 are common, with some ranging up to $400 or more.

Rebates amount to billions of dollars each year. And consumers love them. In a survey of female shoppers by the Promotion Marketing Association in 2003, 76 percent said a rebate would make them more likely to buy a product. Manufacturers love rebates as well, for more reasons than you might think. According to Mark Bergen, the Carlson Professor of Marketing at the University of Minnesota's Carlson School of Management, the percentage of consumers who actually collect their rebates ranges from less than 10 percent to about 30 percent, depending on the product and the dollar amount involved. "You're talking some low numbers. You would be stunned," says Professor Bergen. "That's one reason rebates are so exciting to firms. They get the price-discount effect without actually having to lower their price."

Companies count on a certain percentage of buyers not redeeming their rebates because they misplaced forms, lost receipts, missed deadlines, or forgot about them. Failure to meet multiple rebate requirements—filling out forms, clipping bar codes, making photocopies of receipts, and mailing them—adds another percentage of disqualified rebates. Then there's what the industry calls "slippage"—the percentage of people who get a check and forget to cash it.

Amazingly, some companies, through their mishandling of rebates, are turning their customers off of using rebates. Karen Paczkowski, a fifty-three-year-old nurse, said she got the rebate runaround three separate times: on a laptop computer, a printer, and a cell phone. Each product promised rebates of $100 to $150, and each proved challenging to collect. After filing her paperwork twice, she finally got the $100 rebate on a Hewlett-Packard printer. But she's still waiting for a $150 rebate from Best Buy on her laptop and $100 from T-Mobile for the cell phone, despite repeated phone calls, letters, and resubmissions of documents. "I'm not buying another thing with a rebate," Paczkowski says. "Next time, I'm going on store price only." And her experience is not unique. "We get a lot of complaints on rebates—hundreds a year," says Jane Driggs, president of the Better Business Bureau of Minnesota and North Dakota.

Timothy Silk, an assistant professor of marketing at the University of South Carolina who is studying rebates, says what appear to be overly complicated procedures often are how manufacturers combat rebate fraud, in which criminals mass-produce rebate forms and redeem them. The Promotion Marketing Association estimates rebate fraud at more than $500 million per year. So it's understandable why businesses have become more careful in honoring requested rebates. Nonetheless, businesses must be careful not to ruin a good thing.

Source: Excerpted in part from Don Oldenburg, "The Rebate Check May Not Be in the Mail," *Washington Post* (February 1, 2005), C10; John Reinan, "Let the Rebate Buyer Beware," www.startribune.com/stories/535/4973394.html (September 11, 2004).

McDonald's decided to include miniature Beanie Babies in its Happy Meals (see Market Facts 8.3), it produced nearly 100 million of the toys, its largest order ever for a promotion. Yet that number still wasn't enough. Consumer demand was so overwhelming that McDonald's recommended to its restaurants that they limit sales to ten meals per customer after some customers began buying the meals by the caseload![79]

## When Coupons Cost You Money

Supposedly the first grocery coupon, worth one cent, was offered by Grape Nuts cereal in 1895. Since then, grocers have relied heavily on coupons for motivating consumers to shop at their stores. Sunday newspapers usually carry freestanding inserts loaded with coupons for products available at the local grocery store. More recently, coupons have been made available at the point-of-purchase, such as electronic dispensers located on the shelves or peel-off coupons on the packages themselves. Point-of-purchase coupons are undeniably convenient and help save money on the products to which the coupons apply, but these coupons may have a hidden cost.

In an in-store experiment, some of the shoppers were handed a one-dollar-off coupon; others were not. Those receiving the coupon made, on average, 11.4 unplanned purchases at a cost of $27.26. Those that were not given the coupon made fewer unplanned purchases (7.8) and spent less money on these purchases ($19.58). Thus, the coupon stimulated significantly more unplanned spending on items other than the one to which the coupon applied.

Further analysis revealed that the coupon recipients were more likely to make unplanned purchases of a particular nature. Coupon recipients, compared to those not receiving the coupon, made significantly more purchases of items that were (1) cognitively related to the product featured in the coupon, (2) in close proximity on the grocery shelf to the product featured in the coupon, (3) on sale, and (4) considered to be treats (e.g., ice cream). Presumably, receiving this unexpected coupon enhanced shoppers' moods, thereby making them more likely to buy treats, and also priming them to pay more attention to similar items, such as those also available at a price discount. These mood and cognitive effects, in turn, determined the particular unplanned purchases made by the coupon recipients.

So the next time you're in a grocery store and accept an unexpected coupon, be careful. The savings you realize from using the coupon may pale in comparison to the money you spend on the additional items that end up in your shopping cart.

Source: Carrie M. Heilman, Kent Nakamoto, and Ambar G. Rao, "Pleasant Surprises: Consumer Response to Unexpected In-Store Coupons," *Journal of Marketing Research*, 39 (May 2002), 242–252.

Premiums are a popular tool for attracting new business in the banking industry these days.[80] Typically, banks offer relatively inexpensive items that are cheaper than offering cash incentives or paying higher interest rates on accounts. "When you offer a gift, it lowers the acquisition cost to the bank," explains James Gresham of Rennhack Marketing Services, a financial-services marketing company that provides premiums to the banking industry. And these premiums work. One bank's campaign targeting college students doubled the number of new accounts normally opened by offering, among other things, lava lamps. Another bank went so far as to offer consumers a free Cadillac SRX. Just one catch: a minimum of $400,000 had to be deposited in a five-year CD offering an interest rate of 1 percent. So much for being "free."

Just as there are potential limitations with price reductions, premiums also have their share of possible shortcomings (indeed they do; see Buyer Beware 8.4), both for the promoted product and the product used as the premium. First, a particular premium may actually hurt a product's sales. This result can occur when the number of consumers motivated by the premium are outweighed by an even greater number of consumers who are motivated not to purchase the product because of the premium.[81]

### Whale Hunting in Las Vegas

Sometimes the size of the incentives used to motivate potential customers is much larger than the free toy offered in a McDonald's Happy Meal. Has a company ever wanted your business so much that it offered you a $25,000 shopping spree for free? Probably not—unless you're a whale. Whale is the term used by casinos for gamblers who have lots of money and are willing to wager hundreds of thousands, even millions, of dollars during their visit to the casino. Some casinos reserve their best penthouse suites, sometimes large enough to accommodate four average-sized homes, for whales only. Cost? There is none. In fact, virtually everything is free except, of course, the money wagered. Food, drinks, a butler for the suite who is available twenty-four hours a day, sightseeing trips to nearby attractions, and shopping sprees are used as bait during whale hunting.

Casinos are betting that they'll recoup more than enough money from a whale's losing wagers to offset the thousands of dollars in incentives given away. And a whale is much more valuable than a regular customer. According to one industry insider, a single whale can make more money for a casino than one thousand regular customers over the long run. But beware. In the short run, catching a whale can be risky business. One Las Vegas casino lost $20 million during a whale's forty-minute visit to its blackjack table!

In addition, the **value-discounting hypothesis** predicts that *products offered as a free premium will be valued less.*[82] Prior exposure to an item used as a premium has been shown to reduce consumers' purchase intentions for a similar item from the same product category. Moreover, the perceived value of the product offered as a premium is dependent on the particular product it's being used to promote. Consumers indicated that they would be willing to pay nearly $29, on average, for a Cross pen offered as a free premium for purchasing a bottle of Royal Salute whiskey (retail price of $90). But when this same pen served as a premium for Bombay Sapphire gin (retail price of $16), the price consumers were willing to pay for the pen dropped to little more than $21. Thus, both the promoted product and the premium product need to be careful in whom they choose as a partner.

Contests and sweepstakes are other types of incentives used to motivate consumers. The Toyota Corporation offered a contest in which visitors to its website competed to win a pickup truck.[83] Publishers Clearing House has built its reputation and business (selling magazine subscriptions) through its famous sweepstakes drawing, which gives consumers the chance of becoming an instant millionaire. And Figure 8.13 displays two sweepstakes offers. By registering online or simply using a Capital One Visa credit card, consumers were entered for a chance to win a Daytona 500 VIP Trip package. Pepsi's "Call upon Yoda" sweepstakes offered consumers the chance to win $1 million in prizes.

But certainly one of the most exotic sweepstakes ever offered was by Volvo. A commercial during the 2005 Super Bowl informed consumers that they could go to www.boldlygo.com and enter a sweepstakes offering a flight into space aboard Virgin Galactic, the fledgling company you were first introduced to in Chapter 4. The grand prize, which includes three days of preflight training, is valued at $200,000. The sweepstakes is promoting Volvo's XC90 sports utility vehicle, which is the company's best-selling model in the United States.[84]

## New Definition of Free

The e-mail messages are tantalizing: "Join now and receive a free IBM laptop." "Your complementary iPod with free shipping is waiting." These offers and similar ones on the Internet promise gifts for buying products or services. Are they for real?

Apparently some are. Gratis Internet, a Web marketer, has developed a system in which it buys pricey products like iPods and gives them away. To receive the iPod, participants are asked to sign up for one of about ten different offers and to persuade five others to do the same. Rob Jewell, cofounder of Gratis, says the company gives away five hundred iPods a week. The company provided the names and e-mail addresses of about two dozen people who had received free iPods. One of these people, Jacob Snyder, says "I did a lot of research because I didn't trust it." But after finding what he deemed to be legitimate success stories, he decided to make a run at a free iPod. He signed up for a forty-five-day free offer for Internet service provider AOL, which he discontinued after a short trial, and he also convinced five of his friends to participate in one of the offers. Within a month, he received his iPod.

Yet others, dealing with different companies, report different experiences. Let me tell you about my own personal experience that started with an e-mail I received from BizRate.com and one of its "special partners." According to this e-mail, "eMarket Research

Group is currently looking for new product testers. Simply complete the evaluation survey and get a free Dell Laptop." No problem, I thought. I can certainly take the time to complete a survey for a free computer that I wanted to give to my brother-in-law. The so-called evaluation survey was nothing more than a sham. I didn't evaluate anything. Instead, I had to indicate which offers (e.g., signing up for a new credit card or putting my name on someone's e-mail list) I would accept. I was able to satisfy the requirements of accepting offers without spending any money for the first two sets of offers, so I did. But then came the deal killer. Satisfying the requirements of the last set of offers required spending far more money than I could possibly justify for this so-called free computer. I can't begin to tell you how annoyed I was. I had not only wasted my time, but by accepting those initial offers I had helped this company. Nor is my experience unique. While doing research for the book, I ran across a website, www.ripoffreport.com, which lists complaints from others who had the misfortune of dealing with eMarket Research Group, as well as other companies. Unlike myself, these unhappy consumers had actually completed all of the requirements to receive their free product, but in most cases were still waiting. The lesson to be learned here is perhaps best summarized by Vic, who wrote on www.ripoffreport.com's message board, "The lesson is that the only thing on this earth that is truly free is your mother's love. Everything else has a string or catch attached."

Source: Excerpted in part from Barbara Whitaker, "A Web Offer Too Good to Be True? Read the Fine Print," *New York Times* (December 26, 2004), 3, 8.

### Implementing a Loyalty Program

Beyond motivating initial or trial purchasing, companies are also interested in motivating repeat business. Health clubs have been successful at recruiting new members, but less so at retaining them because 30 percent of new members fail to renew their memberships.[85] Similarly, the number of league bowlers peaked at 9 million in 1980 but has since declined to 3.5 million.[86] Obviously, it's difficult for businesses to grow when their ability to retain customers is limited.

**Loyalty programs** try to *motivate repeat buying by providing rewards to customers based on how much business they do with a company.*[87] The origins of loyalty programs can be traced to at least 1876, when a retailer began issuing S&H Green Stamps. The more the customer bought, the more stamps he or she received. Once the customer had accumulated enough stamps, the stamps could be redeemed for gifts.[88]

FIGURE 8.13  Capital One Uses a Sweepstakes to Motivate Usage of Its Credit Cards and Pepsi Uses a Sweepstakes to Motivate Product Purchase

| TABLE 8.7 | Consumers' Participation In and Usage of Loyalty Programs | |
|---|---|---|
| CATEGORY | PARTICIPATE IN LOYALTY PROGRAM (%) | USE IT EVERY TIME THEY SHOP (%) |
| Supermarket | 58 | 84 |
| Credit cards | 29 | 68 |
| Drugstore | 27 | 79 |
| Entertainment | 24 | 81 |
| Travel | 23 | 68 |
| Bookstore | 20 | 73 |
| Restaurant | 19 | 62 |
| Greeting card store | 16 | 68 |

Source: John Fetto. "The Loyal Treatment," *American Demographics* (July/August 2003). 16. Reprinted with permission from July/August 2003 issue of *American Demographics*. Copyright Crain Communications. Inc., 2003.

One of the most popular loyalty programs today is the airline industry's frequent-flyer program, in which passengers earn credits toward future flights. More than 32 million Americans have frequent-flyer accounts.[89] Free airline mileage is so enticing to consumers that it's featured in the loyalty programs of many different products, including hotels (e.g., Travelodge Hotels), rental cars, credit cards, and florists. The most successful loyalty card in the world, by almost any measure, is AirMiles in Canada, an example of an *omnibus* card, which encourages consumers to select one retailer over its competitors in a wide variety of retail sectors. More than 50 percent of the households in Canada participate regularly in the AirMiles program.

Loyalty programs are offered by a variety of businesses. Table 8.7 identifies American adults' participation and usage rates for loyalty programs in various industries. The popularity of loyalty programs has led at least one person to suggest the following consumer mantra: "If you reward them, they will come."[90] But unlike other approaches for motivating consumers, loyalty programs have the distinct advantage of providing useful information to marketers. The tracking of consumers' purchasing behavior needed for implementing these programs provides the data needed for estimating their lifetime value (the CLV concept introduced in Chapter 2). Tracking can also help identify customer segments that can be targeted with special offers or perks more likely to be of value to them.[91]

Loyalty programs are becoming an important element in the marketing mix for Internet businesses. "You can expect that more and more businesses are going to be introducing loyalty programs of all sorts," says Irving Wladawsky-Berger, general manager of IBM's Internet division. "Over the Internet there is going to be a major push for businesses to differentiate themselves with loyalty programs."[92] And consumers are all for this. In a survey of online consumers, more than half said that they're more likely to buy from an e-commerce site if it offers a loyalty program.[93]

Loyalty programs can be highly effective when implemented well.[94] The Passport program of Chico's, described in Chapter 2 (see Consumer Behavior and Marketing 2.2), accounts for 93 percent of total sales at Chico's and is an important tool in converting its customers into fans. Department stores are in various states of decline, but a notable exception is Neiman-Marcus, and part of its success is attributed to InCircle Rewards®, which has been "simply rewarding for twenty years." If you visit the Neiman-Marcus website (www.neimanmarcus.com), you'll see that, in addition to invitations to special events for its best customers, Neiman-Marcus provides rewards ranging from perfume, Neiman-Marcus gift cards, and resort accommodations for 5,000 points (reflecting $5,000 of purchases) to a private NetJet tour taking customers to lunch and shopping sprees in Neiman-Marcus cities around the nation for 5,000,000 points (yes, for customers who have spent $5,000,000 at Neiman-Marcus).

### Enhancing Perceived Risk

Another way of motivating consumers is to enhance the perceived risk of product purchase and consumption. Perceived risk represents consumers' apprehensions about the consequences of their behavior.[95] Consumers may have reservations about whether a product will live up to their expectations. They will be concerned when they think that purchase and consumption bring negative consequences. Ultimately, perceived risk depends on consumers' beliefs about the consequences of buying and consuming the product, whether the consequences are good or bad, and the consequences' importance to the consumer. If a consumer is leery that an expensive vacation that offers a supposedly unique consumption experience will turn out to be another ordinary but overpriced experience, perceived risk will be greater. The overwhelming medical evidence about the health risks of smoking has certainly increased the perceived risk of this consumption activity.

As you learned in Chapter 4, perceived risk influences consumer search. Greater risk causes more search, because of its influence on consumer motivation. Usually, consumers are motivated to not put themselves at risk, especially when the outcomes are important. One way consumers try to reduce risk is by acquiring more information about the purchase decision. In essence, perceived risk affects the need for information. Depending on what is learned during search, consumers' choices may turn out differently than if less extensive search had been undertaken. Moreover, greater perceived risk may cause consumers to become more risk averse when choosing products.

Educating consumers about their risks may motivate them to make more informed choices that reduce their exposure to risk. According to the headline of one car ad, "Most accidents happen in the showroom." The ad went on to describe the negative consequences (e.g., spending too much for too little) that consumers might experience for doing a less than thorough search. Presumably, the ad tries to motivate consumers to undertake greater external search as a way of increasing the chances of the advertised carmaker being considered during decision making.

Similarly, the ad in Figure 8.14 emphasizes the deadly risk posed by heart disease to women by informing the reader that heart disease claims the lives of one out of every two women. The ad goes on to say how the advertised product, specifically designed for women, can reduce their risk. Those women to whom this ad would be personally relevant (e.g., those with a history of heart attacks or those with risk factors, such as high cholesterol, high blood pressure, diabetes, and family history) should be especially motivated to respond. Those consumers who accept the ad's claims as

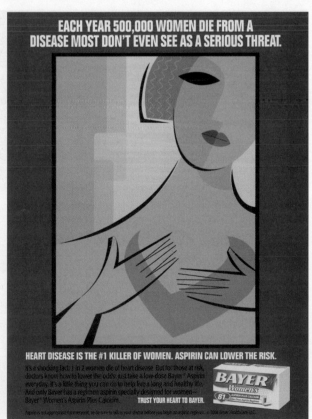

**FIGURE 8.14** Informing Consumers of Their Risks May Motivate Them to Take Action

true will become motivated to purchase and consume those products that enable them to minimize their risks. More skeptical consumers may decide that additional information is needed and undertake external search, perhaps by talking to their doctor. Depending on what is learned, the consumers will then decide what to do.

Beyond educating consumers about risks, companies may be able to shape consumers' risk perceptions simply by changing the temporal frames used when conveying risk information. Rather than only reporting the number of heart attacks that occur each year, for example, this information could be broken down to the number of heart attacks that occur each day. Temporal framing of risk information on a daily basis increases perceived risk relative to temporal framing on a yearly basis.[96] You'll learn more about the use of framing for influencing consumers' opinions in Chapter 15.

### Arousing Consumers' Curiosity

People, like cats, are curious creatures. Our curiosity often motivates us to learn more about what has aroused our interest. For new products (e.g., electrical cars, digital cameras, and web TVs), which need to educate potential customers about the product's benefits and attributes, motivating consumers to acquire and learn product information is critical. Arousing consumers' curiosity may activate their need for information. One way of doing this is by advertising a benefit that is not normally associated with the product (such as a camera that allows the user to delete part of the picture).[97]

Companies sometimes try to arouse consumers' curiosity when introducing new products into the marketplace. When Anheuser-Busch was test marketing its new Bud Select, it used billboards to tell consumers to be on the lookout for a new beer that would soon be coming to their area.[98] Similarly, one automobile manufacturer tweaked consumers' curiosity when the company was preparing to roll out its new product. Prior to the new car's arrival at car dealerships, consumers were exposed to advertisements such as the one in Figure 8.15, in which the car's identity was hidden. Accompanying this ad was a postcard that told consumers, "You give us your name, we'll give you ours." This approach, of course, allowed the company to collect vital information about potential car buyers. The so-called "mystery car" turned out to be the Chrysler 300, recipient of Motor Trend's 2005 Car of the Year, the most recognized and coveted award in the automotive industry.

One day a salesperson in Chrysler's Los Angeles office received the following voicemail: "Yo, what up? This is big Snoop Dogg, trying to put these new legs down for this new 300C. What I gotta' do to get that brand new 300 up outta you? Get back in contact with my nephew so you can make it happen, then it's official like a referee's whistle. If you want this car to blow, give it to me. This is Snoop Dogg. Preach!" So did Snoop snag a free set of wheels? He did. In return, he included the car in one of his music videos.[99] (Wait a minute! Snoop just gave me an idea. Look at all the free advertising Chrysler is getting here. Excuse me, I have a call to make.)

TheMysteryCar.com

FIGURE 8.15 This Car Company Aroused Consumers' Curiosity during the Market Introduction of Its New Product

## Summary

One of the most fundamental questions about consumer behavior is, "Why do people buy?" The answer to this question is found in an understanding of consumer motivation. Consumers are motivated to purchase and consume products to satisfy their needs. As you have seen in this chapter, consumers have a variety of needs. Some (e.g., physiological, safety, and health) are fundamental to our survival. Others (e.g., financial security, pleasure, and giving to others) may be less essential for existing but are still critical to the consumer's sense of well-being. Those companies that better understand consumers' needs stand a greater chance of attracting and retaining customers.

Sometimes, consumers' purchase motivation is driven by a single need. Other times, motivation is more complex and fueled by multiple needs. Satisfying certain needs may come at the expense of others, thus leading to motivational conflict. In deciding which needs take precedence, consumers must prioritize them based on a need's importance at that particular moment in time.

Although essential, understanding consumer motivation is not easy. When asked why they buy, consumers may distort their answers. In the case of unconscious motivation, consumers themselves are not fully aware of why they behave the way they do. And because motivation can change over time, companies should continually monitor the reasons why people buy and consume.

Companies can enhance consumers' motivation to fill their needs through product purchase and consumption in several ways. Price reductions and other types of incentives (e.g., a loyalty program) are important motivators for many. Messages that enhance perceived risk or arouse curiosity also hold the potential for motivating consumers.

## Review and Discussion Questions

1. Why is it important for companies to understand consumer motivation?

2. Beyond understanding consumer motivation, what else does a company need to know to fully appreciate the reasons that consumers buy specific products and brands?

3. A manufacturer of household cleaning products is interested in learning what motivates consumers to buy its products. What needs do you think consumers are trying to satisfy when buying and using these products?

4. Although water is free, many consumers choose to pay. What needs do you think consumers are seeking to satisfy when they purchase bottled water?

5. What is Maslow's hierarchy of needs? How do differences in need priorities influence consumer behavior?

6. What are the potential advantages and disadvantages for a product that fulfills multiple needs?

7. Some suggest that it is important to distinguish between a need and a want. From this perspective, a need is something we must have, whereas a want represents something we desire but can live without. Do you think this is a meaningful distinction? Why or why not?

8. It has been suggested that products represent "symbols for sale." What does this mean to you?

9. A business is perplexed by the unexpected results of its recent advertising campaign and has turned to you for help in understanding what is going on. This new campaign was designed to increase the advertised product's personal relevance to consumers by emphasizing its ability to fill previously underappreciated needs. Yet, the campaign had no noticeable effect on sales of the advertised product. Rather, it appeared to stimulate the sales of a competitor. Why might this have occurred?

## Notes

[1] Harold W. Berkman, Jay D. Lindquist, and M. Joseph Sirgy, *Consumer Behavior* (Chicago: NTC Publishing Group, 1997).

[2] See, for example, Ernest Dichter, *Handbook of Consumer Motivations: The Psychology of Consumption* (New York: McGraw-Hill, 1964); Jeffrey F. Durgee, "Interpreting Dichter's Interpretations: An Analysis of Consumption Symbolism in the *Handbook of Consumer Motivations*," in Hanne Hartvig-Larsen, David Glen Mick, and Christian Alstead, eds., *Marketing and Semiotics: Selected Papers from the Copenhagen Symposium* (Copenhagen, 1991), 52–74; Morris B. Holbrook and Elizabeth C. Hirschman, "The Experiential Aspects of Consumption: Consumer Fantasies, Feelings, and Fun," *Journal of Consumer Research*, 9 (September 1982), 132–140; Abraham H. Maslow, *Motivation and Personality* (New York: Harper & Row, 1970); David C. McClelland, *Personality* (New York: William Sloane, 1941); William J. McGuire, "Psychological Motives and Communication Gratification," in J. G. Blumer and C. Katz, eds., *The Uses of Mass Communications: Current Perspectives on Gratification Research* (New York: Sage, 1974), 167–196; A. H. Murray, *Explorations in Personality* (New

York: Oxford University Press, 1938).

3 Amy Cortese, "The Sleep of Forgetfulness (And The Bed Remembers)," *New York Times* (September 12, 2004), 3, 8; Joyce Gempertein, "Boomers Go Beddy-Buy; Can't Sleep without $4,000 Mattresses and Water-Pocket Pillows," *Washington Post* (September 19, 2004), F1.

4 Michele Chandler, "Viagra: A Drug-Business Boost, But No Cure-All," *Miami Herald's Business Monday* (July 13, 1998), 7.

5 Bruce Japsen, "Hey, Guys, So You Don't Need Help in Bedroom?" *Knight Ridder Tribune Business News* (January 23, 2005), 1. Also see Christopher Snowbeck, "Despite TV Ad Blitz, Sales of Erectile Drugs Lack Vigor," *Knight Ridder Tribune Business News* (January 23, 2005), 1.

6 James Zoltak, "Poll: Safety a Main Concern in Travel Plans," *Amusement Business* (March 22, 2004), 7.

7 Ross Fadner, "Phishing Attacks Skyrocket in October," www.mediapost.com (November 22, 2004).

8 "Tough But Sensitive," *American Demographics* (March 1999), 56.

9 Ed Blazina, "GM Hoping That Safety Sells," *Knight Ridder Tribune Business News* (February 6, 2005), 1.

10 David Perry, "Volvo's Safety Mission," *Furniture Today* (January 24, 2005), 38.

11 Ibid.

12 Karen Matthews, "Ad Campaign Selling the Need for SUV Safety; Young Males Are Primary Targets," www.marketingpower.com (February 1, 2005).

13 Cambridge Consumer Credit Index, www.cambridgeconsumerindex.com (January 28, 2005).

14 Erika Niedowski, "Red Meat Newly Linked to Colorectal Cancer," www.sunsentinel.com (January 12, 2005).

15 Anthony Faiola, "Japanese Are Old Hands at Fitness," *Miami Herald* (October 28, 2004), A24.

16 "U.S. Prescription Drug Sales Increase 8.3 Percent in 2004," *Los Angeles Times* (February 15, 2005), C5; "Leading 10 Corporations by U.S. Sales,

2000," Press Room, IMS Health, Inc., www.imshealth.com.

17 Susan Chandler, "Air Concerns Breathe Life Into Purifier Sales," www.seattletimes.com (November 26, 2004).

18 Chad Terhune, "Tropicana to Squeeze Sugar Out of Orange Juice," *Jacksonville Times Union* (November 29, 2003), D8.

19 All the information in this paragraph comes from "Restaurants Scramble for a More Nutritional Menu," www.wusa9news.com (June 30, 2004).

20 For a classic article on the symbolic meaning of products, see Sidney J. Levy, "Symbols for Sale," *Harvard Business Review* (July/August 1959), 117–124. For an interesting history of the motivation research era, see Sidney J. Levy's comments in *ACR Newsletter* (March 1991), 3–6.

21 "Pet Popularity Race Has New No. 2," *Parade Magazine* (January 4, 1998), 16.

22 *Life Insurance: Consumer Attitudes and Ownership*, MetLife (August 2002), www.metlife.com/WPSAssets/1315895 3111079722286V1FFinal%20 ExecSummary%20%20Post%20911% 20.pdf

23 Ibid.

24 Ibid.

25 "New MetLife Survey Finds Consumers Are Highly Concerned about Need for Life Insurance, Yet Most Remain Underinsured," Press Release, MetLife (September 21, 2004), www.metlife.com.

26 Melanie Gilder, "Jewelers Get Ready for Big Sales Weekend," *Knight-Ridder Tribune Business News* (February 11, 2005), 1.

27 Mary Connelly, "Dodge Will Vary Charger Advertising Messages," *Automotive News* (January 31, 2005), F56.

28 Juliet Chung, "For Some Beta Testers, It's about Buzz, Not Bugs," *New York Times* (July 22, 2004), G1.

29 Kate MacArthur, "UK Not Feeling the Love; McD's Puts Slogan on Ice," *Advertising Age* (October 25, 2004), 45.

30 "Tattooed Emotions," *Marketing News* (February 1, 2004), 3.

31 "More Than 7 Million Americans Partici-

pate in Online Fantasy Sports, According to comScore Media Metrix," www.comscore.com (July 19, 2004).

32 Angus McCrone, "How Poker Web Sites Hold a Winning Hand," *Evening Standard* (February 18, 2005), 1.

33 Jonathan Krim, "Poker's Popularity Proves a Hot Hand for Gaming Industry," *Washington Post* (September 6, 2004), A1.

34 Ibid.

35 Leslie Miller, "Survey: Homes Have More Cars and Drivers," *Miami Herald* (August 30, 2003), A23.

36 June Fletcher, "Latest Sign of Status: Big Garage," *Miami Herald* (March 14, 1999), H1, H8; personal communication with Elyass Gawhary of the American Moving and Storage Association, January 24, 2005.

37 Brigid Schulte, "Big: It's Bigger Than Ever," *Miami Herald* (December 10, 1997), D1, D2.

38 Ibid.

39 "The People Column," *Miami Herald* (February 9, 1999), A2.

40 Rafael Lorente, "Coin Collecting Gets Some Added Oomph," *Sun-Sentinel* (January 9, 2000), A1, A15.

41 Russell W. Belk, "Possessions and the Extended Self," *Journal of Consumer Research*, 15 (September 1988), 139–168. Also see Joel B. Cohen, "An Over-Extended Self?" *Journal of Consumer Research*, 16 (June 1989), 125–128; Russell W. Belk, "Extended Self and Extending Paradigmatic Perspective," *Journal of Consumer Research*, 16 (June 1989), 129–132.

42 For additional information about the self-concept, see M. Joseph Sirgy, "Self-Concept in Consumer Behavior: A Critical Review," *Journal of Consumer Research*, 9 (December 1982), 287–300; M. Joseph Sirgy, "Using Self-Congruity and Ideal Congruity to Predict Purchase Motivation," *Journal of Business Research*, 13 (1985), 195–206.

43 Dennis W. Rook, "The Buying Impulse," *Journal of Consumer Research*, 14 (September 1987), 189–199.

44 David Glenn Mick and Michelle DeMoss,

"Self-Gifts: Phenomenological Insights from Four Contexts," *Journal of Consumer Research*, 17 (December 1990), 322–332.

45 Sandra Yin, "Give and Take," *American Demographics*, 25 (November 2003), 12.

46 Ross Fadner, "Analyst: Users Turn to Web for Information, Not Entertainment," www.mediapost.com (September 24, 2004).

47 Leigh McAlister, "A Dynamic Attribute Satiation Model of Variety Seeking Behavior," *Journal of Consumer Research*, 12 (September 1982), 141–150.

48 Barbara E. Kahn and Brian Wansink, "The Influence of Assortment Structure on Perceived Variety and Consumption Quantities," *Journal of Consumer Research*, 30 (March 2004), 519–533.

49 "Japan's New Fad: Mobile Phones that Ring Musically," *Miami Herald (*March 15, 1999), A16.

50 Todd Richissin, "'Vive le Big Mac!' French Gourmets Say," *Miami Herald* (April 1, 2004), A18.

51 Paul Simao, "Coke, Rivals Betting on Flavored Water," www.washingtonpost.com (December 12, 2004).

52 Steve Jones, "Packages Lose out As Tourists Seek Variety," *Travel Weekly* (December 11, 2004), 29.

53 Shankar Vedantam, "Warnings about Medications' Risks Add Worry to Pain," www.washingtonpost.com (December 23, 2004).

54 Marc Kaufman, "Arthritis Drug Study in 2000 Found Risks," *Washington Post* (February 1, 2005), A10; Marc Kaufman, "New Study Criticizes Painkiller Marketing; Arthritis Drug Ads a Factor in Overuse," *Washington Post* (January 25, 2005), A1; "Pfizer's Bid to Save Celebrex May Get Boost From Data," www.business.bostonherald.com (December 21, 2004); "Pfizer Pulling Advertising for Celebrex," www.business.bostonherald.com (December 20, 2004).

55 "Status Unconscious," *American Demographics* (March 1999), 28.

56 Maslow, *Motivation and Personality.*

57 Richard L. Celsi and Jerry C. Olson, "The Role of Involvement in Attention and Comprehension Processes," *Journal of Consumer Research*, 15 (September 1988), 210–224.

58 Peter H. Bloch, Daniel L. Sherrell, and Nancy M. Ridgway, "Consumer Search: An Extended Framework," *Journal of Consumer Research*, 13 (June 1986), 119–126; Judith Lynne Zaichkowsky, "Measuring the Involvement Construct," *Journal of Consumer Research*, 12 (December 1985), 341–352.

59 Martha Rogers, "Nintendo Plays for Keeps," www.1to1.com (October 14, 2004).

60 Nancy Klingener, "Treasure Hunter Passes into Legend," *Miami Herald* (December 21, 1998), A1, A18.

61 Cambridge Consumer Credit Index, www.cambridgeconsumerindex.com (January 28, 2005).

62 Rebecca Piirto, "Beyond Mind Games," *American Demographics* (December 1991), 52–57.

63 Ibid. For those interested in learning more about Dichter's thinking, see Ernest Dichter, *Handbook of Consumer Motivations.*

64 Dichter, *Handbook of Consumer Motivations.*

65 Tara Parker-Pope, "Dial Soap Aims at Soothing Fear of Germs," *Wall Street Journal* (January 20, 1998), B7.

66 Rob Walker, "Unstained Masses," *New York Times Magazine* (May 2, 2004), 40.

67 "Women Say *Sayonara* to Valentine Chocolates," *Miami Herald (*February 13, 1999), A20.

68 For a very interesting discussion of the history of promotions, see David Vaczek and Richard Sale, "100 Years of Promotion," *PROMO Magazine* (August 1998), 32–41, 142–145.

69 Tom Belden, "It's More Than Fare: Airlines Yield Key Data," *Miami Herald's Business Monday* (July 14, 1997), 12.

70 Kelly K. Spors, "Shoppers Get Web Rebates," *Wall Street Journal* (November 14, 2004), F5.

71 Vaczek and Sale, "100 Years of Promotion."

72 Margaret Webb Pressler, "Use of Coupons Cuts Both Ways," www.washingtonpost.com (September 12, 2004).

73 *Insights*, NPD Research, Inc., 1979–1982.

74 Katherine Zoe Andrews, "Do Marketing Policies Change Consumer Behavior in the Long Run?" *Insights from MSI* (Winter/Spring 1997), 1–2.

75 Joseph B. White and Lee Hawkins Jr., "GM's Sales Drop As Discounts Fade; Decline of 16.7 Percent Leads Automaker to Cut Output; Ford Reports 7.4 Percent Decrease," *Wall Street Journal* (December 2, 2004), A3.

76 Warren Brown, "Rebates Please Consumers but Squeeze Suppliers," www.washingtonpost.com (December 12, 2004).

77 Priya Raghubir and Kim P. Corfman, "When Do Price Promotions Affect Brand Evaluations?" *Journal of Marketing Research*, 36 (May 1999), 211–222. Note, however, that the adverse effect of coupons on brand evaluations may not always be present. Raghubir and Corfman's research shows that the effect disappears when price promotions are offered by multiple firms. For more recent research, see Priya Raghubir, "Coupons in Context: Discounting Prices or Decreasing Profits? *Journal of Retailing*, 80 (2004), 1–12.

78 Mike Phillips, "NBA Learning Art of Self-Promotion," *Miami Herald (*February 5, 1999), D4.

79 "McDonald's Runs Low on Teenie Beanie Toys," *Miami Herald* (April 16, 1997), B11.

80 Jane J. Kim, "Beyond the Toaster: Banks Step up Freebies; Flat-Screen TVs, Even Cars Are Latest Perks as Industry Focuses on Consumer Accounts," *Wall Street Journal* (October 14, 2004), D1.

81 Itamar Simonson, Ziv Carmon, and Suzanne O'Curry, "Experimental Evidence on the Negative Effect of Product Features and Sales Promotions on Brand Choice," *Marketing Science* 13 (Winter 1994), 23–40.

82 Priya Raghubir, "Free Gift with Purchase: Promoting or Discounting the Brand?" *Journal of Consumer Psychology*, 14 (2004), 181–186.

[83] Jess McCuan, "Auto Companies Head Online in Search of Sales Leads," *Wall Street Journal* (July 6, 1999), A20.

[84] Jean Halliday, "Super Bowl to Ground Control: Win a Ride into Space with Volvo," www.adage.com (February 3, 2005).

[85] Michelle Chandler, "More Than Just Dumb Bells," *Miami Herald's Business Monday* (April 20, 1998), 18–20.

[86] "So Who Needs Leagues? AMF Wants You and Your Family," *New York Times* (August 8, 2002), C4.

[87] For research on loyalty programs, see Joseph A. Bellizzi and Terry Bristol, "An Assessment of Supermarket Loyalty Cards in One Major U.S. Market," *Journal of Consumer Marketing,* 21 (2004), 144–154; Ran Kivetz and Itamar Simonson, "Earning the Right to Indulge: Effort as a Determinant of Customer Preferences toward Frequency Program Rewards," *Journal of Marketing Research,* 39 (May 2002), 155–170; Mark D. Uncles, Grahame R. Dowling, and Kathy Hammond, "Customer Loyalty and Customer Loyalty Programs," *Journal of Consumer Marketing,* 20 (2003), 294–316; Brian Wansink, "Developing a Cost-Effective Brand Loyalty Program," *Journal of Advertising Research* (September 2003), 301–309.

[88] Vaczek and Sale, "100 Years of Promotion."

[89] Dorothy Dowling, "Frequent Perks Keep Travelers Loyal," *American Demographics* (September 1998), 32–36.

[90] John Fetto, "The Loyal Treatment," *American Demographics* (July/August 2003), 16.

[91] C. B. Bhattacharya, "When Customers Are Members: Customer Retention in Paid Membership Contexts," *Journal of the Academy of Marketing Science,* 26 (Winter 1998), 31–44.

[92] David Poppe, "How Do Internet Retailers Foster Customer Loyalty?" *Miami Herald's Business Monday* (February 8, 1999), 13.

[93] Jennifer Lach, "Carrots in Cyberspace," *American Demographics* (May 1999), 43–45.

[94] Michael Lewis, "The Influence of Loyalty Programs and Short-Term Promotions on Customer Retention," *Journal of Marketing Research,* 41 (August 2004), 281–293.

[95] James R. Bettman, "Perceived Risk and Its Components: A Model and Empirical Test," *Journal of Marketing Research,* 10 (May 1973), 184–190; Raymond A. Bauer, "Consumer Behavior as Risk Taking," in Robert S. Hancock, ed., *Dynamic Marketing for a Changing World* (Chicago: American Marketing Association, 1960), 389–398; Grahame R. Dowling, "Perceived Risk: The Concept and Its Measurement," *Psychology and Marketing,* 3 (Fall 1986), 193–210; Lawrence X. Tarpey and J. Paul Peter, "A Comparative Analysis of Three Consumer Decision Strategies," *Journal of Consumer Research,* 2 (June 1975), 29–37.

[96] Sucharita Chandran and Geeta Menon, "When a Day Means More Than a Year: Effects of Temporal Framing on Judgments of Health Risk," *Journal of Consumer Research,* 31 (September 2004), 375–389.

[97] Katherine Zoe Andrews, "The Power of Curiosity: Motivating Consumers to Learn," *Insights from MSI* (Summer 1999), 1, 6.

[98] Gregory Cancelada, "Anheuser-Busch Puts More Hops on Its Budweiser Fastball," *Knight Ridder Tribune Business News* (January 26, 2005), 1.

[99] Stephen Power and Neil E. Boudette, "Auto Reverse: Slide in Mercedes's Performance Dents Chrysler's Recent Revival; DaimlerChrysler Fixes a Unit, While Another Stumbles; Fuel for Merger Critics; Snoop Dogg Gets a 300C," *Wall Street Journal* (February 9, 2005), A1.

# Chapter 9

# Consumer Knowledge

## Opening Vignette

If it looks like a duck and quacks like a duck, then maybe it should shut up for a while. Aflac, the insurance company that rose to pop-cultural heights on the wings of a waterfowl, is launching a $50 million advertising campaign that partly muzzles its web-footed friend and instead seeks to better define what the company does. The move is a risky one, given the iconic status the feathered creature has reached since being introduced in January 2000.

Known for its loud "AFLAC" quack, the duck has become one of the country's most recognizable ad icons. Before the duck's first appearance, most people had never heard of the Columbus, Georgia, purveyor of supplemental workplace insurance. Since that time, however, Aflac brand awareness has skyrocketed from 12 percent to 90 percent, says the company. But name recognition alone isn't enough. "Consumers were saying, 'I know you are insurance and you have this duck that quacks, but what can you do for me?'" says Al Johnson, Aflac's vice president of advertising and branding.

Aflac says it was prompted to redo its advertising after increases in sales began to slow down and consumer research found that people were confused about the company. Survey research revealed that 60 percent of the respondents weren't exactly sure what Aflac insurance was. Other research found that about half of the respondents said that the current advertising doesn't explain what Aflac is. Hence, the change.

In one new commercial, dubbed "Pet Store," comedian Gilbert Gottfried, the voice of the Aflac duck, tries to return the duck to a pet store. "He just says the same thing over and over," complains Mr. Gottfried, who becomes frustrated when the duck fails to quack. A parrot weighs in with the Aflac name and what the company does. In a surprising twist, this commercial represents one of the few times the duck doesn't reveal the company name. Aflac hopes to tone down the duck's call, but the company says the familiar squawk might return. "You don't want to annoy consumers," adds Mr. Johnson. "The duck is evolving."

Source: Excerpted in part from Suzanne Vranica, "Aflac Partly Muzzles Iconic Duck; Ensurer Begins Campaign of $50 Million to Improve Understanding of Business," *Wall Street Journal* (December 2, 2004), B8.

The opening vignette captures several key concepts covered in this chapter. The first is brand awareness. The initial Aflac advertising campaign was extremely successful in creating awareness of the company's existence in the marketplace. Yet it fell short in creating sufficient knowledge about the product offering, a shortcoming that the new campaign intends to overcome. Product knowledge is another key concept that you will learn about in the following pages.

This chapter focuses on **consumer knowledge,** which can be defined as the *information stored in memory that's relevant to the purchase, consumption, and disposal of goods and services.* For example, what does the SPF number found on sunscreens represent? What differences are there between Rolex and Timex watches? "We must protect this house!" is the slogan for which product? Should young children drink large quantities of juices? Should diabetics minimize consumption of foods that contain salt or sugar? What product category contains a brand named Topol? What comes to mind when you think about Volvo automobiles?

Although these questions cover a broad range of topics, each question taps into your consumer knowledge. SPF stands for "sun protection factor," and the number represents the product's strength in protecting skin from the harmful rays of the sun. Rolex and Timex watches differ in their prices, quality, and the prestige of product ownership. The slogan comes from Under Armour sports apparel. Drinking twelve ounces or more of juice each day may cause children to be shorter and fatter.[1] Diabetics should avoid foods that contain sugar. Topol is a brand of toothpaste. And only you can answer the question concerning Volvo automobiles.

How important is consumer knowledge? How does it influence consumer behavior? The answers to these questions can be found in the following section.

## The Importance of Consumer Knowledge

What we know or don't know strongly influences our decision-making processes. You've already seen some examples of this in Chapter 4 in which we considered how knowledge impacts internal (see Figure 4.8) and external (see Figure 4.13) information search. But there's much more. Consider two individuals preparing to buy a used car. One person, an experienced buyer, is very knowledgeable about automobiles. The other is an inexperienced, first-time buyer with very limited product knowledge. These knowledge differences may lead each buyer down a different path. The knowledgeable individual feels confident in his ability to reasonably assess the strengths and weaknesses of the used cars he examines during search. The less knowledgeable individual does not. Given this inability to evaluate the product, the less knowledgeable individual may elicit the aid of a "purchase pal," someone seen as being better equipped for evaluating the choice alternatives and willing to provide the necessary assistance.

Beyond affecting how a decision is made, consumer knowledge may also determine the final decision itself.[2] Those used cars available for purchase but unknown to the buyer cannot be chosen. Or a telltale sign of engine problems, though undetected by a novice, may cause an expert to eliminate the car from further consideration. Knowledgeable consumers are more capable of evaluating a product's true merits. They have a better understanding of what attributes to look at and how to evaluate the product on these attributes.[3] These abilities give knowledgeable consumers a greater chance of making better choices than their less knowledgeable counterparts.

To further illustrate the impact of consumer knowledge, let's consider how it impacts the intended consumption of a particular food, soy. A random sample of American consumers responded to a survey assessing their knowledge about soy.[4] Their responses were used to classify the consumers into one of four groups: (1) those whose knowledge was limited to soy's attributes, (2) those whose knowledge was limited to the consequences or benefits of consuming soy, (3) those possessing both types of knowledge, and (4) those lacking either type of knowledge. Each group's intention to consume a soy-related product within the next three weeks was then compared. The results of this comparison, shown in Figure 9.1, clearly show that greater product knowledge can facilitate product demand.

**FIGURE 9.1**     Consumers' Soy Knowledge Determines
Their Soy Consumption Intentions

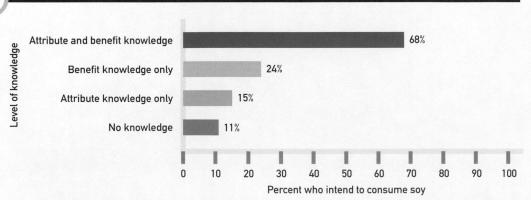

Source: Brian Wansink, Randall E. Westgren, and Matthew M. Cheney, "The Hierarchy of Nutritional Knowledge that Relates to the Consumption of a Functional Food," *Nutrition* (2005), in press.

Source: A. Belen del Rio, Rodolfo Vacquez, and Victor Iglesias, "The Effects of Brand Associations on Consumer Response." *Journal of Consumer Marketing.* 18 (2001), 410–425.

The influence of consumer knowledge extends beyond product choice and consumption. To see how, let's turn our attention to a study about sports shoes that examined the relationships between specific brand associations and various types of consumer responses.[5] **Brand associations** are *the linkages in memory between the brand and other concepts.* These linkages, representing what consumers know (or at least what they think they know), are typically referred to as beliefs or perceptions. Brand associations include the beliefs about a brand's attributes and its consumption benefits, beliefs that were examined in the aforementioned soy study. We will further explore brand associations later in the chapter, when we delve more deeply into the concept of product image. But for now, let's turn to the study about sports shoes.

The study, conducted in Spain, measured various brand associations for sports shoes. Of particular interest here are two of these associations: perceptions about the brand's quality and perceptions about the brand as a social status symbol. The study also measured various consumer responses, such as the willingness to (1) purchase brand extensions (i.e., products carrying the same brand name as the sports shoes but in different product categories), (2) recommend the brand to others, and (3) pay a higher price for the brand. The relationship between these responses and brand associations was then tested. Figure 9.2 shows those relationships found to be significant. On the one hand, a brand's quality associations were positively related to each of the responses, indicating that higher quality enhances consumers' acceptance of brand extensions, willingness to recommend the brand, and willingness to pay a price premium. On the other hand, a brand's status associations only facilitate the likelihood of consumers buying brand extensions, thus indicating that different associations are likely to vary in their influence on consumer behavior.[6]

Consumer knowledge is important in many other ways. It can shape the inferences consumers make about unknown product attributes using known product attributes.[7] Consumers' acceptance of a product's price will depend on their knowledge about competitors' prices.[8] Consumer knowledge affects the learning and subsequent retrieval (we'll talk more about retrieval later on in Chapter 16) of new information.[9] Consumer knowledge can influence how consumers respond to salespeople, something we'll touch on later in the chapter. It often necessitates different strategies for persuading those who are more versus less knowledgeable, another issue covered later in the chapter. The list goes on and on.

You should now possess a better sense of why we've devoted an entire chapter to this topic. Consumer knowledge is a powerful individual difference variable that affects consumer behavior in so many ways. Now it's time to expand your knowledge about this subject in another direction—the many types of consumer knowledge.

## Types of Consumer Knowledge

Consumer knowledge is a very broad term that collectively refers to many different types of knowledge. In the following sections, we discuss five main types of consumer knowledge: (1) product knowledge, (2) purchase knowledge, (3) consumption or usage knowledge, (4) persuasion knowledge, and (5) self-knowledge.

### Product Knowledge

**Product knowledge** represents *the information stored in consumers' memory about products.* In discussing this type of knowledge, we distinguish between consumers' knowledge about a product category versus their knowledge about members (i.e., brands) of this category.

#### PRODUCT CATEGORY KNOWLEDGE

Although consumers buy brands, not product categories, product category knowledge is the prerequisite starting point for developing demand in the marketplace. Take, for example, casket stores. Consumers have traditionally purchased caskets from funeral homes. Stores specializing in caskets have recently emerged to compete with the funeral homes. Creating knowledge about this new category is essential. "Business is going well and the more people that learn about casket stores, the better business will be," says one store owner.[10] A similar sentiment is voiced by Sonja Tuitele, a spokeswoman for Wild Oats, a natural-foods store chain: "When people ask us who's your competition, we always say its lack of awareness."[11]

To illustrate the concept of product category knowledge, we want to ask you a few questions. What is a television set? Easy question, right? Unless you're a member of a nomadic tribe that wanders along the Amazon River shunning modern civilization, you know what a TV is. Next question: What is the difference between analog and digital TV? A little more challenging question? It's the difference between the traditional, fat TV sets and the new, flat TV sets that have stormed the market the past few years.[12] Okay. It's time to take the gloves off. Try these questions on for size: What are the two basic types of flat-panel TVs? What's the difference between HDTV and EDTV? What is "burn-in"? An HD format of 720p means what? What is a DLP microchip?

So how'd you do in answering these last few questions? Let's see. The two basic types of flat-panel TVs are plasma and LCD (which stands for liquid-crystal display). HDTV stands for high-definition TV and is a subcategory of digital TV. EDTV (enhanced-definition TV) is another subcategory of digital TV. EDTV offers fewer lines of resolution than HDTV, meaning the picture is not as sharp or detailed. Burn-in is the problem that currently plagues plasma TVs. If a plasma TV stays tuned to the same station for too long, the network logo may begin to etch itself into the screen, leaving a faint ghost image even when you switch to another channel. The 720p format refers to 720 progressively scanned lines of resolution. Progressive indicates that a screen image is replenished sixty times per second. DLP stands for digital light processing. An employee of Texas Instruments invented the DLP microchip, which noticeably improves picture clarity while eliminating the burn-in problem. Texas Instruments is creating product category knowledge by educating consumers about the technology through advertising and a dedicated website (www.dlp.com) in the hopes that, along the lines of Intel's success in computers, consumers will buy TVs with DLP.[13] As Texas Instruments' slogan says, "Be sure your next TV has DLP."

All the knowledge necessary for answering these questions would be contained within a mental category we could call "television sets." Depending on the consumer's degree of knowledge, this category may be very simple in its content and structure. For some, the category may contain little more than information about what the product is and its most basic features or attributes. For others, the category may be extremely rich with information, containing multiple subcategories (e.g., LCD versus plasma TVs) within a complex memory structure. The terms product novice and expert are often used to refer to such knowledge differences. **Product novices** *possess very simple levels of product category knowledge.* **Product experts** *possess vast amounts of product category knowledge.* Product experts' extensive knowledge also includes what they know about particular members of a category, called brands. Let's now turn our attention to brand knowledge.

## BRAND KNOWLEDGE

Whereas product category knowledge involves what consumers know about a general product category such as televisions, brand knowledge focuses on what consumers know about a specific brand within the product category (e.g., the Sony brand in the product category of televisions). The most fundamental aspect of brand knowledge involves whether or not consumers are aware of the brand's existence. In our discussion of consumer decision making in Chapter 4, we noted that, before a product can enter the consideration set, the product must gain entrance into the awareness set, which comprises those products known to the consumer. Until a person learns about a product's existence, converting her or him into a customer is impossible.

Obviously, one of the challenges facing new products is creating an awareness of the products' existence in the marketplace. How successful were some of the new products in 2004 in achieving awareness? One answer to this question was provided by an online survey of one thousand consumers conducted in December 2004.[14] These consumers reported whether they were aware of each of the new products listed in Table 9.1. As you can see, these products differed substantially in how successful they were in achieving consumer awareness of their existence.[15]

Absolut Raspberri liquor does not appear in Table 9.1, but it is a new product that created awareness (unlike any of the company's previous products) on American television (see Figure 9.3 and Market Facts 9.1 to learn more about Absolut). Although the four major broadcast networks (ABC, CBS, Fox, and NBC) continue to refuse to accept liquor advertising, numerous cable networks and local TV stations are willing to do so. In the fall of 2004, Absolut Raspberri's commercials ran on BET, E!, FX, Spike TV, VH-1, and USA. The commercials feature various street artists working their magic as they transform an ordinary Absolut bottle into a work of art. The decision to depart from Absolut's traditional reliance on print advertising and include television is because of TV's ability to "work faster as a medium to get the word out," says Patrick O'Neil, the group creative director for Absolut at TBWA/Chiay/Day, Absolut's advertising agency since 1981.[16] This campaign is supported by a website (Absolut.com) that allows visitors, once they've located the secret passage (it's in the upper left-hand corner of the computer screen), to render their own artistic version of the Absolut Raspberri bottle, which can then be signed and posted on the website. Absolut, in turn, posts one of these new pieces of art every ten seconds, along with the creator's initials and country of origin.[17]

Even established brands and companies often find themselves needing to create awareness. Do you know what TIAA-CREF is? Probably not. It's a $300 billion financial services company. Yet in a recent survey, only 1 percent of respondents recognized

**TABLE 9.1**  Americans' Awareness of New Products in 2004

| NEW PRODUCT | AMERICANS AWARE OF PRODUCT (%) |
|---|---|
| Coca-Cola C2 | 59 |
| Pepsi Edge | 56 |
| Swiffer Sweep + Vac | 55 |
| Gillette's M3Power | 55 |
| Glad Press 'n Seal plastic wrap | 53 |
| Clorox ToiletWand | 53 |
| Hershey's Swoops | 51 |
| Apple iPod mini | 47 |
| Oral-B's Brush Ups | 46 |
| Tide with a Touch of Downy | 46 |
| 7Up Plus | 40 |
| Mustang 2005 | 39 |
| Lysol Ready Brush | 39 |
| Febreze Scentstories | 37 |
| Progresso Rich & Hearty Soups | 35 |

Source: Schneider/Stagnito Communications, "Most Memorable New Product Launch Survey," conducted by InsightExpress (2004). Copyright 2004 InsightExpress LLC.

the TIAA-CREF name.[18] A $300 billion company that sells to consumers and yet only one in a hundred can even recognize its name? And that's not the only problem the company is facing, as you will see in our discussion of companies with image problems later in the chapter.

Established brands that move into new markets will need to create awareness. Saturn is very familiar to American consumers as a supplier of automobiles, but the company was virtually unknown to Japanese consumers when it entered Japan in 1997. Only 1 percent of Japanese surveyed even mentioned Saturn when asked to identify familiar automobile makers.[19] Overcoming this lack of awareness is essential for gaining a toehold in the Japanese automobile market.

Or think about the challenges facing local retailers who attempt to develop their business on the Internet. Even those with excellent reputations founded on years of business in their local market are essentially unknown entities to anyone outside their area. The retailer J&R has been selling to New Yorkers for more than three decades. The company began in 1971 when Joe and Rachelle Friedman (who took the initials of their first names to form the J&R name) opened their first store with their wedding money. From that humble beginning J&R has grown into a mini-empire with its own mail-order catalog business. Yet this success means little to those Internet users unfamiliar with the company. "We were just another site," says Ms. Friedman. "People didn't know who we were, how big we were, and whether we were reputable." One way J&R overcame this problem was to sign up as a merchant at Amazon.com. "The Amazon partnership is a great way for J&R to build brand identity and brand familiarity," says Donna Hoffman, codirector of the Sloan Center for Internet Retailing at Vanderbilt University. "People think 'If it's on Amazon, it must be good.'"[20]

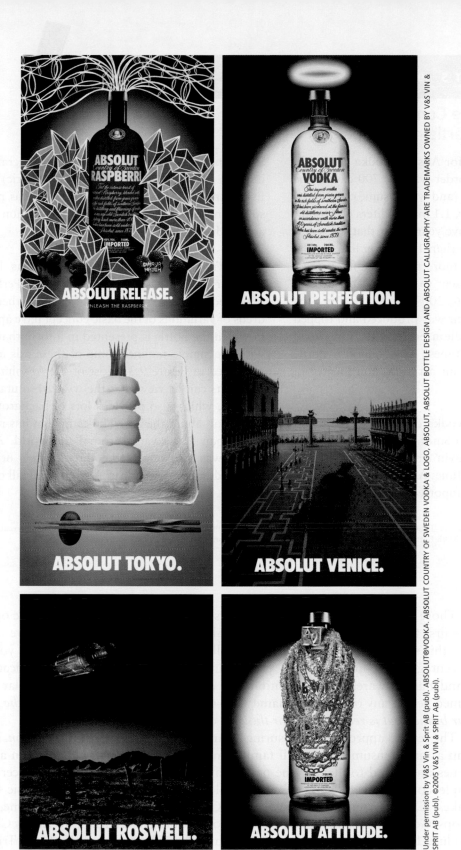

**FIGURE 9.3** Absolut Advertisements: A Classic Advertising Campaign
for More Than Twenty-Five Years

## Absolut Vodka: The Company, the Brand, and a Classic Advertising Campaign

In 1979, the first order for Absolut vodka arrived in the United States. The order was for 700 cases. The very first bottle was sold (and we presume consumed) in Boston. One year later, 1.1 million liters of Absolut were sold in America. Five years after that, the company was shipping more than 10 million liters to the United States. In 2003, more than 72 million liters of Absolut vodka were sent to 126 markets around the globe. On March 16, 2004, at 10:30 a.m., the billionth bottle of Absolut was produced and topped with a gold cap. One billion bottles lined up would circle the Earth—two times! This billionth bottle is now part of the Absolut art collection located in New York.

The origins of Absolut vodka can be traced back to 1879, when Lars Olsson Smith created its predecessor, Absolut Rent Brannvin (translation: Absolutely Pure Vodka). Since that time, Absolut has gone on to become the best-selling imported vodka in the United States and the number three liquor brand overall, trailing only Bacardi rum and Smirnoff (domestic) vodka. Every drop of Absolut is made in the Ahus plant in southern Sweden, where nearly a half-million bottles are produced every day.

Absolut's print advertising campaign has become legendary. The first ad, entitled Absolut Perfection, appeared in 1980 (see Figure 9.3). Since then, hundreds of variations of the basic concept have appeared in which the bottle is presented in a form that ties in with the simple tagline. Some of these ads are also presented in Figure 9.3. Most of the Absolut advertisements can be viewed at the www.absolutads.com website, which also provides lots of background information about the ads. The campaign has received more than 350 awards around the world. Absolut vodka was also one of the three brands originally inducted into the American Advertising Hall of Fame in 1993.

Sources: Stuart Elliott, "Absolut to Try Television Ads," www.nytimes.com (September 3, 2004); "Absolut Vodka Turns 25 Tomorrow," www.absolut.com (April 19, 2004); "The 1,000,000,000th Bottle of Absolut Left Ahus Today," www.absolut.com (March 16, 2004).

Those interested in assessing consumers' brand awareness have two basic options. The first focuses on what consumers are able to *recall* from memory. Before reading past this sentence, stop and write down all the brands of cereal familiar to you. The percentage of people naming a particular brand would provide one indication of brand name awareness. In addition, we could also examine the particular brand named before any other brand name. **Top-of-the-mind awareness** refers to *the particular brand that is remembered or thought of first.*

The second approach to measuring awareness focuses on name *recognition*. Rather than asking consumers to recall familiar names, consumers would be given a list of names and asked to identify the names familiar to them. Continuing the cereal example, consider the following cereals: Apple Jacks, Banana Nut Crunch, Basic 4, Bran Flakes, Cap'n Crunch, Cheerios, Chex, Cocoa Pebbles, Crispix, Fiber One, Froot Loops, Golden Grahams, Grape Nuts, Kellogg's Corn Flakes, Kix, Life, Lucky Charms, Product 19, Raisin Bran, Rice Krispies, Shredded Wheat, Special K, Total, Trix, and Wheaties. It's probably a safe bet that you recognized at least one of these cereals but that you didn't recall it when asked to do so in the preceding paragraph. For this reason, recognition-based estimates typically indicate higher levels of awareness than estimates based on recall. So which indicator of awareness is most appropriate? As we discussed in Chapter 4, choosing the better indicator ultimately depends on whether consumers construct their consideration sets based on recall (such as the consumer

**TABLE 9.2**     *Current and Classic Product Slogans*

How many of these slogans represent a brand association in your memory?

| | |
|---|---|
| 1. | We bring good things to life. |
| 2. | The ultimate driving machine. |
| 3. | Can you hear me now? |
| 4. | Melts in your mouth, not in your hands. |
| 5. | Where you at? |
| 6. | What's in your wallet? |
| 7. | Is it in you? |
| 8. | Like nothing else. |
| 9. | Sometimes you feel like a nut, sometimes you don't. |
| 10. | Be big. Be meaty. Be frank. |
| 11. | The best a man can get. |
| 12. | There are some things money can't buy. For everything else there's . . . |
| 13. | Let your fingers do the walking. |
| 14. | Live the friendly skies. |
| 15. | Whassup?! |
| 16. | Where the rubber meets the road. |
| 17. | Like no vacation on Earth. |
| 18. | How do you wear it? |
| 19. | It takes a lickin', but it keeps on tickin'. |
| 20. | Are you gellin'? |

Note: The identity of the products, companies, and retailers associated with these slogans can be found at the end of the chapter after the Summary.

deciding which fast-food restaurant to patronize and forms the consideration set from memory) or recognition (such as the grocery shopper who develops the consideration set based on products recognized at the point-of-purchase).

Earlier we introduced the concept of brand associations, which represent the linkages between other informational nodes and the node representing the brand in memory. Each brand within the awareness set is likely to have a set of associations. These associations may include not only product attributes and benefits that we discussed previously, but they may include many other aspects as well. Many brands have successfully linked their name with various symbols. McDonald's is the home of the Golden Arches and Ronald McDonald. Goodyear has its blimp, Pillsbury has the Doughboy, and Tony the Tiger thinks that Kellogg's Frosted Flakes are great. Product slogans, such as those appearing in Table 9.2, are another type of brand association. Brand associations come in many shapes and forms, including product endorsers, sponsorships, advertising campaigns, logos, and so on. The concept of **brand image** refers to the *entire array of associations that are activated from memory when consumers think about the brand.*

**Image analysis** involves *examining the current set of brand associations that exist in the marketplace.* The initial step of an image analysis is to identify these associations, usually by asking consumers, "What comes to mind when you think about [brand or product name]?" This approach assumes (some would say that *hopes* is the

## Neuromarketers Scan the Mind to See What They Can Find

Read Montague, a neuroscientist at the Baylor College of Medicine, found some fascinating results when he monitored the brain activity of people drinking soda with an MRI machine. When people were unaware whether they were drinking Pepsi or Coke, Pepsi tended to produce a stronger response in their brain's ventral putamen, a region thought to process feelings of reward. Among those who preferred Pepsi, the ventral putamen was five times more active when drinking Pepsi than that of Coke fans when drinking Coke. But when Montague repeated the test and told the participants which of the taste samples they were drinking was Coke, the brain activity was remarkably different. Now there was activity in the medial prefrontal cortex, an area of the brain that scientists say governs high-level cognitive powers. Apparently, people were meditating in a more sophisticated way on the taste of Coke, allowing memories and other impressions of the drink—in a word, its brand—to shape their preference. In contrast, Pepsi did not achieve the same effect when participants were told which samples were Pepsi. The conclusion: the Coke brand name was much more powerful, at least for these participants, than the Pepsi name; powerful enough to override an objective preference.

Dr. Montague is just one of a growing breed of researchers who are applying the methods of the neurology lab to the questions of the marketing world. Researchers at the Mind of the Market Laboratory at Harvard Business School work as full-fledged "neuromarketers." In the summer of 2003, the BrightHouse Institute for Sciences at Emory University Hospital became the first neuromarketing firm to boast a Fortune 500 consumer-products company as a client. BrightHouse's client list now includes Home Depot, Pepperidge Farm, and Kmart. The institute will scan the brains of a representative sample of its client's prospective customers, assess their reactions to the company's products and advertising, and tweak the corporate image accordingly.

The BrightHouse Institute's techniques are based, in part, on an experiment conducted by Clint Kilts, a professor of psychiatry and behavioral sciences at Emory and the institute's scientific director. Professor Kilts asked test subjects to look at some products and rate how strongly they liked or disliked them. Then, while scanning their brains in a MRI machine, he showed them the products again. When he looked at the images of their brains, he was struck by one particular

more appropriate term) that consumers are willing (i.e., they'll be honest in their answers) and able (i.e., they have the self-knowledge—something we'll talk about later in the chapter—needed for answering this question) to accurately report their brand images. Directly asking consumers to report their brand associations is not, however, the only approach available for understanding brand image. Some advocate examining consumers' brainwave activity. You can learn more about this procedure in Consumer Behavior and Marketing 9.1.

Not all associations are equally linked to a brand. Some associations will be more salient and stronger than others. Disney has created numerous cartoon characters over the years. Yet few of them, if any, rival the association between the company and Mickey Mouse. The second step, then, of an image analysis is to assess the strength of a brand's associations. This step can be achieved in a couple of ways. One way is to simply count how many consumers report a particular association when responding to the question about what comes to mind when they think about the brand. The stronger the association, the more often it will be reported.

Another approach involves asking consumers to indicate the extent to which they perceive the brand as being linked to an association. For example, we could ask consumers to indicate their perceptions of a brand's quality on a scale ranging from "high quality" to "low quality." This is essentially the approach used by the Reputation

result: whenever a subject saw a product he had identified as one he truly loved—something that might prompt him to say, "That's just so *me!*"—his brain would show increased activity in the medial prefrontal cortex. An immediate, intuitive bond between consumer and product is one that every company dreams of making. "If you like Chevy trucks, it's because that has become the larger gestalt of who you self-attribute as," says Professor Kilts. "You're a Chevy guy." With the help of neuromarketers, Professor Kilts claims companies can now know with certainty whether their products are making that special connection.

MRI scanning offers the promise of an unbiased glimpse at a consumer's mind in action. You cannot misrepresent your responses to an MRI machine. Your medial prefrontal cortex will start firing when you see something you adore, even if you claim not to like it. "Let's say I show you *Playboy*," says Professor Kilts, "and you go, 'Oh, no, no, no!' Really? We could tell you actually like it."

MRI scanning may also give insight on how consumers react to products in ways that even they may not be entirely conscious of. Scientists working with DaimlerChrysler scanned the brains of a number of men as they looked at pictures of cars and rated the cars for attractiveness. The scientists found that the most popular vehicles, the Porsche- and Ferrari-style sports cars, triggered activity in a section of the brain called the fusiform face area, which governs facial recognition. "They were reminded of faces when they look at the cars," says Henry Walter, a psychiatrist at the University of Ulm in Germany who ran the study. "The lights of the cars look a little like eyes."

Not all are convinced, however. James Twitchell, a professor of advertising at the University of Florida, wonders whether neuromarketing isn't just the next stage of scientific pretense on the part of the advertising industry. Professor Twitchell recently attended an advertising conference in which a marketer discussed neuromarketing. The entire room sat in awe as a speaker suggested that neuroscience will finally crack open the mind of the shopper. "A lot of it is just garbage," he says, "but the garbage is so powerful."

Sources: Excerpted in part from Clive Thompson, "There's a Sucker Born in Every Medial Prefrontal Cortex," *New York Times Magazine* (October 26, 2003), 54–57; and Linda Tischler, "The Good Brand," *Fast Company* (April 2004), 47–49.

Institute and Harris Interactive to assess corporate image (or, using their terminology, corporate reputation).[21] Consumers rate selected companies along twenty different attributes representing six main dimensions: products and services, financial performance, workplace environment, social responsibility, vision and leadership, and emotional appeal. These ratings are then combined to derive a *reputation quotient* (RQ), with higher ratings representing more favorable corporate images.

To learn the top corporate images, at least according to the RQ procedure, and how the top performers have changed over time, let's take a look at the top ten for each year between 1999 (the first year that RQ scores were calculated) and 2004. These top ten scores are summarized in Table 9.3.

First order of business: a big round of applause to Johnson & Johnson, which has maintained the top spot every year since 1999, a truly exceptional achievement. Next order of business: let's consider how much stability there is in the top ten. One way to measure this is to estimate the percentage of companies on one year's list that also make it on the following year's list. This percentage varies considerably, ranging from a low of 30 percent for the 2001–2002 time period (indicating that only three of the companies on the 2001 list were on the list in 2002) to a high of 80 percent for the 2003–2004 time period. The average stability measure is 52 percent. And if we look at how many companies on the 1999 list were in the top ten in 2004, we see that only

### 2004

| RANK | SCORE | COMPANY |
|---|---|---|
| 1 | 79.8 | Johnson & Johnson |
| 2 | 79.1 | 3M |
| 3 | 78.9 | Coca-Cola |
| 4 | 78.3 | Procter & Gamble |
| 5 | 78.2 | United Parcel Service (UPS) |
| 6 | 78.0 | Microsoft |
| 7 | 78.0 | Sony |
| 8 | 77.5 | FedEx |
| 9 | 77.4 | General Mills |
| 10 | 76.2 | Honda |

### 2003

| RANK | SCORE | COMPANY |
|---|---|---|
| 1 | 79.5 | Johnson & Johnson |
| 2 | 78.5 | United Parcel Service (UPS) |
| 3 | 78.0 | Coca-Cola |
| 4 | 78.0 | Walt Disney |
| 5 | 77.9 | Microsoft |
| 6 | 77.4 | General Mills |
| 7 | 77.0 | FedEx |
| 8 | 76.7 | 3M |
| 9 | 76.5 | Procter & Gamble |
| 10 | 76.0 | Dell |

### 2002

| RANK | SCORE | COMPANY |
|---|---|---|
| 1 | 82.1 | Johnson & Johnson |
| 2 | 80.7 | Harley-Davidson |
| 3 | 79.0 | Coca-Cola |
| 4 | 78.7 | United Parcel Service (UPS) |
| 5 | 78.6 | General Mills |
| 6 | 78.5 | Maytag |
| 7 | 78.5 | Eastman Kodak |
| 8 | 78.2 | Home Depot |
| 9 | 78.2 | Dell |
| 10 | 77.9 | 3M |

### 2001

| RANK | SCORE | COMPANY |
|---|---|---|
| 1 | 82.5 | Johnson & Johnson |
| 2 | 81.8 | Microsoft |
| 3 | 80.8 | Coca-Cola |
| 4 | 80.8 | Intel |
| 5 | 80.2 | 3M |
| 6 | 79.4 | Sony |
| 7 | 79.2 | Hewlett-Packard |
| 8 | 78.3 | FedEx |
| 9 | 78.1 | Maytag |
| 10 | 78.1 | IBM |

### 2000

| RANK | SCORE | COMPANY |
|---|---|---|
| 1 | 81.6 | Johnson & Johnson |
| 2 | 80.6 | Maytag |
| 3 | 80.5 | Sony |
| 4 | 80.0 | Home Depot |
| 5 | 79.9 | Intel |
| 6 | 79.4 | Anheuser-Busch |
| 7 | 78.6 | IBM |
| 8 | 78.5 | Disney |
| 9 | 78.5 | Microsoft |
| 10 | 78.2 | Procter & Gamble |

### 1999

| RANK | SCORE | COMPANY |
|---|---|---|
| 1 | 83.4 | Johnson & Johnson |
| 2 | 81.6 | Coca-Cola |
| 3 | 81.2 | Hewlett-Packard |
| 4 | 81.0 | Intel |
| 5 | 81.0 | Ben & Jerry's |
| 6 | 80.5 | Wal*Mart |
| 7 | 79.9 | Xerox |
| 8 | 79.7 | Home Depot |
| 9 | 78.8 | Gateway |
| 10 | 78.7 | Disney |

Source: The Reputation Institute, www.reputationinstitute.com; The Reputation Practice at Harris Interactive, www.harrisinteractive.com/RQ.

Note: Maximum possible score is 100.

two were on the list. This latter observation further underscores just how impressive Johnson & Johnson's stay at the top has been.

Now let's journey outside the United States and see what consumers in other countries think. Table 9.4 contains the top ten corporate reputations in 2004 for eight more countries: France, Germany, the United Kingdom, Denmark, Norway, Sweden, Australia, and the Netherlands. A couple of points can be made here. Notice that Microsoft has been the most successful U.S. company in fostering its corporate image abroad, making the list of five of these countries. Interestingly, some U.S. companies that are absent from the top ten list in their home country are present on this list abroad. McDonald's is on the list in Germany and Sweden, and Wal*Mart is on the United Kingdom's list, for example. Apparently Wal*Mart's domestic problems (we'll say more about this later in the chapter), which are reflected in the company's fall from the number six ranking with a score of 80.5 in 1999 to a ranking of number twenty-eight with a score of 70.6 in 2004, have not followed the company abroad. Finally, considerable variety exists across the countries in the type of company that occupies the top spot: the world's largest cosmetic company, L'Oréal, in France; an automotive company, Porsche, in Germany; the conglomerate Virgin Group in the United Kingdom (the company headed by Sir Richard Branson, who you might remember from Chapter 4 as one of the men behind Virgin Galactic, which seeks to fly passengers into outer space in the not-too-distant future); the world's largest container-shipping line, A. P. Moller-Maersk, in Denmark; the 124-year-old cooperative, Tine, which supplies most of the milk in Norway; the ready-to-assemble furniture company, IKEA, in Sweden; an airline company, Virgin Blue, in Australia, one of the companies in the U.K.-conglomerate Virgin Group; and a beer company with the largest brewery in Europe, Heineken, in the Netherlands.

How important is a company's reputation? In answering this question, stop and think about how important your reputation is. Do you think it affects how others would respond to you? Of course. And the same is true for companies. Harris Interactive reports that a strong relationship exists between reputation and a number of key consumer behaviors.[22] Not only does a positive reputation enhance the odds of consumers buying a company's products and services, but it also makes consumers more likely to recommend the company to other people. But that's not all. A positive corporate reputation facilitates consumers buying a company's stock and recommending the stock to other investors.

A complete understanding of a brand's image often requires more than looking at the set of associations linked to the product. The exploration of what a particular association represents in the consumer's psyche may also be necessary; in other words, what's associated with the brand's associations. Consider Budweiser's long-standing association with Clydesdale horses. Understanding consumers' associations with the horses gives one a better insight into Budweiser's brand image. For some consumers, the horses may be associated with power, strength, and tradition: "They're working horses . . . that's the way they used to deliver beer."[23] Others might think the horses symbolize the working-class man: "Strong, hard working, and proud." The end result of this type of probing is an enriched appreciation of the brand's meaning to the consumer.

Before we move on to the next type of consumer knowledge, we want to acquaint you with one more approach to image analysis: perceptual mapping.[24] **Perceptual mapping** is *a form of image analysis that derives brand images from consumers' similarity judgments.* In this approach, consumers are asked to judge the similarity of those brands examined in the image analysis. This process is followed, two brands at a time (e.g., respondents are asked "How similar are brands A and B?" and report their

TABLE 9.4

**TABLE 9.4**  The Top Ten Corporate Reputations for Countries Around the Globe, 2004

### France

| RANK | SCORE | COMPANY |
|------|-------|---------|
| 1 | 76.1 | L'Oréal |
| 2 | 73.5 | Danone |
| 3 | 69.8 | Microsoft |
| 4 | 69.2 | PSA Peugeot Citroen |
| 5 | 68.2 | Carrefour |
| 6 | 67.5 | EDF |
| 7 | 67.3 | Renault |
| 8 | 64.4 | Air France |
| 9 | 61.1 | La Poste |
| 10 | 59.2 | Total |

### Germany

| RANK | SCORE | COMPANY |
|------|-------|---------|
| 1 | 75.4 | Porsche |
| 2 | 75.2 | ALDI |
| 3 | 73.2 | BMW |
| 4 | 70.0 | Microsoft |
| 5 | 69.0 | Siemens |
| 6 | 68.7 | BASF |
| 7 | 68.7 | DaimlerChrysler |
| 8 | 68.5 | Volkswagen |
| 9 | 67.1 | Bayer |
| 10 | 62.8 | McDonald's |

### United Kingdom

| RANK | SCORE | COMPANY |
|------|-------|---------|
| 1 | 77.2 | Virgin Group |
| 2 | 76.1 | Sony |
| 3 | 74.4 | The Body Shop |
| 4 | 74.1 | Microsoft |
| 5 | 72.8 | Tesco |
| 6 | 72.4 | John Lewis Partnership |
| 7 | 69.3 | Wal*Mart |
| 8 | 67.5 | J. Sainsbury PLC |
| 9 | 64.6 | United Co-op |
| 10 | 62.7 | British Airways |

### Denmark

| RANK | SCORE | COMPANY |
|------|-------|---------|
| 1 | 82.4 | A. P. Moller-Maersk |
| 2 | 82.4 | Danfoss |
| 3 | 81.6 | Grundfos |
| 4 | 80.7 | Bang & Olufsen |
| 5 | 80.4 | Novo Nordisk |
| 6 | 78.3 | Lego Company |
| 7 | 78.3 | Vestas |
| 8 | 72.9 | Dansk Supermarked |
| 9 | 70.9 | Danske Bank |
| 10 | 70.4 | Arla Foods |

opinions on a scale ranging from "extremely similar" to "extremely dissimilar"), for all pairwise combinations of the brands being examined. The similarity judgments are then submitted to a statistical program that produces a perceptual map. Brands that are perceived as being similar will be located close to one another on the perceptual map. Those brands viewed as different are located farther apart.

To illustrate, in Figure 9.4 we've constructed a perceptual map for a set of hypothetical food brands, identified as brands A through E. The map contains two dimensions, representing calories and taste. (Perceptual maps do not come with their dimensions labeled as in Figure 9.4. Rather, this is something that the analyst must figure out.) Where a brand is located on the perceptual map indicates how the brand is perceived by consumers on the caloric and taste dimensions. Brands A and B are viewed as great tasting but high in calories. Even worse is brand C, which is seen as being high in calories with a plain taste. Brands D and E are also seen as plain tasting, but at least have the benefit of low calories.

| Norway | | | Sweden | | |
|---|---|---|---|---|---|
| RANK | SCORE | COMPANY | RANK | SCORE | COMPANY |
| 1 | 75.0 | Tine | 1 | 79.3 | IKEA |
| 2 | 72.2 | REMA 1000 | 2 | 76.5 | Nokia |
| 3 | 70.1 | Hydro | 3 | 74.2 | Microsoft |
| 4 | 69.8 | Coop | 4 | 70.7 | Volvo |
| 5 | 69.2 | Statoil | 5 | 69.9 | ICA |
| 6 | 67.7 | Coca-Cola | 6 | 67.9 | Saab |
| 7 | 66.0 | DnB NOR | 7 | 64.1 | Coop |
| 8 | 65.8 | RIMI | 8 | 60.4 | Ericsson |
| 9 | 65.4 | Telenor | 9 | 58.9 | ABB |
| 10 | 64.4 | El-Kjop | 10 | 57.0 | McDonald's |

| Australia | | | The Netherlands | | |
|---|---|---|---|---|---|
| RANK | SCORE | COMPANY | RANK | SCORE | COMPANY |
| 1 | 79.5 | Virgin Blue | 1 | 79.1 | Heineken |
| 2 | 79.2 | Microsoft | 2 | 76.9 | IKEA |
| 3 | 75.5 | Toyota | 3 | 75.1 | Sony |
| 4 | 75.0 | Quantas | 4 | 73.4 | Unilever |
| 5 | 74.9 | Bunnings | 5 | 71.2 | TPG |
| 6 | 74.8 | Holden | 6 | 71.0 | Shell |
| 7 | 73.6 | Harvey Norman | 7 | 70.3 | Hennes & Maurtiz |
| 8 | 72.9 | Woolworths | 8 | 70.3 | Akzo Nobel |
| 9 | 72.3 | Bendigo Bank | 9 | 69.7 | Philips |
| 10 | 72.3 | NRMA motorists (NSW) | 10 | 68.8 | ABN Amro |

Sources: The Reputation Institute, www.reputationinstitute.com; The Reputation Practice at Harris Interactive, www.harrisinteractive.com/RQ; Maria Akerhielm, "Top Swedish Firms Hurt by Others' Woes," *Wall Street Journal Europe* (November 15, 2004), A7.

Note: Maximum possible score is 100.

9.4 FIGURE 9.4 A Hypothetical Perceptual Map of Food Brands

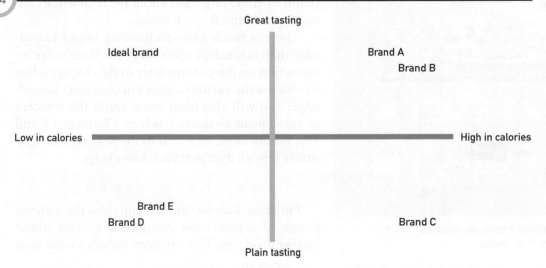

What is the advantage of this form of image analysis? Perceptual mapping doesn't require identifying the particular set of important attributes that drive consumers' brand image and having consumers respond to measures based on these various attributes. Those measures are replaced by the similarity judgments required to produce the perceptual map. Moreover, perceptual mapping is very attractive for its ability to suggest new products. How does it do this? By asking consumers about their ideal brand. In addition to reporting their similarity judgments about existing brands, consumers can also be asked about the similarity between each of these existing brands and their ideal brand. This ideal brand is then located on the perceptual map along with the existing brands. When this ideal brand is located in a position on the perceptual map that is unoccupied by existing brands, companies can see an opportunity to introduce a product in the vacant perceptual space. For example, an ideal brand that was located in the upper left-hand quadrant of Figure 9.4 would indicate that a food brand offering a great taste with few calories would be well received by consumers.

Beyond acknowledging the different approaches to measuring brand knowledge or image, we also want to say a few words about building this knowledge or image. The building of brand knowledge essentially entails building an association between the brand and some other concept. Sometimes this other concept already exists in consumers' memory; all that's missing is the linkage between it and the brand name. For example, all consumers know what a late fee is, often because they have had to pay one. When Blockbuster decided to stop charging customers for returning their video rentals late, the company "only" needed to establish a previously nonexistent association between its name and the concept of no late fees (see Figure 9.5).

At other times, knowledge about the concept itself as well as the concept's association with the brand must be built. Reebok, for instance, discovered that many consumers were unfamiliar with its vector logo. "For whatever reason, the vector had not been front and center as a marketing effort," says Peter Amell, CEO of the advertising agency Amell Group, which created a multimillion-dollar global campaign focusing on the vector logo. "The importance of the campaign is to clarify the name of the vector and to allow the consumer to have an insight into the reason why they have that fantastic badge."[25] In so doing, Reebok will build consumers' knowledge about its brand by educating them about the logo while connecting it to the Reebok name.

There is much more to building brand knowledge than is touched upon here. You'll see more information on the concept later in the chapter when we discuss the various sources of consumer knowledge. You will also learn more about this concept in subsequent chapters (such as Chapters 15 and 16). But for now, let's turn to the next type of consumer knowledge: purchase knowledge.

### Purchase Knowledge

**Purchase knowledge** encompasses the *various pieces of information consumers possess about buying products*. This category includes what con-

**FIGURE 9.5** Blockbuster Builds Knowledge about Its "No More Late Fees" Policy

sumers know about the product's price, whether it can be bought more cheaply at certain times, and where the product can be purchased.

## HOW MUCH DOES IT COST?

Certainly one of the most critical aspects of purchase knowledge involves the product's price, because price can often make or break a sale.[26] The perception of being reasonably priced goes a long way in determining a product's success in the marketplace. Such perceptions depend not only on knowledge about the product's price, but on knowledge about the typical range of prices within the product category.[27] An exorbitant price may not seem so unreasonable to the uninformed. This same price may appear outrageous when one knows that a competitor offers a product of comparable quality for half the price.

Given the importance of price, businesses need to have a clear understanding of consumers' price knowledge. Of particular concern is the accuracy of this knowledge. Let's use an example that we're sure you can relate to: the cost of college tuition. A national survey by the U.S. Department of Education asked juniors and seniors in high school along with their parents to estimate the cost of tuition and fees for one year's attendance at a public institution in their state.[28] Figure 9.6 shows the distribution of these estimates for both the high school students and their parents. These distributions are remarkably similar. The figure also shows the distribution of the actual costs in the United States at the time of the study. A comparison of this distribution with those from the students and parents reveals a major difference: many students and parents substantially overestimate the true costs. Whereas around a quarter of the students and parents believe that the cost would equal or exceed $8,000, in reality not a single public institution in the country charged this amount of money. This survey is an example of the misperception concept, which we will cover later in the chapter. And as you will also see, the existence of such misperceptions typically evokes efforts to correct this inaccurate knowledge.

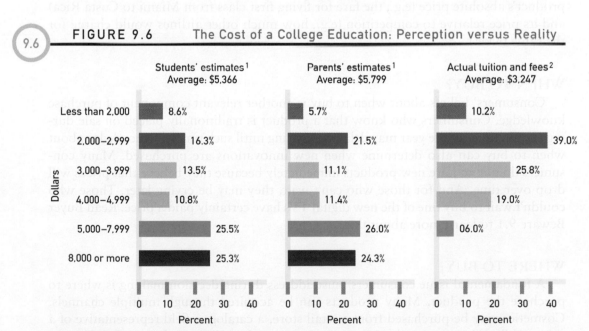

**FIGURE 9.6**  The Cost of a College Education: Perception versus Reality

Source: National Household Education Survey, Parent Interview and Youth Interview, nces.ed.gov/quicktables/Detail.asp?Key=1049 (1999).

[1] Does not include those who reported room and board in their estimates. Includes respondents who were undecided about where to attend but estimated tuition and fees for public four-year institutions in their state.

[2] Does not include room and board costs.

# Do the math.

How much will it cost to fill up your player?

iTunes® + [iPod] = **$10,000**
10,000 songs to fill an iPod®

napster TO GO + [MP3 players] = **$15** Per Month
Creative Zen Micro, Dell Pocket DJ, iriver H10

Your choice of a million songs to fill your compatible MP3 player*

Introducing *Napster To Go*®. Now you can fill and refill your compatible MP3 player with your choice of over one million songs for only $14.95 per month.
**All the music you want. Any way you want it.**

**Try *Napster To Go* for free at Napster.com**

napster™

The breakthrough technology behind *Napster To Go* works with great players from iriver, Dell, Creative, Samsung, Gateway and others.

*It is necessary to maintain a subscription in order to continue access to songs downloaded from *Napster To Go*.
© 2003-2005 Napster, LLC. Napster, Napster To Go and the Kitty Head Design are trademarks of Napster. Other trademarks are the property of their respective owners.

**FIGURE 9.7** Creating Relative Price Knowledge

Businesses not only need to understand consumers' knowledge about their prices, but they also need to examine consumers' knowledge about their competitors' prices. After all, consumers might accurately know your price but if they falsely believe that a competitor is less expensive, you're at a disadvantage. For this reason, understanding consumers' relative price knowledge is important. **Relative price knowledge** is *what consumers know about one price relative to another.*[29] Take, for example, a recent study that examined consumers' relative price knowledge of online versus bricks-and-mortar retailers. The study found that many consumers estimate that books are around 3 percent cheaper when purchased online. Yet a survey of thirty book retailers revealed that the price advantage was actually 10 percent.[30] Businesses that enjoy a relative price advantage will find it in their best interests to communicate this advantage to consumers. An example of this is the ad for Napster appearing in Figure 9.7, which focuses on its price superiority over a specific competitor.

Managers' pricing decisions may depend on their perceptions of how well informed consumers are about prices.[31] Managers are more motivated to hold prices down and respond to competitors' price cuts when the managers believe that consumers are knowledgeable about the prices charged by the market. Low levels of price knowledge, however, enable companies to be less concerned about price differences relative to the competition. If consumers are largely uninformed about relative price differences, companies may exploit this ignorance through higher prices. Accordingly, a key part of a product's image analysis involves understanding consumers' knowledge about the product's absolute price (e.g., the fare for flying first class from Miami to Costa Rica) and its price relative to competition (e.g., how much other airlines would charge for the same ticket).

## WHEN TO BUY?

Consumers' beliefs about when to buy is another relevant component of purchase knowledge. Consumers who know that a product is traditionally placed on sale during certain times of the year may delay purchasing until such times.[32] Knowledge about when to buy can also determine when new innovations are purchased. Many consumers do not acquire new products immediately because they believe that prices will drop over time. And for those who can't wait, they may be crying later. Those who couldn't wait to buy one of the new digital TVs have certainly paid a price. Read Buyer Beware 9.1 to learn more about this.

## WHERE TO BUY?

A fundamental issue consumers must address during decision making is where to purchase the product. Many products can be acquired through multiple channels. Cosmetics may be purchased from a retail store, a catalog, a field representative of a cosmetic firm that uses a sales force (e.g., Avon or Mary Kay), or the Internet. Flowers can be bought from traditional retail florists, discount stores like Wal*Mart and Costco, grocery stores, over the phone from vendors (many of whom are nothing more

## Buy Now, Cry Later

The price of liquid-crystal display (LCD) televisions fell between 30 percent and 50 percent last year—with the larger screens dropping more—a decline that will likely be repeated in 2005, said Douglas Woo, president of Westinghouse Digital Electronics. Westinghouse introduced a twenty-seven-inch LCD TV for $2,499 in January 2004. A year later it was selling for $1,299. A thirty-seven-inch LCD TV that cost $7,000 a year ago now sells for about $3,000, says Sean Wargo, director of industry analysis at the Consumer Electronics Association manufacturers trade group.

New factories and improved manufacturing techniques are expected to contribute to significant price declines this year. Sharp, the world's biggest supplier of LCD TVs, is investing $1.45 billion to build a Japanese plant designed to produce panels forty inches and larger by October 2006. Liquid-crystal displays, which are also used in notebook computers as well as, increasingly, desktop monitors, still cost far more per-inch than plasma televisions. Higher manufacturing costs are the reason.

But Michael Heiss, a consumer electronics consultant in Los Angeles, says LCD prices will keep falling after prices for plasma tumbled last year. Plasma TVs, which use a charged gas to eliminate pixels on the screen, are expected to cost an average of $2,485 in 2005, down from $4,649 in 2003, according to the Consumer Electronics Association. Ken Cranes Home Entertainment, a chain of eight stores in Southern California, cut the price of its lowest-priced forty-two-inch high-definition plasma TV to $3,500 from $4,400 in January 2005. The lowest price a year ago was about $7,000.

Doug Zenz, a Newport Beach, California, mortgage banker who dropped $5,400 last month on a fifty-inch Sony plasma television, knows his new toy can only get cheaper. "Most people cannot afford five or seven thousand dollars for a TV set," says Zenz. "It's like all new technology: the first people to jump in pay top dollar."

Source: Excerpted in part from Elliott Spagat, "Want a Huge TV? Your Wallet Says to Wait," www.washingtonpost.com (January 28, 2005). Copyright 2005 The Washington Post. Reprinted by permission.

than third-party order takers), on the Internet, directly from growers, and from street vendors who peddle their wares while motorists are stopped at traffic lights. This proliferation of competitors and middlemen (the third-party order takers who connect traditional retail florists with customers but at a substantial cost to the retailer) has caused many traditional retailers to go under. The number of floral shops operating in the United States has shrunk from nearly 24,000 in 2001 to less than 22,000 in 2004.[33]

Decisions about where to buy depend on purchase knowledge, and a lack of awareness precludes purchase consideration. Taco Bell®, through advertisements such as the one in Figure 9.8, is creating awareness of its new Mountain Dew Baja Blast™ as well as purchase knowledge with the ad copy indicating that the drink is available only at Taco Bell. The U.S. Postal Service has mailed brochures to consumers informing them of the variety of ways for buying postage stamps, including by mail, over the phone, and through the Internet (www.usps.com).

The Internet has been the catalyst for tremendous sales growth for many product categories, but American consumers continue to be reluctant to buy prescription drugs online. Depending on the source, somewhere between 4 percent to 6 percent of consumers have ever done so.[34] The major barrier? Purchase knowledge. Sixty-two percent of consumers believe that the prescription drugs available online are not as safe as those

**FIGURE 9.8** Creating Knowledge about Where to Buy

**FIGURE 9.9** Creating Knowledge about How to Use a Service

available at the local pharmacy.[35] Until this belief is changed, the future of online prescription drug sales will be limited. Apparently doctors' attitudes will need to be changed as well. Many consumers resist the temptation of lower prices because of doctors' instructions not to fill prescriptions online.[36]

For traditional bricks-and-mortar retailers, another component of purchase knowledge involves where the product is located within the store. In one study, shoppers were shown floor plans of a supermarket and asked to identify the location of various products. Shoppers were more accurate for products placed on peripheral or exterior aisles than for those items located along central or interior aisles. Accuracy was also greater for smaller stores and for shoppers reporting higher levels of store patronage.[37]

Knowledge about a product's location within a store can affect buying behavior.[38] When consumers are unfamiliar with the store, they have to rely more heavily on in-store information and displays for identifying product locations. This increased processing of in-store stimuli may activate needs or desires previously unrecognized, thereby leading to unplanned purchases.

## Consumption and Usage Knowledge

**Consumption and usage knowledge** encompasses the *information in memory about how a product can be consumed and what is required to actually use the product*. This knowledge is important for several reasons. First, consumers are unlikely to buy a product when they lack sufficient information about how to use it. Marketing efforts designed to educate the consumer about how to consume the product are then needed. For example, some consumers avoid making conference calls simply because of a lack of knowledge about how to do so. One way AT&T overcame this barrier was to provide consumers with the necessary information on a plastic card that can be stored for future reference (see Figure 9.9). Similarly, phone companies seeking to increase consumers' use of their services when making collect phone calls have spent lots of money educating consumers about what numbers they should dial (e.g., 1-800-CALLATT, 1-800-COLLECT).

Earlier in the chapter we talked about Absolut vodka's introduction of the newest addition to its product line to the American market. If we travel around the globe we'll find that Absolut is also busy in the Chinese market. The size of the vodka market

PART 3 [ INDIVIDUAL DETERMINANTS OF CONSUMER BEHAVIOR

in China is less than 1 percent of the American market, but it is a growth market with considerable upside potential. For this reason, Absolut, currently the market leader in China, is busily developing this market. Because many Chinese consumers are unfamiliar with vodka, creating usage knowledge is essential. Absolut has developed a website in China that features tips on mixing and consuming vodka. The company is also planning to educate bartenders on the fine art of serving Absolut vodka.[39]

Another barrier to purchase occurs when consumers possess incomplete information about the different ways or situations in which a product can be consumed. Educational efforts are warranted again, as is the case for the Bounce ad in Figure 9.10. The ad describes how Bounce, traditionally found in clothes dryers, can be used throughout the home as a freshener. Such efforts are quite common, because businesses often identify and promote new product uses to enhance demand, particularly in the case of mature products.

Note, however, that care must be taken in selecting new uses. A major concern is that a new use may actually lower a product's attractiveness to consumers. For example, Avon employed a multiple-usage positioning for its bath oil, Skin-So-Soft. In addition to describing the bath oil's use as an after-shower moisturizer, Avon suggested that the product could remove tar spots on automobiles. Some consumers were less than enthusiastic about using a skin moisturizer that also removed tar from a car!

Even if inadequate consumption knowledge does not prevent product purchase, it can still have detrimental effects on consumer satisfaction. Limitations in usage knowledge may prevent consumers from realizing all of the possible benefits offered by a product, thereby undermining the full amount of satisfaction that could be derived from using the product. Some of today's products, such as digital cameras, have become so complicated because of the multiple features they offer that many consumers never learn how to use them fully. A misused product may not perform properly, causing customers to feel dissatisfied. As you can see in Consumer Behavior and Marketing 9.2, both laundry detergent and appliance makers are concerned that consumers' inadequate usage knowledge might cause consumers to blame the companies' products for less-than-sterling laundry. Even worse, the misuse of some products may lead to bodily injury, such as accidents involving handheld power saws.[40]

## Persuasion Knowledge

**Persuasion knowledge** represents *what consumers know about the goals and tactics of those trying to persuade them.*[41] Let's test your persuasion knowledge. Look at Figure 9.11, which reproduces a road sign posted by campaigners who support a candidate's election to the local school board. Can you identify the goals and tactics of this persuasion attempt?

If you have ever voted in an election in which numerous candidates were competing for numerous positions, there is a very good chance that at least some of the names shown in the voting booth were unfamiliar to you. And sometimes you are forced to

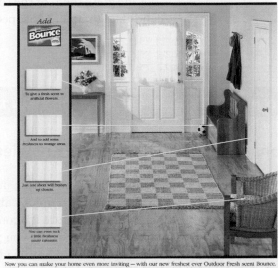

How to make a fresh entrance.

Now you can make your home even more inviting — with our new freshest ever Outdoor Fresh scent Bounce. Tuck a new sheet anywhere you like and get a crisp, clean time released freshness that keeps working day after day. It's freshness that's nice to come home to. Bounce. A fresh idea right under your nose.

Introducing our freshest Outdoor Fresh scent ever.

Keep out of reach of children and pets. Hang sheets freely or place in an open envelope to avoid direct contact with fabrics.

With Permission of the Procter & Gamble Company.

**FIGURE 9.10** Expanding Consumers' Knowledge about Different Ways to Use a Product

make a choice between two or more unknown individuals. Yet this choice might easily change if one of the candidates was familiar to you. Consequently, enhancing voters' familiarity with a candidate's name may tip the scales in the candidate's favor.

One goal, then, of the road sign appearing in Figure 9.11 is to build awareness of the candidate's name. Most people probably recognize this. What may escape most people

## CONSUMER BEHAVIOR AND MARKETING 9.2

## Consumers' Laundry Usage Knowledge Needs Some Brightener

Americans own more clothing than any culture in the history of mankind. Americans are also finicky about wearing something more than once before it's considered dirty. Put these together and what do you get? Laundry, lots of it! An estimated 35 billion loads of wash are done in the United States each year. The average American woman spends seven to nine hours a week just doing laundry.

You might think that most consumers would be rather knowledgeable about such a commonplace activity, right? How about you? Think you know how to do the laundry correctly? Let's find out. First question: In which order should the clothing, detergent, and water be added to the washing machine? Next question: Should bleach and detergent be added at the same or different times? Last question: For removing stains, is it better to use cold or hot water?

According to the industry, the optimal order is water, then detergent, then clothing. If you didn't know that, you are not alone. Procter & Gamble (P&G) estimates that fewer than half of Americans load their washing machines in the proper order. Bleach and detergent should not be added at the same time. The resulting chemical reaction weakens the bleach. P&G recommends adding the bleach five minutes after the detergent. And for removing stains, a detergent lathers more easily in hot water, thereby boosting its stain-removing power.

Deficiencies in usage knowledge are not limited to what goes inside the washing machine; deficiencies exist for the machine as well. Washers now come in a dazzling array of choices, some with twenty-plus cycles, including hand-wash, jeans, and silk, as well as others that can be custom-programmed by the consumer. But much of this progress has been lost on Americans. Many simply don't take advantage of the features and, instead, stick with a basic warm wash–cold rinse routine, regardless of the fabric or type of dirt.

Detergent manufacturers such as P&G (which produces, among other brands, Tide) are very interested in how consumers use its products when doing the laundry. P&G is so interested that it actually pays consumers to let its researchers come to the consumers' homes and observe them do laundry. The company also sends its representatives to educate appliance makers about the proper laundry advice the makers should be giving consumers.

Why does P&G go to such efforts? Because it doesn't want consumers blaming its products when the laundry doesn't turn out as clean as they expect. And this happens far too often. Industry research shows that Americans' clothes are coming out dirtier than in other developed countries. The reason? Inadequate knowledge about how to use the detergent and the machine. Both appliance manufacturers and detergent makers share a common need: educating consumers about the proper usage of their products.

Source: Emily Nelson, "Wash and Wear: In Doing Laundry, Americans Cling to Outmoded Ways—Machines, Detergents Evolve, But Clothes Still Don't Get as Clean as They Could—Shying Away from Hot Water," *Wall Street Journal* (May 16, 2002), A1. Copyright 2002 by Dow Jones & Co. Reproduced with permission of Dow Jones & Co., Inc., in the textbook format via Copyright Clearance Center.

is the sign's use of visual imagery for increasing voters' memory of the candidate's name. In particular, the red heart provides a visual representation of the name. As we shall see in Chapter 16, visual representations of semantic concepts (e.g., the name of a person or product) can be a very effective tactic for enhancing memory.

The use of the red heart within the sign has another potential benefit, depending on whether the heart evokes in the viewer particular feelings or associations that are favorable. If these associations are evoked, then these feelings and associations may carry over to the candidate. By simply pairing the candidate with a liked stimulus, voters' liking of the candidate may be increased. In Chapter 15, we will discuss how simply associating one object with another may influence consumers' beliefs, attitudes, and choices.

Persuasion knowledge is important because it influences how consumers respond to persuaders and persuasion attempts. One study has shown, for example, that persuasion knowledge adversely affects consumers' perceptions of a salesperson's sincerity and enhances inferences about a salesperson's ulterior motives.[42] Bearden, Hardesty, and Rose have developed the items in Table 9.5 as a way of measuring consumers' persuasion knowledge.[43]

**FIGURE 9.11** Do You Recognize the Persuasion Tactics Used by This Sign?

Courtesy of author

### Self-Knowledge

How well do know yourself? The answer to this question is the essence of self-knowledge, also referred to as metacognition. **Self-knowledge** represents *the person's understanding of her or his own mental processes.*[44] Let's illustrate what self-knowledge is and why it's important with an example. Companies often ask consumers to report the importance of various product attributes in evaluating and choosing products. In so doing, these companies are assuming that consumers actually know what's important to them. So long as this assumption is a reasonable one, no problem. But what

| 9.5 | TABLE 9.5 | Measuring Persuasion Knowledge |
|---|---|---|

Consumer indicates the extent to which each of the following statements is characteristic of her or him on a five-point scale ranging from "extremely uncharacteristic" (1) to "extremely characteristic" (5).

1. I know when an offer is "too good to be true."
2. I can tell when an offer has strings attached.
3. I have no trouble understanding the bargaining tactics used by salespersons.
4. I know when a marketer is pressuring me to buy.
5. I can see through sales gimmicks used to get consumers to buy.
6. I can separate fact from fantasy in advertising.

Source: William O. Bearden, David M. Hardesty, and Randall L. Rose, "Consumer Self-Confidence: Refinements in Conceptualization and Measurement," *Journal of Consumer Research*, 28 (June 2001), 121–134.

**TABLE 9.6**     A Comparison of Mobile Phone Attribute Importance Estimates Based on Consumers' Subjective Judgments versus Estimates Derived from Conjoint Analysis

| ATTRIBUTE | SUBJECTIVE | CONJOINT |
|---|---|---|
| Access fee | (1) 29.09 | (1) 33.03 |
| Call rates | (2) 20.05 | (3) 18.91 |
| Telephone features | (3) 16.17 | (4) 11.09 |
| Free calls | (4) 14.89 | (5) 11.01 |
| Mobile-to-mobile phone rates | (5) 13.05 | (2) 19.38 |
| Connection fee | (6) 6.96 | (6) 7.15 |

Source: Herman Riquelme, "Do Consumers Know What They Want?" *Journal of Consumer Marketing*, 18 (2001), 437–448.

Note: Numbers in parentheses represent the rank order of importance for the attribute. The next number represents the attribute's average importance score estimated by either the subjective or conjoint approach. The higher this number, the greater the attribute's importance.

if consumers lack the self-knowledge needed to accurately report what's important to them? Companies relying on such information when designing products may miss their intended targets.

One assessment of consumers' self-knowledge involved existing mobile phone users.[45] Consumers were asked to distribute 100 points across six different attributes in terms of relative importance. The more important the attribute, the more points it would be assigned. The study also used a well-known procedure, conjoint analysis, which, among other things, statistically derives the importance of the various attributes based on consumers' ratings of product descriptions. Table 9.6 presents the average importance for each attribute based on consumers' subjective estimates and conjoint analysis. Both approaches agree on what's most important (access fee) and least important (connection fee) to these consumers. But differences exist for the attributes between these two extremes. Whereas consumers' subjective estimates indicate that call rates and telephone features were the second and third most important attributes, the conjoint analysis says that mobile-to-mobile phone rates and call rates were the second and third most important attributes.

So how do we know which estimates are most accurate? By looking at which set of estimates is most accurate in predicting the mobile phone actually purchased by consumers. In this case, the conjoint-based estimates performed much better.[46] Accordingly, the study concluded that, to most effectively match products to the attributes actually used by consumers in their choices, "companies are better off relying on mathematically-derived utilities than those reported by consumers."[47]

## Sources of Consumer Knowledge

Consumer knowledge is acquired from a number of different sources. These sources can be classified along two major dimensions: (1) personal versus impersonal, and (2) business- versus non-business-controlled. The first dimension, personal versus impersonal, pertains to whether or not the knowledge source is another human being. The second dimension, business- versus non-business-controlled, refers to whether or

**TABLE 9.7**     Consumers' Sources of Knowledge

|  | BUSINESS-CONTROLLED | NON-BUSINESS-CONTROLLED |
|---|---|---|
| **PERSONAL** | Sales personnel | Family and friends |
|  | Service personnel | Coworkers |
|  | Paid product endorsers | Other shoppers |
|  |  | Experts, opinion leaders, and influentials |
|  |  | Internet forums and bulletin boards |
| **IMPERSONAL** | Products | Television and radio shows |
|  | Point-of-purchase materials | Noncorporate websites |
|  |    (e.g., displays, store signage, |    (e.g., blogs, government sites) |
|  |    advertising circulars) | Books |
|  | Advertising | Government reports |
|  | Catalogs | Newspapers |
|  | Corporate websites | Magazines |
|  | Yellow Pages |  |

not the knowledge source originates from the business community. The various sources of knowledge as a function of these two characteristics are summarized in Table 9.7.

Of course, not all sources of knowledge are created equal. Indeed, some are more influential than others. Because of their vested interest, business sources of knowledge are often viewed with a suspicious eye. Consumers have more faith in knowledge sources that are not attempting to make a profit from them. This holds especially true for personal sources of knowledge that are not controlled by business. Such sources will usually have the greatest impact on consumers, especially when they are perceived as more knowledgeable. But these days, telling the difference between a business versus non-business source may not be as easy as you think. To find out why, you'll have to read Buyer Beware 9.2.

Even within a particular knowledge source considerable variation may exist in the amount of confidence consumers have. As one indication of how consumers' confidence in knowledge sources can vary, let's look at the results of an online poll that asked consumers which news media (e.g., newspapers, radio, TV, and so forth) they generally found the most credible.[48] These results are presented in Table 9.8. There was a two-way tie for first place between newspapers and local TV news. Even so, less than one-third of the respondents found these knowledge sources to be the most credible.

Importantly, the relative influence of knowledge sources depends on the type of information being conveyed. A doctor's opinion about medical issues matters a lot. The doctor's opinion about fashion probably matters very little. Consumers' skepticism toward advertising reduces how much they rely on advertising as a source of information about how well the product will perform. On the other hand, as a source of information about the product's existence, many find advertising very useful. When college students were asked about how they prefer to learn about products and services, as shown in Table 9.9, television advertising was second only to word-of-mouth. Indeed, advertising in the three major forms of media accounted for three of the top five spots on the list.

Typically, one of the most useful sources of knowledge is that which comes from product consumption itself. The knowledge acquired from other sources may be very useful, but there's no substitute for the real thing. We often learn most of what we

## Buzz Marketers Hire Others to Tell You What They Want You to Hear

That friendly person you just talked to may not be who you think he or she is. Just another consumer like yourself? Maybe. And maybe not. Why? Because some marketers are using a new approach to create buzz about their products: paying people to pose as consumers and talk up products.

This approach has been around since the mid-1990s, when Kirshenbaum Bond & Partners created an effort for Hennessy, the cognac brand, that involved hiring 150 actors to drink at trendy bars and chat with patrons about the pricey product. In 2002, the U.S. arm of Sony Ericsson Mobile Communications promoted its new camera phone by hiring 60 actors to hang out at tourist attractions and act like tourists. The actors' task: ask an unsuspecting passerby to take their pictures with the Sony Ericsson devices. The agency behind the effort, Omnicom Group's Fathom Communications, told the actors to identify themselves only when asked directly. And in 2004, TMR Multimedia, a small marketing firm in Hollywood, Florida, was hired by a major snack-food company to conduct a pilot project for a healthy snack, which included having people hang around clinics while munching on the new product.

As you might imagine, not everyone is happy about this. "Some of these practices are deceptive because people think they are talking to a real person and they are talking to a shill," says Gary Ruskin, executive director of Commercial Alert, a Portland, Oregon, watchdog group. "It's about the commercializing of human relationships." Sony Ericsson received wide criticism for its approach to promoting its new camera phone. "That campaign is shilling, and it violates the 'honesty of identity' rule," says Andy Sernovitz, chief executive officer of the Word of Mouth Marketing Association, a Chicago trade group with forty marketing firms and advertisers as members. The Association has announced a new set of rules and guidelines for word-of-mouth advertising, one of the fastest-growing advertising practices. But getting every company to buy into self-regulation might not be easy. "I can't begin to imagine how one can regulate an industry that thrives on its covert nature," says Margaret Kessler, project coordinator at TMR Multimedia.

Source: Excerpted in part from Suzanne Vranica, "Getting Buzz Marketers to Fess Up," *Wall Street Journal* (February 9, 2005), B9. Copyright 2005 by Dow Jones & Co. Reproduced with permission of Dow Jones & Co., Inc., in the textbook format via Copyright Clearance Center.

| TABLE 9.8 | Consumers' Perceptions of Media Credibility |
|---|---|
| **MEDIA** | **PERCENTAGE** |
| Newspapers | 30 |
| Local television news | 30 |
| Cable news networks | 24 |
| Online news sites | 21 |
| Broadcast television network news | 20 |
| News magazines | 16 |
| News radio | 13 |
| Talk radio | 13 |
| Blogs (Web logs) | 4 |
| Other | 9 |

Source: Joe Mandese, "Papers, Local TV Seen As More Credible Than Network News; Consumers, Trade Split on Bias," www.mediapost.com (November 1, 2004). Copyright 2005 MediaPost Communications. All rights reserved.

Note: Percentages represent the number of consumers choosing each news media as the most credible in general. The numbers sum to greater than 100 percent because respondents were allowed to choose more than one news media as most credible.

**TABLE 9.9**　　　How College Students Prefer to Learn about
Products and Services (percent)

| KNOWLEDGE SOURCE | TOTAL | MALES | FEMALES |
|---|---|---|---|
| Word-of-mouth | 59 | 54 | 64 |
| Advertising on television | 58 | 55 | 60 |
| Advertising in a magazine | 42 | 37 | 47 |
| Free samples in a store | 37 | 31 | 43 |
| Advertising on radio | 32 | 30 | 35 |
| Information on the Internet | 30 | 33 | 27 |
| Product reviews in magazines | 28 | 30 | 25 |
| Free samples on campus | 27 | 25 | 29 |
| Advertising banner on the Internet | 24 | 25 | 24 |
| Free gift with purchase | 22 | 14 | 30 |
| Free samples sent in the mail | 22 | 16 | 28 |

Source: Student Monitor. www.studentmonitor.com (Fall 2004).

really need to know by simply consuming the product. For this reason, purchase and consumption are sometimes chosen as a way of learning about a product rather than engaging in effortful information search. A consumer may decide, for instance, that the easiest way to learn about a new food item discovered at the grocery store is to take it home and try it.

Whether or not a consumer's knowledge is based on the direct experience that comes from consumption is important. Direct experience typically makes us feel more confident about what we know.[49] Your mother may say that you're going to love her new recipe, but you really don't know until you actually taste it. Greater confidence, in turn, means that you are more likely to rely on this knowledge during decision making, thereby reducing external search. Finally, those interested in changing consumer knowledge face a greater challenge when this knowledge is based on direct experience. Compared to knowledge based on indirect experience (e.g., what you might learn from an ad or a friend), knowledge derived from actual experience is more resistant to change.[50]

Companies sometimes have to adjust their marketing strategies when targeting consumers who lack direct experience with the product. One example comes from the cruise line industry. Many consumers have never taken a cruise because they're apprehensive about whether they'll enjoy the consumption experience. To alleviate this concern, Carnival Cruise Lines once offered a money-back guarantee for any unused portion of a cruise. During the first three months in which the guarantee was offered, only thirty-seven of the more than a quarter of a million passengers applied for a refund.[51]

Now that you are acquainted with the sources of consumer knowledge, let's consider a couple of the reasons why businesses find it important to understand these sources. Chapter 14 (called "Making Contact") focuses on what companies must do when delivering their messages to consumers. In developing their "contact" strategies, companies need to consider which "transmission" channels provide them with their best chance of reaching their target consumers. In other words, companies need to decide which knowledge sources to use for delivering their messages. The quality of this decision improves with the quality of information a company possesses about target consumers' sources of knowledge.

Companies also find it essential to monitor what is being transmitted about the company to the consumer through these sources. This process requires tracking the content and favorability of consumers' word-of-mouth and word-of-mouse communication as well as media coverage of the company and its products. Of these three avenues of communication, monitoring word-of-mouth communication is the most challenging simply because, unlike the other two, there is rarely a permanent record of it. Broadcast media can be recorded. Print media and word-of-mouse rely on the written word, and therefore can be readily examined. Companies can (and should) visit websites such as complaints.com, planetfeedback.com, and thesqueakywheel.com, which are dedicated to providing consumers a forum for voicing their complaints. But understanding word-of-mouth typically requires asking consumers to report what they have heard and what they have said. We'll come back to word-of-mouth communication in Chapter 13's discussion of personal sources of influence on the consumer.

One example of how all companies can monitor what's being said about them in the media is the Delahaye Index. This index, estimated quarterly by Medialink Worldwide, represents how and how often a company is discussed across a number of televised and print news sources. Companies are scored based on the number of positive or negative statements about them on certain key reputation-driving dimensions (products and services, financial management, stakeholder relations, organizational integrity, and organizational strength) as well as the frequency of such coverage.[52] Table 9.10 lists the ten companies that received the highest scores, indicating the most favorable coverage, in the second quarter of 2004. Wal*Mart should be especially pleased with its appearance on this list (although its number seven ranking is down from the number one ranking the company received in the first quarter of 2004) given, as we discuss subsequently, the image problems the company has endured in recent times.

One last point before we leave this section. We have covered the major sources of information that consumers rely on, but how information (something that is external to the consumer) becomes knowledge (something that resides inside of the consumer's memory) has not been addressed. This transformation of information into knowledge is covered in Chapter 16 ("Helping Consumers to Remember"). Chapter 16 presents the concept of cognitive learning, which deals with how information becomes knowl-

**TABLE 9.10**  The Ten Companies That Receive the Most Favorable Media Coverage, According to the Delahaye Index

| RANK | COMPANY |
| --- | --- |
| 1 | Microsoft |
| 2 | Walt Disney |
| 3 | Verizon Communications |
| 4 | General Motors |
| 5 | Intel |
| 6 | Boeing |
| 7 | Wal*Mart |
| 8 | Ford |
| 9 | General Electric |
| 10 | Wachovia |

Source: "Microsoft Earns Best Corporate Reputation in the Media, According to Delahaye Index," news release, Medialink Worldwide, www.medialink.com (September 7, 2004).

edge, as well as the various ways companies can facilitate the initial learning of information and its subsequent retrieval from memory.

## The Benefits of Understanding Consumer Knowledge

We hope you have already started to develop an appreciation of the potential benefits that come from understanding consumer knowledge. We have touched on some of these benefits while introducing you to the fundamentals of consumer knowledge. Now it's time to focus your thinking on the business and public policy benefits that come from such an understanding.

### Implications for Business

An understanding of consumer knowledge is useful to companies in at least five different ways: (1) it allows them to gauge whether the positioning intended for their products actually exists in the consumer's mind; (2) it allows them to identify purchase barriers; (3) it helps in discovering new product uses that in turn stimulate sales; (4) it helps them gauge the potential threat posed by competitors to their existing customer base; and (5) it can enhance the effectiveness of customer recruitment activities.

### GAUGING THE PRODUCT'S POSITIONING SUCCESS

One of the most important benefits derived from an analysis of consumer knowledge is that this knowledge provides an acid test of a company's success in achieving its desired product positioning in the marketplace. Don't be misled into thinking that a product's sales are the "real" acid test. They're not. Sales depend on many things besides the product's image. A company can be right on target with its product's image and yet sales may not be on target. And a product's image may not be exactly where it needs to be and yet sales can still roll in. The one way to really know if the product has achieved the desired positioning is to compare the actual image with the desired image. **Desired image** refers to *the image that a company seeks to create in the marketplace for its product*. A company's marketing efforts have succeeded in carving out the desired positioning for the product when the actual and desired images are in sync.

Yet differences often exist between the desired and actual images, a reality that reinforces the wisdom of undertaking image analyses along the lines discussed earlier in the chapter. When the actual and desired images are out of alignment, corrective actions will be needed. And such actions are commonplace. The following is just a tiny fraction of the efforts undertaken in recent times to close the image gap (and for a look at one such effort that's still on the drawing board, go to Consumer Behavior and Marketing 9.3).

- "I'm lovin' it" is McDonald's latest slogan. Apparently, many British consumers are not. Complaints range from bad food (many call it "rubbish") to the staff being less than friendly.[53] So in late 2004, McDonald's initiated a new advertising campaign for the United Kingdom called "Changes," which replaces the company's Golden Arches with a yellow question mark and the tagline, "McDonald's. But not as you know it." The campaign is "to encourage people to think of us differently," says Larry Light, McDonald's chief global marketing officer.[54]
- Cisco, the networking equipment brand, put $150 million into a 2005 global advertising campaign to change its image. Deb Mielke, managing director for Treillage Network Strategies, says, "Based on where Cisco's heading [into consulting], I think this is a nice first step in getting them to change their image. They always had a technical sell, this makes them more of a business solution. It absolutely makes sense for them right now."[55]

## Sugar Seeks to Sweeten Its Image

Life is not so sweet in the sugar bowl these days. The competition is growing stronger and more aggressive (see the Sugar Lite ad in Figure 9.12), sugar is losing sales, and consumers' reservations about sugar at a time of escalating health and dietary concerns are the ingredients of a not-so-tasty future. In 2004, while sugar sales were dropping 4 percent, sales of sucralose, also known as Splenda, skyrocketed 47 percent. From the industry's perspective, the popularity of these alternative forms of sweeteners, the low-carb diet craze, and concerns about obesity and diabetes all contributed to the decline in sugar sales. Indeed, concerns about the growing number of obese Americans,

particularly children, has produced a double whammy for the sugar industry. Not only are consumers cutting down on the use of sugar at their dining tables, food companies are also cutting back on sugar in their manufacturing processes and emphasizing this reduction to consumers. As shown in Figure 9.12, Hawaiian Punch has introduced a "Light" version with less sugar, while some cereals have changed their packaging to communicate sugar's reduced presence.

So for the second time ever in its history, the Sugar Association is funding another advertising campaign. Starting in May 2005 and continuing for the next

**FIGURE 9.12** Examples of the Pressures the Sugar Industry Is Feeling These Days

FIGURE 9.12 (Continued)

three years, between $3 million and $5 million will be spent per year on radio, print, and television advertisements. "We want the consumer to know that [sugar] is all natural, and it's only 15 calories a teaspoon," said Melanie Miller, a spokeswoman for the Sugar Association. "In moderation, it's not evil. We'd like to take back our identity. Instead of 'Splenda and spice and everything nice,' we'd like to go back to 'sugar and spice and everything nice.'"

To help craft its "sugar is not evil" message, the sugar industry selected Marriner Marketing Communications, in part because of the firm's experience with other food companies, including Perdue Farms, Campbell Soup, and Kellogg. Marriner already has started collecting information from consumers about their

sugar purchasing habits, said Carol Whitman, the firm's director of business development. The company is most interested in what compels consumers to buy sugar instead of alternative sweeteners. "After consumer input, we will come to an agreement on a strategy we want to use," Whitman said. "We're definitely going to attack it from a consumer standpoint."

Whatever the final strategy, the industry hopes that the approach will prove as successful as the industry's first advertising campaign. This initial campaign, launched twenty years ago, also came at a time when sugar sales and consumption were waning. But by the time the campaign ended in the early 1990s, sales were up 12 to 15 percent.

Sources: Excerpted in part from Dina ElBoghdady, "Sweetening Sugar's Image; Association Picks Columbia Firm to Run Ad Campaign," *Washington Post* (January 20, 2005), T8; Caroline E. Mayer and Dina ElBoghdady, "Sugar, Vending Groups Take Action against Obesity Claims," *Washington Post* (January 13, 2005), E1.

• After several years of bad press over its hiring practices, stance toward labor unions, actions against smaller competitors, and community impact, Wal*Mart's image has taken a bit of a beating. In early 2005, the company launched a national advertising campaign to repair its corporate image. Full-page ads in over a hundred newspapers touted the wages and benefits Wal*Mart pays to company employees. A website was launched to support the campaign. President and CEO Lee Scott re-iterated the message in personal interviews and television appearances.[56]

• TIAA-CREF, the aforementioned multibillion-dollar company with the minus-cule awareness, is in the process of fixing this deficiency as well as another prob-lem: its image. "We've been viewed as paternalistic and a little old-fashioned with a narrow product line," says its president, Herb Allison. So the company has hired an edgy advertising company to assist in creating a hipper image, changed its slo-gan, and expanded its product line.[57]

• At the end of 2004, several old-school brands were trying to become cool again. Kahlúa, the iconic coffee liqueur from the disco days of the 1970s, launched its largest global television advertising campaign ever, using exotic images such as a woman walking an alligator instead of a dog. Tia Maria, another coffee liqueur, be-gan a new campaign as well. The company's customer base, composed mostly of women, has been aging because of the company's limited success in attracting younger women. Courvoisier, a cognac, started a print campaign targeting urban men aged twenty-five to thirty-five. The company is hoping to recapture the popu-larity it enjoyed in 2002 thanks to the hit song "Pass the Courvoisier," by Busta Rhymes and P. Diddy.[58]

• States are also in the image game. Louisiana discovered through market research that many Americans perceive the state as a place to party, but little else. It has launched a $6.5 million ad campaign, featuring the state's cul-ture and environment, to broaden its image and appeal.[59] When potential tourists were asked what came to mind about Utah, one word kept popping up: *dry*. Not in reference to the climate, but dry as in difficult to get an alcoholic drink. Not an enticing image for many. So water became a big part of the state's sum-mer 2004 advertising campaign. People boating on lakes and rivers were prominent features in the print advertisements.[60]

• When asked about whether various companies were "con-cerned with my health," only 10 percent reported that Pepsi was so inclined, placing the company far behind most of the other companies rated by consumers. So PepsiCo developed its new "Smart Spot" symbol, which includes the text "Smart choices made easy," to go on product packaging (see Fig-ure 9.13). Only those products that meet certain nutritional standards receive the symbol. More than one hundred prod-ucts, including brand names such as Dole, Gatorade, Quaker, and Tropicana, carry the new symbol. Sales of products carry-ing the Smart Spot have increased by 8 percent, well ahead of the company's 5 percent growth in the United States overall.[61]

• What comes to mind when you hear the name La-Z-Boy? Comfortable? Fashionable? If you're like most consumers, yes to the first, no to the second. Thus, the seventy-seven-year-old furniture maker is trying to tweak its image. To this end, the company has added a new line of furniture designed by Todd Oldham, who has designed clothes for celebrities such as Julia Roberts. "We own comfort in the consumers' minds when it

**FIGURE 9.13** PepsiCo Hopes to Enhance the Healthiness Image of Its Products with the New Smart Spot

comes to home furnishings," says Jennifer Sievertsen, La-Z-Boy's director of brand and retail marketing. But she adds that the company now wants consumers to know that "we also have a fairly wide variety of very stylish, trendy products." [62]

Why does a product's actual image differ from its desired image? The answer to this question overlaps with the reasons why knowledge can serve as a barrier to product purchase. So let's move on to that topic.

## IDENTIFYING PURCHASE BARRIERS

Sometimes the reason consumers don't buy a company's product can be traced back to their knowledge. Or, in some cases, their lack of knowledge. **Knowledge gaps** refer to *an absence of information in memory*. These gaps can be detrimental to a product's success. When consumers are unaware of a product's existence, a deadly knowledge gap exists. But knowledge gaps are not limited to simply whether consumers are familiar with what products and retailers are available. Even if the product's or retailer's existence is known, consumers still may have significant gaps in other aspects of their knowledge. Perhaps they are unaware of some important association or attribute, such as when consumers do not know which product charges the lowest price or which product offers the best warranty. Maybe they are ignorant of some valuable product use. Many different types of knowledge gaps may exist in the minds of target consumers. And these gaps usually represent a purchase barrier. For example, despite the appearance of Charmin on supermarket shelves in the United States for many years, the brand was introduced in the United Kingdom only five years ago and remains unfamiliar to many of the consumers in that market. The vice president of family care for Western Europe at Procter & Gamble himself would stand in the grocery aisle and ask consumers why they were buying a competitor's product instead of P&G's Charmin brand. "I don't know anything about Charmin" is what he would typically hear.[63] Or consider the state of New Hampshire, which has been around far longer than any of the consumers alive today. When the state commissioned an image study, it discovered knowledge gaps even among prior visitors and vacationers who fail to have much knowledge about the state other than in the area that attracted them initially.[64]

From a business perspective, the key is to identify gaps whose existence undermines the likelihood of consumers choosing the product when making their purchase decisions. Knowledge gaps are rampant for new products. A major hurdle for Web TV, in which consumers can gain access to the Internet through their television set instead of a computer, has been getting consumers to understand what Internet television really is.[65]

Knowledge gaps exist even for well-known products. When CBS's *60 Minutes* aired a segment that stated that moderate consumption of red (but not white) wine reduces the risk of heart disease, sales of red wine skyrocketed by 40 percent! One company later placed tags on its red wine bottles carrying excerpts from the program.[66] Similarly, Kellogg's hopes that educating consumers about the additional antioxidants in its Smart Start cereal (see Figure 9.14) will enhance demand for the product.

Even when knowledge gaps do not exist, barriers to purchase may still reside within consumers' knowledge. These barriers will exist when consumers hold certain product associations that are less than attractive. Mercedes-Benz has certain associations detrimental to its image. According to the chief creative officer of Mercedes' advertising agency, some consumers view the brand as too "cold and Germanic."[67] Others are put off by the company's snobby image. BMW has experienced similar image problems. "Before, I think we were a little cold and aloof," says Jim McDowell, vice president of marketing for BMW's U.S. sales unit. "We have been working hard to project a more human side to BMW. We want it to be a smiling brand."[68]

SWEET FLAKES, OAT CLUSTERS
AND NOW MORE ANTIOXIDANTS
TO BOOT. HOW MUCH SMARTER
OF A START CAN YOU GET?

With vitamins A, C, & E to help boost your immune system.

SMART
START

START AGING SMART

**FIGURE 9.14** Kellogg's Wants to Educate Consumers about the Extra Antioxidants in Its Cereal

Once undesirable associations in the actual product image have been identified, a key issue is understanding the extent to which these associations are justifiable. Sometimes consumers' negative perceptions are justifiable because the perceptions reflect a true limitation in the product offering. Remember TIAA-CREF and La-Z-Boy's recent attempts to change their images? Consumers' perceptions of these companies' limited product lines caused the companies to offer consumers more choices. Mercedes' image has been tarnished recently by problems with the quality of its automobiles. After years of being consistently rated at the top in studies of automobile quality, the company has seen its ratings dropping since 2002. So has the company's share of the luxury car market. In the late 1990s, Mercedes outsold all of its competitors in the luxury car market. As of 2005, the company had dropped to fourth place in this market. One of the ways Mercedes responded to this situation involved launching the "Zero Defect Initiative" aimed at improving its product quality.[69]

At other times, however, undesirable associations do not correspond to reality. When this is so, misperception is said to exist. **Misperception** is simply *inaccurate knowledge*. Companies have a misperception problem when consumers believe something that is not true. And depending on the nature of this misperception, the belief may serve as a major purchase barrier. For example, many Americans hold incorrect knowledge about some brands' country of origin.[70] Nearly two-thirds of consumers believe that Grey Poupon mustard is from France. Nearly half think Yoplait yogurt is French. Both are American brands. Similarly, 70 percent say Heineken beer is from Germany; it's from the Netherlands. So what's the problem with these seemingly harmless misperceptions? The problem is that these brands may unfairly suffer, as when some consumers boycotted French and German products in protest over these countries not sending troops to support the United States in its war with Iraq.[71]

But unlike the case when negative perceptions are grounded in reality, fixing misperceptions does not require changing the product. Rather, the process requires changing how the product is perceived. Auto makers say that one of consumers' biggest misconceptions about hybrid vehicles, which draw power from two energy sources, gas and electricity, is that the battery needs to be plugged in to an electrical socket to recharge.[72] The early models introduced years ago needed this type of recharging, but surplus engine power is now used to continually recharge the vehicle's battery. So now the industry has to correct this misperception. At the 2005 North American International Auto Show, prominent signs informed consumers that hybrid vehicles no longer needed to be plugged in.[73] The same point was conveyed in advertising that appeared during the 2005 Super Bowl.

Similarly, Lever Brothers, the maker of Dove soap, identified several undesirable misperceptions about its product. The company addressed this inaccurate knowledge by mailing target households a packet that contained, among other things, the brochure appearing in Figure 9.15. These misperceptions were listed inside the brochure, followed by an explanation about why each was incorrect.

**FIGURE 9.15** One Company's Effort to Fight Product Misperception

One area of particular concern to companies is price misperception. When consumers believe that a company's prices are higher than they truly are, correcting this inaccurate knowledge will almost always be in the company's best interests. Hallmark encountered this situation when the company discovered that many consumers overestimated the prices of its cards, in some cases by as much as 50 percent more than the actual price. The company responded by launching a $10 million advertising campaign promoting its lower-end cards selling for less than two dollars.[74]

Another example comes from the lawn care industry. Consumers were asked to estimate the price of one company's service. Although customers gave very accurate estimates, nonusers did not. Nonusers' average price estimate was twice the actual price, and many exaggerated the price by a factor of three or four. This discovery of nonusers' unfavorable price misperceptions resulted in a change in the company's advertising strategy. A new campaign centering on the theme, "It's not as expensive as you might think," was soon launched. Mercedes Benz also used advertising to correct consumers' price misperceptions. One ad said: "Perception—$50,000. Fact—$31,425." Our last example of dealing with price misperception comes from a brochure sent by Publix Super Markets to target households. Apparently many of the consumers residing within these households overestimated the cost of shopping at Publix, thus prompting the claim, "Prices that are lower than you think," within the brochure.

There is much more to shaping consumers' product images than what we have discussed so far. In fact, we devote an entire chapter (Chapter 15) to this topic later on.

**TABLE 9.11**     Consumers Find Multiple New Uses for Products

| PRODUCT | TYPICAL USE | NEW USE |
|---|---|---|
| Paper towels | Cleaning spills or drying | Use as an emergency coffee filter. |
| | | Strain fat from broth. |
| | | Line refrigerator vegetable bin to soak up moisture. |
| | | Write school lunchbox notes for children. |
| Shaving cream | Moistening whiskers for a shave | Clean your hands at the tool bench—needs no water. |
| | | Remove spilled latex paint in emergencies. |
| | | Clean decorative stones or rocks in yard. |
| Mayonnaise | Cooking ingredient or spread | Helps remove a ring from a finger. |
| | | Removes white rings from wood furniture. |
| | | Removes crayon marks from furniture. |
| Dental floss | Clean teeth | Hang pictures. |
| | | Cut cheese. |
| | | Use as emergency thread for heavy fabrics. |
| Bar soap | Wash hands and body | Lubricate zippers. |
| | | Make bubbles for bubble bath. |
| | | Soap nails and screws. |
| | | Take the sting and itch from insect bites. |

Source: Brian Wansink, "How Resourceful Consumers Identify New Uses for Old Products," *Journal of Family and Consumer Science*, 95 (November 2003), 109–113.

But for now, let's continue our discussion of why companies should be interested in understanding consumer knowledge.

### DISCOVERING NEW USES

Consumers are often ingenious at coming up with new ways of using an old product (see Table 9.11). As such, consumers can be an invaluable source of ideas about new product uses. A classic example is Kimberly-Clark's Kleenex tissue, which was sold originally as a product to be used along with cold cream for removing makeup. Eventually, the tissue was repositioned as a disposable handkerchief after the company had received numerous letters from consumers describing new uses for the product. At one point, the company included a package insert listing nearly fifty other uses that consumers had found.[75] By understanding usage knowledge, companies may discover new uses that can be promoted as a means of broadening their products' appeal.

### GAUGING THE SEVERITY OF COMPETITIVE THREATS

An assessment of consumer knowledge regarding competitors is useful for gauging competitive threats to one's business. To illustrate, suppose that a food company surveyed its customers about their opinions of the company's brand as well as competitors' brands. Now suppose that the survey found that competitor A is perceived as highly similar to the company's offering, and the rest of the competition is viewed as inferior. Consequently, the company should be much more concerned about competitor A's potential for stealing customers and may wish to undertake activities that would help further differentiate the company's brand from competitor A's brand in the minds of its customers.

## ENHANCING THE EFFECTIVENESS OF CUSTOMER RECRUITMENT ACTIVITIES

Finally, an examination of consumer knowledge can assist in the development of customer recruitment activities. Consider attempts to steal a competitor's business. In this situation, focusing on the brand images held by the competitors' customers is necessary. Ideally, this method would be followed for the customers of each separate competitor, because different competitors' customers may hold very different images. There are reasons why consumers decided to do business with the competition. These reasons should become apparent when you compare how a competitor's customers rate the product they currently buy and the product you want them to buy. Perhaps they think your product costs more. Maybe your product is seen as possessing lower quality. Whatever the reason, you will have a better understanding of those deficiencies in your product that must be remedied to convert the competitor's customers into your customers.

Identifying what needs to be changed is only part of the story. A company also needs to identify how such changes might best be accomplished. Should the company rely on advertising to carry a message? If so, should the advertising target customers, or should it focus on a particular knowledge source such as pharmacists? Maybe salespeople would be more successful in carrying the company's message. By understanding which knowledge sources consumers rely on, companies can more effectively and efficiently direct their efforts in the proper direction.

Consumer knowledge also carries implications concerning whether sales messages should focus on technical information regarding product attributes versus emphasizing product benefits that may be more easily understood by target consumers. Whereas knowledgeable consumers are able to use technical information when forming product evaluations, unknowledgeable consumers are less able to do so. Instead, unknowledgeable consumers may be more persuaded by messages conveying easily understood product benefits.[76] Finally, the nature of consumers' persuasion knowledge may suggest the need to avoid persuasion tactics that are blatantly obvious to the target market.

## Implications for Public Policy

From a public policy perspective, consumer welfare is the primary concern. The goal is to help consumers rather than the business goal of selling to consumers. So consumer knowledge needs to be examined to see if there are either knowledge gaps or misperceptions that impair consumers' ability to operate in the marketplace. AARP recognized the need to educate Florida homeowners who suffered at the hands of multiple hurricanes during the fall of 2004 about what to look out for when repairing their damaged homes. The organization sent members a booklet of informational materials, the first page of which is shown in Figure 9.16.

Governmental agencies such as the Federal Trade Commission may survey consumers about their knowledge to help guide policies aimed at protecting the uninformed consumer. When consumers

**Putting Things Back Together!**
**Advice on Disaster Repair**

Get the facts before a bad contractor or a bad loan gets you.

Your home is worth a lot to you...but dishonest home contractors see the value in it, too. After disasters, people spend billions of dollars for home repairs. Usually the work is done well, but each year many homeowners are victims of poor, overpriced, or never-completed work. Some people posing as home repair specialists are simply con artists looking for easy money. Others are front men for predatory lenders.

If you are planning on making repairs to your home, it is important to pick the right contractor and the right financing. Here's how...

**AARP** Florida
www.aarp.org/fl

Courtesy of AARP Florida

**FIGURE 9.16** AARP Sent This Material to Its Florida Members to Educate Them about Unscrupulous Contractors

## Health Illiteracy in America

Consider the following two sentences taken from actual documents that consumers encounter in the health field. The first comes from an informed consent form: "A comparison of the effectiveness of educational media in combination with a counseling method on smoking habits is being examined." From a consumer privacy notice comes the following: "Examples of such mandatory disclosures include notifying state or local health authorities regarding particular communicable diseases." Do you understand what these sentences are saying? We would think so. Yet millions of Americans do not. In fact, 40 million Americans cannot read such complex sentences at all.

But the problem is far more widespread and goes much deeper than the inability to read complicated material. According to a report issued by the Institute of Medicine of the National Academies, nearly half of all American adults—90 million people—have limited health literacy. These individuals have problems following instructions on drug labels, interpreting hospital consent forms, even understanding a doctor's diagnosis and instructions. "It's a shocking figure," says Dr. Carolyn Clancy, director of the government's Agency for Healthcare Research and Quality.

What is health literacy? It is the degree to which one can obtain, process, and understand basic informa-

tion and services needed to make appropriate health decisions. Health literacy is more than simply reading skills and includes writing, listening, speaking, arithmetic, and conceptual knowledge. Health literacy skills are needed for discussing care with health professionals; reading and understanding medical terms, patient information sheets, consent forms, and advertising; and using medical tools such as a thermometer. More than three hundred studies indicate that health-related materials cannot be understood by most of the people for whom they are intended. Such understanding is almost impossible for the millions who can't read well, aren't fluent in English, or have vision or cognitive problems caused by aging.

There is a higher rate of hospitalization and use of emergency services among those with limited health literacy. "Health literacy is fundamental to quality care," says David A. Kindig, chair of the Committee on Health Literacy and professor emeritus of population health sciences, University of Wisconsin-Madison. "The public's ability to understand and make informed decisions about their health is a frequently ignored problem that can have a profound impact on individuals' health and the health care system. Most professionals and policy makers have little understanding of the extent and effects of this problem."

Sources: Excerpted in part from Lauran Neergaard, "Many Can't Tell What the Doctor Ordered," *Miami Herald* (April 9, 2004), A7; *Health Literacy: A Prescription to End Confusion,* Institute of Medicine of the National Academies (April 2004); "Press Release: 90 Million Americans Are Burdened with Inadequate Health Literacy; IOM Report Calls for National Effort to Improve Health Literacy," www.nationalacademies.org (April 8, 2004).

are thought to lack sufficient information to make an informed choice, policy makers may enact legislation that requires the disclosure of appropriate information. This was the motivation behind the government's requiring the cigarette industry to replace the original warning required by law ("The Surgeon General has determined that cigarette smoking is dangerous to your health"). Cigarette manufacturers are now required to rotate periodically a series of warning labels describing specific dangers (e.g., "Smoking causes lung cancer, heart disease, emphysema, and may complicate pregnancy"). Similarly, the Centers for Disease Control and the American Academy of Dermatology have tried to educate consumers about the cancer risk of excessive exposure to the sun.[77] Most recently, an urgent call has been made to improve millions of Americans' health literacy. To learn about the severity of this knowledge gap and its consequences, read Market Facts 9.2.

Not only does Americans' health literacy need to be improved, but their financial literacy needs improvement as well. A nationwide survey of high school seniors shows that they could, on average, answer correctly only about half of a series of questions about personal finance and economics.[78] Similarly, the fourteenth annual Retirement Confidence Survey revealed a number of significant knowledge gaps and misperceptions about retirement among adults.[79] "They think they can get full Social Security benefits earlier than they can, they think they have more pension coverage than they do," explains Alicia Munnell, director of the Center for Retirement Research at Boston College. "They think they are saving more than they are, and they think they will work longer than they will."[80] One clear indicator of problems ahead is the common misperception about needing less income during one's retirement years. About 75 percent of Americans currently employed believe that they can get by on less income when they retire. Yet when you ask those who are retired, half of them will tell you that they need the same amount of money as their preretirement income, if not more.[81] The lesson for you? Start saving. Start saving now.

## Summary

Consumer knowledge consists of the information stored within memory. This chapter discusses five major types of consumer knowledge: (1) product knowledge (consisting of product category and brand knowledge), (2) purchase knowledge, (3) consumption and usage knowledge, (4) persuasion knowledge, and (5) self-knowledge. Awareness and image analyses help companies to better understand consumer knowledge. And this understanding may yield many benefits, including the identification of knowledge gaps or undesirable knowledge (such as misperceptions) that undermine the odds of a product being chosen. Examining consumer knowledge sheds light on a product's positioning success, and may lead to the discovery of previously unappreciated product uses. Analyzing consumer knowledge is also useful for gauging the severity of competitive threats and helping companies become more effective in their customer recruitment activities. Finally, companies should understand the sources of consumer knowledge and be especially attentive to whether this knowledge is based on direct experience.

## Product Slogans

The identities of the product, company, or retailer associated with the slogans in Table 9.2 are as follows: (1) GE, (2) BMW, (3) Verizon, (4) M&Ms, (5) Boost Mobile, (6) Capital One, (7) Gatorade, (8) Hummer, (9) Peter Paul Almond Joy, (10) Ball Park Franks, (11) Gillette, (12) MasterCard, (13) Yellow Pages, (14) United Airlines, (15) Budweiser, (16) Firestone, (17) Royal Caribbean, (18) Gap, (19) Timex, (20) Dr. Scholl's.

## Review and Discussion Questions

1. Why might a company care about top-of-the-mind awareness? When might it not care about this?

2. Consider the following set of results from an image analysis in which the customers of a competitive food product (brand A) rated their own brand, your brand (B), and another competitor (brand C). What conclusions can you draw from this information?

good tasting    C: __ : B: __ : __ : __ poor tasting
high in nutrition C: __ : __ A: B: __ : __ low in nutrition
expensive     C: __ : __ A: __ : B: __ inexpensive
easy to cook    __ : B: A: __ : __ : __ C difficult to cook

3. What suggestions do you have for improving what could be learned from the information presented in Tables 9.3 and 9.4 about a company's image?

4. Describe how advertising strategy may depend on consumer knowledge.

5. A grocer recently completed a study of consumers who patronize the store. One of the more intriguing findings was that the amount spent during a shopping trip depended on the number of times a

consumer had shopped at the store. Consumers spent much more money when shopping for only the first or second time at the store. How can you explain this finding?

6. You are developing some brochures that describe a fairly sophisticated and technically oriented product. Results of market research indicate that the two primary target markets hold very different beliefs about how much product knowledge they possess. One segment perceives itself as very knowledgeable, whereas the other sees itself as quite ignorant about the product. What implications does this difference in perceived knowledge carry for developing the brochures?

7. The chapter discusses the importance of understanding consumers' price knowledge but ignores when this type of knowledge may be more or less important. Do you think there are circumstances in which consumers' price knowledge becomes more or less important? Is so, what are these?

8. A recent survey of various target markets reveals important differences in both their level of product knowledge and their use of friends' recommendations during decision making. Consumers having limited knowledge relied heavily on others' recommendations, whereas knowledgeable consumers did not. How can you explain this difference?

## Notes

[1] Fran Brennan, "Limit Kids' Juice Intake, Experts Say," *Miami Herald* (January 31, 1997), F1.

[2] Christine Moorman, Kristin Diehl, David Brinberg, and Blair Kidwell, "Subjective Knowledge, Search Locations, and Consumer Choice," *Journal of Consumer Research*, 31 (December 2004), 673–680.

[3] Joseph A. Alba and J. Wesley Hutchinson, "Dimensions of Consumer Expertise," *Journal of Consumer Research*, 13 (March 1987), 411–454. Also see Mita Sujan, "Consumer Knowledge: Effects on Evaluation Strategies Mediating Consumer Judgments," *Journal of Consumer Research*, 12 (June 1985), 31–46.

[4] Brian Wansink, Randall E. Westgren, and Matthew M. Cheney, "The Hierarchy of Nutritional Knowledge That Relates to the Consumption of a Functional Food," *Nutrition* (2005), in press.

[5] A. Belen del Rio, Rodolfo Vacquez, and Victor Iglesias, "The Effects of Brand Associations on Consumer Response," *Journal of Consumer Marketing*, 18 (2001), 410–425.

[6] For additional research on the influence of brand associations on consumer behavior, see M. K. Agarwal and V. R. Rao, "An Empirical Comparison of Consumer-Based Measures of Brand Equity," *Marketing Letters*, 7 (1996), 237–247; Rajeev Batra and Pamela Miles Homer, "The Situational Impact of Brand Image Beliefs," *Journal of Consumer Psychology*, 14 (2004), 318–330; C. J. Cobb-Walgren, C. A. Ruble, and N. Donthu, "Brand Equity, Brand Preference, and Purchase Intent," *Journal of Advertising*, 24 (1995), 25–40; C. S. Park and V. Srinivasan, "A Survey-Based Method for Measuring and Understanding Brand Equity and Its Extendibility," *Journal of Marketing Research*, 31 (May 1994), 271–288; B. Yoo, N. Donthu, and S. Lee, "An Examination of Selected Marketing Mix Elements and Brand Equity," *Journal of Academy of Marketing Science*, 28 (2000), 195–211.

[7] Alexander Cherenev and Gregory S. Carpenter, "The Role of Market Efficiency Intuitions in Consumer Choice: A Case of Compensatory Inferences," *Journal of Marketing Research*, 38 (August 2001), 349–361.

[8] Akshay R. Rao and Wanda A. Sieben, "The Effect of Prior Knowledge on Price Acceptability and the Type of Information Examined," *Journal of Consumer Research*, 19 (September 1992), 256–270.

[9] Elizabeth Cowley and Andrew A. Mitchell, "The Moderating Effect of Product Knowledge on the Learning and Organization of Product Information," *Journal of Consumer Research*, 30 (December 2003), 443–454.

[10] Carol Park, "Coffin Makers in California Unearth Ways to Compete for Boomers' Bones," *Knight Ridder Tribune Business News* (January 10, 2005), 1.

[11] Lisa Biank Fasig, "Wild Oats Tweaking Brand as Customers Go Natural," *Business Courier* (July 16, 2004), 5.

[12] Mike Musgrove, "To Be Picture-Perfect, a Choice of 3," *Washington Post* (August 29, 2004), F1.

[13] Beth Snyder Bulik, "Texas Instruments Super Bowl Ad Ends Campaign," www.adage.com (February 3, 2005).

[14] Schneider/Stagnito Communications, "Most Memorable New Product Launch Survey," conducted by InsightExpress, www.schneiderpr.com (2004).

[15] For insight on how to improve the success rate of new product introductions, see Joan Schneider, *New Product Launch: 10 Proven Strategies*, Stagnito Communications, www.schneiderpr.com (2004).

[16] Stuart Elliott, "Absolut to Try Television Ads," www.nytimes.com (September 3, 2004).

[17] Tobi Elkin, "Absolut Hit: Raspberri," www.mediapost.com (August 30, 2004).

18 Robin Sidel, "How Do You Get Hip When Your Name Is TIAA-CREF?" *Wall Street Journal* (June 29, 2004), C1.

19 Alan L. Adler, "Saturn Faces Difficult Launch in Japan," *Miami Herald* (May 15, 1997), G4.

20 Andrew Blackman, "A Strong Net Game: J&R Electronics Didn't Have Much of a Chance of Finding Growth Online; So, What's Its Secret?" *Wall Street Journal* (October 25, 2004), R6.

21 The information reported here was downloaded from Harris Interactive's website, www.harrisinteractive.com.

22 Ronald Alsop, "A Good Corporate Reputation Draws Consumers and Investors," *Wall Street Journal Books* (2004). Also see Zeynep Gurhan-Canli and Rajeev Batra, "When Corporate Image Affects Product Evaluations: The Moderating Role of Perceived Risk," *Journal of Marketing Research*, 41 (May 2004), 197–205.

23 Sal Randazzo, "Build a BIP to Underst and Brand's Image," *Marketing News* (September 16, 1991), 18. This article contains an interesting discussion of image analysis.

24 Tammo H. A. Bijmolt and Michel Wedel, "A Comparison of Multidimensional Scaling Methods for Perceptual Mapping," *Journal of Marketing Research*, 36 (May 1999), 277–235. Perceptual mapping can be used for more than examining brand image. See R. Kenneth Teas and Terry A. Grapentine, "Is Your Message Getting Across?" *Marketing Research*, 14 (Spring 2002), 34–39.

25 Rich Thomaselli, "Reebok Logo Gets $50 Million Global Campaign," www.adage.com (August 25, 2003).

26 For research concerning the measurement of price knowledge, see Marc Vanhuele and Xavier Dreze, "Measuring the Price Knowledge Shoppers Bring to the Store," *Journal of Marketing*, 66 (October 2002), 72–85.

27 Akshay R. Rao and Wanda A. Sieben, "The Effect of Prior Knowledge on Price Acceptability and the Type of Information Examined," *Journal of Consumer Research*, 19 (September 1992), 256–270.

28 For more information on education statistics, go to www.nces.ed.gov.

29 An example of examining consumers' relative price knowledge can be found in Michael J. Barone, Kenneth C. Manning, and Paul W. Miniard (2004), "Consumer Response to Partial Price Comparisons in Retail Environments," *Journal of Marketing*, 68 (July), 37–47.

30 Bob Tedeschi, "Cheaper Than It Seems," *New York Times* (January 10, 2005), C9.

31 Joel E. Urbany and Peter R. Dickson, "Consumer Information, Competitive Rivalry, and Pricing in the Retail Grocery Industry," working paper, University of South Carolina (1988).

32 For research on how consumer knowledge about deals affects purchase behavior, see Aradhna Krishna, "The Effect of Deal Knowledge on Consumer Purchase Behavior," *Journal of Marketing Research*, 31 (February 1994), 76–91.

33 Mike Schneider, "Florists Wither," *Miami Herald* (February 12, 2005), C1, C3.

34 The 4 percent estimate is reported by Anick Jesdanun, "In U.S. Few Buy Drugs Online," *Marketing News* (November 1, 2004), 22. A 6 percent estimate is reported by James Frederick, "Shift in Public Attitudes Seen As Rising Health Care Costs Take off," *Drug Store News* (October 11, 2004), 21–22.

35 Jesdanun, "In U.S. Few Buy Drugs Online."

36 Christopher Conkey, "States' Bid for Cheaper Medicine Sputters; Official Web Sites for Buying Drugs from Canada Are Slow to Take off with Consumers," *Wall Street Journal* (February 14, 2005), A4.

37 Robert Sommer and Susan Aitkens, "Mental Mapping of Two Supermarkets," *Journal of Consumer Research*, 9 (September 1982), 211–215.

38 C. Whan Park, Easwar S. Iyer, and Daniel C. Smith, "The Effects of Situational Factors on In-Store Grocery Shopping Behavior: The Role of Store Environment and Time Available for Shopping," *Journal of Consumer Research*, 15 (March 1989), 422–433.

39 Christopher Lawton, "Absolut Seeks Growth through 'Fu'; Timed to Lunar New Year, Ads with Chinese Flavor Target Burgeoning Market," *Wall Street Journal* (February 14, 2005), B8.

40 For an example of research concerning product safety knowledge, see Richard Staelin, "The Effects of Consumer Education on Consumer Product Safety Behavior," *Journal of Consumer Research*, 5 (June 1978), 30–40.

41 Marian Friestad and Peter Wright, "The Persuasion Knowledge Model: How People Cope with Persuasion Attempts," *Journal of Consumer Research*, 21 (June 1994), 1–31. For recent research in this area, see Rohini Ahluwalia and Robert E. Burnkrant, "Answering Questions about Questions: A Persuasion Knowledge Perspective for Understanding the Effects of Rhetorical Questions," *Journal of Consumer Research*, 31 (June 2004), 26–42; Christina L. Brown and Aradhna Krishna, "The Skeptical Shopper: A Metacognitive Account for the Effects of Default Options on Choice," *Journal of Consumer Research*, 31 (December 2004), 529–539; Margaret C. Campbell and Amna Kirmani, "Consumers' Use of Persuasion Knowledge: The Effects of Accessibility and Cognitive Capacity on Perceptions of an Influence Agent," *Journal of Consumer Research*, 27 (June 2000), 69–83.

42 Campbell and Kirmani, "Consumers' Use of Persuasion Knowledge."

43 William O. Bearden, David M. Hardesty, and Randall L. Rose, "Consumers' Self-Confidence: Refinements in Conceptualization and Measurement," *Journal of Consumer Research*, 28 (June 2001), 121–134. Their persuasion knowledge measure has been used recently by Ahluwalia and Burnkrant, "Answering Questions about Questions."

44 See Joseph W. Alba and J. Wesley Hutchinson, "Knowledge Calibration: What Consumers Know and What They Think They Know," *Journal of Consumer Research*, 27 (September 2000), 123–156.

45 Herman Riquelme, "Do Consumers Know What They Want?" *Journal of Consumer Marketing*, 18 (2001), 437–448.

46 It has long been recognized that statisti-

cal models outperform those based on human judgment. See Paul Slovic, "Psychological Study of Human Judgment: Implications for Investment Decision Making," *Journal of Finance,* 27 (September 1972), 779–799.

[47]Riquelme, "Do Consumers Know What They Want?"

[48]Joe Mandese, "Papers, Local TV Seen as More Credible Than Network News; Consumers, Trade Split on Bias," www.mediapost.com (November 1, 2004).

[49]Lawrence J. Marks and Michael A. Kamins, "The Use of Product Sampling and Advertising: Effects of Sequence of Exposure and Degree of Advertising Claim Exaggeration on Consumers' Belief Strength, Belief Confidence, and Attitudes," *Journal of Marketing Research,* 25 (August 1988), 266–281.

[50]Chenghuan Wu and David R. Shaffer, "Susceptibility to Persuasive Appeals as a Function of Source Credibility and Prior Experience with the Attitude Object," *Journal of Personality and Social Psychology,* 52 (April 1987), 677–688.

[51]Dale K. DuPont, "Carnival Cruisers Just in Time for Money-Back Offer," *Miami Herald* (November 21, 1996), C1, C5.

[52]"Microsoft Earns Best Corporate Reputation in the Media, According to Delahaye Index," news release, Medialink Worldwide, www.medialink.com (September 7, 2004).

[53]Ronald Alsop, "Corporate Reputation Survey: Best-Known Companies Aren't Always the Best Liked; McDonald's Takes Pounding for Menu Items, Surly Staff; Cheers and Jeers for Microsoft," *Wall Street Journal* (November 15, 2004), B4.

[54]Kate MacArthur, "UK Not Feeling the Love, McD's Puts Slogan on Ice," *Advertising Age* (October 25, 2004), 45; Arthur De Montesquiou, "Fallen Arches: McDonald's to Drop Logo in 'Change' British Ad Campaign," Canoe Money, www.money.canoe.ca/News/

Sectors/Media/2004/10/13/pf-667688 .html (October 13, 2004).

[55]Diane Anderson, "Cisco Reboots Image with $150M Effort," *Brandweek* (January 10, 2005), 4.

[56]David Wethe, "Wal-Mart Lashes Back at Critics with Newspaper Advertisements," *Knight Ridder Tribune Business News* (January 14, 2005), 1; "Wal-Mart Starts Campaign to Improve Image," www.washingtonpost.com (January 13, 2005).

[57]Sidel, "How Do You Get Hip When Your Name Is TIAA-CREF?"

[58]Robert Guy Matthews, "Spirits Makers Aim to Juice Their Old-School Beverages; Kahlúa and Courvoisier Are among the Brands Getting Image Makeovers," *Wall Street Journal* (November 11, 2004), B5.

[59]Jonathan Betz, "State Tries to Change Image with Ad Campaign," www.wwltv .com (January 23, 2005).

[60]Mike Gorrell, " 'Dry' Utah Whets Ad Campaign," *Salt Lake Tribune* (May 8, 2004).

[61]Chad Terhune, "Pepsi, Discovery in Smart-Snack Push," *Wall Street Journal* (December 6, 2004), B3; Chad Terhune, "PepsiCo to Identify, Promote Its More-Healthful Products," *Wall Street Journal* (July 30, 2004), B3.

[62]Sarah Karush, "La-Z-Boy Will Not Suffer Stodgy Image Sitting Down," *Miami Herald* (May 28, 2004), C8.

[63]Erin White, "P&G's British Ad Gets Back to Basics; More Creative Cartoon Bear 'Hibernates' As Charmin Gets Old-Fashioned Pitch," *Wall Street Journal* (August 20, 2004), B2.

[64]Lauri Klefos, "Defining New Hampshire's Image in the Travel Market," *New Hampshire Business Review* (April 16, 2004), A28.

[65]Michel Marriott, "Will Computers on TV Go the Way of the 8-Track?" *Miami Herald* (March 1, 1998), H16.

[66]Carole Sugarman, "Wine's Benefits, Risks Argued on Labels," *The State* (November 10, 1992), D4.

[67]Sally Goll Beatty, "Mercedes Hopes Duckie, Child Broaden Appeal," *Wall Street Journal* (May 21, 1997), B1, B8.

[68]Oscar Suris, "Now, BMW and Mercedes Seem Sensible," *Wall Street Journal* (November 6, 1996), B1, B8.

[69]Stephen Power and Neil E. Boudette, "Auto Reverse: Slide in Mercedes's Performance Dents Chrysler's Recent Revival; DaimlerChrysler Fixes a Unit, while Another Stumbles; Fuel for Merger Critics; Snoop Dogg Gets a 300C," *Wall Street Journal* (February 9, 2005), A1.

[70]"American Consumers Split over Substitutions and Boycotts of French, German, and Canadian Products," www .fleishman.com (April 17, 2003).

[71]"American Consumers Delaying Major Purchases, Negative toward Products from Countries Opposed to US Actions in Iraq," www.fleishman.com (March 31, 2003).

[72]D-Ann Durban, "Hybrid Vehicle Market Hasn't Accelerated Yet," *Miami Herald* (January 11, 2005), C5.

[73]Ibid.

[74]Calmetta Y. Coleman, "Hallmark Campaign Focuses on Card Costs," *Wall Street Journal* (February 12, 1998), B6.

[75]The authors thank Professor Jim Burroughs of Rutgers University for this example.

[76]Joseph A. Alba and J. Wesley Hutchinson, "Dimensions of Consumer Expertise," *Journal of Consumer Research,* 13 (March 1987), 411–454.

[77]Shannon Dortch, "There Goes the Sun," *American Demographics* (August 1997), 4–7.

[78]Jeannine Aversa, "Students 'Dismal but Improving,' " *Miami Herald* (April 2, 2004), C4.

[79]Harriet Johnson Brackey, "Many Will Find Gold Scarce in Golden Years," *Miami Herald* (April 5, 2004), A1, A2.

[80]Ibid.

[81]Ibid.

# Chapter 10

# Consumer Beliefs, Feelings, Attitudes, and Intentions

## Opening Vignette

In Chapter 6 we told you about the many challenges facing the orange juice industry (see Consumer Behavior and Marketing 6.1). Especially disturbing has been the declining consumption of orange juice. One of the ways the industry hoped to reverse its recent decline was to reinforce orange juice's image as a healthy drink. A $7 million advertising campaign was conducted in 2004 with this objective in mind. So did the campaign meet this objective? Let's look at the report card.

In the beginning of 2005, a market research study surveyed a random sample of consumers about their orange juice beliefs, attitudes, and behaviors. Rather than showing the hoped-for improvement in consumers' beliefs and attitudes, the survey revealed just the opposite had occurred on several key measures. Only 62 percent rated orange juice as "good for your health," down from 70 percent the previous year. The survey also showed that declines had occurred for the statements "a drink you feel good about drinking" and "being 100 percent pure." Other measures, such as "reducing the risk of certain diseases" and "providing important nutrients, vitamins, and minerals" showed no significant changes over the year-long period, but fell below historical levels.

Deterioration in consumers' beliefs and attitudes were detected in other areas as well. Only 53 percent rated orange juice as "tasting great," a decline from 63 percent a year earlier. The survey further revealed a declining trend among consumers who rated orange juice as "thirst quenching," "able to drink without getting tired of it," and "enjoyed by everyone in the household." Moreover, the number of consumers who reported purchasing orange juice in the past thirty days fell to 75 percent, down from 77 percent the prior year and below levels reported in most quarters since 2000.

Orange juice sales in supermarkets have declined for the past three citrus seasons, and the Florida Department of Citrus projects another 0.5 percent decline in the 2004–2005 season. Through January 22, 2005, however, department figures showed a 2.4 percent decline in retail sales. "We don't have a clear indication advertising is what's driving the purchasing of juice," says Paul Cragin III, the senior vice president for market research at Data Development Worldwide, the company that conducted the survey. "We got good purchasing levels, but it doesn't seem to be a function of the advertising."

Source: Kevin Bouffard, "Orange Juice Ads Fare Poorly," *Knight Ridder Tribune Business News* (February 17, 2005), 1.

Before the orange juice industry can stop the bleeding at the checkout counter, it must first stop the erosion in consumers' beliefs and attitudes toward its product.

For these attitudes are what strongly affect consumers' purchasing behavior. As you well know, rarely do we give a company our money without first giving it our stamp of approval in the form of holding favorable attitudes toward the product it's trying to sell us.

The purpose of this chapter is to develop your understanding of attitudes as well as the closely related concepts of intentions, beliefs, and feelings. Let's begin by clarifying what we mean by each of these terms. **Attitudes** are *global evaluative judgments.* When we say that someone has a favorable attitude toward, say, a product, we mean that he likes the product; he evaluates the product to be good and desirable. A negative attitude connotes the opposite: he dislikes the product; the product is evaluated as being bad and undesirable. **Intentions** are *subjective judgments by people about how they will behave in the future.* Hopefully you intend to read the rest of this chapter. Afterwards, you may intend to watch some television, work on the computer, call a friend, or eat some food. It's also possible that you haven't formed any immediate intentions on what you'll do next.

**Beliefs** are also subjective judgments, but they *are subjective judgments about the relationship between two or more things.* Ideally, after you finish this chapter, you will believe that it was informative. You may also form beliefs about whether the chapter was interesting (versus boring) and easy (versus difficult) to understand. Finally, **feelings** can be defined as an *affective state* (such as the mood you currently are in) *or reaction* (such as the feelings experienced during product consumption or processing an advertisement). Feelings may be positive (e.g., feeling happy) or negative (e.g., feeling disappointed). They may be overwhelming (such as feelings that occur during or after a near-death experience), or they may be virtually nonexistent (such as feelings that occur when taking a vitamin pill).

The relationships between intentions, attitudes, beliefs, and feelings are represented diagrammatically by Figure 10.1. Beliefs and feelings are the building blocks on which attitudes are built. If you believe that a brand has desirable attributes, you'll have a more favorable attitude toward the brand. Similarly, if you associate the brand with positive feelings, your attitude also becomes more favorable. Attitudes, in turn, determine intentions.[1] Your intention to buy a particular brand, for example, should grow stronger as your attitude toward this brand becomes more favorable. The figure also indicates a relationship between intentions and actual behavior, thereby reflecting the notion that people typically do what they intend to do.

Figure 10.1 is your roadmap for Chapter 10. We begin our journey with consumer beliefs. We will then travel southward and visit the other determinant of attitudes: feelings. Next, we'll move eastward on our map to consumer attitudes. After exploring this area, we'll resume our eastward journey to our final stop of consumer intentions. So all aboard. First stop: consumer beliefs.

**FIGURE 10.1**    The Relationships between Consumer Beliefs, Consumer Feelings, Consumer Attitudes, Consumer Intentions, and Consumer Behavior

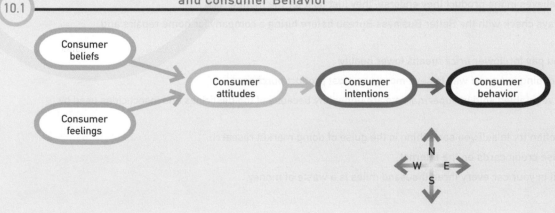

## Consumer Beliefs

You have already encountered a couple of the most important type of beliefs in previous chapters of the book. In Chapter 9 we discussed the beliefs about a brand's associations that determine brand image. And we are far from done in our coverage of these brand beliefs. Indeed, we'll return to them later in this chapter when we introduce you to multiattribute attitude models, the dominant approach over the last three decades for understanding the beliefs that determine consumers' attitudes. We also talked about beliefs in the form of expectations and the critical role they play in determining post-consumption satisfaction in Chapter 6. **Expectations** are *beliefs about the future*. There are other types of expectations besides those about brands and products that are important to understand. We will get to these very soon. But first, a few words about beliefs in general.

Given our emphasis in Part II of the book on the decision-making process that drives consumers' product and store choices and the focus on product knowledge in Chapter 9, it is understandable why our coverage of consumer beliefs thus far has been dominated by those beliefs that pertain to products in general and brands in particular. Yet many other types of beliefs held by consumers affect how the consumers behave in the marketplace. Table 10.1 lists a few of the countless beliefs consumers may hold. How many of these beliefs are held by you?

| TABLE 10.1 | A Sampling of Consumer Beliefs |
| --- | --- |

1. If a deal seems to be too good to be true, it probably is.
2. You can't trust a salesperson, no matter what he or she is selling.
3. Downloading music for free is stealing from the musicians and recording companies.
4. Many businesses mark up products' prices before putting them on sale.
5. The health care system needs improvement.
6. You can't believe what most advertising says these days.
7. Extended warranties are worth the money.
8. Prescription medicines bought online are of lower quality than those bought at a local store.
9. People need less money to live on once they retire.
10. Auto repair shops take advantage of women.
11. Appliances today are not as durable as they were twenty years ago.
12. Larger-sized packages of a product are always a better per-unit buy than a smaller-sized package of the same item.
13. No one really believes in the product they endorse; they just do it for the money.
14. One should always check with the Better Business Bureau before hiring a company for home repairs and improvements.
15. You get what you pay for; lower price means lower quality.
16. Comparison shopping is a good way to save money on most product purchases.
17. Most fruits and vegetables sold in supermarkets are unhealthy because of the pesticides and insecticides used by farmers.
18. Telemarketers often try to sell you something in the guise of doing market research.
19. It's not safe to use credit cards on the Internet.
20. Changing the oil in your car every three thousand miles is a waste of money.

Although covering all of the beliefs relevant to consumer behavior is impossible, highlighting a few of the beliefs of particular significance is possible. Let's begin with consumers' beliefs about something considered so important that the Survey Research Center at the University of Michigan has been measuring it for more than half a century.[2]

### The Indices of Consumer Expectations and Consumer Sentiment

Whereas consumers' ability to spend is a function of their income and financial assets, their willingness to spend is determined, in part, by their beliefs about their financial future. Consumers feel more comfortable in making the financial commitments typically required by major purchases when they are optimistic about the future. Discretionary purchases are likely to be delayed when these expectations are pessimistic. For this reason, the Indices of Consumer Expectations and Consumer Sentiment were created as a way of anticipating consumers' buying behavior in the immediate future.

Every month a sample of five hundred Americans respond to these three measures of their expectations: (1) whether they think they will be better off financially one year into the future, (2) whether they think the country will be better off financially one year into the future, and (3) whether they think the country will be better off financially five years into the future. Responses to these measures form the Index of Consumer Expectations (ICE). The ICE was considered to be important enough that in 1989 it was included by the U.S. Commerce Department as a component in its Index of Leading Economic Indicators to help forecast future trends in the U.S. economy.[3]

The ICE responses, along with responses to measures assessing consumers' current financial situation (whether they are better off financially than they were a year ago) and their beliefs about current buying conditions (whether they believe now is a good time for buying major household items), are combined to form the widely reported Index of Consumer Sentiment (ICS). Each month the financial news media report the latest ICS score and how it differs from the prior month. You can see how the ICS has fluctuated, sometimes dramatically, over the past fifty years by looking at Figure 10.2.

**FIGURE 10.2**   The Index of Consumer Sentiment, 1954–2004

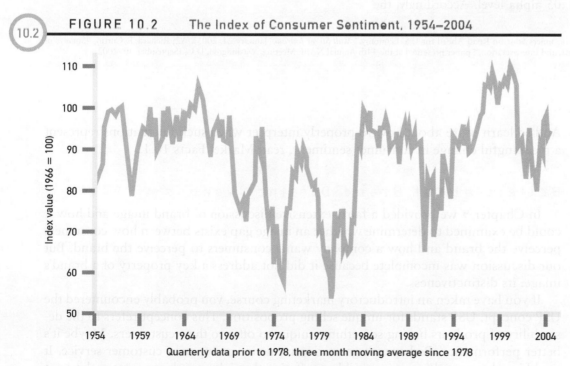

Quarterly data prior to 1978, three month moving average since 1978

Source: Surveys of Consumers, Survey Research Center, University of Michigan, www.sca.isr.umich.edu

## The Index of Consumer Sentiment: Misperceptions and Misrepresentations

In January 2005, the mid-month report on the Index of Consumer Sentiment showed a score of 95.8, down from 97.1 in December 2004. Shortly thereafter, in a story titled "Consumers Sour on Road Ahead for U.S. Economy," the *Wall Street Journal* reported: "The slight decline in the University of Michigan sentiment index doesn't suggest consumers are feeling overly gloomy, according to Steve Stanley, chief economist at RBS Greenwich Capital. Consumer spending was 'stellar' in the second half of last year, 'so the current levels of sentiment are certainly not an impediment to robust advances and actual outlays,' he said in a note to clients."

In a paper written by Dr. Richard T. Curtin, director of the Surveys of Consumers at the University of Michigan, he laments about common misperceptions and misrepresentations of the sentiment index. First, a slight change in the numbers does not necessarily indicate a significant change in consumer sentiment. As Dr. Curtin states in his paper, "This is perhaps the most frustrating and most common misinterpretation of the data." A change of nearly five points in the index score must take place before it reaches significance at the conventional .05 alpha level. Accordingly, the most appropriate interpretation of the numbers reported in December 2004 and January 2005 is that consumer sentiment remained unchanged, not that there has been a decline, not even a slight one.

Moreover, even if a significant change in consumer sentiment had taken place during this time period (December 2004 to January 2005), it is inappropriate to relate the change to sales activity during this time period or, even worse, to sales activity during an earlier time period. Again we refer to Dr. Curtin's paper: "There would be no reason to measure consumer expectations if they did not predict future spending and saving behavior. Nonetheless, it is rather typical to read that, for example, the September data was not consistent with September retail sales. I have never read a report that compared consumer confidence data from say six months ago with current sales. Indeed, there is no reason to expect a relationship of this month's confidence data with this month's sales data although there is usually some correspondence. The empirical evidence has consistently found that the data from the Surveys of Consumers does provide accurate forecasts six to twelve months in advance."

Source: Agnes T. Crane, "Consumers Sour on Road Ahead for U.S. Economy," *Wall Street Journal* (January 24, 2005), A2; Richard T. Curtin, "Surveys of Consumers: Theory, Methods, and Interpretation," paper presented at the 44th Annual NABE Meeting, Washington, D.C. (September 30, 2002).

And to learn more about how to properly interpret when such fluctuations represent a meaningful change in consumer sentiment, read Market Facts 10.1.

### Beliefs about Brand Distinctiveness

In Chapter 9 we provided a fairly extensive discussion of brand image and how it could be examined to determine whether an image gap exists between how consumers perceive the brand and how a company wants consumers to perceive the brand. But our discussion was incomplete because it did not address a key property of a brand's image: its distinctiveness.

If you have taken an introductory marketing course, you probably encountered the USP concept. USP stands for unique selling proposition. This concept refers to the desirability of products having something unique to offer to their customers. Maybe it's better performance. Perhaps it's greater convenience or superior customer service. It could involve something as intangible as offering the right social image, something we talked about in Chapter 8. Whatever it is, the USP should represent why consumers would want to buy your product rather than your competitor's product. And this USP should be represented in a company's communications with consumers. For example, it's easy to see from the comparative advertisement in Figure 10.3 what the makers of Yoplait Light believe is its unique selling proposition. Comparative advertising that describes the advertised brand's superiority over its competitors is an excellent way of conveying the USP. Ivanabitch vodka, on the other hand, is relying on a pickle to help communicate the product's distinctiveness to consumers. To learn more about how the company got itself into a bit of a pickle, stop for a moment and take a look at Consumer Behavior and Marketing 10.1.

Brand distinctiveness is considered important enough that it's included in Harris Interactive's EquiTrend measurement system. You might recall our discussion of EquiTrend from Chapter 6 in which we presented its findings about the extent to which different brands fulfill consumers' expectations. EquiTrend also assesses a brand's distinctiveness in terms of its perceived uniqueness relative to its competition.[4] Table 10.2 presents the average distinctiveness ratings for twenty-five of the more than one thousand brands examined by EquiTrend.

FIGURE 10.3 This Advertisement Communicates the Product's Unique Selling Proposition to Consumers

Courtesy of Yoplait USA

Oreo cookies top the list with an average of 7.21, with 10 being the maximum possible score a brand could receive. Four of the top five brands are products, the single exception being eBay, the highest-rated online brand in the ratings released by Harris Interactive for public consumption on its website.[5] At the bottom of the list is AT&T Long Distance Services, with a very mediocre average of 4.30. This relative lack of distinctiveness is a characteristic of the telecommunications market as a whole. Brands in the financial services market don't have much to brag about, either. The most appropriate use of this information entails comparing competitors within the same market, such as Barnes & Noble and Borders bookstores. Table 10.2 reveals a noticeable difference in the companies' ratings in favor of Barnes & Noble (6.52 versus 5.64). Nonetheless, it's interesting to note that this superiority largely evaporates for Barnes & Noble's website (5.79 rating), thus indicating an area for future improvements.

Why is distinctiveness so important? Brands perceived as undifferentiated from their competitors will face greater challenges in attracting and keeping customers. When a brand is seen as similar to the rest of the field, consumers have little reason to prefer it over another. When New Hampshire commissioned an image study to assist in the development of its tourism business, the state discovered that consumers had difficulty differentiating it from other New England states. Consumers perceived New Hampshire and its neighboring states as being very similar in what they had to offer a tourist.[6]

Moreover, a lack of distinctiveness means that consumers have less reason to repurchase the same brand. Without distinctiveness, customer loyalty becomes unlikely. Distinctiveness also enables a business to charge more money for its offering. When all brands are believed to be similar, price competition intensifies. But when a brand has successfully differentiated itself from the rest, consumers should be more willing to pay for what can only be obtained by buying the brand. This usually means more profit for the firm. For all of these reasons, then, creating a brand image that is meaningfully

## Ivanabitch Vodka Sticks with Its Pickle to Create Brand Distinctiveness

Ivanabitch vodka is distilled in the Netherlands and imported by International Spirits, a division of the Itera Group, which is based in Moscow. The vodka was launched in 2004, yet advertising was delayed until February 2005, when its distribution system was completed.

Empire Communications Group, an advertising company based in Jacksonville, Florida, developed an advertising campaign that includes advertisements with a pickle propped up inside a cocktail glass. Empire's managing partner, Pete Helow, says the pickle is part of the campaign because Russians commonly eat pickles while drinking vodka. So Empire's marketing strategy is designed to link the Ivanabitch brand name with the image of a pickle. The vodka is now being marketed in four Florida cities: Jacksonville, Miami, Orlando, and Tampa.

Not all are enamored, however, with the pickle. Empire's billboard campaign for the vodka was rejected by Florida's two major billboard owners, Viacom Outdoor and Clear Channel Outdoor, in all four cities. The billboard companies had no objection to the name of the vodka, according to Helow. He added, "They said, 'If you remove the pickle we'll run the [bill]-board.'" Officials from both companies said the pickle was too suggestive and recommended laying it horizontally on a plate or chopping it up instead. "I saw several creative executions for outdoor advertisements for Ivanabitch vodka and I didn't approve any of them," says Rod Firestone, Clear Channel Outdoor's Jacksonville division president. "I did not think they were appropriate copy for the streets of Jacksonville."

Empire has refused to remove the pickle because, as Helow notes, doing so would undermine the focus of the advertising campaign. International Spirits president Steve Koegler said he was surprised by the reaction of the billboard companies. But he plans to keep the pickle as the vodka's signature mark. "To be honest with you, I never thought of it as a phallic symbol until [Viacom and Clear Channel] brought it up," says Koegler. "It was amazing." Helow adds, "It made no sense to remove the pickle to appease the billboard companies. We're introducing the authentic Russian way to drink vodka. That sets us apart from every other vodka." Empire is now running the advertisement using mobile billboards on the sides of trucks.

Source: Christopher Calnan, "Ad Company Determined to Keep Its Vodka Pickle," *Florida Times-Union* (February 23, 2005), 1.

differentiated from the competition is an important objective in managing consumers' beliefs.

### Inferential Beliefs

Another type of consumer belief is the **inferential belief,** in which *consumers use information about one thing to form beliefs about another thing.* Consumers often form inferential beliefs, such as when product information is incomplete[7] or when consumers interpret certain product attributes as signals of product quality. Some of the most common inferential beliefs are **price-quality inferential beliefs,** in which *consumers use price information to form beliefs about a product's quality.*[8] Products that charge higher prices are believed to possess greater quality than lower-priced products. One cosmetics manufacturer learned about price-quality inferential beliefs the hard way when it introduced a new line of cosmetics of comparable quality to existing brands but at a significantly lower price. Yet target consumers relied on price as an indicator of quality and were unwilling to run the risk of a "facial meltdown" to save

| BRAND | BRAND DISTINCTIVENESS |
|---|---|
| Oreo cookies | 7.21 |
| WD-40 spray lubricant | 7.03 |
| Hershey's milk chocolate candy bars | 7.00 |
| eBay | 6.97 |
| Reynolds Wrap aluminum foil | 6.70 |
| Google.com | 6.65 |
| Ziploc food bags | 6.53 |
| Barnes & Noble bookstores | 6.52 |
| Heinz ketchup | 6.48 |
| Yahoo! | 6.36 |
| Amazon.com | 6.33 |
| Duracell batteries | 6.29 |
| Toys "R" Us stores | 6.27 |
| Wal*Mart discount stores | 6.27 |
| Kleenex facial tissues | 6.06 |
| Sam's Club | 5.91 |
| BarnesAndNoble.com | 5.79 |
| Borders bookstores | 5.64 |
| Visa | 5.53 |
| Office Depot office supply stores | 5.32 |
| MasterCard | 5.23 |
| Verizon Communications | 5.11 |
| Citibank | 4.69 |
| Cingular Wireless | 4.57 |
| AT&T Long Distance Services | 4.30 |

Source: "Reynolds Wrap Aluminum Foil Ranks #1 in Overall Brand Equity," Harris Interactive, www.harrisinteractive.com (June 22, 2004). Reprinted with permission from Harris Interactive, Inc. All Rights Reserved.

Note: Higher numbers indicate greater distinctiveness, with 10 being the maximum possible score.

themselves a little bit of money. The new line went nowhere and eventually was withdrawn from the market. To find out how a Chinese manufacturer adjusted its marketing strategy when entering India to accommodate consumers' price-quality inferential beliefs, read Consumer Behavior and Marketing 10.2.

Another example of inferential beliefs involving price comes from retailers' use of partially comparative pricing. **Partially comparative pricing** is *when a retailer features price comparisons for some but not all of the products it carries.* You've probably encountered this practice in a grocery store where every so often a shelf tag indicates the more expensive price charged by a competitor for a particular product. These comparisons enhance consumers' beliefs about the store's price superiority for the comparatively priced items,[9] but what inferential beliefs might consumers form about how the store's prices compare with its competitor for the noncomparatively priced items?

## Indian Consumers' Price-Quality Beliefs Shape Marketing Strategy

Chinese consumer-electronics maker Haier Group, with operations in the United States, Europe, the Middle East, Africa, and elsewhere in Asia, is making a big push into India, trying to win a slice of one of the world's fastest-growing markets after earlier bids by rivals Konka Group and TCL Corp. failed. Konka's and TCL's entry into India proved disastrous due to a misjudgment of the Indian consumer, an ineffective entry strategy, and troubled relationships with the companies' local partners. Haier is determined not to repeat those companies' mistakes. To begin with, Haier's India operation will be fully owned. And it won't pitch its products as "cheap."

Shortly after India began dropping its import barriers in the late 1990s, low-priced Chinese toys, batteries, and other consumer goods began flooding the Indian market. These goods came at a steep discount to those produced by Indian manufacturers, prompting charges of "dumping." But the threat of trade penalties never materialized. Instead, stories began to circulate of defective Chinese products; one story told of batteries losing their charge after a single use. Konka and TCL didn't understand the association of quality and price in the mind of the Indian consumer, so the companies' efforts to sell products cheaply merely earned them a reputation of being substandard, say market watchers. Soon, both Konka and TCL ended up shutting down their Indian operations. "There is a perception among the Indian consumers that China is a technologically backward country," says Richie Liu, director of TCL India Holdings, a fully owned subsidiary of TCL that's making a bid to reenter India with a $12 million initial investment.

Haier, however, is seeking to make over the Chinese image in India. So rather than selling its television sets, refrigerators, and air conditioners as affordable, Haier is positioning its products as premium quality with price tags on par with those of its competitors or, in some cases, even higher. This approach matches a business model that has reaped huge profits in India for South Korean giants LG Electronics and Samsung Electronics.

Haier believes that India will become its second-largest market after China in the next five years, contributing 10 percent of the global sales. Haier plans to invest $15 million in the country in the next year, and long-term plans include a local research-and-development center for consumer products.

Source: Excerpted in part from Rasul Bailay, "A Haier Price," *Far Eastern Economic Review,* 167 (May 27, 2004), 44.

Might they think that the promoted price advantages on some items would apply to the rest of the items? If so, consumers would use the price superiority conveyed by the comparatively priced products to infer a similar superiority for the noncomparatively priced products. Retailers certainly wouldn't mind this happening. But what if consumers were more skeptical and cynical in their thinking? Might they infer that the reason why other items are priced noncomparatively is because these items are actually more expensive than what the competitor would charge? In this case, the consumers would infer that the noncomparatively priced products are more expensive, an obviously undesirable outcome for the retailer.

To answer these questions, Barone, Manning, and Miniard conducted a series of studies in which participants reported their relative price beliefs (i.e., their beliefs about the price charged by one retailer relative to the price charged by its competitor) after processing a set of materials containing the prices charged by the retailer for a select group of products.[10] These products and their prices are presented in Table 10.3. Some of the participants received only the noncomparative prices identified in the table. Others received the set of prices identified in the partially comparative pricing

TABLE 10.3

10.3

**TABLE 10.3** Description of the Prices Used in the Partially Comparative Pricing and the Noncomparative Pricing Conditions of Barone, Manning, and Miniard's Research

| PRODUCT | NONCOMPARATIVE PRICING MATERIALS | PARTIALLY COMPARATIVE PRICING MATERIALS |
|---|---|---|
| Cranberry juice[a] | $2.88 | $2.88 versus $3.39 at the competitor's store |
| Cup-of-noodles[a] | $0.40 | $0.40 versus $0.51 at the competitor's store |
| Pickles[b] | $2.24 | $2.24 |
| Potato chips[b] | $1.19 | $1.19 |

Source: Michael J. Barone, Kenneth C. Manning, and Paul W. Miniard, "Consumer Response to Retailers' Use of Partially Comparative Pricing," *Journal of Marketing*, 68 (July 2004), 37–47, Study 1.

[a] Comparatively priced products only in the partially comparative pricing materials.
[b] Noncomparatively priced product in both sets of materials.

column. For these participants, two of the products are comparatively priced, whereas the remaining two products are noncomparatively priced. Notice, then, that a comparison of the relative price beliefs for pickles and potato chips allows us to determine what happens when comparatively priced products are present. So what did happen? Participants reported less favorable relative price beliefs for the noncomparatively priced products when comparatively priced products were present, thus indicating that partially comparative pricing may have the undesirable effect of making the retailer seem more expensive than its competitor for noncomparatively priced products.

Although the examples of inferential beliefs have involved the use of price information thus far, it is certainly not the only basis by which consumers make inferences. Product packaging is sometimes used. One grocer decided to wrap its fresh fish in the same way meats are packaged. This decision proved to be a costly mistake as consumers interpreted the wrapping as an indication of the fish being less than fresh, and sales declined. The presence of color granules in products ranging from laundry detergents to cold medicines have prompted inferences of greater product effectiveness.

Advertising can also shape consumers' inferences. Comparative advertising claims about the advertised brand's superiority over its competitor on those attributes featured in the advertisement have been found to influence consumers' inferences about the advertised brand's superiority on attributes never discussed in the advertisement.[11] The pictures featured in an advertisement can be a potent basis for the formation of inferential beliefs. Suppose the producer of a tissue product wants to encourage consumers to believe that the product is soft. Beyond explicitly stating that the tissue is soft, how else might the producer encourage such beliefs in its advertising? How about including a picture of something known for its softness? A picture of a fluffy little kitten should do the trick. Indeed, it does. One study compared the beliefs about a tissue's softness after participants were shown either an ad explicitly claiming the product was soft versus an ad making no such claim, but containing a picture of the kitten. Remarkably, beliefs about the product's softness were significantly greater after participants had seen the ad with the kitten.[12] These findings support the wisdom of including visual elements within advertising—such as in the Verizon advertisement in Figure 10.4, which uses images of an old-time locomotive versus a modern bullet train to visually convey the difference in speed between Verizon's product and that of its competition—that encourage the formation of favorable inferential beliefs about the advertised product.

Other Wireless Networks

verizonwireless BroadbandAccess

Makes laptop
connections wireless

Check email or access
corporate intranet

Easy to set up
and install

Verizon Wireless PC 5220 Card

Introducing Verizon Wireless Broadband**Access**. The power to wirelessly download with speeds like your office LAN.

Now your workforce can download wirelessly at unbelievable speeds in the greater Miami–Ft. Lauderdale area and top cities across the country. So they can connect to the Internet, intranet, or email and download at speeds comparable to your office LAN with the rich experience of broadband. With our wireless PC card in their laptop and typical speeds between 300 and 500 kbps, your employees can work as efficiently outside the office as they do inside. Broadband**Access** gives them the freedom to effortlessly download critical information, complex files, and applications. So they have the power to quickly get answers while in the field for better customer service and even close sales right on the spot. And with our wide-area mobility and secure CDMA technology, business can be conducted anywhere within our Broadband**Access** coverage area without the need for a hot spot connection. It's one more reason why for all your company's wireless needs, we mean business.

Network
Enabled
By
Lucent Technologies

Contact our business representatives at 1.800.VZW.4BIZ or log on to verizonwireless.com.
Coverage not available in all areas. Claims based on published speeds. Actual speeds vary. ©2004 Verizon Wireless

verizonwireless
We never stop working for you®

**FIGURE 10.4** Visual Advertising Elements That Encourage Favorable Inferential Beliefs about the Advertised Product

The potential for inferential belief activity sometimes requires protecting consumers from themselves. In the dietary supplement market, for example, using a particular brand name may cause consumers to make unwarranted inferences about a product. Consumers might infer that a product named Herbal Prozac might serve as an effective substitute for the prescription drug Prozac. Or Hepatacure might be believed to help treat liver problems. To prevent these mistaken inferences, the Food and Drug Administration passed a ruling that prohibits the makers of dietary supplements from using suggestive names.[13]

## Consumer Confusion

So far our focus has been on what consumers believe. But sometimes, consumers just don't know what to believe. Consider homeowners who want to turn their unfinished basement with its cinderblock walls into a more habitable living space. This process often requires first eliminating the potential for moisture to seep in and through the basement walls. A number of small companies and one-man operations claim they can prevent this seepage using a variety of methods that vary substantially in cost. And once companies discover that you are looking at different companies and ways of handling this problem, some may tell you why you'll be sorry if you go with another company. Given these conflicting claims about which approach is best, homeowners can easily end up being confused about which approach to use. I know I certainly was when I went through this decision process for my first home many years ago.

Confusion comes in many shapes and forms.[14] There's the confusion that arises because of conflicting information and knowledge, like that experienced by the homeowners trying to decide which method to use for preventing water problems in their basement. There's the confusion that occurs because of insufficient information. After three hundred incidents involving Firestone tires that resulted in forty-six deaths, Firestone announced that it was recalling 6.5 million of its tires, the second-largest recall in history. Initially, there was an incredible amount of confusion, with many owners of Firestone tires unaffected by the recall demanding replacements. At least one auto service center owner felt that much of the problem was due to Firestone not providing adequate information during the early days of the product recall.[15]

Confusion may stem from mistaken identity, such as when consumers mistakenly believe that one company's product is actually the product of a different company. Maybe the names are too similar (for an example, see Buyer Beware 10.1). Maybe the packaging of one is much like the packaging of another. Maybe particular product features are so similar that confusion may result. Whatever the source, legal actions are often taken by the company who perceives its product being infringed upon. DaimlerChrysler sought an injunction against General Motors on grounds that GM's Hummer H2's grille design was so similar to the grille used on DaimlerChrysler's Jeep Wrangler that consumer confusion would arise. GM's response: no one is going to confuse a Hummer with a Jeep. The courts sided with GM and refused to grant the injunction.[16] This type of confusion, in which consumers believe something

## Brand Name Confusion in the Pharmacy

The Food and Drug Administration is warning health care professionals and consumers about prescribing and dispensing errors between two drugs with similar names. The errors have occurred between Zyprexa, an antipsychotic drug made by Eli Lilly, and Zyrtec, an antihistamine made by Pfizer, used to treat allergies. In addition to having similar names, Zyprexa and Zyrtec are often stored close together on pharmacy shelves. The drugs also are both taken once daily and share some of the same dose strengths.

In a letter sent to health care professionals that was posted on the FDA's website, Lilly said the company had received reports of the drugs being given incorrectly to consumers. "These reports include instances where Zyprexa was incorrectly dispensed for Zyrtec and vice versa, leading to various adverse events in some instances," the letter said. "These errors could result in unnecessary adverse events or potential relapse in patients suffering from schizophrenia or bipolar disorder." Heather Lusk, a Lilly spokeswoman, said the company has received seventy-nine reports of prescribing or dispensing errors since both drugs came on the market in 1996. She said that a "few" hospitalizations have been possibly related to the mix-ups but that the company is not aware of anyone who suffered a relapse of their bipolar disorder or schizophrenia.

Lilly said that it would make changes to the label for the 10-mg bottle of Zyprexa to reduce the potential for error and would conduct an advertising campaign directed at health care professionals. The label changes include capitalizing all letters of *Zyprexa*, except for the letter *y*, and offsetting the last five letters in yellow highlights.

Source: Excerpted from Jennifer Corbett Dooren, "FDA Warns of Drug Confusion," *Wall Street Journal* (February 9, 2005), D5. Copyright 2005 by Dow Jones & Co. Reproduced with permission of Dow Jones & Co., Inc., in the textbook format via Copyright Clearance Center.

that's incorrect, is analogous to the concept of misperception you learned about in Chapter 9.

In fact, consumer confusion may exist for many different reasons. Changes in a product's image and positioning may leave consumers confused until the old image gives way to the new one. When Procter & Gamble changed the name of its Sunny Delight drink for kids to Sunny D and repositioned it as a healthy alternative to soft drinks, efforts were necessary for eliminating confusion among consumers in the United Kingdom.[17] Some reports have claimed that America Online has confused consumers with its multiple marketing messages covering a spectrum of topics and services.[18] A comparative advertisement for the Duracell Coppertop brand of batteries showed consumers that these batteries lasted up to three times longer than so-called heavy-duty batteries (the old-fashioned zinc-carbon batteries) by depicting the use of different batteries in different toys. Whereas the toys containing the heavy-duty batteries eventually became powerless, the cute yellow duck powered by the Duracell brand continued going strong. Apparently many consumers became confused about just who Duracell was being compared against. When rival Energizer conducted a consumer survey, nearly half of the respondents thought the ad was claiming superiority over Energizer's alkaline batteries. Energizer filed a federal lawsuit that eventually led to the phrase "excluding alkaline batteries" being added to the commercial when touting Duracell's superiority.[19]

How do consumers respond to confusion? It depends. When confused about which product best serves their needs, consumers may try to resolve the confusion through further information search if they believe such activity will be fruitful. If additional search is not viewed as potentially useful and a choice is needed, the choice will likely be made based on those things that are perfectly clear, such as price. When I finally had to make a decision about which company to hire for making my basement walls moisture resistant, the only thing clear to me was that some companies were going to charge me a lot more money than others. I had no idea whether the expensive methods for handling this problem would be any more effective than the cheaper approaches. So I decided to go with one of the cheaper methods. And for the few years that I lived in the house before moving, I never had a problem with moisture in the basement.

In other situations, however, confusion can cause consumers to defer product purchase indefinitely. In late 2004, the Merck drug company pulled its widely prescribed painkiller medication Vioxx off the market because of safety concerns. Many consumers switched to nonprescription pain relievers, causing double-digit sales gains for these products. Others stopped taking pain medications altogether. "Whenever there is press around drug safety, you will see that people will sit it out for a while trying to figure out what to do," observes Lisa Morris, global marketing director at IMS, a pharmaceutical research and consulting firm.[20] Adds William Rowe, executive director of the American Pain Foundation, "It is disconcerting because it could mean there are people, due to the confusion, who are doing nothing and experiencing pain."[21]

## Consumer Feelings

As we noted near the beginning of the chapter, beliefs are only one of the two primary determinants of consumer attitudes. Attitudes may also depend on feelings. To illustrate the importance of feelings in shaping consumer attitudes, let's consider the influence exerted by the most pervasive of all feelings: the consumer's mood state. **Mood state** refers to *how people feel at a particular moment in time.*[22] For example, how do you feel right now? Happy? Sad? Energized? Tired? Bored (we certainly hope not!)?

Did you know that the attitudes you form may depend on your mood state at the time of attitude formation?[23] Indeed, a number of studies have found that people will evaluate products more favorably when they are in a good mood than when they are not. Let's pause for a moment and ponder the implications of this finding. Participants' mood states are peripheral or irrelevant to the product and its performance. Nonetheless, despite this irrelevance, mood states affect how products are evaluated. Recognize, then, the opportunity this affords companies for shaping consumer opinions about their products in ways that do not require changing the product's attributes or benefits. This means, for just one example, that a retailer can sway shoppers' evaluations of the desirability of the products it carries by configuring its shopping environment to evoke more favorable mood states.[24]

Feelings, including mood states, are far richer in nature than simply whether they are good or bad. One study identified more than sixty different feelings that were grouped into three major categories: upbeat, negative, and warm.[25] Table 10.4 lists the different feelings within each of these three categories. The value of distinguishing between different feelings, including those that fall into the same category, is illustrated by recent research showing that disgust and sadness, although both negative emotions, produced very different effects on participants' economic decisions.[26]

There are three principal occasions during which feelings may shape consumers' attitudes and possibly their behaviors. Depending on the nature of the television commercial and the program in which it appears, feelings may be activated when consumers encounter and process advertising that, in turn, influences their post-message

| UPBEAT | NEGATIVE | WARM |
|---|---|---|
| Active | Angry | Affectionate |
| Adventurous | Annoyed | Calm |
| Alive | Bad | Concerned |
| Amused | Bored | Contemplative |
| Attentive | Critical | Emotional |
| Attractive | Defiant | Hopeful |
| Carefree | Depressed | Kind |
| Cheerful | Disgusted | Moved |
| Confident | Disinterested | Peaceful |
| Creative | Dubious | Pensive |
| Delighted | Dull | Sentimental |
| Elated | Fed-up | Touched |
| Energetic | Insulted | Warm-hearted |
| Enthusiastic | Irritated | |
| Excited | Lonely | |
| Exhilarated | Offended | |
| Good | Regretful | |
| Happy | Sad | |
| Humorous | Skeptical | |
| Independent | Suspicious | |
| Industrious | | |
| Inspired | | |
| Interested | | |
| Joyous | | |
| Light-hearted | | |
| Lively | | |
| Playful | | |
| Pleased | | |
| Proud | | |
| Satisfied | | |
| Stimulated | | |
| Strong | | |

Source: Julie A. Edell and Marian Chapman Burke. "The Power of Feelings in Understanding Advertising Effects." *Journal of Consumer Research*, 14 (December 1987), 421–433.

attitudes. Similarly, depending on the store, consumers may experience certain feelings during shopping that affect their attitudes and behaviors within the retail environment. Finally, product consumption itself may trigger certain feelings that determine post-consumption attitudes. In the remainder of this section, we examine each of these occasions more closely.

Cottonelle. Lab tested for comfort.

Give your family the ultimate in comfort with our very best. Cottonelle® Ultra toilet paper.

Cottonelle. Looking out for the family.™

**FIGURE 10.5** Advertising That Evokes Positive Feelings

Although much of the advertising consumers encounter in the marketplace does not evoke any type of emotional response on the part of viewers, some advertising does. Advertising sometimes amuses us and makes us laugh, if only for a fleeting moment. You've probably chuckled once or twice while watching one of the commercials from the "Battle of the Beers" advertising campaigns, in which Miller and Budweiser are taking shots at each other. At other times, advertising may evoke a warm and fuzzy feeling inside. We suspect that many of the parents who encountered the advertisement for Kimberly-Clark's Cottonelle bathroom tissue (Figure 10.5) experienced such feelings. And every once in a while, advertising may move us in ways usually reserved for reality. Anheuser-Busch's "Applause" commercial, which appeared during the 2005 Super Bowl, shows American troops walking through an airport terminal. A single civilian begins to clap. Then another joins in. Soon, the terminal is filled with the sound of appreciative Americans applauding those who risk their lives for all of us. The editor of AdAge.com, a Vietnam veteran, wrote a story about this commercial in which he tells of the tears it brought to his eyes.[27] He was not the only person that the commercial touched in this way: it was rated the most-liked commercial by viewers in February 2005.[28]

Of course, not all of the feelings experienced while processing advertising will be positive. Sometimes advertising annoys us, such as when it contains an overbearing spokesperson or it wears out its welcome because of being repeated too often.[29] Sometimes advertising offends people. Certain segments of the population, for example, find sexually themed advertising to be highly inappropriate and experience strongly negative feelings when they encounter advertising of this nature. The Hardee's commercial for its Western Bacon Thickburger featured model and actress Cameron Richardson seductively riding a mechanical bull while holding on to a Thickburger. At a website featuring this commercial, the majority of consumers who posted an opinion reported how much they enjoyed the commercial. But this opinion was not shared by everyone. One poster thought it was "very vulgar and suggestive." Another announced that one of the "family values" watchdog organizations was calling for a boycott of Hardee's.

The feelings activated by an advertisement are important because of their potential to influence the attitudes formed about the product featured in the advertisement.[30] Attitudes toward the advertised product become more favorable after viewing an ad that evokes positive feelings. Conversely, ads that elicit negative feelings may cause consumers to hold less favorable product attitudes.

Beyond the feelings induced by advertising, the feelings induced by the program in which a commercial appears are also important. This occurs because some programs influence viewers' moods. Some television programs make us feel happy; others may have the opposite effect. Because mood states influence the product attitudes formed after processing an advertisement,[31] advertisers may benefit by placing their messages in television shows that evoke positive moods while avoiding those that depress consumers' mood states.[32] Coca-Cola has avoided advertising during TV news programs because "there's going to be some bad news in there and Coke is an upbeat, fun product."[33]

## Feelings as Part of the Shopping Experience

Just like advertisements, retail environments differ in the types of feelings they may elicit from consumers during the shopping experience. Many retail environments are rather plain and ordinary. Little effort is made to configure the environment in such a way that consumers are likely to feel the types of positive emotions that can be so beneficial, for reasons we will cover shortly. Your local supermarket is probably a good example of this. As one business consultant observes, if you want to feel like it's 1964, step inside your average supermarket.[34] Of course, it could be worse, and sometimes it is. Some retail environments are much worse than ordinary. They evoke negative feelings from those who dare to enter them. They can be so bad that the shopper leaves the store in a much worse mood state compared to the one he or she had upon entering the store.[35] But for those retailers that "get it right," just the opposite can happen: being in the store puts shoppers in a much better mood.[36] Consumers don't just go shopping at the store; they experience the store.

Total customer experience drives Victoria's Secret retail formula. Not only does management want the store atmosphere to make people feel welcome, comfortable, and "in the mood," management wants the clothing to make women feel sexy, desirable, and good about themselves. Nowhere is Victoria's Secret's brand better executed than at its new, two-story flagship store in New York City's Herald Square, a 25,000-square-foot stage of sexy images of silky lingerie and enticing colors, luscious fragrances and scents, and romantic music, all configured to make shopping a most pleasurable experience. Publix supermarkets may claim, "Where shopping is a pleasure." At Victoria's Secret's Herald Square location, it truly is.

In the past, researchers have relied quite heavily on Mehrabian and Russell's PAD conceptualization for understanding the influence of store environments on consumer behavior.[37] From this perspective, environments evoke three primary types of emotional response: pleasure, arousal, and dominance. **Pleasure** represents *positive feelings*, **arousal** reflects *feelings of excitement and stimulation*, and **dominance** indicates *feelings of being in control*. These three basic responses, in turn, determine how an individual acts in an environment, such as staying in or leaving the environment. Donovan and Rossiter's assessment of the PAD's relevance to retail environments found pleasure to be by far the most influential determinant. Pleasure was related to consumers' attitude toward the store, their intention to spend time browsing in the store, and whether they would spend more than they had originally planned on spending.[38]

Researchers are continuing to explore the impact of feelings on consumer response to retail environments, although not necessarily within the confines of the PAD framework. Some researchers have simply distinguished between positive versus negative feelings.[39] Others have looked at the influence of retail environments in terms of how an environment affects consumers' mood states.[40] Regardless of the particular orientation taken by researchers, they have consistently found that how a retail environment makes consumers feel is important. Indeed, the feelings experienced during shopping can have far more profound effects than influencing attitudes toward a particular retailer[41] or the products carried by the retailer.[42] These feelings can also determine consumers' shopping and spending behaviors. Retail environments that make people feel good are rewarded with shoppers staying longer, buying more items, and spending more money.[43] Given these benefits, it's rather surprising how often retailers fail to take full advantage of this potent influence on consumer behavior.

## TABLE 10.5  Measuring Feelings

How often, if at all, do you experience the following feelings as a result of *eating chocolate?*

| | | | | | | | | | |
|---|---|---|---|---|---|---|---|---|---|
| Happy | never | 1 | 2 | 3 | 4 | 5 | 6 | 7 | very often |
| Excited | never | 1 | 2 | 3 | 4 | 5 | 6 | 7 | very often |
| Delighted | never | 1 | 2 | 3 | 4 | 5 | 6 | 7 | very often |
| Joyous | never | 1 | 2 | 3 | 4 | 5 | 6 | 7 | very often |
| Satisfied | never | 1 | 2 | 3 | 4 | 5 | 6 | 7 | very often |
| Proud | never | 1 | 2 | 3 | 4 | 5 | 6 | 7 | very often |
| Annoyed | never | 1 | 2 | 3 | 4 | 5 | 6 | 7 | very often |
| Depressed | never | 1 | 2 | 3 | 4 | 5 | 6 | 7 | very often |
| Guilty | never | 1 | 2 | 3 | 4 | 5 | 6 | 7 | very often |
| Regretful | never | 1 | 2 | 3 | 4 | 5 | 6 | 7 | very often |

Courtesy, Yogi Tea. Used with permission.

**FIGURE 10.6** Promoting the Advertised Product's Ability to Evoke Desired Feelings

### Feelings as Part of the Consumption Experience

In Chapter 6, we noted that consumption experiences often evoke feelings. Indeed, some experiences are liked primarily for their ability to induce certain feelings, whether it be the tranquility that comes from listening to the waves caress the shore at a tropical resort or the thrills of skydiving. Even for products whose consumption is relatively free of emotion (e.g., a plastic garbage bag), feelings in the form of frustration and regret may still occur if the product fails to perform properly (e.g., a garbage bag that bursts, leaving quite a mess to be cleaned up). For this reason, then, feelings have the potential to be a part of virtually all consumption experiences. And given this potential, companies should examine what feelings exist during consumption. An example of measuring the feelings experienced during consumption (in this example, eating chocolate) appears in Table 10.5. Note that a slight change in the wording of the question is all that would be needed to adapt this measure for use in assessing the feelings experienced when processing an advertisement or shopping.

It is well documented that feelings experienced during consumption of a product will influence consumers' post-consumption evaluations.[44] Consumers are more satisfied when product consumption leads to positive feelings while avoiding negative feelings. Greater satisfaction, in turn, leads to many desirable outcomes, many of which were described in Chapter 6's coverage of why customer satisfaction is so important to companies.

Companies may therefore find it beneficial to promote their products based on the positive feelings experienced during consumption. Automobile manufacturers, for example, often emphasize the thrills awaiting those who sit behind the steering wheel of their vehicles. Amusement parks communicate how much fun awaits you. The advertisement for Yogi Tea in Figure 10.6 suggests that the product will exhilarate users as they are "energized by healing herbs." In contrast, getaway vacation packages targeting the overworked executive promise a weekend of relaxation and tranquility. Sometimes products are promoted as a way for consumers to achieve favorable mood states. Two examples of advertising that emphasize the advertised product's mood-altering qualities can be found in Figure 10.7.

Helping consumers avoid or reduce the negative feelings that might otherwise occur during consumption is another approach sometimes used for enhancing a product's desirability. One car rental company has promoted itself through advertising showing the frustration and irritation consumers may experience when renting from the competition—feelings that are, of course, avoided when renting from the advertised company. Similarly, many consumers experience tremendous guilt when eating food considered to be less than healthy. As shown in Figure 10.8, French's recognizes these concerns by highlighting the credentials of their products, allowing consumers to avoid the guilt they might otherwise feel.

Just as moods play a role when consumers are processing advertisements and shopping in retail environments, moods may also be important during product consumption, although this may depend on the nature of the consumption experience. To illustrate, consider the study in which college students tasted peanut butter while listening to music that put them in a more or less favorable mood state.[45] The students then tasted one of three different versions of peanut butter: (1) peanut butter mixed with honey, (2) peanut butter mixed with baking soda, or (3) unaltered peanut butter. The students' post-consumption product attitudes as a function of their mood and peanut butter version are presented in Figure 10.9. Mood affected the ratings of the unaltered peanut butter, with a more favorable mood producing more favorable evaluations of the product. Yet this influence disappeared when either honey or baking soda was added to the peanut butter. Many loved the sweeter taste from using honey; nearly all hated the bitter taste produced by the baking soda. Apparently, when consumption activates such intense feelings, these

**FIGURE 10.7** These Advertisements Emphasize the Advertised Product's Mood-Altering Properties

**FIGURE 10.8** This Product Attempts to Build Positive Attitudes by Emphasizing How It Avoids the Negative Feelings That May Arise During Consumption

feelings can overpower the influence of less intense affective states like mood.

At this point, we are halfway through our journey that we mapped out in Figure 10.1. We have visited beliefs and feelings, the two major determinants of attitudes. It's now time for us to head eastward on our map so that we may explore the concept of attitudes more fully.

## Consumer Attitudes

Just to remind you, attitudes are global or overall evaluative judgments. If I ask you whether you like or dislike my product, if you have a favorable or unfavorable opinion of my product, or if you think my product is the best, I'm asking you to tell me your attitude toward my product. And because attitudes influence consumers' purchase and consumption intentions, companies are very interested in knowing about consumers' attitudes toward their products.

So let's take a look at one indicator of consumers' product attitudes: which brands they think are the best. Each year the Harris Poll of "best brands" asks consumers, "Considering everything, which three brands do you consider the best?"[46] The ten brands identified most often in 2004 are reported in Table 10.6. The number one brand, Sony, has enjoyed the top spot since 2000. New to this year's top ten lists are Toyota and Honda.

**FIGURE 10.9** Mood Can Shape Consumers' Interpretation of Consumption Experiences That Do Not Evoke Strong Affective Reactions

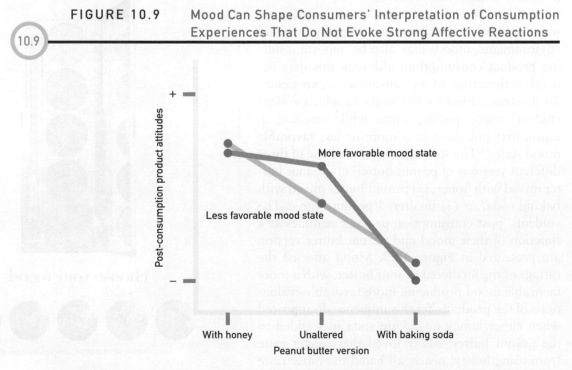

Source: Paul W. Miniard, Sunil Bhatla, and Deepak Sirdeshmukh, "Mood as a Determinant of Post-Consumption Evaluations: Mood Effects and Their Dependency on the Affective Intensity of the Consumption Experience," *Journal of Consumer Psychology,* 1 (1992), 173–195.

**TABLE 10.6**     Consumers' "Best Brands": The Top Ten

1. Sony
2. Coca-Cola
3. Dell
4. Kraft
5. Toyota
6. Ford
7. Honda
8. Procter & Gamble
9. General Electric
10. General Motors

Source: "Sony Tops the List in Annual Best Brands Survey for Fifth Consecutive Year," Harris Interactive, www.harrisinteractive.com (July 7, 2004). Reprinted with permission from Harris Interactive, Inc. All Rights Reserved.

Their presence gives the automobile industry four brands on the list, the most of any industry and the industry's best showing ever.

Recognize that this list of best brands only speaks to a brand name's overall standing from the consumer's point of view. The list does not tell us about consumers' attitudes toward specific products carrying the brand name. The Sony name, for example, exists in many different product categories. It's highly unlikely that consumers would hold the same attitudes regardless of the product category in which the name appears. For this reason, understanding consumers' attitudes toward a specific branded product requires a more focused assessment approach.

Such an assessment is offered by Harris Interactive's EquiTrend system, which we discussed earlier in the chapter when we covered brand distinctiveness. The EquiTrend system evaluates the brand equity of more than one thousand brands in thirty-five product categories.[47] This evaluation is based on consumers rating the brands in three areas: (1) familiarity, (2) perceived product quality, and (3) purchase intent—the likelihood of buying the brand regardless of its price.[48] These ratings are combined to form a total brand equity score, representing the brand's overall attractiveness to consumers.

Would you care to venture a guess about which branded product earned the top spot in 2004? We'll even give you a hint: it's sold in supermarkets, it's non-edible, and it's very shiny. To find out if you're right, go to Table 10.7. This table contains the ten branded products with the highest brand equity scores. The table also presents the products' individual scores in each of the three areas used to derive the equity scores. You will readily notice that this list is dominated by products found on supermarket shelves. Not a single electronic or mechanical product made it into the top ten. The top-ranked product received an equity score of 75.1 out of a possible 100. Inspection of this product's scores shows excellent ratings were achieved in familiarity (only 1 percent below the highest score any product received) and purchase intent (in which it was the highest rated product). And even though the difference between the top-ranked product's quality score (7.47) and that given to the product receiving the highest quality score (Hershey's candy bars with a 7.51) is certainly too small to represent a meaningful difference, there clearly is room for improvement, in an absolute sense, given the difference between the product's quality score and the maximum possible

**TABLE 10.7**  The Top Ten Branded Products

| PRODUCT | RANK[a] | EQUITY[b] | FAMILIARITY[c] | QUALITY[d] | PURCHASE INTENT[d] |
|---|---|---|---|---|---|
| Reynolds Wrap aluminum foil | 1 | 75.1 | 96 | 7.47 | 9.00 |
| Hershey's milk chocolate candy bars | 2 | 74.0 | 97 | 7.51 | 8.67 |
| Ziploc food bags | 3 | 73.6 | 97 | 7.44 | 8.85 |
| Heinz ketchup | 4 | 72.9 | 97 | 7.36 | 8.72 |
| Duracell batteries | 5 | 72.5 | 97 | 7.36 | 8.75 |
| WD-40 spray lubricant | 6 | 72.3 | 92 | 7.48 | 8.67 |
| Kleenex facial tissues | 7 | 72.3 | 94 | 7.30 | 8.73 |
| Kraft | 8 | 72.2 | 95 | 7.30 | 8.69 |
| Clorox bleach | 9 | 72.1 | 95 | 7.36 | 8.60 |
| Oreo cookies | 10 | 71.6 | 96 | 7.37 | 8.36 |
| Top ten average score | | 72.9 | 96 | 7.40 | 8.70 |

Source: "Reynolds Wrap Aluminum Foil Ranks #1 in Overall Brand Equity," Harris Interactive, www.harrisinteractive.com (June 22, 2004). Reprinted with permission from Harris Interactive, Inc. All Rights Reserved.

[a] Rank based on equity score.
[b] Equity score based on quality, familiarity, and purchase intent scores. Maximum score is 100.
[c] Percentage indicating somewhat, very, or extremely familiar with brand.
[d] Maximum score of 10; the higher the number, the better.

score of 10. Indeed, this "limitation" applies to all of the products identified in Table 10.7. Apparently the quality dimension largely accounts for the equity scores not being even closer to the maximum of 100.

We don't want the retailers of the world to feel that we are neglecting them. Table 10.8 presents the ten retailers receiving the highest equity scores. The top-ranked store is Wal*Mart with an equity score of 70.8. This score did not earn Wal*Mart a position in the overall top ten list shown in Table 10.6, but it's good enough to place Wal*Mart at the head of the class in the retail brands category. Although a number of the retailers achieved higher quality scores than Wal*Mart, none of them surpassed Wal*Mart's familiarity and purchase intentions scores. The one number that really jumps out of Table 10.8 is the substantial number of consumers unfamiliar with Borders bookstores, especially in comparison to competitor Barnes & Noble.

Finally, let's take a look at EquiTrend's results for those retail brands that make their living online. Table 10.9 contains the scores for the top ten online brands. Yahoo! has the greatest familiarity among consumers, but it doesn't have the greatest equity. That honor belongs to Google.com. One of the more interesting things about Table 10.9 is how the average scores for the top ten online brands, shown in the last row of the table, compare with the average scores for the top ten retail brands in Table 10.8. Although online sellers trail the bricks-and-mortar retailers in familiarity and purchase intent, their average quality scores are essentially the same, indicating that consumers do not believe that the quality of goods offered through one channel is any better than the quality of goods sold through the other channel, at least for the set of products carried by these retailers. Nonetheless, you might remember from Chapter 9 that many consumers are reluctant to purchase prescription drugs online because of concerns about product quality, which suggests that the perceptions of parity observed here may not extend to all product categories.

**TABLE 10.8**     The Top Ten Retail Brands

| RETAILER | RANK[a] | EQUITY[b] | FAMILIARITY[c] | QUALITY[d] | PURCHASE INTENT[d] |
|---|---|---|---|---|---|
| Wal*Mart | 1 | 70.8 | 96 | 6.94 | 8.52 |
| Home Depot | 2 | 68.9 | 90 | 7.08 | 8.42 |
| Target | 3 | 68.0 | 93 | 6.96 | 8.29 |
| Barnes & Noble | 4 | 67.2 | 88 | 7.24 | 8.13 |
| Best Buy | 5 | 66.1 | 89 | 6.95 | 8.19 |
| Lowe's Home Improvement | 6 | 65.5 | 82 | 7.02 | 8.10 |
| Borders bookstores | 7 | 63.9 | 61 | 7.07 | 7.93 |
| Office Depot | 8 | 63.8 | 88 | 6.79 | 8.01 |
| Sam's Club | 9 | 63.1 | 82 | 6.92 | 7.68 |
| Toys "R" Us | 10 | 62.5 | 93 | 6.95 | 7.54 |
| Top ten average score | | 66.4 | 86 | 6.99 | 8.08 |

Source: "Reynolds Wrap Aluminum Foil Ranks #1 in Overall Brand Equity," Harris Interactive, www.harrisinteractive.com (June 22, 2004). Reprinted with permission from Harris Interactive, Inc. All Rights Reserved.

[a] Rank based on equity score.
[b] Equity score based on quality, familiarity, and purchase intent scores. Maximum score is 100.
[c] Percentage indicating somewhat, very, or extremely familiar with brand.
[d] Maximum score of 10; the higher the number, the better.

**TABLE 10.9**     The Top Ten Online Brands

| BRAND | RANK[a] | EQUITY[b] | FAMILIARITY[c] | QUALITY[d] | PURCHASE INTENT[d] |
|---|---|---|---|---|---|
| Google.com | 1 | 69.3 | 85 | 7.43 | 8.23 |
| Yahoo! | 2 | 68.0 | 93 | 7.20 | 7.98 |
| Microsoft.com | 3 | 63.2 | 88 | 6.88 | 7.67 |
| HistoryChannel.com | 4 | 62.7 | 79 | 7.20 | 7.69 |
| BarnesAndNoble.com | 5 | 61.8 | 75 | 7.03 | 7.60 |
| Hallmark.com | 6 | 61.6 | 68 | 7.14 | 7.51 |
| Amazon.com | 7 | 61.5 | 77 | 6.94 | 7.55 |
| Discovery.com | 8 | 60.7 | 62 | 7.11 | 7.43 |
| eBay | 9 | 60.3 | 85 | 6.89 | 7.35 |
| BestBuy.com | 10 | 59.9 | 78 | 6.76 | 7.50 |
| Top Ten Average Score | | 62.9 | 79 | 7.06 | 7.65 |

Source: "Reynolds Wrap Aluminum Foil Ranks #1 in Overall Brand Equity," Harris Interactive, www.harrisinteractive.com (June 22, 2004). Reprinted with permission from Harris Interactive, Inc. All Rights Reserved.

[a] Rank based on equity score.
[b] Equity score based on quality, familiarity, and purchase intent scores. Maximum score is 100.
[c] Percentage indicating somewhat, very, or extremely familiar with brand.
[d] Maximum score of 10; the higher the number, the better.

Attitudes can vary along several dimensions or properties. Two fundamental properties of attitudes are their valence and extremity. **Attitude valence** refers to *whether the attitude is positive, negative, or neutral.* A consumer may like Coke and Pepsi, dislike Shasta cola, and be fairly indifferent toward RC cola. **Attitude extremity** reflects *the intensity of the liking or disliking.* Even though the consumer has a positive attitude toward both Coke and Pepsi, he or she may be much more favorable toward one brand than another.

Attitude valence and extremity are important in several ways. To illustrate, suppose we segment consumers in terms of the favorability of their attitudes toward sports. We could place those who like a particular sport in one segment, those who dislike the sport in another segment, and those who are indifferent in yet another segment. We could further refine this simple segmentation approach by further subdividing the favorable and unfavorable segments into smaller segments based on the extremity of attitudes. For instance, among those holding a positive attitude toward a certain sport, we could differentiate between those for whom the sport is their favorite one versus those who like it even though it's not their favorite. Table 10.10 identifies the percentage of Americans choosing a sport as their favorite. Why would this information be important? Because

**TABLE 10.10**     Americans' Favorite Sports, 1985–2004 (percent)

| SPORT | 1985 | 1994 | 2004 |
|---|---|---|---|
| Pro football | 24 | 24 | 30 |
| Baseball | 23 | 17 | 15 |
| College football | 10 | 7 | 11 |
| Men's pro basketball | 6 | 11 | 7 |
| Auto racing | 5 | 5 | 7 |
| Men's college basketball | 6 | 8 | 6 |
| Men's golf | 3 | 5 | 4 |
| Hockey | 2 | 5 | 4 |
| Men's soccer | 3 | 3 | 3 |
| Women's tennis | NA | NA | 2 |
| Boxing | NA | NA | 2 |
| Track & field | 2 | 2 | 1 |
| Men's tennis | 5 | 3 | 1 |
| Horse racing | 4 | 2 | 1 |
| Bowling | 3 | 1 | 1 |
| Women's college basketball | NA | NA | 1 |
| Women's soccer | NA | NA | 1 |
| Women's pro basketball | NA | NA | * |
| Women's golf | NA | NA | * |
| Not sure | * | 2 | 2 |

Source: "Professional Football Leads Baseball by 2-to-1 as Nation's Favorite Sport," The Harris Poll, Harris Interactive, www.harrisinteractive.com (October 13, 2004).

Note: Numbers represent the percentage of Americans choosing the sport as their favorite.

NA = not available; * < 1.

**TABLE 10.11**      Sports Disliked by Americans, 1993–2003 (percent)

| SPORT | 1993 | 2003 |
|---|---|---|
| Dog fighting | NA | 81.4 |
| Pro wrestling | 42.5 | 55.7 |
| Bullfighting | NA | 46.2 |
| Pro boxing | 34.7 | 31.3 |
| PGA Tour | 31.9 | 30.4 |
| PGA Seniors | 31.4 | 29.9 |
| LPGA Tour | 34.0 | 29.2 |
| NASCAR | 16.9 | 27.9 |
| Soccer | 18.1 | 27.6 |
| ATP men's tennis | 20.8 | 26.5 |

Source: "Not Bowling?" *Marketing News* (October 10, 2003), 16.

Note: Numbers represent the percentage of Americans indicating they disliked or hated the sport.

NA = not available.

it identifies the size of the market for products and services that cater to a sport in terms of the best prospects—those holding attitudes most conducive to buying and using these products and services. For example, the potential demand for products and services related to the most popular sport, professional football, such as football equipment, products carrying team logos, and television and radio broadcasts of football games, is tied to the number of these best prospects. Increasing the number of "true fans" translates into more business for these products and services. Conversely, the size of the segment holding unfavorable attitudes represents a constraint to the size of the potential market. Table 10.11 reports the percentage of Americans who dislike, even hate, a particular sport. Unless these attitudes are changed, there is no chance of converting these consumers into customers.

Attitudes are not carved in stone. Indeed, they are often rather fickle. Today's craze may easily become tomorrow's has-been, as clothing and toy manufacturers know all too well. Even long-established attitudes can change over time. A tradition that started back in the mid-1800s involved going out into the woods and chopping down that season's Christmas tree. Slowly but surely, that tradition gave way to families driving to a local vendor to find a Christmas tree. But over the last twenty years or so, nature's contribution to the Christmas holidays has been increasingly replaced by man-made counterfeits. You can find out more about this and how tree growers are responding to this competitive threat in Consumer Behavior and Marketing 10.3.

This potential for attitudes to change brings us to our next attitude property: attitude resistance. **Attitude resistance** is the *degree to which an attitude is immune to change.*[49] Some attitudes are highly resistant to change; others are much more malleable. Ideally, companies want their customers' product attitudes to be highly resistant, which makes the customers less vulnerable to competitive attacks. One indication of a company's vulnerability to competitive attacks is the resistance of its customers' attitudes toward its product. Take, for example, the Oust air freshener comparative advertisement that claims that Oust, unlike Lysol products, can kill bacteria in the air. This advertisement's success in courting Lysol users will depend on their resistance to such an attack on their brand. Typically, users of the comparison

## Consumers' Changing Attitudes Threaten a Holiday Tradition

The National Christmas Tree Association (NCTA), which represents thousands of Christmas tree growers nationwide, has conducted an annual consumer survey since 1990. Between then and 2002, the sales of Christmas trees had seen a steady increase. Good news, right? Not really. Why? Because this increase went almost exclusively to the Association's competitor: artificial trees. In 1990, the Association found that Americans displayed 35.4 million fresh trees and 36.3 million artificial trees (most of which are imported from China)—roughly a fifty-fifty split. By 2002, the balance had tipped decidedly in favor of the tree that comes out of a box. By then, 57.2 million artificial trees were on display in the United States, compared to only 22.3 million real trees. So in little more than a decade, fresh tree sales had declined by nearly 40 percent. This shift from natural to artificial was especially prevalent among baby boomers, those born between 1946 and 1964. To make matters even worse, another menacing number turned up in the 2002 survey. Nearly one-third of U.S. households did not display any Christmas tree at all, real or artificial. The growers were obviously in a battle for their very existence.

Market research was undertaken. "We've had focus groups to ask people what they like and don't like about a real tree versus a fake tree," says Chal Landgren, an Oregon State University professor and extension forester. Consumers hated those messy brown needles. According to Landgren, forestry researchers several years earlier had begun tackling the needle problem with Douglas firs. Oregon growers are working with Oregon State and Washington State university researchers to breed trees with the most desirable characteristics. These growers and researchers are even doing experimental breeding to produce real trees that, like artificial ones, won't drop brown needles.

The Internet was also enlisted to help in the battle. The Association's website (www.realchristmastrees.org)

has areas for both children and teachers. The children's section is designed to foster knowledge and favorable attitudes among these future consumers and current influencers of their parents' decisions. And to make buying a real tree more convenient for consumers, some sellers have opened sites on the Internet for easy ordering and delivery. In 2004, the Association launched a market expansion campaign, which promoted the benefits of buying a fresh tree. Among other things, a cross-promotion with *The Polar Express* holiday movie was initiated, in which moviegoers could redeem their tickets for a discount on the purchase of a tree at participating vendors.

These efforts have paid off the last couple of years. The sales decline has been not only stopped but reversed. In 2003, 23.4 million Americans purchased a fresh tree. This number jumped to 27.1 million consumers in 2004, the largest single-year sales increase since the Association began tracking such things. At the same time, sales of artificial trees declined, as 9 million households reported buying one of these in 2004, a decrease of 600,000 from the previous year.

"This is great news for those in the Real Christmas Tree industry, both growers and retailers," says Erwin Loiterstein, chairman of the NCTA Market Expansion Task Force. "Consumers are obviously demanding more of the traditional, farm-grown, natural trees instead of the fake ones from China. Our research indicates that several factors contributed to this increase. Mostly, there is a growing trend in the U.S. for having a natural, traditional product to celebrate the holidays, especially among younger adults. In fact, among households headed by members of Generation Y (people from the ages of eighteen to twenty-nine), fifteen Real Christmas Trees were purchased for every one fake tree." Apparently the "real thing" has become the "in thing" again.

Sources: Excerpted in part from Michelle Cole, "Disturbing Trends Needle Christmas Tree Growers in Oregon," *Knight Ridder Tribune Business News* (December 4, 2003), 1. Also see "U.S. Consumers Purchase More Real Trees," press release, National Christmas Tree Association, www.realchristmastrees.org (January 25, 2005).

brand in a comparative advertisement are more resistant to changing their attitudes than are users of a different brand.[50] Later in the chapter we'll talk about alternative strategies for changing consumers' attitudes. When we do so you should keep in mind that the success of any given strategy ultimately depends on attitude resistance. Resistance is the barrier that attitude change strategies must overcome.

So what determines attitude resistance? Ultimately, if the foundation on which the attitude is built is strong, then resistance will be strong. The salesperson for a competitor's offering may have some rather unflattering things to say about the product you currently prefer. Among other things, your ability to resist this attack depends on your product knowledge. To the extent that you are able to poke holes in the salesperson's arguments (e.g., by being knowledgeable about the weaknesses of the competitor's offering), your preference is less likely to change. Product knowledge in the form of direct experience with the attitude object usually leads to firmly entrenched attitudes that are highly resistant to change. In contrast, attitudes based on indirect experience, such as those formed after seeing an advertisement or hearing what someone else has to say about the attitude object, are normally more susceptible to change.[51]

Attitudes may also vary in terms of the degree of confidence with which they are held. **Attitude confidence** represents *a person's belief that her or his attitude is correct.*[52] Some attitudes may be confidently held, whereas others may exist with a minimal degree of confidence. Attitudes based on direct experience with the product are usually held with more confidence than those derived from indirect experience, such as those that might be formed after seeing an ad for new product.[53] Attitude confidence is important for two reasons. First, it can affect the strength of the relationship between attitudes and behavior.[54] Confidently held attitudes will usually be relied on more heavily to guide behavior. When confidence is low, consumers may not feel comfortable with acting on their existing attitudes. Instead, consumers may search for additional information before deciding how to act. Second, confidence can affect an attitude's susceptibility to change. Attitudes associated with greater confidence are more resistant to change.[55]

The last property considered here, **attitude accessibility**, refers to *how easily the attitude can be retrieved from memory.* Attitudes reside in memory. Just like anything else that lives there, attitudes must first be remembered before they can be influential. Attitudes that are more accessible will exert a greater influence on behavior.[56] Accessibility also influences the odds that an attitude will be spontaneously activated when the attitude object is encountered, such as when shoppers encounter a product in the retail environment.[57] How companies can enhance the accessibility of attitudes and other things that exist in the consumer's memory is the subject of Chapter 16.

## Types of Attitudes

Attitudes come in many shapes and forms. The preceding discussion concerning consumers' opinions about different products and retailers has focused on what is referred to as **attitude toward the object ($A_o$)**. $A_o$ represents an *evaluation of the attitude object,* such as a product. For example, judgments about which product is liked the most, which product has the highest quality, and which product is the "best" are based on a person's overall evaluation of the product. Of course, products and retailers are just some of the attitude objects of relevance in understanding consumer behavior. Take, for example, consumers' attitudes toward advertising. A study by the Advertising Research Foundation indicates that viewers' liking of a television commercial is an important predictor of the ad's success in the marketplace.[58] And many studies have examined the role played by consumers' **attitude toward the ad ($A_{ad}$)**, representing their *global evaluation of an advertisement.* The studies unanimously show that $A_{ad}$ is a significant determinant of the product attitudes held after viewing the ad.[59]

Suppose a consumer has a very favorable attitude toward a product. Is it safe to think that this consumer will buy the product? Not necessarily. Favorable attitudes toward a product do not necessarily translate into purchase behavior. Why? Because liking one product does not preclude the possibility that another product is liked even more. For this reason, attitudes are sometimes measured in the form of preferences. **Preferences** represent *attitudes toward one object in relation to another.* For example, which cola do you prefer, Coke or Pepsi?

Suppose that a product is the most preferred. Is it now safe to think that it will be purchased? Again, not necessarily. A person might prefer a Porsche automobile over all other brands but still not buy it if the price tag is outside the person's financial reach. In this case, the person will have an unfavorable attitude toward buying a Porsche. This possibility leads us to another type of attitude known as **attitude toward the behavior ($A_b$)**. $A_b$ represents an *evaluation of performing a particular behavior involving the attitude object,* such as buying the product. Although $A_o$ and $A_b$ are usually related, they are not the same. As we have just seen, someone can have a very favorable attitude toward some product (i.e., a positive $A_o$) but still have an unfavorable attitude toward buying the product ($A_b$). To further reinforce the distinctions between $A_o$, $A_b$, and preferences, examples of how to measure each are shown in Table 10.12.

Given $A_b$'s focus on behavior, it is not surprising that $A_b$ is related more strongly than $A_o$ to behavioral intentions[60] and, consequently, behavior. Accordingly, when one is interested in understanding the attitudes that drive a particular behavior, focusing on $A_b$ will be more appropriate. For it is $A_b$ rather than $A_o$ that will more strongly determine how consumers behave. And many behaviors beyond what consumers buy can determine a product's degree of success. You have already encountered one such behavior in Chapter 4 when we discussed consumer search behavior. What consumers discover during external search can determine what they buy. But here's another example. Take the products needed for playing tennis. The demand for such products is tied directly to the popularity of the sport. Figure 10.10 shows the number of Americans playing tennis between 1987 and 2003. Even with the rebound that's occurred the last couple of years with the emergence of some young American tennis stars like Serena and Venus Williams and Andy Roddick, the 17.3 million players in

| 10.12 | TABLE 10.12 | Measuring Attitudes and Preferences |
|---|---|---|

**ATTITUDE TOWARD THE BEHAVIOR:**

| Buying a Dell personal computer would be: | Very good | 1 | 2 | 3 | 4 | 5 | 6 | 7 | Very bad |
|---|---|---|---|---|---|---|---|---|---|
| | Very rewarding | 1 | 2 | 3 | 4 | 5 | 6 | 7 | Very punishing |
| | Very wise | 1 | 2 | 3 | 4 | 5 | 6 | 7 | Very foolish |

**ATTITUDE TOWARD THE OBJECT:**

| How much do you like or dislike Dell personal computers? | Like very much | 1 | 2 | 3 | 4 | 5 | 6 | 7 | Dislike very much |
|---|---|---|---|---|---|---|---|---|---|

**PREFERENCE:**

| Compared to Apple personal computers, how much do you like Dell personal computers? | Like Dell much more than Apple | 1 | 2 | 3 | 4 | 5 | 6 | 7 | Like Apple much more than Dell |
|---|---|---|---|---|---|---|---|---|---|

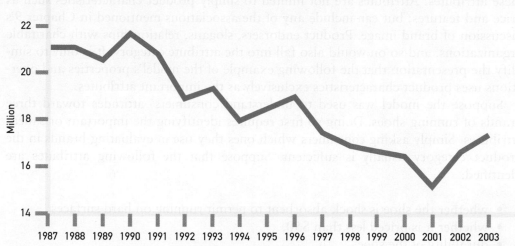

Source: Douglas Hanks III, "Tennis? Anyone?" *Miami Herald* (October 23, 2004), Cl, C3.

2003 is substantially below the nearly 22 million players in 1990.[61] Only 6 percent of vacationers report that tennis is an important part of their vacation, a percentage that's nearly half of what it was almost a decade earlier.[62] As these numbers indicate, this industry has not been able to maintain the favorable attitudes toward playing tennis that it once enjoyed. Rekindling these favorable attitudes in today's youth must be a top priority for the tennis industry.

Early in the chapter we made reference to something called multiattribute attitude models, the dominant approach over the last three decades for understanding the beliefs that determine attitudes. The time has now arrived for us to examine these models up close and personal.

## Using Multiattribute Attitude Models to Understand Consumer Attitudes

According to multiattribute attitude models, beliefs about a product's attributes or characteristics are important because they determine the favorability of one's attitude toward the product. Two different multiattribute models are discussed next.[63]

### THE FISHBEIN MULTIATTRIBUTE ATTITUDE MODEL

Martin Fishbein's formulation has been used extensively by consumer researchers since its conception more than forty years ago.[64] Symbolically, the formulation can be expressed as

$$A_o = \sum_{i=1}^{n} b_i e_i$$

where

$A_o$ = attitude toward the object,
$b_i$ = the strength of the belief that the object has attribute $i$,
$e_i$ = the evaluation of attribute $i$, and
$n$ = the number of salient or important attributes.

The model proposes that attitude toward an object (such as a product) is based on the summed set of beliefs about the object's attributes weighted by the evaluation of these attributes. Attributes are not limited to simply product characteristics such as price and features, but can include any of the associations mentioned in Chapter 9's discussion of brand image. Product endorsers, slogans, relationships with charitable organizations, and so on would also fall into the attribute category. It is only to simplify the presentation that the following example of the model's properties and operations uses product characteristics exclusively as the important attributes.

Suppose the model was used to understand consumers' attitudes toward three brands of running shoes. Doing so first requires identifying the important or salient attributes. Simply asking consumers which ones they use in evaluating brands in the product category usually is sufficient. Suppose that the following attributes are identified:

- whether the shoe is shock absorbent to permit running on hard surfaces,
- whether it is priced less than $50,
- durability of the shoe,
- how comfortable the shoe is to wear,
- whether the shoe is available in a desired color, and
- amount of arch support.

Next, the appropriate $b_i$ and $e_i$ measures must be developed. The $e_i$ component, representing the evaluation of an attribute, is measured on a seven-point evaluative scale ranging from "very good" to "very bad," as in the following example.

Buying running shoes priced at less than $50 is
very good __ : __ : __ : __ : __ : __ : __ very bad
$\phantom{}$+3 +2 +1 0 −1 −2 −3

This evaluation would be done for each of the six salient attributes identified previously.

The $b_i$ component represents how strongly consumers believe that a particular brand of running shoes possesses a given attribute. Beliefs usually are measured on a seven-point scale of perceived likelihood ranging from "very likely" to "very unlikely," as in the following example.

How likely is it that brand A running shoes are priced at less than $50?
very likely __ : __ : __ : __ : __ : __ : __ very unlikely
$\phantom{}$+3 +2 +1 0 −1 −2 −3

For each brand, an assessment of consumers' beliefs for each attribute must be performed. Given three brands and six attributes, a total of eighteen belief measures would be necessary.[65]

A survey containing the $b_i$ and $e_i$ measures would then be administered to a sample of consumers. An average response would be calculated for each measure. A set of hypothetical results appears in Table 10.13. When interpreting the numbers in Table 10.13, keep in mind that the $b_i$ and $e_i$ scales range from a maximum score of +3 to a minimum score of −3.

The results for $e_i$ indicate that durability and comfort are the most desirable product attributes, followed by shock absorbency and arch support, with color a relatively minor although still salient consideration. Unlike the remaining attributes, low price (less than $50) receives a negative score. This finding does not mean that price is

**TABLE 10.13**  Hypothetical Results for Fishbein's Multiattribute Model

| ATTRIBUTE | EVALUATION ($e_i$) | BELIEFS ($b_i$) | | |
|---|---|---|---|---|
| | | BRAND A | BRAND B | BRAND C |
| Shock absorbent | +2 | +2 | +1 | −1 |
| Price less than $50 | −1 | −3 | −1 | +3 |
| Durability | +3 | +3 | +1 | −1 |
| Comfort | +3 | +2 | +3 | +1 |
| Desired color | +1 | +1 | +3 | +3 |
| Arch support | +2 | +3 | +1 | −2 |
| Total $\sum b_i e_i$ score | | +29 | +20 | −6 |

unimportant. Rather, it indicates that low price is viewed as undesirable. This result is to be expected when consumers perceive a price-quality relationship and are willing to pay a little more for higher quality.

The results for $b_i$ indicate that brand A is viewed favorably because it receives positive belief ratings on all desired attributes. Brand A attains maximum ratings on both durability and arch support, and is not believed to cost less than $50. Given that low price is undesirable, this latter belief works in favor of brand A.

As a rule of thumb, companies want consumers to perceive their products as (1) possessing desirable attributes (when $e_i$ is positive, $b_i$ should be positive), and (2) not possessing undesirable attributes (when $e_i$ is negative, $b_i$ should be negative). The Lipton tea advertisement in Figure 10.11 illustrates the former by touting the tea's great taste and antioxidants. The Horizon Organic milk advertisement in Figure 10.12 illustrates the latter by communicating that the product is not tainted with such undesirables as antibiotics, added growth hormones, and dangerous pesticides.

Although brand B outperforms brand A on comfort and color in Table 10.13, brand B is perceived as inferior to brand A on the remaining attributes. Brand C is viewed as low priced, a belief that undermines attitude, given the negative evaluation of low price. The results further indicate that brand C is not believed to perform well in terms of durability, arch support, and absorbing shock. On the positive side, brand C is seen as somewhat comfortable and having a desired color.

To estimate brand attitude, we first multiply the belief score by its corresponding evaluation score for each attribute ($b_i \times e_i$). For example, the brand A belief score of +2 for shock absorbency is multiplied by the evaluation of +2, which produces a value of +4 for this attribute. This procedure is repeated for each of the five remaining attributes. The $b_i e_i$ scores are then summed. This produces a total $\sum b_i e_i$ score of +29 for brand A. For brands B and C, the total $\sum b_i e_i$ values are +20 and −6,

**FIGURE 10.11** Communicating the Presence of Desirable Attributes Can Create Favorable Attitudes toward the Product

My goodness.

HORIZON ORGANIC

Horizon Organic® Milk is produced without the use of antibiotics, added growth hormones or dangerous pesticides.

That's why Horizon Organic milk is as wholesome as it gets. Not only does it taste creamy, fresh and delicious, but it's also very good for you. And that'll have you feeling good inside and out.

HORIZON
ORGANIC
Good from the beginning.

**FIGURE 10.12** Communicating the Absence of Undesirable Attributes Can Also Create Favorable Attitudes

respectively. The score for brand A is very good, considering that the maximum score, given the current set of evaluations, is +36. The maximum score is derived by assuming the "ideal" belief score (+3 or −3, depending on whether the attribute is positively or negatively evaluated) and combining it with the existing evaluation scores.

## THE IDEAL-POINT MULTIATTRIBUTE ATTITUDE MODEL

Whereas the Fishbein model was developed to understand all different kinds of attitudes, the ideal-point model was designed specifically for understanding consumer attitudes toward products.[66] This model can be represented symbolically as

$$A_p = \sum_{i=1}^{n} W_i |I_i - X_i|$$

where

$A_p$ = attitude toward the product,
$W_i$ = the importance of attribute $i$,
$I_i$ = the "ideal" performance on attribute $i$,
$X_i$ = the belief about the product's actual performance on attribute $i$, and
$n$ = the number of salient attributes.

Under the ideal-point model, consumers indicate where they believe a product is located on scales representing the various degrees or levels of salient attributes. Consumers also report where the "ideal" product would fall on these attribute scales. According to the model, the closer a product's actual rating is to the ideal rating, the more favorable the attitude.

As an illustration, suppose we applied the ideal-point model to soft drinks and that the following attributes are identified as salient:

- sweetness of taste,
- degree of carbonation,
- number of calories,
- amount of real fruit juices, and
- price.

Next, we would develop a scale representing various levels of each salient attribute. Using sweetness as an example, the scale could look like the following.

very sweet taste __ : __ : __ : __ : __ : __ : __ very bitter taste
             1   2   3   4   5   6   7

Consumers would report their ideal or preferred taste by placing an $I$ in the appropriate response category (the $I_i$ from the model equation). They'd also indicate their beliefs about where various brands fall along this taste continuum (the $X_i$ from the

**TABLE 10.14**  Hypothetical Results for the Ideal-Point Multiattribute Attitude Model

| ATTRIBUTE | IMPORTANCE ($W_i$) | IDEAL POINT ($I_i$) | BELIEFS ($X_i$) BRAND A | BELIEFS ($X_i$) BRAND B |
|---|---|---|---|---|
| Taste: | | | | |
| sweet (1) – bitter (7) | 6 | 2 | 2 | 3 |
| Carbonation: | | | | |
| high (1) – low (7) | 3 | 3 | 2 | 6 |
| Calories: | | | | |
| high (1) – low (7) | 4 | 5 | 4 | 5 |
| Fruit juices: | | | | |
| high (1) – low (7) | 4 | 1 | 2 | 2 |
| Price: | | | | |
| high (1) – low (7) | 5 | 5 | 4 | 3 |
| Total $\sum W_i |I_i - X_i|$ score | | | 16 | 29 |

model equation). Finally, consumers would provide ratings of attribute importance on a scale such as the following.

not at all important __ : __ : __ : __ : __ : __ extremely important
                            0   1   2   3   4   5   6

Suppose we found the results presented in Table 10.14. The first column specifies the attributes on which the ideal (the third column) and actual brand (the fourth and fifth columns) ratings were taken. Attribute importance ratings appear in the second column.

In this example, taste is the most important attribute; carbonation is the least important. The ideal-point ratings indicate that the ideal soft drink should be sweet tasting, somewhat carbonated, fairly low in calories, very high in fruit juices, and toward the low side on price. Brand A is perceived as matching or being very close to the ideal brand for all attributes. Brand B is thought to perform well on some attributes (calories) but not on others (carbonation).

Total brand attitude scores are estimated by first taking the difference between the ideal and actual brand ratings on an attribute. For taste, brand A has a difference of 0 (2 − 2), and the difference for brand B is −1 (2 − 3). This difference is converted to an absolute value, as indicated by the vertical-line symbols surrounding $I_i - X_i$ in the model equation. This absolute value is multiplied by the importance score. This operation produces scores of 0 for brand A (0 × 6) and 6 for brand B (1 × 6) on the taste attribute. We would repeat this process for the remaining attributes and sum the scores. For brand A, the total score is 16; brand B's score is 29. Unlike Fishbein's multiattribute model, in which higher scores indicate more favorable attitudes, lower scores are better under the ideal-point model. In fact, the best score a brand can receive is 0, indicating that the brand matches perfectly the ideal attribute configuration.

## BENEFITS OF USING MULTIATTRIBUTE ATTITUDE MODELS

A major attraction of these models is their substantial diagnostic power. Attitude measures tell us whether consumers like or dislike a product but are silent about *why*

**TABLE 10.15        The Stimulus Importance–Performance Grid**

| ATTRIBUTE IMPORTANCE | OUR PERFORMANCE | COMPETITOR'S PERFORMANCE | SIMULTANEOUS RESULT |
|---|---|---|---|
| High | Poor | Poor | Neglected opportunity |
| High | Poor | Good | Competitive disadvantage |
| High | Good | Poor | Competitive advantage |
| High | Good | Good | Head-to-head competition |
| Low | Poor | Poor | Null opportunity |
| Low | Poor | Good | False alarm |
| Low | Good | Poor | False advantage |
| Low | Good | Good | False competition |

Source: Alvin C. Burns, "Generating Marketing Strategy Priorities Based on Relative Competitive Position," *Journal of Consumer Marketing*, 3 (Fall 1986), 49–56.

the product is liked or disliked. Such an understanding requires looking at what consumers believe about a product's attributes and the importance of these attributes.

One useful way of thinking about the information derived from multiattribute models is the stimulus importance–performance grid shown in Table 10.15. A brand's performance along a particular attribute is classified into one of eight cells. This classification depends on the attribute's importance (high versus low), the brand's performance on the attribute (good versus poor), and a competitive brand's performance on the attribute (good versus poor). Marketing implications are then drawn for each cell. For example, when a company's brand is truly superior to competitors on an important attribute, the company holds a competitive advantage that should be exploited, perhaps through a comparative advertising campaign.

Poor performance by all brands on an important attribute signals a neglected opportunity. By enhancing our brand's performance on this attribute, we could turn the neglected opportunity into a competitive advantage. Poor performance by all brands on an unimportant attribute, however, represents little opportunity. Improving the brand's performance would have little, if any, impact on product attitudes and choices as long as the attribute remained unimportant to consumers.

Multiattribute attitude models can also provide the information necessary for some types of segmentation. As an example, segmenting consumers based on the importance they place on various attributes might be useful. Marketing activities differ considerably when target consumers are primarily concerned with low price rather than high quality.

Another benefit of these models is their usefulness for new product development.[67] Discovering that current offerings fall short of the ideal brand reveals an opportunity for introducing a new product that more closely resembles the ideal. A multiattribute model has also been used successfully by the Lever Brothers Company to forecast the market shares of Tone moisturizing soap and Coast deodorant soap before their market introduction.[68]

The last, but certainly not the least, benefit offered by multiattribute attitude models is the help they provide in the identification of attitude change strategies. In the following section we describe the basic attitude change strategies suggested by these models and how the models can be used to estimate the potential payoff of each strategy in terms of how much improvement in consumers' attitudes each may provide.

## ATTITUDE CHANGE IMPLICATIONS FROM MULTIATTRIBUTE ATTITUDE MODELS

From a multiattribute model perspective, there are three basic ways for changing consumer attitudes: (1) changing beliefs, (2) changing attribute importance, and (3) changing ideal points.[69]

**Changing Beliefs**  Changing consumers' beliefs is a common business objective. Do you remember all of those examples we gave in Chapter 9 about companies trying to change their products' images? (I certainly hope so because I'm not about to describe all of them again!) Each example represented an attempt to change beliefs to not only improve a product's image, but to improve consumers' attitudes toward the product as well. So let's take a look at the guidance offered by multiattribute attitude models in identifying belief changes.

Returning to the soft drink example and Table 10.14, suppose we wanted to increase consumers' attitudes toward brand B relative to brand A. The model suggests two basic belief change options for doing this: (1) increase brand B's beliefs, and (2) decrease brand A's beliefs. Starting with brand B's beliefs, the model is useful for identifying which beliefs are in need of repair and which beliefs are just where they need to be. Such is the case for brand B's calorie beliefs, which are in perfect harmony with the ideal point; any change here would only hurt attitudes toward the brand. In contrast, the model indicates that changes in the beliefs about any of the remaining attributes in the direction of the ideal point would improve brand attitudes.

In addition to pulling its attitude up, brand B should consider pulling brand A's attitude down. How can brand B do this? By going on the offensive. Comparative advertising—touting the advantages of the advertised brand over a competitor—can undermine beliefs about the competitor's brand.[70] Consequently, to the extent brand B possesses important advantages over brand A, brand B should consider undertaking a comparative advertising campaign that communicates these advantages as a way of reducing consumers' beliefs about brand A.

**Changing Attribute Importance**  Another way of altering attitudes is to change the importance consumers attach to various attributes. Depending on how a brand is perceived, one might wish either to increase or to decrease an attribute's importance. Research has demonstrated the potential to enhance the salience of an attribute already viewed as somewhat important.[71] Nonetheless, as a general rule, changing an attribute's importance is more difficult to accomplish than changing beliefs.

For brand B in Table 10.14, what changes in attribute importance would you recommend? In answering this question, you need to consider how each brand is perceived relative to the ideal performance. When the beliefs for both brands match the ideal point, nothing can be gained by altering the attribute's importance. For instance, no matter what importance is attached to fruit juices, the relative preference between brands A and B will not change given the current set of beliefs.

When, however, brand A is seen as closer to the ideal point for a particular attribute than brand B, decreasing the attribute's importance is to brand B's advantage. The categories of taste, carbonation, and price would all benefit from this strategy. Anything that can be done to make these attributes even less important to consumers helps reduce preferences for brand A relative to brand B.

Increasing attribute importance is desirable when the competitor's brand is farther from the ideal point than your offering. In Table 10.14, brand A is farther than brand B

**FIGURE 10.13** This Ad Attempts to Change Consumers' Ideal Point for Alcohol in Mouthwash

from the ideal point along the calories attribute. Consequently, enhancing the importance of calories would benefit brand B.

Another variant of changing attribute importance involves efforts to add a new attribute. That is, a company may try to create salience for an attribute that is currently unimportant. Flame broiling is unimportant to many consumers in selecting a fast-food burger restaurant, although Burger King's advertising has attempted to alter this opinion. Adding a new attribute to the set of salient attributes essentially amounts to increasing the importance of something that previously was nonsalient.

**Changing Ideal Points** Another option for changing attitudes suggested by the ideal-point model involves altering consumers' preferences about what the ideal product would look like. For example, would your ideal brand of mouthwash contain a lot of alcohol, some alcohol, or no alcohol? Based on the belief that alcohol increases the mouthwash's effectiveness, some people prefer this ingredient in their mouthwash. The ad for Rembrandt mouthwash shown in Figure 10.13, however, argues otherwise. The ad claims that though alcohol does kill bacteria, it may actually irritate a person's mouth. If believed, this ad would cause a change in the ideal point for many consumers.

There are several ideal-point changes in Table 10.14 that would help brand B. Attitudes toward brand B would become more favorable if consumers preferred either a more bitter taste, less carbonation, or a higher price. Such changes could also reduce attitudes toward brand A, depending on whether the changes broadened the gap between perceptions of brand A's performance and the ideal performance.

Changes for the remaining attributes, calories and fruit juices, would not be attractive to brand B. Given that brand B is seen as having the ideal number of calories, altering the ideal point would be self-destructive. Although attitude toward brand B would improve if consumers preferred a little less fruit juice in their beverage, this change produces the same attitudinal impact for both brands. Given that the two brands are perceived as being the same on this attribute, any change in the preferred level of fruit juices cannot alter consumers' brand preferences.

**Estimating the Attitudinal Impact of Alternative Changes** As you have seen, brand B might consider implementing a number of alternative changes to increase consumers' liking of brand B relative to its competitor. Decisions about which changes to pursue should depend on several considerations. Some changes will be discarded because they will require product modifications that are prohibitively expensive to implement or that are virtually impossible to accomplish (such as greatly improving product quality while maintaining a price lower than the competitor's).

Consumer resistance to change should also be considered, because some changes may be more likely than others. A belief based on inaccurate product information about the brand's price can be corrected fairly easily. In the absence of an actual product change, for example, changing beliefs derived from actual consumption about the taste of Spam may be nearly impossible. Nor should one underestimate how difficult changing attribute importance and ideal points can be. An airline with a poor safety record may wish that consumers placed less importance on safety in selecting a carrier, but it is impossible for the company to accomplish this.

Another consideration in deciding which changes should be implemented is the potential attitudinal payoff that each change might deliver. Multiattribute attitude models help estimate this payoff. Let's go back to brand B in Table 10.14 one last time. Can you identify the single change that, if successful, would have the most favorable attitudinal impact from brand B's point of view?

Changing the ideal point for carbonation from 3 to 6 would be the single best change. The total multiattribute score for brand B would drop from 29 to 20 (remember, lower total scores are better for the ideal-point model). This same change would increase the total score for brand A from 16 to 25. This is the only single change that would give brand B a more favorable total score than brand A.

The next best change would involve shifting the ideal point for taste from 2 to 3. The new total scores for brands A and B would be 22 and 23, respectively. This process would continue for each of the possible changes, thus yielding information about their relative attitudinal impact. All else being equal, those changes offering the most favorable impact should be pursued.

Although multiattribute attitude models are valuable in suggesting and prioritizing potential attitude change strategies, these models certainly should not be viewed as offering a complete specification of all potential strategies. In some circumstances, the models may not even represent the most fruitful perspective on changing consumers' attitudes. Persuasion researchers have learned much more about the art and science of influencing consumer opinion than what we have covered here. It is for this reason that we devote an entire chapter to this subject (see Chapter 15) later in the book. But for now, it's time to complete the final leg of the trip we began long ago in the roadmap of Figure 10.1. Next and final stop: consumer intentions.

## Consumer Intentions

One of the most important skills a company can possess is the ability to predict how people will act as consumers (see Market Facts 10.2). Doing so helps the company answer such fundamental questions as "How much of my existing product should be produced to meet demand?" and "How much demand will there be for my new product?" Companies that underestimate demand have shortchanged their opportunities for greater sales and profits. Those that overestimate demand usually end up having to sell the surplus at a discount, thereby hurting profitability.

Yet answering these questions is far from easy. The rather dramatic failure rate of new products (by some estimates, around 90 percent) provides compelling testimony to the difficulties of forecasting consumer behavior. And just about every Christmas there is at least one toy so popular that it quickly sells out, leaving frantic parents desperately searching in hope of finding just one more. The dissatisfaction that arose when consumers were unable to purchase a Furby toy advertised as available at Walgreens led this retailer to quickly apologize in writing.

Beyond what consumers buy, companies are also interested in predicting where they'll buy, when they'll buy, and how much they'll buy. And this interest goes beyond just buying. Customer service departments must determine the number of personnel needed for handling consumer inquiries and complaints. Such determinations should be based at least partly on estimates of the number of consumers that will require daily attention. Industries that live off consumption activities (e.g., television networks) are interested in predicting consumption behavior (e.g., whether a new show will attract a large enough audience to justify the show being placed on the schedule).

## The 2004 Christmas Season Predictive Scorecard in the Toy Retail Market

With one week left until Christmas day in 2004, customers could still find some of the season's hottest toys, such as Dora's Talking House and Bella Dancerella, a ballet kit, at Toys "R" Us. But it was a different story at rival Wal*Mart stores, where inventory of many of the popular items was depleted, according to some analysts. Toys "R" Us, the nation's second-largest toy retailer behind Wal*Mart, had a lot at stake during Christmas 2004. The previous year, Wal*Mart had spoiled Toys "R" Us's Christmas with earlier and heavier discounts than in the past. This strategy had certainly contributed to the plummeting of profits at Toys "R" Us by more than 60 percent in 2003.

To help reverse its fortunes during the 2004 holiday season, Toys "R" Us stocked its shelves earlier than it did the previous year, carried more exclusive merchandise, and beat the discounters on price during November. Toys "R" Us also enjoyed a competitive advantage in its ability to predict the hottest toys of the season and have them in stock during the final stretch. According to Sean McGowan, an analyst at investment research firm Harris Nesbitt, a spot check of twenty-five "hot" toys showed that Toys "R" Us was in stock on 68 percent of the items less than two weeks before Christmas. That number compared with 56 percent for Target and 48 percent for Wal*Mart. Mark Rowan, an analyst at Prudential Equity Group, reported that Toys "R" Us was in stock on 82 percent of the items on his list of twenty-eight hot toys. Target was also second on his list with 72 percent. Wal*Mart was a distant third at only 44 percent. Once its competitors began to run out of certain items, Toys "R" Us no longer needed to reduce prices for items that couldn't be found on its rivals' shelves. Having product that your competitors don't and selling it for more money are the rewards enjoyed by Toys "R" Us for outperforming its rivals in anticipating consumer demand during the 2004 Christmas season.

Source: Anne D'Innocenzio, "Toy Shortages Seen at Some Stores," www.washingtonpost.com (December 17, 2004). Copyright 2004, The Washington Post. Reprinted with permission.

So how can we predict what people will do? A common practice is to rely on past behavior to forecast future behavior. If sales have increased steadily at a rate of 15 percent annually over the past few years, one might reasonably anticipate a similar increase next year. If a consumer has bought the same brand of coffee each of the last ten trips to the grocery store, it would seem a safe bet that the same brand will be purchased during the next trip.

But things change, and what happened in the past may become far less relevant than what is happening today. Sales of American flags soared like an eagle during the Gulf War of 1991 as a wave of patriotism flooded the country, a tidal wave that eventually subsided. Sales trends are sometimes erratic, jumping up and down. Cigar consumption in the United States peaked in 1973 at a little more than 11 billion cigars. In 1993, only 3.4 billion cigars went up in smoke. Sales then rebounded, fueled heavily by female consumers. Consumption rose to 5 billion cigars by 1997.[72] These fluctuations, unless of a regular nature, reduce the forecasting power of past behavior. And, of course, past behavior is not even an option for forecasting first-year sales of new products.

An alternative approach to predicting consumer behavior involves asking consumers what they intend to do. Consider, for example, the results presented in Table 10.16. These results come from a poll conducted by the Boston Consulting

**TABLE 10.16**   Consumers' Spending Intentions: Winners and Losers (percent)

| PLAN TO SPEND MORE | | PLAN TO SPEND LESS | |
|---|---|---|---|
| 1.  Sit-down restaurants | 57.6 | 1.  Car insurance | 53.7 |
| 2.  Home or apartment items | 57.3 | 2.  Fast-service restaurants | 51.1 |
| 3.  Computer | 52.4 | 3.  Bottled water | 48.2 |
| 4.  Cars | 51.9 | 4.  Accessories (handbags, wallets) | 45.0 |
| 5.  Furniture | 51.3 | 5.  Takeout/frozen meals | 43.6 |
| 6.  Home entertainment | 50.2 | 6.  Mobile phone | 41.2 |
| 7.  Kitchen appliances | 49.9 | 7.  Bath and body products | 39.6 |
| 8.  Bedding | 49.3 | 8.  Bath linens | 38.8 |
| 9.  Washer/dryer | 48.6 | 9.  Hair care | 38.5 |
| 10.  Travel | 43.3 | 10.  Clothing | 35.2 |

Source: Michael Malone, "Face Value," *Restaurant Business* (January 15, 2004), 30–36.

Note: Numbers represent the percentage of consumers indicating they intend to spend more or less in this product category.

Group that asked consumers whether they intended to spend more or less money in a number of different product categories. In essence, these consumers reported a form of spending intentions. **Spending intentions** reflect *how much money consumers think they'll spend*. But this is not the only type of consumer intentions. There are **purchase intentions** representing *what consumers think they'll buy*. A special type of purchase intentions is **repurchase intentions,** which indicate *whether consumers anticipate buying the same product or brand again*. **Shopping intentions** capture *where consumers plan on making their product purchases*. **Search intentions** indicate consumers' *intentions to engage in external search*, a topic covered in Chapter 4. **Consumption intentions** represent consumers' *intentions to engage in a particular consumption activity* (e.g., watch television, exercise, browse the Internet). Table 10.17 contains examples of how these different types of intentions can be measured.

People usually do what they intend to do. Grocery shoppers intending to buy the items on their shopping list usually do. This is not to say that intentions are always fulfilled. One might travel to the local video store intending to rent a particular movie only to discover that all copies have been checked out. Nonetheless, intentions have been shown repeatedly to be a significant predictor of how people behave.[73]

One example of intentions' ability to predict purchase behavior comes from the barbecue grill industry. In 2003, the industry shipped more than 14 million barbecue grills for a total of nearly $3 billion. Nonetheless, this represented a decline of 7 percent relative to the previous year. The Hearth, Patio & Barbecue Association surveyed consumers about their purchase intentions and, based on their responses, predicted a rebound in 2004.[74] Shipments did increase to nearly 14.5 million units, a 2.5 percent improvement over the 2003 numbers.[75]

Another demonstration of intentions' predictive power comes from the 2004 presidential election between the incumbent, Republican George W. Bush, and the challenger, Democrat John Kerry. Based on polls of voters' intentions shortly before the election, projections were made on a state-by-state basis as to which candidate each state would end up supporting on Election Day. These projections appear in Figure 10.14. Nine of the states were classified as "too close to call." The remainder

**TABLE 10.17**   Measuring Different Types of Consumer Intentions

1. PURCHASE INTENTIONS:

Will you buy a Mercedes-Benz automobile
during the next 12 months?               No chance   1   2   3   4   5   6   7   I definitely will

2. REPURCHASE INTENTIONS:

The next time you purchase coffee,
will you buy the same brand?             No chance   1   2   3   4   5   6   7   I definitely will

3. SHOPPING INTENTIONS:

Will you shop at Wal*Mart during
the next 30 days?                        No chance   1   2   3   4   5   6   7   I definitely will

4. SPENDING INTENTIONS:

Will you spend at least $1,000 on
Christmas gifts this year?               No chance   1   2   3   4   5   6   7   I definitely will

5. CONSUMPTION INTENTIONS:

Will you watch the next Super Bowl?      No chance   1   2   3   4   5   6   7   I definitely will

6. SEARCH INTENTIONS:

The next time you need to be hospitalized,
will you speak to your doctor before
choosing a hospital?                     No chance   1   2   3   4   5   6   7   I definitely will

were projected to vote for either the Republican or the Democratic candidate, although the strength of this projection varied from "safe" to "leans." The actual results of the presidential race are shown in Figure 10.15. Comparison of the two figures reveals that the polls accurately forecasted every single state, including those that were only tentatively classified as "leans."

## Constraints on the Predictive Power of Intentions

Although intentions are a significant predictor of behavior, they are far from being a perfect predictor. We intended to have this textbook completed much earlier than it actually was. Have you kept all of your New Year's resolutions? Sometimes even the best intentions go unfulfilled. And sometimes businesses are happy when intentions miss their mark. Earlier in the chapter we told you about the battle between growers of fresh Christmas trees and makers of the artificial version (see Consumer Behavior and Marketing 10.3). What we didn't tell you about was the use of purchase intentions measures to forecast sales during the 2004 holiday season. The intentions measures did accurately predict a sales increase.[76] But rather than buying the 24 to 24.5 million trees forecasted by these measures, consumers actually purchased a little more than 27 million trees. A pleasant surprise, indeed.

Intentions can change. Unanticipated circumstances may cause them to change.[77] Suppose you fully intend at this moment to purchase a particular product. Yet later on during information search, you learn something that changes your intentions. Obviously, intentions measured prior to this change are unlikely to provide an accurate

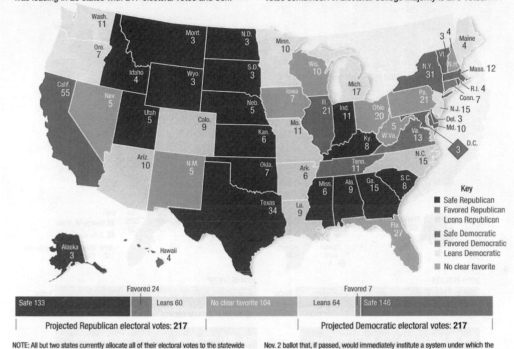

## At the Moment, It's a Tie

Congressional Quarterly's assessment of the presidential campaigns across the nation — for the 51 sets of votes in the Electoral College — shows that, as of Oct. 22, President Bush was leading in 25 states with 217 electoral votes and Sen.

John Kerry was ahead in 16 states (plus Washington, D.C.) with 217 electoral votes. That means the presidency will be decided mainly in the nine remaining states, which have 104 electoral votes combined. An Electoral College majority is 270 votes.

**Key**

- Safe Republican
- Favored Republican
- Leans Republican
- Safe Democratic
- Favored Democratic
- Leans Democratic
- No clear favorite

Favored 24

| Safe 133 | Leans 60 | No clear favorite 104 | Leans 64 | Safe 146 |

Favored 7

Projected Republican electoral votes: **217**        Projected Democratic electoral votes: **217**

NOTE: All but two states currently allocate all of their electoral votes to the statewide winner of the presidential popular vote; in Maine and Nebraska, some votes are allocated to the winner in each congressional district. Colorado has an initiative on the Nov. 2 ballot that, if passed, would immediately institute a system under which the state's electoral votes would be divided proportionately to the presidential candidates based on their statewide vote percentages.

**FIGURE 10.14** Pre-Election Forecasts for the 2004 Presidential Race

Source: "At the Moment, It's a Tie." www.CQ.com (October 23, 2004).

prediction of behavior. Similarly, you may not intend on buying a product yet end up doing so. Grocery shoppers often buy items that are not on their grocery list. Consumers enter a clothing store wanting to buy a shirt and tie and walk out carrying an entire suit.

Despite these limitations, consumer intentions may still be a company's best bet for predicting future behavior. When Quaker State tested the potential of a new engine treatment product, purchase intentions were a key factor in forecasting future demand for the product. "You can project that data into future market share and trial usage," says Bob Cohen, former executive vice president of the innovations center at Quaker State. "It's the best information you can have to evaluate whether or not to go forward and invest more money."[78]

Although we cannot control whether consumers act upon their intentions, we can control some things or at least be aware that these things will influence intentions' predictive accuracy. The measurement of intentions is important. Intention measures should fully correspond to the to-be-predicted behavior. If a company wants to predict whether consumers will buy its product at a particular time, then the intention measure should specify all this information (e.g., "Do you intend to buy Campbell's soup the next time you go grocery shopping?"). As the correspondence between the intention measures and the to-be-predicted behavior becomes weaker, so does the intention's predictive power.[79]

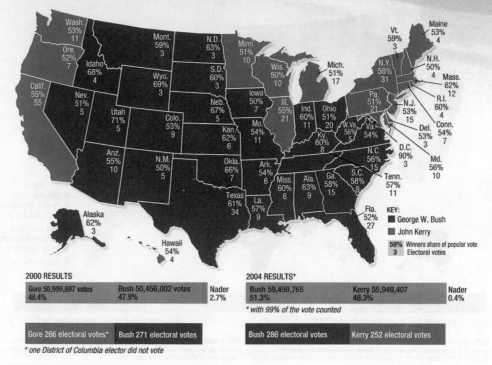

**PRESIDENTIAL RESULTS**

# A Clear If Close Outcome, No Matter How It's Counted

Unlike four years ago, when George W. Bush won the presidency with a bare Electoral College majority and 500,000 fewer votes than Al Gore, his re-election triumphs Nov. 2 were clear on both counts. He won the popular vote by 3.5 million. And he won 286 electoral votes. He carried two Gore states, Iowa and New Mexico, and picked up extra electoral votes because of reapportionment gains in states he carried both times. John Kerry picked up one Bush state from 2000, New Hampshire.

**KEY:**
- George W. Bush
- John Kerry
- **59%** Winners share of popular vote
- **3** Electoral votes

**2000 RESULTS**

| Gore 50,999,897 votes 48.4% | Bush 50,456,002 votes 47.9% | Nader 2.7% |
|---|---|---|

**2004 RESULTS***

| Bush 59,459,765 51.3% | Kerry 55,949,407 48.3% | Nader 0.4% |
|---|---|---|

*\* with 99% of the vote counted*

| Gore 266 electoral votes* | Bush 271 electoral votes |
|---|---|

| Bush 286 electoral votes | Kerry 252 electoral votes |
|---|---|

*\* one District of Columbia elector did not vote*

**FIGURE 10.15** State-by-State Results for the 2004 Presidential Race

Source: "At the Moment, It's a Tie," www.CQ.com (October 23, 2004)

Measuring what people intend to do may sometimes be less predictive of their future behavior than measuring what they expect to do.[80] If you ask cigarette smokers whether they intend to become nonsmokers, many will answer with a resounding "yes!" Yet fulfilling these intentions is far from easy. Sometimes habit is more powerful than willpower. A more realistic assessment might be obtained by measuring behavioral expectations. **Behavioral expectations** represent the *perceived likelihood of performing a behavior.* Although smokers may hold very strong intentions to quit, they may report more moderate expectations of doing so because of past failures.

In addition to how intentions are measured, when they're measured is also important. How accurate do you think you would be in forecasting what you will be doing five minutes, five days, or five years from this moment? You probably feel confident about what you'll be doing five minutes from now (reading this chapter, right?). And you may even have a pretty good idea about what you'll be doing five days from now. But it is almost certain that you would feel rather uncertain about forecasting your behavior five years into the future.

Forecasting accuracy depends on how far into the future one is trying to predict. If we ask consumers today what they intend to do tomorrow, our forecast should be right on target. Prediction of even more distant behavior can be achieved. But as the time interval between when intentions are measured and when the to-be-predicted behavior occurs, there is a greater opportunity for intentions to change. People may learn something that reverses their previously stated intentions. Whatever the reason, forecasts based on the original intentions become less accurate. Thus, as the time interval between the measurement of intentions and the behavior itself increases, the opportunity for change becomes greater, thereby undermining prediction.[81]

The predictive power of intentions further depends on the to-be-predicted behavior. If a person always buys the same coffee brand, intentions to buy this brand during the next shopping trip should be very accurate. The same is true for the family that visits Disney World every summer. Behaviors repeated with regularity usually can be forecasted with greater precision.

Also important is whether the behavior is under volitional control. **Volitional control** represents *the degree to which a behavior can be performed at will.* Many behaviors are under complete volitional control. For example, you control whether you will continue to read the rest of this paragraph. Some behaviors, however, may not be under our complete control. You can't rent a video if it's not available. You may intend to get an A on your next exam, but whether you do depends at least somewhat on how difficult the professor makes the exam.

The existence of uncontrollable factors interferes with our ability to do what we intend to do. When this disruption occurs, intentions become less accurate predictors of behavior. Consequently, **perceived behavioral control**, representing the *person's belief about how easy it is to perform the behavior,* is sometimes used along with intentions to predict behavior.[82]

### Other Uses of Consumer Intentions

Consumer intentions are helpful as an indicator of the possible effects of certain marketing activities. In the hemp industry, for example, there are conflicting opinions about the wisdom of reminding consumers about hemp's association with marijuana. Some companies emphasize this association when marketing their products; others avoid it. To determine whether this association helps or hinders, consumers were surveyed about whether they would be more or less likely to purchase a product made of hemp knowing it comes from the same plant as marijuana. For every person reporting that he or she would be more likely to buy a hemp product knowing that it was made from the same plant as marijuana, eight others said the knowledge would make them less likely to purchase a hemp product.[83]

Similarly, consider a company contemplating a significant change in its product because it believes that doing so will lead to greater sales. Nonetheless, the company recognizes that this change may not work and might even hurt sales. Before actually implementing this change, the company could first explore whether the change influences consumers' intentions in the desired direction. This precaution could prevent a costly mistake. Evaluating the impact of potential marketing activities makes good business sense. Although no one knows for sure what will happen until something is implemented in the market, this does not eliminate the value of testing the waters. And given the strength of the intention-behavior relationship, intentions provide a reasonable test.

Repurchase intentions should also provide a better indication of a company's likely success in retaining customers than offered by satisfaction measures. You might remember from Chapter 6 that even satisfied customers may switch to a competitor that offers a better deal. As such, simply relying on customer satisfaction measures for estimating customer retention is tenuous at best. Customers who appear to be satisfied may still have little intention of buying the same product again. The best way to know this is by measuring repurchase intentions.

Finally, intention measures may actually influence consumer behavior. Considerable research shows that simply answering a measure about what you intend to do in the future can significantly affect your future behavior, thus creating the opportunity for companies to influence consumers by asking them to report their intentions.[84] To learn more about this finding, read Buyer Beware 10.2.

## Market Surveys Can Do More Than Simply Record Your Opinions

Have you ever participated in a market research survey or an opinion poll in which you were asked your intentions? Such surveys and polls are quite common. Consumers are asked which products they intend to purchase, which stores they intend to patronize, and even which political candidates they plan to vote for. You might think that the only costs of participating in these activities are the time you give and whatever discomfort you might feel in disclosing your personal preferences to a complete stranger, but there is a hidden cost: the simple act of reporting your intentions actually affects your subsequent behavior. Research has shown that, compared to those not asked their intentions, responding to purchase intention measures (1) increases the probability of making an initial purchase, (2) increases the likelihood of repeat buying, (3) accelerates how quickly repurchase occurs, and (4) can influence the brand actually chosen. As one example, Chandon, Morwitz, and Reinartz (2004) report that 26.7 percent of consumers who stated their intentions to repurchase from an online

grocer actually did so within the two-month period following the measurement of their intentions. In contrast, only 16.4 percent of the consumers not asked their intentions repurchased from the online grocer.

Why would responding to intention measures have such effects? Because doing so increases the accessibility of the rendered judgments in memory. Increased accessibility, in turn, means that these judgments are more available for influencing subsequent judgments and behaviors.

So does this mean you need to avoid answering such questions? Not at all. Williams, Fitzsimons, and Black (2004) show that simply educating people about the effect of intention measurement on purchase behavior is sufficient to eliminate its influence. You have now been so educated. Consequently, as long as you remember this lesson, it should be safe for you to tell others your intentions.

Sources: Pierre Chandon, Vicki G. Morwitz, and Werner J. Reinartz, "The Short- and Long-Term Effects of Measuring Intent to Repurchase," *Journal of Consumer Research,* 31 (December 2004), 566–572; Patti Williams, Gavan J. Fitzsimons, and Lauren G. Black, "When Consumers Do Not Recognize 'Benign' Intention Questions as Persuasion Attempts," *Journal of Consumer Research,* 31 (December 2004), 540–550.

## Chapter Summary

## Summary

This chapter covers some of the most important constructs in consumer behavior: beliefs, feelings, attitudes, and intentions. We make this claim for both predictive and diagnostic reasons. Efforts to forecast future consumer behavior typically rely on what consumers have done in the past. Yet when using past behavior as a predictor is not possible or inappropriate, what consumers intend or expect to do will be the most potent predictor available. At the same time, however, intentions possess limited diagnostic power. We may feel rather confident in predicting what consumers may or may not do based on their stated intentions, but intention measures do not tell us why consumers hold such intentions. To understand the reasons why consumers

hold particular intentions, we need to dig deeper and look at their attitudes, beliefs, and feelings.

One especially powerful diagnostic tool covered in the chapter is the multiattribute attitude model, which focuses on the set of beliefs that determine a particular attitude. Multiattribute attitude models come in many forms, including the Fishbein and ideal-point versions. An important advantage of the ideal-point model is its identification of consumers' preferred or ideal configuration of product attributes. Not only are multiattribute attitude models useful for understanding why consumers hold the attitudes that they do, these models are also helpful in identifying and prioritizing alternative strategies for improving consumers' attitudes.

Multiattribute attitude models emphasize consumers' beliefs about a product's attributes, but these are not the only important consumer beliefs. Indeed, many different types of consumer beliefs shape how consumers behave in the marketplace, from what they believe about future economic conditions to what they believe about the trustworthiness of alternative information sources. And sometimes consumers aren't sure what to believe. Such confusion also influences consumer behavior.

Consumers' attitudes depend not only on beliefs, but on feelings as well. How products make consumers feel during consumption can be just as influential, if not more, in determining how much consumers like the product. Feelings may exist in different marketplace activities beyond product consumption. They may occur when consumers are processing advertisements. They may occur when consumers are shopping. And beyond how a product, advertisement, or store makes consumers feel, the mood state carried by consumers into each of these marketplace activities is also important.

## Review and Discussion Questions

1. A marketing research study undertaken for a major appliance manufacturer disclosed that 30 percent of those polled plan on purchasing a trash compactor in the next three months, and 15 percent plan on purchasing a new iron. How much confidence should be placed in the predictive accuracy of these intention measurements? More generally, will predictive accuracy vary across products? Why or why not?

2. You are interested in predicting whether a person will purchase a new Chrysler from the Bob Caldwell dealership in the next month. Someone suggests the following phrasing for the intention measure: "How likely is it that you will buy a new automobile soon?" Why is this measure unlikely to predict the behavior of interest?

3. In January 2005, before market introduction, Mr. Dickson conducted a survey of consumers' attitudes toward his new product. The survey revealed that 80 percent of those interviewed held favorable attitudes toward the product. The product was introduced in June 2006, and product

sales have been very disappointing. What explanations can you offer for this discrepancy between the attitude survey and product sales?

4. Consider the following results for a television set, based on Fishbein's multiattribute model.

| ATTRIBUTE | EVALUATION | BRAND BELIEF |
| --- | --- | --- |
| Clear picture | +3 | +2 |
| Low price | +2 | −1 |
| Durable | +3 | +1 |
| Attractive cabinet | +1 | +3 |

First, calculate the overall attitude score. Second, calculate the maximum overall score a brand could receive given the current set of attribute evaluations. Third, describe the product's strengths and weaknesses as perceived by consumers.

5. Using the multiattribute results presented in question 4, identify all possible changes that would enhance brand attitude. Which change would lead to the greatest improvement in attitude?

6. Discuss the tradeoffs between multiattribute attitude models, measures of attitude toward a product, and measures of purchase intentions in terms of (a) their relative predictive power, and (b) their usefulness in understanding consumer behavior.

7. Assume a company is trying to decide which consumer segments represent its best bet for future expansion. To help in this decision, the research department has collected information about segment members' product attitudes. The results show the following average attitude scores on a ten-point scale ranging from "bad product" (1) to "good product" (10).

| | |
| --- | --- |
| Segment A | 8.2 |
| Segment B | 7.5 |
| Segment C | 6.1 |

Based on this information, segment A has been chosen as the best bet for expansion. Do you agree? What problems might exist with making this decision based on the current information?

## Notes

[1] Other factors beyond attitudes may also influence intentions. See Icek Ajzen, "The Theory of Planned Behavior," *Organizational Behavior and Human Decision Processes*, 50 (1991), 179–211; Icek Ajzen and Martin Fishbein, *Understanding Attitudes and Predicting Social Behavior* (Englewood Cliffs, NJ: Prentice-Hall, 1980); Martin Fishbein and Icek Ajzen, *Belief, Attitude, Intention, and Behavior: An Introduction to Theory and Research* (Reading, MA: Addison-Wesley, 1975); Paul W. Miniard and Joel B. Cohen, "Modeling Personal and Normative Influences on Behavior," *Journal of Consumer Research*, 10 (September

1983), 169–180; Paul R. Warshaw, "A New Model for Predicting Behavioral Intentions: An Alternative to Fishbein," *Journal of Marketing Research,* 17 (May 1980), 153–172.

[2] For more information about the Survey Research Center and the Indices of Consumer Expectations and Consumer Sentiment, go to www.sca.isr.umich.edu.

[3] Richard T. Curtin, "Surveys of Consumers: Theory, Methods, and Interpretation," paper presented at the 44th Annual NABE Meeting, Washington, D.C. (September 30, 2002).

[4] "EquiTrend's 5 Key Measures," Harris Interactive, www.harrisinteractive.com.

[5] "Reynolds Wrap Aluminum Foil Ranks #1 in Overall Brand Equity," Harris Interactive, www.harrisinteractive.com (June 22, 2004).

[6] Lauri Klefos, "Defining New Hampshire's Image and the Travel Market," *New Hampshire Business Review* (April 16, 2004), A28.

[7] Alexander Cherenev and Gregory S. Carpenter, "The Role of Market Efficiency Intuitions in Consumer Choice: A Case of Compensatory Inferences," *Journal of Marketing Research,* 38 (August 2001), 349–361; Gary T. Ford and Ruth Ann Smith, "Inferential Beliefs in Consumer Evaluations: An Assessment of Alternative Processing Strategies," *Journal of Consumer Research,* 14 (December 1987), 363–371.

[8] Frank R. Kardes, Maria L. Cronley, James J. Kellaris, and Steven S. Posavac, "The Role of Selective Information Processing and Price-Quality Inference," *Journal of Consumer Research,* 31 (September 2004), 368–374; Donald Lichtenstein and Scott Burton, "The Relationship between Perceived and Objective Price-Quality," *Journal of Marketing Research,* 26 (November 1989), 429–443; Erian Gerstner, "Do Higher Prices Signal Higher Quality?" *Journal of Marketing Research,* 22 (May 1985), 209–215.

[9] Larry D. Compeau and Dhruv Grewal, "Adding Value by Communicating Price Deals Effectively: Does It Matter How You Phrase It?" *Pricing Strategy &* *Practice,* 2 (1994), 28–36; Dhruv Grewal, Howard Marmorstein, and Arun Sharma, "Communicating Price Information through Semantic Cues: The Moderating Effects of Situation and Discount Size," *Journal of Consumer Research,* 23 (September 1996), 148–155; Donald R. Lichtenstein, Scot Burton, and Eric J. Karson, "The Effect of Semantic Cues on Consumer Perceptions of Reference Price Ads," *Journal of Consumer Research,* 18 (December 1991), 380–391.

[10] Michael J. Barone, Kenneth C. Manning, and Paul W. Miniard, "Consumer Response to Retailers' Use of Partially Comparative Pricing," *Journal of Marketing,* 68 (July 2004), 37–47.

[11] Cornelia Pechmann, "Do Consumers Overgeneralize One-Sided Comparative Price Claims, and Are More Stringent Regulations Needed?" *Journal of Marketing Research,* 33 (May 1996), 150–162.

[12] Andrew A. Mitchell and Jerry C. Olson, "Are Product Attribute Beliefs the Only Mediators of Advertising Effects on Brand Attitudes?" *Journal of Marketing Research,* 18 (August 1981), 318–332.

[13] "FDA Restricts Claims Made by Dietary Supplements," *Miami Herald* (April 25, 1998), A27.

[14] To learn more about consumer confusion, see Marcel Cohen, "Insights into Consumer Confusion," *Consumer Policy Review,* 9 (November/December 1999), 210–213; Vincent-Wayne Mitchell and Vassilios Papavassiliou, "Marketing Causes and Implications of Consumer Confusion," *Journal of Product and Brand Management,* 8 (1999), 319–334; Dan Sarel and Howard Marmorstein, "Designing Confusion Surveys for Cyberspace Trademark Litigation: The Admissibility vs. Weight Debate," *Intellectual Property & Technology Law Journal,* 14 (September 2002), 12–17.

[15] Timothy Aeppel and Norihiko Shirouzu, "Bridgestone/Firestone's Handling of Recall Results in Consumer Confusion, Chaos," *Wall Street Journal* (August 11, 2000), A3.

[16] "Daimler Is Set Back on Bid to Stop GM on Grille Design," *Wall Street Journal* (November 19, 2002), 1.

[17] Sam Solly, "Sunny D Tells Parents to Get Real with Vitamin C Message," *Marketing* (August 7, 2003), 19.

[18] Claire Atkinson, "AOL's 'Gut-Wrenching' Overhaul," *Advertising Age* (February 23, 2004), 1–2.

[19] Daniel Golden and Suzanne Vranica, "Duracell's Duck Ad Will Carry Disclaimer," *Wall Street Journal* (February 7, 2002), B7.

[20] Linda A. Johnson, "Painful Decisions," *Miami Herald* (February 15, 2005), C1, C5.

[21] Ibid.

[22] For a general discussion of the role of mood in consumer behavior, see Meryl Paula Gardner, "Mood States and Consumer Behavior: A Critical Review," *Journal of Consumer Research,* 12 (December 1985), 281–300.

[23] Michael J. Barone, Paul W. Miniard, and Jean Romeo, "The Influence of Positive Mood on Consumers' Evaluations of Brand Extensions," *Journal of Consumer Research,* 26 (March 2000), 386–400; Rajeev Batra and Douglas M. Stayman, "The Role of Mood in Advertising Effectiveness," *Journal of Consumer Research,* 17 (September 1990), 203–214; Daniel J. Howard and Thomas E. Barry, "The Role of the Thematic Congruence between a Mood-Inducing Event in an Advertised Product in Determining the Effects of Mood on Brand Attitudes," *Journal of Consumer Psychology,* 3 (1994), 1–27; Alice M. Isen, Thomas E. Shalker, Margaret Clark, and Lynn Karp, "Affect, Accessibility of Material, and Behavior: A Cognitive Loop?" *Journal of Personality and Social Psychology,* 36 (1978), 1–12; Richard E. Petty, David W. Schumann, Stephen A. Richman, and Alan J. Strathman, "Positive Mood and Persuasion: Different Roles for Affect under High- and Low-Elaboration Conditions," *Journal of Personality and Social Psychology,* 64 (January 1993), 5–20.

[24] Carl Obermiller and Mary Jo Bittner, "Store Atmosphere: A Peripheral Cue for Product Evaluation," in David C. Stew-

art, ed., *American Psychological Association Annual Conference Proceedings* (American Psychological Association, 1984), 52–53.

25 Julie A. Edell and Marian Chapman Burke, "The Power of Feelings in Understanding Advertising Effects," *Journal of Consumer Research,* 14 (December 1987), 421–433.

26 Jennifer S. Lerner, Deborah A. Small, and George Loewenstein, "Heartstrings and Purse Strings: Carryover Effects of Emotions on Economic Decisions," *Psychological Science,* 15 (2004), 337–341.

27 Hoag Levins, "Defending Anheuser-Busch's Applause Spot," www.adage.com (February 14, 2005).

28 "Month's Top 10 Most-Liked, Most-Recalled New TV Spots," www.adage.com (March 7, 2005).

29 Arno J. Rethans, John L. Swasy, and Lawrence J. Marks, "Effects of Television Commercial Repetition, Receiver Knowledge, and Commercial Length: A Test of the Two-Factor Model," *Journal of Marketing Research,* 23 (February 1986), 50–61.

30 Marian Chapman Burke and Julie A. Edell, "The Impact of Feelings on Ad-Based Affect and Cognition," *Journal of Marketing Research,* 26 (February 1989), 69–83; Julie A. Edell and Marian Chapman Burke, "The Power of Feelings in Understanding Advertising Effects," *Journal of Consumer Research,* 14 (December 1987), 421–433; Thomas J. Olney, Morris B. Holbrook, and Rajeev Batra, "Consumer Responses to Advertising: The Effects of Ad Content, Emotions, and Attitude toward the Ad on Viewing Time," *Journal of Consumer Research,* 17 (March 1991), 440–453; Douglas M. Stayman and Rajeev Batra, "Encoding and Retrieval of Ad Affect in Memory," *Journal of Marketing Research,* 28 (May 1991), 232–239. Also see Jennifer Edson Escalas, Marian Chapman Moore, and Julie Edell Britton, "Fishing for Feelings? Hooking Viewers Helps!" *Journal of Consumer Psychology,* 14 (2004), 105–114.

31 Batra and Stayman, "The Role of Mood in Advertising Effectiveness"; Howard and Barry, "The Role of Thematic Congruence between a Mood-Inducing Event and an Advertised Product in Determining the Effects of Mood on Brand Attitudes"; Punam Anand Keller, Isaac M. Lipkus, and Barbara K. Rimer, "Affect, Framing, and Persuasion," *Journal of Marketing Research,* 40 (February 2003), 54–64; Petty, Schumann, Richman, and Strathman, "Positive Mood and Persuasion."

32 Marvin E. Goldberg and Gerald J. Gorn, "Happy and Sad TV Programs: How They Affect Reactions to Commercials," *Journal of Consumer Research,* 14 (December 1987), 387–403; John P. Murry Jr., John L. Lastovicka, and Surendra N. Singh, "Feelings and Liking Responses to Television Programs: An Examination of Two Explanations for Media-Context Effects," *Journal of Consumer Research,* 18 (March 1992), 441–451. For additional research on context effects, see Patrick De Pelsmacker, Maggie Geuens, and Pascal Anckaert, "Media Context in Advertising Effectiveness: The Role of Context Appreciation and Context/Ad Similarity," *Journal of Advertising,* 31 (Summer 2002), 49–61.

33 "GF, Coke Tell Why They Shun TV News," *Advertising Age* (January 28, 1980), 39.

34 Adam Hanft, "How Super Is Your Market?" *Wall Street Journal* (March 1, 2005), B2.

35 Kordelia Spies, Friedrich Hesse, and Kerstin Loesch, "Store Atmosphere, Mood and Purchasing Behavior," *International Journal of Research in Marketing,* 14 (1997), 1–17.

36 Ibid.

37 A. Mehrabian and James H. Russell, *An Approach to Environmental Psychology* (Cambridge, MA: MIT Press, 1974).

38 Robert J. Donovan and John R. Rossiter, "Store Atmosphere: An Environmental Psychology Approach," *Journal of Retailing,* 58 (Spring 1982), 34–57.

39 Changjo Yoo, Jonghee Park, and Deborah J. MacInnis, "Effects of Store Characteristics and In-Store Emotional Experiences on Store Attitude," *Journal of Business Research,* 42 (1998), 253–263.

40 Spies, Hesse, and Loesch, "Store Atmosphere, Mood and Purchasing Behavior."

41 Donovan and Rossiter, "Store Atmosphere: An Environmental Psychology Approach"; Elaine Sherman, Anil Mathur, and Ruth Belk Smith, "Store Environment and Consumer Purchase Behavior: Mediating Role of Consumer Emotions," *Psychology and Marketing,* 14 (July 1997), 361–378; Yoo, Park, and MacInnis, "Effects of Store Characteristics and In-Store Emotional Experiences on Store Attitude."

42 Obermiller and Bittner, "Store Atmosphere: A Peripheral Cue for Product Evaluation."

43 Robert J. Donovan, John R. Rossiter, Gilian Marcoolyn, and Andrew Nesdale, "Store Atmosphere and Purchasing Behavior," *Journal of Retailing,* 70 (Fall 1994), 283–294; Sherman, Mathur, and Smith, "Store Environment and Consumer Purchase Behavior"; Spies, Hesse, and Loesch, "Store Atmosphere, Mood and Purchasing Behavior."

44 Morris B. Holbrook and Elizabeth C. Hirschman, "The Experiential Aspects of Consumption: Consumer Fantasies, Feelings, and Fun," *Journal of Consumer Research,* 9 (September 1982), 132–140; Haim Mano and Richard L. Oliver, "Assessing the Dimensionality and Structure of the Consumption Experience: Evaluation, Feeling, and Satisfaction," *Journal of Consumer Research,* 20 (December 1993), 451–466; Richard L. Oliver, "Cognitive, Affective, and Attribute Bases of the Satisfaction Response," *Journal of Consumer Research,* 20 (December 1993), 418–430; Robert A. Westbrook, "Product/Consumption-Based Affective Responses and Postpurchase Processes," *Journal of Marketing Research,* 24 (August 1987), 258–270; Robert A. Westbrook and Richard L. Oliver, "The Dimensionality of Consumption Emotion Patterns and Consumer Satisfaction," *Journal of Consumer Research,* 18 (June 1991), 84–91.

45 Paul W. Miniard, Sunil Bhatla, and Deepak Sirdeshmukh, "Mood as a Determinant of Post-Consumption Evaluations: Mood Effects and Their Dependency on the Affective Intensity of the Consumption Experience," *Journal of Consumer Psychology*, 1 (1992), 173–195.

46 "Sony Tops the List in Annual Best Brands Survey for Fifth Consecutive Year," Harris Interactive, www.harrisinteractive.com (July 7, 2004).

47 "Reynolds Wrap Aluminum Foil Ranks #1 in Overall Brand Equity," Harris Interactive, www.harrisinteractive.com (June 22, 2004).

48 "EquiTrend's 5 Key Measures," Harris Interactive, www.harrisinteractive.com.

49 For an excellent review of the literature concerning attitude resistance, see Alice H. Eagly and Shelly Chaiken, *The Psychology of Attitudes* (Fort Worth, TX: Harcourt Brace Jovanovich, 1993).

50 Michael J. Barone and Paul W. Miniard, "How and When Factual Ad Claims Can Mislead Consumers: Examining the Deceptive Consequences of *Copy X Copy* Interactions for Partial Comparative Ads," *Journal of Marketing Research*, 36 (February 1999), 58–74; Michael J. Barone, Kay M. Palan, and Paul W. Miniard, "Brand Usage and Gender as Moderators of the Potential Deception Associated with Partial Comparative Advertising," *Journal of Advertising*, 33 (Spring 2004), 19–28.

51 Russell H. Fazio and Mark P. Zanna, "On the Predictive Validity of Attitudes: The Roles of Direct Experience and Confidence," *Journal of Personality*, 46 (June 1978), 228–243; Lawrence J. Marks and Michael A. Kamins, "The Use of Product Sampling and Advertising: Effects of Sequence of Exposure and Degree of Advertising Claim Exaggeration on Consumers' Belief Strength, Belief Confidence, and Attitudes," *Journal of Marketing Research*, 5 (August 1988), 266–281; Robert E. Smith and William R. Swinyard, "Attitude-Behavior Consistency: The Impact of Product Trial versus Advertising," *Journal of Marketing Research*, 20 (August 1983), 257–267.

52 Ida E. Berger, "The Nature of Attitude Accessibility and Attitude Confidence: A Triangulated Experiment," *Journal of Consumer Psychology*, 1 (1992), 103–124; Ida E. Berger and Andrew A. Mitchell, "The Effect of Advertising on Attitude Accessibility, Attitude Confidence, and the Attitude-Behavior Relationship," *Journal of Consumer Research*, 16 (December 1989), 269–279.

53 Fazio and Zanna, "On the Predictive Validity of Attitudes"; Marks and Kamins, "The Use of Product Sampling and Advertising"; Smith and Swinyard, "Attitude-Behavior Consistency."

54 Berger, "The Nature of Attitude Accessibility and Attitude Confidence"; Fazio and Zanna, "On the Predictive Validity of Attitudes"; Smith and Swinyard, "Attitude-Behavior Consistency."

55 Marks and Kamins, "The Use of Product Sampling and Advertising."

56 Berger and Mitchell, "The Effect of Advertising on Attitude Accessibility, Attitude Confidence, and the Attitude-Behavior Relationship"; Russell H. Fazio, Martha C. Powell, and Carol J. Williams, "The Role of Attitude Accessibility and the Attitude-to-Behavior Process," *Journal of Consumer Research*, 16 (December 1989), 280–288.

57 Russell H. Fazio, David M. Sanbonmatsu, Martha C. Powell, and Frank R. Kardes, "On the Automatic Activation of Attitudes," *Journal of Personality and Social Psychology*, 40 (February 1986), 229–238.

58 Cyndee Miller, "Study Says 'Likability' Surfaces as Measure of TV Ad Success," *Marketing News* (January 7, 1991), 6, 14. Also see Cyndee Miller, "Researchers Balk at Testing Rough Ads for 'Likability,'" *Marketing News* (September 2, 1991), 2.

59 Keith S. Coulter, "An Examination of Qualitative vs. Quantitative Elaboration Likelihood Effects," *Psychology and Marketing*, 22 (January 2005), 31–49; Scott B. MacKenzie, Richard J. Lutz, and George E. Belch, "The Role of Attitude toward the Ad as a Mediator of Advertising Effectiveness: A Test of Competing Explanations," *Journal of Marketing Research*, 23 (May 1986), 130–143; Paul W. Miniard, Sunil Bhatla, and Randall L. Rose, "On the Formation and Relationship of Ad and Brand Attitudes: An Experimental and Causal Analysis," *Journal of Marketing Research*, 27 (August 1990), 290–303; Andrew A. Mitchell and Jerry C. Olson, "Are Product Attribute Beliefs the Only Mediators of Advertising Effects on Brand Attitudes?" *Journal of Marketing Research*, 18 (August 1981), 318–332.

60 Fishbein and Ajzen, *Belief, Attitude, Intention, and Behavior*.

61 Douglas Hanks III, "Tennis? Anyone?" *Miami Herald* (October 23, 2004), C1, C3.

62 Ibid.

63 Discussion of additional multiattribute models can be found in Frank A. Bass and W. Wayne Talarzyk, "Attitude Model for the Study of Brand Preference," *Journal of Marketing Research*, 9 (February 1972), 93–96; Jagdish N. Sheth and W. Wayne Talarzyk, "Perceived Instrumentality and Value Importance as Determinants of Attitudes," *Journal of Marketing Research*, 9 (February 1973), 6–9; Milton J. Rosenberg, "Cognitive Structure and Attitudinal Affect," *Journal of Abnormal and Social Psychology*, 53 (November 1956), 367–372; Olli T. Ahtola, "The Vector Model of Preferences: An Alternative to the Fishbein Model," *Journal of Marketing Research*, 12 (February 1975), 52–59.

64 Martin Fishbein, "An Investigation of the Relationships between Beliefs about an Object and the Attitude toward That Object," *Human Relations*, 16 (August 1963), 233–240; Fishbein and Ajzen, *Belief, Attitude, Intention, and Behavior*; Ajzen and Fishbein, *Understanding Attitudes and Predicting Social Behavior*. For general reviews of multiattribute models in consumer research, see Richard J. Lutz and James R. Bettman, "MultiAttribute Models in Marketing: A Bicentennial Review," in Arch G. Woodside, Jagdish N. Sheth, and Peter D. Bennett, eds., *Consumer and Industrial Buying Behavior*

(New York: North-Holland, 1977), 137–149; William L. Wilkie and Edgar A. Pessemier, "Issues in Marketing's Use of Multi-Attribute Models," *Journal of Marketing Research,* 10 (November 1973), 428–441.

[65] Evidence suggests that the order in which beliefs are measured (by attribute across brands versus by brand across attributes) can be important. See Eugene D. Joffee and Israel D. Nebenzahl, "Alternative Questionnaire Formats for Country Image Studies," *Journal of Marketing Research,* 21 (November 1984), 463–471. Certain characteristics of the response scale may also affect elderly consumers' responses. See Rama K. Jayanti, Mary K. McManamon, and Thomas W. Whipple, "The Effects of Aging on Brand Attitude Measurement," *Journal of Consumer Marketing,* 21 (2004), 264–273.

[66] Examples of applying the ideal-point model can be found in James L. Ginter, "An Experimental Investigation of Attitude Change and Choice of a New Brand," *Journal of Marketing Research,* 11 (February 1974), 30–40; Donald R. Lehmann, "Television Show Preference: Application of a Choice Model," *Journal of Marketing Research,* 8 (February 1972), 47–55.

[67] For research on the model's usefulness in new product development, see Morris B. Holbrook and William J. Havlena, "Assessing the Real-to-Artificial Generalizability of Multiattribute Attitude Models in Tests of New Product Designs," *Journal of Marketing Research,* 25 (February 1988), 25–35.

[68] "Lever Brothers Uses Micromodel to Project Market Share," *Marketing News* (November 27, 1981).

[69] For an empirical demonstration of changing attitudes from a multiattribute perspective, see Richard J. Lutz, "Changing Brand Attitudes through Modification of Cognitive Structure," *Journal of Consumer Research,* 1 (March 1975), 49–59.

[70] Paul W. Miniard, Randall L. Rose, Michael J. Barone, and Kenneth C. Manning, "On the Need for Relative Measures When Assessing Comparative Advertising Effects," *Journal of Advertising,* 22 (September 1993), 41–58; Paul W. Miniard, Randall L. Rose, Kenneth C. Manning, and Michael J. Barone, "Tracking the Effects of Comparative and Noncomparative Advertising with Relative and Nonrelative Measures: A Further Examination of the Framing Correspondence Hypothesis," *Journal of Business Research,* 41 (February 1998), 137–143; Cornelia Pechmann and S. Ratneshwar, "The Use of Comparative Advertising for Brand Positioning: Association versus Differentiation," *Journal of Consumer Research,* 18 (September 1991), 145–160; Randall L. Rose, Paul W. Miniard, Michael J. Barone, Kenneth C. Manning, and Brian D. Till, "When Persuasion Goes Undetected: The Case of Comparative Advertising," *Journal of Marketing Research,* 30 (August 1993), 315–330.

[71] Scott B. MacKenzie, "The Role of Attention in Mediating the Effect of Advertising on Attribute Importance," *Journal of Consumer Research,* 13 (September 1986), 174–195.

[72] Gregg Fields, "Blowing Smoke?" *Miami Herald* (January 25, 1998), F1, F3.

[73] For research on the intention-behavior relationship, see Donald H. Granbois and John O. Summers, "Primary and Secondary Validity of Consumer Purchase Probabilities," *Journal of Consumer Research,* 4 (March 1975), 31–38; Paul W. Miniard, Carl Obermiller, and Thomas J. Page Jr., "A Further Assessment of Measurement Influences on the Intention-Behavior Relationship," *Journal of Marketing Research,* 20 (May 1983), 206–212; David J. Reibstein, "The Prediction of Individual Probabilities of Brand Choice," *Journal of Consumer Research,* 5 (December 1978), 163–168; Paul R. Warshaw, "Predicting Purchase and Other Behaviors from General and Contextually Specific Intentions," *Journal of Marketing Research,* 17 (February 1980), 26–33.

[74] Chuck Elliott, "Fire Up the Grill," *LP-Gas* (May 2004), 12–14.

[75] "Barbecue and Grill Unit Shipments," Hearth, Patio & Barbecue Association, www.hpba.org.

[76] "US Consumers Plan to Buy More Real Trees," press release, National Christmas Tree Association, www.realchristmas trees.org (November 26, 2004).

[77] Joseph A. Cote, James McCullough, and Michael Reilly, "Effects of Unexpected Situations on Behavior-Intention Differences: A Garbology Analysis," *Journal of Consumer Research,* 12 (September 1985), 188–194.

[78] Jennifer Lach, "Meet You in Aisle Three," *American Demographics* (April 1999), 41–42.

[79] For an excellent discussion of the importance of measurement correspondence, see Icek Ajzen and Martin Fishbein, "Attitude-Behavior Relations: A Theoretical Analysis and Review of Empirical Research," *Psychological Bulletin,* 84 (September 1977), 888–918. For an empirical demonstration, see James Jaccard, G. William King, and Richard Pomozal, "Attitudes and Behavior: An Analysis of Specificity of Attitudinal Predictors," *Human Relations,* 30 (September 1977), 817–824.

[80] Paul R. Warshaw and Fred D. Davis, "Disentangling Behavioral Intention and Behavioral Expectation," *Journal of Experimental Social Psychology,* 21 (1985), 213–228.

[81] Ajzen and Fishbein, *Understanding Attitudes and Predicting Social Behavior;* E. Bonfield, "Attitude, Social Influence, Personal Norms, and Intention Interactions as Related to Brand Purchase Behavior," *Journal of Marketing Research,* 11 (November 1974), 379–389.

[82] Icek Ajzen, "From Intentions to Actions: A Theory of Planned Behavior," in J. Kuhland and J. Beckman, eds., *Action Control: From Cognitions to Behavior* (Heidelberg: Springer-Verlag, 1985), 11–39; Ajzen, "The Theory of Planned Behavior"; Thomas J. Madden, Pamela Scholder Ellen, and Icek Ajzen, "A Comparison of the Theory of Planned Behavior and the Theory of Reasoned Action," *Personality and Social Psychology Bulletin,* 18 (February 1992), 3–9.

[83] Cyndee Miller, "Hemp Is Latest Buzz-word," *Marketing News* (March 17, 1997), 1, 6.

[84] Pierre Chandon, Vicki G. Morwitz, and Werner J. Reinartz, "The Short- and Long-Term Effects of Measuring Intent to Repurchase," *Journal of Consumer Research,* 31 (December 2004), 566–572; Gavan J. Fitzsimmons and Vicki G. Morwitz, "The Effect of Measuring Intent on Brand-Level Purchase Behavior," *Journal of Consumer Research,* 23 (June 1996), 1–11; Vicki G. Morwitz and Gavan J. Fitzsimons, "The Mere-Measurement Effect; Why Does Measuring Intentions Change Actual Behavior?" *Journal of Consumer Psychology,* 14 (2004), 64–74 ; Vicki G. Morwitz, Eric Johnson, and David Schmittlein, "Does Measuring Intent Change Behavior?" *Journal of Consumer Research,* 20 (June 1993), 46–61; Patti Williams, Gavan J. Fitzsimons, and Lauren G. Black, "When Consumers Do Not Recognize 'Benign' Intention Questions as Persuasion Attempts," *Journal of Consumer Research,* 31 (December 2004), 540–550.

# Environmental Influences on Consumer Behavior

No person is an island. This statement certainly is true in the study of consumer behavior. Individuals come in all shapes, sizes, and colors, and behave in a variety of ways, as seen in the previous sections of this book. These characteristics are what make you unique as an individual. But what causes you to be the way you are? Is it genetic predisposition, the environment, or some combination thereof that has guided you in your evolution as a unique individual? Even scientists from many disciplines disagree on the answers to such basic questions.

One thing is clear—consumers are shaped to some extent by the environment in which they live, and they in turn affect their environments through their behaviors. The following chapters show you how this process occurs and addresses the impact of environmental influences on purchase and consumption decisions.

Fundamental to the discussion of environmental influences is the topic of culture. Chapter 11 focuses on the role of culture and ethnic influences on consumer behavior, including religion, values, and social class. Family and household influences are discussed in Chapter 12, including the changing roles of women and men in society and the changing makeup of the family unit. The final chapter in this section, Chapter 13, focuses on personal and group influences that shape the way we behave and live.

# Chapter 11

# Culture, Ethnicity, and Social Class

## Opening Vignette

"Hmm. That sounds fine if the customer arrives from the right side, but what about people approaching from the opposite direction? Wouldn't they see only the backs of the mannequins?" a retail merchandising manager asks.

"Yes," replies Paco Underhill, the twenty-first-century anthropologist of shopping, "but they'll be outnumbered because research shows that most mall pedestrians follow a counterclockwise loop through a mall—except in Britain, where people drive on the left side of the road and thus prefer a clockwise path as pedestrians."

Another suggestion involves the otherwise barren and discreet public restrooms. Underhill proposes handing their management over to shops that sell soaps and other bath products as a way of showcasing their products and improving the ambience of the entire mall. "Talk to any woman and you quickly learn how pleasant bathrooms make prolonged shopping trips possible," he writes in his popular book, *Call of the Mall.*

Just as the legendary anthropologist Margaret Mead lived with, observed and interviewed Somoan girls to learn more about the role of women in society, Paco Hill studies customers where they dwell—the suburban shopping center—and helps merchants figure out the best way to capture customers' minds and wallets. Clients of Envirosell, his consulting firm, range from Sunglass Hut to Saks Fifth Avenue. Underhill's research identifies "ways that merchants shoot themselves in the foot," such as a women's clothing store with aisles too narrow for baby strollers or barebones fitting rooms. "Why don't we do a better job of romancing the dressing room?" he asks, going on to recommend adjustable lighting that simulates outdoor and indoor environments. "The dressing room is often the least glamorous part of a store, and yet it's where so much of the decision making happens."

Similarly, many department stores locate perfume counters near the entrance—a throwback to pre-automobile days when fragrance sections were "a bulwark against the stench of horse manure coming in from the street"—rather than in clothing sections where consumers are making complete wardrobe decisions.

When asked which stores do the best job of avoiding the types of blunders described in his book, Underhill cites home and kitchen stores Crate & Barrel and Williams-Sonoma. They are "wonderful" with visuals, music, even scents, he says. They appeal to aging baby boomers who want to "feather their nests" with luxury goods.

In his book, Underhill devotes a short chapter to kiosks, which originated in Boston's Faneuil Hall Marketplace and have become cash cows for mall owners, with annual leases running as high as $50,000 for a forty-five-square-foot cart. Other chapters explore the psychology behind mall food courts, shoe departments, parking garages, and cosmetics counters. One conclusion concerns the "six-second greeting," in which clerks greet shoppers no later than six seconds after they've entered the store, on the theory that customers who talk with employees are more likely to buy. But that can backfire. If a cosmetics clerk approaches a shopper within the first 30 seconds, the approach scares the person off, according to Underhill's research. "The trick is to let the customer browse unaided, then watch her carefully for the first time she raises her head, even for a second. . . . It's the equivalent of a jerk on a fishing line—that's the moment the sales associate needs to start reeling her in."

Other findings from studying the culture of consumer behavior include the following.

- On a city street, men walk faster than women. In a mall, it's the opposite. Slowpoke walkers are known in the industry as "Neanderthals."
- By age fifty, the human eye lets in 20 percent less light, but store and restaurant designers are typically young, and "what they think looks bright enough is too dark for customers middle-aged and older."
- To remember where their cars are parked, men prefer numbers and letters, women like colors, and kids respond to symbols such as animals or fruit.
- The most expensive items on store shelves are placed at eye level. Look above or below that shelf for bargains.
- Products on tables sell better than those on shelves or racks.
- The average consumer sizes up a store and decides whether or not to shop there just ten seconds after walking in.
- Almost all the music you hear in stores is instrumental—no words. Store owners don't want you to consciously listen to (and be distracted by) the music. The exception: music stores.

To understand the effects of culture on consumption, researchers go to stores to do "field work." They count how many people are buying what types of products. They keep track of how many people walk into a store and how many people leave with a shopping bag, and where people go inside the store. They look at how parking lots are arranged, and other variables, such as the ones you saw in Chapter 3 in the section on "Consumer Logistics."

Source: Paco Underhill, *Call of the Mall* (New York: Simon & Schuster, 2004). Excerpts from Gina Ferrazi, "He's Got It Covered: Underhill," *Los Angeles Times* (February 17, 2004); and Rachel Dickinson, "They Want to Know Why You Buy; Here Are Some of the Ways Companies Figure Out How to Get You into Their Stores and Spend a Lot of Money," *Christian Science Monitor* (April 13, 2004).

Many factors affect how we, as individuals and as societies, live, buy, and consume. External influences such as culture, ethnicity, and social class influence how *individual* consumers buy and use products, and in the search for effective segmentation strategies, also help explain how *groups of consumers* behave.

The historical focus of consumer behavior has been individual differences and individual decision making, which are more important than ever because, as consumer segments are becoming more defined, marketers have a greater need to reach smaller segments of consumers. Understanding the *independent self* is important for marketing in the *individualistic* culture of North America,[1] but in a global economy we mustn't also forget *the interdependent self*,[2] especially because 70 percent of the world's consumers live in *collectivist* cultures. Culture and ethnicity affect how individuals make decisions and are useful for developing segmentation strategies because they influence groups of individuals.

## What Is Culture?

**Culture** refers to a *set of values, ideas, artifacts, and other meaningful symbols that help individuals communicate, interpret, and evaluate as members of society.* Culture has been described as the blueprint of human activity, determining the coordinates of social action and productive activity.[3] Culture has also been defined as a set of socially acquired behavior patterns transmitted symbolically through language and other means to the members of a particular society.[4] Culture does not include the instincts or erratic behavior revealed in an individual's one-time solution to a unique problem. Culture is, however, influenced by factors such as ethnicity, race, religion, and national or regional identity, as seen in Figure 11.1. As some of these elements change within a society, so then changes the culture.

Cultures can be described, evaluated, and differentiated according to their abstract and material elements. **Abstract elements** include *values, attitudes, ideas, personality types, and summary constructs, such as religion or politics.* Some cultures also believe in myths or have superstitions, as seen in Consumer Behavior and Marketing 11.1. A symbol might also evolve to represent a culture, such as the bald eagle, which represents the characteristics of independence, courage, and strength that mark the culture of the United States. This type of symbol embodies three central components—language, aesthetic styles, and story themes[5]—that become short-hand for a culture, defining its characteristics and values similar to how brands define the characteristics of a company or product.

Your self-esteem as an individual, and therefore much of your personality and ability to function well in life, is derived from the culture in which you are raised. Anthropologists have long known that when a tribe of people lose the feeling that their way of life is worthwhile, they may stop reproducing, or in large numbers simply lie down and die beside streams full of fish. Food is not the primary nourishment of people; it is their self-esteem.[6] When members of a family, a gender, an ethnic or national background, or other cultural grouping manifest with low self-esteem, dysfunction and perhaps depression is often the result. This pattern is why many universities offer courses

**FIGURE 11.1**     Influences on Culture

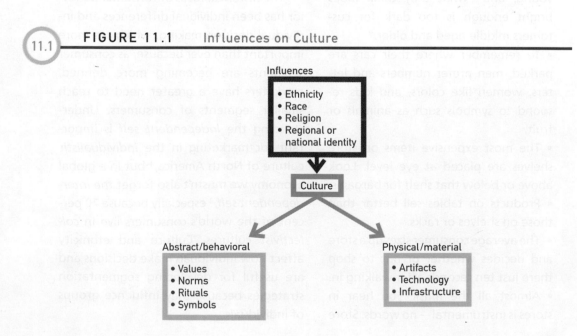

## Superstition Can Affect Behavior in a Macroculture

Superstition has always had a big impact on human behavior, sometimes yielding macroeconomic effects for even the most industrialized societies. An example of the effects of superstition is the rate of Japanese births from 1960 to 1990. A general, steady decline is evident in recent decades. But what jumps out is the single-year 25 percent drop in 1966. Such a sudden dip and recovery in birthrates meant all kinds of problems for companies selling baby cribs in 1966 or bicycles in 1972, for colleges and universities in 1984, and for employers in 1988.

Why did the number of births plunge 25 percent for only one year? In much of Asia (where Chinese influences are strong), each year is associated with one of twelve animals. For example, 1996 was the year of the Rat. Both 1990 and 1978 were years of the Horse, as was 1966. In Japanese culture, there is a traditional belief about *heigo,* or the year of the Fire Horse, which occurs once every sixty years, the last time in 1966. According to this long-standing superstition, a female born in a year of the Fire Horse is destined both to live an unhappy life and to kill her husband if she marries. Judging by the birthrate that year in Japan, superstitions about the year of the Fire Horse deterred people from having children. The relevant point here is that superstitions can substantially affect behavior on a macroeconomic scale in industrialized countries.

Source: Excerpted from Cathy Anterasian, John L. Graham, R. Bruce Money, "Are U.S. Managers Superstitious about Market Share?" *Sloan Management Review* (Summer 1996), 67–77.

focused on self-development or cultural sensitivity, which are intended to reverse such effects. For consumers, times of depression or sadness may cause them to lose hope in the future and overspend, often charging excessive amounts to their credit cards, or overeat, gaining excessive weight. The cycle thus perpetuates, as inescapable debt and poor health are also leading causes of depression.

**Cultural artifacts** include the *material components of a culture,* such as books, computers, tools, buildings, and specific products, such as a pair of designer jeans or the latest hit CD. Computers, cell phones, and Starbucks coffee shops all are artifacts of postmodern culture, as is piercing various body parts for some segments. For other segments, business suits and air conditioners are the signs of global cosmopolitanism and modernity.[7] Products also provide *symbols of meaning* in a society[8] and often represent family relationships, as in the case of a pearl necklace handed down through generations, or are associated with one's national or ethnic identity. Products sometimes are used in *ritual behavior,* such as foods eaten on certain holidays (like hot dogs and apple pie on the Fourth of July) or as a part of special religious ceremonies (such as a bar mitzvah or first communion). Occasionally, products become so much of a symbol in a society that they become *icons,* as in the case of brands such as McDonald's arches and Coca-Cola's distinctive bottle.

In Brazil, belief in the mystical properties of guarana (a plant believed to enhance power, spirit, and sexual prowess) represents an abstract element of Brazilian culture, and guarana-based drinks available throughout Brazil are cultural artifacts. Even today, Brazilian consumers like Coke but they also love guarana-based drinks, as shown in Figure 11.2a.[9] Similarly, Unicum, a traditional Hungarian herb liqueur, has become part of the Hungarian culture and acts as a Hungarian cultural icon in the ad seen in Figure 11.2b.

FIGURE 11.2a Guarana-based drinks are reflective of Brazilian culture.

FIGURE 11.2b Unicum Liqueur is a cultural icon in Hungary.

Culture provides people with a sense of identity and an understanding of acceptable behavior within society. Some of the more important characteristics influenced by culture follow.[10]

1. Sense of self and space

2. Communication and language

3. Dress and appearance

4. Food and feeding habits

5. Time and time consciousness

6. Relationships (family, organizations, government, and so on)

7. Values and norms

8. Beliefs and attitudes

9. Mental processes and learning

10. Work habits and practices

These characteristics can be used to define and differentiate one culture from another and identify cultural similarities. Marketers use cultural characteristics in global segmentation strategies. For example, McDonald's global expansion required the company to address the food and eating habits of various cultures. Although research showed that basic menu items would sell well in most markets, the company had to add some foods to reflect the cultural preferences of local markets. In Japan, McDonald's restaurants added rice (the country's staple food) to the menu. In Holland, it offered packets of mayonnaise instead of ketchup for fries. And in India, it addressed the sacred beliefs of the Hindu culture (that prohibit eating cows) by putting lamb burgers on the menu. In fact, such a large portion of India is vegetarian that adding a veggie burger to the menu would also have made sense.

## Values and Norms

Two important elements of culture are values and norms. **Norms** are *rules of behavior held by a majority or at least a consensus of a group about how individuals should behave.* Cultural or social values are those shared broadly across groups of people, whereas personal values, as you read in Chapter 7, are the terminal (goals) or instrumental (behavior) beliefs of individuals.

Societal and personal values are not always the same; in fact, values may vary among people of the same culture. To illustrate this point, examine societal values about how we should treat others. Although societal values generally condemn stealing another person's property, a thief's personal values may make an exception for such behavior in their unique circumstances. For instance, the thief may justify stealing if he has a legitimate need for the item or if he believes the owner is undeserving.

Further, look at vegetarians around the globe. Many vegetarians in the United States differ in behaviors from the cultural norms, perhaps for health reasons, often without disapproving of people who believe eating meat is acceptable. By contrast, in India, vegetarianism is a cultural norm and part of the value system of many of the nation's consumers. These types of social values, described in this chapter, are closely related to the personal values described in Chapter 7 and can sometimes be measured with psychographic (AIO) or Rokeach (RVS) scales.[11] Values that reflect the individualism or collectivism of a nation, discussed in Chapter 7, can affect product evaluation as well. Research was conducted in the United States and Japan in which subjects were given attribute information about a mountain bike manufactured in either Japan or the United States. The product was described as either superior or inferior to competition. Respondents in Japan evaluated the product that originated in their home country (versus the foreign country) more favorably regardless of actual product superiority. In contrast, respondents in the United States evaluated the product that originated in their home country more favorably only when the product was clearly superior to the competition, indicating that individualism and collectivism explains country-of-origin effects.[12]

Values and norms represent the beliefs of various groups within a society. **Macroculture** refers to *values and symbols that apply to an entire society or to most of its citizens.* **Microculture** refers to *values and symbols of a restrictive group or segment of consumers, defined according to variables such as age, religion, ethnicity, or social class.* Microcultures are sometimes called subcultures, but we use the term microculture to avoid concern that calling ethnic groups subcultures connotes inferiority, dissent, or exclusion.

Some countries, such as the United States, Switzerland, and Singapore, have national cultures made up of many microcultures, whereas other countries, such as Japan and South Korea, are more homogeneous. Countries like the United States reflect diverse ethnic components of their cultures, meaning that marketers have to be ready to adapt to the changing needs of the market as influenced by the changes in the diverse ethnic groups and many microcultures. For example, hamburgers are a U.S. cultural icon, but the ethnic influences of the increasing Latino market have caused a change in what condiment is put on hamburgers—from ketchup to salsa. In contrast, a marketer in Tokyo can look out the corporate window and know that most Japanese consumers will have similar beliefs about honor, family, religion, education, and work habits—all important in understanding consumer behavior. Cultures endow individuals with different rules or principles that provide guidance for making decisions, and a need to provide reasons activates such cultural knowledge. Principles of compromise, for example, are more prevalent in East Asian cultures than North American culture.[13]

## How Do People Get Their Values?

Unlike animals, whose behavior is governed largely by instinct, humans learn their norms by imitating others and observing the process of reward and punishment of people who adhere to or deviate from the group's norms. *The processes by which people develop their values, motivations, and habitual activity* are referred to as **socialization.** Another way to think about socialization is that it is the process of absorbing a culture. Parental practices, often determined by cultural norms, affect consumer socialization. For example, Japanese consumer socialization is characterized by benevolent dependence, consistent with a collectivist, interdependent society, whereas American consumer socialization is characterized by directed independence, consistent with an individualistic society.[14] Although most studies focus on how people learn consumer skills when they are young, consumer socialization is a process that occurs throughout life.[15]

The process of how values are transferred from one generation to the next and where individuals get their values is summarized in Figure 11.3. The values transfusion model shows how the values of a society are reflected in families, religious institutions, and schools, all of which expose and transmit values to individuals. These institutions and early lifetime experiences combine to affect which values individuals internalize and which ones they disregard.

Also important in the adoption process is the influence of peers and media. Media not only *reflects* societal values, but it can significantly *influence* the values of

**FIGURE 11.3**    The Values Transfusion Model

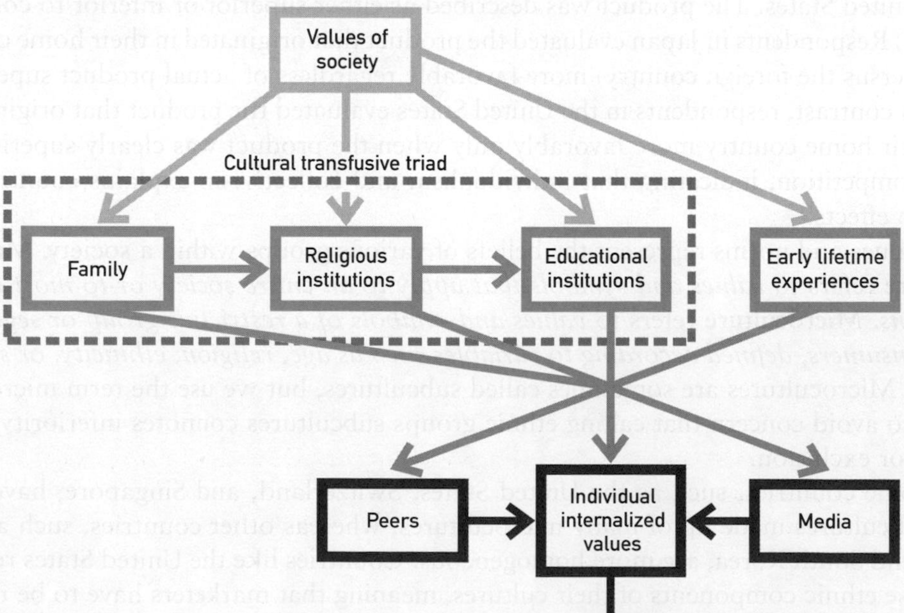

individuals. For example, a movie might portray using illegal drugs or driving drunk (values that society does not condone) as being "cool" or "funny," thereby potentially undermining social norms in influencing the values of individuals. Media can also reinforce cultural values important to a society such as success, hard work, or patriotism, passing them onto another generation. The German culture, for example, emphasizes the importance of children in families. The streets and parks of many German cities are adorned with sculptures or statutes reflecting the "ideal family," children playing with each other, a baby being embraced by his mother, or a young couple walking hand-in-hand. Similarly, the advertisement in Figure 11.4 reminds mothers that there are many reasons for taking care of their health, but none more important than their duty to their children, referring to the mother's love for her young daughter and unborn baby.

Through the socialization process depicted in Figure 11.3, people adopt values that influence how they live, how they define right and wrong, how they shop, and what is important to them—such as pleasure, honesty, financial security, or ambition. These life forces produce preferences relating to color, packaging, location, operating hours, interactions with salespeople, and many other variables, as you saw in the opening vignette of this chapter. Further, the values adopted by individuals today shape the values of society in the future. But just as individuals adopt certain values, they also abandon values when the values no longer meet the needs of society. In fact, some anthropologists view culture as an entity serving humans in their attempts to meet their most basic biological and social needs. When norms no longer provide gratification to a society, the norms lose their relevance to the majority of people.

FIGURE 11.4 Media Both Reflects and Influences Social Values

Courtesy of Sara Lee Food & Beverage

## Adapting Strategies to Changing Cultures

Culture is adaptive, which means that marketing strategies based on the values of society must also be adaptive. When cultural changes occur, trends develop and provide marketing opportunities to those who spot the changes before their competitors do. As culture evolves, marketers may associate product or brand benefits with new values, or they may have to change the product if that value is no longer gratifying in society. For example, a hearty breakfast of steak and eggs, sugar-cured ham, sausage gravy, and a mile-high stack of pancakes used to be a staple in the mass American culture. When most consumers worked on a farm or in strenuous manufacturing and labor jobs, high-energy and high-calorie foods were valued and gratifying. As those jobs were replaced by largely sedentary desk jobs, the food industry had to shift its appeal to lean meats with fewer calories and less fat and cholesterol. Today, Americans consume more pounds of poultry per year than either beef or pork.

Sometimes cultural norms change easily, and sometimes they remain the same for decades. Marketers must address **consumer socialization,** *the acquisition of consumption-related cognitions, attitudes, and behavior.* Norms learned early in life may be highly resistant to promotional efforts. When an advertiser is dealing with deeply ingrained, culturally defined behavior (about, for example, food, sex, basic forms of clothing, and so on), changing the marketing mix to conform to cultural values is easier than changing the values through advertising. As an example, eating dogs, horses, sheep eyes, live fish, and even the brain of a live monkey is considered normal and healthy behavior in some cultures. Advertising would have great difficulty, however, convincing typical North American consumers to try these products. The result of consumer socialization learned early in life and the cultural stability it produces is probably the reason why many Americans still prefer ketchup in a glass bottle instead of more efficient plastic packaging.

## How Culture Affects Consumer Behavior

Culture has a profound effect on why and how people buy and consume products and services. It affects the specific products people buy as well as the structure of consumption, individual decision making, and communication in a society.

### Influence of Culture on Pre-Purchase and Purchase

Culture affects the need, search, and alternative evaluation stages of how individuals make purchase decisions in a variety of ways. Although marketers can influence these stages through point-of-purchase displays, print and television advertising, and retailing strategies, certain cultural forces are difficult to overcome, at least in the short term.

Cultures view differently what is needed to enjoy a good standard of living. For example, North American households used to contain one television, around which family members gathered to watch live shows. Now, consumers often buy several televisions for one household, and having a second television in the bedroom or the kitchen has become the cultural norm, with similar norms developing for personal computers. However, other cultures see this type of consumption as frivolous; their definition of *need* dictates that one television or computer per household is adequate.

Culture also affects how consumers are likely to *search* for information. In some cultures, word-of-mouth and advice from a family member about product or brand choice are more important than information found in an advertisement. And in other cultures, consumers are more likely to search the Internet for unbiased third-party recommendations. To formulate the most effective information strategy, marketers must understand which method is valued more in a particular culture. At one time, holiday shopping meant visiting many stores; cultural norms shifted to reflect changes in cultural artifacts (computers and the Internet), but the socialization process also required consumers to learn ways of protecting themselves from technology (see Buyer Beware 11.1).

During *alternative evaluation,* some consumers place more weight on certain product attributes than on others, often due to the consumer's culture. For example, some wealthy consumers may think low price is the most important attribute, not because they lack money but because thrift (a cultural value) influences their choices, taught to them by the middle-class values associated with newly affluent consumers.[16] Conversely, a poor consumer may purchase an expensive pair of shoes because of personal or group values that persuade the individual to follow a fashion trend, perhaps believing that other people will regard them as part of a higher social status than might otherwise be conferred.

During *purchase* processes, the amount of price negotiation expected by both seller and buyer is culturally determined. For many people, shopping is not just a transaction, but the *experience* of searching for a "perfect self" or finding a "community" like a market, a coffee shop, or a neighborhood store where interaction among customers

## Holiday Gift Buying: Do You Know Where Your Credit Card Is?

Online buying continues to snowball, according to the results of an America Online survey, as Americans are doing more of their holiday shopping on the Internet. Fifty-three percent of those polled, AOL reports, said they planned to spend more than half their holiday budget shopping online. Make that 58 percent in the Washington, D.C., area, where the regular online shoppers are expected to buy an average of eleven gifts while sitting in the festive glow of their computer screens. AOL doesn't know how many online shoppers can be considered this devoted, but the retail research firm NPD Group says that before the last strains of "Auld Lang Syne" ring in the New Year, more than 40 percent of all Americans will have shopped the e-biz aisles at least once, spending almost $145 billion online.

Fear of getting ripped off still makes many shoppers uneasy about online purchasing, because of all that commotion about e-Grinchy identity theft. Clicking the "submit" icon when ordering and then realizing your credit card number has flitted off into Never-Never Land may feel a little like the adrenaline jolt that comes the moment you first think your wallet's missing. To reduce that risk, the following are hints to keep the Grinch from stealing your Christmas.

• Buy from established online retailers and Internet offspring of brick-and-mortar companies you trust. But a growing number of shopper sites—such as Yahoo! Shopping, BizRate, AOL's inStore, Froogle, Shopzilla, Cairo.com, and Shopping.com—assist consumers in comparison shopping. These sites not only search online retailers for good deals but rate the sellers for dependability, service, customer care, and so forth.

• Stick with online stores that give at least one telephone number, maybe even a physical address—and not just an e-mail contact. Some experts suggest calling the number before ordering.

• Check the site's shipping calendar of drop-dead order dates for guaranteed on-time holiday deliveries.

• Check the return policies. Online retailers tend to be more lenient about returned items, but "some merchants set a deadline for returns or charge a fee to accept returned merchandise," warns the Visa USA and Better Business Bureau guidelines.

• When going from browsing products to the Web page where you submit credit card data and personal info to actually order the products, make sure the site is secure. The Privacy Rights Clearinghouse and the Identity Theft Resource Center's online shopping guide says indicators that such pages are secure include a padlock icon on the browser's status bar, an unbroken key icon, or a URL for the website that begins with "https" (the s stands for "secure") when you make an order. E-mail is not secure.

• Document all online purchases by printing and saving a copy of the order page—before you click the "submit" icon. Once you press that button, more often than not, you just get a confirmation code.

• Use one credit card exclusively for online purchases so fraudulent or unauthorized charges are easier to monitor. And never use your bank account debit card. Debit cards lack protections credit cards provide, such as limited liability for losses.

Source: Excerpted from Don Oldenburg, "The Year Shoppers Left the Mall Behind," *Washington Post* (December 14, 2004), C9. Copyright 2004, The Washington Post. Reprinted with permission.

occurs.[17] Elements of the purchase process, such as price expectations, are culturally defined. In Greece and some Middle Eastern countries, for instance, even the price of a physician's services is subject to negotiation, whereas in North American markets, a physician's fee is generally predetermined and nonnegotiable. In Hong Kong, consumers are accustomed to walking through crowded marketplaces, examining and buying freshly slaughtered meat that is hanging in the open air (see Figure 11.5).

**FIGURE 11.5** Hong Kong Market

North American consumers would be fearful of bacteria or insects that might accumulate on the meat from exposure to the open air.

## Influence of Culture on Consumption and Divestment

Culture also affects how consumers use or consume products. Consumers buy products to obtain function, form, and meaning, all of which marketers must address because each is defined by the cultural context of consumption.

When consumers use a product, they expect it to perform a function. In the case of washing machines, the function is to clean clothes. But consumers' expectations about function and form often vary between cultures. In European cultures, washing machines are expected to last for decades. Space is often sparse, causing the washing machine to be located in a cellar or under the countertop in a kitchen or bathroom. Water is limited in many European cities, so the washing machines must be efficient. In addition, most European households do not have the fifty-gallon water heaters found in many American homes but rather rely on instantaneous hot water generated by small electrical appliances attached directly to a spigot. As a result, European washers must be self-heating. Given these requirements, highly efficient, front-loading machines costing more than $1,000 are marketed successfully throughout Europe and Asia by firms such as Miele, a German-based manufacturer and supplier of household appliances. Yet, when Miele introduced this product in North America, the product found only limited success, primarily in upscale urban dwellings. Hot water is ample in most American homes, so a self-heating washer is superfluous. Americans also move more frequently than Europeans and do not want to invest in a machine they will have for only a few years; further, Americans are accustomed to the more convenient but less efficient cleaning ability of top-loading machines.[18]

Culture also influences how individuals dispose of products in the divestment stage of the CDP model. In the United States, washing machines are almost a disposable product. Relatively inexpensive and awkward to move, when they break or if the consumer moves, they are often discarded or left behind. Other cultures promote reselling products after use, giving them to others to use, or recycling them and their packaging when possible.

## How Core Values Affect Marketing

Successful retailers know that *a basic group of products is essential to a store's traffic, customer loyalty, and profits.* These products are known as **core merchandise.** Likewise, **core values** are basic to understanding the behavior of people and can be helpful to marketers in several ways.

- *Core values define how products are used in a society.* Not only do core values determine what foods should be eaten, but they also determine with what other foods they are appropriate, how they are prepared, and the time of day to eat them.
- *Core values provide positive and negative valences (attraction or aversion) for brands and communications programs.* Marketers may use celebrity athletes or musicians such as LeBron James or Madonna to achieve positive valences to their brands, a successful strategy provided the image of the celebrity doesn't turn negative.
- *Core values define acceptable market relationships.* A firm's native culture (and values) influences its business strategies, tactics, and practices in the global marketplace,[19] and it affects international buying practices as well.[20] For example, in Japan, a company will often do business with small suppliers or distribution companies owned by former employees, with whom they have a relationship or similar cultural backgrounds. But in the United States, where the culture favors impersonal relationships and equality, developing the trust needed for effective relationship marketing may be more difficult.[21]
- *Core values define ethical behavior.* The ethics of a particular firm are influenced by the values or ethics of the individuals it employs, just as the ethical climate of a country is influenced by the core values of its people and institutions. The United States has been characterized as a "money culture" in which business executives operate principally by greed.[22] Some people might find various corporate goals incompatible with their own personal ethics,[23] causing stress and job dissatisfaction. Sales managers can decrease the likelihood of ethical conflict by selecting and hiring individuals who have values and beliefs consistent with, or are willing to accept, the organization's values.[24]

Brands, as you read in Chapter 2, can turn customers into "fans," especially when they connect with consumers' culture. That's why brand managers must evaluate, emulate, and infiltrate the core culture of their customers. Many years ago, Chevrolet management evaluated America's core culture and, recognizing hot dogs and apple pie as the culture's comfort foods and baseball as its national pastime, developed a slogan that lasted for decades. What could be more culturally relevant than the refrain with which Chevy infiltrated the mass market psyche of an entire generation, teaching them to sing, "Hot dogs, baseball, apple pie, and Chevrolet." Music made the brand memorable but cultural relevance made it enduring. Both the culture and music changes, of course, and for nearly a decade Chevrolet has pounded away with a Bob Seger classic, instilling the belief that Chevy trucks are built "like a rock."

Culturally relevant brands are ones that resonate with important values of target markets. They reach down deep not only into the minds of consumers, but into their hearts as well. Building brands on key values causes consumers to connect with the brand on more than a "liking" level, but at a "feeling" level. Key consumers know, perhaps without knowing why, "This brand is for me." Culturally relevant brands evoke strong responses, often at unspoken but emotional levels. Investing in relationships with customers and their culture ultimately leads to behavioral loyalty, a finding verified in cross-cultural research in a three-country (United States, Belgium, and Netherlands) comparative study.[25]

## Changing Values

Society's values change continuously even though core values are relatively permanent. Marketers should pay special attention to values in transition because they affect the size of market segments. Changes in values may alter responses to advertising, service offerings, and retailing formats. Changes that occurred in the late twentieth century (see Table 11.1) represented a paradigm shift or a fundamental reordering of the way consumers and marketers viewed the world[26] and set the stage for the current marketing environment. Looking at the right column of Table 11.1, you might want to consider how values will change in the next few decades, guiding your individual decisions as a consumer or manager.

Changes in a society's values can be forecast on the basis of a **life-cycle explanation,** meaning that *as individuals grow older, their values change.* In other words, societal values in the future will be similar to today as younger people grow older and grow into the values of their parents. This is a theory of behavioral assimilation. **Generational change,** by contrast, suggests that *there will be gradual replacement of existing values by those of young people who form the leading generation in value terms.* When today's young people grow old, they will retain the values of their youth and replace societal values of today's older consumers.[27] What do you think? In thirty

| TABLE 11.1 | Changing Values in Western Civilization |
|---|---|

Developed Western societies are gradually discarding traditional values and are beginning to embrace emerging new values on an ever-widening scale.

| TRADITIONAL VALUES | NEW VALUES |
|---|---|
| Self-denial ethic | Self-fulfillment ethic |
| Higher standard of living | Better quality of life |
| Traditional sex roles | Blurring of sex roles |
| Accepted definition of success | Individualized definition of success |
| Traditional family life | Alternative families |
| Faith in industry, institutions | Self-reliance |
| Live to work | Work to live |
| Hero worship | Love of ideas |
| Expansionism | Pluralism |
| Patriotism | Less nationalistic |
| Unparalleled growth | Growing sense of limits |
| Industrial growth | Information and service growth |
| Receptivity to technology | Technology orientation |

Source: Joseph T. Plummer, "Changing Values," *Futurist* 23 (January/February 1989), 10.

11.1

years, will you be more like your peers or your parents? Your answer will depend on how your values will be affected by the **cultural transfusive triad** of *families, religious organizations, and schools,* as well as early lifetime experiences. The effectiveness of persuasive communications will be affected by whether values, often assumed to be relatively stable and driven by culture-based norms and traditions, are in fact flexible and driven more by your own individual personality.[28]

## Changing Family Influences

Family is the dominant agent for transmitting values in most cultures. Many changes are occurring in the family (this subject is examined more closely in Chapter 12, but some of the most significant include the following.

- *Less time for in-home or parent-child influence.* With many mothers working outside the home, today a majority of young children attend preschool or daycare, as compared to 5.7 percent in 1965. Today, children are increasingly learning their values outside the family from babysitters, nannies, schools, and the media. The increase in births to unmarried women also diminishes potential parental influence on children.
- *Increasing divorce rates.* Many children are now raised part of their lives in single-parent households, contributing to decreased family influence. These children are often less likely to form and live in traditional families, influencing values of the future generation.
- *The isolated nuclear family.* Geographic separation of the nuclear family from grandparents and other relatives (due to increased mobility of jobs and education) contributes to a lack of heritage or a yearning for roots.

## Changing Religious Influences

Religious institutions can play a significant role in transmitting values, and the degree to which individuals believe in God or a "higher power" may affect many areas of behavior. Market Facts 11.1 shows some of these effects on voting and other behavior and the variation of the effects by age group and geography. Judeo-Christian religious institutions have historically played an important role in shaping the values of the United States and other Western cultures, although this has become more diversified in recent years. Slightly over half (52 percent) of U.S. adults identify themselves as Protestants, about one-fourth Roman Catholic, 1.3 percent Jewish, 0.5 percent Muslim, and the remainder more than one hundred different categories.[29] The proportion of consumers who do not identify with any religion (including atheists, agnostics, humanists, and secularists) has grown from 8 percent of the U.S. population in 1990 to 14 percent in 2001.

The following summarizes some of the trends in religion occurring in the United States.

- *Traditional churches and religions have seen a decline in loyalty.* The decline of institutionalized religion began after World War II as the baby boomers began to question the status quo and forge their own values. In 1958, only one in twenty-five adult Americans had left the denomination in which they were raised, but the American Religious Identification Survey reported that 16 percent had changed their religious preference in 2001.[30] The fastest-growing church denominations are high-involvement, socially conservative groups, with the Church of Jesus Christ of Latter-day Saints (Mormon), Churches of Christ, and Assemblies of God each

# The Influence of Religion and Core Values on Voting

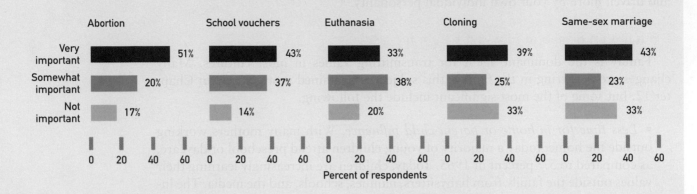

|  | Abortion | School vouchers | Euthanasia | Cloning | Same-sex marriage |
|---|---|---|---|---|---|
| Very important | 51% | 43% | 33% | 39% | 43% |
| Somewhat important | 20% | 37% | 38% | 25% | 23% |
| Not important | 17% | 14% | 20% | 33% | 33% |

Percent of respondents

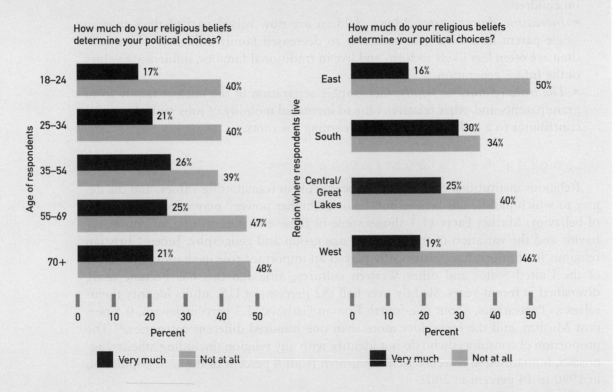

**How much do your religious beliefs determine your political choices?**

Age of respondents:
| 18–24 | 17% / 40% |
| 25–34 | 21% / 40% |
| 35–54 | 26% / 39% |
| 55–69 | 25% / 47% |
| 70+ | 21% / 48% |

■ Very much   ▨ Not at all

**How much do your religious beliefs determine your political choices?**

Region where respondents live:
| East | 16% / 50% |
| South | 30% / 34% |
| Central/ Great Lakes | 25% / 40% |
| West | 19% / 46% |

■ Very much   ▨ Not at all

Source: Louis Witt, "Whose Side Is God On?" *American Demographics*, 26, no. 1 (2004), 18. Reprinted with permission from February 2004 issue of *American Demographics*. Copyright Crain Communications, Inc., 2004.

growing 19 percent since 1990. Losing the most members are the Presbyterians and the United Church of Christ, declining 12 percent and 15 percent, respectively, since 1990.[31]

• *An increase in non-Christian religions has taken place.* With the increase in ethnic diversity has come an increased number of practicing Buddhists, Muslims, and Hindus, among others. These religions, like rapidly growing Christian groups, are often socially conservative and promote respect for family members.

• *There has been a shift from traditional religion to spirituality.* Many Americans, especially aging baby boomers, are searching for experiential faith and spirituality rather than traditional religion. Spirituality is more personal and practical, involves stress reduction more than salvation, and is about feeling good, not just being good.[32] Under this loose definition of faith and religion, millions of Americans have a sudden passion for spirituality,[33] and are defining themselves as "religious," even if they rarely attend an organized religious service. As a result, 90 percent of Americans say religion plays a significant role in their everyday life, and only 10 percent consider religion "not at all important."[34]

• *Women are more religious.* Women tend to express their religious beliefs and spirituality more than men, often joining Bible studies and women's groups to support each other in these efforts and accepting more responsibility for inculcating religious values to children or grandchildren. Women are also more likely than men to define success in religious terms.[35] Celebrities including Paris Hilton, Britney Spears, Demi Moore, and Madonna have been prominently identified with Kabbalah, a form of Jewish mysticism.[36]

• *Religion and spirituality are big business and influence big business.* With the increase in spirituality has come an increase in the sales of religious books, spiritual retreats, religious logos on apparel, alternative health care, spiritual education, religious broadcast stations, overseas missions trips, and crossover religious music ranging from U2 to MercyMe. Mel Gibson's *Passion of the Christ* became one of the all-time highest-grossing films through grassroots marketing efforts aimed mostly at Christians, and Rick Warren's book *The Purpose-Driven Life* has sold more than 21 million copies, spawning thousands of home and church study groups.[37] Consumer Behavior and Marketing 11.2 describes how the values of religious consumers sometimes affect major retailers and their suppliers.

## Changing Educational Institutions

The third major institution that transmits values to consumers is education. The influence of education appears to be increasing, due in part to the increased participation of Americans in formal education as well as the vacuum left by absent families and declining participation in religious institutions. There is also concern among many about the nature of this increased influence.

• *A dramatic increase in formal education has taken place.* Today, one in four workers in the United States is a college graduate, up from about one in eight in 1970. Although fewer working women than men are college graduates currently, that ratio is changing rapidly because today more women are enrolled in colleges and universities than are men. Weekend and evening MBA programs, satellite campuses, Internet courses, and other innovations encourage pursuit of higher education among a greater number of people, including working parents and senior citizens. The University of Phoenix is one such institution dedicated to the needs of working professionals and their employers. The university's founder, Dr. John

## VeggieTales: Taking Evangelical Christian Values Mainstream

Until five years ago, few people other than evangelical Christians had heard of VeggieTales, a small company's series of cartoon videos starring talking cucumbers and tomatoes learning biblical lessons. That, however, was before the VeggieTales went to Wal*Mart. "We found out that many of the buyers at the big box chains were already fans of the shows, experiencing it at church," said Dan Merrell, senior vice president for marketing at Big Idea Productions, which makes VeggieTales. The latest VeggieTales cartoon, *Jonah,* has been one of the best-selling videos in the country with 2.7 million copies sold, of which about half were in mass merchandise stores, and about 25 percent in Wal*Mart alone.

Major chains like Costco, Target, and Wal*Mart have also helped turn country performers like the Dixie Chicks, Toby Keith, and Faith Hill into superstars and helped produce national best sellers by conservative authors such as Bernard Goldberg, Ann Coulter, and Bill O'Reilly.

Wal*Mart and other big discount chains often now account for more than 50 percent of sales of best-selling albums, more than 40 percent of best-selling books, and more than 60 percent of best-selling DVDs. This situation brings criticism from authors, musicians, and civil liberties groups who argue that major chains are censoring and homogenizing popular culture by appealing to traditionalist customers. "They have obviously reached the Bush-red audience in a big way," said Laurence J. Kirshbaum, chairman of AOL Time Warner's books unit, referring to the color coding used on television news reports to denote states voting for President George W. Bush during the last election. "It has been a seismic shift in the business, and to some of us in publishing it has been a revelation."

Buyers at Wal*Mart and some other retailers screen content to avoid selling material likely to offend their conservative customers. Wal*Mart has banned everything from the rapper Eminem's albums to the best-selling diaries of the rock star Kurt Cobain and has stopped selling men's magazines *Maxim* and *Stuff.* Critics say the stores' policies make it harder for excluded works to become best sellers. "It is going to hurt sales of anything that is at all controversial, and if the stores are not going to put the CDs on the shelves, then the record companies are not going to make them," said Jay Rosenthal, a lawyer who represents the Recording Artists Coalition, a lobbying organization. But conservative groups praise the stores' selection policies. Dr. A. William Merrell, a vice president of the Southern Baptist Convention, said the stores were performing a public service in that "they have said, 'Don't send us smut.'"

Source: Excerpted from David Kirkpatrick, "Shaping Cultural Tastes at Big Retail Chains," *New York Times* (May 18, 2003). Copyright 2003 by The New York Times Co. Reprinted with permission.

Sperling, believed that lifelong employment with a single employer would be replaced by lifelong learning and employment with a variety of employers. After observing a large number of baby boomers interested in completing their degrees, but deterred by the difficulty of older Americans parking, registering, and attending classes at traditional universities designed for eighteen to twenty-two year olds, Sperling founded the University of Phoenix in 1976. Today, more than 230,000 students are served through 163 campuses and learning centers in thirty-three states. The University of Phoenix is regarded as a pioneer of new approaches to curricular and program design, teaching methods, and student services—something that has inspired change in more traditional universities while generating handsome profits for its owner, the for-profit Apollo Group.

- *Teaching has evolved from memorization to questioning.* In the past, teaching often emphasized description and memorization of facts, with no latitude for questioning. Rather than evaluating different points of view and determining how they best fit together in solving a problem, students merely regurgitated preprogrammed answers. In recent years, the trend has been toward analytical approaches emphasizing questioning of the old and the formulation of completely new approaches and solutions. Consumers taught in this new environment may reject rigid definitions of right or wrong, dismiss marketing programs as attempts to manipulate, and put more thought into their buying decisions. In turn, marketing organizations must revise sales programs and product information formats to provide answers when customers ask questions.

- *Digital learning has increased in popularity.* More students are experiencing some form of distance learning over the Internet, whether by actual instruction from teachers in digital formats or performing research on the Internet for courses in a traditional classroom format. Given the expense of paying for educational facilities and transportation to a common location, many companies are employing technology to deliver up-to-date training in the workplace. Best Buy is one of a growing number of firms that offers a wide variety of courses digitally to its employees, covering product, technology, management, and customer service topics. Gen Y and younger consumers have been exposed to computers and the Internet for much of their lives, and have developed high expectations about websites and electronic marketing for the firms that seek their patronage and loyalty.

## The Influences of Age-Related Microcultures on Values

In addition to families, religious institutions, and educational institutions, culture and values are shaped by early life experiences. As you saw in Chapter 3, consumer analysts employ **cohort analysis** to *investigate the changes in patterns of behavior or attitudes in a cohort, which is a group of individuals linked as a group in some way—* often by age. Cohort analysis focuses on actual changes in the behavior or attitudes of a cohort, the changes that can be attributed to the process of aging, and changes that are associated with events of a particular period, such as the Great Depression, Watergate, or September 11, 2001.[38] The 1960s was an era in which countercultures challenged the past, bringing increased concern about civil rights and feminist and immigrant values. Some observers believe that America has entered a postmodern era, in which cultural contradictions are celebrated and blended.[39] Although fads may change (flat-top haircuts in the 1950s and body piercing or tattoos in the 1990s), the cultural dynamic is the same—minority groups start changes while the majority are still in the "I don't get it" category.[40] A little bit of daring and breaking away from a "squeaky clean" image is probably what the advertiser in Figure 11.6 hopes to accomplish.

What were the defining influences on the cohorts you read about in Chapter 7? Although slightly different ages of cohorts are presented than the Muppies and Gen Y ages given in Chapter 7, Table 11.2 highlights the major influences on each cohort. As you study these cohort descriptions, think about how each cohort's early experiences affect values and how American culture might change as the cohorts evolve over their lives. Among consumers between the ages of eighteen to thirty-four, 23 percent of men and 26 percent of women report they "always or frequently" covet the money of the rich and famous, whereas only 6 percent of older consumers report that response, apparently relinquishing that wish years ago.[41] Keep in mind that these influences are

**CAUTION: 245 HORSEPOWER**

SIDE EFFECTS MAY INCLUDE HOOTING, HOLLERING, WHITE KNUCKLES, SPINE TINGLING, INCREASED HEART RATE AND SWEET GIRLFRIEND. IN CLINICAL TRIALS, MOST FREQUENTLY REPORTED ADVERSE EFFECTS INCLUDED JEALOUSY AND ENVY AMONG FRIENDS PLUS MISAPPROPRIATION OF SICK DAYS. INDIVIDUAL RESULTS MAY VARY. USE ONLY AS DIRECTED. KEEP OUT OF REACH OF SMALL CHILDREN.

*MOTOR TREND*
2005 TRUCK OF THE YEAR

TACOMA  2005 MOTOR TREND TRUCK OF THE YEAR.  With an available awe-inspiring 245-hp V6, 282 lb.-ft. of torque and the TRD Off-Road Package, it's no wonder the all-new Toyota Tacoma is a force to be reckoned with. toyota.com

**FIGURE 11.6** Younger age cohorts often defy cultural norms in having fun

only part of the set of influences on an individual's values. Family, peer, and religious influences may be more important when predicting the effects on values and consumption behavior of individual consumers.[42]

## National Culture

Culture has always had a profound impact on the way consumers perceive themselves, the products they buy and use, the purchasing processes they follow, and the organizations from which they purchase. Today, marketers are giving more attention to understanding macrocultures and how they affect consumer behavior. One researcher, Gert Hofstede, found four dimensions of culture that are common among sixty-six countries.[43] These dimensions serve as a foundation for characterizing, comparing, and contrasting specific national cultures, and are helpful in identifying environmentally sensitive segments of the market.[44] As a consumer analyst who some day may be responsible for global marketing strategies, consider these values when developing appropriate strategies for each nation.

- *Individualism versus collectivism.* Individualism describes the importance of the individual and the virtues of self-reliance and personal independence, and in some cases this classification signifies that the interests of individuals should take precedence over those of the social group. Collectivism, by contrast, emphasizes the interrelationship of persons, the importance of relationships in connecting people, and the need for individuals to assimilate into the social group. Table 11.3 summarizes the attitudinal and behavioral differences associated with individualism and collectivism.
- *Uncertainty avoidance.* Uncertainty avoidance concerns the different ways in which societies react to the uncertainties and ambiguities inherent in life. Some societies rely upon well-defined rules or rituals to guide behavior, whereas others tolerate deviant ideas and behavior.
- *Power distance.* Power distance reflects the degree to which a society accepts inequality in power at different levels of organizations and institutions. This dimension can affect preferences for centralization of authority, acceptance of differential rewards, and the ways people of unequal status work together.
- *Masculinity-femininity.* This factor defines the extent to which societies hold values traditionally regarded as predominantly masculine or feminine. Assertiveness, respect for achievement, and the acquisition of money and material possessions are identified with masculinity; and nurturing, concern for the environment, and championing the underdog are associated with a culture's femininity.

## Geographic Culture

Although national cultural characteristics may exist for an entire nation, geographic areas within a nation sometimes develop their own culture. For example, the

**TABLE 11.2**     Consumer Age Cohorts

*Depression cohort*
Born: 1912–1921
Age in 2004: 83–92
Coming of age: 1930–1939
Percentage of population in 2001:
6% (13 million)
Sex mindset: Intolerant
Favorite music: Big band
and swing

This group's coming-of-age experience consisted of economic strife, elevated unemployment rates, and the need to take menial jobs to survive. Financial security—which they lacked most when coming of age—rules their thinking. The major defining event is the Great Depression.

*World War II cohort*
Born: 1922–1927
Age in 2004: 77–82
Coming of age: 1940–1945
Percentage of population in 2001:
8% (17 million)
Sex mindset: Ambivalent
Favorite music: Boogie woogie,
Bugle Boy patriotic, and
Frank Sinatra

Sacrifice for the common good was widely accepted among members of the World War II cohort, as evidenced by women working in factories for the war effort and men going off to fight. Overall, this cohort was focused on defeating a common enemy, and their members are more team oriented and patriotic than those of other generational cohorts. The major defining event is World War II.

*Postwar cohort*
Born: 1928–1945
Age in 2004: 59–76
Coming of age: 1946–1963
Percentage of population in 2001:
41% (47 million)
Sex mindset: Repressive
Favorite music: Frank Sinatra
until the birth of rock & roll
(Elvis, Chuck Berry)

These individuals experienced a time of remarkable economic growth and social tranquility, a time of family togetherness, school dress codes, and moving to the suburbs. There were some elements of unrest (e.g., the Korean conflict, McCarthyism), but overall this was a pretty tranquil time, which is why this is such a long cohort. Defining events include the end of World War II, the Korean War, the emergence of rock & roll, good economic times, the civil rights movement, moving to the suburbs, and the Cold War.

*Leading-edge baby boomer cohort*
Born: 1946–1954
Age in 2004: 50–58
Coming of age: 1963–1972
Percentage of population in 2001:
14% (31 million)
Sex mindset: Experimental
Favorite music: Rock & roll,
protest, and folk

This group remembers the assassinations of John and Robert Kennedy and Martin Luther King Jr. The loss of JFK first shaped this cohort's values. The members of this group became adults during the Vietnam War and watched as the first man walked on the moon. Leading-edge boomers are very aware of their cohort grouping, and are very self-assured and self-centered. They championed causes with fervor because they were sure of being right (e.g., Greenpeace, civil rights, women's lib), and felt equally justified in being hedonistic and self-indulgent (e.g., with marijuana, "free love," and sensuality). Because of their position following the "birth dearth" of the Depression years, members of this group had (and continue to have) an influence on society disproportionate to their numbers, being smaller as a group than the later boomer cohort that followed. Defining moments include the assassinations of JFK, RFK, and Martin Luther King Jr., the Vietnam War, and the first man on the moon.

*(continued)*

**TABLE 11.2**        (Continued)

| | |
|---|---|
| *Trailing-edge baby boomer cohort*<br>Born: 1955–1965<br>Age in 2004: 39–49<br>Coming of age: 1973–1983<br>Percentage of population in 2001: 22% (49 million)<br>Sex mindset: Permissive<br>Favorite music: Classic rock, disco, funk, and glam | This group witnessed the fall of Vietnam, Watergate, and Nixon's resignation. The oil embargo, raging inflation rate, and the more than 30 percent decline in the S&P Index led these individuals to be far less optimistic about their financial future than the leading-edge boomers, whom they feel got the biggest opportunities in jobs, houses, and investments. Defining events include the fall of Vietnam, Watergate, the resignation of Nixon, and the energy crisis of the late 1970s. |
| *Generation X cohort*<br>Born: 1966–1976<br>Age in 2004: 27–38<br>Coming of age: 1984–94<br>Percentage of population: 19% (42 million)<br>Sex mindset: Cautious<br>Favorite music: Pop, alternative rock, and rap | These are the latchkey children of the 1980s, who have received the most negative publicity. Perhaps because many have seen first-hand the trauma of divorce, this cohort has delayed marriage and children, and members of this group don't take those commitments lightly. More than other groups, this cohort accepts cultural diversity and puts quality of personal life ahead of work life. They're "free agents," not "team players." Despite a rocky start into adulthood, this group shows a spirit of entrepreneurship unmatched by any other cohort, as evidenced by the many technology startups of the late 1990s that captured this spirit. Defining events include the Challenger explosion, the stock market crash of 1987, the fall of the Berlin Wall, the AIDS epidemic, and the Gulf War. |
| *N generation cohort (Gen Y, millennials, or echo boomers)\**<br>Born: 1977–1984<br>Age in 2004: 20–26<br>Coming of age: 1995–present<br>Percentage of population: 12% (26 million)<br>Sex mindset: Tolerant<br>Favorite music: Hip-hop and dance | The youngest cohort is called the N Generation cohort or the N-Gens, because the advent of the Internet is a defining event for them, and because they will be the engine of growth over the next two decades. Members of this group are also known as Gen Y or Millennials, and while still a work in progress, their core value structure seems to be quite different from that of Gen X. They are more idealistic and team oriented than the cynical, "What's in it for me?" free-agent mindset of many Generation Xers. Defining moments include the impeachment of President Clinton, the Columbine school shootings, the September 11, 2001, terrorist attacks, and the war on Iraq. |

Source: Adapted from Meredith Geoffrey, Charles Schewe, and Janice Karlovich, *Defining Markets, Defining Moments* (2002).

*Note: This definition of N Gen (Gen Y) is more narrow than the definition given in Chapter 7.

**TABLE 11.3**        Individualism Versus Collectivism

| | INDIVIDUALISM<br>(E.G., UNITED STATES, AUSTRALIA, CANADA) | COLLECTIVISM<br>(E.G., HONG KONG, TAIWAN, JAPAN) |
|---|---|---|
| Self-construal | Defined by internal attributes, personal traits | Defined by important others, family, friends |
| Role of others | Self-evaluation (e.g., standards of social comparison, sources of appraisal regarding self) | Self-definition (e.g., relationships with others define self and affect personal preferences) |
| Values | Emphasis on separateness, individuality | Emphasis on connectedness, relationships |
| Motivational drives | Focus on differentiation, relatively greater need to be unique | Focus on similarity, relatively greater need to blend in |
| Behavior | Reflective of personal preferences, needs | Influenced by preferences, needs of close others |

southwestern United States is known for casual lifestyles featuring comfortable clothing, outdoor entertainment, and physical recreation such as hiking. People in the Southwest may also be more receptive to new products, such as modern art and alternative health therapies, compared to the conservative, inhibited attitudes that characterize other areas of the nation. Climate, religious affiliations of the population, nationality influences, and other variables are interrelated to produce a core of cultural values in a geographic area. Yet research indicates that culture can cut across national, state, and provincial borders, and incorporate the culture, climate, institutions, business organizations, and resources of each region.[45] A recent study by Harris Interactive of 2,013 respondents found that money is a highly coveted value, but the value varies greatly by geographic region. In the West, 40 percent of respondents cite other people's money as the object of their affection versus 28 percent in the Northeast.[46] Understanding the values of various regions may guide marketers' efforts to position products to various regions.

Perhaps the best-known example of geographic cultures is the "Red-Blue" dichotomy of U.S. states, frequently reported in connection with the 2004 election of President George W. Bush. Figure 11.7 shows this dichotomy on a county-by-county basis (probably a more insightful way to look at the dichotomy than state-by-state). The Red counties are populous, but more rural oriented, with above-average income. Blue counties are more populous, but with below-average income. Looking at the United States at night (see Figure 11.8), lights visible from outer space reveal the urban nature of Blue geographic regions. For political marketing, the values of each area are critically important. Most other marketers will also find significant differences in brand choices between Red and Blue segments. Red markets are more favorable to Wal*Mart and Microsoft, and Blues are likely to be fans of Target and Dell. But when the choice comes to remodeling, there is no political divide—everybody likes Home Depot. Kroger, Sears, and Lowe's all performed significantly better among Red-state respondents, but brands doing well in both groups include Johnson & Johnson, Disney, and Harley-Davidson.[47]

## North American Core Values

Core values can be observed in Canada and the United States, even though both countries encompass values reflecting diverse national origins within their populations. Values are less rigid in North America because these countries are so young compared with most Asian and European countries.

### The Foundation of American Values

The United States was largely an agrarian nation just two generations ago. Although the country is now primarily urbanized and suburbanized, understanding its origin helps analyze today's culture. Much of the religious and ethical tradition is believed to have come from sixteenth-century Calvinist (Puritan) doctrine, which emphasizes individual responsibility and a positive work ethic. Anglo-Saxon civil rights, the rule of law, and representative institutions were inherited from the English background; ideas of egalitarian democracy and a secular spirit sprang from the French and American Revolutions. The period of slavery and its aftermath, and the European immigration of three centuries, have affected the American character strongly. American values emphasize an ownership society, not surprising perhaps because the nation was founded by marketers, accounting for entrepreneurial values being a pervasive part of contemporary American culture.[48] Even though most people are employees of large,

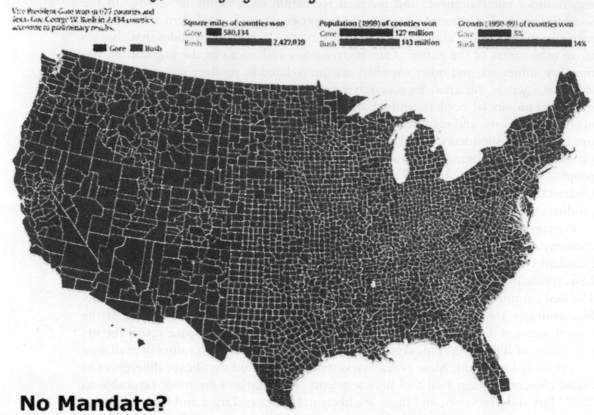

# The vote Tuesday, county by county

Vice President Gore won in 677 counties and Texas Gov. George W. Bush in 2,434 counties, according to preliminary results.

■ Gore ■ Bush

| Square miles of counties won | | Population (1999) of counties won | | Growth (1990-99) of counties won | |
|---|---|---|---|---|---|
| Gore | 580,134 | Gore | 127 million | Gore | 5% |
| Bush | 2,427,039 | Bush | 143 million | Bush | 14% |

## No Mandate?

**FIGURE 11.7**  Red State versus Blue State Geographic Cultures

Source: Angry Bear, www.angrybear.blogspot.com/fourmaps.html

**FIGURE 11.8**  Major U.S. Metropolitan Areas as Seen from Outer Space at Night

Source: Angry Bear, www.angrybear.blogspot.com/fourmaps.html

complex organizations rather than farmers or shopkeepers, and goods are purchased rather than produced, many American values retain the agrarian base—emphasizing good work ethics, self-sufficiency, and the philosophy that any one individual can make a difference.

### American Values and Advertising

What are the core values that provide appeals for advertising and marketing programs? Eight of the most basic are described in Table 11.4. Sometimes advertisers are accused of appealing mostly to fear, snobbery, and self-indulgence, but after reviewing the values in Table 11.4, you can see how such an approach would have limited appeal. Marketers are more successful when they appeal to core values based on hard work, achievement and success, optimism, and equal opportunity for a better material standard of living. These values may explain why the highest-rated television ad during the 2005 Super Bowl was a Budweiser commercial depicting an airport crowd applauding and giving homage to American troops returning from war.[49]

Advertisers must understand values to avoid violating standards. Benetton, the Italian apparel retailer, developed a famous and controversial set of ads, most too provocative to be used in the United States. Figure 11.9 features some of these ads. In one, readers are presented with pastel-colored balloon-type images. A closer look reveals that they are condoms, part of a safe-sex blitz in which some stores gave away condoms. This ad, considered a religiously offensive ad by some, ran throughout Europe, as did an ad showing a black woman nursing a white baby, designed to promote harmony among the races. Both were deemed as too provocative for the United States. Still another Benetton ad showed a black man and a white man chained together to promote the "united colors" theme. This ad was withdrawn in the United States after minority groups complained that the ad implied that the black man was a criminal and accused the company of racism.[50]

### U.S. and Canadian Variations in Values

Canada and the United States are similar in many ways, but their values and institutions vary in important ways. For one, Canadianism has less of an ideology than Americanism does. America's emphasis on individualism and achievement can be traced to the American Revolution, an upheaval that Canada did not support. Canada presents a more neutral, affable face that distinguishes the country from its more exuberant and aggressive neighbor. Canadians have greater awareness of American media and institutions than conversely.

Canada and the United States have different situations and different histories. For example, law and order enforced by the centrally controlled Northwest Mounted Police (now the Royal Canadian Mounted Police) tamed Canada's frontier much earlier than was the case in the wild, wild western United States. Seymour Lipset, one of the most prolific analysts of Canadian-U.S. relationships, believes that this is the reason Canadians generally have more respect for law and order today than do U.S. citizens.[51] In Table 11.5, some of the differences between the values of the two countries are described, based on Lipset's research.

## Ethnic Microcultures and Their Influences on Consumer Behavior

Ethnicity is an important element in determining culture and predicting consumer preferences and behaviors. It is a process of group identification in which people use ethnic labels to define themselves and others. A *subjectivist* perspective reflects ascriptions people make about themselves. An *objectivist* definition is derived from

### Material Well-Being

Achievement and success are measured mostly by the quantity and quality of material goods. There is display value in articles that others can see, such as designer clothing, luxury cars, and large homes. Although rebellion against such values is sometimes expressed, well-being is fundamental to the American value system. Americans believe in the marvels of modern comforts (good transportation, central heating, air conditioning, and labor-saving appliances) and believe in the "right" to have such things.

### Twofold Moralizing

Americans believe in polarized morality, in which actions are either good or bad. Twofold judgments are the rule: legal or illegal, moral or immoral, and civilized or primitive. Consumers cast these judgments on public officials and companies, deeming them either ethical or unethical, not a little of both. Similarly, advertising that is "a little deceptive" is considered bad even if the overall message is largely correct. However, some conditions exist making the same behavior right or wrong depending on the situation. Gambling in many instances is illegal or "wrong," but when organized as a state lottery to benefit a good cause, it can be legal or "right."

### Importance of Work over Play

Although work is associated in American values with purpose and maturity, play is associated with frivolity, pleasure, and children. In other cultures, festivals and holidays and children having fun are the most important events in society, whereas in the United States, even socializing is often work related.

### Time Is Money

Americans view time differently from many other cultures. In the United States, time is more exact in nature, whereas in countries such as Mexico, time is approximate. Americans tend to be punctual, schedule activities at specific times, and expect others to keep appointments based on set times.

### Effort, Optimism, and Entrepreneurship

Americans believe that problems should be identified and effort should be made to solve them. With proper effort, one can be optimistic about success. Europeans sometimes laugh at their American friends who believe that for every problem there is a solution. This attitude is based on the concept that people are their own masters and can control outcomes. In American culture, effort is rewarded, competition is enforced, and individual achievement is paramount. Entrepreneurship is one result of American values of effort, optimism, and the importance of winning.

### Mastery over Nature

American core values produce a conquering attitude toward nature, which is different from Buddhism and Hinduism, in which people and nature are one and work with nature. Americans' conquering attitude stems from three assumptions: the universe is mechanistic, people are the masters of the earth, and people are qualitatively different from all other forms of life. American advertising depicts people who are in command of their natural environments when they show men fighting hair loss or women fighting wrinkles.

### Egalitarianism

American core values support the belief that all people should have equal opportunities for achievement. Though some discrimination does occur, the core values, codified legislatively and judicially, favor equality of all people, especially those accepting the values and behaviors of the social majority.

### Humanitarianism

American values support assistance of those less fortunate. Assistance expresses itself in the giving of donations to unknown individuals and groups needing aid because of natural disasters, disabilities, or disadvantages. Organizations such as the American Lung Association or the American Cancer Society benefit from Americans' beliefs in humanitarianism. For corporations, humanitarianism is not only a social responsibility but an important means through which to communicate with consumers.

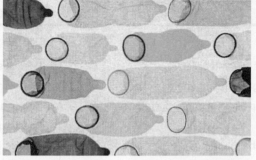

**FIGURE 11.9** How Social Values Affect Advertising

Courtesy of Benetton; David Ellis, "Benetton Ads: A Risqué Business," *Time* (March 25, 1991), 13.

sociocultural categories. In consumer research, ethnicity is best defined as some combination of these, including the strength or weakness of affiliation that people have with the ethnic group.[52] To the degree that people in an ethnic group share common perceptions and cognitions that are different from those of other ethnic groups or the larger society, they constitute a distinct ethnic group that may be useful to treat as a market segment.[53]

Specific consumers may not reflect the values of the ethnic group with which they are commonly identified. To believe that a given individual necessarily adheres to all the values of any specific microculture would make the observer guilty of stereotyping. Consumer behavior is a function of "felt ethnicity" as well as cultural identity, social surroundings, and product type.[54]

## America's Ethnic Microcultures

The United States, like Switzerland, Singapore, and South Africa, is a montage of nationality groups. Recent figures register fifty-four countries represented by 100,000 or more American residents. In Canada, the proportion of foreign-born residents, at 18 percent of the population in 2001, is at its highest levels in seventy years. However, many of these immigrants migrate to Canada's three largest cities, such as Toronto, where as many as 46 percent of residents speak a native language other than English. Look back at Figure 7.3 in Chapter 7 and you will see the importance of immigration in the United States and how country of origin has changed, affecting the makeup of the population but also influencing the U.S. culture. In the early 1900s, U.S. immigrants were mostly from European nations, but more recently are mostly from Latin and Asian nations. In either case, immigrants arriving from other nations bring with them new religions, cultures, and languages.

Some immigrants identify with much of their culture of origin; others do not. A variable closely associated with national ethnic identity is the language spoken at

**TABLE 11.5**   Variations in Values Between Canada and the United States

| CANADA | UNITED STATES |
|---|---|
| More observance of law and order | Less observance |
| Emphasis on the rights and obligations of community | More emphasis on individual rights and obligations |
| Courts are perceived as an arm of the state | Courts perceived as a check on the powers of the state |
| Lawful society | Greater propensity to redefine or ignore rules |
| Use the system to change things | Employ informal, aggressive, and sometimes extra-legal means to correct what they think is wrong. "The greater lawlessness and corruption in the U.S. can also be attributed in part to a stronger emphasis on achievement" |
| Canadians find success in slightly bad taste | "Americans worship success" |
| Greater value of social relationships | Greater importance of work |
| | Higher commitment to work ethic |
| | Greater value of achievement (Goldfarb study) |
| Canadians more cautious | Americans take more risks |
| Corporate network denser in Canada. 1984—80% of companies on TSE controlled by 7 families; 32 families and 5 conglomerates control about 33% of all nonfinancial assets | One hundred largest firms own about 33% of all nonfinancial assets, few controlled by individuals |
| 5 banks hold 80% of all deposits | Literally thousands of small banks in the United States |
| Anticombines legislation weakly enforced | Business affected by antielitist and anti–big business sentiments |
| Favor partial or total government ownership | Strong antitrust laws |
| | Anti–big business, pro competition |
| Business leaders more likely to have privileged upbringing and less specialized education | Business leaders more likely to have a specialized education |
| Emphasis on social programs and government support | More laissez-faire |
| Canadian labor union density more than twice that of the American | |
| Fewer lobbying organizations in Canada even in proportion to smaller Canadian population. Since politicians toe party line, lobbying not as important | Seven thousand lobbying organizations registered with Congress—since congresspersons can vote as they choose on a bill, lobbying can be effective |

Source: Summarized from Seymour Martin Lipset, *Continental Divide: The Values and Institutions of the United States and Canada* (New York: Routledge, 1990).

home. Two groups of Americans who often speak a language other than English are Chinese and Latinos. Eighty-one percent of Chinese Americans speak Chinese at home, whereas 43 percent of Latinos speak Spanish at home.[55] Values, however, determine the degree to which immigrants embrace traditional American core values and how the immigrants contribute to the cultural diversity of North America. When an immigrant family becomes American, the members usually manifest and reinforce the work ethic that is at the core of American values.[56] When marketing programs call attention to consumers' cultural identity, making them aware of their membership in a group, this mindset leads the consumers to make decisions that minimize the risk of negative outcomes to both themselves and others, creating a tendency to compromise their individual consumer choice situations.[57]

As individuals are exposed to various ethnic microcultures, they often adapt to or take on characteristics of that culture. **Acculturation** measures the *degree to which a consumer has learned the ways of a different culture compared to how they were raised.* Individuals adapt to cultural changes in both social and professional situations—as they live among, befriend, and work with others. Managers and salespersons faced with the challenge of global business, find more success when they respond and adapt to the cultural differences of their business partners.[58] Individuals adapt to cultural changes, but so do companies and organizations. A study of Latino, Asian, Middle Eastern, and Anglo retailers found that when they adapted to the cultures of their customers, changes occurred to themselves, their firms, their consumers, and ultimately, the marketplace.[59] Consumer Behavior and Marketing 11.3 describes how a marketer is developing marketing strategies to reach the increasing number of consumers emigrating from India. Some universities and businesses are now offering courses to help their employees learn the basics of Hindi.

### Euro-Descent Americans

More than 200 million Americans are of European descent; England is the background nation for 26.34 percent of Americans, followed closely by Germany with 26.14 percent and Ireland with 17.77 percent. European immigration, which had been on a decline since the 1950s, increased dramatically from 1985 to 1995, experiencing a 155 percent increase over the period.[60] According to the Immigration and Naturalization Service, more than 1.2 million European immigrants came to the

**CONSUMER BEHAVIOR AND MARKETING 11.3**

## Acculturation Leads to New Recruiting Practices

In efforts to tap into the growing market of Indian Americans, Puneet Seth, managing director of Mutual of New York Life Insurance's New Jersey branch, is looking for new recruits in nontraditional places. In an age of electronic resumes and Web-based recruiting, Seth is visiting Hindu temples in search of employees able to speak the language and specific dialect of the markets he is targeting. On a recent visit to the Bochasanwasi Akshar-Purshottam Sanstha Temple in Edison, New Jersey, he encountered four hundred worshipers, many of whom still speak Gujarati, the original language of the niche to which he is seeking to sell insurance. In this instance, Seth's goal is to recruit a high-profile member of the community who would have influence in the market and understand the culture. Overall, he hopes to hire "a Punjabi, a

Gujarati, and a Bihari" to reach other segments of the Indian American market.

Indian Americans, among the fastest-growing ethnic cultures in the United States, have a median household income of $44,696 and perceive insurance to be the single most important investment tool to protect against unforeseen events. Yet, even with this desire for insurance, this ethnic market is more likely to buy from a salesperson who speaks the same language and understands their culture because of an implied, underlying level of trust. But finding a salesperson who can speak the language of the Indian American customer can be tricky because eighteen official Indian languages exist.

Source: Based on "Insurers Court Indian-American Market," *Wall Street Journal* (October 12, 1999), B1.

United States during those ten years, primarily stemming from the fall of Communism and the resulting freedom of Eastern Europeans. Recent immigrants and native-born Americans with close ties to their European heritage are defined as Euro-American ethnics.

Traditionally, Euro-American ethnics have displayed a "work hard, play hard" mentality and have been willing to work extended hours to save money for things like education, housing, and retirement. Their thriftiness is exhibited in their high coupon usage rate—75 percent versus 64 percent of all non-Hispanic whites—to reach their primary goal of creating security for themselves and their families. When asked about attitudes toward money, Russian Americans stated that the ability to make material purchases today was more important than long-term financial security.[61] Although European ethnics like to save money, this does not mean they don't spend it on material items. According to Mediamark Research, 92 percent of Euro-American ethnics owns VCRs and stereos, compared to 60 percent of all non-Hispanic whites. Some of this conspicuous consumption is born from a desire to become "American," a status quickly attained through the acquisition of American symbols of success.

## Native American Culture

In a sense, the one truly "American" culture is that of Native Americans, although marketers view Native Americans as a minority ethnic group in today's majority culture. After nearly a century of assimilation into white society, there is a resurgence of identification with the classification "Native American" by American Indians, Alaskan Eskimos, Native Hawaiians, and the nearly one million aboriginals in Canada. Almost 2.5 million people in the United States identified themselves as American Indian in the 2000 census, and more than seven million claim some American Indian ancestry. Some American Indians dislike the idea of sharing their culture and spiritual practices with white people, but others welcome people of any race into their culture. The interest in Native American culture has increased consumer demand for products that reflect their ancient crafts and skills, some now available online rather than in shops historically located near areas of Native American residences. In recent years, some entrepreneurial leaders of Native American groups have "reclaimed" tribal lands, sometimes opening casinos, hotels, shopping centers, and other tourist attractions that provide employment for members of the tribe while raising the standard of living for the entire community.

## Multiethnic Microcultures

Increased ethnic diversity within a nation often leads to interracial relationships and marriages, resulting in children belonging to multiple ethnic microcultures. When this occurs, it is difficult to determine which of the influences will affect behavior and values more. For example, which is the greatest influence on golf superstar Tiger Woods' values and behaviors—his father's race (African American) or his mother's race (Asian American)? Knowing all of his ethnic and cultural influences allows marketers to reach him and other multiethnic consumers more effectively with diverse messages. A consumer's ethnic self-awareness—a temporary state during which a person is more sensitive to information related to his or her own ethnicity—moderates consumer response to targeted advertising, using cues from the advertisement that draw attention to ethnicity.[62]

In 2000, the Bureau of the Census began collecting multiracial information on U.S. citizens for the first time in its history. When asked to describe one's race, individuals were allowed to mark multiple boxes, such as Asian, Black, and Native American, in-

## FIGURE 11.10   U.S. Population by Race and Ethnic Group, 1970, 2000, and 2050

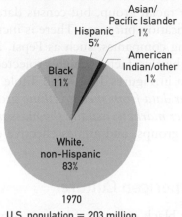

1970
U.S. population = 203 million

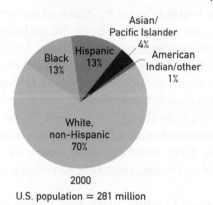

2000
U.S. population = 281 million

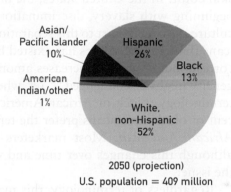

2050 (projection)
U.S. population = 409 million

### TABLE 11.6     U.S. Households and Average Incomes

| 2003 | ALL RACES | AFRICAN AMERICAN | ASIAN | WHITE (NON-HISPANIC) | HISPANIC |
|---|---|---|---|---|---|
| Number of households (millions) | 112 | 14 | 4.2 | 92 | 11.7 |
| Median income | $43,318 | $29,689 | $55,262 | $47,777 | $32,997 |

Source: U.S. Census Bureau: Historical Income Tables—Households, www.census.gov/hhes/income/histinc/inchhdet.html.

stead of being forced to select only one of the possible five categories. The difficulty is in tabulation—with the new format, sixty-four possible racial categories exist.[63] In spite of the complications, this information yields more detailed and accurate data on specific racial groups, and identifies needs for specialized advertising and market research.[64] The Association for MultiEthnic Americans (AMEA) estimates that 2 to 3 percent of Americans identify themselves with more than one racial group.

Marketers focus most of their attention on three ethnic groups: African Americans, Latinos, and Asian Americans. Figure 11.10 shows current and projected population breakdown by race and ethnicity, and Table 11.6 shows the number of households and corresponding incomes for each major ethnic segment. Household size and structure explains why some groups have more people but fewer households. The U.S. Census Bureau collects data using the term "Hispanic," making it necessary to use that term when discussing census data, although Latino is the term normally used in this book. Hispanics can be of any racial group, but census data also uses the term "non-Hispanic whites" for classification purposes. There is increasing interest in transcultural marketing among leading companies, such as Pepsi, McDonald's, and Coca-Cola.[65] Their interest is caused by two factors: high projected growth rates and substantial buying power, as shown in Figures 11.10 and Table 11.6. **Transcultural marketing research** is used to *gather data from specific ethnic groups and compare these data to those collected from other markets, usually the mass market.* The information identifies differences between groups, and guides effective communication and marketing strategies.

## Black or African American Culture

African American or black culture refers to a common heritage rather than to a skin color. In the United States, the black heritage is conditioned by a shared history beginning with slavery, discrimination, suffering, and segregation from the majority culture. Owing in part to this separation, a greater homogeneity among African Americans than among whites has existed historically, although as the education level and corresponding income increases among segments of this group, the notion of homogeneity might be challenged.[66] Yet, when defining this market, controversy over proper terminology (black or African American) still exists, even though more than 70 percent of black Americans prefer the term *black,* compared with 15 percent preferring *African American.* Most marketers opt for the term *black/African American,*[67] although this changes over time and with regional variation, requiring sensitivity to the issue.

Regardless of terminology, this market is worthy of serious marketing attention. This market has a population base of more than 32 million people with growing buying power, especially among the middle class.[68] However, black consumers have also been underrepresented in advertisements and have often been shown in stereotypical or menial roles.[69] That African Americans compose 12.1 percent of the U.S. population and 11.3 percent of the readership of all magazines[70] has created more use of black actors in ads.

### Structural Influences on Black/African American Markets

The primary structural influences shaping African American markets include income, education, families, and environment. These factors help marketers to understand and predict consumer behavior among African American consumers.

### INCOME

The number of affluent black households has risen sharply in recent years, with the number of households making over $50,000 at more than 25 percent, up from 9 percent in 1967.[71] Yet people who reported black as their only race had a poverty rate of 24.4 percent in 2003, compared to 22.5 percent for Hispanics, 11.8 percent for Asians, and 8.2 percent for non-Hispanic whites. Although non-Hispanic whites had the lowest rates of any racial groups, they account for 44 percent of the people in poverty, the largest number of any group. Marketers are recognizing that despite the high levels of poverty, the purchasing power of blacks is substantial.[72] The number of African Americans grew 21 percent from 1990 to 2000, and their buying power increased from $318 billion a year in 1990 to $688 billion in 2002, according to the University of Georgia's Selig Center for Economic Growth. The center projects that black purchasing power will reach $921 billion in 2008, an increase of 189 percent in 18 years, versus a 128 percent rise for whites, and a 148 percent rise in buying power for all Americans.[73]

Two factors related to low income among black families are significant in the study of consumer behavior. First, there is the reality of low spending power for a large portion of this market. Black consumers often buy from stores that compete on price and welcome food stamps, and they must spend a large portion of their income on staple products. Dollar stores and discount grocers, such as Aldi, benefit from their patronage. The second factor is the separation of the effects of low income versus ethnicity and culture on consumer behavior. Because many studies report only the consumption differences between black and white consumers without separating the influence of income differences, marketers may mistakenly minimize the importance of middle- and higher-income black market targets. When examined from a cultural standpoint, more similarities than differences in black and white spending exist, with a majority of the differences due to lower incomes and living in central cities.[74]

## EDUCATION

The level of education among blacks varies greatly. A large number of children living below the poverty line and in crime-ridden urban neighborhoods receive inferior education and lack the skills needed to get jobs, earn incomes, and acquire consumer skills. Many of these children learn skills and behaviors on the streets rather than from teachers or parents. Yet among blacks age twenty-five and over, the proportion that had at least a high-school diploma in 2003 was 80 percent, a record high. This proportion rose by 10 percentage points from 1993 to 2003. For blacks ages twenty-five to twenty-nine, the proportion is considerably higher, 88 percent. Higher education has become a priority for a significant portion of this segment, as seen in the increase in the number of African American college students over the last two decades.

## FAMILY CHARACTERISTICS

The African American culture is influenced by a variety of family characteristics. A high proportion of African American families are headed by women, about two times higher than in white families. Only 38 percent of black children live with two parents, compared with 77 percent of white children.[75] Therefore, black women influence many purchases traditionally purchased by male householders and have a great deal of authority in the family, which marketers must understand and portray correctly in ads. What's more, the average black family is younger than its white counterparts. The median age is about five years younger, a factor accounting for differences in preferences for clothing, music, shelter, cars, and many other products and activities.[76] Research studies indicate that actors used in ads targeting this market should be consistent with the expectations of the market[77] and portrayed realistically if the ads are to influence the market.

Related to family characteristics is personal health. Statistics show that African Americans as a group have a greater risk of diabetes, heart disease, stroke, glaucoma, arthritis, kidney disease, and certain types of cancer than other ethnic groups. Sickle-cell anemia, a genetic condition, is found almost exclusively among African Americans and must be considered when planning a family. When it comes to health issues, people can assimilate or not assimilate, join the mainstream or a microculture, get an education or not—but none of these activities will change their DNA. Many black women today actively seek information on health issues affecting their segment, and public health groups frequently target such segments to assess the availability of care and prevention for various diseases.

## DISCRIMINATION

The effects of discrimination on the African American culture are so massive and enduring that they cannot be ignored in the analysis of consumer behavior. Even after years of affirmative action programs, about which substantial controversy over effectiveness exists, employment parity for African Americans has not been achieved. Some studies show that underrepresentation of minorities in higher- and lower-status occupations is still due to discrimination.[78]

As a result of years of discrimination, some black consumers have substantial skepticism toward white businesses—some of which acted as bankers for slave merchants, supported segregated housing, limited employment opportunities, and restrained the use of blacks in the media until recent years. Today, firms that make a special effort to show sensitivity to black culture, use black media wisely, and stand against discrimination may be able to turn a problem into an opportunity. To create better relationships with this segment, many companies create public relations programs and special promotions in conjunction with Black History Month, sponsoring scholarships and other programs. Living in a large, racially segregated city where black liberal and black nationalist political ideologies are discussed affects shopping habits, ranging from housing to food.[79]

### African American Consumption Patterns

How do African Americans differ in their consumption patterns from other market segments? Consumer research has focused on this topic and on the similarities and differences between whites and blacks in the United States for decades.[80] Because most of these studies failed to control for socioeconomic status or other structural variables,[81] consumer researchers are faced with the dilemma of deciding which of the studies are still valid.

Many factors must be considered in developing marketing programs for African Americans. African American Markets Group (AAMG), a unit of Ketchem Public Relations Worldwide, and other leading researchers provide guidelines for developing effective communications programs[82] that consider both cultural and structural elements.

Among magazines with the highest credibility ratings are the black publications *Essence* and *Ebony,* as well as *Consumer Reports.* Although approximately 85 percent of those surveyed indicated that their leading source of information regarding products and companies is local television news, 82 percent also said they look for information from magazines aimed specifically at the African American market.[83] Respondents said they trust these publications more than other sources, which researchers attribute to their trust in black reporters and advice givers. Black-owned television news and local black-owned newspapers also ranked higher than other sources in terms of trustworthiness.[84] Although the Black Entertainment Television (BET) network delivers large audiences of black consumers, magazines are still the preferred medium for many mainstream advertisers, including those shown in Figure 11.11a and b.

The consequences of ignoring the impact of black-owned media on consumers can be devastating. Home Depot currently spends $4.7 million per year advertising in black-owned newspapers, and millions more are spent by retailers like Office Depot,

**FIGURE 11.11a** Advertisements Appealing to the African American Market

T-Mobile Wireless, Wal*Mart, and Target. When it was discovered that a policy at Kohl's department stores, which bought $86.4 million in newspaper advertising in 2004, prohibited advertising in black-owned newspapers, these papers called for a boycott. Despite the public relations snafu, because Kohl's target market is young mothers, the company's advertising dollars may still be better spent with black radio stations, which have greater influence over its target market.[85]

Retailers and product manufacturers alike have become more aware of the African American market. Retailers, including J. C. Penney and Sears, have introduced merchandise targeted specifically to black consumers. Sears named a line of clothing Essence, and Spiegel launched "E Style" catalogs of women's clothing, geared toward readers of *Ebony* magazine. Tommy Hilfiger crossed ethnic market lines by taking baggy pants and hip-hop styles mainstream, only to be supplanted by brands such as Sean John and Phat Farm. Cosmetic giants such as Avon, Revlon, Procter & Gamble's Cover Girl, and L'Oréal make special efforts to target women of color with products for dark skin tones. Cosmetic ads have also changed in recent years by featuring African American models, and black supermodels such as Tyra Banks have become some of the most effective spokespersons for such companies as lingerie marketer Victoria's Secret.

**FIGURE 11.11b**

## Asian American Culture

Asian Americans have a strong give-and-take relationship with traditional American culture. Although they contribute to American culture (influencing everything from foods and tastes to values and education), Asian Americans also adopt many Western philosophies into their own lifestyles and culture. In advertisements, Asian consumers from Confucian and Buddhist philosophies focus on reality as flexible and constant and have little problem accepting contradictions. By contrast, western cultures influenced by Judeo-Christian philosophies tend to reject this duality, seeing things in more absolute terms of "right" and "wrong." Combining positive and negative emotions in advertisements is effective for East Asian consumers, not for consumers of European descent.[86] Combine their willingness to adopt U.S. products (such as fashion apparel) with the fact that more than one-quarter of all immigrants to the United States are from Asia, and you can see why Asian Americans have become a desirable target for marketing organizations. In 2003, India and China had the second- and third-most number of emigrants to the United States, surpassed only by Mexico.[87]

Asian Americans are usually defined to include Chinese, Japanese, Koreans, Vietnamese, Cambodians, Laotians, Filipinos, Asian Indians, Pakistanis, Hawaiians, Samoans, Guamanians, Fiji Islanders, and other Asians and Pacific Islanders living in the United States. As a whole, this market is expected to continue growing in size and percentage of U.S. population, perhaps reaching up to 20 million consumers early this century. Keep in mind as you read the following pages that there can be great variation in preferences and lifestyles among Asian Americans of varied national backgrounds.

### Structural Influences

#### INCOME

As you saw in Table 11.6, Asian Americans have substantially higher incomes than any other group, nearly double the incomes of African American consumers. Fifty-three percent of Asian households have at least two income earners—with 74 percent of men and 59 percent of women in the work force. With a projection by the Selig Center that Asian American buying power will hit $526 billion in 2008, you can see why marketers are reaching out to this segment.

Asian Americans are also more likely to own a business than other minorities.[88] In fact, Koreans dominate entrepreneurial ventures, owning more than 113 businesses per 1,000 population, far more than any other minority or non-minority population group.[89] Koreans also have a higher rate of business success, due in part to their higher than average level of education and diligent work ethic. A study of Korean immigrants concluded that the values of hard work and merchant ability have been developed as a result of coming to America, rather than because of their Korean background.[90]

#### EDUCATION

Asian Americans believe strongly in education. They have the highest rate of education among any U.S. population category, correlated, of course, with a higher education level.

#### FAMILY CHARACTERISTICS

The Asian American culture is characterized by hard work, strong family ties, appreciation for education, and other values that lead to success in entrepreneurship, technical skills, and the arts. Family is a priority for this ethnic group, and they tend to keep close ties with family members at home and abroad. Children are very important to the family structure. Some Asian Americans tend to have more children than the majority culture, contributing to the rapid growth of this segment. From early ages, children are taught to respect elders, parents, and other family members. In turn, parents often sacrifice to provide the best possible education and opportunities for their children.

Family influences are also very strong among many Asian Americans. For example, Chinese American consumers often prefer shopping in large family groups for important purchases, with buying decisions approved by family elders. Though a product such as a car might be intended for a teenager or a middle-aged engineer, a successful sales approach might include communications directed to the grandfather or elderly uncle.

### Asian American Consumption Patterns

Among Asian Americans, 54 percent shop as a leisure activity compared with 50 percent of the general population. Asians also think quality is more important than price when they choose a store. They are far more likely than other groups to use technology such as automated teller machines, and many more own VCRs or DVDs, CD players, microwave ovens, home computers, and telephone answering machines.[91] Read Market Facts 11.2 to see other differences.

Cultural sensitivity is essential in marketing to Asian Americans—sometimes firms need to look to multicultural marketing firms for advice. For example, a marketer might not know the importance of numbers to Asian Americans, particularly the number 8, which symbolizes prosperity. Colors are also important in symbolizing different

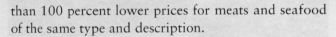

**MARKET FACTS 11.2**

## Comparing Consumers from Different Cultures

Research comparing samples of American and Chinese culture finds these two cultural groups have dramatically different shopping patterns. Chinese consumers use multiple senses when examining unpackaged food, and do so far more than American shoppers. Chinese consumers also inspect many more items and take much more time to shop. The differences in shopping behavior correspond to clear differences in prices between grocery stores serving the two cultural groups. Chinese supermarkets have substantially lower prices across a range of food products than mainstream American supermarkets. These differences ranged from 37 percent lower prices for packaged goods of the same brand and size to more than 100 percent lower prices for meats and seafood of the same type and description.

How do bilingual consumers process bilingual information? When asking Chinese-English bilinguals to evaluate dual brand names, proficient consumers prefer sound translation when the English name is emphasized, but meaning translation when the Chinese name is emphasized. In contrast, less proficient bilinguals engage in semantic processing of the dual names. These results suggest that proficiency must be added as a key concept to a framework that addresses bilingual consumer environments.

Source: Abstracted from David Ackennan and Gerald Tellis, "Can Culture Affect Prices? A Cross-Cultural Study of Shopping and Retail Prices," *Journal of Retailing,* 77 (Spring 2001), 57–83; and Shi Zang and Bernd Schmitt, "Activating Sound and Meaning: The Role of Language Proficiency in Bilingual Consumer Environments," *Journal of Consumer Research,* 31 (June 2004), 220–229.

things—especially red, which is associated with good luck. Many Asian Americans believe that white envelopes should not be used around a holiday because white usually symbolizes death. Citibank adapted one of its ads celebrating the traditional American New Year's holiday to one celebrating the Chinese New Year by replacing images of corks from champagne bottles with dragons, which have spiritual significance. Celebrities, especially those of Asian background, can also be very effective in appealing to this market. When Reebok featured tennis star Michael Chang in ads, its shoe sales among Asian Americans greatly increased,[92] and Tiger Woods shares appeal from his Asian and African American heritage, emerging as a celebrity who appeals to nearly all cultural groups. Marketers need to reach Asian American consumers in different ways—not just through mass media, but also through cultural and foreign language publications. National- and language-oriented media may promote greater loyalty among readers and listeners, as well as provide excellent "cost-per-thousand" of concentrated market targets. For example, Vietnamese overwhelmingly prefer to read and hear ads in Vietnamese. They watch more native language television (about 9.5 hours per week) than other Asian Americans, making it more important for a firm to communicate in their native tongue.[93] But not all Asian Americans are the same. Recent immigrants from India may prefer to speak with each other in Hindi, but prefer to read English. Marketers may find better results with English-language publications, such as *India Abroad*.[94]

Even with effective advertising and communication strategies, the sales process doesn't end with bringing consumers into the store. Some Asian Americans, especially the Chinese, expect to bargain over price—to them, bargaining is a normal part of the business culture, which may be the reason for the lower prices described in Market Facts 11.2. But to someone more accustomed to American business—even a car salesperson—the exchange can seem downright cutthroat. One San Francisco Volkswagen dealer tells his salespeople, "When the guy comes in here and makes a ridiculous offer on a car, you don't get mad. You come back with something equally ridiculous and have a good laugh. Then start your real negotiation."[95]

The Asian American culture is so successful in America that many of the products have become adopted by the major culture—Chinese food, sushi, and Japanese cars such as Honda, Toyota, and Lexus come to mind. Is it also possible to use symbols of Asian culture to promote products among the majority market? In Figure 11.12, Gillette uses Spicy Green Tea, a traditional Japanese beverage shared at women's social gatherings, as the feminine basis for women's shaving cream, encouraging women to "throw your legs a tea party".

## Latino (Hispanic) Culture

Latinos are now the largest minority group in the United States, recently surpassing African Americans in numbers. This group's members make the United States one of the largest Spanish-speaking nations in the world, with Latinos making up the

Courtesy of The Gillette Company

Don't just shave. Throw your legs a tea party.

NEW SATIN CARE SPICY GREEN TEA SHAVE GEL Its exotic re-energizing fragrance has moisture-rich skin nourishing vitamins that leave legs feeling soft and satiny smooth.

LEGS LOVE SATIN

**FIGURE 11.12** Advertising Appealing to the Asian American Market

majority of many communities in Texas, California, and Florida. The combination of rapid growth, size, and distinctive language is at the heart of the group's interest to marketers. The Hispanic market is 88 percent concentrated in cities, an attractive fact for media plans, distribution facilities, and other elements of marketing programs. Businesses such as San Juan–based Banco Popular have found opportunity in this trend, using its U.S. banking charter and Spanish-speaking call centers to open full-service banking offices in primarily Latino communities in New York, New Jersey, Illinois, and Florida. Diversity in culture and other variables within this segment dictate that the market should be regarded as a heterogeneous set of wants and behaviors rather than the "Latino segment," [96] and can be compared with other minority and majority segments using the Rokeach Value System (RVS).[97]

## Who Is Latino?

Language and cultural identity, rather than national origin, are the key elements in Latino culture, which may include any color or race. Whether the term *Hispanic* or *Latino* is more appropriate is a controversial question. The Census Bureau uses the term *Hispanic* to describe Americans whose origins are in the Spanish-speaking countries of the Western world, and media and marketers typically use the term Hispanic. Outside Texas and the southwestern United States, however, the term *Latino* is usually preferred, and increasingly, country of origin, such as *Mexican American, Puerto Rican American,* or *Cuban American* is preferred. Academic groups and recent immigrants tend to prefer *Latino* to *Hispanic,* whereas affluent and older immigrants tend to use *Hispanic.*[98] In this text, the term *Hispanic* is mostly used to reflect usage in government statistics and the media. *Latin* is also used increasingly to reflect, not only a music style, but a form of culture with appeal to many consumers beyond the Latino segment. U.S.-based television networks, such as Univision and Telemundo, reach many in the Hispanic market with programming that includes variety shows, soap operas, and dramatic series that appeal more to Latin culture than do situation comedies and game shows. Internet sites, such as www.quepasa.com, www.miami.com, and www.el-mundo.es also provide up-to-date information of interest to the Hispanic market.

Latino consumers are often segmented into four groups: Mexicans, Puerto Ricans, Cubans, and others. Mexicans account for about 60 percent of all Latinos (53 percent born in the United States), are concentrated in the Southwest states, and tend to be young with large families. Puerto Ricans account for 15 percent of Latinos and are concentrated in large cities in the Northeast, most notably New York City but also Cleveland and Chicago. Most Puerto Ricans arrived in the United States during the past twenty-five years, and many are now in middle age, with young children born in the United States. Cubans make up about 7 percent of all Hispanics (7 percent born in the United States) and are concentrated in urban areas of the Southeast, primarily South Florida. Cubans are the oldest group, have fewer children, and tend to be the aristocracy in terms of occupation, education, and income. Other Latinos (which constitute 18 percent) are primarily from Central America or the Caribbean and are dispersed geographically. Ninety-three percent of them are foreign-born and are mostly young adults with few children.[99]

The diversity within the Latino market provides differences in values and motivations. Mexican Americans are more likely to be assimilated into the U.S. culture. Although Cubans who fled the oppressive regime of Fidel Castro may not want to return anytime soon, they are more likely to think of themselves as Latino first and American second.[100] Language varies between segments. The word for beans may be *frijoles,* but can also be translated with many other words more common among consumers from Argentina, Puerto Rico, or other countries. A "sale" may be *venta* or *promoción* or other words.

## INCOME

Latinos represent the fastest-growing ethnic market in the United States, purchasing over $340 billion annually[101] and projected by the Selig Center to have buying power that will triple, to slightly more than $1 trillion by 2008. Within the market, Cuban average income is higher than that of any other Latino group, whereas Puerto Ricans have the lowest average of any Latino group.

## EDUCATION

The number of Latinos attending college and receiving bachelor's degrees has increased in recent years. In the early 1980s, Latino students made up 2.3 percent of the university population, but this number more than doubled by 2000 and is expected to grow more rapidly in the future, fueling continued income growth.

## FAMILY CHARACTERISTICS

The family is extremely important in Latino culture and differs from non-Latino whites not only in values but also in size (larger) and age (younger).[102] Latino youth make up the largest ethnic youth population in the United States, a figure expected to increase because of higher fertility rates.[103] Latino families tend to do lots of things together, not only with the immediate family but the extended family. Market Facts 11.3 describes how "Latino urbanism" affects cities with high Latino concentrations and may be a pattern for other urban markets.

Many young and middle-aged Latino immigrants still have close ties to family and extended family still living in their native countries. Feeling an obligation to care for them, immigrants share their newfound prosperity by sending monthly wire transfers back home. In 2004, $45.8 billion was sent electronically from the United States to Latin America and the Caribbean, making Latin America the single largest destination for cash remittances in the global market. Cash remittances provided an additional $16.6 billion to Mexico's economy in 2004. At one time as many as 5,000 "dollar stores" operated in Cuba, where consumers could buy a wide range of merchandise using U.S. currency sent from American family and friends. Many Latino consumers use money-transfer companies such as Western Union with hassle-free locations in neighborhood convenience stores, pawnshops, and check-cashing outlets. As transaction fees range from 8 to 15 percent, however, many banks are now getting into the business, and greater competition is bringing prices down, which benefits immigrants and their families. The end result is consumers who contribute to, and participate in, two economies and two cultures simultaneously.

## RELIGION

The majority of Latin American cultures are influenced by Catholicism, but many immigrants from nations like Mexico have abandoned the Roman Catholic Church in favor of other forms of Christianity. According to one report, each year more than 60,000 Latino Catholics convert to Protestantism. The largest benefactor is the Pentecostal movement, in which small, storefront churches in urban areas like Los Angeles combine contemporary Latin-inspired music with a "born again" message of hope and empowerment—things immigrants cannot do without. Not only can the trials and

### Building for the Latino Market

Amid sprawling suburban gated communities with three-car garages and mega-malls, Santa Ana, California, is building an antidote to suburban sprawl, a hub based on a "new urbanism" of dense, walkable neighborhoods where people live, work, and play. But it's a new urbanism with a twist: Latino new urbanism.

In California, where Latinos are projected to be the majority of the population by 2050, many consumers grew up in Mexico with compact neighborhoods, large public places, and a sense of community. Builders and planners have largely ignored the cultural identity of this new wave of home buyers, says planner Michael Mendez, who coined the term "Latino new urbanism." The National Association of Home Builders plans to publish a book on designing homes for the Latino market, now the nation's largest minority group.

For Latinos who celebrate events with family dinners and festivals, homes are being remodeled to include large front porches, fountains, and wrought iron with nearby neighborhood parks as a social place outside the home. In San Ysidro, near the Mexican border, facades of new homes are vibrant red, blue, yellow, and green. Three-bedroom, two-bathroom homes are selling for $270,000, about half the local median price. Former Secretary of Housing and Urban Development Henry Cisneros now heads a company developing homes that fit the needs of Latino families, from big kitchens with gas stoves for grilling tortillas to courtyards for social gatherings, multiple bedrooms for large and extended families, and driveways that accommodate numerous cars.

Dowell Myers, a demographer at the University of Southern California, says, "Who's to say Latino new urbanism should be just for Latinos? Maybe it's a general model for the whole region."

Source: Based on Haya El Nasser, "'New Urbanism' Embraces Latinos," *USA Today* (February 16, 2005), A3. Copyright 2005 USA Today, a division of Gannett Co., Inc.

tribulations of immigrant life be forgotten at the exuberant nightly prayer meetings offered by many of these churches, but there is also a sense of community and personal belonging. Despite 70 percent of the Roman Catholic Diocese of Los Angeles being Latino, many Catholic congregations still have difficulty accommodating the large number of immigrants—from finding Spanish-speaking priests to celebrate Mass and administer sacraments, to raising funds to expand churches in ethnic neighborhoods. The sheer size of many Catholic churches also leads immigrants to feel disconnected. But in neighborhoods like L.A.'s Peakwood Union, where the poverty rate is 50 percent, Pentecostal congregations (which rely heavily on lay leadership) often act like extended families, helping members with practical needs like jobs or just plain survival.[104]

Pentecostal churches aren't the only ones attracting large numbers of Latino immigrants. The Church of Jesus Christ of Latter-day Saints (Mormon) has seen its number of Spanish-speaking congregations quadruple to more than 200,000 Spanish-speaking members in the United States. The emphasis of the Mormon faith on family, hard work, and humility, which experts say parallel the Latino culture's focus on family values, fuels the Latino inclination to join the religion. In Ventura County, California (population 800,000), twenty-six full-time, Spanish-speaking missionaries scour Latino neighborhoods daily, offering an alternative for individuals disenchanted with their traditional faiths or seeking fresh spiritual guidance.[105]

On a recent PBS documentary, Carlton College professor Luis Leon said, "Immigrants who come to the United States are seeking a new sense of self. They want a new identity. They want a new way to be in the world, and in many ways, converting to evangelicalism is a fulfillment of that expectation. It gives them a new sense of who they are. It gives them a new God." [106]

## Latino Consumption Patterns and Characteristics

Many firms have adapted product lines to meet the needs of the Latino segment. Pavion, which has a successful line of cosmetics for black consumers called Black Radiance, added Solo Para Ti (Only For You) for Latinas (*Latina* is the word used for female Latinos). All aspects of Solo Para Ti (products, promotions, and even the name) were designed with the Latina culture in mind. The products are available in high-shine and in bright shades to appeal to Latinas. To reach this market, Pavion advertises on Spanish-language television and radio and features in-store promotions in both Spanish and English.[107] Similarly, Latino culture is affecting the tastes and preferences of the majority culture, causing companies to reformulate their product offerings.

In 2005, Target began targeting Latinos with a website in Spanish and repositioning of its brand. The general market was so accustomed to Target ads that the retailer had omitted its name from the ads, relying instead on its signature red color and bull's-eye logo. However, the emblem wasn't relevant to Latinos, who thought Target sold clothing only or that it was a higher-priced store, and who felt the logo was a little distant. The reason Latinos felt Target was "too American" was that the concept of the store was never explained to them. The solution was new TV ads with the look and feel of the general market but introducing Spanish-speakers to the Target brand and affordable design promise. Bright colors and sleekly designed products swirl across the screen, with lines like "Designer tea kettles at the price of regular tea kettles," and "Isaac Mizrahi shoes at the price of regular shoes." Paco Olavarrieta, creative partner at Target's Spanish market ad agency, concludes, "Once a Hispanic goes [to Target] and understands they can get Isaac Mizrahi shoes and they cost $30, they say 'Wow.'" [108]

Latinos watch television about the same amount as the average American, but they watch Spanish-language programming a majority of the time. Hispanics watch, on average, 15.3 hours of Spanish programming per week and 10 hours of English programming.[109] A popular talk show, especially among the 5.4 million stay-at-home Latina mothers, is *Cristina,* which generates a worldwide television audience of more than 100 million viewers. Such wide viewership led the esteemed Pulaski Furniture Company to partner with the show's host to be the first major furniture manufacturer to market a line addressed to the Latino market. Among other things, the furniture must have the flexibility of adding many chairs to appeal to the family size and extended family setting of Hispanic meal time. (Remember how the family of Carlos expected him to attend a family gathering in the opening vignette in Chapter 1?) Almost 13 million Latinos are also online, 42 percent of which are Spanish-dominant and 31 percent bilingual. Yet 81 percent of Fortune 100 companies don't have Spanish-language websites, and even the other 19 percent often fail to offer really useful Spanish-language navigation and content online, according to a survey by Forrester Research.[110]

Differences among segments of the Latino market affect purchase behavior in many ways, including the use of coupons. Proud that they are now making a better living, some Latino consumers are reluctant to use coupons that they believe are "for people who can't afford to pay the full price." [111] One study found that Spanish-speaking Latinos who identify closely with their microculture do not rely on printed sources of information as much as English-language Latinos do, but do rely on couponing, in-store point-of-purchase displays, and word-of-mouth.[112] As the Latino market is assimilated into an older non-Latino market, however, many characteristics of this microculture—such as higher brand loyalty, lower coupon usage, and more shopping enjoyment—are increasingly questionable.[113] Brand loyalty is increasingly questioned as typical behavior, although price, product quality, and shopping ease appear to be constant attributes of importance to Latinos.[114]

Figure 11.13 displays four ads directed to Latinos. Notice some of the themes and strategies revealed in the ads. In Figure 11.13, the Volkswagen ad's asterisked message of "family required" appeals to the value of the entire family doing things together as well as the generally larger family size of Latinos. Volkswagen reaches the Latino market in a variety of ways, including its website. What's cool is that instead of www.vw.com/es, VW announced a website called www.agarracalle.com, with *Agarra calle* ("road grabbing") intended to be a Spanish-language version of Volkswagen's tagline "Drivers wanted." You can see the same basic appeal to large Latino families in the Chrysler ad, but with the addition of a Latina showing that the new Town & Country "has a place for everyone and everyone has a place." The Latina in the ad also demonstrates (and the copy explains) how easy it is to fold the seats into the floor. Ads are often more effective when they include people, communicating how products fit consumer lifestyles. The Wal*Mart ad, for instance, reveals how much of what a young woman needs for her home she can purchase at Wal*Mart. "Loyalty" is Wal*Mart's message—to its employees, communities and customers. The Nissan ad, by contrast, challenges the status quo by showing this group of Latinas how to set their own style and find a "new way of living."

## Avoiding Marketing Blunders

Failure to understand the Latino culture can lead to marketing blunders. These blunders can be divided into three main types: translation blunders, culture misunderstandings, and Hispanic idiosyncrasies.[115]

**FIGURE 11.13** Advertisements Appealing to the Latino Market

Los hijos traen grandes satisfacciones.

*Familia requerida.

Sharan  VW

NUEVA TOWN & COUNTRY DEL 2005. TIENE LUGAR PARA TODOS Y TODO TIENE SU LUGAR.

Todo cambia, hasta lo totalmente nuevo Chrysler Town & Country del 2005. Ahora disponible con el exclusivo sistema de asientos y compartimientos DOBLA FÁCIL dos filas de compartimientos y asientos que desaparecen totalmente en el piso. Así tienes espacio de carga cuando lo necesitas, y cuando no, tienes espacio de sobra para cargar con quien quieras.

CHRYSLER
INSPIRACIÓN INCLUIDA

ABRÓCHATELO  Chrysler Financial  Financiando Tu Paseo

*Lealtad*

"En Wal-Mart me siento como en mi casa. Aquí encuentro todo y Wal-Mart me llena la imaginación. El 70% de las cosas que compro para mi casa son de Wal-Mart."
—Nihosotty Mozas

Todo empezó cuando Nihosotty Mozas compró su casa. "Cambiarme a mi casa nueva fue maravilloso, pero luego cuando vi todo el espacio pensé que me volvía loca. Pero con los precios bajos de Wal-Mart siempre me alcanza para todo, y todo hace juego, me encanta. Compré la mesa para el televisor, mi teléfono, vasos, vajilla, sábanas, toallas, secadora, licuadora, florecitas, cortinas, en fin, con los precios que me dan puedo comprar cantidad de cosas. Es una maravilla."

WAL★MART
Para Su Familia, De Todo Corazón.

Siempre.

**FIGURE 11.13** (Continued)

## TRANSLATION BLUNDERS

Although most Latinos are bilingual, about 94 percent speak Spanish in the home and think in Spanish—creating the need for marketers to communicate in Spanish.[116] This situation can lead to translation blunders. For example, one cigarette advertisement wanted to read the brand contained "less tar," but the translation actually read "less asphalt." Even market researchers make a blunder when they ask for the *dama de la casa* (madam of the house) rather than the *señora de la casa* (lady of the house). In addition to conveying the wrong message, translation mistakes can offend and alienate an ethnic culture. Read Consumer Behavior and Marketing 11.4 to see how Hershey's made an agonizing choice about this issue.

## CULTURE MISUNDERSTANDINGS

Misunderstandings occur when marketers use stereotypes of their own self-reference criteria for designing marketing and communication strategies. For example, a telephone company commercial portrayed a wife telling her husband to "run downstairs and phone Maria" and "tell her we'll be a little late." Two cultural errors

## What's The Right Spanish Name for a Product?

Hershey's made a controversial choice in promoting its new U.S. Hispanic line with language familiar to Mexicans, but not to other Spanish-speakers. La Dulceria Thalia products—a range of Hershey's kisses, wafer bars, and lollipops backed by Mexican entertainer Thalia—are described in print and radio ads and on packaging as made from *cajeta*, the Mexican version of the caramel flavor known as *dulce de leche* in the rest of Latin America.

Marketers often agonize over when to segment their Hispanic marketing by ethnic group and when to target all Latinos. "We use the term *(cajeta)* because 67 percent of all Hispanics are Mexican and we're targeting Mexicans," said a Hershey spokeswoman. In some Latin countries, the word *cajeta* exists with a different meaning. In Argentina, for example, the word has a very sexual meaning. In an unscientific office poll, speakers of Mexican Spanish all were familiar with *cajeta;* Puerto Ricans and Dominicans weren't. "It could be some kind of box," speculated an Ecuadorean, thinking of *caja*, the Spanish word for box.

"There is Walter Cronkite Spanish," said Jose Cancela, principal of a new Miami-based consulting firm, Hispanic USA. "Using a word that is not known to 40 percent of the market is not smart marketing. The U.S. Hispanic market is a convergence of different people from all over the world. We all use the same dictionary and that's the Hispanic USA dictionary."

Not everyone cares. Cristina Benitez, president of Chicago-based marketing services agency Lazos Latinos and a speaker of Puerto Rican Spanish, said,

Hershey's leverages the popularity of Thalia, a Mexican pop star.

© AP/W de World Photos

"Thalia is a great spokesperson and the ads are really cute." Other marketers are also targeting the Hispanic sweet tooth. Entenmann's is introducing its own range of products with flavors like *dulce de leche* and pineapple under the brand name Delicias.

Source: Laurel Wentz, "Hershey's Name Sparks Hispanic Controversy," Adage.com (February 22, 2005). Reprinted with permission from February 2005, www.adage.com. Copyright Crain Communications, Inc., 2005

were committed. First, it is not customary for a Latina wife to give her husband orders, especially among traditional families. Second, Latinos do not normally call to say they will not be on time; it is customary to arrive a little late. Misunderstandings about the meaning of time may be one of the reasons Mexican Americans have more complaints about the delivery service of retailers than do other consumers.[117]

## LATINO IDIOSYNCRASIES

Marketing blunders sometimes occur from failure to understand the idiosyncrasies of each segment of the total Latino market. A beer company filmed a Latino advertisement using the *Paseo del Rio* (Riverwalk) in San Antonio, Texas, as a background. The ad was well received among Latinos living on the West Coast, who liked the Spanish atmosphere. In San Antonio itself, however, Latinos did not like the ad because they considered the *Paseo del Rio* to be an attraction for non-Latino white tourists rather than for Latino residents. In another example, a version of the slogan, "With us, you travel with leather" worked well for some forms of Spanish, but for Cubanos, was translated as "With us, you travel naked." Likewise, it may be acceptable for a person from Mexico to be described as a *chicano,* but not for someone from Cuba.

## French Canadian Culture

One of the largest and most distinct cultures in North America is the French Canadian culture, which is centered mostly in Quebec. French Canadians can be considered a nationality group or a geographic culture. The 7.5 million residents of Quebec account for more than 23 percent of the Canadian population, and about 20 percent of workers in Canada speak only French.[118] For years, the French culture was somewhat ignored by English-oriented advertisers, thereby creating a social problem and limiting the potential effectiveness of communications to the French market. Some of the differential treatment may have been caused by different social class groupings compared with Anglo markets.[119]

Is advertising transferable between the French Canadian (FC) culture and the English Canadian (EC) culture? Some marketers believe that separate advertising material must be developed to be effective in the FC microculture. Others believe that materials can be developed that are effective with both groups. In this latter case, a minimum of verbal material is used, with emphasis on the visual. One study, which compared communications with FC and EC consumers on a cross-cultural basis, indicated the potential for increasing effectiveness in advertising communications by targeting FCs with people-oriented ads and ECs with message-oriented ads.[120]

Because of the size and importance of the FC market to Canada's economy, the segment has attracted the attention of many marketers. The process of understanding communications in a cross-cultural setting, however, is applicable to other situations in which diverse ethnic groups are the target for marketing programs. Psycholinguistic research on bilingual consumers suggests that advertisements in an individual's second language are not retained as well as ads in their first language, but when there is a high level of congruity between picture and text, the retention for second-language ads is increased.[121]

## Social-Class Microcultures

Microcultures can also be described in terms of social class. **Social class** is defined as *relatively permanent and homogeneous divisions in a society into which individuals or families sharing similar values, lifestyles, interests, wealth, status, education, economic positions, and behavior can be categorized.* Class membership exists and can be described as a statistical category whether or not individuals are aware of their common situation. Some of the concrete variables that define various social classes include occupation, education, friendships, ways of speaking, and possessions. Perceived variables that define social classes include power and prestige.[122] Marketing research often focuses on social-class variables because the mix of goods that consumers are *able* to buy is determined in part by social class.

For marketers and sociologists, status groups are of primary interest because they influence what people buy and consume. **Status groups** reflect *a community's expectations for style of life among each class as well as the positive or negative social estimation of honor given to each class.* Simply stated, whereas classes are stratified based on their relations to the production and acquisition of goods, status groups are stratified according to lifestyles and the principles of the consumption of goods.[123] For practical purposes, however, it is usually adequate in the study of consumer behavior to treat the terms status and class interchangeably, recognizing that status may also be used in other contexts to describe differential respect given to individuals within a group.

If the 1980s were about greed and ostentation for upper-social-class groups and the 1990s were about value and self-fulfillment, what will be the legacy of the 2000s? The experts observe that in recent years, affluent tastes have run more toward the utilitarian with a penchant toward frugality. Range Rovers, Lincoln Navigators, and Ford Explorers, rather than Porsches, have been the vehicles of choice of upper-income consumers,[124] prompting Mercedes, Lexus, and BMW to develop and market SUVs to their utilitarian, upper-social-class consumers. The new status symbol of upper-class consumers, at least in Red states, is shopping at dollar stores, Aldi, Wal*Mart, or "Tar-zhay"—Target with a fake French accent.

## What Determines Social Class?

Your social class is influenced mostly by the family in which you were raised. Your father's occupation probably had a significant effect, since that has historically been the most important determinant, followed closely by your mother's occupation.[125] Variables that determine social class have been identified in social stratification studies since the 1920s and 1930s. Today, social-class research includes thousands of studies dealing with the measurement of social class in large cities; movement between social classes; interactions of social class with gender, race, ethnicity, and education; and the effects of social class on poverty and economic policy. From extensive research, nine variables have emerged as most important in determining social class,[126] as shown in Table 11.7.

For consumer analysts, six of these variables are especially useful in understanding a consumer's social class. These variables are occupation, personal performance, interactions, possessions, value orientations, and class consciousness.

## OCCUPATION

Occupation is the best single indicator of social class in most consumer research. The work that consumers perform greatly affects their lifestyles and consumption patterns. For example, blue-collar workers spend a large percentage of their income on food, whereas managers and professionals spend a greater share of their income on eating out, clothing, and financial services.[127]

| TABLE 11.7 | Economic, Interaction, and Political Variables | |
| --- | --- | --- |
| **ECONOMIC VARIABLES** | **INTERACTION VARIABLES** | **POLITICAL VARIABLES** |
| Occupation | Personal prestige | Power |
| Income | Association | Class consciousness |
| Wealth | Socialization | Mobility |

Sometimes, people make the mistake of equating social class with income. Social class is not determined by income, even though there may be a correlation due to the relationship between income and other variables that determine social class. A senior garbage collector, for example, might earn more than an assistant professor of history. The professor typically would be ascribed higher social class, however. You can probably think of more examples of how income and social class are not necessarily related.

## PERSONAL PERFORMANCE

A person's status can also be influenced by his or her success relative to that of others in the same occupation—that is, by an individual's personal performance. Even though income is not a good indicator of overall social class, income may serve as a gauge of personal performance within an occupation. Personal performance also involves activities other than job-related pursuits. Perhaps your father has a lower-status occupation, but your family may still achieve higher status if your father is perceived as one who helps others in need, is unusually kind and interested in fellow workers, or is a faithful leader in civic or religious organizations. A reputation as a good mother or a good father may also elevate one's status.

## INTERACTIONS

People feel most comfortable when they are with people of similar values and behavior. Group membership and interactions are considered a primary determinant of a person's social class. The interaction variables of personal prestige, association, and socialization are the essence of social class. People have high **prestige** *when other people have an attitude of respect or deference to them.* **Association** is a *variable concerned with everyday relationships, with people who like to do the same things they do, in the same ways, and with whom they feel comfortable.* Social-class behavior and values are clearly differentiated in children by the time they have reached adolescence, in variables that vary by social class such as self-esteem.[128] Social interactions ordinarily are limited to one's immediate social class even though opportunities exist for broader contact. Most marriages occur within the same or adjacent social classes.

## POSSESSIONS

Possessions are symbols of class membership—not only the number of possessions, but also the nature of the choices. Conspicuous consumption (people's desire to provide prominent visible evidence of their ability to afford luxury goods) helps explain why different classes buy different products. Thus, a middle-class family may choose wall-to-wall carpeting, whereas an upper-class family is more likely to choose Oriental rugs.[129]

Possessions and wealth are closely related. Wealth is usually a result of an accumulation of past income. In certain forms, such as ownership of a business or stocks and bonds, wealth is the source of future income that may enable a family to maintain its (high) social class from generation to generation. Thus, possessions that indicate a family's wealth are important in reflecting social class. Some products and brands are positioned as symbols of status—as products used by upper-middle or upper classes. For people who are striving to become associated with those classes, the purchase of such brands may be partially based on the desire for such affiliation or identification.

## VALUE ORIENTATIONS

Values indicate the social class to which one belongs. When a group of people share a common set of abstract convictions that organize and relate many specific attributes, it is possible to categorize an individual in the group by the degree to which he or she possesses these values. Some observers believe that in countries other than the United

States, values are more important than possessions. Class is indicated more by merit derived from expressions in art, science, religion and even in such mundane things as dressing and eating properly. In contrast, people in the United States are believed to practice the "religion of money."[130]

Although a person may be of great wealth, involvement in criminal activity, exploitation of the poor, outrageous public behavior, or abuse of alcohol or other drugs may relegate him or her to a lower social class in American culture, in which upper classes are generally expected to conduct themselves with dignity and respect.

## CLASS CONSCIOUSNESS

One of the important political variables of social class is class consciousness—the degree to which people in a social class are aware of themselves as a distinctive group with shared political and economic interests. To some extent, a person's social class is indicated by how conscious that person is of social class. Lower-social-class individuals may recognize the reality of social class but may not be as sensitive to specific differences. Thus, advertising for goods selling to upper-class market targets are often rich with social-class symbols, but ads to middle- and lower-social-class targets may not be well received if they use a direct class appeal.

### Social Stratification

Have you noticed that in many contexts, like school or work, some people are ranked higher than others and are perceived to have more power or control? Americans may hope that everyone has the same opportunity to access products and services; however, the reality is that some people have either "more luck" or are better "positioned" to attain than others. **Social stratification** refers to the *perceived hierarchies in which consumers rate others as higher or lower in social status.* Those who *earn a higher status due to work or study* have **achieved status,** whereas those who are *lucky to be born wealthy or beautiful* have **ascribed status.**

Regardless of how status is achieved, social class can be classified into six distinct segments, as defined by W. Lloyd Warner in 1941: upper upper, lower upper, upper middle, lower middle, upper lower, and lower lower.[131] The Gilbert and Kahl definitions,[132] shown in Table 11.8, provide generally accepted estimates on the size of various social classes, and emphasize economic distinctions, especially the recent emphasis on capitalism and entrepreneurship. The Coleman-Rainwater approach emphasizes how people interact with each other as equals, superiors, or inferiors, especially in their work relationships.

One complexity in measuring social class is the problem of *status inconsistency*—when people rate high on one variable but low on another. Highly paid athletes and popular musicians often fit this category. The other end of the spectrum of status inconsistency would include some professors who have average or below-average income but a lot of education and many other cultural advantages. These people do not fit into many of the generalizations about social class.

### Social Class Dynamics

Is it possible to change your social class? **Social mobility** refers to the process of *passing from one social class to another,* but includes more than just changing your occupation or income level. In England, citizens can rarely change class rapidly and can never be royalty unless born into it. In India, the family doesn't change class, but it's believed that individuals may do so in future lives through reincarnation. In countries such as Russia, China, and Hungary, consumers formerly subscribed to the working-class ideologies of Communism and Socialism. In those countries today, there

## Two Recent Views of the American Status Structure

| THE GILBERT-KAHL NEW SYNTHESIS CLASS STRUCTURE: A SITUATIONS MODEL FROM POLITICAL THEORY AND SOCIOLOGICAL ANALYSIS | THE COLEMAN-RAINWATER SOCIAL STANDING CLASS HIERARCHY: A REPUTATIONAL BEHAVIORAL VIEW IN THE COMMUNITY STUDY TRADITION |
|---|---|
| *Upper Americans* | *Upper Americans* |
| Capitalist Class (1%)—Their investment decisions shape the national economy; income mostly from assets earned inherited; prestige university connections | Upper Upper (0.3%)—"Capital S society" world of inherited wealth, aristocratic names |
| Upper Middle Class (14%)—Upper managers, professionals, medium businessmen; college educated; family income ideally runs nearly twice the national average | Lower Upper (1.2%)—Newer social elite drawn from current corporate leadership |
|  | Upper Middle (12.5%)—Rest of college graduate managers and professionals; lifestyle centers on private clubs, causes, and the arts |
| *Middle Americans* | *Middle Americans* |
| Middle Class (33%)—Middle-level white-collar, top-level blue-collar; education past high school typical; income somewhat above the national average | Middle Class (32%)—Average-pay white-collar workers and their blue-collar friends; live on "the better side of town," try to "do the proper things" |
| Working Class (32%)—Middle-level blue-collar; lower-level white-collar; income runs slightly below the national average; education is also slightly below | Working Class (38%)—Average-pay blue-collar workers; lead "working class lifestyle" whatever the income, school background, and job |
| *Marginal and Lower Americans* | *Lower Americans* |
| Working Poor (11–12%)—Below mainstream America in living standard but above the poverty line; low-paid service workers, operatives; some high school education | "A lower group of people but not the lowest" (9%)—Working not on welfare; living standard is just above poverty; behavior judged "crude," "trashy" |
| Underclass (8–9%)—Depend primarily on welfare system for sustenance; living standard below poverty line; not regularly employed; lack schooling | "Real lower lower" (7%)—On welfare, visibly poverty-stricken, usually out of work (or have "the dirtiest jobs"); "bums," "common criminals" |

Abstracted by Coleman from Dennis Gilbert and Joseph A. Kahl, "The American Class Structure: A Synthesis," Chapter 11. *The American Class Structure: A New Synthesis* (Homewood, Ill.: The Dorsey Press, 1982); drawn from Chapters 8, 9, and 10 of Richard P. Coleman and Lee P. Rainwater, with Kent A. McClelland, *Social Standing in America: New Dimensions of Class* (New York: Basic Books, 1978).

are new stirrings and the emergence of a consumer culture that is demonstrated in homes, electronic equipment, cars, household help, and clothes that no longer reflect the stereotyped view of a person as a cog in the societal mechanism.[133]

Although in the United States it is possible to climb upward (upward mobility) in the social order, the probabilities of this actually happening are not very high.[134] Children's social class usually predicts their social class as adults,[135] with factors such as access to good education and racial discrimination ultimately limiting social mobility for men and women.[136]

Although individuals might not change their social status easily, they often display behaviors or symbols of other social classes. **Parody display** describes *the mockery of status symbols and behavior,* whereby an upper-class individual might intentionally use the word *ain't* to proclaim distaste for class or his or her own security in the social status system. Though some people think about upholding their social class, others rebel against it by becoming part of the counterculture, perhaps displaying their distaste for their class with body piercing or tattooing.

## Social Class and Consumer Behavior

Social class affects consumer behavior in a variety of ways. Certain consumers read magazines, such as *Town & Country* and *Architectural Digest,* because the contents reflect the interests of the higher social classes to which the readers belong or to which they aspire. The magazines advertise upscale products for affluent consumers and contain articles that reflect the themes and motivations of special significance to affluent social classes—articles about arts and craftsmanship, interior decoration, dominance of nature, the triumph of technology, fashion trends, and the ideology of affluence.[137]

Consumers associate brands of products and services with specific social classes. For example, Heineken and Amstel Light are considered to be upper-middle-class drinks, whereas Budweiser is perceived as a beer for "every person" and is consumed mainly by middle- and lower-class drinkers. In the United States fifty years ago, beer was perceived as a lower-class beverage, but today it is popular with all classes—perhaps as a result of marketing efforts and the introduction of upscale microbrews and imported beers.

## Market Segmentation

Social class can be used to segment markets. The procedures for market segmentation include the following steps.

1. Identification of social class usage of product

2. Comparison of social class variables for segmentation with other variables (e.g., income, life cycle, and so on)

3. Description of social-class characteristics identified in market target

4. Development of marketing program to maximize effectiveness of marketing mix based on consistency with social-class attributes

Analysis of market segments by socioeconomic profile helps in the development of a comprehensive marketing program to match the preferences and behavior of the market target. This program would include product attributes, media strategy, creative strategy, channels of distribution, and pricing.

Targeting various zip codes facilitates social class segmentation. Zip codes estimate status without the need to collect additional data from respondents other than addresses, classifying households into segments such as the "suburban elites" who live in Scarsdale, New York; Winnetka, Illinois; or similar locations. Each segment is described in terms of typical leisure time activities, frequently read publications, and favored brands.[138]

## Positioning Based on Social-Class Characteristics

Social class is an important concept in developing positioning strategies, which create perceptions in consumers' minds about the attributes of a product or organization. To accomplish positioning effectively requires a good understanding of the class characteristics of the target market and the class attributes desired for the product. As marketers, it is important to note that the number of consumers who aspire to higher social classes is much larger than those who are in them. Currently many of the middle class can buy products with the symbols and allure of higher social classes—and often do for products as diverse as those of Coach or Godiva. Wanting it all is a hallmark of the middle class. Buying the best on at least a few occasions is a way to set them apart and bolster their self-image. Ads for premium-priced products need to be sensual, provocative, and elegant for these products,[139] such as the examples in Figure 11.14. Dominant culture and microculture consumers respond favorably to ads that feature dominant culture source and non-source cues, leading to favorable ad attitudes.[140]

**FIGURE 11.14** Advertisements of Premium-Priced Products

## Summary

Culture is the complex of values, ideas, attitudes, and other meaningful symbols that allow humans to communicate, interpret, and evaluate as members of society. Culture and its values are transmitted from one generation to another, and individuals learn values and culture through socialization and acculturation. The core values of a society define how products are used, with regard to their function, form, and meaning. Culture also provides positive and negative valences for brands and for communication programs and defines the ideology of consumption.

The fundamental forces that form values are included in the cultural transfusive triad (family, religion, and schools). In addition to these influences, early lifetime experiences, such as depressions, wars, and other major events, also affect values.

North America is a multicultural society composed of basic core values in the macroculture and many microcultures. With organizations striving to understand consumers better, many marketers are studying microcultures more closely, including how cultural icons and trends transcend from one microculture to another. These segments may be either age, religious, geographic, or ethnic microcultures.

Marketing to consumers in North America must be done in an environment of multicultural diversity. Ethnic groups may be formed around nationality, religion, physical attributes, or geographic location. Major microcultures in North America include Native Americans, Asian Americans, African Americans, Latinos, and French Canadians.

Another type of microculture is defined by social class. Social classes are relatively permanent and homogeneous groupings of people in society, permitting them to be compared with one another. For marketers, the most important determinants of social class are usually considered to be occupation, personal performance, interactions, possessions, value orientations, and class consciousness.

Social classes in the United States are traditionally divided into six groups: upper upper, lower upper, upper middle, lower middle, upper lower, and lower lower. Newer classification systems emphasize the enlarged capitalist or professional classes in the upper-middle or lower-lower classes. Each group displays characteristic values and behaviors that are useful to consumer analysts in designing marketing programs.

## Review and Discussion Questions

1. What is meant by the term *culture?* Why does this term create confusion about its meaning?
2. Where do consumers get their values?
3. Examine the American core values described in this chapter. Consider how they are changing, what might influence them, and how they might influence a marketer of consumer electronics products.
4. Select the topic of family, religious institutions, or schools, and prepare a report documenting the changes that are occurring in the institution you chose.
5. Describe values of the various age cohorts. What appeals or methods of marketing are likely to be effective with various market segments?
6. Select one of the dimensions of culture identified by Hofstede, and describe how it might be used in market segmentation.
7. Are there really differences between the consumption patterns of black and white individuals? Explain your answer.
8. Asian Americans still represent a small proportion of the total population of the United States. Why should they be given much importance in marketing research and strategies? What types of adaptations should be made to a marketing plan to reach Asian Americans?
9. Describe some influences of the Latino culture on the American macroculture.
10. Assume that the American Cancer Society wanted to target the Hispanic population with a campaign about the importance of cancer screenings and early detection. What types of recommendations would you make for reaching this market effectively?
11. What variables determine an individual's social class? In what order of importance should they be ranked?
12. In what way does income relate to social class? Why is it used so infrequently as an indicator of social class? What should be its proper value as an indicator?
13. A marketing researcher is speculating on the influence of the upper classes on the consumption decisions of the lower classes for the following products: automobiles, food, clothing, and baby-care products. What conclusions would you expect for each of these products? Describe a research project that could be used to answer this question.

Chapter Summary

14. In what social class would you place professional athletes? Actors and actresses?

15. What's your opinion on Consumer Behavior and Marketing 11.2? Should consumers' religious views be allowed to affect product selection and marketing by firms such as Wal*Mart?

## Notes

[1] Harry C. Triandis, "Cross-Cultural Studies of Individualism and Collectivism," in John Berman, ed., *Nebraska Symposium on Motivation* (Lincoln: University of Nebraska Press, 1989), 41–133.

[2] Hazel Rose Markus and Shinobu Kitayama, "Culture and the Self: Implications for Cognition, Emotion, and Motivation," *Psychological Review*, 98 (March, 1991), 224–253.

[3] Grant McCracken, "Culture and Consumption: A Theoretical Account of the Structure and Movement of the Cultural Meaning of Consumer Goods," *Journal of Consumer Research*, 13 (June 1986), 71–81.

[4] Melanie Wallendorf and M. Reilly, "Distinguishing Culture of Origin from Culture of Residence," in R. Bagozzi and A. Tybout, eds., *Advances in Consumer Research*, 10 (Association for Consumer Research, 1983), 699–701.

[5] Dana L. Alden, Jan-Benedict E. M. Steenkamp, and Rajeev Batra, "Brand Positioning through Advertising in Asia, North America and Europe: The Role of Global Consumer Culture," *Journal of Marketing*, 63 (January 1999), 75–87.

[6] Daniel Liechty, *The Ernest Becker Reader* (Seattle: University of Washington Press, 2005), 166.

[7] Alden, Steenkamp, and Batra, "Brand Positioning through Advertising in Asia, North America and Europe."

[8] James H. Leigh and Terrance G. Gabel, "Symbolic Interactionism: Its Effects on Consumer Behavior and Implications for Marketing Strategy," *Journal of Consumer Marketing*, 9 (Winter 1992), 27–38.

[9] Matt Moffett and Nikhil Deogun, "Brazilians Like Coke, But What They Love to Drink Is Guarana," *Wall Street Journal* (July 8, 1999), A1.

[10] Phillip R. Harris and Robert I. Moran, *Managing Cultural Differences* (Houston: Gulf Publishing Company, 1987), 190–195.

[11] P. Valette-Florence and A. Jolibert, "Social Values, A.I.O., and Consumption Patterns," *Journal of Business Research*, 20 (March 1990), 109–122.

[12] Zenap Gurgan-Canli and Duraijaj Maheswaran, "Cultural Variations in Country of Origin Effects," *Journal of Marketing Research*, 37 (August 2000), 309–318.

[13] Donnel Briley, Michael Morris, and Itamar Simonson, "Reasons as Carriers of Culture: Dynamic versus Dispositional Models of Cultural Influence on Decision Making," *Journal of Consumer Research*, 27 (September 2000), 157–179.

[14] Gregory M. Rose, "Consumer Socialization, Parental Style, and Developmental Timetables in the United States and Japan," *Journal of Marketing*, 63 (July 1999), 105–109.

[15] George P. Moschis, *Consumer Socialization* (Lexington, MA: Lexington Books, 1987), 9.

[16] Coreen Bailor, "The Young and the Rich: The New Thrifty," *Destination CRM* (February 9, 2005).

[17] Sharon Zukin, *Point of Purchases: How Shopping Changed American Culture* (New York: Routledge, 2003).

[18] Roger Blackwell, "Miele," in Roger D. Blackwell, Kristina S. Blackwell, and W. Wayne Talarzyk, *Contemporary Cases in Consumer Behavior* (Hinsdale, IL: Dryden Press, 1993), 452–462.

[19] Johny Johansson and Ikujiro Nonaka, *Relentless: The Japanese Way of Marketing* (New York: HarperBusiness, 1996).

[20] R. Bruce Money, Mary C. Gilly, and John L. Graham, "Explorations of National Culture and Word of Mouth Referral Behavior in the Purchase of Industrial Services in the United States and Japan," *Journal of Marketing* (October 1998), 76–87.

[21] Angela da Rocha, Rebecca Arkader, and Antonio Barretto, "On Networks and Bonds: A Cultural Analysis of the Nature of Relationships," in David W. Cravens and Peter R. Dickson, eds., *Enhancing Knowledge Development in Marketing* (Chicago: American Marketing Association, 1993), 92–96.

[22] William Taylor, "Crime? Greed? Big Ideas? What Were the '80s About?" *Harvard Business Review* (January/February 1992), 32–45.

[23] Foo Nin Ho, Scott J. Vitell, James H. Barnes, and Rene Desborde, "Ethical Correlates of Role Conflict and Ambiguity in Marketing: The Mediating Role of Cognitive Moral Development," *Journal of the Academy of Marketing Science* (Spring 1997), 117–126.

[24] Charles H. Schwepker, O. C. Ferrell, Thomas N. Ingram, "The Influence of Ethical Climate and Ethical Conflict on Role Stress in the Sales Force," *Journal of the Academy of Marketing Science* (Spring 1997), 99–108.

[25] Kristol De Wulf, Gaby Odekerken-Schroeder and Dawn Iacobucci, "Investments in Consumer Relationships: A Cross-Industry Exploration," *Journal of Marketing*, 65 (October 2001), 33–51.

[26] Joseph T. Plummer, "Changing Values," *Futurist* 23 (January/February 1989), 8–13.

[27] Sheena Ashford and Noel Timms, *What Europe Thinks: A Study of Western European Values* (Aldershot: Dartmouth, 1992).

[28] Jennifer Aaker, "Accessibility or Diagnosticity? Disentangling the Influence of Culture on Persuasion Processes and Attitudes," *Journal of Consumer Research*, 26 (March 2000), 340–358.

[29] "One Nation, Under God?" *American Demographics* (January 2002), 16.

30 Pamela Paul, "Religious Identity and Mobility," *American Demographics* (March 2003), 20–21.

31 Ibid.

32 Richard Cimino and Don Lattin, "Choosing My Religion," *American Demographics* (April 1999), 62–65.

33 David B. Wolfe, "The Psychological Center of Gravity," *American Demographics* (April 1998), 16.

34 Louise Witt, "Whose Side is God On? *American Demographics* (February 2004), 18–19.

35 "A Measure of Success," *American Demographics* (April 1999), 9.

36 Cathleen Falsani, "Nothing Phony about Madonna's Spiritual Journey," *Chicago Sun-Times* (September 17, 2004).

37 Jon Fine, "How a 'Pyromarketing' Campaign Sold over 21 Million Books," www.adage.com (March 1, 2005).

38 Norval D. Glenn, *Cohort Analysis* (Beverly Hills, CA: Sage Publications, 1977).

39 John Robinson and Nicholas Zill, "Matters of Culture," *American Demographics* (September 1997), 24.

40 Ibid.

41 Christopher Reynolds, "Up on the Envy Meter," *American Demographics* (June 2004), 6–7.

42 Stephanie Noble and Charles Schewe, "Cohort Segmentation: An Exploration of its Validity," *Journal of Business Research*, 56 (December 2003), 979–987.

43 Gert Hofstede, "Culture's Consequences: International Differences in Work-Related Values" (Beverly Hills, CA: Sage Publications, 1984).

44 Roger P. McIntyre, Martin S. Meloche, and Susan L. Lewis, "National Culture as a Macro Tool for Environmental Sensitivity Segmentation," in David Cravens and Peter Dickson, eds., *Enhancing Knowledge Development in Marketing* (Chicago: American Marketing Association, 1993), 153–159.

45 Joel Garreau, *The Nine Nations of North America* (Boston: Houghton Mifflin, 1981).

46 Reynolds "Up on the Envy Meter."

47 Martin Wolk, "Brand Names Split along Red-Blue Lines," www.msnbc.com (January 19, 2005).

48 Walter McDougal, *Freedom Just Around the Corner: A New American History, 1585–1828* (New York: Harper/Collins, 2004).

49 "Month's 10 Most-Liked, Most Recalled TV Spots," www.adage.com (March 7, 2005).

50 David Ellis, "Benetton Ads: A Risque Business," *Time* (March 25, 1991), 13.

51 Seymour M. Lipset, *North American Cultures: Values and Institutions in Canada and the United States* (Orono, ME: Borderlands, 1990), 6.

52 Rohit Deshpande, Wayne D. Hoyer, and Naveen Donthu, "The Intensity of Ethnic Affiliation: A Study of the Sociology of Hispanic Consumption," *Journal of Consumer Research*, 13 (September 1986), 214–219.

53 Elizabeth C. Hirschman, "An Examination of Ethnicity and Consumption Using Free Response Data," in *AMA Educators' Conference Proceedings* (Chicago: American Marketing Association, 1982), 84–88.

54 Johanna Zmud and Carolos Arce, "The Ethnicity and Consumption Relationship," in John F. Sherry Jr., and Brian Sternthal, eds., *Diversity in Consumer Behavior* (Provo, UT: Association for Consumer Research, 1992), 443–449.

55 Edith McArthur, "What Language Do You Speak?" *American Demographics* (October 1984), 32–33.

56 Nathan Caplan, John K. Whitmore, and Marcella H. Choy, *The Boat People and Achievement in America: A Study of Family Life, Hard Work, and Cultural Values* (Ann Arbor, MI: University of Michigan Press, 1989).

57 Donnel Briley and Robert Wyer Jr., "The Effect of Group Membership Salience on the Avoidance of Negative Outcomes: Implications for Social and Consumer Decisions," *Journal of Consumer Research*, 29 (December 2002), 400–416.

58 Douglas W. LaBahn and Katrin R. Harich, "Sensitivity to National Business Culture: Effects on U.S.–Mexican Channel Relationship Performance," *Journal of International Marketing*, 5 (Winter 1997), 29–51.

59 Lisa Penaloza and Mary C. Gilly, "Marketer Acculturation: The Changer and the Changed," *Journal of Marketing* 63 (July 1999), 84–104.

60 Shelly Reese, "When Whites Aren't a Mass Market," *American Demographics* (March 1997), 51–54.

61 Ibid.

62 Mark Forehand and Rohit Deshpande, "What We See Makes Us Who We Are: Priming Ethnic Self-Awareness and Advertising Response," *Journal of Marketing Research*, 38 (August 2001), 336–349.

63 William O'Hare, "Managing Multiple-Race Data," *American Demographics* (April 1998), 42–44.

64 Christy Fisher, "It's All in the Details," *American Demographics* (April 1998), 45–47.

65 Juan Faura, "Transcultural Marketing No Longer an Afterthought," *Marketing News* (January 4, 1999), 16.

66 Reynolds Farley and Suzanne M. Bianchi, "The Growing Gap between Blacks," *American Demographics* (July 1983), 15–18.

67 Jerome D. Williams, "Reflections of a Black Middle-Class Consumer: Caught between Two Worlds or Getting the Best of Both?" in Sherry and Sternthal, *Diversity in Consumer Behavior*, 850–855.

68 Cyndee Miller, "Research on Black Consumers," *Marketing News* (September 13, 1993), 1ff.

69 Mark Green, *Invisible People: The Depiction of Minorities in Magazine Ads and Catalogs* (New York: City of New York Department of Consumer Affairs, 1991).

70 Tommy E. Whittler, "The Effects of Actors' Race in Commercial Advertising: Review and Extension," *Journal of Advertising*, 20 (September 1991), 54–60; Tommy E. Whittler and Joan DiMeo, "Viewers' Reactions to Racial Cues in Advertising Stimuli," *Journal of Advertising Research*, 31 (December 1991), 37–46.

71 "Affluence Is at Record Level," *American Demographics Magazine Supplement* (November 1999), 8.

72 Chris Sandlund, "There's a New Face to America," *Success* (April 1999), 40.

73 Susan Thea Posnock, "The Color of the Magazine Industry," *Folio Magazine* (January 5, 2004).

74 William O'Hare, "Blacks and Whites: One Market or Two?" *American Demographics* (March 1987), 44–48.

75 Nancy Ten Kate, "Black Children More Likely to Live with One Parent," *American Demographics* (February 1991), 11.

76 A collection of articles on this topic is found in Harriette Pipies McAdoo, ed., *Black Families* (Newbury Park, CA: Sage Publications, 1988).

77 William J. Qualls and David J. Moore, "Stereotyping Effects on Consumers' Evaluation of Advertising: Impact of Racial Difference between Actors and Viewers," *Psychology and Marketing*, 7 (Summer 1990), 135–151.

78 Frank McCoy, "Rethinking the Cost of Discrimination," *Black Enterprise*, 24 (January 1994), 54–59.

79 David Crockett and Melanie Wallendorf, "The Role of Normative Political Ideology in Consumer Behavior," *Journal of Consumer Research*, 31 (December 2004), 511–519.

80 Raymond A. Bauer and Scott M. Cunningham, *Studies in the Negro Market* (Cambridge, MA: Marketing Science Institute, 1970). See also Donald Sexton, "Black Buyer Behavior," *Journal of Marketing*, 36 (October 1972), 36–39.

81 Thomas E. Ness and Melvin T. Stith, "Middle-Class Values in Blacks and Whites," in Robert E. Pitts Jr. and Arch G. Woodside, *Personal Values and Consumer Psychology* (Lexington, MA: Lexington Books, 1984), 255–270.

82 Parke Gibson, *$70 Billion in the Black* (New York: Macmillan, 1978); B. G. Yovovich, "The Debate Rages On: Marketing to Blacks," *Advertising Age* (November 29, 1982), M-10; David Astor, "Black Spending Power: $140 Billion and Growing," *Marketing Communications* (July 1982), 13–18; P. A. Robin-son, C. P. Rao, and S. C. Mehta, "Historical Perspectives of Black Consumer Research in the United States: A Critical Review," in C. T. Tan and J. Sheth, eds., *Historical Perspectives in Consumer Research* (Singapore: National University of Singapore, 1985), 46–50.

83 Jake Holden, "The Ring of Truth," *American Demographics* (October 1998), 14.

84 Ibid.

85 "Black Newspapers Push Kohl's Boycott over Lack of Advertising," *Milwaukee Journal-Sentinel,* March 9, 2005.

86 Patti Williams and Jennifer Aaker, "Can Mixed Emotions Peacefully Coexist?" *Journal of Consumer Research*, 28 (March 2002), 636–650.

87 United States Bureau of Citizenship and Immigration Services, United States Department of Homeland Security, www.uscis.gov, most recent data for 2003.

88 Wendy Manning and William O'Hare, "Asian-American Businesses," *American Demographics* (August 1988), 35–39.

89 William O'Hare, "Reaching for the Dream," *American Demographics* (January 1992), 32–36.

90 Ivan Light and Edna Bonacich, *Immigrant Entrepreneurs: Koreans in Los Angeles, 1965–1982* (Los Angeles: University of California Press, 1988).

91 Dan Fost, "California's Asian Market," *American Demographics* (October 1990), 34–37.

92 Cyndee Miller, "Hot Asian-American Market Not Starting Much of a Fire Yet," *Marketing News* (January 21, 1991), 12.

93 Marcia Mogelonsky, "Watching in Tongues," *American Demographics* (April 1998), 48–52.

94 Chris Sandlund, "There's a New Face to America," *Success* (April 1999), 44.

95 Joel Kotkin, "Selling to the New America," *Inc.* (July 1987), 46–47.

96 Geraldine Fennel, Joel Saegert, Francis Piron, and Rosemary Jimenez, "Do Hispanics Constitute a Market Segment?" in Sherry and Sternthal, *Diversity in Consumer Behavior*, 28–33.

97 Humberto Valencia, "Hispanic Values and Subcultural Research," *Journal of the Academy of Marketing Science*, 17 (Winter 1989), 23–28; Van R. Wood and Roy Howell, "A Note on Hispanic Values and Subcultural Research: An Alternative View," *Journal of the Academy of Marketing Science,* 19 (Winter 1991), 61–67.

98 Quandary over One Term to Cover Myriad People," *Wall Street Journal* (January 18, 1994), B1.

99 Daniel Yankelovich, *Spanish USA* (New York: Yankelovich, Skelly & White, 1981). See also the reports on a repetition in 1984 of the same study in "Homogenized Hispanics," *American Demographics* (February 1985), 16.

100 Yankelovich, *Spanish USA.*

101 "Soccer Plays to Growing Hispanic Market," *Population Today* (April 1999), 5.

102 Lisa Penaloza Alaniz and Marcy C. Gilly, "The Hispanic Family-Consumer Research Issues," *Psychology and Marketing* (Winter 1986), 291–303.

103 Helene Stapinski, "Generacion Latino," *American Demographics* (July 1999), 65.

104 "Latino Pentecostals," *PBS Religion and Ethics Newsweekly* (March 18, 2005).

105 "Latino Mormons Grow in Numbers Nationwide," *Ventura County Star,* (March 7, 2005).

106 Ibid.

107 Lisa Jones Townsel, "Cosmetics Go Ethnic," *St. Louis Post-Dispatch* (August 26, 1997), C8.

108 Laurel Wentz, "Target Broadens Hispanic Marketing Efforts," www.adage.com (February 28, 2005).

109 Marcia Mogelonsky, "Watching in Tongues," *American Demographics* (April 1998), 48–52.

110 Laurel Wentz, "Big Markets Get It Wrong with Hispanic Websites," www.adage.com (February 24, 2005).

111 Luiz Diaz-Altertini, "Brand-Loyal Hispanics Need Good Reason for Switching," *Advertising Age* (April 16, 1979), SX–23.

112 Cynthia Webster, "The Effects of Hispanic Subcultural Identification on Information Search Behavior," *Journal of Advertising Research*, 32 (September/October 1992), 54–62.

113 Robert E. Wilkes and Humberto Valencia, "Shopping-Related Characteristics of Mexican-Americans and Blacks," *Psychology and Marketing*, 3 (Winter 1986), 247–259.

114 Joel Saegert, Robert J. Hoover, and Marye Tharp Hilger, "Characteristics of Mexican American Consumers," *Journal of Consumer Research*, 12 (June 1985), 104–109.

115 Humberto Valencia, "Point of View: Avoid Hispanic Market Blunders," *Journal of Advertising Research*, 23 (January 1984), 19–22.

116 Jim Sondheim, Rodd Rodriquez, Richard Dillon, and Richard Parades, "Hispanic Market: The Invisible Giant," *Advertising Age* (April 16, 1979), S-20. See also Martha Frase-Blunt, "Who Watches Spanish Language TV?" *Hispanic* (November 1991), 26–27.

117 T. Bettina Cornewell and Alan David Bligh, "Complaint Behavior of Mexican-American Consumers to a Third-Party Agency," *Journal of Consumer Affairs*, 25 (Summer 1991), 1–18.

118 Statistics Canada, www.statcan.ca (March 2005).

119 Pierre C. Lefrancois and Giles Chatel, "The French-Canadian Consumer: Fact and Fancy," in J. S. Wright and J. L. Goldstrucker, eds., *New Ideas for Successful Marketing* (Chicago: American Marketing Association, 1966), 705–717; Bernard Blishen, "Social Class and Opportunity in Canada," *Canadian Review of Sociology and Anthropology*, 7 (May 1970), 110–127.

120 Robert Tamilia, "Cross-Cultural Advertising Research: A Review and Suggested Framework," in Ronald C. Curhan, ed., *1974 Combined Proceedings of the AMA* (Chicago: American Marketing Association, 1974), 131–134.

121 David Luna and Laura Peracchio, "Moderators of Language Effects in Advertising to Bilinguals: A Psycholinguistic Approach," *Journal of Consumer Research*, 28 (September 2001), 284–296.

122 Daniel W. Rossides, *Social Stratification* (Englewood Cliffs, NJ: Prentice-Hall, 1990).

123 Max Weber, in H. H. Gard and C. Wright Mills, eds., *From Max Weber: Essays in Sociology* (New York: Oxford University Press, 1946), 193.

124 Excerpts from Kenneth Labich, "Class in America," *Fortune* (February 7, 1994), 114–126.

125 Stephen L. Nock, "Social Origins as Determinants of Family Social Status" (paper presented to the Mid-South Sociological Association, 1980).

126 Reprinted with permission of Wadsworth, Inc., from Dennis Gilbert and Joseph A. Kahl, *The American Class Structure: A New Synthesis*, 3rd ed. (1982). Although not cited in each instance, this excellent book has influenced the content of this chapter in numerous other points.

127 Robert Cage, "Spending Differences across Occupational Fields," *Monthly Labor Review*, 112 (December 1989), 33–43.

128 David H. Demo and Ritch C. Savin-Williams, "Early Adolescent Self-Esteem as a Function of Social Class," *American Journal of Sociology*, 88 (November 1983), 763–773; Viktor Gecas and Monica A. Seff, "Social Class and Self-Esteem: Psychological Centrality, Compensation, and the Relative Effects of Work and Home," *Social Psychology Quarterly*, 53 (1990), 165–173.

129 Elizabeth C. Hirschman, "Secular Immortality and the American Ideology of Affluence," *Journal of Consumer Research*, 17 (June 1990), 31–42.

130 Michael Useem and S. M. Miller, "The Upper Class in Higher Education," *Social Policy*, 7 (January/February 1977), 28–31.

131 W. Lloyd Warner, *Social Class in America: A Manual of Procedure for the Measurement of Social Status* (New York: Harper, 1960).

132 The Gilbert-Kahl estimates are also accepted in Daniel W. Rossides, *Social Stratification* (Englewood Cliffs, NJ: Prentice-Hall, 1990), 406–408. Class publications that even today are still valuable reading for consumer analysts include Pierre Martineau, "Social Classes and Spending Behavior," *Journal of Marketing*, 23 (October 1958), 121–130; Sidney Levy, "Social Class and Consumer Behavior," in Joseph W. Newman, ed., *On Knowing the Consumer* (New York: Wiley, 1966), 146–160; Richard R. Coleman and Bernice L. Neugarten, *Social Status in the City* (San Francisco: Jossey-Bass, 1971).

133 Natalya Prusakova, "Dress to Impress," *Business in the USSR* (December 1991), 90–93.

134 Andrea Tyree and Robert W. Hodge, "Five Empirical Landmarks," *Social Forces*, 56 (March 1978), 761–769. Some of the methodological issues in these studies are discussed in C. Matthew Snipp, "Occupational Mobility and Social Class: Insights from Men's Career Mobility," *American Sociological Review*, 50 (August 1985), 475–492.

135 John R. Snarey and George E. Vaillant, "How Lower- and Working-Class Youth Become Middle-Class Adults: The Association between Ego Defense Mechanisms and Upward Social Mobility," *Child Development*, 56 (1985), 904–908.

136 Ivan D. Chase, "A Comparison of Men's and Women's Intergenerational Mobility in the United States," *American Sociological Review*, 40 (August 1975), 483–505.

137 Hirschman, "Secular Immortality and the American Ideology of Affluence."

138 Kenneth Labich, "Class in America," *Fortune* (February 7, 1994), 114–126.

139 Jaclyn Fierman, "The High-Living Middle Class," *Fortune* (April 13, 1987), 27.

140 Anne Brumbaugh, "Source and Non-Source Cues in Advertising and Their Effects on the Activation of Cultural and Subcultural Knowledge on the Route to Persuasion," *Journal of Consumer Research*, 29 (September 2002), 258–270.

# Chapter 12

# Family and Household Influences

## Opening Vignette

"We are Family!" If reading that phrase brings to mind a song by the same title, you already understand one of the most important realities about families and their influence on consumer behavior. Families are just not what they used to be—a fact disclosed in a type of consumer research called **content analysis,** which examines *how communicated messages reflect people's attitudes and beliefs.* To get a better understanding of how American families have changed the past few decades, let's look at how they're portrayed in one of the most influential media—television.

Go back to the 1950s and there's no question as to which family member influenced decision making on *Father Knows Best.* In the 1960s, the most important influence was visible as June Cleaver shaped the minds of her kids and everyone else on *Leave It to Beaver.* Both *Beaver* and *Father Knows Best* were described in their day as "reality" shows, depicting a father at work (earning a wage) and a mother taking care of the home and children—a reality for most American families in the 1950s and 1960s.

In the early 1970s, America was exposed to a new reality—blended families—with shows like *The Brady Bunch* depicting a family consisting of a man and woman, each with children from a previous marriage, reflecting the reality of at least 20 to 30 percent of U.S. families at that time. About the same time, the Partridge Family

hit the airwaves with another new reality— a fatherless family of six who decided to form a rock band and tour the country in a psychedelically painted school bus, under the leadership of "supermom" Shirley Partridge (Shirley Jones).

The 1970s TV show that forced America to face a different view of reality was *All in the Family,* which pioneered a new brand of realistic, frank satire based on real-world social issues, from the perspective of blue-collar worker Archie Bunker. Bigoted, opinionated, and uneducated, Archie made no bones about his racial and political views, reflecting every negative stereotype imaginable. Archie was the king of his world, casting judgment from his easy chair throne with supermarket beer in hand. Catering to Archie's every whim was his faithful wife, homemaker Edith, who was the peacemaker—always looking on the bright side, soothing over feelings hurt by Archie. "Too Good Edith" never complained, continuing to serve Archie and others even when she was grappling with illness—a detail she didn't want to bother Archie with on the final episode. Edith, the epitome of the "1950s housewife," and Archie, the chauvinistic "man of the house," were cast as relics of times past— challenged by equality, inclusion, feminism, and other new ideals introduced by daughter Gloria and son-in-law Michael.

The 1980s saw the forerunner of the new American "family"—not a family in the traditional meaning, but rather a close group of acquaintances who gathered in an intimate Boston pub named *Cheers* ("where everybody knows your name"). Although the characters of *Cheers* all had families outside the bar, including the heavyset beer-adoring Norm Peterson's wife Vera and the jovial aging postman Cliff Claven's mother (who he still lived with), these characters were not a part of the cast. In fact, Vera never appeared on the show, although Norm spoke often of his adoration of her—telling us that she has a face like Ed Asner, that they sleep in different rooms, and that their sex life is nonexistent. *Cheers* began to earn high ratings during its third season (1984–1985), when NBC placed it in its Thursday night primetime lineup with two other shows about families: *Family Ties* and *The Cosby Show.*

*Cheers* paved the way for the decade of the 1990s, and the growing reality that family functions were increasingly performed by *Friends,* a group of twenty-somethings who lived together and shared closer relationships than the families in which they were born. The 1990s and early 2000s had a few other famous TV families, including the *Simpsons,* the *Sopranos,* and a retired widower living with his son on *Frasier.* In 2005, there aren't many television families like the Bunkers, the Bradys, or the Andersons in *Father Knows Best,* but there are plenty of *Desperate Housewives.*

Source: Fifty years of watching television—and the help of websites celebrating the shows described above.

---

Who or what is a family? The definition has changed over the past fifty years, and not just on television, as you'll see in this chapter. If people were paying close attention to *Lassie,* perhaps they would have realized what firms like PETsMART and Mars (maker of Pedigree dog food) assert in their marketing strategies: "Pets are family, too." A generation ago, dogs slept in backyard doghouses or on tattered blankets on the porch, but today, dogs sleep in specially constructed indoor dog "palaces," sometimes furnished with satin pillows and linens. They receive holiday gifts and watch their owners spend over $36 billion a year on products and services. Even trips to veterinarians, who are often more customer-centric than medical doctors, result in total pampering. According to the American Pet Products Manufacturers Association, Americans now own more than 236 million dogs, cats, reptiles, birds, fish, and small animals, with 56 percent of all households owning a pet and 61 percent of all pet-owning households having no children at home. Animals may be expensive, but they're still cheaper than children. Look at Figure 12.1 and you'll probably conclude that for some consumers, pets rule families and their decisions.

FIGURE 12.1 When It Comes to Holiday Gift Giving, Dogs Are Family Members, Too

## The Importance of Families and Households on Consumer Behavior

If you were in charge of marketing breakfast cereal, to whom would you direct your advertising campaign? Is it mothers, fathers, teens, children, or some combination of family members? Kix cereal in the United States appeals to both children (by tasting good) and mothers (by being nutritious), thus deserving its tagline, "Kid tested, mother approved." The importance of the family or household unit in consumer behavior arises for two reasons: (1) many products are purchased by a family unit; and (2) individual buying decisions may be heavily influenced by other family members.

How families or households make purchase decisions depends on the roles of various family members in the purchase, consumption, and influence of products. Products such as milk and toothpaste may be purchased by one person but consumed by the entire household, whereas personal care items such as cosmetics or shaving cream are often purchased by an individual family member for his or her own personal consumption. Homes and cars, on the other hand, are often purchased by both partners, perhaps with involvement from children or members of the extended family. As one researcher[1] explains, "A husband may buy a station wagon, given the reality of having to transport four children, despite his strong preference for a sports car," and a father may ask his daughter or son about colors and options before he and his wife purchase a car the entire family might use. Visits to shopping malls may involve multiple family members buying clothing and accessories simultaneously, often influencing each other's decisions—children may buy clothing paid for and approved of by parents, whereas teenagers may influence the clothing purchases of a parent.

Regardless of how many family members are present when items are being purchased, the other family members play an important role in the purchase. For example, the parent of two young children who is responsible for buying food for the family may act as an individual in the market, but his or her decisions are still influenced by the preferences and power of other family members. Even when people live alone, they may prefer the same (or perhaps the opposite) style of furniture or brand of laundry detergent as the family in which they were raised. Although marketing communications are usually directed to individuals, marketers should consider the consumption circumstances and the family structure before deciding on specific communication or advertising methods to attract their target segment.[2]

### What Is a Family?

In spite of the realities described in the opening vignette, statistical data define a **family** as *a group of two or more persons related by blood, marriage, or adoption who reside together.* The **nuclear family** is *the immediate group of father, mother, and child(ren) living together.* The **extended family** is *the nuclear family, plus other relatives, such as grandparents, uncles and aunts, cousins, and parents-in-law.* The *family into which one is born* is called the **family of orientation,** whereas *the one established by marriage* is the **family of procreation.**

### What Is a Household?

The term **household** is used to describe *all persons, both related and unrelated, who occupy a housing unit.* There are significant differences between the terms *household* and *family,* even though they are sometimes used interchangeably. Distinguishing between these terms when examining data is important, because the average family size is 3.14 people and household size is 2.59 people.

Households are becoming a more important unit of analysis for marketers because of the rapid growth in nontraditional families and nonfamily households. Among non-family households, many are single adults living alone (25.8 percent of all households in the 2000 census). The remaining nonfamily households include those consisting of elderly people living with nonfamily members, persons of opposite sex sharing living quarters, friends living together, and same-sex couples. Any of these households may or may not include children. Families are the largest category of households (68 percent in the 2000 census), but nonfamily households are the fastest growing. One way to avoid the question of whether to study families or households is to simply use the term *consumer unit* (CU) or *minimal household unit* (MHU) in describing buying behavior.[3]

## Structural Variables Affecting Families and Households

Family or household variables affect consumer purchasing. **Structural variables** include the *age of the head of household or family, marital status, presence of children, and employment status*. For example, consumer analysts have enormous interest in whether families have children and how many they have. Children increase family demand for clothing, food, furniture, homes, medical care, and education, and children decrease demand for many discretionary items, including travel, higher-priced restaurants, and adult clothing.

## Sociological Variables Affecting Families and Households

Marketers can understand family and household decisions better by examining the sociological dimensions of how families make consumer decisions. Three **sociological variables** that help explain how families function include *cohesion, adaptability, and communication.*

- **Cohesion** is *the emotional bonding between family members*. It measures how close family members feel to one another. Cohesion reflects a sense of connectedness to or separateness from other family members.
- **Adaptability** measures *the ability of a family to change its power structure, role relationships, and relationship rules in response to situational and developmental stress*. The degree of adaptability shows how well a family can meet the challenges presented by changing situations.
- **Communication** is *a facilitating dimension, critical to movement on the other two dimensions*. Positive communication (such as empathy, reflective listening, and supportive comments) enables family members to share their changing needs as they relate to cohesion and adaptability. Negative communication (such as double messages, double binds, and criticism) minimizes the ability to share feelings, thereby restricting movement in the dimensions of cohesion and adaptability. Understanding whether family members are satisfied with family purchases requires communication within the family.[4]

## Family Celebrations and Gift Giving

Marketers frequently reference sociological research on "resilient" families—those that emphasize time spent together through family traditions, rituals, and celebrations. Not only are resilient families better able to deal with transitions and tragedies,

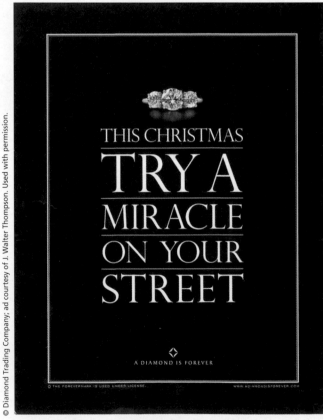

**FIGURE 12.2** Marketers appeal to the different ways market segments celebrate the holidays

they also affect consumer demand for many products.[5] Family celebrations help families survive crises and fuel retail sales, with Hanukkah and Christmas generating 50 percent or more of yearly sales[6] (and an even higher percentage of profits) for many retailers. Today gift giving and family holidays are an important area of study,[7] with Halloween becoming the second most popular holiday in the United States in terms of retail sales of gifts and home decorations—two consumer behavior activities that convey a family's holiday spirit.[8] Other holidays that are being celebrated more frequently than in the past include Cinco de Mayo (among Mexican Americans), Kwanzaa (among African Americans), and Chinese New Year. Retail promotions that were once focused exclusively on the traditional December holidays are increasingly starting on Super Bowl Sunday or Valentine's Day and continuing throughout the year.

Changes in family and household structures can be blamed in part for the decline in traditional holiday spending as well as shifts to other holidays throughout the year celebrated more with friends. Greater numbers of divorced parents may force children to spend holidays between two households, taking some of the joy out of the celebrations and making the physical movement of large gifts difficult,

FIGURE 12.2 (Continued)

thus increasing sales of gift certificates, gift cards, and Internet gift purchases. When households have fewer children, fewer gifts need to be purchased. Members of affluent families may buy items when they want rather than wait until a holiday to receive them as gifts, meaning it's difficult for family members to buy gifts for one another because many consumers (especially forty-five- to sixty-year-olds) already have most everything they want.[9] Some families react to the commercialization of the holidays by reestablishing the religious or familial meaning of traditions and celebrations—perhaps buying a real Christmas tree instead of an artificial tree, as you read in Consumer Behavior and Marketing 10.3 and as you will learn in the case about the National Christmas Tree Association at the end of this book.

Advertisements that relate holiday spending to consumer behavior are shown in Figure 12.2.

## Who Determines What the Family Buys?

Families use products even though individuals usually buy them. Determining what products should be bought at which retail outlet, how and when products are used, and who should buy them is a complicated process involving a variety of roles and actors.

### Role Behavior

Families and other groups exhibit what are known as instrumental and expressive role behaviors. **Instrumental roles,** also known as functional or economic roles, involve *financial, performance, and other functions performed by group members.* **Expressive roles** involve *supporting other family members in the decision-making process and expressing the family's aesthetic or emotional needs, including upholding family norms.* How individual family members perform each of these roles may influence how family income gets allocated to different types of products or retailers. These roles may be dynamic over time, depending upon spousal post-purchase satisfactions with previous decisions.[10]

## INDIVIDUAL ROLES IN FAMILY PURCHASES

Family consumption decisions involve at least five definable roles, which may be assumed by spouses, children, or other members of a household. Having both multiple roles and multiple actors is normal.

1. *Initiator or gatekeeper:* Initiator of family thinking about buying products and gathering information to aid the decision.

2. *Influencer:* Individual whose opinions are sought concerning criteria the family should use in purchases and which products or brands most likely fit those evaluative criteria.

3. *Decider:* The person with the financial authority or power to choose how the family's money will be spent and on which products or brands.

4. *Buyer:* The person who acts as the purchasing agent by visiting the store, calling suppliers, writing checks, bringing products into the home, and so on.

5. *User:* The person or persons who use the product.

Marketers need to communicate with consumers in each of these roles, remembering that different family members will assume different roles depending on the situation and product. Children, for example, are users of cereals, toys, clothing, and many other products although they may not be the buyers. One or both of the parents may be the decider and the buyer, although the children may be important as influencers and users. Parents may act as gatekeepers by preventing children from watching some television programs or attempting to negate television's influence. And those with the most expertise in an area may take on influencer roles.

**Family marketing** focuses on the relationships between family members based on the roles they assume, including the relationship between purchaser and family consumer and between purchaser and purchase decision maker. Family marketing differentiates scenarios in which some purchases might have more than one decision maker from those that have more than one consumer. Sometimes the purchaser and the consumer are the same person; sometimes they are different people. The family purchase decision-making process can be complex, but answering the following questions helps identify different purchaser-consumer relationships:

1. Who's buying for whom?

2. Who are the principal characters?

3. What's the plot for the purchase?

4. Who wants what when?

5. What can we assume? [11]

In the restaurant industry, the trend has been to focus on marketing to the family as a single unit.[12] Several decades ago, "going out for dinner" described a special night out for dating or married couples, but today it describes a typical evening's solution for eating dinner for many American families. A few days after the tragedy of September 11, 2001, sales soared at casual dining restaurants nationwide as families put a greater priority on spending quality time together. Restaurants are monitoring closely the changes occurring in the modern family, noting a trend toward "fast casual," which offers the convenience and speed of quick service restaurants (QSRs) but with upgraded and perhaps healthier food selections. Kroger (a national grocery chain) now offers freshly made, take-home pizzas in some stores, knowing that the pizzas appeal to the entire family. Likewise, Wild Oats Market (a chain of natural and organic food stores) offers a variety of foods in the home meal replacement (HMR) arena, providing a solution to singles who don't want to cook for one person and time-rushed families who don't have time to prepare meals from scratch.

Some fast-food chains like Wendy's and Chick-Fil-A appeal directly to health-conscious adults with salads and chicken sandwiches, but they also play to the "veto power" of children by creating an environment that is kid friendly with prizes, games, and special children's menus. These restaurants may not be the first choice of many kids, but children are unlikely to protest if their parents choose to take them there. By contrast, McDonald's has achieved much of its success by being kid focused—appealing directly to children who will influence their parents to visit Ronald McDonald and his playground. But how does McDonald's reach consumers in another part of the globe? With a Prosperity Burger, as you can see in Consumer Behavior and Marketing 12.1.

## SPOUSAL ROLES IN BUYING DECISIONS

Which spouse has greater influence in family buying decisions? How does this vary by product category, stage of decision-making process, and individual household? Generally, the following role structure categories are used to analyze these questions.

1. *Autonomic:* an equal number of decisions is made by each spouse, but each decision is individually made by one spouse or the other

2. *Husband dominant:* the husband or male head-of-household makes a majority of the decisions

3. *Wife dominant:* the wife or female head-of-household makes a majority of the decisions

4. *Joint* (syncratic): most decisions are made with equal involvement by both spouses

These categories are sometimes simplified to "husband more than wife," "wife more than husband," "both husband and wife," or simply "husband only" or "wife only." The type of product, stage in the decision process, and nature of circumstances surrounding the decision influences which situation exists. And keep in mind that the terms *husband* and *wife* apply to roles performed by members of the household and may exist even though the family members might not be married.

A landmark study investigating husband-wife influences conducted by Harry Davis and Benny Rigaux[13] is presented in a triangular configuration in Figure 12.3. Their findings have greatly influenced thinking about the relative influence of husbands and wives on decision making and the extent of role specialization. Are there some roles in family decision making that one spouse typically performs? The study seems to indicate yes, but you can apply some of the information examined throughout this text to identify how the roles of household members are changing.

### Influences on the Decision Process

How do husbands and wives perceive their relative influence on decision making across the decision stages? And what does this mean for marketers? Figure 12.3 shows how some product-service categories are traditionally wife dominant, including

## McDonald's Adapts to Asian Tastes

McDonald's is going regional in its Asian marketing, a first for the world's largest restaurant chain as it seeks economies of scale while appealing to local tastes in the battle for Asian palates. In nine countries from South Korea to Indonesia, McDonald's is rolling out the Prosperity Burger, a nod to the Lunar New Year celebrated with different holidays across the region. The campaign brings the same promotional spicy burger, as well as shared television advertisements, to all 2,200 restaurants around the region, outside of Japan.

The regional campaign is part of McDonald's struggle with a problem that vexes multinational marketers: Should advertising be local, global—or somewhere in between? McDonald's abandoned its long-standing strategy of creating independent advertising for each country when the company united all of its markets under the "I'm Lovin' It" theme (shown in Figure 1.5), which continues today, even in the prosperity campaign. But one-size-fits-all is a pickle in Asia, where ads that don't make sense across different cultures and tastes can translate into bad business. Even under "I'm Lovin' It," local Asian markets have continued to make some local ads, occasionally sharing resources—between Hong Kong and Taiwan, for example. The Asian prosperity campaign is McDonald's attempt to have its cake and eat it, too.

The challenge for McDonald's was to develop a single regional campaign that could work as well as past local ones. Only in greater China and its diaspora do consumers celebrate Chinese New Year. Rather than focusing on a particular celebration, McDonald's decided to focus on the consumer, looking for a universal human insight linking people that can transcend nationalities and borders.

Most Asian cultures mark the Lunar New Year with some event that looks toward good luck in the future. The resulting product: an ad featuring a boy who needs better luck fishing. His brother passes him a Prosperity Burger—which looks like a variation on the restaurant's McRib sandwich—and his fortunes change, culminating in the arrival of a computer-generated whale. After ad testing with each local market, numerous tweaks were made to the language, music, icons (e.g., firecrackers), and frequency of product shots.

The inspiration for the campaign came from Malaysia, a multiethnic country in Southeast Asia that includes large populations of Malays, Chinese, and Indians. McDonald's restaurants in Malaysia had been selling and marketing a version of the Prosperity Burger in recent years as a unified way to promote the season for customers who celebrated Chinese New Year as well as other holidays.

Another obstacle: McDonald's customers in markets like Korea and China don't physically look like the customers far away in the Philippines and Indonesia. Again, Malaysia provided an answer: McDonald's ad agency filmed and hired its cast there, emphasizing a spectrum of ethnicities.

Source: Excerpted from Geoffrey Fowler, "McDonald's Asian Marketing Takes on a Regional Approach," *Wall Street Journal* (January 26, 2005), 1.

women's clothing, children's clothing, and groceries. Two categories that are husband dominant are lawn mowers and hardware. Joint decisions tend to be made about vacations, televisions, refrigerators, and upholstered living room furniture. Autonomic decision making tends to be present in decisions about women's jewelry, men's leisure and business clothing, sporting equipment, lamps, toys and games, indoor paint and wallpaper, and luggage. By understanding where on this "map" the decision to buy particular products falls, marketers can begin to determine which product attributes

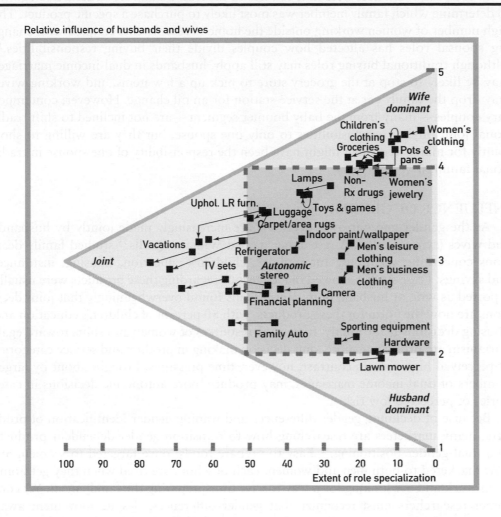

INFLUENCE BY DECISION STAGE

Spouses exert different degrees of influence when passing through the different stages of the decision-making process, as indicated in Figure 12.3 by the direction of the arrows, which shows the movement from information search to final decision. Movement may be minimal for many low-involvement goods and more pronounced for goods that are risky or have high involvement for the family. The decision process tends to move toward joint participation and away from autonomic behavior as a final decision nears. Movement is most pronounced for refrigerators, family automobiles, upholstered living room furniture, and carpets or rugs. Vacations are perhaps the most democratic of a family's purchase decisions.

The information search stage is more autonomic than joint when compared to final decisions. Marketing plans thus require specialized use of media having a strong appeal to husbands or wives rather than both. Product or store design must reflect the evaluative criteria of both husband and wife since consensus must be achieved in the final decision. Separate campaigns may be timed to coincide with specialized interests, especially for products with a long planning cycle.

## INFLUENCE OF EMPLOYMENT

In the past, marketers were able to refer to the traditional role structure categories to determine which family member was most likely to purchase a specific product. The high number of women working outside the home in recent years coupled with changing spousal roles has affected how couples divide their buying responsibilities.[14] Although traditional buying roles may still apply, husbands in dual-income marriages may be likely to stop at the grocery store to pick up a few items, and working wives may drop the family car at the service station for an oil change. However, contemporary couples—many from the baby boomer segment—are not inclined to shift traditional joint buying responsibilities to only one spouse, but they are willing to shop jointly for major items that might have been the responsibility of one spouse in traditional families.

## INFLUENCE OF GENDER

As the gender gap narrows, decisions are increasingly made jointly by husbands and wives (syncratically). A researcher named William Qualls[15] studied family decisions concerning vacations, automobiles, children's education, housing, insurance, and savings. Prior studies showed that decisions regarding these products were usually reported as wife or husband dominant. Qualls found overwhelmingly that joint decisions are now the norm for these products, with 80 percent of children's education and housing decisions made jointly. Increasing resources of women and shifts toward egalitarianism are producing more joint decision making in product and service categories of perceived high risk. In contrast, however, time pressures, brought about by larger numbers of dual-income marriages, may produce more autonomic decisions in categories of perceived low risk.

Because of declining gender differences and waning gender identification of products, many marketers are researching how to transition gender-dependent products to a dual-gender positioning.[16] Easy-to-prepare foods, once targeted to women, are now marketed to both men and women, each of whom are tired when they get home from work and are looking for a way to save time preparing the family meal. Yet consumer researchers must recognize that gender differences, despite movement away from sex role dominance, still exist for some products and in some situations,[17] such as personal care products. Literature reviews of these areas are available in Jenkins[18]; Bums and Granbois[19]; Gupta, Hagerty, and Myers[20]; and Roberts.[21] Although gender-related consumer behavior still exists, the roles are not determined by biological sex so much as the socialization experiences that teach men and women different consumer activities.[22] As you read the Family Furniture case at the end of this book, consider the possibility that consumers, especially younger ones, may be more androgynous. Education and career are important influences and, in an era when male and female consumers under age thirty have essentially the same educations and careers, gender roles in purchasing food and other products may be much more blurred than in the past, becoming what might be called the *androgynous consumer*.

## Family Life Cycles

Families pass through a *series of stages that change them over time*. This process historically has been called the **family life cycle** (FLC). The concept may need to be changed to **household life cycle** (HLC) or **consumer life cycle** (CLC) in the future to reflect changes in society. However, we will use the term FLC[23] to show how the life cycle affects consumer behavior.[24]

The traditional FLC describes family patterns as consumers marry, have children, leave home, lose a spouse, and retire. These stages are described in Table 12.1, along with consumer behaviors associated with each stage. But consumers don't necessarily have to pass through all these stages—they can skip multiple stages based on their lifestyle choices. When reviewing this information, think about how contemporary developments such as divorce, smaller family size, and delayed age of marriage affect the consumption activities of these stages.[25]

The family life cycle can be depicted graphically by using a curve similar to that of the product life cycle. Figure 12.4 shows how income, on average, changes during life and how saving behavior affects income in latter stages, demonstrating the point in Chapter 1 that what you have (wealth) is determined not so much by what you earn as it is by what you save, an axiom that greatly impacts your lifestyle when you retire. As household leaders enter their thirties and forties, often their income levels increase (because they begin to reach higher earning positions and their spouse is also working), but so do their spending levels (especially if they have children). This development decreases their disposable income during these life stages, making it more difficult for them to save money or splurge on luxury items. As the number of U.S. households headed by people between the ages of twenty-five and fifty declines in the next few years (remember Chapter 3?) and householders over age fifty increase, changes in life stage and family life cycle will affect the demand for products ranging from home furnishings to travel. Older consumers working for firms that have "quasi-retirement" programs may work instead of retiring to earn the income they failed to save in earlier years, and older baby boomers are increasingly doing short-term consulting and project work, sometimes for more pay and less stress than the corporate grind they left behind.[26]

Marketers use descriptions of these FLC stages when analyzing marketing and communication strategies for products and services, but the marketers often add additional information about consumer markets to analyze consumers' needs, identify niches, and develop consumer-specific marketing plans. Marketers can add socioeconomic data (such as income, employment status, financial well-being, and activities) to family life stages to improve predictions about product choices and help explain further consumer activities.[27]

The data resulting from this type of analysis permit a quantitative analysis of market sizes. Additional data can be collected concerning preferences, expenditures, and shopping behaviors of each segment to identify and help attract core customers in the life stage most profitable to the firm. With Generation Y choosing new spring break destinations such as Panama City and Daytona Beach over traditional venues like Ft. Lauderdale or Cancun, some older resorts are changing their marketing to target older consumers, hoping to replace college students with the students' parents, who probably have more money to spend and cause less disruption.[28] Keep in mind that life stage can be different for different consumers. For example, according to federal statistics, the number of older, second-generation fathers (men who remarry and have second families later in life) is growing.[29] Though these men may be in their fifties, their life stage is similar in many ways to that of a thirty-year-old father—paying for one child's day care but with the extra burden of paying for another child's wedding. The FLC helps explain how families change over time and, when modified with market data (including individuals' life stages), the FLC is useful in identifying core market targets. Reaching these markets may require a blend of new and old marketing tactics, including the "retro marketing" of Procter & Gamble described in Consumer Behavior and Marketing 12.2.

### Young singles (S)

Young singles may live alone, with their nuclear families, or with friends, or they may co-habitate with partners—translating into a wide range of how much disposable income is spent on furniture, rent, food, and other living expenses in this stage. Although earnings tend to be relatively low, these consumers usually don't have many financial obligations and don't feel the need to save for their futures or retirement. Many of them find themselves spending as much as they make on cars, furnishings for first residences away from home, fashions, recreation, alcoholic beverages, food away from home, vacations, and other products and services involved in the dating game. Some of these singles may have young children, forcing them to give up some discretionary spending for necessities such as day care and baby products.

### Newly married couples (NM)

Newly married couples without children are usually better off financially than they were when they were single, since they often have two incomes available to spend on one household. These families tend to spend a substantial amount of their incomes on cars, clothing, vacations, and other leisure activities. They also have the highest purchase rate and highest average purchases of durable goods (particularly furniture and appliances) and appear to be more susceptible to advertising.

### Full nest I (FN I)

With the arrival of the first child, parents begin to change their roles in the family, and decide if one parent will stay home to care for the child or if they will both work and buy daycare services. Either route usually leads to a decline in family disposable income and a change in how the family spends its income. In this stage, families are likely to move into their first homes; purchase furniture and furnishings for the child; buy a washer and dryer and home maintenance items; and purchase new items such as baby food, cough medicine, vitamins, toys, sleds, and skates. These requirements reduce families' ability to save, and the husband and wife are often dissatisfied with their financial position.

### Full nest II (FN II)

In this stage, the youngest child has reached school age, the employed spouse's income has improved, and the other spouse often returns to part- or full-time work outside the home. Consequently, the family's financial position usually improves, but the family finds itself consuming more and in larger quantities. Consumption patterns continue to be heavily influenced by the children, since the family tends to buy large-sized packages of food and cleaning supplies, bicycles, music lessons, clothing, sports equipment, and a computer. Discount department stores (such as Kohl's and Target), mass merchandisers (such as Wal*Mart and Carrefour), and warehouse club stores (such as Costco and Sam's Club) are popular with consumers in this stage.

### Full nest III (FN III)

As the family grows older and parents enter their mid-40s, their financial position usually continues to improve because the primary wage earner's income rises, the second wage earner is receiving a higher salary, and the children earn spending and education money from occasional and part-time employment. The family typically replaces some worn pieces of furniture, purchases another automobile, buys some luxury appliances, and spends money on dental services (braces) and education. Families also spend more on computers in this stage, buying additional PCs for their older children. Depending on where children go to college and how many are seeking higher education, the financial position of the family may be tighter than other instances.

### Married, no kids (M-NK)

Couples who marry and do not have children are likely to have more disposable income to spend on charities, travel, and entertainment than either couples with children or singles in their age range. Not only do they have fewer expenses, these couples are more likely to be dual-wage earners, making it easier for them to retire earlier if they save appropriately.

**TABLE 12.1          (Continued)**

*Older singles (OS)*

Singles, age 40 or older, may be *Single Again* (ending married status because of divorce or death of a spouse) or *Never Married* (because they prefer to live independently or because they co-habitate with partners), either group of which may or may not have children living in the household. *Single Again* families often find themselves struggling financially due to the high cost of divorce and the expense of having to raise a family on one income. They often have to set up a new household (usually not as big as their previous home); buy furnishings accordingly; pay alimony and/or child support; and sometimes increase travel expenditures if the children live in another city, state, or country. They also pay for clothing and leisure activities conducive to meeting a future mate. On the other hand, many *Never Married Single* households are well-off financially since they never had to pay child-related costs and often live in smaller homes than large families require. This group now has more available income to spend on travel and leisure but feels the pressure to save for the future, since there is no second income on which to rely as they get older.

*Empty nest I (EN I)*

At this stage, the family is most satisfied with its financial position. The children have left home and are financially independent allowing the family to save more. In this stage, discretionary income is spent on what the couple wants rather than on what the children need. Therefore, they spend on home improvements, luxury items, vacations, sports utility vehicles, food away from home, travel, second homes (or smaller but nicer homes than were needed to house large families), and products for their grandchildren. This group is also more educated than generations in the past and are looking for fun educational opportunities, including eco-tourism and computer-related skills.

*Empty nest II (EN II)*

By this time, the income earners have retired, usually resulting in a reduction in income and disposable income. Expenditures become health oriented, centering on such items as medical appliances and health, sleep and digestion medicines. They may also move to climates more suitable to their medical requirements. But many of these families continue to be active and in good health, allowing them to spend time traveling, exercising, and volunteering. Many continue working part time to supplement their retirement and keep them socially involved.

*Solitary survivor (SS)*

Solitary survivors may be either employed or not employed. If the surviving spouse has worked outside the home in the past, he or she usually continues employment or goes back to work to live on earned income (rather than savings) and remain socially active. Expenditures for clothing and food usually decline in this stage, with income spent on health care, sickness care, travel, entertainment, and services, such as lawn care and house cleaning. Those who are not employed are often on fixed incomes and may move in with friends to share housing expenses and companionship, and some may choose to re-marry.

*Retired solitary survivor (RSS)*

Retired solitary survivors follow the same general consumption patterns as solitary survivors; however, their income may not be as high. Depending on how much they have been able to save throughout their lifetimes, they can afford to buy a wide range of products. But for many, spending declines drastically due to lack of need for many new products and higher medical expenses. These individuals have special needs for attention, affection, and security.

**FIGURE 12.4**     Income Available to Spend by Life Cycle Stage

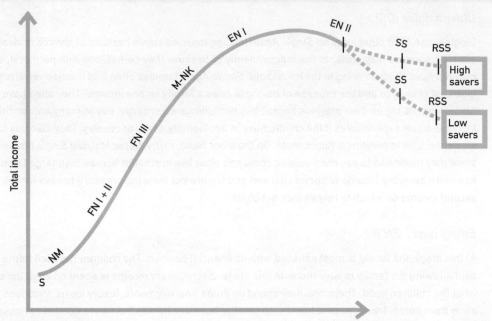

Life Cycle Stages are defined in Table 12.1

## CONSUMER BEHAVIOR AND MARKETING 12.2

### Reviving Retro Marketing Tools from the Past

Procter & Gamble, one of the biggest proponents of new marketing techniques, is relying on one of the oldest in its latest Charmin ad campaign: a jingle, featuring the virtues of Charmin's new Mega Roll toilet paper. The use of a jingle, a marketing tactic that dates back to the 1950s, could be perceived as sappy or outdated, given that most firms are working overtime to find newfangled, stealthy ad tactics to reach hard-to-reach consumers. But the saturation of today's advertising airwaves with recycled pop songs could mean that old-fashioned jingles work as well.

The jingle in P&G's "Busy Bear" jingle goes, "It's soft and strong in mega amounts. When it comes to Charmin, size counts. I'm on a roll, I'm on a mega roll." Television ads feature Charmin's animated bears frolicking while the tune plays in the background. To the kids who wished they were Oscar Mayer wieners in 1963 to McDonald's servers singing, "You deserve a break today," jingles are part of a baby boomer background in which they rivaled hit songs in popularity. Toe-tapping tunes written expressly for ads

have declined since then, but record labels, struggling to find new sources of revenue to offset weak CD sales, are focusing on ads as a growth medium. The most spectacular success has been a Cadillac ad that included Led Zeppelin singing "It's been a long time since I rock and rolled," to rejuvenate an aging Cadillac brand.

In the age of the iPod, jingles run the risk of sounding corny, but P&G believes jingles still work, saying "If they are humming it, they are buying it." In 2004, Charmin used another jingle called "Dylan Song," and much to executives' surprise, sales soared, immediately rising 7 percent after release of the jingle and maintaining double-digit percentage increases since then. That TV ad was the best-recalled consumer product ad in 2004, according to Intermedia Advertising Group, a New York research firm. P&G says it received e-mails from consumers who found the song, well, charming—and the Charmin brand racked up $1.5 billion in sales.

Source: Excerpted from Susanne Vranica, "P&G Goes Retro to Tour Charmin," The Wall Street Journal, March 3, 2005, B2. © 2005 by Dow Jones & Co. Reproduced with permission of DOW JONES & CO., INC. in the format textbook via Copyright Clearance Center, Inc.

Family life cycle stage is an important predictor of family or household spending. The late 1990s brought economic growth and prosperity to many industrialized nations, including North America. At first glance, one might think that consumer spending must have skyrocketed during this time—especially because the number of households grew and baby boomers entered their peak spending years. But when examined from a household standpoint, the analysis reveals that the average American household spent cautiously during this time even though unemployment levels were down and wage rates were up. In fact, it wasn't until the last few years of the decade that spending by individual households was restored to the levels of 1987. The average household spent 13 percent less on food away from home, 25 percent less on major appliances, and 15 percent less on clothing in 1997 than in 1987.[30] Between 1997 and 2002, spending by the average household grew 5 percent to $40,677, after adjusting for inflation, much less than the 11 percent growth in household income during those years. Contrary to popular perception, Americans are cautious spenders at the individual household level. Older Americans learned the lesson of caution during the Depression. Boomers learned it during the recession of the early 1990s, and the booming economy that followed failed to convince most of them to spend beyond their means. The recession of 2001 and the sluggish recovery in employment have reinforced economic conservatism in most households, hurting the bottom line of many businesses that provide discretionary products and services.[31] The aging of boomers and soaring health care costs will tighten household budgets even more in the future, and marketers will have to adapt.

Table 12.2 shows how household spending changed for major categories during the last decade. When examining these numbers, analyze why you think spending changed by thinking about demographic, lifestyle, and family issues. For the most part, consumers changed their spending from "things" to "services," with the biggest increases found in health insurance, pharmaceuticals, and personal care services (many of which are health related). America faces a $2 trillion crisis in its health care spending, which, if not solved, is projected to explode to $3.6 trillion by 2014, or nearly 19 percent of the entire U.S. economy, up from 15.4 percent now.[32] One category of "things" that has increased for the average household is cars and trucks, but much of that is for high-quality used vehicles (many purchased using eBay), apparently reflecting a strategy that many consumers find useful to cope with increased spending on services.

## Changing Family and Household Structure

The basic structure of families and households is changing in the United States, as you observed in the opening vignette. Many of these trends are also happening in Canada, Europe, and other parts of the world. Marketers and consumer analysts should evaluate how these changes can affect marketing strategy by asking questions like: What is the structure of contemporary families? How is that structure changing? How does structure affect the various stages of the consumer decision process? Are the changing realities of family structure a problem or an opportunity for growth? For answers, marketers should analyze marriage and living patterns, information that can be found through primary research and data from government agencies such as the U.S. Census Bureau and Statistics Canada.

### To Marry or Not to Marry? That Is the Question

Over the past thirty years, some of the most dramatic changes in American society have been related to marriage and the family. These changes include delays in first marriage and higher rates of divorce and nonmarital cohabitation. The projected number

**TABLE 12.2**  Family Spending Trends, 1990–2000 (in 2000 dollars)

|  | 2000 | 1990 | PERCENT CHANGE, 1990–2000 |
|---|---|---|---|
| Number of consumer units (in thousands) | 109,367 | 96,968 | 12.8 |
| Average income before taxes | $44,649 | $42,014 | 6.3 |
| Average annual spending | 38,045 | 37,393 | 1.7 |
| Food | $5,158 | $5,660 | −8.9 |
| Food at home | 3,021 | 3,274 | −7.7 |
| Food away from home | 2,137 | 2,386 | −6.6 |
| Alcoholic beverages | 372 | 386 | −3.6 |
| Housing | 12,319 | 11,446 | 7.4 |
| Shelter | 7,114 | 6,372 | 11.7 |
| Utilities, fuels, public services | 2,489 | 2,490 | 0.0 |
| Household services | 684 | 588 | 16.4 |
| Housekeeping supplies | 482 | 535 | −9.9 |
| Household furnishings and equipment | 1,549 | 1,482 | 4.5 |
| Apparel and services | 1,856 | 2,132 | −12.9 |
| Men, 16 and over | 344 | 427 | −19.4 |
| Boys, 2 to 15 | 96 | 9 | 4.1 |
| Women, 16 and over | 607 | 772 | −21.4 |
| Girls, 2 to 15 | 118 | 115 | 2.9 |
| Children under 2 | 82 | 92 | −11.1 |
| Footwear | 609 | 717 | −15.1 |
| Transportation | 7,417 | 6,746 | 10.0 |
| Cars and trucks, new | 1,605 | 1,527 | 5.1 |
| Cars and trucks, used | 1,770 | 1,249 | 41.7 |

of single 18- to 34-year-olds is expected to grow modestly to 38.4 million by the year 2010.[33] In the United States, the average age at which people get married for the first time is 26.9 for men and 25.3 for women. Regardless of these changes, most adults eventually marry and "try it" at least for a few years. In 1970, the divorce rate was only one-third the marriage rate, but by 2000, the divorce rate was well over half the marriage rate. The 2000 census reported that 54 percent of all households were married, but more recent data indicate that 50.8 percent are single and 49.2 percent are married.

When consumers marry later, they usually have to buy fewer basic furnishings and products needed for housekeeping; in fact, they often have to consolidate two households, which means divesting of duplicate items. But what they *do* buy tends to be better quality. Delayed marriages also produce more extensive travel capabilities; a higher probability of owning two cars; and firmer preferences for styles, colors, and product designs.

Of those marriages that do occur, 59 percent of marriages to brides under age eighteen end in divorce within fifteen years, compared to 36 percent of those married at age twenty or older. A recent study, however, indicates that the effects of divorce on children are not as great as in the past because divorce has become more socially acceptable.[34] Today's children of divorce are much more likely to marry than their counterparts of twenty years ago. Those that do divorce ("single again" consumers) often carry with them preferences and shopping patterns learned in marriage even though they are classified as single households. Divorced consumers may also have financial

| | 2000 | 1990 | PERCENT CHANGE, 1990–2000 |
|---|---|---|---|
| Vehicle rental, leases, licenses, other | 551 | 250 | 120.1 |
| Public transportation | 427 | 398 | 7.3 |
| Health care | 2,066 | 1,950 | 6.0 |
| Health insurance | 983 | 765 | 28.4 |
| Medical services | 568 | 740 | −23.3 |
| Drugs | 416 | 332 | 25.3 |
| Medical supplies | 99 | 112 | −11.6 |
| Entertainment | 1,863 | 1,874 | −0.6 |
| Fees and admissions | 515 | 489 | 5.4 |
| Television, radios, sound equipment | 622 | 598 | 4.0 |
| Pets, toys, playground equipment | 334 | 364 | −8.1 |
| Other entertainment products and services | 393 | 423 | −7.1 |
| Personal care products and services | 564 | 480 | 17.6 |
| Reading | 146 | 202 | −27.6 |
| Education | 632 | 535 | 18.2 |
| Tobacco products and supplies | 319 | 361 | −11.6 |
| Miscellaneous | 776 | 1,109 | −30.0 |
| Cash contributions | 1,192 | 1,075 | 10.9 |
| Personal insurance and pensions | 3,365 | 3,415 | −1.5 |
| Life and other personal insurance | 399 | 455 | −12.2 |
| Pensions and Social Security | 2,966 | 2,962 | 0.1 |

Source: *Household Spending: Who Spends How Much on What,* 7th ed. (Ithaca, NY: New Strategist Publications, 2003). Copyright 2003 New Strategist Publications, Inc.

problems that restrict their ability to buy the things that married couples or never-married singles might buy.[35] But divorce does create markets, because one family becomes two households that need furnishings—good news for mass retailers selling home goods at bargain prices. Should people who divorce remarry, they are also likely to re-divorce, returning to single status yet again. "Blended families" make consumer analysis more complex because of influences from stepchildren, siblings of the multiple families, and former spouses.

The trend toward half of marriages ending in divorce that began in the 1970s and 1980s results in half of all grandchildren having divorced grandparents in the 2000s. "The upside of all of this is that children can have more grandparents who love them," said Andrew Cherlin, a sociologist specializing in divorce at Johns Hopkins University.[36] For some new parents, the extra grandparent support is a boon, a kind of long-delayed silver lining emerging from the cloud of their parents' divorce. Stepparents who may have once been objects of resentment are cast in a new light when they offer free babysitting and a shared fascination with the minute details of a child's development. Some stepparents, too, are finding new pleasures as they age into a grandparent role free from the conflicts that so often marked their relationships with stepchildren. Children tend to embrace those who love them, without heed to biology or court papers. More grandparents and step-grandparents may mean more markets for buying gifts, with perhaps eight grandparents purchasing graduation, wedding, and holiday gifts.

**FIGURE 12.5** It's Okay to Be Single

## The Singles Boom

Individuals who delay marriage, get divorced, or lose a spouse are fueling the rise in the number of single households in developed nations. More than 100 million American adults (over age fifteen) are not in married relationships, according to the 2000 U.S. Census, a major change from the past.

Individuals who choose not to marry often choose to cohabitate, either with opposite or same-sex partners. Legally composed of singles, but functioning more as families, cohabitating singles are the fastest-growing segment of the singles market. Cohabitating couples made up 1 percent of the population in 1970, rising to about 5 percent in 2000, with 43 percent of unmarried couples including children in the household. The 2000 census reported about 25 percent of all households are householders living alone. It's okay to be single, which is what is communicated by actress Sarah Jessica Parker and the cast of the HBO original series, *Sex in the City*, shown in Figure 12.5.

### MATURE SINGLES MARKETS

Of all individuals living single, 61 percent are women, with a median age of sixty-six years. For the men, the median age is forty-five years. The demographics of single men and women are dramatically different because they are single for different reasons. Many women live alone because their husbands have died, and nearly half of all women older than seventy-five are widows. Men live alone mostly because they have not yet married or they are divorced, evolving from "wild and crazy" to "tired and pudgy" bachelors.[37] Of women who live alone, 43 percent are widowed and 30 percent are divorced or separated, but only 13 percent of men who live alone are widowers and 38 percent are divorced or separated. Nearly half of men who live alone have never been married.[38]

Women, especially older women, are spending their money, time, and energy creating a new kind of singles market, ripe with opportunities for firms focusing on travel, financial services, social activities, entertainment, and religious involvement. In time, the "booming singles market" will eventually become a market for home-security devices, treatment for chronic health problems, and perhaps bus trips to nearby tourist destinations.

## YOUNGER SINGLES MARKETS

Specialized media and products (such as *Living Single* magazine and single-serving food products, usually microwaveable) are often directed to the younger portions of the singles market. Home builders are also adapting because singles account for 36 percent of first-time home buyers.[39] Design changes include fewer bedrooms, less dining room space, and bigger kitchens—the "living room" for many in this segment. Master bedrooms are more luxurious, bathrooms more spa-like, and living space better equipped for high-tech entertainment.[40]

### Gay and Lesbian Markets

Gay and lesbian consumers represent a segment of the market receiving greater attention by marketers. Most are classified as singles (although some jurisdictions may recognize the married status of some same-sex households), sometimes living in traditional family settings at some point in their lives. Reliable data concerning the size of the market are scarce, although it is estimated that as little as 6 percent or as many as 16 percent of adult Americans may be part of this market.[41] To add even more confusion to the subject, the Alan Guttmacher Institute estimates that only 1 percent of men consider themselves exclusively homosexual,[42] a fact corroborated by the 2000 U.S. Census, which revealed that less than 1.8 percent of men and 0.6 percent of women identify themselves as "gay/lesbian." Only recently has the U.S. Population Census provided information on the number of same-sex couples by including a question in which gay couples have the opportunity to designate each other as an "unmarried partner" as opposed to "housemate/roommate." Chicago's Overlooked Opinions was among the first research institutions to conduct ongoing panels reporting data on gay and lesbian consumers, finding most to be affluent and image conscious.[43]

According to Simmons Market Research, gay and lesbian households have a median income of $55,670, and about 70 percent of gays and lesbians have at least a college education and work in either professional or managerial jobs.[44] Gays and lesbians are likely to live in urban areas, travel extensively, spend considerable money on clothing, and express more interest in the arts. Often they are more aware of current social issues and are more politically active than their heterosexual counterparts. But targeting all gay men is like targeting all heterosexual men, often contradictory and conflicting. The microculture of the gay and lesbian market is based on sexuality, camaraderie, and gender flexibility—all in opposition to the mainstream culture, which is often orthodox and unsympathetic.[45] The issue for some marketers is how to target effectively the gay and lesbian market without alienating heterosexual customers. Some firms do this with websites designed especially for these markets.[46]

The primary marketing technique in reaching the gay and lesbian market is simply to recognize that the market exists and establish a relationship with this segment. This approach can be accomplished by participation in or sponsorship of activities considered important by gay consumers, such as AIDS research or community events relating to gay rights. Corporations can also create awareness by sponsorship of operas, ballets, classical concerts, and museums that attract high participation among the gay community, while also reaching the community at large.

## Marketing to Gays

The Fab Five from television's *Queer Eye for the Straight Guy* have worked wonders with the hair and threads of America's most fashion-challenged stiffs, but can they do the same for General Motors? Whether by luck or foresight, the GMC Yukon XL Denali is prominently displayed in each episode. The *Queer Eye* promotion stands out as GM's first high-profile attempt to reach buyers in the gay community. GM is considering a broader campaign to capture more of the $450 billion spending power of the gay and lesbian community, as well as broadening its appeal to diverse communities. Subaru has courted gay buyers for several years, and DaimlerChrysler is running some tailored ads overseas. Ford is using ads tailored to gays for its Jaguar and Volvo luxury brands. "The Big Three have only come along in the last couple of years, but they were not among the first to try it," said Michael Wilke, marketing analyst and founder of Commercial Closet (www.commercialcloset.org), a website for gay and lesbian-related advertising.

On *Queer Eye,* Carson, Ted, Kyan, Jai, and Thom—dubbed the Fab Five—dash to the rescue of hapless heterosexuals, treating them to salons, luxury clothiers, and high-end grocers in hopes of making them more attractive to their mates. Before the show's debut, GM won the right to be the featured ride by providing the truck to the show—complete with a New York license plate reading "FAB 5." GM has achieved exposure with an estimated 2 million mostly young and cosmopolitan viewers getting a peek at the Denali every time the show is aired. The company says it has received thousands of requests for information on the vehicle directly as a result of the show. Overall, sales of GMC Yukon models were up 3.3 percent compared to the previous year while GM's overall unit sales have fallen 3.1 percent.

In 2002, Jaguar introduced a tailored magazine ad that featured a curving road with the caption, "Life is full of twists and turns. Care for a partner?" Volvo has since introduced ads with a number of same-sex couples, some with children, others with pets, with the caption, "Whether you're starting a family or creating one as you go"—with an SUV and convertible version of its cars pictured.

Other major marketing campaigns aimed at gays and lesbians include the following.

- Avis Rent-A-Car: Runs ads in targeted magazines trumpeting the company's treatment of domestic partners as family members.
- Earthlink: Runs print ads with same-sex couples and the text, "Your Internet service should be as fabulous as you are."
- Bridgestone Tires: Runs a series of Internet ads on gay- and lesbian-related websites with same-sex couples pictured.
- Subaru of America: One of the first auto companies to target gays and lesbians; featured targeted magazine ads in 1996 that read, "It's not a choice. It's the way we're built."

Source: Excerpted from Mike Hudson, "Big 3 Slowly Tests Gay Market," *Detroit News* (October 9, 2003).

Marketers may also advertise in gay-oriented media at both local and national levels. Gay-oriented publications such as *The Advocate* and *Genre,* along with numerous websites like www.gay.com, attract advertisers such as Banana Republic, Wells Fargo, American Airlines, Philip Morris, and Calvin Klein. Some analysts believe that advertisers generate high loyalty among gay readers for advertising in such targeted media without alienating the mass market. Carillon Importers began advertising Absolut vodka in *The Advocate* in 1979. After many years of clever Absolut ads and targeting the gay market in addition to its traditional straight market, patrons of gay bars tended to ask for Absolut rather than just vodka. A Volkswagen TV ad featuring two young men driving together, who stopped to pick up a discarded chair, only to discard it

**TABLE 12.3**  Median Income by Household Type

| ALL HOUSEHOLDS | MEDIAN INCOME, 2003 | PERCENT CHANGE IN REAL INCOME, 2002–2003 |
|---|---|---|
| Family households | $53,991 | 0.1 |
| Married couples | 62,405 | −0.4 |
| Female householder (no husband present) | 29,307 | −1.2 |
| Male householder (no wife present) | 41,959 | −1.7 |
| Nonfamily householder | 25,741 | −1.0 |
| Female householders | 21,313 | −0.4 |
| Male householders | 31,928 | −0.6 |

Source: U.S. Census Bureau, Current Population Reports, "Income, Poverty, and Health Insurance Coverage in the United States: 2003." www.census.gov/prod/www/abs/popula.html.

themselves later, was recognized by gay men as a gay-oriented ad and perceived as straight by other consumers. Volkswagen used mass media but designed ads with a sensitivity that attracted the gay market.[47] For additional ways marketers target gay consumers, see Consumer Behavior and Marketing 12.3. Brands attain legitimacy (social fitness) through the framing processes, and some brands connect with the gay market's shared ways of interpreting meanings and social interaction, providing a connection between the community and the brand. Consumers who are sensitive to these frames ascribe to those brands the frames of the gay and lesbian community, thus creating a social fit with meanings important to the gay community.[48]

## Household Characteristics

Average household size has fallen in most industrialized countries. In the United States, the average dropped to 2.59 persons in 2000, down from 3.14 in 1970. One-person households account for about 25 percent of the total, compared with 18 percent in 1970, and households with six or more persons dropped from 19.5 percent of all households to less than 6 percent today. The 2000 census discloses that only 23.5 percent of American households consist of a married couple living with their own child(ren) younger than eighteen years, compared with 31 percent in 1980 and 40 percent in 1970. Nonfamily households are projected to grow much more rapidly than families over the next few decades, but the highest incomes are found among family households, as you see in Table 12.3, explained of course by the reality that married couples typically have two incomes, in sharp contrast to the Bunkers, Andersons, or Cleavers described in the opening vignette.

Marketers are increasingly interested in single-parent households because of the rapid growth of this category. Most are headed by a female with no husband present (more than 12 percent of all households), but there is also growth in the number of male householders with children and no wife present. Women without husbands is highest among black family households, at about 48 percent of all black family households, but the rate of growth slowed during the past decade to 3.8 percent per year. Meanwhile, the growth rate of Latino single-parent households has more than doubled to 7 percent per year, the highest rate of increase for any ethnic group. About 26 percent of white children, 64 percent of black children, and 37 percent of Latino children live in a single-parent household.[49] And of course, "household with pet" may

## "We'll Leave the Lights On, and a Milkbone"

The W Hotel at Union Square not only welcomes pets arriving with two-legged guests, but occasionally celebrates its connection with the animal world. Recently, the hotel was host to a dog fashion show. Pet-friendly policies—once the preserve of the top end of the business—have become a more common tactic in the hotel marketing wars, along with extra-comfortable beds and high-speed Internet access, according to industry executives and analysts.

This heightened marketing to pet owners has increased since the attacks of September 11, 2001, as more travelers drive rather than fly, often taking their animals with them. In some properties, this change amounts to no more than a grudging willingness to accept an animal, usually with a size limit and an additional cleaning charge tacked on. But other hotels offer elaborate welcomes with personalized greetings and services, including, at the Ritz-Carlton Hotel in New York, the loan of a Burberry raincoat if it happens to be raining when the need for a walk arises.

Demographics and the changing role of pets in the family affects marketing, according to Emily Goldfischer, a vice president of the Loews Corporation, who explains, "People are getting married later and delaying having kids, so they have pets. Also, pets have become part of the family and people want them to travel with the family." Loews has no restriction on the size or weight of a pet, although some hotels charge $25 to cover extra costs.

"Our PAWS program can accommodate dogs as well as human guests," says Ross Klein, manager of the W Hotels. "We have beds for dogs, special meals, wellness and massage services, and a veterinarian on call." Hotels often place guests with pets on a limited number of floors to avoid contact with small children, who might be scared by a large dog, or with people who do not like animals or might be allergic to them.

More and more hotels are finding ways to accommodate both pets and their owners.

Associated Press/AP

Other problems can arise, such as barking that annoys other guests. Cleaners and service people may be reluctant to enter a room with a large unsupervised dog inside. To deal with this, Loews has a special doorknob sign to alert housekeepers that there is a pet in the room, and the chain asks for a cell phone number or provides guests with a "puppy pager" so that the hotel can contact them if there is a problem with a pet.

Source: Excerpted from John Holusha, "We'll Leave the Lights On, and a Milkbone," *New York Times* (March 9, 2005). Copyright 2005 by The New York Times Co. Reprinted with permission.

be an increasingly important market target, as you see in Consumer Behavior and Marketing 12.4.

## Changing Roles of Women

Marketing managers have always been interested in lifestyle changes that occur among women because female consumers buy so many products—for themselves and for families. Women's lifestyles have changed dramatically during the last century, especially since Gloria Steinem made feminism a household word and singer Helen Reddy sang the 1970s smash hit, "I Am Woman." Those times brought with them a fight for equality between the sexes in terms of job opportunity, respect, and pay. And women never looked back. In fact, interest in female consumers continues to intensify because of greater proportion of women in the population, improved purchasing ability, and greater importance in the workplace.

Female consumers now outnumber male consumers by about 5.5 million because women tend to live longer than men do. Some experts say this is due to physiological differences between men and women, and others say it's because women have traditionally not dealt with the same career stresses as men. In fact, some researchers speculate that as women move up the corporate ladder and manage households, they may begin to mirror the life expectancy of men. And many women do mirror the lifestyles of their male counterparts, especially as they take on androgynous roles in the work force or in social activities.

Feminine roles are of great concern today to consumer analysts and marketers. A **role** *specifies what the typical occupant of a given position is expected to do in that position in a particular social context*.[50] Consumer analysts are especially concerned with gender roles of women in the family and in their position as purchasing agents for the family. One of the challenges women face today is balancing their roles as wife or partner, mother, wage-earner, and consumer. Figure 12.6 is an ad that portrays multiple roles facing women with multiple responsibilities.

### Female Employment

Women in developed nations have much higher rates of employment outside the home than in the past. Of the 138 million[51] women in the United States, the majority (about 71 percent) have traded a kitchen apron for work clothes, in contrast to the less than 25 percent who worked outside the home in 1950 and 13 percent in 1870. This trend is occurring on a global scale as well, with the percentages of working women reaching 52 percent in Canada, 49 percent in Japan, 47 percent in Great Britain, and 46 percent in Australia.[52] In 2003, 82 percent of families had at least one employed member. Both the husband and wife work in 50.9 percent of married-couple families, and the rate for mothers with children under age eighteen is 71.1 percent.

Women can choose to work full time or part time outside the home or to stay at home, managing the household or perhaps as one of the 430,000 people who make their living as traders on eBay.

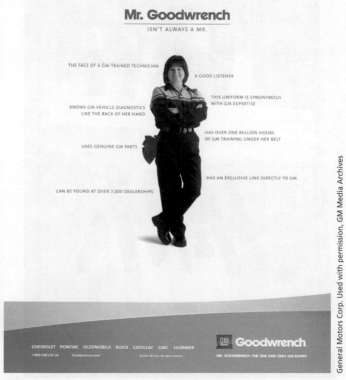

FIGURE 12.6 Women Today Play Multiple Roles with Multiple Responsibilities

Families in which the wife works full time have much higher average incomes than households with only one person working, which affects greatly the total amount of money the family has to spend.[53] Though employment increases family income, working outside the home also increases family expenditures on specific items such as child care, clothing, food away from home, and gasoline. This finding is why retailers such as H&M (shown in Figure 12.7) that sell fashion on a budget have enjoyed considerable success. Families with two incomes also spend more on housing than do one-earner families.[54]

## Career Orientation

Employed individuals are sometimes classified by orientation toward their careers. A researcher named Rena Bartos described two groups of working women: those who think of themselves as having a career and those to whom work is "just a job." There are also housewives who prefer to stay at home but have worked outside the home in the past and plan to work outside the home again in the future. For marketers, this distinction may be important because homemakers and just-a-job women are more likely to read traditional women's magazines, whereas professional women are more likely to read general interest and business-oriented magazines and newspapers.[55] As with other consumer classifications, working or nonworking wives should not be treated as homogeneous segments[56] because many differences exist and account for different purchasing behaviors within these groups. The increasing number of career women making more money than their husbands may attract the attention of marketers of dis-

**FIGURE 12.7** Working Families Want Fashion. But on a Budget

**FIGURE 12.8** In a reversal of traditional gender roles, this woman gives a gift to show her affection.

PART 4 [ ENVIRONMENTAL INFLUENCES ON CONSUMER BEHAVIOR

cretionary goods. Armed with their own spending money, many women may choose to splurge on acts of self-indulgence while others may reverse traditional gender roles and buy a special gift for the men in their lives, as illustrated by the couple in Figure 12.8.

## Women and Time

Married working women experience many time pressures. These women often have two jobs: household responsibilities, including children, plus their jobs in the marketplace. Studies show they have significantly less leisure time than either their husbands or full-time homemakers.[57] This finding would suggest that working wives would buy more time-saving appliances, use more convenience foods, spend less time shopping, and so forth. Actually, research shows that working and nonworking wives are similar in such behavior if income, life stage, and other situational variables are held constant,[58] and that working-wife families appear to spend more on food away from home, child care, and household services.

FIGURE 12.9 Moments of Relaxation or Self-Indulgence

## Role Overload

Role overload exists when the total demands on time and energy associated with the prescribed activities of multiple roles are too great to perform the roles adequately or comfortably.[59] Sex-role ideology and other forces create pressures toward more equality in workloads between men and women, but research shows that employed women work more hours each day than husbands who are employed and wives who are not employed, resulting in role overload for many women.[60] As women contribute more to the family income, they expect in return a more equal division of the household responsibilities.[61] There is evidence, especially among younger families, that attitudes toward work and housework have shifted, causing a move toward more household equality between the sexes.[62] This finding is why working wives may respond positively to marketers who offer moments of relaxation and self-indulgence,[63] as seen in the ad for cozy warm bedroom slippers in Figure 12.9.

## Marketing to Women

Consumer researchers are interested in women's multiple roles, time pressures, and changing family structures so that the researchers can develop effective marketing and communication programs to reach them. With such information, marketers can look beyond the one-size-fits-all description of general segments of women to more descriptive and specific descriptions.

The "mother" category has been relatively understudied because of incorrect assumptions about this market segment. Leo Burnett, the Chicago-based advertising agency, studied the premise that "all mothers must be the same and can be reached through similar advertising because they are all concerned with the same issues (health and well-being of their children)." Through Leo*She*, the agency's unit focusing on marketing to women, the company found four major groups of mothers, each with unique characteristics (see Figure 12.10).[64] An executive from Leo Burnett also found the

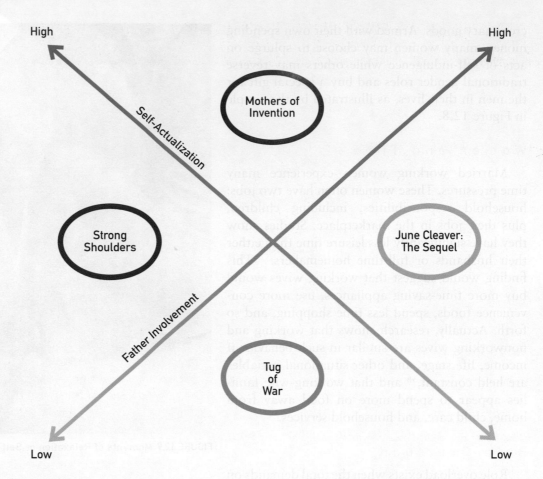

High  High

Mothers of
Invention

Self-Actualization

Strong
Shoulders

June Cleaver:
The Sequel

Father Involvement

Tug
of
War

Low  Low

**June Cleaver: The Sequel**

These women believe in the traditional roles of "stay-at-home" moms and "bread-winner" dads. They tend to be white, highly educated, and from upscale backgrounds. Slightly more than half of them stay at home full time to care for their families, compared to the national average of 30 percent.

**Tug of War Moms**

They share some of the same traditional notions of motherhood, but are forced to work—and they aren't happy about that. These moms, 79 percent of whom work outside the home, are full of angst and anxiety.

**Strong Shoulders**

More than a third of this group are single mothers, who have a positive view of their lives, despite their lower income levels and little support from their children's dads. Thirty-four percent of these women are between 18 and 24 years old.

**Mothers of Invention**

These women enjoy motherhood, work outside the home, and have help with their child-rearing responsibilities from helpful husbands. Unlike the Tug-of-Wars, this group—a mix of gen xers and boomers—has developed new and creative ways to balance career with a happy home life.

**FIGURE 12.10** Multiple Moms: Four Types

roles of working women in China to be changing substantially, as described in Market Facts 12.1.

Different mother segments look at advertising, the Internet, products, time, and brands differently. For example, time-strapped Tug-of-War moms are the most brand conscious because buying recognized brands saves time and simplifies their shopping

## Changing Roles of Women In China

On a recent visit to the Shanghai offices of a major toothpaste company, Linda Kovarik, associate director for strategic planning at ad agency Leo Burnett, noticed that many of the female employees kept framed glamour shots on their desks. The most frequent subject: themselves. "I'm not talking about group hug with mom, dad, and grandpa; it's just themselves," said Ms. Kovarik. These glamour shots are a telling portrait of the changing mindset of female consumers in China. "We are seeing a rise in materialism and ego. Women are expressing themselves in a way their mothers couldn't," she says. "Brands need to offer them room to be vain and to explain who they are."

In a study of the mindset of Chinese women in their 30s and 50s in Chengdu and Shanghai, the stereotypes of Chinese women as traditionalists were absent. Instead, one young woman wrote: "I am the center of the world, I am the focal point. Draw a circle and you can find me. I'm quite realistic, but sometimes I daydream. I'm a little bit selfish, but I'm always there for my friends."

To understand how much the economic clout of Chinese women has changed, consider the following figures. The average annual income in China's urban centers soared 315 percent between 1990 and 2000 to 6,317 yuan ($764), according to the China Statistical Yearbook. Chinese officials don't break down income growth between sexes, but women's slice of the pie has clearly grown. The portion of the female work force in managerial positions rose to 6.1 percent in 2000 from 2.9 percent in 1990, and the portion of women employed in professional or technical jobs rose to 22.8 percent from 17.4 percent, according to the National Bureau of Statistics of China.

Companies are taking note. In 1998, for example, Procter & Gamble's marketing strategy for Rejoice shampoo, one of the country's top-selling brands, pulled an ad that featured an airline hostess and replaced it with one of a woman working as an airline mechanical engineer. The change was driven by consumer surveys that showed that women had become more career focused, says P&G's Rejoice brand manager, Jacky Cheng. Since then, women have again raised the bar, and the latest ad for Rejoice Refresh shampoo, running now on Chinese television, features a girl playing beach volleyball.

A key driver of this new attitude, besides rising incomes, is the dramatic change in the retail landscape itself: women are more fashion focused because there's simply more fashion available to them. "The offerings have increased dramatically," said Jacques Penhirin, a partner at McKinsey & Co. in Shanghai. "For example, there was shampoo, but you had three or five to choose from. You've got 300 today." At the same time, quality has gone up and price has gone down.

During this period of rapid change, the income gap between women and men has actually grown. China's urban women make 62.7 percent of what men make for similar work, 7.4 percentage points lower than in 1990, according to a July 2001 survey by the All China Women Federation. Nonetheless, women's attitudes are evolving at a breakneck pace. One-quarter of urban, unmarried woman say they want to marry, but not have kids, according to a survey conducted by Sinofile Information Services. Another 11 percent of unmarried women say they would prefer to stay single.

Source: Cris Prystay, "As China's Women Change, Marketers Notice—Procter & Gamble, Like Others, Tries to Appeal To Evolving Sensibilities," *Wall Street Journal* (May 30, 2002), A1. Copyright 2002 by Dow Jones & Co. Reproduced with permission of Dow Jones & Co., Inc., in the format textbook via Copyright Clearance Center.

trips. Consumer products companies targeting these women should spotlight the values of their brands. But new brands or brands that are in trouble can benefit from targeting the emerging groups of Strong Shoulders moms (perhaps via inspirational television or career personalities) and Mothers of Invention (via the Internet), according to Leo*She*. The key is not to treat all moms the same or expect to capture all of them with one single message, but rather to understand the intergenerational impact in the mother-daughter dyad on product decisions, brand extensions, pricing, place-related decisions, and promotion.[65]

Firms can use such information to augment existing strategies to better reach, keep, and service clients. For example, many retailers are open twenty-four hours a day, seven days a week, to accommodate conflicting work schedules. One study found that, among mothers who work full time, 45 percent work different shifts than their husbands, and 57 percent of part-time working women work different shifts than their husbands, a strategy to add two incomes without additional child care costs.[66] Increased time pressures may make Internet retailers attractive for many items, especially gifts. Doncaster, a direct marketer of upscale women's clothing, adapts to women's busy schedules and hectic lifestyles by showing its products in the comfort of associates' homes. Clients can make appointments during their lunch hours, evening hours, or weekends to view and try on clothing in the comfort of clients' homes or offices.

## Changing Masculine Roles

Roles of men in families are changing substantially as well. It is not uncommon in the United States for the woman of the household to buy new tires for the car while the husband stays home to cook dinner or watch the kids. As men's share of family income decreases and as values shift in society, men are free to participate more fully in family functions and are taking on new roles in consuming and purchasing products.[67] In a survey of one thousand American men by the advertising agency Cunningham & Walsh, more and more could be termed *househusbands*. The privately published survey disclosed that 47 percent of men vacuum the house, 80 percent take out the garbage, 41 percent wash dishes, 37 percent make beds, 33 percent load the washing machine, 27 percent clean the bathroom, 23 percent dust, 23 percent dry dishes, 21 percent sort laundry, 16 percent clean the refrigerator, and 14 percent clean the oven. More than 50 percent of men take part in regular shopping trips, suggesting that men are important targets for many types of household products. Men are not only participating in household activities but are increasing their rate of participation.[68] Men now do one-fifth of the cooking, cleaning, and laundry, and married men now do more housework than unmarried men. Many men still express their masculinity, however, by trading their SUVs for big pickup trucks.[69] And they visit different gyms, as you can see in Consumer Behavior and Marketing 12.5.

Much literature has focused on the new roles of men.[70] Joseph Pleck, a leading researcher, notes that, although the "new father" image is increasingly portrayed in the media, there *is*, in reality, substantive change in men's behaviors.[71] The new father is present at the birth, is involved with his children as infants (not just when they are older), participates in the actual day-to-day work of child care, and is involved with his daughters as much as his sons. Men in the twenty-first century see themselves as being more sensitive. Men remain interested in romance, but they also express increased interest in fitness, health, helping raise the children, helping out with household chores, and finding a better balance between work and leisure. Stereotypes of men's shopping in the past characterized men as "grab and go," "whine and wait," and "fear of the feminine," but recent research indicates these stereotypes contradict actual facts. Many men have achieved gender role transcendence and evaluate alternatives, bargain, and even shop in "feminine" stores.[72] Among other things, men are increasingly a market for personal care appearance products,[73] as illustrated in the ad in Figure 12.11. Some professional football players even wear panty hose under their uniforms on cold winter days because they find that nylon stockings provide warmth and absorb perspiration without the added bulk of long thermal underwear. Increasingly doctors also

## Where Do You Work Out?

Husband and wife Warren Korkie and Sandra Hagen believe in gender equality. Even their five-year-old twins are evenly split, one boy and one girl. So when Hagen opened a women-only gym in August 2002, not much time passed before Korkie started pondering a men-only facility to match. The result: Second Wind Circuit Training, a men-only gym that sits just three storefronts away from his wife's Curves for Women in North Raleigh's Pinecrest Point shopping center.

"The same day she opened Curves, I started my MBA at UNC," Korkie said. "I was looking at some of the reasons Curves has been so successful, and I started thinking of how you could do something like that for men." Korkie took elements from Curves, such as its space-efficient design. The equipment is arranged in a circuit, alternating rest stations and machines, and the workouts are created to be quick thirty-minute visits. Korkie made some changes to make the gym more appealing to men. Unlike Curves, which uses hydraulic equipment, Second Wind places much more emphasis on weight resistance and building muscle mass.

The gyms work because being in a single-sex environment is a little less intimidating. Curves members like the social atmosphere of a women-only facility, and men like working out without having to try to impress women. Gym owners admit that there are some members for whom interaction with the opposite sex is a draw, but say that there's a large percentage of people who prefer a men-only or women-only model.

Hagen and Korkie say that there's no real competition between their businesses, and they work together behind the scenes on the operations of both. But from the outside, they appear to be two entirely separate businesses. "I try to avoid going over there," Korkie said. "They don't really want me there."

Curves took a lot less marketing because it is a nationally recognized franchise. In its first week, Hagen's Curves franchise had sixty-eight members, and it's up to seven hundred now. After nearly four months, Korkie's membership sits at about forty, though he said it's growing. "It's tough when you're trying to build a new brand," he said.

Source: Excerpted from Sue Stock, "Husband, Wife, Open Gender-Specific Gyms," *Knight Ridder Tribune Business News* (April 20, 2005), 1.

recommend tight fitting socks, similar to ladies knee-highs, to prevent blood cots in legs on long airline flights. There was an underground culture of men wearing panty hose, but forced to buy women's brands until an innovative marketer brought out ACTIVSKIN legwear with male-specific features, such as a fly in front, to appeal to men and using the slogan, "ComfiLons are not your mother's panty hose." [74]

As economic conditions and men's roles in the home change, men are redefining themselves. Whereas the man of the 1950s wanted a settled, stable, suburban existence, and the man of the 1970s cared more about power than fitting in, today's "organization man" carries a briefcase in one hand and pushes a baby carriage with the other. And although he considers his career important, he doesn't want to sacrifice time with his family. [75] Businesses will have to adapt to changes that men are facing, such as having to stay home with a sick child. The compromises today's organization man is making are similar to those made by working women, and firms that do not address these changing roles and needs could lose some of their best and brightest employees. [76]

A new **androgynous consumer** that *has the characteristics of both male and female consumers (or no distinguishing masculine or feminine characteristics at all)* may be

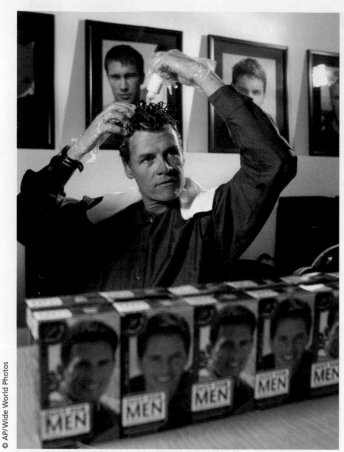

**FIGURE 12.11** Not Just For Women: A Complete Line of Men's Hair Coloring Products

emerging, especially among young, educated professionals. Careers and education shape much of consumer behavior and, for consumers under thirty, women and men have similar careers and education. Cultural definitions of roles for parenting and household tasks may not be changing as rapidly, but clearly they are changing. If careers and household roles are evolving to be similar across genders, it is reasonable to expect consumer behavior to be androgynous in many product and retail purchase categories. Additional details are explained in Market Facts 12.2.

## Children and Household Consumer Behavior

Children change dramatically how the family functions—in terms of relationships, employment, and purchases—and their influence is changing family spending throughout much of the world. Studies based on Canadian data indicate that young children reduce parents' participation in the labor force, change how families spend their money, and reduce the amount of time and money available for leisure.[77] Research in Asia-Pacific regions indicates that 81 percent of children receive monetary gifts from relatives, and 53.6 percent receive a regular allowance. When it comes to buying, 66 percent of children are influenced by television advertising, and 15.5 percent are influenced by the Internet.[78]

### Influence of Children

The children's market has captured the attention of marketers worldwide because of the increasing dollars, euros, and pounds they spend on products and because of the enormous influence they exert over spending power in a growing number of product categories such as footwear and clothing.[79] The fastest-growing purchase category for children has been apparel, due in part to children assuming greater responsibility for their own necessities.[80] Armed with money received from allowances, chores, and gifts from grandparents, children average just more than two hundred store visits per year, either alone or with parents. A typical ten-year-old goes shopping with parents two to three times per week (directly influencing about $188 billion of household purchases) and shops alone around once a week. In a cross-cultural analysis of Tweens (eight–fourteen-year-olds) in fifteen countries in Europe, Asia, and North and South America, researchers conclude that Tweens around the globe spend $300 billion directly and influence $1.88 trillion in sales.[81]

But their influence on household spending varies by product user and by degree.[82] Children tend to have greater influence in purchase decisions involving products for their own use,[83] whereas their influence is more limited on more expensive, higher-risk products. Children exert *direct influence* over parental spending when they request specific products and brands. Direct influence also refers to joint decision making— actively participating with family members to make a purchase. Children's influence

# MARKET FACTS 12.2

## The Androgynous Consumer

### When Two Become One

Men and woman are about to become one sex, at least in the eyes of industry and advertising, a new consumer trends report claims. Changes in the structure of society have blurred traditional distinctions between men and women, according to research group Datamonitor. This development has forced manufacturers and advertisers to adopt new marketing strategies to win consumers.

Datamonitor says it has revealed the all-important consumer trends that manufacturers must follow to keep up with consumer "mega-trends." "Gender complexity" has made men become more feminized, taking an active role in parenting while becoming more fashion conscious and spending more money on beauty products. Women, meanwhile, have more earning power, marry later in life or stay single, while catching up with men in drinking.

The changes in gender attitudes are already reflected in advertising. Ads for Pampers nappies feature a father, and All Bar One bars sport a lighter female-friendly decor.

Source: Excerpted from Guy Robarts, "Gender Blur Impacts Sales Tactics," BBC News, www.bbc.co.uk (December 12, 2004).

---

might also be *indirect,* which occurs when parents buy products and brands that they know their children prefer, without being asked or told to make that specific purchase. These kinds of transactions account for almost $300 million in U.S. household spending. Automakers target kids in magazines and point-of-purchase displays because children indirectly influence about $17.7 billion in auto purchases.[84] Market research firm Just Kid of Stamford, Connecticut, estimates that 76 percent of mothers of seven- to twelve-year-olds consult their children about what to have for breakfast or let them choose it outright, and 36 percent involve them in dinner decisions.[85] And the influence of children on computer purchases is just beginning to blossom, as the "system administrator" of many home computers is often the household's teenager.

Not only do children influence choices, but they also are actually making purchases, with family money and with their own. Just as children affect family purchases, families affect young consumers' perception and evaluation of product and brand choices.[86] Children's consumer behavior is absorbed at very young ages from familial examples, so if parents exhibit brand loyalty to a specific brand, children perceive that brand and product to be good.[87] A family's influence on a child's brand choices is important to marketers because the influence affects purchase decisions later in life as well. Children evaluate brand extensions more on surface cues (such as brand names) and less on deep cues (similarities between parent brand and brands extension).[88]

Where do children like to shop best? Convenience stores rank at the top of children's shopping lists because they sell a lot of snack food and other products children like and because their neighborhood locations are easily accessible. In fact, most children will make their first independent purchases at convenience stores. As children reach ages eight to ten years, they prefer mass merchandisers because of the breadth of products in the toy, snack foods, clothing, and school supplies categories. They also like to shop specialty stores because of the depth of toys, music, or shoes offered. Children usually have a favorite grocery store and recommend their mothers shop there when they shop together. Finally, children find drugstores and department stores cold, boring, and very adult oriented.

## Childhood Socialization

Much of consumer behavior is learned as a child.[89] Family communication about purchases and consumer behavior is the key in children's consumer socialization process. Children who buy Pepsi when they are young are more likely to buy Pepsi when they are older. They are also more likely to react negatively to product changes but are less affected by price increases. And single consumers tend to be more loyal to the brands they learned to buy as children. Children learn from siblings and parents how exchange relationships work and that benefits are given when the children show concern for other's needs.[90]

So how do children learn their consumer behaviors? They learn primarily from shopping with parents—known as co-shopping. Co-shoppers tend to be more concerned about their children's development as consumers. They place more value on children's input in family consumer decisions, including decisions on products not encountered on typical co-shopping trips such as automobiles, major appliances, life insurance, and vacations.[91] Co-shoppers explain more to their children why they don't buy products and discuss the role of advertising, which to some extent may mediate the influence of advertising. In the free-market environment of the United States, advertising is an important influence, despite parental concern and repeated but generally unsuccessful attempts to regulate the influence of advertising on children.[92] Advertising has significant influences on how younger children form product trial experience, but for older children, advertising serves more to frame the interpretation of product usage.[93]

Different types of mothers communicate consumer skills and knowledge to their children in different ways. Researchers found that mothers who are restrictive and warm in their relationships with their children tend to monitor and control children's consumption activities more, whereas mothers who respect and solicit children's opinions use messages that promote purchasing and consumption decision-making abilities.[94] Consider what influences a parent may have on the food choices children make in Buyer Beware 12.1.

Retailers can benefit from understanding the role of children in buying. Some retailers may consider children an interference with parents' shopping time. Retailers such as IKEA, the Swedish furniture manufacturer with stores around the world, provides play areas for children while parents shop. A more proactive approach is found in Japanese department stores, which encourage children and parents (principally mothers) to interact with toys found in the store, making the stores fun places for children to visit. This approach is shown in Figure 12.12.

Many changes in family structure directly affect how marketers communicate to children and their families. For example, higher education and delayed marriage are increasing the number of families with *only children* (who are accustomed to communicating with adults more than with siblings or peers). Their preferences may be more

## Do You Know What Your Kids Are Eating?

If you become a parent, you will become aware of the many advertising messages that attempt to persuade kids to eat unhealthy foods. Now food fights are breaking out, led by groups such as the Center for Science in the Public Interest (CSPI), which has called for a halt to promoting soda, caffeinated drinks, and sugary drinks; foods largely devoid of nutrients; foods high in fats or added sugars; and large-portion products. In addition to advocating guidelines, the group hired a director of litigation to develop lawsuits against food industry practices such as marketing fruit snacks by implying that there is a lot of fruit in the product when there is really more sugar than fruit. The advocacy group wants to stop advertising junk food on television shows with more than a quarter of the audience under age eighteen; halt the use of toys, games, contests, or other incentives to promote nutritionally poor foods; and completely stop the marketing of unhealthy food in schools.

"Clearly, parents bear the primary responsibility for feeding their children a healthy diet," said Margo G.

Wootan, CSPI's nutrition policy director. But, she said, "parents are fighting a losing battle against food marketers," which have more than doubled their marketing spending in the past ten years to $15 billion. Every day, children see about fifty-eight commercial messages from television alone, and about half of those are for food products, she said.

Food and advertising officials disagreed with CSPI facts and proposals. Daniel Jaffe, executive vice president of the Association of National Advertisers, which represents more than three hundred companies that advertise more than eight thousand brands, said his group's research has shown that food and restaurant advertising aimed at children dropped between 1993 and 2003. "By narrowly focusing on advertising and marketing, CSPI misses the point," the Grocery Manufacturers of America said in a statement. "Effective solutions must incorporate sound nutrition, increased physical activity, consumer and parent education, and community support."

Source: Caroline Mayer, "Group Takes Aim at Junk Food Marketing," *The Washington Post* (January 7, 2005), E3. Copyright 2005, The Washington Post. Reprinted with permission.

"adult" than marketers have traditionally expected. Adult communications will be more effective when directed to children with higher verbal and creative skills associated with only children. Further, families in which both parents are employed have less time to spend with children and may be willing to spend more money on consumer products for children to compensate.

## Research Methodology for Family Decision Studies

When preparing an analysis of family influences on buying or the consumption decisions of families, most of the research techniques are similar to other marketing research studies. However, a few unique aspects of family decisions should be considered.

The study of family consumer decisions is less common than that of individual consumer decisions because of the difficulty of researching and studying the family as a unit. Administering a questionnaire simultaneously to an entire family requires accessing all members (difficult in today's hectic environment), using language that has the same meaning to all family members (difficult with discrepancies in age or education), and interpreting results when members of the same family report conflicting opinions about family purchases or influences on decisions.

**FIGURE 12.12** Involving Children in Shopping in a Japanese Department Store

## Measuring Influences

Role structure studies have often viewed purchasing as an act rather than a process and have based findings on questions such as "Who usually makes the decision to purchase?" or "Who influences the decision?" Yet, the role and influence of family members vary by stage in the decision process. The following questions might be useful for measuring family influence.[95]

1. Who was responsible for initial need recognition?

2. Who was responsible for acquiring information about the purchase alternatives?

3. Who made the final decision on which alternative should be purchased?

4. Who made the actual purchase of the product?

Husbands and wives are more likely to have similar perceptions about their relative influence on a given phase when questioning focuses on the decision stages.

The relevant role structure categories in a research project depend on the specific product or service under consideration, but in many product categories, only the husband or wife is involved. In other categories, it is useful to measure the amount of influence of different family members and other variables, such as family life cycle stage and lifestyles.[96]

## Interviewer Bias

The gender of the interviewer or observer may influence the roles husbands and wives say they play in a purchase situation. To overcome this bias, either self-administered questionnaires (such as mail or Internet questionnaires) should be used or the observer should be randomly assigned to respondents, with an equal number of male and female interviewers.

## Respondent Selection

In measuring family buying, it is necessary to decide which members of the family unit should be asked about the influence of various family members. Results often vary considerably depending on which family members are interviewed. Most often, wives are the ones interviewed, but the percentage of couples whose responses agree is often so low that it makes interviewing only one family member unacceptable. Some studies indicate that husbands' responses concerning purchase intentions are better predictors of number of items and total expenditures planned, although wives predicted better for certain products such as appliances, home furnishings, and entertainment equipment.[97]

## Summary

Families or households are consumer units of critical importance in the study of consumer behavior for two reasons. First, families or households are the unit of usage and purchase for many consumer products. Second, the family is a major influence on the attitudes and behavior of individuals. As consumers, we as individuals are the creation of our families to a large extent.

A family is a group of two or more persons related by blood, marriage, or adoption who reside together. A household differs from a family by describing all the persons, both related and unrelated, who occupy a housing unit. Thus, households outnumber families and are smaller in size; the average income is higher for families than households.

Family (or household) members occupy various roles, which include initiator (gatekeeper), influencer, decider, buyer, and user. The influence of spouses, children, or other family members varies depending on the resources of family members, the type of product, the stage in the family life cycle, and the stage in the buying decision. These variables are more important in understanding family decisions than traditional roles ascribed to one gender or the other.

Families and households are changing in their structure and composition. Among more important recent changes are increases in the number of single households, smaller average family size, later marriages, divorce, remarriage and redivorce, cohabitating singles, and increased awareness of the gay and lesbian market. The increasing number of employed women has created role overload for employed women who work more hours (combining paid work and family work) each week than their husbands or nonemployed women.

Marketers are concerned with the roles performed by women, men, and children. Advertising to women increasingly reflects themes of increasing income and responsibility and drives for self-fulfillment and self-enhancement. Masculine roles increasingly reflect shared performance of household activities. The blurring of traditional gender roles that existed in the past may be creating androgynous consumers, especially among young, well-educated professionals.

**Chapter Summary**

Children learn much of their consumption and buying behavior from parents and exert considerable influence on family purchases.

Marketing research techniques useful in studying families and households give special consideration to the decision process framework, questioning techniques, role structure categories and relative influence, interviewer bias, and respondent selection. A methodological problem is created because husbands and wives often differ in their responses to questions about how their families buy consumer goods and services.

## Review and Discussion Questions

1. What is meant by the term *family?* What is the importance of studying families to the understanding of consumer behavior?
2. Some studies of consumer behavior maintain that the family rather than the individual should be the unit of analysis in consumer behavior. What are the advantages and disadvantages of using the family as the unit of analysis?
3. Do husbands or wives have the most influence on buying decisions? Outline your answer.
4. Explain the changes occurring in the home meal replacement (HMR) market, and describe why you think demand for these types of products will increase or decrease in the future.

5. Will there be more or fewer women employed outside the home in the future? What variables should be considered in answering this question? How does the answer affect demand for consumer products?
6. Analyze the statement, "Working women buy products and services in essentially the same ways as nonworking women."
7. What is meant by the "singles" market? How would a travel company (such as an airline, resort, or cruise line) appeal to the singles market?
8. Assume that an airline has asked for a research project to understand how families make vacation decisions. You are asked to prepare a research design for the project. What would you suggest?
9. Assume that you are the marketing manager for a clothing firm that wishes to attract the gay and lesbian market. How would you assess the size of this market? Outline the marketing program you would recommend.
10. Children do not have much purchasing power, relative to other markets. Yet they are believed to be very important in the understanding of consumer behavior. Why? What might firms do to be more profitable as a result of understanding the role of children in family buying?

## Notes

1. Harry L. Davis, "Decision Making within the Household," *Journal of Consumer Research*, 2 (March 1976), 241–260.
2. Terry Childers and Akshay Rao, "The Influence of Familial and Peer-Based Reference Groups on Consumer Decisions," *Journal of Consumer Research*, 19 (September 1992), 198–221.
3. For a discussion of these issues on a global perspective, see Nico Keilman, Anton Kuitsten, and Ad Vossen, eds., *Modeling Household Formation and Dissolution* (New York: Oxford University Press, 1988).
4. David H. Olson, et al., *Families: What Makes Them Work?* (Beverly Hills, CA: Sage Publications, 1983).

5. Hamilton I. McCubbin and Marilyn A. McCubbin, "Typologies of Resilient Families: Emerging Roles of Social Class and Ethnicity," *Family Relations*, 37 (July 1988), 247–254.
6. Tibbett Speer, "Stretching the Holiday Season," *American Demographics* (November 1997), 43.
7. Russell Belk, "A Child's Christmas in America: Santa Claus as Deity, Consumption as Religion," *Journal of American Culture*, 10 (Spring 1987), 87–100; David Cheal, *The Gift Economy* (London: Routledge, 1988); Elizabeth Hirschman and Priscilla LaBarbera, "The Meaning of Christmas," in Elizabeth Hirschman, ed., *Interpretative Consumer Research* (Provo, UT: Association for Consumer Research), 136–147.

8. Russell Belk and Gregory Coon, "Gift Giving as Agapic Love: An Alternative to the Exchange Paradigm Based on Dating Experiences," *Journal of Consumer Research*, 20 (December 1993), 393–417.
9. "Holiday Finale Disappoints Retailers—Again," *Wall Street Journal* (December 26, 1997).
10. Chenting Su, Edward Fern, and Keying Ye, "A Temporal Dynamic Model of Spousal Family Purchase-Decision Behavior," *Journal of Marketing Research*, 40 (August 2003), 268–282.
11. Robert Boutilier, "Pulling the Family's Strings," *American Demographics* (August 1993), 44–48.
12. Theresa Howard, "Family Marketing Values: Beyond Toys and Coloring Books," *Nation's Restaurant News* (April 22, 1996).

[13] Harry L. Davis and Benny R. Rigaux, "Perception of Marital Roles in Decision Processes," *Journal of Consumer Research,* 1 (June 1974), 5–14.

[14] Marilyn Lavin, "Husband-Dominant, Wife-Dominant, Joint: A Shopping Typology for Baby Boom Couples?" *Journal of Consumer Marketing,* 10 (1993), 33–42.

[15] William J. Qualls, "Changing Sex Roles: Its Impact upon Family Decision Making," in Andrew Mitchell, ed., *Advances in Consumer Research,* 9 (Ann Arbor, MI: Association for Consumer Research, 1982), 267–270.

[16] Joseph Bellizzi and Laura Milner, "Gender Positioning of a Traditionally Male-Dominated Product," *Journal of Advertising Research,* 31 (June/July 1991), 72–79.

[17] For research on this topic from a wide variety of disciplines, see Beth B. Hess and Myra Marx Ferree, *Analyzing Gender* (Newbury Park, CA: Sage Publications, 1987).

[18] Roger Jenkins, "Contributions of Theory to the Study of Family Decision-Making," in Jerry Olson, ed., *Advances in Consumer Research,* 7 (Ann Arbor, MI: Association for Consumer Research, 1980), 207–211.

[19] Alvin Bums and Donald Granbois, "Advancing the Study of Family Purchase Decision Making," in Olson, *Advances in Consumer Research,* 221–226.

[20] Sunil Gupta, Michael R. Hagerty, and John G. Myers, "New Directions in Family Decision Making Research," in Alice M. Tybout, ed., *Advances in Consumer Research,* 10 (Ann Arbor, MI: Association for Consumer Research, 1983), 445–450.

[21] Mary Lou Roberts, "Gender Differences and Household Decision-Making: Needed Conceptual and Methodological Developments," in Thomas C. Kinnear, ed., *Advances in Consumer Research,* 11 (Provo, UT: Association for Consumer Research, 1984), 276–278.

[22] Eileen Fischer and Stephen J. Arnold, "More than a Labor of Love: Gender Roles and Christmas Gift Shopping," *Journal of Consumer Research,* 17 (December 1990), 333–343.

[23] William D. Wells and George Gubar, "The Life Cycle Concept," *Journal of Marketing Research,* 2 (November 1966), 355–363.

[24] Fred D. Reynolds and William D. Wells, *Consumer Behavior* (New York: McGraw-Hill, 1977).

[25] Patrick E. Murphy and William Staples, "A Modernized Family Life Cycle," *Journal of Consumer Research,* 6 (June 1979), 12–22.

[26] Erin White, "Focus on Recruitment, Pay and Getting Ahead," *Wall Street Journal* (February 22, 2005), B8.

[27] Janet Wagner and Sherman Hanna, "The Effectiveness of Family Life Cycle Variables in Consumer Expenditure Research," *Journal of Consumer Research,* 10 (December 1983), 281–291.

[28] Avery Johnson, "Spring-Break Party Destinations Try Bringing In the Grown-Ups," *Wall Street Journal* (February 22, 2005), D6.

[29] Joanne Y. Cleaver, "Good Old Dad," *American Demographics* (June 1999), 59–63.

[30] Cheryl Russell, "The New Consumer Paradigm," *American Demographics* (April 1999), 52–53.

[31] *Household Spending: Who Spends How Much on What* (Ithaca, NY: New Strategist Publications, 2005), 1.

[32] Julie Appleby, "Health Care Tab Ready to Explode," *USA Today* (February 24, 2005), A1.

[33] Kendra Darko, "A Home of Their Own," *American Demographics* (September 1999), 35–38.

[34] Jennifer Lach, "The Consequences of Divorce," *American Demographics* (October 1999), 14.

[35] For a thorough analysis of the financial and other decision-making capabilities of these families, see Frank Furstenbert and Graham B. Spanier, *Recycling the Family* (Beverly Hills, CA: Sage Publications, 1984).

[36] Amy Harmon, "Ask Them (All 8 of Them) about Their Grandson," *New York Times* (March 20, 2005).

[37] "The Future of Households," *American Demographics* (December 1993), 39.

[38] Peter Francese, "Well Enough Alone," *American Demographics,* 24 (November 2003), 32–34.

[39] Kendra Darko, "A Home of Their Own," *American Demographics* (September 1999), 35–38.

[40] Anne McGrath, "Living Alone and Loving It," *U.S. News and World Report* (August 3, 1987).

[41] W. Wayne Delozier and C. William Roe, "Marketing to the Homosexual (Gay) Market," in Robert L. King, ed., *Marketing: Toward the Twenty-First Century* (Richmond, VA: Southern Marketing Association, 1991), 107–109.

[42] Felicity Barringer, "Sex Survey of American Men Finds 1 percent Are Gay," *New York Times* (April 15, 1993), A1.

[43] "Gay Community Looks for Strength in Numbers," *American Marketplace* (July 4, 1991), 134.

[44] Rachel X. Weissman, "Gay Market Power," *American Demographics* (June 1999), 32–33.

[45] Steven Kates, "The Protean Quality of Subcultural Consumption: An Ethnographic Account of Gay Consumers," *Journal of Consumer Research,* 29 (December 2002), 383–400.

[46] Weissman, "Gay Market Power."

[47] Cyndee Miller, "Gays Are Affluent but Often Overlooked Market," *Marketing News* (December 24, 1990), 2.

[48] Steven Kates, "The Dynamics of Brand Legitimacy: An Interpretive Study in the Gay Men's Community," *Journal of Consumer Research,* 31 (September 2004), 455–465.

[49] U.S. Bureau of the Census, No. 75, "Family Groups with Children Under 18 Years Old, by Race and Hispanic Origin, 1997."

[50] David Wilson, "Role Theory and Buying-Selling Negotiations: A Critical Review," in Richard Bagozzi, ed., *Marketing in the 1980s* (Chicago: American Marketing Association, 1980), 118–121.

[51] U.S. Department of Labor, Bureau of Labor Statistics, data.bls.gov (March 2005).

[52] Salah Hassan and Roger Blackwell, *Global Marketing Perspectives and Cases* (Fort Worth, TX: Dryden Press, 1994), 122.

[53] Rose M. Rubin, Bobye J. Riney, and David J. Molina, "Expenditure Pattern Differentials between One-Earner and Dual-Earner Households: 1972–1973 and 1984," *Journal of Consumer Research*, 17 (June 1990), 43–52.

[54] Eva Jacobs, Stephanie Shipp, and Gregory Brown, "Families of Working Wives Spending More on Services and Nondurables," *Monthly Labor Review*, 112 (February 1989), 15–23.

[55] Rena Bartos, *The Moving Target: What Every Marketer Should Know about Women* (New York: Free Press, 1982).

[56] Charles Schaninger, Margaret Nelson, and William Danko, "An Empirical Evaluation of the Bartos Model of Wife's Work Involvement," *Journal of Advertising Research*, 33 (May–June 1993), 49–63.

[57] Marianne Ferber and Bonnie Birnbaum, "One Job or Two Jobs: The Implications for Young Wives," *Journal of Consumer Research*, 8 (December 1980), 263–271.

[58] Charles B. Weinberg and Russell S. Winer, "Working Wives and Major Family Expenditures: Replication and Extension," *Journal of Consumer Research*, 7 (September 1983), 259–263.

[59] Patricia Voydanoff, *Work and Family Life* (Newbury Park, CA: Sage Publications, 1987), 83.

[60] Alvin C. Burns and Ellen Foxman, "Role Load and Its Consequences on Individual Consumer Behavior," in Terence A. Shimp, et al., eds., *1986 AMA Educators' Proceedings* (Chicago: American Marketing Association, 1986), 18.

[61] B. Townsend and I. C. O'Neil, "American Women Get Mad: Women's Attitudes Are Changing and Here's What You Can Expect in the 1990's," *American Demographics* (August 1990), 26–32.

[62] F. Thomas Juster, "A Note on Recent Changes in Time Use," in R. Thomas Juster and Frank P. Stafford, eds., *Time, Goods, and Well-Being* (Ann Arbor, MI:

Institute for Social Research, 1985), 313–332.

[63] Done Bellante and Ann C. Foster, "Working Wives and Expenditure on Services," *Journal of Consumer Research*, 11 (September 1984), 700–707.

[64] Cristina Merrill, "Mother's Work Is Never Done," *American Demographics* (September 1999), 29–32.

[65] Elizabeth Moore, William Wilkie, and Richard Lutz, "Passing the Torch: Intergenerational Influences as a Source of Brand Equity," *Journal of Marketing*, 66 (April 2002), 17–38.

[66] Alan Otten, "People Patterns," *Wall Street Journal* (June 14, 1988), 33.

[67] Linda Jacobsen and Brad Edmondson, "Father Figures," *American Demographics* (August 1993), 22–27.

[68] John P. Robinson, "Who's Doing the Housework," *American Demographics* (December 1988), 24–28ff.

[69] Danny Hakim, "Big Pickup Trucks Eclipsing S.U.V.'s," *New York Times* (February 8, 2005), C1.

[70] Michael S. Kimmel, ed., *Changing Men: New Directions in Research on Men and Masculinity* (Newbury Park, CA: Sage Publications, 1987).

[71] Joseph H. Pleck, "American Fathering in Historical Perspective," in Kimmel, *Changing Men*, 93.

[72] Cele Otnes and Mary McGrath, "Perceptions and Realities of Male Shopping Behavior," *Journal of Retailing*, 77 (Spring 2001), 111–138.

[73] "Real Men Get Waxed," *Economist*, 368 (July 5, 2003), 57.

[74] Kevin Helliker, "Kingsize, Not Queen: Some Men Have Taken To Wearing Pantyhose—Mainstay for Cross Dressers Is Boon to Athletes and Guys On Their Feet All Day Long," *Wall Street Journal* (February 19, 2002), A1.

[75] Michael Kimmel, "What Do Men Want?" *Harvard Business Review* (November/December 1993), 50–63.

[76] Ibid.

[77] Robert E. Wilkes, "Husband-Wife Influence in Purchase Decisions: A Confirmation and Extension," *Journal of Marketing Research*, 12 (May 1975), 224–227.

[78] David Evans and Olivia Toth, "Parents Buy, But Kids Rule," *Media Asia* (November 14, 2003), 22–24.

[79] J. Gregan-Paxton and John Roedder, "Are Young Children Adaptive Decision Makers? A Study of Age Differences in Information Search Behavior," *Journal of Consumer Research*, 21 (March 1995), 567–580.

[80] James McNeal, "Tapping the Three Kids' Markets," *American Demographics* (April 1998), 37.

[81] Martin Lindstrom and Patricia Seybold, *Brand Child* (London: Kogan Page, 2003).

[82] Sharon Beatty and Salil Talpade, "Adolescent Influence in Family Decision Making: A Replication with Extension," *Journal of Consumer Research*, 21 (September 1994), 332–341.

[83] Chankon Kim and Hanjoon Lee, "Development of Family Triadic Measures for Children's Purchase Influence," *Journal of Marketing Research*, 34 (August 1997), 307–321.

[84] James McNeal, "Tapping the Three Kids' Markets," *American Demographics* (April 1998), 37–41.

[85] Margaret Pressler, "Kids Rule for Back to School," *Washington Post* (August 15, 2004), F5.

[86] Margaret Hogg, Margaret Bruce, and Alexander Hill, "Fashion Brand Preferences among Young Consumers," *International Journal of Retail & Distribution Management*, 26 (August 1998), 293.

[87] C. E. Hite and R. E. Hite, "Reliance on Brand by Young Children," *International Journal of Market Research*, 37 (March 1995), 185–193.

[88] Shi Zhang and Sanjay Sood, "'Deep' and 'Surface' Cues: Brand Extension Evaluations by Children and Adults," *Journal of Consumer Research*, 29 (June 2002), 129–142.

[89] Scott Ward, "Consumer Socialization," in Harold Kassarjian and Thomas Robertson, eds., *Perspectives in Consumer Behavior* (Glenview, IL: Scott Foresman, 1981).

[90] June Cotte and Stacy Wood, "Families and Innovative Consumer Behavior: A

Triadic Analysis of Sibling and Parental Influence, *Journal of Consumer Research,* 31 (June 2004), 78–87.

[91] Sanford Grossbart, Les Carlson, and Ann Walsh, "Consumer Socialization and Frequency of Shopping with Children," *Journal of the Academy of Marketing Science,* 19 (Summer 1991), 155–163.

[92] Gary Cross, "Valves of Desire: A Historian's Perspective on Parents, Children, and Marketing," *Journal of Consumer Research,* 29 (December 2002), 441–448.

[93] Elizabeth Moore and Richard Lutz, "Children, Advertising, and Product Experiences: A Mulltimethod Inquiry," *Journal of Consumer Research,* 27 (June 2000), 31–49.

[94] Les Carlson, Sanford Grossbart, and J. Kathleen Stuenke, "The Role of Parental Socialization Types on Differential Family Communication Patterns Regarding Consumption," *Journal of Consumer Psychology,* 1 (1992), 31–52.

[95] Robert E. Wildes, "Husband-Wife Influence in Purchase Decisions: A Confirmation and Extension," *Journal of Marketing Research,* 12 (May 1975), 224–227.

[96] Rosann L. Spiro, "Persuasion in Family Decision-Making," *Journal of Consumer Research,* 9 (March 1983), 393–401.

[97] Donald H. Granbois and John O. Summers, "Primary and Secondary Validity of Consumer Purchase Probabilities," *Journal of Consumer Research,* 1 (March 1975), 31–38.

# Group and Personal Influence

## Opening Vignette

Digital connectivity has replaced the need for visitors to a new city to ask a hotel concierge or taxi driver which restaurants and night clubs are the most popular hangouts for all different types of people. Face-to-face interaction has always been the most frequent source of information for consumers making purchasing decisions ranging from food and clothing to cars and computers, but the Internet has added new methods of seeking the opinions of others. Technology expands personal influence from conversations with neighbors across the fence and coworkers around the water cooler to chats with Web friends around the world at transmission speeds measured in nanoseconds.

More than five million bloggers go public with their opinions on everything from politics and religion to consumer products and customer service, with the number rapidly spreading across segments of society. People ranging from students to CEOs can easily use weblogging services like Google's Blogger (blogger.com), Live Journal (livejournal.com), or TypePad (typepad.com) to share their experiences and learn from the experiences of others. Many blogs relate to consumer and financial topics such as BudgetingBabe .blogspot.com, dedicated to "all the young working women who want to spend like Carrie in a Jimmy Choo store, but have a

budget closer to Roseanne" ("Carrie" referring, of course, to Sarah Jessica Parker's character in the HBO hit series, *Sex and the City*).

"GodCasting" is now an established way of propagating established religions, with preachers converting their sermons to a digital format that can be downloaded and heard on iPods and other portable MP3 players. "Pod preachers," including Christians and Buddhists, are among the most prolific users of this new communication technology, just as sermons were among the first types of broadcasts when radio was the rapidly growing innovation of the 1920s. Recently launched podcasts range from *Catholic Answers Live,* a daily program run by a San Diego–based lay group, to *Teachings for the New Age,* which offers thoughts on "following your inner self and achieving true perfection." Religious podcasters say they like the medium because it's an inexpensive way to reach the masses. A spokesman for The Vineyard, an evangelical Christian fellowship, explains, "It takes a lot of money to run a TV show but podcasting is basically free. There is never a mention of asking for money. There's no need." A 2004 Pew Internet Project reported that 82 million Americans have used the Internet for spiritual and religious purposes (Religion News Service, March 21, 2005). It's not just religious podcasting that's catching on; political parties are involved as well as news organizations like Air America, a liberal-oriented radio network. According to Ipodder.org, a podcasting software organization, nearly 4,000 podcasts have sprung up around the world.

E-mail is another way people communicate their opinions. But are you frustrated by hundreds of junk e-mails every time you open Microsoft Outlook? Junk e-mail costs Internet service providers as much as $500 million a year in extra network capacity and infuriates consumers to the point of blocking all messages except those from authorized senders. Firewalls and antivirus programs need regular updates to prevent fast-moving hackers and new viruses from compromising computers, but these programs aren't foolproof, sometimes allowing in unwanted worms and trojans. Some experts say you should use two antivirus programs and two anti-spyware programs, but that could lead to a dramatic slowdown in your computer's processing speed. And sometimes when consumers buy online or download something "free" (such as a screensaver), they've also granted permission (buried in the fine print) to download software that causes advertisements to later pop up on their screens. Uses cause abuses. Phishing refers to a scam that dupes consumers into disclosing financial information, such as their bank account numbers, to fraudulent websites that resemble those of legitimate banks, brokerages, and online retailers. In September 2003, computer-security firm MessageLabs counted 279 phishing e-mails for the month. By November 2004, the number of phishing messages jumped to more than 100,000 a day from 1,707 sites identified by the Anti-Phishing Working Group, a collection of banks, security firms, and retailers. Problems such as these are reasons telecommunication hasn't completely replaced "telling a friend" as the primary source of personal influence.

Going on vacation or spring break doesn't mean you're out of contact with friends anymore, or limited to travel guides to find things to do. In addition to essentials like swimsuits, beach towels and sunglasses, your luggage likely includes an iPod, digital camera, a wireless connected laptop, and accessories to go along with each of them. When you arrive, you may locate a restaurant or a lively club with your Web-browsing "smart phone," such as T-Mobile's Sidekick, marketed as a "hiptop" computer. A smart phone is the size of a candy bar with a miniature "typewriter" keyboard and built-in Web browser. Going on vacation a decade ago meant escaping from the office and, to track you down, your boss had to know exactly where you would be at which times. Not anymore: Internet calling, known as VoIP (voice over Internet protocol) turns any computer into a phone connection, reducing or eliminating long-distance charges and allowing (or forcing) you into VoIPing by the swimming pool. With today's ubiquitous cell phones and an array of new technologies, it's difficult to get away from your friends, coworkers, or neighbors, and group and personal influence has been extended into a new space—cyberspace.

Sources: Various media reports including Jon Van, "Fraud, Hassles May Put Net in Not Worth It Mode," *Chicago Tribune* (January 2, 2005), 1; Jim Carlton, "What to Pack On Your Next Vacation," *Wall Street Journal* (March 21, 2005), R1; and Kate Zernike, "Tired of TiVo? Beyond Blogs? Podcasts Are Here," *New York Times* (February 19, 2005).

## Group and Personal Influences on Individuals

Other people, whether as individuals or in groups, exert enormous influence on consumers. Belonging to groups, trying to "fit in," and striving to please others affects every stage of the consumer decision process. Input from people with whom consumers identify and aspire to emulate enhances credibility about product and retail choices while also stimulating the trial and adoption of new products. In the past, interpersonal influences were concentrated among individuals with whom consumers had daily contact or perhaps learned about from mass media. Increasingly, however, our "friends" may be virtual friends, existing mostly in cyberspace, as you read about Carlos in the opening vignette of Chapter 1. The Internet widens the scope of interpersonal influence and permits instant-messaging ("IM-ing") group members, whether they are next door, across campus, or on another continent. "Getting together" increasingly means communication by mobile technology, yet the communication can still be individualized, which is the theme of the advertisement in Figure 13.1, allowing you to "do whatever."

The process of group and interpersonal influence has been studied for decades by sociologists and communication researchers as well as consumer analysts. Even though technology widens and accelerates interpersonal influence, the process is still understood by studying fundamental concepts and research, the topic of this chapter. Group influences begin in childhood, affecting consumer beliefs as well as how consumers respond to other media. As an example of research on this topic, a group of ninth graders were exposed to one of eight videos showing stimulus advertising (cigarette ads, antismoking ads, both, and neither) along with images of unfamiliar teenagers who either did or did not smoke. During adolescence, stereotypic beliefs about cigarette smoking, alcohol use, and illicit drug use sometimes change from negative to neutral or even positive. In the study, seeing the cigarette ads in conjunction with images of peers smoking strengthened positive perceptions about smoking and caused subjects to seek out favorable information about tobacco use. By contrast, antismoking ads shown in conjunction with cigarette ads led to unfavorable feelings about peers who smoked.[1]

### What Are Reference Groups?

A **reference group** is any *person or group of people who significantly influences an individual's behavior.*[2] The values, attitudes, behaviors, and norms of this group are perceived to have relevance upon the evaluations, behaviors, and aspirations of another individual.[3] Reference groups might be individuals, such as celebrities, athletes, and political leaders, or they might be groups with which individuals identify, such as rock bands, political parties, and sports teams. Most people are averse to behavior that contradicts group consensus,[4] and young people tend to seek the approval of their peers more than older adults do. Wearing clothing from

Courtesy of Nokia

**FIGURE 13.1** Wireless Communications Expand Our Scope of Personal Influence While Providing Greater Individual Freedom

**FIGURE 13.2**  Personal and Group Influence on Individuals

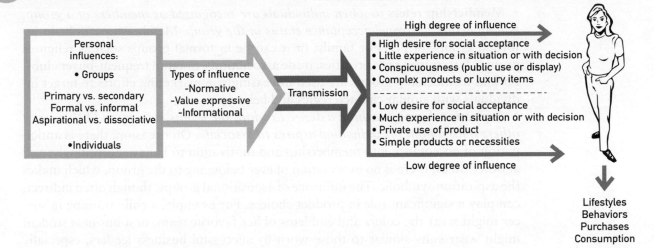

Abercrombie & Fitch (or other brands, such as Old Navy and Tommy Hilfiger) decreases the risk adolescent consumers feel during the purchase process while increasing their comfort level by helping them look the same as their friends. Figure 13.2 depicts the influence process, beginning with the source and type of influence, proceeding through the transmission of influence and degree of effect, and ending with the influence on behaviors, lifestyles, purchases, and consumption. This model can serve as a pictorial outline of the first half of this chapter.

## Types of Reference Groups

Social groups can take many forms, and individuals can belong to a variety of groups. Regardless of the type of reference group, input from others can be viewed as binding, in which case the input is referred to as *normative* influence, or at other times input can be viewed as *comparative,* which serves only as yet another source of information in decision making. These roles can occur in many types of groups, including the following.

- The greatest influence and impact usually is exerted by **primary groups**—*a social aggregation that is sufficiently intimate to permit and facilitate unrestricted direct interaction.* Because there exists cohesiveness and motivated participation, members exhibit marked similarities in beliefs and behavior.[5] The family is the most obvious example of a strongly influential primary group.
- **Secondary groups** also *have direct interaction, but it is more sporadic, less comprehensive, and less influential in shaping thought and behavior.*[6] Examples are professional associations, trade unions, and community organizations.
- **Formal groups** are *characterized by a defined structure (often written) and a known list of members and requirements for membership.* Examples are religious groups, fraternal bodies, and community service organizations. The influence exerted on behavior varies, depending on the motivation of individual members to accept and comply with the group's standards. Moreover, there are wide latitudes in the degree to which specific conformity is expected and enforced.
- In contrast to formal groups, **informal groups** *have far less structure and are likely to be based on friendship or interests.* Though their norms can be stringent, they seldom appear in writing, but the effect on behavior can be strong if individuals are motivated by social acceptance. There also is a high degree of intimate, face-to-face

interaction, which further strengthens the power with which expectations and sanctions are expressed and enforced.

- **Membership** refers to *when individuals are recognized as members of a group, having achieved formal acceptance status in the group.* Membership can be in informal groups of peers or family, or it can be in formal groups such as religious groups, fraternities and sororities, trade associations, or retail frequent-buyer clubs. Formal membership groups are used increasingly in marketing efforts to target individuals with similar characteristics and behaviors.

- **Aspirational groups** *exhibit a desire to adopt the norms, values, and behavior of others with whom the individual aspires to associate.* On occasion, there is anticipation of acceptance into membership and motivation to behave accordingly, and at other times, there is no expectation of ever belonging to the group, which makes the aspiration symbolic. The influence of aspirational groups, though often indirect, can play a significant role in product choices. For example, a child training in soccer might wear the colors and emblems of her favorite team, or a business student might wear suits similar to those worn by successful business leaders, especially during pre-graduation job recruiting.

- Influence also can be exerted by **dissociative groups**—*groups from which an individual tries to avoid association.* An example of this situation occurs when someone changes his or her social class by abandoning certain behaviors and brand choices for upscale alternatives. Some teens also disassociate themselves from their peers and parents by dressing in counterculture clothing, dying their hair purple, or tattooing their bodies. By disassociating themselves from one group, however, people associate themselves with another.

- **Virtual membership groups** have evolved through chat rooms and other associations on the Internet, as *virtual communities rather than geographic ones.* Internet communities are based on sets of social relations among people[7] rather than face-to-face relationships. Chat rooms allow individuals with similar interests to connect, interact with each other, and share information on topics from figure skating to deep-sea diving. The flow of information on the Internet is often less inhibited than during other encounters because individuals don't usually meet face to face,[8] and individuals feel more comfortable writing things to one another that they would have difficulty saying in person.

The relevant social context in any of these groups affects how consumers will respond to marketing efforts on the basis of group membership traits. Studies of consumers demonstrate the importance of social status within the group to understanding the influence of group membership on consumer behavior.[9]

## Types of Group Influence

Three primary types of influence affect individuals' decisions, behaviors, purchases, and lifestyles. **Normative influence** occurs *when individuals alter their behaviors or beliefs to meet the expectations of a particular group.* In this instance, the norms of the group influence behaviors, such as how an individual dresses or what brand of car he or she drives. Often the goal of the individual is conformity. **Value-expressive influence** occurs when *a need for psychological association with a group causes acceptance of its norms, values, attitudes, or behaviors.* Even though there may be no motivation to become a member, individuals often enhance their image in the eyes of others, or achieve identification with people they admire and respect. Because consumers often accept the opinions of others as providing credible and needed evidence about reality,[10] they often seek the advice of others before making a purchase or life decision.

**Informational influence** occurs *when people have difficulty assessing product or brand characteristics by their own observation or contact.* In this instance, they will accept recommendations or usage by others as evidence about the nature of the product[11] and use the information in their own product or brand decisions.

## How Reference Groups Influence Individuals

Reference groups affect individual consumers in different ways and to different degrees, depending on individual characteristics and product purchase situations. First, reference groups create socialization of individuals. Second, they are important in developing and evaluating one's self-concept and provide a benchmark for comparing oneself to others. Third, reference groups are a device for obtaining compliance with norms in a society.

### Socialization

Socialization occurs under the influence of various reference groups, as discussed in Chapter 11. A company manual may explain the formal dress code to a new employee, for example, but informal work groups teach the employee which styles are the most comfortable and easiest to maintain, as well as which stores to purchase the clothes. The process of socialization and acculturation permits an individual to know what behavior is likely to result in stability for both the individual and the group.

Going shopping with friends is one way of learning about what others perceive is important and appropriate. While overall mall patronage in the United States has been declining for several years, patronage among U.S. adolescents (especially females) has risen sharply. An in-depth study of this phenomenon indicates some factors specifically relevant to adolescent females (ages twelve to nineteen) help explain the process as social education within the cohort,[12] as well as learning about trends, comfort, safety, companionship, and "freedom" as mall-patronage motivation.

### Self-Concept

People protect and modify their self-concept by their interactions with others in reference groups. What we think of ourselves is influenced in our social interactions by the reactions of others whose values we share or opinions we respect. One form of social interaction is the consumption of products. We communicate meaning to others when we buy and use products. Our clothing, transportation, and career choices make statements about us, and our behaviors and lifestyle are the presentation of ourselves (or an idealized view of ourselves) to our reference groups. By wearing a sports team's logo on a shirt, consumers blend their personal identities with the cultural milieu surrounding the product[13] and assume an altered social identity. People also maintain their self-concept by conforming to roles they have learned. When individuals belong to many groups, they take on numerous roles, and feel pressure to act in certain ways expected by someone in that particular role. Look at Figure 13.3

**FIGURE 13.3** Reference Groups Help Define the Self-Concept of Individuals

© AP/Wide World Photos

and you see the use of one of the first groups many people join—community sports teams—as a source of defining one's self-concept.

Testimonial advertising is a direct application of understanding the social consequences of the self-concept. A child sees athletic megastars Tiger Woods and LeBron James wearing Nike apparel and either consciously or subconsciously attributes to the Nike brand (at least in part) the respect and strength that he or she desires. Testimonials from respected movie stars, politicians, or sports figures can be very effective if the self that is projected by the reference person in the testimonial is consistent with the idealized self of the consumer in the target audience.

## Social Comparison

Most individuals have a need to evaluate themselves by comparing themselves to others. How successful, healthy, or wealthy people perceive themselves to be often depends on how they fare in comparison to their peers or other reference group members. In addition to learning from groups, individuals use reference groups as benchmarks or yardsticks to measure their own behaviors, opinions, abilities, and possessions. But individuals select different comparison groups at different times. When an individual and his or her reference group are similar, confidence in the accuracy of information received is greater.[14] However, consumers tend to value differing views only when they are highly confident in their own opinions and abilities.[15]

Comparison is not limited to groups with which consumers have personal contact. Advertising and television can be sources of social comparison. For example, when some professional baseball players were reported to be using steroids and other supplements to enhance their natural abilities, some high school athletes who compared themselves with those individuals began to alter their own consumption behavior to include those substances, despite the fact that they were illegal. Women are bombarded daily with airbrushed images of professional models gracing the pages of fashion magazines around the world. As women see these images, many of them feel increased dissatisfaction with their own bodies,[16] contributing perhaps to an increase in the number of women suffering from anorexia and bulimia or seeking liposuction, artificial breast implants, and other plastic surgery. Sadly, only the positive benefits of these choices are visible—the media often doesn't show the grave dangers associated with many private choices of public figures.

## Conformity

The desire of an individual to fit in with a reference group often leads to **conformity**—*a change in beliefs or actions based on real or perceived group pressures.* Two types of conformity exist: compliance and acceptance. **Compliance** occurs *when an individual conforms to the wishes of the group without accepting all its beliefs or behaviors,* whereas **acceptance** occurs *when an individual actually changes his or her beliefs and values to those of the group.* Sometimes a consumer makes a conscious effort to emulate the behavior of others in the group or to be identified with the group's behavior to receive a reward (such as social acceptance). And sometimes the influence of the group is more subtle, occurring without the conscious effort of the individual being influenced. For example, some consumers might not know how to behave in a particular situation and use group norms as a guide on how to behave correctly. Knowing how to get people to conform to the norms of a group or an individual within the group, such as a salesperson, is an important determinant of successful communication, but understanding the process is just as important to you as an individual in knowing how to resist such communications, as you can read in Buyer Beware 13.1, which describes the research of Robert Cialdini.

Reference groups influence individuals to conform to group norms in varying degrees depending on the characteristics of the group, the individual, and the situation, as seen in Figure 13.2. The more cohesive a group is, the more influence it is likely to have on individual members, with much of the influence coming from loyal members of the group. Further, the size of the group affects its ability to influence; the old belief that there is "safety in numbers" holds true in many instances of group influence. An individual might turn to a group with expertise in a particular area to help him or her make product decisions, especially if the consumer has limited information available. A consumer is also more likely to conform to group norms if the person likes the group or possesses a strong desire to belong to the group. Individuals who have a strong need for social acceptance might be more likely to be influenced by others than those who are more independent and do not place as much importance on social acceptance. Similarly, individuals who plan on using items publicly (displaying them) are more likely to be influenced by others so as to decrease the risk of choosing the "wrong" brand or product. Individuals are less swayed by group influences when purchasing necessity items to be used in private or items not requiring much thought or pre-purchase search. Yet normative influence can extend across many situations.[17]

## PROFITS OF CONFORMITY

Conformity is most likely to occur when the rewards of compliance exceed its costs, concludes sociologist George Homans, who shed light on the dynamics of normative compliance and the relationship between its rewards and costs.[18] Rewards, such as self-esteem or acceptance, can reinforce behavior and encourage repetition, whereas costs can discourage certain behaviors. The degree of influence on final outcome is determined by an individual's perception of the "profit" inherent in the interaction (i.e., rewards minus costs). For example, if someone is asked to join another person for a cup of coffee, there will be rewards (e.g., companionship, coffee, esteem stemming from the invitation), but there may also be costs (e.g., lost time, money, and perhaps missed opportunity to go with someone else).

## CONSPICUOUSNESS

Several studies over the years have demonstrated that conformity pressures are not sufficient to induce behavior unless the product or service is publicly conspicuous in its purchase and use.[19] Furthermore, luxury goods are more susceptible to social influence than necessities.[20] Conspicuousness affects conformity in two ways. First, because others (including group members) will see the product, a desire to be accepted and identified as part of the group causes many consumers to conform rather than risk public ridicule or embarrassment. Second, individuals (such as fashion-conscious teenagers) receive clear signals from their peers about product alternatives, which make further information search unnecessary.[21]

Conformity is not a fixed product characteristic—it depends on the situation and the ways in which the product is used. For example, normative influence on brand choice is important when beer is to be served to friends but not when it is consumed privately.[22] Table 13.1 explains how reference groups influence product and brand choice in different situations. In one study,[23] more than eight hundred respondents

## Defend Yourself Against Manipulation

Life's decisions are affected by who you influence or persuade and the people who influence or persuade you. If you know how to persuade people, your likelihood of success improves measurably. For this reason, organizations spend millions on training people to improve their selling and negotiation skills and to become highly skilled at persuading you to spend your money. Do you spend as much effort in understanding what they are persuading you to do and learning how to make good decisions in response?

John Mariotti, an influential management consultant and former CEO, encourages people to study the work of social psychologist Robert Cialdini to understand compliance and why people respond the way they do. In his book, *Influence: The Psychology of Persuasion,* Dr. Robert Cialdini explains six psychological principles that drive your powerful impulse to comply to the pressures of others and shows how to defend against manipulation or put the principles to work for you. These principles (reciprocation, commitment and consistency, social proof, likeability, authority, and scarcity) are consciously or subconsciously employed by people to persuade other people, sometimes with "automatic, mindless compliance." Being aware of these principles increases defense against them, and Cialdini gives practical advice on "How to Say No."

Influences that create a powerful urge to respond include the following.

- *Reciprocation*—the old give-and-take and take-and-take. This is the principle behind the Hare Krishna practice of handing out free flowers or books in airports, and the basis for the entire ad specialty business (e.g., free pens, coffee mugs, and so forth). When someone gives you something, you feel obliged to reciprocate. Nothing says the exchange must be fair or equitable, and the intent of someone using this principle to his or her advantage is that it won't be.
- *Commitment and consistency*—false hobgoblins of the mind. After people make a carefully considered decision or analysis, and then a commitment, they have a strong tendency to defend and reinforce that position consistently—regardless of how right or wrong it was. Think of the last car or computer you bought, and how strongly you became a vocal supporter of that brand or model, even noticing that "there's a lot more of these sold now than there used to be." Many people remain loyal to their initial decisions even if they have ample reason to be dissatisfied. This explains why some people continue to hold bad investments, even when it's clear they won't recover their money.

---

13.1 **TABLE 13.1**  Reference Group Influence on Product and Brand Purchase Decisions

| | PRODUCT | |
|---|---|---|
| **BRAND** | **WEAK REFERENCE GROUP INFLUENCE** | **STRONG REFERENCE GROUP INFLUENCE** |
| | Public necessities | Public luxuries |
| Strong reference group influences (+) | *Influence:* Weak product and strong brand | *Influence:* Strong product and strong brand |
| | *Examples:* Wristwatch, automobile, suits | *Examples:* Golf clubs, snow skis, sailboat |
| | Private necessities | Private luxuries |
| Weak reference group influences (−) | *Influence:* Weak product and weak brand | *Influence:* Strong product and weak brand |
| | *Examples:* Mattress, floor lamp, refrigerator | *Examples:* TV or computer game, trash compactor, icemaker |

Source: William O. Bearden and Michael J. Etzel, " Reference Group Influence on Product and Brand Purchase Decisions," *Journal of Consumer Research* 9 (September 1982), 1985.

- *Social proof*—truths are "us." This principle explains why people laugh along with laugh tracks on TV sitcoms, why riots erupt in otherwise peaceful demonstrations, and why bystanders allow a person to be mugged in full view of a crowd with no one helping the victim. The reason is that no one wants to break out of the crowd. Studies indicate that after a widely reported suicide, suicide rates increase the following week. The publicized suicide legitimizes suicide for others, according to the doctrine of social proof. When a website reported alleged errors in President Bush's National Guard service record during the 2004 presidential campaign, CBS Evening News anchor Dan Rather considered it legitimate to do the same although the report was later proven inaccurate and Rather subsequently left his job.

- *Likeability*—the friendly thief. Physical attractiveness and likeability increase a person's influence. That's why the use of attractive models in ads and the friendly salutations of telephone solicitors increase the probability of persuasion. People like people similar to themselves in interests, lifestyles, and culture, but they can have an even greater influence on you when they compliment and are nice to you. Watch out for situations such as joining a health club or considering a timeshare purchase when you find yourself liking the salesperson too much.

- *Authority*—directed deference. Uniforms are not a coincidence. They impart an unspoken message of influence based on authority, as do titles, offices, and other trappings. In Cialdini's book, hospital patients did not ask any questions when a total stranger dressed in a doctor's coat asked to change their medications. Many quack medical practitioners will use the same titles, appearance, and vocabulary as legitimate professionals, but the quacks lack the same level of training, expertise, and skill and can sometimes inflict harm.

- *Scarcity*—the rule of the few. When products like stamps or currency are misprinted or popular toys like Beanie Babies are produced in limited quantity, their value goes up. Even the illusion of scarcity is very powerful. Realtors who have other (often imaginary) prospective buyers use this leverage regularly. If you don't buy the product now, it may be gone tomorrow. When competing buyers for a used car "coincidentally" show up at the same time to look at the car, the competition may increase the price buyers are willing to pay for it.

Learning to be persuasive honestly is a valuable tool, but don't count on everyone following that practice. Others will use these techniques to influence you. When you are aware of the techniques, you are ready to evaluate and respond to them. Forewarned is forearmed!

Source: Robert Cialdini, *Influence: The Psychology of Persuasion* (New York: Perennial Currents, 1998); and John L. Mariotti, *The Enterprise and Economic Week in Review*, www.shape-shifters.com/new.shtml#blog (March 5, 2005).

were asked to consider sixteen products that differed along the private-public and necessity-luxury dimensions. For each product, respondents rated the extent of reference group influence on product category and brand choice. The study showed how to classify the types of product and brand choices that are most likely to be swayed by group influences. For example, before people began using the alarm clocks on their cell phones, wristwatches were often worn out of necessity with little regard as to what other people did. But brand choice is quite different—for example, the high social acceptability in some quarters garnered by wearing a Swatch or Rolex. Table 13.1 offers insights into the ways in which social influence becomes expressed.

## Appealing to Normative Influence in Marketing Strategy

Marketers have learned the potency of appealing to the "in thing." Wearing a yellow wristband to demonstrate cancer awareness (recognizing the courage and heroism of bicyclist Lance Armstrong) or a pink wristband to signify concern over breast cancer gains greatest acceptance among groups with high susceptibility to normative influence. High product visibility also increases reference group influence. You can see how this is translated into marketing strategy for a not-for-profit organization selling multicolored bracelets for HIV/AIDS awareness at leading retailers in Figure 13.4.

Normative compliance may be less important now than in the past in industrialized nations.[24] The reason is that urbanization is creating a society where grandparents, aunts, uncles, and other members of extended families are less likely to have face-to-face interactions, putting the personal needs of individual consumers ahead of group loyalty. Furthermore, urban living in anonymous cities minimizes the long-term social interaction that is characteristic of rural communities and small towns. Virtual groups on the Internet may exert influence on specific topics, but it's a little difficult to get information about what your virtual friend is wearing, eating, or driving, and it's difficult to have a face-to-face conversation with friends if you're listening to your iPod. Television and other media represent social reality with such power that the media themselves may be a more important source of normative influence than other people on beliefs and behavior.[25]

Another consideration leading to diminished normative compliance is *a weakened respect for social norms,* referred to by sociologists as **anomie**.[26] Some people feel an ambivalence toward social norms that causes them to conform grudgingly or, in certain instances, not conform at all. Some marketers appeal to people who want to be different and express their individuality rather than be considered just "one of the group." Buell, Harley-Davidson's series of high performance motorbikes designed by racing champion Erik Buell, appeals to professionals and others with sufficient disposable income to spend on a sport bike, yet who also want to live in the "fast lane". As illustrated in Figure 13.5, Buell provides a break from the social norms of "sex, money, and down-shifting."

FIGURE 13.4 High Product Visibility Raises Reference Group Influence

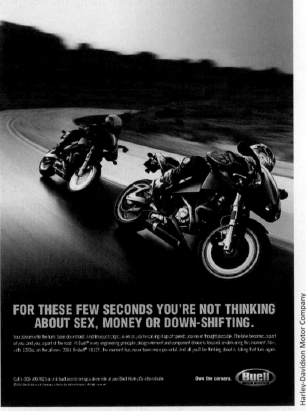

FIGURE 13.5 Sometimes People Express Themselves Outside Social Norms

PART 4 [ ENVIRONMENTAL INFLUENCES ON CONSUMER BEHAVIOR

Celebrities, especially movie stars, television actors, entertainers, and sports figures, can be powerful assets to marketing and advertising campaigns. Celebrities grab attention, create awareness, and communicate effectively with consumers who admire them or aspire to be like them. Consumers may relate to a common problem they share with the celebrity in the ad, or they may hope to emulate him or her by using the endorsed product. In either case, marketers hope that consumers will relate, in a positive light, the product to the celebrity endorser. The variety of products influenced by celebrities may surprise you (see Market Facts 13.1).

Celebrities can appear in advertisements in four primary ways. They can give *testimonials,* in which they tout the benefits of the product based on their personal usage, or *endorsements,* in which they lend their name or likeness to a product without necessarily being an expert in the area. A celebrity can also be an *actor* in a commercial or a company *spokesperson,* in which he or she represents the brand or company for an extended time period. After his unsuccessful 1996 presidential campaign, Senator Bob Dole endorsed Visa credit cards and began a testimonial campaign promoting Viagra as a remedy to erectile dysfunction. Tiger Woods' role as an endorser is obvious for golf-related products, but for other products ranging from credit cards to

## MARKET FACTS 13.1

## Celebrity Marketing

If you believe that celebrities only influence sales of products such as clothing and music, you may get a smile from learning that Hollywood A-listers such as Gwyneth Paltrow or Halle Berry are now the influencers of Chiclet-style smiles with prosthetic choppers. It's a snap-on smile, a kind of white-enameled cousin to press-on nails, another example of the public sinking its incisors into celebrity culture to attain a Julia Roberts' million-dollar smile. The product to which we refer is a resin appliance that fits over existing teeth and sells for $1,000 to $3,000.

Cosmetic teeth reflect the changing nature of the benefits from a dentist's services. "It's not for health," says Jeff Golub-Evans, a New York cosmetic dentist. "More and more patients go to dentists to look better rather than to feel better." His Red Carpet Smile comes in several Oscar-winning models ranging from the "square, sexy" Gwyneth model to the "sophisticated," and most requested, Halle model in a range of

shades. Business has grown rapidly since he started selling the custom-molded products.

A typical customer might be a teen having her senior picture shot soon, says Lawrence Addleson, president of the American Academy of Cosmetic Dentistry. "My wife says I used to talk like a ventriloquist because I didn't want to show my teeth," says Arvid Saunatis of Woodridge, Illinois. Now he says his speech has improved and he looks ten years younger. New Yorker Deborah Day, age thirty-four, owns the Gwyneth model to cover a dental feature associated with another A-lister, the Madonna gap. Portland, Oregon, television personality Nicolle Camarata had multiple Madonna gaps until she bought her new smile, modeled after Sarah Jessica Parker's grin, but limits use to her television appearances. On dates, she says, she would hate to be the kind of woman for whom "the wig comes off, the fake eyelashes come off, the teeth pop out," and the guy is horrified.

Source: Excerpted from Olivia Barker, "Snap On, Snap Off-Celebrity Choppers," *USA Today* (March 22, 2005), D1. Copyright 2005 USA Today, a division of Gannett Co., Inc.

**FIGURE 13.6** Tiger Woods as Celebrity Endorser of a Variety of Products

watches and cars to breakfast cereal, he attracts attention based on consumer awareness and general admiration of him, rather than any specific expertise with the product (notice in both ads shown in Figure 13.6, Tiger Woods is wearing his own line of Nike apparel, thus indirectly endorsing yet another brand and product).

Key to the success of any advertising campaign, even in the case of celebrity advertising, is credibility of the endorser—in this case, the celebrity. Most celebrities lose credibility with audiences when they promote too many products simultaneously because consumers conclude the celebrity is indiscriminate in his or her sponsorship—motivated by financial incentives more than belief in the product.

In addition to celebrities, other reference group appeals, including expert appeals and "common-person" appeals, are effective in reaching consumers. An **expert** is *any person who possesses unique information or skills that can help consumers make better purchase decisions than other types of spokespersons.* Doctors who sell pain relievers, service repairpersons who recommend one brand of appliance over another, or professional mountain guides who represent a particular brand of outdoor clothing are examples of expert appeals. In contrast, the **common-person appeal** features *testimonials from "regular" consumers with whom most individuals can relate.* Slice-of-life ads show how consumers use advertised products to solve everyday problems and make it easy for consumers to picture themselves in that specific purchase or usage situation.

## Transmission of Influence through Dyadic Exchanges

Group influences are transmitted to individuals in many ways. People often observe how a group behaves or dresses and emulate what they see. Children do this when they watch their older siblings and parents behave and consume products, copying what they see in efforts to be "older" or more like their parents. Television, movies, and music videos are a significant source of information on fashion trends, such as the ragged Madonna look of the 1980s (which some fans still wear) or the style of urban clothing worn by Sean "P. Diddy" Combs, a rap music artist who turned his flair for fashion into the successful clothing line, Sean John. Consumers pick up new words and phrases from TV shows or websites such as Jib Jab (www.jibjab.com) and copy gestures, motions, sayings, or dances from TV and movie personalities such as Jerry Seinfeld and Adam Sandler. Formal groups may communicate through their websites and e-mail lists as well as traditional publications such as newsletters and magazines. Using a Bayesian (remember Chapter 2?) model of dyadic interaction, researchers have shown that group member preferences are influenced by two distinct elements—preference revision and concession—and vary across product attributes, individuals, and product categories. Converging preferences affect a member's concession, which in turn affects members' satisfaction with the joint decision. More importantly, a member's satisfaction is higher when his or her concession is reciprocated.[27]

Although the media transmit group influences and the Internet can accomplish transmission very fast, the most effective is still person-to-person exchange. Not only do individuals receive personal communication from someone about behaviors and lifestyles, but also they receive feedback on their own behaviors, which may further modify or reinforce behavior. Individuals may choose to adopt a new behavior, and then decide to continue it or drop it based on the opinions of their peers and other primary reference groups. These *exchanges of resources (in this instance, opinions and comments) between two individuals that influence these individual's behaviors or beliefs* represent **dyadic exchanges.** Two forms of dyadic exchanges, word-of-mouth communication and service encounters, deserve additional consideration.

## Word-of-Mouth Communication

How often do you base a decision, at least in part, to go to a movie, try a new restaurant, or buy a new brand on what your friends or family have told you about it? When individuals hear about, observe, or experience things, they often tell others. This is word-of-mouth (WOM) communication—the informal transmission of ideas, comments, opinions, and information between two people, neither one of which is a marketer. For example, it is easy to imagine that, before widespread availability of television, radio, and other means of mass communication, individuals relied heavily on the advice of their neighbors and families when making buying decisions. But even in today's age of e-commerce, advertising, and television, WOM is still a powerful behavior and purchase influencer for many categories of goods and services. E-mail, in fact, is often a fast way to transmit those WOM communications, stimulated perhaps by marketers. Consumer Behavior and Marketing 13.1 explains how this can be an effective marketing tool, in a process described in popular business books *The Tipping Point* by Malcolm Gladwell and *Unleashing the Idea Virus* by Seth Godin.[28]

In the WOM process, there exists a *sender* and a *receiver*, each of whom gains something from the exchange. The **receiver** *gains information about behaviors and choices, which is valuable to the receiver in the decision process.* The receiver also receives feedback about current behaviors, which can be used to determine whether or not to continue them. Of particular value is the ability of WOM to reduce cognitive dissonance (doubts) after a major purchase decision.[29] Similarly, the **sender** *increases his or her confidence in the personal product or behavior choice by persuading others to do the same.* The sender also receives the psychological benefits of prestige, power, and helpfulness of supplying information and opinions that others accept in their decision process. The WOM process further increases the group's cohesion by increasing

## Interactive Viral Campaigns

Viral marketing is the new weapon in an arsenal of marketing techniques. Companies try to create messages so compelling and often so funny or suggestive that consumers are motivated to share them with other people in their reference groups. The goal is the exponential spread of ads that have the added weight of personal endorsement by friends. The sharing may be the discussion of favorite Super Bowl ads with coworkers, but increasingly the sharing takes the form of friends e-mailing or text-messaging each other about websites such as political satirists www.jibjab.com.

An example of how marketers use this technique is the offbeat "Subservient Chicken" site, which was created to promote a Burger King chicken sandwich. The site, which shows a person in a chicken suit who seems to follow typed commands from Web surfers, has drawn 14 million unique visitors, according to the agency that created it, Crispin Porter & Bogusky in Miami.

Georgia-Pacific used a viral campaign to promote Brawny paper towels to women between the ages of twenty-five and fifty-four. To "seed" the campaign, Georgia-Pacific sent a blast of e-mail messages to consumers who had signed up for newsletters from www.allyourrooms.com, a Georgia-Pacific site that provides information on topics such as decorating, entertaining, and cleaning. Visitors to the site found a section of tongue-in-cheek "Innocent Escapes" videos in which a strong but sensitive Brawny Man offers compliments like, "By the way, you look beautiful today—something about your eyes." Visitors not only found a "play" button next to the ad, but also a "send to a friend" button. Although Georgia-Pacific spent less than 1 percent of its advertising budget on this medium, the campaign produced millions of impressions with the added value of endorsement by friends.

The success of Brawny's "Innocent Escapes" depends on the entertainment value it brings visitors, says Stephen Strong, director for interactive at Foot Cone & Belding advertising agency. "It's human nature to share that stuff," he said. "People will be sending each other stuff online until the Internet shuts down."

Source: Excerpts from Nat Ives, "Interactive Viral Campaigns Ask Consumers to Spread the Word," *The New York Times* (February 18, 2005). Copyright 2003 by The New York Times Co. Reprinted with permission.

the number of individuals adopting similar lifestyle, purchase, or behavior philosophies and actions. Table 13.2 summarizes the benefits of WOM for both senders and receivers.

### Opinion Leadership

The sender of information and opinions in the WOM process is often referred to as the opinion leader. This person, by definition, influences the decision of another person. But opinion leaders also change roles and seek advice from others when they do not have experience with or expertise in a specific area. Personal influence in the form of opinion leadership is most likely to occur in the following situations.

- An individual has limited knowledge of a product or brand. However, if internal search for information proves to be adequate, WOM has less impact on decision making.[30]
- The person lacks ability to evaluate the product or service.
- The consumer does not believe or trust advertising and other sources of information.
- Other information sources have low credibility with the consumer.

TABLE 13.2       Benefits of Word-of-Mouth

|  | HEDONIC BENEFITS | FUNCTIONAL BENEFITS |
|---|---|---|
| Receiver | Decrease risk of new behavior | More information about options |
|  | Increase confidence of choice | More reliable/credible information |
|  | Decreased cognitive dissonance | Less time spent on search |
|  | Increase likelihood of acceptance by a desired group or individual | Enhanced relationship with another individual |
| Sender | Feeling of power and prestige of influencing others' behaviors | Potential reciprocity of exchange |
|  | Enhanced position within a group | Increased attention and status |
|  |  | Increase in number of individuals with similar behaviors |
|  |  | Increased cohesion within group |
|  |  | Satisfaction of verbal expression |

- The individual has a high need for social approval.
- Strong social ties exist between sender and receiver.[31]
- The product is complex.
- The product is difficult to test against objective criteria. Therefore, the experience of others acts as a "vicarious trial."[32]
- The product is highly visible to others.

Generally people will not share their experience with products or services unless the conversation produces some type of gratification. In addition to the benefits and rewards of giving opinions shown in Table 13.2, opinion leaders have additional reasons to offer opinions. Telling others about a new purchase can be pleasurable and exciting for the opinion leader, making him or her the center of attention during the discussion and positioning the individual as having some expertise in a particular area. Through WOM, the opinion leader gains attention, shows connoisseurship, suggests status, and asserts superiority.[33] Also, spreading positive WOM may reinforce the purchaser's own buying decision, perhaps reducing any "buyer's remorse" or uncertainty from the transaction. Although these motivations exist, often people just want to help a friend or relative make a better purchase decision, especially if they are very satisfied with a product or service of interest to another person[34] or a "fan" of a firm.

## CHARACTERISTICS OF OPINION LEADERS

Extensive research has been conducted over the years in many countries regarding the characteristics of opinion leaders.[35] Research indicates that opinion leaders and receivers often share similar demographic characteristics and lifestyles (i.e., they are *homophilous*),[36] yet they may have a greater social status within the same group as followers. This seems logical considering that individuals with similar characteristics might live in the same neighborhoods and belong to the same groups, having frequent contact with one another.

In general, researchers conclude that the most common characteristic of opinion leaders across categories is that they are very involved with a particular product category. They tend to read specialized publications about a specific category and actively seek information from mass media and other sources. They also possess greater self-confidence; are more outgoing and gregarious; and want to share information, talk with others, and seek other opinions.[37] Accordingly, opinion leaders' tendency to initiate conversations is directly proportional to the extent of interest or involvement in the topic under consideration.[38]

Similar to opinion leaders are **product innovators**—*individuals who are the first to try new products.* These consumers are more adventurous than opinion leaders and are less concerned about deviating from group norms because they are less likely to be integrated into social groups. As you will see in the next section of this chapter, each of us has some degree of innovativeness and over the course of our lives has adopted some objects or ideas that we perceive as new.[39]

## OVERLAPPING OPINION LEADERSHIP

An individual may be classified as an opinion leader in one area, but not in another. For example, you may seek advice from a parent as to which financial institution to establish checking and savings accounts, while your best friend might give better advice on cosmetic and clothing purchases. Individuals are deemed opinion leaders based on their perceived knowledge (or expertise) of a product category (or subject), and the greater the perceived expertise, the more likely that person's opinions are to influence decisions.[40] This influence may spill over to other related areas,[41] which is termed *opinion leadership overlap.* An electronics salesperson, for example, might sell stereo equipment, but might also be considered by some an opinion leader for televisions, speakers, and DVDs, all of which are product categories that involve similar interests.

A recently identified source of personal influence possesses a large amount of information about a variety of products, categories, retail concepts, and markets. **Market mavens**[42] *gather much of their information from shopping experiences, openness to information (including direct mail and the Internet), and general market awareness, making them more aware of new products than other people.* Like opinion leaders, market mavens have high levels of brand awareness and like to share their information with others. However, their knowledge base includes information on a vast variety of products (not just high-involvement items), allowing them to disseminate information on low- and medium-involvement items, such as shampoo and deodorant.[43]

Another source of personal influence in the marketplace is the **surrogate consumer** (or surrogate shopper)—*an individual who acts as an agent to guide, direct, and conduct activities in the marketplace.*[44] Although a surrogate consumer's expertise does lie in specific product and related categories, it also crosses over to various activities involving these related categories. For example, a new homeowner may hire an interior decorator to source furniture and fixtures from Italy and coordinate wallpaper and paint from the United States with rugs from Pakistan and upholstery from Hong Kong. In addition to ordering all the products, the decorator will deliver and install them in the consumer's home. Surrogate consumers, such as realtors (buyers' agents) and financial advisors, add an additional layer in the distribution process of high-involvement products, but surrogates often increase the efficiency of the decision process by assuming some of the search, evaluation, and purchase activities. Firms that sell a large volume of product to surrogate consumers have to design and maintain relationships with them, which may differ from programs that foster relationships with consumers.[45] As minority markets increasingly command the majority of marketer's minds, identifying and enlisting opinion leaders in those markets becomes increasingly important. Consumer Behavior and Marketing 13.2 describes how this process can be accomplished.

### Service Encounters

Consumers encounter marketers and salespeople every day, whether they visit a doctor, purchase a car, return a dress to a store, or take a camera in for repairs. Whenever there is *personal communication between a consumer and a marketer,* a

## Enlisting Opinion Leaders to Reach Minority Markets

McDonald's was ahead of most marketers decades ago when it began to identify and recruit opinion leaders in minority markets to become restaurant franchisees. During the civil unrest of the 1960s in the Watts section of Los Angeles and other urban areas, entire blocks of business were left in embers due to rioting and looting, but the arches of McDonald's kept glowing brightly because they were part of the neighborhood that residents did not want destroyed. Residents knew the franchise owners—opinion leaders in the community in many instances—and they knew the firm was the employer of many of those residents. Destroy the business and you destroy the jobs of neighbors, they realized.

Bringing the principle of reaching minority markets by enlisting neighborhood opinion leaders is a strategy brought up to date by firms such as MetroPCS Communications, a Dallas-based company that sells cell phones that feature the flat-fee MetroPCS system. The company sells phones through independent dealers and has 1.5 million customers in cities such as Miami, San Francisco, Sacramento, and Atlanta.

Competing in a market dominated by wireless giants, MetroPCS uses a strategy it calls micromarketing zones. Michael Johnson, MetroPCS's regional vice president in Atlanta says, "We try to identify a community and find someone there who's interested in starting a business and selling our service. Or find an existing dealer with ties to the community. Early adopters were in the ethnic neighborhoods, but we've seen tremendous growth on the north side of Atlanta, too."

The approach is a micro grass-roots strategy in which the company's dealers reflect the ethnic and racial makeup of their neighborhoods. "Diversity makes a lot of sense," said Jeff Thomas, whose first MetroPCS store was in a heavily African American area. "A lot of times people simply relate better to people they're more familiar with." Nearly one-quarter of these locations are owned by minorities, from African Americans to Latinos to Koreans to Indians, reflective of company forays into diverse neighborhoods. The company spends time understanding the lifestyle and culture of those groups. Commenting on the strategy, Kennesaw State University's Paola Diaz-Torres said that other companies would do well to adopt a similar grass-roots approach in an increasingly diverse metro marketplace. If a foreign language is involved, "sometimes companies believe that translating their marketing campaign is enough," she said. "If that's the approach, they're wasting their time, because much can be lost in the translation."

One of the PCS dealers is Zion Cordeiro, a native of Brazil who speaks English, Spanish, Portuguese, and French, and is learning Russian from his Russian wife. Cordeiro, who owns three stores in Atlanta (some serving a heavily Latino clientele), says, "The company understands that communities have their own flavor, their own culture. And it's not just the language people speak, but the way they shop and how they make decisions."

Source: Tom Barry, "Grass-Roots Game Plan," *Atlanta Business Chronicle* (March 18–24, 2005), B1ff. Copyright 2005 American City Business Journals, Inc., and its licensors. All rights reserved.

service encounter occurs, often a key to successful marketing.[46] A service encounter can be the various transactions that occur during a retail purchase (from being greeted with a smile at the door to speedy checkout or home delivery) or the experience of consuming the specific services a consumer purchases (such as dining, transportation, or financial services).

During a service encounter, the buyer and the seller assume specific roles,[47] as if they had studied and are acting out parts in a play, with the store acting as the stage.[48] Deviation from expected roles can result in dissatisfaction with the purchase or service encounter, depending on when the interaction between the two parties occurs. Because this is a form of dyadic exchange, both parties gain something from the exchange and can therefore become dissatisfied with the process if expectations are not met.[49] For example, if an employee at the service counter is rude or underestimates how long a repair will take, the consumer will be unhappy with the exchange. And if the consumer does not bring a proper method of payment or yells at the employee for something out of his or her control, the employee will likewise become dissatisfied with the process.

One challenge for service providers is how to understand the needs of different types of customers and match the appropriate sales associate or sales approach to each individual customer. Some customers might desire a great deal of assistance with product evaluations and choice, whereas others prefer little interaction with salespeople. Firms such as Wal*Mart, Home Depot, and Target are known for training employees to be friendly and greet store guests, but these employees still may wait for a customer to ask for assistance or information. Because the product mix at these mega-retailers ranges from low-involvement to high-involvement items, customers can expect more assistance from outgoing associates in departments selling high-involvement products. Specialty stores, such as Bath & Body Works, or apparel stores such as Neiman-Marcus, Nordstrom, and Canada's famed Harry Rosen, teach their employees to ask customers if they need assistance. Employees are trained to take cues from customers and assume an active role in product coordination and choice, if that is what the customer desires. However, some exclusive boutiques, such as Chanel or Escada, keep a respectable distance from their customers, who might include celebrities who want to be "left alone." Yet these sales associates can quickly alter their strategies and become very involved in the service encounter depending on the cues they receive from the customer.

The salesperson plays an important role in fostering a relationship between buyer and seller—which can include the retailer and the brand that is being sold. The extent of the relationship depends in part both on *how* the salesperson communicates with the customer and *what* is communicated. Good sales associates listen to their customers, evaluate what is said and observed, and determine what products or services will best satisfy the customers' needs or desires.[50] When a consumer develops a close relationship with a salesperson, a friendship may result, which can transform a mere marketing encounter into a social encounter[51] and motivate consumers to maintain relationships with these service providers.[52] For example, many consumers are very loyal to their hairstylists—clients and hairstylists share personal information and see each other regularly over time, thereby creating a friendship that fosters loyalty and positive word-of-mouth.[53] Variations in the dyadic abilities of salespeople account for great variations in their effectiveness, especially for automobiles, insurance, and other products in which the salesperson is a key component in the firm's marketing strategy. People are the brand for many retailers or in organizations such as hospitals where consumers may have difficulty assessing the quality of services received. Ohio State University marketing professor Neeli Bendapudi explains, "People are crucial. They are critical. They are your living brand. When a customer comes into your store and interacts with your associates, that's a moment of truth. Employees can enhance or destroy your brand. Experience always trumps a brand—people remember how they were treated, not your advertising."[54]

**Customer intimacy** refers to *the detailed understanding and focus on customers' needs lifestyles and behaviors in an effort to create a deep cultural connection with the customers*,[55] but **reverse customer intimacy**—*how well marketers facilitate customers knowing the marketer*— may also be a key to customer loyalty. Achieving reverse customer intimacy is accomplished when Steven Tyler of Aerosmith participates in high school drug prevention programs or members of the band participate in a "meet and greet" before local concerts. Letting fans "behind the scenes" on touring events or revealing details of a rock star's personal life through website diaries is a strategy used by legendary entertainers ranging from Neil Diamond to Maroon 5.[56]

Several models that theorize how personal influence is transmitted between individuals and from groups to individuals have been developed. **Trickle-down theory,** the oldest theory, theorizes that *lower classes often emulate the behavior of their higher-class counterparts.*[57] According to this theory, influence is transmitted vertically through social classes, when higher classes express wealth through conspicuous consumption, and lower social classes copy their behavior. This theory used to explain the dissemination of new fashions and styles, but it rarely occurs today because new fashions are disseminated overnight through mass media and quickly copied on a mass scale. And in reality, little direct, personal contact is made between social classes. The trickling down of influence still occurs, however, in some developing economies where access to mass media is restricted. Even here, however, it appears to be decreasing as media access increases.

## TWO-STEP FLOW

At one time, advertisers and other commercial persuaders affected the masses through opinion leaders. The **two-step flow of communication** model, shown in Figure 13.7, indicates *that opinion leaders are the direct receivers of information from advertisements and that they interpret and transmit the information to others through word-of-mouth.*[58] But rarely does the opinion leader mediate the flow of mass media content as the two-step theory assumes. Current understanding shows that opinion leaders and seekers are also legitimate targets, and both are affected by mass media. In fact, mass media can motivate the seeker to approach someone else for advice rather than vice versa.

## MULTISTEP FLOW

Recognizing that mass media can reach anyone in a population and influence them directly, the **multistep flow of communication** model was developed. This model indicates *that information can flow directly to different types of consumers, including opinion leaders, gatekeepers, and opinion seekers or receivers.* Gatekeepers, who neither influence nor are influenced by others, decide whether other group members should receive information or not. For example, a parent may monitor and restrict the television programs or websites a child can access, thereby acting as a gatekeeper. Figure 13.8

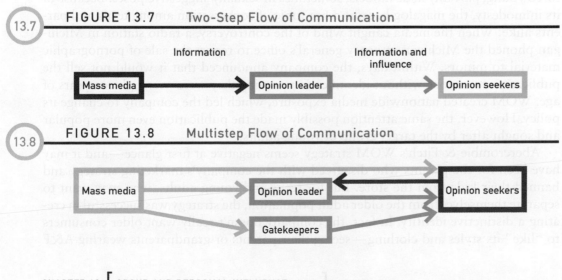

**FIGURE 13.7**     Two-Step Flow of Communication

**FIGURE 13.8**     Multistep Flow of Communication

shows how opinion leaders can receive information, pass it on to seekers, and receive feedback, and how information can reach seekers directly.

## WOM and Opinion Leaders in Advertising and Marketing Strategy

How much advertising has Apple used to gain acceptance of the iPod? Relatively little, because opinion leaders told others about the product and because iPod users with white cords dangling from their ears were visible members of the "club." How much advertising did Napster and other peer-to-peer file sharing services do in their beginning years? None, partly because the major use of the services (digital music swapping) was illegal. People told other people how to use the program, making Napster one of the most rapidly diffused innovations in history.

For Google, the most successful Internet search engine, a majority of the early "promotion" was word-of-mouth communication among "nerdy" Net insiders. Although many consumers don't know exactly how Google works, "Googling" has still become a household word. WOM and personal influence can have a more decisive role in influencing behavior than advertising and other marketer-dominated sources[59] and is usually much less expensive, as you saw in Consumer Behavior 13.1. At the heart of the issues are individuals' views that WOM is a more trustworthy and credible source of information than salespeople or paid advertising. As a result, a large proportion of consumer buying decisions are influenced by direct (or personal) recommendations from others.[60] Although advertising provides information individuals might not get from other sources, consumers don't always trust that the advertiser has their best interests in mind. Often consumers believe that the advertiser will stretch the truth (known as *puffing*) or exaggerate the benefits of a product to benefit the company.

### The Advertising-WOM Relationship

Advertising influences the effectiveness of WOM and vice versa. First, advertising can provide information to consumers about products and brands that they might not seek from other sources (such as peers or family members). If a consumer trusts a brand or product and its advertising, an individual's need for and receptiveness to WOM decreases. However, if an ad or marketer is unfamiliar to a consumer or is not perceived as trustworthy, reliance on WOM increases. Second, advertising can create WOM among consumers and peer groups, the goal of viral marketing. Abercrombie & Fitch released a provocative version of its *A&F Quarterly* "magalog" prior to the 2003 holiday season. Called the "Sex Ed Edition," the combination magazine and catalog featured young, partially nude models, sometimes in sexually suggestive poses. Because of its immodesty, the magalog became a hot topic of conversation among teens and parents alike. When the media caught wind of the controversy, a radio station in Michigan phoned the Michigan attorney general's office to report the sale of pornographic material to minors. Within days, the company announced that it would not sell the publication to anyone without identification proving they were over eighteen years of age. WOM created nationwide media exposure, which led the company to change its policy. However, the same attention possibly made the publication even more popular and sought after by the target group of young adults.

Abercrombie & Fitch's WOM strategy seems negative at first glance—and it may have been for the parents who disagreed with the company's marketing strategy and banned their kids from the store. But for teens and young adults, who may want to separate themselves from the older adult population, the strategy was successful in creating a distinctive identity. In fact, the company doesn't really want older consumers to "like" its styles and clothing—seeing their parents or grandparents wearing A&F

clothes would "turn off" much of the company's younger, independent market target, as would the presence of younger kids in the stores. In fact, to reach consumers other than the college age target of A&F, the company developed the Hollister brand for high school–age consumers and the Ruehl 925 brand for young working adults.

### Primary Reliance on Word-of-Mouth

On some occasions, companies can rely on word-of-mouth communication as a substitute for advertising. This was the strategy for Victoria's Secret for many years, relying on WOM among consumers and WOM occurring in dialog between actors in television shows. Not until the late 1990s did the company undertake much formal advertising, which focused primarily on brand and image with its "Angels" campaign. Admittedly, it is highly unusual to omit advertising and sales efforts entirely, and few would risk this step, but retailers as diverse as Wal*Mart[61] and Victoria's Secret have demonstrated that advertising can be sharply reduced when word-of-mouth is strong. When Wal*Mart began receiving negative WOM because of allegations that Wal*Mart stores hurt communities by limiting competition and shortchanging labor, the company began an advertising campaign addressing these issues. The ads featured employees who felt a sense of ownership in the company standing in front of their stores saying, "This is *my* Wal*Mart," as well as a website (www.walmartfacts.com) that describes in detail pay rates, employee health benefits, the economic benefits of low prices to middle-class families, and corporate contributions to communities across the nation.

### Targeting Opinion Leaders

Opinion leaders are sensitive to various sources of information, including advertising,[62] and if opinion leaders can be identified, marketing to them as a distinct segment may be feasible. This approach is challenging because of the similarity between sender and receiver, even in media exposure patterns. Hence, mounting strategies that reach only this segment may be difficult, although exceptions may occur when certain types of social or organizational leaders act as opinion leaders, such as coaches, physicians, and clergy. In addition to targeting their leadership roles and responsibilities through mass media, firms can reach them individually through association memberships, direct mail, and publicity in trade or special-interest magazines.

### Stimulating Word-of-Mouth

WOM about a new product or service can be stimulated in many ways. For example, a company may lend or give opinion leaders a product to display and use. When Toyota launched the Lexus brand in the United States, local dealerships mailed invitations to known community leaders to test-drive the new models of their choice. Even though the number of immediate purchases was not great, individuals told their friends about the experience, creating positive WOM, and stored information for future purchase decisions. Companies also provide free products for physicians and dentists to give to patients (e.g., Oral-B brand toothbrushes and dental floss) and for athletes to use when training and competing (e.g., Adidas and Nike shoes and clothing). In both cases, opinion leaders help foster relationships between sellers and consumers.

Another familiar option is to induce the opinion leader to open his or her home for product demonstrations. The classic example is the Tupperware party and its contemporary equivalent, a Longaberger basket party. The most enthusiastic participants are often recruited to host parties in their own homes, receiving merchandise and discounts in exchange for inviting their friends. Not-for-profit organizations rely on this method of stimulating WOM to generate interest in fundraising events. These organizations often ask community leaders to host events in their homes, hoping to capture interest and secure participation of potential donors and volunteers. Republicans used this strategy in the 2004 presidential election, organizing neighborhood "block parties" that registered voters and distributed literature, yard signs, bumper stickers, and other items that identified people to their friends as supporters of George W. Bush.

### Creating Opinion Leaders

Organizations sometimes hire or directly involve individuals who display characteristics of opinion leaders to influence consumers. Banana Republic, Abercrombie & Fitch, and other clothing retailers often hire popular and attractive young people to work in their stores. These opinion leaders receive substantial discounts on clothing and are encouraged (sometimes required) to dress according to a particular style when working, to promote the "in-ness" of the brand.

Companies can also create opinion leaders by providing incentives for new customers to attract others to the stores. The companies can offer attractive product premiums or even outright financial rebates for additional sales that new customers influence. Some long-distance and cellular telephone companies offer "friends and family" plans that provide discounted rates and free minutes if consumers refer and enroll others in the service. E*Trade gained part of its early acceptance by giving commission-free stock trades and frequent-flyer miles to individuals who referred their friends to open new accounts.

At times, companies can activate information search and dissemination through advertising that encourages word-of-mouth. An ad might use a phrase, such as "ask a person who owns one," to cause people to seek information from others. Sam's Club, a chain of retail membership warehouses owned by Wal*Mart, sometimes provides coupons that encourage members to invite their friends and family to "experience the savings for themselves." Normally customers are required to purchase a membership to shop at Sam's Club but the coupon allows users to try the store without such a commitment. Sam's Club hopes to enlist its fans and opinion leaders to attract additional customers, who after trying the club may decide to become members themselves. Realizing that many people dine with family and friends rather than alone, the ad in Figure 13.9 reminds Red Lobster "fans" to "share the love" by bringing others to Red Lobster. Demonstrations, displays, and product trials can help generate WOM, consumer interest, and information search as well. For example, flat-screen TVs have been offered to airline clubs and luxury hotels because such high-visibility locations encourage trial usage among opinion leaders. Similarly, automobile manufacturers make deals with car rental companies on new products such as GPS and satellite radio, about which they want to stimulate trial and WOM.

### Managing Negative WOM

"I would never buy a car from that dealer again. The salesperson was eager to sell me the car, but then made me wait for hours while he did the paperwork. He didn't tell me everything I needed to know about the financing and never called to follow up on the sale. I've since had some problems with the car and when I took it to the

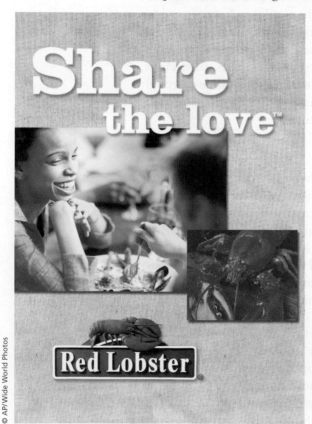

© AP/Wide World Photos

**FIGURE 13.9** Some Firms Provide Coupons and Other Incentives to Refer Friends and Family

service department, four days passed before they could even tell me what was wrong with it. The people aren't friendly and the service is terrible . . . I'll never go back there." If your best friend were to relay these opinions to you, how likely would you be to buy a car from this dealer?

Just as positive word-of-mouth can be one of a marketer's greatest assets, the opposite can be true when the content is negative. More than one-third of all WOM information is negative WOM, which is usually given high priority and weighs heavily in decision making.[63] This prioritizing occurs because marketer-dominated communication is uniformly positive, thus alerting the potential buyer to anything that provides a different perspective. Moreover, the dissatisfied buyer is more motivated to share information.[64]

## MONITORING THE CONTENT OF WORD-OF-MOUTH

Although a business firm cannot directly control the influence of WOM, the presence and impact of WOM can be monitored. For example, Coca-Cola examined the communication patterns of people who had complained to the company.[65] The company found that more than 12 percent told twenty or more people about the response they had received from the company. Those who were completely satisfied with the company's response told four to five others about their positive experience, whereas those who thought they were not treated fairly told nine to ten people about their experience. Nearly one-third of those who thought their complaints were not dealt with adequately refused to buy any more of the company's products, and another 45 percent reduced their purchases, showing how negative WOM can affect even low-involvement products. Manufacturers of automobiles and other high-involvement products often evaluate dealers and gauge customer satisfaction with extensive surveys. Southwest Airlines, which has the greatest customer satisfaction of all domestic carriers, announces at the end of each flight, "If you enjoyed your flight today, please tell a friend. If not, please tell us."

Companies must also monitor rumors circulating about their brands and products. Usually not based at all on facts but rather fears and anxieties, rumors can change as they are transmitted from one person to another and take on lives of their own. The greater the degrees of anxiety and uncertainty, the more rapidly a rumor will spread throughout a population. Large and small firms around the world have been victims of rumors, including giants such as Procter & Gamble, Coca-Cola, and McDonald's. A few years ago, a rumor circulated that fast-food firms advertising "100 percent pure beef" in their hamburgers actually used 100 percent *of the beef,* including the tongue, eyeballs, and intestines. McDonald's, Burger King, and Wendy's became aware of the rumor but could not issue a statement that "there are no intestines in our hamburgers" because doing so would draw attention to the rumor and spread it to individuals who might not have heard it. Instead, they changed the description to "100 percent USDA Choice ground beef," which by law cannot have anything added to it. Attention was focused on what the hamburgers contained rather than on what they didn't contain.

## CURBING NEGATIVE WORD-OF-MOUTH

Imagine you have just started your car and suddenly it surges out of control, forward or backward. This is exactly what happened to owners of the 1986 Audi 5000S, according to more than five hundred complaints made to the National Highway Traffic Safety Administration. Audi management initially refused to acknowledge any culpability for this problem, even after a *60 Minutes* television exposé activated public outrage. A drastic drop in sales had to occur to induce Audi's acknowledgment of a problem, product recall, and remedial repair.[66] Audi management was later vindicated in their claims of innocence, but the company never fully recovered from this unfortunate attitude of insensitivity to consumers.

What should a company do when something goes terribly wrong? Certainly, stonewalling (denying the problem) is not the answer. The best strategy usually is an immediate acknowledgment of the problem by a credible company spokesperson, as Johnson & Johnson did when cyanide-laced Tylenol (the result of tampered packages) caused seven deaths in Chicago. The company's president went on national television to express sympathy for the victims' families and describe what the company was doing to assure consumer safety. An important point to recognize is that negative word-of-mouth rarely goes away by itself. If matters are not dealt with promptly, the financial results could be immediate and catastrophic. In 2005, Wendy's faced another challenge, this time not just a rumor, when a one-and-a-quarter-inch piece of a human finger (complete with manicured nail) was found cooked in the chili at one of its restaurants in San Jose, California. Wendy's acknowledged the incident, scrutinized its manufacturing processes, offered a reward for information on who the finger might belong to, and vowed to work with local officials in DNA and fingerprint searches.[67] The "victim" was later prosecuted for the fraud when the finger was identified as belonging to a family friend who lost it in an industrial accident. Public-relations professionals say there are just two major moves a company can make when bad news strikes: make sure you have all your facts straight and tell the truth.

## Diffusion of Innovations

Just as influence diffuses between people, products and innovations diffuse through the marketplace. Marketers bombard consumers with thousands of new products each year. Compound that with new retail concepts, new product positioning, and new variations of existing products, and it is a wonder that consumers are able to make any buying and consumption decisions at all. Some new products succeed, adopted by enough customers to achieve profitability. Such new products are the key to increased sales, profits, and competitive strength for most organizations. Yet 50 percent or more of new products fail, often because the product satisfies needs or desires no better than existing products.

Organizations need to innovate consistently to remain competitive, but innovation is so risky and expensive that many form business alliances with other firms to quicken the pace and reduce risks of new product development (NPD). Although alliances or external NPD may allow for greater access to resources and spread out risks (by sharing resources), 70 percent of such alliances fail[68] and such projects have lower success rates than internal NPD. Ultimately, firms must understand how to improve competencies in innovation projects. In research that investigated twenty-four predictors of new product performance, the most significant variables associated with success were identified as product advantage, market potential, meeting customer needs, predevelopment task proficiencies, and dedicated resources.[69] The remainder of this chapter focuses on how new products diffuse through the marketplace, why some are rejected and others are accepted, and the role of consumer insight.

### Innovations and New Products

An **innovation** can be defined in a variety of ways, but the most commonly accepted definition is *any idea or product perceived by the potential adopter to be new.* It follows then that a **product innovation** (or new product) is *any product recently introduced to the market or perceived to be new when compared to existing products.* An organization may define a new product by the percentage of potential market that has adopted the product or the amount of time in the market, but consumers use *subjective* definitions of innovation, derived from the thought structure of a particular individual or entity.

Innovations can also be defined *objectively*, based on criteria external to the adopter. According to this definition, innovations are *ideas, behaviors, or things that are qualitatively different from existing forms*. But what constitutes a "qualitative difference" is not concrete. Marketers use the word *new* on packaging and in advertising to call attention to products recently introduced to the marketplace, but the Federal Trade Commission limits the use of the word *new* in advertising to products available in the marketplace for less than six months. Certainly, the Internet was qualitatively different from existing communication forms available at the time of its introduction, but is Liquid Tide a new product compared with the existing powder form of Tide?

Innovation affects firms in many ways, including increased profits and enhanced shareholder value (ESV). But innovation is not limited to new products. Innovative ideas, innovative people, and innovative processes exist in thriving organizations throughout the world. Research indicates that winning firms generate "idea power" that provides the competitive advantage, not only in new products but also in new ideas in every area: better packaging, more efficient invoicing techniques, new planning systems, and lower-cost manufacturing processes.[70] It is important to recognize that underlying needs may not be changed, just the technology of meeting those needs. Look in Figure 13.10 for Canon, the desire for clear, crisp shots of family and friends has not changed, the images are now just captured digitally rather than on film.

As significant as the effects on organizations, new products affect consumers' lives in many ways as well. Introducing new products may attempt to change consumers'

**FIGURE 13.10** Underlying Needs Don't Always Change although the Technology to Fulfill Those Needs Does

behaviors beyond simply switching from one brand to another—the new products can change the way consumers live. Sometimes the changes have profound effects (both positive and negative) on the people who buy the new product. Though silicone breast implants have allowed many cancer patients to regain positive self-image, the implants have jeopardized the lives of many other patients who have experienced severe tissue scarring and other problems including alleged leaks in the implants. Sometimes the changes have profoundly negative effects on the people who do not adopt them, as may be true for those who fail to adopt e-mail or vaccines. Perhaps more significant than any of these effects, the introduction of a new product can change how society is organized—as was the case with electricity, cars, and computers.

## Types of Innovations

One system of classifying innovations is based on the impact of the innovation on behavior in the social structure, which classifies innovations as continuous, dynamically continuous, and discontinuous.[71] These classifications are presented as follows in the order of least to most disruptive to existing behavior patterns.

A **continuous innovation** is the modification of the taste, appearance, performance, or reliability of an existing product rather than the establishment of a totally new one. Most new products fall into this category. Examples include adding baking soda and mouthwash to Colgate toothpaste, adding spam filters to Microsoft's Outlook software, or reducing carbohydrates in Lay's potato chips. A firm might also consider a product-line extension as a continuous innovation, as is the case with Gillette's addition of women's razors and shaving cream, which have the same functional attributes as men's products but are designed and packaged specifically for women. These are the appeals in Figure 13.11, targeted to French-speaking consumers.

A **dynamically continuous innovation** may involve either the creation of a new product or a significant alteration of an existing one, but does not generally alter established purchase or usage patterns. Examples include electric toothbrushes, compact disc players, organic foods, 3M's Post-it Notes, and washable food containers. Figure 13.12 shows such an innovation in oral care. Another example is Mentadent toothpaste, presented in an innovative package (which you saw in Chapter 3 as Figure 3.16).

A **discontinuous innovation** involves *the introduction of an entirely new product that significantly alters consumers' behavior patterns and lifestyles.* Examples include automobiles, televisions, videocassette recorders, and computers. The Internet is discontinuous when it fundamentally changes shopping behavior for products such as airline tickets, transferring sales from travel agents to websites, thus producing really new products.[72] Existing knowledge and innovation continuity are major factors influencing consumers' adoption process. When consumers can transfer knowledge from other areas, consumers have higher comprehension and perceive more net benefits of new products, especially for continuous innovations. Only when entrenched knowledge is accompanied by relevant information from a supplementary knowledge base are consumers able to use their expertise to understand and appreciate discontinuous innovations.[73]

**FIGURE 13.11** Continuous Innovation Yields Product Line Extensions

Innovations are usually considered in terms of new products, but innovations might also be *usage based*—finding new uses for old products. For many years, consumers bought Swanson's chicken broth to use as stock in soups and gravies. To increase sales, the company introduced an ad campaign that showed consumers how to use Swanson broth, instead of oils and fats, in cooking healthy. Arm & Hammer baking soda faced a problem when most consumers quit baking. The solution was to get consumers to use baking soda in other ways—from fighting odors in the refrigerator and litter box to removing laundry stains and brushing teeth. Individuals sometimes take the lead and invent their own new uses for existing products, as has been the case with duct tape—used by consumers not only for home repairs, but to tow cars, make signs, create prom dresses and tuxedos, and even repair pet ducks! Finding new usages that may lead to product innovations can be accomplished by "listening in" to dialogues between customers and Web-based virtual advisers. Using Kelley Blue Book's Auto Choice Advisor, consumers can enter and search feedback on the features, design, comfort, reliability, and quality of nearly any make and model of car or truck. These data are available at little incremental cost and have been shown to generate billions of dollars of opportunities for products such as pick-up trucks.[74]

Put down the ordinary.
Pick up the extraordinary.

**FIGURE 13.12** Dynamically Continuous Innovation Results in New Products for Existing Uses

Courtesy of Oral-B

## Why Some Innovations Succeed and Others Don't

Some new products are winners in the marketplace and others are losers. For every success story such as compact discs or MP3 players, there are failures such as early picture phones, quadraphonic audio systems, and (pre-Internet) PC home banking.[75] Successful products are those that become *culturally anchored*—so inextricably a part of a consumer's life and sociocultural surroundings that the person-product interface is an important part of the individual's self-concept.[76] Imagine doing without personal computers, cell phones, or microwave ovens with today's values and lifestyles. But why did these innovations succeed when others failed? Research by Everett Rogers and others[77] indicate five main characteristics associated with successful new products: (1) relative advantage, (2) compatibility, (3) complexity, (4) trialability, and (5) observability.

### Relative Advantage

The most important factor to examine when evaluating the potential success of a new product is its relative advantage—the degree to which consumers may *perceive* it to offer substantially greater benefits than the product they currently use. Analysts may ask to what degree the new product will be a substitute for existing ones or complement the array of products already in consumers' inventories.

New products most likely to succeed are those that appeal to strongly felt consumer needs. In banking, automatic teller machines (ATMs) gave consumers twenty-four-hour access to cash and thus diffused through the social system quickly because of their high, perceived relative advantage over traditional banking hours. In contrast, debit cards, which act as cash or checks during the purchase process, have been slow to diffuse. Although they generate transaction revenue and offer other advantages to banks, including decreased costs associated with processing checks, many consumers perceive little relative advantage of debit cards over cash or credit cards, appealing mostly to consumers who want the convenience of credit cards but who either do not have established credit or have difficulty managing their personal debt.

## Compatibility

Compatibility refers to the degree to which a new product is consistent with an individual's existing practices, values, needs, and past experiences of the potential adopters. Computer software and hardware product decisions are usually based on compatibility of the new product with an existing system, a central part of Microsoft's marketing strategy. The introduction of Mentadent's peroxide-based whitening toothpaste that you saw in Figure 3.16 was well received by U.S. consumers looking for a way to brighten their smiles. The new toothpaste did not require any new equipment or new learning and was consistent with existing norms that value white teeth. DVDs, although different from videotapes in form, are compatible in usage for consumers who are accustomed to using a computer CD-ROM drive.

Similarly, Radio Shack was successful in introducing personal computers to America in the 1980s because of the company's existing distribution system of thousands of stores. Customers whose normal behavior favored technologically innovative products were already in the stores buying products. Computers, though technically different in function from Radio Shack's core product mix, were still related to consumers' product interests. The combination of distribution, personal service, and related product interests was compatible with the existing values and experiences of early adopters of computers. Compatibility with usage should be an important design consideration and is the featured appeal in the Fujitsu tablet PC shown in Figure 13.13.

## Complexity

Complexity is the degree to which an innovation is perceived as difficult to understand and use. The more complex the new product, the more difficult it will be to gain acceptance. Microwave ovens diffused rapidly because they are easy to use. The complexity principle makes it advantageous for companies to build products that are as simple as possible to understand and use, especially during initial introduction so that consumers can understand them. Instructions play an important role as well—the more complex the use or assembly instructions, the less likely the product will succeed. That's why many Web shoppers are attracted to a website and interested in buying the product or service, but get to the checkout stage and abandon purchase because of complex procedures or difficult questions and timing issues.

Complexity is a significant deterrent of trying new technology, including using computers and buy-

© AP/Wide World Photos

**FIGURE 13.13** Compatibility with Existing Uses Is an Important Attribute of New Products

## Make It Better and Make It Simple—and It Will Diffuse

Who's the most powerful woman in business? According to business magazines, it's the CEO of eBay, Meg Whitman, who runs one of history's fastest-growing companies. The first version of what became eBay went online in September 1995, founded by Chairman Pierre Omidyar. Since then, the company has grown to $3.3 billion in revenue (in 2004), reaching that mark faster than Dell, Microsoft, or Cisco Systems. The company has 135 million users worldwide, a cybernation larger than the combined population of Germany and France. However, eBay's basic service is not new—auctions have been popular for centuries—but the Internet made it better, providing a huge relative advantage over geographically limited auctions.

CEO Whitman, along with Chairman Omidyar, believes the Internet is the perfect marketplace, where everyone is on an equal footing and the marketplace sets the price. Part of the company's success is the process of creating an ever-exploding community of buyers and sellers. Once when the system crashed from overuse, each of eBay's employees called lists of users personally to apologize, winning raves from users. The company's emphasis on customer service has helped it become the world's biggest used car dealer and expand into Europe and Asia. Originally the community was mostly individuals, but increasingly sellers range from individuals to major corporations. The global consultancy Accenture, for instance, has created software that allows consumer product manufacturers to sell

excess inventories on eBay. Whitman believes eBay could have developed a set of complicated websites, but her philosophy is to keep it simple so that anyone can understand how to use it.

Where does eBay go in the future? According to Whitman, the company will keep expanding globally. Today, in about 15 percent of the transactions, the buyer and seller are in different countries. "I'd be surprised if that's not 50 percent to 60 percent ten years from now," Whitman says. "And think what that means about connecting the Third World with the industrialized world." The newest service is called Kijiji (which means "village" in Swahili), a classified ad–type service overseas. Making it easy for consumers to use eBay is also the reason eBay acquired PayPal, a financial services website that enables individual sellers to accept credit cards for purchases. As broadband becomes more widespread, eBay listings may eventually have sound and video.

What's the most significant lesson learned from eBay (besides the enormous profits that can be made from providing a product with a large relative advantage and simplicity in usage)? Omidyar, the founder, says, "The remarkable fact that 135 million people have learned they can trust a complete stranger—that's had an incredible social impact. People have more in common than they think."

Source: Excerpts from Kevin Maney, "10 Years Ago, eBay Changed the World, Sort of By Accident," *USA Today* (March 22, 2005), B1. Copyright 2005 USA Today, a division of Gannett Co., Inc.

ing over the Internet. Read Consumer Behavior and Marketing 13.3 and you'll observe that, in addition to high relative advantage, eBay is successful because the company keeps its process simple—and compatible with the auction process that consumers have used for centuries.

### Trialability

New products are more apt to succeed when consumers can experiment with or try the idea on a limited basis, with limited financial risk. For example, Procter & Gamble and General Foods give away millions of new products each year to allow consumers to easily try the products without economic risk. Sampling, couponing, and trial-sized products all induce consumers to use new soaps, foods, deodorants, and other low-unit-value, consumer-packaged goods. But these methods also work for expensive, complex, high-involvement discontinuous innovations, even though a bit more creativity is required.

Leasing is a strategy widely used by auto manufacturers to introduce consumers to new car models. Auto manufacturers will sometimes make special offers to rental car companies on redesigned models or cars equipped with innovative features to give consumers an opportunity to try the new product or new feature, as Chrysler did when it redesigned the (unsuccessful) Neon to be the "new" PT Cruiser. Perhaps to the extreme, America Online (AOL) gave away millions of discs containing free software that, when installed, gives consumers hundreds of hours of free Internet access.

### Observability

Observability (and communicability) reflects the degree to which the results of using a new product are visible to friends and neighbors. If consumers can see others benefiting from the use of a new product, then the product is more likely to be successful and diffuse faster. For example, a young adult might see the social acceptance and compliments a peer receives when wearing a particular fashion, clothing brand, hairstyle, or fragrance, and choose to buy the product to receive the same benefit. The use of celebrities walking down a red carpet at the Emmys or Oscars often enhances the visibility of designer fashions, and at the Super Bowl new Cadillacs (including the Escalade) are positioned for spectators and viewers to observe. The Super Bowl is also the highest-visibility venue for introducing new ads and marketing campaigns.

These five characteristics of relative advantage, compatibility, complexity, trialability and observability can be used to rate the likelihood of adoption in the marketplace. Innovations that rate high in multiple areas are most likely to diffuse through the desired market target. For further competitive analysis, you might want to study the product life cycle and examine the advantages and disadvantages of introducing a new product in the various stages.[78] An example is shown in Consumer Behavior and Marketing 13.4, which compares the success of CompuServe and AOL on these variables. Although CompuServe was introduced more than a decade earlier than AOL, it was eclipsed and eventually acquired by AOL—in part because AOL was positioned better on some of the critical determinants of new product success.

## The Diffusion Process

The most important contribution to the study of diffusion of innovations was a book of the same name, written by Everett Rogers in 1962 and updated several times.[79] According to Rogers, **diffusion** is defined as the *process by which an innovation (new idea) is communicated through certain channels over time among the members of a social system.* Using this definition, a product might be around for a long time but still be perceived as new in a given market. The Internet, for example, was introduced in 1969 but was considered new in many markets as late as the 1990s. Rogers' research identifies product characteristics and other variables that influence the diffusion process and explains how consumers individually adopt new products and innovations.

The diffusion of an innovation includes many stages, as seen in Figure 13.14:

- Diffusion of information and communication—involves the communication between a consumer and an organization, a marketer, or a group or personal influencer
- Consumer decision process for an innovation—the process by which an individual consumer decides to adopt or reject an innovation

## AOL versus CompuServe: How Consumers Evaluate Competitive Innovations

By 2005, America Online (AOL) dominated and in fact owned CompuServe, its early competitor that started in the late 1970s and offered a full range of modern e-commerce services. CompuServe began by offering information online to technology- and information-based professionals but by 1984 was selling everything from apparel and airline tickets to software and music online, as well as a wide range of financial, news, entertainment, and e-mail services. Even though its text-based user interface (no graphics) and slow-transmission dial-up access was anything but user friendly, CompuServe became a leader in e-commerce among technology-oriented individuals, and scored high on content and quality of service. America Online joined the cyber-race a decade later, but positioned its user-friendly service as a communication-based tool for the mass market. Although CompuServe expected its users to figure out how to navigate and use its products and services, AOL made the technology easy for the mass market to use in everyday life. In head-to-head competition in the marketplace, AOL was the big winner because it designed its product from the perspective of everyday consumers. The accompanying chart examines how consumers probably compared the two firms on Rogers' key factors of new product success, eventually causing a majority to adopt AOL.

### Market Acceptance: Specialty vs. Mass Market

|  | Technology | Relative Advantage | Compatability | Complexity | Trialability | Observability |
|---|---|---|---|---|---|---|
| Compu-Serve (specialty) | A+ for tech-oriented market—others should just figure it out | Concise, extensive data access | Specialty: technology fits savvy market well and databases fit users | Difficult to use, even for tech-oriented consumers | Low | Limited to tech areas and specialty markets |
| AOL (mass) | Make technology easy for mass market to use in everyday life | Cheaper and time flexible way to communicate | Mass technology easy for those with existing computer | Easy to use for all consumers | High—free samples to mass market | Vast—consumers observe others through chat rooms and through brand |

**(13.14)**    **FIGURE 13.14**    Adoption and Diffusion of Innovation Process

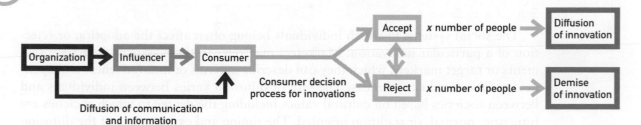

- Diffusion of innovation or demise of innovation—the cumulative effect of how many consumers either adopt or reject an innovation over time, leading to its diffusion or demise in the marketplace

Rogers' model includes the diffusion process, which is societal in nature, and the adoption process, which is individual in nature, and shows their roles in the overall diffusion of innovation process.

The diffusion process is influenced by many factors, many of which have been identified in thousands of diffusion studies. From these studies, the primary success factors in the diffusion of innovations are:

- Innovation (new product, service, or idea)
- Communication (through formal and informal channels)
- Time (for individuals' adoption decisions and rate)
- Social system (interrelated people, groups, or other systems)

### Communication

Communication is critical to the diffusion process. How consumers learn about new products, either through consumer-marketer communication or consumer-consumer communication, influences the rate at which new products are identified and tried by consumers. As discussed earlier in this chapter, word-of-mouth plays an important role in product trial and diffusion.

In addition to interpersonal communication, marketers must also address the influence of advertising, Internet presence, salespersons, and opinion leaders in new product marketing strategy. Only when consumers become aware of a new product can trial be encouraged and the diffusion process initiated. Advertising can accelerate the diffusion process.[80] Effects on profitability are optimal if a firm advertises heavily when the product is introduced and reduces advertising as the product moves through its life cycle—at which time interpersonal communications begin to take effect.

### Time

Another factor influencing the diffusion process is time. How long an individual takes to move from product awareness to product purchase or rejection indicates how long a product will take to diffuse through the market. In this instance, time is dependent upon external factors (e.g., availability of product and economic resources) and internal factors (e.g., personality and adopter category). Some consumers will quickly decide a new product is not what they want, perhaps because of brand loyalty and satisfaction with current products. Other consumers may want a product but may not buy it for a variety of reasons.[81] Understanding the temporal process of adoption is very important. Otherwise, a firm might introduce a product, advertise it heavily, and commit large amounts of resources to the project only to see it "fail." In actuality, the firm may have underestimated the time required for the new product to diffuse through the market, which is what occurred with many of the "dot bombs" of the late 1990s.[82]

### Social System

The social systems to which individuals belong often affect the adoption or rejection of a particular innovation. Marketers may refer to these systems as market segments or target markets, which they can describe in terms of innovativeness and openness to new products or ideas. The rate of diffusion varies between individuals and between societies based on cultural values including the degree to which societies are futuristic, normal, or tradition oriented. The timing and expectations of the diffusion can be modified for each market.[83] Although modern or contemporary social systems are likely to try and accept new products, traditional societies are not.

As with any targeted marketing plan, communicating to consumers based on the characteristics and orientation of their social system is important in the adoption process. That's why certain age cohorts (described in Chapters 7 and 12), such as aging baby boomers, may be targets for new fitness, health, and beauty products that promise better bodies or a younger appearance.

## Speed of Diffusion

Although WOM is very important to the innovation diffusion process, marketers have little control over this variable. However, marketers have more control over some factors, such as product characteristics, pricing, and resource allocations, that contribute to the speed of diffusion. The speed of global diffusion of innovations increases with the number of countries that have adopted an innovation and with the length of the international experience with an innovation.[84] These and other variables that affect the speed of diffusion are represented in the following propositions.[85]

The greater the *competitive intensity* of the supplier, the more rapid the diffusion and the higher the diffusion level. Highly competitive firms have more aggressive pricing strategies and allocate greater resources to the product introduction. Intense competition frequently leads to price wars and an increase in demand due to the more price-sensitive customers entering the market. And the more innovative a new product is, the more likely a competitive firm is to retaliate with additional product-based innovations.[86]

The better the *reputation of the supplier* (breeding confidence among potential adopters), the faster the initial diffusion will be. A good reputation leads to source credibility, which in turn may reduce uncertainty and risk while increasing confidence in the purchase decision.

Products also diffuse more rapidly when *standardized technology* is used. Consumers may believe a purchase to be more risky if they are unsure which technology will become standard—perhaps this is why it takes from five to fifteen years before new electronic technologies catch on among consumers.[87] When this risk is reduced or avoided, more consumers are likely to adopt the product.

**Vertical coordination,** a *high degree of dependence and interlocking relationships among channel members,* also increases the rate of diffusion. Coordination increases the information flow from supplier to consumer, thereby increasing diffusion.

*Resource commitments,* such as greater research and development expenditures, are positively related to innovations. As technologies become enhanced and more alternatives become available, diffusion becomes broader and more rapid. And as advertising, personal selling, sales promotion activities, and distribution support increases, diffusion also increases. Marketing research allocations can help guide research and development (R&D) expenditures as well as develop a positioning strategy for the new technology, both of which are instrumental in the diffusion process. Some research shows that an increasing rate of adoption of innovations has resulted in a rapidly shortened product life cycle,[88] which translates into less time for management to approve moving to the next phase of product introduction.[89] Often there is a "saddle" in which sales reach an initial peak, then decline into a trough before returning to levels exceeding the initial peak. Researchers have explained this by a dual-market phenomenon, differentiating early market adopters and main market adopters as two separate markets. If these two segments—the early market and the main market—adopt at different rates and the difference is pronounced, then the overall sales to the two markets exhibit a temporary decline at the intermediate or "saddle" stage.[90]

New product adoption is the result of a decision process, in many ways similar to the general consumer decision process described throughout this book. But what makes the consumer decision process for new products different from that for other products? The main distinction lies in the emphasis on communications within the social structure rather than individual information processing. Examining diffusion variables represents a *relational approach,* analyzing communication networks and how social-structural variables affect diffusion flows in the system, in contrast to a *monadic approach,* which focuses on the personal and social characteristics of individual consumers.

The most widely adopted model for understanding the adoption process of innovations is again that of Everett Rogers, which includes knowledge, persuasion, decision, implementation, and confirmation, as seen in Figure 13.15. As you examine this model, keep in mind that not only does an individual consumer move through the stages of adopting or rejecting a new product, but other consumers also move through the process, the combined effects of which determine ultimate diffusion or demise.

## KNOWLEDGE

The knowledge stage begins when a consumer receives physical or social stimuli that give exposure and attention to the new product and how it works. Knowledge of the new product is more likely to occur through media than in later stages, but can be influenced by opinion leaders as well. How a person receives and interprets the knowledge is affected by his or her personal characteristics. Consumers have greater uncertainty when estimating the usefulness of really new products than they have with continuous innovations, and they cope with this through mental simulation and analogies with other preferences.[91]

## PERSUASION

Persuasion, in the Rogers paradigm, refers to the formation of favorable or unfavorable attitudes toward the innovation. If the innovation is a new brand, consumers may attach attributes of the product category to it to persuade their evaluation.[92] The consumer may imagine how satisfactory the new product might be in some anticipated future-use situation, perhaps giving the product a "vicarious trial" in the consumer's mind.

**FIGURE 13.15**  Rogers's Model of Innovation Decision Process

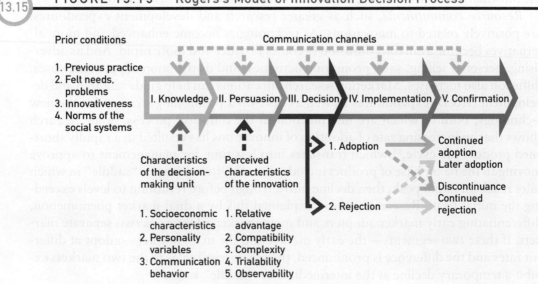

Persuasiveness is related to perceived risks and consequences of adopting and using the new product. When an individual considers a new product, he or she must weigh the potential gains from adoption against the potential losses of switching from the product now used. If the new product is adopted, it may be inferior to a present product or cost more than the increased value gained by using the new product.

## DECISION

The decision stage involves a choice between adopting and rejecting the innovation. Some members of the social system are **adopters**—*people who have made a decision to use a new product*—whereas others are **nonadopters**. Adoption involves both psychological and behavioral commitment to a product over time.[93] Ordinarily, this means continued use of the product unless situational variables (including lack of availability) prevent or interrupt usage. Consumers might also reject the innovation, and thus decide not to adopt. Active rejection involves the consideration of adoption, or perhaps even a trial, but a final decision not to adopt. Passive rejection consists of never really considering use of the innovation. Some consumers will not be exposed to information about the product whereas others will wait until other people have tried the product before doing so themselves.

## IMPLEMENTATION

Implementation occurs when the consumer puts an innovation to use. Until the implementation stage, the process has been a mental exercise, but now behavioral change is required. The strength of the marketing plan may be the critical determinant in whether a good product that has been communicated effectively results in a sale.

Price, new product information, advertising, and communication play important roles in determining a sale. 3M's Post-it Notes, which consist of notepaper with an adhesive strip on the back, are an example of a simple, new product. The product has diffused throughout the world as a replacement for paper clips, notepads, and loose pieces of paper. 3M gave away significant numbers of workplace samples that employees took home. Family members began using them for many purposes, creating rapid diffusion of the product in the consumer as well as the business market.

## CONFIRMATION

During confirmation, consumers seek reinforcement for their innovation decision. Consumers sometimes reverse previous decisions, especially when exposed to conflicting messages about the innovation, causing dissonance. Those who adopt products can reject them after short or long periods, and vice versa. Discontinuance is a serious concern to marketers. Pringles, stacked potato crisps that are similar to potato chips, were introduced by Procter & Gamble and were successful in attracting many adopters. The product eventually failed in its original form, however, because the degree of discontinuance was so high, a fact that went undetected until after the firm had invested millions of dollars in marketing and building additional manufacturing plants. Recently, Pringles gained renewed acceptance in the marketplace, with a "new, better-tasting" product, "fun designs" printed directly on each crisp, and an upbeat marketing campaign appealing to younger consumers.

Similarly, many early purchasers of digital cameras found them so time consuming to use that they returned to analog (film) cameras, except for special uses in which the digital camera had advantages over film. Then, Hewlett-Packard, Lexmark, and others introduced printers that allowed consumers to easily use memory cards and photographic paper.

In the development process, marketers need to determine who is most likely to buy the new product. Determinants include individuals' personalities, social status, education level, and aversion to or acceptance of risk. In addition to individual characteristics, the role within the family also affects adoption behavior. Research studies indicate that there are times and situations in which wives' needs may be the driving factor behind much of the innovative behavior decision making that occurs in the family [94] for several product categories. These characteristics, combined with "degree of innovativeness," cause different adopter classifications to behave differently during the various decision process stages [95] and for new products and new brands. [96]

Consumers can be classified according to the time it takes for them to adopt a new product relative to other consumers. Figure 13.16 depicts the five major categories of consumers based on their adoption cycle time in relation to other adopters in their social system or market segment. **Innovators** are *the first consumer group to adopt products.* They tend to be adventuresome, enjoy some risk, have an above-average education, and socialize with other innovators—sometimes being "experts" in the product category of the innovation. Innovators are less likely to seek solutions within the context of previous solutions to a problem. [97] Innovators often are the main market target for firms introducing new products because they influence additional potential adopters. [98] People may be innovators for some products but not for others. Consumers who are *innovators for many products* are said to be **polymorphic,** whereas those who are *innovators for only one product* are **monomorphic.**

Additional classifications of adopters are early adopters, early and late majority, and laggards. **Early adopters** tend to be *opinion leaders and role models for others, with good social skills and respect within larger social systems.* Some research indicates that early adopters use both mass media and interpersonal sources more than later adopters. [99] The **early majority** consists of *consumers who deliberate extensively before buying new products, yet adopt them just before the average time it takes the target population as a whole.* The **late majority** tends to be *cautious when evaluating innovations, taking more time than average to adopt them, and often at the pressure of peers.* **Laggards,** the last group to adopt innovations, tend to be *anchored in the past, are suspicious of the new, and exhibit the lowest level of innovativeness among adopters.* Some consumers may actively reject the new product from the very beginning. Unlike

(13.16)   **FIGURE 13.16**   Adopter Classes

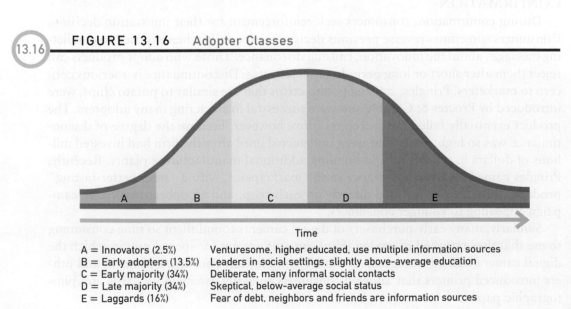

Time

A = Innovators (2.5%)      Venturesome, higher educated, use multiple information sources
B = Early adopters (13.5%) Leaders in social settings, slightly above-average education
C = Early majority (34%)   Deliberate, many informal social contacts
D = Late majority (34%)    Skeptical, below-average social status
E = Laggards (16%)         Fear of debt, neighbors and friends are information sources

laggards, they might best be described as early rejecters. For that reason and others, adoption may be less than the 100 percent shown in Figure 13.16.

After some innovators have adopted a new product, others may follow, depending on the value of the innovation and other characteristics of the product. In fact, the rate of adoption increases as the number of adopters increases,[100] causing the bell curve in Figure 13.16 to be taller and thinner. It is clear from this analysis that marketers must focus their attention on innovators and early adopters—if marketers do not succeed in winning adoption of the new product by these people, there is not much hope for the rest of the population.

Innovativeness is another benchmark to measure likelihood to adopt an innovation. **Innovativeness** is the *degree to which an individual adopts an innovation earlier than other members of a social system*. Degree of innovation can be measured based on time of adoption or based on how many prespecified new products an individual has purchased by a specific point in time. Innovators and early adopters have higher degrees of innovativeness than do late majority and laggards, which affects their brand loyalty, decision making, preference, and communication. Without characteristics such as innovativeness, consumer behavior would consist of a series of routine buying responses to a static set of products.

Innovators can be segmented into cognitive innovators and sensory innovators. **Cognitive innovators** have *a strong preference for new mental experiences*, whereas **sensory innovators** have *a strong preference for new sensory experiences*.[101] Some innovators prefer both. Advertising and other communication messages can be targeted accordingly. Communication aimed at cognitive innovators should emphasize the advantages of the innovation over other existing products and services. Communication targeted to sensory innovators should emphasize the uniqueness of the product and reduce its complexity, performance, and economic risks with long warranties, manufacturer-supported service centers, and easy-to-read-and-understand instructions. Understanding the differences between these types of innovators allows marketers to select the media and tailor the messages to fit the attributes of the segment.[102]

## Managerial Perspectives on Adoption and Diffusion of Innovation

Senior executives around the world understand that the successful introduction of new products is critical to their profitability and long-term financial success. Although development groups are producing primarily line and brand extensions or slight improvements to existing products, management teams need *breakthroughs* to fuel growth and profits. For some firms, these breakthroughs will not come because of the firms' short-term focus on how to increase sales and customers today.[103] Even for those firms with long-term strategic vision, a poor track record of market acceptance can leave even the best CEOs scratching their heads, wondering how to bolster new product development.

New product development requires the coordination of marketing, engineering, research, and other parts of the firm[104] along with extensive knowledge about the *end user*. This type of market knowledge is a strategic asset[105] and a core organizational competence.[106] As you read in Chapter 2, consumer insight is key to developing products that consumers are likely to adopt and decreasing the amount of time and money spent on failed new product trials, as shown in Figure 13.17. Intuition and information about a consumer need leads to the formation of an insight, which is analyzed through research of end users. For example, Kodak positioned digital technology based on consumer insight that people want to turn special moments into "memories"

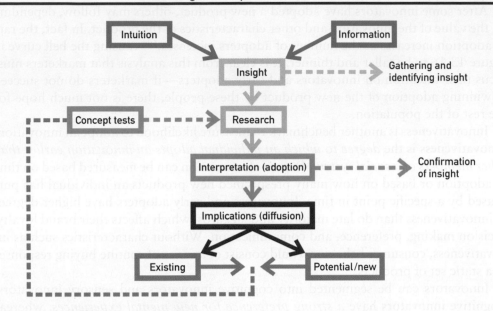

(Figure 13.18) using Internet connectivity, wireless, and peripherals such as color photo printers and CD-writers. After interpretation of the research, the insight is either dismissed or confirmed—beginning product design and development.[107] Involving customers in the design process can lead to designs that customers find more appealing.[108] Implications of the insight and information about the diffusion and adoption processes are analyzed for existing products and potential products, which can lead to concept tests, depending on management's predictions about market adoption. Concept test results and additional research are again analyzed before resources are committed to full-scale production. Test market data and simulation models (as well as other mathematical models)[109] can help forecast future sales and profitability of new products as well as help marketing managers understand why consumers consider or reject them.[110]

Important to the innovation development process is research. Studies indicate that a lack of research delays managers' decision-making process[111]

FIGURE 13.18  Kodak Positions on Insight Rather Than Technology

and causes them to rely on what is already known about how new products are accepted, based on other products and theory. In addition to formal research, marketing managers need grassroots ways of understanding consumer reaction to new products. Silicon Graphics turned to computer-aided design and animation experts for knowledge in designing a new generation of supercomputers used in modeling and visualization.[112] Sony's managers talk with dealers and consumers constantly to get their reactions to its new products, and Wal*Mart's managers to spend lots of time in not only their own stores, but also those of competitors, listening to consumers and gaining insights.

3M has taken the new product development process outside its walls and entered the minds, offices, and lives of its lead customers to discover what types of innovations they want to purchase. 3M adopted a lead-user strategy, which focuses on collecting information from the leading edges of a company's target market rather than from its center.[113] In other words, 3M interviews innovators rather than early adopters or early majority about either how they have "invented" their own solutions to a problem or how they have adapted existing products to meet their specific requirements. 3M's goal, also, is to target lead users from markets that face similar problems in a more extreme form. Development teams at 3M have found that some lead users had developed product innovations that were ahead of those available in the marketplace. Not only do they gain information and insight into what their customers' needs are, they develop closer relationships with them, stimulating sales.

## Summary

Personal and group influences often play an important role in consumer decision making, especially when there are high levels of involvement and perceived risk, and the product or service has public visibility. This influence is expressed both through reference groups and through word-of-mouth communication, often aided by the Internet with e-mail, blogging, podcasting, and other interactive methods for stimulating viral communications.

Reference groups are any type of social aggregation that can influence attitudes and behavior, including primary (face-to-face) groups, secondary groups, and aspirational groups. The influence occurs in three ways: (1) normative (pressures to conform to group norms in thinking and behavior), (2) value-expressive (reflecting a desire for psychological association and a willingness to accept values of others without pressure), and (3) informational (beliefs and behaviors of others are accepted as evidence about reality). When there is motivation to comply with group norms, it is important to make this a feature in marketing appeals.

Personal influence also is expressed through what has traditionally been referred to as "opinion leadership." What this means is that a credible person, referred to as an "influential," is accepted as a source of information about purchase and use. The greater the credibility of the influential, the greater his or her impact on other people.

The diffusion of innovations deals with how a new product or innovation is adopted in a society. This is important to marketing organizations because new products must be brought out continuously for

firms to survive. The elements of the diffusion process include the innovation, the communication of the innovation, time, and the social system. The diffusion process begins with the dissemination of information or communication to individuals, which leads them to make individual decisions about the adoption or rejection of an innovation. Finally, as more and more individuals adopt a new product, the innovation diffuses throughout a given social system.

Everett Rogers, the most influential change agent in the area of diffusion, identified the types of consumers adopting a new product as innovators, early adopters, early majority, late majority, and laggards. If products are to be successful in the marketplace, they must be accepted by innovators and early adopters, and marketers increasingly research these groups for insights and target communication to them.

## Review and Discussion Questions

1. For which of the following products would you expect personal and group influence to be a factor in buying decisions: soft drinks, motor oil, designer jeans, eyeliner, house paint, breakfast cereals, wine, carpeting, a dishwasher, and a digital camera? What are your reasons in each case?

2. Regarding each product listed in question 1, do you think there could be a variation between personal influence on product choice and on brand name? Why do you say this?

3. Recall the last time you volunteered information to someone about a brand or product that you purchased. What caused you to share in this way? How does your motivation compare with the

motivations mentioned in the text? Have you used the Internet to be a part of viral communications?

4. Your company manufactures a full line of mobile homes in all price ranges. Several studies have indicated that word-of-mouth communication plays a role in the buying decision. Prepare a statement indicating the alternative strategies that can be used to harness and capitalize on this source of consumer influence. Which strategy do you think would be most effective?

5. Assume that you are a public relations consultant for an employer or a financial institution offering health savings accounts (HSAs), an innovative financial product. What could either organization do to stimulate the type of word-of-mouth that would stimulate diffusion of the product?

6. Explain as precisely as possible the differences between continuous, dynamically continuous, and discontinuous innovations. Give some examples of each, other than those mentioned in the text.

7. What are the main competitive challenges facing firms in which understanding of diffusion of innovations might be helpful?

8. Prepare a short essay that explains how to pick winners from the many candidates for new product introduction.

9. The manufacturer of a new wireless communication device is attempting to determine who the innovators for the product might be. How would you describe the target market and influencers of this market? What would the communication strategy be in terms of word-of-mouth and advertising? What appeals would you suggest be used in promoting the product?

10. A large manufacturer of health and beauty products wants to introduce a new toothpaste brand in addition to the three already marketed by the manufacturer. Evaluate for the firm what information might be used for innovation studies to guide introduction of the product.

# Notes

1 Cornelia Pechmann and Susan Knight, "An Experimental Investigation of the Joint Effects of Advertising and Peers on Adolescents' Beliefs and Intentions about Cigarette Consumption, " *Journal of Consumer Research*, 29 (June 2002), 5–20.

2 William O. Bearden and Michael J. Etzel, "Reference Group Influence on Product and Brand Purchase Decisions," *Journal of Consumer Research*, 9 (September 1982), 184.

3 C. Whan Park and V. Parker Lewsig, "Students and Housewives: Differences in Susceptibility to Reference Group Influence," *Journal of Consumer Research*, 4 (September 1977), 102–110.

4 For information on important studies in this area, see Solomon E. Asch, "Effects of Group Pressure on the Modification and Distortion of Judgments," in H. Guetzkow, ed., *Groups, Leadership, and Men* (Pittsburgh, PA: Carnegie Press, 1951); Lee Ross, Gunter Bierbrauer, and Susan Hoffman, "The Role of Attribution Processes in Conformity and Dissent: Revisiting the Asch Situation,"

*American Psychologist* (February 1976), 148–157; and M. Venkatesan, "Experimental Study of Consumer Behavior Conformity and Independence," *Journal of Marketing Research*, 3 (November 1966), 384–387.

5 Robert E. Witt and Grady D. Bruce, "Group Influence and Brand Choice," *Journal of Marketing Research*, 9 (November 1972), 440–443.

6 James C. Ward and Peter H. Reingen, "Sociocognitive Analysis of Group Decision Making among Consumers," *Journal of Consumer Research*, 17 (December 1990), 245–262.

7 Cara Okleshen and Sanford Grossbart, "Usenet Groups, Virtual Community and Consumer Behavior," in Joseph W. Alba and J. Wesley Hutchinson, eds., *Advances in Consumer Research*, 25 (Provo, UT: Association of Consumer Research, 1998), 276–282.

8 Eileen Fischer, Julia Bristor, and Brenda Gainer, "Creating or Escaping Community? An Exploratory Study of Internet Consumers' Behaviors," *Advances in Consumer Research*, 23 (Provo, UT: Association of Consumer Research, 1996), 178–182. See also Siok Kuan Tambyah,

"Life on the Net: The Reconstruction of Self and Community," *Advances in Consumer Research*, 23 (Provo, UT: Association of Consumer Research, 1996), 172–177.

9 Sonya Grier and Rohit Despande, "Social Dimensions of Consumer Distinctiveness: The Influence of Social Status on Group Identity and Advertising Persuasion," *Journal of Marketing Research*, 38 (May 2001), 216–227.

10 Robert Burnkrant and Alain Cousineau, "Informational and Normative Social Influence in Buyer Behavior," *Journal of Consumer Research* (December 1975), 206–215. Also see H. C. Kelman, "Processes of Opinion Change," *Public Opinion Quarterly*, 25 (Spring 1961), 57–78.

11 Bobby Calder and Robert Burnkrant, "Interpersonal Influence on Consumer Behavior: An Attribution Theory Approach," *Journal of Consumer Research*, 4 (June 1977), 29–38.

12 Diana Haytko and Julie Baker, "It's All At the Mall: Exploring Adolescent Girls' Experiences," *Journal of Retailing*, 80 (Spring 2004), 67–84.

13 Richard L. Oliver, "Whence Consumer Loyalty?" in George S. Day and

David B. Montgomery, eds., *Journal of Marketing,* 63 (Special Issue 1999), 33–44.

[14] Abraham Tesser, Murray Millar, and Janet Moore, "Some Affective Consequences of Social Comparison and Reflection Processes: The Pain and Pleasure of Being Close," *Journal of Personality and Social Psychology,* 54 (January 1988), 1, 49–61.

[15] L. Wheeler, K. G. Shaver, R. A. Jones, G. R. Goethals, J. Cooper, J. E. Robinson, C. L. Gruder, and K. W. Butzine, "Factors Determining the Choice of a Comparison Other," *Journal of Experimental Social Psychology,* 5 (April 1969), 219–232.

[16] Marsha L. Richins, "Social Comparison and the Idealized Images of Advertising," *Journal of Consumer Research,* 18 (June 1991), 71–83.

[17] See William O. Bearden and Randall L. Rose, "Attention to Social Comparison Information: An Individual Difference Factor Affecting Consumer Conformity," *Journal of Consumer Research,* 16 (March 1990), 461–472; and William O. Bearden, Richard G. Netemeyer, and Jesse E. Teel, "Measurement of Consumer Susceptibility to Interpersonal Influence," *Journal of Consumer Research,* 15 (March 1989), 473–481.

[18] George Homans, *Social Behavior: Its Elementary Forms* (New York: Harcourt, 1961).

[19] Gwen Rae Bachmann, Deborah Roedder John, and Akshay R. Rao, "Children's Susceptibility to Peer Group Purchase Influence: An Exploratory Investigation," in Leigh McAllister and Michael L. Rothschild, eds., *Advances in Consumer Research,* 20 (Provo, UT: Association for Consumer Research, 1992), 463–468; Stephen A. LaTour and Ajay K. Manrai, "Interactive Impact of Information and Normative Influence on Donations," *Journal of Marketing Research,* 26 (August 1989), 327–335; Paul W. Miniard and Joel E. Cohen, "Modeling Personal and Normative Influences on Behavior," *Journal of Consumer Research,* 10 (September 1983), 169–180;

C. Whan Park and V. Parker Lessig, "Students and Housewives: Differences in Susceptibility to Reference Group Influence," *Journal of Consumer Research,* 4 (September 1977), 102–109.

[20] Bearden and Etzel, "Reference Group Influence on Product and Brand Purchase Decisions."

[21] David E. Midgley, Grahame R. Dowling, and Pamela D. Morrison, "Consumer Types, Social Influence, Information Search and Choice," in T. K. Srull, ed., *Advances in Social Cognition* (Mahwah, NJ: Lawrence Erlbaum Associates, 1990), 137–143.

[22] Miniard and Cohen, "Modeling Personal and Normative Influences on Behavior."

[23] Bearden and Etzel, "Reference Group Influence on Product and Brand Purchase Decisions."

[24] "31 Major Trends Shaping the Future of American Business," *Public Pulse,* 2 (1986), 1; Park and Lessig, "Students and Housewives"; Robert E. Burnkrant and Alan Cousineau, "Informational and Normative Social Influence in Buyer Behavior," *Journal of Consumer Research,* 2 (December 1975), 206–215.

[25] L. J. Shrum, Thomas C. O'Guinn, Richard J. Semenik, and Ronald J. Faber, "Processes and Effects in the Construction of Normative Consumer Beliefs: The Role of Television," in Rebecca H. Holman and Michael R. Solomon, eds., *Advances in Consumer Research,* 18 (Provo, UT: Association for Consumer Research, 1991), 755–763.

[26] Emile Durkheim, *Suicide,* trans. by George Simpson (New York: Free Press, 1951). For a cultural perspective, see Robert Merton, "Anomie, Anomia, and Social Interaction: Contexts of Deviate Behavior," in M. B. Clinard, ed., *Anomie and Deviate Behavior* (New York: Free Press, 1964).

[27] Anocha Aribarg, Neeraj Arora, and Onur Bodur, "Understanding the Role of Preference Revision and Concession in Group Decisions," *Journal of Marketing Research,* 39 (August 2002), 336–350.

[28] Malcolm Gladwell, *The Tipping Point* (Boston: Back Bay Books, 2002); Seth Godin, *Unleashing the Ideavirus* (Dobbs Ferry, NY: Do You Zoom, 2000). See also Malcolm Gladwell, *Blink: The Power of Thinking Without Thinking* (New York: Little, Brown, 2005).

[29] Hubert Gatignon and Thomas S. Robertson, "A Propositional Inventory for New Diffusion Research," *Journal of Consumer Research,* 11 (March 1985), 849–867.

[30] Paul M. Herr, Frank R. Kardes, and John Kim, "Effects of Word-of-Mouth and Product-Attribute Information on Persuasion: An Accessibility Diagnosticity Perspective," *Journal of Consumer Research,* 17 (March 1991), 458–462.

[31] Jacqueline Johnson Brown and Peter H. Reingen, "Social Ties and Word-of-Mouth Referral Behavior," *Journal of Consumer Research,* 14 (December 1987), 350–362.

[32] William L. Wilkie, *Consumer Behavior* (New York: Wiley, 1986), 160.

[33] Ernest Dichter, "How Word-of-Mouth Advertising Works," *Harvard Business Review* (November/December 1966), 147–166.

[34] Paula Fitzgerald Bone, "Determinants of Word-of-Mouth Communications during Product Consumption," in John F. Sherry and Brian Sternthal, eds., *Advances in Consumer Research,* 19 (Provo, UT: Association for Consumer Research, 1992), 579–583.

[35] See, especially, Everett M. Rogers, *Diffusion of Innovations,* 3rd ed. (New York: Free Press, 1983).

[36] See Brown and Reingen, "Social Ties and Word-of-Mouth Referral Behavior."

[37] Laura J. Yale and Mary C. Gilly, "Dyadic Perceptions in Personal Source Information Search," *Journal of Business Research,* 32 (March 1995), 225–237.

[38] Meera P. Venkatraman, "Opinion Leadership: Enduring Involvement and Characteristics of Opinion Leaders: A Moderating or Mediating Relationship," in Marvin E. Goldberg, Gerald Gorn, and Richard W. Pollay, eds., *Advances in Consumer Research,* 17 (Provo, UT:

Association for Consumer Research, 1990), 60–67.

[39] Elizabeth Hirschman, "Innovativeness, Novelty Seeking, and Consumer Creativity," *Journal of Consumer Research,* 7 (December 1980), 283–295.

[40] Mary C. Gilly, John L. Graham, Mary Finley Wolfinbarger, and Laura J. Yale, "A Dyadic Study of Interpersonal Information Search," *Journal of the Academy of Marketing Science,* 26 (April 1998), 83–100.

[41] Charles W. King and John O. Summers, "Overlap of Opinion Leadership across Product Categories," *Journal of Marketing Research,* 7 (February 1970), 43–50.

[42] Lawrence F. Feick and Linda L. Price, "The Market Maven: A Diffuser of Marketplace Information," *Journal of Marketing,* 51 (January 1987), 85.

[43] Michael T. Elliott and Anne E. Warfield, "Do Market Mavens Categorize Brands Differently?" in Leigh McAlister and Michael L. Rothschild, eds., *Advances in Consumer Research,* 20 (Provo, UT: Association for Consumer Research 1993), 202–208; and Frank Alpert, "Consumer Market Beliefs and Their Managerial Implications: An Empirical Examination," *Journal of Consumer Marketing,* 10 (April 1993), 56–70.

[44] King and Summers, "Overlap of Opinion Leadership across Product Categories."

[45] Stanley C. Hollander and Kathleen M. Rassuli, "Shopping with Other People's Money: The Marketing Management Implications of Surrogate-Mediated Consumer Decision Making," *Journal of Marketing,* 63 (April 1999), 2.

[46] Leonard Berry, *Discovering the Soul of Service* (New York: Free Press, 1999).

[47] Michael R. Solomon, Carol Surprenant, John A. Czepiel, and Evelyn G. Gutman, "A Role Theory Perspective on Dyadic Interactions: The Service Encounter," *Journal of Marketing,* 49 (Winter 1985), 99–111.

[48] Stephen Grove and Raymond Fisk, "The Service Encounter as Theater," in John F. Sherry Jr., and Brian Sternthal, eds., *Advances in Consumer Research,* 19 (Provo, UT: Association for Consumer Research, 1992), 455–461.

[49] Glenn B. Voss, A. Parasuraman, and Dhruv Grewal, "The Roles of Price, Performance, and Expectations in Determining Satisfaction in Service Exchanges," *Journal of Marketing,* 62 (October 1998), 46–61.

[50] Rosemary P. Ramsey and Ravipreet S. Sohi, "Listening to Your Customers: The Impact of Perceived Salesperson Listening Behavior on Relationship Outcomes," *Journal of the Academy of Marketing Science,* 25 (Spring 1997), 2, 127–137.

[51] Neeli Bendapudi, and Leonard L. Berry, "Customers' Motivations for Maintaining Relationships with Service Providers," *Journal of Retailing,* 73 (January 1997), 15–37.

[52] Kevin P. Gwinner, Dwayne D. Gremler, and Mary Jo Bitner, "Relational Benefits in Service Industries: The Customer's Perspective," *Journal of the Academy of Marketing Science* 26 (April 1998), 101–114.

[53] Linda L. Price and Eric J. Arnould, "Commercial Friendships: Service Provider-Client Relationships in Context," *Journal of Marketing,* 63 (October 1999), 38–56.

[54] Neeli Benapudi, "Where Does the Wow in Wawa Come From," *NACS Magazine* (November 2004). See also Leonard Berry and Neeli Bendapudi, "Clueing in the Customers," *Harvard Business Review,* 81 (February 2003) 100–106, 126.

[55] Michael Tracey and Fred Wersema, *The Disciple of Market Leadership* (Philadelphia: Perseus Book Group, 1997).

[56] Roger Blackwell and Tina Stephan, *Brands That Rock* (New York: Wiley, 2003).

[57] Thorstein Veblen, *The Theory of the Leisure Class* (New York: Macmillan, 1899); George Simmel, "Fashion," *International Quarterly,* 10 (1904), 130–155.

[58] Paul E. Lazarsfeld, Bernard R. Berelson, and Hazel Gaudet, *The People's Choice* (New York: Columbia University Press, 1948), 151.

[59] For a review of relevant research, see Herr, Kardes, and Kim, "Effects of Word-of-Mouth and Product-Attribute Informa-

tion on Persuasion"; Linda L. Price and Lawrence F. Feick, "The Role of Interpersonal Sources and External Search: An Informational Perspective," in Thomas C. Kinnear, ed., *Advances,* 11 (Provo, UT: Association for Consumer Research, 1984), 250–255; and Theresa A. Swartz and Nancy Stephens, "Information Search for Services: The Maturity Segment," in Kinnear, *Advances,* 244–249.

[60] Barbara B. Stern and Stephen J. Gould, "The Consumer as Financial Opinion Leader," *Journal of Retail Banking,* 10 (Summer 1988), 43–52.

[61] Christy Fisher, "Wal-Mart's Way," *Advertising Age* (February 18, 1991), 3.

[62] Jonathan Gutman and Michael K. Mills, "Fashion Lifestyle and Consumer Information Usage: Formulating Effective Marketing Communications," in Bruce J. Walker, et al., eds., *An Assessment of Marketing Thought and Practice* (Chicago: American Marketing Association, 1982), 199–203.

[63] Herr, Kardes, and Kim, "Effects of Word-of-Mouth and Product-Attribute Information on Persuasion"; Marsha L. Richins, "Word of Mouth Communication as Negative Information," in Kinnear, *Advances,* 697–702; and Richard W. Mizerski, "An Attribution Explanation of the Disproportionate Influence of Unfavorable Information," *Journal of Consumer Research,* 9 (December 1982), 301–310.

[64] John H. Holmes and John D. Lett Jr., "Product Sampling and Word of Mouth," *Journal of Advertising Research,* 17 (October 1977), 35–40.

[65] Measuring the Grapevine: Consumer Response and Word-of-Mouth, The Coca-Cola Co. (1981).

[66] John E. Pluennecke and William J. Hampton, "Can Audi Fix a Dented Image?" *Business Week* (November 17, 1986), 81–82.

[67] Barnet Wolf, "Wendy's Got on Top of Story," *Columbus Dispatch* (March 26, 2005), C1.

[68] Euene Sivadas and Robert Dwyer, "An Examination of Organizational Factors Influencing New Product Success in

Internal and Alliance-Based Processes," *Journal of Marketing,* 64 (January 2000), 31–50.

[69] David Henard and David Szymanski, "Why Some New Products Are More Successful Than Others," *Journal of Marketing Research,* 38 (August 2001), 362–376.

[70] Rosabeth Moss Kanter, "Highlights," in Kanter, ed., *The Change Masters: Innovation and Entrepreneurship in the American Corporation* (New York: Free Press, 1987).

[71] Thomas S. Robertson, "The Process of Innovation and the Diffusion of Innovation," *Journal of Marketing* (January 1967), 14–19.

[72] Lee G. Cooper, "Strategic Marketing Planning for Radically New Products," *Journal of Marketing,* 64 (January 2000), 1–16.

[73] C. Page Moreau, Donald Lehmann, and Arthur Markman, "Entrenched Knowledge Structures and Consumer Response to New Products," *Journal of Marketing Research,* 38 (February 2001), 14–30.

[74] Glen Urban and John Hauser, "'Listening In' to Find and Explore New Combinations of Customer Needs," *Journal of Marketing,* 68 (April 2004), 72–98.

[75] Thomas McCarroll, "What New Age?" *Time* (August 12, 1991), 44–45.

[76] Michael S. Latour and Scott D. Roberts, "Cultural Anchoring and Product Diffusion," *Journal of Consumer Marketing,* 9 (Fall 1991), 29–34.

[77] Salah Hassan, "Attributes of Diffusion Adoption Decisions," Proceedings of the Academy of Marketing Science (1990).

[78] For a good discussion on this subject, please see Venkatesh Shankar, Gregory S. Carpenter, and Lakshman Krishnamurthi, "The Advantages of Entry in the Growth Stage of the Product Life Cycle: An Empirical Analysis," *Journal of Marketing Research,* 36 (May 1999), 269–276.

[79] Everett M. Rogers, *Diffusion of Innovations,* 3rd ed. (New York: Free Press, 1983), 5.

[80] Dan Horsky and Leonard S. Simon, "Advertising and the Diffusion of New Products," *Marketing Science,* 2 (Winter 1983), 1–17.

[81] John O'Shaugnessy, *Why People Buy* (New York: Oxford University Press, 1987), 25–38.

[82] Roger Blackwell and Kristina Stephan, *Customers Rule! Why the E-Commerce Honeymoon is Over and Where Winning Firms Go From Here* (New York: Random/Crown Business, 2001).

[83] James Wills, A. C. Samli, and Laurence Jacobs, "Developing Global Products and Marketing Strategies: A Construct and a Research Agenda," *Journal of the Academy of Marketing Science,* 19 (Winter 1991), 1–10.

[84] Marnik Dekimpe, Phillip Parker, and Miklos Savary, "Global Diffusion of Technological Innovations: A Coupled-Hazard Approach," *Journal of Marketing Research,* 37 (February 2000), 47–60.

[85] Thomas S. Robertson and Hubert Gatignon, "Competitive Effects on Technology Diffusion," *Journal of Marketing,* 50 (July 1986), 1–12.

[86] Sabine Kuester, Christian Homburg, and Thomas S. Robertson, "Retaliatory Behavior to New Product Entry," *Journal of Marketing,* 63 (October 1999), 90–106.

[87] "New Technologies Take Time," *Business Week* (April 19, 1999), 8.

[88] Richard Olshavsky, "Time and the Rate of Adoption of Innovations," *Journal of Consumer Research,* 6 (March 1980), 425–428.

[89] Milton D. Rosenau Jr., "Speeding Your New Product to Market," *Journal of Consumer Marketing,* 5 (Spring 1988), 23–35.

[90] Jacob Goldenberg, Barak Libai, and Eitan Muller, "Riding the Saddle: How Cross-Market Communications Can Create a Major Slump in Sales," *Journal of Marketing,* 66 (April 2002), 1–16.

[91] Steve Hoeffler, "Measuring Preferences for Really New Products," *Journal of Marketing Research,* 40 (November 2003), 405–421.

[92] Thomas C. Boyd and Charlotte H. Mason, "The Link between Attractiveness of 'Extrabrand' Attributes and the Adoption of Innovations," *Journal of the Academy of Marketing Science,* 27 (Summer 1999), 306–319.

[93] John M. Antil, "New Product or Service Adoption: When Does It Happen?" *Journal of Consumer Marketing,* 5 (Spring 1988), 5–15.

[94] David J. Bums, "Husband-Wife Innovative Consumer Decision Making: Exploring the Effect of Family Power," *Psychology and Marketing,* 9 (New York: Wiley, 1992), 175–189.

[95] Gordon R. Foxall and Seema Bhate, "Cognitive Style and Personal Involvement as Explicators of Innovative Purchasing of 'Healthy' Food Brands," *European Journal of Marketing,* 27 (February 1993), 5–16.

[96] Gordon Foxall and Christopher G. Hawkins, "Cognitive Style and Consumer Innovativeness: An Empirical Test of Kirton's Adaption-Innovation Theory in the Context of Food Purchasing," *European Journal of Marketing,* 20 (March 1986), 63–80.

[97] M. J. Kirton, "Adaptors and Innovators: A Theory of Cognitive Style," in K. Gronhaug and M. Kaufman, eds., *Innovation: A Cross-Disciplinary Perspective* (New York: Wiley, 1986).

[98] Vijay Mahajan and Eitan Muller, "When Is It Worthwhile Targeting the Majority Instead of the Innovators in a New Product Launch?" *Journal of Marketing Research,* 35 (November 1998), 488–495.

[99] Linda Price, Lawrence Feick, and Daniel Smith, "A Re-Examination of Communication Channel Usage by Adopter Categories," in Richard Lutz, ed., *Advances in Consumer Research,* 13 (Provo, UT: Association for Consumer Research, 1986), 409–412.

[100] Ram C. Rao and Frank M. Bass, "Competition, Strategy, and Price Dynamics: A Theoretical and Empirical Investigation," *Journal of Marketing Research,* 24 (August 1985), 283–296.

[101] Hirschman, "Innovativeness, Novelty Seeking, and Consumer Creativity"; M. P. Venkatraman and L. P. Price, "Differentiating between Cognitive and Sensory Innovativeness: Concepts, Measurement and Their Implications," *Journal of*

*Business Research*, 20 (June 1990), 293–315.

102 Meera P. Venkatraman, "The Impact of Innovativeness and Innovation Type on Adoption," *Journal of Retailing*, 67 (Spring 1991), 51–67.

103 Eric von Hippel, Stefan Thomke, and Mary Sonnack, "Creating Breakthroughs at 3M," *Harvard Business Review* (September/October 1999), 47–57.

104 John P. Workman Jr., "Marketing's Limited Role in New Product Development in One Computer Systems Firm," *Journal of Marketing Research*, 30 (November 1993), 405–421.

105 Rashi Glazer, "Marketing in an Information-Intensive Environment: Strategic Implications of Knowledge as an Asset," *Journal of Marketing*, 55 (October 1991), 1–19.

106 James M. Sinkula, "Market Information Processing and Organizational Learning," *Journal of Marketing*, 58 (January 1994), 35–45. For more information, see Gary Hamel and C. K. Prahalad, *Competing for the Future* (Boston: Harvard Business School Press, 1994).

107 Lisa Susanne Willsey, "Taking These 7 Steps Will Help You Launch a New Product," *Marketing News* (March 29, 1999), 17.

108 Darren W. Dahl, Amitava Chattopadhyay, and Gerald J. Gorn, "The Use of Visual Mental Imagery in New Product Design," *Journal of Marketing Research*, 36 (February 1999), 18–28.

109 Space does not permit more detailed discussion of these models. If you are interested, you will find them described, along with appropriate citations to source materials, in earlier editions of this text. See James Engel and Roger Blackwell, *Consumer Behavior*, 4th ed. (Homewood, IL: Dryden Press, 1982), 401–409. For a review of these models, see C. Naqrasimhan and S. K. Sen, "Test Market Models for New Product Introduction," in Yoram Wind, Vijay Mahjan, and Richard Cardozo, eds., *New Product Forecasting— Models and Applications* (Lexington, MA: Lexington Books, 1981); and Vijay Mahjan and Robert A. Peterson, *Innovation Diffusion: Models and Applications* (Beverly Hills, CA: Sage Publications,

1985). See also Vijay Mahjan, Eitan Muller, and Frank M. Bass, "New Product Diffusion Models in Marketing: A Review and Directions for Research," *Journal of Marketing*, 54 (January 1990), 1–26.

110 Glen L. Urban, John S. Hulland, and Bruce D. Weinberg, "Premarket Forecasting for New Consumer Durable Goods: Modeling Categorization, Elimination, and Consideration Phenomena," *Journal of Marketing*, 57 (April 1993), 47–63.

111 Booz-Allen & Hamilton, *New Products Management for the 1980's* (New York: Booz-Allen & Hamilton, 1982).

112 Tiger Li and Roger J. Calantone, "The Impact of Market Knowledge Competence on New Product Advantage: Conceptualization and Empirical Examination," *Journal of Marketing*, 62 (October 1998), 13–29.

113 Eric von Hippel, Stefan Thomke, and Mary Sonnack, "Creating Breakthroughs at 3M," *Harvard Business Review* (September/October 1999), 47–57.

# Influencing Consumer Behavior

In the prior sections of this text, we focused on those aspects of consumer behavior essential for building a basic understanding of consumers. But beyond understanding consumers, companies also need to know how to influence consumers. Companies try to influence what consumers buy, when they buy, and where they buy. Obviously, a company's long-term success depends heavily on its ability to influence consumer behavior.

The purpose of this section is to discuss the requirements that companies must satisfy if they are to be successful in their efforts to influence consumers. Chapter 14 begins this section with the most fundamental prerequisite—making contact with potential buyers. Making contact requires not only being at the right place at the right time, it also requires gaining that most valuable consumer resource: attention.

After making contact, companies typically try to shape the product opinions held by consumers. In Chapter 15 we focus on how opinion shaping can be achieved. Finally, Chapter 16 explores how companies help consumers remember things that increase the odds of them becoming customers, or, for those who already are, becoming even better customers (i.e., buying more often).

PART 5

# Chapter 14

# Making Contact

## Opening Vignette

Once upon a time, a marketer's life in America was so much easier. In the 1960s, a commercial that aired simultaneously on ABC, CBS, and NBC could reach 80 percent of American women. The Big Three weren't just the major TV networks, they were the only TV networks. The country was far more uniform in terms not only of ethnicity—the great Latino influx had not yet begun—but also of aspiration. The governing idea was not merely to keep up with the Joneses, but to be the Joneses—to own the same model of car or dishwasher or lawnmower. Mass marketing was in its prime.

Those days are but a distant memory now. As levels of affluence rose markedly in the 1970s and 1980s, status was redefined. "From the consumer point of view," says Larry Light, McDonald's chief marketing officer, "we've had a change from 'I want to be normal' to 'I want to be special.'" America today is a far more diverse and commercially self-indulgent society than it was in the heyday of the mass market. And the mass market has fragmented into a vast array of market segments with their own unique requirements.

At the same time, the almost-universal audience assembled long ago by network television is fragmenting at an accelerating rate. Prime-time network ratings and newspaper circulation have been sliding since the 1970s. But only in more recent times have we witnessed the proliferation of digital and wireless communication channels that are spreading the mass audience of yore ever-thinner across hundreds of narrowcast cable-TV and radio channels, thousands of specialized magazines, and millions of computer terminals, video-game consoles, personal digital assistants, and cell-phone screens. In 1994, the average U.S. household received twenty-seven TV channels. Ten years later, the average is one hundred channels.

Another contributor to mass marketing's decline is cost. "Mass marketing is based upon low-cost for thousands, the ability to reach people cheaply," says marketing guru Erwin Ephron of Ephron, Papazian & Ephron. "When television is cheap, you can let it do everything. But when television becomes expensive, it opens the door to less-than-mass media." According to the Television Bureau of Advertising, the networks' average cost per thousand viewers, or CPM, was $1.96 in 1972. By 2002, CPM had soared to $16.79 in prime time. The same fate has befallen print. Daily newspaper readership fell from a high of 81 percent in 1964 to 55 percent of households in 2002. Yet the cost of newspaper advertising per unit of circulation has increased tenfold since the mid-1960s.

The result of all these changes has been a shift away from mass marketing to micromarketing, a shift from selling to the vast, anonymous crowd to selling to millions of particular consumers. What's happened at McDonald's is not atypical.

McDonald's now devotes one-third of its U.S. marketing budget to television, compared with two-thirds five years ago. Money that used to go for thirty-second network spots now pays for closed-circuit sports programming piped into Latino bars and for ads in *Upscale,* a custom-published magazine distributed to black barbershops. To sharpen its appeal to young men, another of its prime target audiences, McDonald's advertises on Foot Locker's in-store video network. The company zeroes in on mothers through ads in women's magazines such as *O: The Oprah Magazine* and *Marie Claire* and on websites like Yahoo! and iVillage. "We are a big marketer," says Larry Light. "We are not a mass marketer."

In the competition for advertising dollars, the new digital media—especially the Internet—are blessed by two intrinsic advantages over mass media. First, digital media are interactive. This capability enables marketers to gather reams of invaluable personal information directly from customers and adjust their sales pitches accordingly, in some cases in real time. Second, in part because digital media are interactive, they permit a fuller and more precise measuring of advertising's impact. "Advertisers want to exactly know what they are paying for and what they are getting for it, and you really get metrics on the Web," says David Verklin, CEO of Carat North America, a media-buying agency. "Clients really believe in the Web now."

In the 2002 movie *Minority Report,* there's a scene that symbolizes the ultimate in micromarketing. As the character played by Tom Cruise makes his way through a city of the not-too-distant future, electronic billboard advertisements talk to him by name as he passes by. As you will see later in the chapter, this level of personalization is one of the reasons why businesses have been attracted to the Internet and some of its interactive forms of communication.

The progress of micromarketing appears to be inexorable, favored as it is by economics and demographics. Certainly there is no stopping media proliferation, for it is providing consumers with what they crave: a wealth of new content and innovative modes of consuming it. The mass market will not disappear, nor will the mass media. But the fortunes of many of America's best-known companies now will rise or fall depending on how well they adapt to what is shaping up as a long and chaotic transition from the fading age of mass marketing to the dawning era of micromarketing.

Source: Excerpted in part from Anthony Bianco, Tom Lowry, Robert Berner, Michael Arndt, and Ronald Grover, "The Vanishing Mass Market," *BusinessWeek Online,* www.businessweek.com (July 12, 2004). Copyright July 12, 2004. Reprinted by permission of McGraw-Hill Companies, Inc. All Rights Reserved.

Just as businesses must offer products that meet consumers' needs in order to succeed, so too must they make contact with their potential customers. Advertisements that are not seen by the right people will prove to be a poor investment. Even if the ads reach target consumers, they may still prove to be a poor investment if the cost of making contact is too great. Purchase incentives that get overlooked can't motivate buying. Products that sit unnoticed on the grocer's shelf will never know the joy of being scanned. Websites ignored while traveling the information highway cannot prosper. Somehow, someway, companies must find a way of making contact without wasting money that would otherwise go to their bottom lines. Doing so requires two things. The first is getting exposure.

## Exposure

**Exposure** occurs when *there is physical proximity to a stimulus that allows one or more of a person's five senses the opportunity to be activated.* This activation happens when a stimulus meets or exceeds the **lower threshold:** *the minimum amount of stimulus intensity necessary for sensation to occur.* Given a stimulus of sufficient strength (e.g., a noise loud enough to be heard), sensory receptors are activated, and the encoded information is transmitted along nerve fibers to the brain.

Getting exposure essentially means entering the person's sphere of existence. I can't teach my students if I'm in the classroom and they're not. Similarly, television commercials that appear only in programs you never watch cannot influence you. Products offered at stores never entered can't be noticed either. Consequently, businesses must find a way to bring their messages and products into sufficient physical proximity for consumers to have the opportunity to notice them.

A nice illustration of the importance of exposure comes from a company that discovered it could secure a higher placement in Internet search engines by changing how it listed itself. This higher placement, in turn, increased the number of potential customers exposed to the company's offering. Four months after changing its listing, monthly sales jumped from $25,000 to $65,000.[1] A similar demonstration is provided by a study of supermarket sales flyers. Consumers exposed to the flyers spent more than twice as much on the products promoted in the flyers than did those not exposed.[2]

### Reaching the Consumer

In seeking exposure, companies must decide which pathways its messages and products will travel in the pursuit of customers. As indicated by the vignette at the beginning of this chapter, companies have more choices than ever before. This section reviews a number of these.

### TRADITIONAL MEDIA AND DISTRIBUTION CHANNELS

Until recent times, companies' choices for reaching consumers were confined to the traditional forms of media and distribution channels. Television, radio, newspapers, magazines, the mail, and the phone were the primary message carriers used by companies to inform and persuade target consumers. Bricks-and-mortar retailers and mail-order catalogers were the dominant means by which consumers purchased products.

But as is always the case, things changed. For a number of reasons, some of them described in the chapter's opening vignette, mass media and traditional methods of reaching consumers became less effective but more expensive, not an attractive combination for those interested in profits. The media giants have made changes that enable them to satisfy their clients' desires for more flexibility in their ability to deliver different messages to different sections of the country. *Time* magazine, for example, can produce an incredible number of ad-customized versions of its national edition. "We've done as many as 20,000 versions, but that's not something we want to do every week," says Edward R. McCarrick, publisher of *Time*.[3] Similarly, as described in Consumer Behavior and Marketing 14.1, many companies are hoping that new technology will soon allow the same thing to happen for television advertising.

In an attempt to enhance the effectiveness of television advertising, tactics popular long ago are making a comeback. One such tactic is the **product placement,** in which *companies pay to have their products embedded within an entertainment vehicle.* Another tactic is having a single advertiser sponsor a television program. Both tactics are reflected in the Fox television series *24* starring Kiefer Sutherland. The Ford F-150

## Television Hopes to Soon Offer Customized Advertising

As the advertising industry worries about the effectiveness of traditional television advertising, venture capitalists are betting that the thirty-second spot has a bright future. Since 2000, venture-capital firms have poured millions of dollars into fledgling companies that are developing software designed to get America's couch potatoes to watch television ads. Television operators are starting to roll out those services, which enable advertisers to broadcast commercials tailored to appeal to specific groups of viewers. With the technology, a car dealership, for example, no longer is limited to a one-size-fits-all TV commercial. Instead, the dealer can air ads for its luxury brands in an affluent neighborhood, while marketing its lower-priced models in zip codes where residents may have less purchasing power.

"This is the future of TV advertising," says Dan Nova, a managing general partner at Highland Capital Partners, a venture-capital firm that has an investment in Navic Networks, a start-up specializing in the technology. "If I were to factor what TV advertising may be like in three to five years, I think today's concept of producing blanket TV ads will be analogous to dropping leaflets out of an airplane." "This is absolutely the kind of technology that is going to stem the tide of marketing dollars flowing out of TV into other mediums and help television survive as a viable marketing medium," says Lance Maerov, senior vice president at Grey Ventures, the independent venture-capital arm of New York marketing-services holding company Grey Global Group. "From a VC [venture capital] perspective, this is a huge opportunity. In the U.S. alone,

$50 billion-plus a year is spent on TV advertising. All we need to do is capture a little of that."

Grey Ventures has its money riding on Visible World, a start-up that has raised about $28 million in funding since its launch in February 2000. Visible World has developed a software in partnership with SeaChange International that, within seconds, can produce thousands of versions of a TV commercial, changing features such as music, voiceover, and graphics to enhance its appeal with specific groups of viewers. Currently, the technology helps deliver customized ads to specific TV programs and designated markets. But Visible World also has initial agreements with two cable operators that could begin sending commercials to individual households in the near future. "With the advent of digital set-top boxes, you can go all the way down to the user," says Norman Flore, a partner at RVC, the former venture-capital arm of Reuters Group. "Just like direct marketing, which sends mail that would be more attractive to you, the same publicly available information can be used to show a commercial that's more relevant."

Time Warner, which began deploying customized ad capabilities across its cable systems in Hawaii in 2002 with technology developed by Navic, has seen a high level of interest from Madison Avenue, says Larry Fischer, president of advertising sales for Time Warner Cable. "When I pick up the phone and say I want to talk about advanced advertising, it's on everyone's radar screen," he says.

Source: Excerpted in part from Janet Whitman, "VCs Try to Tailor TV Ads to Meet Specific Taste," *Wall Street Journal* (October 20, 2004), 1. Copyright 2004 by Dow Jones & Co. Reproduced with permission of Dow Jones & Co., Inc., in the textbook format via Copyright Clearance Center, Inc.

truck was the sole sponsor when the show premiered. And Sutherland's character drives around in a Ford Explorer.

### THE INTERNET

Certainly one of the major contributors to the declining influence of traditional media has been the emergence of the Internet. In Chapter 4, we gave considerable discussion to the importance the Internet now plays in consumers' lives. We previously have described a number of aspects of the Internet, such as its role during information search and product purchase and how billions of dollars that used to be paid to

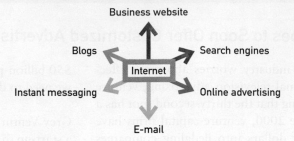

bricks-and-mortar retailers are now being spent online. Neglected in our earlier discussions was the Internet's usefulness to companies in terms of making contact with existing and potential customers, a deficiency we now correct. As indicated in Figure 14.1, companies can use the Internet for making contact with their customers in at least six different ways: websites, search engines, e-mail, online advertising, instant messaging, and blogs.

**Business Websites** A company's website is the launching pad of its Internet presence. And the website's effectiveness ultimately determines the payoff received from the remaining methods for making contact over the Internet. An e-mail campaign that drives large numbers of consumers to the company's website is wasted if these consumers leave empty-handed. When done properly, a company's Internet strategy should succeed in not only satisfying its existing customer base, consisting of those who shop at its bricks-and-mortar stores and/or those who have made a prior purchase at its website, but it should also succeed in recruiting new customers to its business. The ability of a company's online presence to attract new business is demonstrated by Saks Fifth Avenue's recent experience. When Saks examined whether online buyers in 2004 had purchased from the retailer previously, it discovered that more than 40 percent were making their first purchase from the company.[4]

Rather than viewing its Internet presence as a competitor to its bricks-and-mortar presence, a company should appreciate the role each plays in facilitating the other's success. In talking about Best Buy's online accomplishments in 2004, in which sales increased between 50–100 percent depending on the product category, Sam Taylor, senior vice president of online stores, asked "Is it [the Internet] a channel that supports our other channels, or is it the ideal sales channel? It should be both."[5] The support function is reflected by the fact that half of Best Buy's buyers had conducted online research before going to the store. And inside the store shoppers find signs directing them to the retailer's website.

This same sort of support function exists in the new car market, in which over half of new-car buyers search the Internet before visiting a dealership.[6] As such, car manufacturers' websites have considerable opportunity to influence consumers' shopping and purchase behaviors. Car manufacturers are interested in knowing what consumers think of their websites, especially in relation to the competition. One indication of this is provided by J. D. Power & Associates, the market research company you learned about way back in Chapter 6's Market Facts 6.2. The company surveyed more than 11,000 new-car buyers for their evaluations of the manufacturers' sites in terms of relevance, navigability, and appearance/presentation.[7] The ten highest rated sites, along with the number of points that each site earned out of a possible 1,000 points, are shown in Table 14.1. And the winner is . . .

. . . Hummer. Hummer's website relies on Macromedia Flash, an animation program that delivers streaming video content. Liz Vanzura, Hummer's marketing director,

| TABLE 14.1 | Consumers' Ratings of Automobile Manufacturers' Websites: The Top Ten | |
|---|---|---|
| BRAND | WEBSITE | SCORE |
| Hummer | www.hummer.com | 828 |
| Acura | www.acura.com | 821 |
| Honda | www.honda.com | 820 |
| Pontiac | www.pontiac.com | 817 |
| Cadillac | www.cadillac.com | 816 |
| Lexus | www.lexus.com | 816 |
| Suzuki | www.suzukiauto.com | 815 |
| BMW | www.bmwusa.com | 814 |
| Kia | www.kia.com | 814 |
| Mini Cooper | www.miniusa.com | 814 |

Source: Dale Buss. "Hummer.com Is Top Web Site in J. D. Power Survey." *Automotive News* (February 21, 2005), 20. Copyright Crain Communications, Inc., 2005.

Note: The maximum possible score was 1,000.

explains that the website was designed to reflect the product's attributes: "Visually, all the cues and the creativity look and feel like Hummer." [8] Hummer earned the top spot, but a comparison of the scores shows relatively little difference among these ten websites. Indeed, the difference between the top and the tenth-ranked site is only 14 points, not that much considering that we're dealing with a 1,000-point scale. It's probably fair to say that these sites are quite similar in their effectiveness. And just how effective a website can be in this market is the focus of Consumer Behavior and Marketing 14.2, which describes the sales a website has brought to one car dealership.

**Search Engine Marketing** Unlike the subjects that follow, we have already devoted a fair amount of attention to the importance of search engines in determining any website's success in making contact. We noted in Chapter 4, for example, that the large majority of Internet users find websites through search engines such as Google, MSN, Yahoo!, and others (see Market Facts 4.3). For this reason, websites should be built with both consumers and search engines in mind. We refer you back to Consumer Behavior and Marketing 4.2 to refresh your memory about search engine marketing and the increasing emphasis that companies are placing on it in their efforts to reach new customers.

**Online Advertising** Online advertising is on the rebound. Following two years of declining revenues, online advertising registered a hefty increase of 21 percent in 2003.[9] Much of this growth was due to what's known as keyword advertisements. Keyword ads look nothing like conventional advertisements. Rather, they appear as "sponsored links" or "sponsored search results" that appear alongside the regular search results generated by search engines such as Google in response to a consumer's inquiry. In 2002, keyword advertising accounted for 15 percent of ad revenues. The following year, their share skyrocketed to 35 percent.[10]

Online advertisements come in several forms: static, pop-ups, and floaters. Static ads, such as keyword ads, are stationary. Pop-up ads open new windows, causing clutter on the user's computer screen. Consumers' general dislike of pop-ups and the emergence of software that blocks them has caused some advertisers to move away from

## Website Upgrade Increases Web Sales

During the depth of the dot-com collapse, Bill Marsh Auto, northern Michigan's largest auto dealer, was in the midst of rebuilding its website. The dealership had thousands of customers within the Traverse City, Michigan, area, but looked to its website as a way to easily reach even more potential customers. Yet according to marketing director Dean Rose, the company site at the time was little more than a Yellow Pages advertisement. "We didn't even list our inventory," he says. A chance encounter at a sports event, however, introduced him to a solution that would eventually accelerate its Web-based car sales nearly sixfold. "I was at a hockey game at the University of Michigan and I was sitting under what appeared to be a camera," Rose says.

After a little search, Rose discovered that the camera, SilkRoad TrueLook, was allowing online spectators to not only view but also control the images of the game they saw. Recognizing the potential, the dealership implemented the IP-based camera management platform in 2000, which enables customers to do virtually anything associated with the car shopping experience, except to test-drive the cars. Potential customers can view the actual showroom, zoom in on cars that they like for more detail, and actually see the no-haggle prices of cars marked on the windshields. By taking this "one price" or no price-negotiating approach, Rose says, "we found that our ability to sell cars online became much greater, because now [customers are] seeing the price." In fact, using the LIVEcard feature, customers can save and e-mail pictures of cars they like along with a text message to the sales team.

According to Rose, the technology has shifted the company's mindset. "When we first started . . . just to get [salespeople] to answer their e-mails five or six years ago was very difficult to do. They'd rather see the tire kickers out on the lot, because they feel that they are here—I can go sell them a car," he explains. "Now we [find] that people walk into the dealership with pictures printed out of the car they want. That makes it a little bit more easy to sell."

Since implementing SilkRoad TrueLook, Bill Marsh's Web-based sales have jumped from about seven cars per month to more than forty cars per month. The dealership's reach has expanded from Northern Michigan to as far as Florida and New Mexico, and even to overseas military personnel. Traffic on the company's website has also seen an uptick: more than 65 percent of its customers have visited the website before coming in, and about 60 percent of those used the camera. "That's a huge number, especially when the average age of our customers is 51 years old," says Rose. He also notes that SilkRoad allows the dealership to provide customers with a level of comfort. "Helping them know that we're around, helping them know that the car they want is there, knowing that they can drive two hours in the snow and not have the cars sold from under them when they get here—that's a huge, huge thing."

Source: Excerpted in part from Coreen Bailor, "Revving up Web Sales," *Customer Relationship Management* (March 2005), 51–52.

them. Of increasing popularity among advertisers are floater ads, which overlay the content of the page instead of creating new windows. Their frequency of appearance on the Internet has increased nearly one-third between December 2003 to December 2004.[11] Particularly attractive to advertisers is their immunity to the software that blocks pop-ups. Although many consumers find pop-ups and floaters intrusive and annoying, their "click-through rates," representing the percentage of people that click on the advertisement to learn more, is somewhere between 3 and 5 percent, far greater than the 0.5 percent rate achieved by static advertising.[12] And to increase the effectiveness of online advertising, many companies have started using adware, the subject of Buyer Beware 14.1.

## Beware of Adware

Chuck Harris remembers when the Internet was fun and he'd spend hours reading his favorite news sites, checking the church calendar, browsing the shops. Then, a few weeks ago, he lost control of his computer. It turned into a giant electronic billboard. The Web browser had been taken over by a company he didn't recognize. Pop-up windows tried to download stuff he didn't ask for. Strange icons kept appearing offering low home mortgage loans and other stuff he didn't want. Harris spent days trying to fix the computer, but the programs had multiplied to the point where he couldn't run anything else and he decided to give up on the machine. Last week, the sixty-eight-year-old retired aerospace engineer shelled out $1,000 for a new computer, but now he and his wife, Dorothy, use it only when absolutely necessary. "We have just about quit using the computer," he said. "It isn't worth the aggravation."

As if computer users didn't have enough to worry about with hackers, viruses, spam, and other online menaces, now there's a new scourge. Millions of consumers like Harris have been struggling with a recent surge in what computer experts call spyware or adware. The terms apply to a broad range of programs that users download from the Internet, usually unintentionally. Unlike the occasional pop-up ad, these electronic hitchhikers are hidden programs that stay on the computer's hard drive. When consumers' online behavior indicates that they're looking for a certain type of product, the adware activates the sponsor's advertisement for consumers' viewing pleasure. Spyware, on the other hand, tracks and reports on the user's movements and personal information.

Telecommunications giant Verizon Communications has been using adware for nearly two years to draw prospective customers to its high-speed Internet business. Claria, the leading adware provider, names Sprint, Motorola, and online travel company Orbitz among its clients in a recent Securities and Exchange Commission filing. Claria's chief rival, WhenU, says British Airways and Bank of America are among the big-name companies that have used its service. Advertisers like adware because they believe it works, delivering more customers at a lower cost than many other forms of online advertising. "We find that it's much more efficient than other means of direct advertising," says John Bonomo, a Verizon spokesman.

Experts estimate that tens of thousands of spyware and adware programs circulate on the Internet. The National Cyber Security Alliance, a partnership between the tech industry and the Homeland Security Department, estimates that 90 percent of computers using high-speed Internet connections have collected at least one spyware or adware program, causing a loss in productivity and a need for extra customer support and repairs. Colleen Ryan, a spokeswoman for Dell, says that since August 2003 customer support calls to Dell related to spyware have gone from slightly more than 2 percent to between 10 and 15 percent.

Adware is typically downloaded, often without the user's knowledge, along with music-sharing programs, such as Kazaa, or with free screensavers, toolbars, or desktop weather services. The more reputable adware companies tell consumers what the programs do and ask for permission to download to their computer—but usually the notice is buried deep in fine print. You know, the type of fine print that most people just skip over.

Consumers are not alone in their objections to these programs. Even the Interactive Advertising Bureau, the online-advertising industry's standards group, is uncomfortable with the system. "Marketers always tell me the same thing: It's effective," says Greg Stuart, president and chief executive of the New York group. "I say the same thing: 'Yeah, and Tony Soprano's management techniques are effective, but we don't accept them in a civilized society.'"

FYI: You can download free anti-spyware software such as Spybot, Search & Destroy, and Ad-Aware at www.download.com.

Sources: Excerpted in part from Ariana Eunjung Cha, "Computer Users Face New Scourge," *Washington Post* (October 10, 2004), A1; Michael Totty, "Pesky Pop-up Internet Ads Go Mainstream, As 'Adware' Gains Acceptance," *Wall Street Journal* (June 22, 2004), B1.

In 2003, online advertising took the next step toward the future of advertising as depicted in the film *Minority Report*. When Israeli consumers who had previously given their permission to receive electronic messages visited certain websites, they encountered advertisements built specifically for them and that addressed them by their name. The allure of these personalized ads was so strong that the click-through rate registered a staggering 34 percent! As the novelty wore off, the click-through rates tapered off. Even so, they stabilized in the 7–12 percent range, a click-through rate clearly superior to that achieved by nonpersonalized online ads. This technology was scheduled for adoption by certain American companies in the summer of 2004.[13]

**E-mail Marketing** In 2003, $2.1 billion was spent on e-mail marketing in the United States, representing an increase of 38 percent over the prior year.[14] This figure is projected to nearly triple to $6.1 billion by 2008.[15] One of the major attractions to this method of reaching consumers is that it's relatively inexpensive. An outbound e-mail can cost as little as half a cent to deliver. By comparison, mailing a letter at bulk rates costs about 18 cents.[16]

Making contact with e-mails faces two major challenges. First, there's achieving delivery and avoiding what's called "bounce-back." Some bounce-back is unavoidable, such as when mailboxes are full or servers are down. But bounce-back due to invalid e-mail addresses indicates problems with the mailing list, whereas being blocked by the recipient's mail server suggests a deficiency in the e-mail itself.

The next challenge is getting the recipient to open the e-mail. What appears in the sender and subject lines is critical at this stage. A survey asked one thousand e-mail users: "What most compels you to open a permission-based e-mail?"[17] A **permission-based e-mail** is *one which recipients have previously granted permission to a commercial sender to contact them in this fashion*. In contrast, **spam** is *unsolicited commercial e-mail*. As shown in Figure 14.2, what appears in the sender line (i.e., the "from" line) has a greater impact than the subject line by a margin of two to one.

What do consumers look for in the sender line? A familiar name. Because when the name is unfamiliar, an e-mail is viewed by most consumers as a piece of spam. That survey of e-mail users also asked: "Which of the following do you consider junk mail or spam?" When e-mails came from unknown senders, 93 percent categorized the e-mails as spam.[18] Why would that matter? It matters because of how consumers respond to spam. Figure 14.3 shows the different ways consumers respond to spam.

**FIGURE 14.2**  The Importance of Sender and Subject Lines in Consumers' Decisions to Open E-Mails

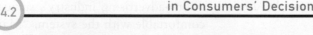

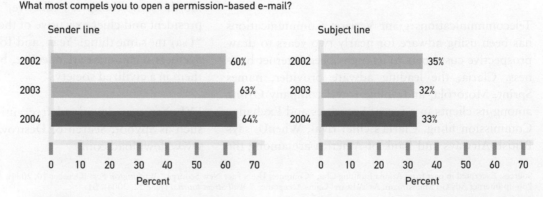

What most compels you to open a permission-based e-mail?

| Sender line | | Subject line | |
|---|---|---|---|
| 2002 | 60% | 2002 | 35% |
| 2003 | 63% | 2003 | 32% |
| 2004 | 64% | 2004 | 33% |

**FIGURE 14.3**  How Consumers Respond to Spam

When you receive an unsolicited promotional e-mail (spam), are you most likely to . . .

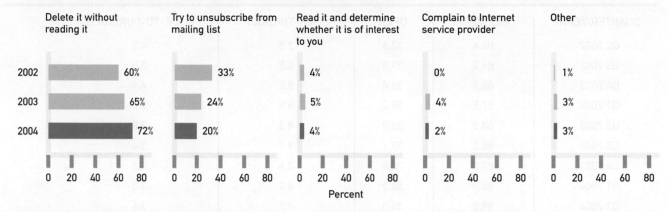

**FIGURE 14.4**  Subject Line Content That Motivates Consumers to Open Their E-Mails

What type of subject line content compels you to open a permission-based e-mail?

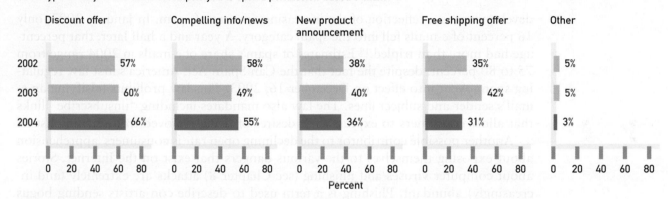

In 2004, only 4 percent bothered to read such e-mail. And for every person that reads a piece of spam, eighteen others simply deleted it without ever opening it.

Regarding the subject line, some subjects are more enticing than others. Again we return to our survey of one thousand e-mail users. These users were asked: "What type of subject line content compels you to open a permission-based e-mail?" Their responses are summarized in Figure 14.4. Consistent with our discussion in Chapter 8 about the money motivator, subject lines containing a discount offer were viewed as providing the most compelling reason to open the e-mail.

So how successful are companies in making contact through e-mails? Evidence that speaks to this question appears in Table 14.2. The table presents the percentage of e-mails successfully delivered and opened for much of 2002 and all of 2003 and 2004. During this time the delivery rate has steadily increased, reaching an all-time high of 90.6 percent in the fourth quarter of 2004.

The percentage of e-mails opened is, of course, much lower than the delivery rate. And there's been some deterioration in the open rate during 2004. Perhaps this

**TABLE 14.2**  Delivery, Open, Click-Through, and Click-to-Purchase Rates for E-mail (percent)

| QUARTER/YEAR | DELIVERY | OPEN | CLICK-THROUGH | CLICK-TO-PURCHASE |
|---|---|---|---|---|
| Q2 2002 | 86.4 | 37.6 | 7.5 | 4.3 |
| Q3 2002 | 86.7 | 37.3 | 8.5 | 3.5 |
| Q4 2002 | 86.5 | 36.4 | 8.0 | 4.9 |
| Q1 2003 | 87.5 | 39.2 | 8.9 | 3.5 |
| Q2 2003 | 88.5 | 38.8 | 8.3 | 3.8 |
| Q3 2003 | 88.2 | 37.1 | 9.2 | 3.4 |
| Q4 2003 | 87.3 | 36.8 | 8.4 | 4.2 |
| Q1 2004 | 88.8 | 38.2 | 8.4 | 3.3 |
| Q2 2004 | 89.5 | 36.0 | 7.7 | 3.6 |
| Q3 2004 | 89.3 | 34.3 | 8.2 | 4.4 |
| Q4 2004 | 90.6 | 32.6 | 8.0 | 4.8 |

Source: *DoubleClick 2004 Email Trend Report*, DoubleClick, www.doubleclick.com (March 2005).

development is a reflection of the increasing amount of spam. In January 2002, only 16 percent of e-mails fell into the spam category. A year and a half later, that percentage had more than tripled.[19] Estimates of spam's share of e-mails in 2004 range from 75 to 80 percent, despite the fact that the Can-Spam Act, America's first law regulating spam, went into effect on December 16, 2003. This law prohibits falsifying an e-mail's sender and subject lines. The law also mandates including "unsubscribe" links that allow consumers to express their desires of being removed from mailing lists.[20]

Another possible contributor to the declining open rate is consumers' apprehension about exposing themselves to the various dangers that exist on the Internet. Stories about computer viruses and phishing (see Chapter 8) attacks are extremely (and increasingly) abundant. Phishing is a term used to describe con artists sending bogus e-mails to consumers, usually under the guise of originating from a well-known company, asking for personal information that allows the thief to steal the consumer's identity. Identity theft has grown so rapidly that a coalition consisting of the federal government and leading consumer organizations and financial institutions launched a campaign to educate consumers about phishing scams in the summer of 2004.[21] To learn more about how to protect yourself from becoming a victim of identity theft, read Buyer Beware 14.2.

Returning to Table 14.2, the final two columns present the click-through rate and the click-to-purchase conversion rate. The click-through rate represents how often recipients click on the website link contained within the e-mail. This rate has shown some small up-and-down fluctuations during 2004. The click-to-purchase conversion rate indicates the percentage of those clicking through to the website that made a purchase during their visit. This rate has climbed steadily during 2004 and ended the year only slightly below its highest level achieved in the last quarter of 2002.

**Instant Messaging**  Instant messaging (IM) is one of the new kids on the block. But this kid is growing up fast. And according to one IM executive, here's why: "This is a heightened level of interaction and awareness," says Frazier Miller, director of product management of Yahoo! Messenger. "In terms of interactivity, when you compare

## Identity Theft in America

According to the Federal Trade Commission (FTC), more than three million Americans become victims of identity theft each year. For four consecutive years, identity theft has been the most frequent complaint filed with the FTC. In 2004, nearly 250,000 complaints about identity theft, representing 39 percent of the total complaints, were lodged with the FTC. By comparison, around 31,000 complaints were filed in 2000. Phishing attacks cost U.S. banks and credit-card issuers an estimated $1.2 billion in 2003. The problem has become serious enough that a growing number of companies are offering identity-theft insurance coverage as an employee benefit, in part to cut down on the lost time when a worker is a victim.

In today's phishing environment, no company should be sending you an e-mail asking for personal information. If you do receive such an e-mail that appears to be legitimate, do not cut and paste material from it. Either open a new Internet browser window and type in the company's Web address or pick up the phone and call the company directly. Be on the lookout for messages that begin with "Dear customer." Most companies send personalized messages using your name.

Identity theft is, of course, not limited to Internet scams. Solicitations for your personal information can come over the telephone or by mail. "Dumpster diving," in which identity thieves search through trash looking for personal information or steal people's mail out of their mailboxes, are other ways identity theft can occur.

Officials suggest that consumers take the following precautions to reduce their risks.

• Never provide your Social Security number, credit card and debit card numbers, PINs (personal identification numbers), passwords, or other personal information in response to an unsolicited phone call, fax, letter, or e-mail, no matter how friendly or official the circumstances may appear.

• Keep your important documents and checkbook locked up in a secure place within your home.

• Be extra careful if you have housemates in your home or let workers inside. They sometimes are in the best position to find personal information and use it without your knowledge. As much as we regret saying it, even relatives, friends, and neighbors pose a potential risk. According to the 2005 Identity Fraud Survey Report, they represent an astounding 50 percent of all known identity thieves.

• Don't reprint your Social Security number, phone number, or driver's license number on your checks. You have the right to refuse requests for your Social Security number from merchants and service providers.

• Protect your incoming and outgoing mail. Those who live in rural areas where mailboxes are out on a county highway or an apartment complex where the mailboxes are accessible to passersby are particularly vulnerable to theft.

• Be careful with how you dispose of important documents. Papers containing important information such as credit card or bank account numbers should be shredded before being trashed.

• More frequent monitoring of your financial accounts online will allow you to detect a potential problem more quickly.

The Better Business Bureau and Javelin have created the Identity Safety Quiz so consumers can assess their vulnerability. You can find this quiz at www.idsafety.net. After taking the quiz, you'll receive some advice on how to better protect yourself. And if you do fall victim to identity theft, call 866-ID-HOTLINE for advice on what to do.

Sources: Pete Bach, "Simple Precautions Head off Identity Theft," *Appleton (Wisconsin) Post-Crescent* (January 9, 2005), 1; Jeanette Borzo, "E-Commerce: Something's Fishy: Online Identity-Theft Scams Are so Effective That They Threaten to Steal a Vital Ingredient of E-Commerce: Trust," *Wall Street Journal* (November 15, 2004), R8; Colleen DeBaise, "Firms Begin to Offer Employees Insurance against Identity Theft," *Wall Street Journal* (January 18, 2005), D3; Brian Krebs, "How to Fend Off Phishing," www.washingtonpost.com (November 18, 2004); Michelle Singletary, "When ID Theft Starts at Home," *Washington Post* (February 13, 2005), F1; "Losing Your Life Online," eMarketer, www.emarketer.com (March 22, 2005); "Overview of the Identity Theft Program: October 1998–September 2003," *Federal Trade Commission Report* (September 2003).

IM to watching TV or driving past a billboard, it's at the other end of the scale, where people are engaging in something that they like to do while they've got these brand images around them."[22] What brand images? The brand images that are embedded within Yahoo!'s "IMVironments." IMVironments, now numbering more than thirty, feature a particular product within the IM service. For example, there's one for Major League Baseball in which users receive real-time updates of games while messaging with others. Polaroid, Kraft, Dentyne, Disney's *The Incredibles,* and Kellogg's Pop Tarts recently have advertised on Yahoo! Messenger.[23]

Companies are attracted to instant messaging because of its popularity among that difficult-to-reach market of young consumers. Nearly three-fourths of teenagers use IM every day. But they're not alone. In fact, they're not even the largest user group. Consumers thirty-five years of age and older represent 45 percent of IM users; those between the ages of eighteen and thirty-four account for 35 percent; those under eighteen account for the remaining 20 percent. In September 2004, almost 64 million Americans sent an instant message. One last statistic: Yahoo!'s IM users average nearly an hour a day sending and receiving messages.[24]

Business is not the only one using IM to make contact with consumers. During the 2004 presidential election, both political parties made their presence known on the Internet. Websites for each political candidate attracted millions of visitors. Online ads promoting one candidate and/or attacking the opponent were commonplace. At one point, the Democrats had placed online ads on more than one hundred different websites. Shortly before Election Day, AOL's Instant Messenger program joined the fray. When users logged on they found an image of Senator John Edwards, the Democratic vice presidential candidate, above the list of their messaging "buddies." A pop-up window then appeared, playing a video attacking Senator Edwards.[25]

**Blogs** In Chapter 6 we introduced you to blogs, short for Web logs, which are websites that contain an online personal journal with reflections, comments and often hyperlinks provided by the writer.[26] You won't find this word in the dictionary (at least not yet), but you'll find millions of blogs on the Internet. More than 8 million Americans had created a blog by 2004. And 32 million Americans spent time reading blogs in 2004, an increase in readership of nearly 60 percent.[27]

Most bloggers take pride in their domain being free of corporate influence, but this has started to change. When Dr Pepper/Seven Up rolled out its new product, Raging Cow, a milk-based drink aimed at young consumers, the company created a blog and recruited teenagers to write about the product in exchange for free product samples. When this undisclosed relationship between the teenage bloggers and the company was discovered, consumers began boycotting the product. "People were upset with the premise that marketing dollars were invading the blog community," explains Todd Copilevitz, who at the time worked for the Richards Group, the advertising agency behind the campaign. "We were one of the first down the path and suffered a slew of arrows."[28]

Yet the invasion of corporate America into blog land continues. GreenCine is an online DVD-rental company. The company launched its own blog, GreenCine Daily, containing stories of interest to film buffs. The blog is credited with causing a twenty-fold increase in traffic to its website and with playing a major role in helping the company to double its membership and revenues in the past year.[29] A similar success is reported by Nerve.com, an online magazine and dating service, which actually turned its blog over to some of its dating customers to write about their experiences. Less than a year later, more people are stopping by its website and its revenues are up by 50 percent.[30]

Some companies have entered the blog community by getting their employees to write about their company. High-profile corporate executives such as Sun Microsystems CEO Jonathan Schwartz and owners such as Mark Cuban, who owns the Dallas Mavericks basketball team, are blogging. Craig Flannagan, a marketing manager for the Microsoft Developer Network, says that he created a blog as another way of making contact with his customers.[31]

## ADDITIONAL MODES OF CONTACT

There are, of course, other ways of reaching consumers beyond traditional media and the Internet. Certainly one of the hottest forms of marketing these days is viral marketing.

**Viral Marketing** **Viral marketing** occurs when *a company creates something (linked sometimes only tangentially to the company's product) that is so compelling that consumers spontaneously pass the "something" along to others they know.* In the parlance of the marketing and advertising industry, viral marketing is all about creating "buzz." **Buzz** refers to *how much attention has been generated by a marketing activity.* Buzz is reflected in the amount of word-of-mouth and word-of-mouse activity occurring in the marketplace. In essence, viral marketing relies primarily on consumers for making contact with other consumers.

Procter & Gamble's online component of its "Coldwater Challenge" campaign exemplifies viral marketing. This campaign supports its newest laundry detergent, Tide Coldwater, which, as the name implies, is formulated for use in cold water. In January 2005, in partnership with the Alliance to Save Energy, a nonprofit organization, P&G sent e-mails to more than 10,000 consumers asking them to take the challenge and encouraging them to get their friends involved as well.[32] Taking the challenge required going to the product's website and signing up to receive a free sample. On the site is a pulsating map representing the number of consumers who have signed up to take the challenge. Consumers that provide e-mail addresses of others to be contacted about the challenge also get to see their own personal map representing their contribution to the campaign. As of March 25, 2005, the website reported that 773,856 people had accepted the challenge. And visits to Tide.com jumped 900 percent once the campaign started.[33]

Some have taken the generating of buzz one step further. Rather than hope that consumers will talk about a product, a new company called BzzAgent enlists consumers to spread the buzz. If you want to learn more about this company and its BzzAgents, read Market Facts 14.1.

Our next example has been described as the "automotive marketing coup of 2004."[34] On September 13, 2004, Pontiac gave away 276 brand new G6 sedans to audience members of Oprah Winfrey's television show. The impact of this event was immediately evident in consumers' online behaviors. Relative to the prior week, search engines registered a 1,000 percent increase for Oprah and Pontiac.[35] Visits to Pontiac's and Oprah's websites showed huge increases as well (see Table 14.3). "The giveaway buzz was clearly a winner in breaking through the clutter on every media channel and in the workplace, where word-of-mouth is a particularly valuable marketing tool," says Dan Hess, senior vice president of comScore Networks. "With the majority of new-car buyers researching online before they buy, the impact of this event in drawing Americans—including those in-market for a new car—to Pontiac online can't be overlooked."[36] General Motors reports that, in just the first week following the giveaway, more than seven hundred stories were broadcast on television. It's been estimated that over $100 million worth of publicity has been generated by this event.[37]

Companies have discovered other ways of generating buzz and making contact using what's been labeled "branded entertainment"[38] or "advertainment,"[39] in which advertising uses Hollywood-style production techniques. In 2001, BMW pioneered the

## BzzAgent: Buzz for Hire

Companies have long recognized that word-of-mouth is one of the most potent weapons in a marketer's arsenal. The trick has been to harness that power in a disciplined, strategic way. A new company, BzzAgent, aims to do just that. The company has assembled a nationwide volunteer army of natural-born buzzers and will channel their chatter toward products and services they deem worth talking about. BzzAgent's method is simple: once a client signs on, the company searches its database of more than 60,000 volunteers (that's right, volunteers; none of them are paid money for their services) for "agents" matching the demographic and psychographic profile of target customers of the product or service. Those folks are offered a chance to sign up for a buzz campaign. Volunteers receive a sample product and a training manual for buzz-creating strategies. These strategies include talking about the product to friends, chatting up salespeople at retail outlets, or e-mailing influential people on the product's behalf. Each time agents complete an activity, they're expected to file a report describing the nature of the buzz and its effectiveness. BzzAgent coaches respond with encouragement and feedback on additional techniques.

To give you a better sense of what BzzAgents do, consider a few scenes from the life of Gabriella, an agent who worked on a campaign for Al Fresco sausages. At one grocery store, she asked a manager why no Al Fresco sausages were available. At a second store, she dropped a card touting the product into the suggestion box. At a third, she talked a stranger into buying a package. She suggested that the organizers of a neighborhood picnic serve Al Fresco. She took some sausages to a friend's house for dinner and "explained to her how the sausage comes in six delicious flavors." Talking to another friend whom she had already converted into an Al Fresco customer, she noted that the product is "not just for barbecues" and would be good at breakfast, too. She even wrote to a local priest known for his interest in Italian food, suggesting a recipe for Tuscan white-bean soup that included Al Fresco sausage. The priest wrote back to say he'd give it a try.

Hiring such busy buzzers doesn't come cheap. BzzAgent's fees vary according to the size and nature of the campaign. A twelve-week campaign involving one thousand agents, for example, runs about $95,000, excluding product samples. But results can be impressive. According to Rick Pascocello, vice president of advertising and promotions for the Penguin Group, the BzzAgent community managed to revive *The Art of Shen Ku*, a book that had gotten lost in the non-stop news blitz following September 11, 2001. A year after publication, backed by a preholiday BzzAgent schmoozefest, the book sold two-and-a-half times its original printing, a near miracle for a backlist title. Rock Bottom Restaurants' sales grew by $1.2 million in one quarter after four hundred members of its frequent-diner program became BzzAgents. And the campaign for Al Fresco sausages that Gabriella worked on? She was one of two thousand agents that helped Al Fresco boost its sales by 100 percent in some stores.

Sources: Excerpted in part from Linda Tischler, "What's the Buzz?" *Fast Company* (May 2004), 76–77; Rob Walker, "The Hidden (In Plain Sight) Persuaders," *New York Times Magazine* (December 5, 2004), 68–75, 104, 130–131.

technique with a series of short films available on the Internet in which its automobiles played a leading role along with some Hollywood notables. This technique proved so successful in generating buzz that others have followed suit, often adding their own wrinkle. Jerry Seinfeld sold American Express on the idea of creating "webisodes," five-minute video clips of Jerry hanging out with Superman and both of them being "rescued" by an American Express credit card. Converse invited consumers to submit their own short films, many of which can be seen at www.conversegallery.com, with $10,000 being paid to those used in a television commercial.[40] And we would be remiss not to acknowledge Burger King's www.subservientchicken.com, which features a

| | SUNDAY 9/12/04 | MONDAY 9/13/04 | TUESDAY 9/14/04 | WEDNESDAY 9/15/04 |
|---|---|---|---|---|
| **Pontiac.com** | | | | |
| Number of visitors | 26,000 | 85,000 | 141,000 | 76,000 |
| Increase over average[a] | 135% | 322% | 636% | 406% |
| **Oprah.com** | | | | |
| Number of visitors | 56,000 | 346,000 | 634,000 | 290,000 |
| Increase over average[a] | 192% | 551% | 864% | 374% |

Source: "Oprah Giveaway Drives Massive Traffic Increase at Oprah and Pontiac Sites, According to comScore Networks," press release, comScore Networks, www.comscore.com (September 17, 2004).

[a]Represents the increase in Web traffic for this particular day versus the average Web traffic for this day in the prior month.

webcam-type view of a person in a chicken suit that, within reason, follows the viewer's typed commands. Barely one year was needed before the site had registered 215 million hits![41] Now that's one busy chicken!!

**Mobile Marketing** The mobile market consists of cell phones, personal digital assistants (PDAs), and any other wireless communication device. Mobile marketing is in its infancy, especially in the United States, which as of 2004 represented less than 5 percent of the $61 billion global market for wireless communication devices.[42] A 2004 survey of cell phone users revealed that only 20 percent had received a text advertisement through their phone.[43] This low percentage reflects not only the market's embryonic stage of development, but also the fact that users must first give their permission to receive such messages. This permission is required by the same Can-Spam law discussed previously that prohibits unsolicited commercial messages. And given that sending and receiving text messages cost consumers money, spammers are likely to be even less tolerated in this medium than on the Internet.

One indication of this medium's potential is the recent success enjoyed by cable television's History Channel.[44] To support its new special *The Barbarians,* text messages promoting the program were sent to 100,000 cell phones the same day the show was to be broadcast. A follow-up survey several days later revealed that 88 percent read the message, 18 percent watched the program, and 12 percent bothered to forward the message on to someone else. The History Channel was sufficiently impressed with these results that it used similar text messages to support two additional new shows.

In the hopes of growing the audience for its TV reality series *The Simple Life* starring Paris Hilton and Nicole Richie, Fox is teaming up with Verizon Wireless to offer video clips called "mobisodes" that can be viewed on cell phones.[45] These mobisodes will show one minute of show footage that ended up on the editing floor. But to view these clips, Verizon customers will need a video-enabled cell phone and be willing to pay a monthly subscription fee of $15 plus a charge of 99 cents for each downloaded mobisode. Whether Paris Hilton's popularity will induce consumers to pay these prices remains to be seen. Meanwhile, in India, a cell phone company broadcast an entire new movie for its users to watch for free as a way of promoting its video-streaming service.[46]

**Advergaming** Another new advertising medium is **advergaming,** which are *games containing product associations.* Advergames are popping up on dozens of commercial websites. Kraft's Nabiscoworld.com offers players more than fifty games to choose from, many of them laden with images of the company's various brands. For example, there's a basketball game called Oreo Dunk 'N Slam, which shows banners reading "Oreo Lick 'em!!!" and "Oreo Dunk 'em!!!" behind the virtual basket. One mother reports that after her seven-year-old son finished playing the game, he told his mother that he was hungry and asked for, of course, some Oreos.[47]

Advergaming has several benefits. The cost of making contact through this medium is a fraction of many other mediums. Players are often exposed to dozens of brand images and messages for a considerable amount of time. A typical player will spend thirty minutes with a game.[48] And not to be overlooked is the fact that the product is being paired repeatedly with fun and excitement. In Chapter 15 we will discuss how such associations are useful to companies in shaping consumers' product attitudes and beliefs.

Advergaming is not limited to the Internet. Companies have found advergames useful in attracting and educating potential customers at trade shows. Solvay Pharmaceuticals had a racing game developed for its testosterone replacement therapy product that the company used at trade shows for attracting physicians and generating sales leads. The game proved so popular that the company had to shorten the playing time to accommodate all who wanted to play.[49]

## Selective Exposure

Even if an advertiser is successful at getting its message to the right people at the right place at the right time, exposure still may not occur. Rather than sitting passively, consumers may select a different course of action and deliberately try to avoid exposure. The concept of selective exposure embodies this reality. As such, selective exposure essentially reduces the size of the audience that is truly reached. Numbers about a magazine's readership size or a TV program's audience size should not be interpreted as the number of consumers that actually will come into contact with advertising carried by these media.

Selective exposure is everywhere. In the early days of the Internet, one consumer told how she put tape across her computer screen to block out the ads she would otherwise encounter. Another consumer confessed how he and his coworkers used hacker software to eliminate advertisements.[50] Today, many consumers use software that is widely available for blocking certain forms of Internet advertising.

Selective exposure happens when consumers watch television. As shown in Figure 14.5, consumers usually find something to do during the commercial break besides watch advertising (unless this commercial break just happens to be during the Super Bowl, something we'll talk about later in the chapter). Many consumers *grab the remote control and switch to another station*. This behavior, undertaken by millions of viewers, is called **zapping**.[51] Of the minority that do continue watching television, they typically do so without giving their full attention. Later in the chapter we'll discuss why this is a problem.

The cousin of zapping is **zipping,** in which a person *fast-forwards through commercials when watching recorded programming*. Back when VCRs were the sole option for recording television programming, an estimated 50 percent of advertising was zipped.[52] Things did not get any better with the arrival of TiVo and DVR (digital video recorder) technology. One source reports that zipping depends on how long the consumer has been using a DVR.[53] For those owning a DVR less than a year, 56 percent say they always zip through the commercials. This number increases to 72 percent for those owning a DVR for one year or longer. A different source suggests even greater losses in exposure have occurred and estimates that consumers with DVRs typically fast-forward through 92 percent of the advertising.[54]

**FIGURE 14.5**     What Are Consumers Doing during TV Commercial Breaks?

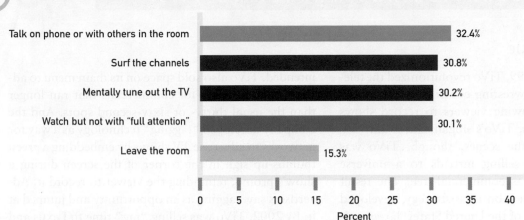

| | |
|---|---|
| Talk on phone or with others in the room | 32.4% |
| Surf the channels | 30.8% |
| Mentally tune out the TV | 30.2% |
| Watch but not with "full attention" | 30.1% |
| Leave the room | 15.3% |

Percent

Source: Don E. Schultz, "TV Advertisers Defy Logic, Pay More for Less." *Marketing News* (June 9, 2003), 14–15.

Note: Numbers represent the percentage of people who say they regularly do this activity when a television commercial comes on.

Moreover, the adverse influence of DVRs on advertising exposure rates should be amplified as their ownership becomes more commonplace. DVRs had penetrated only 5 percent of American homes in 2004, but they're expected to be in 41 percent of homes within five years.[55] Yet all is not bad news. You'll find out about some recent changes in TiVo's product strategy and much more when you read Consumer Behavior and Marketing 14.3.

### The Danger of Overexposure

As the saying goes, sometimes too much of a good thing is bad. Though exposure is a good thing to have, too much of it may not be so good. New or novel stimuli typically command attention. As these stimuli become more familiar through repeated exposure, however, habituation sets in. **Habituation** occurs *when a stimulus becomes so familiar and ordinary that it loses its attention-getting ability.* Consider the couple who moves from a quiet, small town to an apartment in the middle of New York City. Initially, they'll find the noise levels very noticeable and disturbing. But before too long, they'll grow accustomed (i.e., become habituated) to the noise to the point that it's hardly noticed.

The same phenomenon occurs in advertising. In the beginning, a new ad may be very effective at grabbing attention. But after seeing the ad over and over again, consumers grow tired of it and stop paying attention. **Advertising wearout** is the term used to describe *ads that lose their effectiveness because of overexposure.*[56] One advertising researcher offers the following rule of thumb: commercials lose half their effectiveness after accumulating 1,000 gross rating points (the sum of all the ratings that a commercial gets based on the programs in which it appears). At the 1,000 mark, the ad has reached nearly half of all U.S. households with TV sets at least ten times.[57]

Overexposure may not only cause ads to lose their ability to attract attention, it can have an even more detrimental impact. The tedium of seeing the same ad repeatedly sometimes causes consumers to become more critical and argumentative during ad processing.[58] This outcome, in turn, may result in consumers holding less favorable attitudes toward the ad and the product.[59]

One solution to the wearout problem involves using ads that differ in their executions but that carry the same basic message.[60] One ad campaign for Energizer batteries featuring the drum-banging pink bunny consisted of more than twenty commercials.

## TiVo to the Rescue

When it debuted in 1999, TiVo revolutionized the television experience by wresting control of screen time from advertisers, allowing viewers to record shows and skip commercials. TiVo's slogan said it all: "TV your way." Behind the scenes, though, TiVo was courting advertisers, selling inroads to a universe most customers saw as commercial-free. The result is a groundbreaking new business strategy, developed with more than thirty of the United States' largest advertisers, that in key ways circumvents the very technology that made TiVo famous. TV "your way" is quickly becoming TV "their way," too.

In early 2005, TiVo viewers began seeing "billboards," or small logos, popping up over TV commercials as they fast-forwarded through them, offering contest entries, giveaways, or links to other ads. If viewers "opt in" to the ad, their contact information will be downloaded to that advertiser—exclusively and by permission only—so even more direct marketing can take place. By late 2005, TiVo expects to roll out "couch commerce," a system that enables viewers to purchase products and participate in surveys using their remote control.

For viewers though, TiVo's new strategy means the technology famously christened "God's machine" by Federal Communications Commission chairman Michael Powell is rapidly becoming a marketer's best friend, proving that try as they might, consumers cannot hide from marketing. "TiVo looked like it was going to be the weapon of mass destruction of Madison Avenue," says Robert Thompson, professor of television and pop culture at Syracuse University. "However, we knew that the [TV] spot ad would not go gently into the night, and this is the next battle strategy."

Yet from its inception, TiVo engineered its system with advertisers and networks in mind. Rather than allowing consumers to skip commercials entirely, TiVo restricted its fast-forward capabilities so viewers could still see the commercial, albeit eight times faster than intended. TiVo also sold space on its main menu to advertisers as a venue for commercials that ran longer than the usual thirty- or sixty-second spots. And the company developed "tagging" technology as a way for networks to advertise TV shows by embedding a green thumbs-up sign in the corner of the screen during a show's promo, reminding the viewer to record it. Advertisers saw tagging as an opportunity and jumped at it. By 2002, TiVo was selling "tag" time to Lexus and Best Buy. The thumbs-up icons appeared during live commercials, inviting the viewer to "click here" for a chance to enter a contest, receive a DVD or brochure, or watch a glossy, long-form commercial. Over time, General Motors, Nissan Motor, Coca-Cola, Walt Disney World, and Royal Caribbean cruise line paid their way into the program.

TiVo's shift underscores what industry observers have been saying since TiVo started: that TV advertising and programming must change dramatically to survive. These are anxious times for marketers who are faced with commercial-busting technology that's evolving faster than they can keep up. Broadcast-ready cell phones, hyper-real video games, interactive DVDs, and the Internet give consumers the on-demand, often commercial-free entertainment they crave. "The message we really want to get across," says Davina Kent, TiVo's advertising and research sales manager, "is that we now have a dedicated road map for advertising." And TiVo's research shows that between 5 and 20 percent of its viewers voluntarily "participate" in an ad—either by clicking on a tag or by selecting a long-form commercial from a main menu—when given the opportunity to do so.

"I look at TiVo being the first generation of the TV advertising of the future," says Tim Hanlon, a vice president at Starcom MediaVest Group, one of the world's largest media-buying companies, with clients such as General Motors, Procter & Gamble, and Best Buy. "There's a whole witch's brew of change coming to the linear television form."

Source: Excerpted from Gina Piccalo, "TiVo: A Marketer's (New) Best Friend," www.seattletimes.com (November 22, 2004). Copyright 2004 by the Seattle Times. Reproduced with permission of Tribune Media Services.

Not to be outdone, competitor Duracell developed more than forty spots in which different battery-operated toys were shown to run longer when powered by a Duracell battery.[61] Although additional expenses are incurred from the production of multiple ad executions, this cost usually is a worthwhile investment for reducing the problem of advertising wearout.

Overexposure extends beyond advertising to the product itself. The successful Ron Jon surf shops recognize the potential payoff from increasing its stores and locations. Nonetheless, Ron Jon is worried that, in so doing, it'll lose some of the mystique provided by its limited availability. The latest clothing fashions often become less appealing to trendsetters as the items become more commonplace. Overexposure may be one reason why the sales of Abercrombie & Fitch have slowed dramatically. As Megan Murray, a student at the University of Michigan, explains, "I hate the way it has its name all over everything. I guess the image is starting to wear off because it is everywhere."[62]

Although essential, exposure alone is insufficient for making contact. As noted earlier, simply because advertisers are successful in gaining exposure to their commercials does not necessarily mean that consumers are paying attention to them. The second requirement for making contact, then, is gaining attention.

## Attention

According to Webster's dictionary, attention is "the act of keeping one's mind closely on something or the ability to do this; mental concentration."[63] This definition reflects a fundamental element of attention—namely, its *focus* (i.e., the direction of attention). Right now your focus is here. If your phone or doorbell rings, or if somebody interrupts you, the focus of your attention will be redirected.

Yet focus is only part of attention. *Intensity* (i.e., the degree of attention) is the other. Sometimes we think about something as much as we possibly can. We give it our full and undivided attention. More often, we are less generous. Something may occupy our thoughts only for a fleeting moment. With all due respect to Mr. Webster, we define **attention** as the *amount of thinking focused in a particular direction.*

Before companies can get consumers to pay their product's price, they must first get consumers to pay attention. Obviously, people don't buy products they have never thought about. Do you remember the concept of the consideration set (those alternatives considered during decision making) from Chapter 4? Being a member of the consideration set means being thought about as a possible choice. Moreover, alternatives within the consideration set that become the focus of attention during decision making may stand a better chance of being chosen. When given the choice between frozen yogurt and a fruit salad, only 25 percent selected frozen yogurt when their attention was focused on the fruit salad. This percentage doubled, however, when attention was focused on the yogurt.[64]

Similarly, before the messages companies transmit through their salespeople and advertising can work, consumers must pay attention. As the saying goes, a message that falls on deaf ears can't be heard. Ads and salespeople that are ignored can neither inform nor persuade.

The amount of attention or thinking is also important. Rather than undertaking the thinking necessary to carefully compare choice alternatives, consumers may opt for simpler decision strategies such as buying the cheapest or most familiar alternative. These strategies may lead consumers to make different choices than if they had given more attention to the decision at hand. And as you'll learn in Chapters 15 and 16, the amount of thinking (as well as the content of this thinking) during information processing strongly influences how consumers respond to persuasive messages as well as what they remember.

Understanding humans' mental capacity is the domain of the social science called cognitive psychology. Cognitive psychologists traditionally decompose mental capacity into three parts: sensory memory, short-term memory, and long-term memory. **Sensory memory** refers to *that part of mental capacity used when initially analyzing a stimulus detected by one of our five senses*. If the stimulus passes through this phase, it receives further processing using short-term memory. **Short-term memory** is *where thinking occurs*. Here the stimulus is interpreted and contemplated using concepts stored in long-term memory. **Long-term memory** is *the mental warehouse containing all of our knowledge*. Depending on what occurs in short-term memory, new information may be passed along for storage into long-term memory. In Chapter 16, you'll read about how companies try to implant information in consumers' long-term memory. But for now, we'll focus on short-term memory, because it's this part of mental capacity that's being allocated when something catches our attention.

Short-term memory is a limited mental resource. *The length of time short-time memory can be focused on a single stimulus or thought* (i.e., the **span of attention**) is not very long. You can demonstrate this to yourself by testing just how long you are able to concentrate on a particular thought before your mind begins to wander. In advertising, the use of shorter commercials is one way to overcome consumers' limited attention spans.[65]

Nor can information survive very long in short-term memory without efforts to keep it activated. Suppose you were shown a phone number long enough to process it and then were prevented from rehearsing the number. How much time would elapse before the number faded away? Without rehearsal, information typically fades from short-term memory in thirty seconds or less.[66]

The size or capacity of short-term memory is also limited. We can process only a certain amount of information at a time. The size of short-term memory is often measured in terms of an informational chunk, which represents a grouping or combination of information that can be processed as a whole unit. Depending on which source one chooses to draw on, capacity varies from four or five chunks to as many as seven.[67]

Whereas consumer advocates usually urge businesses and regulators to disclose more product information so that consumers can make more informed (and presumably better) choices, some suggest that more information may actually have the opposite effect. The concern is that consumers may become confused and make poorer choices when the amount of information processed during decision making exceeds cognitive capacity.[68] This outcome may be particularly true for inexperienced buyers. According to Brian Wansink, professor of marketing and director of the Food and Brand Research Lab at Cornell University, "It depends on the consumer shopping cycle. At the start of the cycle, a shopper faced with too many products will not make a careful choice because he or she is too bewildered. Not until the shopper is comfortable within the category can he or she make good product choices."[69]

## Grabbing Consumers' Attention

The world of the consumer is more cluttered than my five-year-old daughter's bedroom. The average person is bombarded by hundreds of advertisements each and every day, a number that will only grow as advertisers find new ways to reach us.[70] Mailboxes are stuffed with catalogs and junk mail. One of the biggest complaints of Internet users is sorting through the spam that fills their e-mail inbox. Stores are stocked with thousands upon thousands of products wanting our attention, with new ones arriving each day.

Even if consumers wanted to, it is simply impossible for them to pay attention to all the products and companies frantically waving their hands at them. Consumers have to be selective in what receives their attention because, as was just pointed out, attention draws upon a limited cognitive resource. Some things gain entry into our thought processes; many do not. We drive by numerous retail establishments without noticing their existence. We rush past countless products during shopping trips oblivious to their presence. We ignore advertisements. We toss junk mail. Internet users delete e-mail messages without ever opening them up.

In the quest for consumers' attention, businesses face an uphill battle. Consumers have far more important things in their lives to be contemplating than the multitude of ordinary, low-involvement products that they buy and use with little thought. This partly explains why consumers, during an average shopping trip at the grocery store, spend less than three seconds looking at each product.[71]

For all these reasons, grabbing consumers' attention is one of the most formidable challenges facing business today. It's kind of like fishing when the lake is cluttered with fishermen and the fish aren't hungry—not the best circumstances for catching tonight's dinner. Yet despite these obstacles, it's still possible to catch something, especially if you use the right bait or lure and know where to cast it. The same is true for businesses trying to hook attention. They need to know what bait to use. And their options are numerous. Indeed, as described in the following pages, companies have an array of approaches at their disposal for grabbing attention.[72]

## CONNECT WITH CONSUMERS' NEEDS

Have you ever gone grocery shopping when you were extremely hungry? We imagine everybody has. You probably paid a lot more attention to products on the grocer's shelves than you might normally. And you probably ended up with items in your shopping cart that otherwise would not have been purchased. In this instance, your heightened need for food made you allocate more cognitive resources to processing objects perceived as satisfying this need.

More generally, people are particularly attentive to stimuli perceived as relevant to their needs. "The most important thing with any e-mail is the quality of the list and the relevance of the message," says Red Eye chief executive Paul Cook.[73] Relevance affects what e-mails consumers open. It affects what advertisements and products are given attention. And the more relevant they become, the more attention these ads and products receive.

Connecting to consumers' needs may require reminding them of their needs before showing them how the product can satisfy these needs. A TV commercial for Snickers candy bars started with the question, "Hungry?" Viewers are then instructed to "grab a Snickers" as they watch the palm of a human hand voraciously devour the product.

## PERMISSION MARKETING

The term **permission marketing** refers to *asking consumers for their permission to send them product-related materials.* For those interested in marketing to consumers over the Internet, the Can-Spam Act requires gaining such permission. But beyond this legal requirement, getting consumers' permission makes good business sense. Figure 14.6 shows the difference in how consumers respond to e-mails from an unknown sender versus a company they had previously granted permission to contact them in this fashion. Virtually none of the permission-based e-mails are deleted without being read, a fate suffered by more than half of the e-mails received without the consumer's permission. Moreover, consumers were far less likely to be annoyed by permission-based e-mails than by those that did not first get their permission.

FIGURE 14.6    The Advantage of Gaining Consumers' Permission

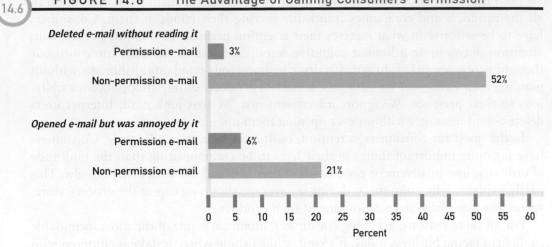

Source: Arundhati Parmar, "You Have Our Permission," *Marketing News* (January 6, 2003), 3. Reprinted with permission from The American Marketing Association

## PAYING CONSUMERS TO PAY ATTENTION

Companies have paid consumers for their attention. The Aristotle Publishing Company offers qualified web users between 50 and 75 cents for each piece of e-mail from political candidates that they read. More than one million voters have signed up for the service, a number expected to double within a year. Unlike a direct mailing that may be opened by only 2 or 3 percent of recipients, "you get a 98 percent open rate because you are by definition operating with permission," explains John Aristotle Phillips, the company's cofounder.[74] Similarly, Broadpoint Communications offered its customers two free minutes of long-distance calling for each ten- to fifteen-second commercial they listened to over the telephone. An average customer heard around 150 ads a month, which translated into three hundred minutes of free long-distance time.[75]

## LOOK! IT MOVES!

Thousands of years ago when humans had to worry about becoming some predator's next meal, the ability to detect something moving in the bushes was an essential survival skill. Although this threat has long since vanished, our sensitivity to movement has not. Stimuli in motion are more likely to attract attention than stationary objects. As described in Market Facts 14.2, one company was happy to learn how the sales effectiveness of its point-of-purchase displays was enhanced greatly by including movement. Even the suggestion or appearance of movement can draw attention. Advertisers often use quasi-motion in print advertisements for this purpose.

## USE ISOLATION

Another way advertisers try to gain attention is to use isolation. **Isolation** involves *placing only a few stimuli in an otherwise barren perceptual field*. Other objects that, if present, would compete for attention are eliminated. The ad in Figure 14.7 illustrates the isolation principle.

## MAKE IT BIGGER

In general, the larger the stimulus, the more it tends to stand out and draw attention. Consequently, an easy way for companies to attract attention is to simply make things bigger. Larger print ads are more likely to grab attention than their smaller

## Gaining Attention (and Sales) with Movement

Point-of-purchase (POP) displays are often used by companies for attracting consumers' attention in a retail environment that is increasingly crowded with new products. The Olympia Brewing Company conducted a study to determine the effects of POP displays on purchase behavior. The research involved food and liquor stores located within two California cities. Some of the stores received a display; others did not. These latter stores provided a baseline for determining whether the displays influenced sales. Further, two types of POP displays were tested: motion displays (those with some movement being generated by the display) and static displays (those without movement).

Sales in the stores were then monitored over a four-week period. The results (numbers represent the increase in sales over stores without displays) are presented as follows.

| | Static displays | Motion displays |
| --- | --- | --- |
| Food stores | 18 percent | 49 percent |
| Liquor stores | 56 percent | 107 percent |

These findings clearly reveal the effectiveness of POP displays in generating sales. The presence of a display produced an average sales increase of more than 50 percent. The greater improvement in sales found for liquor stores suggests that POP displays become more effective when consumers are already inclined to purchase the product (it seems safe to believe that those visiting the liquor store were so inclined). Finally, including movement within the display substantially improved its effectiveness. Motion displays nearly tripled the sales increase of the static displays in food stores and nearly doubled the sales increase in liquor stores.

---

cousins. One demonstration of the importance of ad size comes from the yellow pages telephone directory. As consumers flip the pages, they're more likely to notice the bigger ads. Doubling the size of one ad in the yellow pages improved sales a reported 500 percent. When the ad quadrupled in size, sales increased 1500 percent.[76]

Things get a bit more complicated when considering the size of individual ad elements, such as pictures, text, and the advertised brand. Advertising textbooks have often recommended that bigger pictures cause consumers to devote more attention to an advertisement.[77] Yet a recent study of more than 3,600 consumers' eye movements while looking at more than 1,300 print advertisements failed to support this conventional wisdom.[78] Although pictures were by far the most important determinant of the attention given to an ad, increases in their size did not lead to more attention. Rather, more attention was elicited by increasing the amount of ad space allocated to the text.

The effectiveness of free-standing inserts (FSIs) also depends on their size. FSIs are those ads containing coupons that are grouped together and inserted into the Sunday newspaper. In one

Until tomorrow.

The best sleep you ever got with a cold...medicine.

VICKS NyQuil MULTI-SYMPTOM COLD/FLU Relief

**FIGURE 14.7** This Ad Uses Isolation to Grab Attention

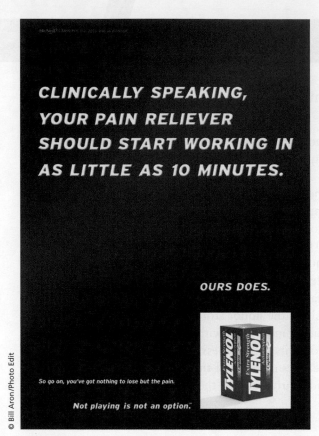

CLINICALLY SPEAKING,
YOUR PAIN RELIEVER
SHOULD START WORKING IN
AS LITTLE AS 10 MINUTES.

OURS DOES.

*So go on, you've got nothing to lose but the pain.*

*Not playing is not an option.*

**FIGURE 14.8** Red Is an Effective Attention-Getting Color

advertisement sponsored by the industry's trade association, full-page FSIs were reported to be 20 percent more effective than half-page FSIs in generating trial and repeat purchasing.

Bigger may be better in the store as well. Products have a greater chance of being noticed as the size or amount of shelf space allocated to them increases. This reality can be especially important for impulse items, whose sales may depend partly on how much space they receive.[79]

## COLORS ARE NICE

The attention-getting and holding power of a stimulus may be increased sharply through the use of color.[80] In a field study involving newspaper advertising, one-color ads produced 41 percent more sales than did their black-and-white counterparts.[81] Color ads cost more, so their incremental effectiveness must be weighed against the additional expense.

Moreover, some colors may be more attention getting than others. Did you know that red cars get more speeding tickets than cars of any other color? Although people who choose to drive a red car may be more inclined to speed, their odds of being noticed by police officers are heightened by the color of their car. The same is true for advertising. Many print advertisements use red as a background color as a way of drawing attention (see Figure 14.8). Companies placing ads in the yellow pages are encouraged to use red as a way of attracting attention.

## MAKE IT MORE INTENSE

Have you ever noticed that the volume of a commercial is sometimes much louder than the programming that preceded it? This volume change is far from accidental. To the contrary, it's a deliberate attempt to get your attention by increasing stimulus intensity. Intense stimuli stand out relative to their weaker counterparts. Consequently, ads containing intense elements, such as loud sounds and bright colors, are more likely to be noticed. Radio and television commercials sometimes begin with a loud noise to attract attention.

## LOCATION! LOCATION! LOCATION!

An old real estate joke goes something like this: "What are the three most important things to know about real estate? Location! Location! Location!" Though overstated (what about price?), the point being made is that location is critical. This point is also true for attention. Stimuli may be more noticeable simply because of where they are located in the environment.

Grocery vendors know very well the importance of location. The sales for some products, especially those purchased more impulsively, are quite sensitive to where they are located in the retail environment. Many of the items at the grocery checkout would be bought far less frequently if displayed in more remote areas of the store. For years the conventional wisdom has been that products located at the end of the aisle or on shelves at eye level (there's an old adage, "eye level is buy level") stand a better chance of being noticed and purchased. Recently, however, this conventional wisdom has been challenged. It's been suggested that consumers actually gaze fifteen to thirty degrees lower than eye level while shopping.[82] And at least one market study has found greater sales from promotional materials located within the grocery aisle rather than at the end of the aisle.[83]

A commercial's location within the commercial break affects attention.[84] The first commercial is most likely to receive some attention before viewers start tuning out during the commercial break. And the last commercial is the next most valuable position because of viewers paying more attention in anticipation of the program resuming. Location is also important for print media. Greater attention is given to ads located in the front part than in the back part of a magazine, on right-hand pages than left-hand pages, and on the inside front, inside back, and outside back covers.[85] Presumably, this attention occurs because of the manner in which consumers typically flip through magazines. For smaller ads that do not occupy an entire page, attention may depend on where they are located on the page. A rule of thumb in advertising is that the upper left-hand corner of the page is the most likely to receive attention, whereas the lower right-hand corner is least likely.[86]

## THE SURPRISE FACTOR

In Chapter 6, we talked about the importance of consumers' expectations as a determinant of their post-consumption evaluations. Expectations are also important in the domain of attention. All of us have certain expectations about what we are likely to encounter during our daily routine. Stimuli congruent with our expectations may receive less attention than those that deviate from what's expected. Something that deviates from what we expect creates a mental incongruity. It's almost like a silent alarm in our head. Our attention is allocated to the source of the incongruity as we attempt to understand and resolve it.

The surprise factor is a popular tactic for gaining consumers' attention. This tactic is an obvious aspect of the ads presented in Figure 14.9. We don't expect to see cordless phones with wings. Nor do we expect to see a human ear protruding from a machine. Showing the unexpected was considered an essential element in ads introducing Sea-Doo's new personal watercraft. These ads pictured the product in some unusual situations around the house (e.g., soaking in a bubble-filled bathtub, resting on satin bed sheets). As one of the advertising executives in charge of the campaign explains, "For Sea-Doo to perform in the market as expected, we have to create advertising that is unexpected. We need to surprise the reader. Intrigue him enough to stop turning pages, so he spends a few minutes learning about how great this product really is."[87]

One of the most surprising commercials to hit the airwaves in 2004 was by SourceNext to promote its StarSuite software product. The commercial shows a consumer, played by actress Norika Fujiwara, who's so amazed by the product's low price that she gives birth to a baby horse in the store! "We convey a concept of our $18 strategy as surprising and moving in the ad," says Nori Matsuda, the president and CEO of SourceNext. "The ad basically says, 'Anything can happen.'"[88]

In the same way, unusual product packaging helps the product stand out on the shelf. One manufacturer made a fortune selling hosiery in an oversized, plastic egg-shaped package that was very different from what women had grown accustomed to seeing in this product category.

CATCHING THE PHONE HAS NEVER BEEN EASIER.

With up to four handsets, Uniden's new 2.4 GHz digital cordless phones offer amazing coverage, clarity and convenience all from a single jack. Finally technology has emerged in a beautiful new form. www.uniden.com

**Uniden**
A World Without Wires

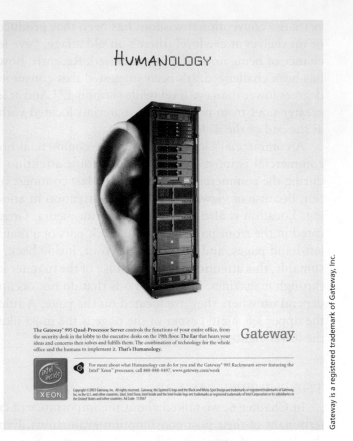

HUMANOLOGY

The Gateway® 995 Quad-Processor Server controls the functions of your entire office, from the security desk in the lobby to the executive desks on the 19th floor. The Ear that hears your ideas and concerns then solves and fulfills them. The combination of technology for the whole office and the humans to implement it. That's Humanology.

**Gateway.**

For more about what Humanology can do for you and the Gateway® 995 Rackmount server featuring the Intel® Xeon™ processor, call 888-888-0497. www.gateway.com/work

**FIGURE 14.9** Unexpected Stimuli Are Effective at Getting Attention

## DISTINCTIVENESS

Suppose you looked at a picture of five people dressed in suits. Four are wearing dark suits; the fifth has on a white suit. Which person do you think you would look at first? Typically, the person dressed in white. Why? Attention is often drawn to the distinctive stimuli within a perceptual field. When everyone else wears dark colors, the white suit stands out. But dress everyone in the same color and this distinctiveness disappears.

As suggested by this example, one way to make an object appear distinctive is to contrast it with other elements within the perceptual field in which the object appears. For example, if the packaging of competitors tends to be similar in colors or shapes, then using different colors or shapes can help the company's package stand out.

## THE HUMAN ATTRACTION

In fishing, sometimes it's necessary to use one fish as bait for another. Similarly, companies often use people for catching consumers' attention. Famous individuals or celebrities are popular bait. The ad for MAC makeup that appears in Figure 14.10 features Pamela Anderson in a rather revealing pose to attract attention. Many companies hire celebrities to endorse their products. Certainly one of the most sought-after endorsers is basketball superstar Michael Jordan, who has appeared as a spokesperson in advertising for numerous companies, including Nike, McDonald's, Quaker Oats, Sara Lee, General Mills, Wilson Sporting Goods, and MCI. In one year alone, Michael Jordan earned an estimated $40 million for endorsing products.[89] Movie stars, even deceased ones, are used to attract attention. In an effort to break through the clutter of products on supermarket shelves, one company developed a line of common grocery products (including cereal, trash bags, and light bulbs) named Star Pak, which features

FIGURE 14.10  MAC Makeup Uses a Celebrity
to Gain Attention

FIGURE 14.11  Chicken of the Sea Hopes to Attract Women's Attention

the faces of some very famous movie stars (e.g., Marilyn Monroe, Clark Gable) on its product packaging.[90]

Retailers sometimes have celebrities make personal appearances as a way of attracting attention and generating store traffic. One car dealer arranged for some of the cast members from the HBO show *The Sopranos* to spend a few hours at its dealership. This promotion drew about 5,000 consumers and sold 187 automobiles.[91]

As you well know, even noncelebrities can grab attention, especially if they are attractive.[92] Good-looking individuals with barely covered toned bodies usually attract a lot of attention. This is true on the beach, and it's also true in advertising. This is why advertisers use this attention-getting device so frequently. One study of the advertising appearing in *Time, Newsweek, Cosmopolitan, Redbook, Playboy,* and *Esquire* found that 40 percent of the ads using adult models contained females dressed in a revealing manner.[93]

The makers of Chicken of the Sea tuna are hoping that the human attraction factor will help the product gain attention and sales. In 2005, the company launched its first TV and print advertising campaign in fourteen years, appropriately named the "Hunk" campaign. An example of the print component appears in Figure 14.11. "We want to poke a little fun at ourselves and break out of the normal boring food ads," explains Don George, vice president of marketing. "We're an all-American brand. We don't want to be controversial but we want to create brand buzz."[94]

## THE ENTERTAINMENT FACTOR

How many times have you watched a familiar television commercial simply because you enjoyed doing so? Probably more times than you even remember. Stimuli

## Quiet Please, the Commercials Are Coming On!

The Super Bowl is unlike any other television event in several ways. First, it's the most expensive advertising buy in television. A thirty-second spot in the 2005 Super Bowl cost $2.4 million. Second, it delivers the largest viewing audience of any televised program. During the period from 2000 to 2004, the average Super Bowl audience in the United States was nearly 88 million. Third, it's the only television event in which millions of consumers actually look forward to seeing the commercials. Indeed, for some consumers, the commercials are the primary reason to watch the Super Bowl.

A survey by the Retail Advertising and Marketing Association asked consumers about their reasons for watching the Super Bowl. Seeing the advertising was ranked as the main reason by 16 percent of consumers. For young adults, this number increases to 25 percent. Another survey asked consumers which aspect they enjoyed the most: watching the game, watching the ads, or spending time with friends and family. For males, two-thirds of them enjoyed watching the game the most, followed by watching the ads (18 percent) and spending time with friends and family (16 percent). But for females, watching the ads (38 percent) came in first, followed by the game (31 percent) and friends and family (30 percent). And when TiVo examined the viewing habits of 10,000 of its subscribers during the 2002 Super Bowl, the company discovered there were more instant replays of the commercials than of the game itself.

This sort of viewing environment is what leads advertisers to spend so much money for so little time. The number of consumers reached is exceptional, but it's always possible to put together a media plan that can deliver similar numbers, although not at one shot. What is truly unique, and what advertisers find so enticing, is the level of viewer involvement when the commercials come on.

The benefits of advertising during the Super Bowl extend well beyond the numbers reached and their level of involvement with the commercials. An analysis of website activity immediately following a commercial's broadcast in 2005 showed that some of the commercials were causing consumers to surf the Web during the game. A Cadillac commercial for its high-performance V-series that promoted its Cadillac Under5.com site increased traffic at that website by more than 1700 percent. A commercial for GoDaddy .com featuring a buxom spokeswoman in a tank top boosted the site's Web traffic by 1600 percent. CEO Bob Parsons reported a 70 percent increase in business during the following week.

The buzz created by Super Bowl commercials is another benefit. When consumers were asked what they talked about with their coworkers the day after the Super Bowl, 47 percent of them talked about the game. And the commercials? They were the subject of conversation for 58 percent.

Sources: Mercedes M. Cardona, "Study: Super Bowl Has Become a National Holiday," AdAge.com, www.adage.com (February 2, 2005); Rick Romell, "Super Bowl Is Still the Premier Venue of the Advertising Game," *Milwaukee Journal Sentinel* (January 30, 2005), 1; May Wong, "TiVo Monitors Habits of Super Bowl Fans," *Miami Herald* (February 5, 2002), C1, C4; "Americans Geared up for Ad Bowl 2005," press release, comScore, www.comscore.com (February 4, 2005); "Hot Points! A Weblog ("Blog") by Bob Parsons," www.bobparsons.com (February 17, 2005); "Super Bowl Ad Campaigns Send Viewers Rushing to the Web," press release, comScore, www.comscore.com (February 8, 2005); "30 Years of Super Bowl Ad Stats," AdAge.com, www.adage.com (February 5, 2005).

that entertain and amuse us draw our attention, even if they happen to come in the form of an advertisement.[95] The OfficeMax commercial with the office clerk sporting an oversized afro as he dances to the "Rubber Band Man" tune while passing out office supplies from his supply cart scored high in entertainment value. Many have chuckled while watching the series of commercials in which Budweiser and Miller have taken shots at each other (you'll learn more about this in the "Battle of the Beers" case in the cases section of the book). And for some, watching the Super Bowl is as much about seeing the newest commercials as it is about the game itself (see Consumer Behavior and Marketing 14.4).

## "LEARNED" ATTENTION-INDUCING STIMULI

Some stimuli attract our attention because we have been taught or conditioned to react to them. A ringing phone or doorbell, for example, typically elicits an immediate response from the person. Ringing phones or wailing sirens are sometimes included in the background of radio and TV ads to capture attention.

Certain words or phrases may also attract consumers' attention because they have learned that these words are associated with things they desire. The word *free* is a good example. Consumers love freebies; the Clorox ad in Figure 14.12 capitalizes on this with its pronouncement of "FREE" in bold, red letters (remember our discussion earlier in the chapter about the attention-getting power of red) and its offer of a free bottle of Clorox with the purchase of its other offerings. Consumers also love saving money. Shoppers browsing through a store may be drawn to those products lying beneath signs that proclaim "Clearance Sale," "Special Sale," or "Fifty Percent Off." A similar approach is used to grab consumers' attention as they sort through their junk mail for the day. On more than one occasion, I have been enticed to open a piece of mail that otherwise would have been deposited directly into the trash can because I saw the phrase "Pay to the order of" through the envelope's cellophane window.

**FIGURE 14.12** Free Things Attract Attention

## LOOK FOR A LESS CLUTTERED ENVIRONMENT

The likelihood that a particular stimulus receives attention is diminished as the number of stimuli competing for this attention increases. This finding is one reason (we'll talk about the other reason in Chapter 16) why clutter in the marketplace amplifies the challenge businesses face in courting consumers' attention. By gaining exposure in less cluttered environments, a company can enhance its chances of being noticed.

Advertisers have entered all sorts of domains in their pursuit of less cluttered environments, such as elevators and bathroom stalls.[96] Movie theaters have become increasingly popular with advertisers. Companies such as Coca-Cola, Nike, and Mars spent a tad over $300 million in 2003 so that moviegoers could see their advertisements, an increase of 34 percent in just one year.[97] These locations are attractive because they reach a "captive audience" at a place where there is little else to compete for their attention. "Being able to get into an environment where you're not competing with other advertising out there is important," counsels one businessman.[98]

Another such environment is the beach. Snapple sculpted mini-billboards into the sand using a rubber mat attached to a roller. On an average beach, 5,000 of these ads measuring 12 feet by 4 feet can be imprinted. Or consider consumers placed on hold when calling a business. Nearly 60 percent of those placed on "silent" hold will hang up in less than one minute.[99] To fill this void, many companies now fill the silence with

## Fox Goes to the Shopping Mall in Search of a Less Cluttered Environment

As Hollywood grapples with the skyrocketing cost of television advertising, one studio is heading down a new avenue to push its movies: shopping malls. "We are looking for places where we'll really stand out rather than just be one of six or seven movies," explains Pamela Levine, Twentieth Century Fox's co-president of marketing. Fox says the company has wrapped up Hollywood's first long-term partnership with a mall owner. Under the exclusive deal, the company's movies will be promoted in shopping centers owned by General Growth Properties, America's second-biggest operator.

In a typical campaign, shoppers will be bombarded with advertisements for the latest Fox movie on everything from huge banners in the garage to tray liners in the restaurants. In some cases, characters from the studio's movie will wander around the malls. In others, retailers will give premiere tickets to loyal customers. Teens will be one of the main targets. Fox's *I, Robot* was the first movie promoted under the partnership. Four-by-six-foot banners of the star, Will Smith, dangled from mall ceilings. Double-sided stickers adorned store windows, posters hung in elevators and alongside escalators, and various ad placements appeared in food courts.

Movie-marketing costs soared 30 percent in 2003. Television has been the main culprit: Major studios typically spend about 80 percent of their marketing budgets on TV advertising for big event movies, and the networks have driven up their rates accordingly. Television historically has been the most effective means of reaching a wide audience, but its power has been diminished as the broadcast networks have lost viewers and new technology like TiVo has made skipping ads easy.

Fox says its campaign presents a cost-efficient way to reach a similarly broad audience. General Growth Properties says the 125 malls covered by the deal, 95 of which include movie theaters, receive 1.5 billion visits a year. Malls are also an inroad to the biggest category of moviegoers: teenagers. "It's very difficult to reach teenagers and young adults with television; they change their programming habits so quickly. You can count on them being at the mall, though," says Jean Pool, chief operating officer at Interpublic Group's Universal McCann, North America. "Ultimately, we envision doing more dramatic things, using technology both inside and outside the properties," says John Bucksbaum, chief executive of General Growth Properties. That strategy could include audiovisual monitors showing trailers and interviews with stars. Images of the movie might also be projected on the walls of malls.

Television advertising will still remain an important part of Fox's marketing mix. "Movies are an audiovisual medium, and television is still one of the key ways to communicate the images and the spectacle of a movie," says Ms. Levine.

Source: Merissa Marr, "Fox to Pitch Its Movie at the Mall; As TV-Ad Costs Escalate, Studio Says New Approach Avoids Broadcast Clutter," *Wall Street Journal* (July 15, 2004), B6. Copyright 2004 by Dow Jones & Co. Reproduced with permission of Dow Jones & Co., Inc., in the textbook format via Copyright Clearance Center, Inc.

messages aimed at selling their products and services. And, as described in Market Facts 14.3, one movie maker has recently turned to shopping malls to promote its movies and avoid the clutter on television.

One of the newest tactics for avoiding clutter, which also incorporates the surprise factor discussed earlier in the chapter, involves using the human body as a walking billboard. In 2001, Bernard Hopkins, the reigning middleweight champion, entered the ring sporting a tattoo on his back that was the website address of an online casino. Since then, advertisers have used all sorts of body parts to promote their products.[100]

One enterprising young man auctioned his forehead for thirty days to SnoreStop for $37,375! Millions of dollars in free publicity were generated by this story, leading to a 50 percent increase in retail sales and a 400 percent increase in Web sales of the product.[101]

Of course, in many cases advertisers have little choice but to place their messages in a cluttered environment, such as when TV commercials are an important part of an advertising campaign. Yet even within a particular medium, there can be considerable variance in the amount of clutter. For example, not all TV networks are the same in the amount of advertising that appears during the commercial break or, in advertising terminology, the commercial pod. Table 14.4 shows the average number of commercial and promotional (commercials for the network's own programs) spots for the different TV networks during the 2003–2004 prime-time season. Whereas a commercial appearing on the Weather Channel would, on average, be accompanied by about two other commercials, a commercial shown on Lifetime would, on average, be accompanied by seven other commercials.

Beyond where it advertises, *when* a company advertises may influence the amount of clutter it faces. Rather than face stiff competition during the holiday season, iVillage, a website that targets women, decided to wait until after Christmas before resuming its $40 million advertising campaign. "Our strategy was to avoid the holiday clutter," explains a company spokesperson.[102]

## Attracting Attention: Some Additional Observations and Recommendations

In the preceding section, we reviewed a number of ways in which companies can try to get your attention. At the risk of stating the obvious, the need for using attention-getting stimuli depends on consumers' intrinsic motivation to pay attention. When consumers freely give their attention, the necessity of including stimuli that attract attention is diminished greatly. Given that such stimuli cost money and absorb precious ad space, they should be used only when necessary.

Moreover, the use of attention-getting stimuli carries some risk. For example, suppose that a well-known celebrity is so effective at gaining attention that the remainder of the advertisement is ignored. When this occurs, advertising effectiveness suffers. Indeed, a stimulus that dominates viewers' attention, while leaving the remainder of the message ignored, is self-defeating. Companies must try to use stimuli that capture attention initially but that do not inhibit processing of the entire message.

Even if the attention-getting device does not cause the remainder of the ad to be ignored, the device may still interfere with ad processing. Because short-term memory has limited capacity, allocating cognitive resources to one thing reduces the amount available for thinking about something else. If during class you start thinking about something that happened earlier in the day, you have reduced your mental capacity for processing what the instructor is saying. If your thoughts are fixated on the celebrity appearing in the commercial, there is less capacity for processing the rest of the ad (i.e., the advertised product and its claims).

To illustrate the adverse effects that may arise when attention is divided, consider the findings from so-called shadowing experiments.[103] In a typical experiment, participants wear headphones and receive a different message in each ear. While listening to both messages, participants are instructed to repeat out loud (i.e., shadow) the content of one of the messages. Despite hearing two different messages simultaneously, people can easily shadow one of them although doing so requires nearly all of their cognitive capacity. This means that little capacity remains for processing the message that is not

TABLE 14.4

Television Networks' Average Number of Commercial and Promotional Spots per Commercial Pod: 2003–2004 Prime-time Season

14.4

| TELEVISION NETWORK | TOTAL UNITS PER POD | COMMERCIAL UNITS PER POD | PROMOTIONAL UNITS PER POD |
|---|---|---|---|
| Weather Channel | 3.53 | 3.28 | 0.25 |
| Speed | 3.96 | 3.00 | 0.96 |
| Headline News | 4.12 | 3.15 | 0.97 |
| ESPN2 | 4.21 | 3.60 | 0.61 |
| ESPN | 4.44 | 3.82 | 0.62 |
| Golf | 4.63 | 3.68 | 0.95 |
| Fox News Channel | 4.67 | 4.16 | 0.51 |
| Outdoor Life Network | 4.83 | 3.84 | 0.99 |
| CNN | 4.91 | 3.93 | 0.98 |
| ESPN Classic | 5.23 | 3.90 | 1.33 |
| CNBC | 5.51 | 4.63 | 0.88 |
| AMC | 5.64 | 3.69 | 1.95 |
| Spike | 5.73 | 5.17 | 0.56 |
| Court TV | 5.80 | 4.67 | 1.13 |
| Fox | 5.95 | 4.46 | 1.49 |
| HGTV | 6.24 | 3.87 | 2.37 |
| NBC | 6.29 | 4.85 | 1.44 |
| UPN | 6.33 | 4.82 | 1.51 |
| TV Land | 6.38 | 5.72 | 0.66 |
| CBS | 6.42 | 4.79 | 1.63 |
| Comedy Central | 6.48 | 4.25 | 2.23 |
| Animal Planet | 6.50 | 4.52 | 1.98 |
| Cartoon Network | 6.67 | 5.06 | 1.61 |
| WB | 6.70 | 5.09 | 1.61 |
| Discovery | 6.71 | 5.13 | 1.58 |
| Game Show Network | 6.85 | 5.98 | 0.87 |

shadowed. And this greatly impairs what is remembered about the nonshadowed message even though it is delivered directly into the person's ear. Indeed, recall of the nonshadowed message's content is virtually nonexistent. Even changes in the message from normal speech to a nonsense speech sound (e.g., normal speech played backwards) escape detection.

Interestingly, reducing the capacity available for processing an ad's claims does not mean necessarily that its persuasiveness is reduced. The degree of persuasiveness will depend on whether the ad claims are strong (i.e., providing compelling reasons for buying the product) or weak (representing less than compelling reasons for purchase). A reduction in the processing of strong claims means that the consumer is less likely to appreciate just how strong they are. Consequently, persuasion is reduced. On the other hand, less processing of weak claims should be beneficial because consumers are less likely to think about the inadequacies of the claims. This result, in turn, may improve the ad's persuasiveness.

TABLE 14.4          (*Continued*)

| TELEVISION NETWORK | TOTAL UNITS PER POD | COMMERCIAL UNITS PER POD | PROMOTIONAL UNITS PER POD |
|---|---|---|---|
| Nickelodeon | 6.91 | 5.73 | 1.18 |
| E! | 6.95 | 5.47 | 1.48 |
| A&E | 6.97 | 5.75 | 1.22 |
| Pax | 7.12 | 5.95 | 1.17 |
| ABC | 7.13 | 5.42 | 1.71 |
| MSNBC | 7.17 | 6.18 | 0.99 |
| Travel Channel | 7.18 | 4.98 | 2.20 |
| Hallmark Channel | 7.21 | 5.61 | 1.60 |
| FX | 7.21 | 5.59 | 1.62 |
| Food | 7.24 | 5.26 | 1.98 |
| Bravo | 7.72 | 5.92 | 1.80 |
| MTV | 8.03 | 6.74 | 1.29 |
| USA | 8.18 | 6.81 | 1.37 |
| TNT | 8.19 | 6.07 | 2.12 |
| TBS | 8.20 | 6.00 | 2.20 |
| Sci-Fi | 8.21 | 6.71 | 1.50 |
| TLC | 8.29 | 5.16 | 3.13 |
| BET | 8.29 | 6.67 | 1.62 |
| WE | 8.29 | 6.87 | 1.42 |
| Oxygen | 8.56 | 6.60 | 1.96 |
| CMT | 9.01 | 8.03 | 0.98 |
| ABC Family | 9.03 | 7.59 | 1.44 |
| VH1 | 9.37 | 8.00 | 1.37 |
| Lifetime | 9.50 | 8.02 | 1.48 |

Source: Joe Mandese, "Report Sends Message to Advertisers: Too Many Messages per TV Break," MediaPost's MediaDailyNews, www.mediapost.com (November 15, 2004).

Beyond interfering with the processing of advertising claims, attention-getting stimuli may affect an ad's persuasiveness in other ways. Rather than helping persuasion, such devices can actually backfire and reduce advertising effectiveness when consumers perceive the stimuli as a tactic to manipulate them.[104] Moreover, something used to attract attention may simply be disliked. A very famous endorser may serve as a powerful hook, but if this person is disliked, these negative feelings may rub off on consumers' product opinions. Models attired in bathing suits, although seen as appropriate endorsers for suntan products, may evoke unfavorable reactions when used to promote other types of products. For example, consider *Travel & Leisure Golf*'s use of supermodel Heidi Klum on its cover as a way of drawing younger males' attention to the magazine when sitting on the newsstand shelf. The cover shows a revealing and provocative picture of Heidi along with the cover line, "Playing with Heidi." Yet the average reader is a fifty-two-year-old male. And females account for 39 percent of the magazine's readers. The cover runs the risk of alienating some readers.[105]

Thus far we have emphasized the importance of getting attention as a fundamental prerequisite for influencing consumer behavior. Nonetheless, some individuals suggest that this may not be necessary. According to them, stimuli that are so weak that they cannot be perceived consciously may still be influential at an unconscious or subliminal level. *The notion that people are influenced by stimuli below their conscious level of awareness* is often referred to as **subliminal persuasion.**

Interest in subliminal persuasion can be traced to the late 1950s when Jim Vicary, the owner of a failing research business, claimed he discovered a way of influencing consumers without their conscious awareness. Vicary reported that Coca-Cola sales increased by 18 percent and popcorn sales grew by 52 percent when the words *DRINK COKE* and *EAT POPCORN* were flashed on a movie theater screen at speeds that escaped conscious detection. When an independent replication did not duplicate his findings, however, Vicary confessed to fabricating his results in the hope of reviving his business.[106]

For years, the subject lay dormant until Wilson Bryan Key contended in a popular book that erotic subliminal cues are implanted in advertisements (e.g., the juxtaposition of ice cubes in a liquor ad) designed to appeal to subconscious sex drives.[107] Today, the use of subliminal stimuli is prevalent. Consumers spend millions of dollars each year on self-help tapes that contain subliminal messages. Horror films occasionally include subliminal death masks and other scary images to enhance their ability to frighten viewers. Retailers sometimes embed subliminal messages within their in-store music to motivate employees and undermine shoplifting. Some resorts also have tried subliminal messages to help vacationers relax.[108]

Despite their prevalent use, the ability of subliminal stimuli to affect consumer behavior is highly questionable. Admittedly, some research does suggest that, in certain situations, subliminal stimuli may have modest effects.[109] Even so, an analysis of the complete literature examining the potential for subliminal stimuli to influence consumer choice led to the conclusion that such influence was "negligible."[110] As one writer on this subject observes,

A century of psychological research substantiates the general principle that more intense stimuli have a greater effect on people's behavior than weaker ones. . . . Subliminal stimuli are usually so weak that the recipient is not just unaware of the stimulus but is also oblivious to the fact that he/she is being stimulated. As a result, the potential effects of subliminal stimuli are easily nullified by other on-going stimulation in the same sensory channel.[111]

And even if the effects of subliminal stimuli were not nullified by the stimuli that are being processed consciously, we would wonder why someone would bother with, at best, a weak method of persuasion when much more effective methods can be used.

## Summary

Making contact with consumers requires two things. The first requirement is exposure. Exposure is defined as the achievement of proximity to a stimulus such that an opportunity exists for activation of one or more of the five senses. For businesses, achieving exposure means making sure that their messages and products are exposed to the right people at the right time and place. The Internet has greatly expanded the options available for making contact. One obstacle to achieving exposure is that consumers are often selective about what they choose to be exposed to. Companies should also be alert to the dangers of overexposure.

The second requirement for making contact is attention. Attention represents the amount of thinking focused in a particular direction. Because attention draws on our limited cognitive resources, we must be selective in what receives our attention. Unfortunately for business, products and advertising are rarely a top priority. Moreover, the competition for consumers' attention has created an extremely cluttered marketplace. These factors together make gaining consumers' attention a most formidable business challenge.

Fortunately, companies have at their disposal an array of techniques and strategies for grabbing attention, many of which were covered in the chapter. Nonetheless, the use of such techniques and strategies can be risky. Ad stimuli that attract attention may interfere with consumers' processing of the rest of the advertisement.

Finally, we examined the potential to influence consumers without their attention. Subliminal persuasion refers to efforts to influence consumers with stimuli beneath their conscious level of awareness. The current consensus is that subliminal stimuli have, at best, minimal effects and that fears of their persuasiveness are largely unfounded.

## Review and Discussion Questions

1. Consider the statement, "Exposure is a necessary but, by itself, insufficient condition for making contact." What does this mean?
2. What is the danger of overexposure? How can this danger be reduced?
3. What is meant by the expression, "a cluttered marketplace"? Why is this important to businesses? How has this influenced business strategy and tactics?
4. One business executive recently commented, "We're going to see advertising become closer to entertainment and entertainment become more like advertising." What does this mean?
5. Consider the advertiser that is concerned about how much DVRs have reduced the percentage of a particular television show's audience that is likely to have been exposed to commercials appearing in this show. How might this advertiser go about calculating how much of the show's audience is unlikely to see its commercial because they record the show on their DVR and fast-forward through the commercials when they eventually watch the show?
6. The following is a set of recommendations for designing yellow pages ads that appeared in *Link*, a trade magazine for the yellow pages industry:
   a. Use color wisely. Don't feel compelled to put every image or block of text into color. And don't just "colorize" your existing ad.
   b. Incorporate material from other media. If you advertise in other media, use the images from these ads in your yellow pages to create an integrated marketing approach.
   c. Beat the ho-hum pattern on the page. Use irregular borders to draw users away from your cookie-cutter competitors. And notice how copy is arranged in most ads and do the opposite.
   d. Use an illustration wherever appropriate. A visual image is an essential eye-catcher. Use something with a contemporary feel and avoid dated clip art.
   e. Use more "yellow space." Cluttered ads confuse and repel users. Words with a little space around them are more attractive and are more likely to be read.

   What principles for gaining attention are reflected in these recommendations?
7. Two consumers are exposed to the same ad. One is in the market for this product, but the other is not. How might these two consumers differ in their processing of this ad?
8. Suppose a company is considering one of two alternative attention-getting devices for use in its

advertising. How should the company decide which device to use?

9. Following the recommendation of its advertising agency, a company modified its current advertising campaign to include a famous celebrity as a way of enticing consumers to pay attention. Yet market research has challenged the wisdom of doing this because its advertising became less, not more, effective. Why might this result have happened?

## Notes

1. "Getting Good Listing Attracts Volumes," *Marketing News* (January 3, 2000), 9–10.

2. Scot Burton, Donald R. Lichtenstein, and Richard G. Netemeyer, "Exposure to Sales Flyers and Increased Purchases in Retail Supermarkets," *Journal of Advertising Research,* 39 (September/October 1999), 7–14.

3. Anthony Bianco, Tom Lowry, Robert Berner, Michael Arndt, and Ronald Grover, "The Vanishing Mass Market," *BusinessWeek Online,* www.businessweek.com (July 12, 2004).

4. John Gaffney, "Retailers Hungry for Customer Data: NRF Wrap-Up," *inside 1to1,* www.1to1.com (January 31, 2005).

5. Ibid.

6. Dale Buss, "Hummer.com Is Top Web Site in J. D. Power Survey," *Automotive News* (February 21, 2005), 20.

7. Ibid.

8. Ibid.

9. Anick Jesadun, "Advertisers Track, Target Website Visitors," *Miami Herald* (June 15, 2004), C8.

10. Ibid.

11. Jonathan Miller, "Floater Ads, the Cousins to Pop Ups, Evade the Blockers," *New York Times* (February 24, 2005), G5.

12. Ibid.

13. Bob Tedeschi, "A Handful of Marketers Get Personal, Summoning Consumers by Name with Customized Ads on the Internet," *New York Times* (June 28, 2004), C2.

14. Suzanne Vranica, "Direct Mail; Agency to Promote Tactic as More-Modern Techniques Like E-Mail Ads Take Hold," *Wall Street Journal* (February 15, 2005), B4.

15. "US Email Marketing to Hit $6BN But Overload Looms," *Precision Marketing* (April 2, 2004), 9.

16. Vranica, "Direct Mail."

17. "DoubleClick's 2004 Consumer Email Study," DoubleClick, www.doubleclick.com (October 2004).

18. Ibid.

19. Beatrice E. Garcia, "Spam Haters Seek Relief," *Miami Herald* (September 30, 2003), C1.

20. David McGuire, "A Year after Legislation, Spam Still Widespread," *Washington Post* (January 4, 2005), E5.

21. David McGwire, "Feds, Private Groups to Educate Consumers about 'Phishing' Scams," www.washingtonpost.com (June 17, 2004).

22. Scott Van Camp, "OMG! Instant Messaging Is Becoming an Ad Vehicle," *Brandweek* (November 1, 2004), 14.

23. Ibid.

24. All of the statistics reported in this paragraph are drawn from Van Camp, "OMG! Instant Messaging Is Becoming an Ad Vehicle."

25. Leslie Walker, "Pop-Up Videos Hit Instant Messengers," *Washington Post* (October 31, 2004), F7.

26. Jesse Oxfeld, "Blogs Rolling in 2005," *Editor & Publisher,* 138 (January 2005), 36–40.

27. Lee Rainie, "The State of Blogging," *Data Memo,* Pew Internet & American Life Project, www.pewinternet.org/PPF/r/144/report_display.asp (January 2005).

28. Mike Hughlett, "Ad Companies Probe Potential of Blog World," *Chicago Tribune* (February 22, 2005), 1.

29. Riva Richmond, "Enterprise: Blogs Keep Internet Customers Coming Back; Small Firms Find Tool Useful for Recognition, Connecting with Buyers," *Wall Street Journal* (March 1, 2005), B8.

30. Ibid.

31. Keith McArthur, "Flog on a Blog: The Next Ad Frontier," www.globetechnology.com (December 7, 2004).

32. Christina Cheddar Berk, "P&G Will Promote 'Green' Detergent," *Wall Street Journal* (January 19, 2005), 1.

33. Neal Leavitt, "No Degrees of Separation—from Tide," www.imediaconnection.com (February 14, 2005).

34. Marty Bernstein, "Pontiac Makes Another Talk Show Giveaway," *Automotive News* (January 31, 2005), D56.

35. "Oprah Giveaway Drives Massive Traffic Increase at Oprah and Pontiac Sites, According to comScore Networks," press release, comScore Networks, www.comscore.com (September 17, 2004).

36. Ibid.

37. Suzanne Vranica and Brian Steinberg, "The Feathers Did Fly; A Year in Ads That Wasn't for Chickens," *Wall Street Journal* (December 20, 2004), B1.

38. Hank Kim, "AMEX Plans Jerry Seinfeld Meets Superman Internet Show," www.adage.com (February 4, 2004).

39. Michael Snider, "Internet: Watch out for Adver-tainment," *Maclean's* (May 17, 2004), 54.

40. Greg Gatlin, "Shorts Are Big for Converse: Fans, Filmmakers Produce Ads," www.bostonherald.com (December 14, 2004).

41. Rob Walker, "Poultry-Geist," *New York Times Magazine* (May 23, 2004), 18.

42. Ross Fadner, "Wireless Messaging Market Catches on Faster in Europe Than US," MediaPost's MediaDaily News, www.mediapost.com (September 9, 2004).

43. Cynthia H. Cho, "For More Advertisers, the Medium Is the Text Message," *Wall Street Journal* (August 2, 2004), B1.

44. Ibid.

45. Brooks Barnes, "Coming to Your Cell: Paris Hilton; TV Firms Will Try to

Widen Shows' Viewers by Enabling Phone Users to Watch Clips," *Wall Street Journal* (March 17, 2005), B3.

46 "Indian Movie to Debut on Cell Phones," *Boston Herald,* www.business .bostonherald.com (December 8, 2004).

47 Joseph Pereira, "Online Arcades Draw Fire for Immersing Kids in Ads," *Miami Herald Business Monday* (May 17, 2004), 1.

48 Ibid.

49 Catherine Arnold, "Just Press Play," *Marketing News* (May 15, 2004), 1, 15.

50 David E. Kalish, "Million Sign Up for Free Internet, But Not All Use It," *Miami Herald* (January 19, 2000), C7.

51 "Background on Zapping," *Marketing News* (September 14, 1984), 36.

52 Michael G. Harvey and James T. Rothe, "Video Cassette Recorders: Their Impact on Viewers and Advertisers," *Journal of Advertising Research* (December 1984/ January 1985), 10–19.

53 Joe Mandese, "Magna: Nielsen Data an 'Eye-Opener,' Reveals Ravages of DVRs over Time," MediaPost's MediaDaily News, www.mediapost.com (November 12, 2004).

54 This estimate comes from a report discussed by Gina Piccalo, "TiVo: A Marketer's (New) Best Friend," www .seattletimes.com (November 22, 2004).

55 Ibid.

56 Margaret Henderson Blair and Michael J. Rabuck, "Advertising Wearin and Wearout: Ten Years Later—More Empirical Evidence and Successful Practice," *Journal of Advertising Research,* 38 (September/October 1998), 7–18; Connie Pechmann and David W. Stewart, "Advertising Repetition: A Critical Review of Wearin and Wearout," *Current Issues and Research in Advertising,* 11 (1988), 285–330; Douglas R. Scott and Debbie Solomon, "What Is Wearout Anyway?" *Journal of Advertising Research,* 38 (September/October 1998), 19–28; David W. Stewart, "Advertising Wearout: What and How You Measure Matters," *Journal of Advertising Research,* 39 (September/October 1999), 39–42.

57 Laura Bird, "Researchers Criticize Overuse of Ads," *Wall Street Journal* (January 3, 1992), B3.

58 Richard E. Petty and John T. Cacioppo, "Effects of Message Repetition and Position on Cognitive Responses, Recall, and Persuasion," *Journal of Personality and Social Psychology,* 37 (January 1979), 97–109; Arno J. Rethans, John L. Swasy, and Lawrence J. Marks, "Effects of Television Commercial Repetition, Receiver Knowledge, and Commercial Length: A Test of the Two-Factor Model," *Journal of Marketing Research,* 23 (February 1986), 50–61.

59 Ibid.

60 Robert E. Burnkrant and Hanumantha R. Unnava, "Effects of Variation in Message Execution on the Learning of Repeated Brand Information," in Melanie Wallendorf and Paul F. Anderson, eds., *Advances in Consumer Research,* 14 (Provo, UT: Association for Consumer Research, 1987), 173–176; H. Rao Unnava and Robert E. Burnkrant, "Effects of Repeating Varied Ad Executions on Brand Name Memory," *Journal of Marketing Research,* 28 (November 1991), 406–416.

61 Bird, "Researchers Criticize Overuse of Ads."

62 Rebecca Quick, "Is Ever-So-Hip Abercrombie & Fitch Losing Its Edge With Teens?" *Wall Street Journal* (February 22, 2000), B1, B4.

63 *Webster's New World Dictionary,* Second College Edition, s.v. "attention."

64 Ravi Dhar and Itamar Simonson, "The Effect of the Focus of Comparison on Consumer Preferences," *Journal of Marketing Research,* 29 (November 1992), 430–440.

65 For research on the effect of using shorter commercials, see Surendra N. Singh and Catherine A. Cole, "The Effect of Length, Content, and Repetition on Television Commercial Effectiveness," *Journal of Marketing Research,* 30 (February 1993), 91–104.

66 Richard M. Shiffrin and R. C. Atkinson, "Storage and Retrieval Processes in Long-Term Memory," *Psychological Review,* 76 (March 1969), 179–193.

67 Herbert A. Simon, "How Big Is a Chunk?" *Science,* 183 (February 1974), 482–488; George A. Miller, "The Magical Number Seven, Plus or Minus Two: Some Limits on Our Capacity for Processing Information," *Psychological Review,* 63 (March 1956), 81–97.

68 Jacob Jacoby, "Information Load and Decision Quality: Some Contested Issues," *Journal of Marketing Research,* 15 (November 1977), 569–573; Jacob Jacoby, "Perspectives on Information Overload," *Journal of Consumer Research,* 10 (March 1984), 432–435; Kevin Lane Keller and Richard Staelin, "Effects of Quality and Quantity of Information on Decision Effectiveness," *Journal of Consumer Research,* 14 (September 1987), 200–213; Naresh K. Malhotra, "Information Load and Consumer Decision Making," *Journal of Consumer Research,* 8 (March 1982), 419–430; Naresh K. Malhotra, "Reflections on the Information Overload Paradigm in Consumer Decision Making," *Journal of Consumer Research,* 10 (March 1984), 436–440; Naresh K. Malhotra, Arun K. Jain, and Stephen W. Lagakos, "The Information Overload Controversy: An Alternative Viewpoint," *Journal of Marketing,* 46 (Spring 1982), 27–37.

69 Marcia Mogelonsky, "Product Overload?" *American Demographics* (August 1998), 64–69.

70 For research on advertising clutter, see Tom J. Brown and Michael L. Rothschild, "Reassessing the Impact of Television Advertising Clutter," *Journal of Consumer Research,* 20 (June 1993), 138–146; Raymond R. Burke and Thomas K. Srull, "Competitive Interference and Consumer Memory for Advertising," *Journal of Consumer Research,* 15 (June 1988), 55–68; Kevin Lane Keller, "Memory and Evaluation Effects in Competitive Advertising Environments," *Journal of Consumer Research,* 17 (March 1991), 463–476; Robert J.

Kent and Chris T. Allen, "Competitive Interference Effects and Consumer Memory for Advertising: The Role of Brand Familiarity," *Journal of Marketing,* 58 (July 1994), 97–105; Peter H. Webb, "Consumer Initial Processing in a Difficult Media Environment," *Journal of Consumer Research,* 6 (December 1979), 225–236; and Michael L. Ray and Peter H. Webb, "Three Prescriptions for Clutter," *Journal of Advertising Research,* 26 (February/March 1986), 69–77.

71 Mogelonsky, "Product Overload?"

72 For an interesting discussion of how an ad's executional elements can affect attention, see Deborah J. MacInnis, Christine Moorman, and Bernard J. Jaworski, "Enhancing and Measuring Consumers' Motivation, Opportunity, and Ability to Process Brand Information," *Journal of Marketing,* 55 (October 1991), 32–53.

73 Rob Gray, "Marketing Inspires Email Innovation," *Revolution* (May 2004), 52–54.

74 Paul O'Donnell, "Read My Pitch! Earn Big Bucks!" *American Demographics* (November 1998), 13, 14, 18.

75 Jennifer Lach, "First, a Word from Our Sponsor," *American Demographics* (January 1999), 39–41.

76 W. F. Wagner, *Yellow Pages Report* (Scotts Valley, CA: Mark Publishing, 1988).

77 John Rossiter and Larry Percy, *Advertising Communications & Promotion Management,* 2nd ed. (New York: McGraw-Hill, 1997); William Wells, John Burnett, and Sandra Moriarty, *Advertising Principles & Practice,* 5th ed. (Upper Saddle River, NJ: Prentice Hall, 2000).

78 Rik Pieters and Michel Wedel, "Attention Capture and Transfer in Advertising: Brand, Pictorial, and Text-Size Effects," *Journal of Marketing,* 68 (April 2004), 36–50.

79 Keith K. Cox, "The Effect of Shelf Space upon Sales of Branded Products," *Journal of Marketing Research,* 7 (February 1970), 55–58.

80 Adam Finn, "Print Ad Recognition Readership Scores: An Information Processing Perspective," *Journal of Marketing Research,* 25 (May 1988), 168–177.

81 Larry Percy, *Ways in Which the People, Words and Pictures in Advertising Influence Its Effectiveness* (Chicago: Financial Institutions Marketing Association, July 1984), 19.

82 Brenda Soars, "What Every Retailer Should Know about the Way into the Shopper's Head," *International Journal of Retail & Distribution Management,* 31 (2003), 628–637.

83 Siobhan Adams, "Putting Your Pop Where It Counts," *Promotions & Incentives* (February 2004), 41–42.

84 Joe Mandese, "Report Sends Message to Advertisers: Too Many Messages per TV Break," *MediaPost's MediaDailyNews,* www.mediapost.com (November 15, 2004).

85 Finn, "Print Ad Recognition Readership Scores."

86 Sandra E. Moriarty, *Creative Advertising: Theory and Practice* (Englewood Cliffs, NJ: Prentice-Hall, 1986). For research indicating that changes in the position of elements within an ad can also influence the ad's persuasiveness, see Chris Janiszewski, "The Influence of Print Advertisement Organization on Affect toward a Brand Name," *Journal of Consumer Research,* 17 (June 1990), 53–65.

87 Cynthia Corzo, "Centerfold Ad Campaign Makes Quite a Splash," *Miami Herald's Business Monday* (March 8, 1999), 11.

88 Ashlee Vance, "Open Source Miracle Horse Stuns MS Japan," *Register,* www.theregister.co.uk (July 6, 2004).

89 Dave Sheinin, "Tiger Has World by Tail," *Miami Herald* (May 20, 1997), A1, A6.

90 Joe Agnew, "Shoppers' Star Gazing Seen as Strategy to Slash Supermarket Shelf Clutter," *Marketing News* (January 16, 1987), 1, 16.

91 Bob Popyk, "Celebrities Bring in Traffic and They Can Turn a Slow Weekend into a Blockbuster Event," *Furniture World Magazine,* www.furninfo.com (February 1, 2003).

92 For research in this area, see M. Wayne Alexander and Ben Judd Jr., "Do Nudes in Ads Enhance Brand Recall?" *Journal of Advertising Research,* 18 (February 1978), 47–50; Michael J. Baker and Gilbert A. Churchill Jr., "The Impact of Physically Attractive Models on Advertising Evaluations," *Journal of Marketing Research,* 14 (November 1977), 538–555; M. Steadman, "How Sexy Illustrations Affect Brand Recall," *Journal of Advertising Research,* 9 (March 1969), 15–18; Lynn R. Kahle and Pamela M. Homer, "Physical Attractiveness of the Celebrity Endorser: A Social Adaptation Perspective," *Journal of Consumer Research,* 11 (March 1985), 954–961; Penny M. Simpson, Steve Horton, Gene Brown, "Male Nudity in Advertisements: A Modified Replication and Extension of Gender and Product Effects," *Journal of the Academy of Marketing Science,* 24 (1996), 257–262.

93 Lawrence Solely and Gary Kurzbard, "Sex in Advertising: A Comparison of 1964 and 1984 Magazine Advertisements," *Journal of Advertising,* 15 (1986), 46–54, 64.

94 Sonia Reyes, "Chicken of the Sea Casts Net for Women Shoppers," *Brandweek* (January 31, 2005), 6.

95 Josephine L. C. M. Woltman Elpers, Michel Wedel, and Rik G. M. Pieters, "Why Do Consumers Stop Viewing Television Commercials? Two Experiments on the Influence of Moment-to-Moment Entertainment and Information Value," *Journal of Marketing Research,* 40 (November 2003) 437–453; Thomas Madden and Marc Weinberger, "The Effect of Humor on Attention in Magazine Advertising," *Journal of Advertising,* 22 (September 1982), 8–14; Marc G. Weinberger and Charles S. Gulas, "The Impact of Humor in Advertising: A Review," *Journal of Advertising,* 32 (December 1982), 35–61.

96 Karen Jacobs, "Elevator Maker to Add Commercial Touch," *Wall Street Journal* (December 7, 1999), B8; Edward D. Murphy, "Portland Entrepreneur Carves

Out Niche with Bathroom Billboard Ads," *Portland Press Herald* (February 18, 2005), 1; Skip Wollenberg, "Advertisements Turn up on Beach, in Bathrooms," *Miami Herald* (June 1, 1999), B8, B10.

[97] David Ranii, "Number of Advertisement in Theaters during Movies Surges," *News & Observer* (October 26, 2004), 1.

[98] Jacobs, "Elevator Maker to Add Commercial Touch."

[99] "Firm Makes Ad Messages for Waiting Callers," *Marketing News* (April 15, 2004), 12.

[100] Arundhati Parmar, "Maximum Exposure," *Marketing News* (September 15, 2003), 6, 8; "Pregnant Woman's Belly Gets $4,000 on eBay," www.washington post.com (February 3, 2005); "Rent This Space: Bodies Double As Billboards," www.beverageworld.com (March 3, 2005).

[101] "Rent This Space: Bodies Double As Billboards."

[102] Jennifer Rewick, "iVillage Holds Ads Until After Christmas," *Wall Street Journal* (December 23, 1999), B10.

[103] E. C. Cherry, "Some Experiments on the Recognition of Speech with One and Two Ears," *Journal of the Acoustical Society of America*, 25 (1953), 975–979.

[104] Margaret C. Campbell, "When Attention-Getting Advertising Tactics Elicit Consumer Inferences of Manipulative Intent: The Importance of Balancing Benefits and Investments," *Journal of Consumer Psychology*, 4 (1995), 225–254.

[105] Heather Chaplin, "Fore, Baby!" *American Demographics* (October 1999), 64–65.

[106] Walter Weir, "Another Look at Sublimi-

nal 'Facts,'" *Advertising Age* (October 15, 1984), 46.

[107] Wilson Bryan Key, *Subliminal Seduction: Ad Media's Manipulation of a Not-So Innocent America* (Englewood Cliffs, NJ: Prentice-Hall, 1972). See also Wilson Bryan Key, *Media Sexploitation* (Englewood Cliffs, NJ: Prentice-Hall, 1976). Key's claims have been strongly challenged. See Jack Haberstroh, "Can't Ignore Subliminal Ad Charges," *Advertising Age* (September 17, 1984), 3, 42, 44; Weir, "Another Look at Subliminal 'Facts.' Research continued in this area. See Ronnie Cuperfain and T. Keith Clark, "A New Perspective on Subliminal Advertising," *Journal of Advertising*, 14 (July 1985), 36–41; Myron Gable, Henry T. Wilkens, Lynn Harris, and Richard Feinberg, "An Evaluation of Subliminally Embedded Sexual Stimuli in Graphics," *Journal of Advertising*, 16 (1987), 26–31; Philip M. Merikle and Jim Cheesman, "Current Status of Research on Subliminal Perception," in Melanie Wallendorf and Paul Anderson, eds., *Advances in Consumer Research*, 14 (Provo, UT: Association for Consumer Research, 1987), 298–302.

[108] Jo Anna Natale, "Are You Open to Suggestion?" *Psychology Today* (September 1988), 28, 30.

[109] Jon A. Krosnick, Andrew L. Betz, Lee J. Jussim, and Ann R. Lynn, "Subliminal Conditioning of Attitudes," *Personality and Social Psychology Bulletin*, 18 (April 1992), 152–162; Robert B. Zajonc and Hazel Markus, "Affective and Cognitive Factors in Preferences," *Journal of Consumer Research*, 9 (September 1982), 123–131. See also Punam Anand and Morris B. Holbrook, "Reinterpreta-

tion of Mere Exposure or Exposure of Mere Reinterpretation," *Journal of Consumer Research*, 17 (September 1990), 242–244; Punam Anand, Morris B. Holbrook, and Debra Stephens, "The Formation of Affective Judgments: The Cognitive-Affective Model versus the Independence Hypothesis," *Journal of Consumer Research*, 15 (December 1988), 386–391; Timothy B. Heath, "The Logic of Mere Exposure: A Reinterpretation of Anand, Holbrook, and Stephens (1988)," *Journal of Consumer Research*, 17 (September 1990), 237–241; Chris Janiszewski, "Preconscious Processing Effects: The Independence of Attitude Formation and Conscious Thought," *Journal of Consumer Research*, 15 (September 1988), 199–209; Chris Janiszewski, "The Influence of Print Advertisement Organization on Affect toward a Brand Name," *Journal of Consumer Research*, 17 (June 1990), 53–65; Carl Obermiller, "Varieties of Mere Exposure: The Effects of Processing Style and Repetition on Affective Response," *Journal of Consumer Research*, 12 (June 1985), 17–31; Yehoshua Tsal, "On the Relationship between Cognitive and Affective Processes: A Critique of Zajonc and Markus," *Journal of Consumer Research*, 12 (December 1985), 358–362.

[110] Charles Trappey, "A Meta-Analysis of Consumer Choice and Subliminal Advertising," *Psychology and Marketing*, 13 (August 1996), 517–530.

[111] Timothy E. Moore, "Subliminal Advertising: What You See Is What You Get," *Journal of Marketing*, 46 (Spring 1982), 38–47.

# Shaping Consumers' Opinions

## Opening Vignette

At the turn of the twenty-first century, American Airlines thought it could gain a competitive advantage by eliminating some of the seats in its airplanes in an effort to give its passengers more room to spread out. Apparently not. In 2005, the airline decided to put an end to its "More Room Throughout Coach" campaign. The company announced that it would reconfigure the seating on its fleet to put more than 12,000 seats back into its jets, hoping the move would raise revenue by some $100 million a year.

Its main competitor, United Airlines, is attempting to capitalize on American's reversal with a move more commonly seen from beer companies and packaged goods marketers. United launched a $15–20 million advertising campaign to promote the legroom of its Economy Plus seating section. Television and radio spots will continue to feature *Rhapsody in Blue,* the Gershwin song that United has used in its commercials since 1987. But the twist to this campaign is that, starting in Chicago, where the two airlines have hubs and are extremely competitive, and later rolling out to other cities, United pokes fun at American Airlines by name. United is tweaking its rival in several print ads for abandoning its more-room campaign. One of United's Chicago-specific print ads shows an illustration of a man bent into a cube. The caption reads, "Fly American, and you could kick yourself. Literally."

Another ad shows a man sitting in a seat with his legs straight up in the air, trying to read a book. The caption on that one reads, "Tired of flying American?" The text under each caption points out that American is putting seats back in its planes, whereas United continues to offer extra leg room in its premium economy class, Economy Plus.

"American handed us this opportunity on a silver platter," says Jerry Dow, United's vice president for marketing. "They made a big deal about seat comfort for their best customers, and then by reversing themselves it gave us a great opportunity and a great competitive advantage that we want to draw people's attention to in Chicago." Mr. Dow said the Chicago portion of the campaign will also include some unspecified guerrilla marketing, and that the airline plans to utilize the approach in other cities depending on its success in Chicago. "The 'gloves off' approach came from a sincere desire and need to stop the perception that American has more room on coach," he said. "They're putting seats back on their planes, and the soft glove approach did not seem to be as effective or as fast as simply pulling that aspect out and making people aware of the fact that we have a differentiated product." Mr. Dow said that American actually started the issue when its "More Room Throughout Coach" campaign began, pointing out an ad that said, "Your knees don't care who your hometown airline is"—a reference, however vague, to United.

American is aware of United's upcoming campaign and seemed amused by the whole thing. A spokesman, however, pointed out that the airline still has a "sizable number of seats" in which the pitch (or legroom) is thirty-three inches, more than the industry standard of thirty-one inches. The spokesman indicated that American has no plans for a counterattack. "I suspect that we'll continue to focus on the aspects of our own business," the spokesman said.

Source: Excerpted in part from Rich Thomaselli, "United Airlines Ads Attack American Airlines," AdAge.com, www.adage.com (March 17, 2005). Also see Scott McCartney, "News for the Knees: AMR Will Expand Coach-Seat Legroom," *Wall Street Journal* (February 4, 2000), A3.

---

Initially, it was American Airlines that wanted to use legroom as a way of shaping consumers' opinions about how comfortable flying with American would be. Now United hopes to differentiate itself from its rival on this attribute. But as United's vice president of marketing points out, doing so requires changing consumers' opinions about which airline is more likely to give passengers' legs a happy flight.

The purpose of this chapter is to examine more closely the ways in which companies can shape consumers' opinions in order to enhance their chances of gaining consumers' business. In Chapter 14, you learned about the exposure and attention requirements for making contact with target consumers. Yet even if contact is established, marketing's job is far from done. Beyond getting consumers to think about their products, companies must also get consumers to think and feel about their products in a certain way. In other words, companies want to shape consumers' product opinions. This means influencing what consumers believe and how they feel about the products in order to achieve the desired product image and a favorable product attitude. Companies that understand how to do so will see the benefits on their bottom lines.

Though we have emphasized repeatedly the importance of shaping consumers' opinions in Chapters 9 and 10, the question of how to do so has, for the most part, been ignored. Until now, that is. In this chapter you will gain a better understanding of how this task can be accomplished. In building this understanding, we start at the beginning: opinion formation.

## Opinion Formation

*The first time we develop a belief, feeling, or attitude about something* is called **opinion formation.** As discussed in Chapter 10, people's attitudinal opinions are based on their beliefs and feelings about the attitude object. To the extent the object is associated with favorable beliefs and feelings, attitudes become more positive. We did not discuss, however, what happens between exposure to some object or stimulus and the subsequent formation of beliefs, feelings, and attitudes. This is the domain of comprehension. **Comprehension** involves *the interpretation of a stimulus.* It's the point at which meaning is attached to the stimulus. This meaning depends on what occurs during stimulus processing. Different aspects of this processing are discussed next.

### Stimulus Categorization

Initially, the person tries to answer the question, "What is it?" Answering this question involves **stimulus categorization** in which *the stimulus is classified using the mental concepts and categories stored in memory.* How a stimulus is categorized is important because the particular mental categories to which a stimulus is assigned affect the opinions formed about the stimulus.[1] For example, the advertisement in Figure 15.1 attempts to influence consumers' opinions about the advertised product by activating two very different mental categories: NASCAR and U-Haul. One category is associated with speed and power; the other is linked to storage and transporting objects. Put them together and you get a powerful automobile with lots of cargo space.

An example of how stimulus categorization can affect product demand occurred when Toro introduced a lightweight snow blower named Snow Pup. The name led many to categorize the product as a toy. Even those who classified it into the proper product category often interpreted the brand name as indicating that it wasn't powerful enough for the job. Changing the name (first to Snowmaster and then simply Toro) eliminated these problems and helped sales.[2]

Unfortunately, consumers often make mistakes during stimulus categorization. The package used by Planters Fresh Roast peanuts looked so similar to the vacuum packaging used for coffee that many consumers miscategorized the product. Grocers were not happy with the mess shoppers made when they errantly poured the peanuts into coffee grinding machines.[3] When Frito-Lay introduced Cheetos Paws, a snack food in the shape of a cheetah's foot, in-store displays were located near the pet food aisle, leaving some consumers uncertain about the product category to which it belonged. In the words of one confused consumer, "Are Paws for my cat or for me?"[4] Nor is advertising immune to miscategorization. Early advertisements for Claritin, an antihistamine, used the tag line, "A clear day with Claritin." Yet many mistakenly categorized the product as an antidepressant.[5]

FIGURE 15.1 Dodge Encourages the Activation of Particular Mental Categories When Consumers Process This Advertisement for Its Magnum Automobile

## Spyware? No! Researchware? Yes!

Way back in Chapter 4 we discussed a study that detected spyware in 80 percent of consumers' personal computers. Spyware, as you might recall, is software downloaded onto a computer (without the permission of the owner) that collects personal information such as the user's online activities, financial records, and passwords. Addressing the 2004 InfoSecurity conference in New York, Roger Thompson, director of content research security management at Computer Associates International, announced, "The only things multiplying faster than definitions for what constitutes spyware is the malware itself." He believes that the threat from spyware will make mass-mailing viruses seem like a minor nuisance. Beyond invading one's privacy, spyware can result in a significant degradation of network performance and an increase in storage consumption.

Related to spyware, although different in several important ways, is U.S. Internet research service provider comScore Networks' Marketscore software. comScore's Marketscore application is installed in over a million personal computers in America and is

the foundation of the company's research services. The software tracks e-commerce trends and website traffic of the company's customers, referred to as "panelists." Unlike spyware, however, consumers must first give their permission, usually induced by offers of increased download speed or sweepstake prizes, before comScore's software is downloaded to their computers. Moreover, the software collects information pertaining only to the user's Web surfing habits. The software further protects the privacy of comScore's customers by making available only aggregated data after scrubbing information that could go back to any individual.

Given these critical differences between spyware and its software, comScore is trying to get Internet service providers and security outfits to accept a new label, researchware, to clearly distinguish its software from spyware. Obviously, this new classification would allow comScore to distance itself from the negative connotations associated with the spyware category and provide the company with a label far more palatable to consumers.

Sources: Excerpted in part from "Microsoft Bid to Turn Spyware Threat into Sales Too!" *Businessline* (January 17, 2005), 1; Ted Bridis, "Internet Users: Think Your Secure Surfing Net? Click Again," *Miami Herald* (October 25, 2004), A1.

---

Stimulus categorization is relevant to one Internet company's current efforts to develop an entirely new classification for its software, a classification far less threatening in its meaning than existing software labels. Take a look at Consumer Behavior and Marketing 15.1 to learn more about this situation.

### The Amount of Processing

Consider the Arm & Hammer laundry detergent advertisement that claims: "For Laundry that's 50% Whiter, 50% Brighter*." Those consumers processing this claim in a rather casual manner might walk away with the impression that the advertised brand is more effective than the rest of the competition, assuming they find such claims credible. Yet suppose someone had taken the time to check out why the ad's performance claim has an asterisk and read the small print along the right-hand edge of the ad, which says: "In Laboratory Testing Versus #4 Liquid Detergent and #3 Powder Detergent." Now what impressions about the advertised brand are likely to be formed? Probably not the same as those held without reading the small print. Take note what this says about the advertiser's expectations concerning how many consumers are likely to invest enough effort to process the small print. Indeed, it's safe to think that this advertiser believes that very few consumers will process the ad carefully enough to discover that the company is essentially admitting there are other brands of detergent which its product cannot claim superiority over.

But this is not the principal reason we give this example. We use this example to illustrate how the amount of processing can shape comprehension and, consequently, opinion formation. Many stimuli, especially those categorized as an advertisement, will receive minimal processing. Having determined what the stimulus is, we decide to allocate our cognitive resources elsewhere. When this happens, there's little chance of the stimulus being influential.

At other times, we might pay enough attention to a commercial to follow what's happening and, perhaps, to notice what's being advertised, but that's about it. In so doing, we may *experience certain thoughts* (called **cognitive responses**) *and feelings* (called **affective responses**). We might think about how tired we are of seeing the same commercial over and over. Or maybe we'll feel amused by a commercial's humor. In any case, processing is far from extensive.

On some occasions, we allocate considerable amounts of our cognitive resources during processing. A commercial may be so engaging that we carefully follow everything it says and shows. Or maybe we listen closely to what the commercial has to say about the product, perhaps because the ad is perceived as containing relevant information useful for a forthcoming and important purchase decision. Claims about the advertised product's benefits and competitive advantages are carefully scrutinized, with prior knowledge germane to the claims' validity being activated from long-term memory. Thinking may extend to product attributes beyond those discussed in the message. A direct mail advertisement that emphasizes high product quality without mentioning price may lead consumers to infer that the price must be high; otherwise, why wouldn't it be shown?

Just how much processing is needed to derive meaning from a stimulus depends on how easily it can be processed. Some stimuli are processed easily; others are far more demanding, requiring much greater amounts of our cognitive resources. Look at the two ads shown in Figure 15.2. The Tilex ad can be comprehended quite easily in only a few seconds. This is not the case for the Prudential Financial ad. Consumers must engage in much more processing of this ad before they can grasp what it communicates. Given the reality that consumers are usually unwilling to invest much of their cognitive resources into processing advertising messages, advertisers typically opt for simple messages that can be comprehended easily. Only when companies believe that consumers will give the time and effort needed for processing more complex messages does it make sense to use such messages.

We do not wish to create the impression that extensive processing is necessary before a stimulus can affect comprehension and opinion formation. To the contrary, even relatively superficial processing may be sufficient for a stimulus to be influential. According to **classical conditioning**, *simply pairing one stimulus that spontaneously evokes certain meanings and feelings with another stimulus can cause a transfer of these meanings and feelings from one to the other.*[6]

## Classical Conditioning

For many, the term *classical conditioning* elicits thoughts of Pavlov and his dogs. Pavlov, the father of classical conditioning and winner of a Nobel Prize, showed how a stimulus acquires new meaning simply by its association with another stimulus. In his famous experiments with dogs, Pavlov started with *a stimulus* (called the **unconditioned stimulus**) *known to evoke automatically a particular response* (called the **unconditioned response**). Specifically, food was used because it causes dogs to

© Bill Aron/Photo Edit

**FIGURE 15.2** Advertisements That Differ in How Easily Each Can Be Processed

salivate. To show that this response could be transferred to a *new stimulus* (called the **conditioned stimulus**) *previously unassociated with this response,* Pavlov began ringing a bell whenever the dogs were given food. Eventually, simply hearing the bell caused the dogs to salivate. Because this response *arises from the conditioning that has taken place,* it's called the **conditioned response.**

Many advertisements rely on the power of simple association for shaping consumers' opinions. This was the case for a Cracker Barrel cheese advertisement that paired knives, a symbol of sharpness, with the product in the hope that this meaning could be conditioned to the product. If it succeeds, the cheese will be perceived as having a sharper flavor. These ad elements and the desired response are represented diagrammatically, from a classical conditioning perspective, in Figure 15.3. And just in case you have doubts about how effective such associations might be, let us remind you of the study we covered in Chapter 10 that showed that a tissue

**FIGURE 15.3**     The Classical Conditioning Approach to Influencing Consumers' Opinions

15.3

| Unconditioned stimulus (US) | Knives | → | Sharpness | Unconditioned response (UR) |
|---|---|---|---|---|
| Conditioned stimulus (CS) | Cheese product | → | Sharp flavor | Conditioned response (CR) |

THE CHILDREN'S **PLACE** Where Fashion Plays.

**FIGURE 15.4** Product-Irrelevant Stimuli Are Often Used to Enhance Consumers' Product Liking

advertisement was able to create more favorable beliefs about the advertised product's softness when the ad simply paired the tissue with a cuddly little kitten than when it explicitly claimed the tissue to be soft.[7]

Beyond a transfer of meaning, simple association may also cause a transfer of feelings and liking. Products are often paired with stimuli that, though devoid of product-relevant meaning, are well liked and evoke favorable feelings. Look at the little girl happily eating (and wearing) a chocolate candy bar in the ad appearing in Figure 15.4. The parents touched by this visual image may transfer this positive affect to the retailer named at the bottom of the ad.

The potential for product-irrelevant stimuli to affect product choice has been illustrated by Gerald Gorn's pioneering research, in which participants are given a choice between two similar pens. One pen is paired with well-liked music. What does music say about a pen's qualities? Not a thing. Nonetheless, pairing it with favorable music causes it to be chosen most often. And when this same pen is paired with music that's disliked, the other pen becomes the most popular choice.[8]

Subsequent research indicates that the potential for product-irrelevant stimuli to alter consumer choice depends on the nature of the choice set. In this study, participants were given a choice between three supposedly new (actually fictitious) soft drinks. They were offered a free six-pack of the brand of their choice. But before choosing, they're shown advertisements for each brand and given taste test ratings. In the ads given to some participants, the ad for one brand called Sunburst had a beautiful tropical sunset; for others, this ad had a picture of some rather ugly iguanas. The taste test ratings describing the brands' performance also varied between participants. Some received ratings indicating that all brands taste virtually the same. These ratings essentially replicated Gorn's setting of virtually identical pens. Others received ratings revealing that one of the brands besides Sunburst is clearly the superior drink. In this situation, Sunburst was dominated by a competitor. Whereas Gorn's findings suggest that the choice of Sunburst will be affected by whether its ad contained the attractive or unattractive picture when the taste ratings indicated that all brands are similar, what happens when the ratings revealed the presence of a dominant brand? The results are graphed in Figure 15.5. Consistent with Gorn's findings, a brand's choice was strongly affected by whether it was paired with a liked or disliked stimulus when the taste ratings indicated that all brands were similar. In this situation, Sunburst was chosen more than twice as often when its ad contained the attractive picture than when it contained the unattractive picture. Yet when Sunburst was dominated by another brand in the choice set, the picture no longer exerted a significant influence on choice. This research tells us that when consumers are choosing among alternatives lacking a dominant brand, association with a well-liked stimulus may tip the scales in favor of the brand making the association. If a brand is clearly inferior to another brand in the choice set, however, it may not be able to offset this competitive disadvantage by pairing itself with some favorable but irrelevant stimulus.[9]

FIGURE 15.5    The Influence of Product-Irrelevant Stimuli on Brand
Choice Depends on the Presence of a Dominant Brand
in the Choice Set

15.5

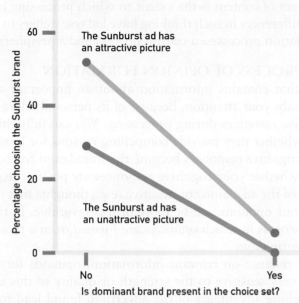

Source: Paul W. Miniard, Deepak Sirdeshmukh, and Daniel E. Innis, "Peripheral Persuasion and Brand Choice," *Journal of Consumer Research*, 19 (September 1992), 226–239.

The power of association to shape consumers' opinions is invaluable to the marketing of products for at least two reasons. First, simple association frees companies from the constraints imposed by how well the product actually performs. Even if the product is inferior to a competitor, by selecting the appropriate stimuli for association with the product, favorable opinions can still be encouraged. Consider the example of Topol toothpaste. Although better than many of its competitors at removing stains, the most effective stain remover (at least during this particular time) was Zact HP, a competitive advantage heavily emphasized in Zact's advertising. For obvious reasons, Topol needed to stay away from talking about its relative performance. Instead, its advertising associated the product with stimuli designed to convey the idea that it removed stains and whitened teeth. Smiling male and female models decked out in all white clothing showing their pearly whites dominated Topol's advertising.

The other reason simple association is so attractive is that it works without requiring consumers to undertake extensive thinking during processing. Consumers usually have better things to think about than many of the products and advertisements that clutter the marketplace. Consequently, extensive thinking is more the exception than the rule. As a result, efforts to shape opinions that require less processing have a greater chance of succeeding.

### The Content of Processing

In addition to the amount of processing, it's also important to understand the content of processing. A critical aspect of this content is the favorableness of the cognitive and affective responses that occur during processing. Favorable responses are a fundamental prerequisite for the formation of favorable product opinions. When responses are unfavorable, companies will not be happy with the opinions that are formed. As a case in point, consider the negative reaction expressed by a fifty-four-year-old woman who found one advertiser's efforts to persuade consumers in her age group to be way off target: "How can they tell me what I need when they clearly don't know who I am? They created an image of old people that's safe for young people, but has nothing to do with us. If it's aimed at me, they missed by a country mile. The inauthenticity of the ad convinced me the product was bull." [10] Ouch.

Another key aspect of content is the extent to which processing involves product-relevant thinking. Differences in such thinking have led researchers to propose two different opinion formation processes: a central process and a peripheral process. [11]

## THE CENTRAL PROCESS OF OPINION FORMATION

Suppose an ad that contains information about an important and forthcoming product purchase grabs your attention. Because of its personal relevance, you allocate considerable cognitive resources during processing. You carefully think about the ad claims, evaluating whether they provide compelling reasons for buying this product. These thoughts or cognitive responses become the foundation for building opinions. And depending on whether your cognitive responses are positive (e.g., thoughts that indicate acceptance of the ad claims) or negative (e.g., thoughts that indicate rejection of the ad claims), your opinions will be more or less favorable. In this instance, you followed a **central process** in which *opinions are formed from a thoughtful consideration of relevant information.*

Because of their reliance on relevant information, opinions formed through the central process are very sensitive to the strength or quality of this information. Ads that describe compelling advantages of the advertised brand lead to more favorable opinions than ads that do not. This simple fact is well documented by research that examined how the opinions formed after ad processing depend on the strength of the ad claims. In a typical study, some people process an ad that contains strong, compelling claims; others process a similar ad in which the strong claims are replaced by weaker versions. If a central process is followed, those given the stronger claims should develop more favorable product opinions than those given the weaker claims. As product-relevant thinking decreases, however, the ad claims should become less influential. At some point, this thinking is so minimal that the opinions formed may be unaffected by the claims' strength.

Research findings that demonstrate how the persuasiveness of an ad's claims depends on the thinking undertaken during processing are presented in Figure 15.6. In this study, participants processed an advertisement for a fictitious product containing either strong or weak claims under conditions designed to influence the degree of product-relevant thinking. [12] Some participants are told that they'll make a choice

**FIGURE 15.6** The Influence of Advertising Claims Depends on the Thinking That Occurs during Ad Processing

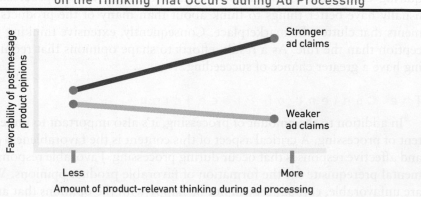

Paul W. Miniard, Sunil Bhatla, Kenneth R. Lord, Peter R. Dickson, and H. Rao Unnava. "Picture-Based Persuasion Processes and the Moderating Role of Involvement." *Journal of Consumer Research*, 18 (June 1991), 92–107.

among various brands, including the advertised brand, and receive a free sample of whichever brand they choose. This knowledge should motivate more thinking about the product and its attributes during processing. Others were not informed about the forthcoming choice. Consequently, they had less reason to think about the ad claims.

As shown in Figure 15.6, the extent to which opinions about the advertised product were affected by the ad claims depended on the amount of product-relevant thinking during processing. In the condition in which such thinking was most likely to occur, those given the ad containing stronger claims formed much more favorable opinions than did those given the weaker claims. Yet the magnitude of this difference declines noticeably in the condition in which product-relevant thinking was less likely to occur. In fact, the product opinions formed in this condition were essentially the same regardless of the ad claims.

Although the preceding study focused on product-relevant information conveyed by advertising claims, such information can be communicated through other advertising elements. Take a look at the ad shown in Figure 15.7. Do you think that the advertiser's use of the visual image of coffee beans fosters more favorable beliefs about its brand of coffee? It sure does. What study did we discuss earlier in the chapter that supports the potential for pictures to impact consumers' opinions about a product's attributes? The study showing how including a picture of a kitten within an ad made people think a tissue was softer.

FIGURE 15.7 An Advertisement's Visual Elements Can Be Used to Effectively Convey Product-Relevant Information

Further evidence of the potential for an ad's visual elements to convey product-relevant information as well as how this influence depends on the nature of consumers' ad processing comes from the following study.[13] Some participants received an ad that contained a picture designed to reinforce certain beliefs about the product's attributes; the ad given to others contained a picture devoid of product-relevant information. The study also manipulated the likelihood of product-relevant thinking in the same manner as the prior study. Following ad processing, participants reported their product opinions, the results of which appear in Figure 15.8. Notice how the pattern of results strongly resembles those previously presented in Figure 15.6. When relatively little thinking about the product occurred during ad processing, opinions were unaffected by the particular picture included in the ad. In contrast, when product-relevant thinking occurs, those shown the ad with a picture providing relevant information formed more favorable opinions than did those shown the ad with a picture lacking relevant information.

## THE PERIPHERAL PROCESS OF OPINION FORMATION

Whether extensive thinking about relevant information occurs during processing depends on both the person's motivation and ability to do so. If you're getting ready to spend thousands of dollars on something, you're probably very motivated (if not, you're probably very rich) to carefully evaluate relevant information. And if you're also able to perform this evaluation (meaning that you have the knowledge necessary for understanding the information as well as the opportunity to do so), you probably

**FIGURE 15.8**    The Influence of Pictures That Convey Product-Relevant Information Also Depends on the Thinking That Occurs during Ad Processing

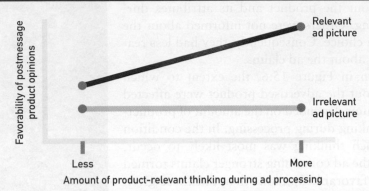

Paul W. Miniard, Sunil Bhatla, Kenneth R. Lord, Peter R. Dickson, and H. Rao Unnava, "Picture-Based Persuasion Processes and the Moderating Role of Involvement," *Journal of Consumer Research*, 18 (June 1991), 92–107.

will. But motivation or ability is often lacking. Just think of the countless commercials you have watched without trying to carefully evaluate the strengths and weaknesses of the advertised product. For whatever reason, you weren't motivated to undertake this type of thinking.

Nonetheless, limited thinking about relevant information does not preclude opinion formation. It simply means that opinions are formed through a different mental process. *Opinions that arise without thinking about relevant information* follow a **peripheral process.** For example, consumers may form opinions about the advertised product based on how much they like and enjoy the commercial itself. A considerable amount of research documents the influence of consumers' attitude toward the ad as an important determinant of advertising effectiveness in shaping their opinions.[14] That a commercial's humor or entertainment value is irrelevant to evaluating the product's true merits doesn't matter when opinions are formed through a peripheral process. As emphasized in our earlier discussion about classical conditioning, simply activating favorable feelings in conjunction with the product can cause these feelings to be transferred over to the product.

To better illustrate the peripheral process of opinion formation, let's return to the research discussed in the prior section that tested the influence of advertising pictures that conveyed product-relevant information. This same research also tested the effect of advertising pictures that served as peripheral cues.[15] **Peripheral cues** are *stimuli devoid of product-relevant information.* Because they lack relevant information, peripheral cues should not be influential when opinion formation follows a central process. Rather, any influence they exert is limited to when opinion formation follows a peripheral process.

In this study, some people received an ad that contained a very attractive picture of a tropical beach at sunset. The ad given to others was identical except that the attractive picture was replaced with one of some ugly iguanas perceived as unattractive. As before, some participants were informed about a forthcoming choice involving the advertised product as a way of encouraging more extensive thinking about the product. Other participants did not anticipate making this product choice.

Figure 15.9 displays the results involving the product opinions formed after ad processing. The attractive picture caused participants to develop more favorable product opinions than did the unattractive picture, but only when thinking about the product's merits was minimal. When such thinking was more likely, opinions were unaffected by

PART 5 [ INFLUENCING CONSUMER BEHAVIOR

**FIGURE 15.9**    Peripheral Pictures Become More Influential When
Product-Relevant Thinking Declines during Ad Processing

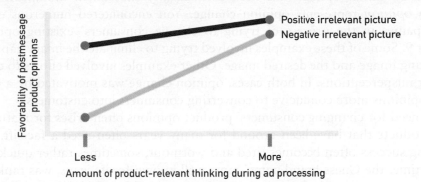

Paul W. Miniard, Sunil Bhatla, Kenneth R. Lord, Peter R. Dickson, and H. Rao Unnava, "Picture-Based Persuasion Processes and the Moderating Role of Involvement," *Journal of Consumer Research*, 18 (June 1991), 92–107.

the pictures. Notice that the pattern of results in this figure differs from the patterns shown earlier in Figures 15.6 and 15.8. These differences are to be expected, depending on whether or not an ad element provides information relevant to evaluating the product. When it does, the ad element should have more influence as product-relevant thinking increases, as evidenced in Figures 15.6 and 15.8. When the ad element does not convey product-relevant information, then its influence should increase as product-relevant thinking decreases, as reflected in Figure 15.9.

## THE INFLUENCE OF BIASED PROCESSING

Even though a person may be highly motivated and able to engage in thoughtful consideration of relevant information, the opinions formed may depend on more than simply the information itself. This happens because other factors may bias or alter information processing, thereby causing a change in how the information is interpreted. One such factor is expectations. To illustrate, take a look at Figure 15.10. What do you see?

Some perceive the stimulus (known as the "broken B") in Figure 15.10 as the letter B. Some interpret it as the number 13. It depends on how you look at it. And how you look at it can be altered by causing you to anticipate seeing either a letter or a number. Suppose that, prior to viewing the broken B, you first processed either four different capital letters or four pairs of numbers. Doing so primes you to expect a letter or a number. This expectation, in turn, strongly affects your interpretation. Those expecting numbers interpret the broken B as 13. Those anticipating letters interpret it as B.[16]

This same phenomenon takes place when consumers are forming their product opinions. We may interpret product information collected during search as being consistent with our prior expectations, especially if this information is ambiguous (i.e., open to multiple interpretations).[17] Expectations can even alter consumers' interpretations of their consumption experiences (see Chapter 6). When consumers ate an energy bar purportedly containing soy protein, they perceived it as tasteless and grainy. Yet the same energy bar consumed without the soy label was rated more favorably.[18] Later in the chapter you'll see how brand names and descriptive labels can induce biased processing.

Similarly, consumers' mood states at the time of information processing may also bias their interpretation and opinion formation in a mood-congruent manner (see Chapter 10). Consumers in a good mood may be more likely to interpret information more favorably than consumers in a less positive mood, thereby causing more favorable opinions to be formed. We will come back to how mood can be used for shaping consumers' opinions later in the chapter.

**FIGURE 15.10** The "Broken B" Stimulus: Prior Expectations Affect Current Perceptions

## Opinion Change

Once an initial opinion has been formed, *any subsequent modification in an existing opinion* represents **opinion change.** You encountered numerous examples of companies in the process of trying to change consumers' existing opinions in Chapter 9. Some of these examples involved trying to eliminate the image gap between an existing image and the desired image. Other examples involved efforts to eliminate product misperceptions. In both cases, opinion change was motivated by a desire to create opinions more conducive to converting consumers into customers.

The need for changing consumers' product opinions often arises for mature products. Products that have been around for many years often need a facelift. Today's smashing success often becomes tired and worn out, sometimes rather quickly. Once upon a time, the Guess brand name, most well known for its jeans, was ranked third by teenagers in terms of its "coolness." Just two years later, it had dropped to twenty-third.[19] To avoid, minimize, or overcome such declines in how they are perceived, companies frequently attempt to revitalize their mature products. After Aurora Foods purchased Duncan Hines baking mixes from Procter & Gamble, Aurora modernized the packaging and rolled out a new advertising campaign.[20] Rock City, a tourist attraction that offers fourteen acres of some of nature's most intriguing handiwork atop Lookout Mountain in Chattanooga, Tennessee, updated its positioning and product image to attract more visitors.[21] Family Circle, the women's magazine, has been changing its content and appearance for several years to attract a younger readership. "We got the boomer," says the magazine's editor-in-chief. "I need the Gen Xer and the younger set to see their lives reflected in this magazine. I'm trying to give us a new attitude, a new look and relevance so women will say, 'This is not our mother's magazine.'"[22]

Sometimes changing consumers' product opinions requires changing the product itself. As shown by the ad in Figure 15.11, the makers of Brawny paper towels want consumers to know that the product is "Massively Improved." Product improvements are common in the marketplace. The MGM Grand Hotel in Las Vegas discovered that its main entrance, in which customers walk through the mouth of a giant lion's head, was a turnoff for many of its Asian customers. Walking through this entrance was viewed symbolically as being devoured by the lion, a symbolism that did not portend good fortune at the gambling table. Consequently, MGM developed a secondary entrance to accommodate those wishing not to be eaten.

Sometimes changing consumers' product opinions does not require actually changing the product. Instead, it requires changing how the product is perceived. Apparently this was the motivation behind a recent advertisement for Equal sweetener. The ad informs consumers that "so many experts say it's [referring to the product] safe" and goes on to present an impressive list of organizations, including the World Health Organization and the American Medical Association, that have endorsed the sweetening ingredient used in Equal as being safe.

An excellent example of changing consumers' product opinions without actually changing the

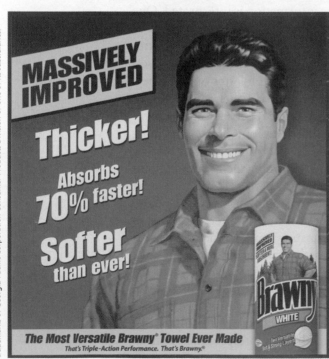

**FIGURE 15.11** Companies Often Improve Their Products to Improve Consumers' Product Opinions

product is the makeover once given to Mountain Dew. For many years, owner PepsiCo pitched the brand as a hillbilly drink with commercials that urged consumers to "tickle your innards." The brand was then repositioned as an alternative soft drink for the savvy young males depicted in the "Do the Dew" campaign that began in 1995. Action-packed commercials featured four young men who had never met a mountain high enough to keep them from grabbing a snowboard. "PepsiCo has done an extraordinary job of positioning Mountain Dew," says Peter Sealey, a marketing professor at the University of California and a former Coca-Cola executive. "It's probably Pepsi's most successful positioning since the Pepsi Generation." [23] Pepsi was able to change consumers' opinions of Mountain Dew, not by altering the product, but by altering how the product was represented in its advertising.

In those instances in which companies find it necessary to actually modify the product itself, an important question involves how much change is necessary before consumers notice that a change has taken place. Suppose, for example, that a manufacturer wishes to cut its product's price just enough so that consumers perceive it as less expensive. How much of a price cut is necessary? Answering this question requires consideration of the differential threshold.

## The Differential Threshold

The **differential threshold** represents *the smallest change in stimulus intensity that will be noticed.* This change is often referred to as the just noticeable difference (jnd). According to **Weber's law,** *perceptions of change depend on more than simply the absolute amount of change.* To illustrate, suppose that a product that normally sells for $2 is offered for $1. Most consumers would perceive this as a significant price savings. Now suppose that a product that normally sells for $200 is offered for $199. Although the absolute amount of price savings ($1) in this situation is the same as that in the prior situation, consumers are unlikely to hold the same opinions about the significance of the savings. This is because perceptions of change depend on the initial starting point before the change as well as the amount of change itself. In particular, Weber's law predicts that it's the absolute amount of change ($1) divided by the initial starting point (either $2 or $200) that ultimately determines people's perceptions of change. Mathematically, this can be expressed as $\Delta I / I$, where $\Delta I$ represents the absolute amount of change, and I represents the initial starting point prior to the change.

Accordingly, in the first situation, the $1 price reduction is judged relative to the initial selling price of $2. In the second situation, however, the $1 price reduction is considered relative to the $200 selling price. The former represents a 50 percent price reduction; the latter represents a price reduction of less than 1 percent. Ultimately, whether each is perceived as representing a significant price reduction depends on the minimum percentage change needed for activating the differential threshold. One rule of thumb is that a price reduction of at least 15 percent is necessary for attracting consumers to a sale. [24] Consequently, the item costing $200 would need to be reduced by $30 to reach this 15 percent threshold. Of course, the size of the differential threshold can vary from one consumer to the next and from one product decision to another. Only through market research can companies determine the size of the differential threshold relevant to their particular situation.

Realize that companies are sometimes interested in changing their products or prices *without* consumers noticing such changes. In these situations, companies wish to stay beneath the differential threshold. Price increases and reductions in product size (such as a shrinking candy bar) are changes that companies often attempt to make without activating the just noticeable difference.

Typically, influencing opinions at the time they are being formed is much easier than changing preexisting opinions, especially if these prior opinions are confidently held. Why? Because efforts to change opinions may face considerable resistance due to the original opinion, a potential roadblock that doesn't exist in opinion formation.

Nonetheless, the size of this roadblock varies from one opinion to the next. Some opinions are held so strongly that changing them is virtually impossible. For example, opinions about the desirability of a democratic society are untouchable in America and many other countries. Other opinions, however, are much less resistant to change, as demonstrated by Mountain Dew's successful repositioning discussed earlier. Ultimately, the amount of resistance depends on the foundation of the opinion. For example, imagine you notice a new product on the grocer's shelf and decide to buy it and try it. The opinions held following consumption are based on direct or first-hand experience with the product. You know whether you liked the product's taste. And if you don't, nothing short of actually improving the product's taste is likely to change your opinion. No matter how much advertising claims otherwise, you'll hold on to those opinions founded in your actual experiences. Suppose, however, that the first time you learn about this new product is during a conversation with another person in which he describes how much he disliked its taste. Any opinions formed from this conversation are based on indirect or secondhand experience. In this instance, you may be less confident in the veracity of your opinions, particularly if you're uncertain about whether your taste buds are similar to this person's. Consequently, you may be less resistant to efforts aimed at changing your opinions.

These differences in an opinion's resistance to change are documented by the following study. Some of the participants formed an initial opinion of a brand of peanut butter by actually tasting it. Others were not given this opportunity. Instead, they were simply given written information about the product. Everyone then processed a persuasive communication for the product that was delivered by a source possessing either high or low credibility. When initial opinions were based on indirect experience, the opinions held after message processing were significantly more favorable if the source was credible. Yet when initial opinions were based on direct experience, post-message opinions were unaffected by the source's credibility, thus revealing that such opinions were more resistant to the persuasive communication.[25]

Although the challenge of altering consumers' opinions should never be taken lightly, we do not want to leave you with the impression that opinion change rarely occurs. To the contrary, consumers change their product opinions quite often. One indication of this is provided by the results of the American Interactive Consumer Survey conducted by the Dieringer Research Group, a market research company. One of the questions in this survey asks consumers whether online information had changed their product opinions in ten different product categories. Figure 15.12 shows the percentage indicating that online information had changed their opinions in at least one of the ten product categories each year the survey was conducted between 1998 and 2004. Applying this percentage to the total number of adult Internet users in the United States produces estimates of the number of American adults that have changed their minds as a result of surfing the Web. These estimates are also shown in Figure 15.12. These numbers give testimony to both the prevalence of opinion change and the power of the Internet in creating such change.

**FIGURE 15.12**  Online Information Has Triggered Changes in Many Internet Users' Product Opinions

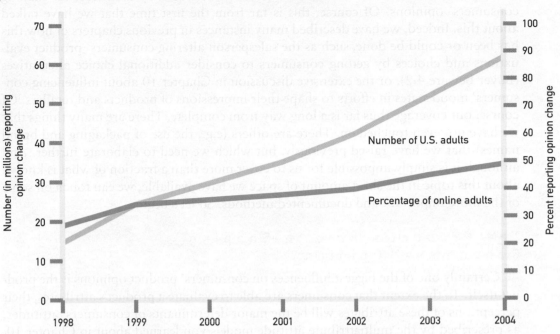

Source: American Interactive Consumer Survey, Dieringer Research Group, www.thedrg.com (2004).

## The Danger of Changing Consumers' Opinions

One complicating factor in the opinion change game is that making changes to improve the opinions of some can hurt the opinions of others, something politicians know all too well. Changing voters' opinions about a candidate's stance on a particular issue (e.g., abortion, gun control, protecting the environment) may be good news for those on one side of the issue but bad news for those on the other side.

This factor is also true for consumers' opinions about products. Changes in a product or its image may be necessary for attracting one segment, but may alienate another segment. This possibility was a concern for Borden Foods when updating the look of Sailor Jack, the treasured mascot of its Cracker Jack's brand of snack food. This change was necessary for attracting today's youthful consumers, many of whom perceived the product as an "old" person's snack. At the same time, however, it was important not to alienate those who had been loyal customers for half a century or more.[26] This same concern faces the makers of Woolite fabric wash as it attempts to deal with its need to update an aging customer base. "The challenge is: How do we keep our base and attract younger customers?" says Woolite's brand manager.[27]

Yet major changes usually produce casualties. This certainly happened many years ago when the Coca-Cola Company decided to drop its original formula in favor of a new formulation. The wave of consumer protest that engulfed the company quickly caused it to reverse its decision and bring back its original formula. Mountain Dew's movement away from its hillbilly image surely cost the company some of those consumers that were attracted by the drink's prior positioning. Nonetheless, Mountain Dew more than compensated for these losses as evidenced by the sales growth the product experienced following this transformation.[28] Thus, changes may alienate some customers, but such sacrifices are acceptable so long as these losses are more than offset by the new customers gained.

# How Businesses Shape Consumers' Opinions

We now turn our attention to the variety of tactics used by businesses for shaping consumers' opinions. Of course, this is far from the first time that we have talked about this. Indeed, we have described many instances in previous chapters of how this has been or could be done, such as the salesperson altering consumers' product evaluations and choices by getting consumers to consider additional choice alternatives (Buyer Beware 4.2), or the extensive discussion in Chapter 10 about influencing consumers' mood states in efforts to shape their impressions of products and retailers. Of course, our coverage thus far is a long way from complete. There are many things that we have not even touched on. There are others (e.g., the use of packaging and brand names) that we have raised previously, but which we need to elaborate further. And although it is simply impossible for us to cover more than a fraction of what is known about this topic in the short amount of space we have available, we can touch on some of the more important and documented methods. So let's begin.

## The Product's Role in Shaping Consumers' Opinion

Certainly one of the biggest influences on consumers' product opinions is the product itself. To the extent that consumers are able to evaluate a product's attributes, their perceptions of these attributes will be the major determinants of consumers' attitudes, as prescribed by the multiattribute attitude models you learned about in Chapter 10. And when consumers lack the product knowledge (Chapter 9) needed for judging a product's attributes, they are more likely to rely on certain product signals (Chapter 4), such as price or warranty, when making their product evaluations. Thus, depending on what consumers rely on when forming their product evaluations, companies can shape these evaluations by either strong product attributes or strong product signals.

As suggested previously in the book, particular elements, such as a product's name and its packaging, can be potent sources of influence for molding consumer opinion into the desired form. We now revisit these and, when appropriate, discuss their potential to alter opinions other than those pertaining to products. We'll also introduce you to a few new things in the following pages.

### THE NAME GAME

In the immortal words of William Shakespeare, "A rose by any other name would smell as sweet." But would consumers' perceptions of a product be the same regardless of its name? You might remember from Chapter 6 the beer-tasting study in which consumers rated the same beer much more favorably when they were informed of its brand name prior to consumption than when they were unaware of the name.[29] Moreover, when consumers were ignorant of a beer's brand name, all the tasted brands were rated the same. But once their identities were revealed, consumers reported significant differences in their ratings. Apparently, a beer by any other name doesn't taste the same. Similarly, consumers' opinions of spaghetti depends on its name. You'll learn about this influence and the retirement of a brand name in existence since 1887 by reading Market Facts 15.1. In these cases, the brand name is creating an expectation that colors consumers' product opinions.

Another demonstration of a brand name's ability to evoke certain expectations that shape consumers' product opinions comes from research on composite branding. **Composite branding** refers to *the use of two well-known brand names on a product*. For example, one of Orville Redenbacher's popcorn flavors is popcorn coated with Cinnabon frosting. Both the Orville Redenbacher and Cinnabon brand names are featured prominently on the package. One study of composite branding examined con-

## Goodbye Franco-American

Franco-American, the brand name that has adorned cans of kids' mealtime favorite SpaghettiOs and other foods for more than a century, is being consigned to history. Campbell Soup is retiring the brand in favor of the better-known Campbell's brand. Market research revealed that the Campbell's brand name was better recognized and regarded by consumers than the Franco-American brand name. "The Campbell's name scored much higher in terms of quality and nutritional profile, so it made sense to leverage the equity that's in the Campbell brand and associate it with some of our other products," explains Juli Mandel Sloves, a spokeswoman for Campbell Soup. The transition, basically replacing the Franco-American banner with the red-and-white Campbell's logo and other labeling changes, began in July 2004. "There's been no change to the products, just to the brand," according to Mandel Sloves.

Mandel Sloves adds that the change is meant to boost sales of SpaghettiOs, RavioliOs, and regular spaghetti, along with beef, chicken, and turkey gravy varieties sold in cans and jars. Campbell Soup had $121 million in revenues from SpaghettiOs and its other canned pastas in 2004, or about 22 percent of the $543 million annual canned pasta market. That number was down slightly from sales of $132 million in the prior year, and well behind Chef Boyardee, which dominates the market with about $295 million in yearly canned pasta sales.

The Franco-American brand got its start in Jersey City, New Jersey, in 1887. That's when French immigrant Alphonse Biardot opened a commercial kitchen to introduce Americans to gourmet foods from his native country. Campbell Soup purchased that company back in 1915.

Source: Linda A. Johnson, "Oh-oh! SpaghettiOs Drops Franco-American Brand," *Miami Herald* (November 19, 2004), C4. Copyright 2004 by the Miami Herald. Reproduced with permission of Tribune Media Services.

---

sumer reaction to a hypothetical chocolate cake mix carrying the Godiva and Slim-Fast brand names.[30] One version of the product was called Godiva chocolate cake mix by Slim-Fast. Another version was labeled Slim-Fast chocolate cake mix by Godiva. Participants were asked to rate these two versions in terms of how well the cake mix would perform in terms of being low in calories and fat, having a good taste, and richness. Significant differences were observed in the ratings across the two versions. As illustrated in Figure 15.13, the Slim-Fast by Godiva version produced the best ratings in terms of calories and fat. In contrast, the Godiva by Slim-Fast version received the better ratings on the taste and richness attributes. Thus, whichever brand name appeared first had the strongest influence on those attributes most closely associated with that particular name.

One of our favorite stories illustrating the importance of a product's name comes from a company selling cricket manure as a fertilizer for gardeners and growers.[31] Initially, the product was named "CC-84." The CC stood for cricket crap; the 84 represented the year the product was first offered. Yet the name failed to convey the organic origins of the product. Rather, the product was more likely to be viewed as a chemical than an organic fertilizer. Product sales went nowhere until its name was changed to "Kricket Krap," a name that better communicated the product's organic origins. Thus, the meaning derived from a product's name may influence the opinions formed about the product. Even the way a name sounds has been shown to convey meaning that affects consumers' impressions of the product.[32] And when a name conveys the wrong meaning, sales are likely to suffer.

The American shrimp industry has entered the name game recently. To help differentiate their product from cheaper foreign imports, domestic shrimpers are pushing

**FIGURE 15.13** The Order of Composite Brand Names Determines
Consumers' Product Opinions

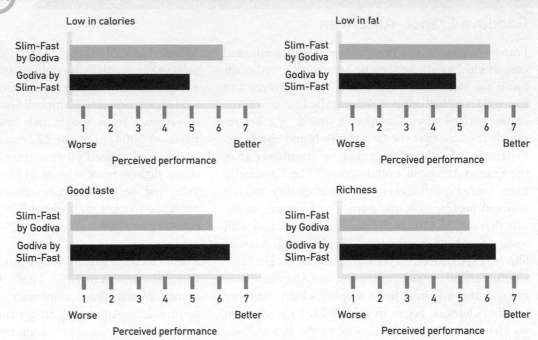

Source: C. Whan Park, Sung Youl Jun, and Allan D. Shocker, "Composite Branding Alliances: An Investigation of Extension and Feedback Effects," *Journal of Marketing Research*, 33 (November 1996), 453–466.

**TABLE 15.1** Labels Used in the Cafeteria Study

| REGULAR MENU-ITEM NAMES | DESCRIPTIVE MENU-ITEM NAMES |
| --- | --- |
| Red beans with rice | Traditional Cajun red beans with rice |
| Seafood filet | Succulent Italian seafood filet |
| Grilled chicken | Tender grilled chicken |
| Chicken parmesan | Home-style chicken parmesan |
| Chocolate pudding | Satin chocolate pudding |
| Zucchini cookies | Grandma's zucchini cookies |

Source: Brian Wansink, James Painter, and Koert Van Ittersum, "Descriptive Menu Labels' Effect on Sales," *Cornell Hotel and Restaurant Administration Quarterly*, 42 (December 2001), 68–72.

such names as "local West Texas white shrimp" and "Wild and Wonderful Florida Shrimp." [33] The ability of such descriptive labels to influence consumers' opinions and behavior has been documented in a cafeteria setting. [34] Researchers varied whether six different menu items were described with either a basic label or a descriptive label. These items and labels are described in Table 15.1. The descriptive labels increased sales by 27 percent. These labels also altered eaters' interpretation of their consumption experience as they reported that the food was of higher quality. In addition, they indicated that they were more likely to eat the item in the future.

## PRODUCT PACKAGING

The potential for a product's package to influence consumers' opinions about what's inside the package has been recognized in earlier chapters. Consumer Behavior and

Marketing 6.4 described how the packaging for some telescopes created unrealistic expectations about what consumers would actually be able to see through the telescope. And in Chapter 10 we told you the story about how a grocer lost sales when it decided to wrap its fresh fish in plastic, thereby causing consumers to perceive the fish as less than fresh.

Packaging also plays an important role in shaping consumers' impressions of the amount of product inside the package. In Chapter 6, we reviewed research that showed how larger packages cause consumers to use more of the product per consumption occasion. Apparently, larger packages lead consumers to believe that more product is inside. Beyond this, plastic containers are perceived as holding more product than their glass counterparts.[35] Taller but thinner packaging creates the illusion of more product inside than shorter but wider packaging,[36] although this difference may disappear when other packaging features, such as the package's ability to attract attention, come into play.[37] Packages that are effective at drawing attention, perhaps because of their unusual shape, have a positive influence on perceptions of the amount of product inside, even when compared to taller packages with less attention-getting capabilities.[38]

Companies occasionally use packaging that's very similar to that of a leading competitor. This is the so-called me-too product that tries to create favorable opinions by using stimulus generalization. **Stimulus generalization** occurs when, *for an existing stimulus-response relationship, the more similar a new stimulus is to the existing one, the more likely it will evoke the same response.* By designing its packaging to resemble the packaging of a well-liked competitor, a company hopes that these favorable opinions will transfer, at least in part, to its product. The next time you are shopping at a grocery or drugstore, take a close look at the packaging of over-the-counter medicines. You'll find many examples of an established brand's packaging being imitated.

Whereas some companies may model their packaging after that of a well-known competitor, others have discovered the benefits that come from using their packaging to differentiate themselves from the competition. A case in point is Hovis, a brand of bread in the United Kingdom. Paula Moss, divisional marketing director at RHM Bread Bakeries, explains: "The packaging had become so totally generic that the differences between bread brands had been lost. We wanted to assert Hovis's personality through the packaging."[39] So it did so using patterns of baked beans and chopped cucumbers to decorate its packaging. Shoppers were intrigued, and sales doubled in two years.[40]

A number of beer and wine producers are relying on packaging these days for shaping consumers' opinions. An excellent example of the ability for packaging to change consumers' perceptions of the product comes from Diageo's Smirnoff Ice. Many men were turned off by the product's image of being a "woman's drink." Yet this barrier was overcome in the United Kingdom when the company packaged the drink in slim aluminum cans.[41] Heineken has recently supplemented its distinctive green glass bottle by selling the product in aluminum cans shaped like beer kegs. And at least one wine-maker has gone metal. The Niebaum Coppola Estate Winery in California's Napa Valley started selling its Sophia Blanc de Blancs in a four-pack of sleek pink metal cans. "It's putting the wine into places where wine traditionally hasn't had an easy opportunity," says Erie Martin, president of the winery.[42]

Unfortunately, not all is good in the world of packaging. Indeed, sometimes packaging can have fatal consequences. You can learn more about this by reading Buyer Beware 15.1.

## DIFFERENT COLORS EVOKE DIFFERENT MEANINGS

An organization known as the Institute of Color Research has performed research that indicates that people make subconscious judgments within the first ninety seconds of encountering a new object. What's the most important determinant of these

## The Risks Posed by Product Packaging

To toddlers who can't read, a white plastic bottle of citrus-scented Clorox bleach with a sliced orange on its label is hard to distinguish from a white plastic bottle of Tropicana orange juice with a sliced orange on its label. Pediatricians and poison control specialists say children often are poisoned when they mistake home chemicals for "look-alike" consumables. The problem is especially acute, the specialists say, when packaging on highly toxic products such as drain cleaners, lamp oil, furniture polish, or antifreeze looks like packaging for juices and soft drinks. "Children are exploring the world by putting things into their mouths. We don't want to add a chance of confusion," says Meredith K. Appy, the president of the Home Safety Council, an alliance of home products companies led by Lowe's, the home-improvement firm.

There's often more than a chance of confusion. "We have a gazillion cases of bleach poisoning," says Rose Ann Soloway, the director of the American Association of Poison Control Centers in Washington, D.C. In 2002, the latest year for which figures are available, U.S. poison control centers reported 20,801 bleach-poisoning cases among children younger than six. Drinking bleach rarely causes more than irritation of the mouth and throat, but it's the most common form of toxic exposure for American children.

How much look-alike labels contribute to toddler poisonings is unknown, but there are lots of opportunities. Pine-Sol cleaners in clear bottles contain liquid the color of apple juice, says Sue Kell of the Blue Ridge Poison Center in Charlottesville, Virginia. Blue window-washing fluid in a clear bottle looks a lot like Frost Gatorade. Comet cleanser in a green canister looks a lot like Kraft parmesan cheese in a green canister.

Dr. Fred Henretig, the medical director of the Poison Control Center at Philadelphia Children's Hospital, says his center has reported two deaths from children drinking furniture polish or lamp oil, which can cause pneumonia, choking, and death. In a third case, a two-year-old survived after drinking lamp oil from a container he had mistaken for a fruit juice bottle. Among the home products most dangerous to children are medicines, pesticides, caustic cleaning products such as drain and oven cleaners, antifreeze, window-washing solutions, and hydrocarbons such as furniture polish, lamp oil, gasoline, and kerosene. The Consumer Product Safety Commission requires kid-proof containers for about thirty household chemicals and most medicines. Manufacturers also must provide the cautionary labels that include first-aid instructions, says Ken Giles, a spokesman for the commission. Clorox voluntarily tops its scented bleaches with child-resistant caps, says Vicky Friedman, a spokeswoman at Clorox's headquarters. Several years ago, the company recalled and reformulated Armor All QuickSilver Wheel Cleaner after two deaths were reported among preschoolers who drank the clear liquid product. To reduce the hazards of look-alike home chemicals, the Home Safety Council recommends storing them carefully and out of children's reach.

Source: Excerpted from Anastasia Ustinova, "'Look-Alike' Products Are a Risk to Kids," *Miami Herald* (March 10, 2004), A8. Copyright 2004 by the Miami Herald. Reproduced with permission of Tribune Media Services.

judgments? Color. Color alone accounts for somewhere between 62 and 90 percent of these initial reactions.[43] Moreover, as described in Table 15.2, these reactions can vary from one country to another.

Because colors convey meaning, consumers' product judgments may depend on its color. Suppose that we add chocolate coloring to vanilla pudding. Most who taste the pudding after being blindfolded so that they cannot see its color will report correctly that it has a vanilla flavor. Yet if consumers are allowed to see the pudding prior to tasting it, its color will cause many to think that it has a chocolate flavor.

Appliance makers have learned that consumers perceive their products such as a vacuum cleaner as being lighter in weight when colored with pastel rather than darker

*White:* The color for weddings in Europe and North America. The traditional mourning color in China and South America. The most important priestly color in India, where religious color associations are more important than in the West.

*Black:* The European and North American color for funerals. The color of mourning for distant relatives when combined with blue in China. Generally viewed as representing high quality among consumers around the world.

*Red:* The color of prohibition and warnings in Europe. Unpopular in Ireland when used with blue and white because this combination represents the British flag. Very popular in China as the color of communism. In India, red is a Hindu symbol of love and generally denotes life, action, and gaiety. Red is also a wedding dress color for Sikhs. Should be avoided in Paraguay, along with green and blue, because these colors are political.

*Pink:* The color for baby girls in the United Kingdom and baby boys in Belgium and eastern France. Seen as a male color in Japan.

*Blue:* The color for baby boys in the United Kingdom and baby girls in Belgium and eastern France. Seen as informative and trustworthy in Europe. In Sweden, blue combined with yellow represents the national flag, but it's not acceptable to use the national colors for commercial purposes. Dark blue has associations with the Kuomintang army in China and may give offense. In India, blue means truth and has intellectual appeal, although dark blue is unpopular as the color of the lowest castes. In Japan, blue is a female color.

*Yellow:* The color of caution in Europe. An Imperial Chinese color that denotes grandeur and mystery. In India, yellow is the color of merchants and second only to white in terms of sanctity. Used along with white at mourning anniversaries in Japan, becoming brighter year after year. In Malaysia, yellow is the color of the Sultans and can never be worn by Malays. The color of despair in Brazil.

*Orange:* Popular in Holland, where orange is the national color, but unpopular in southern Ireland, where it stands for the Protestant church. Orange is a symbol of Thursday in Thailand.

*Green:* The color of the environment in Europe and a significant color for all Muslims. Green has religious significance in Malaysia but is used commercially too. Popular in Mexico as a national color.

*Purple:* The color of royalty, especially in the United Kingdom. The color of soothing in India, but also associated with sorrow. The overall color for sorrow in Brazil. Has religious connotations in Peru, especially in October, and is otherwise best avoided.

*Brown:* Unpopular in Germany for clothing as too political following Hitler's Germany. Brown is thought to bring bad luck in Brazil.

Source: Excerpted from "Branding & Colour: The Colour of Money," *Brand Strategy* (October 6, 2004), 24–27.

tones. When Gateway computers updated its logo, a green color was added to "communicate growth, momentum and vitality."[44] When Apple introduced its teal iMac to the otherwise putty-colored world of computers, consumers took notice. This innovative coloring and a lower price helped Apple sell more than 800,000 iMacs in less than five months.[45] Sears apparently is hoping for a similar success with its introduction of three new colors for its new line of Kenmore washing machines (see Figure 15.14). Manufacturers of laundry soaps and cold capsules recognize the benefits of including colored granules as a visual cue of their products' effectiveness. To convey the idea that it sold inexpensive hot dogs, Wienerschnitzel, a 350-outlet hot dog chain, modified the colors of one outlet to include orange, a color often seen as connoting cheapness. When sales increased 7 percent, every outlet was redone using this color.[46]

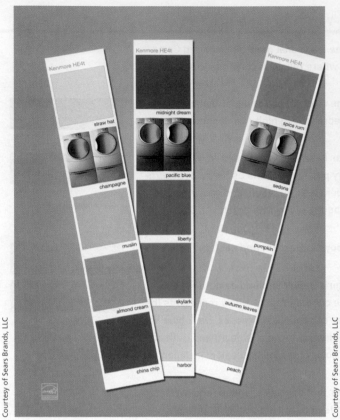

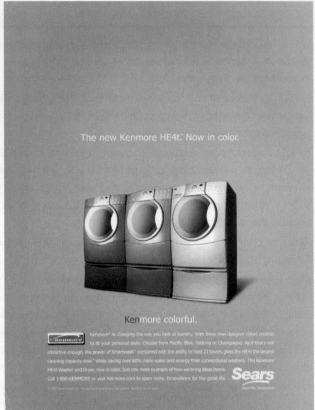

**FIGURE 15.14** Sears Uses Color to Enhance the Appeal of Its New Kenmore Washing Machine

Color has recently been shown to affect consumer response on the Internet. The color blue is quite effective in creating feelings of relaxation, unlike other colors such as yellow. In addition, people perceive that time passes more quickly when they are relaxed. Putting these two findings together, the prediction is that consumers will perceive downloading to occur more quickly when the computer screen is blue rather than yellow. And this is what was found. The enhanced relaxation and reduced perceptions of download time produced by the blue screen resulted in more favorable attitudes toward the website.[47]

## SHAPING CONSUMERS' PRICE PERCEPTIONS

Companies have discovered two basic strategies for influencing consumers' opinions about their products' prices. The first strategy involves the use of **nine-ending prices,** in which *the last digit of a product's price is the number 9*. Following this strategy, a company would charge $19.99 rather than $20.00. Odd-ending prices are effective because they are either interpreted as signaling low price or mentally rounded down to a lower price. This perception, in turn, produces more sales than would be earned otherwise.[48]

The second strategy is called **reference pricing,** in which *information about a price other than that actually charged for the product is provided*. The price tags that a retailer places on the products it carries may list both the actual price charged by the retailer and a higher price, typically described as either the price recommended by the product manufacturer or the price previously charged (e.g., "Was $19.99. Now $14.99"). Similarly, companies that operate over the airwaves such as QVC and Home Shopping Network often list higher reference prices. This same tactic is employed by commercials that ask viewers, "How much would you be willing to pay for this fantastic product? $59? $79? $99? It can be yours for only $29.99!" Or maybe the commercial uses a competitor's much more expensive price as a point of reference. Regardless of the particular reference price used, the idea behind this strategy is to encourage consumers to form more favorable impressions about the actual price's reasonableness. And research documents the ability of reference pricing to do so.[49]

## FREE PRODUCT SAMPLES

Giving consumers free product samples (or, as it's sometimes called, *gifting*; to learn more about gifting, read Consumer Behavior and Marketing 15.2), is one way companies encourage favorable opinions of their products. When Coca-Cola introduced its Surge soft drink to the marketplace, nearly seven million free samples were

## CONSUMER BEHAVIOR AND MARKETING 15.2

### Gifting: Free Samples Hollywood Style

Director David Slade learned a new word at the 2005 Sundance Film Festival, where he had a film, *Hard Candy,* in the competition. "Do you want to be gifted?" he was asked. The debt-laden director soon learned that one of the latest rituals of attending Sundance is being showered with free stuff, a practice known as gifting. "There's cell phones, hair dryers, jewelry, jeans, makeup," he marveled. "You feel a mountain of guilt. You feel immoral. Then it's, 'Sure, I'll take it!' And the joke of it is, I walked away with more money than I got paid for the movie."

The festival, created to celebrate independent, seat-of-the-pants filmmaking, has been invaded by corporate America, which sees an irresistible marketing opportunity in the confluence of talent, celebrity, and world media that gathers for the festival. An entire area on Main Street is now devoted to giving away goods that companies hope to establish as favorites among celebrities, and numerous storefronts and chalets are commandeered by companies promoting (and sometimes gifting) cars, cell phones, fur-lined boots, fur-trimmed parkas, and cameras. Companies like Philips, Fred Segal, Motorola, Sony, Kenneth Cole, and Yahoo! were represented in 2005.

Companies hope that the giveaway will help establish relationships with celebrities and influential taste-makers. "People who are coming to the store are being introduced to the brand," says Mary Filar, marketing director of the upscale Fred Segal department store, which attended for the second year in a row. "It's not about the swag, it's about education." Cast members from the HBO series *Entourage* toured the Fred Segal "store" (nothing there is for sale), collecting jeans, shoes, and whatever else struck their fancy, while the rap star Ludacris stopped by the William Morris chalet to get his free boots and cell phone. "Pamela Anderson, she picked G-strings; Carmen Electra preferred lace bras," says Heather Patt, a spokeswoman for Le Mystere lingerie at the Fred Segal store. Near her booth, another stylist was giving away $600 Walter tweed overcoats. "Everyone is very appreciative, though I'm sure it's a little overwhelming," continued Ms. Patt. "For us it's great brand exposure."

Given such an atmosphere, it's not surprising that people sometimes get a bit carried away. "We've had a lot of people come in and say, 'I want a plasma,' says Nichole Woodcock, a representative for the Philips lounge at the festival, referring to the flat-screen plasma television sets that adorn the suite. "But we're used to it. It's our second year here, so we're used to people expecting a lot." She paused, then added: "Sometimes people expect a little much. But that's what Sundance is all about."

Source: Excerpted in part from Sharon Waxman, "Forget about All Those Films, This Year It's the Sundance Free Stuff," *New York Times* (January 28, 2005), E1, E3. Copyright 2005 by The New York Times Co. Reprinted with permission.

**FIGURE 15.15** Free Samples Are Often Used to Shape Consumers' Product Opinions

distributed.[50] Similarly, Glad distributed a number of free bags, such as the one shown in Figure 15.15, to encourage adoption of its new Odor Shield garbage bags. Free samples are also used for well-established products. Internet provider AOL offered consumers two months of free Internet access (see Figure 15.15) in the hope that potential customers will become actual customers.

The effectiveness of providing free samples when rolling out a new product is documented by market research examining the samples' impact on sales. Figure 15.16 summarizes the findings based on eight new product introduction tests conducted by NPD, a major market research firm, in which one group of consumers received a free sample whereas another group did not. The effect of free samples is revealed by a comparison of the two groups' purchasing behavior. The top graph in Figure 15.16 represents the results involving initial or trial purchasing. As can be seen, nearly 50 percent more households receiving a free sample made an initial purchase relative to "control" households (those not receiving a free sample). Moreover, as indicated by the bottom graph in Figure 15.16, those who purchased after receiving the free sample were slightly more likely to buy it again.

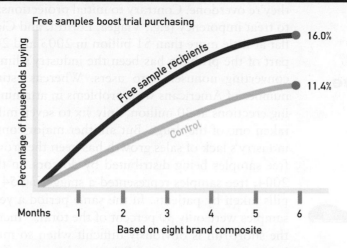

Free samples boost trial purchasing

Free sample recipients — 16.0%

Control — 11.4%

Months 1 2 3 4 5 6

Based on eight brand composite

*Percentage of households buying* (y-axis)

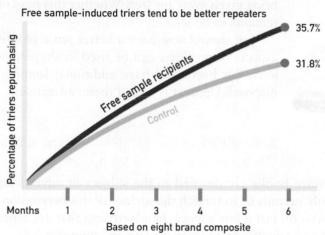

Free sample-induced triers tend to be better repeaters

Free sample recipients — 35.7%

Control — 31.8%

Months 1 2 3 4 5 6

Based on eight brand composite

*Percentage of triers repurchasing* (y-axis)

To estimate the impact of offering free samples on total market penetration, simply multiply the trial rate times the repurchase rate for those who did or did not receive a free sample. Free samples yielded a total penetration of 5.7 percent after six months (trial rate of 16.0 percent times the repurchase rate of 35.7 percent). This compares to a level of 3.6 percent (11.4 percent times 31.8 percent) when free samples were not used. Free samples increased market penetration for these new products by nearly 60 percent ([5.7 – 3.6]/ 3.6). Accordingly, as long as the product delivers, providing consumers with a free product sample can be a very effective way of shaping their opinions.

Of course, giving consumers a free sample is not feasible for many products, not if the company wants to stay in business for very long. It's one thing to give consumers a free month of Internet service or a free bottle of your product. It's quite another to give them a free car (unless your name happens to be Snoop Dogg, as we discussed at the end of Chapter 8). Even so, companies can do the next best thing: let consumers take the product home for a limited time and try it out. This is precisely what General Motors did with its "GM 24-Hour Test Drive" program (see Figure 15.17), which offered consumers the opportunity to take home a GM automobile of their choice for a day. This tactic for shaping consumers' opinions goes back to at least 1984 when Apple allowed consumers to take home one of its Macintosh computers for twenty-four hours.

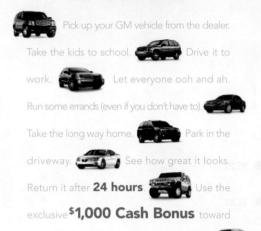

The GM **24 Hour** Test Drive

## Finally, the world's first real-life test drive.
### (It's about time.)

Pick up your GM vehicle from the dealer.

Take the kids to school. Drive it to

work. Let everyone ooh and ah.

Run some errands (even if you don't have to).

Take the long way home. Park in the

driveway. See how great it looks.

Return it after **24 hours**. Use the

exclusive **$1,000 Cash Bonus** toward

a purchase. Then, take it home again.

**FIGURE 15.17** GM Offers Consumers Free Samples,
but Only for a Day

So when might free samples actually hurt sales? When they're overdone. Contrary to initial projections, sales of drugs to treat impotency (e.g., Viagra, Levitra, and Cialis) have been flat at little more than $1 billion in 2003 and 2004. Certainly part of the problem has been the industry's limited success in converting nonusers into users. Whereas estimates put the number of Americans with problems in attaining or maintaining erections at 30 million, only six to seven million men have taken one of the drugs. But another major contributor to the industry's lack of sales growth has been the growth and size of free samples being distributed by doctors. In the first half of 2004, free samples represented a staggering 54 percent of the pills taken by patients. In the same period a year earlier, free samples were only 30 percent of the total.[51] Increasing sales in the short-run is obviously difficult when so much product is being given away for free. Whether this pays off in the long run remains to be seen.

You should now have a better sense of how many different aspects of products can be used in shaping consumers' opinions. But businesses have additional shaping devices at their disposal. Up next is one of these: advertising.

### Advertising's Role in Shaping Consumers' Opinion

Given that entire books are devoted to the subject of advertising, the few pages available here only permits us to scratch the surface of this persuasion technique. Consequently, we focus on just a few aspects of advertising that are especially relevant to those wishing to use advertising to sway consumers' opinions.

### TYPE OF ADVERTISING APPEAL

One key decision facing those who want to use advertising's power to mold consumers' opinions is the type of appeal to feature in such advertising. A number of different ways to distinguish among various types of advertising appeals have been proposed over the years. One of these ways involves the distinction between informational versus emotional appeals. **Informational advertising appeals** *attempt to influence consumers' beliefs about the advertised product.* **Emotional advertising appeals** *try to influence consumers' feelings about the advertised product.* Does this distinction sound familiar? It should, because it parallels the notion that beliefs and feelings are the two primary determinants of attitudes, something we devoted considerable attention to in Chapter 10. For this reason, we won't reiterate it here.

Advertising can also be classified on the basis of whether it uses a utilitarian or value-expressive advertising appeal.[52] Utilitarian advertising appeals are those that focus on the functional features of the product. The advertisement in Figure 15.18 uses a utilitarian appeal. The ad communicates the advertised product's primary function of providing double protection for stored items through visual images intended to foster favorable beliefs about the product along this attribute. More generally, **utilitarian advertising appeals** *aim to influence consumers' opinions about the advertised product's ability to perform its intended function.*

Now take a look at the billboard advertisement presented in Figure 15.19. What does this ad say about the product's attributes and quality? Not a thing. What does it say about the type of people who use this product? Quite a bit. Think about it this way: How many consumers over the age of fifty, versus those under twenty-five years old, would identify with the individuals depicted in this advertisement? Or how about cowboys? Any chance of them identifying with this ad? (OK, you can stop laughing now!) What about college students? It's a safe bet that the advertiser thinks so.

**Value-expressive advertising appeals** *attempt to influence consumers' opinions about the advertised product's ability to communicate something about those who use the product.* Maybe the ad implies that the product can communicate to consumers something about the type of person they are (i.e., the person's actual self-image) or desire to be (i.e., the person's desired self-image). Maybe the ad attempts to convey how the product can communicate a social image intended for public consumption. In either case, the product's symbolic properties, not its functional properties, are emphasized when using value-expressive advertising appeals.

The appropriateness of using a particular type of appeal depends heavily on what's important to consumers when they form their product evaluations. For those products that help consumers to define or achieve their actual or desired self-images, value-expressive appeals should be particularly effective. This strategy is also effective when products are valued for their ability to fulfill

**FIGURE 15.18** A Utilitarian Advertising Appeal

**FIGURE 15.19** A Value-Expressive Advertising Appeal

consumers' social image needs, something we discussed way back in Chapter 8. In contrast, when products are valued for their ability to satisfy consumption needs that are independent of the consumer's self-image or social image needs, utilitarian advertising appeals that communicate the products' functional utility are likely to be more effective.

Finally, we need to acknowledge the overly simplistic view we have presented thus far. The utilitarian and value-expressive properties of advertisements and products is not simply one or the other. In some cases, both are present. Products can be valued for both utilitarian and value-expressive reasons (e.g., automobiles). By the same token, both utilitarian and value-expressive appeals can be present, albeit to varying degrees, in the same advertisement. A car ad, for example, could promote both the advertised product's functional attributes (e.g., safety, durability, gas mileage, and so forth) and its symbolic properties (e.g., the status that ownership confers).

## ADVERTISING CLAIMS

As illustrated earlier in the chapter in our coverage of the central process of opinion formation, ads that make stronger claims about the advertised brand's merits are better at creating favorable product opinions than those containing weaker claims, so long as consumers engage in sufficient thinking about product-relevant information during ad processing. But what makes a claim stronger or weaker? Let's start with the relevancy of claims. Claims about things unrelated to the consumer's needs lack personal relevance. Relevant claims are those that connect with the person's life in some meaningful way. One industry study found that relevancy was the most important determinant of new product advertising's success in persuading consumers to try the product.[53]

The strength of an advertising claim also depends on what it conveys about the advertised product's characteristics and benefits. Consider the ad for Duracell Ultra that claims that it's "the most powerful alkaline battery in the world." If believed, consumers should form more favorable opinions about this product than would be the case when the ad contains more modest claims.[54] Similarly, the comparative ad that describes an important advantage over a well-known competitor represents a stronger advocacy for the advertised brand than a noncomparative ad that's silent about how the advertised brand stacks up relative to its competition. Consequently, comparative ads may lead consumers to form more favorable opinions about the advertised brand relative to the competitor used as a point of comparison.[55]

The extent to which advertising provides substantiation or support for its claims is important.[56] Product demonstrations are an effective way to substantiate claims. When St. Regis wanted to demonstrate the strength of its corrugated paper, the company built a bridge of the material and showed a 2.5-ton Rolls Royce automobile driving over it. One study reports a significant relationship between the use of product demonstrations in TV commercials and their ability to persuade.[57] Testimonials from consumers about their consumption experiences with the product may also help reinforce advertising claims. Ads for weight-loss products often feature individuals talking about how many pounds they have lost.

Another characteristic of advertising claims that may affect consumers' opinions about the advertised product involves whether and when consumers can verify a claim's accuracy or truthfulness. **Search claims** are *those that can be validated before purchase by examining information readily available in the marketplace.* An ad that claims that the advertised product has the lowest price or best warranty can be verified by checking out the competition. **Experience claims** *can also be verified but require product consumption in order to do so.* If an ad for a new brand of salad dressing claims to have a better taste than the brand you currently use, you don't really know if this is true until you have tried it. Sometimes advertising claims are such that *verification of their accuracy is either impossible or unlikely because they require more effort than consumers are willing to invest*. These claims are called **credence claims.** A good example of this is Tylenol's long-running claim, "Used by more hospitals than any other brand of pain reliever." We think it's a safe bet that no consumer has ever surveyed enough hospitals to determine the truthfulness of this claim. Perhaps because they believe that companies are more motivated to tell the truth when their claims can be verified prior to product purchase, consumers perceive search claims to be much more truthful than either experience or credence claims.[58]

Whether a claim is stated in an objective or a subjective manner is also important. **Objective claims** are *claims that focus on factual information that is not subject to individual interpretations*. **Subjective claims,** however, are *claims that may evoke different interpretations across individuals*. Claims such as "low-priced" or "lightweight" would be considered subjective, inasmuch as what is low or light for one person may not be for the next. These same attributes could be expressed objectively by giving the actual price and weight. Because objective claims are more precise and more easily evaluated, they are perceived as more believable, they evoke more favorable thinking during processing, and they facilitate more favorable beliefs and attitudes about the advertised product.[59]

Although the preceding discussion of how advertising claims can influence opinion formation presumes that a sufficient level of thinking about these claims will occur during ad processing, advertising claims may still be influential even if such thinking is rather minimal. This influence can occur when the sheer number of claims serves as a peripheral cue. Under the peripheral route, simply increasing the quantity (rather than quality or strength) of claims can lead to more favorable opinions, even if these additional claims contain unimportant information.[60]

### ADVERTISING'S EXECUTIONAL ELEMENTS

Beyond the written or spoken claims about the advertised product, other elements used in giving advertising form and substance also play a role in the persuasion process. Some of these elements have already been covered in this chapter, when we described how pictures, both those conveying product-relevant information and those devoid of such information (i.e., peripheral cues), can impact the beliefs and attitudes created by an advertisement. Other aspects of an ad's visual elements beyond their product relevance and attractiveness are also important.[61] The particular camera angle reflected by a picture of the advertised product, for instance, has been found to affect the attitudes formed about the product. Pictures that give the appearance of looking up at the product produce more favorable attitudes than either straight-on shots or ones that appear to be looking down on the product.[62]

Even seemingly small details may be influential. Take, for example, the typeface design element of printed materials. There are hundreds of typefaces that vary in their symmetry, elaborateness, and naturalness. Consumer researchers have just started to explore the influence of typeface design.[63] Initial research is suggestive of the potential to influence consumers' product opinions with an ad's typeface design.[64] Such research has implications not only for advertising, but in other areas such as the typeface design most appropriate for a company's logo. As one example, Hilton redesigned its logo from block lettering to a scripted look in an effort to create the impression of being more friendly.[65]

### PRODUCT ENDORSERS

As explained in Chapter 14, advertisers often use product endorsers to attract attention. They also use endorsers for shaping consumers' product opinions. Indeed, simply associating a product with the right endorser can make the product seem more valuable. Think of how many pairs of sneakers have been sold simply because they had Michael Jordan's name on them. When the latest offering bearing his name, the Nike Air Jordan Retro 13, was released, hundreds of eager buyers willing to spend $150 started lining up as early as 4 a.m. outside stores.[66] Demand exceeded supply so much that the Retro 13 was selling over the Internet for as much as $300.[67] His name alone transforms an otherwise ordinary product into a status symbol that must be possessed, a fact that some people find disturbing (see Buyer Beware 15.2). Even though years have passed since he's played (at a professional level) the game that turned him into a household name, Jordan emerged as Americans' favorite sports star in a Harris Poll conducted in January 2005, a spot he has held each year the poll has been conducted since 1993.[68] So powerful is his appeal that retail sales for the Michael Jordan fragrance exceeded $75 million less than one year after its introduction.[69] In 2005, the third cologne bearing his name, called 23 (the number he wore during his playing days), was

## The Dark Side of Marketing

During the past two decades, ever since Michael Jordan signed as the pitchman for Nike in 1985, the craze over Jordan shoes has been much discussed. This craze is especially heightened in black urban areas where the popularity of Jordan shoes and other brand-name apparel has been associated with thefts, armed robberies, and even homicides. The public could stand to know more about the marketing strategies that fuel these desires and the socioeconomic implications of having consumers under a spell.

On March 11, 2005, scholars from around the country gathered at Howard University to share their knowledge on the subject at a three-day conference called "Consuming Kids: How Marketing Undermines Children's Health, Values & Behavior." Alvin Poussaint, professor of psychiatry at Harvard Medical School and president of the Campaign for a Commercial-Free Childhood, moderated panel discussions on such subjects as the sexualization of childhood in advertisements, the economics of obesity, and the commercial branding of children in public schools. "Even parents who are trying to do the right thing must realize what they're up against," says Velma LaPoint, professor of child development at Howard and one of the conference organizers. "They

may be trying to promote positive child development, but at the same time, you've got a marketing industry trying to hire people like me to tell them what a child's vulnerabilities might be at certain ages. In very scientific ways, they set out to capitalize on a child's need to belong and to create in them a feeling that they must always have something new to be accepted."

Sonny Vaccaro, a Nike executive in 1985 and the man credited with bringing Jordan onboard, dismissed talk of marketing boogiemen and said that classic Jordan shoes, like old Frank Sinatra recordings, help keep a glorious past alive. "What we saw happen with Michael [Jordan], and to carry on to other individuals, was a legacy and a myth wrapped up into one thing: a shoe," says Vaccaro, now a consultant to Reebok. "It was incomprehensible, and it grew to mystical proportions. What we are seeing now is a new generation wanting to be a part of that. All humans want to be connected to greatness and glory, and now people are connecting with that, and each other, through the shoe." When one reporter noted that $160 seemed a lot to pay for such a connection, Vaccaro replied, "And they'll pay $260 and $270 when it's time to pay that number." He's undoubtedly right. But, somehow, that just doesn't seem right, does it?

Source: Excerpted in part from Courtland Milloy, "Selling Sneakers Violating Young Minds," *Washington Post* (March 2, 2005), B1. Copyright 2005 The Washington Post. Reprinted by permission.

introduced.[70] As discussed in Consumer Behavior and Marketing 15.3, using celebrities to peddle fragrances (see Figure 15.20) is quite popular these days.

To find out what consumers around the globe think about the effectiveness of celebrity endorsers, Global Market Insite, a market research firm, surveyed one thousand consumers in each of eight different countries. These consumers were asked whether a celebrity endorsement made them think a product was more valuable, less valuable, cheap, or had no effect at all. The results, presented in Table 15.3, reveal substantial differences across the countries in consumers' opinions about the impact of celebrity endorsements. More than half of the Chinese, Japanese, and Russian respondents felt that a celebrity made the product more valuable to them. For the remaining countries, there's a substantial drop-off in the numbers, all the way down to less than 10 percent of the German respondents feeling that celebrities make products

## CONSUMER BEHAVIOR AND MARKETING 15.3

## Using Celebrities to Sell Smells

Several young girls grab bottles of Paris Hilton's new perfume (see Figure 15.20) and spritz themselves and one another in a Macy's department store. Manager Grace Chen rolls her eyes and shrugs. It's impossible to keep the sweet, fruity scent stocked, she says. "It all has to do with image. They all want to be like her."

Paris is not the only celebrity consumers want to make a connection with, even if the connection is only through a scent bearing the celebrity's name or her or his endorsement. Here are some other celebrities that are currently hawking fragrances: Ashley Judd, Beyoncé, Britney Spears, Celine Dion, Charlize Theron, Donald Trump, J. Lo, Jessica Simpson, and Nicole Kidman. Soon to be added to this list are Andy Roddick, Sarah Jessica Parker, and Sean "P. Diddy" Combs, all of whom have fragrances in the works.

Just like any other product category, celebrity fragrance has its share of winners and losers. Certainly one of the most successful fragrances tied to a celebrity has been White Diamonds, with its association with Elizabeth Taylor. Launched in September 1991, White Diamonds remains the number-one-selling brand during the annual Mother's Day gift-buying

spree. J. Lo's Glow fragrance, aimed at the fifteen to twenty-five age group, was the top-selling newcomer when it debuted it 2002, with sales exceeding $40 million internationally that year. Her next scent, Still, launched in 2003 and targeted women over twenty-five. Still cracked the top five of new fragrances for the year.

But many a famous name has been linked with a not-so-successful fragrance over the years: Catherine Deneuve, Cher, Dionne Warwick, Elvira, Elvis Presley, Joan Collins, Julio Iglesias, Kermit the Frog, Linda Evans, Luciano Pavarotti, Martina Navratilova, Mike Ditka, Prince, Salvador Dali, and Sophia Loren. More recently, Naomi Campbell's Naomagic has been far from a best seller. The same for Donald Trump's current entry. "Trump is not doing well," says Grace Chen. "Men don't seem to go for the image thing the way women do." Perhaps not. But that certainly didn't prevent Michael Jordan from racking up the sales. And John Demsey, president of Estée Lauder's MAC cosmetics division, which is developing P. Diddy's new scent, expects the scent to reach global sales in excess of $100 million. Apparently not all stars are equal when it comes to celebrity scents.

Source: Excerpted in part from Gloria Goodale, "Celebrity Scents: Who Do You Smell Like?" *Christian Science Monitor* (January 10, 2005), 11. Also used: Christina Cheddar Berk, "Scent of a Diva: More Pop Stars Peddle Perfume," *Wall Street Journal* (June 30, 2004), B4; Karen-Janine Cohen, "Scent of Success Britney Spears Tie-in Helps Rejuvenate Elizabeth Arden," *South Florida Sun-Sentinel* (December 23, 2004), D1; David Colman, "Celebrity Scents: Simply Resistible," *New York Times* (June 9, 1996), 49; Bruce Horovitz, "Scent of a Showman Michael Jackson Repackages Old Line of Fragrances," *Los Angeles Times* (June 11, 1993), 1; Nat Ives, "A Second Scent Is Hitched to the Fortunes of a Hollywood Star," *New York Times* (July 23, 2003), C8; Sonia Purnell, "Like George Foreman, Some British Celebrities Become Brands for Hire," *London Evening Standard* (November 19, 2004), 1; Sharon Harvey Rosenberg, "Andy Roddick to Have Own Scent," *Miami Herald* (December 15, 2004), C3; Soo Youn, "P. Diddy Gets a Fragrant Twist," *New York Daily News* (May 22, 2004), 38; "Coty Inc. Partners with Sarah Jessica Parker to Develop and Market Fragrances," *PR Newswire Europe* (February 8, 2005).

**FIGURE 15.20** Many Products Hope to Benefit by Associating Themselves with Popular Celebrities

| TABLE 15.3 | Consumers from around the Globe Report Their Opinions about the Impact of Celebrity Endorsers |
| --- | --- |

**Celebrity endorsement makes consumers think a product is:**

| COUNTRY | MORE VALUABLE | LESS VALUABLE | CHEAP | NO EFFECT AT ALL |
| --- | --- | --- | --- | --- |
| Canada | 17.7 | 3.7 | 3.9 | 74.7 |
| China | 51.9 | 8.0 | 3.6 | 36.5 |
| France | 22.7 | 3.0 | 1.7 | 72.6 |
| Germany | 8.7 | 6.2 | 4.8 | 80.3 |
| Japan | 59.2 | 14.0 | 15.1 | 11.7 |
| Russia | 57.7 | 12.5 | 2.4 | 27.4 |
| United Kingdom | 15.9 | 4.2 | 6.9 | 73.0 |
| United States | 13.8 | 3.4 | 3.1 | 79.7 |

Source: GMIPoll, Global Market Insite (December 8, 2004). Copyright 2004 Global Market Insite, Inc.

Note: Numbers represent the percentage of one thousand consumers in each country expressing this opinion about how a celebrity endorsement affects their impression of a product.

more valuable. Curiously, the country containing the greatest number of consumers impressed by celebrities, Japan, is also by far the country with the biggest segment of consumers reporting that celebrity endorsements actually reduce a product's value to them (those reporting it makes the product less valuable or cheapens it). The size of this segment is important because it speaks to the risks incurred by using celebrities, risks that should be weighed against the potential rewards afforded by celebrity endorsers.

Endorsers can be a rich source of meanings that companies may wish to associate with their products.[71] Apparently many American celebrities have the right set of meanings, especially as a symbol of Western culture, for advertisers courting Japanese consumers. Table 15.4 presents just some of the American stars and the products they have pitched in recent times in Japan. On the domestic front, one reason the makers of Tic Tac breath mints chose actress Kimberly Quinn to serve as a spokeswoman in its commercials was that she "reflects the attributes of the brand in terms of being friendly, approachable and trustworthy."[72] Similarly, NASCAR driver Tony Stewart conveys brash masculinity and high endurance, qualities that help Old Spice Red Zone antiperspirant court its youthful target audience.[73] Yet despite their popularity, not all are thrilled about how frequently celebrities are used in advertising. Bob Garfield, a noted writer for *Advertising Age,* contends that "celebrities are seldom used in support of an advertising idea; they are used in place of an advertising idea."[74]

This notion of using celebrities to support an advertising idea takes us to the match-up hypothesis. According to the **match-up hypothesis,** *endorsers are most effective when they are perceived as appropriate spokespeople for the endorsed product.*[75] In other words, the endorser should support or fit with what's being advertised. A supermodel may be a great choice for a cosmetics' manufacturer but less so for an investment company. Lance Armstrong is the six-time winner of the Tour de France and the Associated Press's top male athlete in 2004, an honor he received for the third year in a row and an accomplishment equaled only by Michael Jordan. Yet when it was announced that Discovery Communications, the parent company for the Discovery Channel, the Travel Channel, and others, had decided to sponsor Armstrong's racing team, which had become available when the U.S. Postal Service decided not to renew its sponsorship, some marketers questioned the move. "If they want to increase their global presence, a cycling team would not be the first investment I would suggest," said Jeff Bliss, president of the Javelin Group, a sports marketing firm. "Sports is not their primary focus. It's not as strong a fit as it could be."[76] And who's appropriate for

| TABLE 15.4 | American Stars in Japanese Commercials |
|---|---|
| **CELEBRITY** | **APPEARS IN COMMERCIAL FOR** |
| Antonio Banderas | Subaru Forester |
| Arnold Schwarzenegger | DirecTV |
| Beavis and Butthead | Mintia |
| Christian Slater | Toyota |
| Demi Moore | Jog Mate |
| Keanu Reeves | Suntory Reserve |
| Leonardo DiCaprio | Suzuki Wagon-R |
| Sean Connery | Mazda |

Source: "Whaddaya Know?" *Marketing News* (December 8, 2003), 15, 22.

**FIGURE 15.21** Endorsers That Are Living Proof of a Product's Effectiveness Can Be Especially Persuasive

one segment may not be for another. Rapper Ludacris has his following, but he also has opponents who objected to his association with Pepsi, which led the company to discontinue its TV commercial featuring him.[77]

Endorsers may represent living proof of a product's effectiveness. Trimspa has banked heavily on Anna Nicole Smith's weight loss of nearly seventy pounds while using its product (see Figure 15.21) in its efforts to persuade consumers wanting to shed some pounds. In one of the early commercials featuring Anna, she's asked, "What's your secret?" Her reply: "Trimspa, baby." And then there's Jared Fogle, Subway's spokesperson. You can find out how Jared landed this position in Market Facts 15.2.

Product endorsers can facilitate the acceptance of advertising claims. A source's trustworthiness is critical here. Trusted sources evoke more favorable opinions than sources of questionable trustworthiness. The source's expertise is also important because consumers may be more accepting of claims supported by someone perceived as more knowledgeable, although this influence may easily evaporate when questions exist about the source's trustworthiness.[78]

Finally, endorsers may serve as a peripheral cue. In this case, their attractiveness,[79] how much they are liked,[80] or their celebrity status,[81] regardless of how

## MARKET FACTS 15.2

### Jared Fogle, Subway's Product Endorser

Jared Fogle, a student at Indiana University who had been overweight most of his life, noticed Subway's advertising campaign called "7 Under 6," which promoted the seven sandwiches on its menu with six grams of fat or less. A diet consisting mostly of low-fat Subway sandwiches along with exercise allowed Jared to shed 245 of his original 435 pounds. In 1999, Jared's mother wrote Subway founder Fred DeLuca a letter of thanks and DeLuca immediately saw marketing gold. But others in the organization weren't so sure. Individual cases of extreme weight loss are typically the province of snake-oil diet pills, they pointed out. The letter wound up in the trash.

Then one day Jared ran into a buddy, a reporter for the college newspaper, who had not seen him for a year. The reporter wrote a story about Jared's remarkable transformation that appeared in the college newspaper, which prompted an article in *Men's Health* magazine, a copy of which landed in the mailbox of a Subway franchisee in Chicago. "He (the franchisee) said, 'Let's call this kid,'" recalls DeLuca, "'maybe he can make an ad for us here in Chicago.'" Jared agreed, and DeLuca saw an increase in sales after the ad began airing. Other franchisees started calling. Before long, Jared quit his airline-marketing job, hired an agent, and became a full-time Subway spokesman and an advertising legend.

Sources: Excerpted in part from Matthew Kauffman, "Fat Chance: Weight Loss Brings a Dose of Renown," *Miami Herald* (December 14, 2003), E8; Brian Steinberg, "Sandwich Pitchman Speaks on Being a 'Real' Character," *Wall Street Journal* (December 8, 2004), 1.

relevant any of this may be to evaluating the claims and advertised product, can lead to more favorable opinions being formed.

Although endorsers offer many potential benefits, products tied to a celebrity have a unique risk factor that separates them from other products. They can rise and fall with the fortunes of the endorser. "It's hard to predict the shelf life of someone like Britney Spears," says Carl Sibilski, an industry analyst at investment research firm Morningstar.[82] "Witness what happened with Martha Stewart," says Kathy Feakins, senior partner at Lippincott Mercer, a design and brand strategy agency.[83] A sexual assault charge ended Kobe Bryant's $45 million endorsement deal with Nike.[84]

One way companies can protect their products from such risks is to employ multiple endorsers rather than a single endorser. The Hanes campaign of the 1990s featuring the "Just wait'll we get our Hanes on you" slogan was one of the first campaigns by a major company to use multiple endorsers including, among others, Michael Jordan. In 2005, Hanes launched a $50 million advertising campaign that also used multiple celebrities, including Jordan again, along with Damon Wayans, Matthew Perry, and Marisa Tomei to promote its underwear, sleepwear, socks, and other clothing.[85] Reebok's new "I am what I am" campaign also features multiple celebrities such as movie star Lucy Liu, rappers Jay-Z and 50 Cent, and sports stars Allen Iverson, Yao Ming, and Andy Roddick.[86]

Some marketers also believe that the effectiveness of a celebrity endorser is diminished when the celebrity chosen to endorse one product is in such demand that he or she endorses other products as well. Yet if the celebrity is not also endorsing a competitor, why would this be a problem? Jonathan Asher, a brand consultant explains: "You are paying money to try and build a link between your brand and this person. Advertisers run the risk they won't get the association they are trying to get with their spokesperson. It will just become a blur."[87] One way advertisers might overcome this problem would be to make sure that the desired association is repeatedly reinforced through repetition, although doing so does incur the expense of paying for more advertising exposures. In sum, the benefits of using celebrity endorsers are substantial, but there are potential pitfalls as well.

At this point we have highlighted some of the main product and advertising factors that businesses often use in their efforts to influence consumers' opinions. But we're not done yet. We also want to give you an appreciation for a few more persuasion tactics that do not neatly fit into the product and advertising categories. So hang in there for a few more pages and you will learn about some things that, if nothing else, may help you save some money in the future.

## Framing

As is often the case, there's more than one way to look at things. Take the glass that's filled halfway. I could describe or frame it as half empty. In so doing the emphasis is placed on what's missing. I could also describe or frame the glass as half full. This description emphasizes what's available. Both frames are equally applicable. But they may not be equal in the opinions they create about the desirability of the half-filled glass.

As a simple example of this, consider meat products. Because the percentage of lean meat plus the percentage of fat content always equals 100 percent, information about the percentage of one automatically provides information about the other. If meat is described as 80 percent lean, this means that it has a fat content of 20 percent. Conversely, if meat is described as 20 percent fat, then you know that it's 80 percent lean. Thus, descriptions about either the meat's leanness or fat percentage are equally informative. Even so, they're not equally influential. When asked their opinions about a meat product described as either 80 percent lean or 20 percent fat, those consumers who received the description of the meat's leanness formed much more favorable product opinions than those who received the description of the meat's fat content.[88]

Whether persuasive communications adopt a gain versus loss frame is important in determining how consumers respond to such messages.[89] **Gain-framed messages** *emphasize what is attained by following the messages' recommendations*. In contrast, **loss-framed messages** *emphasize what costs may be incurred if the messages' recommendations are not followed*. An example of these two types of message frames in the context of why women should get mammograms is presented in Table 15.5. The gain-framed message describes the advantages of getting a mammogram. The loss-framed message converts these advantages into disadvantages of not getting a mammogram. Which of these two message frames do you think would be most effective in persuading women to get a mammogram?

If you thought the loss-framed message would be most effective, you are correct. And if you thought the gain-framed message would be most effective, you are also correct. How can this be? Because each type of message frame is most effective under different circumstances. Starting with the loss-framed message, its effectiveness stems from the principle of **loss aversion** (see Buyer Beware 15.3), which says that *losses loom larger than gains*.[90] This means that a loss of a given size (e.g., losing $500) is more painful than a gain of the same size (e.g., finding $500) is pleasurable. For this reason, then, consumers will be more persuaded to adopt loss-framed messages' recommendations in order to avoid the potential losses they risk by not doing so. But this advantage exists only when consumers engage in sufficient levels of thinking during message processing,[91] as in the central process of opinion formation described earlier in the chapter. Loss-framed messages have also been found to be more effective when consumers are in a positive mood state.[92]

| TABLE 15.5 | Examples of Gain-Framed and Loss-Framed Messages |
| --- | --- |

**The Gain-Framed Message**

You can feel confident and have the peace of mind that you are doing the best you can to find breast cancer early.

If breast cancer is found early, it is more likely to be curable.

By finding breast cancer early, women have more treatment options and may need less extreme medical procedures. For example, women whose breast cancers are found early usually have the choice of surgery that spares the breast.

If you get a mammogram, you are using the best method to find out if your breasts are healthy.

**The Loss-Framed Message**

You cannot feel confident nor have the peace of mind that you are doing the best you can to find breast cancer early.

If breast cancer is not found early, it is less likely to be curable.

By not finding breast cancer early, women have fewer treatment options and may need more extreme medical procedures. For example, women whose breast cancers are not found early usually do not have the choice of surgery that spares the breast.

If you do not get a mammogram, you are not using the best method to find out if your breasts are healthy.

Source: Punam Anand Keller, Isaac M. Lipkus, and Barbara K. Rimer, "Affect, Framing, and Persuasion," *Journal of Marketing Research*, 40 (February 2003), 54–64.

## Shaping Consumers' Evaluations of Product Options

A car dealership is deciding how it should present the various options—such as an extended warranty, road hazard insurance, and payment insurance (to cover payments in the event of a disabling illness)—that it offers customers who have just purchased a vehicle. One approach would be to show the customer a list of the options and their prices and ask the customer which, if any, of these options they would like to add to their sales contract. Alternatively, all of the options and their respective prices could be included into a single plan that would be added to the sales contract. Customers would then be asked which, if any, of these options they want to drop. Which approach would you recommend, and why?

Recent research supports the wisdom of the second approach. In one study, some of the research participants were asked which set of options they wished to add to an automobile. The rest were given the fully loaded automobile and had to decide which options to delete. Participants added fewer options than they deleted. Consumers' tendency to buy more when they have to decide what to delete than what to add has been shown across various product categories ranging from the expensive durable items of cars to inexpensive items such as pizzas and salads. The obvious benefit to the company is that it ends up with more of the customer's money.

So why does this happen? Having consumers delete an option makes it more salient what they are giving up or "losing." In essence, having consumers delete an option frames the decision as a loss. When consumers are asked to add an option, the decision is framed as a gain. Because of the loss aversion principle described in the chapter, dropping an option is less likely than adding an option.

One last comment. The next time you are presented with a marketplace decision of this nature, you should be aware of our psychological aversion toward perceived losses and its potential influence on the choices you make when presented with fully loaded products. You are likely to save yourself some money if you start with the basic product and then decide, one option at a time, what you want to add. Doing so should help you recoup the cost of this textbook!

Sources: Irwin P. Levin, Judy Schreiber, Marco Lauriola, and Gary J. Gaeth, "A Tale of Two Pizzas: Building Up from a Basic Product versus Scaling Down from a Fully-Loaded Product," *Marketing Letters,* 13 (November 2002), 335–344; C. Whan Park, Youl Jun Sung, and Deborah J. Macinnis, "Choosing What I Want versus Rejecting What I Do Not Want: An Application of Decision Framing to Product Choice Options," *Journal of Marketing Research,* 37 (May 2000), 187–202.

In contrast, when consumers engage in relatively low levels of thinking during processing (i.e., as in the peripheral process of opinion formation),[93] or when they are in a negative mood state,[94] gain-framed messages are more persuasive. Why? Because the favorable tone of such messages essentially serve as a positive peripheral cue. As we discussed earlier, positive peripheral cues enhance persuasion when thinking is limited during message processing. And for those in a negative mood state, positive-valence stimuli are preferred because of their potential to help the person get out of an undesirable mood state.

Framing is also used to shape consumers' opinions of a product's affordability by reframing a product's total cost into smaller costs over time. One example of this is the **"pennies-a-day" strategy**, which *decomposes a product's price into its cost on a daily basis.*[95] For example, a health club membership that costs $30 a month could be framed as costing one dollar a day. Even though the total cost remains the same, consumer response is not the same. Framing the cost of a magazine subscription on a per-issue price versus a per-year price reportedly increases the number of subscriptions sold by 10–40 percent.[96] Similarly, participants in a research study indicated a greater likelihood of renting a more expensive apartment when they were reminded about how much more they would be paying on a weekly basis. But when they were reminded about how much more they would be paying on a yearly basis, they were less likely to rent the apartment.[97]

Another way of enhancing a product's perceived affordability is by framing its cost in terms of another inexpensive product. For example, a cereal advertisement tells consumers that "for less than the cost of a postage stamp, you can address a bowl of Kellogg's Corn Flakes." This approach to framing a product's cost has produced effects comparable to those achieved by using the pennies-a-day strategy.[98]

### Perceived Scarcity

Consider the consumer watching one of the many shows on cable TV these days selling products that can be purchased on the spot by calling the number on the screen. After a few minutes of viewing, a product appears on the screen that activates the consumer's interest. While debating whether to make the call, a voice announces, "Less than twenty of these items are left in our inventory." The consumer immediately grabs the phone and places an order.

Our hypothetical consumer was propelled to action because the seller successfully created the perception of scarcity by announcing how few of the items remained. According to what's known as the **scarcity effect,** *an object is viewed as more desirable as its perceived scarcity increases.*[99] As we grow up, we learn that valuable objects are often scarce, and that scarce objects are often valuable. Knowledge that an object is scarce may cause it to be seen as more valuable and, consequently, desirable. This effect, in turn, heightens demand.

Support for perceived scarcity's influence on consumer behavior is provided by Jung and Kellaris' recent study. Participants were asked to imagine that they enter a store looking to buy a bottle of wine to give as a gift. Some participants are told that the retailer has only two bottles left of the particular wine they are considering to purchase. Others are told that the retailer has an abundant supply of this wine. Everyone is then told that the shop owner suggests an alternative wine that's actually cheaper. Participants then report their intention to purchase the wine originally being considered. As predicted by the scarcity effect, purchase intentions were significantly greater in the situation where the wine was described as being less plentiful.[100]

Accordingly, providing information about a product's scarcity is another way of shaping consumers' opinions about its desirability. The most obvious way of doing this is to communicate how little of the product is actually available. But this approach may not be the only way. Consider the ad for Laughing Cow cheese that says: "Is the Laughing Cow® shortage driving you crazy? Yeah, us too. We're making 3 times more cheese than we did last year—but there doesn't seem to be enough to go around." Thus, even large amounts of a product may still engender scarcity perceptions by suggesting that consumer demand exceeds product supply.

### Purchase Restrictions

In the late 1970s, the U.S. government reintroduced metal dollars into circulation in the hopes of saving some of the expense incurred by replacing paper dollars, whose average life expectancy is eighteen months. These one dollar coins featured Susan B. Anthony, a pioneer in the women's liberation movement. Yet because this new dollar was very similar in size to a quarter and both had a silver color, concerns over committing transaction errors (i.e., thinking a dollar was a quarter) when money was changing hands severely hampered the coin's acceptance by consumers and retailers. The U.S. Post Office was recruited to help get the new dollars into circulation. Postal clerks were instructed to use the new dollars when making change, but only when people asked for them. Very few did. Then one day an enterprising clerk posted a sign next to his window: "Susan B. Anthony dollars—limit two per customer." People immediately began lining up. One person even asked if he could get back in line and get two more!

Let's move from the post office to the supermarket. Grocers commonly impose purchase restrictions for those items being promoted at a discount price. Shelf tags listing the promotion price also specify a limit on the number of items that can be purchased (e.g., "Limit two per customer"). And just like the restriction conveyed by the postal clerk's sign resulted in increased demand for Susan B. Anthony dollars, the restriction conveyed by a grocer's shelf tag can increase product sales. One analysis of consumers' purchase behavior while grocery shopping over an eighty-week period found that purchase restrictions increased product sales by more than 250 percent.[101]

Think about it. By limiting how much consumers can buy, the grocer actually sold far more product. Why would this happen? Maybe such severe purchase restrictions are interpreted as an indication of product scarcity. Yet as we will discuss shortly, perceived scarcity cannot explain the effectiveness of more relaxed purchase restrictions. Maybe consumers simply interpret the restriction as a signal of the deal's popularity and value without necessarily thinking that there are limited amounts of the product available. They think that the deal is so good that many consumers will purchase and stockpile large amounts of the product unless a restriction is imposed. In either case, purchase restrictions have been shown to shape consumers' opinions of a deal's attractiveness.[102]

Purchase restrictions have been found to work even when they limit the number of items that can be purchased to a number far greater than what consumers would normally buy. This effect is illustrated by a study in which researchers rotated the type of sign placed on supermarket displays of sale-priced Campbell's soups.[103] Sometimes the sign announced "No limit per person." Sometimes the sign stated "Limit of 4 per person." And sometimes the sign stated "Limit of 12 per person." The number of cans bought by consumers as a function of these three signs is presented in Figure 15.22.

As can be seen, the greatest amount of product was purchased when consumers encountered the displays containing a sign restricting them to no more than twelve cans of soup. In this case, sales more than doubled relative to when the sign was absent. And although more cans of soup were sold when the sign restricted purchase to four cans or less compared to when the sign did not impose a purchase restriction, this difference did not reach statistical significance. Note that this pattern of results is

**FIGURE 15.22**  The Influence of Purchase Restrictions on Supermarket Sales of Campbell Soup

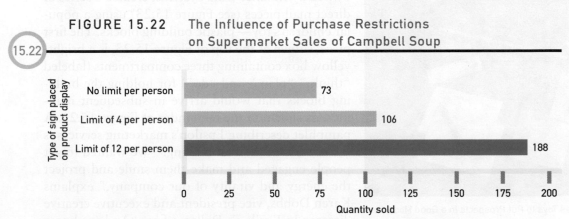

Source: Brian Wansink, Robert J. Kent, and Stephen J. Hoch, "An Anchoring and Adjustment Model of Purchase Quantity Decisions," *Journal of Marketing Research*, 35 (February 1998), 71–81.

CHAPTER 15 [ SHAPING CONSUMERS' OPINIONS

645

difficult to explain from a scarcity perspective. Presumably, consumers would interpret the sign allowing fewer items to be purchased as signaling greater scarcity. If so, greater sales should have been observed when the sign limited purchase to four items than twelve items. Yet just the opposite was found.

What, then, explains why consumers purchased more product when the purchase restriction is more generous in the amount allowed? Apparently, in making their decisions about how much to buy, the maximum number of units identified on purchase restriction signage becomes the starting point, and consumers adjust downwards based on other considerations (such as the deal's attractiveness, budget constraints, and so forth). In the absence of any externally supplied starting point, consumers rely on their "normal" starting point, which in most cases will be relatively low. They then adjust upwards based on other considerations. Because the starting point typically has a powerful influence on where they end up, starting high (such as when the sign limits consumers to twelve items) leads consumers to decide that more should be purchased than starting low.

The use of purchase restrictions is not limited to retailers' signs. It's not uncommon to find similar restrictions imposed by direct marketers attempting to sell their goods through the mail. The U.S. Mint has, on occasion, limited the number of coins or mint sets that can be ordered per household.

## Put Consumers in a Good Mood

In Chapter 10 and previously in this chapter we have acknowledged the benefits of having consumers in a good mood. Happy consumers are more likely to interpret information in a mood-congruent manner, meaning that those processing product information have a greater chance of forming more favorable product opinions when they are in a positive mood state. Given this desirable influence, how might businesses go about putting consumers in that happy frame of mind?

Salespeople have long recognized the usefulness of humor in "warming up" prospects to their sales pitches. Telling a joke or humorous story is an easy way of inducing a more favorable mood state in the consumer. Play is another way. When promoting its services, Epsilon, a relationship marketing firm owned by Alliance Data Systems, created a series of direct mail pieces (see Figure 15.23) using a popular children's toy—plastic building blocks. The first piece, shown at the top of Figure 15.23, is a bright-yellow box containing three compartments (labeled "think," "plan," and "do") for holding the building blocks that would arrive in subsequent mailings, as shown in the remainder of Figure 15.23. A pamphlet describing Epsilon's marketing services is included with the first mailing. "We wanted to get people engaged and make them smile and project the energy and vitality of our company," explains Karen Dobbs, vice president and executive creative director in Epsilon's Dallas office. "And we know that people are always engaged in toys of some

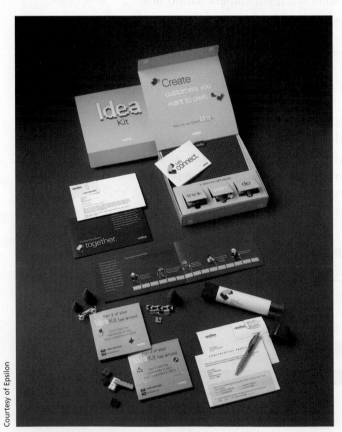

Courtesy of Epsilon

**FIGURE 15.23** Epsilon Uses Toys to Put Prospects in a Good Mood

Source: Paula Andruss, "Lo-Tech DM Pieces Still Draw Customers in Info Age." *Marketing News* (September 1, 2004), 10–11.

manner. We think they [the mailers and building blocks] create such a good feeling that people will be more receptive to hearing what we have to say." [104] Epsilon is mailing between thirty and fifty of the kits each month to the Fortune 1000 companies it has targeted. And the toys certainly seem to be opening doors because 49 percent of recipients have accepted an Epsilon sales call.[105]

## Summary

Shaping consumers' opinions is a fundamental business activity. Sometimes this process requires encouraging consumers to form favorable product opinions, such as when introducing a new product or taking an established product into new markets and making contact with new customers. At other times, this process requires changing previously formed opinions, such as when a product is actually modified or repositioned in efforts to enhance its appeal.

The product opinions formed by consumers depend heavily on what happens during the comprehension stage of information processing. The particular mental categories to which a product is assigned affect these opinions. So do the cognitive and affective responses that occur during processing.

As you have seen in this chapter, there are many different ways and routes to shaping consumers' opinions. Depending on the nature of thinking during opinion formation, stimuli that say something versus stimuli that say nothing about the product and its attributes may be influential during opinion formation. Consistent with the concept of classical conditioning, simple association with the "right" stimuli can cause consumers to form favorable product opinions. And, of course, there are many other ways to encourage favorable opinions. A product's name, its price, its packaging, its advertising, free samples, the way information is framed, purchase restrictions, and creating perceptions of product scarcity can all be used to foster favorable product opinions.

## Review and Discussion Questions

1. Explain how classical conditioning can be used to shape consumers' opinions.

2. What are the central and peripheral processes of opinion formation?

3. Suppose you were faced with the choice between an ad that attempts to create favorable attitudes by making several strong claims about the product and an ad devoid of such claims but filled with attractive visuals and favorable music. How might your preference for a particular ad depend on (a) consumers' involvement at the time of ad exposure, (b) consumers' product knowledge at the time of ad exposure, and (c) the product's performance relative to competition?

4. An advertiser wants to include some well-liked music in its commercials that describe the results of independent laboratory tests that support the product's effectiveness. Do you think this music should occur prior to the product claims, after the product claims, or does it matter where it occurs during the commercial?

5. To determine which of two celebrities should be used as the endorser for an upcoming ad campaign, a company assessed how much target consumers liked each celebrity. Based on these results, one of the celebrities was selected and the campaign was launched. Shortly thereafter, the campaign was withdrawn, because it proved ineffective. Interestingly, when the campaign was reintroduced using the celebrity who was liked less, the campaign was quite effective. How can you explain the greater effectiveness of the less liked endorser?

6. A retailer of computer goods is puzzled by consumers' response to her recent fall sale. There was only one purchase of the $3,000 model (sale priced at $2,750). The $1,000 model (sale priced at $875), despite having only half the $250 savings offered by the more expensive model, sold out. How can you explain these results?

7. In an effort to enhance its product's appeal to younger consumers, a company replaces the celebrity used for many years as its product endorser with a much younger celebrity. To its surprise,

product sales actually declined after the change was made. Why might this have happened?

8. A retailer is trying to decide what level of purchase restriction it should impose during its upcoming sale of a particular product. One school of thought is that a severe restriction should be imposed of limiting shoppers' purchases to one unit per customer. A very different approach would be to set the restriction to a much higher level, such as ten units per customer. How might the relative effectiveness of these two different levels of restriction depend on the product being promoted?

# Notes

[1] Susan Fiske and Mark A. Pavelchak, "Category-Based versus Piecemeal-Based Affective Responses: Developments in Schema-Triggered Affect," in Richard M. Sorrentino and E. Tory Higgins, eds., *The Handbook of Motivation and Cognition: Foundations of Social Behavior* (New York: Guilford, 1986), 167–203. For an application of categorization theory in the context of brand extensions, see Michael J. Barone, Paul W. Miniard, and Jean B. Romeo, "The Influence of Positive Mood on Brand Extension Evaluations," *Journal of Consumer Research*, 26 (March 2000), 387–401.

[2] J. Neher, "Toro Cutting a Wide Swath in Outdoor Appliance Marketing," *Advertising Age* (February 25, 1979), 21.

[3] Robert M. McMath, "Chock Full of (Pea)nuts," *American Demographics* (April 1997), 60.

[4] Robert Johnson, "In the Chips," *Wall Street Journal* (March 22, 1991), B1–B2.

[5] Rachel X. Weissman, "But First, Call Your Drug Company," *American Demographics* (October 1998), 27, 28, 30.

[6] For research on classical conditioning in a product context, see Chris T. Allen and Thomas J. Madden, "A Closer Look at Classical Conditioning," *Journal of Consumer Research*, 12 (December 1985), 301–315; Chris Janiszewski and Luk Warlop, "The Influence of Classical Conditioning Procedures on Subsequent Attention to the Conditioned Brand," *Journal of Consumer Research*, 20 (September 1993), 171–189; Terence A. Shimp, Elnora W. Stuart, and Randall W. Engle, "A Program of Classical Conditioning Experiments Testing Variations in the Conditioned Stimulus and Context," *Journal of Consumer Research*, 18 (June 1991), 1–12; and Elnora W. Stuart, Terence A. Shimp, and Randall W. Engle, "Classical Conditioning of Consumer Attitudes: Four Experiments in an Advertising Context," *Journal of Consumer Research*, 14 (December 1987), 334–349.

[7] Andrew A. Mitchell and Jerry C. Olson, "Are Product Attribute Beliefs the Only Mediators of Advertising Effects on Brand Attitudes?" *Journal of Marketing Research*, 18 (August 1981), 318–332.

[8] Gerald J. Gorn, "The Effects of Music in Advertising on Choice Behavior: A Classical Conditioning Approach," *Journal of Marketing*, 46 (Winter 1982), 94–101.

[9] Paul W. Miniard, Deepak Sirdeshmukh, and Daniel E. Innis, "Peripheral Persuasion and Brand Choice," *Journal of Consumer Research*, 19 (September 1992), 226–239. See also Timothy B. Heath, Michael S. McCarthy, and David L. Mothersbaugh, "Spokesperson Fame and Vividness Effects in the Context of Issue-Relevant Thinking: The Moderating Role of Competitive Setting," *Journal of Consumer Research*, 20 (March 1994), 520–534.

[10] Heather Chaplin, "Centrum's Self-Inflicted Silver Bullet," *American Demographics* (March 1999), 68–69.

[11] Richard E. Petty and John T. Cacioppo, *Communication and Persuasion: Central and Peripheral Routes to Attitude Change* (New York: Springer-Verlag, 1986); Richard E. Petty and John T. Cacioppo, "The Elaboration Likelihood Model of Persuasion," in Leonard Berkowitz, ed., *Advances in Experimental Social Psychology*, 19 (New York: Academic Press, 1986), 123–205. A similar conceptualization is offered by Shelly Chaiken, "Heuristic versus Systematic Information Processing and the Use of Source versus Message Cues in Persuasion," *Journal of Personality and Social Psychology*, 39 (November 1980), 752–766. See also Alice H. Eagly and Shelly Chaiken, *The Psychology of Attitudes* (Fort Worth, TX: Harcourt Brace Jovanovich, 1993).

[12] Paul W. Miniard, Sunil Bhatla, Kenneth R. Lord, Peter R. Dickson, and H. Rao Unnava, "Picture-Based Persuasion Processes and the Moderating Role of Involvement," *Journal of Consumer Research*, 18 (June 1991), 92–107.

[13] Ibid.

[14] Interest in attitude toward advertisements was largely sparked by the following two articles: Mitchell and Olson, "Are Product Attribute Beliefs the Only Mediators of Advertising Effects on Brand Attitudes?" and Terence Shimp, "Attitude toward the Ad as a Mediator of Consumer Brand Choice," *Journal of Advertising*, 10 (1981), 9–15. Also see Stephen P. Brown and Douglas M. Stayman, "Antecedents and Consequences of Attitude toward the Ad: A Meta-Analysis," *Journal of Consumer Research*, 19 (June 1992), 34–51; Scott B. MacKenzie, Richard J. Lutz, and George E. Belch, "The Role of Attitude toward the Ad as a Mediator of Advertising Effectiveness: A Test of Competing Explanations," *Journal of Marketing Research*, 23 (May 1986), 130–143; Paul W. Miniard, Sunil Bhatla, and Randall L. Rose, "On the Formation and Relationship of Ad and

Brand Attitudes: An Experimental and Causal Analysis," *Journal of Marketing Research,* 27 (August 1990), 290–303.

15 Miniard, Bhatla, Lord, Dickson, and Unnava, "Picture-Based Persuasion Processes and the Moderating Role of Involvement."

16 Jerome S. Bruner and A. Leigh Minturn, "Perceptual Identification and Perceptual Organization," *Journal of General Psychology,* 53 (July 1955), 21–28.

17 Young-Won Ha and Stephen J. Hoch, "Ambiguity, Processing Strategy, and Advertising Evidence Interactions," *Journal of Consumer Research,* 16 (December 1989), 354–360.

18 Brian Wansink and Se-Bum Park, "Sensory Suggestiveness and Labeling: Do Soy Labels Bias Taste?" *Journal of Sensory Studies,* 17 (November 2002), 483–491.

19 Frederick Rose and John R. Emshwiller, "Guess, Coolness Fading, Plans Sultry Ads," *Wall Street Journal* (November 19, 1997), B8.

20 Dana James, "Rejuvenating Mature Brands Can Be Stimulating Exercise," *Marketing News* (August 16, 1999), 16–17.

21 "Chattanooga Attraction Gets Revamped Image," *Marketing News* (September 14, 1998), 33.

22 Lisa Granatstein, "Attitude Change," *Mediaweek* (October 4, 2004), 37.

23 Greg Johnson, "Dewing It," *Miami Herald* (October 22, 1999), C1, C4.

24 Albert J. Della Bitta and Kent B. Monroe, "A Multivariate Analysis of the Perception of Value from Retail Price Advertisements," in Kent B. Monroe, ed., *Advances in Consumer Research,* 8 (Ann Arbor, MI: Association for Consumer Research, 1980), 161–165.

25 Chenghuan Wu and David R. Shaffer, "Susceptibility to Persuasive Appeals as a Function of Source Credibility and Prior Experience with the Attitude Object," *Journal of Personality and Social Psychology,* 52 (April 1987), 677–688. See also Lawrence J. Marks and Michael A. Kamins, "The Use of Product Sampling and Advertising: Effects of Sequence of Exposure and Degree of Advertising Claim Exaggeration on Consumers' Belief Strength, Belief Confidence, and Attitudes," *Journal of Marketing Research,* 25 (August 1988), 266–281; Robert E. Smith and William R. Swinyard, "Attitude-Behavior Consistency: The Impact of Product Trial versus Advertising," *Journal of Marketing Research,* 20 (August 1983), 257–267.

26 Ian P. Murphy, "All-American Icon Gets a New Look," *Marketing News* (August 18, 1997), 6.

27 Micheline Maynard, "Wrapping a Familiar Name around a New Product," *New York Times* (May 22, 2004), C1.

28 Johnson, "Dewing It."

29 Ralph I. Allison and Kenneth P. Uhl, "Influence of Beer Brand Identification on Taste Perception," *Journal of Marketing Research,* 1 (August 1964), 36–39. For a demonstration of the importance of brand name in car buying, see Mary W. Sullivan, "How Brand Names Affect the Demand for Twin Automobiles," *Journal of Marketing Research,* 35 (May 1998), 154–165.

30 C. Whan Park, Sung Youl Jun, and Allan D. Shocker, "Composite Branding Alliances: An Investigation of Extension and Feedback Effects," *Journal of Marketing Research,* 33 (November 1996), 453–466.

31 "Fertilizer by Any Other Name Doesn't Sell as Well, by Jiminy," *The State* (September 28, 1991), A9.

32 Richard R. Klink, "Creating Brand Names with Meaning: The Use of Sound Symbolism," *Marketing Letters,* 11 (February 2000), 5–20; Richard R. Klink, "Creating Meaningful New Brand Names: A Study of Semantics and Sound Symbolism," *Journal of Marketing: Theory and Practice,* 9 (Spring 2001), 27–34; Eric Yorkston and Getta Menon, "A Sound Idea: Phonetic Effects of Brand Names on Consumer Judgments," *Journal of Consumer Research,* 31 (June 2004), 43–51.

33 Katy McLaughlin, "Shrimp Gets a Makeover, As Foreign Imports Rise; US Fishermen Try Giving Prawns Regional Identities; The 'Iodine-y Aftertaste,'" *Wall Street Journal* (August 19, 2004), D1.

34 Brian Wansink, James Painter, and Koert Van Ittersum, "Descriptive Menu Labels' Effect on Sales," *Cornell Hotel and Restaurant Administration Quarterly,* 42 (December 2001), 68–72. Also see Brian Wansink, Koert Van Ittersum, and James Painter, "How Descriptive Food Names Bias Sensory Perceptions in Restaurants," *Food Quality and Preference,* 16 (2005), 393–400.

35 Priya Raghubir and Aradhna Krishna, "Vital Dimensions in Volume Perception: Can the Eye Fool the Stomach?" *Journal of Marketing Research,* 36 (August 1999), 313–326.

36 Ibid.

37 Valerie Folkes and Shashi Matta, "The Effect of Package Shape on Consumers' Judgments of Product Volume: Attention as a Mental Contaminant," *Journal of Consumer Research,* 31 (September 2004), 390–401.

38 Ibid.

39 "Branding & Colour: The Colour of Money," *Brand Strategy* (October 6, 2004), 24–27.

40 Ibid.

41 Paul Glader and Christopher Lawton, "Beer and Wine Makers Use Fancy Cans to Court New Fans," *Wall Street Journal* (August 24, 2004), B1.

42 Ibid.

43 "Branding & Colour: The Colour of Money."

44 Sally Beatty, "Gateway 2000 Plans Shorter Name, Longer Client Talks and No Cows," *Wall Street Journal* (April 24, 1998), B6.

45 Arundhati Parmar, "Marketers Ask: Hues on First?" *Marketing News* (February 15, 2004), 8, 10.

46 Randall Lane, "Does Orange Mean Cheap?" *Forbes* (December 23, 1991), 144–146.

47 Gerald J. Gorn, Amitava Chattopadhyay, Jaideep Sengupta, and Shashank Tripathi, "Waiting for the Web: How Screen Color Affects Time Perception," *Journal of*

*Marketing Research*, 41 (May 2004), 215–225.

[48] For a concise review of this literature, see Keith S. Coulter, "Odd-Ending Price Underestimation: An Experimental Examination of Left-to-Right Processing Effects," *Journal of Product & Brand Management*, 10 (2001), 276–292.

[49] See, for example, Joel E. Urbany, William O. Bearden, and Dan C. Weilbaker, "The Effect of Plausible and Exaggerated Reference Prices on Consumer Perceptions and Price Search," *Journal of Consumer Research*, 15 (June 1988), 95–110.

[50] Nikhil Deogun, "Coca-Cola Plans Splashy Rollout of Citrus Soda," *Wall Street Journal* (December 16, 1996), B1, B11.

[51] Scott Hensley, Jeanne Whalen, and Leila Abboud, "Demand Lags for Viagra and Its Rivals," *Wall Street Journal* (January 11, 2005), B1.

[52] J. S. Johar and Joseph Sirgy, "Value-Expressive versus Utilitarian Advertising Appeals: When and Why to Use Which Appeal," *Journal of Advertising*, 20 (September 1991), 23–33. See also C. Whan Park, Bernard J. Jaworski, and Deborah J. MacInnis, "Strategic Brand Concept-Image Management," *Journal of Marketing*, 50 (October 1986), 135–145; Mark Snyder and Kenneth G. DeBono, "Appeals to Image and Claims about Quality: Understanding the Psychology of Advertising," *Journal of Personality and Social Psychology*, 49 (March 1985), 586–597.

[53] David Olson, "The Characteristics of High-Trial New-Product Advertising," *Journal of Advertising Research*, 25 (October/November 1985), 11–16.

[54] Although stronger claims generally produce more favorable opinions than weaker claims, there may be situations in which weaker claims are actually better. For a demonstration of this, see Marvin E. Goldberg and Jon Hartwick, "The Effects of Advertiser Reputation and Extremity of Advertising Claim on Advertising Effectiveness," *Journal of Consumer Research*, 17 (September 1990), 172–179.

[55] Dhruv Grewal, Sukumar Kavanoor, Edward F. Fern, Carolyn Costley, and James Barnes, "Comparative versus Noncomparative Advertising: A Meta-Analysis," *Journal of Marketing*, 61 (October 1997), 1–15; Paul W. Miniard, Randall L. Rose, Michael J. Barone, and Kenneth C. Manning, "On the Need for Relative Measures When Assessing Comparative Advertising Effects," *Journal of Advertising*, 22 (September 1993), 41–58; Paul W. Miniard, Randall L. Rose, Kenneth C. Manning, and Michael J. Barone, "Tracking the Effects of Comparative and Noncomparative Advertising with Relative and Nonrelative Measures: A Further Examination of the Framing Correspondence Hypothesis," *Journal of Business Research*, 41 (February 1998), 137–143; Randall L. Rose, Paul W. Miniard, Michael J. Barone, Kenneth C. Manning, and Brian D. Till, "When Persuasion Goes Undetected: The Case of Comparative Advertising," *Journal of Marketing Research*, 30 (August 1993), 315–330.

[56] James M. Munch, Gregory W. Boller, and John L. Swasy, "The Effects of Argument Structure and Affective Tagging on Product Attitude Formation," *Journal of Consumer Research*, 20 (September 1993), 294–302.

[57] Cyndee Miller, "Demonstrating Your Point: Showing How the Product Works Adds Authenticity," *Marketing News* (September 13, 1993), 2.

[58] Gary T. Ford, Darlene B. Smith, and John L. Swasy, "Consumer Skepticism of Advertising Claims: Testing Hypotheses from Economics of Information," *Journal of Consumer Research*, 16 (March 1990), 433–441.

[59] See William K. Darley and Robert E. Smith, "Advertising Claim Objectivity: Antecedents and Effects," *Journal of Marketing*, 57 (October 1993), 100–113; Julie A. Edell and Richard Staelin, "The Information Processing of Pictures in Print Advertisements," *Journal of Consumer Research*, 10 (June 1983), 45–61; Ford, Smith, and Swasy, "Consumer Skepticism of Advertising Claims"; and Morris B. Holbrook, "Beyond Attitude Structure: Toward the Informational Determinants of Attitude," *Journal of Marketing Research*, 15 (November 1978), 545–556.

[60] Richard E. Petty and John T. Cacioppo, "The Effects of Involvement on Responses to Argument Quantity and Quality: Central and Peripheral Routes to Persuasion," *Journal of Personality and Social Psychology*, 46 (January 1984), 69–81. See also Joseph W. Alba and Howard Marmorstein, "The Effects of Frequency Knowledge on Consumer Decision Making," *Journal of Consumer Research*, 14 (June 1987), 14–25.

[61] Val Larsen, David Luna, and Laura A. Peracchio, "Points of View and Pieces of Time: A Taxonomy of Image Attributes," *Journal of Consumer Research*, 31 (June 2004), 102–111; Laura A. Peracchio and Joan Meyers-Levy, "How Ambiguous Cropped Objects and Ad Photos Can Affect Product Evaluations," *Journal of Consumer Research*, 21 (June 1994), 190–205.

[62] Joan Meyers-Levy and Laura A. Peracchio, "Getting an Angle in Advertising: The Effect of Camera Angle on Product Evaluation," *Journal of Marketing Research*, 29 (November 1992), 454–461.

[63] Terry L. Childers and Jeffrey Jass, "All Dressed Up with Something to Say: Effects of Typeface Semantic Associations on Brand Perceptions and Consumer Memory," *Journal of Consumer Psychology*, 12 (2002), 93–106; Pamela W. Henderson, Joan L. Giese, and Joseph A. Cote, "Impression Management Using Typeface Design," *Journal of Marketing*, 68 (October 2004), 60–72; Michael S. McCarthy and David L. Mothersbaugh, "Effects of Typographic Factors and Advertising-Based Persuasion: A General Model and Initial Empirical Test," *Psychology and Marketing*, 19 (July–August 2002), 663–691.

[64] Childers and Jass, "All Dressed Up with Something to Say."

[65] Tony Spaeth, "Powerbrands," *Across the Board*, 36 (1999), 23–28.

[66] Jeffery S. Solochek, "Shoe Shoppers Take Over Tampa, Fla., Mall," *St. Petersburg Times* (December 23, 2004), 1.

67 Courtland Milloy, "Selling Sneakers Violating Young Minds," *Washington Post* (March 2, 2005), B1.

68 "Michael Jordan Remains Nation's Favorite Sports Star, Closely Followed by Peyton Manning and Tiger Woods," Harris Interactive, The Harris Poll, www.harrisinteractive.com (March 2, 2005).

69 Robin Givhan, "$75 Million! Smell of Cash Rising Quickly from Jordan Fragrance," *Miami Herald* (May 22, 1997), F5.

70 Matthew W. Evans, "Jordan's 3rd Scent is a 23," *WWD* (February 4, 2005), 15.

71 For recent research on this meaning transfer, see Rajeev Batra and Pamela Miles Homer, "The Situational Impact of Brand Image Beliefs," *Journal of Consumer Psychology*, 14 (2004), 318–330.

72 Suzanne Vranica, "Tic Tac Maker Hopes Fresh Face Breathes New Life into Campaign," *Wall Street Journal* (December 13, 1999), B25.

73 James Tenser, "Endorser Qualities Count More Than Ever," *Advertising Age* (November 8, 2004), S2–S3.

74 Robert Garfield, "TD Waterhouse Makes Trade with Celebs," *Advertising Age* (November 29, 1999), 79.

75 Michael A. Kamins, "An Investigation into the 'Match-Up Hypothesis' in Celebrity Advertising: When Beauty Only May Be Skin Deep," *Journal of Advertising*, 19 (1990), 4–13.

76 Annys Shin, "With Armstrong, Discovery Puts Marketing on Wheels; Star Power, Global Reach Cited in Sponsorship Deal," *Washington Post* (January 27, 2005), T26.

77 "PepsiCo Pulls Ad by Rap Musician," *New York Times* (August 29, 2002), C8.

78 For a general review, see Brian Sternthal, Lynn Phillips, and Ruby Dholakia, "The Persuasive Effect of Source Credibility: A Situational Analysis," *Public Opinion Quarterly*, 42 (Fall 1978), 285–314. See also Danny L. Moore, Douglas Hausknecht, and Kanchana Thamodaran, "Time Compression, Response Opportunity, and Persuasion," *Journal of Consumer Research*, 13 (June 1986), 85–99; S. Ratneshwar and Shelly

Chaiken, "Comprehension's Role in Persuasion: The Case of Its Moderating Effect on the Persuasive Impact of Source Cues," *Journal of Consumer Research*, 18 (June 1991), 52–62; Arch G. Woodside and J. William Davenport Jr., "The Effect of Salesman Similarity and Expertise on Consumer Purchasing Behavior," *Journal of Marketing Research*, 11 (May 1974), 198–202; Chenghuan Wu and David R. Shaffer, "Susceptibility to Persuasive Appeals as a Function of Source Credibility and Prior Experience with the Attitude Object," *Journal of Personality and Social Psychology*, 52 (April 1987), 677–688. We should note that less credible sources on occasion induce more persuasion. See Robert R. Harmon and Kenneth A. Coney, "The Persuasive Effects of Source Credibility in Buy and Lease Situations," *Journal of Marketing Research*, 19 (May 1982), 255–260; and Brian Sternthal, Ruby Dholakia, and Clark Leavitt, "The Persuasive Effect of Source Credibility: Tests of Cognitive Response," *Journal of Consumer Research*, 4 (March 1978), 252–260.

79 Michael J. Baker and Gilbert A. Churchill Jr., "The Impact of Physically Attractive Models on Advertising Evaluations," *Journal of Marketing Research*, 14 (November 1977), 538–555; Shelly Chaiken, "Communicator Physical Attractiveness and Persuasion," *Journal of Personality and Social Psychology*, 37 (August 1979), 752–766; Lynn R. Kahle and Pamela M. Homer, "Physical Attractiveness of the Celebrity Endorser: A Social Adaptation Perspective," *Journal of Consumer Research*, 11 (March 1985), 954–961.

80 Kahle and Homer, "Physical Attractiveness of the Celebrity Endorser."

81 Richard E. Petty, John T. Cacioppo, and David Schumann, "Central and Peripheral Routes to Advertising Effectiveness: The Moderating Role of Involvement," *Journal of Consumer Research*, 10 (September 1983), 135–146.

82 Karen-Janine Cohen, "Scent of Success Britney Spears Tie-in Helps Rejuvenate Elizabeth Arden," *South Florida Sun-Sentinel* (December 23, 2004), D1.

83 Nat Ives, "A Second Scent Is Hitched to the Fortunes of a Hollywood Star," *New York Times* (July 23, 2003), C8.

84 James Tenser, "Endorser Qualities Count More Than Ever," *Advertising Age* (November 8, 2004), S2–S3.

85 Stuart Elliot, "Hanes Revives and Adapts a Successful Campaign from the 90's," *New York Times* (February 24, 2005), C7.

86 Christopher Rowland, "Reebok Rolls Out Marketing Drive," *Boston Globe* (February 10, 2005), 1.

87 Brian Steinberg, "This Carmen Is a Three-Way Act; Multiple Ad Campaigns Bring Risk of Overexposure of Ms. Electra as Endorser," *Wall Street Journal* (September 28, 2004), B5.

88 Irwin P. Levin and Gary J. Gaeth, "How Consumers Are Affected by the Framing of Attribute Information Before and After Consuming the Product," *Journal of Consumer Research*, 15 (December 1988), 374–378.

89 Lauren G. Block and Punam Keller, "When to Accentuate the Negative: The Effects of Perceived Efficacy and Message Framing on Intentions to Perform a Health-Related Behavior," *Journal of Marketing Research*, 32 (May 1995), 192–203; Rajesh K. Chandy, Gerard J. Tellis, Deborah J. MacInnis, and Pattana Thaivanich, "What to Say When: Advertising Appeals in Evolving Markets," *Journal of Marketing Research*, 38 (November 2001), 399–414; Punam Anand Keller, Isaac M. Lipkus, and Barbara K. Rimer, "Affect, Framing, and Persuasion," *Journal of Marketing Research*, 40 (February 2003), 54–64; Durairaj Maheswaran and Joan Myers-Levy, "The Influence of Message Framing and Issue Involvement," *Journal of Marketing Research*, 27 (August 1990), 361–367; Alexander J. Rothman and Peter Salovey, "Shaping Perceptions to Motivate Healthy Behavior: The Role of Message Framing," *Psychological Bulletin*, 121 (1997), 3–19; Baba Shiv, Julie A. Edell Britton, and John W. Payne, "Does Elaboration Increase or Decrease the Effectiveness of Negatively versus Positively

Framed Messages?" *Journal of Consumer Research,* 31 (June 2004), 199–208; Baba Shiv, Julie A. Edell, and John W. Payne, "Factors Affecting the Impact of Negatively versus Positively Framed Ad Messages," *Journal of Consumer Research,* 24 (December 1997), 285–294.

90 Amos Tversky and Daniel Kahneman, "Loss Aversion in Riskless Choice: A Reference-Dependent Model," *Quarterly Journal of Economics,* 106 (November 1991), 1039–1061.

91 Block and Keller, "When to Accentuate the Negative"; Maheswaran and Myers-Levy, "The Influence of Message Framing and Issue Involvement"; Shiv, Britton, and Payne, "Does Elaboration Increase or Decrease the Effectiveness of Negatively versus Positively Framed Messages?"

92 Keller, Lipkus, and Rimer, "Affect, Framing, and Persuasion."

93 Maheswaran and Myers-Levy, "The Influence of Message Framing and Issue Involvement"; Shiv, Britton, and Payne, "Does Elaboration Increase or Decrease the Effectiveness of Negatively versus Positively Framed Messages?"

94 Keller, Lipkus, and Rimer, "Affect, Framing, and Persuasion."

95 John T. Gourville, "Pennies-a-Day: The Effect of Temporal Reframing on Transaction Evaluation," *Journal of Consumer Research,* 24 (March 1998), 395–408. See also John T. Gourville, "The Effect of

Implicit versus Explicit Comparisons on Temporal Pricing Claims," *Marketing Letters,* 10 (May 1999), 113–124.

96 Ibid.

97 Paul C. Price, "Installment Training: The Mental Aggregation and Disaggregation of Monetary Cost over Time," poster presented at the annual meeting of the Society for Judgment and Decision Making, St. Louis (November 13, 1994), as cited in Gourville, "Pennies-a-Day."

98 Gourville, "The Effect of Implicit versus Explicit Comparisons on Temporal Pricing Claims."

99 For research on scarcity effect, see Laura A. Brannon and Timothy C. Brock, "Limiting Time for Responding Enhances Behavior Corresponding to the Merits of Compliance Appeals: Refutations of Heuristic-Cue Theory in Service and Consumer Settings," *Journal of Consumer Psychology,* 10 (May 2001), 135–146; Laura A. Brannon and Timothy C. Brock, "Scarcity Claims Elicit Extreme Responding to Persuasive Messages: Role of Cognitive Elaboration," *Personality & Social Psychology Bulletin,* 27 (March 2001), 365–375; Jae Min Jung and James J. Kellaris, "Cross-National Differences in Proneness to Scarcity Effects: The Moderating Roles of Familiarity, Uncertainty Avoidance, and Need for Cognitive Closure," *Psychology and Marketing,* 21 (September 2004), 739–753; Michael Lynn, "Scarcity Effects on Desirability: Mediated by

Assumed Expensiveness?" *Journal of Economic Psychology,* 10 (June 1989), 257–274; Michael Lynn, "Scarcity Effects on Value: A Quantitative Review of the Commodity Theory Literature," *Psychology and Marketing,* 8 (Spring 1991), 43–57; Soo-Jiuan Tan and Seow Hwang Chua, "'While Stocks Last!' Impact of Framing on Consumers' Perception of Sales Promotions," *Journal of Consumer Marketing,* 21 (2004), 343–355; Theo M. M. Verhallen and Henry S. J. Robben, "Scarcity and Preference: An Experiment on Unavailability and Product Evaluation," *Journal of Economic Psychology,* 15 (June 1994), 315–331.

100 Jung and Kellaris, "Cross-National Differences in Proneness to Scarcity Effects."

101 J. Jeffrey Inman, Anil C. Peter, and Priya Raghubir, "Framing the Deal: The Role of Restrictions in Accentuating Deal Value," *Journal of Consumer Research,* 24 (June 1997), 68–79.

102 Ibid.

103 Brian Wansink, Robert J. Kent, and Stephen J. Hoch, "An Anchoring and Adjustment Model of Purchase Quantity Decisions," *Journal of Marketing Research,* 35 (February 1998), 71–81.

104 Paula Andruss, "Lo-Tech DM Pieces Still Draw Customers in Info Age," *Marketing News* (September 1, 2004), 10–11.

105 Ibid.

# Chapter 16

# Helping Consumers to Remember

## Opening Vignette

"Super heavy duty" AA batteries sell four for about a dollar at Wal*Mart. Sounds like a deal? Depends on who you ask. The Gillette Company, maker of the nation's top-selling Duracell brand, recently launched an aggressive advertising campaign to tell consumers that, despite the impressive-sounding name, so-called heavy-duty batteries go dead much faster than their more-expensive alkaline counterparts. "Why do you think they are so cheap?" asks the text of a Gillette advertisement appearing in newspapers and magazines. Pictured in the ads are heavy-duty batteries made by Energizer, under the Eveready brand, and by Rayovac.

"The consumer is being, in effect, duped by the nomenclature," says Mark Leckie, Duracell's president. Duracell's signature black-and-copper batteries, the most expensive alkaline batteries on the market, cost an average of $3.25 for a pack of four AAs. That's a little more than triple the price at Wal*Mart, but the batteries will last four times longer, according to Gillette. At Energizer, spokeswoman Jacqueline Burwitz acknowledges that the old-fashioned heavy-duty battery is a "very inferior product" and is substantially outperformed by both Duracell and Energizer's own alkaline batteries. Promotions of Eveready in Wal*Mart and Target were done in response to Rayovac's marketing of its own heavy-duty brand. The promotions were "more about protecting our brand," says the spokeswoman.

Driven by demand from bargain-hunting consumers, heavy-duty batteries capture about 10 percent of the U.S. market, up from 7 percent just a few years ago, according to Gillette. Gillette, which doesn't sell heavy-duty batteries in the United States, is now scrambling to combat its rivals' newfound popularity. The company's newest ads underscore a central problem for the industry: shoppers really can't tell batteries apart. After all, batteries are designed to be interchangeable, and few people keep track of how many months pass before the remote control goes cold. As a result, consumers usually snap up cheap batteries or load up when they go on sale or when they are sold in less-profitable jumbo packs. Consumers want bargains, not necessarily high quality, when it comes to batteries. The problem is most acute for Gillette, best known for its razors but which in 2003 rang up $2.02 billion, or 22 percent of its $9.25 billion in revenue, from battery sales.

Gillette's recent television and print advertising campaign, called "Trusted Everywhere," tries to fight that urge by showing people using batteries in critical situations: rescue workers scouting for lost hikers with battery-powered headlamps; and Jon Bon Jovi in concert, crooning into a battery-operated microphone in front of a stadium crowd. The suggestion is that

Duracell's batteries will be working when you need them. "Unless we are continually educating consumers about the difference," Mr. Leckie says, "they tend to forget over time."

---

The difference between various types of batteries is not the only thing consumers tend to forget. Have you ever returned from grocery shopping and suddenly realized that you forgot to buy something that you needed and had intended to purchase? Hasn't everybody? Nor is this forgetting limited to supermarket products. Failure to remember is a recurring theme of consumer behavior. We often forget that it's time for our car's next oil change or our teeth's next cleaning. Each time a consumer forgets to buy something, some company has lost a sales opportunity.

Or maybe the problem is not one of remembering to buy, but rather remembering who to buy from. A consumer may have been very pleased with the work done by a repair person a few years ago and now wants to use this same person again because a new need for his services has arisen. Unfortunately, the consumer can no longer remember his name or the name of his business.

This failure to remember extends to product consumption as well. How many times have you forgotten to watch some television program that you wanted to see? Many people who take medications often forget that it's time for their next pill.[1] The orange juice industry discovered that many purchasers forget about the juice in their refrigerator.[2] And the less often products such as medications and orange juice are consumed, the less often they need to be purchased, which means fewer sales at the cash register.

Even when consumers do remember to make purchase and consumption decisions, memory and what's remembered from it can still play an important role during the decision-making process. You might recall from Chapter 4 our coverage of the consideration set and how consumers' ability to remember choice alternatives (called the retrieval set) often determines whether these alternatives gain entry into the consideration set. Products that are not retrieved from memory won't be considered when making choices unless they're physically present during decision making. Thus, when consideration sets are formed from memory, simply increasing the likelihood that a brand is remembered can significantly enhance its chances of being chosen.[3]

Similarly, what's remembered about the alternatives receiving consideration initially may determine what receives consideration subsequently. Consider the process of buying a home. Initially, people usually search a number of homes for sale prior to purchase. They may then narrow the field down to a handful of homes for a second round of visits. In many cases, whether a home makes the cut depends on what the person remembers about the home. For this reason, some realtors recommend to their clients that they bring a camera to take pictures during house hunting trips. Polaroid snapshots are particularly attractive because their margins provide space for writing notes. Interior decorators recognize the importance of creating "memory points" when decorating a builder's model homes. These memory points help a model stand out and become memorable. One decorator, for example, used a barnyard motif in a room with a sensor that triggered barnyard noises when someone entered the room.[4]

Unless consumers are judging choice alternatives using information physically in front of them, evaluations of the considered alternatives depends completely on what's retrieved from memory. Maybe overall evaluations previously formed about the choice alternatives are retrieved and compared when making the decision (see Chapter 4). Or maybe the decision is made based on what is remembered about the alternatives' attributes. In either case, what's remembered determines what's chosen.[5] What's remembered can also determine where the purchase will be made. Imagine two individuals looking to buy a television. The first person goes to the closest store and buys the TV judged best for the money. The other person goes to the same store and buys nothing because he remembers seeing an advertisement in which the TV most attractive to him is available for a lower price at a competitor's store.

Helping consumers remember is also useful for enhancing advertising effectiveness in several ways. First, to the extent that advertising effects extend over time, consumers' memory becomes a more important determinant of advertising effectiveness. To illustrate, consider a commercial that attempts to get consumers to order the advertised product by phone. If this commercial's influence is limited to only those who call while the ad is being aired, it doesn't matter much whether consumers remember the product and phone number later on. But their memory for such information would be important if advertising had the ability to motivate action hours or even days later. So does it?

Indeed it does. In fact, advertising's influence may actually become stronger as time passes. A compelling demonstration of this was provided recently in a field experiment conducted by Continental Airlines and DoubleClick. The experiment, which involved millions of consumers, manipulated whether they were exposed to online advertising for Continental.[6] Figure 16.1 shows the increases observed in ticket purchases among those who saw the online ad relative to the control group (i.e., those who were not exposed to the online ad) as a function of how much time had elapsed since ad exposure. As can be seen, the increase in ticket buying observed one hour after viewing the ad is but a fraction of the increase found weeks later. The existence of such long-term advertising

**FIGURE 16.1**    Advertising's Long-Term Effects Underscore the Value of Helping Consumers to Remember

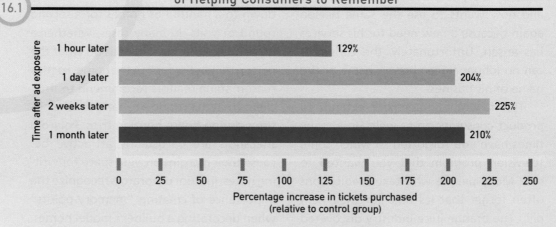

Percentage increase in tickets purchased (relative to control group)

Source: Kris Oser, "Web Ads Get Results Weeks Later," *Advertising Age,* 75 (July 26, 2004), 18.

effects underscores the value of helping consumers remember the appropriate information until they choose to act upon it.

Another way stimulating consumers' memory can facilitate advertising effectiveness is through the use of **nostalgia advertising appeals,** which *attempt to persuade by evoking positive memories of the past.* These memories may be of one's own personal experiences, such as a high school prom or a childhood Christmas. Nostalgic memories can be activated by objects or people strongly associated with the past.[7] During the 2005 Super Bowl, a number of advertisers incorporated nostalgic elements into their advertisements, including music (e.g., the Bee Gees hit, "Stayin' Alive," from the 1977 film *Saturday Night Fever*) and stars (e.g., Gladys Knight, Burt Reynolds, MC Hammer) from yesteryear.[8] Nostalgia appeals also encompass references to times before the person was born. Though nostalgia advertising appeals come in many forms, they share the common objective of encouraging consumers to remember something positive from the past. Why? Because the positive thoughts and feelings attached to such memories may then be transferred to the product opinions held after ad processing, thereby enhancing consumers' product opinions.[9] And in some cases, advertising may focus on activating the consumer's memory of past consumption experiences. An ad for Cap'n Crunch cereal showed a picture of an adult holding a bowl of the cereal with the headline "Taste Buds Never Forget." In so doing, the company hopes that past users will recall favorable memories of eating the cereal and decide to try it again.

For these reasons, businesses' best interests usually lie in helping consumers to remember. This chapter considers how to improve consumers' ability to remember. But first, we need to cover some background material that will provide you with a better understanding of the task faced by businesses. Remembering consists of two basic processes: cognitive learning (getting information into long-term memory) and retrieval (pulling it back out).

## Cognitive Learning

In Chapter 14, we covered cognitive capacity and the distinction between short-term memory (where thinking and interpretation occurs) and long-term memory (the mental warehouse in which knowledge resides). **Cognitive learning** occurs *when information processed in short-term memory is stored in long-term memory.* Obviously, how well something can be remembered depends on how well it was learned to begin with. After all, you can't remember something you don't know! So what determines cognitive learning? Rehearsal and elaboration are two key factors.

### Rehearsal

**Rehearsal** *involves the mental repetition of information or, more formally, the recycling of information through short-term memory.* Some people describe rehearsal as a form of inner speech.

Rehearsal serves two main functions. First, it allows for the maintenance of information in short-term memory. An example is when we mentally repeat a telephone number that we looked up just long enough for us to dial the number. Rehearsal is undertaken to keep the information activated long enough for the person to dial the number. The second function of rehearsal involves the transfer of information from short-term memory to long-term memory. Greater rehearsal increases the strength of the long-term memory trace, thereby enhancing the likelihood that the trace can be later retrieved.

### Elaboration

The amount of **elaboration** *(the degree of integration between the stimulus and existing knowledge)* that occurs during processing influences the amount of learning that takes place. At low levels of elaboration, a stimulus is processed in much the same form in which it's encountered. For example, a person wanting to remember a license plate numbered AJN268 might encode this stimulus without any elaboration by simply repeating "A-J-N-2-6-8."

A more elaborate encoding of this license plate number could involve rearranging the letters into the name JAN, adding the numbers (which total sixteen), and then visualizing a sixteen-year-old girl named Jan. This, in fact, was what a person reported doing in an effort to remember the license number of a car he witnessed leaving the scene of a bank robbery. After realizing he had seen the getaway car, he telephoned the police and gave them the license number. The suspects were apprehended, and he received the reward money offered for information leading to their arrest.

Greater elaboration generally leads to greater learning.[10] The more a person elaborates on a piece of information (or the more "deeply" it is processed), the greater the number of linkages formed between the new information and information already stored in memory. This, in turn, increases the number of avenues or paths by which the information can be retrieved from memory. In essence, the memory trace becomes more accessible given the greater number of pathways (linkages) available for retrieval. Many of the techniques suggested by memory experts and performers for increasing one's ability to learn and remember new information rely on the benefits of elaboration.[11]

The amount of elaboration that occurs during information processing depends on the person's motivation and ability to do so.[12] Each is discussed next.

## MOTIVATION

A person's motivational state at the time of exposure to new information has a considerable influence on what's learned. Sometimes people *deliberately try to learn so that they can later remember* the information, as might be the case for the student reading this text in preparation for a forthcoming exam or someone trying to absorb and remember a salesperson's suggestions on what to look for when buying the product. Such learning is called **intentional learning.**

Of course, sometimes we learn even when we're not trying. If you read this morning's newspaper or watched the news on television, you probably learned a thing or two even though this was not your intention. *Learning that occurs despite the absence of the intention to do so* is called **incidental learning.** As one would expect, learning is greater when it's intentional than incidental.[13]

## ABILITY

Knowledge is an important determinant of learning because it enables the person to undertake more meaningful elaboration during information processing. In a classic study of how prior knowledge enhances learning, chess masters and novices were shown chess games in progress.[14] Masters generally held a substantial advantage over novices in remembering the board positions of the chess pieces. Interestingly, this superiority disappeared when subjects were exposed to games in which the pieces were organized randomly. Thus, the beneficial effect of knowledge materialized only when the information conformed to the expert's knowledge structures and expectations (i.e., when the pieces' placement "made sense").

Even when knowledge is high, ability may be low. This is because the ability to learn depends on both individual and environmental factors.[15] A knowledgeable person may be unable to engage in much elaboration of an ad appearing on television if the room is filled with distractions (such as a crying baby). Similarly, the aging process reduces our ability to learn.[16]

## Mental Representations

**Mental representations** refer to *the particular manner in which information is stored in long-term memory.* Sometimes a stimulus is stored in the same form in which it initially appears, as would be the case when consumers focus on learning the specific price of a product. Alternatively, a stimulus may be translated into a different form for storage. Rather than a product's specific price, consumers may store the price perceptions formed during processing (e.g., "too expensive," "cheap," "about average").[17]

The same piece of information may be represented within long-term memory in different forms. The concept of **dual coding** proposes that *information can be stored in both semantic* (i.e., its meaning) *and visual* (i.e., its appearance) *forms.*[18] Consider the child trying to learn state capitals. For Arkansas, the capital is Little Rock. Beyond presenting this information verbally, one could also represent it visually, as shown in Figure 16.2. Doing so enhances the chances of this information being stored semantically and visually.

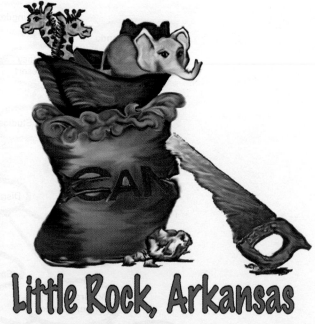

**FIGURE 16.2** Pictures That Evoke Visual Mental Representations Can Increase Learning

The advantage of having multiple representations in memory is that it increases the number of possible mental pathways that can be traveled when trying to remember. The child who is shown the picture in Figure 16.2 has an additional way (i.e., the picture itself) for remembering the state capital of Arkansas. This, in turn, improves the odds of remembering. Later in this chapter, we'll talk about how companies can encourage multiple representations as a way of helping consumers to remember.

Another aspect of mental representations involves the manner in which they are organized in long-term memory.[19] Although there are many theories about memory organization, the literature favors the view of memory being organized in the form of an **associative network**.[20] This perspective proposes that *memory nodes containing bits of information are linked to other memory nodes in a series of hierarchical networks.* Consider, for example, the hypothetical associative network presented in Figure 16.3

(16.3)    **FIGURE 16.3**    An Associative Network for Disney

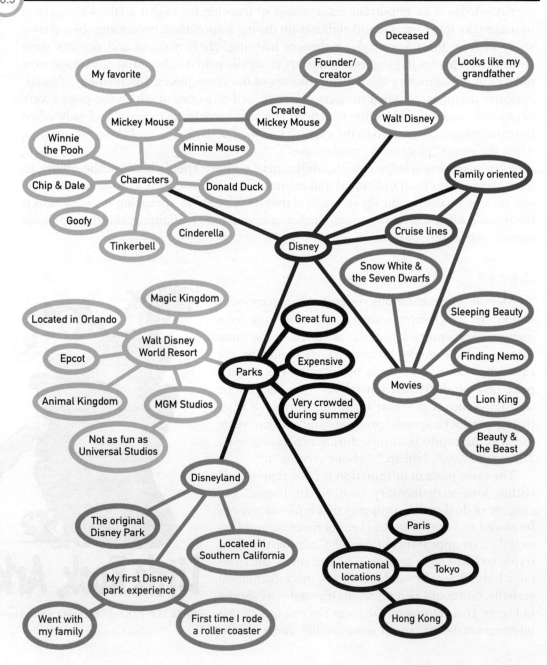

for the memory node representing "Disney." This central node is linked to many other nodes that represent the set of associations that may be activated when the person hears or thinks about Disney. Recognize that it is this set of associations which the image analysis discussed in Chapter 9 attempts to identify. Also recognize that Figure 16.3 displays a simplified representation of the associative network likely to exist for Disney, as many other nodes and linkages that, although not depicted in the figure, are likely to exist. Moreover, the Disney node is likely to be part of other associative networks, such as those representing "famous names" or "vacation parks," with the latter being part of an associative network representing "entertainment options."

## Retrieval

Learning is but one part of remembering. It only addresses getting information from short-term memory into long-term memory, but ignores getting this information back out. The other part of remembering is retrieval. **Retrieval** involves the *activation of information stored in long-term memory that's then transferred into short-term memory*. Together, learning and retrieval are the two fundamental requirements for remembering (see Figure 16.4).

The likelihood that retrieval is successful depends on a couple of things. A key factor is the strength of the memory trace of the to-be-remembered information. Some information is so well known and strongly represented in memory that it can be recalled easily and spontaneously (e.g., the names of your family members). The memory trace for other information, however, may be much weaker. Greater effort and concentration is required before retrieval is successful. Sometimes the memory trace is so weak that retrieval may succeed only if helped by retrieval cues. A **retrieval cue** is a *stimulus that activates information in memory relevant to the to-be-remembered information*. For example, do you remember the name of your first-grade teacher? Many people cannot without assistance. But if shown a picture of their first-grade classroom, their classmates, or their teacher, their memory may be stimulated. Although still in their

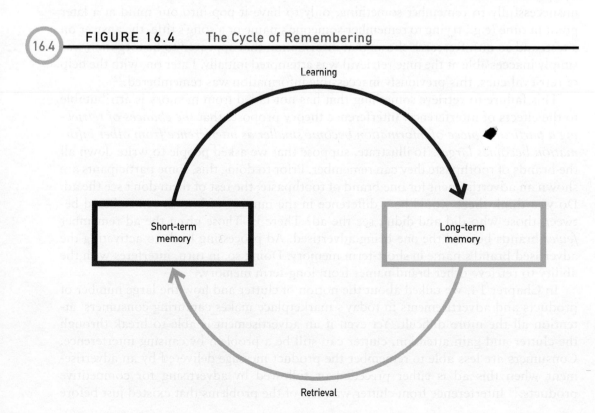

FIGURE 16.4    The Cycle of Remembering

head, the to-be-remembered information was not accessible until activated by its linkage to the memory node activated by the picture. Later on, we'll talk more about retrieval cues and their usefulness in helping consumers remember.

Successful retrieval also depends on the number and strength of linkages between the to-be-remembered item and other memory nodes. According to the concept of **spreading activation,** *activating one memory node causes a ripple effect that spreads throughout its linkages to other nodes.*[21] This, in turn, increases the chances that other nodes are activated, depending on the strength of the linkages. Consequently, if the to-be-remembered node is strongly associated with another, then retrieving the latter may help in retrieving the former. Take the product that has forged a strong relationship with a celebrity spokesperson. Thinking about the celebrity will facilitate retrieval of the product (and vice versa). Moreover, as linkages become more prevalent, there's a greater opportunity for activating the to-be-remembered node while searching memory. Assume one memory node has five strong linkages. Activating any of the five linkages may lead to successful retrieval. Now suppose there's only one strong linkage. Obviously, the chances of remembering are much less.

## Forgetting

As we know all too well, people's efforts at remembering are not always successful. The *failure to retrieve something from memory* is commonly known as **forgetting.**

Why does forgetting occur? According to **decay theory,** *memories grow weaker with the passage of time.* Just like the paintings of famous artists that have faded over the centuries, so too does information painted on the canvas of the brain. Unless information is reactivated after initial learning, decay sets in and the memory trace becomes weaker. At some point, the memory becomes so weak that retrieval may not be possible.

Yet forgetting also occurs even when the memory trace is far from being weak. This happens because not everything stored in long-term memory is accessible for retrieval at a particular moment in time. All of us have experienced situations in which we tried unsuccessfully to remember something, only to have it pop into our mind at a later point in time (e.g., trying to remember someone's name or a song's title, the answer on a test, and so on). Research shows that information that appeared to be forgotten was simply inaccessible at the time retrieval was attempted initially. Later on, with the help of retrieval cues, this previously inaccessible information was remembered.[22]

This failure to retrieve something that has not faded from memory is attributable to the effects of interference. **Interference theory** proposes that *the chances of retrieving a particular piece of information become smaller as interference from other information becomes larger.* To illustrate, suppose that we asked people to write down all the brands of toothpaste they can remember. Prior to doing this, some participants are shown an advertisement for one brand of toothpaste; the rest of them don't see the ad. Do you think there would be a difference in the number of brands remembered between those who did and didn't see the ad? There is. Those given the ad remember *fewer* brands beyond the one being advertised. Ad processing leads to activating the advertised brand's name in short-term memory. Doing so, in turn, interferes with the ability to retrieve other brand names from long-term memory.[23]

In Chapter 14, we talked about the notion of clutter and how the large number of products and advertisements in today's marketplace makes capturing consumers' attention all the more difficult. Yet even if an advertisement is able to break through the clutter and gain attention, clutter can still be a problem by causing interference. Consumers are less able to remember the product message delivered by an advertisement when this ad is either preceded or followed by advertising for competitive products.[24] Interference from clutter was one of the problems that existed just before the dot-com bust at the turn of the twenty-first century. Dot-com advertising was everywhere, leading one advertising executive to observe at the time, "There's just too much out there now. I don't see how people can remember them. It's like being introduced to forty persons at a party." [25]

The presence of competitors' advertising is not the only source of interference. Interference effects can also arise when an endorser used to promote one product appears in advertising for a different product. In one study, 56 percent of the participants could recall having previously seen a commercial for Hallmark that featured Snoopy and the Charlie Brown gang. For those participants exposed to this Hallmark commercial and a commercial for MetLife featuring the same characters, however, recall of the Hallmark commercial dropped to 36 percent. [26] Findings such as these reinforce apprehensions about using celebrity endorsers that appear on behalf of multiple products, something we talked about in the "Product Endorsers" section of Chapter 15.

### Recognition and Recall

Beyond the strength of the memory trace, retrieval also depends on whether the to-be-remembered information requires recognition or recall. For recognition, we simply need to identify whether we're familiar with something because we've seen it before. Students taking an exam, for example, would rely on recognition when answering multiple-choice questions. Similarly, consumers would rely on brand recognition when given a list of brand names and asked to indicate those names familiar to them. Or maybe they're shown an advertisement and asked whether they'd seen it before, thus representing ad recognition. Note, then, that recognition measures provide the strongest possible retrieval cue: the to-be-remembered information itself.

Recall, on the other hand, is more cognitively demanding than recognition. As you well know, it's usually easier to answer multiple-choice questions than short answer questions (e.g., a question asking you to define retrieval) and essay questions (e.g., a question asking you to describe the various ways in which companies can help consumers to remember). This is also true when examining consumers' memory for ads and brands. Asking consumers to indicate those brands of cereal familiar to them from an exhaustive listing of these brands is not the same as asking them to write down all the brands they can think of (as you might remember from our example of this in Chapter 9). Typically, people appear to have a better memory of something when it's measured using recognition rather than recall. [27]

Recall measures come in two basic types. The first, called **free recall** (or unaided recall), *does not contain any retrieval cues*. An example would be asking consumers to remember all the brands advertised during the Super Bowl. A second type is **cued recall** (or aided recall), in which *certain types of retrieval cues are provided*. For example, after telling consumers that an ad appeared during the Super Bowl for a certain type of product (e.g., soft drinks), they'd be asked to recall the particular brand. Given the beneficial effect of retrieval cues noted earlier, people remember more when they answer aided rather than unaided recall measures.

## PRODUCT AWARENESS

In Chapters 4 and 9, we discussed product awareness and how it's an important prerequisite for gaining consideration during decision making. We also acknowledged that this awareness could be assessed using either brand recognition or brand recall measures. We didn't discuss, however, when recognition or recall is the most appropriate indicator of product awareness. We do so now.

Think about when consumers are forming their consideration sets and deciding which brands are worthy of purchase consideration. Sometimes these sets are developed using only internal search (covered in Chapter 4), in which case choice alternatives must be freely recalled from memory. In this instance, whether consumers can recognize a brand name is much less relevant than whether they can recall it. Because unless they do recall it, the brand won't be considered, no matter how recognizable the name may be. Recall is the most appropriate indicator of product awareness for consideration sets generated inside the consumer's head.[28]

At other times, consideration sets are formed at the point of purchase. Indeed, purchase decisions involving grocery and health and beauty aid products are often made in the store.[29] Nonhabitual grocery shoppers may quickly scan the shelf to see what's available and what to consider further. In this case, they need only recognize rather than freely recall the product. Consequently, product awareness in the form of recognition is most relevant. The Adolph Coors Company tracked recognition of its Coors brand of beer as one indicator of its "Blast to Cash" promotional giveaway. "As a result of running this promotion, brand recognition of Coors has gone up for two years in a row, rising from the No. 3 spot to the No. 1 spot in brand awareness," explains an executive with SCA Promotions, a provider of assorted promotional games.[30]

Brand recognition should include more than simply the product's name because recognition of its packaging may also play an important part in gaining entry into the consideration set. One benefit of prominently showing the product packaging in the ad appearing in Figure 16.5 is that it facilitates consumers' ability to recognize the product on the grocer's shelf.

Determining whether recall or recognition is the most relevant measure of product awareness therefore requires understanding which type of retrieval is required for entering the consideration set. Making this determination is important to businesses for two reasons. First, dollars are likely to be wasted if only brand recognition is needed and brand recall is used as the advertising objective.[31] This is because fewer ad and product exposures (and hence dollars) are typically required to achieve a certain level of recognition than is needed to reach the same level of recall. Second, the usefulness of certain business tactics may depend on whether the decision process is based on brand recognition or brand recall. Educating consumers about a product's packaging so that they can more easily recognize it should pay greater dividends for decisions that rely on brand recognition.[32]

## ADVERTISING AWARENESS

Companies are also interested in what consumers remember about their advertising messages. Sometimes this interest leads companies to examine those advertisements consumers remember seeing. During one holiday season, online shoppers were asked to name the most memorable dot-com advertisement they'd seen. Despite heavy spending by Internet companies on advertising during this time, nearly one-fourth couldn't recall even a single ad, leading some companies to question the value of such advertising.[33] Realize, however, that questioning an ad's effectiveness because consumers can't recall it implicitly assumes that memory of an ad's existence is necessary before it can be influential. Yet there's reason to wonder about the validity of this assumption. After processing an ad,

FIGURE 16.5 Showing the Product Increases Product Recognition

© Bill Aron/Photo Edit

someone might remember certain pieces of information about the product (e.g., what it looks like, how much it costs) without remembering the source of this information. And just because an ad is remembered need not mean that it's effective. Obnoxious or offensive ads can be very memorable, but the negative feelings they generate can also have an adverse influence on consumers' product opinions.

Rather than being concerned about *how many* people remember seeing a company's ad, emphasis should be placed on *what* is remembered from the ad. Do consumers, for example, remember the name of the advertised product? What, if anything, do they remember about the claims made in the ad? Questions such as these were asked by Kraft Foods when evaluating a new advertising campaign for its DiGiorno brand of frozen pizza. Copy tests revealed that 64 percent could recall the commercial's main message (an average commercial scored only 24 percent), and 52 percent could recall the brand name.[34] Contrast this with findings concerning what's remembered from the banner ads that appear on websites. One market research firm reports that, of those online consumers who have even bothered to click on a banner ad, more than two-thirds couldn't remember what they saw.[35]

Probably the most commonly used indicator of advertising effectiveness that's based on consumers' memory is the **day-after recall (DAR) measure,** which *assesses consumers' ability to recall the advertised brand twenty-four hours after being exposed to the advertisement.* Table 16.1 presents the ten commercials that debuted in early 2005 with the highest DAR scores. In terms of creating a strong memory trace of the brand name, the America Online campaign running during this time period was extremely successful, as evidenced by its spots receiving the top four DAR scores.

**TABLE 16.1**    **Day-After Recall Rankings for New Commercials Debuting February 28–March 27, 2005: The Top Ten**

| RANK | BRAND | DESCRIPTION | RECALL INDEX |
|------|-------|-------------|--------------|
| 1 | America Online | Two men in cafeteria do ham and tuna sandwich comparison of spam and virus protection. (sixty-second spot) | 232 |
| 2 | America Online | Two men in cafeteria do ham and tuna sandwich comparison of spam and virus protection. (thirty-second spot) | 221 |
| 3 | America Online | Comprehensive Virus Protection—Man asks why he should be worried about new viruses. | 221 |
| 4 | America Online | Comprehensive Virus Protection—Hacked like Kung Pao Chicken, wants to share private e-mail with public. | 217 |
| 5 | Home Depot | Box appears in variety of rapidly changing, colorful designs; employees build chest. | 210 |
| 6 | Blockbuster | All You Can Watch—People celebrate outside store. | 204 |
| 7 | Crayola | Erasables—Girl thinks Mississippi is the hardest state to spell. | 204 |
| 8 | Charmin | MegaRoll—No one likes changing the roll; family of bears lines up. | 204 |
| 9 | Sears | Ty Pennington takes men to check out lawn care equipment. | 203 |
| 10 | Burger King | TenderCrisp Bacon Cheddar Ranch—Rock star Hootie sings about fantasy ranch and lotto tickets. | 190 |

Source: "Month's Top 10 Most-Liked, Most-Recalled New TV Spots," AdAge.com, www.adage.com (April 4, 2005). Reprinted with permission from April 4, 2005, www.adage.com. Copyright Crain Communications, Inc. 2005.

Note: Only new campaigns considered, airing weeks of February 28–March 27, 2005. Recall index is based on the percentage of television viewers who can recall within twenty-four hours the brand of an ad they were exposed to during the normal course of viewing television indexed against the mean score for all ads during the time period. 100 equals average.

Whether consumers remember the particular brand being advertised and the claims made about it is important for the following reasons. If they don't remember the brand, then it's unlikely that anything else that's remembered will be linked to this brand in memory. Even worse, if consumers are confused about which brand was featured in the advertisement, they may mistakenly link the ad claims to a competitor's brand.[36] And because product information conveyed by an ad is intended to make the product more attractive to consumers, remembering this information should increase its chances of being chosen.

Nonetheless, the fact that an ad effectively instills information in consumers' memory should not be interpreted as also indicating that the ad is effective at creating more favorable attitudes toward the advertised product. Remembering something and liking something are not the same thing. This difference is illustrated by a comparison of ad recall and ad liking. Let's take a look at the ten most-liked commercials that debuted during the same time period as those reported in Table 16.1. These most-liked commercials are presented in Table 16.2. A comparison of Table 16.1 and 16.2 reveals minimal overlap between those commercials with high DAR scores and those that are most liked. Only one commercial makes the top ten in terms of memory and liking: the Crayola ad for its Erasables product.

Moreover, the fact that consumers can remember an ad's claims does not mean that they *believe* the claims. And if they don't believe the claims, then they're unlikely to

TABLE 16.2    Most Liked New Commercials Debuting February 28–March 27, 2005: The Top Ten

| RANK | BRAND | DESCRIPTION | LIKEABILITY INDEX |
|------|-------|-------------|-------------------|
| 1 | Office of National Drug Control Policy | Freevibe.com—Girl in pink sweater recites poem about resisting peer pressure and drug use. | 159 |
| 2 | Sony PlayStation | PlayStation Portable (PSP)—Man in red shirt morphs into musical performer. | 157 |
| 3 | Gillette Tag | Body spray—Mrs. Drake answers door, smells Steven, and hits on him. | 155 |
| 4 | Mountain Dew | Man gets soda from vending machine; car remote turns vehicles into new shapes. | 155 |
| 5 | Papa John's | Sicilian Meat Pizza—Woman dances and eats pizza. | 150 |
| 6 | Coca-Cola | With Lime—Scientist thinks of adding lime; scenes of a board meeting and factory; news anchor put lime in Coke. | 150 |
| 7 | Quiznos | Steakhouse Beef Dip Sub—Baby Bob on chair; close-up of food. | 147 |
| 8 | Unilever Axe | Shower Gel—Plumber pulls earring, bra and riding crop out of bathtub drain. | 145 |
| 9 | Crayola | Erasables—Girl thinks Mississippi is the hardest state to spell. | 144 |
| 10 | Home Depot | Flooring—Family plays cards on the floor; doesn't want to spend a lot on floors but wants it to look that way. | 141 |

Source: "Month's Top 10 Most-Liked, Most-Recalled New TV Spots," AdAge.com, www.adage.com (April 4, 2005). Reprinted with permission from April 4, 2005, www.adage.com. Copyright Crain Communications, Inc. 2005.

Note: Only new campaigns considered, airing weeks of February 28–March 27, 2005. Likability index is based on the percentage of television viewers who report to like "a lot" an ad they were exposed to during the normal course of viewing television (among those recalling the brand of the ad) indexed against the mean score for all ads during the time period. 100 equals average.

hold product attitudes as favorable as if they did believe the claims. For this reason, greater recall of the claims may not translate into more favorable attitudes.[37]

## How Companies Can Help Consumers to Remember

For reasons given earlier in the chapter, businesses usually find it's in their best interests to help consumers to remember (although at least one business, as described in Buyer Beware 16.1 on page 669, has no such interest). We now turn our attention to how this might be done. Consumers, of course, have their own ways of helping themselves to remember, such as writing a list of things to do or a list of things to buy on their next shopping trip.[38] But our focus here is on how companies can help consumers remember. Some of the following suggestions are effective because they facilitate the learning process, thereby leading to stronger memory traces. Others work by assisting the retrieval process. In either case, the ultimate outcome is an improvement in consumers' ability to remember.

### Get More Attention

The more attention given to a stimulus, the greater its chances of being remembered. As you well know, if you're thinking about something else while your professor is talking (i.e., your attention is divided), there's little chance you'll remember what the professor said. But when you allocate your full attention to the professor's words, your memory for them is greatly enhanced.

In Chapter 14, we described a number of ways in which companies can enhance consumers' attention to their messages, so we need not reiterate that discussion here. But we did save discussion of one more attention-getting technique for this chapter because of recent research demonstrating its potential for improving consumers' memory. Unlike the visually oriented techniques discussed in Chapter 14, this technique relies on smells. Ambient scents are being used in a number of marketplace locations, including retail stores,[39] supermarkets,[40] restaurants,[41] and casinos.[42] And the potential for scents to influence consumer behavior has been the subject of a number of investigations in recent years.[43]

Of particular relevance here is research showing that the presence of a pleasant ambient scent in a room while participants were evaluating a set of familiar and unfamiliar brands enhanced their brand recall and recognition as evidenced by their performance on an unexpected memory test twenty-four hours later. This research further showed that, at least in the case of brand recognition, scent's beneficial influence was due to participants paying more attention to the brands.[44] So the next time you're studying for a test, you might consider lighting some incense or a scented candle and see if this works for you as well.

### Use Reminders

One obvious way to help consumers remember involves reminding them of what it is the company wants them to remember. Doctors and dentists usually send postcards to their patients reminding them that it's time for their annual checkup (see Figure 16.6). Reminding consumers to take their prescription medications has become a top priority for the pharmaceutical industry (see Consumer Behavior and Marketing 16.1).

Another example of companies finding it profitable to help consumers remember involves consumers' fallible memory about when it's time to change the oil in their automobiles. Without being reminded, many would forget to change their oil until well past the recommended time. To reduce such forgetting, many automobile shops place a small sticker on the inside windshield that indicates when the next oil change is due.

**FIGURE 16.6** Helping Consumers to Remember with Reminders

And those shops that don't use the sticker have wasted an opportunity for increasing their future sales. Jiffy Lube takes this a step further by sending past customers a post-card to remind them that they're overdue for their next service.

Providing consumers with simple reminders of the company's name and contact information is an effective way of helping consumers to remember. "There are two common reasons why businesses never see customers again," says Sharron Senter, a small-business marketing consultant. "First, the customer forgot about them. Second, the customer can't find the company's contact information." Her solution? "Sticker everything! It's the most effective and affordable marketing strategy I know to bring customers back. If you're an electrician, sticker circuit breaker boxes in the customer's home. If you're an accountant, sticker invoices and copies of clients' tax returns. They're miniature billboards. Customers see your message and can't avoid reading it." [45]

Free products bearing the company's name and contact information is another, more expensive way of accomplishing the same thing. "Everybody likes to get something for nothing, and it's a great way to build goodwill," says Steven Sands, president of Sandman Productions, a company that specializes in such promotional items. [46] The company's catalog contains more than three hundred different products that can be customized, ranging from the standard pen to radios and calculators.

The Internet is a useful tool for delivering reminders to consumers. Staples, for example, sends e-mails to customers reminding them to replenish those consumable items (e.g., ink cartridges) they had purchased previously. [47] Gift merchants such as 1-800-FLOWERS send their customers e-mails reminding them of upcoming birthdays, anniversaries, and other special occasions. These e-mails, of course, also contain recommendations for possible gifts. Evidence of the effectiveness of reminder e-mails comes from a gambling website that sends out a reminder to new customers if they

## Here's Hoping You Forget

How would you like to buy something costing thousands of dollars with an opportunity of getting some, perhaps all, of your money back in three years? That's what consumers who enroll in the Cashable Voucher Program are told. Consumers who purchase from retailers participating in the program will receive a voucher potentially worth as much as the price paid for the purchased product that can be redeemed in three years' time. The value of the voucher ultimately depends on the number of consumers that submit a valid voucher relative to the size of the fund that was formed three years previously based on payments retailers are required to make each time they issue a voucher. If, for example, the fund equaled 100 percent or more of the total value of the valid vouchers submitted, then each person submitting a valid voucher would receive the voucher's full value. On the other hand, if the fund equaled only 50 percent of the total value of the valid vouchers submitted, then each person submitting a valid voucher would receive only 50 percent of the voucher's value.

According to the program's website, www.cashable vouchers.com, "The Cashable Voucher is a financial memory test or challenge and we know that a very high percentage of vouchers will never be redeemed. People forget, lose their vouchers or simply fail to claim validly for any number of reasons. In effect, the voucher holders who do not claim validly help pay for those that do. The important thing is that each of the steps appearing in the voucher terms and conditions of agreement section must be satisfied for a valid claim to exist—WILL YOU REMEMBER?"

But in February 2005, Missouri's attorney general Jay Nixon filed a lawsuit claiming that thousands of consumers had been duped out of more than $24 million nationwide. Nixon claims that consumers in as many as thirty-six states were promised rebates of up to 100 percent on big-ticket items such as jewelry, cars, hot tubs, swimming pools, and even cosmetic surgery. But complex and vaguely worded rules kept most consumers from ever getting rebates, the lawsuit claims. "The whole program is set to frustrate claims, pure and simple," Nixon said at a news conference. "The wording in the rules is intentionally vague, intimidating, and cumbersome—virtually ensuring that consumers' claims will be rejected."

According to Nixon, the alleged scheme works like this: the promoters approached retailers with a plan to issue cashable vouchers to consumers. The retailers paid 15 percent of the value of the voucher to the Consumers Trust, a British company that issues the vouchers. The carrot for retailers was that they could charge the consumers whatever they wanted and use the rebate as a promotion to get consumers into their stores. Consumers were told that if they prepared the vouchers properly, mailed them in, and complied with other rules, they could redeem them in three years for up to 100 percent of their purchases. But Nixon said that many consumers were told after three years that they hadn't complied. He said the fine print included vague statements. One such statement said consumers must submit "third-party proof of payment," but did not explain what that meant. Nixon said one voucher warned consumers that their vouchers would be invalidated if anyone assisted them with the claims process. "When the purpose of a promotional program is to frustrate consumers, that's not a promotion—that's a fraud," says Nixon.

Source: Paul Wenske, "Rebate Deal a Fraud, Nixon Says," *Kansas City Star* (February 17, 2005), A1. Copyright 2004 by the Kansas City Star. Reproduced with permission of Tribune Media Services.

have not used the site within seven days of registration. Their research shows that those receiving these reminders are five times more likely to use the website than those who do not receive reminder e-mails.[48]

### Use Retrieval Cues

Earlier in the chapter we introduced the concept of retrieval cues, which are stimuli that activate information in memory that's linked to the to-be-remembered

## Don't Forget Your Meds

In the world of pharmaceutical drugs, getting new customers is only part of the challenge facing drug companies. Getting customers to take their medications, referred to as compliance or adherence, is the other part. "The pharmaceutical industry has been calling [the lack of patient adherence] the $100 billion problem," says Barry Green, chief marketing officer at PharmaCentra, a marketing firm that specializes in compliance. "In the past, patient adherence has not been in the forefront, but that thinking has moved on and it's become more of a hot button," observes Dr. Cameron Durrant, CEO of children's drug company PeriaMed. Next to price controls, Novartis Pharmaceuticals CEO Thomas Ebeling ranks drug adherence as the industry's single biggest issue. "Customer acquisition costs are going up," he says. "Therefore, [we have to get] the patients we have to stay on therapy, if that's the right thing medically." Even a single pill can have tremendous impact, particularly with a blockbuster drug. If every patient on a $2 billion cardiovascular medication took just one additional pill each day, that would represent $17 million in new revenue, says Loreen Babcock, head of LLKFB, a health care direct marketing unit of Omnicom with clients including BristolMyers Squibb, Pfizer, and Abbott Laboratories.

People do not take their medications as directed for many reasons, ranging from the high price of prescription drugs to people simply forgetting. And it is this last problem that has been the focus of some of the efforts designed to enhance adherence. Companies have begun to monitor the consumption patterns of their customers. When customers are reordering at a pace less than that expected on the basis of what the doctor has prescribed, Caremark sends its customers a letter and a brochure about the importance of taking medications as prescribed as a way of getting consumption back on schedule. Doing so should not only benefit the customer's health but should also benefit the company's sales.

Although the primary purpose of DTC (direct-to-consumer) advertising is to raise brand awareness and prompt consumers to ask their physicians for the advertised drug by name, DTC can also be used to help consumers remember to take their medications. "DTC is a reminder to take the medicine or refill your prescription," says Stu Klein, president of the Quantum Group. In some instances, television commercials address drug adherence with a single sentence worked into the copy. These "reminder" advertisements simply mention the drug name for the sake of brand retention. Schering-Plough used the tactic several years ago for its Claritin medication. More recently, GlaxoSmithKline has run commercials for its nasal allergy drug Flonase that tell users of the medication "Don't forget to use Flonase" or "Don't forget to refill your Flonase before you run out."

Source: Christine Bittar, "Take As Directed," *Brandweek,* 45 (July 26–August 2, 2004), 24–27.

information. Because of the typical delay between when an advertisement is processed and when a purchase is made, any relevant product information learned from the ad may not be readily accessible at the point of purchase.[49] One method for encouraging the activation of such information from memory is to place retrieval cues on the product's packaging.[50] These cues consist of some image strongly associated with the advertising itself. A classic example of this is Energizer batteries and the drum-playing pink bunny featured in its commercials. Although these commercials were well received, many consumers had difficulty remembering just what brand was being advertised. Consequently, the favorable feelings generated by the commercials were not linked very strongly to the Energizer name. To overcome this, the packaging was modified to include the pink bunny as a retrieval cue (see Figure 16.7). One indication of the potential payoff of using advertising retrieval cues comes from the Campbell Soup Company. Its sales increased by 15 percent when its point-of-purchase materials were tied directly to its television advertising.[51]

FIGURE 16.7 Energizer Modified Its Packaging to Help Consumers Remember

Companies sometimes include retrieval cues in one commercial that activate memories generated by a different commercial for the same product. One advertising campaign for pre-mixed liquor drinks used two different commercials, each emphasizing a different young couple enjoying themselves dancing at the same party. Each commercial briefly showed the couple featured in the other commercial. By doing this, the advertiser encourages reactivation of the memories supplied by the other commercial. This reactivation helps build a stronger memory trace. It also strengthens the linkages in memory between the mental representations held after processing each commercial.

Interestingly, different types of retrieval cues may be most effective depending on the language of communication. In a recent investigation of this possibility, the relative effectiveness of visual versus auditory retrieval cues was examined for an advertisement that was written using either Chinese logographs or the English alphabet.[52] Because Chinese logographs rely more on visual than auditory processing, researchers anticipated that visual retrieval cues (e.g., such as pictures used in the advertisement) would be most effective for enhancing recall. In contrast, because the English alphabet depends more heavily on auditory than visual processing, researchers expected that auditory retrieval cues (e.g., such as the music played in a commercial) would be best. Bilingual students from Singapore viewed either the Chinese or English version of two different advertisements, one for a tennis racket and the other for a restaurant, on a computer screen. The advertisements contained visual images (e.g., the interior of a restaurant in the case of the restaurant advertisement) and played continuous background music while shown on the computer screen. After viewing the advertisement and engaging in a task designed to clear short-term memory, participants were asked to recall the ad claims. Some participants were shown the same visual images that appeared in the advertisements during ad recall. Others heard the same background music during ad recall. The average recall as a function of whether the advertisement used

**FIGURE 16.8**  Visual Retrieval Cues Are Best for Chinese-Language Communications, Whereas Auditory Retrieval Cues Are Best for English-Language Communications

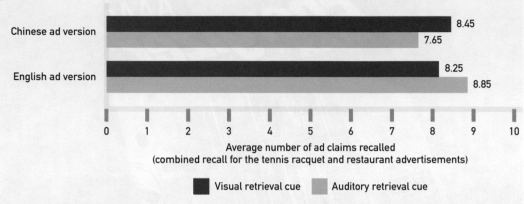

Average number of ad claims recalled
(combined recall for the tennis racquet and restaurant advertisements)

■ Visual retrieval cue    ■ Auditory retrieval cue

Source: Nader T. Tavassoli and Yih Hwai Lee, "The Differential Interaction of Auditory and Visual Advertising Elements with Chinese and English," *Journal of Marketing Research*, 40 (November 2003), 468–480.

Chinese or English and whether a visual or auditory retrieval cue was present during retrieval is shown in Figure 16.8. As expected, more information was remembered when participants that had processed the Chinese-language version of the ads were given a visual retrieval cue. For those that had received the English-language version of the ads, however, recall was superior when they were given the auditory retrieval cue.

### Say It Over and Over: The Value of Repetition

Earlier we noted that greater rehearsal leads to stronger memories. Although students preparing for an upcoming exam may be highly motivated to rehearse their notes, they're unlikely to do so when watching television commercials. Usually our thoughts linger on the commercial for no longer than the time it appears on the screen before us. Only when we perceive the commercial as providing relevant information for an important purchase decision are we likely to take the time and effort to rehearse this information.

To overcome this lack of rehearsal, companies rely on repetition by showing their advertisements repeatedly. Consumers are "forced" into rehearsal each time they process the ad. Repetition essentially represents externally induced rehearsal.

The beneficial influence of repetition on learning has been well substantiated.[53] The standard finding is that learning grows with additional exposures, although at a diminishing rate (i.e., each successive exposure contributes less to memory than the preceding one), until it plateaus, at which point further repetition is unproductive. Moreover, the effectiveness of repetition in building long-term memory is enhanced when repetitions are spread out rather than clustered closely together.[54]

Just how much repetition is necessary for maximizing learning depends on both the person and the to-be-learned information.[55] Those highly motivated to remember what the ad says may do so after a single exposure as long as the ad doesn't say too much. But if it conveys a large or complex set of information, consumers may be unable to fully comprehend and learn the ad information during a single exposure to the ad. Additional exposures to the ad would then be necessary for greater learning. This is also true for even simple messages when consumers lack the motivation for intentional learning.

Recognize that this beneficial influence of repetition on learning has its limits. Because learning plateaus after a certain number of repetitions, further repetition beyond this point is a waste of money. And, as you learned in Chapter 14, too many repetitions can cause advertising to wear out. The negative responses from seeing the same ad over and over again may hurt consumers' product opinions. It is for this reason that companies should develop multiple ad executions carrying the same basic message. Rather than, say, showing the same ad twenty times, the company is better off developing at least two different versions of the ad and showing each ten times.

The potential benefits of repetition may also be limited by advertising clutter. One study reports that repetition enhanced recall when advertising for competitive products was minimal or nonexistent. Yet this increase disappeared under higher levels of competitive advertising.[56]

Beyond repeating the same ad over and over, repetition can also be used within a single ad. This tactic occurs in many of the humorous commercials for AFLAC, the supplemental insurance company. In one of these commercials, a man tries to remember the company's name while oblivious to the helpful duck that repeatedly shouts "AFLAC." When Kraft developed its DiGiorno brand of pizza, an Italian name was chosen in an effort to "lend authenticity to the product." But consumers had trouble pronouncing the name, which raised concerns about their ability to remember it. Consequently, Kraft made sure that the brand name was repeated several times in its commercials.[57]

## Encourage Elaboration

Previously in the chapter we covered how elaborative processing, in which a stimulus is linked or related to various concepts in memory, promotes learning. By encouraging consumers to engage in elaboration during processing, companies can make it easier for consumers to remember. How can this be done? One example is the radio advertisement for an automotive parts supplier called Kar Part Outlet. The ad encouraged listeners to elaborate on the name by linking each word in the name to a different concept in memory. This was done by having the spokesperson say, "Kar, as in what you drive; Part, as in what you do to your hair; Outlet, as in what you stick a plug in."

Another way to encourage elaboration is through self-referencing. **Self-referencing** involves *relating a stimulus to one's own self and experiences.* Suppose we ask some people whether each word in a list describes them. In making this determination, they're likely to engage in self-referencing as they reflect on the type of person they are and whether their behaviors and experiences are consistent with the word's implications. Now suppose we give another group of people the same list of words but ask this group to perform a different task (e.g., such as identifying a synonym for the word). If we later test everyone's memory for the words, those asked to self-reference have greater recall.[58]

This facilitating effect of self-referencing is attributed to a more elaborate encoding of the information. The representation of the self in memory is a complex, highly organized structure. The activation of this richer structure during encoding enhances the number and strength of potential linkages that can be made between the to-be-remembered information and other stored information that, in turn, increases the likelihood of retrieval.

Research supports the potential for encouraging self-referencing through advertising copy. By using the word *you* and ad copy that prompted the retrieval of prior relevant product experiences, recall of the ad information was enhanced.[59] We should point out, however, that some researchers have found that self-referencing reduces retrieval of information conveyed by advertising claims, at least in some circumstances.[60] Further research is needed to clarify when self-referencing helps or hurts.

## Encourage Multiple Representations in Memory

Suppose you just opened up a new business called "Jack's Camera Shoppe" or "Arrow Pest Control" and you want consumers in your target market to learn and remember your company's name. The concept of multiple representations discussed previously, which reflects the notion that information can be stored in both semantic and visual forms in long-term memory, suggests that consumers are more likely to remember your company's name if it is represented in both forms rather than a single form because this provides additional pathways for retrieving the information. Support for this prediction comes from studies in the literature that show that pictures that provide a visual representation of the to-be-remembered semantic information improves memory for this information.[61] Thus, in the case of "Jack's Camera Shoppe" and "Arrow Pest Control," visual representations of these names, perhaps along the lines of those shown in Figure 16.9, should help consumers remember the names. Similarly, consumers exposed to the ad for Curve perfume shown in Figure 16.10 should be more likely to remember the Curve brand name because of the ad's visual elements that reinforce the name.

There is, however, an important limitation to this beneficial effect of including pictures. This limitation is contingent on whether the semantic information spontaneously activates visual imagery when the information is being processed. For example, consider a print ad that contains copy of such vividness that it evokes visual imagery during processing. Because this visual imagery will be a part of the mental representation for any stored information, using actual pictures (of the imagery suggested by the ad copy) in the ad may not help much, if at all. On the other hand, if the ad copy does not evoke imagery, then including pictures will be beneficial because it encourages the formation of visual representations and, consequently, improves retrieval.[62]

## Be Consistent

In a print ad for a brand of vodka, the copy reads, "SMOOTH AS ICE . . . Icy cold. Icy clear. Imported Icy Vodka of Iceland. Why can't everything in life be this smooth?" The ad picture shows a bottle with the brand name ICY that appears to be made of smooth clear ice. In this ad, the brand name, the copy, and the picture convey the same meaning.

Consistency facilitates remembering. Greater consistency among elements within an advertisement, as in the Icy vodka ad, increases what consumers remember about the ad and advertised product.[63] The product benefits described within an ad are better remembered when these benefits are consistent with those suggested by the ad-

**FIGURE 16.9** Visual Representations Can Increase the Memorability of Brand Names

vertised product's name. Similarly, pictures that convey a meaning similar to that attached to the brand name enhance memory of the name (as would be expected given our earlier discussion concerning dual coding and multiple representations). Moreover, when the ad copy also conveys the same meaning as the name and picture, brand name recall improves even further.

To further illustrate the importance of consistency, consider the following study that tested preschoolers' memory for new brand names.[64] Children are told that they are going to play a game called "Remember the Name." They are then shown a cardboard cutout representing the shape of a particular product (e.g., a candy bar) and hear the product's name (e.g., Sky). At the same time, the children are exposed to a color or picture that is either consistent or inconsistent with the concept represented by the brand name. For example, the consistent (inconsistent) color used for the Sky brand name was blue (orange), and the consistent (inconsistent) picture was of an airplane (clock). Figure 16.11 shows the average number of the five brand names that were remembered as a function of the type of stimulus that accompanied the brand name. Compared to the control group, where no color or picture was presented, the presentation of an inconsistent color or picture did not significantly help the children remember the brand names. In contrast, there was a significant increase in their memory of these names when they were accompanied by a consistent color or picture.

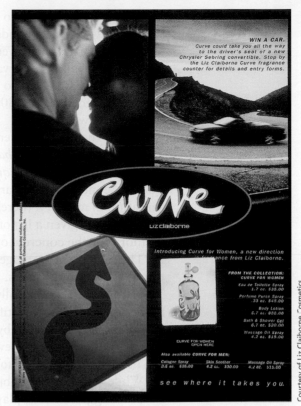

**FIGURE 16.10** Encouraging Visual Representations of the Brand Name in Advertising

*Courtesy of Liz Claiborne Cosmetics*

## Use Easy-to-Remember Stimuli

Which phone number do you think would be the easiest for consumers to remember the next time they want to order some flowers: 1-800-356-9377 or 1-800-FLOWERS? The answer's pretty obvious, isn't it? The latter phone number, by virtue

**FIGURE 16.11** Consistency Enhances Preschoolers' Memory of Brand Names

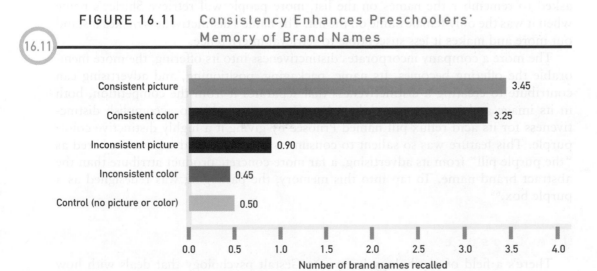

Source: M. Carole Macklin, "Preschoolers' Learning of Brand Names from Visual Cues," *Journal of Consumer Research*, 23 (December 1996), 251–261.

of requiring consumers to remember a single word rather than seven digits, imposes significantly fewer demands on memory. As such, it's easier to remember. The same basic idea underlies the advertisement for Doubletree Hotels that features its telephone number for making reservations, which is printed in big bold numbers and letters as 1-800-222-TREE. And to further reinforce this number and its linkage to the hotel name, the zeros in the "800" part of the telephone number are replaced by a colored drawing of two trees.

Words themselves differ in how easily they are remembered. **Concrete words** (such as *tree* or *dog*) are *those that can be visualized rather easily*. In contrast, **abstract words** (such as *democracy* or *equality*) are *less amenable to visual representation*. Consequently, concrete words are more likely than abstract words to evoke a visual representation in memory, thereby providing an additional pathway for later retrieval. This is why people given a list of both concrete and abstract words will demonstrate greater memory for the concrete ones.[65]

The memory advantage held by concrete words should be considered when developing new brand names. Names using concrete words (e.g., Easy Off, Head and Throat, Move Free) usually will be easier to remember than names using abstract or made-up words (e.g., Actifed, Advil, Ascriptin, Encaprin, Nuprin). Unless this memory advantage is negated by other considerations (e.g., such as when an abstract brand name is more effective in evoking favorable product opinions), concrete names may be the most sensible choice for a brand.

While we're on the subject of brand names, we should also point out that a brand name's suggestiveness plays an important role in shaping consumers' memory of advertising claims. **Brand name suggestiveness** is *the extent to which a brand name conveys or reinforces a particular attribute or benefit offered by the brand*.[66] For example, the DieHard brand name placed on automobile batteries suggests a long-lasting, durable battery. Research has shown that long-term recall of advertising claims is greater when these claims pertain to the same benefit as suggested by the brand name. When these claims involve benefits unrelated to those suggested by the brand name, however, brand name suggestiveness has no effect on recall of the claims.[67]

Stimuli that are distinctive or unique are also easier to remember. For example, suppose we gave people a few minutes to learn a list of one hundred names. The list given to some contains only female names, including Shirley as one of them. Others are given a list containing Shirley's name along with ninety-nine male names. When asked to remember the names on the list, more people will retrieve Shirley's name when it was the only female name on the list. The name's distinctiveness makes it stand out more and makes it less susceptible to retrieval interference.

The more a company incorporates distinctiveness into its offering, the more memorable the offering becomes. Its name, packaging, positioning, and advertising can contribute to creating a distinctiveness that separates it from the competition, both in its image and in its memorability. AstraZeneca was able to accomplish distinctiveness for its acid reflux pill named Prilosec by giving it a highly distinctive color: purple. This feature was so salient to consumers that the brand was remembered as "the purple pill" from its advertising, a far more concrete product attribute than the abstract brand name. To tap into this memory, the packaging was redesigned as a purple box.[68]

## Use Closure

There's a field of psychology known as Gestalt psychology that deals with how people organize or combine stimuli into a meaningful whole during stimulus comprehension. Gestalt psychology has formulated a number of principles about stimulus organization. One of these, closure, is relevant here. **Closure** refers to *the tendency to develop a complete picture or perception when elements in the perceptual field are missing.* Because of this drive to "fill in" the missing parts, the presentation of an incomplete stimulus provides businesses with a mechanism for increasing the amount of thinking that consumers undertake during stimulus processing.

An example of the use of closure in advertising appears in Figure 16.12. Notice how the letters O and C are omitted from the headline and replaced with pieces of the product itself. The value of such omissions has been supported by research showing that, when the missing element relates to the brand name, consumers' memory of the name is improved.[69] And there's an added benefit: closure may not only enhance brand name recall, but it may also lead to more favorable attitudes toward the advertised product.[70]

FIGURE 16.12 The Use of Closure in Advertising Can Enhance Consumers' Brand Memory

Courtesy of Nonnis Food Company

## Put Consumers in a Good Mood

In Chapter 10, we covered the concept of mood, which refers to how people feel at a particular moment in time, and discussed its significance during opinion formation. Another reason mood is important is that it influences retrieval. In general, a positive mood increases retrieval. Moreover, the favorableness of retrieved memories depends on whether mood is positive or negative. Positive moods increase the chances of remembering favorable information; negative moods trigger the retrieval of unfavorable information.[71]

It follows, then, that putting consumers in a good mood increases their chances of remembering positive things about the product. Researchers studying mood effects have sometimes induced positive mood states by giving research participants a small bag of candy.[72] As discussed in Consumer Behavior and Marketing 16.2, some companies have taken this a step further by using candy to carry their names and messages. Advertisements can include mood-altering stimuli such as humor or music to evoke favorable mood states. Doing so facilitates the retrieval of positive product information from memory that, in turn, should make consumers more receptive to the commercial messages. Or think about the businessperson preparing to close the deal with a potential customer. Doing something that improves the prospect's mood (perhaps a free meal at a nice restaurant) should increase the retrieval of information that helps the businessperson accomplish her or his objective.

Before we leave this section on how businesses can help consumers to remember, we would like to make one more point. As you have seen, advertising often plays an important role in helping consumers to remember. It can serve as a simple reminder. It can be repeated as a way of encouraging rehearsal. Its contents can be designed in ways that enhance its impact on consumer memory (e.g., including pictures, encouraging elaboration, and so forth). Yet as a consumer you should be aware that beyond advertising's potential to improve your memory, it may also reshape your memories as well. Indeed, as discussed in Buyer Beware 16.2, advertising may distort consumers' memories of their past experiences.

## Candy Makers Help Consumers Remember

Willy Wonka sang of a world made of candy and "pure imagination." State-of-the-art technology such as lasers, and tasty accessories such as edible ink, now enable marketers to leverage the feel-good effect of candy by arranging to insert logos, images, and brand messages inside hard candy or on chocolate. The hope is that word-*in*-mouth will create word-*of*-mouth. According to Mike Wodke, CEO of LightVision Confections, "When people are looking for something that is going to be remembered and something that is sort of fun and exciting, [branded candy] meets that" need.

LightVision, a Cincinnati-based company, uses technology developed by an MIT physicist to create holographic images embedded in lollipops, a line the company calls holopops. A laser beam etches the image, logo, or message onto the lollipop's sugar crystals in such a way that a three-dimensional, shimmery hologram is created. The hologram, embedded deep within the candy using proprietary technology, is tempting because people can't help but be drawn to the image in the hope of reaching it and licking it off, Wodke says. "In the promotional products business, one of our main objectives is to really emblazon in the end-user whatever the message is," explains Wodke. "As a person begins to lick the lollipop, the image doesn't go away. The thing about the [holopop] is that it's impossible to not look at the image—about sixty times as you eat the candy. So you keep licking and looking, and I guarantee that whatever messages the company wants to get across, by the time the person has finished the lollipop, he will have the message 100 percent memorized."

Also in this business is Melbourne-based Say It on Chocolate (owned by RKR Enterprises), a promotional marketing company that uses edible ink to print images, logos, and messages on high-quality dark and milk chocolate. The ink is made entirely of food materials, which allows it to bond with the chocolate to ensure that the chocolate will have a stable image, instead of a faded or runny one. The logos and images are high resolution, because the way that the image is printed and transferred onto the chocolate mimics standard paper printing procedures—so much so that a company executive calls Say It on Chocolate a "printing company."

Management Information Systems (Minfos), a software development company specializing in the pharmacy industry, wanted to add pizzazz to its booth at the Annual National Conference for Pharmacists. Some four hundred other booths with a host of products and services would be competing for attendees' attention, and Minfos needed to make an impression. So the company turned to Say It on Chocolate, which produced three thousand chocolates with the message, "Minfos: Sweetest software in pharmacy." "We wanted the message to be fun and reflect the item that it was printed on," explains Lisa Roberton, product manager of Minfos. "Some could argue that you don't want your message eaten, but I think it is a message that stays longer in the mind than, say, a piece of direct mail or a pen, as it evokes emotion."

Source: Arundhati Parmar, "How Sweet It Is," *Marketing News* (June 15, 2004), 11–12. Reprinted with permission from the American Marketing Association.

## Products That Help Consumers to Remember

In addition to developing strategies designed to enhance consumers' ability to remember, companies also find it profitable to develop and market products that help consumers remember. A number of dietary and nutritional supplements on the market these days claim their consumption will improve the user's memory. One of these products appears in the advertisement shown in Figure 16.13.

Of course, products that are valued because of their ability to help consumers remember extend well beyond those taken to improve memory. Consider, for example,

## Advertising May "Rewrite" Your Memories of Your Consumption Experiences

Consumers' memories are filled with countless recollections of their consumption experiences. There are memories of the products that we have consumed: how something tasted, how something felt on our skin, how something smelled, how it felt to drive a particular car, whether a product performed as expected, and so on. There are memories of the restaurants and retailers we have patronized. We remember the places we have visited and the things we have done. For example, think back to the first time you experienced a Disney theme park. What do you remember? For many who first visited a Disney park as a child, this memory is truly special. Indeed, many will say that this experience is remembered as one of the most pleasant and treasured memories from their childhood days.

So is it possible that advertising has the power to "rewrite" what you remember about these consumption experiences, especially those as treasured as the first time we experienced the magic of Disney? Apparently so, according to the findings of recent research examining this possibility. In one of the studies, participants are exposed to an advertisement encouraging people to visit a Disney theme park. The ad uses a nostalgia-based appeal in which readers are asked to remember their first visit to a Disney park and includes a variety of descriptions about what may have happened during this experience, such as shaking hands with a cartoon character. One version of this ad uses Mickey Mouse as the cartoon character. Another version uses Bugs Bunny, a Warner Bros. character, not a Disney character. Thus, this ad version attempts to implant a false memory. Following ad exposure, participants are given a series of measures, including those that assess their memories of visiting a Disney

theme park during their childhood days. The potential for advertising to alter consumers' memories is reflected by how many of the participants falsely remember seeing Bugs Bunny during their childhood visits to a Disney park.

For those exposed to the ad version containing Mickey Mouse, 7 percent falsely remembered seeing Bugs Bunny when they visited Disney. So this shows that some degree of error exists in this memory independent of advertising's effect. At issue is whether this percentage increases significantly among those given the false ad version containing Bugs Bunny. It does. Among those given the Bugs Bunny version, 22 percent report that they saw Bugs Bunny when they visited Disney. This reveals that advertising can reshape what we remember about our consumption experiences. Nor is this effect limited to falsely inserting memories of events that could not have possibly happened. Other research shows that advertising can rewrite the favorability of a remembered consumption experience, causing consumers to remember an experience, such as drinking orange juice, as being more favorable than it actually was.

The importance of such findings extends beyond their demonstration of advertising's ability to invade and, in a sense, deprive us of our own memories. These findings further reinforce advertising's potential for influencing consumer behavior. Indeed, consumers typically rely most heavily on their own experiences during decision making. Yet, as you have just seen, these remembered experiences may not truly be their own, but a combination of what truly happened and what advertising says has happened.

Sources: Kathryn A. Braun, "Postexperience Advertising Effects on Consumer Memory," *Journal of Consumer Research*, 25 (March 1999), 319–334; Kathryn A. Braun-LaTour, Michael S. LaTour, Jacqueline E. Pickrell, and Elizabeth F. Loftus, "How and When Advertising Can Influence Memory for Consumer Experience," *Journal of Advertising*, 33 (Winter 2004), 7–25.

the advertisement appearing in Figure 16.14. This appliance manufacturer, with its claim of "We bring back warm memories," uses styles from yesteryear to appeal to those wishing to relive times that have long since passed. And perhaps the ultimate product for helping consumers to remember the past is the camera. Ever since the Eastman Kodak Company introduced its $1 Brownie camera in 1900, consumers have been taking photographs and filling albums that are passed along from one generation to the

**FIGURE 16.13** This Product Promises to Improve Consumers' Memory

**FIGURE 16.14** This Manufacturer Designs Its Products to "Bring Back Warm Memories"

next as a visual record of the family tree. And while the rapid transition from traditional film cameras to digital cameras has brought with it some new challenges for the industry (such as getting consumers to print the digital images stored in their cameras and computers, the topic of Chapter 6's Consumer Behavior and Marketing 6.2), consumers' fascination with photography remains strong. Americans purchased millions of digital cameras in the fourth quarter of 2004 as the digital camera replaced the DVD player as the most popular electronics gift during that holiday season.[73]

In recognition of the power of pictures, toy maker Fisher-Price has partnered with Polaroid in its pursuit of the Latino market. The company has sponsored street fairs where parents and their children can play with its toys in giant playpens plastered with the Fisher-Price logo. Photographers then snap Polaroid pictures of the children playing with the toys that families can take with them as a way of creating an "instant memory" of the event.

Retailers are also starting to appreciate the value of helping shoppers to remember. At the forefront of this movement is the Metro Group, the world's fifth-largest retailer, and its Extra Future Store, a grocery store in Rheinberg, Germany.[74] Here shoppers benefit from the latest technology designed by IBM, Intel, and Microsoft. Customers began their shopping trip by swiping their loyalty card through a "personal shopping assistant," a small computer attached to a shopping cart. Information collected during prior shopping trips is used to formulate a recommended shopping list, such as items that the customer normally purchases or items that may need to be replenished given the amount of time that's passed since the last time they were purchased. Can't remember where a certain item is located in the store? No problem. Just type in what you're looking for on the computer and its navigation system displays a diagram on how to get there from the shopper's current location.

Some products and services that will help consumers remember are currently in the developmental and testing phases. Do you remember the Tamagotchi virtual pet that was so popular a few years ago? This electronic device required owners to push buttons to take care of their virtual pet. Otherwise, it would "die." Researchers at MIT's Age Lab are working on a version of this, called the "pill pet," intended to help older consumers remember their medicines.[75] These consumers would

## The National Family Archives™

In almost all cultures, various items are used to help remember and honor our ancestors. For those long past, the item may be no more than their name written on a gravestone. If we are lucky, perhaps there's a personal item that belonged to the individual that's been passed from one generation to the next. In more modern times, photographic memoirs have become commonplace. Yet virtually all of these run the risk of being lost, destroyed, or deteriorating with the passage of time. Relatively few of us can trace our family lineage back more than a few generations. Many of our ancestors have been forgotten, lost in the sands of time.

But this may soon change. Consider the following concept: Imagine a National Family Archives online computer service in which generations from now your descendants could easily find your personal history, along with a video or audio clip of you talking to those who have yet to be born. Your personal history could contain a written story about your past, treasured photos, and whatever documents you deem worth saving, such as your resumé, medical records, and family tree. This file would be archived in a failsafe computer network with copies of the entire archive stored at several prominent university libraries. The archive would be maintained by a not-for-profit foundation supervised by reputable not-for-profit personal history and archiving associations and highly respectable universities that would study the archives and ensure that your personal history would be preserved for perpetuity.

Suppose that such a service was offered at a cost of a one-time payment of $30. Do you think consumers would be interested in such a service? How might this interest compare with other ways of being remembered? To gauge consumer interest, a study was undertaken that asked, among other things, which, if any, of the following would be ways you would like to be remembered by your descendants. The percentages were as follows.

Be remembered by your personal items passed down from children to grandchildren: 70 percent

Be remembered by an attractive gravestone or plaque: 10 percent

Be remembered in the National Family Archives: 22 percent

Be remembered by a named prize or scholarship at a school or college: 17 percent

None of these: 21 percent

These findings, along with the popularity of websites dedicated to genealogy such as Genealogy.com, Ancestor.com, and MyFamily.com (which combined have more than 1.5 million subscribers), suggest that considerable potential for this service exists in the marketplace. So if one day you encounter an advertisement for National Family Archives, remember that you heard about it here first.

Source: Peter R. Dickson and Sarah White, "Adult Interest in Creating Personal Histories and the National Family Archives Concept: Initial Research Working Paper," report prepared for the Association of Personal Historians. The study was conducted December 2004 by Synovate.

push buttons whenever they take their medicines in order to keep their pet alive and healthy. Market Facts 16.1 describes a service (still on the drawing board) that consumers could use to memorialize family members in cyberspace.

Finally, sometimes products are created not to help consumers remember, but to compensate for their forgetfulness. In late 2004, Procter & Gamble introduced the newest member of the Tide laundry detergent family: Tide with Downy fabric softener. When explaining its reasons for introducing this product extension, the company said it had "identified an unmet need among a subset of women who want clean and soft laundry, but for various reasons are either unwilling to add liquid fabric softener or are inconsistently adding it because they simply forget." [76]

## Summary

Remembering is a fundamental part of consumer behavior and decision making. We have to remember the particular purchase and consumption needs that must be filled. And the alternatives considered during decision making, as well as our opinions of them, may heavily depend on what we remember.

Before something can be remembered, it must be learned. Material processed in short-term memory is transferred to long-term memory given sufficient rehearsal or elaboration. But getting something into long-term memory is only half of the requirements for remembering. The other half is getting it back out (retrieval). But retrieval is not always successful. Memories grow weaker as time passes since their last activation. Even if a memory has not decayed, other memories may interfere with its retrieval.

Thus, by influencing learning and retrieval, companies can help consumers to remember. This chapter identifies a number of ways for doing this, ranging from obvious strategies such as using reminders to perhaps less obvious strategies like putting consumers in a good mood. Companies also need to understand which type of retrieval, recall or recognition, is most relevant during consumer decision making. Finally, we considered how some products are valued because of their ability to help consumers remember.

## Review and Discussion Questions

1. What are the various ways in which companies can help consumers remember?

2. Consider the print ad for Isle of Capri casino, in which the copy says, "Isle have fun. Isle get lucky. Isle get rich." Explain why this ad may increase memory of the casino's name.

3. The product manager for a new brand of skin softener is considering two possible names: Soft Skin versus Dickson's Skin Moisturizer. Which name would you recommend? Why?

4. A canned-goods manufacturer is interested in comparing the effectiveness of two very different commercials. The first commercial repeatedly shows pictures of the product sitting on the grocer's shelves, riding in the grocery cart, and being placed in the buyer's pantry. The second commercial briefly shows the product one time. Instead, this second commercial focuses on images that provide a visual representation of the brand name. When each commercial was examined in a market test, the second commercial was better at increasing brand name recall. Yet it was not as effective as the first commercial for increasing sales. Why might the commercial that's inferior in generating brand name recall prove superior in generating sales?

5. After learning about the potential benefits of including retrieval cues on a product's packaging for stimulating memory of its advertising, a company modified its packaging to include a scene from one of its current commercials. To its dismay, this change didn't seem to help much because sales were unaffected. How might one explain the apparent ineffectiveness of this retrieval cue?

6. In Buyer Beware 16.1, we gave an example in which a company hopes that consumers won't remember. Can you think of other situations in which this would also be true?

7. A company is attempting to reposition one of its products from a positioning the product has held successfully for many years. To do so, the company is relying on a new advertising campaign to convey the new product positioning. In one test of this new campaign's effectiveness, consumers who had seen the ad are asked to remember what the ad says about the product. In looking at the results, the company decided to separate those unfamiliar with the brand from those who are familiar with the brand. Interestingly, those unfamiliar with the brand had a much better memory of the advertising claims than those familiar with the brand. Why might this difference occur?

## Notes

[1] Kathryn Kranhold, "Drug Makers Prescribed Direct-Mail Pitch," *Wall Street Journal* (December 16, 1999), B16.

[2] Lynda Edwards, "Web Zine Claims Citrus Department Stole Its Ham Sandwich," *Miami Herald's Business Monday* (May 10, 1999), 7.

[3] Prakash Nedungadi, "Recall and Consumer Consideration Sets: Influencing Choice Without Altering Brand Evaluations," *Journal of Consumer Research*, 17 (September 1990), 263–276. See also Wayne D. Hoyer and Stephen P. Brown, "Effects of Brand Awareness on Choice for a Common, Repeat-Purchase Product," *Journal of Consumer Research*, 17 (September 1990), 141–148.

4 Alan J. Heavens, "Model Home Says, 'Buy Me.'" *Miami Herald* (May 30, 1999), H1, H4.

5 Gabriel Biehal and Dipankar Chakravarti, "Information Accessibility as a Moderator of Consumer Choice," *Journal of Consumer Research,* 10 (June 1983), 1–14; Gabriel Biehal and Dipankar Chakravarti, "Consumers' Use of Memory and External Information in Choice: Macro and Micro Perspectives," *Journal of Consumer Research,* 12 (March 1986), 382–405; John G. Lynch Jr., Howard Marmorstein, and Michael F. Weigold, "Choices from Sets Including Remembered Brands: Use of Recalled Attributes and Prior Overall Evaluations," *Journal of Consumer Research,* 15 (September 1988), 169–184.

6 Kris Oser, "Web Ads Get Results Weeks Later," *Advertising Age,* 75 (July 26, 2004), 18.

7 Morris B. Holbrook and Robert M. Schindler, "Echoes of the Dear Departed Past: Some Work in Progress on Nostalgia," in Rebecca H. Holman and Michael R. Solomon, eds., *Advances in Consumer Research,* 18 (Provo, UT: Association for Consumer Research, 1991), 330–333. For more on nostalgia, see Russell W. Belk, "The Role of Possessions in Constructing and Maintaining a Sense of Past," in Marvin E. Goldberg, Gerald Gorn, and Richard W. Pollay, eds., *Advances in Consumer Research,* 17 (Provo, UT: Association for Consumer Research, 1990), 669–676; William J. Havlena and Susan L. Holak, "The Good Old Days: Observations on Nostalgia and Its Role in Consumer Behavior," in Rebecca H. Holman and Michael R. Solomon, eds., *Advances in Consumer Research,* 18 (Provo, UT: Association for Consumer Research, 1991), 323–329; Susan L. Holak and William J. Havlena, "Feelings, Fantasies, and Memories: An Examination of the Emotional Components of Nostalgia," *Journal of Business Research,* 42 (July 1998), 217–226; Barbara Stern, "Historical and Personal Nostalgia in Advertising Text: The Fin de Siecle Effect," *Journal of Advertising,* 21 (December 1992), 11–22.

8 Suzanne Vranica and Brian Steinberg, "Crotch Jokes Are Out as Super Bowl Ads Tap into Nostalgia," *Wall Street Journal* (February 3, 2005), B1.

9 Darrel D. Muehling and David E. Sprott, "The Power of Reflection: An Empirical Examination of Nostalgia Advertising Effects," *Journal of Advertising,* 33 (Fall 2004), 25–35; Mita Sujan, James R. Bettman, and Hans Baumgartner, "Influencing Consumer Judgments Using Autobiographical Memories: A Self-Referencing Perspective," *Journal of Marketing Research,* 30 (November 1993), 422–436.

10 Terry L. Childers and Michael J. Houston, "Conditions for a Picture-Superiority Effect on Consumer Memory," *Journal of Consumer Research,* 11 (September 1984), 643–654; Fergus I. M. Craik and Endel Tulving, "Depth of Processing and the Retention of Words in Episodic Memory," *Journal of Experimental Psychology: General,* 104 (September 1975), 268–294; Fergus I. M. Craik and Michael J. Watkins, "The Role of Rehearsal in Short-Term Memory," *Journal of Verbal Learning and Verbal Behavior,* 12 (December 1973), 599–607; Meryl Paula Gardner, Andrew A. Mitchell, and J. Edward Russo, "Low Involvement Strategies for Processing Advertisements," *Journal of Advertising,* 14 (1985), 4–12; Scott A. Hawkins and Stephen J. Hoch, "Low-Involvement Learning: Memory Without Evaluation," *Journal of Consumer Research,* 19 (September 1992), 212–225; Joel Saegert and Robert K. Young, "Comparison of Effects of Repetition and Levels of Processing in Memory for Advertisements," in Andrew A. Mitchell, ed., *Advances in Consumer Research,* 9 (St. Louis: Association for Consumer Research, 1982), 431–434.

11 There is some indication that too much elaboration may actually reduce learning. See David Glen Mick, "Levels of Subjective Comprehension in Advertising Processing and Their Relations to Ad Perceptions, Attitudes, and Memory," *Journal of Consumer Research,* 18 (March 1992), 411–424.

12 Richard E. Petty and John T. Cacioppo, "The Elaboration Likelihood Model of Persuasion," in Leonard Berkowitz, ed., *Advances in Experimental Social Psychology,* 19 (New York: Academic Press, 1986), 123–205.

13 Gabriel Biehal and Dipankur Chakravarti, "Information-Presentation Format and Learning Goals as Determinants of Consumers' Memory Retrieval and Choice Processes," *Journal of Consumer Research,* 8 (March 1982), 431–441; James H. Leigh and Anil Menon, "Audience Involvement Effects on the Information Processing of Umbrella Print Advertisements," *Journal of Advertising,* 16 (1987), 3–12; Barry McLaughlin, "Intentional and Incidental Learning in Human Subjects: The Role of Instructions to Learn and Motivation," *Psychological Bulletin,* 63 (May 1965), 359–376; Bernd H. Schmitt, Nader T. Tavassoli, and Robert T. Millard, "Memory for Print Ads: Understanding Relations among Brand Name, Copy, and Picture," *Journal of Consumer Psychology,* 21 (1993), 1, 55–81.

14 William G. Chase and Herbert A. Simon, "Perception in Chess," *Cognitive Psychology,* 4 (January 1973), 55–81. For a more general discussion, see Joseph W. Alba and J. Wesley Hutchinson, "Dimensions of Consumer Expertise," *Journal of Consumer Research,* 13 (March 1987), 411–454.

15 Rajeev Batra and Michael Ray, "Situational Effects of Advertising: The Moderating Influence of Motivation, Ability and Opportunity to Respond," *Journal of Consumer Research,* 12 (March 1986), 432–445; Danny L. Moore, Douglas Hausknecht, and Kanchana Thamodaran, "Time Compression, Response Opportunity, and Persuasion," *Journal of Consumer Research,* 13 (June 1986), 85–99; James M. Munch and John L. Swasy, "Rhetorical Question, Summarization Frequency, and Argument Strength Effects on Recall," *Journal*

of *Consumer Research,* 15 (June 1988), 69–76.

16 Catherine A. Cole and Michael J. Houston, "Encoding and Media Effects on Consumer Learning Deficiencies in the Elderly," *Journal of Marketing Research,* 24 (February 1987), 55–63. See also Gary J. Gaeth and Timothy B. Heath, "The Cognitive Processing of Misleading Advertising in Young and Old Adults," *Journal of Consumer Research,* 14 (June 1987), 43–54.

17 For recent research on the mental representation of product information, see Terry L. Childers and Madhubalan Viswanathan, "Representation of Numerical and Verbal Product Information in Consumer Memory," *Journal of Business Research,* 47 (February 2000), 109–120.

18 Allan Paivio, *Mental Representations: A Dual Coding Approach* (New York: Oxford University Press, 1986).

19 For research on how consumer-related knowledge is organized, see Gabriel Biehal and Dipankar Chakravarti, "Information-Presentation Format and Learning Goals as Determinants of Consumers' Memory Retrieval and Choice Processes," *Journal of Consumer Research,* 8 (March 1982), 431–441; Eric J. Johnson and J. Edward Russo, "The Organization of Product Information in Memory Identify by Recall Times," in H. Keith Hunt, ed., *Advances in Consumer Research,* 5 (Chicago: Association for Consumer Research, 1978), 79–86; J. Edward Russo and Eric J. Johnson, "What Do Consumers Know about Familiar Products?" in Jerry C. Olson, ed., *Advances in Consumer Research,* 7 (Ann Arbor, MI: Association for Consumer Research, 1980), 417–423.

20 John R. Anderson, *The Architecture of Cognition* (Cambridge, MA: Harvard University Press, 1983).

21 A. M. Collins and E. F. Loftus, "A Spreading Activation Theory of Semantic Processing," *Psychological Review* (November 1975), 407–428. For a recent investigation of spreading activation in the context of brand extensions, see

Maureen Morrin, "The Impact of Brand Extensions on Parent Brand Memory Structures and Retrieval Processes," *Journal Marketing Research,* 36 (November 1999), 517–525.

22 Endel Tulving and Zena Pearlstone, "Availability versus Accessibility of Information in Memory for Words," *Journal of Verbal Learning and Verbal Behavior,* 5 (August 1966), 381–391.

23 Joseph W. Alba and Amitava Chattopadhyay, "Effects of Context and Part-Category Cues on Recall of Competing Brands," *Journal of Marketing Research,* 22 (August 1985), 340–349; Joseph W. Alba and Amitava Chattopadhyay, "Salience Effects in Brand Recall," *Journal of Marketing Research,* 23 (November 1986), 363–369. See also Paul W. Miniard, H. Rao Unnava, and Sunil Bhatla, "Investigating the Recall Inhibition Effect: A Test of Practical Considerations," *Marketing Letters,* 2 (January 1991), 290–303.

24 Raymond R. Burke and Thomas K. Srull, "Competitive Interference and Consumer Memory for Advertising," *Journal of Consumer Research,* 15 (June 1988), 55–68. See also see Carolyn L. Costley and Merrie Brucks, "Selective Recall and Information Use in Consumer Preferences," *Journal of Consumer Research,* 18 (March 1992), 464–474; Kevin Lane Keller, "Memory and Evaluation Effects in Competitive Advertising Environments," *Journal of Consumer Research,* 17 (March 1991), 463–476; Rik G. M. Pieters and Tammo H. A. Bijmolt, "Consumer Memory for Television Advertising: A Field Study of Duration, Serial Position, and Competition Effects," *Journal of Consumer Research,* 23 (March 1997), 362–372. Interference effects may depend on consumers' familiarity with the advertised brand. See Robert J. Kent and Chris T. Allen, "Competitive Interference Effects and Consumer Memory for Advertising: The Role of Brand Familiarity," *Journal of Marketing,* 58 (July 1994), 97–105. The effects of advertising clutter also depend on whether memory is measured using recall or

recognition. See Tom J. Brown and Michael L. Rothschild, "Reassessing the Impact of Television Advertising Clutter," *Journal of Consumer Research,* 20 (June 1993), 138–146.

25 John Dortschner, "Ads!Are!Everywhere! .Com," *Miami Herald* (January 30, 2000), E1, E2. See also Cynthia Corzo, "Field of Ads," *Miami Herald* (January 25, 2000), C1, C3.

26 Kathryn A. Braun-LaTour and Michael S. LaTour, "Assessing the Long-Term Impact of a Consistent Advertising Campaign on Consumer Memory," *Journal of Advertising,* 33 (Summer 2004), 49–61.

27 For research on recall and recognition measures, see Adam Finn, "Print Ad Recognition Readership Scores: An Information Processing Perspective," *Journal of Marketing Research,* 25 (May 1988), 168–177; Surendra N. Singh and Gilbert A. Churchill Jr., "Using the Period of Signal Detection to Improve at Recognition Testing," *Journal of Marketing Research,* 23 (November 1986), 327–336; Surendra N. Singh and Catherine A. Cole, "Forced-Choice Recognition Tests: A Critical Review," *Journal of Advertising,* 14 (1985), 52–58; Surendra N. Singh and Michael L. Rothschild, "Recognition As a Measure of Learning from Television Commercials," *Journal of Marketing Research,* 20 (August 1983), 235–248; and Surendra N. Singh, Michael L. Rothschild, and Gilbert A. Churchill Jr., "Recognition versus Recall as Measures of Television Commercial Forgetting," *Journal of Marketing Research,* 25 (February 1988), 72–80.

28 James R. Bettman, *An Information Processing Theory of Consumer Choice* (Reading, MA: Addison-Wesley, 1979).

29 John A. Quelch and David Kenny, "Extend Profits, Not Product Lines," *Harvard Business Review,* 72 (September/October 1994), 153–160.

30 Kathleen V. Schmidt, "Marketers Win Big in Giveaway Gamble," *Marketing News* (February 28, 2000), 7.

31 Singh, Rothschild, and Churchill, "Recognition versus Recall as Measures of Television Commercial Forgetting."

32 For a discussion of advertising tactics to enhance brand recognition and recall, see John R. Rossiter and Larry Percy, "Advertising Communication Models," in Elizabeth C. Hirschman and Morris B. Holbrook, eds., *Advances in Consumer Research*, 12 (Provo, UT: Association for Consumer Research, 1985), 510–524.

33 Dorschner, "Ads!Are!Everywhere!.com."

34 "Upper Crust," *American Demographics* (March 1999), 58.

35 Katherine Yung, "Advertisers Find the Net a Hard Nut to Crack," *Miami Herald's Business Monday* (July 12, 1999), 11.

36 For a demonstration of mistaken brand identity, see Cornelia Pechmann and David W. Stewart, "The Effects of Comparative Advertising on Attention, Memory, and Purchase Intentions," *Journal of Consumer Research*, 17 (September 1990), 180–191.

37 Amitava Chattopadhyay and Joseph W. Alba, "The Situational Importance of Recall and Inference in Consumer Decision Making," *Journal of Consumer Research*, 15 (June 1988), 1–12; Barbara Loken and Ronald Hoverstad, "Relationships between Information Recall and Subsequent Attitudes: Some Exploratory Findings," *Journal of Consumer Research*, 12 (September 1985), 155–168. Note, however, that the relationship between recall and attitude is stronger when attitudes are not formed during ad processing but are formed at a later time based on retrieval of the ad information. For a discussion of this issue, see Reid Hastie and Bernadette Park, "The Relationship between Memory and Judgment Depends on Whether the Judgment Task Is Memory-Based or On-Line," *Psychological Review*, 93 (June 1986), 258–268; Meryl Lichtenstein and Thomas K. Srull, "Processing Objectives as a Determinant of the Relationship between Recall and Judgment," *Journal of Experimental Social Psychology*, 23 (March 1987), 93–118.

38 For an excellent example of research on consumers' shopping lists, see Lauren G. Block and Vicki G. Morwitz, "Shopping Lists as an External Memory Aid for Grocery Shopping: Influences on List Writing and List Fulfillment," *Journal of Consumer Psychology*, 8 (1999), 343–375.

39 Steve Helmsley, "Scents and Sensibility," *Marketing Week*, 20 (November 20, 1997), 45–50.

40 Jane Bainbridge, "Scenting Opportunities," *Marketing* (February 19, 1998), 36–37.

41 Meredith Petran, "Bakes Great, Less Filling," *Restaurants & Institutions*, 108 (April 1, 1998), 100.

42 Victor D. Chase, "Making Stereophonic Scents," *Appliance Manufacturer* (1998), 12.

43 Paula Fitzgerald Bone and Pam Scholder Ellen, "Scents in the Marketplace: Explaining a Fraction of Olfaction," *Journal of Retailing*, 75 (Summer 1999), 243–262; Charles S. Gulas and Peter H. Bloch, "Right Under Our Noses: Ambient Scent and Consumer Responses," *Journal of Business and Psychology*, 10 (1995), 87–98; Deborah J. Mitchell, Barbara E. Kahn, and Susan C. Knasko, "There's Something in the Air: Effects of Congruent or Incongruent Ambient Odor on Consumer Decision Making," *Journal of Consumer Research*, 22 (June 1995), 229–238; Eric R. Spangenberg, Ayn E. Crowley, and Pamela W. Henderson, "Improving the Store Environment: Do Olfactory Cues Affect Evaluations and Behaviors?" *Journal of Marketing*, 60 (April 1996), 67–80.

44 Maureen Morrin and S. Ratneshwar, "Does It Make Sense to Use Scents to Enhance Brand Memory?" *Journal of Marketing Research*, 40 (February 2003), 10–25.

45 Glenn Singer, "Memory Joggers," *South Florida Sun-Sentinel's Your Business* (August 25, 2003), 16–17.

46 Ibid.

47 Keith Wardell, "Spam Wars: The Second Front," *Catalog Age* (March 2005), 26–27.

48 Rob Gray, "Marketing Inspires Email Innovation," *Revolution* (May 2004), 52–54.

49 Cathy J. Cobb and Wayne D. Hoyer, "The Influence of Advertising at Moment of Brand Choice," *Journal of Advertising* (December 1986), 5–27.

50 Kevin Lane Keller, "Memory Factors in Advertising: The Effect of Advertising Retrieval Cues on Brand Evaluations," *Journal of Consumer Research*, 14 (December 1987), 316–333. For additional research on retrieval cues, see Marian Friestad and Esther Thorson, "Remembering Ads: The Effects of Encoding Strategies, Retrieval Cues, and Emotional Response," *Journal of Consumer Psychology*, 2 (1993), 1–24; Kevin Lane Keller, "Cue Comparability and Framing in Advertising," *Journal of Marketing Research*, 28 (February 1991), 42–57; and Kevin Lane Keller, "Memory and Evaluation Effects in Competitive Advertising Environments," *Journal of Consumer Research*, 17 (March 1991), 463–476.

51 Joseph O. Eastlack Jr., "How to Get More Bang for Your Television Bucks," *Journal of Consumer Marketing*, 1 (1984), 25–34.

52 Nader T. Tavassoli and Yih Hwai Lee, "The Differential Interaction of Auditory and Visual Advertising Elements with Chinese and English," *Journal of Marketing Research*, 40 (November 2003), 468–480.

53 Research on repetition effects can be found in Rajeev Batra and Michael Ray, "Situational Effects of Advertising: The Moderating Influence of Motivation, Ability and Opportunity to Respond," *Journal of Consumer Research*, 12 (March 1986), 432–445; George E. Belch, "The Effects of Television Commercial Repetition on Cognitive Response and Message Acceptance," *Journal of Consumer Research*, 9 (June 1982), 56–65; Arno J. Rethans, John L. Swasy, and Lawrence J. Marks, "Effects of Television Commercial Repetition, Receiver Knowledge, and Commercial Length: A Test of the Two-Factor Model," *Journal of Marketing Research*, 23 (February 1986), 50–61; Surendra N. Singh and Catherine A. Cole, "The Effects of Length, Content, and Repetition on Television Commercial Effectiveness," *Journal of Marketing Research*, 30 (February 1993), 91–104; Surendra N. Singh,

Michael L. Rothschild, and Gilbert A. Churchill Jr., "Recognition versus Recall as Measures of Television Commercial Forgetting," *Journal of Marketing Research,* 25 (February 1988), 72–80; and Esther Thorson and Rita Snyder, "Viewer Recall of Television Commercials: Prediction from the Propositional Structure of Commercial Scripts," *Journal of Marketing Research,* 21 (May 1984), 127–136.

54 Surendra N. Singh, Sanjay Mishra, Neeli Bendapudi, and Denise Linville, "Enhancing Memory of Television Commercials through Message Spacing," *Journal of Marketing Research,* 31 (August 1994), 384–392. For a meta-analysis of the literature on message spacing, see Chris Janiszewski, Hayden Noel, and Alan G. Sawyer, "A Meta-Analysis of the Spacing Effect in Verbal Learning: Implications for Research on Advertising Repetition and Consumer Memory," *Journal of Consumer Research,* 30 (June 2003), 138–149.

55 Punam Anand and Brian Sternthal, "Ease of Message Processing as a Moderator of Repetition Effects in Advertising," *Journal of Marketing Research,* 27 (August 1990), 345–353.

56 Burke and Srull, "Competitive Interference and Consumer Memory for Advertising."

57 "Upper Crust," *American Demographics* (March 1999), 58.

58 See, for example, T. B. Rogers, N. A. Kuiper, and W. S. Kirker, "Self-Reference and Encoding of Personal Information," *Journal of Personality and Social Psychology,* 35 (September 1977), 677–688; and Polly Brown, Janice M. Keenan, and George R. Potts, "The Self-Reference Effect with Imagery Encoding," *Journal of Personality and Social Psychology,* 51 (November 1986), 897–906.

59 Robert E. Burnkrant and H. Rao Unnava, "Self-Referencing: A Strategy for Increasing Processing of Message Content," *Personality and Social Psychology Bulletin,* 15 (December 1989), 628–638. Also see Kathleen Debevec, Harlan E. Spotts, and Jerome B. Kernan, "The Self-

Reference Effect in Persuasion: Implications for Marketing Strategy," in Melanie Wallendorf and Paul Anderson, eds., *Advances in Consumer Research,* 14 (Provo, UT: Association for Consumer Research, 1987), 417–420.

60 Sujan, Bettman, and Baumgartner, "Influencing Consumer Judgments Using Autobiographical Memories."

61 Terry L. Childers and Michael J. Houston, "Conditions for a Picture-Superiority Effect on Consumer Memory," *Journal of Consumer Research,* 11 (September 1984), 643–654; Siew Meng Leow, Swee Hoon Ang, and Lai Leng Tham, "Increasing Brand Name Recall in Print Advertising among Asian Consumers," *Journal of Advertising,* 25 (Summer 1996), 65–81; Kathy A. Lutz and Richard J. Lutz, "Effects of Interactive Imagery on Learning: Application to Advertising," *Journal of Applied Psychology,* 62 (August 1977), 493–498.

62 H. Rao Unnava and Robert E. Burnkrant, "An Imagery-Processing View of the Role of Pictures in Print Advertisements," *Journal of Marketing Research,* 28 (May 1991), 226–231.

63 Roberta L. Klatzky, *Human Memory: Structures and Processes* (San Francisco: W. H. Freeman, 1975), 230.

64 M. Carole Macklin, "Preschoolers' Learning of Brand Names from Visual Cues," *Journal of Consumer Research,* 23 (December 1996), 251–261.

65 Kevin Lane Keller, Susan E. Heckler, and Michael J. Houston, "The Effects of Brand Name Suggestiveness on Advertising Recall," *Journal of Marketing,* 62 (January 1998), 48–57; Schmitt, Tavassoli, and Millard, "Memory for Print Ads."

66 Kevin Lane Keller, Susan E. Heckler, and Michael J. Houston, "The Effects of Brand Name Suggestiveness on Advertising Recall," *Journal of Marketing,* 62 (January 1998), 48–57.

67 Ibid.

68 Christine Bittar, "'Purple Pill' on Counters No Source of Indigestion," *Brandweek* (June 21, 2004), S60.

69 Jaideep Sengupta and Gerald J. Gorn, "Ab-

sence Makes the Mind Grow Sharper: Effects of Element Omission on Subsequent Recall," *Journal of Marketing Research,* 39 (May 2002), 186–201.

70 Laura A. Peracchio and Joan Meyers-Levy, "How Ambiguous Cropped Objects in Ad Photos Can Affect Product Evaluations," *Journal of Consumer Research,* 21 (June 1994), 190–204.

71 P. H. Blaney, "Affect and Memory: A Review," *Psychological Bulletin,* 99 (March 1986), 229–246; Alice M. Isen, "Some Ways in Which Affect Influences Cognitive Processes: Implications for Advertising and Consumer Behavior," in Alice M. Tybout and P. Cafferata, eds., *Advertising and Consumer Psychology* (Lexington, MA: Lexington Books, 1989), 91–117; Patricia A. Knowles, Stephen J. Grove, and W. Jeffrey Burroughs, "An Experimental Examination of Mood Effects on Retrieval and Evaluation of Advertisement and Brand Information," *Journal of the Academy of Marketing Science* (Spring 1993), 135–143.

72 Michael J. Barone, Paul W. Miniard, and Jean Romeo, "The Influence of Positive Mood on Consumers' Evaluations of Brand Extensions," *Journal of Consumer Research,* 26 (June 2000), 386–400; Barbara E. Kahn and Alice M. Isen, "The Influence of Positive Affect on Variety Seeking among Safe, Enjoyable Products," *Journal of Consumer Research,* 20 (September 1993), 257–271.

73 "Americans Enticed by Digital Cameras," *Boston Herald,* www.bostonherald.com (December 14, 2004); "Americans Lured More Than Ever to Look at Hot-Selling Digital Cameras," *Boston Herald,* www.bostonherald.com (December 21, 2004).

74 Elaine Walker, "Bits, Bytes and Grocery Buying," *Miami Herald* (January 18, 2004), E1.

75 Bob Moos, "Specialty Companies Focus on Senior Consumers' Needs," *Dallas Morning News* (July 10, 2004), 1.

76 Deborah Ball, Sarah Ellison, and Janet Adamy, "Just What You Need!; It Takes a Lot of Marketing to Convince Consumers What They're Lacking," *Wall Street Journal* (October 28, 2004), B1.

## World's Most Customer-Centric Company?

In its 2005 presentations to financial analysts and at its shareholders meeting, Amazon.com described itself as having a new mission—to be the earth's most customer-centric company, which the company defined as "starting with the customer and working backwards." As a result, the company announced goals that included

- relentlessly improving the customer experience by expanding selection and convenience while lowering prices;
- demonstrating sustained operating progress;
- positioning for growth;
- making innovation the foundation of everything the company does; and
- focusing on optimizing free cash flow per share.

These goals are much different from when Amazon started in 1995 with the simple mission of becoming the "earth's largest bookstore."

## The Origins of Amazon

Amazon.com was born as a result of Jeff Bezos's quest to be an entrepreneur. His search began with a focus on the Internet, which was growing at 230 percent a year in the 1990s. Bezos, a graduate of Princeton University with degrees in electrical engineering and computer science, didn't start out specifically wanting to open a bookstore, but he realized that the demand for such a wide array of books could never be met by local bookstores, and he incorporated Amazon.com in 1994 and opened its website for business in July 1995.

In the massive jungle of retail concepts that appear around the globe, Jeff Bezos created a unique bookstore—Amazon in both proportion and significance. Command central for this innovative online retailer is located in Seattle, Washington, a city known for being on the progressive edge in a variety of areas including coffee (the home of Starbucks), computer software (Microsoft), retail (Costco), and rock music (Nirvana). The company's headquarters were originally located in a nondescript office, chosen for logistical reasons because it was near Ingram Books' warehouse, the largest book wholesaler in the United States and still a major Amazon vendor. This proximity allowed Amazon initially to keep the warehousing function of its inventory at the wholesaler level, rather than absorb those costs internally. In fact, Amazon originally stocked only four hundred or so of the most popular titles at any given time. The plethora of intelligent, computer-literate workers also made Seattle a logical choice for the company's homestead. Today, however, Amazon has invested hundreds of millions of dollars in its own warehouses in states such as Nevada and Kentucky, partly to handle the "reverse logistics" (returns) problem that plagues both catalog and Internet retailers. Amazon built an infrastructure of warehouses and skilled workers that achieves inventory turns (cost of goods sold divided by average inventory) of over 16 compared to 3 at Barnes and Noble, 11 at Costco, and 7 at Wal*Mart.

By January 2000, Amazon had increased its offerings to 4.7 million book, music, and movie titles and had become the leading online retailer in all of these categories. It quickly became one of the most widely known, used, and cited commerce websites, boasting an online auction house, free electronic greeting cards, and more than 18 million unique items in categories including books, CDs, toys, electronics, videos, DVDs, home-improvement products, lawn and patio furniture, kitchen products, software, baby care, beauty products, video games, and the introduction of the Segway™ human transporter.

Today, Amazon.com includes these offerings, over 45 million books in print, plus a marketplace that includes partners such as Target, Office Depot, Babies "R" Us, and Nordstrom, and plenty of marketers are worried about their future in competition with a store where customers can find and discover most anything they want to buy. At Amazon, this service is accomplished with an American Customer Satisfaction Index of 88, the highest ever achieved in the service industry.

## Marketing, Advertising, and Promotion

By leaving the majority of the warehousing and physical distribution aspects of the business to his supply chain partners, Bezos was able to focus on the marketing side of the venture—undertaking a variety of marketing strategies, including advertising, strategic alliances, and customer-interactive promotions to grow and maintain its customer base. Mark Breier, vice president of marketing for Amazon, explained, "The Internet is all about branding. It's more important here than it is offline. People have to remember your name and type it in. There are no Golden Arches or Coke cans to remind them." Because of Amazon's consumer appeal and the media's curiosity about electronic commerce, the company received extensive news coverage almost from the beginning, including *Time* magazine featuring Bezos as "Person of the Year" in 1999.

In the late 1990s, Amazon also engaged in a coordinated program of print advertising in specialized and general circulation newspapers and magazines, such as the *New York Times Book Review,* the *Wall Street Journal,* and *Wired.* The company placed banner ads on more than fifty high-profile and high-traffic-count websites, including CNET, Yahoo!, Excite, Lycos, Quote.com, and CNN, encouraging readers to click through directly to the Amazon.com bookstore to shop or browse.

To increase its exposure among current Internet users, Amazon.com forged an alliance with AOL, which accounted for 54 percent of Internet users at the time. AOL provided a link to Amazon.com on the home page accessed by AOL members when they logged on. Amazon also formed alliances with other online book retailers through its "Affiliate Program," which consists of several thousand enrolled members. Each affiliate embeds a hyperlink to Amazon's website with books recommended for that affiliate's targeted customer base. The customer is automatically connected to Amazon's site and may place his or her order. The affiliated company is able to offer enhanced services and recommendations, avoids the expenses associated with ordering and fulfillment (absorbed by Amazon), and receives up to a 15 percent commission for all orders.

### Involving Consumers

Amazon's online community attracts and nurtures consumers. Readers, customers, authors, and publishers are invited to post book reviews, and the company sponsors review competitions and provides a forum for author interviews—all designed to entertain and engage readers, enhance the shopping experience, and encourage purchases. The goal is to make Amazon.com consumers first choice for book, music, and video titles, local movie times, yellow page listings, and other information.

Amazon has developed many methods for interacting with consumers. The site provides book reviews from its editorial staff, consumers, and publications to help consumers make informed buying decisions. The company's sophisticated data mining technique customizes offerings to individual customers. And when customers don't come to Amazon.com, it goes to them, e-mailing messages to consumers when their favorite authors release new books, or new titles are released that interested similar customers. The introduction of a Harry Potter book during July 2005 brought about an almost military-style operation to ensure that most of the one million copies ordered in advance would be shipped by UPS to Amazon customers the same day the books were first available in stores.

From its beginning, Amazon has relied on its relationship-building capabilities to capture and keep its customers. Bezos's formula is simple—offer customers an authoritative selection of titles, competitive prices, and outstanding customer service to achieve a preeminent position among online retailers. Bezos explains his philosophy, "The question for all of us is are you creating value? The Web is a great place for companies of all kinds that are creating genuine value for customers, and it is a terrible place for companies that are not."

### Pricing and Costs

Due to increased competition, Amazon began slashing its prices early in its corporate life. Initially, it discounted its "Amazon.com 500" (a list that features the books the company believes will become bestsellers) by a whopping 40 percent, as compared to its standard discount of 10 percent. Today, many sites offer new and used books at lower prices than Amazon, causing the company to shift its promotional pricing to free shipping over a specified amount or unlimited free shipping for customers who subscribe to its membership service, called AmazonPrime™.

## Electronic Competition

Amazon faces plenty of competition online as well as the rock-bottom prices for best sellers that can be found in Costco, Sam's Club, and Wal*Mart stores. In Canada, Indigo Books & Music, which recently merged with Canada's top retail brand, Chapters, offers strong competition both in its stores and online. Walmart.com also sells books on its website, with orders fulfilled by its partners and usually at lower prices than Amazon. Barnes & Noble not only competes online through barnesandnoble.com but also at its stores by giving customers a chance to sip their favorite Starbucks brew while browsing the latest magazines, newspapers, and books. Amazon.com's current and potential competitors include bricks-and-mortar retailers for nearly every product it sells and, of course, public libraries. Numerous specialty booksellers partner with existing distributors (such as Baker & Taylor and Ingram Book Group) that help establish and operate online sites for booksellers. Some of these websites are featured on Amazon.com, often with lower prices than orders fulfilled by Amazon. Half.com, eBay's book and music affiliate, offers a robust selection of used media, although some sellers also list their goods on Amazon.com. Traditional, location-based retailers of music and DVDs still command most of the sales in the book, music, and video categories, and location-based retailers also dominate in most other categories.

## Location-Based Book Retailers

Bezos and his team believe that several characteristics of the traditional book industry have created inefficiencies for all participants—creating opportunity for an alternative channel. Physical store–based book retailers must make significant investments in inventory, real estate, and personnel for each location. This capital and real estate business model, among other things, limits the amount of inventory that can be economically carried in any location. Even book superstores can offer their customers only a small proportion of the total books in print because of limited retail shelf space. In addition, publishers typically offer generous rights of return for their customers and, as a result, effectively bear the risk of their customers' demand forecasting, which encourages overordering. As a result, returns in the book industry are high, creating substantial additional costs. Finally, publishers and traditional book retailers are not as readily equipped, at this time, to collect demographic and psychographic (and behavioral) data about their customers, limiting opportunities for direct marketing and personalized services, compared to the sophisticated customer relationship management (CRM) programs developed by Amazon.

## Customer Service

Amazon relies heavily on its supply chain partners for accurate fulfillment and on-time delivery, thereby entrusting many components of customer satisfaction to its partners. But ultimately, it is Amazon that is responsible for the service that consumers experience. Although the company lists, and effectively advertises, millions of titles, consumers must read the fine print when it comes to fulfillment of orders. Some titles are available for shipment within forty-eight to seventy-two hours, and the remainder of in-print titles are generally available within four to six weeks; out-of-print titles generally are available in two to six months, but some of these may not be available at all.

## Electronic Commerce: Where It's Been and Where It's Going

Electronic retailing has a well-documented history of both failures and successes, and it has been the topic of many academic articles, dating back to the 1960s. A famous *Harvard Business Review* article over two decades ago predicted that supermarkets would soon be "shopped" at home through electronic connections. In fact, many online grocery projects such as Peapod and Webvan were attempted in the United States and failed. The history of electronic retailing includes the early experiments in interactivity such as Qube, owned by Time Warner Cable, which stimulated interest in entertainment but not shopping. Viewtron, a Knight Ridder and AT&T project in Florida, included the ability to run shopping carts through local supermarkets from a television set at home, in the manner of Pacman and Ms. Pacman, which were popular at the time. This project was backed by millions of dollars but failed. CompuServe started an online shopping mall in the early 1980s, but its retailing successes were limited, and the company was later acquired by AOL. The primary reason Prodigy was started and funded by Sears (along with IBM) was to be a shopping service. Although Prodigy achieved limited success as an Internet service provider, its shopping capabilities never took off.

Most of the Internet-based forms of retailing failed during the dot-bomb era of the late 1990s because they did nothing better than bricks-and-mortar stores. Today, according to the Census of Business, after nearly two decades of Internet retailing experiments, Internet shopping accounts for less than 2 percent of total retail sales. This finding has caused some observers to label electronic retailing as a strategy that has great potential and always will be exactly that—a form of retailing with great potential. Is the Internet primarily for selling by retailers or searching by consumers? Amazon's future lies in the hands and minds of consumers. Is it good for aggregating demand for specialty or niche products or will consumers use it for everyday purchases? The Internet's success in retailing will in part be determined by how many consumers (who have historically used traditional means of commerce to purchase merchandise) accept and utilize electronic shopping and buying.

In 2000, Amazon announced that the majority of its sales are now from items other than books. Sales outside the United States (through the company's country-based subsidiaries) are also now growing faster than in the U.S., with nearly half of Amazon's sales coming from the United Kingdom, Germany, France, Japan, and China.

## Amazon's Financial Performance

After reading this case, go to a financial website or Amazon.com's own website in its "Investor Relations" section, and you'll find that financial performance has been anything but stellar. Sales have risen rapidly, but profits have been elusive. The company's investments in technology, physical plants, and marketing have been so extensive that in 2005, the company's balance sheet still reported negative worth and its profit and loss statement showed profits that only recently were even positive and still minuscule.

The first chapter of Amazon.com's future has been written. It's a story of consumer enthusiasm and media attention. Now, consumer lifestyles and the realities of the electronic marketplace as well as Amazon's mission and management will determine if that story will end with Amazon living "happily ever after" or becoming another dot.com tragedy. To prepare your analysis of this case, search online to determine the trends of recent years and your projections of the future.

FOCAL TOPICS

1. What does it mean to have the mission, "the earth's most customer-centric company"? How well is Amazon achieving this mission?

2. What are the supply chain or demand chain elements essential to the operations and marketing of Amazon? Where are its warehouses located and why are they located there? How can the lessons learned from Amazon be applied to other forms of e-commerce and integrated marketing strategies?

3. Which elements of Amazon's marketing mix (remember the four P's from Chapter 2—product, place, price, and promotion) are most successful and which are least successful?

4. What is the nature of competition faced by Amazon? Who are the major competitors on the Internet? Who are the major competitors in traditional forms of retailing? Who will win?

5. What components of the political-legal environment affect the marketing and operations of Amazon and other online marketers? (State laws? Federal laws? Political and economic developments?)

6. What are the strengths and weaknesses of Amazon's pricing strategy? How do its prices compare with competitors on specific books? On these specific books, how do Amazon's prices compare with bricks-and-mortar retailers such as Wal*Mart or Costco and, ultimately, libraries and electronic reference sources.

7. Which products sold by Amazon are likely to be most successful? Consider both B2C (business-to-consumer) and B2B (business-to-business). Support your analysis with both marketing theory and empirical research.

8. How successful is Amazon's global marketing?

9. How successful is Amazon financially (in terms of profitability, size, debt, stock price, and so forth)? Note: Check the Security and Exchange Commission's Edgar database at www.sec.gov, or other financial news websites, for the latest financial reports.

## Product Design Based on Consumption Analysis

Imagine being given free rein to design a car. Not just any car, but a *concept* car, with the goal of pleasing a group of consumers that car companies have determined is the most demanding—professional women.

Volvo did exactly that with Your Concept Car (YCC), a car project managed and designed by an all-female "think tank" team with the female consumer in mind. The statement, "If you meet the expectations of women, you'll exceed the expectations of men," became the motto for the concept car project. Noting that 54 percent of American Volvo buyers are women—a percentage that continues to increase—Volvo president and CEO Hans-Olov Olsson was an enthusiastic proponent of the project.

## Meeting the Need

Volvo research indicates that in the United States, women purchase about 65 percent of cars and influence about 80 percent of all car sales; yet, for a century, men have made most of the decisions in the design, development, and production of cars. In June of 2002, an all-female team of project managers and automobile designers was assembled, including:

Eva-Lisa Andersson, project manager
Camilla Palmertz, project manager
Elna Holmberg, technical project manager
Maria Widell Christiansen, design manager
Tatiana Butovitsch Temm, communications
 manager
Lena Ekelund, deputy technical project manager
Cynthia Charwick, interior designer
Anna Rosen, exterior designer
Maria Uggla, color and trim designer

After preliminary studies, the project was given the go-ahead in December 2002 and the final product was unveiled March 2, 2004, at the Geneva International Motor Show.

The team determined that women customers in the premium segment want everything that men want in terms of performance, prestige, and style. But they want more as well:

- smart storage solutions
- a car that is easy to get in and out of
- good visibility
- a car that can be personalized
- minimal maintenance
- a car that is easy to park

These needs can be met in a variety of ways, including some simple solutions that immediately draw the question, "Why hasn't anyone done this before?" The design team feels that YCC's strength is its focus on customer needs. To understand how women actually use their cars, the team tapped the consumption patterns of over four hundred female Volvo employees.

The YCC was designed to provide what women want in their primary vehicle. Listening to these target consumers, the team adapted the head restraint to accommodate a ponytail for increased comfort and safety of the driver. In response to drivers who use the back seat more often for groceries, gym bags, and laptop computers than for passengers, YCC's back seats are designed like movie theater seats that fold upright until needed for passengers, freeing room on the back floor for loading and unloading. The gull wing doors are designed so that the consumer never has to climb over a dirty surface to get into the back seat; the sill of the door drops down to expose a clean interior. Improved storage involved moving the gear lever and handbrake. The center console now has a shallow compartment for keys, mobile phones, and so forth, with a sliding back compartment capable of storing a purse out of sight. There is also a space for a notebook computer, a "cool box," and a wastepaper basket.

The appearance of the interior is customizable with eight interchangeable upholstery options ranging from leather, linen, and wool bouclé and a shimmering embroidered seat pad, all with matching carpeting. Consistent with Scandinavian tradition, the interior is light, open, and uses materials associated with fine home interiors.

An "Ergovision" system at the dealership scans drivers' bodies and configures optimum driving positions based on the data. The settings are stored digitally on the key unit. When the customer docks the key unit, the seat, steering wheel, pedals, head restraint, and seat belt all automatically move to the designated positions. The customer can also add additional data sets, but the car watchfully notifies the consumer if a data set creates a less-than-optimal line of vision. The car itself can change ride height, "Hi," for a commanding view of the road, or "Lo," for a sporty low ride. The car automatically goes to the high position when the door is opened—a more comfortable height for passengers entering and exiting.

For visibility and safety, the exterior has been designed with a low front end and a long rear window so that all four corners of the car are visible to the driver. The fenders are within view and covered with a sturdy material. The bumper goes all around the vehicle. YCC's exterior finish is similar to that of a nonstick pan, with easy-clean paint that repels dirt and is easy to wash. The seat covers and carpets are also washable.

Day-to-day car maintenance doesn't require access under the hood of the car. The windshield washer fluid filler is located right beside the gas filling point, both with ball-valve fillers that eliminate the need for caps or latches. The entire car front lifts up so there is no "bonnet" or hood because only service technicians should need access to the engine. When service is due, the car automatically notifies a designated service center and even suggests an appointment time. The car also carries out its own diagnostic checks and informs the service center of what parts and materials will be required when the car arrives for service.

Parallel parking is two button clicks away. The first push of the parking assistance button determines if there is sufficient space between two cars to parallel park. If the answer is "yes," a second push steers the car into the space but leaves the driver in control of braking and accelerating.

AP Topic Gallery

Volvo's 'Your Concept Car' is sleek and low maintenance.

YCC's engine is designed to meet the toughest emission standards, with an Integrated Starter-Generator (ISG). The ISG enables the car to shut off when waiting at lights, but comes to life immediately when the accelerator is pushed. The six-speed gearshift can be set on fully automatic, and gears are changed by a switch on the steering column. Powershift ensures that the gear changes are always at the right revs, making for smooth driving and efficient fuel consumption.

Volvo may never actually take YCC into production, but many of the ideas developed by the female think tank may still appear in more conventional Volvos, as well as the models of other car manufacturers. Volvo is a subsidiary of the Ford Motor Company, and the Swedish carmaker's insistence on practicality and safety is diffusing in concept and production models in all of Ford's divisions.

## FOCAL TOPICS

1. Which design elements of the Volvo YCC are most valuable to female consumers?

2. How will male consumers respond to these design elements?

3. What other elements of consumer consumption of cars should be built into future models?

4. Using the consumer decision process (CDP) model, how would you recommend marketing the Volvo YCC?

5. If you were a marketing executive at another car manufacturer, how would you respond to the Volvo YCC?

Note: This case was prepared with the assistance of Ms. Mary Hiser.

## Data Mining the Consumer Decision Process

In today's marketplace, companies are constantly challenged to deliver results that meet a high level of financial expectations. The question isn't what to do, but how to do it better and how to keep improving it. Profitable growth is no longer driven by expansion alone—and every business is in search of ways to do more with less, including

- increasing market share with a shrinking consumer population,
- boosting operational effectiveness while cutting overhead expenses,
- bringing the greatest value to consumers or businesses at the lowest possible cost, and
- reaching out to customers who have an unprecedented number of purchasing options.

One leader in assisting marketers to accomplish these goals is Equitec, a business solutions provider based in Westlake (a suburb of Cleveland, Ohio) that serves some of the largest global supply chains. Founded in 1995 by CEO Michael Henry, a marketer with an extensive background in retail productivity consulting and information-based technologies, Equitec is dedicated to optimizing client growth and productivity. In 2003, Equitec merged with OPUS Interactive, a multichannel consortia database company, to provide clients with production-based business solutions founded on the most accurate sources of multiple dimensions of consumer data. Equitec's clients include leading demand chains such as Home Depot, Procter & Gamble, General Electric, and Sabre Systems (operator of Travelocity.com and other travel-related services).

Consumer Dynamics, Equitec's proprietary information platform, integrates point-of-sale (POS) and other sales data (e.g., customers, transaction history, and marketing and channel preferences) with external consumer information, creating specific strategies to target consumer segments most responsive to a firm's strategies. Equitec solutions provide retailers and other organizations with data-driven solutions to their most important business initiatives by leveraging the predictive data found in Consumer Dynamics. The company partners with premier providers of syndicated U.S. and proprietary consumer data to offer customer-centric retail solutions to the nation's leading marketing organizations.

Equitec's solutions identify supply chain efficiencies; increase revenues and decrease operational costs; improve incremental sales, profits, and return on investment (ROI); and target marketing at the household or business level. The solutions uncover the correlation between customer behavior and several areas of expenditures, including advertising and marketing, inventory, merchandising, real estate, information technology, sales and service, financial services, and customer relationships. To optimize the process, Equitec integrates with existing processes and systems resulting in a more customer-intelligent enterprise.

Consumer Dynamics is implemented for Equitec clients by a team of pioneers in consumer behavior and consumer-based strategies who have achieved notable industry firsts, including

- building an integrated multidimensional consumer database (including demographic, lifestyle, attitudinal, and behavioral data),
- integrating consumer data with POS data,
- correlating advertising mix and media spending with household (HH)-level consumer behavioral data,
- building an HH-level collaboration system,
- collecting and using self-reported lifestyle information,
- developing and automating consumer profile analysis models, and
- establishing a dynamic data collection system.

Because of Equitec's partnerships with multiple data contributors, the company is able to identify multiple characteristics (approximately 160 different variables) of consumers for most of the nation's households based on a consumer's street address, e-mail address, or phone number. When linked to sales transactions for customers with similar characteristics using SAS advanced analytics software, Equitec enables a business to quantify consumer demand, locate the demand, and identify

- potential new market locations,
- prospect opportunities,

- merchandising trends by local market,
- actionable market segments, and
- optimal marketing and advertising channels.

The content and relationships to the consumer purchase decision of Consumer Dynamics are shown in Exhibit 3.1. Traditional marketing analysis functioned on the base of the pyramid, starting with a database of names and progressively adding demographics, geodemographic variables, lifestyles, and attitudes, leading to propensities to buy and eventually readiness to purchase. The power of Consumer Dynamics is shown in Exhibit 3.2, which describes the "lift" or additional response rates (562:1)

achieved from targeting market segments based on each level of additional information about consumers in that segment. Rather than directing a promotional piece to all consumers on a general mailing list, for example, a promotion to segments defined on each of the variables shown in the pyramid creates "lift" or increased response rate 562 times greater than a general mailing, based on actual POS data from a client firm. Exhibits 3.3 and 3.4 contrast the traditional view of consumers based on basic demographic data compared to a view of the consumer using the Consumer Dynamics database and analytical techniques.

## FOCAL TOPICS

1. Which variables in the consumer decision process (CDP) model are captured in the Consumer Dynamics model?

2. How should a firm use this information to improve
   a. targeted promotions,
   b. store locations,
   c. store inventories and supply chain management, and
   d. return on marketing investments?

3. Which retailers (or other organizations) would be the best target clients for Equitec?

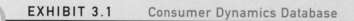

### EXHIBIT 3.1    Consumer Dynamics Database

3.1

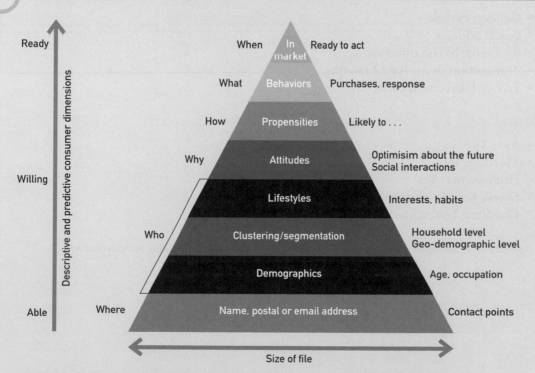

## EXHIBIT 3.2 The Power of Consumer Dynamics

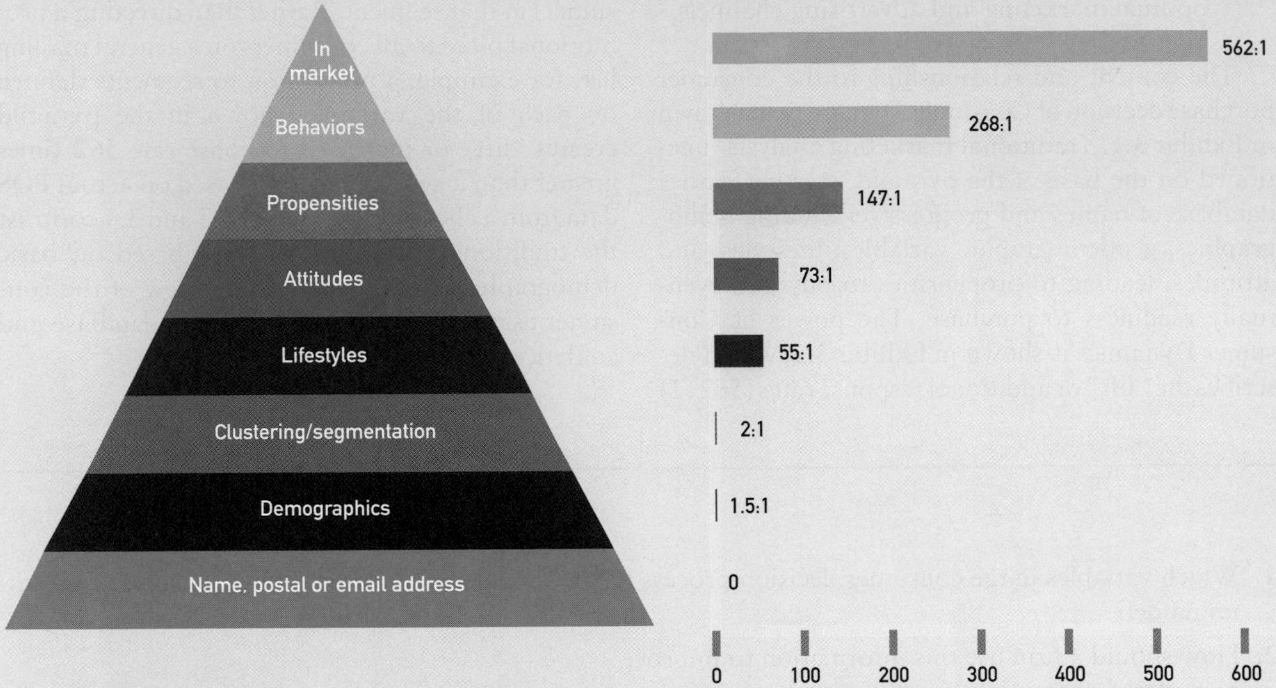
In market
Behaviors
Propensities
Attitudes
Lifestyles
Clustering/segmentation
Demographics
Name, postal or email address
562:1
268:1
147:1
73:1
55:1
2:1
1.5:1
0
0
100
200
300
400
500
600



## EXHIBIT 3.3 Traditional View of Customer

### Internal Information

- Gender: Female
- Postal address
- 0–3 months last purchase
- Transaction detail for 12 months
- Private label credit card

### Demographic Detail Appended

- Age: 31
- Married: Yes
- Homeowner: Yes
- Email: Kclark@ibm.com
- Children: 1 preschooler

**EXHIBIT 3.4**    Consumer Dynamics View of Customer

3.4

- Interests: Theatre/shows, horseracing, spa, and sports
- Lifestyle: Young and professional
- Ambitious
- Stressed mom
- Family centered
- Trendy
- Online: Auto rental, vacation packages, books, and CDs
- Direct Mail: Catalog buyer
- Multisource profile
- Multibuyer profile
- Promotional campaign history
- Total $ spending
- Media preferences
- Channel preferences
- Buying cycle profile
- Life stage events

## Family Owned and Operated

Family Furniture was established in 1953, shortly after the beginning of the building boom that occurred in response to pent-up housing demand after World War II. Founded by Sy Sokol and Patrick O'Reilly, the firm prospered during the latter half of the twentieth century by providing good customer service, an inviting store appearance, extensive selection, and moderate prices.

By 2005, the firm occupied an 80,000-square-foot store, with a large warehouse and shipping facility. It also operated a 50,000-square-foot satellite store in a fast-growing suburb. Its hometown had grown to an area of 600,000 people, a prosperous community with a major state university and several smaller colleges and universities. Although not located in a large city, three other cities with over 1 million residents are located within 150 miles of Family Furniture.

Ownership has changed over the years with the original partners retiring, and ownership eventually ending up in the hands of the current owner, Cheryl Davidson (who is president and CEO but also oversees all marketing operations). Cheryl's brother Greg owns a smaller number of shares in the company and serves as manager of operations, overseeing inbound logistics, the warehouse, and the company's extensive fleet of delivery vehicles. Although descendants of the founders, Cheryl's and Greg's ownership was purchased from the original owners, financed mostly by loans paid off from profits over the years. Profits were excellent in the 1980s and 1990s, but have declined since 2001 due to flat sales, escalating employee health care benefit costs, and increasing inventory and logistics costs.

## Competition

Over the years, Family Furniture's biggest competitors were other furniture stores, as well as the local department store until it stopped selling furniture. Several of the furniture stores have gone out of business or consolidated with the remaining ones. Although some are still effective competitors, none is as large as Family Furniture.

There's no IKEA store in Family Furniture's city, but there's one in a city 125 miles away, and Cheryl is aware that some of her customers drive there to purchase furniture and household accessories. She's also concerned that an increasing number of customers report that they are buying furniture from Pottery Barn and Crate & Barrel, which have stores in the two regional shopping centers serving the city. Cheryl is also concerned that some customers may be buying furniture on the Internet and having it shipped directly to their homes. She knows that mass retailers like Wal*Mart and Target carry numerous furniture items, usually sold *kd* (knocked down, with assembly required), and that warehouse clubs like Sam's and Costco carry a limited selection of top-of-the-line leather sofas and recliners. "Big box" office supply stores also carry desks, chairs, table lamps, and some other items sold by Family Furniture, and specialty carpet stores compete with carpeting lines that Family Furniture has sold well over the years.

## A Changing Market

In recent months, Cheryl has spent time observing and talking to customers in the store, noticing that their ages typically are older—forty-five and up for the most part. Yet the city has many young consumers who graduate from local universities and take jobs in the city or nearby areas. There is also a rapidly increasing number of Latinos living and working in the city and a stable level of about 12 percent African Americans. Because of the university and research orientation of the city, there is also a significant group of well-educated, highly compensated Asian Americans in the community. Unemployment in the city has been low, generally in the 4–5 percent level, even during the recession of the early 2000s, because of the employment base consisting mostly of white-collar, well-educated workers.

Cheryl was particularly interested in what to do about the lack of younger consumers in her store. Family Furniture's market target historically was middle- to higher-income families, who were usually also above age forty-five. Historically, the store targeted females, usually married and making purchasing decisions for the entire family. After reading an article in *Furniture Today*, a trade journal serving the furniture industry, Cheryl began to think of the implications of the U.S. population now consisting of households 50 percent single, and 50 percent married. She also read that those who do marry generally wait until their late twenties. She also wondered if the company was correct to target women rather than men in Family Furniture's marketing plan, especially in a city with many single, young professionals living in the university area and upscale areas of new apartments and condos.

The promotional program of Family Furniture relied on newspaper advertising for much of its early history. More recently, the advertising budget has shifted to television, with commercials placed during or adjacent to local news programs in prime viewing times. A local advertising agency has been responsible for preparing creative content for both print and television, generally showing the location and selection of Family Furniture and emphasizing helpful, friendly service by the store's experienced staff. Although Cheryl emphasizes quality furniture, including well-known national brands, she has been perplexed at how to respond to some competitive furniture stores using "no, no, no" advertising, emphasizing "no down payment, no interest, and no payments until next year." She was recently approached by a small "boutique" advertising agency named Cult Advertising, which suggested the use of nontraditional marketing techniques involving community involvement, a redesigned website, and the purchase of certain key words from Google or other search engines. Cheryl has taken no action on their ideas to incorporate these techniques in the Family Furniture promotional budget.

While talking with a marketing professor at one of the local universities, she asked about the need for research to understand changing markets, how consumers make furniture purchase decisions, and the most effective use of her marketing budget. She also asked the professor's opinion about how to respond to the increasing use of "no, no, no" advertising by competitors. After further discussion, the professor agreed to consider these issues in a research project to be conducted by students in a future class.

## Research Study and Results

Students in the marketing class conducted research consisting of three components: secondary research, focus groups, and a survey of one hundred consumers in the core market targets. The sample was constructed to emphasize consumers in the markets in which Family Furniture historically had low penetration: young (average age thirty), male (75 percent), and well educated (college or graduate degree). Responses indicated that 42 percent had household incomes in the range of $50,000 to $75,000, 25 percent between $75,000 to $100,000, 18 over $100,000, and 15 percent under $50,000. The focus groups and questions to the survey were developed using a multistage consumer decision process (CDP) model measuring need recognition, search processes, pre-purchase, alternative evaluation, purchase, consumption, and post-consumption evaluation and divestment.

Some key findings from this research are presented in Tables 4.1, 4.2, and 4.3, along with a summary of the focus group findings in Table 4.4.

| TABLE 4.1 | What Prompted Your Most Recent Furniture Purchase? |
|---|---|

| MOTIVATION | PERCENTAGE OF RESPONDENTS |
|---|:---:|
| Moving | 36 |
| Need more furniture | 36 |
| Home improvement | 15 |
| Other | 13 |

Note: Study used open-ended questions. *Need more furniture* includes answers such as "necessity," "home office," and "build a CD library." *Home improvement* includes answers such as "need comfort," "organization," "remodeling," "replace old furniture," and "wife wants to redecorate." *Other* includes "having more money," "getting a job," "impulse purchase," "starting to live alone," "great deal," "family expansion," and simply "wife's decision."

**4.2**

TABLE 4.2        Reasons for Choosing a Particular Store

| REASON | PERCENTAGE OF RESPONDENTS |
|---|---|
| Advertising | 3 |
| Previous experience | 28 |
| Sale or promotion | 36 |
| Recommendation of friend | 17 |
| Other | 23 |

Note: *Other* includes a wide range of answers including "type of furniture," "garage sale," "quality," "location," "had styles that I like," "brand," and so forth.

**4.3**

TABLE 4.3        Preferred Financing Offers

| TYPE OF OFFER | PERCENTAGE OF RESPONDENTS |
|---|---|
| Discount for cash payment (e.g., 10 percent, 15 percent) | 8 |
| No interest, no payment for first six months | 1 |
| Eighteen months no payment, no interest | 1 |
| No interest for twelve months | 5 |
| No interest for six months | 12 |
| No interest for three months | 1 |
| No interest for eighteen months | 1 |
| No interest for two years | 2 |
| No payment for six months | 1 |
| No payment for first year | 2 |
| On sale, 20 percent off | 1 |

Note: Forty percent said they would have made the purchase without the financing offer, 11 percent said they would buy some but not all of their purchased items without financing, and 18 percent said they would have made no purchase without financing.

People want to make well-informed, thought-out furniture buying decisions, but often make impulse purchases when they know a furniture purchase is going to be made soon. Respondents frequently reported that their last purchase was made quickly without doing a lot of research because they needed a new piece of furniture, but next time they intend to research; ask family, friends, or coworkers for recommendations; and shop around before making a purchase. When actually faced with a furniture need, consumer intentions are often abandoned if they feel they are getting a good deal on a piece that fits their need.

The most common reasons for new furniture purchases revolved around a life event such as a marriage, birth of a child, a divorce, or moving to a new home. Another common reason was replacing an old or nonfunctional piece. Despite their intentions, buyers make relatively impulsive purchases because the need for the furniture supersedes the need to make a disciplined purchase.

People were most likely to trust information they received from friends or family, and were least likely to trust furniture advertising. One person described furniture ads as "shady." Several people, however, commented that the thing that caused them to enter the store where they eventually made the purchase was a large "SALE" sign. Additionally, people said they would be reluctant to purchase furniture without being able to physically try it out and feel the comfort and workmanship themselves. As a result, many commented that they would search for ideas of styles and brands they like in catalogs and online, but would then look for that brand, or a brand with a similar style, at a store so they could see the furniture in person and try it out themselves.

Regarding the actual purchase, many people said that they had used financing in the past, but would be reluctant to use it again, preferring to save up and pay cash for the item or use a major credit card instead of private label credit. Reasons given for not wanting to use financing included not wanting to lower their credit score, not being sure they understand how financing works, and being worried that charges and interest might end up costing more than the discounts they are receiving. Respondents in this focus group of professional, higher-income consumers were sensitive to the issue of protecting their credit rating. Some indicated that a loyalty or reward program would be preferable to a store credit card. Most people suggested that a store credit card would only be used to get "no,no,no" financing, pay off the balance (even if that meant transferring the balance to another credit card), and then close the account or just cease using the card. The common reason for this statement was perception that store cards may have very high interest and finance charges if items are not paid in full before the end of the promotional period.

Some consumers stated that they will avoid store credit except in cases when they have an "emergency" need for an item and cannot afford to pay cash. On the other hand, several stated that they will use financing for the following reasons: they currently have lower income, but anticipate either a future windfall or increase in income; they desire to feel, or exude the perception, that they can enjoy a lifestyle that is above what they can afford by spreading the payments over a long period of time; or they have a great need because of their current state of life or a life event and lack the resources to afford what they need without financing.

## FOCAL TOPICS

1. Based on your own secondary research, how important as a market target should Gen Y and young professionals be for Family Furniture?

2. Using a multistage CDP model, describe how consumers in this market segment (Gen Y and young professionals) typically make furniture purchase decisions.

3. How should Family Furniture respond to competitors?

4. What promotional strategy and media do you recommend for Family Furniture?

5. What should be the response of Family Furniture to the "no, no, no" advertising used by competitors?

## A War Is Brewing

Ask the management of CrimsonCup Coffee & Tea if they believe "Little David" can take on "Goliath," and you will hear a resounding "YES." Contrary to popular belief, statistics show that small, prepared coffee retailers are growing faster than the mighty Starbucks. And since 1991, CrimsonCup has served independent coffee houses that definitely are not Starbucks, teaching independent coffee shop owners the skills needed to operate a viable and competitive business. If you visit its website (www .crimsoncup.com), oriented toward retailers, you'll find a book (*The Seven Steps to Success: A Common-Sense Guide to Succeed in Specialty Coffee*) written by CrimsonCup's founder Greg Ubert that explains these skills. Consumer information can be found at www.forindependentthinkers.com.

The firm is known for premium coffees that appeal to avid coffee drinkers. From Colombia to Jamaica, from Africa to Hawaii, the firm selects the best coffees from around the world, including Fair Trade certified, organic, signature blends, and flavored coffees in light, medium, and dark roasts. CrimsonCup only purchases Class I Specialty Grade Coffee—the top 5 percent of coffee grown worldwide—and its organic coffees are USDA certified by Quality Certification Services.

CrimsonCup is a small-batch craft-roaster and wholesale distributor offering a full line of coffee and tea products and services. Its expert baristas have opened well over one hundred coffee shops around the country and its Start-up Program includes everything needed to operate independently without the constraints of franchise agreements. This program includes

- comprehensive training,
- merchandising tools,
- professional site evaluation,
- interior space design and layout,
- equipment package,
- continual marketing support,
- award-winning coffee,
- complete drink recipe book, and
- full coffee shop product line.

The nature of coffee consumption has changed considerably over the past decade. Brought on by an insurgence of gourmet coffee retailers, the American coffee culture has evolved to a point where "getting a coffee, going out for coffee, is our little space in the workday to call our own."[1] This evolution in coffee consumption illustrates the importance of coffee in the American culture as more than simply a quick pick-me-up in the morning. According to the 2003 Coffee Consumption Trends Report by the National Coffee Association, 28 percent of daily coffee consumption in the United States is classified as gourmet coffee, up from 18 percent just a few years ago. In a separate study conducted by Mintel Consumer Intelligence, two-thirds of respondents drink coffee away from home at least occasionally.[2] Although Starbucks paved the path for consumer acceptance, independents are now providing the fastest growth.[3] According to a survey of six hundred participants by New York–based brand and customer loyalty research firm Brand Keys, the five most important factors that influence purchasing decisions are

1. recommendations from family or friends,
2. TV commercials,
3. store displays,
4. free samples in the mall, and
5. fliers and newspaper coupons.

Also, according to a U.S. Coffee Shop Market report, the driving factors of consumer demand are quality and convenience. Along these lines the report found the following beliefs and habits among coffee consumers: 58 percent of respondents who regularly buy coffee at a coffee shop said coffee shops offer better-quality coffee. Only 33 percent of all respondents, however, said they think coffee shops sell better coffee than those of their competitors, and only 37 percent of consumers who purchase their coffee at coffee shops instead of brewing it at home normally go to the closest one.[4]

[1] Haidee Allerton, "Ode to a Coffee Urn: When Did It Become All About Coffee?" *T + D* (May 2004), 1.
[2] "Independent Coffeehouse Trade Association Formed," *Gourmet Retailer* (March 2002), 13.
[3] "Starbucks Expansion Plans Full Steam Ahead," *Display & Design Ideas* (April 2004), 12.
[4] "U.S. Coffee Consumption Patterns," *Gourmet Retailer* (March 2002), 13.

CrimsonCup derived its name from the school color of Harvard, Ubert's alma mater. In recent years, the company has added to its brand the slogan, "Coffee for Independent Thinkers"™. This slogan is intended to act as a quality seal of approval. Coffee houses who display this seal in their windows are united in their promise to offer quality drinks in a clean and friendly environment. CrimsonCup's independent retailers report, "People see 'Coffee for Independent Thinkers' and come in to the coffee house. They like the message." Statements like this one have led CrimsonCup management to consider whether or not that might be a better brand than CrimsonCup. To help in this and other decisions, CrimsonCup participated in research designed to understand gourmet coffee consumers better.

## Consumer Research

The consumer research consisted of two phases—focus groups and a survey of several hundred consumers who were university students or closely related to the university environment. The focus groups indicated that the physiological effect from caffeine is a primary reason for coffee consumption. Consumers indicated that they need a boost in the morning and that coffee helps them. Other repeated themes included the desire for something hot and tasty, as well as the routine and tradition of sharing a drink with friends as a social event. When choosing where to buy coffee, most people indicated that they preferred to go the closest location, but the decision to return was based on their own experiences and opinions as well as a combination of taste, price, and location. Speed of service was also mentioned as a factor when deciding where to go. When going for social reasons, atmosphere is important, but less when going alone. People reported getting information on new coffee houses from word-of-mouth based on other people's experiences.

When buying coffee, focus group participants report occasionally buying such things as bagels and sandwiches, although some believed this food was too expensive at coffee shops. Some said they would sometimes "splurge" when tempted by items such as cookies and donuts, even though they had not planned on purchasing these items. Respondents reported that they drink coffee at different times of the day. Most everyone said they drink coffee in the morning, but some mentioned drinking after lunch, in the evening, or to stay awake at night. Most people reported drinking coffee consistently throughout the year, with a few tending to increase consumption in the winter months.

Most everyone reported a bad experience with coffee at some time. When that happened, they stopped going to the store and typically told the people they were with as well as a few friends. Some mentioned obnoxious customers as a negative influence on returning to a store.

A quantitative study was conducted to validate the focus group results. On a 10-point scale, location received the highest score with an average of 6.6, followed by taste at 6.43, and atmosphere at 6.04. Among factors that would discourage return to a store, however, taste was ranked highest at 6.98. Price ranked fifth at 5.19 as a factor influencing choice of a store, but ranked fourth at 6.00 as an attribute that would discourage return to the store. Brand ranked low on both measures with scores of 4.95 for positive attributes and 4.56 as a discouraging factor. Brand, though ranked low as a reason for choosing a store or determining frequency of visits to that store, for a favored brand was a reason to purchase it for office or home use. The most positive items sometimes bought at a coffee shop were breakfast foods such as bagels and muffins (55 percent), followed by sweets such as cookies and cakes (14 percent), and chai tea (8 percent). Only 13 percent indicated not ever purchasing other items from a coffee shop.

As a wholesaler of coffee and tea and a provider of marketing programs to independent coffee shops and retailers, CrimsonCup has experienced growth over the past decade and is within range of becoming the nation's second- or third-largest alternative to Starbucks. Its branding mission has focused on creating the independent retailer as the brand, rather than the product or supplier. The CrimsonCup brand is featured on packaged coffee sold by retailers for office or home consumption, on mugs and cups provided to retailers and in some other promotional materials, and the firm is now considering the issue of whether it should be more aggressive in its promotion of the CrimsonCup or Coffee for Independent Thinkers brands as well as how best to develop its strategy of helping the independent coffee shops it serves.

1. Using the consumer decision process (CDP) model, describe how consumers in different market segments choose retailers of coffee.

2. What additional research should be conducted to validate your assumptions about consumer decisions at each stage of the CDP model?

3. What marketing programs should CrimsonCup provide to its customers, independent coffee shops, and some grocery stores and restaurants?

4. Should the company place its emphasis on the CrimsonCup brand or the Coffee for Independent Thinkers brand?

5. What marketing recommendations would you suggest, both for its primary customers (i.e., coffee shops) and for its ultimate customers (i.e., its customers' customers)?

## A Look Inside a Hard Discounter

When gas prices soar, most consumers have to reduce their spending on other things. If they could buy a $3.50 box of cereal for $1.39 or a $2.99 package of tomatoes for $0.99, and get the same or better quality, the supermarket might be the easiest place to start for frugal consumers. Some consumers don't have the skill to evaluate products of different prices, simply choosing higher-priced items on the assumption that higher price means higher quality. Other households have enough discretionary income that price increases for gasoline don't affect the purchase of other items. This is the environment for a food fight—the battle for consumers' food dollars.

The stakes are high because all consumers must eat. Some retailers, such as Whole Foods, Wild Oats Market, and The Fresh Market stake out a "lifestyle" or "quality" position with niche-oriented strategies appealing to consumers who value gourmet, organic, and specialty products. Others compete on location or convenience, such as Kroger, Publix, and Albertsons, with neighborhood locations across the country. Last, some compete on price, with Wal*Mart looming as the ten-ton gorilla in this arena. A rising star in the battle to appeal to frugal consumers, however, is Aldi.

Traditional grocery retailers are caught in the shrinking middle of the market, which some consumer analysts see as an unsustainable strategy, outflanked by competitors at polar ends of consumer demand. Kroger, Albertsons, Safeway, and others tackle the price issue with promotional programs while also offering a differentiated shopping experience. For Cincinnati-based Kroger, the nation's number-two grocery retailer, the tagline is "Right Store, Right Price." Boise-based Albertsons, with 2,500 stores, tells consumers it "Helps make your life easier," but it has also invested heavily in a shelf tag program dubbed "Compare." Consumers may be asking, "Can the nicest stores in town really have low prices?"

## Low Costs = Low Prices

"You can't lower prices without lowering costs" might be the conclusion of consumer analysts. And if anyone knows how to lower costs, it's Aldi, one of the largest grocery chains in the world and one of the fastest-growing in the United States and other countries.

Aldi is based in Germany, part of a type of retailing known as a "hard discounter." The brand name Aldi is derived from "Albrecht" and "discount." The company was founded in 1946 by two brothers, Karl and Theo Albrecht, and was split into two chains in 1962 over a dispute over whether cigarettes and other tobacco products should be sold at the checkout. Today, Aldi consists of *Aldi Nord* (Aldi North) and *Aldi Sud* (Aldi South), and both of the brothers are annual members of the *Forbes* list of the world's ten richest people. The chains initially covered different regions of Germany, but today operate in many parts of the world. Check the company's website (www.aldi.com) for geographic coverage and the locations of stores nearest you. Aldi Nord operates in northern Germany, Belgium, the Netherlands, Luxembourg, France, Spain, and Denmark; Aldi Sud operates in southern Germany, the United Kingdom, the United States, Ireland, Australia, and Austria (under the name *Hofer*). Despite Aldi's marked emphasis on very low prices, most independent consumer reports suggest that the quality of Aldi products is as high, and sometimes higher, than manufacturers' brands. Aldi carries some manufacturers' brands such as Tyson, Hershey's, and M&M's, but most of Aldi's products are supplied as Aldi private brands by contract manufacturers using the same formula as the number-one selling manufacturer's brand, sometimes actually by the manufacturer of the better-known brand.

Aldi's "strictly no frills" approach is evident everywhere in typical Aldi stores. Stores don't decorate aisles or even stock shelves for that matter. Pallets of products are parked by forklift trucks in the aisles, and the "stocking" function is performed by customers picking products out of the boxes and then picking up the emptied boxes to transport their groceries to their homes, eliminating most labor expense in the store. At checkout, customers place all items on the belt and push the cart to the other end, enabling cashiers to simply scan and transfer the items back into the cart. There's no bagging, no credit cards, and no checks, making the system fast and very inexpensive. Because most products are manufactured and packaged to Aldi's specifications, packages contain barcodes on multiple sides of the package, making scanning faster than in traditional supermarkets where the cashier may have to swipe an item several times before it registers. Only two to three employees may be in the store at a given time, and the cost savings compared to "upmarket" grocery stores are passed on to customers.

Aldi was once ridiculed as being "cheap stores selling poor-quality goods," but first in Germany and now in the United States, a kind of cult of upscale consumers has emerged as "fans" of Aldi because of high-quality products ranging from wines to computers at exceptionally low prices. In a related organization, Trader Joe's, upscale consumers flock to stores with similar operating efficiency that carry organic, vegetarian, and other specialty foods, as well as its own brand of wine students sometimes call "Two Buck Chuck." In the United States, Aldi grew fastest in rural areas and lower-income areas of major cities where food budgets are tight, but today Aldi's stores are opening more suburban locations and are beginning to add a few products under its more upscale private label, Grandessa.

The relationship with Aldi's vendors is unique in that each one, for about 85 percent of products carried, is manufactured specifically for Aldi with product attributes, quality, and packaging nearly the same as the leading manufacturer brand. Through its geographic divisions, Aldi contracts with top-quality manufacturers close to the divisional warehouse, minimizing logistics costs and maximizing speed to store. As a consequence, costs are lower than traditional supermarkets, and products in the store are often fresher (and thus last longer in consumers' homes). Aldi is a favorite customer of many vendors because of its policies of no slotting or advertising allowances, lower packaging and warehousing costs, and an "open book" policy to a firm's financial records in which Aldi expects low prices, but also expects its supply chain partners to earn enough return on capital to delivery quality and maintain the manufacturer as one of the most efficient in the supply chain. Aldi also maintains a policy of maintaining two capable suppliers for each product carried. The entire process works because of "SKU simplification," meaning that the typical Aldi store carries about 700 "stock keeping units," compared to 25,000 or more in the typical super-

market and 150,000 in a Wal*Mart Supercenter. But consumers can satisfy about 85–90 percent of their grocery needs with those 700 SKUs and shop at other stores if they are willing to pay the higher prices associated with wide selection, low inventory turns, and more convenient locations.

When walking through an Aldi store, a skilled marketing analyst can quickly see why Aldi's costs are lower. Customers perform many of the functions paid to employees in competitive stores. Carts are "rented" by customers for a quarter, but the quarter is refunded when the cart is returned, eliminating major labor and cart deterioration costs incurred by competitors—as well as making the parking lot less congested for customers. Don't bother looking for Aldi in a telephone directory; answering phones is too costly and word-of-mouth and a website does the job more effectively. Most stores are not open on Sundays or after 7:00 or 8:00 p.m., concentrating high volume through its highly efficient checkout system with carts filled with one hundred or more items at Aldi compared to smaller quantities at competitors. Look at the accompanying pictures and you'll see these and other cost-reduction tactics. But Aldi doesn't skimp on paying people—usually a few dollars higher per hour than market rate for cashiers (which yields low turnover of store personnel) and some of the highest starting salaries for college graduates entering its retail training program ($62,000 in 2005).

Aldi is a very private firm and thus financial results are not public. Analysts who follow public grocery chains and Wal*Mart have studied Aldi, however, and conclude that its total sales worldwide are around $40 billion and that its profit margins are several times higher than most competitors. An analyst for Bear, Stearns & Co concluded that Aldi's prices were 6.6 percent lower than Wal*Mart's comparable private labels and 36 percent lower than brand-name equivalents at Wal*Mart and, of course, much lower than the major grocery chains. Signage at Aldi features its "Double Quality Guarantee," which says, "Quality, taste and satisfaction are always *Double* guaranteed at Aldi. If for any reason, you are not 100 percent satisfied with any product, we will gladly replace the product AND refund your money," a promise that may be especially important in getting new customers to try the store.

1. What attributes are most important to consumers in determining where they purchase groceries? How does this vary by market segment?

2. If you live near an Aldi store, select a few items and compare prices at Aldi with one of the leading supermarkets and Wal*Mart. How much effect would these price differences have on a typical household's food budget?

3. Aldi does some, but not much, advertising, relying mostly on word-of-mouth and its website. Should this policy be changed? If so, what are your recommendations?

4. What should Aldi's geographic location strategy be? Should it increase stores in its present geographic area or expand to additional areas? Should it concentrate on rural and urban areas or concentrate on suburban stores?

5. What are the "secrets" to Aldi's low prices?

6. If you were responsible for the marketing of a competitor such as Wal*Mart, Kroger, or other grocery chain, how would you respond to the marketing strategy and tactics of Aldi?

Source: This case was developed from a variety of media and public sources, including materials from Christine Augustine, "A Closer Look: Aldi's Limited Assortment Supermarket Model and What It Means for Wal*Mart and the Dollar Stores," Bear Stearns Equity Research (November 22, 2004); and Mya Frazier, "Safeway Chain Shifts Marketing Strategy," AdAge.com (April 6, 2005). Photographs of Aldi by Alan A. Ayers.

At Aldi, carts rent for 25 cents, which is refundable upon return.

## How Do You Say "Christmas?"

When someone mentions the word *Christmas,* many different images can come to mind, depending on who you ask. Some people recall receiving a special gift they had always wanted—perhaps a puppy or a first bicycle. For others the word evokes happy memories of time spent with family and friends, maybe even a grandparent who is no longer with them. A lot of people grow up in homes that don't celebrate Christmas, so they might associate the holiday with brightly colored public light displays, obligatory gift exchanges at the office, or congested shopping malls. Christmas can even stir up negative emotions in some people, bringing to mind the emptiness felt on the first Christmas after a loved one died or their parents divorced. If you ask the National Christmas Tree Association (NCTA), they'll say, "Nothing says *Christmas* like a Real Christmas Tree."

The ways that people celebrate Christmas are very important to the NCTA, a professional organization of thirty-two chartered associations involving four thousand farm, retailer, and related members that exists to promote the use of real Christmas trees and support the industry that provides them.

Although many people think of Christmas trees as home decor, real Christmas trees are actually an agricultural commodity and a leading cash crop of states such as Oregon, North Carolina, and Michigan. In 2004, consumers spent $1.15 billion on real Christmas trees and billions more on decorations, gifts, and holiday cards. Nearly 22,000 farms, 500,000 acres, and 100,000 American workers are supported by this industry. Unlike other cash crops that have an annual harvest (like soybeans and corn), a real Christmas tree can take as long as fifteen years to mature from seedling to sale—requiring not only large amounts of working capital for growers, but also lots of patience and an eye toward the future.

In addition to farms where consumers can select and harvest their own trees, retailers of real Christmas trees include large chain stores like Home Depot and Lowe's, independent hardware and garden centers, as well as neighborhood lots owned by families, commercial enterprises, and non-profit groups (such as church, Scout, and civic associations). Unlike other seasonal products that can be deeply discounted or warehoused until the following year if they don't sell, the perishable nature of real Christmas trees requires retailers who fail to sell their inventories on schedule to recycle them at a loss.

## Not a One-Time Event

Between 1999 and 2003, sales of real Christmas trees dropped from 35.4 million to 23.4 million whereas the number of homes displaying an artificial Christmas tree jumped from 50.6 million to 62.9 million. This was a dramatic change considering that, between 1990 and 1999, sales had been relatively stable at between 31 and 37 million real Christmas trees per year.

At first, industry leaders dismissed the decline in sales as being related to a few isolated "one-time occurrences." The nation was, after all, in economic recession from November 2000 to November 2001. Add to that the tragic events of September 11, 2001, corporate scandals, and wars overseas, and the entire economy suffered. Sales of other consumer products were down—why would those who produce and market real Christmas trees think their situation was any different?

Then some menacing numbers turned up in a 2002 survey. Nearly one-third of U.S. households said they did not display any Christmas tree at all, real or artificial. The changing structure of families (including higher rates of single-parent and divorced households) and increased diversity of the population (introducing new religions and cultures) added to the number of Americans who didn't celebrate Christmas. With two parents working and children involved in multiple extracurricular activities, many families were pressed for time and simply couldn't interrupt their busy schedules to shop for a Christmas tree, take it home, set it up, decorate it, and at the end of the season, take it down. More disheartening, many people didn't think a Christmas tree was a necessary part of celebrating Christmas. These factors all pointed to a dim future for this holiday tradition and, to save the industry, something needed to be done.

## Highlighting the Product Attributes

Modern consumers are savvy and NCTA knew its members had a superior product, so what was the problem? The industry needed to address a number of "myth-conceptions" that consumers held regarding real Christmas trees.

For example, some consumers believed that cutting down a real, living tree was bad for the environment. Worse, many also felt that the reusable nature of an artificial tree was beneficial for the environment. What those consumers didn't realize is that for every real Christmas tree harvested, three seedlings are planted in its place—providing not only a habitat for wild animals, but also protecting the soil and promoting clean air and water. In fact, each acre of real Christmas trees provides enough oxygen to meet the needs of eighteen people. By contrast, the plastics, paints, and other chemicals used in artificial trees require large manufacturing plants that emit thousands of tons of hazardous toxins, polluting air and rivers. Managed farming, which maximizes the usage of available acreage, provides for more total trees and reduces the risk of wildfires and other natural disasters compared to if the land were left undeveloped.

Environmentally conscientious consumers should also be aware that real Christmas trees are fully recyclable, with the by-product often turned into mulch for community playgrounds and parks. Artificial trees overburden landfills (costing all taxpayers) and can take centuries to decompose in the earth. And at a time when American workers are concerned about the security of their own jobs, they should take comfort in buying a domestic product that supports American family farmers—not anonymous factory workers in China and other countries.

NCTA set out on a campaign to understand consumer perceptions of real versus artificial trees and educate consumers on the advantages of real trees. Certainly once consumers understood the characteristics of each product, they would choose a real Christmas tree. But education alone wouldn't suffice in reversing the sales decline—NCTA also had to identify the fastest-growing Christmas tree markets, today and in the future.

## Reaching Generation Y

Generation Y, the cohort of 70 million consumers born between 1979 and 1994, intrigued NCTA for a couple of reasons. Not only were its younger members still living at home and able to influence family purchasing decisions, its older members were advancing to the stage in life in which they would be starting families of their own. NCTA felt that, to be successful in reversing downward trends, it needed to understand the behavior, attitudes, and traditions of younger consumers.

What NCTA found is that, despite growing up in a world of privilege—receiving the full benefits of a stable economy and technological advances—Generation Y struggled with issues involving redefinition of the family, parents who worked outside the home, a lack of affiliation with religious or other community organizations, and rising expectations of teachers, parents, and college admissions offers. The result is that Generation Y longs for a sense of meaning and purpose, which it finds in friends, special interests and hobbies, and consumer products that define one's personal style.

To reach Generation Y, NCTA had to create an image that young people could relate to, while also appealing to their sensibilities as consumers and helping them discover their own personal identities. The goal was to demonstrate to young people, who were in the process of creating their own holiday traditions, that an authentic real Christmas tree should be an integral part of celebrating the holiday season. NCTA also wanted to reinforce the image of real trees as being "genuine," "all natural," and "the real thing."

To achieve its goals, NCTA created an essay contest in which young people submitted photos of their family celebrating Christmas with a real Christmas tree. Grand prizes included a $5,000 scholarship and an all-expense-paid family vacation to Orlando, Florida. "Buzz" was created through fliers (which included the name and address of the nearest tree lot) and point-of-purchase displays.

To generate further visibility, NCTA created a joint marketing promotion with the Warner Brothers Pictures' hit animated movie, *The Polar Express*, starring Tom Hanks. Not only was the movie effective in demonstrating the centrality of a real Christmas tree to celebrating Christmas, joint promotions with local tree lots included taglines in advertising and discounts for consumers who showed their movie ticket stubs.

Understanding that Gen Y spends a lot of time on the Internet for class assignments and communicating with friends via email and instant messaging, NCTA also created an online "advergame" in which visitors to its website could score points by throwing "snowballs" at "mutant fake trees" invading from overseas. Such viral marketing is effective because people who discover and enjoy playing the game send customized messages to their online friends with a link to it. The game not only reinforced the positive product attributes of real Christmas trees (versus hazardous, imported artificial trees), but also linked to websites that provided directions on how to properly buy, display, and dispose of real Christmas trees—as well as addresses of the nearest tree lots.

Last, because NCTA realized the large number of Latinos that make up Generation Y, the organization created print and radio advertisements in both English and Spanish, reinforcing the positive emotions associated with real Christmas trees and informing consumers that real Christmas trees are fully recyclable.

The accompanying charts show some of the results of NCTA's survey of Generation Y consumers.

## The Turnaround

The 2004 campaign proved very successful for NCTA. Between 2003 and 2004, sales of real Christmas trees increased by 3.7 million from 23.4 million to 27.1 million, while at the same time, sales of artificial trees fell by 600,000 to 9 million. More significant is that real Christmas trees were chosen over artificial trees by a ratio of nearly three-to-one, with the ratio reaching fifteen-to-one in Generation Y–headed households.

## FOCAL TOPICS

1. Describe the demographic and cultural changes that led to a decline in real Christmas tree sales.

2. What are the dangers of attributing short-term changes in sales and profitability to current events, rather than looking at long-term trends in consumer behavior?

3. What is the importance of educating consumers on the features of products they buy? How does understanding where a product comes from, how it is made, or how it impacts the environment influence consumer decision making?

4. Why was understanding Generation Y necessary to increase future sales of real Christmas trees? What are some characteristics of Generation Y that may lead to their preference for real over artificial trees?

5. If you were hired by the National Christmas Tree Association to develop a marketing plan for the upcoming holiday season, what elements would your plan include? Describe your target markets, the types of messages you would communicate, and the types of advertising you would use.

Note: This case was written by Alan A. Ayers, MBA, MAcc.

## REFERENCES

Jonathan Brinckman, "Trends Portend Slump in Sales of Holiday Trees," *Portland Oregonian* (October 26, 2004).

National Christmas Tree Association Marketing Tool Kit, National Christmas Tree Association (2005).

"The National Christmas Tree Association," *American Christmas Tree Journal* (May 2004).

"O Christmas Tree," *Cleveland Plain Dealer* (November 28, 2004).

"U.S. Consumers Purchase More Real Trees," press release, National Christmas Tree Association (January 25, 2005).

## 2004: A Great Year for Real Christmas Trees

- 27.1 million consumers purchased a fresh Christmas tree, up 3.7 million from 2003

- $1.15 billion in retail sales, up from $791 million in 2003

- Real trees chosen over fake by more than 3 to 1

- In Generation Y–headed households, the ratio was 15 to 1

# Celebrate Christmas

- **More than 9 out of 10 Gen Yers celebrate Christmas.**

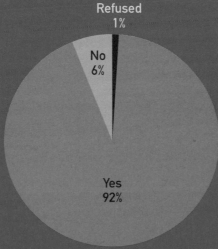

Q: Do you celebrate Christmas?
Base: Total sample (n = 420)

# Tree Type Growing Up

- Nearly two in five Gen Yers celebrated with a real tree every year while growing up; another three in ten sometimes had a real tree over the years.

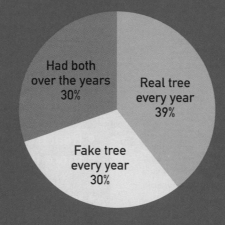

Q: Growing up, was the tree in your home usually . . . ?
Base: Total with tree (n = 373)

# Ways Family Celebrated Christmas

- Nearly three in five Gen Yers (59%) say they celebrated Christmas with a real tree growing up.

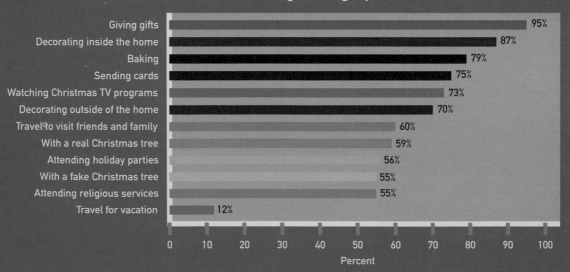

Q: Growing up, what are the ways your family typically celebrated the Christmas holidays?
Base: Total celebrating (n = 387)

# Who Gen Yers Celebrate Christmas With

- **Gen Yers mainly celebrate Christmas with parents, siblings, and extended family.**

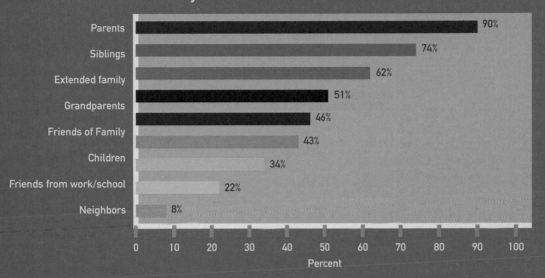

Q: Do you typically share the Christmas holiday with . . . ?
Base: Total celebrating (n = 387)

# Christmas Tree Descriptors

- Leading descriptors of real trees are natural, fun to decorate, messy, and full of life.
- Fake trees are seen as convenient, cost effective, and environmentally friendly.

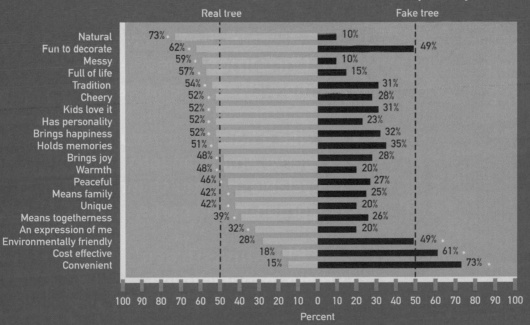

Q: Using a scale of 1 to 7 where 1 means "not descriptive at all" and 7 means "extremely descriptive," please rate how well each of the following terms describes a . . .
Base: Total celebrating (n = 387)

*indicates a statistical difference—95% c.l.

## Reasons for Real Tree Preference

- Fragrance, appearance, and tradition are the leading reasons for preferring a real tree.

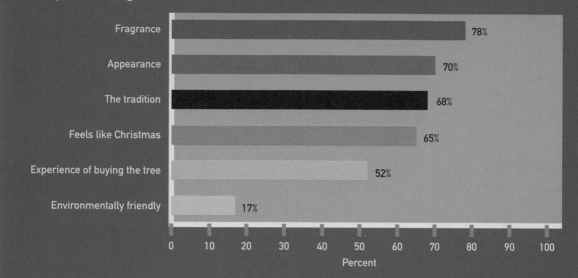

| | |
|---|---|
| Fragrance | 78% |
| Appearance | 70% |
| The tradition | 68% |
| Feels like Christmas | 65% |
| Experience of buying the tree | 52% |
| Environmentally friendly | 17% |

0  10  20  30  40  50  60  70  80  90  100

Percent

Q: Why would you rather have a real Christmas tree?
Base: Total envisioning Christmas with a real tree in future (n = 223)

## Consumer Perceptions: Impact on the Environment

### Real Christmas Trees
- Promote clean air and water
- Protect the soil
- Provide a habitat for nature
- Preserve American jobs
- Recyclable into mulch for playgrounds and parks

### Fake Christmas Trees
- Create manufacturing by-products
- Push jobs overseas
- Overburden landfills

## Is It Profitable to Be Socially Responsible?

If you were asked to name countries where the world's top retailers could be found, would you think of South Africa? Perhaps not, but retail experts would, and chances are that they'd be thinking of Pick 'n Pay.

Pick 'n Pay has evolved from a chain of small upscale grocery stores in Cape Town to one of the largest retail organizations in the Southern Hemisphere with locations as far away as Australia. Its portfolio boasts a variety of retail concepts, including small discount-price stores (offering a limited assortment of basic food items for low-income consumers), neighborhood supermarkets and family hypermarkets, and up-market stores (satisfying the sophisticated tastes of the urban elite with exclusive imported kitchenware and homeware). By 2004, turnover (sales) of the group was $29.3 billion, up 11.8 percent up from the previous year.

Pick 'n Pay's founder, Raymond Ackerman, was the only South African to be rated among the World's Most Respected Business Leaders in the *Financial Times*/PriceWaterhouseCoopers ratings released in November 2004 in New York. Although the founder of one of South Africa's and the world's most enduringly successful retain chains, Ackerman retains his modesty and pragmatism, and is always approachable and in touch with the lives and aspirations of ordinary South Africans. The organization states its mission clearly:

1. WE SERVE
2. With our HEARTS we create a GREAT PLACE to be
3. With our MINDS we create an EXCELLENT PLACE to shop

The company's mission is consumerism, which in simple terms is to interpret and satisfy customers' needs by selling quality products at competitive prices, and to provide courteous service in stores that are well located and pleasing to shop in. A policy of refunding goods without question has enabled Pick 'n Pay to establish long-term customer relationships that bring people back into its stores. Significantly, Ackerman predicted more than a decade ago that the only retailers who would still be in business at the start of the new millennium were those that were pleasing to consumers. "When a business is value driven, it will only ever act in the best interests of its customers, employees, shareholders and supplier," says Ackerman. And the company he founded operates on these values:

1. We are PASSIONATE about our CUSTOMERS and will FIGHT for their rights
2. We CARE for, and RESPECT each other
3. We foster PERSONAL GROWTH and opportunity
4. We nurture LEADERSHIP and vision, and REWARD innovation
5. We live by HONESTY and INTEGRITY
6. We SUPPORT and PARTICIPATE in our COMMUNITIES
7. We take individual RESPONSIBILITY
8. We are all ACCOUNTABLE

Although consumers see stores filled with tempting merchandise, a look behind the scenes of Pick 'n Pay reveals operating principles that focus on efficiency and continued growth and success. Its information systems facilitate order processing, sales reporting, and stock management, while processing some 250,000 payments for third parties and 2 million monthly credit card and debit card transactions. Yet even with superior information technology, Pick 'n Pay's most valuable operating strategy can be traced to Ackerman. The company's guiding operating principles, which graphically describe everything from merchandising philosophies to human relationships, focus on Pick 'n Pay's unique *culture*— distinguishing it from others around the world.

### Counterculture

Pick 'n Pay CEO Sean Summers summarizes the company's approach to satisfying customers and corporate culture. "We always ask: Are we doing things right? Are we doing the right things? We want to get the details right every time and be the first to be what consumers want." Pick 'n Pay's *culture* is evident in its unyielding focus on *consumer value, social responsibility*, and its unique approach to *managing employees*.

### Consumer Value

At a time when few people were courageous enough to question the apartheid government's stifling regulatory policies, Pick 'n Pay developed a reputation for fighting cartels and monopolies on behalf of consumers. These well-publicized fights, often conducted in the courts, demonstrated Ackerman's steely resolve to increase consumer value.

For Pick 'n Pay, consumer value means more than low prices, even though these may win consumer support and admiration. Pick 'n Pay is not satisfied with being the first to discount a price or having the lowest on-shelf prices—its goal is to "save you [consumers] time and money and simplify your life." To fulfill its goals, senior executives travel the world observing how the best retailers serve their customers, return to South Africa, and attempt to build something better than what they've seen abroad. As a result, Pick 'n Pay was the first in its market to introduce hypermarkets, in-store delicatessens, automated teller machines, on-floor customer service managers, baby changing rooms, shopping carts for the disabled, private label brands, branded financial services, and many other innovations.

### Social Responsibility

In addition to promoting consumer value, Pick 'n Pay's culture promotes a social agenda of self-help, feeding the poor, educational programs and environmental projects, and various fund-raising endeavors. These efforts have been directed by Ackerman when he founded the company three decades ago, and the board of directors monitors the firm's social actions closely. In tandem with a fundamental transformation that has taken place in the broad context of South African society over the past decade, significant changes have also taken place within Pick 'n Pay during recent years, based on a fundamental belief that the ability to achieve service excellence for customers is directly proportional to the capacity to establish a climate of dignity, respect, and freedom among every employee in the company.

### Managing People at Pick 'n Pay

"Internal social responsibility" characterizes the firm's humanistic approach to people management.

Although Ackerman located the first Pick 'n Pay stores in affluent suburbs (where managers were normally white, English-speaking males), Pick 'n Pay was among the first to seek out South Africa's historically disadvantaged for management training and development. Ackerman once admitted, "I didn't stand up enough against Apartheid, but what I have done my whole business life is stand up for nondiscrimination." This is evident in Pick 'n Pay's recent Vuselela program (a Xhosa/Zulu word that roughly translates as "process of renewal or rebirth"), which is designed to "reaffirm Pick 'n Pay values of human dignity and mutual respect" and to stimulate employee motivation. Overseen by a black South African director, Issac Motaung, Vuselela is founded on the aforementioned simple and powerful mission statement developed by the staff: "We serve. With our hearts we create a great place to be. With our minds we create an excellent place to shop."

Vuselela has resulted in a spirit of cooperation among individuals to contribute to the betterment of their stores and higher customer service and courtesy levels. Opportunities for self-improvement, including attending university-accredited courses at the Pick 'n Pay Institute, abound. One year, a select group of achievers flew to Orlando, Florida, and attended the Walt Disney Institute. It was the most diverse group ever to participate, and the Disney staff described the initiative as "the most noble act they had ever seen from a company in its commitment to its people."

In addition to its humanistic approach to management, Pick 'n Pay fosters a hands-on culture, in which no manager, regardless of seniority, is above stocking store shelves if that's what's needed to satisfy customers. Every manager comes from within the organization—starting in fruits and vegetables and rotating through every area of operations before receiving any managerial responsibility. Even the most senior managers, clad in season-appropriate shirts without ties, can be found in the stores listening to customers and staff or seated behind their raised desks located at the front of the store near the cash registers.

## Serving Intermarket Segments in Emerging Economies

Emerging markets often are characterized by special problems that affect retail operations, including the formation of dual economies with great disparities in wealth between the "haves" and the "have-nots." Further adding complexity to these markets are higher inflation, unemployment and crime rates, high costs of capital and indirect taxation that fuel growth in informal retail sectors, low labor costs, concentrated supplier power resulting in seller's markets, inefficient distribution channels, and limitation in product knowledge. These economic factors have pushed Pick 'n Pay to become a sophisticated, world-class portfolio retailer.

Each of Pick 'n Pay's retail brands focuses on serving a specific segment of customers, with varying ethnic, economic, and lifestyle characteristics. Score Supermarkets, which emphasizes efficiency, cleanliness, and easy shopping, moves large volumes of basic food and toiletry items through its stores and franchise outlets. Savings are passed on to the lower-income segments served by these stores. Similarly, TM Supermarkets (25 percent held by Pick 'n Pay) is a Zimbabwean chain of residential supermarkets that provides value to its customers. Rite Value convenience supermarkets operate from modern, attractive stores in finely targeted residential areas. Rite Value franchisees usually live within the communities they serve and contribute to their wealth and economic well-being.

Targeted to higher-income segments than served those by Score, Pick 'n Pay Family Supermarkets and Discount Supermarkets stock leading national food and toiletry brands and a limited range of clothing, hardware, and small kitchen appliances. Guided by research that shows that higher-income consumers want better food labeling, extensive nutritional information, fresher foods and more pleasurable shopping experiences with less crowded aisles, Pick 'n Pay Discount Supermarkets' store designs emphasize the shopping *experience* and offer more variety and product choices. Customers can buy prepared foods and fresh fish off ice, order special butcher's cuts, or select from a wide range of fresh fruit and vegetables in a village market walk-through deli (occupying more than one-third of the retail floor space).

Pick 'n Pay Hypermarkets offer an even more extensive range of products, including automotive goods, garden furniture, hardware, toys, major appliances, and electronics. Last, the specialty chain Boardman's offers mainly European kitchenware and homeware to discriminating clients with an emphasis on quality first and value second.

## Product Mix Strategy: From Beans to Jeans

Pick 'n Pay's growth in the midst of a changing environment and focus on a variety of segments has required constant attention to its product mix. Reflecting on Pick 'n Pay's early years in the hypermarket business, one director once said, "We weren't that good in the beginning—clothing is not beans." Taking the consumer's perspective, Pick 'n Pay focuses on usage occasions and attempts to solve consumer problems so that it can manage, market, and sell a large product mix. Pick 'n Pay monitors the different criteria consumers use to determine purchase choices for different product and usage situations. For example, consumers might be willing to pay more for fresh, exotic fruits and vegetables to use in salads and home-prepared desserts, but they may look for lower-priced canned vegetables to use in soups, or inexpensive children's T-shirts that will be worn for one season.

## Private Label Brands That Represent Value

All the stores that boast the Pick 'n Pay name keep on-shelf competition keen by offering five private label brands, each targeted at a different economic stratum and backed by a "twice your money back guarantee." Suppliers who do not update their products to reflect international trends become vulnerable to the private label brands. According to CEO Summers, "We try to stay very close to customers and urge our suppliers to do the same. Over the past decade, people have become less trusting of brands, either because they promise something people don't want anymore or promise something they don't deliver, and manufacturers aren't always able to offer a range of quality products that we believe customers want."

Providing value (lower prices and high quality) to consumers with the Pick 'n Pay *brand* contributes to the chain's uncanny success in a wide range of product categories. Summers adds, "We earn nearly three times more gross profit on private label brands than manufacturer name brands, but our real reason for offering private brands is to ensure that our customers get the quality they expect when they visit a Pick 'n Pay outlet." Today, consumers know that clothing bearing the Pick 'n Pay label often sells elsewhere at much higher prices when marketed under more up-market brand names.

Although he acknowledges the growing demands for convenience and pleasure in shopping, Summers believes that price and safety remain overriding factors for South African shoppers. "Most emerging economies have wealthy and economically challenged segments that live very different lifestyles. There is no doubt in our mind that price is very important to a larger proportion of South African shoppers than is the case in America or Europe. But we also have to look at the variety and quality of the goods we stock. South Africans don't always want all the bells and whistles people want overseas. Sometimes they want a well-made basic product, and we work hard to find it for them." Novelty also is important. Pick 'n Pay buyers were quick to get Teletubbies in-store and say they'll stock yo-yos again, if they become popular.

## The Future

Pick 'n Pay is very different from the chain it was just ten years ago, and more change is on the horizon in the next decade. South Africa's miracle transition has not been without social problems that require management response. For example, security has become more important to most South Africans. Thinking about the financial and psychological price of shopping, managers monitor the local crime situation near their stores. Although Pick 'n Pay believes that social violence may be less severe than the international press suggests, Summers says that "violence in South Africa has risen to unacceptable levels." He adds, "People want to see a security guard in the parking lot and at the entrances of your store in many locations."

Growing spending power in South Africa's historically disadvantaged segments also requires careful thinking about the changing mix of consumers who walk through the doors at Pick 'n Pay. According to Summers, "It's really exciting to be part of a rapidly changing market. We're thinking about differences in culture and demographics that weren't very important a decade ago. If we get it right, we appeal to a wider range of preferences for food, clothing sizes, and the like. When we get it wrong, we sit with stock we have to move at discount prices. Our results suggest that we get it right a lot of the time, but I have no doubt it's going to keep us on our toes."

---

FOCAL TOPICS

1. What evaluative criteria would lead people to choose Pick 'n Pay over its competitors? How important are a firm's practices concerning social responsibility in consumer patronage decisions?

2. To what degree should Pick 'n Pay's marketing strategy vary between ethnic segments in South Africa?

3. What types of internal and external programs could Pick 'n Pay develop to communicate effectively with the various segments of employees and customers, respectively? How would you position advertising or other public relations programs to its many customer segments?

4. Given the hypermarket approach, selling everything from "beans to jeans," how does the consumer decision process (CDP) for clothing differ from that used to choose groceries?

5. Explain how firms that offer such a wide variety of private-label products extend a quality image to products from canned green beans to women's clothing.

## Who Will Capture Your Mind

There's a battle taking place and it's being fought inside your head. The principal weapon? Advertising. Hundreds of millions of dollars of advertising. The combatants? Anheuser-Busch, the world's largest brewer, and SABMiller, the world's second-largest brewer. At stake? Billions of dollars in beer sales.

Although the war has been fought for decades, the current battle began in 2002 when South African Breweries (SAB) purchased Miller Brewing Company from Philip Morris for $3.6 billion to form SABMiller. In the beginning, this new company witnessed erosion in sales and market share for the various Miller brands, the continuation of a trend that had been in existence for over a decade. Its sex-fueled "Cat Fight" advertising campaign featuring Pamela Anderson and other scantily clad beauties was popular among young male drinkers (the industry's primary target market), but it did not stop the bleeding. Indeed, as recently as May 2003, Miller Lite's sales were down 1.3 percent in supermarkets for the year. Although Miller Lite, the first light beer from a major brewer, was once America's best-selling light beer, Bud Light was now the king at the cash register. And the king was growing stronger.

In mid-2003, Miller realized that it was time to get back to the basics, and that it needed to give consumers a reason to choose its beer rather than the competitors' brew. "Anheuser-Busch has operated as America's premier marketing machine over the past three decades," says Robert Mikulay, Miller's executive vice president of marketing. "Their image is incredibly strong, and so our job is to ask people to look closely at the actual beers, and taste for themselves. A-B will try to define 'taste' as half a century of Clydesdale imagery, and we've got to define it based on what's actually in the bottle."

So Miller refocused its advertising to communicate how its beer differs from the competition. During this same time America was caught up in carb mania. Millions of health-conscious consumers were looking to reduce their carbohydrate intake. Miller, hoping to take advantage of this trend, began a comparative advertising campaign emphasizing that Miller Lite has half the carbs of Bud Light. Anheuser-Busch decided to fight back by lowering the carb and calorie count on its sub-premium Natural Light brand of beer to less than that of Miller Lite. Anheuser-Busch also began running advertisements with the message that "all light beers are low in carbs. . . . choose on taste." These moves were intended to negate Miller Lite's product advantage and advertising impact.

In November 2003, Miller attacked the competition on a different front with its "Good Call" campaign. One spot opened with a man holding a generic light-beer bottle that looked suspiciously similar to Bud Light and Coors Light bottles. A moment later, various beer drinkers, panic-stricken, ran around the room yelling, "I can't taste my beer." The ad then cut to three gentlemen drinking Miller Lite, watching the pandemonium while remaining calm. "Next time, try the light beer that actually tastes like beer," the voiceover said.

By the end of 2003, Miller concluded that it was heading in the right direction. After years of sales declines, Miller Lite enjoyed a 2.6 percent increase in its sales volume for the year, giving it an 8.1 percent share of the American market. Although still in third place among light beers, it had gained considerable ground on Coors Light, which held an 8.5 percent market share. Miller Lite's growth had outpaced even Bud Light, which now owned 19.5 percent of the market.

In the spring of 2004, Miller launched a new offensive. Playing off of the 2004 presidential race, Miller unleashed an advertising barrage in which Miller ran for "President of Beers." The campaign lampooned Budweiser for its self-proclaimed title of being the "King of Beers." In one spot an actor takes on one of Budweiser's famous Clydesdales horses in a political debate. "Why won't my opponent debate this issue?" asked the actor as the horse remained silent.

Budweiser lashed back with its "Unleash the Dawgs" marketing effort. This campaign labeled Miller Lite as the "Queen of Carbs" in new store displays and advertising. Frank and Louie, the well-liked animated swamp lizards that appeared in Budweiser ads in the late 1990s, joined the fray. They tell consumers that Miller had to drop out of the presidential race because it had been bought by South African Breweries and was thus a foreign company. "You have to be an American to run for president," says Louie. Budweiser tells consumers that it's been "American brewed since 1876."

Miller responded with ads in which Miller Lite bottles were surrounded by red, white, and blue, and described as "American born since 1855" in "Milwaukee, Wisconsin, USA." Miller filed a lawsuit asserting that the phrase "Queen of Carbs" was "false and misleading" because the phrase implies that Miller Lite is high in carbohydrates when it actually has fewer carbohydrates than Budweiser and Bud Light. Miller also contended that the phrase falsely portrayed Miller Lite as a woman's beer. The lawsuit further objected to Miller Lite being South African–owned because SABMiller is based in the United Kingdom and Miller Lite is brewed in the United States by its Miller Brewing unit. There no longer is an entity known as South African Breweries, the lawsuit points out. A U.S. federal judge granted a preliminary injunction ordering Anheuser-Busch not to refer to Miller as "owned by South African Breweries." The lawsuit was eventually dropped, with Anheuser-Busch agreeing to change some of its ad language.

Remember how Anheuser-Busch wanted drinkers to "choose on taste"? Miller jumped on this tactic with a method made famous in the 1970s during the Coke and Pepsi cola wars: blind taste tests. Since the beginning of 2004, more than one million consumers have participated in the Miller Taste Challenge in which they're asked to choose which sample of unlabeled beer they prefer after tasting each. Participants have chosen Miller Lite or Miller Genuine Draft over Bud Light or Budweiser more than 80 percent of the time, according to Tom Bick, senior brand manager at Miller. "That's something I couldn't do with advertising," he says. But conveying this preference is something advertising can do. One commercial, filmed in Budweiser's hometown of St. Louis, shows a burly beer drinker proclaiming his allegiance to Budweiser just seconds before he chooses Miller Genuine Draft. "It kills me to say it, but Miller Genuine Draft has more flavor," he says. A similar spot was done for Miller Lite. Miller's shift away from emphasizing lower carbs to taste and flavor proved timely as the low-carb craze began to diminish. "They don't want to be stuck with a carb positioning," observes Mike Owens, vice president for sales and marketing at Anheuser-Busch in St. Louis.

Anheuser-Busch executives dismissed Miller's taste attack. "What they're saying is that Miller has more taste," says Owens. "They're not saying Miller tastes better." Concerns were also raised about the validity of the taste tests. A newspaper article published August 31, 2004, by the *New York Times* reported that some people believe the test was biased and that at least one participant lied when choosing Miller because "I was being polite. They were giving us free beer." And some experts question the effectiveness of taste tests these days. "The method is worn and dated," contends one former ad executive.

During the 2004 football season, Miller launched a new advertising campaign attacking Budweiser. The advertisements featured a referee who called mock penalties on people for drinking Bud Light and Budweiser instead of Miller Lite and Miller Genuine Draft. Calling their choice of suds "unbeermanlike" conduct, the referee replaced their Bud Light and Budweiser beers with Miller Lite and Genuine Draft. And for the second time in 2004, Anheuser-Busch launched a direct counterattack. In one Anheuser-Busch advertisement, the referees were seen taking Bud Lights from consumers. But it turns out that the referees are working together to amass a collection of Bud Light for their own enjoyment. In a second spot, the referees were shown being investigated by police over reports of missing Bud Lights and running from the police with their ill-gotten brews.

At this point, the beer battle has become so intense that others are being pulled into the fray. Television networks are refusing commercials on both sides because they're either unduly "disparaging" or appear to contain taste claims that are unsubstantiated and misleading. The consumer watchdog Center for Science and the Public Interest complained to federal regulators and the Beer Institute trade group that the Anheuser-Busch commercials of beer-pilfering referees bolting from police depict lawlessness. "Crime is no joke, nor is the subtext of obtaining one's beer through underhanded means," wrote George Hacker, chief of the center's Alcohol Policies Project, in his complaint letter. "We have no plans to pull the spots," says Francine Katz, an Anheuser-Busch spokeswoman who credited the ads with improved sales of Bud Light and Michelob Ultra, a low-carbohydrate beer marketed to dieters. "We believe there's no doubt the spots are part of our success. I can tell you that people tell us our ads are hysterical and they love them. We look to entertain consumers; we don't worry about what competitors like or don't like about our commercials."

In February 2005, Anheuser-Busch introduced its newest product offering, Budweiser Select, a beer promoted as having no lingering aftertaste. Don Meyer, director of Budweiser Select marketing, says the new beer isn't a response to Miller Lite. "We don't target particular brands," he claims. Others aren't so sure. "I think Budweiser Select was created as a Miller killer," says Harry Schumacher, publisher of *Beer Business Daily,* an Internet-based trade report. He thinks the new brew's marketing strategy involves attempting to pin the "aftertaste" label on Miller Lite.

Meanwhile, Miller's more recent ads continue to press the taste issue. In the latest iteration of its "Good Call" campaign, beer drinkers line up outside an Anheuser-Busch brewery and use a megaphone to inform Budweiser that they chose a Miller beer in a blind taste test. The spots also take a shot at Anheuser-Busch's current advertising campaign emphasizing the freshness of its product by pointing out that all American-brewed beers are fresh. Miller intends to continue its on-premise taste challenges with an objective of having an additional 4 million consumers participate in the test by the end of 2005. "It's been a very powerful tool really bringing home the important differences between our beers and theirs," says Robert Mikulay, executive vice president of marketing. "In fact, in terms of actually prompting reconsideration, it's been one of the most effective marketing investments the beer industry has seen in many years."

Although this battle is far from over, one thing is clear: Miller has been successful in revitalizing its Miller Lite brand. In 2004, Miller Lite's sales volume increased 10.5 percent. That's an extraordinary number when you consider that the entire U.S. beer industry sales increased just 0.6 percent in 2004. Yet despite all of the attention Miller focused on Budweiser, Miller Lite's success has not come completely at Bud Light's expense. To the contrary, Bud Light's sales increased 3.7 percent in 2004.

## FOCAL TOPICS

1. What attributes are most important in determining beer purchasing decisions? How does this vary by market segments?

2. How would you construct a valid taste to determine beer buyers' preferences?

3. Should television networks and stations accept advertising using comparative ads? What standards should (and do) they use in making this decision?

4. If you were in charge of marketing for Budweiser or Miller, to what advertising media would you allocate funds in order to be most effective in the "battle of the beers?"

5. What other marketing activities should Budweiser or Miller use to gain market share?

Sources: Excerpted in part from Tom Daykin, "Budweiser Pops Open New Front in Beer Wars," *Milwaukee Journal Sentinel* (February 28, 2005), 1; Tom Daykin, "Miller Brewing Ads Generate Response from Anheuser-Busch," *Milwaukee Journal Sentinel* (November 23, 2004), 1; Tom Daykin, "New TV Ads by Milwaukee's Miller Brewing Claim Taste-Bud Victory over Bud," *Milwaukee Journal Sentinel* (June 29, 2004), 1; Stuart Elliott, "Battling Ads Pit 'The King of Beers' against 'The Queen of Carbs.' As for Taste? Fuhgeddaboutit," *New York Times* (May 21, 2004), C6; Stuart Elliott, "Miller Brewing Finds That Women Wrestling in Wet Concrete Get Attention but Don't Help It Sell Beer," *New York Times* (June 4, 2003), C5; Nat Ives, "Miller Tones Down Its Low-Carb Focus, Emphasizing Taste Tests to Go after Anheuser-Busch Loyalists," *New York Times* (August 31, 2004), C4; Christopher Lawton, "Coors and Miller Ads May Help Bud; Taking Potshots at Rivals Is Confusing, Sends Buyers to Brand outside the Fray," *Wall Street Journal* (February 20, 2004), A13; Kay MacArthur, "Carb Craze Fuels $300M Beer Battle," *Advertising Age* (March 29, 2004), 1–2; Brian Steinberg and Christopher Lawton, "Anheuser Is Told to Pull Ads Targeting Competitor Miller; Ruling Limits References to 'South African' Links; 'Carb' Issue Is Still Open," *Wall Street Journal* (June 1, 2004), B7; Suzanne Vranica and Christopher Lawton, "New Miller Ads Put Bud to the Test; Taste Trials Will Inflame Beer Wars and May Strike Consumers as Contrived," *Wall Street Journal* (August 12, 2004), B6; "Miller, Anheuser-Busch US TV Ad Battle Getting Nastier," Dow Jones Newswires, www.dowjonesnews.com (January 25, 2005); "Miller Rolls out Latest Ads Focused on Taste, as A-B Reacts with Massive 'Freshness' Campaign," www.BeverageWorld.com (February 28, 2005); James Andorfer, "Miller Brewing Names New CMO," AdAge.com (April 7, 2005).

## The Diffusion of Innovations

The wireless telephone industry is growing at a rapid pace. According to Solomon-Wolff Associates, the strongest user group is the 31–45 age group and the growth trend is expected to peak over the next ten years. Industry analysts have also forecast that the penetration rates from mobile wireless services in the United States will reach 60 to 70 percent of the population by 2005. In spite of its exponential growth, the wireless communications industry is also at its peak of competition. Currently, there are five national service providers in the market: T-Mobile, Cingular Wireless, Verizon Wireless, Sprint PCS, and Alltel.

Because of intense competition and promotions among cellular phone companies, the overall churn rate (how often consumers change service providers) of the industry has been about 1.6 percent, but it's on the rise. The implementation of Local Number Portability, which allows a customer to keep his or her phone number when changing service providers, has been expected to encourage brand switching behavior among cellular subscribers. The increased churn rate could reportedly cost cellular service providers about $20 billion dollars. Consumer brand switching behavior is often related to their overall satisfaction with a company's products and services. A study by J. D. Power & Associates also showed that 26 percent of people who perceived the customer service performance of their respective carrier to be unsatisfactory or less than satisfactory were likely to switch cellular service providers.

## Company Background

T-Mobile USA, based in Bellevue, Washington, is one of the fastest-growing nationwide providers of wireless data, messaging, and voice services. Its annual revenue in 2004 was $11.7 billion, a 40 percent increase from $8.4 billion in 2003. The company has more than 16.3 million subscribers in the United States. With its affiliates, T-Mobile is licensed to provide mobile services to 95 percent of the U.S. population. Internationally, by the third quarter of 2004, almost 109 million people were using cellular services provided by T-Mobile, its German parent company, Deutsche Telekom, and their affiliates.

The success of T-Mobile depends on its clear business strategy, which provides its subscribers with the best value in their cellular services. The slogan "Get more from life" promises to provide T-Mobile subscribers with more services, more minutes, and more features, so they can enjoy the benefits of cellular communication services. T-Mobile branding efforts are executed through its celebrity spokeswomen, the internationally acclaimed actresses Jamie Lee Curtis (starting in 1998) and Catherine Zeta-Jones (starting in 2004). Zeta-Jones has appeared in print, radio, and television advertisements to show consumers the benefits of subscribing to T-Mobile and to associate the brand with its "Get more from life" appeal.

T-Mobile is the only U.S. wireless service provider that operates the widely used digital standard, GSM (Global System for Mobile), in more than 10,000 cities nationwide. The GSM standard also provides wireless subscribers with excellent call reliability and sound quality, in addition to integrated voice, paging and short message, and high-speed data services. Value-added technological innovations have transformed T-Mobile into one of the industry leaders. In 2003, T-Mobile introduced the award-winning color version of the T-Mobile Sidekick, which allows its customers to not only make telephone calls but also surf the Internet, converse using AOL Instant Messenger, write e-mail, play games, and exchange photographs—all using a single device. In 2004, free software was provided to T-Mobile subscribers enabling them to access wireless high-speed broadband Internet (wi-fi) access at over 4,600 T-Mobile Hotspots located in restaurants, hotels, airports, retail stores, and coffee shops nationwide.

Excellent customer satisfaction has helped T-Mobile to build a strong global brand. In 2004, the Wireless Retail Satisfaction Performance Study ranked T-Mobile USA the highest among seven national wireless service providers. The 2004 Customer Care Performance Study also ranked T-Mobile the highest among national carriers by a significant margin. J. D. Power & Associates also honored T-Mobile for its commitment to providing excellent customer satisfaction.

In addition to the excellent performance of its customer service, T-Mobile intends to continue to provide technological innovations in a competitive marketplace. But the company faces a number of recent developments in mobile commerce.

## The State of Mobile Commerce

Mobile commerce (M-commerce) is broadly defined as any commercial activities conducted through various types of mobile equipments via a wireless communication network and wireless devices including digital cellular telephones, pagers, notebook computers, personal digital assistants (PDAs), and automobiles. According to *Wireless Week* (2004), there are currently 94.9 million M-commerce users in 2003 worldwide, and the number of users is expected to grow to 1.67 billion by 2008. Moreover, worldwide revenues from M-commerce were $6.86 billion in 2003 and are expected to reach $554.37 billion by 2008.

Although M-commerce often refers to any commercial transactions of tangible products, recent M-commerce applications have been widely used to deliver a variety of communication and media contents (e.g., mobile advertising, cell-phone ring tones, mp3 music files, and short programming clips). Currently, T-Mobile offers a variety of M-commerce applications such as Caller Tunes (at $1.49 per month), Pictures & Video Messaging (at $2.99 per month), Roadside Assistance (at $2.99 per month), 300 Text Messages (at $2.99 per month), Unlimited T-Zones (at $4.99 per month), and 1,000 Text Messages (at $6.99 per month). Potential new applications include interactive video games, video- and audio-on-demand, and mobile news delivery services. With the explosive growth of the mobile telephone population, combined with developments of wireless technologies, M-commerce has become increasingly important to mobile communication service providers.

---

## FOCAL TOPICS

1. What will be the effect of industry trends on the demand for mobile commerce applications among cellular service providers in the next decade? What killer applications will be most successful?

2. Will the provision of M-commerce applications by T-Mobile help the company build a strong brand and maintain its competitiveness in the marketplace?

3. Will M-commerce applications contribute to T-Mobile present business strategy, "Get more from life"?

4. Will M-commerce applications increase customer satisfaction among T-Mobile subscribers?

5. How will location-based M-commerce applications affect consumer behavior?

6. What effect is mobile advertising likely to have on advertising practices in the next decade?

Note: This case was written by Dr. Kenneth C. C. Yang, Associate Professor, Department of Communication, The University of Texas at El Paso.

## Lessons from the World of Rock and Roll

Establishing a brand that "sings" to consumers, creating undying loyalty and a passionate following, can be accomplished by following examples from a business that literally sings for high profitability. Some rock and roll bands such as the Rolling Stones, Aerosmith, Madonna, Neil Diamond, KISS, and Elton John appeal to both genders, to many age groups—Gen Y through boomers—and to many ethnic backgrounds. The differences in successful brands and bands are as close as their names—only a letter apart. If rock and roll bands can achieve an emotional response that turns customers into fans, how can this process be understood and how can their "secrets" be unlocked to do the same for retailers and vendors or anyone else involved in the process of not just satisfying, but delighting, customers?

Think of what happens when U2, Jessica Simpson, Pearl Jam, or Billy Joel take the stage in front of a 50,000-person crowd. Fans scream as the lead singer walks toward them, cheer at the opening riffs of their favorite tunes, shout, dance, jump, and rock for hours. The power of music is undeniable; the loyalty showered upon those who create it, unmatched; and the lessons for students of consumer behavior, boundless.

## Beyond Customer Loyalty: Creating Singing, Screaming, Money-Spending Fans

Examine the most successful music acts of the last three decades and it's apparent that they've created not just customers, but *fans*—people willing to stand in line for hours to buy the latest CD from their favorite bands or plunk down hundreds of dollars to buy concert tickets. Although all firms in business today have customers, only the most successful have fans. Why all the interest in creating fans? Because of the effect attitudes and buying behavior have on long-term sales and profit levels. In short, *customers* buy from a variety of retailers and choose many brands, often influenced by temporary price breaks or other promotions. Many large consumer products companies spend more promotional dollars securing purchases from cherry-

pickers (whose tendency to buy a specific brand can be described as sporadic at best) than they do capturing more sales from loyal or frequent customers. *Friends* (loyal customers) tend to buy certain brands and shop specific stores more often than others—often because of good past experiences or perhaps advertising that creates empathy for the brand. Loyalty programs have helped retailers and consumer product companies foster relationships with consumers and modify their cherry-picking behavior.

Fans, however, take loyalty to the next level, seeking out specific brands, shopping only certain retailers, and closing their minds to other alternatives. Fans invest time, attention, energy, emotion, and money into building and maintaining a relationship to a brand, and these strong emotional attachments between company and customer are difficult, if not impossible, for others to break. And fans are vocal—they not only tell others about their favorite brands, they recruit others to buy what they buy and shop where they shop. Customers and devotees can be described more on their frequency of behavior, whereas fans are described more on the emotionality and intensity with which they behave. Fans don't drink coffee; they crave Starbucks. Fans don't drive a car or ride a motorcycle; they pilot a Mini Cooper or a Harley-Davidson. For a summary of these differences, study Table 2.2 in Chapter 2.

As the legendary rock bands exhibit, creating brand equity is not a static concept or merely a marketing goal. Rather, it is a dynamic process that requires brands to be engaged in conversation with customers. This type of two-way relationship implies mutual transfer of information, from the brand to the customer and from the customer to the brand. But the relationship between brand and fan goes beyond information flow to become emotion flow.

## Legendary Bands, Legendary Brands

Only a few consumer product brands last so long they might be called legendary. One of those is Wedgwood China, cited by brand historian Nancy Koehn in her book *Brand New*. Dating back to the

1700s, this brand still leads the market in terms of closet-share of the rich and famous, and tops the wish lists of brides-to-be around the globe. By no means exclusive to the world of products and commerce, legends abound in the music world. From Bach, Beethoven, and Brahms (whose music has transcended the centuries) to Al Jolson, Glenn Miller, and Louis "Satchmo" Armstrong (who crossed racial barriers and defined an era of music), artists have connected deeply with people and helped shape culture.

And then there's Elvis—proving that even though an artist may die, a legendary brand lives on and continues to sell, sell, sell. The Elvis brand, like Frank Sinatra and Tony Bennett, has remained a favorite among all sorts of people for decades. Such long-term market presence is amazing, especially considering what's hot one day isn't the next. The question is how to create a brand strong enough to remain popular with customers over time— especially in the wake of a constant onslaught of new competitors armed with new promotional and communication campaigns designed to steal attention and loyalty. An intense look at the music industry sheds some light.

Several common themes, lessons if you will, rise from the close study of why some bands have remained successful decade after decade and why most have had a few hit songs and scurried off into oblivion. Although dozens of strategies leap from studying legendary rock bands, some of the overriding principles learned from analyzing the careers of Elton John, KISS, the Rolling Stones, Aerosmith, Madonna, and Neil Diamond are:

- Emotional connections turn customers into fans
- Maintaining and adapting existing brands is often more profitable than inventing new ones
- Legendary brands evolve to remain culturally relevant
- Passion and energy create brands people want to adopt
- Being the best often evolves by borrowing from the best
- Baby boomers rule much market demand

Marketers looking to create legendary brands— those that capture a place in the fabric of mainstream culture—take note. Famous rock stars have succeeded in ways that few brands have.

## Passion and Energy Create Brands People Want to Adopt

Successful brands project energy and passion— some just project more than others. Victoria's Secret emits an intimate form of passion, and Nike projects passion for exercise and activity. Starbucks CEO Howard Schultz is passionate about coffee. Wal*Mart is passionate about consumers and giving them the best possible value. Energy and passion play the greatest role, perhaps, in personal branding. If someone asked you to describe "the brand called you," what would you say? How would other people describe you? Do you project energy and passion or do you suck it out of others? Whether you explore these questions for personal or professional reasons, your "brand" affects whether or not people want to spend time with you or work with you. Ask yourself, who would you rather hang around— someone who mopes all day, feels sorry for themselves, is lethargic and just generally negative, or someone who smiles, gives off positive energy, and seems to enjoy life? Though the answer seems obvious, it's surprising how many people choose to settle for a personal brand that focuses on the first characteristics rather than the latter.

## Elton John: Music Man, Marketing Man, Architect of a Brand

Elton John has had at least one top-forty hit every year for thirty straight years; not even Elvis, with twenty-three years, matched John's record! From behind his piano, Elton John has reached the hearts and souls of millions of people with a music montage ranging from romantic ballads to toe-tapping rock and roll. "Your Song." "Rocket Man." "The One." Chances are you and people in other generations can name at least three Elton John songs without too much effort. Although baby boomers may remember Elton John from his hits from the 1970s, children today may know him best from Walt Disney's *The Lion King* and *The Road to El Dorado*.

Elton John's appeal has spanned generations as few entertainers' have; fans have watched him transform from what might be described as the Liberace of rock and roll—clad in wild sunglasses, outrageously sequined outfits, and flamboyant hats— to respected artist, British statesman, and AIDS activist.

Born with a name he never liked (Reginald Kenneth Dwight), by the age of eleven he won a scholarship at the Royal Academy of Music in London, where he excelled in mastering the music of Handel, Chopin, and Bach and sang in the school's choir. His mastery of the classics gave way to his love for rock and roll, fueled by the likes of Elvis Presley, Bill Haley, Little Richard, and Jerry Lee Lewis, and he went on to choose a career in rock and roll. He understood that being successful in the classical recordings arena probably meant sales of a few hundred thousand records whereas success in the rock music market meant larger, mass audiences, more market impact, and bigger bucks. Rock and roll was also where his passion resided.

Early in his career, Reginald changed his name to Elton John, teamed up with writer Bernie Taupin, and shifted to a marketing orientation—changing his product, his appearance, and his personality. The result was *Elton John,* his second album, released in 1970. This album could serve as a textbook on consumer behavior, demonstrating how to reach consumers by appealing to basic human emotions and encompassing a wide range of demographic and cultural segments, an approach that served as a blueprint for the brand that Elton John built would build over the next three decades.

The featured track, "Your Song," which became his first number-one hit, spoke about giving the beautiful gift of a song to a lover—a simple sentiment but one that connects with anyone who is in love or wants to be, which is just about everyone. The album also contained other culturally relevant songs, connecting with people of all ages. "Sixty Years On" related to the loneliness of old age, telling with words, harpsichord, and broken piano chords the poignant story of a veteran returning after the war to the isolation of old age. "First Episode at Hienton" spoke directly to the feelings of every teenager, telling the story of a young man's first sexual experience with a girl named Valerie. On "Take Me to the Pilot," the meaning of the words are more cryptic ("I haven't a clue," says Bernie) apparently explained only by Taupin's interest in science fiction at the time. And although the meaning may be foggy, the emotional charge of the music is clear, grabbing the psyche of listeners, taking them to a crescendo of synthesizer-enhanced, full-orchestral climax. "The Greatest Discovery," in contrast, was a piano lullaby describing one of life's most emotional experiences, the birth of a baby.

Elton John's career was progressing modestly, but to become a star, he needed to look and act more like what he aspired to be—a rock star. His first challenge was changing his look. At times he was as rotund as the spectacles he wore as a child. He needed to lose weight, and did. His second challenge was developing a commanding stage presence. In his early live performances, Elton stood on stage or at the piano, awkwardly holding the microphone, devoid of any real personality. Clean-shaven with short bangs across his forehead, this shy guy exuded anything but confidence to his audience—in fact, he appeared somewhat embarrassed to be on stage.

The turning point for John's career came when he appeared at the Troubadour Club in Los Angeles amid much anticipation and hype. Promoters put up billboards and posters, bought radio time, and arranged for Elton to arrive in a British-style double-decker bus. Instead of conservative dress, which would have matched the dark, staid album cover of *Elton John,* the promoters talked him into wearing light-colored bell-bottoms with a huge belt of stars and moons, and a long-sleeved shirt with large letters spelling out "Rock 'n' Roll." Elton's transformation occurred on stage that night when he grabbed a tambourine, involved the audience in a sing-along, and brought down the house with a rousing rendition of "Burn Down the Mission." His new persona connected with the audience as never before, and the experience fueled a transformation that would later include a wide array of costumes, from jumpsuits and bib overalls to white boots and star-spangled T-shirts.

Over the years, Elton John has reached a number of audience types, spanning beyond traditional age, income, and gender boundaries—a transgenerational marketing approach of creating a product that may be designed for a specific segment but whose appeal transcends to a variety of age groups, rather than just Gen Y or just boomers. In the last decade, he has attracted kindergarten-aged fans and their grandparents with "Can You Feel The Love Tonight" and "Circle of Life" from Disney's megahit *The Lion King.* After conquering Hollywood by winning an Academy award for his work on *The Lion King,* he took on Broadway, collaborating with Tim Rice on *Aida.*

Elton John's brand architecture stands as a grand example for how to establish a brand in the marketplace. Developing both the functional and emotional elements of the brand, creating a distinct personality to which customers can relate, formulating a brand promise, and promoting a unique brand position and message to customers are all part of establishing a powerful brand among a host of also-rans.

## KISS: Keep It Simple, Stupid

It's hard to believe that four guys who look like they just ascended from Hell—clad in outrageous makeup, black spandex costumes, and platform shoes—could become an endearing thread in the fabric of American music. KISS invaded the music scene in the 1970s with hard-hitting rock and roll tunes and shows that broke the rules of the concert experience of that day. It wasn't long before legions of kids sang their songs and sported their makeup, much to the dismay of parents wishing they would behave more like those nice Brady kids on TV. But it's safe to say that the impact of KISS on fans and the industry would not have happened were it not for Gene Simmons. His is a story of ambition, vision, ego, and business savvy, and it is as instructive as that of other great entrepreneurs studied in MBA programs.

Chaim Witz was born in 1949 in Israel and came to America with his mother at age eight. Changing his name to Gene (it was more American than Chaim) Klein (his mother's maiden name), he assimilated to his new neighborhood—the Williamsburg area of Brooklyn, New York—and overcame the challenges of living in a single-parent household and having only limited English skills. Gene attended *yeshiva*, where the first half of the day was devoted to the Old Testament, followed by an afternoon of traditional academics, and concluded with Torah studies until 9:30 p.m., with plenty of homework after that. This was young Gene's routine, six days a week, fostering a disciplined lifestyle that served him well during his career.

His life, and the future of rock and roll, would be forever changed in 1964, when Gene and his mother sat together for their Sunday night ritual of eating dinner and watching *Ed Sullivan*. After watching the Beatles perform that night and noticing the attention they got from the girls in the audience, Gene decided to start a band. Though it did bring a lot of attention from friends and girls, Gene continued working whatever jobs were available and saving every dime he could to enter Sullivan County Community College. After getting his associate's degree, he moved back to New York City, lived with

his mother, and attended Richmond College in Staten Island where he completed his bachelor's degree and taught eighth grade briefly. All the time, he played on weekends with his band, recognizing that he really wanted to make it in a rock and roll band.

By 1970, Gene had hooked up with Paul Stanley, a guitarist and songwriter who responded to a newspaper ad Gene placed. In 1972, Gene Klein changed his last name to Simmons (because he liked it better), and he and Paul branched out on their own. They found a drummer, Peter Criss, willing to dress and act as wildly as they did. Finally, Paul Frehley, who changed his name to Ace to avoid the band having two Pauls, joined the group as lead guitarist. KISS was born.

Just as it would be wrong to describe Starbucks as just another brand of coffee, it would be wrong to call the KISS "product" just another rock and roll brand. Admittedly, KISS never set out to be the best musicians the world has ever known. Nor did the band set out to change the world with deep social messages and complex lyrics. KISS did set out, however, to give people an experience, changing the standard for concerts by focusing on the entire entertainment value of the event. They also set out to connect with fans and make gobs of money along the way. Band members connected to audiences, giving them something to talk about for weeks and remember for years, bringing fireworks to the stage, along with fire-breathing tricks, simulated blood, and unleashed craziness—tactics that focused more attention on the musicians and the overall concert experience rather than the music itself.

After all of the pyrotechnics, the stage would be ablaze with fire, smoke, and sometimes brimstone, conjuring up images of another world, especially because band members described themselves as "evil incarnate." Add black costumes and eight-inch platform shoes to already tall band members, and the effect was intimidating—as it was intended to be.

KISS's makeup became an important part of the aura of its brand, creating the illusion among fans that the band wore the makeup all the time. They wanted to believe in the fantasy, and out of respect to what fans wanted, the band decided to keep their makeup on in public—at all times. The makeup became central to the mystique of the brand. For the first time, concertgoers weren't just listening to music; they were seeing it, feeling it, smelling it, and living it. With all senses stimulated, their emotions were heightened as never before, and afterward, they were often left in that awkward state of complete excitement, exhaustion, and shock. After an experience like that, word-of-mouth and repeat patronage was not a problem.

With all four members living in the back of a station wagon and in cheap motels, they took the KISS experience to rural North America, in a strategy very similar to the rise of Wal*Mart, which started in small towns. In his book, *Kiss and Sell*, Chris Lendt explains the roll-out strategy that established KISS's brand. "Performing in out-of-the-way places was a key ingredient to KISS's success." Taking their legendary stage show with all of its trappings—the full arsenal of explosions, fire, smoke, flash pots, flame shooters, bombs, props, lights, and sound—no town was too small for KISS, the most exciting event of the year in towns that big-name bands ignored. Never rude and never turning away kids seeking autographs, KISS built its brand at the grassroots level. Farmers, blue-collar workers, and middle-America appreciated KISS coming to their usually neglected town, where the band stirred up a media frenzy and whirlwind of buying activity. In addition to traditional advertising, contests, and TV and radio interviews, KISS promoted its brand through aggressive merchandising, placing order forms in their albums and selling T-shirts, belt buckles, posters, and anything else they could brand at concerts.

In many respects, KISS had become one of the most successful rock and roll bands in the United States, selling out concert venues wherever it went, but the music industry measured a band's success by the number of records it sold. With poor album sales, expensive shows, and a nearly bankrupted record label, doom loomed dangerously near. In what researchers today would call focus groups, the band talked to its fans and discovered that the first albums didn't really capture what KISS basically was, a live experience. The challenge was capturing the concert experience—energy, explosions, excitement, and all—on a flat piece of vinyl, foregoing the studio-perfect sound of most albums for the raw sound of a live performance.

The only way they thought they could do this would be to record a live album, which producers and label execs insisted never sold well. KISS management fought for what the fans wanted, and the result was *Alive*, not a single disc but a double-album compilation of live recordings of concerts in Iowa, New Jersey, and Michigan, where connection with its audiences and fan appeal were strongest. Immediate success ensued, with the album selling over 4 million copies and projecting KISS to be the biggest band in the country. The album featured a song that would forever become synonymous with the band. "Rock and Roll All Night" was not deep, but it was concise and represented what they stood for at that point, a kind of USP (unique selling proposition) for a whole generation of kids and young adults who wanted to forget about the pressures of life and the deeper meanings hidden in the lyrics of other songs and just have fun.

Today, KISS is everywhere, in nearly every nation and in nearly every medium. Chances are you've seen them either in movies, gracing magazine covers, or on *The Simpsons*, and if you watched the closing ceremonies of the 2002 Winter Olympics, you saw them perform live while famed figure skaters pirouetted around the stage (an odd combination to say the least). KISS's simple strategy was executed with such distinction that since 1972 the band has sold more than eighty million records and is the music industry's all-time merchandising and licensing leader with over a billion dollars in revenue—half of which has been generated in the last five years. The band's merchandise portfolio includes 2,500 licensed products sold around the world.

## Aerosmith: Reinventing a Rock and Roll Brand

After a few years of solidifying their sound, creating music, and playing lots of concerts, Aerosmith released its first album with Columbia Records in 1973, with music and lyrics that represented the collective voice of the kids of their generation. They dressed in funky clothes and wore their hair too long, singer Steven Tyler painted his nails, and guitarist Joe Perry donned a blonde streak in his black mane. The group created a look that was difficult for others to emulate let alone carry off without setting off a tidal wave of snickering. They were different enough to get noticed, but they were so representative of their audience that adoption of the band into their fan's lives was easy. Although Aerosmith cultivated fans superbly, the band found another route for growing its fan base en masse by opening for bands that could still draw a significant audience but ones that Aerosmith could outperform, a kind of lead bait-and-switch type of fan attraction. Big name bands brought fans to concerts, but Aerosmith brought them back. Years of success, hits, and sold-out concerts ensued.

After years of writing, recording, touring, and selling, the band had reached what to most would be the pinnacle of success, selling out major stadiums. But the union of the band was worse for its wear. Drug abuse led to fights, infidelity, and physical problems (no matter how good you are it's difficult to perform when you're passed out back stage). Tyler and Perry, known as the toxic twins, had an intense love-hate relationship, eventually leading to Perry leaving the band and none of the remaining members finding much success.

Rising from the ashes of burned bridges, bruised egos, and thousands of shared joints, came the new Aerosmith, one that would experience more success—both financial and personal—than the original band. Getting clean and sober were key components in restructuring the band, especially because all of the original members were back on board. Today, after twenty years of sobriety, each member is quick to say that life is more rewarding and that they are more focused than ever before, but reinventing the band's brand required co-branding.

As Aerosmith prepared its reinvention, rap music was beginning to emerge from its confined urban market. One group that was getting a lot of attention was Run-DMC, the first rap act to have an album go gold in 1984. Run-DMC and Aerosmith explored the possibility of making a rap version of Aerosmith's song, "Walk This Way," singing together on the record and performing together on the video. The remake would define diversity—part urban rap, part rock and roll; young emerging artists, older, stalled stars; black and white.

In May 1986, the Aerosmith/Run-DMC collaboration hit television and radio, and climbed to number four on the charts. The video depicts Aerosmith in one room with Run-DMC in another, divided only by a wall. Aerosmith is trying to sing and play their music, but the noise coming from the adjacent room is so loud that they can't perform. So, Tyler and crew break down the wall between them and sing the chorus of "Walk This Way" through the shattered plaster and into the world of rap. The video continues with the unified band performing and prancing Tyler-style across the stage together. To this day, the "Walk This Way" video is included in the top ten on both the VH1 and MTV most influential video lists primarily because of the effect the video had on breaking down the real barriers between rap and rock, between black and white kids, and between generations. Aerosmith broke into television music and hasn't looked back, reinforcing the personality of the band and strength of the brand. They also crushed any notion that this middle-aged rock band couldn't be accepted by a new generation of fans. The band members entered rehab, got themselves clean, and rededicated their lives to their families, their art, and eventually themselves. The new version of Aerosmith was healthy and energetic and would go on to write and perform the most critically acclaimed music of their careers.

Since its reinvention, the group has won video awards, fashion awards, teen music awards, and Grammys, proving that some new, improved products are actually new and improved. In 2001 alone, the band headlined the Super Bowl halftime show, played the American Music Awards, hit number one with "Jaded," won best teen rock song, and was inducted into the Rock and Roll Hall of Fame. The band was everywhere, making fans salivate at the chance to see them "live," which fueled ticket sales for the *Just Push Play* tour.

Whereas other bands of their stature choose not to deal with fans one-on-one, Aerosmith still does old-fashioned meet-and-greets. The fans that are lucky enough to get backstage, usually by winning a radio contest, get their pictures taken with the band and have the chance to get something autographed, from album covers to various body parts. But the band doesn't sit stoically behind desks as fans parade by with posters and pens, they mingle in an open room with dozens of fans. Steven Tyler takes time with his fans, looking each one in the eye as he speaks to them, making them feel as if they were the only person in the room at that moment.

During its *Just Push Play* tour, the band devised another way to get close to its fans—a second stage positioned among the lawn seats of outdoor venues. In the middle of the concert, Steven Tyler announced from the stage, "Okay, we're coming out to you." On cue, someone begins a deep-thumping drum-march and the band leaves the stage and moves through the crowd flanked by security. But even a tightly constructed caravan can't prevent the grope-fest the band must endure to get to its hardcore fans. The band then takes to the second stage, giving fans in "the cheap seats," from which the band usually looks like a bunch of ants, a chance to be in the front row for four or five songs. The fans appreciate the gesture; they feel important, valued, and connected.

But the band's attunement to fan relationships doesn't stop there. Aerosmith began offering special backstage experiences to fan club members. For about $400, Aeroforce One members can buy the Velvet Rope package, which includes concert tickets, Aerosmith garb, and a guided backstage tour that explains the inner workings of the stage and crew.

Although management can't guarantee that groups of fans would get to meet the band, they often did. Finally, Velvet Ropers often get to stand at stage-edge during the concert, poised perfectly for Tyler to sing to and for the cameras to capture and project onto the Sony Jumbotron to the rest of the crowd.

## Madonna: The Relevance of Sex in Branding

If it's true that "sex sells," Madonna should be a multibillionaire. Born on August 16, 1958, in Rochester, Michigan, Madonna Louise Veronica Ciccone was a cheerleader and good student during her high school days in suburban Detroit. Her father rewarded her with twenty-five cents for every A she received, so she focused and did well academically as well as in dance and theater. Although she describes herself as an outcast, her classmates describe her as popular, funny, and a bit of a show-off. She received a scholarship for dance and attended the University of Michigan for a few semesters but left for the allure of New York City and the fame and fortune that it offers. Throughout her career, Madonna would use raw ambition and determination to hone her voice, dance, and marketing skills to create a brand personality that is sexy, sexual, sensual, stylish, energetic, sometimes outrageous, always provocative, and usually controversial. She would start, however, as many starving artists before and after her—she did whatever it took to get noticed and get a break, encompassing the sounds, rhythm, and beat of her dance club heritage. Her first album, titled simply *Madonna*, was released in 1983 and its first single, "Holiday," reached the top forty within one month. *Madonna's* second release, "Borderline," spurred a string of seventeen consecutive top ten hits that include "Papa Don't Preach," "Like a Prayer," "Dress You Up," "Justify My Love," "Rescue Me," "Express Yourself," "Like a Virgin," and "Material Girl."

Madonna's second album, *Like a Virgin* (1984), propelled her popularity with the single of the same name becoming her first number-one hit. Rolling around seductively onstage in a wedding gown, she embodied the juxtaposition of virginal and slutty—the fantasy of what every girl wanted to be and what every boy wanted to find. While "Material Girl" and "Crazy for You" sat on the top of the charts, *Playboy* and *Penthouse* magazines published nude photos that Madonna had posed for in 1977. Madonna had established her brand; it stood for self-expression; it begged for breaking the rules; it screamed sex.

The defining musical product for Madonna was her 1989 album, *Like a Prayer*, with the title song creating the greatest buzz among fans, marketers, and casual observers. In a bold step toward marketing and branding innovation, Pepsi-Cola became the first company to debut a hit song and video on a television commercial. Pepsi signed a one-year $5 million contract with Madonna to use the song in its commercial and sponsor the *Blonde Ambition* tour. This new formula of corporate sponsorship and pop music seemed to be a natural win-win marketing strategy. Pepsi could ride on the coattails of the emotional connection Madonna had with her fans; Madonna could debut her music and reach a larger base of fans—the Pepsi Generation.

The two-minute commercial aired on March 2, 1989, amid a buzz of hype and anticipation as viewers turned on their televisions just to see the commercial. The commercial opened with Madonna innocently watching a childhood birthday party and drinking Pepsi, remembering it as the same Pepsi she drank at birthday parties when she was a child. The gospel-infused song and the production served up just the right music-picture image and positioning for Pepsi's core market. The song and the ad were the topic around office watercoolers and high school water fountains the next morning.

Unfortunately for Pepsi, MTV released Madonna's *Like A Prayer* video the next day, featuring scenes of her witnessing the murder of a white girl, defending a black man wrongfully accused, kissing a black saint in church, and dancing in front of a burning cross. The video had a happy ending, which brought the actors together as if it had been a theater production. It appeased her fans who cheered on her ability and willingness to go where others wouldn't and attracted so much attention that both the song and the video catapulted to number one. It was nominated for Best Video of the Year and captured the Viewer's Choice Award at the 1989 MTV Video Music Awards. Pepsi, on the other hand, didn't fare so well with its fans. The positive energy Madonna created with the song was completely zapped by the negative reaction that mainstream America had to her video.

Fast forward to today and Madonna remains sexy, redefining the term according to her life stage. She even appeared on CNN's *Larry King Show* with her husband answering questions on parenting and expressing fairly traditional views on the differences between boys (they love cars) and girls (they love dolls and dressing up with makeup). She doesn't let her children watch television, and she recently completed a deal to write children's books. Even her spirituality has evolved. Raised as a Roman Catholic, she now is a proponent of Kaballah, a form of Jewish mysticism that incorporates the Old Testament and the foundational concepts of "Jesus, the rabbi." Whether you define her as Material Girl or Spiritual Girl, Madonna is a musical superstar—one whose personality often overshadows her musical product. Madonna changes her image nearly as often as she changes her hair color, which has gone from dirty blonde to platinum to black to whatever it is today. Just when fans think they've figured her out, she transforms again, keeping them intrigued, involved, and guessing what could possibly be next.

## The Rolling Stones: Branding Strategies Beyond Satisfaction

Sitting in a meeting with phrases like return on investment, profit and loss statement, business models, and product-pricing flying around the room might make you think you've entered a board meeting for the Fortune 500 company of your choice. Now add to that scene a short whisper of a guy, dressed undoubtedly in tight trousers and an anything-but-conservative shirt, who can dance around a stage even better than any CFO can dance around his or her numbers, and you might conjure up an image of a Rolling Stones "business" meeting. The Rolling Stones organization is a well-oiled money-making machine, and to say it resembles anything less than a Fortune 500 firm would be unjust. In the world of rock and roll, not only would the Rolling Stones likely top the list of legendary bands, but they would most likely top the list of rock businesses as well.

At the helm is CEO Mick Jagger, who attended the London School of Economics, but professes never to have really "studied" business per se. He does, however, have forty years of industry acumen under his tiny belt, along with a keen intellect, a deep understanding of business models, and a knack for turning a profit.

Fans think of a lot of things when they think of the Rolling Stones. There's the music, of course, spanning hits from the 1960s (*Satisfaction* and *Let's Spend the Night Together* jump to mind), 1970s (such as *Jumpin' Jack Flash* and *Honky Tonk*

*Woman*), and 1980s (perhaps *Emotional Rescue* and *She's So Cold*). Gen Xers might think of *Start Me Up*, which was later used to launch Microsoft's Windows 95—the most successful product introduction of all time—for which the Stones reportedly were paid somewhere between $4 and $12 million (secrecy in numbers). Some fans may also think of the infamous lips and tongue logo that adorns T-shirts and biceps around the world. And all fans think of the energetic, ever-gaunt Mick Jagger and his seemingly sleepy, somewhat chemically preserved counterpart Keith Richards. Baby boomers who have found themselves inside corporate America, however, may choose to deem the Rolling Stones as their business, branding, and marketing heroes.

The Rolling Stones, the business, operates like many other large corporations—as a financially driven, global operation based in the Netherlands (because of its more favorable tax laws). The business model focuses on three core revenue-generating areas—album sales, royalties, and touring, each led by a team of competent executives. Regular meetings of the corporate executives examine the effectiveness of managers for each product line in generating revenue and controlling expenses. Although private and secretive, *Fortune* magazine estimates the Stones revenue since 1989 totals $1.5 billion, eclipsing competitors such as U2, Bruce Springsteen, and Michael Jackson. Together, management and band work closely to create the Rolling Stones brand, which combines the image of the band, the personalities of its members, and a diverse array of products, including logo merchandise, touring, royalties, recordings, videos, books, and corporate endorsements. The band is also a master at delivering a consistently satisfying blend of old and new music (more old than new) in an evolving musical experience. This intense combination helps the Rolling Stones brand infiltrate culture at many levels and keep fans engaged and wanting more.

Few bands exceed the staying power and commercial success of the Rolling Stones. In part, it's talent (quality in the world of commerce), hard work, vision, planning, and execution, a basic formula that keeps the band rocking decade after decade, similar to the way brands like Coca-Cola and Cadillac keep rolling through the generations. And in part, it's timing. The Rolling Stones happened to hit the music scene and become part of the collective life soundtrack of the largest demographic segment of our time—the baby boomers. Teenagers of the

1960s listened, made out, danced, smoked, rebelled, and fantasized to Stones music. It was their puberty music, and it was good enough that the kids continued to sing it and the band evolved enough that the kids continued to follow them for decades.

Throughout the 1970s, the Stones released an album every year until 1979. Some years it was one album, often two, sometimes three, and occasionally four. Many went to number one on the U.S. or U.K. sales charts, and often on both. Repeating songs on multiple albums has helped ingrain Rolling Stones music in the minds and hearts of baby boomers across socioeconomic and geographic segments. In addition to the publicity and promotion that accompanies the release of a record, each product introduction gives the band a chance to strengthen the relationship with current fans and create an opportunity to reach new fans. Creating and releasing albums at a rapid rate also creates an aura of demand, popularity, and success with which people want to associate. Among fans, a song they already

know just makes the new material more familiar, an important principle in the theory of how people learn to like something. The band evolves at a rate that doesn't alienate its greatest fans yet keeps the band relevant in the market.

After forty years of hard-hitting rock and roll hits, the Rolling Stones' "senior executives" could trade in their T-shirts and leather for wool cardigans, collect Social Security, and spend their days on the golf course and their nights in front of the television. But Mick Jagger, Keith Richards, Ron Wood, and Charlie Watts are not your stereotypical AARP members. They haven't settled for the passive life; they are still creating, performing, and innovating. Jagger's sixtieth birthday did not bring retirement. Instead, it brought the *Forty Licks* 2002–2003 World Tour, the band's most ambitious to date, which would go on to reach 1 million fans (willing to shell out over $200 million), as the band played thirty-two dates throughout the United States, Canada, Europe, and the Far East.

---

## FOCAL TOPICS

1. Prepare a list of brands that you believe are the most successful and analyze them for the following.
   a. What strategies, tactics, and marketing programs made this brand successful?
   b. What principles from the legendary rock and roll stars described in the case apply to the success of this brand?

2. Of the rock and roll stars described in the case, which does your team believe is the most successful? Why?

3. Of the currently popular musical performers, which are most likely to become "legendary stars"? Why?

4. What principles of branding in this case and other sources should be applied by individual students to "the brand called you" (your personal brand when applying for a career position)?

5. What is the "brand" of your university and your major? What recommendations would you make for improving that brand?

Source: Adapted from Roger Blackwell and Tina Stephan, *Brands That Rock: What Business Leaders Can Learn From Rock and Roll* (New York: Wiley, 2003).

## A

**abstract elements** The elements of culture that include values, attitudes, ideas, personality types, and summary constructs, such as religion or politics.

**abstract words** Words that are not likely to evoke a visual representation in memory.

**acceptance** The fourth stage of information processing, in which a message is accepted or rejected.

**accessibility** The degree to which segments can be reached through advertising or methods of communication and retailing.

**acculturation** The degree to which consumers modify their own behavior as a result of contact with cultures different from the ones in which they were raised.

**achieved status** A higher level of social status attained through personal effort (e.g., career, education, and athletic accomplishments).

**adaptability** A measure of the ability of a family to change its power structure, role relationships, and relationship rules in response to situational and developmental stress.

**adopters** People who have made a decision to use a new product.

**advergaming** The use of games that contain product associations.

**advertising wearout** The loss of advertising effectiveness due to overexposure (i.e., too much repetition).

**affective response** Feelings that are experienced during processing.

**AIO measures** Statements that describe the activities, interests, and opinions of consumers.

**androgynous consumer** A consumer who has the characteristics of both male and female consumers (or no distinguishing masculine or feminine characteristics at all).

**anomie** A weakened respect for social norms that leads to diminished normative compliance.

**approach-approach conflict** A conflict that occurs when a consumer must decide between two or more desirable alternatives.

**approach-avoidance conflict** A conflict that occurs when a chosen course of action has both positive and negative consequences.

**arousal** A primary type of emotional response representing feelings of excitement and stimulation.

**ascribed status** The level of social status that results from factors beyond the direct control of individuals (e.g., age, sex, race, and gender).

**aspirational groups** Groups that the individual seeks to associate with by adopting the group's norms, values, and behavior.

**association** A social class variable concerned with people's everyday relationships with people who like to do the same things they do, in the same ways, and with whom they feel comfortable.

**associative network** A theory of memory organization that proposes that memory nodes containing bits of information are linked to other memory nodes in a series of hierarchical networks.

**attention** The second stage of information processing representing the amount of thinking focused in a particular direction.

**attitude accessibility** How easily an attitude can be retrieved from memory.

**attitude confidence** A person's belief that her or his attitude is correct.

**attitude extremity** A fundamental property of attitudes representing the intensity of liking or disliking.

**attitude resistance** The degree to which an attitude is immune to change.

**attitude toward the ad ($A_{ad}$)** The global evaluation of an advertisement.

**attitude toward the behavior ($A_b$)** An evaluation of performing a particular behavior that involves the attitude object.

**attitude toward the object ($A_o$)** An evaluation of the attitude object, such as a product.

**attitude valence** A fundamental property of attitudes representing whether the attitude is positive, negative, or neutral.

**attitudes** Global evaluative judgments representing what consumers like or dislike.

**attraction effect** When the attractiveness of a given alternative and its odds of being chosen are enhanced by adding a clearly inferior alternative to the set of considered alternatives.

**avoidance-avoidance conflict** A conflict occurring when consumers must decide between two or more undesirable alternatives.

## B

**back-translation** The act of translating, using several translators, a message from its original language to a different language, and then back to the original language.

**behavioral expectations** Consumers' perceived likelihood of performing a behavior.

**beliefs** Subjective knowledge-based judgments about the relationship between two or more things.

**benefit segmentation** Dividing consumers into different market segments based on the benefits they seek from purchasing and consuming products.

**birthrate** The number of live births per 1,000 population in a given year.

**blogs** Short for Web logs; websites that contain an online personal journal with reflections, comments, and often hyperlinks provided by the writer.

**brand** A product or product line, store, or service with an identifiable set of benefits, wrapped in a recognizable personality.

**brand associations** The linkages in memory between the brand and other concepts.

**brand equity** The difference in value created by a brand less the cost of creating the brand.

**brand extensions** The extension of a brand name that is well-known and respected in one product category to another product category for which it had not been known before.

**brand image** The entire array of associations that are activated from memory when consumers think about a brand.

**brand name suggestiveness** The extent to which a brand name conveys or reinforces a particular attribute or benefit offered by the brand.

**brand personality** The personality corresponding to use of a specific brand that consumers see as a reflection of themselves or think that they will develop by using that brand.

**brand promise** The expectation set by a specific brand that a certain outcome will occur in exchange for the consumer's money.

**brand protection** By promising a certain outcome, brands reduce the risk to consumers that a product or service may not deliver as expected.

**buzz** A term used to describe how much attention has been captured by a marketing activity.

# C

**capacity** The cognitive resources that an individual has available at any given time for processing.

**categorization process** When constructing an evaluation of a choice alternative, consumers do so based on the particular category to which the alternative is assigned.

**central process** A process of opinion formation in which opinions are formed from a thoughtful consideration of relevant information.

**classical conditioning** The act of pairing one stimulus that spontaneously evokes certain meanings and feelings with another, causing a transfer of these meanings and feelings from one to the other.

**closure** The tendency to develop a complete picture or perception when elements in the perceptual field are missing.

**cognitive age** The age at which one perceives oneself to be.

**cognitive innovators** Innovators who have a strong preference for new mental experiences.

**cognitive learning** The storing of information in long-term memory.

**cognitive resources** The mental capacity available for undertaking various information-processing activities.

**cognitive response** The thoughts that occur during processing.

**cohesion** The emotional bonding between family members.

**cohort** Any group of individuals linked as a group in some way.

**cohort analysis** A process that investigates the changes in patterns of behavior or attitudes in a cohort.

**common-person appeal** An approach that features testimonials from "regular" consumers with whom most individuals can relate.

**communication** The exchange of thoughts, ideas, messages, and information by speech, writing, behavior, and other means.

**compliance** The act of conforming to the desires of a group without accepting all of its beliefs or behaviors.

**composite branding** The use of two well-known brand names on a product.

**comprehension** The third stage of information processing, involving interpretation of a stimulus.

**compromise effect** When an added alternative causes a preexisting option to become more attractive because it now represents a compromise choice among the set of alternatives.

**compulsive consumption** A response to an uncontrollable drive or desire to obtain, use, or experience a feeling, substance, or activity that leads an individual to repetitively engage in a behavior that will ultimately cause harm to the individual and possibly others.

**concrete words** Those words that can be easily visualized.

**conditioned response** In Pavlov's theory of classical conditioning, the response arising from the conditioning that occurs to the unconditioned stimulus and response.

**conditioned stimulus** In Pavlov's theory of classical conditioning, the new stimulus to which the unconditioned response can be transferred.

**confirmation** When a product's performance meets certain expectations.

**conformity** A change in beliefs or actions based on real or perceived group pressures.

**congruity** How similar members within the segment exhibit behaviors or characteristics that correlate with consumption behavior.

**conjunctive strategy** An evaluation strategy employing a comparison of each brand to cutoffs that are established for each salient attribute of the brand.

**consideration set** Those alternatives considered during decision making.

**consolidated metropolitan statistical area** A grouping of closely related primary metropolitan statistical areas.

**conspicuous consumption** Consumption that is motivated to some extent by the desire to show one's successfulness to other people.

**consumer analysis** The process of understanding consumer trends, global consumer markets, models to predict purchase and consumption patterns, and communication methods to reach target markets most effectively.

**consumer behavior** Activities people undertake when obtaining, consuming, and disposing of products and services. Also, a field of study that focuses on consumer activities.

**consumer confidence** The influence on the consumption process by what consumers think will happen in the future.

**consumer decision process (CDP) model** A road map of consumers' minds that marketers and managers can use to help guide product mix, communication, and sales strategies.

**consumer insight** An understanding of consumers' expressed and unspoken needs and realities that affect how they make life, brand, and product choices.

**consumer knowledge** Information stored in memory that is relevant to purchase, consumption, and disposal of goods and services.

**consumer life cycle** The series of stages that a consumer passes through during life and that change an individual's behavior over time.

**consumer logistics** The speed and ease with which

consumers move through the retail and shopping process.

**consumer motivation** The drive to satisfy both physiological and psychological needs through product purchase and consumption.

**consumer orientation** The process of bringing product design, logistics, manufacturing, and retailing together as a customer-centric demand chain.

**consumer socialization** The acquisition of consumption-related cognitions, attitudes, and behavior.

**consuming** How, where, when, and under what circumstances consumers use products.

**consumption** Consumers' usage of the purchased product.

**consumption analysis** The study of why and how people buy and use products.

**consumption and usage knowledge** The information in memory about how a product can be consumed and what is required to actually use it.

**consumption intentions** What consumers think they will do in terms of engaging in a particular consumption activity.

**consumption norms** Informal rules that govern consumption behavior.

**consumption rituals** A type of expressive, symbolic activity constructed of multiple behaviors that occur in a fixed, episodic sequence and that tend to be repeated over time.

**continuous innovation** The modification of the taste, appearance, performance, or reliability of an existing product rather than the establishment of a totally new one.

**contracyclical advertising** The practice of increasing or at least maintaining advertising during economic slowdowns to gain market share when competitors cut promotional activity.

**core merchandise** A basic group of products that is essential to a store's traffic, customer loyalty, and profits.

**core values** The very basic values of people that, among other things, define how products are used in a society, provide positive and negative valences for brands and communications programs, define acceptable market relationships, and define ethical behavior.

**cost versus benefit perspective** A theory of search behavior that proposes that consumers will search for decision-relevant information when the perceived benefits of the new information are greater than the perceived costs of acquiring the information.

**credence claims** Advertising claims of which validation of accuracy is either impossible or unlikely because more effort is required than consumers are willing to invest.

**cross-cultural analysis** The act of comparing similarities and differences in behavioral and physical aspects of cultures.

**cued recall** A type of recall measure in which certain types of retrieval cues are provided.

**cultural artifacts** Material components of a culture, including such things as books, computers, tools, buildings, and specific products.

**cultural empathy** The ability to understand the inner logic and coherence of other ways of life and refrain from judging other value systems.

**culture** A set of values, ideas, artifacts, and other meaningful symbols that help individuals communicate, interpret, and evaluate as members of society.

**customer-centricity** A strategic commitment to focus every resource of the firm on serving and delighting profitable customers.

**customer intimacy** The detailed understanding and focus on customers' needs lifestyles and behaviors in order to create a deep cultural connection with them.

**customer lifetime value (CLV)** The value to the company of a customer over the whole time the customer relates to the company.

**cutoff** A restriction or requirement for acceptable performance on a product attribute.

# D

**data mining** The creation of a database of names for developing continuous communications and relationships with the consumer.

**day-after recall (DAR) measure** A measure that assesses consumers' ability to recall the advertised brand twenty-four hours after being exposed to an advertisement.

**decay theory** A theory proposing that memories grow weaker with the passage of time.

**demographics** The size, structure, and distribution of a population.

**desired image** The image that a company seeks to create in the marketplace for its product.

**determinant attributes** Features or characteristics (such as price and convenience) that usually determine which brand or store consumers choose.

**differential threshold** The threshold reflecting the smallest change in stimulus intensity that will be noticed.

**diffusion** The process by which an innovation is communicated through certain channels over time among the members of a social system.

**direct marketing** The strategies marketers use to reach consumers somewhere other than a store.

**direct selling** Any form of face-to-face contact between a salesperson and a customer away from a fixed retail location.

**discontinuous innovation** The act of introducing an entirely new product that significantly alters consumers' behavior patterns and lifestyles.

**discretionary time** Time during which consumers are not constrained by economic, legal, moral, or physical compulsion or obligation.

**disposing** How consumers get rid of products and packaging.

**dissatisfaction** A negative post-consumption evaluation that occurs when the consumption experience fails to meet expectations.

**dissociative groups** Groups with which an individual tries to avoid association.

**dominance** A primary type of emotional response representing feelings of being in control.

**dual coding** A concept proposing that information can be stored in both semantic and visual forms.

**dyadic exchanges** Exchanges of resources between two individuals that influence these individuals' behaviors or beliefs.

**dynamically continuous innovation** The act of creating either a new product or a significant alteration of an existing one, but does not generally alter established purchase or usage patterns.

# E

**early adopters** Opinion leaders and role models for others, with good social skills and respect within larger social systems, who adopt new innovations before the masses do.

**early majority** Consumers who deliberate extensively before buying new products, yet adopt them just before the average time it takes the target population as a whole.

**economic demographics** The study of the economic characteristics of a nation's population.

**elaboration** The degree of integration between the stimulus and existing knowledge.

**elimination by aspects strategy** An evaluation strategy resembling the lexicographic strategy but in which the consumer imposes cutoffs.

**emotional advertising appeals** A type of advertising

appeal that attempts to influence consumers' feelings about the advertised product.

**emotional elements** Characteristics of a brand (including image, personality, style, and evoked feelings) that create an emotional connection between customers and the brand.

**endorsements** The act of a celebrity lending his or her name or likeness to a product without necessarily being an expert in the area.

**ethnography** Describing and understanding consumer behavior by interviewing and observing consumers in real-world situations.

**evaluative criteria** The standards and specifications used to compare different products and brands.

**expectancy disconfirmation model** A model that proposes that satisfaction depends on the comparison of pre-purchase expectations with consumption outcomes.

**expectations** Beliefs about the future.

**experience claims** Advertising claims that can be verified following product consumption.

**experimentation** A research methodology that attempts to understand cause-and-effect relationships by manipulating independent variables to determine how these changes affect dependent variables.

**expert** One who possesses unique information or skills that can help consumers make better purchase decisions than other types of spokespersons.

**exposure** The first stage of information processing, in which physical proximity to a stimulus allows one or more of our five senses the opportunity to be activated.

**expressive roles** Roles that involve the support of other family members in the decision-making process and the expression of the family's aesthetic or emotional needs.

**extended family** The nuclear family, plus other relatives, such as grandparents, uncles and aunts, cousins, and parents in law.

**extended problem solving** Problem solving of a higher degree of complexity that influences consumers' actions.

**external search** The act of collecting information from one's environment.

**external search set** Those choice alternatives that consumers gather information about during pre-purchase search.

**exurbs** Areas beyond the suburbs at which consumption may occur and at which population growth is rapidly increasing.

## F

**family** A group of two or more persons related by blood, marriage, or adoption who reside together.

**family life cycle** The series of stages that a family passes through and that change them over time.

**family marketing** Marketing based on the relationships between family members based on the roles they assume.

**family of orientation** The family into which one is born.

**family of procreation** The family established by marriage.

**feelings** An affective state or reaction that can be positive or negative and from which attitudes are developed.

**fertility rate** The number of live births per 1,000 women of childbearing age.

**field experiment** An experiment occurring in a natural setting, such as a home or a store.

**focus groups** Groups consisting of eight to twelve people involved in a discussion led by a moderator skilled in persuading consumers to discuss a subject thoroughly.

**forgetting** The failure to retrieve something from memory.

**formal groups** Social aggregations characterized by a defined structure and a known list of members and requirements for membership.

**free recall** A type of recall measure that does not use any retrieval cues.

**fully planned purchase** A purchase in which both the product and brand are chosen in advance.

**functional elements** Characteristics of a brand (including performance, quality, price, reliability, and logistics) that solve a problem for the consumer.

**"funnel" search strategy** When people begin their Internet search with generic terms but eventually refine their search with terms focusing on specific products.

## G

**gain-framed messages** Messages that emphasize what is attained by following the messages' recommendations.

**generational change** The gradual replacement of existing values by those of young people who form the "leading" generation in terms of value.

**generic need recognition** When the need for an entire product category is stimulated.

**geodemography** Socioeconomic factors affecting

consumption and purchase, including where people live and how they earn and spend their money.

## H

**habitual decision making** A decision to buy based on a past purchase; the least complex of all decision processes.

**habituation** When a stimulus becomes so familiar and ordinary that it loses its attention-getting ability.

**haptic information** Information acquired by touch.

**household** All persons, both related and unrelated, who occupy a housing unit.

**household life cycle** The series of stages that a household passes through and that change it over time.

**hypermarket** A market that incorporates break-through technology in handling materials from a warehouse-operating profile, providing both a warehouse feel for consumers and a strong price appeal.

## I

**image advertising** The use of visual components and words to help consumers form expectations about what kind of experience they will have with a particular product, organization, or store.

**image analysis** An analysis that examines the current set of brand associations that exist in the market-place.

**impulse buying** Buying that is unplanned and occurs when consumers unexpectedly experience a sudden and powerful urge to buy something immediately.

**inbound telemarketing** The use of a toll-free number to place orders directly.

**incidental learning** Learning that occurs despite the absence of the intention to do so.

**income** Money from wages and salaries as well as interest and welfare payments.

**inferential belief** When consumers use information about one thing to form beliefs about something else.

**informal groups** Groups that have far less structure than formal groups and are likely to be based on friendship or common interests.

**information advertising** A method of advertising that provides details about products, prices, hours of store operation, locations, and other attributes that might influence purchase decisions.

**informational advertising appeals** A type of advertising appeal that attempts to influence consumers' beliefs about the advertised product.

**informational influence** The act of accepting recommendations or usage by others as evidence about the nature of a product and using this information in making product or brand decisions.

**in-home observation** Getting inside people's homes to examine exactly how products are consumed.

**information processing** The process by which information is received, processed, and stored in memory.

**innovation** Any idea or product perceived by the potential adopter to be new.

**innovativeness** The degree to which an individual adopts an innovation earlier than other members of a social system.

**innovators** Members of the first consumer group to adopt products.

**instrumental roles** Those functional or economic roles that involve financial, performance, and other functions performed by group members.

**integrated marketing communications (IMC)** A systematic, cross-organizational marketing communication process that is customer-centric, data driven, technically anchored, and branding effective.

**intentional learning** Deliberate learning with the intent of later remembering what is learned.

**intentions** Subjective judgments by individuals about how they will behave in the future.

**interference theory** A theory proposing that the chances of retrieving a particular piece of information become smaller as interference from other information becomes larger.

**intermarket segmentation** The identification of a group of customers that are similar in a variety of characteristics that transcend geographic boundaries.

**internal search** The scanning and retrieval of decision-relevant knowledge from memory.

**interviewer bias** The potential for an interviewer to affect the responses of the interviewee, perhaps because of a desire to please the interviewer.

**involvement** The degree to which an object or behavior is personally relevant or of interest, evoked by a stimulus within a specific situation.

**isolation** When avoiding clutter in advertising, the act of placing an object in a barren perceptual field, eliminating other objects that may compete for attention.

## K

**knowledge gaps** An absence of information in an individual's memory.

# L

**laboratory experiment** An experiment that occurs in a controlled setting such as a laboratory or other research environment, which permits maximum control of variables.

**laddering** In-depth probing directed toward uncovering higher-level meanings at both the benefit and value levels.

**laggards** Consumers who tend to be anchored in the past and suspicious of the new, and who are the last to adopt new innovations.

**late majority** Consumers who tend to be cautious when evaluating innovations, taking more time than average to adopt them, and often at the pressure of peers.

**learning** The process by which experience leads to changes in knowledge and behavior.

**lexicographic strategy** An evaluation strategy in which brands are compared initially on their most important attribute.

**life-cycle explanation** The basis on which society's values are forecast, interpreting that society's values will change as individuals grow older and that individuals will tend to grow into the values that their parents now hold.

**lifestyle** Peoples' patterns of living and spending time and money that reflect their interests, activities, and opinions.

**limited problem solving** Problem solving of a low degree of complexity that influences consumers' actions.

**longitudinal studies** Analysis of repeated measures of consumer activities over time to determine changes in their opinions, buying, and consumption behaviors.

**long-term memory** The mental warehouse containing all of our knowledge.

**loss aversion** Principle that says that losses loom larger than gains.

**loss-framed messages** Messages that emphasize what costs may be incurred if the messages' recommendations are not followed.

**lower threshold** The minimum amount of stimulus intensity necessary for sensation to occur.

**loyalty programs** Programs that strive to motivate repeat buying by providing rewards to customers based on how much business they do with a company.

# M

**macroculture** The values and symbols that apply to an entire society or to most of its citizens.

**macromarketing** The aggregate performance of marketing in society.

**market aggregation** The act of an organization to market and sell the same product or service to all consumers. Also known as mass marketing.

**market analysis** The process of analyzing changing consumer trends, current and potential competitors, company strengths and resources, and the technological, legal, and economic environments.

**market mavens** Individuals who serve as information sources about the marketplace because of their awareness of new products and other marketplace activities.

**market segment** A group of consumers with similar needs, behavior, or other characteristics, which are identified through the market segmentation process.

**market segmentation** The process of identifying groups of people who are similar in one or more ways (based on demographic, psychographic, behavioral, cultural, and/or other characteristics), but somewhat different from other groups.

**marketing** The process of transforming or changing an organization to have what people will buy.

**marketing concept** The process of planning and executing the conception, pricing, promotion, and distribution of ideas, goods, and services to create exchanges that satisfy individual and organizational objectives.

**marketing era** A time when productive capacity exceeded demand, causing firms to change their orientation away from manufacturing capabilities and toward the needs of consumers, thus adopting a marketing orientation.

**marketing orientation** A focus on how an organization adapts to consumers.

**marketing strategy** The allocation of resources to develop and sell products or services that consumers will perceive to provide more value than competitive products or services.

**mass customization** The act of customizing goods or services for individual customers in high volumes and at relatively low costs.

**match-up hypothesis** In product endorsement, the use of endorsers is most effective when the endorsers are perceived as being the appropriate spokespeople for the product to be endorsed.

**measurability** The ability to obtain information about the size, nature, and behavior of a market segment.

**membership** The act of achieving formal acceptance status within a group.

**mental representations** The particular manner in which information is stored in long-term memory.

**metropolitan statistical area** A free-standing metropolitan area that is surrounded by nonmetropolitan counties and that is not closely related to other metropolitan areas.

**microculture** The values and symbols of a restrictive group or segment of consumers, defined according to variables such as age, religion, ethnicity, social class, or another subdivision of the whole.

**midrange problem solving** Problem solving that occurs along the middle of the decision complexity continuum and that affects consumers' actions.

**misperception** Inaccurate knowledge.

**monochromic time** The performance of only one activity at a time for the sole purpose of accomplishing one goal at a time.

**monomorphic** Being an innovator for only one product.

**mood state** How a person currently feels.

**motivation research** The act of uncovering hidden or unrecognized motivations through guided interviewing.

**motivational conflict** What consumers experience when they must make tradeoffs in satisfying their needs.

**motivational intensity** How strongly consumers are motivated to satisfy a particular need.

**multichannel retailing** The act of reaching diverse consumer segments through a variety of formats based on consumers' lifestyles and shopping preferences.

**multistep flow of communication** A model of communication in which information can flow directly to different types of consumers, including opinion leaders, gatekeepers, and opinion seekers or receivers, and in which the gatekeepers decide whether or not other group members should receive information.

# N

**natural increase** The surplus of births over deaths in a given period.

**need recognition** A perception of a difference between the desired state of affairs and the actual situation that is sufficient to arouse and activate the decision process.

**negative disconfirmation** The result that occurs when, after purchase, the product delivers less than what was originally expected.

**negative reinforcement** What occurs when consumption allows consumers to avoid some negative outcome.

**nine-ending prices** Prices in which the last digit of a product's price is the number 9.

**nonadopters** People who decide not to purchase or use a product.

**nondiscretionary time** Time that is constrained by physical, social, and moral obligations.

**nonuser** One who does not consume a particular product at a particular time.

**normative influence** When individuals alter their behaviors or beliefs to meet the expectations of a particular group.

**norms** Rules of behavior held by a majority or at least a consensus of a group about how individuals should behave.

**nostalgia advertising appeals** Messages that attempt to persuade by evoking positive memories of the past.

**nuclear family** The immediate group of father, mother, and children living together.

# O

**objective claims** Advertising claims that focus on factual information that is not subject to individual interpretations.

**observational approach** A method for studying consumer behavior based on observing consumers in real-world situations.

**obtaining** The activities leading up to and including the purchase or receipt of a product.

**ongoing search** Information acquisition occurring on a relatively regular basis regardless of sporadic purchase needs.

**opinion change** Any subsequent modification of an opinion once it has been formed.

**opinion formation** The first time a belief, feeling, or attitude is developed about something.

**opinion leader** In word-of-mouth communication, the sender of information and opinions who influences the decisions of others.

# P

**parody display** The mockery of status symbols and behavior (e.g., an individual from a higher class acting as one from a lower class to display dislike for the higher class).

**partially comparative pricing** When a retailer features price comparisons for some but not all of the products it carries.

**partially planned purchase** A purchase in which intent to buy the product exists but brand choice is deferred until shopping.

**"pennies-a-day" strategy** A persuasion strategy that decomposes a product's price into its cost on a daily basis in order to make the price appear less expensive.

**perceived behavior control** Consumers' beliefs about how easy it is to perform a behavior.

**perceived risk** Consumers' uncertainty about the potential positive and negative consequences of their purchase decisions.

**perceptual mapping** A form of image analysis that derives brand images from consumers' similarity judgments.

**peripheral cues** In the peripheral process of opinion formation, those stimuli that are devoid of product-relevant information.

**peripheral process** A process by which opinions arise without thinking about relevant information.

**permission-based e-mail** An e-mail in which recipients have previously granted permission to a commercial sender to contact them in this fashion.

**permission marketing** Asking consumers their permission to send them product-related materials.

**personal values** Beliefs individuals hold about life and acceptable behavior that transcend situations and events.

**personality** Consistent responses to environmental stimuli that influence how individuals respond to their surrounding environment.

**persuasion knowledge** What consumers know about the goals and tactics of those trying to persuade them.

**phishing** A scam that dupes consumers into disclosing financial information, such as their credit card numbers, to fraudulent websites that resemble those of legitimate banks, brokerages, and online retailers.

**physiological observational methods** Research approaches used by consumer researchers, involving techniques borrowed from medicine, psychology, and other sciences.

**piecemeal process** When constructing an evaluation of a choice alternative, consumers do so by considering the alternative's advantages and disadvantages along important product dimensions.

**place** A phase in which firms decide the most effective outlets through which to sell their products and how best to get them there.

**pleasure** A primary type of emotional response representing positive feelings.

**polychronic time** The simultaneous combining of activities to accomplish several goals at the same time.

**polymorphic** Being an innovator for many products.

**population momentum** Theory based on the fact that the future growth of any population will be influenced by its present age distribution and is the reason that replacement-level fertility does not immediately translate into zero population growth.

**positive confirmation** The result that occurs when, after consumption, the product delivers more than what was originally expected.

**positive reinforcement** What occurs when consumption allows consumers to receive some positive outcome.

**positivism** The process of using rigorous empirical techniques to discover generalizable explanations and laws.

**postmodernism** An approach to understanding consumer behavior that uses qualitative and other forms of nonexperimental research methods.

**preferences** Consumers' attitudes toward one object in relation to another.

**premiums** Products that are offered as an incentive for the purchase of another product.

**pre-purchase evaluation** The third stage of the decision making process that focuses on the manner in which choice alternatives are evaluated.

**pre-purchase search** Search motivated by an upcoming purchase decision.

**prestige** A feeling of pride in oneself that comes when other people have an attitude of respect or deference to them.

**price** The total bundle of disutilities given up by consumers in exchange for a product.

**price-quality inferential beliefs** The result that occurs when consumers use price information to form beliefs about a product's quality.

**primary groups** Groups that are sufficiently intimate to permit and facilitate unrestricted face-to-face interaction.

**primary metropolitan statistical area (PMSA)** A metropolitan area that is closely related to another city.

**product** The total bundle of utilities obtained by consumers in the exchange process.

**product experts** People who possess vast amounts of product category knowledge.

**product innovation** Any product recently introduced to the market or perceived to be new as compared to existing products.

**product innovators** Individuals who are the first to try new products.

**product knowledge** The information stored in consumers' memory about products.

**product novices** Those who possess very simple levels of product category knowledge.

**product placement** A technique in which companies pay to have their products embedded within an entertainment vehicle.

**promotion** The actions of a marketer, including advertising, public relations, sales promotion, and personal sales.

**psychographics** An operational technique of measuring lifestyles that can be used with the large samples needed for definition of market segments.

**punishment** What occurs when consumers receive a negative outcome from consumption.

**purchase intentions** What consumers think they will buy.

**purchase knowledge** The various pieces of information consumers possess about buying products.

# R

**receiver** In word-of-mouth communication, one who gains the information about behaviors and choices, which is useful in the decision process.

**reference group** Any person or group of people that significantly affects or influences another individual's behavior.

**reference pricing** The act of providing information about a price other than that actually charged for the product as a way of influencing consumers' perceptions of the product's expensiveness.

**regret** What consumers experience when they believe that an alternative course of action than the one chosen would have produced a better outcome.

**rehearsal** The mental repetition of information or, more formally, the recycling of information through short-term memory.

**relative price knowledge** What consumers know about one price relative to another.

**repurchase intentions** Whether consumers anticipate buying the same product or brand again.

**retrieval** The activation of information stored in long-term memory.

**retrieval cue** A stimulus that activates information in memory relevant to the to-be-remembered information.

**retrieval set** The recall of choice alternatives from memory.

**reverse customer intimacy** How well marketers facilitate customers knowing the marketer.

**role** What the typical occupant of a given position is expected to do in that position in a particular social context.

# S

**salient attributes** Features of a choice alternative that are important to consumers when evaluating the alternative.

**satisfaction** A positive post-consumption evaluation that occurs when the consumption experience either meets or exceeds expectations.

**scarcity effect** When an object is viewed as more desirable as its perceived scarcity increases.

**search** The motivated activation of knowledge stored in memory or acquisition of information from the environment about potential need satisfiers.

**search claims** Advertising claims that can be validated before purchase by examining information readily available in the marketplace.

**search intentions** Consumers' plans to engage in external search.

**secondary groups** Groups that have face-to-face interaction, but are more sporadic, less comprehensive, and less influential in shaping thought and behavior than are primary groups.

**selective need recognition** When the need for a specific brand within a product category is stimulated.

**self-concept** The mental images or impressions one has of oneself.

**self-gifts** Purchases of items or services by consumers as a means of rewarding, consoling, or motivating themselves.

**self-knowledge** A person's understanding of her or his own mental processes.

**self-referencing** A means of encouraging elaboration by relating a stimulus to oneself and one's experiences.

**sender** In word-of-mouth communication, one who relays information in an attempt to increase the confidence in a product or behavior choice.

**sensory innovators** Innovators who have a strong preference for new sensory experiences.

**sensory memory** That part of capacity used when initially analyzing a stimulus detected by one of our five senses.

**service encounter** The occurrence of a personal communication between a consumer and a marketer.

**shadowing** A method in which a researcher accompanies or "shadows" consumers through the shopping and consumption processes.

**shop-a-longs** Ethnographic technique in which shoppers are accompanied by one or more observers.

**shopping intentions** Where consumers plan on making their product purchases.

**short-term memory** Where thinking occurs; the stimulus is interpreted and contemplated using concepts stored in long-term memory.

**signals** Product attributes that are used to infer other product attributes.

**simple additive** An evaluation strategy by which the consumer counts or adds the number of times each alternative is judged favorably in terms of the set of salient evaluative criteria.

**social class** The relatively permanent and homogeneous divisions in a society into which individuals or families sharing similar values, lifestyles, interests, wealth, status, education, economic positions, and behavior can be categorized.

**social mobility** The process of moving from one social class to another due to changes in occupation, income level, and other factors.

**social stratification** The perceived hierarchies in which people rate others as higher or lower in social status.

**social values** Values held so highly that they almost become stereotypical of a market segment or group and define the behavior held as a norm for a society or group.

**socialization** The processes by which people develop their values, motivations, and habitual activity.

**sociological variables (family)** Three variables—cohesion, adaptability, and communication—that help explain how families function.

**spam** Unsolicited commercial e-mail.

**span of attention** The length of time short-term memory can be focused on a single stimulus or thought.

**spending intentions** How much money consumers think they will spend.

**spreading activation** A concept proposing that activation of one memory node causes a ripple effect that spreads throughout its linkages to other nodes.

**spyware** Software that's downloaded onto a computer without the permission of the owner and collects personal information such as the user's online activities, financial records, and passwords.

**status groups** Groups reflecting a community's expectations for style of life among each class as well as the positive or negative social estimation of honor given to each class.

**stimulus categorization** When a stimulus is classified using the mental concepts and categories stored in memory.

**stimulus generalization** For an existing stimulus-response relationship, the more similar a new stimulus is to the existing one, the more likely it will evoke the same response.

**store atmospherics** The physical properties of the retail environment designed to create an effect on consumer purchases.

**store image** Consumers' overall perception of a store, which they rely on when choosing a store.

**strategy** A decisive allocation of resources (capital, technology, and people) in a particular direction.

**structural variables** Variables that include the age of the head of household or family, marital status, presence of children, and employment status.

**subjective claims** Advertising claims that may be interpreted differently by different consumers.

**subliminal persuasion** The act of influencing people by stimuli below the conscious level of awareness.

**substantiality** The size of a market.

**supply chain** All the organizations involved in taking a product from inception to final consumption.

**surrogate consumer** An individual who acts as an agent to guide, direct, and/or conduct activities in the marketplace.

**surveys** A research method for gathering information from a sample of consumers by asking questions and recording responses.

# T

**testimonials** Using a product endorser to tout the benefits of a product based on that person's positive experience with that product.

**top-of-the-mind awareness** In assessing consumer awareness, the ability of people to remember a given brand before any other brand name.

**total fertility rate** The average number of children that would be born alive to a woman during her lifetime if she were to pass through all of her childbearing years conforming to the age-specific fertility rates of a given year.

**trait** Any distinguishable, relatively enduring way in which one individual differs from another.

**transcultural marketing research** Gathering data from specific ethnic groups and comparing these data to those collected from other markets, usually the mass market.

**trickle-down theory** A theory that alleges that lower classes often emulate the behavior of their higher-class counterparts.

**two-step flow of communication** A model of communication in which the opinion leaders are the direct receivers of information from advertisements and interpret and transmit the information to others through word-of-mouth communication.

## U

**unconditioned response** In Pavlov's theory of classical conditioning, the response evoked by the unconditioned stimulus.

**unconditioned stimulus** In Pavlov's theory of classical conditioning, the stimulus that automatically evokes a particular response.

**unconscious motivation** Being unaware of what really motivates one's behavior.

**unplanned purchase** A purchase in which both the product and brand are chosen at the point of sale.

**usage expansion advertising** Advertising that attempts to persuade consumers to use a familiar product in new or different ways.

**usage volume segmentation** A form of segmentation that divides users into heavy, moderate, and light users.

**user** One who consumes a particular product at a particular time.

**utilitarian advertising appeals** Messages that influence consumers' opinions about the advertised product's ability to perform its intended function.

## V

**value** The difference between what consumers give up for a product and the benefits they receive.

**value-discounting hypothesis** A theory that predicts that products offered as a free premium will be valued less.

**value-expressive advertising appeals** Messages that attempt to influence consumers' opinions about the advertised product's ability to communicate something about those who use the product.

**value-expressive influence** The acceptance of a group's norms, values, attitudes, or behaviors to satisfy a need for psychological association with this group.

**vertical coordination** A high degree of dependence and interlocking relationships among channel members.

**viral marketing** A company's creation of a game, trinket, story, slogan, or other item of interest (linked sometimes only tangentially to the company's product) that is so compelling that consumers spontaneously pass it along to others they know.

**virtual membership groups** Groups based on virtual communities in which individuals from different geographic areas share information without face-to-face contact.

**volitional control** The degree to which a behavior can be performed at will.

## W

**wealth** A measure of net worth or assets, including the value of bank accounts, stocks, and real property, minus any liabilities.

**Weber's law** A theory holding that activating the differential threshold or achieving the just noticeable difference depends on the relative amount of change, not just the absolute amount of change.

**word-of-mouse communication** When consumers communicate with each other over the Internet.

**word-of-mouth communication** The informal transmission of ideas, comments, opinions, and information between two people, neither one of whom is a marketer.

## Z

**zapping** The act of switching channels via remote control during a television program's commercial breaks.

**zipping** The act of fast-forwarding through commercials when watching recorded programming.

Page numbers in *italics* indicate figures and tables

Blair, Margaret Henderson, 603
Blanco, Octavio, 285
Blaney, P. H., 686
Blattberg, Robert, 65
Blazina, Ed, 326
Bleach poisoning, *129, 626*
Blend-a-Med, 268
Blended families, 497
Bligh, Alan David, 479
Blind taste tests, 622, 720
Blishen, Bernard, 479
Bliss, Jeff, 639
Bloch, Peter H., 143, 327, 685
Block, Lauren G., 651, 652, 654, 685
Block, Martin P., 186
Blockbuster, 346, *665*
Blogger, 520
Blogs, 215, 520, 559, 578–79
*Blonde Ambition* (tour), 730
Bluewater, 172
Blumenthal, Richard, 293
BMW
  and advertainment, 579–80
  as advocated brand, 217, *218*
  image problems with, 363
  reputation of, *344*
  and the rich, 261
  website, *571*
Bodur, Onur, 561
Body Shop, The, *344*
Bogart, Leo, 28, 31
Boller, Gregory W., 650
Bolton, Ruth N., 98, 231
Bombay Sapphire, 319
Bon Jovi, Jon, 654
Bonacich, Edna, 478
Bonds, Barry, 305
Bone, Paula Fitzgerald, 284, 561, 685
Bonomo, John, *573*
Boogie woogie, *443*
Boots, 59
Borden Foods, 621
"Borderline" (song), 730
Borders bookstores, 379, *381, 395*
Borgers, Aloys, 186
Borzo, Jeanette, *577*
Boston Consulting Group, 410–11
Bottled water, 310, 312
Bottomley, Paul A., 145
Boudette, Neil E., 328, 372
Bouffard, Kevin, 374
Boulding, William, 145
Bounce fabric softener, 72, 73, 94, 351, *351*
"Bounce-back," 574
Boush, David M., 145
Boutilier, Robert, 516
Bowen, David E., 230
Bowflex fitness machine, *204*
Boxed wine, 194

Boycotts, 457
Boyd, Thomas C., *563*
Brackey, Harriet Johnson, 372
*Brady Bunch, The* (TV program), 480
Brahms, Johannes, 725
Brain, and brand awareness, *340–41*
Brainstorming, 234–35
Brainwave activity, *340*
Branch, Shelley, 134
Brand(s)
  and advertising, promotion, 163
  advocates, *218*
  attributes, 158
  awareness, 266, 331, 336
  and borrowing, 725
  building, 163
  choice, 527, 528, 529
  and coffee, 703
  confusion over, 52, 384–85
  consumer attitudes toward, 392–95, *393–95, 407, 408*
  and cultural relevance, 435–36
  definition of, 51
  distinctiveness of, 378–80, *380, 381*
  easy-to-remember, 677–78
  emotional elements of, 51
  equity, 51, *393*
  evaluation, 96
  evolution of, 725
  expectations about, 206
  exposure, and giveaways, *629*
  extensions, 133–34, *133, 333*
  functional elements of, 51
  global, 63
  ideal, 346
  image analysis of, 276, 339–41, 343–46, *345, 367, 402*
  knowledge, 335–36, 338–46, 369
  legendary, 724–32
  losing appeal of, 134
  loyalty to, 54, 91, 97, 150, 316, 436, 465
  maintenance, 725
  management, global, 269
  in marketing strategy, 50–54
  and memory, 96
  names, 134, *385*, 622–24, 647, 676
  and national promotions, 280
  and passion, 725
  perceptions, 74
  personality, 273
  positioning, 163
  promise, 51
  protection, 52
  ratings, *137*
  recognition, 663–64
  and repurchase intentions, 411
  role of, in shaping consumer opinion, 624–26, *626*
  Rolling Stones as, 731

  store, 280
  strategy, 34, 36, 50
  switching, 91, 92–93, 150, 246, 545–46, 722
  top ten, *344, 393, 393, 394, 395*
  and trust, 717
  and willingness to buy, 238
Brand architecture, 726–27, *727*
Brand associations, 333, 339
Brand equity, 51, 52, *393*
Brand extensions, 133–34, *133*
Brand Keys (research firm), 702
Brand knowledge, 335–46, *336*
Brand names
  advertising and promotion of, 163
  advocated, *218*
  associations, 333, *333*, 339–41, 346
  awareness of, 335–36, *336*, 338–39
  changing, 363–66
*Brand New* (Nancy Koehn), 724–25
Brand personality, 52, 273
Brand promise, 51
Brand strategy, 50, 52
Brand switching, 92–93, 546
"Branded entertainment," 579
Branded products, top ten, *394*
Branding, 63, 622–24, 688, 724
Brannigan, Bonnie, 57
Brannon, Laura, 652
Branson, Sir Richard, 104, 343
Brasel, S. Adam, 228
Bratz dolls, 302
Braun-LaTour, Kathryn A., 679, 684
Braus, Patricia, 144
Brawney, 620, *620*
Brawny, *534*, 618
Brazil, 268, 427
Brennan, Fran, 370
Breast implants, 546
Breier, Mark, 688
Brezen, Tamara S., 186
Bridis, Ted, 142, 609
Bridgestone Tires, *500*
BrightHouse Institute for Sciences, *340*
Briley, Donnel, 476, 477
Brinberg, David, 370
Brinckman, Jonathan, 710
Brio Italian Bistro, 172
Briones, Maricris G., 144
Brislin, Richard W., 66
Bristol, Terry, 328
Bristor, Julie, 560
British Airways, *344, 573*
Britton, Julie A. Edell, 419, 651, 652
Broadband Rocks, 168
Broadpoint Communications, 588
Brock, Timothy, 652
"Broken B" stimulus, 617, *617*
Brooker, George, 99
Brooks, Charles, 185
Brooks, Rick, 186

Conformity, 526–27
Confucianism, 458
Confusion of consumers, 384–86, *385*, 417
Congruity, of market segments, 47
Conjunctive strategies, 137
Conkey, Christopher, 371
Connelly, Mary, 326
Consideration sets, 335, 663–64
  construction of, 131
  determining the, 128–31
  expansion of, *130*
  size of, *129*
Consistency, *528*, 674–75, *675*
Consolidated metropolitan statistical
      area (CMSA), 253
Conspicuous consumption, 300
Conspicuousness, 527, 529
Consumer analysis, 34
  Bayesian analysis, 47–48
  definition of, 47
  of e-commerce, *177–78*
Consumer attitudes, 386, 392–94. *See*
      *also* attitude
Consumer behavior
  activities included in, 5, *5*
  analyzing and predicting, 236–38
  as applied science, 21
  of children, 510–13
  and consumer analysis, 1
  contact, making, 566–2
  cross-cultural, 2–3
  cultural influences on, 432–35, 452–53
  and decisions, 1
  definition of, 4
  demographic analysis and social pol-
      icy, 236–38
  diagnosing, 95
  in Eastern Europe, 268–69
  and economy, 7
  effects of associations on, *333*
  in emerging markets, 265–66
  in European Union, 269–70
  and everyday life, 1, 3
  evolution of, 14–20, *19*
  family influences and, 482
  as field of study, 19
  helping consumers to remember,
      656–84
  and immigration, 243
  individual determinants of, 233
  influence of individual differences on,
      270
  and information, 308
  and intentions, 412–13
  and Internet, 119
  in Latin America, 268
  lifestyles, 277–83
  and marketing programs, success of, 7
  in Pacific Rim, 266–68
  personal values, 273–77, 429

personality, 270
predicting, 273, 409–15
product development, 49
psychographics, 278–79
and psychological processes, 88
and public policy, 11–12
reasons to study, 6–14
and reputation, 343
shaping consumers' opinions, 608–49
social class and, 473
and strategic planning, 1
studying, 6, 20–26
and supply chain, 14
underlying principles of, 26–29
Consumer Behavior Odyssey, 210
Consumer Bill of Rights, 28–29
Consumer characteristics, *43*, 44
Consumer confidence, 257
Consumer databases, 42
Consumer decision process (CDP)
  consumer's mood state, 40, 95
  and consumption, 189
  and consumption evaluations, 227
  culture, 432–35
  and data mining, 694–96
  decision process continuum, 88, 89
  defined, 70
  degree of involvement, 93–94
  described, 67
  development of, 70
  diagnosis of, 95, 96–97
  effect of environmental influences on,
      80, *82*, 83, 87
  extended problem solving, 88–90
  factors influencing, 5, 93–95
  families and, 485–90
  habitual decision making, 88, 91
  impulse buying, 91–92
  individual differences, 86–87
  initial purchase, 88–90, *89*
  for innovations, 545–55
  Internet and, 114–22
  effect of knowledge on, 332
  limited problem solving, 89–90
  and marketing mix strategies, 86
  midrange problem solving, 88–90
  model of, 70–86, *70*
  and need recognition, 70, *70*, 71, *71*, 72–74
  and organizations, 85
  overview, 140
  perceptions of differences among al-
      ternatives, 94
  personal values and, 275–76
  personal variables affecting, 236
  and planning, 150–51
  and postconsumption evaluations,
      227
  and pre-purchase evaluation, 79–81,
      *80*, 127–40
  psychological influences on, 88

and purchase, 81–82, *82*, 150–51,
      *157*
repeat purchases, 91
and research, 86
review and discussion questions on,
      283–84
and risk,123
as road map, 97
and search for information, 74–77,
      *75*, 79, 123
stage one: need recognition, 70–4,
      *70*, *71*
stage two: search for information,
      74–79, *75*
stage three: pre-purchase evaluation
      of alternatives, 67, 70, 79–81,
      *80*, 81–83, 96, 97
stage four: purchase, 70, 81–82, *82*,
      96, 97
stage five: consumption, 82–83, *83*,
      189, 190–10
stage six: post-consumption evalua-
      tion, 83–84, *83*, 210–27
stage seven: divestment, 84–85, *85*
summary of, 283
time availability and, 94–95
types of, 88–93
uses of, 85–86
variables that shape, 86–88
variety seeking, 92
vignette on, 68–69
Consumer decisions, and public policy,
      140
Consumer demand, and geodemogra-
      phy, 253
Consumer Dynamics, 694–97, *696*, *697*
Consumer Electronics Association, *349*
Consumer environment, 37–38
Consumer expectations. *See*
      Expectations
Consumer experience, 206
Consumer Federation of America, *124*,
      218
Consumer feelings. *See* Feelings
Consumer insight, 36, 37
Consumer intentions, 275, 409–15,
      *411*, 416, *416*
"Consumer is king," 7–8
Consumer journey, *208*
Consumer knowledge
  versus ability, 659
  and brand associations, 333
  and consideration sets, 131
  and consumption, 350–51
  and customer recruitment, 367
  defined, 87, 331
  as direct experience, 369
  gaps in, 363, 369
  importance of, 332–34
  and individual differences, 87
  and information, 308
  and internal search, 111